MAINE
Exeter
St. Albans
Palmyra
Orrington
Hartland
Pittsfield
Belfast
Augusta
Camden
Paris/Paris Hill
Woodstock
Richmond
Poland
Brunswick/Topsham
North-Yarmouth
Portland
Gorham
VERMONT
Bershire
Enosburg
Bakersfield
Sutton
St. Albans
Johnson
Stowe
Waterbury
Montpelier
Northfield
Roxbury
Royalton
NEW HAMPSHIRE
Grantham
Claremon
Newport
Concord
Washington
Manchester
West Wilton
New Ipswich
Salem
MASSACHUSETTS
Townsend
Somerville
Boston/West Medford
Lancaster / Clinton
Dorchester/Milton
Albany
Springfield
New Bedford/Fairhaven
Falmouth
Dartmouth
Providence
Hartford
Kensington/Berlin
Rocky Hill
Middletown
West Milton
RHODE ISLAND
CONNECTICUT
NEW JERSEY
N
nw
ne
W
E
sw
se
S

THE

ELLEN G. WHITE

Letters & Manuscripts

WITH ANNOTATIONS

VOLUME 1

1845

1859

THE

ELLEN G. WHITE

Letters & Manuscripts

WITH ANNOTATIONS

VOLUME 1

1845

1859

A PROJECT OF THE TRUSTEES OF
THE ELLEN G. WHITE ESTATE, INC.

REVIEW AND HERALD®
Publishing Association
Hagerstown, MD

Cover Design by Bryan Gray, Review and Herald® Design Center
Interior Design by Heather Hunt Rogers

Library of Congress Control Number: 2014934473

ISBN: 978-0-8280-2789-2

THE ELLEN G. WHITE LETTERS AND MANUSCRIPTS

With Annotations

TABLE OF CONTENTS

ABBREVIATIONS

DF	Ellen G. White Estate Document File
EGW	Ellen G. White
EGWE-GC	Ellen G. White Estate, General Conference
EGWEnc	*Ellen G. White Encyclopedia*
Lt	Ellen G. White letter
Ms	Ellen G. White manuscript
PH	Ellen G. White pamphlet
SDAE	*Seventh-day Adventist Encyclopedia*

SERIES INTRODUCTION

For millions of readers Ellen G. White is best known through her published works, works that include such spiritual classics as *The Desire of Ages* and *Steps to Christ.* The latter volume has circulated in the tens of millions and has been translated into more than 165 languages since it was first published in 1892. But what is not as well known is that much of the writing in both *Steps to Christ* and *The Desire of Ages* originated in letters of heart-stirring appeal to real people who were the beneficiaries of Ellen White's evangelistic fervor. Sentences that many have committed to memory because of their faith-inspiring insights were first penned in the context of personal letters providing hope, encouragement, and timely counsel.

Today we benefit from the works Ellen White produced over the course of her 70-year ministry in which she preserved the core themes of her messages. In addition, compilations published by the Ellen G. White Estate, as she called for in her will, provide a rich spectrum of topical instruction. But in the nineteenth and early twentieth centuries, Ellen White's contemporaries also benefited from interacting with her through correspondence, speaking appointments, and visitation.

Ellen White was more than an author. She was a wife, a mother, an evangelist, a much-sought-after counselor. She had relatives to care for, homes to keep in order, gardens to tend, and bills to pay. She experienced the miserable ailments common to an age predating central heating, air-conditioning, and over-the-counter pain relievers. She traveled for days in cramped, tobacco-smoke-filled railroad cars, which was arguably better than traveling for weeks by horse-drawn carriage. And she knew the life-shattering pain of losing a spouse and two children to sickness and death.

But Ellen White did not live in only a three-dimensional world. The call she received at age 17 compelled her to view every aspect of life in the fuller light of eternity. This is why she agreed to speak to eager audiences when she didn't know if she could stand on her feet, why she wrote letters at 2:00 in the morning, and why public criticism and personal rebuffs did not induce her to hold back or water down her testimonies.

Ellen White's letters and manuscripts give us more than a window into the daily life of a remarkable nineteenth-century female author and religious leader. Those who are convinced of the genuineness of her prophetic claims find in these unpublished writings insights and principles that continue to speak to our generation, even though the original historical setting must guide our interpretation and application (see the introductory article "Interpreting Ellen G. White's Letters and Manuscripts").

This series marks the first effort to publish in chronological order all of Ellen White's previously unpublished writings. Many thousands of pages have been published in various research papers, books, and compilations, but these have been topical selections. Nor have they previously appeared with historical annotations providing the reader with basic information about the persons addressed and issues raised. It is a monumental task, but like all long journeys, it can be completed only if we make a beginning.

An Annotation Supervisory Committee appointed by the White Estate trustees provided guidance and set the parameters for the project. The chief annotator for the pre-1860 documents was Roland Karlman, who, until undertaking this project, served as the director of the Ellen G. White Seventh-day Adventist Research Center at Newbold College, Bracknell, Berkshire, England. The final manuscript also reflects the suggestions of specialists in Adventist history and Ellen White studies in particular, with special thanks to Denis Fortin, George Knight, Jud Lake, Allan Lindsay, Jerry Moon, and Alberto Timm, in addition to the members of the supervisory committee.

It is the hope and desire of the Ellen G. White Estate that the publication of these unique materials will give a greater insight into the life of this phenomenal woman, and that readers will hear and follow the same Spirit who impelled her to commit a lifetime of service to our Lord.

The Trustees of the Ellen G. White Estate

James R. Nix, President

A BIOGRAPHICAL SUMMARY

OF ELLEN G. WHITE'S LIFE UP TO THE TIMES OF THIS VOLUME

Tim Poirier

Within the 15 years spanned by the papers in this volume, an unlettered and unmarried teenager from Maine became a 32-year-old mother of three, a published author, and the unlikely cofounder of what would become an international religious movement that was still, in 1859, without a name.[1]

According to her autobiography, Ellen Gould Harmon was born on November 26, 1827, in Gorham, Maine, she and her twin sister Elizabeth being the last of eight children born to Robert (a hatmaker) and Eunice Harmon (a former schoolteacher). John Quincy Adams was president of the United States, and only 50 years had passed since the 13 American colonies had declared their independence from King George III and the British Empire. Ellen's grandfather had served as a corporal in the Revolutionary War.

Childhood Accident and Conversion

Some time after her family moved to Portland, Maine, Ellen's academic endeavors were tragically cut short at age 9 when an angry schoolmate hurled a stone that struck her in the face, breaking her nose and rendering her virtually unconscious for three weeks. She recalled how physicians declared that "I had lost so much blood my recovery was doubtful; that if I should get better, I could not live long. I was reduced almost to a skeleton."[2]

But Ellen defied the odds. Although her physically debilitated condition ended her hopes of pursuing an education, her life had been preserved and her health slowly improved. After experiencing a spiritual awakening that was sparked by William Miller's visit to her hometown of Portland, Maine, Ellen was baptized into the Methodist Church in 1842.

Miller's message of Christ's imminent return became the focal point of Ellen's religious experience and witness. "I knew it was my duty to continue my efforts for the salvation of precious souls and to pray and confess Christ at every opportunity," she later reflected. "Let come what would, I determined to please God, and live as one who expected the Saviour to come and reward the faithful."[3]

This determination, which other members of the Harmon family shared, led to increasing opposition from their Methodist "brethren and sisters" who

---

Tim Poirier, M.T.S., is vice director and archivist of the Ellen G. White Estate.

were less taken with Miller's viewpoints. A church trial brought about their final separation from the Methodist Church in September 1843.

While initial expectations of Jesus' return looked to the Jewish year beginning with spring 1843 and ending in spring 1844, recalculation of the time prophecies eventually pointed to the fall of 1844, October 22 specifically, as the true date for Christ's second advent. When that date passed—later referred to by followers as the Great Disappointment—confusion and despair took the place of hope and assurance. Some completely abandoned their Advent faith, others looked to new date calculations, while still others searched and waited for an explanation of what they were convinced had been a genuine work of God.

Ellen Harmon's First Vision

It was in that period of uncertainty and perplexity, some two months after the "passing of the time," that Ellen Harmon and four friends gathered for morning prayer in the home of Elizabeth Haines in Portland, Maine. "While praying," she recorded, "the power of God came upon me as I never had felt it before. I was surrounded with light, and was rising higher and higher from the earth"[4]—not physically, but in a vision state. Ellen did not include in her account how long this experience lasted, but it would be the first of many hundreds of visions and prophetic dreams over the course of her life ministry.

Many of these visions took place publicly where supporters and critics alike observed them. Descriptions compiled from eyewitnesses provide the following details (not all necessarily occurring with every vision):

1. As the vision began, she would exclaim "Glory!" or "Glory to God!"—sometimes repeated one or more additional times.

2. She would experience a loss of physical strength.

3. Subsequently, she would often manifest supernatural strength.[5]

4. She would not breathe, but her heartbeat would continue normally, and the color in her cheeks would remain natural.

5. Occasionally she would speak words indicative of the scene she was seeing in vision.

6. Her eyes would remain open, not with a vacant stare, but as if she were intently watching something.

7. Her position might vary. Sometimes she would be seated, sometimes

reclining, and sometimes she would walk about the room and make graceful gestures as she spoke of matters presented.

8. She would be unconscious of what was occurring about her. She would neither see, hear, feel, nor perceive in any way her immediate surroundings or events happening around her.

9. At the close of the vision she would draw a deep breath, followed in about a minute by another, and very soon her natural breathing would resume.

10. Immediately after the vision everything would seem very dark to her.

11. Within a short time she would regain her natural strength and abilities.[6]

The message received in that first vision of December 1844 did not explain their past experience to the small band of disillusioned Millerites, but it provided assurance that God had led them thus far and that He would continue to lead them to the glories of "the city" "if they kept their eyes fixed on Jesus."[7]

Telling the Visions

Despite her ill-health and natural timidity, Ellen Harmon felt constrained to carry out the instruction she had received to share her visions publicly. She recounted, however, that "the idea of a female traveling from place to place caused me to draw back."[8] Finally, through the encouragement of fellow believers in Portland, she set out "to bear my testimony" as "the way opened," leading to an extended itinerary within the New England states of Maine, New Hampshire, and Massachusetts.[9] Little did she know that this would launch a lifetime of travel and speaking that would crisscross the United States of America and also include Europe and Australia.[10]

At first Ellen traveled most often with her older sister, Sarah, and other close friends, sometimes accompanied by former Millerite ministers. Earlier, probably in 1844,[11] she was first introduced to one such leader, Elder James White, and within two years the two would unite their labors together through marriage. James would later describe it in this way: "As she should come before the public she needed a lawful protector, and God having chosen her as a channel of light and truth to the people in a special sense, she could be of great help to me."[12] They were married on August 30, 1846.

Not long after their marriage James and Ellen White began to observe and teach the seventh-day Sabbath, as introduced to them by former Millerite preacher Joseph Bates. Traveling now as a team and without any fixed home of their own, they visited the scattered believers, attended Bible conferences, and began to use the printed page as a means to make known their understanding of Bible prophecy and the importance of the seventh-day Sabbath, and to bring unity among the disparate bands of former Millerites.

Publishing Ventures

While her written works would become Ellen White's lasting legacy, it was not until several months after her first vision that her "trembling hand" was able to hold a pen "steadily"—an accomplishment she attributed to God's special intervention. Her physical condition had become so debilitated by her childhood accident that "up to this time" (early 1845) she "could not write." "While in vision," she wrote, "I was commanded by an angel to write the vision. I attempted it, and wrote readily. My nerves were strengthened, and my hand became steady."[13] Her writing continued for nearly 70 years.

The earliest extant communication of any type by Ellen White (still Ellen Harmon at the time) was a printed letter dated December 20, 1845, addressed to the editor of the *Day-Star*, a Millerite paper published in Cincinnati, Ohio.[14] She concluded her letter, which reported the scenes of her first vision (and a subsequent one concerning the new earth), with the note "This was not written for publication; but for the encouragement of all who may see it, and be encouraged by it." Even so, the editor, Enoch Jacobs, decided to publish her account "at the request of many friends that have heard it read."[15]

As interest increased in this 18-year-old's visionary experiences, supporters circulated her visions inexpensively through "broadsides"—large sheets of paper, usually printed on one side.[16] In May 1847 James White (now married to Ellen) included three communications from his wife in his 24-page pamphlet *A Word to the "Little Flock,"* but it was not until August 1851 that most of Ellen White's earliest writings would be collected into book form and published as *A Sketch of the Christian Experience and Views of Ellen G. White.*[17]

Even prior to her first book, however, several of Ellen's visions reached Sabbatarian Adventists through the "little paper" that James White launched in response to one of his wife's visions. He issued 11 numbers of *The Present Truth* between July 1849 and November 1850, six of which contained communications from Ellen White. Five years later Ellen published her first *Testimony for the Church*—a 16-page pamphlet that launched a series of published "testimonies"[18] that eventually comprised nine volumes and nearly 5,000 pages. Four more *Testimony* numbers would be printed between 1856 and 1859. Several articles also appeared in the *Review and Herald* and the monthly *Youth's Instructor,* the latter having begun in 1852.

Through Turmoil and Travel

During the formative years that followed the 1844 disappointment there was agreement on little and disagreement on much. Had Jesus already returned spiritually? If not, should the time of His return be recalculated? What "door" was "shut" in 1844? Is there a place for charismatic experiences? Who should be recognized as "messengers" (ministers), and how should they be financially supported? Should the publishing effort continue? How should the movement deal with splinter groups, and is some sort of church organization (or "gospel order") appropriate?

Throughout the turmoil James and Ellen White, together with Joseph Bates, emerged as the principal leaders of the growing band of Sabbatarian Adventists. Bates's early publications emphasized the eschatological significance of the Sabbath, and his views largely shaped the theological development of the movement. At the same time, James's editorship of what would become the *Advent Review and Sabbath Herald* (now the *Adventist Review*), along with his wife's influential visions, propelled the message forward. By 1852 the number of followers, by reliable estimation, may have approached 2,000 from a mere 200 in 1850.[19]

Three children were born to the Whites during the times of this volume: Henry Nichols (August 26, 1847), James Edson (July 28, 1849), and William Clarence (August 29, 1854). The demands of James and Ellen's incessant traveling found the boys too often cared for in the homes of close friends—circumstances the parents bemoaned,[20] but which generated frequent correspondence, for which this volume is the richer.

Those friends included the Howland, Hastings, and Nichols families—names that will become very familiar to the readers of the letters from this period. They opened their homes to the Whites, supported them in their ministries, and established such bonds as is evidenced in the naming of their first son, Henry Nichols White.

Shortly after Henry's birth the Howlands invited the young family to share space in their home at Topsham, Maine, where they "commenced housekeeping with borrowed articles." "We were poor and saw close times," wrote Ellen, who recounted James's grueling work handling stone on the nearby railroad before changing his labor to chopping wood "from early morning till dark," earning about 50 cents a day.[21]

Ellen described the desperate times further in her autobiography: "We did not wish to be dependent, and were careful to live within our means. We were resolved to suffer rather than get into debt. I allowed myself and child one pint of milk each day. In the morning before my husband went to his work, he left me nine cents to buy milk for three mornings. It was quite a study with me whether to deny myself and child of milk, or get an apron for him. I gave up the milk, and purchased the cloth for an apron to cover the bare arms of my child."[22]

According to James White,[23] it was not many months later (in the autumn of 1848) that Ellen received her first vision regarding matters of health, specifically the injurious effects of tobacco, coffee, and tea. Other visions received during the times of this volume urged the importance of "cleanliness" and a diet consisting of "more coarse food with little grease,"[24] but it was not until after her major "health reform" vision of June 6, 1863, that Ellen White would begin to focus more extensively on the relationship between physical and spiritual health—a topic soon to become one of the most prominent themes in her public speaking and writings.

For about two and a half years, beginning in the summer of 1849, publishing interests found the Whites transitioning among temporary residences in New England and New York. *The Present Truth,* initially published in July 1849 in Middletown, Connecticut, moved with the Whites to Oswego, New York, before its final number was issued in Paris, Maine. There, in November 1850, James launched the *Second Advent Review and Sabbath Herald,* but the paper's second volume (issued eight months later) hailed from Saratoga Springs, New York.

Continuing westward, the Whites eventually settled in April 1852 in a rented house in Rochester, New York. "You would smile could you look in upon us and see our furniture," Ellen wrote to their longtime friends the Howlands. She continued: "We have bought two old bedsteads for twenty-five cents each. My husband brought me home six old mismatched chairs, for which he paid one dollar, and soon he presented me with four more old chairs, without any seating, paid sixty-two cents for the lot. . . . Butter is so high we do not purchase it, neither can we afford potatoes. We use sauce in the place of butter, and turnips for potatoes. The cherry sauce was provided for us by Sr. Harris. We are willing to endure privations if the work of God can be advanced. We believe the Lord's hand was in our coming to this place."[25]

The following year, after a contentious conference in Jackson, Michigan, the young movement faced its first organized opposition from within—led by Hiram S. Case (an itinerant preacher) and his close friend Charles P. Russell. In 1854 they launched their rival paper, the *Messenger of Truth,* in which Ellen White's visions came under steady attack.

"The *Messenger* Party," as it came to be known, was short-lived (having disbanded by 1857), but it served to advance the growing sentiment advocated by James and Ellen White that "gospel order" was indispensable for the continued unity of the Sabbatarian churches. In the midst of the *Messenger* storm Ellen White would write definitively of this need in a chapter devoted to the topic in her *Supplement to the Christian Experience and Views of Ellen G. White* (1854).[26]

New Beginnings in Battle Creek

The Whites would call Rochester their home until "the brethren in Michigan opened the way for the [*Review*] Office to come to Battle Creek,"

Earliest known photograph of James and Ellen White, circa 1857 (ambrotype)

James and Ellen White with son Willie, circa 1857 (ambrotype)

James and Ellen White, circa 1859

The original James and Ellen White family home (1856-1863) on Wood Street in Battle Creek, Michigan, as restored and open for visitors to Historic Adventist Village

Left to right: sons Henry Nichols, J. Edson, and William C. White, circa 1862

Michigan.[27] Coinciding with the move, a "General Conference" was called in Battle Creek beginning November 16, 1855, "to make choice of those Brethren who shall conduct the *Review,* and to consider other matters of vital interest to the prosperity of the cause."[28] As a result of the conference, the publishing effort was put on solid ground, and the believers reached agreement on a disputed matter of no little significance—the proper hours for Sabbath observance. But it was another topic of "vital interest" that weighed heavily on the minds of the delegates—the "decline of faith and [spirituality] amongst the scattered flock."[29]

In reviewing their "present low state," the delegates found direction in the New Testament's emphasis on the church's appreciation of the gifts of the Holy Spirit. Specifically, they acknowledged their negligence in giving proper regard to Ellen White's visions, in part a result of their "desire to conciliate the feelings of our opponents."[30] The published address set forth the primacy of the Word of God in connection with the prophetic gift and marked a decisive turning point in the movement's affirmation of Ellen White's ministry.

Nevertheless, freedom from criticism was not a common state of affairs for the Whites. The "testimonies" and letters included in this volume reveal the opposition that both James and Ellen encountered, including resistance at times from such prominent Sabbathkeeping leaders as J. H. Waggoner, Uriah Smith, Cyrenius Smith, and J. N. Andrews. These tensions would find resolution, and confidence in Ellen White's visions would be upheld, but not without adding to the tumult of the period.

Soon after the November 1855 conference, perhaps as a visible token of support, church members assisted the Whites in acquiring a 1.5-acre [.6-hectare] lot, and in 1856 they set up house in the first home they could call their own. The financial privations of the past decade were beginning to turn. Today their house stands as the oldest Seventh-day Adventist landmark in Battle Creek.

While living in that home in 1858, Ellen White wrote the account of her March 14 "great controversy" vision, initially published as *Spiritual Gifts,* volume 1, and continued in volumes 3 and 4. As expanded in her later publications, the "great controversy" between Christ and Satan became the central unifying theme of Ellen White's writings.

It was also in that home that 31-year-old Ellen White began in 1859 to keep a day-by-day diary (her earliest known), which is published in full for the first time in this volume. Entries reveal an individual and a home in constant motion—especially at times of general conferences. The day after one such event, which concluded with 35 persons for dinner, Ellen penned only a single entry: "We were all much worn out."[31]

The Whites would remain in Battle Creek for 17 years, little knowing that in the decade ahead they would lose two sons to disease, the nation would be torn asunder by civil war, and the "little flock" that arose from the Millerite disappointment would officially make Battle Creek its headquarters, taking the name "Seventh-day Adventist" (1860).

Major Autobiographical and Biographical Studies Relating to Ellen G. White

Autobiographical Accounts

The earliest biographical account of Ellen White is her own introductory article entitled "Experience and Views," appearing in the July 21, 1851, *Second Advent Review and Sabbath Herald, Extra*, and reprinted the next month in her first book, *A Sketch of the Christian Experience and Views of Ellen G. White* (Saratoga Springs, N.Y.: James White, 1851), pp. 3-9. It begins with her conversion experience and introduction to Millerism, and then describes the receiving and sharing of her first visions up to 1846.

Apart from ongoing reports of meetings and travels in the *Review,* Ellen White's first extended autobiography was published in 1860 as *Spiritual Gifts [vol. 2]. My Christian Experience, Views and Labors in Connection With the Rise and Progress of the Third Angel's Message* (Battle Creek, Mich.: James White, 1860). It consisted of 299 pages (expanded to 304 pages after its first printing), including four pages of "testimonies" from persons attesting to the accuracy of her account. Manuscripts 9 and 10, 1859 [c. 1859], included in this volume, are believed to be part of Ellen White's draft documents for this account.

Between January 6 and May 11, 1876, a 15-part series appeared in the *Signs of the Times* periodical, entitled "Mrs. Ellen G. White: Her Life, Christian Experience, and Labors." Edited by her husband, James, the series was drawn from the *Spiritual Gifts* account, but with editorial variations and some expansion. Four years later saw the publication of *Life Sketches. Ancestry, Early Life, Christian Experience, and Extensive Labors, of Elder James White, and His Wife, Mrs. Ellen G. White* (Battle Creek, Mich.: Steam Press, 1880), again drawn from *Spiritual Gifts [vol. 2],* with yet additional editorial revisions. *Life Sketches* was reprinted and expanded in 1888 (Battle Creek, Mich.: Steam Press, 1888), with only minor changes in Ellen White's account.

In 1885, when the first 30 *Testimonies for the Church* were reprinted as four numbered volumes, volume 1 opened with an autobiographical sketch (pp. 9-112) that took the reader from Ellen White's birth in 1827 to the death of James in 1881 (*Testimonies for the Church* [Oakland, Calif.: Pacific Press, 1885], vol. 1). It served as a primary source—along with the *Spiritual Gifts* (1860) and *Life Sketches* (1880, 1888) accounts—for the narrative published shortly after her death in 1915 by members of her office staff, entitled *Life*

Sketches of Ellen G. White (Mountain View, Calif.: Pacific Press, 1915). The working manuscript for *Life Sketches* also incorporated material gathered from interviews with Ellen White during the closing years of her life (see "Life Sketches" manuscript on www.egwwritings.org).

One further narrative—the last formal autobiographical account undertaken by Ellen White—may be found in *Historical Sketches of the Foreign Missions of the Seventh-day Adventists* (Basel, Switz.: Imprimerie Polyglotte, 1886), pp. 159-249. As the title suggests, the pages record "Notes of Travel" by Ellen White during the first part of her two-year visit to Europe in 1885-1887.

Major Biographical Works

The most comprehensive biography of Ellen White to date is the six-volume series entitled *Ellen G. White,* by Arthur L. White (Hagerstown, Md.: Review and Herald, 1981-1986). The author, Ellen White's grandson, published its last two volumes first (covering the years 1900-1915), because of his interest in interviewing persons still living who knew Ellen White and because issues occurring in the church at the beginning of the twentieth century had "particular relevance to the church at present." In 2000 a one-volume abridgment of the six volumes was published as *Ellen White: Woman of Vision* (Hagerstown, Md.: Review and Herald, 1982, 2000).

Other volumes treat Ellen White's life with narrower focus. Her two years in Europe are chronicled in D. A. Delafield's *Ellen G. White in Europe: 1885-1887* (Washington, D.C.: Review and Herald, 1975). Eleven symposium papers presented on the occasion of the centennial of her European visit are collected in *Ellen G. White and Europe: 1885/1887* (Bracknell, Berkshire, England: Newbold College, 1987).

Dudley M. Canright, a contemporary of Ellen White and a former Seventh-day Adventist, published a critique of her life soon after her death that still forms the basis for the majority of modern criticisms, entitled *Life of Mrs. E. G. White: Seventh-day Adventist Prophet, Her False Claims Refuted* (Cincinnati: Standard Pub. Co., 1919). (For Adventist responses, see F. D. Nichol, *Ellen G. White and Her Critics* [Washington, D.C.: Review and Herald, 1951] and Jud Lake, *Ellen White Under Fire* [Nampa, Idaho: Pacific Press, 2010]).

Ronald L. Numbers examined Ellen White's life from the perspective of her role as health reformer in *Prophetess of Health: A Study of Ellen G. White,* third ed. (Grand Rapids: William B. Eerdmans, 2008). The Ellen G. White Estate prepared a response entitled "A Critique of the Book *Prophetess of Health*" (Takoma Park, Md.: Ellen G. White Estate, 1976, 2008) (www.whiteestate.org/issues/Prophetess-of-Health.pdf).

Two of George R. Knight's four introductory volumes on Ellen White deal primarily with biographical history: *Meeting Ellen White* (Hagerstown, Md.:

Review and Herald, 1996) and *Walking With Ellen White* (Hagerstown, Md.: Review and Herald, 1999). A third volume in the series, *Ellen White's World* (Hagerstown, Md.: Review and Herald, 1998), looks at the historical times in which Ellen White lived, as does *The World of Ellen G. White* (Hagerstown, Md.: Review and Herald, 1987), edited by Gary Land.

Herbert E. Douglass's *Messenger of the Lord* (Nampa, Idaho: Pacific Press, 1998), though not a biography, is still the most comprehensive work covering her life, works, and message.

Notable Encyclopedia Articles and Specialized Studies

Extensive biographical articles may be found in the *Seventh-day Adventist Encyclopedia* (Don F. Neufeld, ed., rev. ed. [Hagerstown, Md.: Review and Herald, 1996], 2 vols.), s.v. "White, Ellen Gould (Harmon)," and in the *Ellen G. White Encyclopedia* (Denis Fortin and Jerry Moon, eds. [Hagerstown, Md.: Review and Herald, 2013]).

For specialized studies regarding more focused topics related to Ellen White's life, the reader is referred to the numerous dissertations, theses, and research papers cited within the annotation footnotes.

---

[1] This article presents only an introductory overview of Ellen White's earliest years—up to 1859. For broader biographical accounts, the reader is referred to the selected works described at the end of this article and in this volume's general bibliography.

[2] Ellen G. White, *Spiritual Gifts [vol. 2]*, p. 9.

[3] *Idem, Testimonies for the Church,* vol. 1, p. 34.

[4] *Idem, Spiritual Gifts [vol. 2]*, p. 30.

[5] Examples include Ellen's picking up a large family Bible weighing 18.5 pounds (8.4 kilograms) and holding it on her outstretched left arm for 20 to 30 minutes. See J. N. Loughborough, *Rise and Progress of the Seventh-day Adventists,* pp. 103, 104.

[6] www.whiteestate.org/issues/faq-egw.html#faq-section-a3

[7] E. G. White, *Spiritual Gifts [vol. 2]*, p. 31.

[8] *Ibid.*, p. 36.

[9] *Ibid.*, pp. 38-49, 67-79.

[10] By 1880 she reported having "crossed the plains fifteen times" ("Incidents by the Way," *Review,* June 17, 1880, p. 386).

[11] James White recalled that she was still 16 years of age when he first met her in Portland, Maine. Ellen White, on the other hand, dated her introduction to James White to early 1845 in Orrington, Maine.

[12] James White and Ellen G. White, *Life Sketches* (1880), p. 126.

[13] E. G. White, *Spiritual Gifts [vol. 2]*, p. 60.

[14] *Day-Star,* Jan. 24, 1846, pp. 31, 32.

[15] *Ibid.*, p. 32. In March Jacobs published a second letter from Ellen—this time one that she specifically requested he print in order to give readers a more complete record "of what God has revealed to me" (*Day-Star,* Mar. 14, 1846, pp. 21, 22). The letter is dated Feb. 15, 1846.

[16] Three broadsides containing her visions are known and included in this collection under the dates of Apr. 6, 1846, Apr. 7, 1847, and Jan. 31, 1849.

[17] Reprinted in 1882 with minor editorial revisions and published since as part of *Early Writings* (Hagerstown, Md.: Review and Herald, 2000).

[18] A term used to refer to "a communication of counsel and instruction given by Ellen

G. White, either orally or in writing, to an individual, to a congregation, or to Seventh-day Adventists in general" (SDAE, s.v. "Testimony").

[19] James White, "A Brief Sketch of the Past" and "The Paper," *Review,* May 6, 1852, pp. 5, 8.

[20] See E. G. White, *Spiritual Gifts [vol. 2],* pp. 211, 212.

[21] *Ibid.,* pp. 87, 88.

[22] *Ibid.,* p. 89.

[23] James White, "Western Tour," *Review,* Nov. 8, 1870, p. 165.

[24] See Ellen G. White, Ms 1, 1854 (Feb. 12) and Ms 2, 1858 (Dec. 27).

[25] E. G. White, *Spiritual Gifts [vol 2],* pp. 160, 161.

[26] Ellen G. White, *Supplement to the Christian Experience and Views of Ellen G. White,* pp. 15-23.

[27] *Idem, Spiritual Gifts [vol. 2],* p. 197.

[28] "General Conference," *Review,* Oct. 16, 1855, p. 64.

[29] Joseph Bates, J. H. Waggoner, M. E. Cornell, "Address of the Conference Assembled at Battle Creek, Mich., Nov. 16th, 1855," *Review,* Dec. 4, 1855, p. 78.

[30] *Ibid.,* pp. 78, 79.

[31] Ellen G. White, Ms 6, 1859 (June 7 entry).

KEY DATES IN ELLEN G. WHITE'S LIFE (1827-1859)

1827, November 26	Ellen White born at Gorham, Maine; moved to Portland, Maine, at early age
1836, late	Accident in Portland, Maine
1840, March	First heard William Miller present the Advent message in Portland, Maine
1840, September	Conversion at Methodist camp meeting in Buxton, Maine
1842, June	William Miller's second preaching series in Portland, Maine
1842, June 26	Baptized into the Methodist Church
1842, September	James White began preaching
1843, September	Disfellowshipped from the Methodist Church
1844, October 22	Great Disappointment
1844, December	First vision (Portland, Maine)
1845, February	"Bridegroom" vision regarding the heavenly sanctuary
1845, spring	"New Earth" vision supporting a literal, visual Second Advent and new earth
1845, spring	Met James White
1845, spring/summer	Relates visions at meetings in Maine, New Hampshire, and Vermont
1845, August	First traveled to Massachusetts
1845, autumn	Longest recorded vision (four hours), at Randolph, Massachusetts
1845, October	"Time of Trouble" vision at Carver, Massachusetts, rejecting time setting
1846, January 24	First vision published in the *Day-Star*
1846, April 6	First "broadside" publication of visions
1846, August 30	Married James White
1846, autumn	James and Ellen White began observance of the seventh-day Sabbath
1847-1848	Resided at Topsham, Maine, with the Howland family
1847, April 3	Vision of the Sabbath's special significance
1847, May 30	James White published *A Word to the "Little Flock"*
1847, August 26	Birth of first son, Henry Nichols
1848, April 20-24	First attended conference of Sabbathkeeping Adventists at Rocky Hill, Connecticut

1848, autumn	Vision regarding the health dangers of tobacco, tea, and coffee
1848, November 18	Vision to begin publishing work
1849, July	First of 11 numbers of *The Present Truth,* published in Middletown, Connecticut
1849, July 28	Birth of second son, James Edson
1849, December 20	William Miller dies
1850, August 24	Vision regarding mysterious "rappings" (spiritualism) and "church order"
1850, November	First number of the *Second Advent Review and Sabbath Herald* published
1851, August	First book published, *A Sketch of the Christian Experience and Views of Ellen G. White*
1852, April	Moved to Rochester, New York
1852, August	First number of the *Youth's Instructor* published
1853	First Sabbath school organized
1853, February 5	Robert Harmon (Ellen White's brother) died
1853, May 6	Nathaniel White (James White's brother) died
1853, late	Offshoot *Messenger* Party formed (continued until about 1857)
1854, January	*Supplement to the Christian Experience and Views of Ellen G. White* published
1854, February 12	Second "health vision" on cleanliness, temperance, and rich foods
1854, August 29	Birth of third son, William Clarence
1854, November 20	Anna White (James White's sister) died
1855, November	Moved to Battle Creek, Michigan
1855, November 16-19	"General Conference" at Battle Creek, Michigan. Affirmation of Ellen White's visions. Sabbatarian Adventists begin to keep Sabbaths at sundown instead of 6:00 p.m.
1855, December	*Testimony for the Church,* no. 1, published
1856, spring	Moved into Wood Street home in Battle Creek, Michigan
1856, August 21	*Testimony for the Church,* no. 2, announced
1856, October	"Laodicean message" applied to the lukewarm spiritual state of the church
1856, December	Whites crossed half-frozen Mississippi River to reclaim discouraged ministers in Waukon, Iowa
1857, April 30	*Testimony for the Church,* no. 3, announced
1857, May/June	Traveled east to meetings in New York and New England

1857, November 19	*Testimony for the Church,* no. 4, announced
1858, March 14	"Great Controversy" vision at Lovett's Grove, Ohio
1858, September 9	*Spiritual Gifts,* vol. 1, announced
1858, September-November	Traveled east to meetings in Ohio, New York, and New England
1859, June	Systematic Benevolence plan officially began
1859, June 16	*Testimony for the Church,* no. 5, announced
1859, August-November	Traveled east to meetings in New York and New England

THE LITERARY RELATIONSHIP BETWEEN ELLEN WHITE'S PUBLISHED AND UNPUBLISHED WORKS

Tim Poirier

The Unpublished Collection

In 1899 Ellen White's son William, referring to his mother's writings, reported to Adventist educator P. T. Magan, "About four years ago the word came to her [Ellen White], 'Gather up the fragments, let nothing be lost,' and this has been repeated many times since."[1] The Ellen G. White Estate is fortunate to have the many letters and manuscripts of Ellen White that it does, mainly the result of her foresight and diligence in preserving her writings years before receiving that special instruction in 1895. By the time of her death, in addition to her books and published articles, Ellen White left as a part of her literary estate more than 3,000 letters and 5,000 manuscripts—some in untranscribed handwritten form—aggregating approximately 50,000 typewritten pages.

While the entire collection is commonly referred to as the "manuscript file," Ellen White specifically referred to her sermons, articles, transcribed interviews, and diaries as "manuscripts," distinguishing them in her file from "letters," which were specifically addressed to individuals, churches, or other groups.

Most of the documents in the file were typed by Ellen White's secretaries from her handwritten drafts. But typewriters (calligraphs) did not come into use by her assistants until 1885. Referring to material that Ellen White was preparing for church leaders in 1882, Arthur L. White wrote: "When these testimonies were written, typewriters and carbon paper had not come into common use. Each document had to be painstakingly copied by hand. If several copies were needed, it was a most forbidding task. The only alternative was to set the matter in type and run off copies on the press."[2]

Under these conditions it is not surprising that in the decades preceding the 1880s often the only copy of a letter would be sent to the addressee, and, unless preserved by the recipient, would be lost to posterity. Writing to readers of the *Review* in 1867, Ellen White referred to "hundreds of letters" and "thousands of pages" of personal testimonies that she had written during the previous two years.[3] Less than 20 such documents are extant.

Tim Poirier, M.T.S., is vice director and archivist of the Ellen G. White Estate.

Relationship to Published Works

Many of the documents in the manuscript file were edited and published by Ellen White and her literary assistants in denominational periodicals, pamphlets, or such books as the nine-volume *Testimonies for the Church.* Others deal with matters of personal or local application, with approximately one fourth of the letters being addressed to family members. As they typically contain no instruction for the church generally, they have largely remained unpublished in book form up to this time, except as cited in biographical or historical works.

Since Ellen White's death in 1915, more than 85 books have been published by her estate, drawing from her published and previously unpublished materials. Ellen White designated this responsibility to her estate in her last will and testament. In addition to topical compilations, 21 volumes of *Manuscript Releases* and two volumes of *Sermons and Talks* have been published, drawn entirely from the manuscript file. These volumes have made available thousands of pages from Ellen White's letters and manuscripts that supplement what she published in her lifetime. This present series, however, is the first effort to publish systematically all of Ellen White's correspondence and manuscripts in chronological order and with annotations.

The Preparation of Books and Articles From Original Manuscripts

Ellen White relied upon trusted editorial assistants, working under her direction, to take what she wrote out by hand and prepare it for publication. Her son W. C. White explained that they were "entrusted with the work of correcting grammatical errors, of eliminating unnecessary repetition, and of grouping paragraphs and sections in their best order." Further, he wrote that her most experienced workers "are authorized to take a sentence, paragraph, or section, from one manuscript where the thought was clearly and fully expressed, and incorporate it with another manuscript, where the same thought was expressed but not so clearly."[4]

Similarly, Ellen White herself described how her editorial assistants made use of her letters and manuscripts in preparing chapters for new publications: "Marian [Davis] greedily grasps every letter I write to others in order to find sentences that she can use in the life of Christ [*The Desire of Ages*].[5]

"She does her work in this way: She takes my articles which are published in the papers, and pastes them in blank books. She also has a copy of all the letters I write. In preparing a chapter for a book, Marian remembers that I have written something on that special point, which may make the matter more forcible. She begins to search for this, and if when she finds it, she sees that it will make the chapter more clear, she adds it.

"The books are not Marian's productions, but my own, gathered from all my writings. Marian has a large field from which to draw, and her ability to arrange the matter is of great value to me. It saves my poring over a mass of matter, which I have no time to do."[6]

In such a process Ellen White's published works reflect the editorial modifications made by her secretaries working under her direction. While some might consider Ellen White's original unpublished drafts to be the most reliable indicators of her thought, the fact that she was engaged throughout the editorial process suggests that later published versions may, in fact, more accurately convey what she wished to express.

One area in which the reader will notice significant differences between the published and unpublished works relates to private and personal communications. Ellen White recognized that sensitive counsel first given to specific individuals or groups often contained principles of value to a wider audience. Much of the material she published in *Testimonies for the Church* traces to personal "testimonies," but with original names and places removed. Changed circumstances might also result in entire sentences or paragraphs added or omitted when reusing a particular letter or manuscript.[7]

Occasionally one will find more than one copy of an Ellen White letter or manuscript in which there are textual differences. These are designated in this series as "variants." In some instances Ellen White prepared a modified version for specific purposes, while others appear to have resulted from the multiple recopying of documents for which the originals are not extant.

Summary

Ellen White was not only called to receive instruction inspired by the Holy Spirit, but was also charged with the task of writing out those messages for the benefit of others. As with any modern author, there is a developmental process that occurs between first putting one's pen to the paper (or one's fingers to the keyboard) and the final desired product. She not only labored to find appropriate human language to describe heavenly things, but also struggled over how best to word a much-needed, divinely inspired rebuke.

Her prophetic calling, however, did not dismiss her day-to-day commitments as a wife, mother, and friend. She was anxious to keep up with the latest news from home (and abroad), enjoying the vital link that correspondence provides in keeping us closely knit in the human family. Both of these dimensions are remarkably preserved in the letters and manuscripts presented in this series.

---

[1] W. C. White to P. T. Magan, May 23, 1899, cited in Arthur L. White, *Ellen G. White: The Australian Years,* p. 451.

[2] Arthur L. White, *Ellen G. White: The Lonely Years,* p. 201.

[3] Ellen G. White, "Questions and Answers," *Review,* Oct. 8, 1867, p. 261.

[4] W. C. White to G. A. Irwin, May 7, 1900. For illustrations of the type of editorial work described by W. C. White, see Tim Poirier, "Exhibits Regarding the Work of Ellen White's Literary Assistants"; James R. Nix, "From Vision to Printed Page."

[5] Ellen G. White, Lt 46a, 1894 (Oct. 25), in *idem, Selected Messages,* book 3, p. 117.

[6] *Idem,* Lt 61a, 1900 (Apr. 23), in *idem, Selected Messages,* book 3, p. 91.

[7] See example of page proofs for *Testimonies for the Church,* vol. 7, pp. 235-239, in DF 194-d.

INTERPRETING ELLEN G. WHITE'S LETTERS AND MANUSCRIPTS

Alberto R. Timm

Ellen G. White was among the most prolific writers of her time. Her classic works have been translated into many languages, reaching an impressive worldwide circulation. Such books tend to deal with universal principles, applicable everywhere and easily understood by the general Christian reader. But when one moves from these books into Ellen White's personal correspondence, the reader encounters particulars of time and place that are foreign to the world we live in today.

Therefore, those unaccustomed to reading such material will find the following insights helpful for interpreting Ellen White's letters and manuscripts, including special attention to their thematic scope and focus, inspiration and authority, context, and practical application.

Thematic Scope and Focus

Ellen White wrote on almost every major area of the Christian life in a challenging world. But the level of importance given to that vast variety of information depends largely on the perspective from which one looks at it. If one looks beyond the mere technical matters and personal concerns addressed in some of the letters, the reader will discover an endless mine of faith-uplifting statements. Her enduring burden—the overriding focus of her life ministry—was to draw people closer to Christ, in whom all her writings centered.

Yet Ellen White's letters dealing with everyday matters are helpful in providing a context to better understand the world in which she lived and carried on her prophetic ministry. By reading Arthur L. White's six volumes titled *Ellen G. White,*[1] one is able to build a historical framework for most of the issues she faced during her lifetime. And by consulting her letters and manuscripts, the reader can often obtain a deeper and more accurate perception of the complexity of the issues, the people involved, and how she reacted to those issues. Furthermore, in dealing with such a variety of issues, she exemplified how to apply religious principles in order to overcome the personal problems of daily life.

Alberto R. Timm, Ph.D., is an associate director at the Ellen G. White Estate.

Inspiration and Authority

The question naturally arises as to whether we should recognize the same inspiration and authority in Ellen White's letters and manuscripts as we do in her published books and articles. Some draw an artificial distinction in authority between prophetic writings that derive from visions and prophetic dreams, and those personal testimonies or counsels making no direct appeal to divine revelation.

Uriah Smith proposed this idea in a letter he wrote in 1883 to D. M. Canright suggesting that the writings of Ellen White comprise both the truly inspired "visions" and the noninspired "testimonies."[2] A century later George E. Rice, in his book *Luke, a Plagiarist?* demonstrated that the Gospel of Luke is a clear example of an inspired book that came into existence through human "research" (reading and oral interviews), under the guidance of the Holy Spirit, but without any known supernatural revelations (prophetic visions and dreams).[3]

Consequently, the above-mentioned distinction does not imply artificial degrees of inspiration within the prophetic writings. The mere fact that an item belongs to the literary category of personal correspondence does not necessarily lower its inspiration and authority. In his book *Messenger of the Lord* Herbert E. Douglass points out that the notion of inspired personal letters derives from the New Testament canon itself. He writes, "Letters to congregations and individuals was the most common method used by New Testament writers. Some of the letters were private; others were meant to be read publicly. It seems most probable that Paul never thought that his letters to Philemon, Timothy, and Titus would become public. But we are all thankful that they did. In these letters we see a mix of common matters with obviously spiritual counsel and instruction. These New Testament letters help us understand better how to relate to Ellen White's many letters that often were private and frequently mixed the common with the sacred.

"If the Lord permitted Paul's private letters to be included in the canon for universal distribution, it would be appropriate to believe that the letters of His modern prophet might also bring encouragement and corrective counsel to those who do not have the benefit of her personal ministry."[4]

However, the reader should recognize that there were also many occasions in which Ellen White addressed "common" subjects with no expectation that the recipients should think she received divine instruction regarding them. Elaborating on this point, she wrote: "But there are times when common things must be stated, common thoughts must occupy the mind, common letters must be written and information given that has passed from one to another of the workers. Such words, such information, are not given under the special inspiration of the Spirit of God. Questions are asked at times that are not upon religious subjects at all, and these questions must be answered.

We converse about houses and lands, trades to be made, and locations for our institutions, their advantages and disadvantages."[5]

Ellen White's statement suggests that it is more the nature of the subject addressed than the literary category of the writing that should guide us on the matter of inspiration and authority. The challenge is that it is not always easy to identify when she dealt with common matters from a noninspired perspective and when she addressed them in an inspired way.

In reality, it is much easier to acknowledge in general terms the existence of noninspired elements than to identify them on a practical level. Only another genuine prophet could handle this task in a trustworthy way. But since none of the canonical prophets ever tried to make such a distinction within the writings of other prophets, it seems evident that such a distinction is not critical for accepting and understanding the essence of Ellen White's prophetic messages.

Fortunately, in most instances Ellen White made it clear when she intended her words to be taken as conveying divine instruction. This is illustrated in a letter she wrote to her son William that began with observations about the weather: "My dear son: This is one of the coldest mornings we have had this winter. The ground is white with frost, and we can hardly keep warm, even with our fireplace packed with long, heavy chunks."

She continued in the first few paragraphs to describe her bookmaking activities, then on page 2 the letter took a different turn: "The light given me now by the Lord is that we are to be careful not to spend our precious time and money unwisely. Many things may suit our fancy; but we are to guard against the expenditure of money for that which is not bread. We shall need much means to advance the work decidedly in our cities. Everyone is to have a part to act in the Lord's work. Parents are to instruct their children in lessons of economy, in order that the younger members of the flock may learn to share the responsibility of supporting the cause of God at this time."[6]

Here we find a clear claim to divine revelation, yet embedded within what at first appears to be a "common" letter. Rather than being an exception, this is what the reader of Ellen White's letters and manuscripts will find again and again throughout her correspondence.

Once we realize that inspiration may be at work in Ellen White's letters and manuscripts as fully as in her published writings, it is important also to understand that inspiration is a supernatural and multifaceted divine assistance that gives to the prophetic writings a trustworthy nature. Not only "the wholistic scope of inspiration" but also the "overall thematic interrelationship" of her writings makes it almost impossible for someone to speak of them "in dichotomous terms as being reliable in some topics and not in others."[7]

This is not to say that in those writings one will not find "orthographical or grammatical mistakes, as well as other kinds of language imperfections such as *lapsus linguae* (a slip of the tongue) or *lapsus memoriae* (a slip of the memory)." But the Holy Spirit was "in control of the inspired message" and always corrected her "in matters important to the church."[8]

Priority Given to Books Published During Ellen White's Lifetime

Even though we might make no distinction between a private letter written under inspiration and one of Ellen White's published articles or books, it is important to recognize that she gave greater editorial attention to material that went into print. What was first written hastily, or in an undeveloped manner, she could refine, clarify, or further expand so that the reader might avoid misunderstanding or misapplying the message. For this reason, when we encounter potentially problematic passages in the writings or teachings of Ellen White, it is her *published* works—specifically those published by her in her lifetime—that we should considered as conveying her views most fully and accurately.

Regarding the authority of Ellen White's prophetic writings, Seventh-day Adventists have understood them as having the same authority that the writings of the noncanonical Bible prophets had for their time. The Bible refers to a number of prophets such as Nathan (1 Chron. 29:29), Huldah (2 Chron. 34:22), Iddo (2 Chron. 9:29), and Agabus (Acts 11:27, 28), some of whom wrote books that Scripture mentions. These prophets communicated divine messages, but their writings (if they wrote) did not become a part of the biblical canon.

Ellen White recognized and taught that the canon of Scripture—those writings that constitute the rule of faith and practice for God's people—is closed.[9] Though she was inspired by the same Holy Spirit who inspired the biblical prophets, her ministry differs in regard to its *purpose* and *scope*. Seventh-day Adventists "do not believe that the writings of Ellen White are an addition to the canon of Sacred Scripture."[10]

Context

When we read Ellen White's letters and manuscripts, it is critical to understand correctly both the *authorial* context and the *original reader's* context of those documents. By authorial context we mean the specific circumstances in which she was living while she penned her messages, with special attention to the interrelationship between the geographical setting, the moment in time, the social-cultural milieu, and the conditions in the church, as well as her own state of health and emotional conditions.

While most of Ellen White's prophetic ministry took place in the United States of America (1844-1885, 1887-1891, 1900-1915), she spent two years in Europe (1885-1887) and almost a decade in Australia (1891-1900), traveling extensively in those places. Most of the time she was surrounded by receptive people, but there were also occasions in which she met strong opposition while rebuking error. Sometimes she was in good health and of good courage; other times she faced health problems. She experienced the grief of losing two sons (1860, 1863) and her own husband (1881) in death. Her personal feelings on such a variety of circumstances showed up in her more personal writings to close friends.

There are two major categories of works that help in understanding the circumstances in which Ellen White penned many of her personal writings.[11] The first category includes her own autobiographical works that provide more specific insights into her daily life and the people with whom she interacted across time. Among those works are *Spiritual Gifts,* volume 2; her later "Biographical Sketch" published in *Testimonies for the Church,* volume 1, pages 9-112; and *Life Sketches. Ancestry, Early Life, Christian Experience, and Extensive Labors of Elder James White, and His Wife, Mrs. Ellen G. White.* Much of the content of these three sources was included in her final and more complete autobiographical work titled *Life Sketches of Ellen G. White.* But her most comprehensive biography is undoubtedly Arthur L. White's six-volume set titled *Ellen G. White.*[12] An abridged version is titled *Ellen White: Woman of Vision.* A more specific study covering the time she spent in Europe (1885-1887) was provided by D. A. Delafield in his *Ellen G. White in Europe.*

Another category of helpful works is comprised of the more general studies that describe the larger scenario in which Ellen White carried on her prophetic ministry. Two of the most insightful works about the specific times in the United States in which she lived are *The World of Ellen G. White,* edited by Gary Land, and George R. Knight's *Ellen White's World.* Additional background can be found in Otto L. Bettmann's *The Good Old Days—They Were Terrible!* and Timothy L. Smith's *Revivalism and Social Reform.* The medical practices of those days are well described in Richard A. Schaefer's *Legacy: Daring to Care,* and D. E. Robinson's *Story of Our Health Message.*

Beyond the authorial context of Ellen White as a writer, it is important to understand the contexts of the original readers to whom her letters and manuscripts were addressed. Since many of those writings were sent to unfamiliar places and even to other countries, it is advantageous to seek some knowledge of what was going on in those places. But to reconstruct such a variety of scattered contexts is not an easy task. One of the most helpful resources in this attempt is Arthur L. White's already-mentioned six-volume set *Ellen G. White.*[13]

Even when a full picture of the original reader's context is not available, the student of Ellen White's correspondence should seek at least some knowledge about the person to whom she sent her message. A good starting point is the second revised edition of the *Seventh-day Adventist Encyclopedia.* An even more specific and detailed source of information is the *Ellen G. White Encyclopedia.* The annotations in the present published volume of her letters and manuscripts are also intended to aid in the task of learning the original reader's context.

Interpretation

After first considering the thematic scope and focus, inspiration and authority, and context of Ellen White's letters and manuscripts, the reader is better prepared to move into the interpretation process. Many helpful principles for interpreting Ellen White's writings are found in George R. Knight's *Reading Ellen White.* Herbert E. Douglass's *Messenger of the Lord*[14] provides additional insights. It is instructive to highlight here a few of those principles that can provide a starting point for interpreting her letters and manuscripts.

The reader should be aware of at least three basic levels of interpretation and their respective sets of principles. One is the *historical* level, in which the specific historical context of the document being studied is reconstructed, with special emphasis on the time, place, and circumstances in which it was produced.

Closely related to this level is the context discovery mentioned above, including the recognition of the personal characteristics of those to whom the document was originally sent. Such historical reconstruction should provide a trustworthy hermeneutical framework in which the reader can distinguish between those elements that are time-conditioned (the particulars of time and place) and those that are applicable to all times and places (universal principles).[15] While contextual studies help to identify particulars of time and place, comparative studies between Ellen White's writings and the Scriptures help to identify universal principles in her writings.

Another basic level of interpretation is *grammatical,* which seeks the correct understanding of the language used in the document under study. Some expressions might carry a uniquely Adventist sense that differs from their most common use. Other terms have changed in meaning over time and mean something today that is quite different from the meaning in Ellen White's day. But usually the literary context itself helps to make clear the likely meaning of the words within the text that is being studied. To avoid imposing artificial meanings on the documents, the reader should define as precisely as possible what the text actually says and what it does not say.

A third hermeneutical level is the *thematic* interpretation. Ellen White's letters are best understood by comparing them with the correspondence to which she was responding. Unfortunately, much of that correspondence is not extant or easily available today. However, in her own letters, she often mentioned the issue to which she was responding.

Additional insights might be found in earlier and later letters she sent to the same person, or even to other people with whom she corresponded about the matter. Furthermore, the reader should be sure that the interpretation of the specific statement is in harmony with the clear teachings of Ellen White's other statements about the same subject. The teaching of the given statement should be kept in balance with correlated themes found in Ellen White's other writings.

Some might suppose that the more Ellen White wrote about a given subject, the more importance we should give to that subject within the overall scope of her writings. As a general rule, one could assume that she wrote more about her favorite topics than about peripheral ones.[16] However, as a prophet, sometimes she had to deal persistently with unbiblical theories (such as pantheism) because of the unwillingness of some people to give them up. Therefore, the reader should not oversimplify the interpretation of Ellen White's writings by suggesting an artificial hierarchy of importance based merely on the amount of time and space she spent on each of the various topics she addressed.

Practical Application

After reconstructing the original context of Ellen White's personal writings and trying to understand what they meant to the original readers, one is better prepared to make a practical application of the message of those writings to the life of the modern reader. But the task of transposing a nineteenth- and early-twentieth-century prophetic message into a twenty-first-century culture has polarized interpreters.

Some, using a *traditionalistic* approach, impose upon the current generation ancient particulars of time and place, making them universal principles. Others, using a *culturalistic* approach, discard universal principles along with the ancient particulars of time and place. Both extremes end up confusing laws, rules, principles, and counsels within the inspired writings.

While traditionalists tend to elevate counsels objectively to the same level as laws and commandments, culturalists tend to lower laws and commandments subjectively to the same level as counsels. To avoid those extremes, one should seek to discern the universal principles that lie behind and support the particulars of time and place.

A classic example of this is found in Ellen White's counsel that girls should "learn to harness and drive a horse" in order to be "better fitted to meet the emergencies of life."[17] A traditionalist would simply overlook any change of context and argue straightforward that since Ellen White stated it at one time, *all* girls of *all* times and places should "learn to harness and drive a horse." On the other hand, a culturalist would assume that since our transportation modes today differ significantly from those in Ellen White's day, her statement should just be disregarded as outdated and senseless.

By contrast, a balanced interpreter would not only acknowledge the modernization of transportation but also ask, "Is there any significant universal principle behind her counsel?" The most natural conclusion would be that girls should learn how to operate the most common transportation means available today. In some places of the world those resources might still be horses, donkeys, or camels, but in others they have been replaced over the years by bicycles, motorcycles, cars, helicopters, and airplanes. It does not matter what kind of device is being used—the basic principle is that girls should be prepared to meet "the emergencies of life," even in matters of transportation.

There is the danger, however, of deriving empty "principles" out of statements that already carry concrete principles previously defined within Scripture in an unchangeable form. For example, from the fourth commandment of the Decalogue (Ex. 20:8-11) one might be tempted to draw the principle that human beings should merely keep one day of the week, but the commandment itself specifies this day as the seventh day of week (verse 10). Therefore, it would not be appropriate to interpret the principle as being merely the choice of any day of the week as the Sabbath.

Furthermore, there are also symbols of religious loyalty that have to be respected even when there is no evident reason for their selection. An example is the command to refrain from eating of the tree of knowledge of good and evil (Gen. 2:15-17), when there was apparently nothing dangerous about the fruit itself (cf. Gen. 3:6). These few examples illustrate the basic principle that divine commandments take precedence over, and even define, how principles are applied.

The reader should also not allow literary and hermeneutical technicalities to take the place of personal commitment to the inspired message. In Ellen White's writings one will find abundant advice and encouragement, warnings, and words of hope. Many of the counsels deal with real circumstances of daily life, such as marital relations, educating children, and living healthfully. The reader should take advantage of the counsels provided by not confining their message merely to their original setting, but also allowing them to speak to our present circumstances.

Summary and Conclusions

A careful study of Ellen White's letters and manuscripts will pay special attention to their thematic scope and focus, inspiration and authority, context, interpretation, and practical application. While covering a broad thematic scope, they continually uplift Christ and His atoning work. From the perspective of divine authorship, her prophetic writings bear the same authority as the noncanonical biblical prophets, but from the perspective of practical function, they are "a lesser light to lead men and women to the greater light"[18] of the Bible. Basic for their interpretation is the understanding of both the authorial contexts and the original readers' contexts. The interpretation should take into consideration the historical, grammatical, and thematic levels. Yet the whole hermeneutical process should culminate in an adequate practical application of those writings in the daily life of the reader.

Within this treasure of counsel and instruction from Ellen White's personal writings the reader will find principles related to almost every circumstance in life. While time has changed life in form, it has not changed in essence. All human beings continue to be sinners in need of the saving grace of God. Therefore, the reader should see this wonderful collection as a valuable tool to help "make Christ first and last and best in everything."[19]

---

[1] Each volume bears a specific title qualifying the respective period of time covered by it, as follows: volume 1: *The Early Years,* 1827-1862; volume 2: *The Progressive Years,* 1862-1876; volume 3: *The Lonely Years,* 1876-1891; volume 4: *The Australian Years,* 1891-1900; volume 5: *The Early Elmshaven Years,* 1900-1905; volume 6: *The Later Elmshaven Years,* 1905-1915.

[2] [Uriah] Smith to [D. M.] Canright, Aug. 7, 1883.

[3] George E. Rice, *Luke, a Plagiarist?* pp. 11, 25.

[4] Herbert E. Douglass, *Messenger of the Lord,* pp. 413, 414.

[5] Ellen G. White, *Selected Messages,* book 1, p. 39.

[6] Ellen G. White to W. C. White, Lt 4, 1911 (Feb. 15), in *Child Guidance,* p. 134.

[7] Alberto R. Timm, "Understanding Inspiration: The Symphonic and Wholistic Nature of Scripture," *Ministry,* August 1999, pp. 12-15.

[8] Juan Carlos Viera, "The Dynamics of Inspiration," *Adventist Review,* spec. ed., May 30, 1996, pp. 27, 28. See also Arthur L. White, *The Ellen G. White Writings,* pp. 47, 48; Roger W. Coon, "Inspiration/Revelation: What It Is and How It Works—Part II," *Journal of Adventist Education* 44 (December 1981-January 1982): 18, 19. In commenting on the question of possible errors in sources used by Ellen White in her writings, W. C. White wrote, "I believe that God has given her discernment to use that which is correct and in harmony with truth regarding all matters essential to salvation" (W. C. White to W. W. Eastman, Nov. 4, 1912, quoted in *Selected Messages,* book 3, pp. 449, 450).

[9] Ellen G. White, *The Great Controversy,* pp. vii, viii.

[10] "The Inspiration and Authority of the Ellen G. White Writings," *Ministry,* February 1983, p. 24. See also "Fundamental Beliefs of Seventh-day Adventists, No. 18: The Gift of Prophecy."

[11] Bibliographic information for the titles referred to may be found in the bibliography.

[12] See note 1 above.

[13] See note 1 above.

[14] Douglass, *Messenger of the Lord,* pp. 371-465.

[15] George R. Knight, *Myths in Adventism: An Interpretative Study of Ellen White, Education, and Related Issues* (Hagerstown, Md.: Review and Herald, 1985), p. 23.

[16] Helpful attempts to identify Ellen White's major themes are found in George R. Knight, *Meeting Ellen White: A Fresh Look at Her Life, Writings, and Major Themes* (Hagerstown, Md.: Review and Herald, 1996); Alberto R. Timm, "Ellen G. White: Side Issues or Central Message?" *Journal of the Adventist Theological Society* 7 (Autumn 1996): 168-179.

[17] Ellen G. White, *Education,* pp. 216, 217.

[18] Ellen G. White, "An Open Letter From Mrs. E. G. White to All Who Love the Blessed Hope," *Advent Review and Sabbath Herald,* Jan. 20, 1903, p. 15. An insightful discussion on the "greater light" / "lesser light" analogy is provided in Coon, pp. 21-24.

[19] Ellen G. White, *Testimonies for the Church,* vol. 7, p. 46.

THE "SHUT DOOR" AND ELLEN WHITE'S VISIONS

Merlin D. Burt

Among the earliest and most persistent criticisms of Ellen White is that she was connected to the shut-door teaching during the first years of her prophetic experience. From 1866 (with the first published critics on the shut door) to the present day, the legitimacy of her visions has been repeatedly challenged because of their apparent support of shut-door views after 1844.[1]

The term *shut door* is a biblical expression taken from Matthew 25:10 and Revelation 3:7. It was used by Millerite Adventists to describe the end of human probation during a brief period just prior to the second coming of Jesus. It is important to remember that Ellen White's early experience is inseparably linked to the Millerite movement. Her first vision came in December 1844 as Millerite Adventists were divided over how to interpret the October 1844 disappointment. The majority, under Joshua V. Himes, concluded that the October date was incorrect. They looked for a future date to fulfill the time prophecies of Daniel and Revelation. A minority of disappointed Millerites remained committed to the October 1844 date, concluding that the prophetic time period had been fulfilled.

All of the principal founders of the Seventh-day Adventist Church, including Ellen White, eventually adopted the minority view. The minority group came to be known as shut-door Adventists because they based their initial explanation for the disappointment on the Matthew 25:1-13 parable of the Bridegroom, which they interpreted as a heavenly wedding. Consequently, they may be referred to as Bridegroom Adventists because their initial interpretation of Matthew 25 involved more than just the idea of a shut door.

Key to understanding this topic must be an examination of the progression of shut-door thinking from 1844 to 1852, with particular focus on the Bridegroom branch of the movement and those who became Sabbatarians. Helpful also is an examination of the progression of Ellen White's own understanding, and particularly the role her visions played in changing the meaning of the shut door. Such a study would be incomplete if it did not also briefly consider some implications concerning divine or special revelation in regard to Ellen White's visions and the shut door.

Merlin D. Burt, Ph.D., is director of the Center for Adventist Research and the Ellen G. White Estate Branch Office at Andrews University.

I. SHUT-DOOR VIEWS FROM 1844 TO 1852

To correctly understand Ellen White's perspective on the shut door, we must understand its origin and development between 1844 and the early 1850s among those who later became Sabbatarian Adventists. During those years the shut-door view progressed through five stages: (1) Millerite disappointment view, (2) Bridegroom view, (3) sanctuary view, (4) sealing message view, and (5) theological integration. The theological meaning of the shut door progressively moved through these five stages, from a simple belief that probation had closed for the world to an open-door view based on the Most Holy Place ministry of Jesus in the heavenly sanctuary, requiring an extensive and distinctive evangelistic mission to the world.

Millerite Disappointment View (October 1844 to About January 1845)

The longstanding Millerite pre-1844-disappointment belief on the shut door originated with William Miller. He first published his view in the seventh lecture of his 1836 *Evidence From Scripture.* He referenced the parable of the ten virgins in Matthew 25 and the close of probation language in Revelation 22:11.[2] Millerites generally believed that probation would close for the world just before the second coming of Jesus. In October, soon after Miller accepted the autumn 1844 date for the fulfillment of the 2300 days, he concluded that probation had already closed.[3] Until early in 1845 he continued to believe that "God in His providence has shut the door; we can only stir one another up to be patient. . . . We are living in the time specified by Malachi 3:18, also Daniel 12:10, and Revelation 22:10-13."[4] The last text, "He that is unjust, let him be unjust still: and he which is filthy, let him be filthy still: and he that is righteous, let him be righteous still: and he that is holy, let him be holy still" (verse 11), is a clear reference to the close of probation. Miller held to this view much longer than his closest associate and publicist, Joshua V. Himes. Miller's position undoubtedly gave strength to the shut-door movement and contributed to the schism that developed among Millerites.

By the end of 1844 Himes concluded that the October 1844 date was incorrect and that Millerites needed to again take up their evangelistic work of proclaiming the soon coming of Jesus. It greatly distressed him that Miller, Apollos Hale, and others whom he respected and with whom he worked continued to hold to a shut-door view. Hale, an associate editor of the *Advent Herald*, even joined Joseph Turner in publishing the *Advent Mirror,* a seminal and definitive paper on the shut door that first defined the Bridegroom view.

Joseph Turner was credited by Himes and Isaac Wellcome as being the principal promoter of the shut-door view after the autumn 1844 disappointment.[5] A Millerite minister from Poland, Maine, and most active in Portland, Maine, Turner served for a time as editor of the *Hope of Israel.*[6] In Turner's paper the idea of a pre-Second Advent judgment and sealing was particularly promoted in the months before the autumn 1844 disappointment. This led to his close of probation position.[7] Turner traveled to various places promoting the shut door, convincing Samuel Snow in New York that the door was still shut.[8] Snow had been the principal promoter of the "seventh-month" movement, becoming through the *Jubilee Standard* an important advocate of the shut door. Interestingly, after Ellen Harmon (later White) rejected Turner's proffered sponsorship, he became her greatest antagonist through the fall of 1845 and during 1846.

The Bridegroom View (January 1845 to About January 1847)

Though Bridegroom Adventists inherited William Miller's original position on the shut door, they significantly modified it. By adding post-1844 details to the Matthew 25 parable of the Bridegroom and ten virgins, they explained why Jesus had not come in 1844. Many argued that though their general work for the world was finished, probation was not closed for everyone.

Joseph Turner and Apollos Hale established the baseline shut-door view for Bridegroom Adventists in their January 1845 *Advent Mirror*. They agreed with Miller that "sinners" who had "rejected the truth" could no longer be converted, but they were more specific in defining who "sinners" were. The *Advent Mirror* did not teach that the "door of mercy" was closed for everyone. It specifically allowed that some individuals could be saved, even from outside the Millerite movement—if they had not spurned the light of the Advent message, and were still "subjects of [God's] mercy."[9] In other words, those who were rebellious against God could not be converted, but those who were walking in the light they had received could still be saved. This shut-door view largely defined Bridegroom Adventism during 1845 and 1846. The *Advent Mirror* also may have influenced Miller's view on the shut door. He wrote in support of its position until March of 1845.[10]

For Bridegroom Adventists the basic theological argument was drawn from the parable of the ten virgins in Matthew 25. They made the parable allegorical of their 1844 experience, and believed that on or about October 22, 1844, Jesus had gone into a heavenly wedding. The *Advent Mirror* divided the marriage into two steps: the actual marriage and the marriage supper. The marriage, it was argued, occurred in heaven and preceded the literal Second Coming. Turner and Hale presented the coming of the Son of man to the Ancient of Days in Daniel 7:9, 10, 13, 14, as describing events connected with a heavenly marriage. The Ancient of Days—God the Father—sat in judgment and gave to the Son of man—Jesus—"dominion, glory and a kingdom." Christ was made king as He received the New Jerusalem at the marriage. Then, as king, Jesus went from the wedding to the "marriage supper," which occurred when He gathered His saints at the Second Coming. Thus they linked the autumn 1844 date to the marriage that they believed confirmed the soon return of Jesus. The *Advent Mirror* placed post-Disappointment Advent believers in the "guest chamber" waiting for the marriage supper. The guest-chamber concept came from another parable found in Matthew 22:1-14. The "guests," or the faithful ones on earth, were waiting for Jesus to come literally to the earth from the heavenly wedding. They further argued that the "guests," or virgins, had responded to the call leading up to the tenth day of the seventh month on October 22, 1844, "Behold, the bridegroom cometh." They had trimmed their lamps and had gone figuratively to meet the Bridegroom.[11]

The foolish virgins, who were not ready, were shut out. "While they [the foolish virgins] went to buy [oil], the bridegroom came; and they that were ready went in with him to the marriage: and the door was shut" (Matt. 25:10). The guests, or Advent believers, were waiting only for the "final examination of the King." Their work was to keep their garments and wait. With emphasis the *Advent Mirror* concluded: "*The judgment is here!*" Interestingly, the paper drew no specific conclusions about just what the judgment was or how it pertained to Advent believers who were waiting in the "guest chamber."[12]

By the summer of 1845 conflict had developed among Bridegroom Adventists over whether the significance of October 22, 1844 (or the "tenth day of the seventh month"), centered on that day alone or on a period of time beginning on that date. O.R.L. Crosier, Emily Clemons, and others began to argue for an extended final atonement period in a heavenly sanctuary, while Samuel Snow aggressively argued for a single-day atonement. He believed that Jesus completed His work as a high priest in the Most Holy Place of the heavenly sanctuary on one day, "the tenth day of the seventh month." Having laid aside His priestly robes, He put on His kingly robes and began to reign. Thus for Snow probation was entirely closed for the world after the tenth day of the seventh month in 1844.[13]

Snow's one-day atonement position was essentially the same as he had presented in August 1844 through his influential *True Midnight Cry*.[14] Crosier's and Clemons' extended atonement view remained more flexible, theologically allowing for individual conversions.[15] Ellen Harmon (later White) was solidly in this second camp and actually was among the first to articulate important aspects of that position. Although there was a great deal of diversity within Bridegroom Adventism during 1845 and 1846, with many ideas on the shut door, there was unity on at least one significant point: the October 1844 experience had been a fulfillment of prophecy.

In addition to differences held regarding the length of the final atonement (one day or "extended"), 1845 Bridegroom Adventists were divided over whether the events predicted for the "tenth day of the seventh month" should be interpreted literally or spiritually. The spiritualizers, who became the dominant group by the end of 1845, held that Jesus had actually come spiritually on the tenth day of the seventh month in 1844. They further argued that the resurrection had taken place and that the saints were spiritually living in the New Jerusalem. Some even argued that Jesus was not a literal person. This view was most clearly expressed through the pages of the *Voice of the Shepherd*, published in Utica, New York.[16]

A minority of Bridegroom Adventists held to a literal view. They agreed that Jesus had done something tangible and real in heaven in connection with a heavenly wedding in 1844, and that soon Jesus would return literally and visibly at the Second Coming. Then there would be a literal resurrection, and the saints would live in a literal city known as the New Jerusalem in the recreated new earth. All of those who later became key leaders in Sabbatarian Adventism and the Seventh-day Adventist Church were opposed to the spiritualizing view. Unfortunately, mainline Adventists like J. V. Himes and Josiah Litch failed to make any distinction among Bridegroom Adventists, and considered all of them to be spiritualizers.[17] This misunderstanding continues to the present among critics of Ellen White and Seventh-day Adventists.

The Sanctuary View (January 1847 to Fall 1848)

After the collapse of spiritualizing Bridegroom Adventism toward the middle of 1846, the only remaining Adventists who still held to the prophetic significance of 1844 were the literalist Bridegroom Adventists. Very quickly, under the influence of Joseph Bates, most adopted the seventh-day Sabbath, so they might more appropriately be named Sabbatarian Adventists. Beginning in January 1847 Bates linked the Sabbath to the heavenly sanctuary and particularly to the Most Holy Place, where the ark of the covenant contains the law of God, of which the Sabbath is central.[18] The open door to the Most Holy Place of Revelation 11:19 revealed the ark of the covenant and the Ten Commandments. The Sabbath, therefore, became "present truth" with eschatological significance.

During 1847 the shut door began to be defined in terms of the heavenly sanctuary, and specifically regarding the door between the holy place and Most Holy Place. The Bridegroom view, based on an allegorical interpretation of the parable of the ten virgins in Matthew 25, became a secondary argument, thus allowing for the developing sanctuary understanding to take the fore. This necessarily gave new emphasis to Jesus' continued work as a high priest, resulting in an increasing discontinuity between the earlier idea of a shut door for "sinners" and the growing realization of the need for an evangelistic proclamation of the Sabbath.

The Sealing Message and the Open Door (1849 Through 1852)

It was the theology of the sealing message that opened to Sabbatarian

Adventists the need for a broader mission to the world and finally removed the earlier restrictive idea regarding the shut door. During 1849 the focus shifted from the shut door of the holy place to the open door of the Most Holy Place of the heavenly sanctuary. The linkage of the Sabbath to the ark in the Most Holy Place during 1847 and 1848 gave rise in 1849 to the understanding of the Sabbath as the seal of God. By 1852 Sabbatarian Adventists had begun to consider the need to evangelize even "sinners" on "present truth," based on Revelation 7 and the sealing of the 144,000. Again Joseph Bates led the way into these important new theological concepts.

For Bates the idea of 144,000 sealed people at the end of time seemed almost unimaginable in light of the "little flock" of Sabbatarian Adventists who numbered a few hundred at most. Connecting the three angels' messages of Revelation 14 to the sealing of the 144,000 in Revelation 7, Bates described two classes of people who comprised the "living saints":[19] "Now all advent believers that have, and do, participate in the advent messages as given in Rev. 14:6-13, will love and keep this covenant with God, and especially his Holy Sabbath, in this covenant; this is a part of the 144,000 now to be sealed.

"The other part are those who do not yet so well understand the advent doctrine; but are endeavoring to serve God with their whole hearts, and are willing, and will receive this covenant and Sabbath as soon as they hear it explained. These will constitute the 144,000, now to be sealed."[20]

With these words Bates argued for an expanded presentation of the sealing message beyond "advent believers." He believed that the sealing message needed to go to the whole world, in a manner similar to the Millerite message of 1843 and 1844. He wrote: "Our judgment hour cry message was to preach to every nation. I ask how this was done? why, by sending publications to every missionary station. We proved that [sending publications] was preaching it to foreign nations, except England and perhaps a few other nations in Europe [that had actual preachers]. Now as this was the way that we have given the *character* of the message to every nation in '43 and '44, so we believe it may be here in the [Rev] vii: chapter [the sealing message]."[21]

Bates even believed that the 144,000 would include slaves in the Southern States who were "living present truth."[22] They were living up to the light they had received and were God's children.

Theological Integration

By 1848 and 1849 the term *shut door* had moved from its original meaning in 1844 (that probation had closed) to an evangelistic term representing "present truth"—as it related to the sealing message and a final proclamation to the world. During the Sabbath Conferences of 1848, James White could triumphantly report: "The brethren are strong on the Sabbath and shut door."[23] What he meant by shut door was very different from the earlier views of Miller or even of the *Advent Mirror*. For Sabbatarian Adventists the shut door had become a general term referring to Jesus' ministry in the Most Holy Place of the heavenly sanctuary.

In 1851 James White defined three categories of people that could be converted—erring brethren, children, and "hidden souls." The hidden souls were those who were "living up to what light they had" and who, when they hear the "third angel . . . will gladly receive the whole truth."[24] For a short time he continued to believe that Sabbatarian Adventists were not to actively evangelize these people. But by 1852 the remaining theological tension between the shut door and the sealing message had dissolved. James White would write: "The Open Door we teach, and invite those who have an ear to hear, to come to it and find salvation through Jesus Christ."[25] He observed that the number of "advent brethren" in the state of New York had grown from "about a score" to "near one thousand."[26] White and others believed that new conversions were occurring because Jesus was before the mercy seat of the Most Holy Place of the heavenly sanctuary.

James White wrote after quoting Revelation 3:7, 8: "This Open Door we teach, and invite those who have an ear to hear, to come to it and find salvation through Jesus Christ. There is an exceeding glory in the view that Jesus has *opened the door* into the holiest of all, or has passed within the second vail, and now stands before the Ark containing the ten commandments. 'And the temple of God was opened in heaven, and there was seen in his temple the ark of his testament.' Rev. xi, 19. If it be said that we are of the Open Door and seventh day Sabbath theory, we shall not object; for this is our faith."[27]

Thus for those Millerites who became Bridegroom Adventists, then Sabbatarian Adventists, and who would eventually become Seventh-day Adventists, the term *shut door* moved from meaning that probation had closed in the autumn of 1844 to an open door evangelistic mission to take the gospel to the world in the context of the Sabbath and the work of Jesus in the Most Holy Place of the heavenly sanctuary. The meaning of the shut door had been progressively redefined to theologically integrate the Millerite movement and the October 1844 experience with the "present truth" of the Sabbath, heavenly sanctuary ministry of Jesus, and the sealing message.

II. ELLEN WHITE'S VIEWS AND ROLE REGARDING THE SHUT DOOR

Ellen White, like other Millerite Adventists, took her initial cue on the shut door from William Miller. She did not originate the view. After the autumn 1844 disappointment and previous to her first vision, she, like Miller, believed that probation had closed for the world. She recollected: "For a time after the disappointment in 1844, I did hold, in common with the advent body, that the door of mercy was then forever closed to the world. This position was taken before my first vision was given me."[28] Related to this statement is another: "With my brethren and sisters after the time passed in '44, I did believe no more sinners would be converted. But I never had a vision that no more sinners would be converted."[29]

In these two statements Ellen White is saying (1) that her shut-door beliefs did not originate with her visions, and (2) that in accepting Miller's views she believed that probation was closed in the weeks following the autumn disappointment. At some point after that, but before her first vision in December, she adopted a position similar to J. V. Himes's—that the October 1844 date was wrong. She believed that Adventists should look to a future date for the coming of Jesus and resume their proclamation to the world. James White wrote in 1847 about her first vision: "When she received her first vision, Dec. 1844, she and all the band in Portland, Maine, had given up the midnight cry, and shut door, as being in the past."[30] Ellen White also recollected in 1847: "At the time I had the vision of the midnight cry I had given it up in the past and thought it future, as also most of the band had."[31] Her first vision countered this position and confirmed the prophetic significance of the Midnight Cry message. In returning to an acceptance of the October 1844 date, she readopted certain aspects of the shut door that she had previously believed.

Ellen White's First Visions and the Close of Probation

The written account of Ellen White's visions, the experience of those closest to her, and her own recollections suggest that she did not readopt her initial prevision view that probation had closed for everyone. She declared in 1874: "I never have stated or written that the world was doomed or damned. I never have under any circumstances used this language to anyone however sinful. I have ever had messages of reproof for those who used these harsh expressions."[32]

This statement is, at least to a degree, in line with that of the *Advent Mirror*, which allowed for the salvation of individuals who had not rejected truth. A second contextual evidence that Ellen Harmon believed that certain people could still be saved is found in the earliest contemporary reference to her visions—the Israel Dammon trial in Maine, as recorded in an area newspaper.[33] Dammon credited his acceptance of the Bridegroom view to the influence of James White.[34] Dammon then traveled with James White and Ellen Harmon from Exeter, Maine, where Ellen Harmon had her Bridegroom vision, to Atkinson. In *Spiritual Gifts* Ellen White gives a lengthy description of the arrest and trial of Israel Dammon.[35] It is reasonable to presume that Dammon and those with him heard Ellen White tell of her vision and were influenced by it.

At the trial of Dammon in March 1845, those Adventists who had met with Ellen Harmon and heard her visions testified that neither Dammon nor their group believed that probation was closed for individuals or even small groups.[36] Isley Osborne, a witness for the defense and an Adventist, was reported to have said regarding Dammon's view of the churches: "He believes there is good, bad, and indifferent in all churches—he thinks it best to come out from them, because there is so many that has [*sic*] fallen from their holy position."[37] Jacob Mason, another Adventist defense witness, also clarified their position on the churches: "Brother Dammon said the churches were of that description—said they were lyers [*sic*], rogues, etc. I did not understand him to include all, but individuals."[38]

Joel Doore, an Adventist from Atkinson, said for the defense: "Elder Dammon said there was [*sic*] bad characters in the churches; I did not understand him to say all."[39] Abel S. Boobar, another Adventist, testified: "Elder D. said the churches were in a fallen state, and he had rather risk himself in the hands of the Almighty as a non-professor, than to be in the place of some of the churches."[40] Even James Ayer, Jr., in whose home the meeting was held, understood that it was "members of the churches who he referred to instead of the whole."[41] Thus Adventist witnesses, who had recently heard Ellen Harmon explain her visions, unanimously testified that individuals could still be saved, even from the "fallen" churches.

One more indication that suggests openness to individual salvation is found in an 1848 issue of the *Girdle of Truth,* in which Eli Curtis included portions of Ellen White's visions. He wrote: "The 'great effectual door' (1 Cor. 16:9) seems to have been closed more than three years since; as our experience very plainly teaches, but not the door of mercy!"[42]

These positions show a consistency with Ellen White's later testimony. Contemporaries such as J. V. Himes and those who later became Advent Christians who accused Ellen White of believing that probation had closed did not differentiate among the divergent and changing positions of Bridegroom Adventists regarding the shut door during 1845.[43]

Although Ellen White abandoned her earlier Millerite view that probation had closed for everyone, evidence suggests that as late as the summer of 1847 she likely still believed that evangelistic work for the unconverted world at large was no longer necessary. Otis Nichols, a close friend and supporter of Ellen White, wrote to William Miller on April 20, 1846, that she encouraged Adventists to "hold on to the faith and the seventh month movement, and that our work was done for the nominal church and the world, and what remains to be done was for the household of faith."[44]

In writing out her first vision, Ellen White used the expression "the wicked world which God had rejected," although she did not elaborate on its meaning.[45] Apollos Hale and Joseph Turner had used the same broad term but in a specifically circumscribed manner when they wrote of "the wicked world" that had "rejected the [Advent] truth" and "turned away their ears with loathing from its warnings and promises."[46] Likewise, William Miller had written of "the wicked world, who had scoffed at the idea of Christ's second coming."[47] Ellen White and those closely associated with her may have attached for a time a broader connotation to "the wicked world," but the designation allows for a less-universal application, as the above examples suggest. Ellen White's own interpretation of the vision, when called upon to explain it in 1883, was that "no reference is made [in the vision] to those who had not seen the light, and therefore were not guilty of its rejection."[48] The biblical principle that a person is responsible for the light they receive through the working of the Holy Spirit was applied by Ellen White to those who had rejected the Advent experience before 1844. The story of the blind man in John 9 articulates this principle. "Jesus said to [the Pharisees], 'If you were blind, you would have no sin; but now you say, "We see." Therefore your sin remains.'"[49] The message and language of Ellen White's first vision remains compatible with this spiritual rejection principle, even though her interpretation and that of her associates may have needed further correction.[50]

In a letter to Joseph Bates on July 13, 1847, she described her February 1845 "Bridegroom" vision. There was a "Sister Durben" who was a "mother in Israel" who did "not believe the door was shut." After Sister Durben arose to speak, Ellen White received her "Bridegroom" vision. She wrote to Bates that when she came out of vision, "my ears were saluted with Sister Durben's singing and shouting with a loud voice. Most of them received the vision, and were settled upon the shut door."[51] While Ellen White did not define how she and those with her understood the shut door at the time of her Bridegroom vision, the vision account itself makes no mention of the door of mercy being closed for the world, but rather depicts the coming of Jesus to the Ancient of Days in the Most Holy Place of the heavenly sanctuary. Her account corresponds closely to the description found in Daniel 7:9, 10, 13, 14.

It would take more time for Sabbatarian Adventists, including Ellen White, to distinguish between the visions' confirmation of the October 1844 date as a fulfillment of prophecy and their preconceptions regarding the shut door. As we will observe below, Ellen White's experience with the developing shut-door teaching may be compared to the manner in which she and other early Sabbatarian Adventists came to understand the correct time to begin the Sabbath. Bible writers likewise had misconceptions that were corrected over time.[52]

Ellen White's Visions Theologically Undermined Initial Shut-Door Views

Ellen White's position on the shut door was influenced and modified by her second major vision, which she received in Exeter, Maine, in February 1845. Known as the Bridegroom vision, it presented a very different idea than that of Samuel Snow and Joseph Turner in the *Jubilee Standard*.[53] As noted previously, Snow would argue that Jesus had ended His work as high priest in the Most Holy Place of the heavenly sanctuary on one day, October 22, 1844. For Snow, Jesus was reigning as king and was no longer a mediator.[54]

In contrast, Ellen White wrote of her vision: "There I beheld Jesus, as He was standing before the Father, a great High Priest."[55] Even her statements about those who remained "bowed before the throne" in the holy place, where she figuratively saw Satan taking God's place, suggest hope. She wrote: "Satan's object was to keep them deceived, and to draw back and deceive God's children."[56] The fact that Satan was working so hard implied that there was hope for those who were deceived. She did not specifically define who the "deceived" ones were. Thus in February 1845 Ellen White was suggesting a post-1844 continuing atonement or intercession, which theologically diverged from the restrictive or one-day atonement idea that probation had closed. Her views were more comparable to those presented by O.R.L. Crosier in the March 1845 *Day-Dawn,* though it is unlikely that she knew, at the time, of this small and obscure publication from western New York.

The Bridegroom vision also seems to have anchored for Ellen White the idea that those who had willfully rejected light could close their own probation. This "shut door" was limited to those who resisted the Holy Spirit and remained indifferent to Jesus' move into the Holy of Holies in the heavenly sanctuary.

Ellen White's time of trouble vision, during the fall of 1845, further confirmed that human probation had not closed. In October 1845 James White was teaching that Jesus would come at the end of the one-year period following the end of the 2300 days. While in Carver, Massachusetts, Ellen White was shown that Jesus could not come yet because the time of trouble had not yet begun.[57] In this vision Ellen White also clarified that God's people had not yet been sealed. She wrote: "Just before we entered it [the time of trouble] we all received the seal of the living God."[58]

The time of trouble vision increased James White's interest in the progression of final events. By 1847 he had developed a three-phase time of trouble beginning in 1844 and continuing until the voice of God at the Second Coming.[59] The three phases were the lesser time of trouble, the greater time of trouble, and Jacob's time of trouble. The lesser trouble began in 1844 while Jesus continued His work as high priest. The greater time of trouble, yet future, would begin when Jesus laid aside His priestly robes and probation closed. Then the seven last plagues would be poured out. Jacob's time of trouble would occur just before the Second Coming. Ellen White's vision of a future time of trouble not only protected against time setting but also provided a theological reason for evangelistic outreach until Jesus ended His work as high priest.

In March and April 1847 Ellen White received visions on the Sabbath. In her

Sabbath halo vision of April 7, 1847, at the home of Stockbridge Howland, she again saw Jesus ministering in the Most Holy Place of the heavenly sanctuary. But her vision added evangelistic dimensions even beyond what Joseph Bates had presented regarding the eschatological importance of the Sabbath. She saw Jesus open the ark in the Most Holy Place and remove the Ten Commandments. She observed that the fourth commandment "shone above them all" and had a "halo of glory" all around it.[60] She was then shown that "God had children, who do not see and keep the Sabbath. They had not rejected the light on it." Then God's people "went forth" and "proclaimed the Sabbath more fully."[61]

This evangelistic call further prepared the way for an understanding of the sealing message and the final collapse of the "probation-closed-for-sinners" view. The Sabbath halo vision so impressed Bates that he published it in a broadside.[62] It is probable that this vision helped him orient his views on the sealing message and the need to proclaim it throughout the world.

Finally, Ellen White's January 31, 1849, broadside, entitled *To Those Who Are Receiving the Seal of the Living God,* and her March 24, 1849, vision of the open door in the Most Holy Place of the heavenly sanctuary placed renewed emphasis on the importance of outreach and the availability of grace to sinners while Jesus remained in the second apartment of the heavenly sanctuary. In one portrayal she saw Jesus "clothed with Priestly garments. He gazed in pity on the remnant, then raised his hands upward, and with a voice of deep pity cried—'My blood, Father, My blood, My blood, My blood.'" Jesus' purpose in this appeal was to delay the release of the "four winds" of trouble until "the servants of God were sealed with the seal of the living God."[63]

Repeating a statement given earlier with one additional sentence connects well the foregoing information on Ellen White's progressive movement toward understanding the open door: "For a time after the disappointment in 1844, I did hold, in common with the advent body, that the door of mercy was then forever closed to the world. This position was taken before my first vision was given me. It was the light given me of God that corrected our error, and enabled us to see the true position."[64]

As Ellen White looked back over her experience leading up to her first vision and then the visions she received in the following months and years, she realized that the visions steadily helped move the "little flock" of early Bridegroom Adventists and then Sabbatarian Adventists toward a more open view. Her visions theologically moved the "little flock" away from the Millerite shut-door view to the Sabbatarian Adventist evangelistic proclamation of the gospel in the context of the three angels' messages to the entire world.

A Shut Door for Those Who Had Rejected the 1844 Message

An additional point needs to be considered. Ellen White continued to believe that a specialized group, those who had rejected the full light of the

Midnight Cry when it was proclaimed before 1844, had closed their own probation.

An often-quoted statement from *Christian Experience and Views* has been used to affirm that as late as 1851 Ellen White believed that the time for the salvation of the world was passed: "I saw that the mysterious signs and wonders, and false reformations would increase, and spread. The reformations that were shown me were not reformations from error to truth. . . . My accompanying angel bade me look for the travail of soul for sinners as used to be. I looked, but could not see it; for the time for their salvation is past."[65]

In 1854 Ellen White clarified what she meant in this statement: "The 'false reformations' referred to on page 27 [of *Christian Experience and Views*] are yet to be more fully seen. This view relates more particularly to those who have heard and rejected the light of the Advent doctrine. They are given over to strong delusions. Such will not have 'the travail of soul for sinners' as formerly. Having rejected the Advent, and being given over to the delusions of Satan, 'the time for their salvation is past.' This does not, however, relate to those who have not heard and have not rejected the doctrine of the Second Advent."[66]

Through the remainder of her life Ellen White continued to believe that probation was closed for those who had rejected the 1844 message after understanding its meaning and seen the moving of God's Spirit. In 1883 she wrote: "I was shown in vision, and I still believe, that there was a shut door in 1844. All who saw the light of the first and second angels' messages and rejected that light were left in darkness."[67] She compared the 1844 experience with that of Noah, Sodom and Gomorrah, and those who crucified Jesus. These each resulted in a limited close of probation.[68]

Misconception and Growing Understanding

A common misconception regarding the gift of prophecy is the belief that prophetic revelation does not allow for correction or growth in understanding on the part of the messenger. Snook and Brinkerhoff both took the position in 1866 that because Ellen White believed in a shut door after receiving her first vision she therefore could not be a true prophet.[69] The next year William Sheldon, the first published non-Sabbatarian Adventist critic of Ellen White, also argued similarly that she could not be a true prophet because she did not believe the Sabbath until more than a year and a half after receiving her first vision and then in later years considered keeping the first day of the week as the "mark of the beast."[70] Snook, Brinkerhoff, and Sheldon did not understand that while God is careful to make sure that His messenger communicates His intended revelation, He allows for growth in their personal understanding and application.

Ellen White's growing understanding of the shut door demonstrates how special revelation functioned in her experience. Can a prophetic messenger be allowed time to advance in his or her understanding? Must God immediately correct or remove every preexisting misconception or incorrect idea? Looking at the biblical model, we find that the prophets and apostles did not always have immediate and perfect understanding, and on occasion even misunderstood aspects of what they were shown.

Daniel is a good example of a prophet needing additional revelations to aid in understanding a vision. After receiving the vision recorded in chapter 8, the prophet "fainted, and was sick certain days;" nor was the vision understood.[71] A significant period of time passed between Daniel 8 and Daniel 9. Daniel had studied the prophecy of Jeremiah 25:10-14 and knew that the Jewish captivity would last only 70 years. But as he contemplated the 2300 days/years of Daniel 8:14 he could not reconcile what he was shown with Jeremiah's prophecy. In answer to his prayer recorded in Daniel 9, the angel Gabriel was sent to explain the previous vision and give the prophet "skill and understanding." This indicates that Daniel initially misinterpreted or misunderstood part of his Daniel 8 vision.

The experience of the apostles after Pentecost is another example. The apostles held incorrect ideas about God's plan for the conversion of non-Jews. It required a vision, recorded in Acts 10, to make Peter willing to eat with and preach to Gentiles. Yet even after that experience others on the Jerusalem Council were reluctant to accept the conversion of Gentiles to Christianity unless they also converted to Judaism. It took time and new circumstances combined with repeated special revelation from God to correct their misunderstanding. The apostles' misconceptions and growing understanding did not invalidate the special revelation previously received. The inspired revelation was always trustworthy and true. It was also progressive.

The apostle Paul sent the runaway slave Onesimus back to Philemon with counsel to treat him like a brother. Paul tempered but did not remove the institution of slavery. Patriarchs in the Old Testament engaged in polygamy as an accepted part of their culture. Even David, who was a man after God's own heart, and Abraham, who was a "friend" of God, apparently engaged in the practice without any thought that it was wrong. They both, with other patriarchs, had the prophetic gift. It is helpful to realize that God does not need to correct every misconception a person has to use him or her to convey special revelation.

Ellen White's experience was similar to these and other Bible prophets. She wrote of her visions: "Often representations are given me which at first I do not understand, but after a time they are made plain by a repeated presentation of those things that I did not at first comprehend, and in ways that make their meaning clear and unmistakable."[72] "For sixty years I have been in communication with heavenly messengers, and I have been constantly learning in reference to divine things."[73]

The interplay between prophetic revelation and mistaken preconceptions is further illustrated in how early Sabbatarian Adventists came to a correct position on the proper time to begin the Sabbath. Both James and Ellen White accepted the Sabbath through reading biblical evidences presented by Joseph Bates in his August 1846 tract, *The Seventh-day Sabbath: A Perpetual Sign*. Bates, who had traveled the world as a sea captain, understood the effect of latitude on sunrise and sunset. He concluded that evening began at 6:00 p.m. and that this was the correct time to begin the Sabbath.[74] His arguments convinced the Whites, who, with most other Sabbatarian Adventists, continued to keep the Sabbath in this way for another nine years. Some, however, suggested that the Sabbath should begin at sunrise, while others thought it should begin at sundown.

In 1847 at Topsham, Maine, Ellen White had a vision that the sunrise time was wrong. The angel said to her, "From even unto even shall ye celebrate your Sabbaths." At the urging of Joseph Bates, those present, including Ellen White, interpreted this to mean that the Sabbath should begin at 6:00 p.m.[75] Ellen White and others drew conclusions from her vision that she had not actually been shown.

During the early 1850s some expressed further questions on the proper time to begin the Sabbath. In the summer of 1855 James White spoke with J. N. Andrews, who agreed to give the matter thorough study.[76] At a November 1855 conference in Battle Creek, Michigan, Andrews' research was presented, giving biblical and historical reasons for beginning the Sabbath at sundown rather than at 6:00 p.m. Most were convinced, but some, including Ellen White, believed that her 1847 vision had confirmed the 6:00 p.m. time.

On Tuesday, November 20, 1855, three days after the discussion of Andrews' paper at the conference, Ellen White had a vision which corrected her longstanding misunderstanding. "I saw that it was in the minds of some [herself included] that the Lord had shown that the Sabbath commenced at six o'clock, when I had only seen that it commenced at 'even,' and it was inferred that even was at six."[77] James White wrote of the misunderstanding of Ellen White's 1847 vision with these words: "Some have the impression that six o'clock time has been taught among us by the direct manifestation of the Holy Spirit. This is a mistake. 'From even to even' was the teaching, from which six o'clock time has been inferred."[78]

The information on Ellen White's vision correcting her and others' understanding was published in her first *Testimony for the Church*. She asked the angel in vision if the "frown of God had been upon His people for commencing the Sabbath as they had." She was shown the "first rise of the Sabbath" and the nine years since and "did not see that the Lord was displeased, or frowned upon them." Then the angel explained why: "If light come, and that light is set aside or rejected, then comes condemnation and the frown of God; but before the light comes, there is no sin, for there is no light for them to reject."[79] Here Ellen White articulated the spiritual rejection principle that a person is not accountable for "light" until it is understood.

As with her corrected understanding of the time to begin the Sabbath, Ellen White's personal preconceptions or possibly mistaken inferences relating to the shut-door teaching do not invalidate her visions, particularly because it was those early visions that provided a theological orientation resulting in a worldwide evangelistic gospel proclamation. Examples of these types of misconception, however, are rare in Ellen White's experience.

III. SUMMARY AND CONCLUSIONS

For those who became Sabbatarian Adventists, and later Seventh-day Adventists, the shut-door idea went through successive stages that progressively changed the meaning of the term. Presented first by William Miller, the shut door was connected to the October 1844 disappointment. For a short time most Adventists believed that the world had been warned of the soon coming of Jesus and had either accepted or rejected the message. Soon, though, Adventism split into two groups. The mainline group abandoned the October 1844 date, looked to a future fulfillment of the prophecies, and resumed evangelistic work. A minority group retained faith in the October 1844 date.

The minority group, described in this article as Bridegroom Adventists, initially adopted a more open view on the shut door than Miller's simple position that probation had closed. They believed that only "sinners" who had rejected truth could no longer be saved and allowed that individuals who had not rejected light could still be saved. This position as presented in the *Advent Mirror* became the new baseline shut-door view.

During 1845 significant theological disagreement developed among Bridegroom Adventists over whether Jesus was still ministering as high priest in the heavenly sanctuary or whether He had laid aside His priestly robes and begun to reign as king. Key individuals such as Samuel Snow and Joseph Turner argued that Jesus had completed His one-day work as high priest in the Most Holy Place on October 22, 1844. Others, such as O.R.L. Crosier, Emily Clemons, and Ellen White, believed that Jesus had begun a final extended atonement as high priest on October 22, 1844. Snow's and Turner's view theologically led to the belief that probation was closed for the world, while Crosier's, Clemons', and White's view suggested a continuation of probation.

By 1846 Crosier and others had connected the idea of a shut door to the partition between the holy place and Most Holy Place of the heavenly sanctuary but continued to believe that "sinners" could not be converted. In January 1847 Joseph Bates linked Jesus' ministry in the Most Holy Place of the heavenly sanctuary to the Sabbath and the Ten Commandments. This linkage suggested that the Sabbath needed to be promoted and shared in light of its eschatological importance. These ideas—the continuation of Jesus as a high priest and the need to proclaim the Sabbath—increased theological tension regarding the meaning of the shut door.

During 1848 and 1849 Bates further refined the eschatological importance of the Sabbath into the sealing message based on Revelation 7 and 14. The Sabbath as the seal of God required that a Sabbath proclamation be given to the world before Jesus could return. This put further strain on the idea of a shut door for "sinners." Sabbatarian Adventists began to emphasize the open door into the Most Holy Place of the heavenly sanctuary, and the term *shut door* was redefined to mean something very different from a shut door of probation. It came to represent the validity of the 1844 experience that Sabbatarian Adventism had embraced. During 1850 and 1851 the movement grew very rapidly, with nearly 1,000 new converts in New York alone.

By 1852 the idea that "sinners" could not be converted was abandoned, and Sabbatarian Adventists acknowledged that Jesus' ministry in the Most Holy Place of the heavenly sanctuary included effecting salvation for sinners. Nevertheless, they continued to believe that the door of probation had closed for those who had persistently resisted the Holy Spirit in the seventh-month movement.

While Ellen White's visions steadfastly affirmed the continued significance of the October 1844 prophetic message, they also suggested that probation had not yet closed for everyone since Jesus was still functioning as a high priest. Ellen White never denied salvation to individuals, but the tenor of her statements and those closely connected with her suggests that for a time she continued to believe that evangelistic work for the unconverted world had ended. Her visions did not require this understanding, however, and theologically led to a more open view. Her first vision, while referring to the "wicked world which God had rejected," can be understood in terms of the spiritual rejection principle. Her February 1845 Bridegroom vision portrayed Jesus as still ministering as a high priest; her October 1845 time of trouble vision indicated that the "sealing" and the great time of trouble had not yet begun and thus suggested that probation had not yet closed; her March and April 1847 Sabbath halo visions revealed that the Sabbath was to be proclaimed more fully before Jesus would return; and her autumn 1848 and March 1849 sealing message visions revealed that Jesus was holding back the winds of strife until God's people could be sealed and that Jesus had opened the door into the Most Holy Place of the heavenly sanctuary.

The theological discontinuity between these visions and the shut door was resolved by 1852. The terms *shut door* and *open door* came to represent the new theological understanding that integrated the Sabbath and the sanctuary, explained the 1844 experience, and gave a reason for a new and distinctive evangelistic outreach to the world.

Perhaps the most important point to be made regarding Ellen White and the shut door is the tenor of her visions. Her first visions pursued a theological path away from previous misconceptions received from William Miller. Her visions also differed from the mainline ideas on the shut door promoted by Joseph Turner and Samuel Snow. It was Ellen White's visions in combination with Joseph Bates's sealing message that helped Sabbatarian Adventists eventually to think in terms of a worldwide mission.

James White reflected in later years on the benefit Sabbatarian Adventists had received by moving more slowly in abandoning some of their misunderstandings concerning the shut door: "Some of this people did believe in the shut door, in common with the Adventists generally, soon after the passing of the time. Some of us held fast this position longer than those did who gave up their Advent experience, and drew back in the direction of perdition. And God be thanked that we did hold fast to that position till the matter was explained by light from the heavenly sanctuary."[80]

From Scripture we understand that special revelation and inspiration do not automatically confer infallibility of understanding to inspired messengers. However, the Holy Spirit makes sure that His intended message is transmitted in a trustworthy and accurate manner. Additionally, God makes sure that His intended result is accomplished. As illustrated by the experience of prophets and apostles in the Bible, this may require repetition and expansion of messages over a period of time through visions and dreams. Thus Scripture provides instructive models on how we should expect the prophetic gift to function in the experience of Ellen White.

---

[1] B. F. Snook and William H. Brinkerhoff, *The Visions of E. G. White, Not of God* (Cedar Rapids, Iowa: Cedar Valley Times, 1866); H. E. Carver, *Mrs. E. G. White's Claims to Divine Inspiration Examined* (Marion, Iowa: published at the "Hope of Israel" Office, 1870); William Sheldon, *The Visions and Theories of the Prophetess Ellen G. White in Conflict With the Bible* (Buchanan, Mich.: W.A.C.P. Association, 1867); Miles Grant, *The True Sabbath: Which Day Shall We Keep? An Examination of Mrs. Ellen White's Visions* (Boston: Advent Christian Publication Society, 1874); A. C. Long, *Comparison of the Early Writings of Mrs. White With Later Publications* (Marion, Iowa: Advent and Sabbath Advocate, 1883); D. M. Canright, *Seventh-day Adventism Renounced After an Experience of Twenty-eight Years: By a Prominent Minister and Writer of That Faith* (Kalamazoo, Mich.: Kalamazoo Pub., 1888); *idem, Life of Mrs. E. G. White, Seventh-day Adventist Prophet: Her False Claims Refuted;* E. S. Ballenger, *Facts About Seventh-day Adventists* (Riverside, Calif.: E. S. Ballenger, c. 1949); Dale Ratzlaff, *Cultic Doctrine of Seventh-day Adventists* (Glendale, Ariz.: Life Assurance Ministries, 1996). Major treatment on the shut door includes: Merlin D. Burt, "The Historical Background, Interconnected Development, and Integration of the Doctrines of the Sanctuary, the Sabbath, and Ellen G. White's Role in Sabbatarian Adventism from 1844 to 1849"; P. Gerard Damsteegt, *Foundations of the Seventh-day Adventist Message and Mission,* pp. 104-124; Herbert E. Douglass, *Messenger of the Lord: The Prophetic Ministry of Ellen G. White,* pp. 500-512, 549-569; Ingemar Lindén, *1844 and the Shut Door Problem;* Francis D. Nichol, *Ellen*

G. White and Her Critics, pp. 161-252; Robert W. Olson, "The 'Shut Door' Documents"; Rolf J. Poehler, "'. . . And the Door Was Shut': Seventh-day Adventists and the Shut-Door Doctrine in the Decade After the Great Disappointment."

[2] William Miller, *Evidence From Scripture and History of the Second Coming of Christ About the Year 1843* (Troy, N.Y.: Kemble & Hooper, 1836), pp. 97, 98.

[3] William Miller, "Brother Miller's Letter, on the Seventh Month," *Midnight Cry,* Oct. 12, 1844, p. 122; *idem,* "Letter From William Miller," *Advent Herald,* Nov. 27, 1844, p. 127.

[4] William Miller, "Letter From Bro. Miller," *Advent Herald,* Dec. 11, 1844, p. 142; see also *idem,* "Letter From Mr. Miller," *Advent Herald,* Feb. 12, 1845, pp. 2, 3.

[5] Joseph Turner, *Hope of Israel,* Jan. 24, 1845, quoted in *Defence of Joshua V. Himes,* pp. 18, 19; Isaac C. Wellcome, *History of the Second Advent Message and Mission, Doctrine and People,* pp. 397, 398.

[6] "The Hope of Israel," *Advent Herald,* Aug. 7, 1844, p. 5.

[7] "The Advent Herald," *Advent Herald,* Oct. 30, 1844, p. 93; see Josiah Litch on the close of probation before the Second Coming: Josiah Litch, "The Doctrine of the Millennium: The Order of the Resurrection and Order of the Judgment," *Second Advent Tracts,* No. XII, June 1841, pp. 11, 12. See also P. Gerard Damsteegt, "Historical Background: Early Nineteenth Century," in *Doctrine of the Sanctuary: A Historical Survey, 1845-1863,* ed. Frank B. Holbrook (Silver Spring, Md.: Biblical Research Institute, 1989), pp. 1-16; Robert Haddock, "A History of the Doctrine of the Sanctuary in the Advent Movement: 1800-1915" (B.D. thesis, Andrews University, 1970), pp. 91-94; C. Mervyn Maxwell, "The Investigative Judgment: Its Early Development," in *The Sanctuary and the Atonement: Biblical, Historical, and Theological Studies,* ed. Arnold V. Wallenkampf and W. Richard Lesher (Washington, D.C.: Review and Herald, 1981), pp. 545-581; *idem, Magnificent Disappointment: What Really Happened in 1844 . . . and Its Meaning for Today* (Boise, Idaho: Pacific Press, 1994), pp. 71-85.

[8] Samuel S. Snow, "Letter From Br. Snow," *Voice of Truth,* Apr. 16, 1845, p. 20.

[9] A. Hale and J. Turner, "Has Not the Savior Come as the Bridegroom?" *Advent Mirror,* January 1845, pp. 3, 4.

[10] William Miller, "Letter From Bro. Miller"; *idem,* "Letter From Mr. Miller"; *idem, Voice of Truth,* Feb. 19, 1845, quoted in James White, *Life Incidents,* p. 201; *idem,* "Letter From Bro. Miller," *Voice of Truth,* Mar. 26, 1845, p. 49; J. V. Himes, "Canadian Tour," *Morning Watch,* Apr. 3, 1845, p. 110.

[11] A. Hale and J. Turner, "Has Not the Savior Come as the Bridegroom?" *Advent Mirror,* January 1845, pp. 1, 2.

[12] *Ibid.,* pp. 1, 3.

[13] Samuel S. Snow, "Behold He Cometh!!" *Day-Star,* Apr. 22, 1845, p. 41. Quoted from *Jubilee Standard.*

[14] Samuel S. Snow, "Behold, the Bridegroom Cometh; Go Ye Out to Meet Him," *True Midnight Cry,* Aug. 22, 1844. For an evaluation of the Bridegroom Adventist struggle over a one-day versus extended atonement, see Merlin D. Burt, "The Extended Atonement View in the *Day-Dawn* and the Emergence of Sabbatarian Adventism," *Andrews University Seminary Studies,* Fall 2006, pp. 331-339.

[15] O.R.L. Crosier and F. B. Hahn, *Day-Dawn* published on last page of *Ontario Messenger,* Mar. 26, 1845, republished in Merlin D. Burt, "The *Day-Dawn* of Canandaigua, New York: Reprint of a Significant Millerite Adventist Journal," *Andrews University Seminary Studies,* Fall 2006, pp. 317-330; O.R.L. Crosier, "From Bro. Crosier," *Hope of Israel,* Apr. 17, 1845, p. 4; Emily C. Clemons, "Letter From Sister Clemons," *Day-Star,* Apr. 15, 1845, p. 35.

[16] Orlando Squires, "Where is Heaven?" *Voice of the Shepherd,* March 1845, pp. 4, 5; C. H. Fenton, "The Harvest of the Earth," *Voice of the Shepherd,* March 1845, p. 1; S. Fenton, "The Resurrection," *Voice of the Shepherd,* March 1845, p. 8; Orlando Squires, "This Same Jesus," *Voice of the Shepherd,* March 1845, p. 5.

[17] J. V. Himes, "A Word to the Advent Brethren Scattered Abroad," *Morning Watch,* Feb. 13, 1845, p. 56. See also *idem,* "A Word to the Advent Brethren Scattered Abroad," *Advent*

Herald, Feb. 19, 1845, p. 13; Josiah Litch, "Did the Bridegroom Come in 1843?" *Morning Watch,* Apr. 10, 1845, p. 119.

[18] Joseph Bates, *The Seventh Day Sabbath,* 2nd ed., pp. iii, iv.

[19] Joseph Bates, *A Seal of the Living God,* pp. 39, 65.

[20] *Ibid.,* pp. 61, 62.

[21] *Ibid.,* p. 34.

[22] Joseph Bates, *A Vindication of the Seventh-day Sabbath,* p. 93.

[23] James White to "My Dear Brother and Sister Hastings," Aug. 26, 1848.

[24] [James White], "Conversions. . . . ," *Review and Herald,* Apr. 7, 1851, p. 64.

[25] [James White], "Call at the Harbinger Office," *Review and Herald,* Feb. 17, 1852, pp. 94, 95.

[26] [James White], "The Work of the Lord," *Review and Herald,* May 6, 1852, pp. 4, 5.

[27] [James White], "Call at the Harbinger Office," *Review and Herald,* Feb. 17, 1852, p. 95.

[28] Ellen G. White, Ms 4, 1883 (c. 1883); *idem, Selected Messages,* book 1, p. 63.

[29] Ellen G. White to J. N. Loughborough, Lt 2, 1874 (Aug. 24); Ellen G. White, *Selected Messages,* book 1, p. 74.

[30] James White, ed., *A Word to the "Little Flock,"* p. 22.

[31] Ellen G. White to Joseph Bates, Lt 3, 1847 (July 13).

[32] Ellen G. White, Lt 2, 1874 (Aug. 24).

[33] "Trial of Elder I. Dammon: Reported for the *Piscataquis Farmer,*" *Piscataquis Farmer,* Mar. 7, 1845, pp. 1, 2.

[34] Israel Dammon, "Letter From Bro. Dammon," *Jubilee Standard,* June 5, 1845, p. 104.

[35] Ellen G. White, *Spiritual Gifts [vol. 2],* pp. 40-42.

[36] See Merlin D. Burt, "Historical Background, Interconnected Development, and Integration of the Doctrines of the Sanctuary, the Sabbath, and Ellen G. White's Role in Sabbatarian Adventism from 1844 to 1849," pp. 136, 137.

[37] "Trial of Elder I. Dammon: Reported for the *Piscataquis Farmer,*" p. 1.

[38] *Ibid.,* p. 2.

[39] *Ibid.*

[40] *Ibid.*

[41] *Ibid.,* p. 1.

[42] Eli Curtis, *Girdle of Truth,* Extra, second ed., Jan. 20, 1848, p. 31; see also M. C. Truesdale, "Statement," Aug. 17, 1875, DF 266.

[43] For an example, see Wellcome, *History of the Second Advent Message,* pp. 397, 398.

[44] Otis Nichols to William Miller, Apr. 20, 1846, letter written on back of broadside *To the Little Remnant Scattered Abroad* (Aurora University).

[45] Ellen G. Harmon, "Letter to Enoch Jacobs," *Day-Star,* Jan. 24, 1846, pp. 31, 32; Ellen G. White to Joseph Bates, Lt 3, 1847 (July 13, 1847). Her first vision was reprinted using the same "wicked world" expression in the broadside *To the Little Remnant Scattered Abroad,* Apr. 6, 1846, and James White, ed., *A Word to the "Little Flock,"* p. 14.

[46] A. Hale and J. Turner, "Has Not the Savior Come as the Bridegroom?" *Advent Mirror,* January 1845, pp. 3, 4.

[47] William Miller, *Evidence From Scripture and History of the Second Coming of Christ About the Year 1843* (Boston: J. V. Himes, 1842), p. 188.

[48] Ellen G. White, Ms 4, 1883 (c. 1883); *idem, Selected Messages,* book 1, p. 64.

[49] John 9:41, NKJV.

[50] Herbert Douglass, *Messenger of the Lord,* pp. 554, 555.

[51] Ellen G. White to Joseph Bates, Lt 3, 1847 (July 13).

[52] See section "Misconception and Growing Understanding" below.

[53] Samuel S. Snow, "Letter From Br. Snow."

[54] See Burt, "Historical Background," pp. 114-117.

[55] Ellen G. Harmon, "Letter From Sister Harmon," *Day-Star,* Mar. 14, 1846, p. 7 (written Feb. 15, 1846).

[56] *Ibid.*

[57] *Ibid.;* James White, "Watchman, What of the Night," *Day-Star,* Sept. 20, 1845, p. 26; James White, ed., *A Word to the "Little Flock,"* p. 22.

[58] Ellen G. Harmon, "Letter From Sister Harmon."

[59] James White, ed., *A Word to the "Little Flock";* see Burt, "Historical Background," pp. 308-312.

[60] E. G. White, "Dear Bro. Bates," *A Vision,* broadside, Apr. 7, 1847, p. 1.

[61] *Ibid.*

[62] *Ibid.*

[63] Ellen G. White, *To Those Who Are Receiving the Seal of the Living God,* broadside, Jan. 31, 1849.

[64] Ellen G. White, Ms 4, 1883 (c. 1883); *idem, Selected Messages,* book 1, p. 63.

[65] Ellen G. White, *A Sketch of the Christian Experience and Views of Ellen G. White,* p. 27 (*Early Writings,* p. 45); see also *idem,* "Dear Brethren and Sisters," *Present Truth,* August 1849, p. 22.

[66] Ellen G. White, *Supplement to the Christian Experience and Views of Ellen G. White,* p. 4 (*Early Writings,* p. 45).

[67] Ellen G. White, Ms 4, 1883 (c. 1883); *idem, Selected Messages,* book 1, p. 63.

[68] *Ibid.*

[69] Snook and Brinkerhoff, *The Visions of E. G. White, Not of God,* pp. 3ff.

[70] William Sheldon, *Visions and Theories,* pp. 3, 4.

[71] Dan. 8:27, KJV.

[72] Ellen G. White, *Selected Messages,* book 3, p. 56.

[73] Ellen G. White, Lt 86, 1906 (Mar. 8); see also *idem, This Day With God,* p. 76.

[74] Bates, *The Seventh Day Sabbath,* p. 32.

[75] Uriah Smith, *The Visions of Mrs. E. G. White, a Manifestation of Spiritual Gifts According to the Scriptures,* p. 90.

[76] James White, "Time of the Sabbath," *Review and Herald,* Dec. 4, 1855, p. 78.

[77] Ellen G. White, *Testimony for the Church* (Battle Creek, Mich.: *Advent Review* Office, 1855), p. 4; *idem, Testimonies for the Church,* vol. 1, p. 116.

[78] James White, "Time of the Sabbath."

[79] E. G. White, *Testimony for the Church,* p. 4; *idem, Testimonies for the Church,* vol. 1, p. 116.

[80] James White, *Life Incidents,* p. 207.

ANNOTATION AND EDITORIAL METHODOLOGY

The intent of this series is to make available, in annotated form, all of Ellen White's extant letters and manuscripts.[1] With few exceptions, writings that are readily available in other published and electronic formats have not been included in this series.[2] The table of contents includes a complete chronological list of Ellen White's writings, with references to excluded published sources printed in *italic* font.[3]

This volume provides a level of historical context for each document through a series of footnotes dealing with such matters as date of composition, identity of addressee, background to events and issues alluded to in the text, and clarification of obscure or archaic expressions. While having succinct notes has been the goal, some letters have required more extensive annotation, particularly those with considerable theological content.

The Text and Transcriptions

The Ellen White text for this series relies primarily on transcripts made by her secretaries under her direction and on those made after her death by the organization responsible for her literary estate.[4] In order to ascertain the reliability of the current transcriptions, a sampling of documents was compared against their handwritten or earliest sources. That examination confirmed that the copyists uniformly opted for what is sometimes called "expanded transcription" in order to improve the readability and clarity of the original. Thus, while remaining true to the meaning and language of the original documents, they corrected or modernized spelling, punctuation, capitalization, and verb tenses, spelled out abbreviations, and inserted paragraph indentations. They also standardized the date and place lines of each letter.

While an entirely new transcription retaining the grammatical idiosyncrasies and archaisms of the original documents might have been attempted for this series, several factors led to the decision to utilize the existing transcriptions. These included practical considerations such as the magnitude and prohibitive cost of retranscribing tens of thousands of manuscript pages and the fact that the current transcriptions are universally used in the many publications in which Ellen White manuscript material is found. More fundamental was the desire to present a text for the general reader that, while remaining true to the meaning and wording of the original manuscripts, was free of the distractions of grammatical imperfections and transcription apparatus. Examples of Ellen White's holographs are reproduced in this volume, enabling interested readers to compare the transcribed text with the handwritten original.

Words that the editors of this series inserted for clarification are enclosed in square brackets—[ ]—and extraordinarily long sentences or paragraphs in existing transcriptions have been split. Also, this edition strives for uniformity in the spelling of a place or person so as to facilitate searching in electronic formats—e.g., "Fannie" versus "Fanny."

A number of the original typescripts contain interlineations penned by Ellen White. In most instances these interlineations have not been included in the text because they typically reflect a later rereading and marking of the document by Ellen White—sometimes years later—and would thus have been unknown to the original recipients. In instances in which the text has included these interlineations they appear between "greater than" and "less than" symbols: < >. So that the reader may know that an interlined copy exists for one of the documents, a plus—+—symbol has been added at the end of the introductory publication line.[5]

Dates, Places, File Numbers, and Publication Data

Letters and manuscripts are in chronological order, making it easier for the reader to follow the development of the narrative and the thinking of Ellen White over the years. Some documents, however, Ellen White left undated, incompletely dated, or, in a few cases, obviously misdated. In such cases dates have been assigned, based on evidence provided in the footnotes. Assigned dates appear in square brackets.

Despite efforts to be exact, some documents could be dated only approximately to the nearest month, year, or even range of years. Such documents appear in the collection at the end of the month, year, or last year in a range of years. Thus letters that can be dated only to "July 1850," "1850," or "1850-1852," for example, would appear at the end of the July 1850, December 1850, and December 1852 sections, respectively.

In cases in which Ellen White has not recorded the address from which her letter was sent, the probable location has been supplied in square brackets. Addresses of diary entries have been dealt with in the same way. The abbreviation "n.p." ("no place") appears where the place of origin is unknown or uncertain. The names of states have been added in square brackets where only the names of towns or villages appear in the original text.

White Estate file number designations are given in parenthesis above the date and place (e.g., "Lt 4, 1849" or "Ms 2, 1885"), while information about the document's previous publication status is found immediately following the name of the addressee or title.

Abstracts

Brief abstracts of the content of each letter or manuscript appear before the body of the document.

Persons

As would be expected in personal letters, Ellen White seldom addresses her correspondents with their full name. Often only the surname (e.g., "Brother Johnson") or the first name (e.g., "Dear Mary") is used. The first task, therefore, has been to attempt to fully identify persons addressed or mentioned. Where the full identity has been established with a high degree of probability, the full name has been inserted into the text within square brackets, with a footnote detailing the evidence. Where, on the other hand, the identity of a person is unclear, a footnote will indicate this. A person is identified only at his or her first mention in the letter or manuscript.

Biographical sketches of persons whose names are **bolded** in the text can be found in the back of this volume. A note at the beginning of the sketches explains the format of the entries.

Contexts

This volume contains a variety of "contextual" notes. Commonly, in order to provide a broader perspective, especially where Ellen White touches on debated issues, a note attempts to place her position in the context of the wider discussion. Thus, for example, a note contrasts her view on the millennium and future persecution of the saints with that of Millerite Adventists and with the early positions that Joseph Bates and James White took.

Notes of another kind involve competing interpretations of certain Ellen White passages or expressions. Most conspicuous among these (involving the pre-1852 period) has been the debate among scholars over how to interpret Ellen White's allusions to some kind of probationary end in 1844. Notes list some of the major contenders in these "shut door" debates, with an evaluation of their respective arguments.

Often the reader is left wondering about the outcome of an event, instruction, or prediction found in a letter. Did the sick person revive? Was Ellen White's instruction heeded or rejected? Were predictions or promises fulfilled? Where known, such information has been supplied. Unfortunately, very few of the letters Ellen White received in response to her communications during this early period have survived, making it more difficult to provide answers to these kinds of questions.

Still other notes describe outcomes or focus on the historical background leading up to a particular event or situation, such as the series of events culminating in the formation of the *Messenger* Party.

Allusions; Obscure or Archaic Expressions

Biblical allusions abound in Ellen White's writings, often woven into their very fabric. No attempt has been made to identify all of these allusions, but identification has usually been limited to instances that are central to the argument or are unusual in some respect. Allusions to hymns, poems, and other literary pieces have been identified where possible, and a few words and expressions that may be puzzling to modern readers, such as "plank road," "carriole," and "snug dealing,"[6] have been explained.

Parameters

While this series is intended primarily for general readers having a basic knowledge of Seventh-day Adventist history and beliefs, researchers will value the substantial investigation into primary sources that underlies the notes, together with their extensive bibliographical references. It is the aim of the editors to thus provide a practical level of annotation that increases the understanding and appreciation of this unique collection for all readers, while suggesting further areas of study for the scholar.

The Trustees of the Ellen G. White Estate

---

[1] On the distinction between Ellen White's "letters" and "manuscripts," see the introductory article "The Literary Relationship Between Ellen White's Published and Unpublished Works." Ellen White's original papers reside at the Ellen G. White Estate, Inc., in Silver Spring, Maryland. Photocopies of the transcriptions are available at numerous Ellen G. White–Seventh-day Adventist Research Centers around the world, the locations of which may be found on the estate's Website: www.EllenWhite.org.

[2] Examples include periodical articles and nonextant letters printed in *An Appeal to the Youth, Spiritual Gifts [vol. 2],* or other publications such as *Testimonies for the Church.* Exceptions included in this volume are Ellen White's two earliest communications (printed in the *Day-Star*), three broadsides, a letter in *A Word to the "Little Flock,"* and "utterances" from a vision printed in a tract by Joseph Bates.

[3] Also indicated by italics are five unauthenticated visions described in Appendix A.

[4] Those transcribed by the Ellen G. White Estate consist of handwritten materials that had not been transcribed by Ellen White's secretaries before her death, as well as additions to the collection that have come to light since 1915. Ellen White's surviving handwritten drafts are preserved at the main office of the White Estate, where upon proper request they may be viewed for scholarly purposes.

[5] Interlined copies may be viewed at the main office of the Ellen G. White Estate.

[6] See Ellen G. White, Ms 5, 1859 (Jan. 18); Lt 8, 1859 (Sept. 15); Lt 1, 1858 (Mar. 3).

LIST OF ILLUSTRATIONS

CHRONOLOGICAL INDEX

OF

ELLEN G. WHITE

LETTERS, MANUSCRIPTS, AND PUBLICATIONS

Date	Addressee/Title	File Number	Page
Dec. 14	Robert Barnes	Lt 5, 1851	317
Dec. 21	Abram and Caroline Dodge	Lt 9, 1851	319
	1852		
Mar. 14	Extracts From Sr. White's Vision in Ballston, New York	Ms 2, 1852	322
Mar. 18	The Nations	Ms 1, 1852	325
Apr. 16	*Stockbridge and Louisa Howland*	*See* Spiritual Gifts [vol. 2], *pp. 160, 161*	
June 2	Brethren and Sisters in Jackson	Lt 2, 1852	328
June 10	*"To the Brethren and Sisters"*	*See* The Advent Review, and Sabbath Herald, *June 10, 1852, p. 2.*	
August	*"Dear Young Friends"*	*See* The Youth's Instructor, *August 1852, pp. 6, 7*	
September	Extract Regarding the Latter Rain	Ms 4, 1852	332
Oct. 25	Dear Friends	Lt 4, 1852	334
October	*"Beauties of the New Earth"*	*See* The Youth's Instructor, *October 1852, pp. 12, 13*	
November	*"Dear Young Friends"*	*See* The Youth's Instructor, *December 1852, pp. 20-22*	
	1853		
Feb. 17	*"To the Saints Scattered Abroad"*	*See* The Advent Review, and Sabbath Herald, *Feb. 17, 1853, pp. 155, 156*	
February	*"Keep the Sabbath Holy"*	*See* The Youth's Instructor, *February 1853, p. 37*	
Mar. 1	The Character That God Requires in His Ministers	Ms 2, 1853	340
March	*Addition of "Notes of Explanation" to* A Sketch of the Christian Experience and Views of Ellen G. White, *pp. 1, 2.*		
Apr. 14	*"Dear Brethren and Sisters"*	*See* The Advent Review, and Sabbath Herald, *Apr. 14, 1853, p. 192*	
May	Mary Chase	Lt 10, 1853	342

Date	Addressee/Title	File Number	Page
May 26	Anna White	Lt 2, 1853	349
June 2	A Vision Given at Jackson, Michigan	Ms 1, 1853	352
June 23	*Extracts from nonextant letter to Robert and Eunice Harmon*	*See* Spiritual Gifts [vol. 2], *pp. 182, 183*	
June 29	Church in Jackson [Michigan]	Lt 3, 1853	365
June 30	Alfred and Adaline Pearsall	Lt 4, 1853	370
July 2	Vision for Commandment Keepers	Ms 3, 1853	372
July 2	Extract From a Vision Given at Rochester	Ms 4, 1853	375
July 5	Abram and Caroline Dodge	Lt 5, 1853	377
July	Extract From a Vision Regarding James White	Ms 5, 1853	382
Aug. 3	Abram and Caroline Dodge	Lt 6, 1853	383
August	*"Dear Brethren and Sisters"*	*See* The Advent Review, and Sabbath Herald, *Aug. 11, 1853, p. 53*	
Aug. 24	Cyrenius and Louisa Smith	Lt 7, 1853	387
Dec. 3	Brother Pierce	Lt 11, 1853	390
Dec. 5	Sister Kellogg	Lt 9, 1853	394
Dec. 16	*"Exhortation to the Young"*	*See* The Youth's Instructor, *January 1854, pp. 5, 6*	

1854

Date	Addressee/Title	File Number	Page
January	*Publication of* Supplement to the Christian Experience and Views of Ellen G. White.		
Feb. 12	Reproof for Adultery and Neglect of Children	Ms 1, 1854	399
Feb. 12	Testimony for Churches in New York State	Ms 3, 1854	408
Feb. 19	Courtesy and Kindness	Ms 6, 1854	417
Mar. 10	Harriet Stevens	Lt 1, 1854	421
Apr. 11	Brother and Sister Pierce	Lt 2, 1854	423
April	Testimony	Ms 4, 1854	425
April	*"He Will Come Again"*	*See* The Youth's Instructor, *April 1854, pp. 28, 29*	
May	*"To the Young"*	*See* The Youth's Instructor, *May 1854, pp. 37, 38*	

Date	Addressee/Title	File Number	Page
c. Jan. 24	*Louisa Howland*	*See* Spiritual Gifts [vol. 2], *pp. 199-202*	
January	*"The New Year"*	*See* The Youth's Instructor, *January 1856, p. 5*	
c. January	David Lamson	Lt 10, 1856	482
Feb. 21	*"Extracts"*	*See* Advent Review, and Sabbath Herald, *Feb. 21, 1856, pp. 166, 167*	
February	*"Thankfulness, and the True Object of Our Affections"*	*See* The Youth's Instructor, *February 1856, p. 13*	
March	*"Watch and Pray"*	*See* The Youth's Instructor, *March 1856, p. 21*	
April	Charles and Rachel Ann Sperry	Lt 11, 1856	772
c. May 27	Testimony for David Arnold, Alexander Ross, and Others	Ms 2, 1856	486
May	*"The Lord Is Good"*	*See* The Youth's Instructor, *May 1856, pp. 37, 38*	
June	*"'Search the Scriptures'"*	*See* The Youth's Instructor, *June 1856, p. 44*	
July 15	Stockbridge and Louisa Howland	Lt 1, 1856	490
July	*"Jesus Says"*	*See* The Youth's Instructor, *July 1856, p. 52*	
August	*"Salvation Through Christ"*	*See* The Youth's Instructor, *August 1856, pp. 62, 63*	
August	*Publication of* Testimony for the Church, *No. 2*		
Dec. 9	Vision Given at Round Grove, Illinois	Ms 1, 1856	495
Dec. 24	Friends at Home	Lt 4, 1856	501
Dec. 24	*Henry, J. Edson, and William C. White*	*See* An Appeal to the Youth, *pp. 40-44*	
c. 1856	Merritt Cornell, Dan Palmer, John P. Kellogg	Lt 6, 1856	503

NUMERICAL INDEX
OF
ELLEN G. WHITE
LETTERS AND MANUSCRIPTS

File Number	Date	Addressee/Title	Page
Lt 6, 1849	Mar. 22	*Same letter as Lt 4, 1849*	
Lt 7, 1849	Sept.	Gilbert and Deborah Collins	186
Lt 8, 1849	May 29	Leonard and Elvira Hastings	171
Ms 1, 1849	Mar. 24	The Open and Shut Door	160
Ms 2, 1849	Jan. 17	The Sealing	140
Ms 3, 1849	Jan. 18	Our Duty in View of the Time of Trouble	145
Ms 4, 1849	Jan. 31	"To Those Who Are Receiving the Seal of the Living God." Broadside.	147
Ms 5, 1849	Sept. 23	Remarks in Vision	181
Ms 6, 1849	June 30	Synopsis of E. G. White's Vision	177
Ms 7, 1849	Mar. 11	Affliction of Sr. Hastings	156

1850

(Only even numbers were assigned for letters, through Lt 30.)

File Number	Date	Addressee/Title	Page
Lt 2, 1850	*undated*	*Refiled as Lt 7, 1849*	
Lt 4, 1850	Feb. 18	Philip and Nancy Collins	197
Lt 6, 1850	*May 18*	*Refiled as Lt 10, 1851*	
Lt 8, 1850	Aug. 4	Harriet Hastings	211
Lt 10, 1850	Mar. 18	Leonard Hastings	199
Lt 12, 1850	Aug. 15	Stockbridge and Louisa Howland	215
Lt 14, 1850	Sept. 1	Prudence Bates	232
Lt 16, 1850	*Feb. 18*	*An extract from Lt 4, 1850*	
Lt 18, 1850	Jan. 11	Leonard and Elvira Hastings	190
Lt 20, 1850	*Jan. 3*	*A James White letter*	
Lt 22, 1850	*Jan. 10*	*A James White letter*	
Lt 24, 1850	*Jan. 11*	*Same letter as Lt 18, 1850*	
Lt 26, 1850	Nov. 1	Reuben and Belinda Loveland	248
Lt 28, 1850	Nov. 27	Church in Br. Hastings' House	252
Lt 30, 1850	Dec. 13	Reuben and Belinda Loveland	263
Lt 31, 1850	Dec.	Mary Nichols	261
Ms 1, 1850	*Apr. 15*	*Unauthenticated; see Appendix A*	
Ms 2, 1850	Jan. 9	The Need for *The Present Truth*	188
Ms 3, 1850	*Mar. 11*	*Refiled as Ms 7, 1849*	
Ms 4, 1850	Jan. 28	A Copy of E. G. White's Vision	192
Ms 5, 1850	July 29	A Vision the Lord Gave Me	203
Ms 5a, 1850	July	To the Church in Your Place	208
Ms 6, 1850	Aug. 22	A Dream	220
Ms 7, 1850	Aug. 24	A Vision the Lord Gave Me	222

File Number	Date	Addressee/Title	Page
Lt 10, 1857	*January*	*Same as Lt 10, 1856*	
Lt 11, 1857	*Dec. 24*	*Same as Lt 5, 1856*	
Lt 12, 1857	Jan. 30	Harriet Stevens	512
Lt 13, 1857	*Jan. 24*	*Refiled as Lt 2a, 1856*	
Lt 14, 1857	July 12	Elon Everts	521
Lt 15, 1857	c. 1857	Stephen Pierce	550
Ms 1, 1857	June	Lack of Appreciation of the Ministry	517
Ms 2, 1857	July 24	Testimony for the Church in Central New York	526
		1858	
Lt 1, 1858	Mar. 3	Mary Loughborough	556
Lt 2, 1858	c. March	Azmon Woodruff	563
Lt 3, 1857	*Mar. 2*	*Copied from* An Appeal to the Youth, *pp. 42-44*	
Ms 1, 1858	*June*	*Refiled as Ms 7, 1854*	
Ms 2, 1858	Dec. 27	Testimony Regarding the Work in Vermont, New Hampshire, and Massachusetts	567
Ms 3, 1858	c. 1858	Testimony for John and Mary Loughborough	575
		1859	
Lt 1, 1859	c. 1859	Brother T.	754
Lt 1a, 1859	Jan. 4	Leonard, Sarah, and Emma Hastings	662
Lt 2, 1859	June 21	John Byington	672
Lt 3, 1859	Sept. 1	Robert and Eunice Harmon	688
Lt 4, 1859	Sept. 2	William Peabody	691
Lt 5, 1859	Sept. 6	Henry White	695
Lt 6, 1859	Sept. 15	W. C. White	703
Lt 7, 1859	Sept. 24	William, Bruce, and Andrew Graham	710
Lt 8, 1859	Sept. 15	Jane Fraser	705
Lt 9, 1859	Sept. 6	W. C. White	701
Lt 10, 1859	September	W. C. White	727
Lt 11, 1859	Oct. 15	J. Edson White	739
Lt 12, 1859	*Nov. 22*	*Refiled as Lt 5, 1857*	
Lt 13, 1859	Jan. 5	Friends	664
Lt 14, 1859	*Oct. 22 ?*	*W. C. White (missing)*	
Lt 15, 1859	c. 1859	Brother and Sister M.	756
Lt 16, 1859	Oct. 28	Samuel Rhodes	741
Lt 17, 1859	Oct. 28	Friends at Roosevelt	746
Lt 18, 1859	Apr. 14	John Naramore	668

1845

(Lt 1, 1845)

DECEMBER 20, PORTLAND, MAINE

LETTER TO

Enoch Jacobs.[1]

Transcribed from the *Day-Star,* vol. 9, nos. 7, 8, January 24, 1846, pp. 31, 32. See Ellen G. White, *Early Writings,* pp. 13-20.

First known published account by 18-year-old Ellen Harmon of her first vision[2] and subsequent "new earth" vision. Written about one year after her first vision,[3] it blends information from these two visions, which have related content. What follows is an unmodified transcription of the printed text.

Letter from Sister Harmon.

Portland, Me., Dec. 20, 1845.

BRO. JACOBS:—

As God has shown me in holy vision the travels of the Advent people to the Holy City, and the rich reward to be given those who wait the return of their

---

[1] *Identity:* Enoch Jacobs was editor of the *Day-Star,* a Millerite paper published in Cincinnati, Ohio. After the October 1844 disappointment, Jacobs's paper became an important publishing venue for those who continued to believe in the relevance of the 1844 experience. Early in 1846 he became sympathetic to the Shaker view of a spiritual second coming of Christ, and by the summer of 1846 he embraced Shakerism. His publication of this letter was just before his theological shift.

See: SDAE, s.v. "Enoch Jacobs," *"Day-Star";* EGWEnc, s.v. "Enoch Jacobs."

[2] James White, however, had included an abbreviated account of the vision five months earlier, in a letter to the editor of the *Day-Star,* where he wrote of "one Sister in Maine who has had a clear vision of the Advent people traveling to the City of God."

See: James White to "Bro. Jacobs," *Day-Star,* Sept. 6, 1845, p. 17 (letter dated Aug. 19, 1845).

[3] The exact date of Ellen White's first vision is unknown. In her July 13, 1847, letter to Joseph Bates, Ellen White gave the date as December 1844. James White gave the same date in his comments about the vision in *A Word to the "Little Flock,"* published a few weeks earlier. In her autobiography Ellen White described the vision as being received while at the home of Elizabeth Haines in Portland, Maine.

See: Ellen G. White, Lt 3, 1847 (July 13); James White, ed., *A Word to the "Little Flock,"* p. 22; Ellen G. White, *Spiritual Gifts [vol. 2],* p. 30.

Lord from the wedding,[4] it may be my duty to give you a short sketch of what God has revealed to me. The dear saints have got many trials to pass through. But our light afflictions which are but for a moment worketh for us a far more exceeding and eternal weight of glory; while we look not at the things which are seen, for the things which are seen are temporal, but the things which are not seen are eternal.[5] I have tried to bring back a good report, & a few grapes from the heavenly Canaan, for which many would stone me, as the congregation bade stone Caleb and Joshua for their report, (Num. 14:10.) But I declare to you, my brother in the Lord, it is a goodly land, and we are well able to go up and possess it. While praying at the famly [*sic*] altar the Holy Ghost fell on me and I seemed to be rising higher and higher, far above the dark world. I turned to look for the Advent people in the world, but could not find them, when a voice said to me, Look again, and look a little higher. At this, I raised my eyes and see [*sic*] a strait and narrow path, cast up high above the world. On this path the Advent people were traveling to the City, which was at the farther end of the path. They had a bright light set up behind them at the first end of the path, which an angel told me was the Midnight Cry.[6] This light shone all along the path and gave light for their feet so they might not stumble. And if they kept their eyes fixed on Jesus, who was just before them, leading them to the City, they were safe. But soon some grew weary, and said the City was a great way off, and they expected to have entered it before. Then Jesus would encourage them by raising his glorious right arm, and from his arm came a glorious light which waved over the Advent band, and they shouted, Hallelujah! Others rashly denied the light behind them, and said that it was not God that had led them out so far. The light behind them went out which left their feet in perfect darkness, and they stumbled and got their eyes off the mark and lost sight of Jesus, and fell off the path down in the dark and wicked world below. It was just as impossible for them to get on the path again & go to the City, as all the wicked world which God had rejected.[7]

---

[4] Although the important concept of "the return of their Lord from the wedding" is inserted here, it does not actually form part of the December 1844 vision, but is part of Ellen Harmon's introductory remarks to Enoch Jacobs, written one year later, reflecting theological insights gained after the December vision. The wedding imagery is first introduced about two months after the first vision, in the vision of February 1845. See notes under Lt 1, 1846 (Feb. 15).

[5] Cf. 2 Cor. 4:17, 18. The report of this vision contains many scriptural allusions, only a few of which are noted in the annotations. James White supplied more than 40 references in his reprint of the vision in *A Word to the "Little Flock,"* pp. 14-18.

[6] The expression "midnight cry" is an allusion to the warning cry "Behold, the bridegroom cometh; go ye out to meet him," given at midnight in the parable of the 10 virgins (Matt. 25:6). As it is used here it refers to the powerful proclamation during the late summer and autumn of 1844 announcing the second coming of Christ on October 22. Even though the predicted Advent failed to materialize, this first vision declares the Midnight Cry to be "a bright light." No information is given at this stage regarding in what way the seemingly discredited Midnight Cry contained light from God.

[7] Two groups are portrayed here as rejected by God: (1) those who had initially accepted

They fell all the way along the path one after another, until we heard the voice of God like many waters, which gave us the day and hour of Jesus' coming.[8] The

---

the Second Advent message ("Midnight Cry") but later rejected it; (2) "all the wicked world," composed of persons who had never professed a faith in the Second Advent. Although we are not told specifically why God "rejected" the members of the second group, the implication is that like the first group, it was because they had wickedly rejected the Advent message.

Concerning members of the first group—those who at first accepted but later rejected the Midnight Cry—William Miller initially took a view similar to that of this vision. They "were crying for mercy a few days since . . . [but] are now scoffing and mocking us." He then added the pointed question "Have not such individuals sinned against the Holy Ghost?" (see William Miller to I. E. Jones, in *Advent Herald,* Dec. 25, 1844, p. 154). For biblical examples of probation closing on certain classes and groups of people, see Francis D. Nichol, *Ellen G. White and Her Critics,* pp. 206-210.

Much discussion has ensued through the years as to the extent and size of the second group—"all the wicked world which God had rejected." Some have held that "the wicked world" refers to the entire population of the world (apart from the loyal Advent believers), since, presumably, in a general sense all humanity is "wicked" and sinful. While this is a reasonable interpretation of the phrase "all the wicked world" taken on its own, the context suggests (as argued above) that "the wicked world" refers to a much more circumscribed group, viz., that which had specifically rejected, maligned, and mocked the Advent proclamation. This would accord with Ellen White's own interpretation of the passage in 1883 when she was called upon to explain its omission in later printings of the vision:

"Two classes are brought to view in the vision—those who declared the light which they had followed a delusion, and the wicked of the world who, having rejected the light, had been rejected of God. No reference is made to those who had not seen the light, and therefore were not guilty of its rejection" (Ms 4, 1883, quoted in Ellen G. White, *Selected Messages,* book 1, p. 64).

An example of the second, more restricted, interpretation of "wicked world" can be seen in another passage from William Miller: "And the wicked world, who have scoffed at the idea of Christ's second coming . . . and laughed and ridiculed the servants of Christ . . . will be silent." Apollos Hale and Joseph Turner likewise used "world" in a very specific manner when they wrote of "the world" that had "rejected the [Advent] truth" and "turned away their ears with loathing from its warnings and promises." (See William Miller, *Evidence From Scripture and History,* p. 188; A. Hale and J. Turner, "Has Not the Savior Come as the Bridegroom?" *Advent Mirror,* January 1845, pp. 3, 4.)

The bibliography of published comment and debate on "the wicked world" passage is extensive. For contrasting interpretations, see, e.g., Uriah Smith, *The Visions of Mrs. E. G. White,* pp. 29-31; W. W. Fletcher, *The Reasons for My Faith,* pp. 188, 205, 206; Francis D. Nichol, *Ellen G. White and Her Critics,* pp. 212-214; Rolf J. Poehler, "'. . . and the Door Was Shut,'" pp. 109, 110, 127, 128; Herbert E. Douglass, *Messenger of the Lord,* pp. 557, 558.

For surveys of the "shut door" debates of the time, see P. Gerard Damsteegt, *Foundations of the Seventh-day Adventist Message and Mission,* pp. 106-112; George R. Knight, *Millennial Fever,* pp. 236-242; Ingemar Lindén, *1844 and the Shut Door Problem,* pp.19-23. See also introductory essay in this volume, "The 'Shut Door' and Ellen White's Visions," and online bibliography by Gary Shearer, "The Shut Door Controversy," at http://library.puc.edu/heritage/bib-ShutDoCon.html.

[8] In *A Word to the "Little Flock"* James White provides an early discussion of this prediction, contrasting it with Millerite thinking on "the voice of God." Note that according to the sequence described in this vision, the "day and hour of Jesus' coming" is announced after the close of probation and apparently only a short time before the Second Advent. When some subsequently alleged that Ellen White claimed to know the day and hour of Jesus' coming, having been shown it in vision, she responded, "I have not the slightest knowledge as to the time spoken by the voice of God. I heard the hour proclaimed, but had no remembrance of that hour after I came out of vision."

living saints, 144,000,[9] in number, know and understand the voice, while the wicked thought it was thunder & an earthquake. When God spake the time, he poured on us the Holy Ghost, and our faces began to light up and shine with the glory of God as Moses did when he came down from Mount Sinai, (Ex. 34:30-34.) By this time the 144,000 were all sealed[10] and perfectly united. On their foreheads was written, God, New Jerusalem, and a glorious Star containing Jesus' new name.[11] At our happy, holy state the wicked were enraged, and would rush violently up to lay hands on us to thrust us in prison,[12] when we would stretch forth the hand in the name of the Lord, and the wicked would fall helpless to the ground. Then it was that the synagogue of Satan[13] knew that God had loved us who could wash one another's feet, and salute the holy brethren with a holy kiss,[14] and they worshipped at our feet. Soon our eyes were drawn to

---

See: James White, "The Voice of God," in *A Word to the "Little Flock,"* pp. 4-8; Ellen G. White, Lt 38, 1888 (Aug. 11).

[9] *See:* EGWEnc, s.v. "144,000."

[10] *See:* EGWEnc, s.v. "Seal of God."

[11] Cf. Rev. 3:12; Rom. 16:16.

[12] That the saints would experience violent persecution just prior to the Second Coming, as portrayed here, was not featured in Millerite prophetic exposition, at least during the final years of the movement. "An idea is abroad that a great time of persecution and martyrdom is before the church," wrote Josiah Litch in 1840, "but I cannot find it in the Bible." Thus, for example, Litch held that the terrors of the seven last plagues would be poured out on the wicked *after* the Second Advent, when the saints had already been delivered, not before. Hale and Jacobs argued that the "time of trouble" predicted in Daniel 12:1 would not touch the saints, who would be delivered *before* it started. On the matter of the seven last plagues, major Millerite expositors such as Apollos Hale, Enoch Jacobs, and C. S. Minor agreed with Litch. William Miller had a different view, holding that six of the seven plagues were already past, being symbolic of the judgments of God on the Papacy going back to the Reformation. While he thought the seventh plague was still future, it did not presage any special persecution for the saints other than what they had always had to endure throughout the centuries. Thus on this point the vision given to Ellen Harmon constituted a major departure from mainstream Millerite thinking. This probably explains why, when this vision was included in the pamphlet *A Word to the "Little Flock"* 16 months later, James White felt it necessary to include a section offering biblical support for the position "that the seven last plagues were all in the future, and that they were all to be poured out before the first resurrection." For White himself, this represented a reversal of his earlier Millerite position.

See: L. [Josiah Litch], "The Battle of Armageddon (concluded)," *Signs of the Times,* Sept. 15, 1840, p. 95; Josiah Litch, *Prophetic Expositions,* p. 175; A. Hale, *Herald of the Bridegroom!* pp. 23, 29; E. Jacobs, "Seventh Seal," *Midnight Cry,* Oct. 26, 1843, p. 82; C. S. M. [C. S. Minor], "His Coming," *Midnight Cry,* Sept. 21, 1843, p. 36; William Miller, *Evidence From Scripture and History,* pp. 219-232; James White, "The Seven Last Plagues," in James White, ed., *A Word to the "Little Flock,"* pp. 1-4.

[13] The imagery used here is taken from Revelation 3:9, in which religious opponents of the people of God ("synagogue of Satan") are finally brought to humbly acknowledge that those they had bitterly opposed were "loved by God." For further comment, see Lt 2, 1847 (Apr. 21), note 5.

[14] It is interesting to note the positive mention, already in this first vision, of the ancient Christian liturgical practices of foot washing and the "holy kiss." It marks an early expression of the restorationist ideal which was to become central to Seventh-day Adventist theological development. Following New Testament admonitions to "salute one another with an holy kiss"

the East, for a small black cloud had appeared about half as large as a man's hand, which we all knew was the Sign of the Son of Man. We all in solemn silence gazed on the cloud as it drew nearer, lighter, and brighter, glorious, and still more glorious, till it was a great white cloud. The bottom appeared like fire, a rainbow was over it, around the cloud were ten thousand angels singing a most lovely song. And on it sat the Son of Man, on his head were crowns, his hair was white and curly and lay on his shoulders. His feet had the appearance of fire, in his right hand was a sharp sickle, in his left a silver trumpet. His eyes were as a flame of fire, which searched his children through and through. Then all faces gathered paleness, and those that God had rejected gathered blackness. Then we all cried out, who shall be able to stand? Is my robe spotless? Then the angels ceased to sing, and there was some time of awful silence, when Jesus spoke, Those who have clean hands and a pure heart shall be able to stand, my grace is sufficient for you. At this, our faces lighted up, and joy filled every heart. And the angels struck a note higher and sung again while the cloud drew still nearer the earth. Then Jesus' silver trumpet sounded, as he descended on the cloud, wrapped in flames of fire. He gazed on the graves of the sleeping saints then raised his eyes and hands to heaven & cried out, Awake! Awake! Awake! ye that sleep in the dust, and arise. Then there was a mighty earthquake. The graves opened, and the dead came up clothed with immortality. The 144,000 shouted, Hallelujah! as they recognized their friends who had been torn from them by death, and in the same moment we were changed and caught up together with them to meet the Lord in the air. We all entered the cloud together, and were 7 days ascending to the sea of glass, when Jesus brought along the crowns and with his own right hand placed them on our heads. He gave us harps of gold and palms of victory. Here on the sea of glass the 144,000 stood in a perfect square. Some of them had very bright crowns, others not so bright. Some crowns

---

(Rom. 16:16, etc.) this practice found its way into the worship services of the early church. "Having ended the prayers, we salute one another with a kiss," Justin Martyr reported in the second century (*First Apology* I. 65). Gradually, however, the "holy kiss" became restricted to a few special ceremonial occasions, such as the consecration of bishops. A somewhat similar historical trajectory can be traced in connection with liturgical foot washing as instituted by Jesus (John 13). With the coming of the Reformation, most Reformers elected not to reinstate these practices; the exception was the Anabaptists, among whom the holy kiss and foot washing were revived. The situation in mid-nineteenth-century America remained largely the same, with only a minority of smaller churches, such as the Mennonites (of the Anabaptist tradition) and the Dunkards, maintaining these practices while the mainline Protestant churches rejected them.

See: The New Schaff-Herzog Encyclopedia of Religious Knowledge, s.v. "Kiss of Peace," by Victor Schultze; *Encyclopaedia of Religion and Ethics,* s.v. "Feet-Washing," by G. A. Frank Knight; *The Mennonite Encyclopedia,* s.v. "Kiss," by James Reusser. For a recent discussion of the restoration motif in Seventh-day Adventist theology, see Hans K. LaRondelle, "The Remnant and the Three Angels' Messages," in *Handbook of Seventh-day Adventist Theology,* pp. 880-889.

appeared hung[15] with stars, while others had but few. All were perfectly satisfied with their crowns. And they were all clothed with a glorious white mantle from their shoulders to their feet. Angels were all about us as we marched over the sea of glass to the gate of the City. Jesus raised his mighty glorious arm, laid hold of the gate and swung it back on its golden hinges, and said to us, You have washed your robes in my blood, stood stiffly for my truth, enter in. We all marched in and felt we had a perfect right in the City. Here we see [*sic*] the tree of life, & the throne of God. Out of the throne came a pure river of water, and on either side of the river was the tree of life.[16] On one side of the river was a trunk of a tree and a trunk on the other side of the river, both of pure transparent gold. At first I thought I see [*sic*] two trees. I looked again and see [*sic*] they were united at the top in one tree. So it was the tree of life on either side of the river of life. Its branches bowed to the place where we stood. And the fruit was glorious, which looked like gold mixed with silver. We all went under the tree, and sat down to

---

[15] In subsequent printings, the apparent error of "hung" was corrected to "heavy."

See: Ellen G. Harmon, Ms 1, 1846 (Apr. 6); James White, ed., *A Word to the "Little Flock,"* p. 15.

[16] The description given in this section leaves no doubt that after the resurrection the saints ascend to heaven, where are "the City," the tree of life, and the river of life. On this point, in interesting ways the account diverges from mainstream Millerism of the time. William Miller's conclusion, accepted almost universally in his movement, was that at Christ's coming both the "living and raised saints will be caught up to meet the Lord in the air. Then the saints will be judged and presented to the Father without spot or wrinkle. . . . And while this is being done in the air, the earth will be cleansed by fire. . . . Then Christ and his people will come down from the heavens, or middle air, and live with his saints on the new earth in a new heaven, or dispensation, forever." The idea that the saints ascend to heaven after the resurrection is not found in Millerite accounts. The saints are "in the air" or "middle air" awaiting the purification of the earth. The focus is on the earth to which the saints descend with the Holy City once the earth has been cleansed, to spend the millennium and beyond.

The Millerite concept of an earthly millennium was retained in the writings of Joseph Bates as late as 1847. Prior to Christ's "second appearing," he wrote in 1847, He receives "the Holy City, which is the capital of his kingdom, that he will bring with him and establish here, and it will ever be the capital of all his dominions under the whole heaven" (*Second Advent Waymarks,* p. 57).

James White likewise maintained in 1846 that "Christ is coming to raise the dead saints and change those who are alive. Christ is coming to restore this earth to its primitive purity. He is coming to set up His everlasting kingdom and reign. Christ is to be king. The Land promised to Abraham and enlarged in Dan. 7: and Isaiah 65: is to be the territory, the spiritual seed of Abram, the subjects, etc." (In a memory statement made 10 years later, in 1855, James White claimed that the Millerite preacher E. R. Pinney had taught "that the Kingdom of God would not be established on the earth till the close of the seventh millennium," and that he, White, had "taught the same since 1845." However, the above extract suggests that it was somewhat later that he took this view.) It would seem, then, that the vision of December 1844 contained hints of a heavenly millennium well before this theme was developed by Sabbatarian Adventists.

See: "Synopsis of Mr. Miller's Views," *Midnight Cry,* Nov. 22, 1842, p. [2]; Joseph Bates, *Second Advent Waymarks and High Heaps,* p. 57; James White to "Brother Collins," Aug. 26, 1846; J. W. [James White], "A Test," *Review,* Oct. 16, 1855, p. 61. For a comparison of Millerite with Seventh-day Adventist views on the millennium, see SDAE, s.v. "Millennium"; Alberto R. Timm, *The Sanctuary and the Three Angels' Messages,* pp. 152, 153.

look at the glory of the place, when Bro. Fitch [Charles Fitch],[17] and Stockman [Levi Stockman],[18] who had preached the gospel of the kingdom, whom God had laid in the grave to save them, came up to us and asked us what we had passed through while they were sleeping. We tried to call up our greatest trials, but they looked so small compared with the far more exceeding and eternal weight of glory that surrounded us, that we could not speak them out, and we all cried out Hallelujah, heaven is cheap enough, and we touched our glorious harps and made heaven's arches ring. And as we were gazing at the glories of the place, our eyes were attracted upwards to something that had the appearance of silver. I asked Jesus to let me see what was within there. In a moment we were winging our way upward and entering in. Here we saw good old father Abraham, Isaac, and Jacob, Noah, Daniel, and many like them. And I saw a veil with a heavy fringe of silver, and gold as a border on the bottom. It was very beautiful. I asked Jesus what was within the veil. He raised it with his own right arm, and bade me take heed. I saw there a glorious ark, overlaid with pure gold, and it had a glorious border resembling Jesus' crowns. On it were two bright angels; their wings were spread over the ark as they sat on each end, with their faces turned towards each other and looking downward. In the ark, beneath where the angels [*sic*] wings were spread, was a golden pot of Manna of a yellowish cast, and I saw a rod, which Jesus said was Aaron's, I saw it bud, blossom, and bear fruit.—And I saw two long golden rods on which hung silver wires, and on the wires most glorious grapes. One cluster was more than a man here can carry. And I saw Jesus step up and take of the manna, almonds, grapes, and pomegranates, and bear them down to the city, and place them on the supper table. I stepped up to see how much was taken away, and there was just as much left, and we shouted Hallelujah. Amen.[19] We all descended from this place down into the city, and with Jesus at our head we all descended from the city down to this earth, on a great and mighty mountain, which could not bear Jesus up, and it parted asunder,

---

[17] *Identity:* Charles Fitch (1805-1844) was a prominent Holiness Millerite minister who died on October 14, 1844, less than two weeks before the anticipated date for the Second Coming.

See: SDAE, s.v. "Charles Fitch"; EGWEnc, s.v. "Charles Fitch."

[18] *Identity:* Levi Stockman (1812-1844) was a respected Methodist Millerite minister who lived in Maine. He helped Ellen Harmon understand the love of God during her conversion process. He contracted tuberculosis and died before the 1844 disappointment. In this vision Ellen White is taken to the future and meets these men after the second coming of Jesus and the resurrection.

See: SDAE, s.v. "Levi Stockman"; EGWEnc, s.v. "Levi Stockman."

[19] From this point forward, Ellen White continues with an account of her "new earth" vision that describes the descent of the New Jerusalem to the earth following the millennium and the restoration of the earth to its Edenic state. The "new earth" vision was probably given in late spring or early summer of 1845. In this and her previous Midnight Cry vision she emphasized the tangible aspects of heaven and the new earth. Ellen White vigorously opposed the spiritualizing view of some Millerites who said that they were now spiritually living in the New Jerusalem. See Ellen G. White, *Spiritual Gifts [vol. 2],* pp. 52-56.

and there was a mighty plain. Then we looked up and saw the great city with twelve foundations, twelve gates, three on each side, and an angel at each gate, and all cried out the city, the great city, it's coming, it's coming down from God, out of heaven, and it came and settled on the place where we stood. Then we began to look at the glorious things outside of the city. There I saw most glorious houses, that had the appearance of silver, supported by four pillars, set with pearls most glorious to behold, which were to be inhabited by the saints. In them was a golden shelf, I saw many of the saints go into the houses, take off their glittering crowns and lay them on the shelf, then go out into the field by the houses to do something with the earth, not as we have to do with the earth here; no, no. A glorious light shone all about their heads, and they were continually shouting and offering praises to God. And I saw another field full of all kinds of flowers, and as I plucked them, I cried out, well they will never fade. Next I saw a field of tall grass, most glorious to behold. It was living green, and had a reflection of silver and gold as it waved proudly to the glory of King Jesus. Then we entered a field full of all kinds of beasts; the lion, the lamb, the leopard and the wolf, altogether in perfect union. We passed through the midst of them, and they followed on peaceably after. Then we entered a wood, not like the dark woods we have here, no, no; but light, and all over glorious. The branches of the trees waved to and fro, and we all cried out, we will dwell safely in the wilderness and sleep in this woods. We passed through the wood, for we were on our way to Mount Zion, as we were traveling along we met a company who were also gazing at the glories of the place: I noticed red as a border on their garments. Their crowns were brilliant—their robes were pure white. As we greeted them, I asked Jesus who they were? He said they were martyrs that had been slain for him. With them was an innumerable company of little ones, they had a hem of red on their garments also. Mount Zion was just before us, and on the Mount sat a glorious temple,[20] and about it were seven other mountains, on which grew roses and lilies, and I saw the little ones climb, or if they chose use their little wings and fly to the top of the mountains, and pluck the never fading flowers. There were all kinds of trees around the temple to beautify the place. The box, the pine, the fir, the oil, the myrtle, the pomegranet [*sic*] and the fig tree, bowed down with the weight of its timely figs that made the place look all over glorious. And as we were about to enter the holy temple, Jesus raised his lovely voice and

---

[20] In his vision of the "holy Jerusalem, descending out of heaven" John wrote, "I saw no temple therein" (Rev. 21:10, 22). Likewise, Ellen Harmon saw no temple in the Holy City in the earth made new. She did, however, see a temple on a mount "outside of the city," although the main function of that temple is not revealed. Since sin and evil have now been eradicated forever, the temple cannot have the soteriological purpose it had served in heaven prior to the eradication of sin. Richard Davidson suggests that "at the consummation of salvation history, the heavenly sanctuary or temple apparently returns to its original doxological function."

See: Richard M. Davidson, "Sanctuary Typology," in *Symposium on Revelation,* pp. 99-130.

said, only the 144,000 enter this place, and we shouted Hallelujah. Well bless the Lord, Bro. Jacobs, it is an extra meeting for those who have the seal of the living God. This temple was supported by seven pillars, all of transparent gold, set with pearls most glorious. The glorious things I saw there, I cannot begin to describe. O, that I could talk in the language of Canaan, then could I tell a little of the glory of the upper world; but if faithful you soon will know all about it. I saw there the tables of stone in which the names of the 144,000, were engraved in letters of gold.—After we had beheld the glory of the temple, we went out. Then Jesus left us and went to the city. Soon we heard his lovely voice again, saying: Come my people; you have come out of great tribulation, and done my will, suffered for me; come in to supper, for I will gird myself, and serve you. We shouted Hallelujah, glory, and entered into the city, and I saw a table of pure silver, it was many miles in length, yet our eyes could extend over it. And I saw the fruit of the tree of life, the manna, almonds, figs, pomegranets [*sic*], grapes, and many other kinds of fruit. We all reclined at the table. I asked Jesus to let me eat of the fruit. He said, not now. Those who eat of the fruit of this land, go back to earth no more. But in a little while if faithful, you shall both eat of the fruit of the tree of life, and drink of the water of the fountain, and he said, you must go back to the earth again, and relate to others, what I have revealed to you. Then an angel bore me gently down to this dark world. Sometimes I think I cannot stay here any longer, all things of earth look so dreary. I feel very lonely here, for I have seen a better land. O, that I had wings like a dove, then would I fly away, and be at rest.

ELLEN G. HARMON.

N.B. This was not written for publication; but for the encouragement of all who may see it, and be encouraged by it.

E. G. H.

THE DAY-STAR. 31

Letter from Bro. Mann.

Randolph, Mass., Dec. 28, 1845.

Dear Bro. Jacobs: —

I want to write a few words about anti-christ and the last time spoken of in 1 John 2: 18–19. Little children, it is the last time: and as ye have heard that anti-christ shall come, even now are there many anti-christs; whereby we know it is the last time. They went out from us, but they were not of us: for if they had been of us; they would no doubt have continued with us; but they went out, that they might be made manifest that they were not all of us. Jude speaks of the same characters, in almost the same words. Jude 13, 19. "A time" in the Bible is one year, or 360 years. The last time cannot be 360 years. therefore it must be one year. 1 Peter 1: 4–5, shows that we are to be delivered in the last time: The same time, or year is spoken of in Isa. 61, 2; 63: 4; 34: 8. In John 2: 22–23, we find who anti-christ is; "he that denieth the Son," he that denies a literal Jesus. Well, these did not become "many" until after this Jewish year commenced, but since that time many have sprang up all around among us. About one half of those who were in the truth when the year commenced have turned antichrist. Well, Praise God! by this "we know that it is the last time," yes, we know it. In Luke 12: 56, we find that these are hypocrites who do not discern this time. The jubilee year, Lev. 25: 10–13, corresponds with the last time. In this year we shall return, every man to his possession. In Luke 12: 36–38, we find that the Lord will come in the second, or third watch, after the wedding time commences; well, we know the first watch reached to the commencement of this year, aud the 2d and 3d watches run parallel with "the last time," and "the jubilee year.— Bro. Jacobs, we read in 2 John 10, 11, if any come unto you and bring not this doctrine, receive him not into your house, neither bid him God speed.

Yours waiting for redemtion in this last time.

T. B. MANN.

Letter from Sister Harmon.

Portland, Me., Dec. 20, 1845.

Bro. Jacobs :—

As God has shown me in holy vision the travels of the Advent people to the Holy City, and the rich reward to be given those who wait the return of their Lord from the wedding, it may be my duty to give you a short sketch of what God has revealed to me. The dear saints have got many trials to pass through. But our light afflictions which are but for a moment worketh for us a far more exceeding and eternal weight of glory; while we look not at the things which are seen, for the things which are seen are temporal, but the things which are not seen are eternal. I have tried to bring back a good report, & a few grapes from the heavenly Canaan, for which many would stone me, as the congregation bade stone Caleb and Joshua for their report, (Num. 14: 10.) But I declare to you, my brother in the Lord, it is a goodly land, and we are well able to go up and possess it. While praying at the family altar the Holy Ghost fell on me and I seemed to be rising higher and higher, far above the dark world. I turned to look for the Advent people in the world, but could not find them, when a voice said to me, Look again, and look a little higher. At this, I raised my eyes and see a strait and narrow path, cast up high above the world. On this path the Advent people were traveling to theCity, which was at the farther end of the path. They had a bright light set up behind them at the first end of the path, which an angel told me was the Midnight Cry. This light shone all along the path aud gave light for their feet so they might not stumble. And if they kept their eyes fixed on Jesus, who was just before them, leading them to the City, they were safe. But soon some grew weary, and said the City was a great way off, and they expected to have entered it before. Then Jesus would encourage them by raising his glorious right arm, and from his arm came a glorious light which waved over the Advent band, and they shouted, Hallelujah! Others rashly denied the light behind them, and said that it was not God that had led them out so far. The light behind them went out which left their feet in perfect darkness, and they stumbled and got their eyes off the mark and lost sight of Jesus, and fell off the path down in the dark and wicked world below. It was just as impossible for them to get on the path again & go to the City, as all the wicked world which God had rejected. They fell all the way along the path one after another, until we heard the voice of God like many waters, which gave us the day and hour of Jesus' coming. The living saints, 144,000, in number, know and understand the voice, while the wicked thought it was thunder & an earthquake. When God spake the time, he poured on us the Holy Ghost, and our faces began to light up and shine with the glory of God as Moses did when he came down from Mount Sinai, (Ex. 34: 30-34.) By this time the 144,000 were all sealed and perfectly united. On their foreheads was written, God, New Jerusalem, and a glorious Star containing Jesus' new name. At our happy, holy state the wicked were enraged, and would rush violently up to lay hands on us to thrust us in prison, when we would stretch forth the hand in the name of the Lord, and the wicked would fall helpless to the ground. Then it was that the synagogue of Satan knew that God had loved us who could wash one another's feet, and salute the holy brethren with a holy kiss, and they worshipped at our feet. Soon our eyes were drawn to the East, for a small black cloud had appeared about half as large as a man's hand, which we all knew was the Sign of the Son of Man. We all in solemn silence gazed on the cloud as it drew nearer, lighter, and brighter, glorious, and still more glorious, till it was a great white cloud. The bottom appeared like fire, a rainbow was over it, around the cloud were ten thousand angels singing a most lovely song. And on it sat the Son of Man, on his head were crowns, his hair was white and curly and lay on his shoulders. His feet had the appearance of fire, in his right hand was a sharp sickle, in his left a silver trumpet. His eyes were as a flame of fire, which searched his children through and through. Then all faces gathered paleness, and those that God had rejected gathered blackness. Then we all cried out, who shall be able to stand? Is my robe spotless? Then the angels ceased to sing, and there was some time of awful silence. when Jesus spoke, Those who have clean hands and a pure heart shall be able to stand, my grace is sufficient for you. At this, our faces lighted up, and joy filled every heart. And the angels struck a note higher and sung again while the cloud drew still nearer the earth. Then Jesus' silver trumpet sounded, as he descended on the cloud, wrapped in flames of fire, He gazed on the graves of the sleeping saints then raised his eyes and hands to heaven & cried out, Awake! Awake! Awake! ye that sleep in the dust, and arise. Then there was a mighty earthquake. The graves opened, and the dead came up clothed with immortality. The 144,000 shouted, Hallelujah! as they recognised their friends who had been torn from them by death, and in the same moment we were changed and caught up together with them to meet the Lord in the air. We all entered the cloud together, and were 7 days ascending to the sea of glass, when Jesus brought along the crowns and with his own right hand placed them on our heads. He gave us harps of gold and palms of victory. Here on the sea of glass the 144,000 stood in a perfect square. Some of them had very bright crowns, others not so bright. Some crowns appeared hung with stars, while others had but few. All were perfectly satisfied with their crowns. And they were all clothed with a glorious white mantle from their shoulders to their feet. Angels were all about us as we marched over the sea of glass to the gate of the City. Jesus raised his mighty glorious arm, laid hold of the gate and swung it back on its golden hinges, and said to us, You have washed your robes in my blood, stood stiffly for my truth, enter in. We all marched in and felt we had a perfect right in the City. Here we see the tree of life, & the throne of God. Out of the throne came a pure river of water, and on either side of the river was the tree of life. On one side of the river was a trunk of a tree and a trunk on the other side of the river, both of pure transparent gold. At first I thought I see two trees. I looked again and see they were united at the top in one tree. So it was the tree of life on either side of the river of life. Its branches bowed to the place where we stood. And the fruit was glorious, which looked like gold mixed with silver. We all went under the tree, and sat down to look at the glory of the place, when Bro. Fitch, and Stockman, who had preached the gospel of the kingdom, whom God had laid in the grave to save them, came up to us and asked us what we had passed through while they were sleeping. We tried to call up our greatest trials, but they looked so small compared with the far more exceeding and eternal weight of glory that surrounded us, that we could not speak them out, and we all cried out Hallelujah, heaven is cheap enough, and we touched our glorious harps and and made heaven's arches ring. And as we were gazing at the glories of the place, our eyes were attracted upwards to something that had the appearance of silver. I asked Jesus to let me see what was within there. In a moment we were winging our way upward and entering in. Here we saw good old father Abrahnm, Isaac, and Jacob, Noah, Daniel, and many like them. And I saw a veil with a heavy fringe of silver, and gold as a border on the bottom. It was very beautiful. I asked Jesus what was within the veil. He raised it with his own right arm, and bade me take heed. I saw there a glorious ark, overlaid with pure gold, and it had a glorious border resembling Jesus' crowns. On it were two bright angels; their wings were spread over the ark as they sat on each end, with their faces turned towards each other and looking downward. In the ark, beneath where the angels wings were spread, was a golden pot of Manna of a yellowish cast, and I saw a rod, which Jesus said was Aarons, I saw it bud, blossom, and bear fruit.— And I saw two long golden rods on which hung silver wires, and on the wires most glorious grapes. One cluster was more than a man here can carry. And I saw Jesus step up and take of the manna, almonds, grapes, and pomegranates, and bear them down to the city, and place them on the supper table. I steped up to see how much was taken away, and there was just as much left, and we shouted Hallelujah. Amen. We all descended from this place down into the city, and with Jesus at our head we all descended from the city down to this earth, on a great and mighty mountain, which could not bear Jesus up, and it parted asunder, and there was a mighty plain. Then we looked up and saw the great city with twelve foundations, twelve gates, three on each side, and an angel at each gate, and all cried out the city, the great city, it's coming, it's coming down from God, out of heaven, and it came and settled on the place where we stood. Then we began to look at the glorious things outside of the city. There I saw most glorious houses, that had the appearance of silver, supported by four pillars, set with pearls most glorious to behold, which were to be inhabited by the saints. In them was a golden shelf, I saw many of the saints go into the houses, take off their glittering crowns and lay them on the shelf, then go out into the field by the houses to do something with the earth, not as we have to do with the earth here; no, no. A glorious light shone all about their heads, and they were continually shouting and offering praises to God. And I saw another field full of all kind of flowers, and as I plucked them, I cried out, well they will never fade. Next I saw a field of tall grass, most glorious to behold. It was living green, and had a reflection of silver and gold as it waived proudly to the glory of King Jesus. Then we entered a field full of all kinds of beasts; the lion, the lamb, the leopard and the wolf, altogether in perfect union- We passed through the midst of them, and they followed on peaceably after. Then we entered a wood, not like the dark woods we have here, no, no; but light, and all over glorious. The branches of the trees waved to and fro, and we all cried out we will dwell safely in the wilderness and sleep in this woods. We passed through the wood, for

Ellen (Harmon) White's earliest known letter, published in the Day-Star, *January 24, 1846. Courtesy of the Center for Adventist Research.*

we were on our way to Mount Zion, as we were traveling along we met a company who were also gazing at the glories of the place: I noticed red as a border on their garments. Their crowns were brilliant—their robes were pure white. As we greeted them, I asked Jesus who they were? He said they were martyrs that had been slain for him. With them was an innumerable company of little ones, they had a hem of red on their garments also. Mount Zion was just before us, and on the Mount sat a glorious temple, and about it were seven other mountains, on which grew roses and lillies, and I saw the little ones climb, or if they chose use their little wings and fly to the top of the mountains, and pluck the never fading flowers. There were all kinds of trees around the temple to beautify the place. The box, the pine, the fir, the oil, the myrtle, the pomegranet, and the fig tree, bowed down with the weight of its timely figs that made the place look all over glorious. And as we were about to enter the holy temple, Jesus raised his lovely voice and said, only the 144,000 enter this place, and we shouted Hallelujah. Well bless the Lord, Bro. Jacobs, it is an extra meeting for those who have the seal of the living God. This temple was supported by seven pillars, all of transparent gold, set with pearls most glorious. The glorious things I saw there, I cannot begin to describe. O, that I could talk in the language of Canaan, then could I tell a little of the glory of the upper world; but if faithful you soon will know all about it. I saw there the tables of stone in which the names of the 144,000, were engraved in letters of gold.—After we had beheld the glory of the temple, we went out. Then Jesus left us and went to the city. Soon we heard his lovely voice again, saying: Come my people; you have come out of great tribulation, and done my will, suffered for me; come in to supper, for I will gird myself, and serve you. We shouted Hallelujah, glory, and entered into the city, and I saw a table of pure silver, it was many miles in length, yet our eyes could extend over it. And I saw the fruit of the tree of life, the manna, almonds, figs, pomegranets, grapes, and many other kinds of fruit. We all reclined at the table. I asked Jesus to let me eat of the fruit. He said, not now. Those who eat of the fruit of this land, go back to earth no more. But in a little while if faithful, you shall both eat of the fruit of the tree of life, and drink of the water of the fountain, and he said, you must go back to the earth again, and relate to others, what I have revealed to you. Then an angel bore me gently down to this dark world. Sometimes I think I cannot stay here any longer, all things of earth look so dreary. I feel very lonely here, for I have seen a better land. O, that I had wings like a dove, then would I fly away, and be at rest.

ELLEN G. HARMON.

N. B. This was not written for publication; but for the encouragement of all who may see it, and be encouraged by it. E. G. H.

Letter from Bro. Wilbur.

West Troy, Dec. 30th, 1845.

Dear Bro. Jacobs:—

I see by your last paper you want all who wish their papers continued, to write to that effect.

I want you to send me the Day Star as long as you publish it. I don't feel positive about all of your positions, but I cannot overthrow them by the Bible, neither have I found any one that could, though many have tried it; but to my mind they have utterly failed, neither have I felt so positive about any thing since the 7th month. But one thing is plain, the wise shall have understanding of how long it will be unto the end of these wonders & what the end of these things will be; for Gabriel told Daniel so. Although I have been shaken on most every thing else, I have never doubted this; and one other saying of the angel I never doubted, that is this, *knowledge shall be increased.*

Now, Bro. Jacobs, I want to tell you some of my feelings since the 7th month. I was then reading the Herald, Midnight Cry, and Voice of Truth, I thought the most of the two former ones. I would get them all at once and would read them if possible before I done any thing else, reading the Voice of Truth last, but I soon found that I had the best of the wine at the last of the feast; and finally, the Herald and Watch drew back so far (as I thought) that I dropped them and feasted on the Voice of Truth; and I have continued to feast on it this last summer, but less and less till now I am obliged to place it on a level with the Herald; and indeed I have good authority for doing so, for I saw a note from the Herald copied in a late number of the Voice of Truth, in which brother Himes could see no difference between the two papers, and brother Marsh acknowledged as much. Ah! thought I, this will account in part for the indifference I have felt of late in reading that paper. When I read the lashing brother Peavy got in that paper, I felt I could not give another dollar to support it. I don't want to find fault with brother Marsh, but I can see he is not the same lovely spirit he was last spring, and that is not strange, for very few of our brethren are out here. Dear brother I hope you will keep humble so the Lord can teach us through you as he has done. I do not worship my brother, but I admire your spirit, and then adore the God who gave it.

I see your weekly receipts are small, and I had saved some money which I had intended to send you, but I have been obliged to put it to other use, but I hope the brethren who can will attend to these matters, and may the Lord bless them. I hope I shall be able to do something soon, though as yet I am not in debt for the paper only to God. I have wished it might be enlarged, but perhaps it is best as it is. The Lord direct you and the rest of the brethren. Amen.

Your brother,

HIRAM WILBUR.

Letter from Bro. Cook.

New York, Jan. 8, 1846.

Dear Bro. Jacobs:—

Your paper of Jan. 3d is read. One good brother said that it was the best number that had ever appeared. Bro Penfield should recollect that my remark concerning Prof. Bush, related to *the resurrection*, including Christ the first fruits and then those who are his "at his coming."

As to the grand theme of your paper, I have no time to write. My engagement in Newark calls me away. I rest in the revealed will of our gracious Lord, as to this subject, just as I do in relation to the Divine Character. My powers are too feeble to attempt to make my God any thing different from what He has revealed himself. For many years my reverence for God has forbiden any irreverent theory as to the Divine existence. Should it seem to be desirable I may give what seems to me, the plain language of revelation on this point.

As to the coming of our Lord and Saviour Jesus Christ, I have no will, nor theory, aside from revelation. My whole being acquiesces in the revealed will of God. I have the fullest conviction that each jot and tittle will be strictly fulfilled, and this utterly precludes the idea that the partial fulfillment of prophecy relating to the 2d Advent, is *the* 2d Advent. Surely God has given me capacity sufficient to see, and grace to confess the distinction between the chesnut bur, and the chesnut. As the season advances and the frost matures the fruit, and opens the bur, I can get the *nut without pricking my fingers.* This requires "patience;" but then the nut is nourishing. The impatient prick their fingers, in plucking the premature fruit, and induce disease. "Be ye patient, brethren, unto the coming of the Lord, for the coming of the *Lord draweth nigh.*" "Grudge not one against another, brethren, lest ye be condemned." "Behold we count them *happy* who *endure.*"

My figure is an homely one; but if it enables any one to see the truth, it will answer my purpose. If we are but "patient" under the refining, purifying process, of present waiting, our faith will be found unto praise and *honor* and *glory* at the *appearing* of (not of the saints, but) Jesus Christ.

If the present "trial of faith" be the praise, and honor and glory, (as it must be, if the appearing of Jesus has taken place,) then I could as readily admit, that the bur is not in nature, distinguished from the naked nutritious nut.

The whole question, of the coming of our Saviour, may be resolved into this. Is there such a being as Jesus Christ? If we admit his distinctive existence, we must admit that He will "appear." "We shall *see Him*," not ourselves! *His actual coming is as certain as his destinctive existence*; and his existence is so much more real than ours, that it is only "because He lives that we shall live." I wrote in each case as I saw and felt. I am glad that I wrote, though it might have been well, had I written all at once, and added something more on the identity, or distinctive existence of our blessed Saviour. My conceptions are more elevated, and as I believe, more correct than formerly; because more scriptural.

His being "in his saints," and glorifying them, does not, I conceive, destroy his distinctive existence, any more than the indwelling of the Holy Spirit destroys his agency or existence. No more than God's dwelling with his people will absorb, or destroy God. This is plain language, which I should not use, but because the occasion demands it: Many have come in Christ's "name saying I am Christ."

Surely I have no will in this matter except to do the will of Jesus. "His counsel will stand and he will do all his pleasure." Amen!

I have no horns to hook at, or heels to kick any one: Should we get out of patience and act an unchristian part, we should give the enemy a triumph over us from which we might never recover. Surely I have wanted to be just right in sentiment and sympathy; and I propose to listen to every one, in whom confidence can be placed, as patiently as I did to friends I saw in Ohio. Then make a final appeal "to the law and the testimony." Lord lead us still. Amen!

We have had some precious good meetings here and in Newark, with those who have "not cast away their confidence,"—who love present truth. Adieu.

Yours in hope as ever.

J. B. COOK.

Bro. Cook, the "Chesnut bur" is open—do not fear "pricking" your fingers because the bur is still there; but eat freely and live forever. I do not claim to have swallowed the *whole* "nut," but to have had a taste and am yet feasting.—Ed.

CORRESPONDENTS.

☞ There are on hand a large number of articles from correspondents, that will appear as fast as they can be published. The deficiency in the receipts for the past two weeks, has left me some $15 in arrears, in consequence of which, the single numbers will have to be resorted to again for awhile.

The gathering of God's people is rapidly going forward, and will soon be done; after which the paper will not be needed.

I shall continue, by the permission of my Heavenly Father, to present to our readers, various branches of this glorious theme—the Kingdom of God set up, and to be received as a little child. The articles of all those who are sincerely opposed to the views presented, will be published, if written in a kind, loving spirit.

The vision of Sister Harmon in the present number, is published at the request of many friends that have heard it read.

LETTERS AND RECEIPTS,

For the week ending Jan. 22d.

Z. W. Hoyt; Eli B Johnson, 1.00; Thomas Bracken, 1.00 Abraham Bartlett, 1.00; S. H. Milner, for Mrs. Dobson, 2.00; Elisabeth S. Willard; Philana Neall; (the paper is sent to you gratis;) Catharine Smith; Henry V. Davis, 2.00; J. D. Pickands; H. C. Townsend, 1.00; D. Smith, .50; E. R. Southwick, .50; Jacob Weston, 1.00; S. S. Rogers, 1.00; C. Burlingham, for Jabez Wood, and James Smith, each .50; Stephen Pratt, for Hollis Twitchell, 1.00; S. R. Lathrop, 50

1846

(Lt 1, 1846)

FEBRUARY 15, FALMOUTH, MASSACHUSETTS

LETTER TO

Enoch Jacobs.[1]

Transcribed from the *Day-Star,* vol. 10, no. 1, March 14, 1846, pp. 7, 8. See Ellen G. White, *Early Writings,* pp. 54-56.

> *Follow-up to Ellen Harmon's December 20, 1845, letter to Enoch Jacobs published in the* Day-Star. *This letter contains descriptions of her mid-February 1845 "Bridegroom" and October 1845 "time of trouble" visions. What follows is an unmodified transcription of the published text.*

Letter from Sister Harmon.

Falmouth, Mass., Feb. 15, 1846.

BRO. JACOBS:—

My vision which you published in the Day-Star[2] was written under a deep sense of duty, to you, not expecting you would publish it. Had I for once thought it was to be spread before the many readers of your paper, I should have been more particular and stated some things which I left out. As the readers of the Day-Star have seen a part of what God has revealed to me, and as the part which I have not written is of vast importance to the Saints; I humbly request you to publish this also in your paper. God showed me the following, one year ago this month:—I saw a throne, and on it sat the Father and his Son Jesus Christ.[3] I gazed on Jesus' countenance and admired his lovely person. The Fathers person I could not behold for a cloud of glorious light covered him. I asked Jesus if his Father had a form like himself; He said he had, but I could not behold it; for, said he, if you should for once see the

---

[1] *Identity:* Enoch Jacobs was editor of the *Day-Star,* a Millerite paper published in Cincinnati, Ohio. See Lt 1, 1845 (Dec. 20), note 1.

[2] Jan. 24, 1846, issue. See Lt 1, 1845 (Dec. 20).

[3] This is Ellen Harmon's first known account of her second major vision, sometimes referred to as her "Bridegroom" vision. According to her July 13, 1847, letter to Joseph Bates, it was received in Exeter, Maine, during her first trip to eastern Maine in mid-February 1845.

See: Ellen G. White, Lt 3, 1847 (July 13).

glory of his person, you would cease to exist.[4] Before the throne was the Advent people, the Church, and the world.[5] I saw a company bowed down before the throne, deeply interested while most of them stood up disinterested and careless. Those who were bowed before the throne would offer up their prayers and look to Jesus, then he would look to his Father and appeared to be pleading with him. Then a light came from the Father to his Son and from him to the praying company. Then I saw an exceeding bright light[6] come from the Father to the Son and from the Son it waved over the people before the throne. But few would receive this great light. Many came out from under it and immediately resisted it. Others were careless and did not cherish the light and it moved off from them. Some cherished it and went and bowed down before the throne with the little praying company. This company all received the light, and rejoiced in it as their countenances shone with its glory. Then I saw the Father rise from the throne and in a flaming chariot go into the Holy of Holies within the vail, and did sit. There I saw thrones which I had not seen before. Then Jesus rose up from the throne, and most of those who were bowed down rose up with him. And I did not see one ray of light pass from Jesus to the careless multitude after he rose up, and they were left in perfect darkness.[7] Those who rose up when Jesus did, kept their eyes fixed on him as he left the throne, and led them out a little way, then he raised his right arm and we heard his lovely voice saying, wait ye, I am going to my Father to receive the Kingdom. Keep your garments spotless and in a little while I

---

[4] The vision's confirmation of the personality of God the Father and God the Son was in direct opposition to spiritualizing views gaining adherents among a small faction of post-1844 Millerites, eventually including Enoch Jacobs.

See: Ellen G. White, *Spiritual Gifts [vol. 2],* pp. 72-74. Enoch Jacobs's transition to Shakerism and related spiritualized views is documented by Merlin Burt in "Sabbatarian Adventism From 1844 to 1849," pp. 231-242.

[5] I.e., the Millerites, the professed Christian churches, and unbelievers. The "praying company" next brought to view appears to represent those among them who are earnestly seeking for truth.

[6] In Ellen White's first vision a "bright light" illumines the pathway of the Advent people, which an angel identified as the "Midnight Cry." See Lt 1, 1845 (Dec. 20), note 6. This affirmation of the "Midnight Cry," the proclamation during the summer and autumn of 1844 pointing to October 22, 1844, as the time of the Second Advent, was at odds with what was rapidly becoming the majority opinion in post-Disappointment Adventism, viz., that the October date was a mistaken calculation of no particular prophetic significance.

[7] Cf. the description in Ellen White's first vision of those on the path who "rashly denied the light behind them," resulting in its going out and leaving their feet "in perfect darkness" (Lt 1, 1845 [Dec. 20]).

This passage has been cited in partial support of the conclusion that this vision teaches the radical idea that the entire world, with the exception of the small Millerite group, was finally rejected by God. Note, however, the repeated qualifier made in this vision that it is those who are "careless," who "resisted" and "did not cherish" light from God, who are left in darkness, not a blanket rejection of all non-Millerites. This "rejection" principle, which is found also in the first vision (Lt 1, 1845) but especially in this vision, undercuts the conclusion that these visions advocate the radical "shut door" standpoint (see Lt 1, 1845 [Dec. 20], note 7).

will return from the wedding, and receive you to myself. And I saw a cloudy chariot with wheels like flaming fire. Angels were all about the chariot as it came where Jesus was; he stepped into it and was borne to the Holiest where the Father sat. Then I beheld Jesus as he was before the Father a great High Priest.[8, 9] On the hem of his garment was a bell and a pomegranate, a bell and a pomegranate. Then Jesus shewed me the difference between faith and feeling. And I saw those who rose up with Jesus send up their faith to Jesus in the Holiest, and praying, Father give us thy spirit. Then Jesus would breathe on them the Holy Ghost. In the breath was light, power and much love, joy and

---

[8] On two points in particular this passage presents an understanding of the wedding parable of Matthew 25 quite at odds with the established Millerite interpretation:

The coming of the Bridegroom to the marriage did not signify Christ's coming in glory to the earth to receive His waiting saints (the bride) at the close of the 2300 years, as the Millerites taught. Instead it signified the coming of Christ at that time to the Father in the Holy of Holies of the heavenly sanctuary, preparatory to the subsequent marriage.

The "marriage" of the parable indicated not Christ's reception of His church at the Second Coming but rather Christ's reception of "the Kingdom" from His Father prior to the Second Coming. Thus the "marriage" precedes the Second Coming. Biblical support for this sequence of events is alluded to in the words "in a little while I will return from the wedding, and receive you to myself," a clear reference to the wedding parable of Luke 12, in which Christ's followers are admonished to be "like unto men that wait for their lord, when he will return from the wedding."

The interpretation of the Matthew 25 marriage parable found in this vision represents one of several competing explanations for the Disappointment circulating among Adventists in the months following October 1844. It was first proposed in print in an extensive article by Apollos Hale and Joseph Turner a few weeks prior to the vision, in January 1845. This circumstance is probably what prompted Joseph Bates, two years later, to inquire whether Ellen Harmon had had "light on the Bridegroom's coming before" she saw it in vision. See notes on Lt 3, 1847 (July 13).

See: A. Hale and J. Turner, "Has Not the Savior Come as the Bridegroom?" *Advent Mirror,* January 1845. For an indication of the range of ideas circulating by February 1845 regarding what really happened on October 22, 1844, see I. E. Jones to William Miller, Feb. 15, 1845, in *The Millerites and Early Adventists,* sec. 5, reel 11.

[9] The theologically significant statement that Jesus was a "great High Priest" was counter to mainline "shut door" thought that emerged by the summer of 1845 and was promoted by Joseph Turner and Samuel Snow. They argued that Jesus reigned as king and was no longer a priest. See introductory article "The 'Shut Door' and Ellen White's Visions."

Although not explicitly stated, there is a strong suggestion here of a two-apartment heavenly sanctuary with Jesus transiting from the holy place to the Holy of Holies in 1844, a theme later to become prominent in Seventh-day Adventist theology. Unlike the theme of the coming of the Bridegroom mentioned earlier, the theme of Jesus coming to the Holy of Holies in 1844 is not known to have appeared in print prior to this vision (mid-February 1845). Probably not until the following month, March 1845, did O.R.L. Crosier and F. B. Hahn publish a similar view. There is some evidence, however, that similar ideas had oral circulation in certain places. Thus I. E. Jones, in a letter to William Miller on February 15, 1845, speaks of some persons in the Boston area who believed that on "the tenth of the 7th month . . . the Saviour then came <u>out</u> of the Holie [*sic*] of Holies . . . others, that he never <u>entered</u> the Holie of Holies till then" (emphasis in original).

See: O.R.L. Crosier and F. B. Hahn, reprint of early 1845 *Day-Dawn* issue published on last page of *Ontario Messenger,* Mar. 26, 1845; I. E. Jones to William Miller, Feb. 15, 1845, in *The Millerites and Early Adventists.*

peace. Then I turned to look at the company who were still bowed before the throne. They did not know that Jesus had left it. Satan appeared to be by the throne trying to carry on the work of God. I saw them look up to the throne and pray, My Father give us thy spirit. Then Satan would breathe on them an unholy influence. In it there was light and much power, but no sweet love, joy and peace. Satan's object was to keep them deceived and to draw back and deceive God's children.[10] I saw one after another leave the company who were praying to Jesus in the Holiest, go and join those before the throne and they at once received the unholy influence of Satan.

About four months since, I had a vision of events, all in the future.[11] And I saw the time of trouble,[12] such as never was,—Jesus told me it was the time of Jacob's trouble, and that we should be delivered out of it by the voice of God. Just before we entered it, we all received the seal of the living God.[13]

---

[10] The vision's depiction of Satan's efforts to *keep* this group deceived implies that the door of probation was still open for believers who had not by faith followed Jesus into the Holy of Holies. It would take more time for the full ramifications of this view to be understood. In a note to "Dear Brethren and Sisters," Ellen White later responded to misrepresentations of her comments about Satan's appearing before God's throne, and her descriptions of the movements of God the Father.

See: E. G. White, "Dear Brethren and Sisters," *Review*, Apr. 14, 1853, p. 192. Merlin D. Burt, "Ellen White and the Shut Door," in *"Ellen White and Current Issues" Symposium*, vol. 1, pp. 82, 83.

[11] There are good reasons to believe that this vision was given Ellen Harmon in October 1845 while on a visit to Carver, Massachusetts. According to James White, she received a vision at Carver, with similar content, in "the 7th month, 1845" of the Hebrew calendar, i.e., about October 1845. This harmonizes well with Ellen Harmon's statement that the vision was received "about four months since" the date of her letter, i.e., about mid-October 1845.

James White recalls in *A Word to the "Little Flock"* that both he and Ellen Harmon were surprised at the main thrust of this vision, viz., "that the saints must pass through the 'time of Jacob's trouble,'" still future but preceding the Second Advent. James White credits this vision with disabusing him of his conviction that Christ would be coming "a few days" later, "at the 7th month, 1845." While most Millerite expositors in 1843-1844 agreed that the "time of trouble" lay in the future, they believed that it would take place after the Advent, not before. The next eschatological event was the Second Advent, or, as Apollos Hale put it in 1843, "We have nothing to look for but the appearing of our Lord." Furthermore, only the wicked would have to suffer the "time of trouble," since the saints had already been delivered.

See: James White, ed., *A Word to the "Little Flock,"* p. 22. For examples of Millerite expositors prior to 1844 who placed "the time of trouble" after the Second Coming, see A. Hale, *Herald of the Bridegroom!*, pp. 21, 29, 33; E. Jacobs, "Seventh Seal," *Midnight Cry*, Oct. 26, 1843, p. 81.

[12] *See:* EGWEnc, s.v. "Time of Trouble."

[13] The predictions made in this passage seem to go counter to a radical shut-door position. First, the assertion that the Second Advent should not be expected momentarily because it would be preceded by "the time of Jacob's trouble." Second, it is significant that the sealing of the saints is also described as a future event. This would directly contradict the most radical shut-door doctrine, i.e., that since October 22, 1844, the saints were permanently sealed and safe.

See: Rolf J. Poehler, "'. . . and the Door Was Shut,'" pp. 113, 134; EGWEnc, s.v. "Seal of God."

Then I saw the four Angels cease to hold the four winds. And I saw famine, pestilence and sword, nation rose against nation, and the whole world was in confusion. Then we cried to God for deliverance day and night till we began to hear the bells on Jesus' garment. And I saw Jesus rise up in the Holiest, and as he came out we heard the tinkling of bells, and knew our High Priest was coming out. Then we heard the voice of God which shook the heavens and earth, and gave the 144,000 the day and hour of Jesus' coming.[14] Then the saints were free, united and full of the glory of God, for he had turned their captivity. And I saw a flaming cloud come where Jesus stood and he laid off his priestly garment and put on his kingly robe, took his place on the cloud which carried him to the east where it first appeared to the saints on earth, a small black cloud, which was the sign of the Son of Man. While the cloud was passing from the Holiest to the east which took a number of days, the Synagogue of Satan worshiped at the saints [*sic*] feet.[15]

ELLEN G. HARMON.

---

[14] *See:* Lt 1, 1845 (Dec. 20), note 8.
[15] *See:* Lt 1, 1845 (Dec. 20), note 13.

1846

(Ms 1, 1846)

APRIL 6, PORTLAND, MAINE

"To the Little Remnant Scattered Abroad."

Broadside.[1] See Ellen G. White, *Early Writings,* pp. 13-20, 54-56.

Ellen G. Harmon's first broadside reprinting similar content to that reported in her two previous letters to Enoch Jacobs in the Day-Star.[2] *It presents her first major visions from 1844-1845: "Midnight Cry," "Bridegroom," "new earth," and "close of probation." What follows is an unmodified transcription of the published text.*

As God has shown me in holy vision the travels of the Advent people to the Holy City, and the rich reward to be given those who wait the return of their Lord from the wedding, it may be my duty to give you a short sketch of what God has revealed to me. The dear saints have got many trials to pass through. But our light afflictions, which are but for a moment, worketh for us a far more exceeding and eternal weight of glory—while we look not at the things which are seen, for the things which are seen are temporal, but the things which are not seen are eternal. I have tried to bring back a good report, and a few grapes from the heavenly Canaan, for which many would stone me, as the congregation bade stone Caleb and Joshua for their report, (Num. 14:10.) But I declare to you, my brethren and sisters in the Lord, it is a goodly land, and we are well able to go up and possess it.

While praying at the family altar, the Holy Ghost fell on me, and I seemed to be rising higher and higher, far above the dark world. I turned to look for the Advent people in the world, but could not find them—when a voice said to me, "Look again, and look a little higher." At this I raised my eyes and saw a straight and narrow path, cast up high above the world. On this path the Advent people were travelling to the City, which was at the farther end of the path. They had a bright light set up behind them at the first end of the path, which an angel told me was the Midnight Cry. This light shone all

---

[1] A broadside was a single-sheet document printed on one side. It was most often used for advertisements and was the simplest form of printing at the time. "To the Little Remnant Scattered Abroad" was a three-column broadside published by James White in Portland, Maine, with the financial assistance of H. S. Gurney, a blacksmith of Fairhaven, Massachusetts. It is believed to be the first broadside by Ellen Harmon.

[2] Jan. 24 and Mar. 14, 1846, issues. For comments on the visions reprinted in this broadside, see notes for Lt 1, 1845 (Dec. 20), and Lt 1, 1846 (Feb. 15).

along the path and gave light for their feet so they might not stumble. And if they kept their eyes fixed on Jesus, who was just before them, leading them to the City, they were safe. But soon some grew weary, and they said the City was a great way off, and they expected to have entered it before. Then Jesus would encourage them by raising his glorious right arm, and from his arm came a glorious light which waved over the Advent band, and they shouted Hallelujah! Others rashly denied the light behind them, and said that it was not God that had led them out so far. The light behind them went out leaving their feet in perfect darkness, and they stumbled and got their eyes off the mark and lost sight of Jesus, and fell off the path down in the dark and wicked world below. It was just as impossible for them to get on the path again and go to the City, as all the wicked world which God had rejected. They fell all the way along the path one after another, until we heard the voice of God like many waters, which gave us the day and hour of Jesus' coming. The living saints, 144,000 in number, knew and understood the voice, while the wicked thought it was thunder and an earthquake. When God spake the time, he poured on us the Holy Ghost, and our faces began to light up and shine with the glory of God as Moses did when he came down from Mount Sinai, (Ex. 34:30-34.)

By this time the 144,000 were all sealed and perfectly united. On their foreheads was written, God, New Jerusalem, and a glorious Star containing Jesus' new name. At our happy, holy state the wicked were enraged, and would rush violently up to lay hands on us to thrust us in prison, when we would stretch forth the hand in the name of the Lord, and the wicked would fall helpless to the ground. Then it was that the synagogue of Satan knew that God had loved us who could wash one another's feet, and salute the holy brethren with a holy kiss, and they worshipped at our feet. Soon our eyes were drawn to the East, for a small black cloud had appeared about half as large as a man's hand, which we all knew was the Sign of the Son of Man. We all in solemn silence gazed on the cloud as it drew nearer, lighter, and brighter, glorious, and still more glorious, till it was a great white cloud. The bottom appeared like fire, a rainbow was over it, around the cloud were ten thousand angels singing a most lovely song. And on it sat the Son of Man, on his head were crowns, his hair was white and curly and lay on his shoulders. His feet had the appearance of fire, in his right hand was a sharp sickle, in his left a silver trumpet. His eyes were as a flame of fire, which searched his children through and through. Then all faces gathered paleness, and those that God had rejected gathered blackness. Then we all cried out, who shall be able to stand? Is my robe spotless? Then the angels ceased to sing, and there was sometime of awful silence, when Jesus spoke. Those who have clean hands and a pure heart shall be able to stand, my grace is sufficient for you. At this, our faces lighted up, and joy filled every heart. And the angels struck a note higher and sung again while the cloud drew still nearer the earth. Then Jesus' silver trumpet sounded, as he descended on the cloud, wrapped in flames of fire. He gazed on the graves of the sleeping saints, then raised his eyes and hands to heaven and cried out, Awake! Awake! Awake! ye that sleep in the dust, and arise. Then there was a mighty earthquake. The graves opened, and the dead came up clothed with immortality. The 144,000 shouted, Hallelujah! as they recognized their friends who had been torn from them by death, and in the same moment we were changed and caught up together with them to meet the Lord in the air. We all entered the cloud together, and were seven days ascending to the sea of glass, when Jesus brought along the crowns and with his own right hand placed them on our heads. He gave us harps of gold and palms of victory. Here on the sea of glass the 144,000 stood in a perfect square. Some of them had very bright crowns, others not so bright. Some crowns appeared heavy with stars, while others had but few. All were perfectly satisfied with their crowns. And they were all clothed with a glorious white mantle from their shoulders to their feet. Angels were all about us as we marched over the sea of glass to the gate of the City. Jesus raised his mighty glorious arm, laid hold of the gate and swung it back on its golden hinges, and said to us, You have washed your robes in my blood, stood stiffly for my truth, enter in. We all marched in and felt we had a perfect right in the City. Here we saw the tree of life, and the throne of God. Out of the throne came a pure river of water, and on either side of the river was the tree of life. On one side of the river was a trunk of a tree and a trunk on the other side of the river, both of pure transparent gold.

At first I thought I saw two trees. I looked again and saw they were united at the top in one tree. So it was the tree of life, on either side of the river of life; its branches bowed to the place where we stood; and the fruit was glorious, which looked like gold mixed with silver. We all went under the tree, and sat down to look at the glory of the place, when brothers Fitch [Charles Fitch] and Stockman [Levi Stockman], who had preached the gospel of the kingdom, and whom God had laid in the grave to save them, came up to us and asked us what we had passed through while they were sleeping. We tried to call up our greatest trials, but they looked so small compared with the far more exceeding and eternal weight of glory that surrounded us, that we could not speak them out, and we all cried out Hallelujah, heaven is cheap enough, and we touched our glorious harps and made heaven's arches ring. And as we were gazing at the glories of the place our eyes were attracted upwards to something that had the appearance of silver. I asked Jesus to let me see what was within there. In a moment we were winging our way upward, and entering in; here we saw good old father Abraham, Isaac, Jacob, Noah, Daniel, and many like them. And I saw a veil with a heavy fringe of silver and gold as a border on the bottom; it was very beautiful. I asked Jesus what was within the veil. He raised it with his own right arm, and bade me take heed. I saw there a glorious ark, overlaid with pure gold, and it had a glorious border, resembling Jesus' crowns; on it were two bright angels—their wings were spread over the ark as they sat on each end, with their faces turned towards each other and looking downward. In the ark, beneath where the angels wings were spread, was a golden pot of Manna, of a yellowish cast; and I saw a rod, which Jesus said was Aarons; I saw it bud, blossom and bear fruit. And I saw two long golden rods, on which hung silver wires, and on the wires most glorious grapes; one cluster was more than a man here could carry. And I saw Jesus step up and take off the manna, almonds, grapes and pomegranates, and bear them down to the city, and place them on the supper table. I stepped up to see how much was taken away, and there was just as much left; and we shouted Hallelujah—Amen. We all descended from this place down into the city, and with Jesus at our head we all descended from the city down to this earth, on a great and mighty mountain, which could not bear Jesus up, and it parted asunder, and there was a mighty plain. Then we looked up and saw the great city, with twelve foundations, twelve gates, three on each side, and an angel at each gate, and all cried out, "the city, the great city, it's coming, it's coming down from God, out of heaven;" and it came and settled on the place where we stood. Then we began to look at the glorious things outside of the city. There I saw most glorious houses, that had the appearance of silver, supported by four pillars, set with pearls, most glorious to behold, which were to be inhabited by the saints; in them was a golden shelf; I saw many of the saints go into the houses, take off their glittering crowns and lay them on the shelf, then go out into the field by the houses to do something with the earth; not as we have to do with the earth here; no, no. A glorious light shone all about their heads, and they were continually shouting and offering praises to God.

And I saw another field full of all kind of flowers, and as I plucked them, I cried out, well they will never fade. Next I saw a field of tall grass, most glorious to behold; it was living green, and had a reflection of silver and gold, as it waved proudly to the glory of King Jesus. Then we entered a field full of all kinds of beasts—the lion, the lamb, the leopard and the wolf, altogether in perfect union; we passed through the midst of them, and they followed on peaceably after. Then we entered a wood, not like the dark woods we have here, no, no; but light, and all over glorious; the branches of the trees waved to and fro, and we all cried out, "we will dwell safely in the wilderness and sleep in this woods." We passed through the wood, for we were on our way to Mount Zion. As we were travelling along, we met a company who were also gazing at the glories of the place. I noticed red as a border on their garments; their crowns were brilliant; their robes were pure white. As we greeted them, I asked Jesus who they were? He said they were martyrs that had been slain for him. With them was an innumerable company of little ones; they had a hem of red on their garments also. Mount Zion was just before us, and on the Mount sat a glorious temple, and about it were seven other mountains, on which grew roses and lilies, and I saw the little ones climb, or if they chose, use their little wings and fly to the top of the mountains, and pluck the never fading flowers. There were all kinds of trees around the temple to beautify the place; the box, the pine, the fir, the oil, the myrtle, the pomegranet [*sic*], and the fig tree bowed down with the weight of its timely figs, that made the place look all over glorious. And as we were about to enter the holy temple, Jesus raised his lovely voice and said, only the 144,000 enter this place, and we shouted Hallelujah.

Well, bless the Lord, dear brethren and sisters, it is an extra meeting for those who have the seal of the living God. This temple was supported by seven pillars, all of transparent gold, set with pearls most glorious. The glorious things I saw there, I cannot begin to describe. O, that I could talk in the language of Canaan, then could I tell a little of the glory of the upper world; but, if faithful, you soon will know all about it. I saw there the tables of stone in which the names of the 144,000, were engraved in letters of gold; after we had beheld the glory of the temple, we went out. Then Jesus left us, and went to the city; soon, we heard his lovely voice again, saying—"Come my people, you have come out of great tribulation, and done my will; suffered for me; come in to supper, for I will gird myself, and serve you." We shouted Hallelujah, glory; and entered into the city; and I saw a table of pure silver, it was many miles in length, yet our eyes could extend over it. And I saw the fruit of the tree of life, the manna, almonds, figs, pomegranets [*sic*], grapes, and many other kinds of fruit. We all reclined at the table. I asked Jesus to let me eat of the fruit. He said, not now. Those who eat of the fruit of this land, go back to earth no more. But in a little while, if faithful, you shall both eat of the fruit of the tree of life, and drink of the water of the fountain; and he said, you must go back to the earth again, and relate to others, what I have revealed to you. Then an angel bore me gently down to this dark world. Sometimes I think I cannot stay here any longer, all things of earth look so dreary—I feel very lonely here, for I have seen a better land. O, that I had wings like a dove, then would I fly away, and be at rest.

In February, 1845, I had a vision of events commencing with the Midnight Cry. I saw a throne and on it sat the Father and the Son. I gazed on Jesus' countenance and admired his lovely person. The Father's person I could not behold, for a cloud of glorious light covered him. I asked Jesus if his Father had a form like himself. He said he had, but I could not behold it, for said he if you should once behold the glory of his person you would cease to exist. Before the throne I saw the Advent people, the church, and the world. I saw a company, bowed down before the throne, deeply interested, while the most of them stood up disinterested and careless. Those who were bowed before the throne would offer up their prayers and look to Jesus; then he would look to his Father, and appeared to be pleading with Him. A light would come from the Father to the Son, and from the Son to the praying company. Then I saw an exceeding bright light come from the Father to the Son, and from the Son it waved over the people before the throne. But few would receive this great light; many came out from under it and immediately resisted it; others were careless and did not cherish the light, and it moved off from them; some cherished it, and went and bowed down with the little praying company. This company all received the light, and rejoiced in it, as their countenances shone with its glory. And I saw the Father rise from the throne, and in a flaming Chariot go into the Holy of Holies, within the veil, and did sit. There I saw thrones that I had never seen before. Then Jesus rose up from the throne, and the most of those who were bowed down arose with Him; and I did not see one ray of light pass from Jesus to the careless multitude after he arose, and they were left in perfect darkness. Those who rose up when Jesus did, kept their eyes fixed on Him as He left the throne and led them out a little way.—Then He raised His right arm and we heard his lovely voice saying, "Wait here—I am going to my Father to receive the Kingdom; keep your garments spotless, and in a little while I will return from the wedding and receive you to myself." And I saw a cloudy chariot, with wheels like flaming fire, and Angels were all around it as it came where Jesus was. He stepped into the chariot and was borne to the Holiest where the Father sat. There I beheld Jesus, as He was standing before the Father, a great High Priest. On the hem of His garment was a bell and pomegranate. Then Jesus shew me the difference between faith and feeling. And I saw those who rose up with Jesus send up their faith to Him in the Holiest, and pray—my Father give us thy Spirit. Then Jesus would breathe upon them the Holy Ghost. In the breath was light, power, and much love, joy and peace. Then I turned to look at the company who were still bowed before the throne; they did not know that Jesus had left it.—Satan appeared to be by the throne, trying to carry on the work of God; I saw them look up to the throne and pray, my Father give us thy Spirit; then Satan would breathe upon them an unholy influence; in it there was light and much power, but no sweet love, joy and peace. Satan's object was to keep them deceived, and to draw back and deceive God's children. I saw one after another leave the company who were praying to Jesus in the Holiest, and go and join those before the throne, and they at once received the unholy influence of Satan.

About four months since I had a vision of events all in the future. I saw the time of trouble, such as never was. Jesus told me it was the time of Jacob's trouble, and that we should be delivered out of it by the voice of God. Then I saw the four angels cease to hold the four winds. And I saw famine, pestilence and sword—nation rose against nation, and the whole world was in confusion. Then we cried to God day and night for deliverance, until we began to hear the bells on Jesus' garment. And I saw Jesus rise up in the Holiest, and as he came out we heard the tinkling of the bells and knew that our High Priest was coming out. Then we heard the voice of God which shook the heavens and the earth, and gave the 144,000 the day and hour of Jesus coming. Then the saints were free, united, and full of the glory of God, for he has turned their captivity. And I saw a flaming cloud come where Jesus stood. Then Jesus laid off his priestly garment and put on his Kingly robe, and took his place on the cloud which carried him to the East, where it first appeared to the saints on earth—a small black cloud which was the sign of the Son of Man. While the cloud was passing from the Holiest to the East, which took a number of days, the synagogue of Satan worshipped at the saint's [*sic*] feet.

ELLEN G. HARMON.

PORTLAND, April 6, 1846.

TO THE LITTLE REMNANT SCATTERED ABROAD.

As God has shown me in holy vision the travels of the Advent people to the Holy City, and the rich reward to be given those who wait the return of their Lord from the wedding, it may be my duty to give you a short sketch of what God has revealed to me. The dear saints have got many trials to pass through. But our light afflictions, which are but for a moment, worketh for us a far more exceeding and eternal weight of glory—while we look not at the things which are seen, for the things which are seen are temporal, but the things which are not seen are eternal. I have tried to bring back a good report, and a few grapes from the heavenly Canaan, for which many would stone me, as the congregation bade stone Caleb and Joshua for their report, (Num. 14: 10.) But I declare to you, my brethren and sisters in the Lord, it is a goodly land, and we are well able to go up and possess it.

While praying at the family altar, the Holy Ghost fell on me, and I seemed to be rising higher and higher, far above the dark world. I turned to look for the Advent people in the world, but could not find them—when a voice said to me, "Look again, and look a little higher." At this I raised my eyes and saw a straight and narrow path, cast up high above the world. On this path the Advent people were travelling to the City, which was at the farther end of the path. They had a bright light set up behind them at the first end of the path, which an angel told me was the Midnight Cry. This light shone all along the path and gave light for their feet so they might not stumble. And if they kept their eyes fixed on Jesus, who was just before them, leading them to the City, they were safe. But soon some grew weary, and they said the City was a great way off, and they expected to have entered it before. Then Jesus would encourage them by raising his glorious right arm, and from his arm came a glorious light which waved over the Advent band, and they shouted Hallelujah! Others rashly denied the light behind them, and said that it was not God that had led them out so far. The light behind them went out leaving their feet in perfect darkness, and they stumbled and got their eyes off the mark and lost sight of Jesus, and fell off the path down in the dark and wicked world below. It was just as impossible for them to get on the path again and go to the City, as all the wicked world which God had rejected. They fell all the way along the path one after another, until we heard the voice of God like many waters, which gave us the day and hour of Jesus' coming. The living saints, 144,000 in number, knew and understood the voice, while the wicked thought it was thunder and an earthquake. When God spake the time, he poured on us the Holy Ghost, and our faces began to light up and shine with the glory of God as Moses did when he came down from Mount Sinai, (Ex. 34: 30-34.)

By this time the 144,000 were all sealed and perfectly united. On their foreheads was written, God, New Jerusalem, and a glorious Star containing Jesus' new name. At our happy, holy state the wicked were enraged, and would rush violently up to lay hands on us to thrust us in prison, when we would stretch forth the hand in the name of the Lord, and the wicked would fall helpless to the ground. Then it was that the synagogue of Satan knew that God had loved us who could wash one another's feet, and salute the holy brethren with a holy kiss, and they worshipped at our feet. Soon our eyes were drawn to the East, for a small black cloud had appeared about half as large as a man's hand, which we all knew was the Sign of the Son of Man. We all in solemn silence gazed on the cloud as it drew nearer, lighter, and brighter, glorious, and still more glorious, till it was a great white cloud. The bottom appeared like fire, a rainbow was over it, around the cloud were ten thousand angels singing a most lovely song. And on it sat the Son of Man, on his head were crowns, his hair was white and curly and lay on his shoulders. His feet had the appearance of fire, in his right hand was a sharp sickle, in his left a silver trumpet. His eyes were as a flame of fire, which searched his children through and through. Then all faces gathered paleness, and those that God had rejected gathered blackness. Then we all cried out, who shall be able to stand? Is my robe spotless? Then the angels ceased to sing, and there was some time of awful silence, when Jesus spoke. Those who have clean hands and a pure heart shall be able to stand, my grace is sufficient for you. At this, our faces lighted up, and joy filled every heart. And the angels struck a note higher and sung again while the cloud drew still nearer the earth. Then Jesus' silver trumpet sounded, as he descended on the cloud, wrapped in flames of fire. He gazed on the graves of the sleeping saints, then raised his eyes and hands to heaven and cried out, Awake! Awake! Awake! ye that sleep in the dust, and arise. Then there was a mighty earthquake. The graves opened, and the dead came up clothed with immortality. The 144,000 shouted, Hallelujah! as they recognised their friends who had been torn from them by death, and in the same moment we were changed and caught up together with them to meet the Lord in the air. We all entered the cloud together, and were seven days ascending to the sea of glass, when Jesus brought along the crowns and with his own right hand placed them on our heads. He gave us harps of gold and palms of victory. Here on the sea of glass the 144,000 stood in a perfect square. Some of them had very bright crowns, others not so bright. Some crowns appeared heavy with stars, while others had but few. All were perfectly satisfied with their crowns. And they were all clothed with a glorious white mantle from their shoulders to their feet. Angels were all about us as we marched over the sea of glass to the gate of the City. Jesus raised his mighty glorious arm, laid hold of the gate and swung it back on its golden hinges, and said to us, You have washed your robes in my blood, stood stifly for my truth, enter in. We all marched in and felt we had a perfect right in the City. Here we saw the tree of lifle, and the throne of God. Out of the throne came a pure river of water, and on either side of the river was the tree of life. On one side of the river was a trunk of a tree and a trunk on the other side of the river, both of pure ransparent gold.

At first I thought I saw two trees. I looked again and saw they were united at the top in one tree. So it was the tree of life, on either side of the river of life; its branches bowed to the place where we stood; and the fruit was glorious, which looked like gold mixed with silver. We all went under the tree, and sat down to look at the glory of the place, when brothers Fitch and Stockman, who had preached the gospel of the kingdom, and whom God had laid in the grave to save them, came up to us and asked us what we had passed through while they were sleeping. We tried to call up our greatest trials, but they looked so small compared with the far more exceeding and eternal weight of glory that surrounded us, that we could not speak them out, and we all cried out Hallelujah, heaven is cheap enough, and we touched our glorious harps and made heaven's arches ring. And as we were gazing at the glories of the place our eyes were attracted upwards to something that had the appearance of silver. I asked Jesus to let me see what was within there. In a moment we were winging our way upward, and entering in; here we saw good old father Abraham, Isaac, Jacob, Noah, Daniel, and many like them. And I saw a veil with a heavy fringe of silver and gold, as a border on the bottom; it was very beautiful. I asked Jesus what was within the veil. He raised it with his own right arm, and bade me take heed. I saw there a glorious ark, overlaid with pure gold, and it had a glorious border, resembling Jesus' crowns; on it were two bright angels—their wings were spread over the ark as they sat on each end, with their faces turned towards each other and looking downward. In the ark, beneath where the angels wings were spread, was a golden pot of Manna, of a yellowish cast; and I saw a rod, which Jesus said was Aarons; I saw it bud, blossom and bear fruit. And I saw two long golden rods, on which hung silver wires, and on the wires most glorious grapes; one cluster was more than a man here could carry. And I saw Jesus step up and take off the manna, almonds, grapes and pomegranates, and bear them down to the city, and place them on the supper table. I stepped up to see how much was taken away, and there was just as much left; and we shouted Hellelujah—Amen. We all descended from this place down into the city, and with Jesus at our head we all descended from the city down to this earth, on a great and mighty mountain, which could not bear Jesus up, and it parted asunder, and there was a mighty plain. Then we looked up and saw the great city, with twelve foundations, twelve gates, three on each side, and an angel at each gate, and all cried out, "the city, the great city, it's coming, it's coming down from God, out of heaven;" and it came and settled on the place where we stood. Then we began to look at the glorious things outside of the city. There I saw most glorious houses, that had the appearance of silver, supported by four pillars, set with pearls, most glorious to behold, which were to be inhabited by the saints; in them was a golden shelf; I saw many of the saints go into the houses, take off their glittering crowns and lay them on the shelf, then go out into the field by the houses to do something with the earth; not as we have to do with the earth here; no, no. A glorious light shone all about their heads, and they were continually shouting and offering praises to God.

And I saw another field full of all kind of flowers, and as I plucked them, I cried out, well they will never fade. Next I saw a field of tall grass, most glorious to behold; it was living green, and had a reflection of silver and gold, as it waived proudly to the glory of King Jesus. Then we entered a field full of all kinds of beasts—the lion, the lamb, the leopard and the wolf, altogether in perfect union; we passed through the midst of them, and they followed on peaceably after. Then we entered a wood, not like the dark woods we have here, no, no; but light, and all over glorious; the branches of the trees waved to and fro, and we all cried out, "we will dwell safely in the wilderness and sleep in this woods." We passed through the wood, for we were on our way to Mount Zion. As we were travelling along, we met a company who were also gazing at the glories of the place. I noticed red as a border on their garments; their crowns were brilliant; their robes were pure white. As we greeted them, I asked Jesus who they were? He said they were martyrs that had been slain for him. With them was an innumerable company of little ones; they had a hem of red on their garments also. Mount Zion was just before us, and on the Mount sat a glorious temple, and about it were seven other mountains, on which grew roses and lillies, and I saw the little ones climb, or if they chose, use their little wings and fly to the top of the mountains, and pluck the never fading flowers. There were all kinds of trees around the temple to beautify the place; the box, the pine, the fir, the oil, the myrtle, the pomegranet, and the fig tree bowed down with the weight of its timely figs, that made the place look all over glorious. And as we were about to enter the holy temple, Jesus raised his lovely voice and said, only the 144,000 enter this place, and we shouted Hallelujah.

Well, bless the Lord, dear brethren and sisters, it is an extra meeting for those who have the seal of the living God. This temple was supported by seven pillars, all of transparent gold, set with pearls most glorious. The glorious things I saw there, I cannot begin to describe. O, that I could talk in the language of Canaan, then could I tell a little of the glory of the upper world; but, if faithful, you soon will know all about it. I saw there the tables of stone in which the names of the 144,000, were engraved in letters of gold; after we had beheld the glory of the temple, we went out. Then Jesus left us, and went to the city; soon, we heard his lovely voice again, saying—"Come my people, you have come out of great tribulation, and done my will; suffered for me; come in to supper, for I will gird myself, and serve you." We shouted Hallelujah, glory; and entered into the city; and I saw a table of pure silver, it was many miles in length, yet our eyes could extend over it. And I saw the fruit of the tree of life, the manna, almonds, figs, pomegranets, grapes, and many other kinds of fruit. We all reclined at the table. I asked Jesus to let me eat of the fruit. He said, not now. Those who eat of the fruit of this land, go back to earth no more. But in a little while, if faithful, you shall both eat of the fruit of the tree of life, and drink of the water of the fountain; and he said, you must go back to the earth again, and relate to others, what I have revealed to you. Then an angel bore me gently down to this dark world. Sometimes I think I cannot stay here any longer, all things of earth look so dreary—I feel very lonely here, for I have seen a better land. O, that I had wings like a dove, then would I fly away, and be at rest.

In February, 1845, I had a vision of events commencing with the Midnight Cry. I saw a throne and on it sat the Father and the Son. I gazed on Jesus' countenance and admired his lovely person. The Father's person I could not behold, for a cloud of glorious light covered him. I asked Jesus if his Father had a form like himself. He said he had, but I could not behold it, for said he if you should once behold the glory of his person you would cease to exist. Before the throne I saw the Advent people, the church, and the world. I saw a company, bowed down before the throne, deeply interested, while the most of them stood up disinterested and careless. Those who were bowed before the throne would offer up their prayers and look to Jesus; then he would look to his Father, and appeared to be pleading with Him. A light would come from the Father to the Son, and from the son to the praying company. Then I saw an exceeding bright light come from the Father to the Son, and from the Son it waved over the people before the throne. But few would receive this great light; many came out from under it and immediately resisted it; others were careless and did not cherish the light, and it moved off from them; some cherished it, and went and bowed down with the little praying company. This company all received the light, and rejoiced in it, as their countenances shone with its glory. And I saw the Father rise from the throne, and in a flaming Chariot go into the Holy of Holies, within the veil, and did sit. There I saw thrones that I had never seen before. Then Jesus rose up from the throne, and the most of those who were bowed down arose with Him; and I did not see one ray of light pass from Jesus to the careless multitude after he arose, and they were left in perfect darkness. Those who rose up when Jesus did, kept their eyes fixed on Him as He left the throne and led them out a little way.—Then He raised His right arm and we heard his lovely voice saying, "Wait here—I am going to my Father to receive the Kingdom; keep your garments spotless, and in a little while I will return from the wedding and receive you to myself." And I saw a cloudy chariot, with wheels like flaming fire, and Angels were all around it as it came where Jesus was. He stepped into the chariot and was borne to the Holiest where the Father sat. There I beheld Jesus, as He was standing before the Father, a great High Priest. On the hem of His garment was a bell and pomegranate. Then Jesus shew me the difference between faith and feeling. And I saw those who rose up with Jesus send up their faith to Him in the Holiest, and pray—my Father give us thy Spirit. Then Jesus would breathe upon them the Holy Ghost. In the breath was light, power, and much love, joy and peace. Then I turned to look at the company who were still bowed before the throne; they did not know that Jesus had left it.—Satan appeared to be by the throne, trying to carry on the work of God; I saw them look up to the throne and pray, my Father give us thy Spirit; then Satan would breathe upon them an unholy influence; in it there was light and much power, but no sweet love, joy and peace. Satan's object was to keep them deceived, and to draw back and deceive God's children. I saw one after another leave the company who were praying to Jesus in the Holiest, and go and join those before the throne, and they at once received the unholy influence of Satan.

About four months since I had a vision of events all in the future. I saw the time of trouble, such as never was. Jesus told me it was the time of Jacob's trouble, and that we should be delivered out of it by the voice of God. Then I saw the four angels cease to hold the four winds. And I saw famine, pestilence and sword—nation rose against nation, and the whole world was in confusion. Then we cried to God day and night for deliverance, until we began to hear the bells on Jesus' garment. And I saw Jesus rise up in the Holiest, and as he came out we heard the tinkling of the bells and knew that our High Priest was coming out. Then we heard the voice of God which shook the heavens and the earth, and gave the 144,000 the day and hour of Jesus' coming. Then the saints were free, united, and full of the glory of God, for he has turned their captivity. And I saw a flaming cloud come where Jesus stood. Then Jesus laid off his priestly garment and put on his Kingly robe, and took his place on the cloud which carried him to the East, where it first appeared to the saints on earth—a small black cloud which was the sign of the Son of Man. While the cloud was passing from the Holiest to the East, which took a number of days, the synagogue of Satan worshipped at the saint's feet.

ELLEN G. HARMON.

PORTLAND, APRIL 6, 1846.

First Ellen (Harmon) White broadside, published by James White, April 6, 1846. Otis Nichols wrote a letter to William Miller on the back of one of these broadsides describing Ellen Harmon's experience. Original dimensions (H x W): 15.75 x 12.25 in. (40 x 31 cm.).

Home of Otis and Mary Nichols, Dorchester, Massachusetts. No longer standing.

Otis Nichols and his wife, Mary

A VISION.

VOL. I. TOPSHAM, (Me.) APRIL 7, 1847. No. 1.

Dear Brother Bates :—Last Sabbath we met with the dear brethren and sisters here, who meet at Bro. Howland's.

We felt an unusual spirit of prayer. And as we prayed, the Holy Ghost fell upon us. We were very happy. Soon I was lost to earthly things, and was wrapped up in a vison of God's glory. I saw an angel swiftly flying to me. He quickly carried me from the earth to the Holy City. In the city I saw a temple, which I entered. I passed through a door before I came to the first veil. This veil was raised, and I passed into the Holy Place. Here I saw the Altar of Incense. Before the altar was the table, on which was the candlestick, with seven lamps, and the showbread, &c. After viewing the glory of the Holy, Jesus raised the second veil, and I passed into the Holy of Holies.

In the Holiest I saw an ark; on the top and sides of it was purest gold. On each end of the ark was a lovely Cherub, with their wings spread out over it. Their faces were turned towards each other, and they looked downwards. Between the angels was a golden censor. Above the ark, where the angels stood, was an exceeding bright glory, that appeared like a throne where God dwelt. Jesus stood by the ark. And as the saints' prayers came up to Jesus, the incense in the censor would smoke, and He offered up the prayers of the saints with the smoke of the incense to His Father. In the ark, was the golden pot of manna, Aaron's rod that budded, and the tables of stone which folded together like a book. Jesus opened them, and I saw the ten commandments written on them with the finger of God. On one table was four, and on the other six. The four on the first table shone brighter than the other six. But the fourth (the Sabbath commandment,) shone above them all; for the Sabbath was set apart to be kept in honor of God's holy name. The holy Sabbath looked glorious—a halo of glory was all around it. I saw that the Sabbath was not nailed to the cross. If it was, the other nine commandments were; and we are at liberty to go forth and break them all, as well as to break the fourth. I saw that God had not changed the Sabbath, for He never changes. But the Pope had changed it from the seventh to the first day of the week; for he was to change times and laws.

And I saw that if God had changed the Sabbath, from the seventh to the first day, He would have changed the writing of the Sabbath commandment, written on the tables of stone, which are now in the ark, in the Most Holy Place of the Temple in heaven; and it would read thus: The first day is the Sabbath of the Lord thy God. But I saw that it read the same as when written on the tables of stone by the finger of God, and delivered to Moses in Sinai, "But the seventh day is the Sabbath of the Lord thy God." I saw that the holy Sabbath is, and will be, the separating wall between the true Israel of God and unbelievers; and that the Sabbath is the great question, to unite the hearts of God's dear waiting saints. And if one believed, and kept the Sabbath, and received the blessing attending it, and then gave it up, and broke the holy commandment, they would shut the gates of the Holy City against themselves, as sure as there was a God that rules in heaven above. I saw that God had children, who do not see and keep the Sabbath. They had not rejected the light on it. And at the commencement of the time of trouble, we were filled with the Holy Ghost as we went forth, and proclaimed the Sabbath more fully. This enraged the church, and nominal Adventists, as they could not refute the Sabbath truth. And at this time, God's chosen all saw clearly that we had the truth, and they came out and endured the persecution with us. And I saw the sword, famine, pestilence, and great confusion in the land. The wicked thought that we had brought the judgments down on them. They rose up and took counsel to rid the earth of us, thinking that then the evil would be stayed.

I saw all that "would not receive the mark of the Beast, and of his Image, in their foreheads or in their hands," could not buy or sell. I saw that the number (666) of the Image Beast was made up; and that it was the beast that changed the Sabbath, and the Image Beast had followed on after, and kept the Pope's, and not God's Sabbath. And all we were required to do, was to give up God's Sabbath, and keep the Pope's, and then we should have the mark of the Beast, and of his Image.

In the time of trouble, we all fled from the cities and villages, but were pursued by the wicked, who entered the houses of the saints with the sword. They raised the sword to kill us, but it broke, and fell, as powerless as a straw. Then we all cried day and night for deliverance, and the cry came up before God. The sun came up, and the moon stood still. The streams ceased to flow. Dark heavy clouds came up, and clashed against each other. But there was one clear place of settled glory, from whence came the *voice of God* like many waters, which shook the heavens, and the earth. The sky opened and shut, and was in commotion. The mountains shook like a reed in the wind, and cast out rugged rocks all around. The sea boiled like a pot, and cast out stones upon the land. And as God spoke the day and hour of Jesus coming, and delivered the everlasting covenant to His people, He spoke one sentence, and then paused, while the words were rolling through the earth! The Israel of God stood with their eyes fixed upwards, listening to the words as they came from the mouth of Jehovah, and rolled through the earth like peals of loudest thunder! It was awfully solemn. At the end of every sentence, the saints shouted, Glory! Hallelujah! Their countenances were lighted up with the glory of God; and they shone with the glory as Moses' face did when he came down from Sinai. The wicked could not look on them, for the glory. And when the never ending blessing was pronounced on those who had honored God, in keeping His Sabbath holy, there was a mighty shout of victory over the Beast, and over his Image.

Then commenced the jubilee, when the land should rest. I saw the pious slave rise in triumph and victory, and shake off the chains that bound him, while his wicked master was in confusion, and knew not what to do; for the wicked could not understand the words of the voice of God. Soon appeared the great white cloud. It looked more lovely than ever before. On it sat the Son of Man. At first we did not see Jesus on the cloud, but as it drew near the earth, we could behold his lovely person. This cloud when it first appeared was the Sign of the Son of Man in heaven. The voice of the Son of God called forth the sleeping saints, clothed with a glorious immortality. The living saints were changed in a moment, and caught up with them in the cloudy chariot. It looked all over glorious as it rolled upwards. On either side of the chariot were wings, and beneath it wheels. And as the chariot rolled upwards, the wheels cried Holy, and the wings as they moved, cried, Holy, and the retinue of Holy Angels around the cloud cried Holy, Holy, Holy, Lord God Almighty. And the saints in the cloud cried Glory, Hallelujah. And the cloudy chariot rolled upwards to the Holy City. Jesus threw open the gates of the Golden City, and led us in. Here we were made welcome, for we had kept the "*Commandments* of God," and had a "right to the tree of life."

From your sister in the blessed hope,

E. G. WHITE.

Remarks.—I do not publish the above vision thinking to add or diminish from the "sure word of prophecy." That will stand the test of men and wreck of worlds! "It is written that man shall not live by bread alone, but by every word of God." Amen.

It is now about two years since I first saw the author, and heard her relate the substance of her visions as she has since published them in Portland (April 6, 1846). Although I could see nothing in them that militated against the word, yet I felt alarmed and tried exceedingly, and for a long time unwilling to believe that it was any thing more than what was produced by a protracted debilitated state of her body.

I therefore sought opportunities in presence of others, when her mind seemed freed from excitement (out of meeting) to question, and cross question her, and her friends which accompanied her, especially her elder sister, to get if possible at the truth. During the number of visits she has made to New Bedford and Fairhaven since, while at our meetings, I have seen her in vision a number of times, and also in Topsham, Me., and those who were present during some of these exciting scenes know well with what interest and intensity I listened to every word, and watched every move to detect deception, or mesmeric influence. And I thank God for the opportunity I have had with others to witness these things. I can now confidently speak for myself. I believe the work is of God, and is given to comfort and strengthen his "scattered," "torn" and "pealed people," since the closing up of our work for the world in October, 1844. The distracted state of lo, heres! and lo, theres! since that time has exceedingly perplexed God's honest, willing people, and made it exceedingly difficult for such as were not able to expound the many conflicting texts that have been presented to their view. I confess that I have received light and instruction on many passages that I could not before clearly distinguish. I believe her to be a self-sacrificing, honest, willing child of God, and saved, if at all, through her entire obedience to His will.

At a meeting in Fairhaven, 6th of the last month, I saw her have a similar vision, which I then wrote down. It may be said that I send this out to strengthen the argument of my late work on the Sabbath. I do in the sense above stated. Respecting that work I entertain no fears. There is no scriptural argument to move it.

The above vision can be had by application, post paid, to James White, Gorham, Me., or to the editor.

JOSEPH BATES,
Fairhaven, Mass.

PRESS OF BENJAMIN LINDSEY—No. 6 NORTH WATER-STREET—NEW-BEDFORD.

Second Ellen White broadside, published by Joseph Bates, April 7, 1847.
Original dimensions (H x W): 13 x 8.3 in. (33 x 21 cm.).

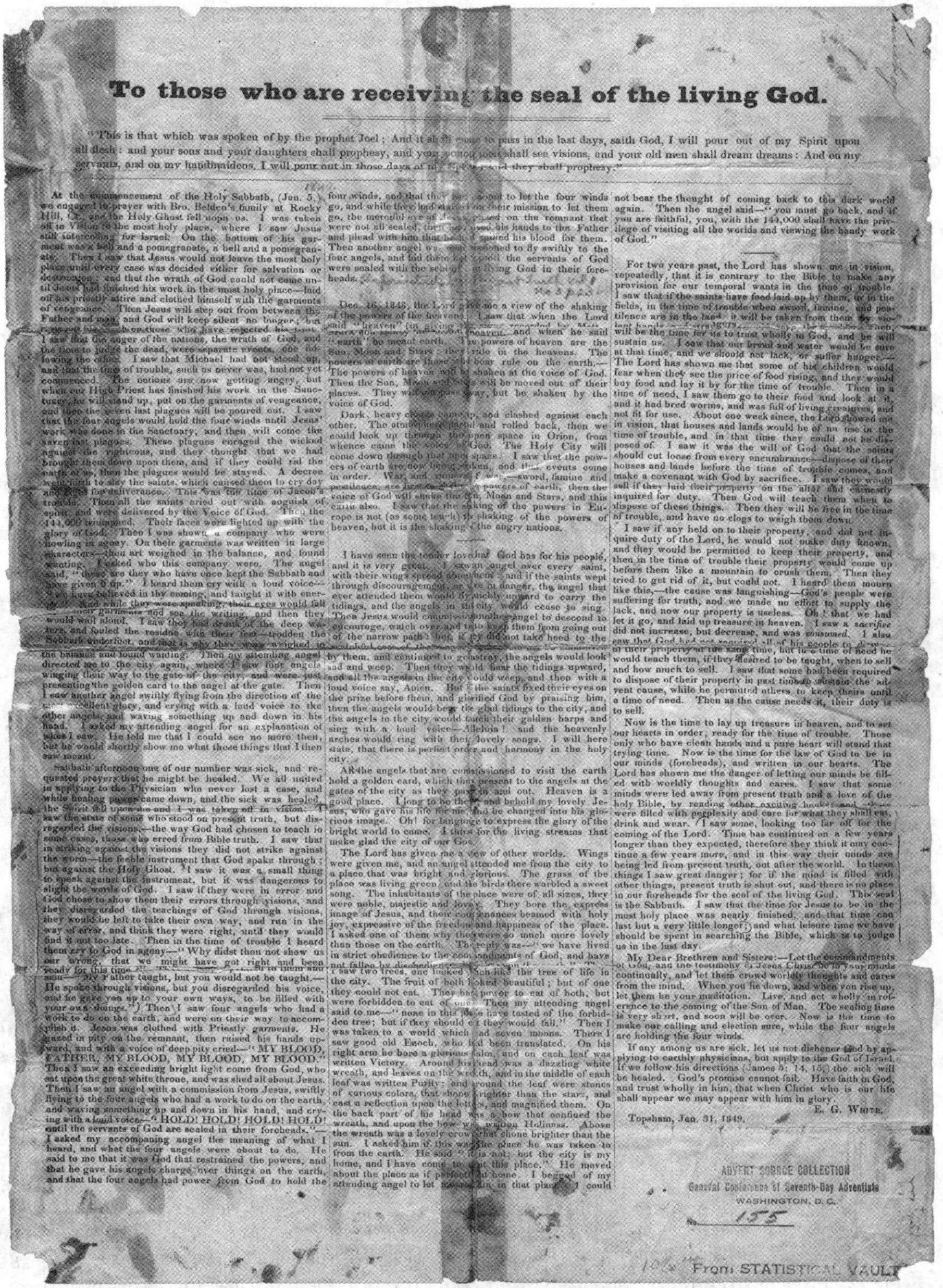

To those who are receiving the seal of the living God.

"This is that which was spoken of by the prophet Joel; And it sh[illegible] come to pass in the last days, saith God, I will pour out of my Spirit upon all flesh: and your sons and your daughters shall prophesy, and your [illegible] shall see visions, and your old men shall dream dreams: And on my servants, and on my handmaidens, I will pour out in those days of my Sp[illegible] and they shall prophesy."

At the commencement of the Holy Sabbath, (Jan. 5,) we engaged in prayer with Bro. Belden's family at Rocky Hill, Ct., and the Holy Ghost fell uopn us. I was taken off in Vision to the most holy place, where I saw Jesus still interceding for Israel. On the bottom of his garment was a bell and a pomegranate, a bell and a pomegranate. Then I saw that Jesus would not leave the most holy place until every case was decided either for salvation or destruction: and that the wrath of God could not come until Jesus had finished his work in the most holy place—laid off his priestly attire and clothed himself with the garments of vengeance. Then Jesus will step out from between the Father and man, and God will keep silent no longer; but [illegible] on those who have rejected his [illegible]. I saw that the anger of the nations, the wrath of God, and the time to judge the dead, were separate events, one following the other. I saw that Michael had not stood up, and that the time of trouble, such as never was, had not yet commenced. The nations are now getting angry, but when our High Priest has finished his work in the Sanctuary, he will stand up, put on the garments of vengeance, and then the seven last plagues will be poured out. I saw that the four angels would hold the four winds until Jesus' work was done in the Sanctuary, and then will come the seven last plagues. These plagues enraged the wicked against the righteous, and they thought that we had brought them down upon them, and if they could rid the earth of us, then the plagues would be stayed. A decree went forth to slay the saints, which caused them to cry day and night for deliverance. This was the time of Jacob's trouble. Then all the saints cried out with anguish of spirit, and were delivered by the Voice of God. Then the 144,000 triumphed. Their faces were lighted up with the glory of God. Then I was shown a company who were howling in agony. On their garments was written in large characters—thou art weighed in the balance, and found wanting. I asked who this company were. The angel said, "these are they who have once kept the Sabbath and have given it up." I heard them cry with a loud voice—"we have believed in thy coming, and taught it with energy." And while they were speaking, their eyes would fall [illegible] their garments and see the writing, and then they would wail aloud. I saw they had drunk of the deep waters, and fouled the residue with their feet—trodden the Sabbath underfoot, and that is why they were weighed in the balance and found wanting. Then my attending angel directed me to the city again, where I saw four angels winging their way to the gate of the city, and were just presenting the golden card to the angel at the gate. Then I saw another angel swiftly flying from the direction of the [illegible]excellent glory, and crying with a loud voice to the other angels, and waving something up and down in his hand. I asked my attending angel for an explanation of what I saw. He told me that I could see no more then, but he would shortly show me what those things that I then saw meant.

Sabbath afternoon one of our number was sick, and requested prayers that he might be healed. We all united in applying to the Physician who never lost a case, and while healing power came down, and the sick was healed, the Spirit fell upon me and I was taken off in vision. I saw the state of some who stood on present truth, but disregarded the visions,—the way God had chosen to teach in some cases, those who erred from Bible truth. I saw that in striking against the visions they did not strike against the worm—the feeble instrument that God spake through; but against the Holy Ghost. I saw it was a small thing to speak against the instrument, but it was dangerous to slight the words of God. I saw if they were in error and God chose to show them their errors through visions, and they disregarded the teachings of God through visions, they would be left to take their own way, and run in the way of error, and think they were right, until they would find it out too late. Then in the time of trouble I heard them cry to God in agony—"Why didst thou not show us our wrong, that we might have got right and been ready for this time?" [illegible] to them and said—"My Father taught, but you would not be taught.—He spoke through visions, but you disregarded his voice, and he gave you up to your own ways, to be filled with your own doings." Then I saw four angels who had a work to do on the earth, and were on their way to accomplish it. Jesus was clothed with Priestly garments. He gazed in pity on the remnant, then raised his hands upward, and with a voice of deep pity cried—"MY BLOOD, FATHER, MY BLOOD, MY BLOOD, MY BLOOD." Then I saw an exceeding bright light come from God, who sat upon the great white throne, and was shed all about Jesus. Then I saw an angel with a commission from Jesus, swiftly flying to the four angels who had a work to do on the earth, and waving something up and down in his hand, and crying with a loud voice—"HOLD! HOLD! HOLD! HOLD! until the servants of God are sealed in their foreheads."—I asked my accompaning angel the meaning of what I heard, and what the four angels were about to do. He said to me that it was God that restrained the powers, and that he gave his angels charge over things on the earth, and that the four angels had power from God to hold the four winds, and that they [illegible] to let the four winds go, and while they had started on their mission to let them go, the merciful eye of Jesus gazed on the remnant that were not all sealed, then he raised his hands to the Father and plead with him that he had spilled his blood for them. Then another angel was commissioned to fly swiftly to the four angels, and bid them hold until the servants of God were sealed with the seal of the living God in their foreheads.

Dec. 16, 1848, the Lord gave me a view of the shaking of the powers of the heavens. I saw that when the Lord said "heaven" (in giving [illegible]) he meant heaven, and when he said "earth" he meant earth. The powers of heaven are the Sun, Moon and Stars; they rule in the heavens. The powers of earth are those who bear rule on the earth.—The powers of heaven will be shaken at the voice of God. Then the Sun, Moon and Stars will be moved out of their places. They will not pass away, but be shaken by the voice of God.

Dark, heavy clouds came up, and clashed against each other. The atmosphere parted and rolled back, then we could look up through the open space in Orion, from whence came the voice of God. The Holy City will come down through that open space. I saw that the powers of earth are now being shaken, and that events come in order. War, and rumors of war,—sword, famine and pestilence, are first to shake the powers of earth, then the voice of God will shake the Sun, Moon and Stars, and this earth also. I saw that the shaking of the powers in Europe is not (as some teach) the shaking of the powers of heaven, but it is the shaking of the angry nations.

I have seen the tender love that God has for his people, and it is very great. I saw an angel over every saint, with their wings spread about them; and if the saints wept through discouragement, or were in danger, the angel that ever attended them would fly quickly upward to carry the tidings, and the angels in the city would cease to sing. Then Jesus would commission another angel to descend to encourage, watch over and to keep them from going out of the narrow path; but, if they did not take heed to the [illegible] by them, and continued to go astray, the angels would look sad and weep. Then they would bear the tidings upward, and all the angels in the city would weep, and then with a loud voice say, Amen. But if the saints fixed their eyes on the prize before them, and glorified God by praising him, then the angels would bear the glad tidings to the city, and the angels in the city would tou[illegible]ch their golden harps and sing with a loud voice—Alleluia! and the heavenly arches would ring with their lovely songs. I will here state, that there is perfect order and harmony in the holy city.

All the angels that are commissioned to visit the earth hold a golden card, which they present to the angels at the gates of the city as they pass in and out. Heaven is a good place. I long to be there, and behold my lovely Jesus, who gave his life for me, and be changed into his glorious image. Oh! for language to express the glory of the bright world to come. I thirst for the living streams that make glad the city of our God.

The Lord has given me a view of other worlds. Wings were given me, and an angel attended me from the city to a place that was bright and glorious. The grass of the place was living green, and the birds there warbled a sweet song. The inhabitants of the place were of all sizes, they were noble, majestic and lovely. They bore the express image of Jesus, and their countenances beamed with holy joy, expressive of the freedom and happiness of the place. I asked one of them why they were so much more lovely than those on the earth. The reply was—"we have lived in strict obedience to the commandments of God, and have not fallen by disobedience [illegible]." I saw two trees, one looked much like the tree of life in the city. The fruit of both looked beautiful; but of one they could not eat. They had power to eat of both, but were forbidden to eat of one. Then my attending angel said to me—"none in this place have tasted of the forbidden tree; but if they should eat they would fall." Then I was taken to a world which had seven moons. There I saw good old Enoch, who had been translated. On his right arm he bore a glorious palm, and on each leaf was written Victory. Around his head was a dazzling white wreath, and leaves on the wreath, and in the middle of each leaf was written Purity; and around the leaf were stones of various colors, that shone brighter than the stars, and cast a reflection upon the letters, and magnified them. On the back part of his head was a bow that confined the wreath, and upon the bow was written Holiness. Above the wreath was a lovely crown that shone brighter than the sun. I asked him if this was the place he was taken to from the earth. He said "it is not; but the city is my home, and I have come to visit this place." He moved about the place as if perfectly at home. I begged of my attending angel to let me remain in that place. I could not bear the thought of coming back to this dark world again. Then the angel said—"you must go back, and if you are faithful, you, with the 144,000 shall have the privilege of visiting all the worlds and viewing the handy work of God."

For two years past, the Lord has shown me in vision, repeatedly, that it is contrary to the Bible to make any provision for our temporal wants in the time of trouble. I saw that if the saints have food laid up by them, or in the fields, in the time of trouble when sword, famine, and pestilence are in the land, it will be taken from them by violent hands [illegible] strangers. [illegible] Then will be the time for us to trust wholly in God, and he will sustain us. I saw that our bread and water would be sure at that time, and we should not lack, or suffer hunger.—The Lord has shown me that some of his children would fear when they see the price of food rising, and they would buy food and lay it by for the time of trouble. Then in a time of need, I saw them go to their food and look at it, and it had bred worms, and was full of living creatures, and not fit for use. About one week since, the Lord showed me in vision, that houses and lands would be of no use in the time of trouble, and in that time they could not be disposed of. I saw it was the will of God that the saints should cut loose from every encumbrance—dispose of their houses and lands before the time of trouble comes, and make a covenant with God by sacrifice. I saw they would sell if they laid their property on the altar and earnestly inquired for duty. Then God will teach them when to dispose of these things. Then they will be free in the time of trouble, and have no clogs to weigh them down.

I saw if any held on to their property, and did not inquire duty of the Lord, he would not make duty known, and they would be permitted to keep their property, and then in the time of trouble their property would come up before them like a mountain to crush them. Then they tried to get rid of it, but could not. I heard them mourn like this,—the cause was languishing—God's people were suffering for truth, and we made no effort to supply the lack, and now our property is useless. Oh! that we had let it go, and laid up treasure in heaven. I saw a *sacrifice* did not increase, but decrease, and was *consumed*. I also saw that God had not required all of his people to dispose of their property at the same time, but in a time of need he would teach them, if they desired to be taught, when to sell and how much to sell. I saw that some had been required to dispose of their property in past times to sustain the advent cause, while he permitted others to keep theirs until a time of need. Then as the cause needs it, their duty is to sell.

Now is the time to lay up treasure in heaven, and to set our hearts in order, ready for the time of trouble. Those only who have clean hands and a pure heart will stand that trying time. Now is the time for the law of God to be in our minds (foreheads), and written in our hearts. The Lord has shown me the danger of letting our minds be filled with worldly thoughts and cares. I saw that some minds were led away from present truth and a love of the holy Bible, by reading other exciting books; and others were filled with perplexity and care for what they shall eat, drink and wear. I saw some, looking too far off for the coming of the Lord. Time has continued on a few years longer than they expected, therefore they think it may continue a few years more, and in this way their minds are being led from present truth, out after the world. In these things I saw great danger; for if the mind is filled with other things, present truth is shut out, and there is no place in our foreheads for the seal of the living God. This seal is the Sabbath. I saw that the time for Jesus to be in the most holy place was nearly finished, and that time can last but a very little longer; and what leisure time we have should be spent in searching the Bible, which is to judge us in the last day.

My Dear Brethren and Sisters:—Let the commandments of God, and the testimony of Jesus Christ be in your minds continually, and let them crowd worldly thoughts and cares from the mind. When you lie down, and when you rise up, let them be your meditation. Live, and act wholly in reference to the coming of the Son of Man. The sealing time is very short, and soon will be over. Now is the time to make our calling and election sure, while the four angels are holding the four winds.

If any among us are sick, let us not dishonor God by applying to earthly physicians, but apply to the God of Israel. If we follow his directions (James 5: 14, 15,) the sick will be healed. God's promise cannot fail. Have faith in God, and trust wholly in him, that when Christ who is our life shall appear we may appear with him in glory.

E. G. White.

Topsham, Jan. 31, 1849.

Third Ellen White broadside, published by James White, January 31, 1849.
Original dimensions (H x W): 16.5 x 11 in. (42 x 28 cm.). Courtesy of the Center for Adventist Research.

1847

(Lt 1, 1847)

APRIL 7, TOPSHAM, MAINE

LETTER TO

Joseph Bates.

Transcribed from "A Vision," vol. 1, no. 1. Broadside.[1] See Ellen G. White, *Early Writings,* pp. 32-35.

> *"Sabbath halo" vision published as a broadside. Bates published the letter with appended comments. This vision confirmed the eschatological importance of the Sabbath based on Jesus' work in the Most Holy Place of the heavenly sanctuary. What follows is an unmodified transcription of the published text.*

Dear Brother Bates:—Last Sabbath we met with the dear brethren and sisters here, who meet at Bro. Howland's [**Stockbridge Howland**].[2]

We felt an unusual spirit of prayer. And as we prayed, the Holy Ghost fell upon us. We were very happy. Soon I was lost to earthly things, and was wrapped up in a vision of God's glory. I saw an angel swiftly flying to me. He quickly carried me from the earth to the Holy City. In the city I saw a temple, which I entered. I passed through a door before I came to the first veil. This veil was raised, and I passed into the Holy Place. Here I saw the Altar of Incense. Before the altar was the table, on which was the candlestick, with seven lamps, and the showbread, &c. After viewing the glory of the Holy,

---

[1] A broadside was a single-sheet document printed on one side. The publication is dated "April 7, 1847," a Wednesday; however, in the opening sentences Ellen White dates the vision to "last Sabbath," presumably April 3.

[2] Ellen White's "Sabbath halo" vision occurred in the home of Stockbridge and Louisa M. Howland in Topsham, Maine. She had a similar vision on March 6, 1847, in Fairhaven, Massachusetts. The Howland home was the location of several significant early Sabbatarian Adventist meetings. The only known record of the March 6 vision is Joseph Bates's mention of it in his remarks found later in this broadside.

Ellen Harmon was at first resistant to the idea of the continuing validity of the seventh-day Sabbath, as urged by Joseph Bates. However, soon after their marriage on August 30, 1846, James and Ellen White became convinced of the biblical evidence for its observance through the reading of Bates's first Sabbath tract.

See: Ellen G. White, *Testimonies for the Church,* vol. 1, pp. 75, 76; Joseph Bates, *The Seventh Day Sabbath: A Perpetual Sign*. For Bates's influence in connection with the historical and theological significance of the "Sabbath halo" vision, see Merlin Burt, "Sabbatarian Adventism From 1844 to 1849," esp. pp. 276-301.

Jesus raised the second veil, and I passed into the Holy of Holies.[3]

In the Holiest I saw an ark; on the top and sides of it was purest gold. On each end of the ark was a lovely Cherub, with their wings spread out over it. Their faces were turned towards each other, and they looked downwards. Between the angels was a golden censor. Above the ark, where the angels stood, was an exceeding bright glory, that appeared like a throne where God dwelt. Jesus stood by the ark. And as the saints' prayers came up to Jesus, the incense in the censor would smoke, and He offered up the prayers of the saints with the smoke of the incense to His Father. In the ark, was the golden pot of manna, Aaron's rod that budded and the tables of stone which folded together like a book. Jesus opened them, and I saw the ten commandments[4] written on them with the finger of God. On one table was four, and on the other six. The four on the first table shone brighter than the other six. But the fourth (the Sabbath commandment,) shone above them all; for the Sabbath was set apart to be kept in honor of God's holy name. The holy Sabbath looked glorious—a halo of glory was all around it. I saw that the Sabbath was not nailed to the cross. If it was, the other nine commandments were; and we are at liberty to go forth and break them all, as well as to break the fourth.[5] I saw that God had not changed the Sabbath, for He never changes. But the Pope had changed it from the seventh to the first day of the week; for he was to change times and laws.[6]

And I saw that if God had changed the Sabbath, from the seventh to the first day, He would have changed the writing of the Sabbath commandment, written on the tables of stone, which are now in the ark, in the Most Holy Place of the Temple in heaven; and it would read thus: The first day is the Sabbath of the Lord thy God. But I saw that it read the same as when written on the tables of stone by the finger of God, and delivered to Moses in Sinai, "But the seventh day is the Sabbath of the Lord thy God." I saw that the holy Sabbath is, and will be, the separating wall between the true Israel of God and unbelievers;[7] and that the Sabbath is

---

[3] Allusions to the existence of a two-apartment heavenly sanctuary are found already two years earlier in the vision of February 1845 (Lt 1, 1846 [Feb. 15]).

[4] The connection made here between the Ten Commandments, including the fourth, and the Most Holy Place of the heavenly sanctuary affirms Joseph Bates's studies of Revelation 11:19, first published some months earlier in January 1847.

See: Joseph Bates, *The Seventh Day Sabbath: A Perpetual Sign,* 2nd ed., pp. iii, iv.

[5] This counterargument to the claim that the Sabbath commandment was "nailed to the cross," together with the arguments that follow regarding the change of the Sabbath, reflect traditional lines of reasoning of the Seventh Day Baptists that were subsequently adopted by early Sabbatarian Adventists such as T. M. Preble and Joseph Bates.

See: Merlin Burt, "Sabbatarian Adventism From 1844 to 1849," pp. 278-281.

[6] Cf. Dan. 7:25.

[7] The vision depicts the composition of the "the true Israel of God" as not yet fixed but enlarging as individuals respond positively to the light of the Sabbath truth. "God's chosen" included those "who do not see and keep the Sabbath," who "had not rejected the light on it," and who in the future "came out and endured the persecution with us."

the great question, to unite the hearts of God's dear waiting saints. And if one believed, and kept the Sabbath, and received the blessing attending it, and then gave it up, and broke the holy commandment, they would shut the gates of the Holy City against themselves, as sure as there was a God that rules in heaven above. I saw that God had children, who do not see and keep the Sabbath. They had not rejected the light on it. And at the commencement of the time of trouble,[8] we were filled with the Holy Ghost as we went forth, and proclaimed the Sabbath more fully. This enraged the church, and nominal Adventists, as they could not refute the Sabbath truth. And at this time, God's chosen all saw clearly that we had the truth, and they came out and endured the persecution with us.[9] And I saw the sword, famine, pestilence, and great confusion in the land. The wicked thought that we had brought the judgments down on them. They rose up and took counsel to rid the earth of us,[10] thinking that then the evil would be stayed.

---

[8] An examination of *A Word to the "Little Flock,"* published the following month, shows that James and Ellen White believed in a three-phase "time of trouble": first, the early time of trouble that began after October 1844, when Jesus began His high-priestly ministry in the Most Holy Place of the heavenly sanctuary; second, the time of trouble after the close of human probation, when Jesus leaves the Most Holy Place and the seven last plagues are poured out; third, the time of Jacob's trouble, which occurs before the voice of God delivers His people immediately preceding the Second Coming. Evidently, the time of trouble referred to in this paragraph is the first phase—after 1844 and before probation closes—since God's people "proclaimed the Sabbath more fully." In the next paragraph Ellen White moved on to describe the events during the great time of trouble after probation closes.

See: James White, "The Time of Trouble" and "The Time of Jacob's Trouble," in *A Word to the "Little Flock,"* pp. 8-10; EGWEnc, s.v. "Time of Trouble."

[9] Although in earlier vision accounts a radical shut-door stance is denied by implication in several places, this is perhaps the first time that a qualified "open door" position is explicitly asserted. It seems justified to infer from this passage that in the future, persons from mainline churches as well as from non-Sabbatarian Adventist bodies would join the Sabbathkeeping Adventists. For Damsteegt this passage is "the first reference that more specifically described the future mission among non-Adventists." Poehler, despite some caveats, agrees. "There can be no question that, as Damsteegt has pointed out, this vision 'contributed significantly to the development of a new theology of mission.'" For a contrasting position, see Lindén, p. 60.

See: P. Gerard Damsteegt, *Foundations of the Seventh-day Adventist Message and Mission,* p. 152; Rolf J. Poehler, "'. . . and the Door Was Shut,'" pp. 114, 115; Ingemar Lindén, *1844 and the Shut Door Problem,* p. 60.

[10] This section of the vision, dealing with the role of the Sabbath in the end-time persecution of the saints, confirms the conclusions of Joseph Bates's Bible study that he had first published three months earlier in the revised edition of his pamphlet *The Seventh Day Sabbath: A Perpetual Sign.* However, it should be noted that the core prediction that God's people would undergo violent persecution just prior to the Second Advent had first appeared among future Sabbatarian leaders in Ellen [Harmon] White's earliest vision of December 1844, with further details given in the vision of October 1845 (Lt 1, 1845 [Dec. 20], note 12, and Lt 1, 1846 [Feb. 15], last paragraph). Thus when it comes to this important aspect of Seventh-day Adventist eschatology (the "great controversy" motif) it seems likely that the original impetus for Bates's 1847 pamphlet came from the visions of 1844 and 1845. The same can be said for James White's articles appearing in the seminal pamphlet *A Word to the "Little Flock,"* published in May 1847. His articles, entitled "The Seven Last Plagues," "The Voice of God," "The Time of Trouble,"

I saw all that "would not receive the mark of the Beast, and of his Image, in their foreheads or in their hands," could not buy or sell. I saw that the number (666) of the Image Beast was made up;[11] and that it was the beast that changed the Sabbath, and the Image Beast had followed on after, and kept the Pope's, and not God's Sabbath. And all we were required to do, was to give up God's Sabbath, and keep the Pope's, and then we should have the mark of the Beast, and of his Image.

In the time of trouble, we all fled from the cities and villages, but were pursued by the wicked, who entered the houses of the saints with the sword. They raised the sword to kill us, but it broke, and fell, as powerless as a straw. Then we all cried day and night for deliverance, and the cry came up before God. The sun came up, and the moon stood still. The streams ceased to flow. Dark heavy clouds came up, and clashed against each other. But there was one clear place of settled glory, from whence came the *voice of God* like many waters, which shook the heavens, and the earth. The sky opened and shut, and was in commotion. The mountains shook like a reed in the wind, and cast out rugged rocks all around. The sea boiled like a pot, and cast out stones upon the land. And as God spoke the day and hour of Jesus coming,[12] and delivered the everlasting covenant to His people, He spoke one sentence, and then paused, while the words were rolling through the earth! The Israel of God stood with their eyes fixed upwards, listening to the words as they came from the mouth of Jehovah, and rolled through the earth like peals of loudest thunder! It was awfully solemn. At the end of every sentence, the saints shouted, Glory! Hallelujah! Their countenances were lighted up with the glory of God; and they shone with the glory as Moses' face did when he came down from Sinai. The wicked could not look on them, for the glory. And when the never ending blessing was pronounced on those who had honored God, in keeping His Sabbath holy, there was a mighty shout of victory over the Beast, and over his Image.

---

and "The Time of Jacob's Trouble," all serve the purpose of examining the biblical case for the predictions of end-time troubles found in the earliest visions. Although it is generally true that in the early development of Seventh-day Adventist doctrine the visions served to confirm prior biblical research, in this case it would seem the opposite was the case.

See: Joseph Bates, *The Seventh Day Sabbath: A Perpetual Sign*, 2nd ed., pp. 58, 59; James White, ed., *A Word to the "Little Flock."* For a divergent position on the contribution of Joseph Bates to the origins of the "great controversy" concept, see George Knight, *Joseph Bates,* pp. 114-117.

[11] What Ellen White meant by the number of the image beast being made up is not clear. The parenthetical (666) is most likely an explanatory insertion by the publisher, Joseph Bates. In 1847 James White similarly identified the number 666 with the image beast described in Revelation 13:11-18, though he would later argue (1860) that it was the number of the first (papal) beast. Nowhere in her writings does Ellen White elaborate on the meaning of the number 666.

For an overview of early Adventist interpretations of the number of the beast, see P. Gerard Damsteegt, *Foundations of the Seventh-day Adventist Message and Mission,* pp. 205-207.

[12] *See:* Lt 1, 1845 (Dec. 20), note 8.

Then commenced the jubilee, when the land should rest. I saw the pious slave rise in triumph and victory, and shake off the chains that bound him, while his wicked master was in confusion, and knew not what to do;[13] for the wicked could not understand the words of the voice of God. Soon appeared the great white cloud. It looked more lovely than ever before. On it sat the Son of Man. At first we did not see Jesus on the cloud, but as it drew near the earth, we could behold his lovely person. This cloud when it first appeared was the Sign of the Son of Man in heaven. The voice of the Son of God called forth the sleeping saints, clothed with a glorious immortality. The living saints were changed in a moment, and caught up with them in the cloudy chariot. It looked all over glorious as it rolled upwards. On either side of the chariot were wings, and beneath it wheels. And as the chariot rolled upwards, the wheels cried Holy, and the wings as they moved, cried Holy, and the retinue of Holy Angels around the cloud cried Holy, Holy, Holy, Lord God Almighty. And the saints in the cloud cried Glory, Hallelujah. And the cloudy chariot rolled upwards to the Holy City. Jesus threw open the gates of the Golden City, and led us in. Here we were made welcome, for we had kept the "*Commandments* of God," and had a "right to the tree of life."[14]

From your sister in the blessed hope,

E. G. WHITE.

---

[13] Millerites and early Adventists often drew parallels of different kinds between the year of jubilee as the climax of the ancient Jewish calendar (Lev. 25) and the climax of earth's history at the coming of Christ and the millennium. Thus, the instruction given that all Hebrew slaves were to be freed in the jubilee year (Lev. 25:10) was seen by William Miller as "typical of the redemption of the people of God from all captivity, bondage, or death into the glorious liberty of the sons of God; Rom. viii.21; and is also typical of the times of the restitution of all things. Acts iii. 21." Likewise J. H. Waggoner, writing in 1859, saw "the fiftieth year, or jubilee . . . [when] bondmen went free . . . [as] typifying the final redemption of God's people . . . now groaning under the curse." It is possible that the passage about "the pious slave" in this vision should be given a similar typological interpretation rather than a literal one. Most readers, however, have assumed that the slave statement should be understood literally. Dudley Canright, archcritic of Seventh-day Adventism, classifies it with "other mistakes" that Ellen White made: "In 1849 she foretold what would happen when Jesus came, and said: 'I saw the pious slave rise.' But now there are no slaves. She had not then dreamed of the abolition of slavery." Considerable discussion of this charge has ensued over the years.

See: William Miller, *A Trilogy,* p. 31; D. M. Canright, *Seventh-Day Adventism Renounced,* p. 146; J.H.W. [J. H. Waggoner], "The Discussion—The Sabbath," *Review,* Feb. 24, 1859, p. 110. For various views on the "pious slave" passage, see: "The Visions—Objections Answered," *Review,* June 26, 1866, p. 26; "Will Slavery Be Again?" *Review,* July 16, 1901, p. 458; Stephen N. Haskell, *The Cross and Its Shadow,* pp. 250, 256, 257; Francis D. Nichol, *Ellen G. White and Her Critics,* pp. 337-341.

[14] Cf. Rev. 22:14: "Blessed are they that do his commandments, that they may have a right to the tree of life, and may enter in through the gates into the city."

Remarks.[15]*—I do not publish the above vision thinking to add or diminish from the "sure word of prophecy." That will stand the test of men and wreck of worlds! "It is written that man shall not live by bread alone, but by every word of God." Amen.*

It is now about two years since I first saw the author, and heard her relate the substance of her visions as she has since published them in Portland (April 6, 1846). Although I could see nothing in them that militated against the word, yet I felt alarmed and tried exceedingly, and for a long time unwilling to believe that it was any thing more than what was produced by a protracted debilitated state of her body.

I therefore sought opportunities in presence of others, when her mind seemed freed from excitement, (out of meeting) to question, and cross question her, and her friends which accompanied her, especially her elder sister, to get if possible at the truth. During the number of visits she has made to New Bedford and Fairhaven since, while at our meetings, I have seen her in vision a number of times, and also in Topsham, Me., and those who were present during some of these exciting scenes know well with what interest and intensity I listened to every word, and watched every move to detect deception, or mesmeric influence. And I thank God for the opportunity I have had with others to witness these things. I can now confidently speak for myself. I believe the work is of God, and is given to comfort and strengthen his "scattered," "torn," and "pealed people," since the closing up of our work for the world in October, 1844.[16] *The distracted state of lo, heres! and lo, theres! since that time has exceedingly perplexed God's honest, willing people, and made it exceedingly difficult for such as were not able to expound the many conflicting texts that have been presented to their view. I confess that I have received light and instruction on many passages that I could not before clearly distinguish. I believe her to be a self-sacrificing, honest, willing child of God, and saved, if at all, through her entire obedience to His will.*

At a meeting in Fairhaven, 6th of the last month, I saw her have a similar vision, which I then wrote down. It may be said that I send this out to strengthen the argument of my late work on the Sabbath. I do in the sense above stated. Respecting that work I entertain no fears. There is no scriptural argument to move it.

The above vision can be had by application, post paid, to James White, Gorham, Me., or to the editor.

JOSEPH BATES.
Fairhaven, Mass.

---

[15] Joseph Bates added these remarks to his publication of the vision, explaining why he accepted Ellen White's visions as a legitimate manifestation of the prophetic gift. At the same time, he remained firm on the Bible as the final authority for what he had written about the seventh-day Sabbath, concluding his remarks with the words: "There is no scriptural argument to move it." Bates's comments were written from Fairhaven, Massachusetts, his longtime city of residence. The text has been italicized in this transcription to distinguish Bates's remarks from the text of the vision.

[16] While recognizing that others would yet respond to the proclamation of the three angels' messages (see note 7 above), Bates still believed that the time had passed for evangelization of the unconverted.

1847

(Lt 2, 1847)

APRIL 21, TOPSHAM, MAINE

LETTER TO
Eli Curtis.[1]

Transcribed from *A Word to the "Little Flock,"* pp. 11, 12.[2]

Clarifies points of agreement and disagreement with Eli Curtis on the progression of final events before the second coming of Jesus. What follows is an unmodified transcription of the published text.

Topsham, April 21, 1847.

To BRO. ELI CURTIS, New York City.

Dear Bro:—In the Day-Dawn, Vol. 1, Nos. 10 and 11, you kindly invite me to address you a communication.

The only apology I have to offer for not writing before is, I have not had a clear duty to write till now. You will, I doubt not, excuse me for addressing you so publicly, at this time. I have been much interested in your writings in the Dawn, and Extra; and fully agree with you on some points, but on others we widely differ.[3]

---

[1] *Identity:* Eli Curtis (fl. 1845-1861). Publisher and editor from New York City who turned from Millerite Adventism to spiritism. In 1847 he began to publish the *Girdle of Truth,* which held minority Adventist views in some ways similar to those of the emerging Sabbatarian Adventists. Ellen White and Eli Curtis exchanged views on various theological issues around this time. Within the next few years, however, Curtis veered toward spiritism, and by 1850 Ellen White declared that she had "no faith in his course." Beginning in 1851 Eli Curtis published several spiritist papers and tracts containing purported spirit communications. In 1870 a certain "Eli Curtis" bought a property at Mount Nebo, Ohio, for the purpose of forming a spiritualist colony. Whether he was the same Eli Curtis here considered is not known.

See: E. G. White, "Eli Curtis," *Present Truth,* May 1850, p. 80; John B. Kachuba, *Ghosthunting Ohio,* p. 205; SDAE, s.v. "Eli Curtis"; EGWEnc, s.v. "Eli Curtis."

[2] *A Word to the "Little Flock"* is the first combined statement of faith by the three original founders of Sabbatarian Adventism and the Seventh-day Adventist Church. Containing material from James and Ellen White and Joseph Bates, it is essentially a representation of the progression of end-time events from 1844 to the final judgment at the end of the millennium. Besides the letter to Eli Curtis, *A Word to the "Little Flock"* also republished the content of Ellen White's first two broadsides, "To the Little Remnant Scattered Abroad" and "A Vision." Many scriptural references are added to the reprinted version of the broadsides.

[3] The *Dawn* is the *Day-Dawn,* published by O.R.L. Crosier in Canandaigua, New York (see note 10 below). Neither of the two issues of the *Day-Dawn* mentioned is extant. The identity

Your Extra is now on the stand before me; and I beg leave to state to you, and the scattered flock of God, what I have seen in vision relative to these things on which you have written. I fully agree with you, that there will be two literal resurrections, 1000 years apart.

I also agree with you, that the new heavens, and the new earth, (Rev. 21:1. Isa. 65:17. 2 Pet. 3:13.) will not appear, till after the wicked dead are raised, and destroyed, at the end of the 1000 years.[4] I saw that Satan was "loosed out of his prison," at the end of the 1000 years, just at the time the wicked dead were raised; and that Satan deceived them by making them believe that they could take the holy city from the saints. The wicked all marched up around the "camp of the saints," with Satan at their head; and when they were ready to make an effort to take the city, the Almighty breathed from his high throne, on the city, a breath of devouring fire, which came down on them, and burnt them up, "root and branch."

And I saw, that as Christ is the vine, and his children the branches: so Satan is the "root", and his children are the "branches;" and at the final destruction of "Gog and Magog," the whole wicked host will be burnt up, "root and branch,"

---

of the Extra is not entirely clear. Given that Ellen White's letter is dated April 21, however, it is likely that she is referring to the Extra that had been published together with the *Day-Dawn* three weeks earlier on April 2. According to the editor, "the Extra which accompanies this number [Apr. 2, 1847] is published for Bro. Eli Curtis, of N. Y. city." Whatever the case, the Extra has not been available for this analysis. Ellen White was concerned that Curtis used her visions to support views she did not hold.

See: "The Advent This Spring," *Day-Dawn,* Apr. 2, 1847, p. 7; Ellen G. White, "Eli Curtis," *Present Truth,* May 1850, p. 80; *idem,* "Eli Curtis," *Review,* Apr. 7, 1851, p. 64; *idem,* Ms 4, 1883 (1SM 60, 61).

[4] According to mainstream Millerite thinking, events at the beginning of the millennium included the second coming of Christ, the resurrection of the righteous dead, the destruction of the wicked, and the purification of the earth by fire, resulting in "a new heaven and a new earth" (Rev. 21:1). Events at the close of the millennium included the resurrection of the wicked dead, the loosing of Satan, the attempted attack on the Holy City, and the final punitive fires. Gradually, over a period of about five years, Sabbatarian Adventists developed a view of the millennium that differed from the above schema on several key points. The earliest break with the Millerite view is found in Ellen Harmon's first vision of December 1844, in which the saints ascend with Christ to heaven at the Second Coming (see Lt 1, 1845 [Dec. 20], note 16). The next major break appears in this 1847 letter with the assertion that the new heavens and new earth would not emerge at the beginning of the millennium as the Millerites had taught, but at the end, thus anticipating the subsequent teaching that the final fires that destroy Satan and the wicked will also purify the earth, making it "new." James White claimed, some years later, that his wife's "view of this subject [the millennium] was not till 1850," his main point being to prove that on this subject, as well as on other unique Sabbatarian teachings, "it should be understood that all these views . . . were brought out from the Scriptures before Mrs. W. had any view in regard to them." However, as can be seen from the visions of 1844 and 1847, Ellen White received instruction on important aspects of the emerging new concept of the millennium well before 1850.

See: J. W. [James White], "A Test," *Review,* Oct. 16, 1855, p. 61. For a summary of William Miller's views on the millennium, see Joshua V. Himes, ed., *Views of the Prophecies and Prophetic Chronology,* pp. 33-35. The development of Seventh-day Adventist teachings on the millennium are summarized in SDAE, s.v. "Millennium," and EGWEnc, s.v. "Millennium."

and cease to exist.[5] Then will appear the new heaven and the new earth. Then will the saints "build houses," and "plant vineyards." I saw, that all the righteous dead were raised by the voice of the Son of God, at the first resurrection; and all that were raised at the second resurrection, were burnt up, and ceased to exist.

You think, that those who worship before the saint's [*sic*] feet, (Rev. 3:9), will at last be saved. Here I must differ with you; for God shew me that this class were professed Adventists, who had fallen away, and "crucified to themselves the Son of God afresh, and put him to an open shame." And in the "hour of temptation," which is yet to come, to show out every one's true character, they will know that they are forever lost; and overwhelmed with anguish of spirit, they will bow at the saint's feet.[6]

You also think, that Michael stood up, and the time of trouble commenced, in the spring of 1844.

The Lord has shown me in vision, that Jesus rose up, and shut the door, and

---

[5] This is the earliest indication in Ellen White's visions that the wicked will not suffer eternal punishment in the lake of fire, but will be annihilated. This went counter to the belief in the immortality of the soul held by William Miller and most mainstream Adventists at the time. The vision, however, affirmed the prior beliefs of Ellen Harmon, who had personally rejected the idea of eternal punishment before she received her first vision (see Ellen G. White, *Testimonies for the Church,* vol. 1, pp. 39, 40). James White and Joseph Bates shared the same belief prior to 1844, having emerged from the Christian Connection movement, some of whom were annihilationists.

For a survey of the divisiveness of the issue of inherent versus conditional immortality within mainstream Adventism of the 1850s, see David Tallmadge Arthur, "'Come Out of Babylon,'" pp. 201-208; George R. Knight, *Millennial Fever,* pp. 283-288. Alberto R. Timm discusses the significance of these issues in the context of Seventh-day Adventist doctrinal development in *The Sanctuary and the Three Angels' Messages,* pp. 156-162. *The Conditionalist Faith of Our Fathers,* by LeRoy Edwin Froom, provides a detailed historical survey of conditionalism through the Christian Era.

[6] Revelation 3:9, a message to the church in Philadelphia, which is quoted from here, reads in full: "Behold, I will make them of the synagogue of Satan, which say they are Jews, and are not, but do lie; behold, I will make them to come and worship before thy feet, and to know that I have loved thee." Throughout the ages beleaguered Christian minorities suffering at the hands of those they perceived as falsely claiming to be Christians have identified with the sufferings of the church in Philadelphia at the hands of "the synagogue of Satan, which say they are Jews, and are not, but do lie." The expression "which say they are Jews, and are not" has been seen as figurative of those who claim to be Christians ("true Jews") but are not. Thus, for example, the Waldenses, as reported by their enemies, held that "the Romish Church has become a Babel, a Synagogue of Satan; it is the Church of the wicked" (Comba, p. 284; for further historical examples of this kind, see Kovacs, pp. 54-56).

The promise given the harassed Philadelphians is that their opponents will "come and worship before thy feet, and to know that I have loved thee," with the indication given in the following verse that this will take place in the time of trial and tribulation that precedes Christ's second coming. It is a theme that is further developed in the writings of Ellen White. Speaking of events just before the Second Coming, she wrote, "[Ministers and people] see that they have rebelled against the Author of all just and righteous law. The setting aside of the divine precepts gave rise to thousands of springs of evil. . . . They realize what they have forfeited by transgression, and they fall at the feet of those whose fidelity they have despised and derided, and confess that God has loved them" (Ellen G. White, *The Great Controversy,* p. 655).

See: Emilio Comba, *History of the Waldenses of Italy,* p. 284; Judith L. Kovacs et al., *Revelation: The Apocalypse of Jesus Christ,* pp. 54-56; Joseph Bates, *A Vindication of the Seventh-day Sabbath,* p. 6.

entered the Holy of Holies, at the 7th month 1844; but Michael's standing up (Dan. 12:1) to deliver his people, is in the future.[7]

This, will not take place, until Jesus has finished his priestly office in the Heavenly Sanctuary, and lays off his priestly attire, and puts on his most kingly robes, and crown,[8] to ride forth on the cloudy chariot, to "thresh the heathen in anger," and deliver his people.

Then Jesus will have the sharp sickle in his hand, (Rev. 14:14) and then the saints will cry day and night to Jesus on the cloud, to thrust in his sharp sickle and reap.

This, will be the time of Jacob's trouble,[9] (Jer. 30:5-8) out of which, the saints will be delivered by the voice of God.

I believe the Sanctuary, to be cleansed at the end of the 2300 days, is the New Jerusalem Temple, of which Christ is a minister. The Lord shew me in vision, more than one year ago, that Brother Crosier [O.R.L. Crosier][10] had the true light, on the cleansing of the Sanctuary, &c; and that it was his will, that Brother C. should write out the view which he gave us in the Day-Star, Extra, February 7, 1846. I feel fully authorized by the Lord, to recommend that Extra, to every saint.

I pray that these lines may prove a blessing to you, and all the dear children who may read them.

E. G. WHITE.

---

[7] Even with the revolutionary turmoil and toppling of kingdoms in Europe the following year, 1848, Ellen White continued to be shown in vision that Michael's standing up and the "time of trouble, such as never was" (Dan. 12:1) were still future. On this point her vision was at odds with the conviction of Joseph Bates, who for a time saw the European turmoil as the beginning of the fulfillment of Daniel 12:1.

See: Ms 2, 1849 (Jan. 17), note 7, and Ms 1, 1848 (Nov. 18, 19), note 7.

[8] For a comment on the theological significance of this change in Jesus' role, see Lt 1, 1846 (Feb. 15), note 9.

[9] *See:* Lt 1, 1847 (Apr. 7), note 8.

[10] *Identity:* Owen Russell Loomis Crosier (Crozier) (1820-1912). Prominent figure during the 1850s and early 1860s in the emerging "age-to-come" Adventist movement led by Joseph Marsh. From 1847 to 1853 Crosier was assistant editor of Marsh's *Advent Harbinger* in Rochester, New York. After "age-to-comers" organized a conference in Michigan, Crosier was appointed state evangelist (1858) and conference secretary (1860). Crosier's significance to Seventh-day Adventism lies especially in his groundbreaking *Day-Dawn* article "To All Who Are Waiting for Redemption" in March 1845, as amplified in "The Law of Moses" in the *Day-Star* Extra of February 7, 1846. In contrast to the Millerite view that on October 22, 1844, Christ would leave the heavenly sanctuary to execute judgment on earth, Crosier argued that that day marked the beginning of an extended work by Christ in the Most Holy Place of the heavenly sanctuary, a paradigm shift that laid the basis for subsequent Seventh-day Adventist sanctuary theology. There is some evidence that Crosier's position built on the insights of Hiram Edson dating back to October 1844. For a time Crosier also kept the Sabbath, but by 1847 he abandoned both the Sabbath and sanctuary doctrines.

See: Richard C. Nickels, *Six Papers on the History of the Church of God*, pp. 117, 118; Merlin D. Burt, "The *Day-Dawn* of Canandaigua, New York: Reprint of a Significant Millerite Adventist Journal," *Andrews University Seminary Studies* 44:317-330; O.R.L. Crosier, "The Law of Moses," *Day-Star* Extra, Feb. 7, 1846, pp. 37-44; George R. Knight, *Millennial Fever*, pp. 304-307; Merlin D. Burt, "Sabbatarian Adventism From 1844 to 1849," pp. 242-250; EGWEnc, s.v. "O.R.L. Crosier."

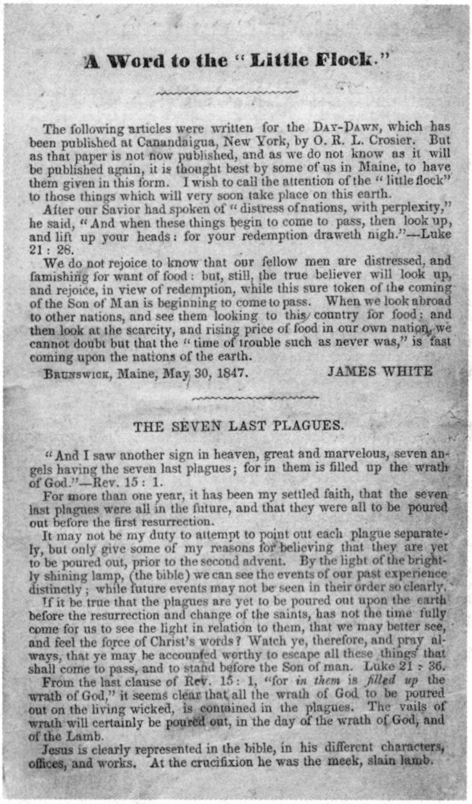

A Word to the "Little Flock."

The following articles were written for the DAY-DAWN, which has been published at Canandaigua, New York, by O. R. L. Crosier. But as that paper is not now published, and as we do not know as it will be published again, it is thought best by some of us in Maine, to have them given in this form. I wish to call the attention of the "little flock" to those things which will very soon take place on this earth.

After our Savior had spoken of "distress of nations, with perplexity," he said, "And when these things begin to come to pass, then look up, and lift up your heads: for your redemption draweth nigh."—Luke 21: 28.

We do not rejoice to know that our fellow men are distressed, and famishing for want of food: but, still, the true believer will look up, and rejoice, in view of redemption, while this sure token of the coming of the Son of Man is beginning to come to pass. When we look abroad to other nations, and see them looking to this country for food: and then look at the scarcity, and rising price of food in our own nation, we cannot doubt but that the "time of trouble such as never was," is fast coming upon the nations of the earth.

BRUNSWICK, Maine, May 30, 1847. JAMES WHITE

THE SEVEN LAST PLAGUES.

"And I saw another sign in heaven, great and marvelous, seven angels having the seven last plagues; for in them is filled up the wrath of God."—Rev. 15: 1.

For more than one year, it has been my settled faith, that the seven last plagues were all in the future, and that they were all to be poured out before the first resurrection.

It may not be my duty to attempt to point out each plague separately, but only give some of my reasons for believing that they are yet to be poured out, prior to the second advent. By the light of the brightly shining lamp, (the bible) we can see the events of our past experience distinctly; while future events may not be seen in their order so clearly.

If it be true that the plagues are yet to be poured out upon the earth before the resurrection and change of the saints, has not the time fully come for us to see the light in relation to them, that we may better see, and feel the force of Christ's words? Watch ye, therefore, and pray always, that ye may be accounted worthy to escape all these things that shall come to pass, and to stand before the Son of man. Luke 21: 36.

From the last clause of Rev. 15: 1, "for *in them* is *filled up* the wrath of God," it seems clear that all the wrath of God to be poured out on the living wicked, is contained in the plagues. The vails of wrath will certainly be poured out, in the day of the wrath of God, and of the Lamb.

Jesus is clearly represented in the bible, in his different characters, offices, and works. At the crucifixion he was the meek, slain lamb.

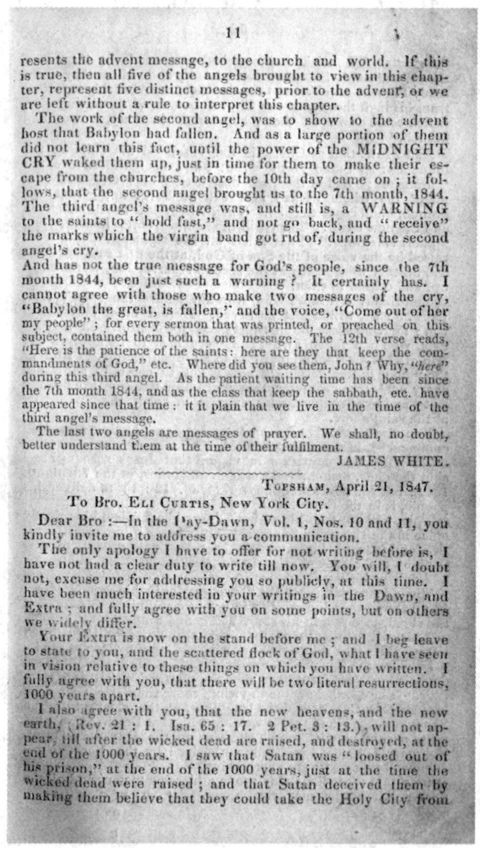

11

resents the advent message, to the church and world. If this is true, then all five of the angels brought to view in this chapter, represent five distinct messages, prior to the advent, or we are left without a rule to interpret this chapter.

The work of the second angel, was to show to the advent host that Babylon had fallen. And as a large portion of them did not learn this fact, until the power of the MIDNIGHT CRY waked them up, just in time for them to make their escape from the churches, before the 10th day came on; it follows, that the second angel brought us to the 7th month, 1844. The third angel's message was, and still is, a WARNING to the saints to "hold fast," and not go back, and "receive" the marks which the virgin band got rid of, during the second angel's cry.

And has not the true message for God's people, since the 7th month 1844, been just such a warning? It certainly has. I cannot agree with those who make two messages of the cry, "Babylon the great, is fallen," and the voice, "Come out of her my people"; for every sermon that was printed, or preached on this subject, contained them both in one message. The 12th verse reads, "Here is the patience of the saints: here are they that keep the commandments of God," etc. Where did you see them, John? Why, "*here*" during this third angel. As the patient waiting time has been since the 7th month 1844, and as the class that keep the sabbath, etc. have appeared since that time: it it plain that we live in the time of the third angel's message.

The last two angels are messages of prayer. We shall, no doubt, better understand them at the time of their fulfilment.

JAMES WHITE.

TOPSHAM, April 21, 1847.

To BRO. ELI CURTIS, New York City.

Dear Bro:—In the Day-Dawn, Vol. 1, Nos. 10 and 11, you kindly invite me to address you a communication.

The only apology I have to offer for not writing before is, I have not had a clear duty to write till now. You will, I doubt not, excuse me for addressing you so publicly, at this time. I have been much interested in your writings in the Dawn, and Extra; and fully agree with you on some points, but on others we widely differ.

Your Extra is now on the stand before me; and I beg leave to state to you, and the scattered flock of God, what I have seen in vision relative to these things on which you have written. I fully agree with you, that there will be two literal resurrections, 1000 years apart.

I also agree with you, that the new heavens, and the new earth, (Rev. 21: 1. Isa. 65: 17. 2 Pet. 3: 13.), will not appear, till after the wicked dead are raised, and destroyed, at the end of the 1000 years. I saw that Satan was "loosed out of his prison," at the end of the 1000 years, just at the time the wicked dead were raised; and that Satan deceived them by making them believe that they could take the Holy City from

A Word to the "Little Flock," *printed May 30, 1847, by James White, contained three communications from Ellen White, including one to Eli Curtis, publisher of the* Girdle of Truth.

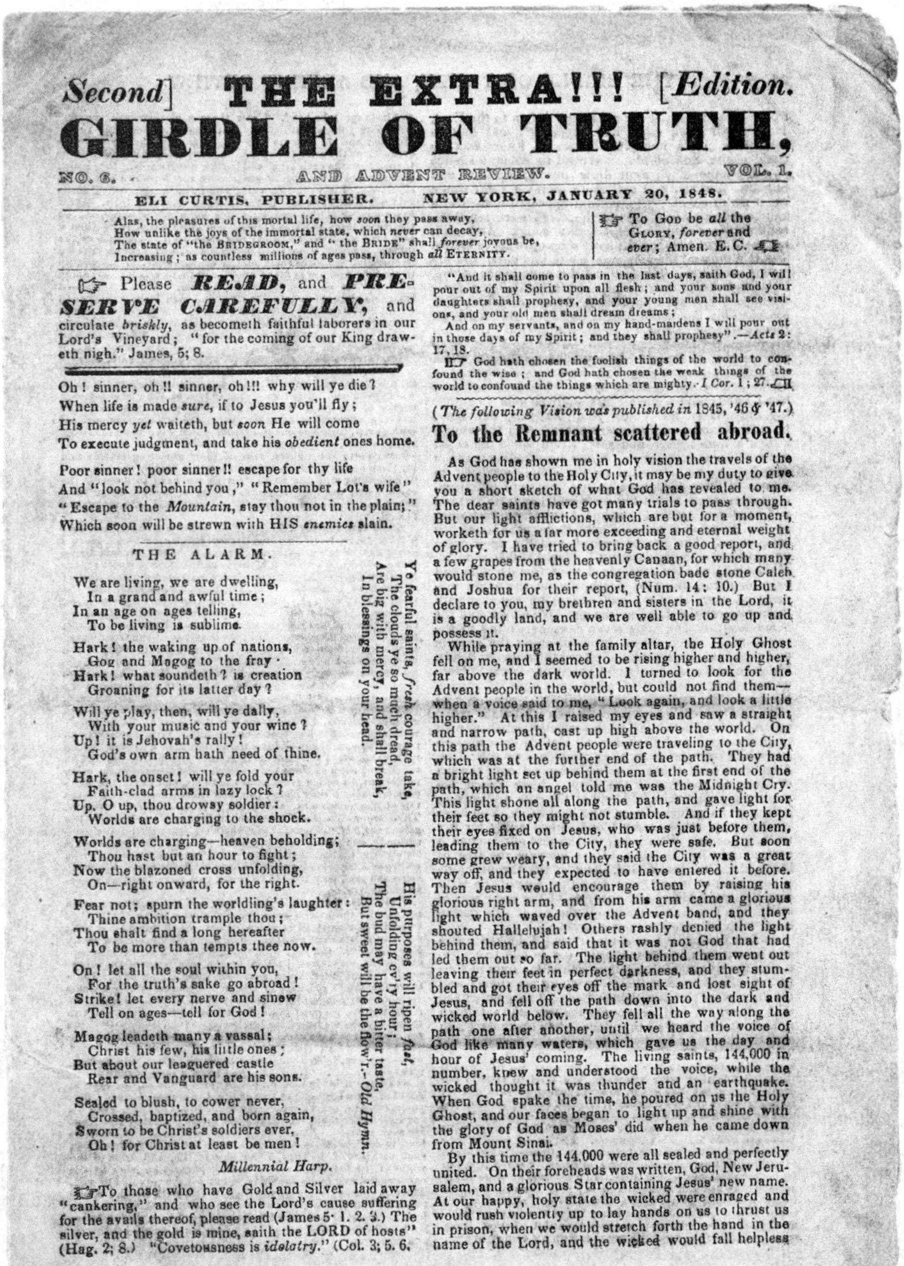

Second] **THE EXTRA!!!** [*Edition.*

GIRDLE OF TRUTH,

NO. 6. AND ADVENT REVIEW. VOL. 1.

ELI CURTIS, PUBLISHER. NEW YORK, JANUARY 20, 1848.

Alas, the pleasures of this mortal life, how *soon* they pass away,
How unlike the joys of the immortal state, which *never* can decay,
The state of "the BRIDEGROOM," and "the BRIDE" shall *forever* joyous be,
Increasing; as countless millions of ages pass, through *all* ETERNITY.

☞ To GOD be *all* the GLORY, *forever* and *ever*; Amen. E. C. ☜

☞ Please ***READ***, and ***PRESERVE CAREFULLY***, and circulate *briskly*, as becometh faithful laborers in our Lord's Vineyard; "for the coming of our King draweth nigh." James, 5; 8.

Oh! sinner, oh!! sinner, oh!!! why will ye die?
When life is made *sure*, if to Jesus you'll fly;
His mercy *yet* waiteth, but *soon* He will come
To execute judgment, and take his *obedient* ones home.

Poor sinner! poor sinner!! escape for thy life
And "look not behind you," "Remember Lot's wife"
"Escape to the *Mountain*, stay thou not in the plain;"
Which soon will be strewn with HIS *enemies* slain.

THE ALARM.

We are living, we are dwelling,
In a grand and awful time;
In an age on ages telling,
To be living is sublime.

Hark! the waking up of nations,
Gog and Magog to the fray·
Hark! what soundeth? is creation
Groaning for its latter day?

Will ye play, then, will ye dally,
With your music and your wine?
Up! it is Jehovah's rally!
God's own arm hath need of thine.

Hark, the onset! will ye fold your
Faith-clad arms in lazy lock?
Up, O up, thou drowsy soldier:
Worlds are charging to the shock.

Worlds are charging—heaven beholding;
Thou hast but an hour to fight;
Now the blazoned cross unfolding,
On—right onward, for the right.

Fear not; spurn the worldling's laughter:
Thine ambition trample thou;
Thou shalt find a long hereafter
To be more than tempts thee now.

Oh! let all the soul within you,
For the truth's sake go abroad!
Strike! let every nerve and sinew
Tell on ages—tell for God!

Magog leadeth many a vassal;
Christ his few, his little ones;
But about our leaguered castle
Rear and Vanguard are his sons.

Sealed to blush, to cower never,
Crossed, baptized, and born again,
Sworn to be Christ's soldiers ever,
Oh! for Christ at least be men!

Millennial Harp.

Ye fearful saints, *fresh* courage take,
The clouds ye so much dread,
Are big with mercy, and shall break,
In blessings on your head.

His purposes will ripen *fast*,
Unfolding ev'ry hour;
The bud may have a bitter taste,
But sweet will be the flow'r.—*Old Hymn.*

☞ To those who have Gold and Silver laid away "cankering," and who see the Lord's cause suffering for the avails thereof, please read (James 5· 1. 2. 3.) The silver, and the gold is mine, saith the LORD of hosts" (Hag. 2; 8.) "Covetousness is *idolatry*." (Col. 3; 5. 6.

"And it shall come to pass in the last days, saith God, I will pour out of my Spirit upon all flesh; and your sons and your daughters shall prophesy, and your young men shall see visions, and your old men shall dream dreams;

And on my servants, and on my hand-maidens I will pour out in those days of my Spirit; and they shall prophesy".—*Acts* 2: 17, 18.

☞ God hath chosen the foolish things of the world to confound the wise; and God hath chosen the weak things of the world to confound the things which are mighty.·*I Cor.* 1; 27. ☜

(*The following Vision was published in* 1845, '46 & '47.)

To the Remnant scattered abroad.

As God has shown me in holy vision the travels of the Advent people to the Holy City, it may be my duty to give you a short sketch of what God has revealed to me. The dear saints have got many trials to pass through. But our light afflictions, which are but for a moment, worketh for us a far more exceeding and eternal weight of glory. I have tried to bring back a good report, and a few grapes from the heavenly Canaan, for which many would stone me, as the congregation bade stone Caleb and Joshua for their report, (Num. 14: 10.) But I declare to you, my brethren and sisters in the Lord, it is a goodly land, and we are well able to go up and possess it.

While praying at the family altar, the Holy Ghost fell on me, and I seemed to be rising higher and higher, far above the dark world. I turned to look for the Advent people in the world, but could not find them—when a voice said to me, "Look again, and look a little higher." At this I raised my eyes and saw a straight and narrow path, cast up high above the world. On this path the Advent people were traveling to the City, which was at the further end of the path. They had a bright light set up behind them at the first end of the path, which an angel told me was the Midnight Cry. This light shone all along the path, and gave light for their feet so they might not stumble. And if they kept their eyes fixed on Jesus, who was just before them, leading them to the City, they were safe. But soon some grew weary, and they said the City was a great way off, and they expected to have entered it before. Then Jesus would encourage them by raising his glorious right arm, and from his arm came a glorious light which waved over the Advent band, and they shouted Hallelujah! Others rashly denied the light behind them, and said that it was not God that had led them out so far. The light behind them went out leaving their feet in perfect darkness, and they stumbled and got their eyes off the mark and lost sight of Jesus, and fell off the path down into the dark and wicked world below. They fell all the way along the path one after another, until we heard the voice of God like many waters, which gave us the day and hour of Jesus' coming. The living saints, 144,000 in number, knew and understood the voice, while the wicked thought it was thunder and an earthquake. When God spake the time, he poured on us the Holy Ghost, and our faces began to light up and shine with the glory of God as Moses' did when he came down from Mount Sinai.

By this time the 144,000 were all sealed and perfectly united. On their foreheads was written, God, New Jerusalem, and a glorious Star containing Jesus' new name. At our happy, holy state the wicked were enraged and would rush violently up to lay hands on us to thrust us in prison, when we would stretch forth the hand in the name of the Lord, and the wicked would fall helpless

Ellen White's first vision was published by Eli Curtis in his Girdle of Truth, and Advent Review, Extra, *January 20, 1848. Original dimensions (H x W): 9.5 x 6.25 in. (24 x 16 cm.). Courtesy James R. Nix.*

1847

MAY 30, BRUNSWICK, MAINE

PUBLICATION OF

A Word to the "Little Flock."

Published by James White. 24 pp. Includes edited reprints of writings above, dated April 6, 7, and 21, 1847.

1847

(Lt 3, 1847)

JULY 13, GORHAM, MAINE

LETTER TO

Joseph Bates.[1]

This letter is published in entirety in Ellen G. White, *Manuscript Releases,* vol. 5, pp. 95-98.

Narrative of circumstances surrounding the "Midnight Cry" and "Bridegroom" visions of December 1844 and February 1845.

Dear Brother Bates:

As James [**James Springer White**] is at work[2] and sisters are from home[3]

---

[1] *Identity:* The letter is addressed "Mr. Joseph Bates, Fairhaven, Mass."

[2] Six weeks later James White wrote to friends, "God has blessed me with health to labor with my hands. . . . I have been able to earn about $25.00 the past six weeks; and my health is much improved. For this I do praise God." The exact nature of his manual labor during these weeks is not known.

See: James White to Elvira Hastings, Aug. 22, 1847.

[3] As is implied in several early sources, Ellen and James White stayed in the home of Ellen's parents in Gorham, Maine, from the time of their marriage in August 1846 until October 1847. At the time of writing, two of Ellen's sisters, Sarah (later Sarah B. Belden) and Elizabeth (later Elizabeth N. Bangs) were still unmarried and presumably living at home.

See: James White to Elvira Hastings, Aug. 22, 1847; Ellen G. White, *Spiritual Gifts [vol. 2],* p. 83; James R. Nix, "Robert Harmon," p. 3; Artemas C. Harmon, ed., *The Harmon Genealogy,* p. 41; 1850 U.S. Federal Census, "Samuel McCann," Maine, Cumberland County,

thought I would employ myself in writing a line to you. My health is quite good for me. My faith is still strong that that very same Jesus that ascended up into heaven will so come in like manner as He went up, and that very, very soon. I have had many trials of late; discouragement at times has laid so fast hold upon me it seemed impossible to shake it off. But thank God, Satan has not got the victory over me yet, and by the grace of God he never shall. I know and feel my weakness, but I have laid hold upon the strong arm of Jehovah, and I can say today I know that my Redeemer liveth, and if He lives I shall live also. Oh, how good it would be to meet with a few of like precious faith to exhort and comfort one another with words of holy cheer from the Word of God.[4] The sheep are now scattered, but thank God they are about to be gathered to a good pasture.

Oh, how sweet it will be to meet all the blood-washed throng in the city of our God. 'Tis then we'll sing the song of Moses and the Lamb as we march through the gates into the city, bearing the palms of victory and wearing the crowns of glory. Brother Bates, you write in a letter to James[5] something about the Bridegroom's coming,[6] as stated in the first published visions. By the letter you would like to know whether I had light on the Bridegroom's coming before I saw it in vision. I can readily answer, No.[7] The Lord showed

---

Poland, p. 34; William C. White, "Sketches and Memories of James and Ellen G. White: XII. Removal to Saratoga Springs," *Review,* May 23, 1935, p. 10.

[4] The implication is that there were no other Sabbathkeepers in Gorham at this time, not even Ellen's parents, in whose house the Whites were living. The first evidence that Robert and Eunice Harmon had accepted the Sabbath is found a year later when James White wrote of "Ellen's parents" that "they are with us in the faith."

See: James White to "Dear Brother and Sister," Aug. 26, 1848.

[5] This letter is not in the White Estate archives.

[6] Prior to January 1845 the general Adventist interpretation of the Bridegroom's coming as portrayed in the parable of the 10 virgins was that it represented the second coming of Christ to the earth to receive His bride, the church. Sometime in January 1845 Apollos Hale (c. 1807-after 1882) and Joseph Turner (1807-1862) published the radically different view that the bride represented the New Jerusalem and the coming of the Bridegroom signified the coming of Christ to the Father to receive the kingdom (represented by the New Jerusalem) prior to His return to earth at the Second Coming. A few weeks later, "about the middle of February," Ellen Harmon was shown in vision a view of the Bridegroom's coming that in some major respects agreed with the position of Hale and Turner.

See: A. Hale and J. Turner, "Has Not the Savior Come as the Bridegroom?" *Advent Mirror,* January 1845, pp. 3, 4; SDAE, s.v. "Apollos Hale," "Joseph Turner"; EGWEnc, s.v. "Joseph Turner."

[7] The question here raised by Joseph Bates whether Ellen White had prior knowledge of matters shown her in vision was destined to become a central issue to those concerned with testing or confirming the genuineness of the visions. In some cases, as with the present one, Ellen White's answer was no, she had no previous acquaintance with the matters shown in vision. In other cases she did have prior knowledge, but as she pointed out, this in itself did not negate the genuineness of the vision. "What if you had said ever so much? Would that affect the visions that God gives me? If so, then the visions are nothing. . . . What you have said, Sister Loveland, influenced me not at all. My opinion has nothing to do with what God has shown me in vision."

me the travail of the Advent band and midnight cry in December,[8] but He did not show me the Bridegroom's coming until February following. Perhaps you would like to have me give a statement in relation to both visions. At the time I had the vision of the midnight cry I had given it up in the past and thought it future, as also most of the band had.[9] I know not what time J. Turner [Joseph Turner] got out his paper. I knew he had one out and one was in the house, but I knew not what was in it, for I did not read a word in it.[10] I had been, and still was, very sick. I took no interest in reading, for it injured my head and made me nervous. After I had the vision and God gave me light, He bade me deliver it to the band, but I shrank from it. I was young, and I thought they would not receive it from me. I disobeyed the Lord, and instead of remaining at home, where the meeting was to be that night, I got in a sleigh in the morning and rode three or four miles [six kilometers] and there I found J. T. He merely inquired how I was and if I was in the way of my duty. I said nothing, for I knew I was not. I passed up chamber and did not see him again for two hours, when he came up, asked if I was to be at meeting that night. I told him, no. He said he wanted to hear my vision and thought it duty for me to go home. I told him I should not. He said no more, but went away. I thought, and told those around me, if I went I should have to come out against his views, thinking he believed with the rest.[11] I had not told any of them what God had shown me, and I did not tell them in what I should cut across his track.

All that day I suffered much in body and mind. It seemed that God had forsaken me entirely. I prayed the Lord if He would give me strength to ride home that night, the first opportunity I would deliver the message He had given me. He did give me strength and I rode home that night. Meeting had been done some time, and not a word was said by any of the family about the meeting.

Very early next morning J. T. [Joseph Turner] called, said he was in haste going out of the city in a short time, and wanted I should tell him all that God had shown me in vision. It was with fear and trembling I told him all.

See: Ellen G. White, Lt 6, 1851 (Apr. 1).

[8] On the significance of the expression "Midnight Cry," see Lt 1, 1845 (Dec. 20), note 6.

[9] In other words, by December 1844 Ellen Harmon no longer believed that the 2300-day prophecy had ended on October 22, 1844, but that its ending was still future.

[10] It is not clear which paper Ellen White refers to here. The vision under discussion in this part of the letter is the first vision of December 1844, which she appears to have related to the Portland "band" within days of receiving it. The *Advent Mirror,* which Joseph Turner edited together with A. Hale, contained the groundbreaking article "Has Not the Savior Come as the Bridegroom?" which was in general agreement with the December vision but was not published until January 1845. Another possibility is that the reference is to the Portland-based *Hope of Israel.* This periodical had begun publication some months earlier and was also coedited by Joseph Turner.

See: A. Hale and J. Turner, "Has Not the Savior Come as the Bridegroom?" *Advent Mirror,* January 1845, pp. 3, 4; "The Hope of Israel," *Advent Herald,* Aug. 7, 1844, p. 5.

[11] That is, she thought Turner had given up the belief that God had led in the proclamation of October 22, 1844.

After I had got through he said he had told out the same last evening. I was rejoiced, for I expected he was coming out against me, for all the while I had not heard anyone say what he believed. He said the Lord had sent him to hear me talk the evening before, but as I would not, He meant His children should have the light in some way, so He took him. There were but few out when he talked, so the next meeting I told my vision, and the band, believing my visions from God, received what God bade me to deliver to them.

The view about the Bridegroom's coming I had about the middle of February 1845.

While in Exeter, Maine, in meeting with Israel Damman,[12] James, and many others, many of them did not believe in a shut door.[13] I suffered much at the commencement of the meeting. Unbelief seemed to be on every hand. There was one sister there that was called very spiritual. She had traveled and been a powerful preacher the most of the time for twenty years. She had been truly a mother in Israel. But a division had risen in the band on the shut door. She had great sympathy, and could not believe the door was shut. (I had known nothing of their differences.) Sister Durben[14] got up to talk. I felt very, very sad. At length my soul seemed to be in an agony, and while she was talking I fell from my chair to the floor.[15] It was then I had a view of Jesus rising from His mediatorial throne and going to the holiest as Bridegroom to receive His kingdom.[16] They were all deeply interested in the

---

[12] *Identity:* Israel Damman [sometimes Damon or Dammon] (c. 1811-1886). A Millerite preacher and subsequent Advent Christian minister, who received notoriety for his arrest and trial reported in several New England newspapers following a meeting in Atkinson, Maine, on February 15, 1845.

See: EGWEnc, s.v. "Israel Damman"; James R. Nix, "Another Look at Israel Damman."

[13] *See:* Introductory article "The 'Shut Door' and Ellen White's Visions" and note 16 below.

[14] This person has not been identified.

[15] For more on Ellen White's physical posture while in vision, see W. C. White to C. A. Zumwalf, Feb. 24, 1936, and James R. Nix, "Another Look at Israel Damman," p. 16.

[16] For the earliest published accounts of this vision, see: Ellen G. Harmon, "Letter From Sister Harmon," *Day-Star,* Mar. 15, 1846 (Lt 1, 1845 [Dec. 20]); *idem,* "To the Little Remnant Scattered Abroad," Ms 1, 1846 (Apr. 6).

Ellen White makes the comment a few lines further on that "most of them received the vision," that is, the vision of the Bridegroom's coming, "and were settled upon the shut door." The conflating of the two events shows that they were not disparate happenings but closely related. According to the parable of the 10 virgins from which this imagery is taken (Matt. 25), "the bridegroom came; and they that were ready went in with him to the marriage: and the door was shut"; that is, to accept that the Bridegroom had come on October 22, 1844 (see note 6 above) also entailed accepting that the "door" had been "shut" in some sense.

Those who accepted that a door had been shut in 1844 had disparate views as to what this meant. A survey of the contemporary literature reveals some who held a moderate position on the "shut door," whereby those consciously rejecting the divinely led "seventh month" preaching in 1844 had sinned against the Holy Spirit. Others held the far more radical position that the door was shut on all non-Millerites on October 22, 1844.

The following discussions of early Sabbatarian shut door beliefs—including those of Ellen

view. They all said it was entirely new to them.[17] The Lord worked in mighty power setting the truth home to their hearts. Sister Durben knew what the power of the Lord was, for she had felt it many times; and a short time after I fell she was struck down and fell to the floor, crying to God to have mercy on her. When I came out of vision, my ears were saluted with Sister Durben's singing and shouting with a loud voice.[18] Most of them received the vision, and were settled upon the shut door. Previous to this I had no light on the coming of the Bridegroom, but had expected Him to this earth to deliver His people on the tenth day of the seventh month. I did not hear a lecture or a word in any way relating to the Bridegroom's going to the holiest. I had but very few privileges in 1842, 1843, & 1844. My sisters both went to the camp meetings in New Hampshire and Maine, while my health prevented me from going to but one, in Maine. I know the light I received came from God, it was not taught me by man. I knew not how to write so that others could read it till God gave me my visions. I went to school but very little on account of my health. I do not think I went to school a day after I was twelve years old, and did not go then but a few days at a time, when sickness would cause me to take [to] my bed for weeks and sometimes for months. The first I wrote anything that could be called writing was after I had been sick [and] the prayer of faith was put up for me, and healing . . . [Here the sheet ends, and the remainder of the letter is gone.]

White—represent a wide range of views: Herbert E. Douglass, *Messenger of the Lord,* pp. 500-511, 554-569; Ingemar Lindén, *1844 and the Shut Door Problem*; Rolf J. Poehler, "'. . . and the Door was Shut'"; Gerard P. Damsteegt, *Foundations of the Seventh-day Adventist Message and Mission,* pp. 149-163; Arthur L. White, "Ellen G. White and the Shut Door Question"; Robert W. Olson, "The 'Shut Door' Documents." For further comment on the rejection motif, see Ms 1, 1849 (Mar. 24), note 13.

See also: Introductory article "The 'Shut Door' and Ellen White's Visions"; EGWEnc, s.v. "Shut Door."

[17] At the time of this meeting, in February 1845, the majority Adventist view rejected the related ideas that the Advent preaching in 1844 was the "midnight cry" of the parable or that the Bridegroom had come or that the door had been shut. The alternative view affirming the prophetic significance of October 22, 1844, the coming of the Bridegroom on that date, etc., was very recent, having first been published by Hale and Turner only a few weeks earlier in January 1845. It is not surprising that Ellen White's vision, broadly affirming the Turner alternative, "was entirely new to them."

[18] On ecstatic phenomena in early Adventism, see Appendix article "Ellen White and Religious Enthusiasm in Early Adventist Experience"; EGWEnc, s.v. "Ecstatic Experiences."

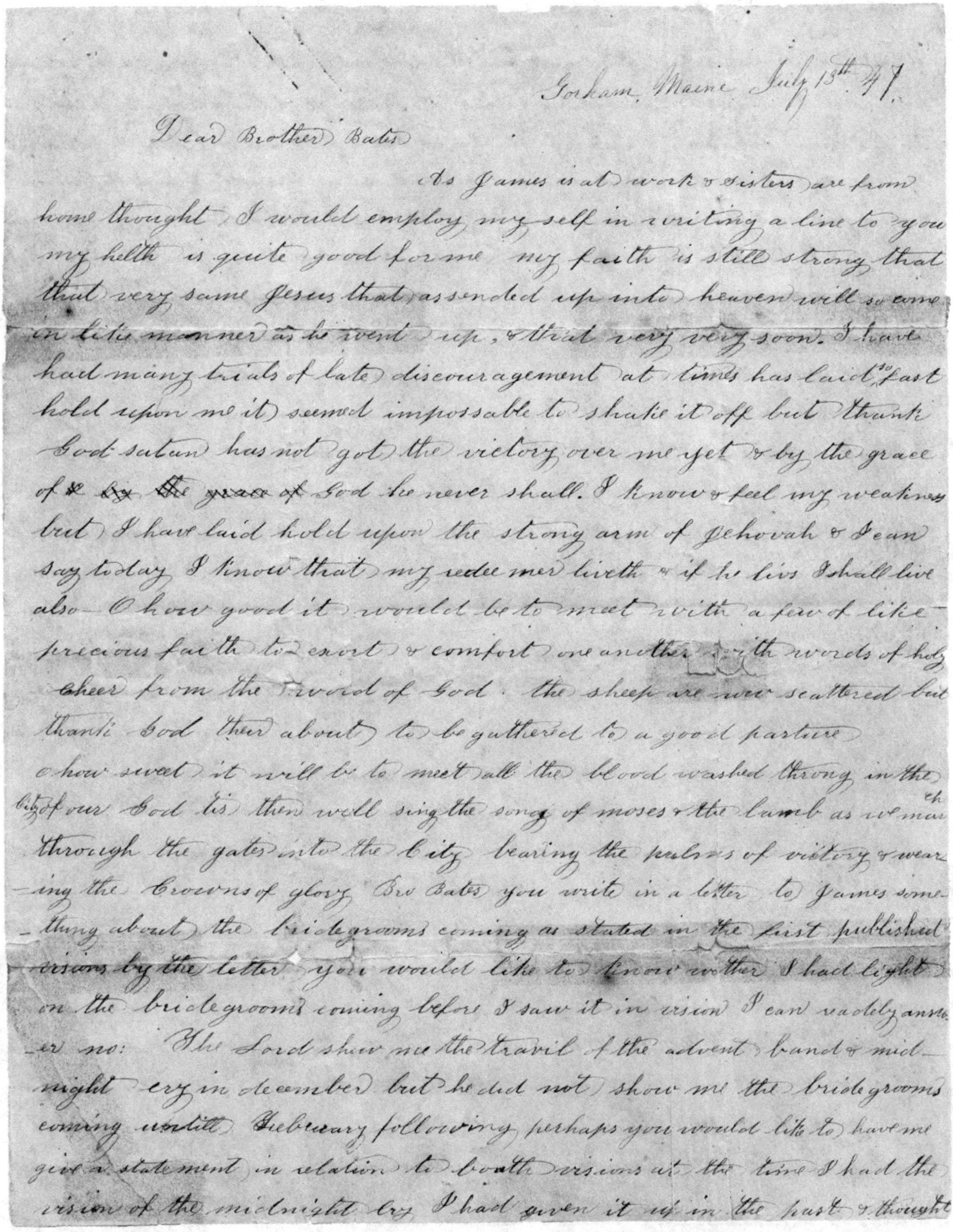

Gorham, Maine July 13th 47.

Dear Brother Bates

As James is at work & sisters are from home thought I would employ my self in writing a line to you my helth is quite good for me my faith is still strong that that very same Jesus that assended up into heaven will so come in like manner as he went up, & that very very soon. I have had many trials of late discouragement at times has laid too fast hold upon me it seemed impossable to shake it off but thank God satan has not got the victory over me yet & by the grace of God he never shall. I know & feel my weakness but I have laid hold upon the strong arm of Jehovah & I can say today I know that my redeemer liveth & if he lives I shall live also— O how good it would be to meet with a few of like precious faith to exort & comfort one another with words of holy cheer from the word of God. the sheep are now scattered but thank God they are about to be gathered to a good pasture o how sweet it will be to meet all the blood washed throng in the city of our God tis then well sing the song of moses & the lamb as we march through the gates into the city bearing the palms of victory & wearing the Crowns of glory Bro Bates you write in a letter to James something about the bridegrooms coming as stated in the first published visions by the letter you would like to know wether I had light on the bridegrooms coming before I saw it in vision I can readily answer no: The Lord show me the travil of the advent band & midnight cry in december but he did not show me the bridegrooms coming untill Febuary following perhaps you would like to have me give a statement in relation to booth visions at the time I had the vision of the midnight cry I had given it up in the past & thought

Ellen White's earliest known handwritten letter, written July 13, 1847 (Lt 3, 1847), and addressed to Joseph Bates

it future as also moast of the band had I knew not what time J. Turner got out
his paper I knew he had one out & one was in the house but I knew not what was in
it for I did not read a word in it I had ben & still was very sick I took no inte
-rest in reading for it injured my head & made me nervous after I had the vision
& God gave me light he bid me deliver it to the band but I srunck from it I was
young & I thought they would not receive it from me I disobeyed the Lord & ins-
-ted of remaining at home where the meeting was to be that night I got in a sleigh
in the morning & rode 3 or 4 miles & their I found J. T. he merely inquired how I was
and if I was in the way of my duty I said nothing for I knew I was not I pas-
sed up chamber & did not see him agan for 2 hours when he came up asked if I was
to be at meeting that night I told him no he said he wanted to hear my vision
& thought it duty for me to go home I told him I should not. he said no more
but went away I thought & told those around me if I went I should have to
come out agunst his veiws thinking he beleived with the rest I had not told
any of them what God had shown me and I did not tell them in what I should
cut across his track all that day I suffered much in body & mind it seemed
that God had forsaken me entirely I prayed the Lord if he would give me strength
to ride home that night the first oppertunity I would deliver the message he had
given me. He did give me strength & I rode home that night meeting had been
done some time & not a word was said by any of the family about the meeting
very early next morning J. T. called said he was in haste going out of the city
in a short time & wanted I should tell him all that God had shown me in
vision it was with fear & trembling I told him all after I had got through
he said he had told out the same last evening I was rejoiced for I expected he
was coming out agunst me for all the while I had not heard any one say what
he beleived he said the Lord had sent him to hear me talk the evening
before but as I would not he ment his children should have the light in some
way so he took him their was but few out when he talked so the next
meeting I told my vision & the band beleiving my visions from God received
what God bid me to deliver to ~~them~~ them The veiw about the Bridegroom,

Turner & Hale's Advent Mirror was dated Jan 1845

coming I had about the midle of February 1845 while in Exeter Main in meeting

The Hope of Israel Extra published about the 20th December

with Israel Damman James & many others. many of them did not beleive in a shut door I suffered much at the commencement of the meeting unbeleif seemed to be on every hand their was one sister their that was called very spiritual she had travild & been a powerfull preacher the most of the time for 20 years she had been truly a mother in israel. but a division had risen in the band on the shut door she had great sympithy & could not beleive the door was shut (I had known nothing of their differances) sister Durben got up to talk I felt very very sad at length my soul seemed to be in an agony & while she was talking I fell from my chair to the floor it was then I had a veiw of Jesus riseing from his meaditoral throne & going to the holiest as bridegroom to receive his kingdom they where all deeply interested in the veiw they all said it was entirely new to them the Lord worked in mighty power setting the truth home to their hearts sister Durben knew what the power of the Lord was for she had felt it many times & a short time after I fell she was struck down & fell to the floor crying to God to have mercy on her when I came out of vision my [illegible] were saluted [illegible] Sis. Durbens singing & shouteing with a loud voice. most of them received the vision & was settled upon the shut door. Previous to this I had no light on the coming of the bridegroom but had expected him to this earth to deliver his people on the tenth day of the 7th month I did not hear a lecture or a word in any way relateing to the bridegrooms going to the holiest I had but very few privalages in 42. 3. & 4 my sisters boath went to the camp meetings in N. Hampshere & Main while my [illegible] th prevented me from going to but one in Main I know the light I [illegible] [illegible] came from God it [illegible] not [illegible] [illegible] man I knew not how to write so that others could read it till God gave it [illegible] I went to school but very little on acount of my helth I do not think I went to school a day after I was 12 years old & did not go then but a few days at a time when sickness would cause me to take my bed for weeks & sometimes for months the first I wrote any thing that could be called writing was after I had been sick the prayer of faith was put up for me & healing

Mr Joseph Bates
Fairhaven
Mass.

1847

(Lt 4, 1847)

AUGUST 25,[1] GORHAM, MAINE

LETTER TO

Elvira Hastings.[2]

Copied from a letter of James White to Elvira Hastings, begun August 22, 1847.[3] Previously unpublished.

Clarification of the prediction that prior to the Second Advent the voice of God will announce the day and the hour of Jesus' coming.

P.S. In your letter[4] you say "Sister White mentions God spoke the day and hour of Jesus' coming," and you inquired "I should like to know if it is to be spoken before we all hear it."[5] To this question I answer by writing Ellen's words that she has just spoken while lying on the bed beside my writing stand.[6] "Tell her that none hear the voice until all hear it. Then every living child of God will hear and know the voice of God as He gives us the day and hour. Then joy and glory will fill every heart." J. W. [James White]

---

[1] James White's letter has the place heading "Gorham." For date, see note 3.

[2] *Identity:* The address on the letter reads "Elvira Hastings, New Ipswich, N.H."

[3] The section of James White's letter appearing below is dated "Aug. 25."

[4] It appears that James White's first contact with Elvira Hastings was in a letter written on May 21, 1847, in which he enclosed "two visions." One of these "visions" was the broadsheet containing Ellen White's first recorded vision on the Sabbath, published by Joseph Bates a few weeks earlier, in April, at a cost of $7.50 for 1,000 copies. White indirectly solicited a contribution to help cover the printing costs. The other "vision" sent by White was probably the broadside "To the Little Remnant Scattered Abroad," which had been published in April the previous year, 1846. Elvira Hastings replied to White a few days later, on May 28, enclosing a $1.00 contribution and also raising the theological question on the "voice of God."

See: James White to Elvira Hastings, May 21, 1847; James White to Elvira Hastings, Aug. 22, 1847; Ellen G. Harmon, "To the Little Remnant Scattered Abroad," Ms 1, 1846 (Apr. 6).

[5] Two of the three visions given in the broadside "To the Little Remnant Scattered Abroad" contained the prediction that prior to the Second Advent the voice of God would announce the day and hour of Jesus' coming to the 144,000. For further comments on this prediction, see Lt 1, 1845 (Dec. 20), note 8.

[6] If this part of James White's letter is correctly dated (Aug. 25, 1847), it was the day before Ellen gave birth to their first child, Henry Nichols White. This may explain why Ellen was "lying on the bed." Three days earlier James reported that Ellen "has been out of health for years, and suffers much at this time."

See: James White to Elvira Hastings, Aug. 22-Sept. 1, 1847.

1848

(Ms 1, 1848)

NOVEMBER 18, 19,[1] DORCHESTER, MASSACHUSETTS

REPORT OF

E. G. White Utterances During Visions of November 18 and 19, 1848.

Transcripted from Joseph Bates's tract *A Seal of the Living God, A Hundred Forty-four Thousand of the Servants of God Sealed*, pp. 24-26, 32.

J. B. Cook's repudiation of the Sabbath. The Seal of God and Time of Trouble.

In a vision in meeting the day before, November 18, she says: "Who has relaxed that fourth commandment?[2] O thou foolish man! thou shalt feel the weight of this commandment when you cannot keep it. That charge shall be held up to thee in the day of judgment, and you will feel it more."

"O, thou wilt wish that those words had never passed thy lips."

"Stand out from him entirely."

When she came out of vision, she said:

"I saw that he rolled, and turned on his bed, to see how he could get round this law of God."

"I saw that he would feel the weight and force of it when he could not keep it."

"I saw he did things on the Sabbath, and wished to justify himself." Who was this you saw? answer: J. B. Cook. "For there is nothing *covered* that shall not be revealed, neither hid that shall not be known."—Luke 12:2. For further information, see *Advent Harbinger*, Sept. 30-Nov. 11, 1848.

---

[1] According to Joseph Bates's introductions to the two visions (included in the text of the manuscript), they took place over two days, November 18 and 19, 1848, in Dorchester, Massachusetts.

[2] The answer to this question, given further down, is "J. B. Cook." John B. Cook, a former Baptist minister and Millerite writer, had kept the Sabbath and defended it in print from 1846 to 1848. However, during the autumn of 1848, shortly before Ellen White's vision, Cook renounced his position on the Sabbath in the course of several articles written for the *Advent Harbinger*. He concluded his article of September 30, 1848, with the words "While the Sabbatic law is thus *relaxed*, every other precept of the Decalogue is *enforced* and embodied in the law of Christ!!" It is likely that the question "who has relaxed that fourth commandment?" relates to Cook's statement in the September 30 *Harbinger*.

See: J.B.C. [J. B. Cook], "The Sabbath, No. II," *Advent Harbinger*, Sept. 30, 1848, p. 113. Cook's abandonment of his former Sabbatarian position is further documented in Merlin Burt, "Sabbatarian Adventism From 1844 to 1849," pp. 344, 345; SDAE, s.v. "J. B. Cook."

Report of E. G. White Utterances During Vision, November 19, 1848

[J. Bates introduction:] A small company of brethren and sisters were assembled in meeting in Dorchester, near Boston, Mass. Before the meeting commenced, some of us were examining some of the points in the sealing message; some difference of opinion existed about the correctness of the view of the word ascending, &c,[3] and whereas we had made the publishing of the

---

[3] The first four verses of Revelation 7 dealing with the seal of God had come under special scrutiny by Sabbatarian Adventists in 1848:

1. And after these things I saw four angels standing on the four corners of the earth, holding the four winds of the earth, that the wind should not blow on the earth, nor on the sea, nor on any tree.
2. And I saw another angel ascending from the east, having the seal of the living God: and he cried with a loud voice to the four angels, to whom it was given to hurt the earth and the sea,
3. Saying, Hurt not the earth, neither the sea, nor the trees, till we have sealed the servants of our God in their foreheads.
4. And I heard the number of them which were sealed: and they were sealed an hundred and forty and four thousand of all the tribes of the children of Israel.

A letter from Joseph Bates dated August 7, 1848, is the first extant source that proposes that the seal of God in this passage is related to the Sabbath. While Bates's interpretation on this central point seems shortly to have gained broad acceptance among Sabbatarian Adventists, there was disagreement on his interpretation of some other features of the passage. Two points of contention were:

1. Whether the angel in verse 2 should be understood literally or symbolically. Bates originally believed the angel "ascending from the east" symbolized Adventist preachers of the Sabbath. That they ascended "from the east" (literally "from the rising of the sun") was taken as corresponding with the fact that they started their proclamation on the East Coast of the United States, later spreading westward. Bates subsequently changed his view, now holding that the angel in verse 2 was literal and modifying his earlier position that "ascending from the east" primarily had a geographical meaning. He attributed his change to this vision that focuses on the manner in which the Sabbath message arose rather than on its location. Like the ascending sun the message gradually increased in strength and glory. (Note expressions such as "Like the sun, first cold, grows warmer and sends its rays.")
2. How to interpret the four angels holding the four winds (verse 1). Bates initially followed other Adventist expositors in taking the four angels to mean national powers. Thus Joseph Turner, editor of *The Bible Advocate,* held that the four angels were the main signatories to the peace treaties at the Congress of Vienna in 1815 after the Napoleonic wars, powers that thereby had the might to hold back the winds of war. Bates's interpretation was a little different, as he included the United States together with the main European powers.

After meeting the objections of "many of those observing the Sabbath," Bates changed his position here also. In May 1849 he published a retraction, holding that "the four messengers [angels], instead of being the four principal governments of earth, are FOUR LITERAL ANGELS commissioned by God to execute His purpose in the destruction of the wicked."

See: Joseph Bates to Brother and Sister Hastings, Aug. 7, 1848; [J. Turner], "The Loosing of the Four Winds," *Bible Advocate,* June 15, 1849, p. 132; Joseph Bates, *A Seal of the Living God,* pp. 4, 24; "Not So," *Review,* Dec. 23, 1851, p. 72. For a detailed historical and theological study of "the sealing message" as it developed in 1848 and 1849, see Merlin Burt, "Sabbatarian Adventism From 1844 to 1849," pp. 360-380.

message a subject of prayer at the Topsham Conference (Me.) a little previous,[4] and the way to publish appeared not sufficiently clear, we therefore resolved unitedly to refer it all to God. After some time spent in earnest prayer for light and instruction, God gave Sister White the following in vision, viz:

"Where did the light break out? Let thine angels teach us where the light broke out! It commenced from a little, then Thou didst give one light after another. The testimony and commandments are linked together, they cannot be separated; that comes first the ten commandments, by God."

"The commandments never would be struck against if it were not to get rid of the Sabbath commandment. That one that has relaxed it is very foolish. It was very small, and when it rose, though it rose in strength, it was weak back there, when it came up it increase, (or increased.) If they won't hear it they are as accountable as though they did hear it."

"He was well pleased when His law began to come up in strength, and the waste places began to be built up."

"Out of weakness it has become strong from searching His Word. The test upon it has been but a short time. All who are saved will be tried upon it in some way.[5] That truth arises and is on the increase, stronger, and stronger. It's the seal! It's coming up! It arises, commencing from the rising of the sun. Like the sun, first cold, grows warmer and sends its rays."[6]

"When that truth arose there was but little light in it, but it has been increasing. O the power of these rays."

"It grows in strength, the greatest weight and light is on that truth for it lasts forever when the Bible is not needed. It arose there in the east, it began with a small light, but its beams are healing. O how mighty is that truth; it's the highest after they enter the goodly land, but it will increase till they are made immortal. It commenced from the rising of the sun, keeps on its course like the sun, but it never sets."

"The angels are holding the four winds."

"It is God that restrains the powers."

"The angels have not let go, for the saints are not all sealed."

"The time of trouble has commenced, it is begun.[7] The reason why the

---

[4] October 20-22, 1848. See James White to Leonard and Elvira Hastings, Oct. 2, 1848.

[5] That the statement "all who are saved will be tried" on the Sabbath in some way does not apply to all earlier generations of believers is apparent from the previous sentence, which points out the recent foundation of this test.

[6] See note 1.

[7] This statement, made in November 1848, at first sight appears to contradict Ellen White's vision some weeks later, in January 1849, where she "saw that Michael had not stood up, and that the time of trouble, such as never was had not yet commenced." But further examination of the two passages makes clear that the time of trouble referred to in November is not the same as that referred to in January. The January vision uses the expression "time of trouble" in the context of Daniel 12:1: "At that time shall Michael stand up . . . : and there shall be a time of trouble, such as never was." This verse was understood as indicating that a time of

four winds have not let go, is because the saints are not all sealed. It's on the increase, and will increase more and more; the trouble will never end until the earth is rid of the wicked."

"At that time neighbor will be against neighbor. That time has not yet come, when brother against brother and sister against sister; but will come when Michael stands up."

"When Michael stands up this trouble will be all over the earth."

"Why they are just ready to blow. There's a check put on because the saints are not sealed."

"Yea, publish the things thou hast seen and heard, and the blessing of God will attend. Look ye! that rising is in strength, and grows brighter and brighter. That truth is the seal, that's why it comes last. The shut door[8] we have had. God has taught and taught, but that experience is not the seal, and that commandment that has been trodden under foot will be exalted. And when ye get that you will go through the time of trouble."

"Yea, all that thou art looking at, thou shalt not see just now. Be careful, let not light be set aside which comes from another way from which thou art looking for."

[Note by J. Bates:] The above was copied word for word as she spake in vision, therefore it's unadulterated; some sentences escaped us, and some which we have not copied here. This probably is sufficient to show the answer to our prayers.

---

trouble would occur immediately after the close of Christ's intercession. In the November vision, however, the time of trouble has already started but the standing up of Michael is still future: "That time has not yet come . . . but will come when Michael stands up." Clearly, a time of trouble that commences before Michael stands up cannot refer to the same time of trouble found in Daniel 12:1, which commences after Michael stands up.

It is interesting that Ellen White's visions on this issue went counter to the views of the senior voice of Sabbatarian Adventism at that time, Joseph Bates. In his book *A Seal of the Living God,* published some weeks later (January 1849) Bates, impressed with the current revolutionary fervor in Europe, insisted that "the time of trouble such as never was, Dan. xii:1 *has* began [*sic*]" (emphasis Bates's).

See: Ellen G. White, Ms 2, 1849 (Jan. 17); Joseph Bates, *A Seal of the Living God,* p. 48; SDAE, s.v. "Michael, the Archangel"; EGWEnc, s.v. "Time of Trouble." For discussions on the issue of a "time of trouble" prior to the close of probation, see Ellen G. White, *Supplement to the Christian Experience and Views of Ellen G. White,* pp. 3, 4 (EW 85, 86); Merlin Burt, "Sabbatarian Adventism From 1844 to 1849," pp. 311-314; SDAE, s.v. "Little Time of Trouble."

[8] *See:* Introductory article "The 'Shut Door' and Ellen White's Visions"; EGWEnc, s.v. "Shut Door."

1848

(Lt 2, 1848)

DECEMBER 18, ROCKY HILL, CONNECTICUT

LETTER TO

the "Scattered Remnant."

Portions of this letter are similar to Ellen G. White, *Early Writings*, p. 41.

The European revolutions of 1848 were not a fulfillment of Christ's prediction that "the powers of heaven shall be shaken."

To the Scattered Remnant—Dear Brethren:

God gave me a [vision] the evening of the 16th. I saw that when the Lord said heaven He meant heaven and when He said earth, He meant earth in giving the signs as recorded by Matt. Mark and Luke.

I saw that the powers of heaven are the sun, moon and stars. They rule in the heavens. I saw that the powers of earth are those who bear rule on earth. I saw that the powers of heaven will be shaken at the voice of God. Then the sun, moon, and stars will be moved out of their places. They will not fall or pass away, but be shaken by the voice of God.

Dark, heavy clouds came up and clashed against each other; the atmosphere parted and rolled back, then we could see the open space in Orion[1] from whence came the voice of God. I saw that the Holy City will come down through that open space. I saw that the powers of earth are now being shaken.

---

[1] This is the first and only specific mention of an "open space" in Orion in Ellen White's writings. Several noted astronomers had reported "openings" in the Great Nebula in Orion, a fact seen by subsequent Adventist writers as confirming Ellen White's vision. Thus, Christian Huygens, in the seventeenth century, interpreted certain dark areas of the nebula as "an opening in the sky." Likewise, most nineteenth-century astronomers interpreted starless, dark portions of the Orion Nebula as "tubes through which we may look into the remotest depths of space" (Alexander von Humboldt, in Sprengel and Martz, *Review*, Apr. 1, 1976, p. 10). However, by the early twentieth century "these blank areas in the sky were discovered to be opaque clouds of dust and gas situated between the earth and the most distant stars" (*ibid.*), not openings leading to the depths of space. These later scientific discoveries do not, of course, disprove the description given in the vision that the new Jerusalem pictured by John as "coming down from God out of heaven" (Rev. 21:2) will make its entrance into our galaxy and view by way of the constellation Orion.

The best historical survey of the intersection of science and theology as regards Ellen White's Orion vision is found in Merton E. Sprengel and Dowell E. Martz, "Orion Revisited," *Review*, Mar. 25, 1976, pp. 4-7; *idem*, "How Open Is Orion's Open Space?" *Review*, Apr. 1, 1976, pp. 9-11; *idem*, "Does the 'Open Space' Exist Today?" *Review*, Apr. 8, 1976, pp. 6-8.

(Lt 2, 1848) December 18, 1848

The Lord showed me that things came in order—war, and rumors of war—sword, famine, and pestilence are first to shake the powers of earth, then the voice of God will shake the heavens and earth—the sun, moon, and stars and this planet also. I saw that the shaking of nations in Europe is not the shaking of the powers of heaven as some teach, but it is the shaking of the powers of earth.[2]

In hope.

---

[2] The last sentence provides a key to understanding this document. Some Adventists interpreted the revolutionary ferment sweeping through Europe in 1848 in which a string of monarchs were overthrown as fulfilling Christ's prediction in Luke 21:26 that "the powers of heaven shall be shaken." They also noted that this event is the last of the signs enumerated by Christ in this passage before the coming of the Son of man: "And there shall be signs in the sun, and in the moon, and in the stars; and upon the earth distress of nations, with perplexity; the sea and the waves roaring; men's hearts failing them for fear, and for looking after those things which are coming upon the earth: for the powers of heaven shall be shaken. And then they shall see the Son of man coming" (verses 25-27). Thus D. Crary wrote in the Adventist *Bible Advocate* of the 1848 events as "this sweeping tornado, which like an electric shock, has passed over Europe" and concludes that this is the event "which the Saviour gave as the last sign of his coming, 'The powers that are in heaven shall be shaken.'" The extent to which Sabbatarian Adventists shared this interpretation is not known, but the fact that the vision contradicts it suggests that it was an issue among them, also.

The obvious difficulty with this interpretation is that it is hard to see why European powers in 1848 should be described as "the powers that are in heaven." Some *Advocate* articles and letters argued that "the powers of heaven" simply meant "the powers and kingdoms of this world," whereas others held that the two are clearly distinguished in the Bible. For J. B. Cook "the heaven" is as distinct from "the earth" in the Bible "as the Creator is from the creature." We should not "confound heaven and earth!"

The debate over the meaning of "heaven" and "earth" in the Bible and over Christ's expression "the shaking of the powers of heaven" in the context of the 1848 revolutions clearly provides the context for Ellen White's statements in this vision. Thus the opening sentences seek to define these terms, and the last sentence concludes that "the shaking of the powers of heaven" applies not to the current crisis in Europe but to future events, when "the voice of God will shake the heavens and earth—the sun, moon, and stars and this planet also."

See: D. Crary, "The Powers That Are in Heaven Shall Be Shaken," *Bible Advocate,* June 1, 1848, p. 116; H. L. Smith, "The Powers of Heaven Shall Be Shaken," *Bible Advocate,* June 8, 1848, pp. 123, 124; H. H. Gross, "Signs of This Time," *Bible Advocate,* June 8, 1848, p. 127; J. B. Cook, "The Opening Heavens," *Bible Advocate,* June 15, 1848, p. 133.

1849

(Ms 2, 1849)

JANUARY 17, TOPSHAM, MAINE

The Sealing.

Portions of this manuscript are published in Arthur L. White, *Ellen G. White: The Early Years,* pp. 157, 158, and compare to the broadside "To Those Who Are Receiving the Seal of the Living God" (Ms 4, 1849 [Jan. 31]). See also Ellen G. White, *Early Writings,* pp. 36-39.

Concerning the sequence of final events.

At the commencement of the holy Sabbath (Jan. 5) I was taken off in vision to the most holy place, where I saw Jesus still interceding for Israel.[1] On the bottom of His garment was a bell and a pomegranate, a bell and a pomegranate.[2] Then I saw that Jesus would not leave the most holy place until every case was decided, either for salvation or destruction. I saw that the wrath of God[3] could not come until Jesus had finished His work in the most holy place, laid off His priestly attire, and clothed Himself with the garments of vengeance. Then Jesus will step out from between the Father and man, and God will keep silent no longer, but pour out His wrath on those who have rejected His truth. I saw that the anger of the nations, the wrath of God, and the time to judge the dead, were separate events, one following the other. I saw that Michael[4] had not stood up, and that the time of trouble,[5] such as never was, had not yet commenced. I saw that the nations are now getting angry, but when our High Priest has finished His work in the sanctuary, then He will stand up, put on the garments of vengeance, and then will the seven last plagues[6] be poured out.[7]

---

[1] It should not be assumed that "Israel" is used here in the restricted sense of only Sabbatarian Adventists who had accepted the three angels' messages. Almost two years earlier Ellen White had indicated that God's "chosen" included those "who do not see and keep the Sabbath. They had not rejected the light on it," and in the future "they came out and endured the persecution with us."

See: Ellen G. White, Lt 1, 1847 (Apr. 7); introductory article "The 'Shut Door' and Ellen White's Visions"; EGWEnc, s.v. "Shut Door."

[2] Ex. 28:34.

[3] *See:* EGWEnc, s.v. "Wrath of God."

[4] *See:* SDAE, s.v. "Michael, the Archangel"; *Questions on Doctrine,* pp. 65-76.

[5] *See:* EGWEnc, s.v. "Time of Trouble."

[6] *See:* EGWEnc, s.v. "Plagues, Seven Last."

[7] This vision focuses on the interpretation and fulfillment of certain biblical passages dealing with end-time events. The first paragraph centers on Revelation 11:18, Revelation 15:1, and

I saw that the four angels would hold the four winds until Jesus' work was done in the sanctuary, then the seven last plagues will be poured out.[8] These plagues enraged the wicked against the righteous, and they thought that we had brought the plagues down upon them, and if they could rid the earth of us, then the plagues would be stayed.

A decree went forth to slay the saints, which caused them to cry day and night for deliverance. This was the time of Jacob's trouble.[9] Then all the saints cried out with anguish of spirit, and were delivered by the voice of God. Then the 144,000[10] triumphed. Their faces were lighted up with the glory of God. Then I was shown a company who were howling in agony.

Daniel 12:1:

- Rev. 11:18—"And the nations were angry, and thy wrath is come, and the time of the dead, that they should be judged."
- Rev. 15:1—"And I saw another sign in heaven, great and marvellous, seven angels having the seven last plagues; for in them is filled up the wrath of God."

Some 18 months earlier James White, referring to Revelation 15:1, had argued that the "wrath of God . . . is contained in the plagues" and would be poured out "in the future" (*A Word to the "Little Flock,"* p. 1). (He had also placed the "time of trouble" of Daniel 12:1 and the releasing of the "four winds" in the future.) By January 1849, however, Joseph Bates had published his conviction that the wrath of God was already beginning to be manifest in the events of Europe in 1848:

- "See the account from the Boston *Times* of Oct. 26, 1848, of the flight of the Emperor of Austria from VIENNA. . . . See also a similar state of things in Berlin. . . . Almost every arrival from Europe shows that these difficulties instead of being settled are breaking out like volcanic eruptions. . . . Well, say the thoughtless ones, these things are nothing more than what has been before. I reply . . . isolated revolutions are trivial, when compared as it were with continental Europe. There things without any doubt are in their progress and order the fulfillment of prophecy, viz: 'The nations are angry, thy wrath has come.' Rev. xi:18" (*A Seal of the Living God,* p. 48).

Joseph Bates was not the only one who was stirred by the revolutionary events of 1848 into thinking that the "wrath of God" and the final events had begun, but his voice was especially significant. Bates's biographer George Knight calls him the "acknowledged leader" of the Sabbatarian Adventists until 1849.

Clearly, this vision of January 5, 1849, placed the "wrath of God" as still future, challenging the position taken by Bates in his tract *A Seal of the Living God,* published the same month. It also challenged Bates on his interpretation of Daniel 12:1:

- "And at that time shall Michael stand up . . . : and there shall be a time of trouble, such as never was . . . : and at that time thy people shall be delivered, every one that shall be found written in the book."

Again Bates was convinced by the events of 1848 that the "time of trouble, such as never was" had begun: "The time of trouble such as never was," Dan. xii:1, *has* began [*sic*]" whereas according to the vision "the time of trouble, such as never was, had not commenced."

See: James White, ed., *A Word to the "Little Flock,"* pp. 1, 8, 3; Joseph Bates, *A Seal of the Living God,* pp. 48, 46; George R. Knight, *Joseph Bates,* p. 167.

[8] The position taken here that the releasing of the four winds was still a future event can also be contrasted with Bates's convictions that the 1848 chaos in France (one of the four angels holding the four winds, according to him) meant that "A WIND [begins] to blow."

See: Joseph Bates, *A Seal of the Living God,* p. 46.

[9] *See:* SDAE, s.v. "Jacob's Trouble, Time of."

[10] *See:* EGWEnc, s.v. "144,000."

On their garments was written in large characters—thou art weighed in the balance and found wanting. I asked who this company were, and the angel said, these are they who have once kept the Sabbath, and have given it up. I heard them cry with a loud voice—we have believed in Thy coming and taught it with energy. And then while they were speaking, their eyes would fall upon their garments, and see the writing—thou art weighed in the balance and found wanting. Then they would wail aloud. I saw they had drunk of the deep waters, and fouled the residue with their feet—trodden the Sabbath underfoot, and that is why they were weighed in the balance and found wanting.

Then my attending angel[11] directed me to the City again where I saw four angels winging their way to the gate of the City, and were just presenting the golden card[12] to the angel at the gate. Then I saw another angel swiftly flying from the direction of the most excellent glory; and crying with a loud voice to the other four angels and waving something up and down in his hand. I asked my attending angel for an explanation of what I saw. He told me that I could see no more then, but he would shortly show me what those things that I then saw meant.

Sabbath afternoon one of our number was sick and requested prayers that he might be healed. We all united in applying to the Physician who never lost a case and while healing power came down, and the sick was

---

[11] As with the interpreting angels who appeared in the visions of Ezekiel (Eze. 40-48), Daniel (Dan. 8-10), Zechariah (Zech. 1; 2; 4), and John (Rev. 17; 21; 22), an angel sometimes explained various features of a scene shown Ellen White while in vision. Mention of an interpreting angel is found already in the account of her first vision. Various designations are employed in her writings, such as "attending angel" (first found in this document), "accompanying angel," and "guide." In an article from 1875 Ellen White related that the "same person has appeared before me in important dreams to instruct me from time to time during the past twenty-six years."

See: Ellen G. Harmon, Lt 1, 1845 (Dec. 20); Ellen G. White, "A Remarkable Dream," *Review*, Nov. 4, 1875, p. 139. For further examples of angelic guidance while in vision, see Ellen G. White, *The Truth About Angels*, pp. 252-257.

[12] One other mention is made in Ellen White's writings of these "golden cards": "All the angels that are commissioned to visit the earth hold a golden card, which they present to the angels at the gates of the city as they pass in and out" (Ms 4, 1849 [Jan. 31]). The question arises, Why would such a system be necessary for heavenly angels? The passage must be read in the context of its previous sentence: "I will here state, that there is perfect order and harmony in the holy city." Thus, the "golden cards" apparently relate to the "perfect order" of heaven rather than to some sort of security procedure.

A related question is whether the presentation of cards by the angels should be understood literally. Not enough information is given for a definitive answer, but in this same vision an angel is seen "waving something up and down in his hand," which is identified in a different vision on the same Sabbath as the "seal of God" (cf. Rev. 7:2). As a literal seal is not to be impressed upon the foreheads of the redeemed, it suggests the possibility that Ellen White's view of angels presenting "golden cards" may also be a visual way of communicating that the city is administered with "perfect order and harmony."

See: Ellen G. White, Ms 4, 1849, "To Those Who Are Receiving the Seal of the Living God," broadside, Jan. 31, 1849.

healed, the power fell upon me and I was taken off in vision.

I saw the state of some who professed to stand on present truth, but disregarded the visions—the way God had chosen to teach, in some cases, those who erred from Bible truth. I saw that in striking against the visions, they did not strike against the worm,—the feeble instrument that God spoke through, but against the Holy Ghost. I saw it was a small thing to speak against the instrument, but it was dangerous to slight the words of God. I saw if they were in error and God chose to show them their errors through visions, and they disregarded the teachings of God through visions, they would be left to take their own way, and run in the way of error, and think they were right until they would find it out too late. Then in the time of trouble I heard them cry to God in agony—why did'st Thou not show us our wrong, that we might have gotten right, and ready for this time? Then an angel pointed to them, and said—my Father taught but you would not be instructed. He spoke through visions but you disregarded His voice, and He gave you up to your own ways to be filled with your own doings.

Then I saw four angels who had a work to do on the earth, and were on their way to accomplish it. I saw Jesus clothed with priestly garments. He gazed in pity on the remnant then raised His hands upward, and with a voice of deep pity cried—"My blood, Father, My blood, My blood, My blood."

Then I saw an exceeding bright light come from God who sat on the great white throne, and was shed all about Jesus. I saw an angel with a commission from Jesus swiftly flying to the four angels who had a work to do on the earth, and waving something up and down in his hand, and crying with a loud voice, "Hold, Hold, Hold, Hold until the servants of God are sealed in their foreheads."[13]

I asked my attending angel the meaning of what I heard, and what the four angels were about to do. He said to me that it was God that restrained the powers,[14] and that He gave His angels charge over things on the earth, and that the four angels had power from God to hold the four winds, and that they were about to let them go, and while they had started to let the four winds go the merciful eye of Jesus gazed on the remnant who were not all sealed, then He raised His hands to the Father, and pleaded with Him that He had spilled His blood for them. Then another angel was commissioned to fly swiftly to the four angels, and bid them hold until the servants of God

---

[13] *See:* EGWEnc, s.v. "Seal of God."

[14] The last two paragraphs seem to undercut the view of Bates and others that "the four angels" holding the four winds symbolized four major nations. For Bates these were Britain, Russia, France, and the United States. Taken together, an important element of this vision is its challenge to the views of Bates (without mentioning him by name) on the prophetic significance of the 1848 events in Europe. No doubt these questions had been discussed at the "Sabbatarian Bible Conferences" during the autumn of 1848.

See: Joseph Bates, *A Seal of the Living God,* p. 4.

were sealed in their foreheads.

I saw that the nations had not power to hold themselves. I also saw that we were not to cry to God to hold the four winds, nor to the nations, but one angel was to cry to other angels equal in power, to hold until the servants of God were sealed in their foreheads.

In hope of being one of the 144,000.

1849

(Ms 3, 1849)

JANUARY 18, TOPSHAM, MAINE

Our Duty in View of the Time of Trouble.

Portions of this manuscript are published in Ellen G. White, *Manuscript Releases,* vol. 5, p. 200, and compare to the broadside "To Those Who Are Receiving the Seal of the Living God" (Ms 4, 1849 [Jan. 31]). See also Ellen G. White, *Early Writings,* pp. 56-58.

Guidance on financial sacrifice before the time of trouble.

Dear Brethren & Sisters:

The Lord has shown me in vision that it is contrary to the Bible to make any preparations for our temporal wants in the time of trouble.[1] I saw that if the saints have food laid up by them, or in the fields in that time of trouble, when sword, famine and pestilence is in the land, it will be taken from them by violent hands.

Then will be the time for us to trust in God, and He will sustain us. I saw that our bread and water would be sure at that time and we shall not lack or suffer hunger. The Lord has shown me that some of His children would fear when they see the price of food rising, and they would buy food and lay it by for the time of trouble. Then in the time of need I saw them go to their food and look at it and it had bred worms, and was full of living creatures and not fit for use.

About one week since the Lord showed me in vision that houses and lands will be of no use in the time of trouble; and that in that time they could not be disposed of. I saw that it was the will of God that the saints should cut loose from every encumbrance, dispose of their houses and lands before the time of trouble comes, and thus make a covenant with God by sacrifice. I saw they would sell if they laid their property on the altar and earnestly inquired for duty. God will teach them when to dispose of these things. Then they will be free in the time of trouble and have no clogs to weigh them down.

I saw if any held on to their property and did not inquire duty of God, He would not make duty plain and they would be left to keep their property, and then in the time of trouble their property would come up before them like a mountain to crush them. Then they tried to get rid of it, but could not.

---

[1] *See:* EGWEnc, s.v. "Time of Trouble."

I heard them mourn like this:—God's people were suffering for truth, the cause was languishing; but we made no effort to supply the lack, and now our property is useless. Oh! that we had let it go, and laid up treasure in heaven. I saw that a sacrifice did not increase, but decreased, and was consumed.

I also saw that God had not required all of His people to dispose of their property at the same time, but in a time of need He would teach them, if they desired to be taught, when to sell, and how much to sell. I saw that some had been required to dispose of their property in past time to sustain the Advent cause; while He had permitted others to keep theirs until a time of need. Then as the cause needs it their duty is to sell.[2]

To the church of God who keep the Sabbath—the seal of the living God.[3]

---

[2] Although the second part of this manuscript calls for financial sacrifice, even to the extent of selling houses and lands, there are a number of qualifying statements expressed in the last paragraph. The whole question of informed as opposed to rash sacrifice should be seen in the context of certain radical voices within the young movement. Most influential was that of Joseph Bates, who, in a tract published the same month, January 1849, urged members to sell their properties and not to delay with the hope that prices would rise. Bates had followed that same stern path himself. James White wrote of Bates that he once "had some eight or ten thousand dollars . . . [but] has spent all his property in the Holy Advent cause." The uncompromising stand taken by Bates in the 1849 tract was probably influenced by his conviction at the time that the contemporary revolutionary events in Europe constituted the beginning of the time of trouble spoken of in Daniel 12:1. Nevertheless, Bates's radical message, according to Ellen White, caused considerable problems in western New York, where poor members sometimes demanded that wealthier members sell their property in order to help support them. James White, writing in January 1850, held that "there has been means enough squandered away, and worse than lost in W. New York, the last nine months to support the paper [*Present Truth*] six months or a year."

See: Joseph Bates, *A Seal of the Living God,* pp. 68, 69; Ellen G. White, Ms 14, 1850 (Sept.); *idem, Spiritual Gifts [vol. 2],* pp. 119-121; James White to "Bro. Bowles," Oct. 17, 1849; James White to Leonard Hastings, Jan. 10, 1850.

[3] *See:* EGWEnc, s.v. "Seal of God."

1849

(Ms 4, 1849)

JANUARY 31, TOPSHAM, MAINE

"To Those Who Are Receiving the Seal of the Living God."

Broadside.[1] See Ellen G. White, *Early Writings,* pp. 36-41, 56-58.

This last of the early Ellen White broadsides emphasized such various practical and theological issues as: Mercy is still available while Jesus is interceding; time continuing until all the remnant are sealed; the availability of divine healing; the danger of not heeding the visions; incorrect views on the "shaking of the powers of the heavens"; what to do with property at the end of time; confirmation that the Sabbath was the seal of God; and to not be discouraged that time has continued longer than expected. What follows is an unmodified transcription of the published text.

"This is that which was spoken of by the prophet Joel; And it shall come to pass in the last days, saith God, I will pour out of my Spirit upon all flesh: and your sons and your daughters shall prophesy, and your young men shall see visions, and your old men shall dream dreams: and on my servants, and on my handmaidens, I will pour out in those days of my Spirit; and they shall prophesy."[2]

At the commencement of the Holy Sabbath, (Jan. 5,) we engaged in prayer with Bro. Belden's [**Albert Belden**] family at Rocky Hill, Ct.,[3] and the Holy Ghost fell upon us. I was taken off in Vision to the most holy place,

---

[1] A broadside was a single-page document printed on one side. Much of the text of this broadside parallels earlier accounts of the same visions, and was reprinted in the August 1849 issue of *The Present Truth* before being included in Ellen White's first book, *A Sketch of the Christian Experience and Views of Ellen G. White* (1851). Three visions are specifically identified: one on December 16, 1848, and two on Sabbath, January 5/6, 1849. For annotations of the January 5 and 6 visions, the first to be recounted in the broadside, see Ms 2, 1849 (Jan. 17).

[2] Acts 2:16-18. Joel's prophecy provided Adventists with a biblical basis for acceptance of the prophetic gift in the "last days," and was seen to be partially fulfilled in Ellen White's experience.

[3] The home of Albert Belden was the site of the first 1848 Sabbatarian Bible Conference. Within a few months of writing this letter, James and Ellen White took up residence with the Belden family.

where I saw Jesus still interceding for Israel. On the bottom of his garment was a bell and a pomegranate, a bell and a pomegranate. Then I saw that Jesus would not leave the most holy place until every case was decided either for salvation or destruction: and that the wrath of God could not come until Jesus had finished his work in the most holy place—laid off his priestly attire and clothed himself with the garments of vengeance. Then Jesus will step out from between the Father and man, and God will keep silent no longer; but pour out his wrath on those who have rejected his truth. I saw that the anger of the nations, the wrath of God, and the time to judge the dead, were separate events, one following the other. I saw that Michael had not stood up, and that the time of trouble, such as never was, had not yet commenced. The nations are now getting angry, but when our High Priest has finished his work in the Sanctuary, he will stand up, put on the garments of vengeance, and then the seven last plagues will be poured out. I saw that the four angels would hold the four winds until Jesus work was done in the Sanctuary, and then will come the seven last plagues. These plagues enraged the wicked against the righteous, and they thought that we had brought them down upon them, and if they could rid the earth of us, then the plagues would be stayed. A decree went forth to slay the saints, which caused them to cry day and night for deliverance. This was the time of Jacob's trouble. Then all the saints cried out with anguish of spirit, and were delivered by the Voice of God. Then the 144,000 triumphed. Their faces were lighted up with the glory of God. Then I was shown a company who were howling in agony. On their garments was written in large characters—thou art weighed in the balance, and found wanting. I asked who this company were. The angel said, "these are they who have once kept the Sabbath and have given it up." I heard them cry with a loud voice—"we have believed in thy coming, and taught it with energy." And while they were speaking, their eyes would fall upon their garments and see the writing, and then they would wail aloud. I saw they had drunk of the deep waters, and fouled the residue with their feet—trodden the Sabbath underfoot, and that is why they were weighed in the balance and found wanting. Then my attending angel directed me to the city again, where I saw four angels winging their way to the gate of the city, and were just presenting the golden card to the angel at the gate. Then I saw another angel swiftly flying from the direction of the most excellent glory, and crying with a loud voice to the other angels, and waving something up and down in his hand. I asked my attending angel for an explanation of what I saw. He told me that I could see no more then, but he would shortly show me what those things that I then saw meant.

Sabbath afternoon one of our number was sick, and requested prayers that he might be healed. We all united in applying to the Physician who never lost a case, and while healing power came down, and the sick was healed, the Spirit fell upon me and I was taken off in vision. I saw the state of some who stood on present truth, but disregarded the visions,—the way God had chosen to teach in some cases, those who erred from Bible truth. I saw that in striking against the visions they did not strike against the worm—the feeble instrument that God spake through; but against the Holy Ghost. I saw it was a small thing to speak against the instrument, but it was dangerous to slight the words of God. I saw if they were in error and God chose to show them their errors through visions, and they disregarded the teachings of God through visions, they would be left to take their own way, and run in the way of error, and think they were right, until they would find it out too late. Then in the time of trouble I heard them cry to God in agony—"Why didst thou not show us our wrong, that we might have got right and been ready for this time?" Then an angel pointed to them and said—"My Father taught, but you would not be taught.—He spoke through visions, but you disregarded his voice, and he gave you up to your own ways, to be filled with your own doings." Then I saw four angels who had a work to do on the earth, and were on their way to accomplish it. Jesus was clothed with Priestly garments. He gazed in pity on the remnant, then raised his hands upward, and with a voice of deep pity cried—"MY BLOOD, FATHER, MY BLOOD, MY BLOOD, MY BLOOD." Then I saw an exceeding bright light come from God, who sat upon the great white throne, and was shed all about Jesus. Then I saw an angel with a commission from Jesus, swiftly flying to the four angels who had a work to do on the earth, and waving something up and down in his hand, and crying with a loud voice—"HOLD! HOLD! HOLD! HOLD! until the servants of God are sealed in their foreheads."—I asked my accompanying angel the meaning of what I heard, and what the four angels were about to do. He said to me that it was God that restrained the powers, and that he gave his angels charge over things on the earth, and that the four angels had power from God to hold the four winds, and that they were about to let the four winds go, and while they had started on their mission to let them go, the merciful eye of Jesus gazed on the remnant that were not all sealed, then he raised his hands to the Father and plead with him that he had spilled his blood for them. Then another angel was commissioned to fly swiftly to the four angels, and bid them hold until the servants of God were sealed with the seal of the living God in their foreheads.

Dec. 16, 1848,[4] the Lord gave me a view of the shaking of the powers of the heavens. I saw that when the Lord said "heaven" (in giving the signs recorded by Matthew, Mark and Luke) he meant heaven, and when he said

[4] For annotations regarding this December 16 vision, see Lt 2, 1848 (Dec. 18).

"earth" he meant earth. The powers of heaven are the Sun, Moon, and Stars: they rule in the heavens. The powers of earth are those who bear rule on the earth.—The powers of heaven will be shaken at the voice of God. Then the Sun, Moon and Stars will be moved out of their places. They will not pass away, but be shaken by the voice of God.

Dark, heavy clouds came up, and clashed against each other. The atmosphere parted and rolled back, then we could look up through the open space in Orion, from whence came the voice of God. The Holy City will come down through that open space. I saw that the powers of earth are now being shaken, and that events come in order. War, and rumors of war,—sword, famine and pestilence, are first to shake the powers of earth, then the voice of God will shake the Sun, Moon and Stars, and this earth also. I saw that the shaking of the powers in Europe is not (as some teach) the shaking of the powers of heaven, but it is the shaking of the angry nations.

I have seen the tender love that God has for his people, and it is very great. I saw an angel over every saint, with their wings spread about them: and if the saints wept through discouragement, or were in danger, the angel that ever attended them would fly quickly upward to carry the tidings, and the angels in the city would cease to sing. Then Jesus would commission another angel to descend to encourage, watch over and try to keep them from going out of the narrow path: but, if they did not take heed to the watchful care of these angels, and would not be comforted by them, and continued to go astray, the angels would look sad and weep. Then they would bear the tidings upward, and all the angels in the city would weep, and then with a loud voice say, Amen. But if the saints fixed their eyes on the prize before them, and glorified God by praising him, then the angels would bear the glad tidings to the city, and the angels in the city would touch their golden harps and sing with a loud voice—Alleluia! and the heavenly arches would ring with their lovely songs. I will here state, that there is perfect order and harmony in the holy city.

All the angels that are commissioned to visit the earth hold a golden card, which they present to the angels at the gates of the city as they pass in and out.[5] Heaven is a good place. I long to be there, and behold my lovely Jesus, who gave his life for me, and be changed into his glorious image. Oh! for language to express the glory of the bright world to come. I thirst for the living streams that make glad the city of our God.

The Lord has given me a view of other worlds.[6] Wings were given me, and

[5] *See:* Ms 2, 1849 (Jan. 17), note 12.

[6] Both James and Ellen White reported that Ellen received a vision of other "planets" in November 1846, at Topsham, Maine. Joseph Bates, a former sea captain, was present and apparently was the one who identified specific planets based on her descriptions. (There is no

an angel attended me from the city to a place that was bright and glorious. The grass of the place was living green, and the birds there warbled a sweet song. The inhabitants of the place were of all sizes, they were noble, majestic and lovely. They bore the express image of Jesus, and their countenances beamed with holy joy, expressive of the freedom and happiness of the place. I asked one of them why they were so much more lovely than those on the earth. The reply was—"we have lived in strict obedience to the commandments of God, and have not fallen by disobedience, like those on the earth." Then I saw two trees, one looked much like the tree of life in the city. The fruit of both looked beautiful; but of one they could not eat. They had power to eat of both, but were forbidden to eat of one. Then my attending angel said to me—"none in this place have tasted of the forbidden tree; but if they should eat they would fall." Then I was taken to a world which had seven moons. There I saw good old Enoch, who had been translated. On his right arm he bore a glorious palm, and on each leaf was written Victory. Around his head was a dazzling white wreath, and leaves on the wreath, and in the middle of each was written Purity; and around the leaf were stones of various colors, that shone brighter than the stars, and cast a reflection upon the letters, and magnified them. On the back part of his head was a bow that confined the wreath, and upon the bow was written Holiness. Above the wreath was a lovely crown that shone brighter than the sun. I asked him if this was the place he was taken to from the earth. He said, "It is not; but the city is my home, and I have come to visit this place." He moved about the place as if perfectly at home. I begged of my attending angel to let me remain in that place. I could not bear the thought of coming back to this dark world again. Then the angel said—"you must go back, and if you are faithful, you, with the 144,000 shall have the privilege of visiting all the worlds and viewing the handy work of God."

For two years past, the Lord has shown me in vision, repeatedly, that it is contrary to the Bible to make any provision for our temporal wants in the time of trouble.[7] I saw that if the saints have food laid up by them, or in the fields, in the time of trouble when sword, famine, and pestilence are in the land, it will be taken from them by violent hands and strangers would reap their fields. Then will be the time for us to trust wholly in God, and he will

---

record of Ellen White's identifying the "worlds" she was shown in vision.) It is not certain whether the view here described is the same 1846 vision or a different one. That she had more than one view of "other worlds" may be inferred from her description of the 1846 vision as being "the first time" that she "had a view of other planets."

See: James White, ed., *A Word to the "Little Flock,"* p. 22; Ellen G. White, *Spiritual Gifts [vol. 2],* p. 83. For a discussion of the question of which "worlds" Ellen White saw in vision, see F. D. Nichol, *Ellen G. White and Her Critics,* pp. 91-101.

[7] For annotations on this segment of the broadside, see Ms 3, 1849 (Jan. 18).

sustain us. I saw that our bread and water would be sure at that time, and we should not lack, or suffer hunger.—The Lord has shown me that some of his children would fear when they see the price of food rising, and they would buy food and lay it by for the time of trouble. Then in a time of need, I saw them go to their food and look at it, and it had bred worms, and was full of living creatures, and not fit for use. About one week since, the Lord showed me in vision, that houses and lands would be of no use in the time of trouble, and in that time they could not be disposed of. I saw it was the will of God that the saints should cut loose from every encumbrance—dispose of their houses and lands before the time of trouble comes, and make a covenant with God by sacrifice. I saw they would sell if they laid their property on the altar and earnestly inquired for duty. Then God will teach them when to dispose of these things. Then they will be free in the time of trouble, and have no clogs to weigh them down.

I saw if they held on to their property, and did not inquire duty of the Lord, he would not make duty known, and they would be permitted to keep their property, and then in the time of trouble their property would come up before them like a mountain to crush them. Then they tried to get rid of it, but could not. I heard them mourn like this,—the cause was languishing—God's people were suffering for truth, and we made no effort to supply the lack, and now our property is useless. Oh! that we had let it go, and laid up treasure in heaven. I saw a *sacrifice* did not increase, but decrease, and was *consumed*. I also saw that God had not required all of his people to dispose of their property at the same time, but in a time of need he would teach them, if they desired to be taught, when to sell and how much to sell. I saw that some had been required to dispose of their property in past time to sustain the advent cause, while he permitted others to keep theirs until a time of need. Then as the cause needs it, their duty is to sell.

Now is the time to lay up treasure in heaven, and to set our hearts in order, ready for the time of trouble. Those only who have clean hands and a pure heart will stand that trying time. Now is the time for the law of God to be in our minds (foreheads), and written in our hearts. The Lord has shown me the danger of letting our minds be filled with worldly thoughts and cares. I saw that some minds were led away from present truth and a love of the holy Bible, by reading other exciting books; and others were filled with perplexity and care for what they shall eat, drink and wear. I saw some, looking too far off for the coming of the Lord. Time has continued on a few years longer than they expected, therefore they think it may continue a few years more, and in this way their minds are being led from present truth, out after the world. In these things I saw great danger; for if the mind is filled with other things, present truth is shut out, and there is no place in our foreheads for the seal of the living God. This seal is the Sabbath. I saw that the time for Jesus to be in the most holy place was nearly finished, and that time can last but a very little longer; and what leisure time we have should be spent in searching the Bible, which is to judge us in the last day.[8]

My Dear Brethren and Sisters:—Let the commandments of God, and the testimony of Jesus Christ be in your minds continually, and let them crowd worldly thoughts and cares from the mind. When you lie down, and when you rise up, let them be your meditation. Live, and act wholly in reference to the coming of the Son of Man. The sealing time is very short, and soon will be over. Now is the time to make our calling and election sure, while the four angels are holding the four winds.

If any among us are sick, let us not dishonor God by applying to earthly physicians, but apply to the God of Israel.[9] If we follow his directions (James 5:14, 15) the sick will be healed. God's promise cannot fail. Have faith in God, and trust wholly in him, that when Christ who is our life shall appear we may appear with him in glory.

E. G. WHITE.

Topsham, Jan. 31, 1849.

---

[8] In 1883 Ellen White addressed the "time" question raised by these and other statements. After quoting several scriptural examples (1 Cor. 7:29, 30; Rom. 13:12; Rev. 1:3; 22:6, 7), she wrote: "The angels of God in their messages to men represent time as very short. Thus it has always been presented to me. It is true that time has continued longer than we expected in the early days of this message. Our Saviour did not appear as soon as we hoped. But has the word of the Lord failed? Never! It should be remembered that the promises and threatenings of God are alike conditional" (Ms 4, 1883 [*Selected Messages,* book 1, p. 67]).

[9] On not applying to "earthly physicians," see Lt 8, 1849 (May 29), note 18.

1849

(Lt 2, 1849)

[CIRCA MARCH 6,[1] FAIRHAVEN, MASSACHUSETTS]

LETTER TO

Elvira Hastings.[2]

Previously unpublished.

Letter to a friend, Elvira Hastings, in which Ellen White gives details of her impending visit together with news of progress of the movement in Connecticut and Massachusetts.

Dear Sister Hastings:

We feel it to be duty to visit you before we return to Maine.[3] We shall take the first train of cars Friday for Townsend [Massachusetts].[4] Your husband, if he pleases, will meet us at the depot.

Brother Bates [**Joseph Bates**] and Brother Gurney [**Heman S. Gurney**] returned from Connecticut last week.[5] Their testimony is that the work of God is going forward there. The saints are setting their hearts in order for the coming of the Lord, and moving forward in union and love as they have not for years. Praise the name of the Lord! My prayer is, Lord, carry on Thy work

---

[1] The arrival of Bates and Gurney on Sunday, February 25 (note 5), is said in the second paragraph to be "last week," so the date of the letter would not be before Sunday, March 4. Since it appears that that Sunday (March 4) is spoken of in the past tense (paragraph 3), the letter probably was not written before Monday, March 5. Presumably, then, the letter was written on March 5 or 6 or shortly thereafter, since the letter is in part a request for Mr. Hastings to meet the Whites at the train station on Friday, March 9.

[2] *Identity:* In the first paragraph Ellen White informs "Sister Hastings" of her intention to visit her, arriving on Friday (March 9, 1849). A few days later, on March 11, Ellen White writes of a vision received "at the house of Brother Leonard Hastings of New Ipswich," whose wife was Elvira.

See: Ellen G. White, Ms 7, 1849 (Mar. 11).

[3] At this point the Whites were about four weeks into a six-week itinerary that had taken them from Topsham, Maine, in early February to several places in Massachusetts. Ellen and James White had been corresponding with the Hastingses for about two years but had not yet met them in person. For an account of this journey, see: Ellen G. White, *Spiritual Gifts [vol. 2],* pp. 108-113; Arthur L. White, *Ellen G. White: The Early Years,* pp. 158, 159.

[4] The railroad station at Townsend, Massachusetts, was probably the closest station to New Ipswich, New Hampshire, about 10 miles (16 kilometers) distant.

[5] James White wrote on February 25, 1849: "Bros. Bates and Gurney have been some three weeks in Ct. We expect them home today." "Home" for Bates and Gurney was Fairhaven, Massachusetts, where the Whites had been based for more than two weeks.

See: James White to Leonard and Elvira Hastings, Feb. 25, 1849.

among Thy people until all discord shall be removed and the hearts of Thy people shall be knit together by high and holy ties.

We have had some powerful seasons here of late. Sabbath and Sunday God moved in mighty power and there was a breaking down before God. There had been wrongs and hard feelings between some of the little company here.[6] God in His mercy gave me a vision of the state of things and showed me that there must be a tearing down and building up. They felt the power of the message and those that were wrong confessed their wrong, were forgiven, and we had a melting time. God's people are preparing and getting ready for the seal of the living God. Brethren Bates and Gurney are strong in God and the power of His might.

I must close and get this in the office to go out in today's mail. Keep up good courage. Lean wholly upon God. He will not leave or forsake us. Love to your husband.

Your sister in haste.

---

[6] The context suggests that Ellen White is referring to the "little company" in Fairhaven. A year later the Whites visited Fairhaven again and mentioned continuing problems: "At Fairhaven we found the brethren in a tried state. . . . Some, who have wounded the precious cause . . . , have been 'purged out from among them' as 'rebels'; but God has raised up others to glorify his name."

See: W. [James White], "Our Tour East," *Advent Review,* August 1850, p. 14.

1849

(Ms 7, 1849)

MARCH 11,[1] [NEW IPSWICH, NEW HAMPSHIRE]

Affliction of Mrs. Hastings [Elvira Hastings].[2]

Previously unpublished.

Vision of the struggle between good and evil forces over the life of Elvira Hastings.

While engaged in prayer at the house of Brother Leonard Hastings [**Leonard Hastings**] of New Ipswich,[3] N.H., the Holy Ghost was breathed upon us, and I was taken off in vision and borne by an angel above this dark world. The angel showed me the afflictions of Sister Hastings.[4] I asked the angel if it was God who had afflicted her. The angel said God *suffered* it to be so.

Then the angel pointed to the earth and shewed me a person who was short and thick. I saw Satan pouring upon this person a stream of darkness, as a sunbeam is poured forth from the sun, and as it came upon him he bloated. His head seemed larger than usual, and his face was red and much bloated. While in this state, Satan used this person as an agent to affect and afflict Sister Hastings. I saw that this was the cause of Sister Hastings' sickness, and that the object of this person was to afflict unto death, so that his iniquity might be covered which might otherwise be exposed.[5]

---

[1] The only source for this manuscript is a typewritten copy with the words "March 11" written on it. No year is indicated. There are good reasons, however, for assigning this document to 1849. According to a letter from Leonard Hastings, "Bro. and sister White made us their first visit in March, 1849." That it was during the March 1849 visit and not the June 1850 or any subsequent visit that Ellen White had the vision recorded here, is apparent from the information about "the afflictions of Sister Hastings." Elvira Hastings died in February 1850.

See: Ellen G. White, *Spiritual Gifts [vol. 2],* pp. 110-112; W. [James White], "Our Tour East," *Advent Review*, August 1850, p. 14.

[2] *Identity:* The address on the letter reads "Elvira Hastings, New Ipswich, N.H."

[3] According to Leonard Hastings, this was Ellen and James White's first visit to the Hastings home in New Ipswich, New Hampshire. They stayed about one week before returning to Dorchester, Massachusetts, and back to Maine.

See: Ellen G. White, *Spiritual Gifts [vol. 2],* pp. 112, 113.

[4] Ellen White described Elvira Hastings as in a "wretched state of health" on this occasion. According to Leonard Hastings, "my wife had been afflicted with a severe illness for two succeeding winters." About one year later, in February 1850, Mrs. Hastings died at age 42 of "cramp colic."

See: Ibid., pp. 110, 112; W. [James White], "Our Tour East," *Advent Review,* August 1850, p. 14.

[5] In a letter to the Hastingses some weeks later on April 21, Ellen White used similar

I saw that Satan had the full control of this person, and that others beside Sister Hastings were affected by him. I saw his garments all covered over with the blood of souls. I saw that this person was a vessel of wrath fitted for destruction, reserved for the seven last plagues, if God can bear with him until that time.

I saw that the angels from God had hovered about Sister Hastings, and comforted and strengthened her, or life would have departed from her. I saw that it was time for God to work and deliver her. I also saw that if God's servants had united in prayer with strong and living faith with Sister Hastings in her dwelling, the power of the enemy would have been broken before this, and that now his power is completely broken.

---

language in a more specific way. She wrote there of some "ministers who had rejected God's truth," "professed Adventists who had rejected present truth," as "agents" through whom "Satan was working." "I saw that some of the agents of the devil were affecting the bodies of those they could not deceive. . . . Some . . . were even trying to afflict some of the saints unto death."

There is a possibility that the particular "agent" referred to here is Jacob Weston, an itinerant Adventist minister living in the same town as Mrs. Hastings (New Ipswich). According to Joseph Bates it was Weston who, under the pseudonym "Barnabas," had written a series of letters against the Sabbath in the Adventist periodical *The Bible Advocate.* Jacob Weston subsequently became hostile to Bates over the latter's allegations that he had attempted to defraud C. Stowe of Washington, New Hampshire. In some way, the details of which are not clear, Elvira Hastings was also involved in the Weston-Bates imbroglio and became a target of Weston's ire.

See: Ellen G. White, Lt 5, 1849 (Apr. 21); Joseph Bates to Leonard and Elvira Hastings, Apr. 7, 1848, Merlin D. Burt, "Sabbatarian Adventism From 1844 to 1849," pp. 335, 336, 350, 351.

1849

(Lt 4, 1849)

MARCH 22,[1] TOPSHAM, MAINE

LETTER TO
Leonard and Elvira Hastings.[2]

Portions of this letter are published in Arthur L. White, *Ellen G. White: The Early Years,* p. 159.

An account of the Whites' return journey after visiting the Hastingses in New Ipswich, New Hampshire.

Dear Brother and Sister Hastings:

I can write but little now as I am weak, but the Lord is very good to poor unworthy me. While riding in the stage Wednesday I thought I should have to stop at a private house and go no farther,[3] but James [**James Springer White**] and I united in faith together that God would give me strength and suddenly I felt a visible change for the better, and arrived here without accident or harm.[4] Praise the name of the Lord. Yesterday I was unable to sit up; today am free from pain, though weak. My faith is strong in God. I am ready to go anywhere He shall send me, knowing He will give me strength.

Keep up good courage, my dear Brother and Sister. God is your helper. A few more days here in toil and then we shall be free. Time is short; let us hold fast unto the end. Pray for poor me. Excuse my [not] writing more; my side pains me much; I cannot write.

E. W.

---

[1] This document is in the form of a postscript to a letter by James White headed "Topsham, March 22, 1849." The second part of James White's letter is dated "March 23."

[2] *Identity:* The letter is addressed to "Leonard Hastings, New Ipswich, N.H." For "Elvira" as his wife's name, see W. [James White], "Our Tour East," *Advent Review,* August 1850, p. 14, together with Elvira Hastings, "My Dear Brother and Sister," *Advent Review,* August 1850, p. 15.

[3] James White adds the detail that the last 16 miles (26 kilometers) from North Yarmouth to Brunswick by stagecoach took three hours, during which they were "shook up and down . . . in snow banks and mud sloughs."

See: James White to Leonard and Elvira Hastings, Mar. 22, 1849.

[4] For a more comprehensive account of the Whites' return journey to Topsham, Maine, after their six-week itinerary in Massachusetts and New Hampshire, see Ellen G. White, Lt 5, 1849 (Apr. 21); James White to Leonard and Elvira Hastings, Mar. 22, 1849. Arthur L. White provides a synopsis of their travels in early 1849 in *Ellen G. White: The Early Years,* pp. 158, 159.

[Note added in James White's handwriting:]

Ellen says, "Do give my love to the children." Her side is so lame she cannot write a word more, "and sign my name," so here it is.

E. G. White

Leonard Hastings

1849

(Ms 1, 1849)

[MARCH 24,[1] TOPSHAM, MAINE]

The Open and Shut Door.[2]

See *The Present Truth,* August 1849, and Letter 5, 1849 (Apr. 21).

The Sabbath as a test. Satan's attempts through mesmerism, spiritualism, and false revivals to deceive God's people.

We had a sweet, interesting meeting with the brethren and sisters at Topsham, Me. [Maine]. The Spirit of God rested upon us, and I was taken off in the Spirit.

I saw that the commandments of God and the shut door[3] could not be separated. I saw that the time for the commandments of God to shine out to His people was when the door was opened in the inner apartment of the heavenly sanctuary where the ark is containing the commandments. This door was not opened until Jesus' mediation was finished in the outer apartment of the sanctuary in 1844.

Then Jesus rose up and shut the door in the outer apartment and opened the holy; and the faith of Israel now reaches within the second veil where Jesus now stands by the ark. I saw that Jesus had shut the door in the Holy Place, and no man can open it. And that He had opened the door in the Most Holy place, and no man can shut it. And that since Jesus has opened the door in the Most Holy place, the commandments have been shining out and God has been testing His people on the holy Sabbath.[4]

---

[1] Although the place and exact date when this manuscript was written is not known, it gives an account of a vision that, according to the opening line, was given to Ellen White at Topsham, Maine. The date of the vision is not given in this document, but two parallel accounts of the vision date it March 24, 1849.

See: Ellen G. White, Lt 5, 1849 (Apr. 21); *idem,* "Dear Brethren and Sisters," *Present Truth,* August 1849, p. 21.

[2] This is a variant account of the same vision recounted in Lt 5, 1849 (Apr. 21).

[3] *See*: Introductory article "The 'Shut Door' and Ellen White's Visions"; EGWEnc, s.v. "Shut Door."

[4] A link between the Sabbath and the sanctuary had been proposed by Joseph Bates as early as 1846 and shown to Ellen White in her April 3, 1847, vision. This vision of March 1849, however, in addition to confirming earlier study and revelation, is of interest since for the first time the imagery of Revelation 3:7 ("he that openeth, and no man shutteth; and shutteth, and no man openeth; . . . behold, I have set before thee an open door, and no man can shut it") is used to describe Christ's transition in 1844 from the holy place to the Most Holy Place of the heavenly sanctuary. Thus the concept of a shut door is not used in the context of the

I saw that the test on the Sabbath could not come until the mediation of Jesus in the Holy was finished, and He had passed within the second veil. Therefore Christians who died before the seventh month 1844, and had not kept the Sabbath, rest in hope; for there was no condemnation until the true light on the Sabbath came. I saw that Satan was tempting God's people on this point because so many good Christians had died in the hope, and had not kept the true Sabbath.

I saw that our adversaries had been trying to open the door in the outer apartment and to close the door in the inner apartment where the ark is containing the two tablets of stone on which were written the ten commandments by God's own finger.[5] I saw that Satan was using every device in this time to keep the minds of God's people from present truth and cause them to waver. I saw a covering that God was drawing over His people to protect them in the time of trouble, and every soul that was decided on the truth was to be covered with this covering of Almighty God. Satan knew this and was also at work in mighty power.

I saw that the mysterious knocking in N.Y. [New York] was the power of Satan clothed in a religious garb to lull the deceived to more security and to draw the minds of God's people, if possible, to look at that and cause them to doubt the teachings of God among His people.[6] I saw that Satan was working through agents in a number of ways. He was at work through ministers who had rejected God's truth, and had been given over to strong delusions to believe a lie that they might be damned.[7] While they are preaching or praying some would fall prostrate and helpless; not by the power of the Holy Ghost, no, no; but by the power of Satan breathed on these agents and through them to the people.

Bridegroom parable of Matthew 25, as it had been used earlier, but in the context of the division between the holy place and Most Holy Place of the heavenly sanctuary.

See: Joseph Bates, *The Opening Heavens*, p. 36; Ellen G. White, Lt 1, 1847 (Apr. 7).

[5] That is, they had tried to divert attention from the claims of the Ten Commandments, especially the Sabbath commandment, and perhaps the sanctuary's two-phased ministry. For a study of anti-Sabbatarian articles published during the previous two years, particularly in the columns of *The Bible Advocate*, see Merlin Burt, "Sabbatarian Adventism From 1844 to 1849," pp. 326-342.

[6] This is the earliest extant warning by Ellen White regarding the claims of the Fox sisters of Hydesville, New York, who from March 1848 professed to have contacted the spirits of the dead through rappings (i.e., "mysterious knocking") in their house. After their first public demonstrations of spirit communication in Rochester, New York, in November 1849, public interest grew very rapidly. Many who became Spiritualists broke with their churches. Probably the most high-profile casualty from Seventh-day Adventist ranks to the Spiritualists was Moses Hull, a minister and writer who defected in 1863.

See: Bret E. Carroll, *Spiritualism in Antebellum America*, pp. 46-62; SDAE, s.v. "Moses Hull"; James R. Nix, "The Life and Work of Moses Hull"; EGWEnc, s.v. "Moses Hull"; "Spiritualism."

[7] Paraphrase of 2 Thess. 2:11, 12: "And for this cause God shall send them strong delusion, that they should believe a lie: That they all might be damned who believe not the truth, but had pleasure in unrighteousness."

I saw some professed Adventists who had rejected present truth while preaching, praying, or in private conversation used mesmerism to gain adherents; and the people would rejoice, thinking it was the power of God; and some that used it were so far in the darkness and deception of the devil that they thought it was the power of God given them to exercise.[8] I saw that these men had made God altogether such a one as themselves and valued His power as a thing of naught. I saw that some of these agents of the devil were affecting the bodies of those that they could not deceive and draw from the present truth.[9] Some of these were even trying to affect some of the saints unto death.[10] Oh, that all could get a view of it as God revealed it unto me,—that they might know more of the wiles of Satan so as to be on their guard.

I saw that Satan was at work in these ways to distract, draw away, and deceive God's people just now in this sealing time.[11] I saw some who were not standing stiffly, their knees were trembling, their feet were sliding because they were not planted on the present truth, and the covering of Almighty God could not be drawn over them while they were thus trembling. Satan was trying his every art to hold them where they were until the sealing was over, and the covering drawn over God's people, and they were left without protection in the time of slaughter. God has begun to draw the covering over

---

[8] Mesmerism had become very popular in America by the 1840s, but little is known about its level of penetration among (first-day) Adventists. One or two specific names of Adventist ministers thought to be involved in mesmerism are mentioned in contemporary Sabbatarian sources. According to J. N. Andrews, a certain P. A. Smith claimed that he "could heal people by Mesmerism, and do other wonders." Joseph Turner, prominent Millerite Adventist minister and editor, was identified by both Ellen White and Joseph Bates as being involved with mesmerism. In one of the more vivid passages of her 1860 autobiography Ellen White recalled a meeting in 1845 at which Turner "had his hand up to his face, and was looking through his fingers, his eyes intently fixed on me." In 1848 Bates charged Turner with using his "mesmeric influence" on "some of the dear sisters" and suggested that mesmerism was involved in Turner's revival meetings in New Bedford, Massachusetts, charges that were subsequently angrily rejected by Turner.

See: J. N. Andrews, "Reply to Mary A. Seymour," *Review,* Mar. 2, 1852, p. 102; Ellen G. White, *Spiritual Gifts [vol. 2],* p. 63; Joseph Bates, *A Vindication of the Seventh-Day Sabbath,* pp. 16, 17; James White to Stockbridge Howland, July 2, 1848; Merlin Burt, "Sabbatarian Adventism From 1844 to 1849," pp. 140-146, 349, 350; EGWEnc, s.v. "Hypnosis and Mesmerism." For a recent study of the intersection of mesmerism and religion in mid-nineteenth-century America, see Ann Taves, *Fits, Trances, & Visions,* pp. 119-165.

[9] For a discussion of the expression "present truth," see Alberto R. Timm, *The Sanctuary and the Three Angels' Messages,* pp. 115, 116, 122-129, 243-252; EGWEnc, s.v. "Present Truth."

[10] Further light is thrown on this somewhat obscure passage in Ms 7, 1849, dated just a few weeks earlier, concerning Elvira Hastings. In a vision Ellen White was shown a certain unnamed person whom "Satan used . . . as an agent to affect and afflict Sister Hastings" "unto death." The closeness in the language of the two passages and the proximity in time between them clearly suggest that Elvira Hastings was one of those referred to in this passage as being affected by an agent of Satan. See note 5 in Ms 7, 1849 (Mar. 11), for further discussion regarding the possible identification of the "agent" affecting Elvira Hastings.

[11] *See:* EGWEnc, s.v. "Seal of God."

His people, therefore it will very soon be drawn over all those who are to have a shelter in the day of the Lord.

I saw that as God worked in power for His people; Satan would also work, and that the mysterious knocking, and signs and wonders of Satan and false reformations would increase and spread. The reformations that were shown me were not reformations from error to truth; no, no; but from bad to worse, for those who professed a change of heart had only wrapped about them a religious garb which covered up the iniquity of a vile heart. Some appeared to have been really converted so as to deceive God's people. But if their hearts could be seen they would appear as black as ever.[12] My accompanying angel bade me to look for the travail of soul for sinners as used to be. I looked, but could not see it, for the time of their salvation is passed.[13]

---

[12] For a study of early Sabbatarian Adventists' attitudes to religious revivals, see P. Gerard Damsteegt, *Foundations of the Seventh-day Adventist Message and Mission,* pp. 184-186.

[13] Some have interpreted the phrase "the time of their salvation is passed" to refer to the "sinners" in the previous sentence and concluded that the vision takes the radical position that there can be no more conversions (Canright, Lindén). That this conclusion is not necessary has been argued by others mainly on two grounds:

- An equally plausible reading of this manuscript is that the statement "the time of their salvation is passed" refers specifically to those mentioned earlier who had "rejected God's truth" and "rejected present truth" (Nichol). Ellen White herself, in a comment made in 1854, explains that this expression "relates more particularly to those who have heard and rejected the light of the Advent doctrine."
- Even if "the time of their salvation is passed" does refer to "sinners," it has been argued that the word "sinners" is used by Ellen White and other contemporary Sabbatarian Adventists in the restricted sense of those who had willfully rejected the gospel and/or the Advent message. They recognized that there were "honest souls" who were not guilty of willful rejection and who would yet take their stand with God's people (Poehler).

See: D. M. Canright, *Seventh-Day Adventism Renounced,* p. 145; Ingemar Lindén, *1844 and the Shut Door Problem,* pp. 56, 57; Francis D. Nichol, *Ellen G. White and Her Critics,* pp. 227, 228; Ellen G. White, *Supplement to the Christian Experience and Views of Ellen G. White,* p. 4 (*Early Writings,* p. 45); Rolf J. Poehler, "'. . . and the Door Was Shut,'" pp. 126-130; introductory article "The 'Shut Door' and Ellen White's Visions"; EGWEnc, s.v. "Shut Door."

1849

(Lt 5, 1849)

APRIL 21, MILTON, MASSACHUSETTS

LETTER TO

Leonard W. and Elvira Hastings.[1]

Portions of this letter are published in Ellen G. White, *Manuscript Releases,* vol. 1, p. 390; vol. 5, pp. 93, 94, 200.

> *News to close friends of recent travels. Account of vision of March 24, 1849: The Sabbath as a test. Satan's attempts through mesmerism, spiritualism, and false revivals to deceive God's people.*

Dear Brother and Sister Hastings:

I now sit down to write you a few lines and give you a little history of our journey and of the dealings of God with us since we left you.[2] It was rather a tedious journey for me from Dorchester [Massachusetts] to Brunswick [Maine].[3] I stood my journey all quite well until we came to the last sixteen miles [26 kilometers]. We were obliged to take the stage from North Yarmouth [Maine] to Brunswick. The roads were very bad. I felt that I could not perform the journey and that I must stop at a private house. The stage shook us round very much. James and I agreed to unite our prayers together, and in faith believing, ask God for strength, and praise His holy name, He heard us pray. I felt a visible change for the better and was enabled in the strength of God to finish the journey without accident or harm.

The first Sabbath we spent in Topsham, was a sweet, interesting time. It seems that Jesus Himself passed through our midst and shed His light and

---

[1] *Identity:* The letter is addressed to "Leonard Hastings, New Ipswich, N.H." For "Elvira" as his wife's name, see W. [James White], "Our Tour East," *Advent Review,* August 1850, p. 14, together with Elvira Hastings, "My Dear Brother and Sister," *Advent Review,* August 1850, p. 15.

[2] Although James and Ellen White had been corresponding with the Hastingses for about two years, it was during the visit here mentioned, in March 1849, that the two families first met in person.

See: Ellen G. White, *Spiritual Gifts [vol. 2],* pp. 112, 113.

[3] The Whites had returned to Topsham, Maine, via Boston and Dorchester. James adds the detail that the last 16 miles (26 kilometers) from North Yarmouth to Brunswick by stagecoach took three hours, during which they were "shook up and down . . . in snow banks and mud sloughs." Ellen White was about five months pregnant at the time.

See: James White to Leonard and Elvira Hastings, Mar. 22, 1849.

glory upon us. We all had a rich draught from the well of Bethlehem. The Spirit came upon me and I was taken off in vision. I saw many important things, some of which I will write you before I close this letter. I saw Brother Stowell [**Lewis B. Stowell**][4] of Paris [Maine] was wavering upon the shut door.[5] I felt that I must visit them. Although it was fifty miles [80 kilometers] off and very bad going, I believed God would strengthen me to perform the journey. We went and found they needed strengthening. There had not been a meeting in the place for above two years.[6] We spent one week with them. Our meetings were very interesting. They were hungry for present truth. We had free, powerful meetings with them. God gave me two visions while there, much to the comfort and strength of the brethren and sisters. Brother Stowell was established in the shut door and all the present truth he had doubted. Strength was given me from on high so that my journey wearied me not at all and my health has been better ever since. Thank God He gives us strength as we need.

After we returned from Paris, we felt that it was time to make up our minds where to go and spend the summer. We were in much perplexity and trial to know how to decide. We had been expecting God to teach in such a way that we could not mistake duty, but we were disappointed and as we had no light to go elsewhere, concluded to go to New York. James wrote them when to come for us at Utica [New York] and I signed my name to the letter after he had signed his. Soon I began to feel distressed and burdened. It seemed that I should be driven to distraction. I found relief by weeping. When in my distress James was afraid I would die, and he threw the letter in the stove, as he told me afterward, then knelt down by my bedside and prayed God to roll off the burden, and I was relieved. The next morning I awoke perfectly free and clear, all my distress was gone, and I felt assured God would open the way before us.

James went to the office and brought in a letter from Brother Belden [**Albert Belden**],[7] Rocky Hill, Connecticut, giving us a strong invitation to come there and live with them; said they should consider it a privilege to

---

[4] *Identity:* Although there were a number of Stowell families in Paris, Maine, at this time, the only known Sabbatarian one was the family of Lewis B. Stowell. "Brother Stowell" could, strictly speaking, be one of Lewis's sons, such as Oswald (age 21), also a Sabbathkeeper, but it is more likely that "Brother Stowell" would be reserved for the father.

See: Search term "Stowell" in *Words of the Pioneers*; William Berry Lapham, *History of Paris, Maine,* p. 738.

[5] *See:* Introductory article "The 'Shut Door' and Ellen White's Visions"; EGWEnc, s.v. "Shut Door."

[6] The beginnings of the group of Sabbathkeeping Adventists in Paris, Maine, can be traced to 1845.

See: Mrs. M. C. Stowell Crawford, "A Letter From a Veteran Worker," *Southern Watchman,* Apr. 25, 1905, p. 278.

[7] *Identity:* Writing to Stephen T. Belden, son of Albert Belden, in 1904, Ellen White recalls

administer to our wants. We felt clear to go and felt that it was the way the Lord had opened. They sent us means to go with.

We came to this place yesterday; found our dear Brother Nichols' [**Otis Nichols**][8] family as well as usual, steadfast in the faith, and strong in all the present truth. Sister Temple [**Elizabeth Temple**][9] continues well and strong. Praise the Lord, she stands out a living monument of the healing power of God.[10] Last week she earned eight dollars cleaning house in Boston [Massachusetts]. Our God is a living God; He is bringing up and reviving His people and preparing them to stand in the battle of the Lord. The work is still going on in Connecticut. The Lord has shown me in vision He was at work there and that what He was doing for His people was only a few drops before a more plentiful shower.

Keep up good courage, my dear Brother and Sister. I do want to hear from you very much, and should rejoice to have the privilege of being in your happy dwelling once more. How is your health, Sister Hastings? And how is your child, the babe?[11] Do let us know. We shall start for Connecticut Monday and settle down. Write us there and direct to James White, Rocky Hill, Ct.

I will now write you the vision God gave me on the Sabbath, the 24th of March.[12] We had a glorious meeting. I was taken off in vision.

I saw the commandments of God and shut door could not be separated. I saw [that] the time for the commandments of God to shine out to His people was when the door was opened in the inner apartment of the heavenly

---

the time that "the paper *Present Truth* was first published" (summer 1849). "We were then living at Rocky Hill, in your father's [Albert Belden's] house."

See: Ellen G. White, Lt 293, 1904 (Oct. 17); 1850 U.S. Federal Census, "Albert Belden," Connecticut, Hartford County, Rocky Hill, p. 13.

[8] *Identity:* The main clue to the identity of "Brother Nichols'" is that he lives in "this place," i.e., Milton, Massachusetts (just south of Boston), as recorded at the top of the letter. The only Sabbatarian Nichols family living in that area during this period is that of Otis Nichols, of Dorchester, Massachusetts. It is uncertain why Ellen White implies here that Otis Nichols lives in Milton. Dorchester and Milton, however, were very close, if not adjacent to each other, so there may well be some natural reason Milton, and not Dorchester, is given as the address.

See: Search term "Otis Nichols" in *Words of the Pioneers.*

[9] *Identity:* The fact that "Sister Temple" worked in Boston is helpful in establishing her identity. The only "Temple" living in Boston mentioned in the *Review* during this period is "E. Temple" or "Elizabeth Temple."

See: Search term "Temple" in *Words of the Pioneers.*

[10] Six weeks earlier, on March 8, 1849, Ellen White had anointed Elizabeth Temple, who was seriously ill. The Whites had returned eight days later and found her "at the wash-tub in the enjoyment of good health."

See: James White to Leonard and Elvira Hastings, Mar. 22, 1849; Ellen G. White, *Spiritual Gifts [vol. 2],* pp. 109, 110, 113.

[11] Ellen and James White's visit to the Hastingses the previous month had been in part occasioned by the "wretched state of health" of Elvira Hastings, together with the affliction of her 8-week-old baby, who "cried continually."

See: Ellen G. White, *Spiritual Gifts [vol. 2],* p. 110.

[12] *See:* Ms 1, 1849 (Mar. 24)—a variant account of the same vision.

sanctuary in 1844. Then Jesus rose up and shut the door in the outer apartment and opened the door in the inner apartment and passed into the Most Holy Place, and the faith of Israel now reaches within the second veil where Jesus now stands by the ark. I saw that Jesus had shut the door in the Holy Place and no man can open it, and that He had opened the door in the Most Holy Place and no man can shut it; and that since Jesus had opened the door in the Most Holy Place the commandments have been shining out and God has been testing His people on the holy Sabbath.[13] I saw that the test on the Sabbath could not come until the mediation of Jesus was finished in the Holy and He had passed within the second veil; therefore Christians who died before the seventh month, 1844, and had not kept the true Sabbath, rest in hope, for there was no condemnation until the true light on the Sabbath came.

I saw that our adversaries had been trying to open the door in the outer apartment and to close the door in the inner apartment where the ark is, containing the two tables of stone on which are written the ten commandments by God's own finger.[14] I saw that Satan was now using every device in this sealing time to keep the minds of God's people from present truth and cause them to waver. I saw a covering that God was drawing over His people to protect them in the time of trouble, and every soul that was decided upon the truth was to be covered with this covering of Almighty God. Satan knew this and was also at work in mighty power. I saw that the mysterious knocking in New York was the power of Satan clothed in a religious garb to lull the deceived to more security and to draw the minds of God's people to look at that and cause them to doubt the teachings of God among His people.[15]

I saw that Satan was working through agents in a number of ways. He was at work through ministers who had rejected God's truth and had been given over to strong delusions to believe a lie, that they might be damned.[16] I saw while they were preaching or praying some would fall prostrate and helpless, not by the power of the Holy Ghost, No, no, but by the power of Satan breathed upon these agents and through them to the people.

I saw that some professed Adventists who had rejected present truth, while preaching, praying or in private conversation used mesmerism to gain adherents, and the people would rejoice, thinking it was the power of God;

---

[13] On the link between the Sabbath and the sanctuary, see Ms 1, 1849 (Mar. 24), note 4.

[14] *See:* Ms 1, 1849 (Mar. 24), note 5.

[15] On this earliest extant warning by Ellen White regarding the claims of the Fox sisters of Hydesville, New York, see Ms 1, 1849 (Mar. 24), note 6.

[16] Paraphrase of 2 Thess. 2:11, 12: "And for this cause God shall send them strong delusion, that they should believe a lie: That they all might be damned who believe not the truth, but had pleasure in unrighteousness."

and even those that used it (mesmerism) themselves were so far in the darkness and deception of the devil that they thought it was the power of God given them to exercise.[17] I saw that these men had made God altogether such an one as themselves.

I saw that some of the agents of the devil were affecting the bodies of those they could not deceive and draw from the present truth.[18] Some of them were even trying to afflict some of the saints unto death.[19] (Oh, that all could get a view of it as God revealed it unto me, that they might know more of the wiles of Satan so as to be on their guard.)

I saw that Satan was at work in these ways to distract, draw away, and deceive God's people just now in this sealing time[20] more than ever before. I saw some who were not standing stiffly, their knees were trembling, their feet were sliding, because they were not planted firmly on present truth, and the covering of Almighty God would not be drawn over them. While they were thus trembling Satan was trying his every art to hold them where they were until the sealing was over and the covering drawn over God's people, and they left out without protection in the time of slaughter. God has begun to draw this covering over His people, therefore it will very soon be drawn over all of those who are to have a shelter in the time of trouble or day of the Lord.

I saw that as God worked for His people, Satan would also work, and that the mysterious knocking and signs and wonders of Satan and false reformations would increase and spread. The reformations that were shown me were not reformations from error to truth, No, no, but from bad to worse, for those who professed a change of heart had only wrapt about them a religious cloak which covered up the iniquity of a vile heart so as to deceive God's people; but if their hearts could be seen they would appear as black as ever.[21] My accompanying angel bade me look for the travail of souls for sinners as used to be. I looked but could not see it for the time for their salvation is past.[22] Dear Brother and Sister, I have now written the vision God gave me. I am tired sitting so long. Our position looks very clear. We know we have the truth, the midnight cry is behind us, the door was shut in 1844 and Jesus is soon to step out from between God and man. The sealing will then be accomplished—finished up. Oh, let us keep on the whole armor of God that we may be ready for battle at any moment. We shall have to fight every inch of ground now.

---

[17] *See:* Ms 1, 1849 (Mar. 24), note 8.

[18] *See:* EGWEnc, s.v. "Present Truth."

[19] *See:* Ms 1, 1849 (Mar. 24), note 10.

[20] *See*: EGWEnc, s.v. "Seal of God."

[21] For a study of early Sabbatarian Adventist attitudes to religious revivals, see P. Gerard Damsteegt, *Foundations of the Seventh-day Adventist Message and Mission,* pp. 184-186.

[22] *See:* Ms 1, 1849 (Mar. 24), note 13.

Satan has come down in great power, knowing his time is short; but with the commandments of God written in our hearts and in our minds [we] will go on strong and bold, and although the sons of Anak be many and tall,[23] yet we will go on crying, The commandments of God and the testimony of Jesus.

Glory be to God, we shall get the victory and enter the goodly land if we keep the commandments. Oh yes, and we shall have right to the tree of life, and drink of those streams that make glad the city of our God, and we shall behold the lovely face of Jesus and be made like Him. Lift up your heads and rejoice, your redemption is nigh.

Arabella [**Harriet Arabella Hastings**],[24] the Lord is coming; are you all ready? Can you meet Him in peace and say, This is our God, we have waited for Him? Oh do take hold on the strength of God and make peace with Him, that you may stand when the earth shall reel to and fro like a drunkard. And the rest of the children,—I cannot call them by name,—Love God with your whole hearts and pray much that you may be sealed. It is of great importance that you secure your soul's salvation. Much love to all.

E. G. White

Much love to Sister Gorham [**Elizabeth Gorham**];[25] tell her, for me, to

---

[23] Cf. Num. 13:33: "And there we saw the giants, the sons of Anak . . . : and we were in our own sight as grasshoppers."

[24] *Identity:* The appeal to Arabella "and the rest of the children" clearly indicates that Arabella was a daughter of Leonard and Elvira Hastings to whom the letter is addressed. Arabella was the oldest of the Hastings children, about 16 at the time. Her name is given as "Harriet A. Hastings" in her 1854 obituary. Ellen White, in her correspondence, sometimes referred to her as "Arabella" and sometimes as "Harriet" (cf. Lt 5, 1849 [Apr. 21], and Lt 10, 1850 [Mar. 18], with Lt 7, 1851 [July 27], and Lt 3, 1851 [Aug. 11]). Presumably the middle initial "A" stands for Arabella. (The 1850 U.S. Federal Census for the Leonard Hastings household lists a 17-year old "Hannah A. Hastings." It is assumed here that this is an error and that "Hannah" should be "Harriet.")

See: Obituary: "Harriet A. Hastings," *Review*, Sept. 5, 1854, p. 31; 1850 U.S. Federal Census, "Leonard Hastings," New Hampshire, Hillsborough County, New Ipswich, p. 272.

[25] *Identity:* In several letters written to the Hastingses in New Ipswich, New Hampshire, Ellen White sent her warm greetings to "Sister Gorham." A clue to her identity comes in a letter fragment from 1851, in which the writer (name unknown) says he "landed by cars at 10 a.m. at Mason Village. Found a Sister Goram [the spelling disparity is probably not significant], took dinner, and then walked five miles [eight kilometers] to Bro. Hastings, New Ipswich." According to the 1850 census there was an Elizabeth Gorham living in Mason but no Gorham at all living in nearby New Ipswich. The probability that Ellen White is greeting Elizabeth Gorham of Mason is raised by the circumstance that the *Review's* only mentions of "Gorham" as a personal name during the 1850s are "E. Gorham," "Elizabeth Gorham," and "J. Gorham."

See: Ellen G. White, Lt 8, 1849 (May 29); Lt 18, 1850 (Jan. 11); Lt 10, 1850 (Mar. 18); Lt 28, 1850 (Nov. 27); Lt 3, 1851 (Aug. 11); Lt 7, 1851 (July 27); (writer unknown) to "the dear disciples of Jesus in Dartmouth," Nov. 7, 1851; 1850 U.S. Federal Census, "Elizabeth Gorham," New Hampshire, Hillsborough County, Mason, p. 299; search term "Gorham" in *Words of the Pioneers.*

hold fast; tell her her deliverance is soon to come and she will soon, if faithful, enjoy the company of Jesus and angels. Tell her to stand stiffly, to let nothing move her from the truth. My love to Sister Eastman, although I have never seen her, and Brother Gardner.[26] I should love to see you all. Pray for poor, unworthy me.

In haste.

[26] The identities of "Sister Eastman" and "Brother Gardner" have not been established.

1849
(Lt 8, 1849)

MAY 29, ROCKY HILL, CONNECTICUT

LETTER TO
Leonard W. Hastings and Elvira Hastings.[1]

Portions of this letter are published in Ellen G. White, *Manuscript Releases,* vol. 4, pp. 323-326; vol. 5, pp. 248, 249.

> *Letter to close friends, the Hastings family, containing news of a dramatic healing and of personal trials and difficulties. Includes words of spiritual encouragement to all members of the family.*

Dear Brother and Sister Hastings:

We received your kind and sweet letter in due time.[2] James [**James Springer White**] was in New York when it came and my health was very poor at that time or I should have written you before his return. He came home last Tuesday, had a good time in western N. Y. feeding the hungry sheep. We have been in a very tried state of late while we see the wrongs in Connecticut. My soul has carried the burden and distress for two weeks past.

Last Sabbath was a trying day to me. As soon as meeting commenced my burden grew heavier. My heart ached almost to bursting. I was obliged to leave the room and not come in again until meeting closed. I cried aloud for

---

[1] The original handwritten draft of this letter carries the date of "May 29, 1848," which is puzzling because it seems to conflict with some of the other assertions found in the letter. Paragraph 5 reveals that the Whites had already visited the Hastings family ("I have not forgotten the good seasons we had together"), whereas Leonard Hastings later recalled that "Bro. and sister White made us their first visit in March, 1849" (Ellen G. White, *Spiritual Gifts* [*vol. 2*], p. 112). In addition, James White is said to have returned recently from "western N.Y." (par. 1), whereas other evidence strongly suggests that James's first visit to western New York was together with Ellen some months later, in August 1848 (James White to Hastings, Aug. 26, 1848). Another anomaly is that the second part of the letter is headed "June 1, Friday" when, in fact, June 1 fell on a Thursday in 1848. June 1 did, however, fall on a Friday in 1849, and this circumstance, together with the testimony of Leonard Hastings, suggests that the letter was actually written in 1849. A closer examination of the handwritten original date "May 29, 1848," reveals that the ink strokes of the "1848" are much lighter and fainter than the "May 29," suggesting—though clearly not demanding—that the year "1848" might have been added at a later time, with the original bearing only the month and day of "May 29." The balance of evidence, it seems, favors the conclusion that the letter was written on May 29, 1849.

[2] This letter is not in the White Estate archives.

a long time, but tears would not relieve me. I thought I must leave Ct. and made up my mind to go to western N. Y.

Last Sunday we were at Bro. Ralph's [**Richard Ralph**][3] and we engaged in prayer for the special teachings of God how to move, whether to go to N. Y. or stay in Ct.[4] The Spirit came and we had a powerful season. Brother and Sister Ralph were both laid prostrate and remained helpless for some time.[5] I was taken off in vision and saw concerning the state of some here, and also saw there would be a conference at your place and that it was duty of my husband to attend[6] and that a conference should be holden in Paris, Maine, and souls would be strengthened and comforted there.[7] I then saw it was not duty to go to N. Y. but that we must tarry and abide where we were,[8] so our minds

---

[3] *Identity:* The only Ralph identified in the *Review* during the 1850s as coming from Connecticut is "R. Ralph," of Berlin, Connecticut. That this is the Ralph Ellen White is speaking of is quite certain, inasmuch as Berlin is only eight miles (13 kilometers) or so from Rocky Hill and she reported that they had visited Berlin "last Sunday." The full first name of "Richard" is obtained from the 1850 census records.

See: Search term "Ralph" in *Words of the Pioneers;* obituary: "The Companion of Bro. R. Ralph," *Review,* Oct. 17, 1854, p. 79; 1850 U.S. Federal Census, "Richard Ralph," Connecticut, Hartford County, Berlin, p. 128; obituary: "Richard Ralph," *Review,* Oct. 5, 1897, p. 639.

[4] Exactly what "the wrongs in Connecticut" (par. 1) were that caused Ellen White to consider moving to New York State are not known, but this section illustrates the intensity with which the Whites sought divine guidance in their moves and travels. Two months earlier they had experienced "much perplexity and trial," not knowing whether to spend the summer in New York, Connecticut, or Massachusetts, before they felt impressed that they should go to Connecticut.

See: James White to Leonard and Elivira Hastings, Feb. 25, 1849; James White to "Beloved Brother and Sister," Mar. 22, 1849, Ellen G. White, Lt 5, 1849 (Apr. 21).

[5] *See:* Appendix article "Ellen White and Religious Enthusiasm in Early Adventist Experience"; EGWEnc, s.v. "Ecstatic Experiences."

[6] Some weeks earlier James White had written to Leonard and Elvira Hastings, of New Ipswich, New Hampshire, asking them of the advisability of holding a conference "in N. H. as soon as June" at which James White and Joseph Bates would lead out. A reference in *Spiritual Gifts* to a journey by James White to New Hampshire and Maine about June 1849 seems to confirm that the conference took place. Ellen White, only a few weeks away from giving birth to Edson (July 28), did not accompany her husband.

See: James White to "Beloved Friends," postscript to Lt 5, 1849 (Apr. 21); Ellen G. White, *Spiritual Gifts [vol. 2],* p. 113.

[7] Whereas James White had planned for a conference in Paris, Maine, in June 1849, it appears to have been postponed till September. Ellen White recalled in her memoirs that the Paris group "had not had a meeting for one year and a half" at the time when the conference opened on September 14. The prediction that "souls would be strengthened and comforted there" was strikingly fulfilled, as related in *Spiritual Gifts.* In particular the conference marked the emergence of 20-year-old J. N. Andrews to a lifetime of ministry and scholarship for the young movement.

See: James White to "Beloved Friends," postscript to Lt 5, 1849 (Apr. 21); Ellen G. White, *Spiritual Gifts [vol. 2],* pp. 116, 117; John N. Andrews, "Dear Brethren and Sisters," *Present Truth,* December 1849 (no. 5), p. 38.

[8] The Whites stayed in Rocky Hill, Connecticut, over the summer of 1849. During this period Edson was born on July 28 and James White started the publication of *The Present Truth.*

are made up what to do, and may God give me strength to endure the trials I shall have to pass through here.

This morning we had a good time; my soul was taken into a sacred nearness to God. I could hold sweet communion with Him, my peace was as a river and my poor heart burned with love to God. Praise His holy name. My soul doth magnify the Lord for His tender kindness unto me.

I was rejoiced to hear of the good time you had at your house with Sister Gorham [**Elizabeth Gorham**][9] and Eastman.[10] I should have loved to [have] been one of your company. I have not forgotten the good seasons we had together,[11] neither have I forgotten your kindness to us. May the Lord reward you for your labors of love unto us. We have had sweet union together.[12] Oh, may it last until Jesus comes. Let nothing cast you down but be encouraged and remember Jesus hath the watchful care over you. Time is very short, deliverance is coming and Satan knows it and is working in great power. I can see the restraint is being taken off from the wicked, and very soon when Jesus steps out from between the Father and man it will be entirely gone. Now is the time we must watch on every hand, against the wiles of Satan and have steady, abiding faith in God, faith that will stand the trial, such faith as Elijah had when he prayed for rain. He prayed once and sent his servant to see if there was any sign of his prayer being answered, and although there was none, outward appearance was against him, yet he did not give up in discouragement but bid his servant to go again yet seven times. Elijah had faith that holds on and that would stand the trials seven times. At last the cloud appeared and the heavens gave rain.

Bless God the prayer of faith will bring the dew of heaven and our souls will be watered by it. Hold on to faith, let your feelings be what they will. Oh, how my soul feels for the flock of God. I long to be out among them. I often awake myself crying to God's people to get ready, get ready that the cloak of Almighty God may be thrown around them and they be hid in the time of trouble. I shall be deprived [of] the privilege of meeting with you in

---

However, by September, when Edson was 6 weeks old, their travels started again, first to conferences in Vermont and Maine, and later in the autumn to western New York. By December 1849 they had settled in Oswego, New York. For an overview of the travels and work of the Whites during 1849, see Arthur L. White, *Ellen G. White: The Early Years,* pp. 158-170.

[9] *Identity:* See Lt 5, 1849 (Apr. 21), note 25.

[10] This person has not been identified.

[11] The Whites had first visited the Hastings family in person some two months earlier, in March 1849.

See: Ellen G. White, *Spiritual Gifts [vol. 2],* p. 112.

[12] In her autobiography Ellen White wrote of the Hastings family, "Our hearts were knit together, especially was the heart of sister Hastings knit with mine, as were David's and Jonathan's. Our union was not marred while she lived."

See: Ibid., p. 111.

conference. I feel the privation but the will of the Lord be done.[13] My heart and mind will be there, and my prayers shall be for you that God would work among you.

How are the children? Do they feel their acceptance with God? Dear children, do not rest a moment if you do not. God loves to hear the prayers of the young. Call upon Him and make your peace with Him that you may stand in the day of slaughter.[14] I do love you, children, and I want you to be saved in the kingdom and enjoy the beauty of the earth made new. Get ready, get ready, love not this world, love not the wicked, but God and those who have His image. Tell Sister Gorham to be of good courage; tell her although she may be in the heated furnace the Lord will not leave her. Tell her to hold fast the truth whatever opposition she may have. It's better to serve God than man, His strength is sufficient for her.

Love to Sister Eastman and Brother Gardner.[15] Should love to see you all. Pray for me. I have trials that none but God knows of, but I have started for eternal life and I cannot stop this side. I must see the inside of glory, stagger not at the promises but believe. Faith, simple faith is what we want, a firm reliance and trust in God. Faith will drive back the powers of darkness; only have faith and you will have a clear, sweet atmosphere to live and breathe in.

Kiss the little morsel[16] for me and do write us [as] often as you can. This is a hasty line. Pray for me.

E. G. White

June 1, Friday

Dear Brother and Sister:

It has been stormy here for some days. Last Wednesday about six o'clock P. M. a brother came from Portland [Connecticut], eleven miles [18 kilometers] from here and wanted we should go and pray for his wife for she was just alive, and that was all. She was taken so violent that they called in a physician. He tried to help her, but could do her no good, and said she must die. Another physician was consulted who said he could do nothing. The last

---

[13] This could be a reference to the New Hampshire conference planned for June 1849. See note 6 above.

[14] Apocalyptic imagery taken from Ezekiel 9, where Ezekiel sees six men with slaughter weapons charged to smite all except those marked on the forehead.

[15] This person has not been identified.

[16] No doubt a reference to John Frederick Hastings, born just a few months earlier.

See: 1850 U.S. Federal Census, "John Hastings," New Hampshire, Hillsborough County, New Ipswich, p. 272; Ellen G. White, *Spiritual Gifts [vol. 2]*, p. 110.

was the most celebrated physician in Middletown, Ct. Sr. Penfield[17] told her husband to go for God's people; she sent for us. It was rather of a trial for me to start. It was rainy and I had been very weak all day, but I concluded to go. James felt he must go too. Brother and Sister Ralph also went according to her request. We prayed for her [at] ten o'clock that night and the Spirit began to settle. She had been in very great agony but we anointed her with oil in the name of the Lord and then our earnest cries went up to God for healing power.

God began to work, the pain ceased, but we did not get the full victory we wanted that night. She rested well that night, was free from pain. In the morn we united in prayer for her again. The power came down like a mighty, rushing wind, the room was filled with the glory of God, and I was swallowed up in the glory and was taken off in vision.

I saw the willingness of God to heal the afflicted and distressed. I also saw that God was displeased when we trusted in or called on earthly physicians.[18] I saw the beauty, the glory and majesty of Jesus. The sun could not shine in His presence any more than a star at noonday when the sun shone in its splendor. O how rich the inheritance of the saints looked to me. How glorious! Tongue cannot describe it. On every side and all around was glory, glory, glory, that cannot be expressed. My soul was enchanted with the sight. I longed to see more and more. It seemed that I could plunge in the glory, that I could swim in it. Praise the name of the Lord. Oh, shall we not go on with perseverance?

---

[17] This person has not been identified.

[18] Ellen White did not understand the affirmation of faith healing found here to exclude the use of simple remedies. For example, the previous summer, when the Whites feared that their infant son, Henry, "would die with consumption," they "used simple herbs," and other medicines, "but they had no effect." It was after these failed that the Whites anointed Henry, who subsequently recovered. This relationship between the use of remedies and prayer for healing was confirmed by vision in 1853: "I saw that it was right to use herbs that are beneficial to the use of man" (Lt 11, 1853 [Dec. 3]).

If the use of remedies per se is not the issue, the question remains why "earthly physicians" should not be consulted. Even though the vision is not explicit on this point, it seems natural to suggest that the problem lay in the dangerous nature of many of the "remedies" so common in mid-nineteenth-century medical practice. In the light of her other counsels, including those in regard to Christian physicians, this statement may also be understood as a warning not to put one's whole trust for healing in human instrumentalities, but to keep God in the equation.

See: Ellen G. White, *Spiritual Gifts [vol. 2],* pp. 104-106; *idem,* Lt 11, 1853 (Dec. 3); EGWEnc, s.v. "Prayer for the Sick." For accounts of the state of nineteenth-century American medicine, see Mervyn G. Hardinge, *A Physician Explains Ellen White's Counsel on Drugs, Herbs, and Natural Remedies,* pp. 19-58; Albert E. Hirst, "Ellen White's Criticism of Nineteenth Century Medicine [part 1]," *Review,* June 30, 1983, pp. 9, 10. An in-depth analysis of alternative medical thought and practice in nineteenth-century America is provided in John S. Haller, *Medical Protestants: The Eclectics in American Medicine, 1825-1939.* The analysis offered above is challenged by Ronald Numbers in *Prophetess of Health,* pp. 76-81. See response to Numbers on this issue in *A Critique of the Book* Prophetess of Health, pp. 42-44.

Shall we sink down now? No, no, we shall soon see Jesus and reign with Him in glory. Hold fast, hold fast, hold fast.

The work of healing was done up well. She grew stronger in body and mind, and while I was in vision the doctor came, he heard the shouting in vision and would not come in. Brother Penfield wanted he should come in, said he would not come in any case, seemed to be afraid and rode off and carried the news that we were making a great noise over that sick woman and he thought if she was kept still she would get well, when he had not seen her since he said she would die. The neighbors, when we left yesterday, were all stirred up and mad at us because we had prayed for Sister Penfield and she had been healed. Sister P. is strong. Praise the Lord.

Love to all, in haste.

1849

(Ms 6, 1849)

[JUNE 30, ROCKY HILL, CONNECTICUT]

SYNOPSIS OF

E. G. White's Vision, June 30, 1849, at Rocky Hill.[1]

Previously unpublished.

Utterances while in vision: Probation almost finished; urgent call for unity, sacrifice, and proclamation.[2]

Chief among ten thousand—hallelujah—glory. Look ye, heaven is in commotion. What is the matter? Just about to bathe His sword in heaven. How long? How long? How long? In commotion, the throng. Swift messengers of Almighty God, withhold not [the means, I suppose].[3] Speed the messengers, speed the messengers (still repeated), speed the messengers. Last work.

Pray for the covering.[4] God cannot be trifled with. Look ye, be careful how thou treadest. The angels are letting go; the sword, famine, and pestilence [are] coming speedily.[5] Cut it down. Is there any danger? None for God's people. Eternal weight of glory (repeated). Little idols[6] must be dropped in

---

[1] The handwritten source for this record, copied by an unknown scribe, adds this title in the same handwriting.

[2] This manuscript is one of the few in the White Estate collection that records the actual words uttered by Ellen White while in public vision. See Ms 1, 1848 (Nov. 18, 19), for another example. Such reports provide valuable insights into the phenomena of the visions themselves and sometimes include information on movements, gestures, facial expressions, etc. However, as far as conveying information on the factual content of the vision, these reports are limited in what they can provide. Not only is the accuracy of the recorder's transcription not guaranteed, but the intermittent character of the utterances means that there is often insufficient context available to make the meaning of individual statements clear or to understand the overall structure of the vision. In the case at hand, Ms 6, 1849, certain themes appear—the shortness of time, the need to spread the message, appeals for unity and self-sacrifice—but we cannot be sure how these elements fit into the overall message. Since, as far as we know, Ellen White never wrote out an account of this vision, our understanding of it remains partial.

[3] The identity of the person who recorded Ellen White's words and added the bracketed remarks has not been established.

[4] Cf. Ms 1, 1849 (Mar. 24): "I saw a covering that God was drawing over His people to protect them in the time of trouble, and every soul that was decided on the truth was to be covered with this covering of Almighty God."

[5] See further down: "The four angels are about to let go; then the time of trouble." Cf. Ms 2, 1849 (Jan. 17): "I saw that the four angels would hold the four winds until Jesus' work was done in the sanctuary, then the seven last plagues will be poured out." "The four angels had power from God to hold the four winds, and . . . they were about to let them go."

[6] Probably includes tobacco. That is how the person recording Ellen White's utterances

the pathway. There will not be disunion much longer. The sealing work[7] will soon be done. Press together (repeated). Love one another as I have loved you. Lay down your life for the brethren. Deny self; it is not dead; it has got to die throughout the camp. He loves His brethren as Himself. If they cannot agree together here, they cannot reign together in heaven.

Have pity; speed them on. There is commotion in heaven! No more proclamation; every case fixed.[8] My Lord and my God! Speed Thy messengers (repeated many times). The mansions are about ready. Heirs of God and joint heirs with Christ. It is high time that self was denied. The mind will be clearer. They are to be done away. The time of trouble[9] is coming; who will stand?

Deny self (repeated) to do others good. Have the eyes wide open; see on the right and on the left, and see if you cannot do someone good. The latter rain[10] is coming; a few drops have fallen (healing the sick). It is coming; open thine eyes. Let the angels hover. Serve God perfectly. It is a great thing to be a Christian, a great thing to be swallowed up in God. They (the wicked) shall not fear as much as they do now. Expect they will make light of it.

He has not forgotten His people. He will place crowns on their heads. That company have denied self—(repeated). Nothing to do with them. Israel brought them away from the Egyptians (meaning the children), while the destroying angel passed by. Their blood shall be upon their garments. Although Noah, Job, and Daniel were in the land, they could deliver but their own souls. God's people are a peculiar people, not like the world—it's poison, it's like an adder. Look ye well lest blood be found upon thy garments, lest thy children be cast down before thine eyes. Have pity, have compassion, spare a little longer. *"Have pity"* (repeated).

"The light is almost gone. You have no desire to meet with them." (Sister Anderson).[11] The jewels are almost made up. They are made up but they do not shine. It is the swift messengers that are to do the work.[12] Think that the

---

in vision three months later interpreted her usage of "idols": "[God] is well pleased in giving up the idols (tobacco, etc.) and calling upon Him. Cut loose from everything that hinders thy progress." (Ms 5, 1849 [Sept. 23]). See also Lt 5, 1851 (Dec. 14): "I have seen in vision that tobacco was a filthy weed. . . . Said my accompanying angel, 'If it is an *idol* it is high time it was given up.'"

[7] *See*: EGWEnc, s.v. "Seal of God."

[8] Undoubtedly pointing to the future declaration of Revelation 22:11 and not to the time then present (as if probation had already closed). Other statements in this document confirm that every case is not yet fixed, e.g., "Speed God's people to save all that can be saved" in the next-to-last paragraph.

[9] *See:* EGWEnc, s.v. "Time of Trouble."

[10] *See:* EGWEnc, s.v. "Latter Rain."

[11] This person has not been identified, nor is anything known of the situation alluded to here.

[12] Cf. the following statement from 1851: "The Lord has often given me a view of the situation and wants of the scattered jewels who have not yet come to the light of the present truth, and that the messengers should speed their way to them as fast as possible" (Ellen G.

reward will not be great enough to pay for all the trials. Yea, God sent thee to that work [meaning Brother Chamberlain (**Ezra L. H. Chamberlain**).[13, 14] Can the leopard change his spots? Hide it from me; take it away that my eyes may not behold. Hide it away. Thou hast lain the burden on me once, twice, and thrice, and has sent Thy servants 100 miles [161 kilometers].

Oh, spare (repeated). Think ye that the ark will move there? It is not a holy place. Look, God will not bear always (repeated). He is great. He is mighty. He has been trifled with; will not bear always. The work will be done up speedily; the burden may be 100 miles [161 kilometers] off. Look, a little. Spare (repeated). Hide away under the covering. Get beneath it. Do not stand outside. Hide away quickly. The four angels are about to let go; then the time of trouble.

Everything has got to be proclaimed upon the housetops. If the sins are confessed before that time. That time will be an awful time. If confessed, it must be done right early. Every secret thing must come to light. If confessed before that time, thy sins will be placed on the scapegoat[15] and borne away.

Time of trouble, it will come right early. The signs shall be reacted over again;[16] the day and hour will then be known. The sea will boil like a pot. Their faces will then shine like Moses'. He appears in the east; His sword

---

White, *A Sketch of the Christian Experience and Views of Ellen G. White,* p. 49 [*Early Writings,* p. 61]).

[13] *Identity:* The only Chamberlain mentioned in the *Present Truth* and the *Review* during this period, up to 1852, is E.L.H. Chamberlain, of Middletown, Connecticut. The identity is confirmed by the fact that the meeting at which this vision was received took place in Rocky Hill, just a few miles from E.L.H. Chamberlain's home town of Middletown. That Chamberlain was an active lay preacher at this time fits the description here that he is one of the "messengers."

[14] Although E.L H. Chamberlain, about 50 years old at this time, had traveled and preached as far afield as western New York and Maine, apparently he was not a very effective public speaker. According to visions received in 1850 and 1852, "it was not his duty to travel." For the remaining five years of his life Chamberlain's sphere of activity was mostly limited to his home town in Connecticut.

See: Search term "E.L.H. Chamberlain" in *Words of the Pioneers*; Ellen G. White, Lt 10, 1850 (Mar. 18); *idem,* Lt 4, 1852 (Oct. 25).

[15] *See:* SDAE, s.v. "Scapegoat"; EGWEnc, s.v. "Investigative Judgment."

[16] Some may see in this statement an assertion that certain biblical prophecies have dual fulfillments. Thus, for example, some may understand it to mean that the predictions of Matthew 24 and Revelation 6 concerning a great earthquake, the sun becoming "black as sackcloth of hair," the moon becoming as blood, and the stars falling were fulfilled a first time during the striking events of 1755, 1780, and 1833 but will receive a second fulfillment in the cataclysmic events just preceding the Second Coming. See, for example, Ellen G. White, *Early Writings,* p. 41. Another interpretation of this statement, however, is that the events of 1755, etc., were a unique fulfillment of Bible prophecy, but that similar catastrophic events will precede the Second Coming.

For examples of approaches to the application of the "cosmic signs" in Adventist understanding, see Hans K. LaRondelle, "The Application of Cosmic Signs in the Adventist Tradition," *Ministry,* September 1998, pp. 25-27, William H. Shea, "Cosmic Signs Through History," *Ministry,* February 1999, pp. 10, 11, and Tim Poirier, "The End of a Sign or a Sign of the End?" *Adventist Review,* Nov. 13, 2008, pp. 18-21.

girded on His thigh. Then deliverance comes, perfect and entire, and God's people will be caught up on the white cloud.

I see it. (Says Brother Chamberlain: Here was silence for some ten minutes, her eyes going quickly each way as if looking at angels. When she came out of vision she accounted it thus: "I saw a large company of angels moving. I was not permitted to tell what they said to me. Each one had a round rod in their hand ten inches [25 centimeters] long.[17] Think they had something to do with the time of trouble, etc.")

How long shall these things be? Where art thou? Do not know. How does thou stand? Don't know. Isn't it thy privilege to know? Every servant can know whether their lives are hid with Christ in God. Did ye not see them speeding quickly? Speed God's people to save all that can be saved. Move, move, move. Not rashly; be sure God sends thee. The work is for God and then nothing can touch thee.

What? Don't thou turn an eye to please self. Live for God. If God's people do not go along, something is wrong. The four angels just ready to let go. His strength will save. Get hold of Jesus. Dark. Lonely. Thou knowest the sadness of the heart. How long shall it be so? Sadness. Have pity, have pity.

---

[17] Perhaps for the purpose of measurement. Cf. Eze. 40:3, 6; Zech. 2:1, 2; Rev. 11:1.

1849

AUGUST 1849

"Dear Brethren and Sisters."

Article published in *The Present Truth,* vol. 1, no. 3, August 1849, pp. 21-24.

1849

(Ms 5, 1849)

SEPTEMBER 23, TOPSHAM, MAINE[1]

Remarks in Vision.

Previously unpublished.

An entreaty to live fully for God in view of the impending crisis. Carried in vision to another planet.

Beautiful and glorious, lovely, lovely, lovely.[2] Haughtiness must come down, pride must fall.[3] Holy, holy, holy, holy. Who shall be able to stand? He

---

[1] Six weeks after their second son, James Edson White, was born on July 28, 1849, the Whites traveled from Connecticut to Paris, Maine, to attend a conference, held September 14-16. A conference followed in Topsham, Maine, probably on September 21-23. According to Joseph Bates, writing on September 25, "Ellen had a vision at each conference." The presumption is therefore that Ellen White's public vision dated September 23, here recorded, was received during the Topsham conference.

See: Ellen G. White, *Spiritual Gifts [vol. 2],* p. 116; "Conferences," *Present Truth,* August 1849, p. 24; Joseph Bates to Leonard and Elvira Hastings, Sept. 25, 1849.

[2] This manuscript is another rare example of a report of actual words uttered by Ellen White in public vision. For comments on the accuracy and limitations of such reports, see Ms 6, 1849 (June 30), note 2. Since, as far as we know, Ellen White never wrote out an account of this vision, our understanding of it remains partial.

[3] The utterances in this vision include an unusually large number of biblical (KJV) expressions and allusions. The following two instances, all taken from the first paragraph, serve to illustrate the tenor of the whole manuscript:

- "Who shall be able to stand? He that hath clean hands and a pure heart" (par. 1). Cf. Ps. 24: 3, 4: "Who shall ascend into the hill of the Lord? or who shall stand in his holy place? He that hath clean hands, and a pure heart."
- "Who hath directed the mind of the Lord, or being His counselor hath taught Him?" (par. 1). Cf. Isa. 40:13: "Who hath directed the Spirit of the Lord, or being his cousellor

that hath clean hands and a pure heart: to those who take Him for the Man of their counsel there is salvation. Who hath directed the mind of the Lord, or being His counselor hath taught Him? In infinite wisdom He hath established the Sabbath in Eden. Behold ye, be careful how ye treat the Sabbath of the Lord your God. It is holy, it is holy to the Lord.

Everything must be sacrificed this side of the (loosing) [of] the four winds.[4] Should anything be considered too dear to sacrifice for God? Behold ye, can ye not see them just ready to let go? Speed thee, hide, beneath the covering.[5] The mind is perplexed. The mind is troubled. Break away (her parents[6] and others).

That seal[7] must be implanted in a clear mind. It is so engrossed there is no place for the seal. Who hath the image of the lovely Jesus? Holy God have mercy, have mercy upon Thy Zion.[8] Heal them, heal them. Watch them carefully, have everything done this side of the standing up of Michael.[9] Those that now get established get fully established not to falter.

Do ye see those men?—1, 2, 3, 4, 5 (pointing to angels who were waiting to write on their rolls the names of those established, and those separated from us). Do you not see those bloody men with their weapons coming on

---

hath taught him?"

[4] The loosing of the "four winds" indicates the time when Christ's intercession has ceased, general probation has closed and a "time of trouble" begins. "I saw that the four angels would hold the four winds until Jesus' work was done in the sanctuary, then the seven last plagues will be poured out" (Ms 2, 1849 [Jan. 17]).

See: EGWEnc, s.v. "Plagues, Seven Last"; "Time of Trouble."

[5] The shortness of the time is a major emphasis of this vision. For Joseph Bates, who was present, it was the dominant theme. Two days later he wrote, "The cry from the holy City is speed the messengers, speed the messengers, the work is almost done. . . . The vision says spare neither money nor anything to do the work now. Soon it will be forever to [*sic*] late." Ellen White was later accused of being a false prophet. In 1883 she responded: "The angels of God in their messages to men represent time as very short. Thus it has always been presented to me. It is true that time has continued longer than we expected in the early days of this message. . . . But has the word of the Lord failed? Never! It should be remembered that the promises and threatenings of God are alike conditional."

See: Joseph Bates to Leonard and Elvira Hastings," Sept. 25, 1849; Ellen G. White, Ms 4, 1883 (c. 1883) (*Selected Messages,* book 1, p. 67).

[6] Ellen White recalled in 1860 that her mother had not attended the Paris conference but was present later in September 1849 for this conference at Topsham. The parentheses suggest that both parents were witnesses to their daughter's vision. There is evidence that as early as August 1848 Robert and Eunice Harmon were keeping the Sabbath. James White writes on August 26, 1848: "Call at Gorham where Ellen's parents live. They are with us in the faith."

See: Ellen G. White, *Spiritual Gifts [vol. 2],* pp. 117, 118; James White to "Dear Brother and Sister," Aug. 26, 1848; Arthur L. White, *Ellen G. White: The Early Years*, p. 119.

[7] *See:* EGWEnc, s.v. "Seal of God."

[8] "Zion" here used metaphorically to denote the people of God.

[9] An event that, according to Daniel 12:1, immediately precedes the "time of trouble, such as never was."

See: SDAE, s.v. "Michael, the Archangel"; *Questions on Doctrine,* pp. 65-76; EGWEnc, s.v. "Time of Trouble."

as soon as the last name is enrolled?[10] Do ye not see the pestilence wasting at noonday? Look ye, look ye, some have been leaning, and they have leaned too long, presumed when the commandments of God were plain in His Word they have leaned on something else. *Beware,* they have presumed on the mercy of God. God save, closing up, closing up, closing up, closing up. But two things—heaven or hell, life or death, now, now.

Behold ye, pleading that blood and after that work is finished. He will hold out no longer. Girds His sword upon His thigh and rides forth for the deliverance of the captive, the destroying angels! Then there will be no buying or selling. He will spread a table in the wilderness faithful just and true. It's the life of the saints they are after, they have not got the seal, it is something else, it's the mark of the beast,[11] and his image. They cry, they agonize. (Who? those who were right once, then they all join with the others, the wicked.) It's too late, too late. Every idle word put a watch before thee.

(Putting the Bible on Augusta Stowell [**Harriet Augusta Stowell**]): Study it, study it, take it, believe it, walk out on it, the Word of God, faith, the Book of books, the all-seeing eye! Tremble before the Lord of hosts. Look ye, the mind has been filled, it has been engrossed with trash. Cast it off, bear it away. Walk carefully before thy God. Keep thine eye steady upon thy God, faith, faith, faith, faith, faith. Take it as the man of thy counsel, take it as a hammer, a fire it will consume the dross, it will consume the tin, too much trash, cast it out.

(Taking the large Bible containing the apocrypha[12]): Pure and undefiled, a part of it is consumed, holy, holy, walk carefully, tempted. The Word of God, take it (Marion Stowell [**Marion Concordia Stowell**[13]]), bind it long upon thine heart, pure and unadulterated. How lovely, how lovely, how lovely. My blood, My blood, My blood. O the children of disobedience, reproved, reproved. Thy word, Thy word, Thy word, a part of it is burned unadulterated, a part of the hidden book, a part of it is burned (the apocrypha).

Those that shall despitefully tread [treat?] that remnant would think that they are doing God service. Why? because they are led captive by Satan at his will. Hidden book, it is cast out. Bind it to the heart (4 times) bind it, bind it,

---

[10] The appeal to escape the coming destruction is here repeated, this time using the imagery of Ezekiel 9. Ezekiel there sees "six men . . . every man a slaughter weapon in his hand" charged to smite all except those marked in the forehead by one of the men "clothed with linen, with a writer's inkhorn by his side."

[11] *See:* EGWEnc, s.v. "Mark of the Beast."

[12] Even Protestant Bibles commonly included the Apocrypha as a separate section between Old and New Testaments, until the British and Foreign Bible Society decided to exclude it from all its Bibles in 1826. See S. L. Greenslade, ed., *The Cambridge History of the Bible,* vol. 3, p. 391.

[13] Second name "Concordia" found in William Berry Lapham, *History of Paris, Maine,* p. 738.

bind it, (laying the Bible on Oswell Stowell [**Lewis Oswald Stowell**][14]) let not its pages be closed, read it carefully. Snares will beset on every side, take the strait truth, bind it to the heart (3 times), let everything be cast out.[15]

It is the youth (here and other places). Critical place. Satan is tempting them, if they go back, if they give up there is, will be no more hope. They have received the knowledge of the truth. Souls hither and thither are hungry, Oh how they would eat the truth. Fly swiftly. It is of God, lay aside the idols, can ye not see it? He is well pleased in giving up the idols (tobacco &c) and calling upon Him. Cut loose from everything that hinders thy progress, too late to be entangled, the Jubilee[16] is coming.

God's people are a tried people. Been trials, large blocks to get over. He is frowning; that's why the wheels could not go.[17] Some are breaking the holy commandments. Since the door was shut[18] those that broke them are in an awful place. After the light shone upon the Sabbath those that have received it and cast it away, there is no hope for them. The condemnation was great for breaking the nine commandments.

(Out of vision she said, But when the light comes on the fourth it would be greater if rejected.)

Press together, press together, how much? to lay down thy life for one another. Money nor nothing should be spared, live for God. Keep the mouth, keep the mouth, light, trifling, wicked conversation. Satan tempts thee, need much grace to stand. Keep thy finger on thy mouth, too apt to speak, lacking in faith, He loves thee (Sister Curtis [**Mercy A. Curtis**][19]). Take it as the

---

[14] The three Stowells mentioned in this manuscript, Oswald (21), Marion (20), and Harriet Augusta (18), were children of **Lewis B.** and **Laura Stowell**, of Paris, Maine.

[15] The intent of the utterances regarding the Apocrypha in the preceding three paragraphs is not clear. What is the significance of its being "consumed," "burned," and "cast out"? Does it constitute a positive evaluation of the Apocrypha—that it has value but has been "despitefully" treated? Or do the words "burned," etc., imply a negative evaluation? Or is, perhaps, no judgment intended at all? Unfortunately, no account of this vision, written by Ellen White, is available to answer some of these questions.

There has been little published comment on this passage. More attention has been given to Ellen White's vision a few months later, in January 1850 (Ms 4, 1850), also dealing with the Bible and the Apocrypha. See the following articles for two somewhat different perspectives. Denis Fortin, "Sixty-six Books—or Eighty-one? Did Ellen White Recommend the Apocrypha?" *Review,* Mar. 28, 2002, p. 9; Ron Graybill, "Under the Triple Eagle. Early Adventist Use of the Apocrypha," *Adventist Heritage,* Winter 1987, pp. 25-32; EGWEnc, s.v. "Apocrypha."

[16] *See:* Siegfried H. Horn, ed., *Seventh-day Adventist Bible Dictionary,* s.v. "Jubilee."

[17] Ellen White occasionally uses the expression "blocking the wheels of progress" or the like (e.g., Ms 15, 1885 [July 17]). This would fit into the present context, since two sentences earlier she speaks of cutting loose "from everything that hinders thy progress."

[18] *See:* Introductory article "The 'Shut Door' and Ellen White's Visions"; EGWEnc, s.v. "Shut Door."

[19] *Identity:* Since "Sister Curtis" witnessed the vision in Topsham it is likely that she belongs to the same Curtis family mentioned by J. N. Loughborough and Ellen White as living in Topsham during the 1840s. Loughborough and White, however, supply only the family

man of thy counsel, let not thy mouth be closed (Henry Nichols [**Henry O. Nichols**]). (Not in vision said, He believes the promises are for every one else but for him.) Glory, the rich reward, the rich reward, glory.

Going to another place or planet.

Majestic, lovely and beautiful, they know the redeemed in that dark spot (this earth) that they shall soon behold them. Hallelujah, lovely as in the garden of Eden of all sizes, as they pass around by the gates they behold their image.[20] They meet every Sabbath holy unto the Lord. It was not there they had never changed it. How could it be? The Pope changed it.

Lovely and majestic person (Christ) comes unto this place. How holy, how holy, holy, how beautiful is His countenance. They can embrace Him. Hallelujah, hallelujah. Beautiful and lovely, brighter than the sun at noonday. Behold put it in the most holy place, in heaven those two lovely angels looking down into the commandments and the golden pot of manna. If Israel had kept them there they would have been as strong as an army with banners. Jerusalem would have stood until now if they had not broken them. Oh, let me remain;[21] go forth quickly. When the law is sealed up and closed with His disciples then He will let go. Drop the curtain, I cannot see it. I cannot behold it, save, save, save, O God have pity, have mercy, save, O save.

---

name—Curtis. Evidence of her full identity comes from an obituary in the *Review* of Mercy A. Curtis, which tells us that she died in Topsham in 1907 and that she and her husband "had accepted the Adventist faith in 1843" and "were among the first to embrace the Sabbath." Census data reveals that Mercy Curtis had been married to Robert G. Curtis, who was listed as a Topsham resident as early as the census of 1840. "R. G. Curtis" is mentioned regularly in the subscriber lists of the *Review*. In summary it is likely that "Sister Curtis" in this manuscript is Mercy A. Curtis, since she was a Sabbatarian Adventist who lived in Topsham during the 1840s.

See: J. N. Loughborough, *The Great Second Advent Movement,* pp. 238, 257, 258; James White and Ellen G. White, *Life Sketches* (1880), p. 199; Ellen G. White, *Spiritual Gifts [vol. 2],* p. 199; obituary: "Mercy A. Curtis," *Review,* Dec. 12, 1907, p. 37; 1840 U.S. Federal Census, "Robert G. Curtis," Maine, Lincoln County, Topsham, p. 13; 1880 U.S. Federal Census, "Mercy A. Curtis," Maine, Sagadahoc County, Topsham, p. 191; search term "R. G. Curtis" in *Words of the Pioneers.*

[20] Cf.: "The Lord has given me a view of other worlds . . . a place that was bright and glorious. . . . The inhabitants of the place were of all sizes, they were noble, majestic and lovely" (Ellen G. White, "To Those Who Are Receiving the Seal of the Living God," broadside, Jan. 31, 1849).

[21] Cf.: "I begged of my attending angel to let me remain in that place. I could not bear the thought of coming back to this dark world again" (*ibid.*).

1849

(Lt 7, 1849)

[SEPTEMBER],[1] N.P.

LETTER TO

Gilbert N. and Deborah L. Collins.[2]

This letter is published in entirety in Ellen G. White, *Manuscript Releases,* vol. 3, pp. 174, 175.

Letter of encouragement and admonition to children of close friends.

Dear Children, Gilbert and Deborah,

I have just laid down my child [**James Edson White**] a few moments to write you a word.[2] Are you good children? Do you keep the commandments of God, and love and obey your parents? If you do you have the promise of entering the holy city where all is harmony and joy. You must pray to God much that He would accept you, and keep you from the pestilence and sickness that is abroad in the land.[3]

God loves the young if their hearts are turned unto Him, and He loves to bless them.

I am now on my way to visit Henry [**Henry Nichols White**], and present

---

[1] Ellen White provides no date for this letter, but does offer a useful clue: "I am now on my way to visit Henry, and present to him his little brother." That she was coming to "present" Edson to his brother Henry strongly suggests that the two were to meet for the first time. It is very likely that this meeting took place in September 1849, when Edson was only 2 months old. According to the account in *Spiritual Gifts,* "when he [Edson] was six weeks old we went to Maine" visiting, during September 1849, among other places a conference at Topsham where Henry lived with the Howland family. Although Ellen White does not specifically state that Edson went with them to Maine, this would seem to be the most natural interpretation.

See: Ellen G. White, *Spiritual Gifts [vol. 2],* pp. 116, 118; Joseph Bates to Leonard and Elvira Hastings, Sept. 25, 1849.

[2] The Whites had a close relationship with Philip and Nancy Collins and their children, which explains the fact that this special letter was written to the children. Correspondence between James White and the Collinses can be traced back to 1846. Six letters from either James or Ellen White to the Collins family have been preserved. In early 1849 the Whites had answered an urgent call to come to Dartmouth when Gilbert Collins was seriously ill. He was dramatically healed in answer to prayer.

See: James White to Philip Collins, Aug. 26, 1846; Ellen G. White, *Spiritual Gifts [vol. 2],* pp. 108, 109.

[3] For background on the 1849 pestilence, see Charles E. Rosenberg, *The Cholera Years: The United States in 1832, 1849, and 1866.*

to him his little brother.[4] I hope you will be good children. Love God. Speak the truth at all times. Be obedient to your parents, and then God will be pleased with you, smile upon and bless you. Be good, be good.

In haste and love.

[4]*See:* Note 1 above.

1849

SEPTEMBER 1849

"Dear Brethren and Sisters."

Article published in *The Present Truth,* vol. 1, no. 4, September 1849, pp. 31, 32.

1850

(Ms 2, 1850)

[JANUARY 9, OSWEGO, NEW YORK][1]

The Need for *The Present Truth.*

This manuscript is published in entirety in Arthur L. White, *Ellen G. White: The Early Years,* p. 172.

The importance of continuing support for The Present Truth *paper.*

I saw the paper and that it was needed.[2] That souls were hungry for the truth that must be written in the paper. I saw that if the paper stopped for want of means, and those hungry sheep died for want of the paper, it would not be James' [**James Springer White**] fault, but it would be the fault of those to whom God had lent His money to be faithful stewards over, and they

---

[1] The only extant copy of this vision is found in James White's letter to "Brother Hastings," headed "Oswego, N.Y., January 10, 1850." The vision, White reports, was received "last night."

[2] The reference here is to *The Present Truth.* One of the earliest Sabbatarian Adventist periodicals, and the first published by the group that later took the name "Seventh-day Adventists," the first issue was published by James White in July 1849. "Very soon," wrote Ellen White, "letters came bringing means to publish the paper." However, by December, six issues later, initial reader enthusiasm and donations had diminished, and James White thought "the poor little paper . . . [would] die." He was further discouraged by Joseph Bates's opposition to the whole project of issuing a periodical, preferring to publish pamphlets instead. It was while James White was "in this depressed, miserable state of mind" that Ellen had the encouraging vision on January 9, 1850, part of which is reported in this manuscript.

See: Ellen G. White, *Spiritual Gifts [vol. 2],* p. 116; James White to Leonard and Elvira Hastings, Jan. 3, 1850; *idem,* "The Paper," *Present Truth,* December 1849, p. 47; *idem,* to Leonard Hastings, Jan. 10, 1850. For an overview of early publishing ventures, see Arthur L. White, *Ellen G. White: The Early Years,* pp. 163-173; EGWEnc, s.v. "*Present Truth.*"

let it lie idle; and the blood of souls would be upon their garments. I saw that the paper should go, and if they let it die, they would weep in anguish soon. I saw that God did not want James to stop yet, but he must *write, write, write, write,* and speed the message and let it go. I saw that it would go where God's servants cannot go.

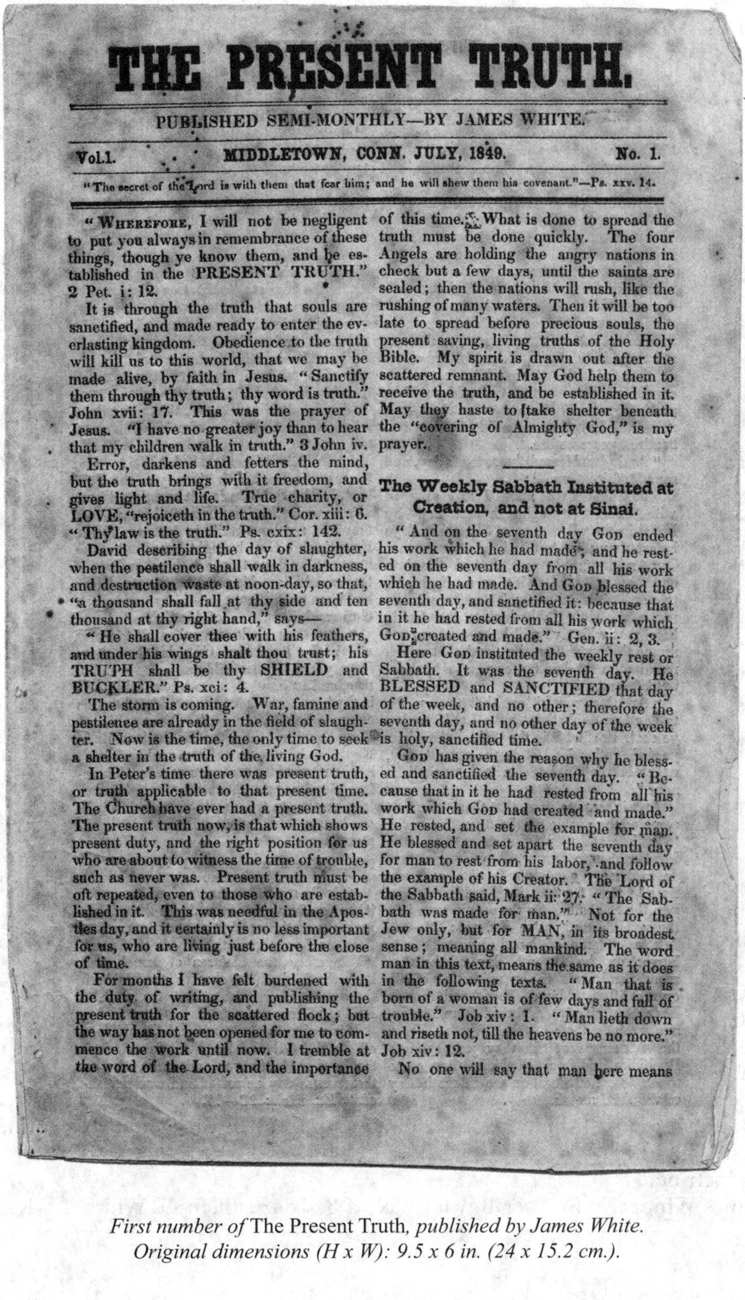

THE PRESENT TRUTH.

PUBLISHED SEMI-MONTHLY—BY JAMES WHITE.

Vol.1. MIDDLETOWN, CONN. JULY, 1849. No. 1.

"The secret of the Lord is with them that fear him; and he will shew them his covenant."—Ps. xxv. 14.

"WHEREFORE, I will not be negligent to put you always in remembrance of these things, though ye know them, and be established in the PRESENT TRUTH." 2 Pet. i: 12.

It is through the truth that souls are sanctified, and made ready to enter the everlasting kingdom. Obedience to the truth will kill us to this world, that we may be made alive, by faith in Jesus. "Sanctify them through thy truth; thy word is truth." John xvii: 17. This was the prayer of Jesus. "I have no greater joy than to hear that my children walk in truth." 3 John iv.

Error, darkens and fetters the mind, but the truth brings with it freedom, and gives light and life. True charity, or LOVE, "rejoiceth in the truth." Cor. xiii: 6. "Thy law is the truth." Ps. cxix: 142.

David describing the day of slaughter, when the pestilence shall walk in darkness, and destruction waste at noon-day, so that, "a thousand shall fall at thy side and ten thousand at thy right hand," says—

"He shall cover thee with his feathers, and under his wings shalt thou trust; his TRUTH shall be thy SHIELD and BUCKLER." Ps. xci: 4.

The storm is coming. War, famine and pestilence are already in the field of slaughter. Now is the time, the only time to seek a shelter in the truth of the living God.

In Peter's time there was present truth, or truth applicable to that present time. The Church have ever had a present truth. The present truth now, is that which shows present duty, and the right position for us who are about to witness the time of trouble, such as never was. Present truth must be oft repeated, even to those who are established in it. This was needful in the Apostles day, and it certainly is no less important for us, who are living just before the close of time.

For months I have felt burdened with the duty of writing, and publishing the present truth for the scattered flock; but the way has not been opened for me to commence the work until now. I tremble at the word of the Lord, and the importance of this time. What is done to spread the truth must be done quickly. The four Angels are holding the angry nations in check but a few days, until the saints are sealed; then the nations will rush, like the rushing of many waters. Then it will be too late to spread before precious souls, the present saving, living truths of the Holy Bible. My spirit is drawn out after the scattered remnant. May God help them to receive the truth, and be established in it. May they haste to take shelter beneath the "covering of Almighty God," is my prayer.

The Weekly Sabbath Instituted at Creation, and not at Sinai.

"And on the seventh day GOD ended his work which he had made; and he rested on the seventh day from all his work which he had made. And GOD blessed the seventh day, and sanctified it: because that in it he had rested from all his work which GOD created and made." Gen. ii: 2, 3.

Here GOD instituted the weekly rest or Sabbath. It was the seventh day. He BLESSED and SANCTIFIED that day of the week, and no other; therefore the seventh day, and no other day of the week is holy, sanctified time.

GOD has given the reason why he blessed and sanctified the seventh day. "Because that in it he had rested from all his work which GOD had created and made." He rested, and set the example for man. He blessed and set apart the seventh day for man to rest from his labor, and follow the example of his Creator. The Lord of the Sabbath said, Mark ii: 27. "The Sabbath was made for man." Not for the Jew only, but for MAN, in its broadest sense; meaning all mankind. The word man in this text, means the same as it does in the following texts. "Man that is born of a woman is of few days and full of trouble." Job xiv: 1. "Man lieth down and riseth not, till the heavens be no more." Job xiv: 12.

No one will say that man here means

First number of The Present Truth, *published by James White. Original dimensions (H x W): 9.5 x 6 in. (24 x 15.2 cm.).*

1850

(Lt 18, 1850)

[JANUARY 11, OSWEGO, NEW YORK][1]

LETTER TO

Leonard W. and Elvira Hastings.

This letter is published in entirety in Ellen G. White, *Manuscript Releases,* vol. 19, p. 128.

Earnest spiritual encouragement to close friends in view of the urgency of the hour.

Dear Brother and Sister Hastings:

I will take time to write you a few lines. I earnestly desire to see you.[2] I pray God to bless and sanctify you. I felt today the necessity of being *all, all* ready, that when the time of trouble[3] such as never was, shall come, we may be hid. O my Brother and Sister, I wish all of God's people could get a sight of it as God has shown it me. The work of the Lord is going on. Souls are coming into the truth[4] and soon the work will be all done. Keep up good courage, hope in God, let nothing weigh thee down. We have the truth. We know it. Praise the Lord. I saw yesterday our work was not to the shepherds who have

---

[1] Although no date and place of writing are given, this information is deduced from the fact that these lines are appended to a letter that James White wrote to "Brother Hastings" from Oswego on January 10 and 11, 1850.

See: James White to Leonard Hastings, Jan. 10, 1850.

[2] Letters from both James and Ellen White to the Hastingses express their affection for that family. When Elvira Hastings died some weeks later, in February 1850, Ellen found the news "overwhelming." According to James, "Ellen has mourned more than to lose one of her children, I think."

See: Ellen G. White, Lt 10, 1850 (Mar. 18); James White to Leonard Hastings, Mar. 18, 1850.

[3] *See:* EGWEnc, s.v. "Time of Trouble."

[4] Sabbatarian Adventism in western New York, where the Whites were located at this time, was experiencing remarkable growth. Writing some weeks earlier, James White enthusiastically reported that "in Western N.Y. the number of Sabbath keepers is increasing fast. There are more than twice the number now than six months ago." Not only was there numerical increase, but some of it was coming from outside the ranks of Adventists. In a letter written the following month, Ellen White noted that some of those "coming out upon the truth" "have not heard the Advent doctrine."

See: James White to "Brother Bowles," Nov. 8, 1849; Ellen G. White, Lt 4, 1850 (Feb. 18).

rejected the former messages,[5] but to the honest deceived who are led astray. I saw the [false] shepherds would soon be fed with judgment. Let the truth come out everywhere we go, the seventh day is the Sabbath of the Lord our God. Cheer up. There are better days coming.

My love to your dear children. Tell them for me to have their lives hid with Christ in God, to have their hearts wholly given to God that they may be hid in the day of the Lord's anger. Pray for us and do write us and let us know how you get along. I am in haste or I would write more. Babe is cutting teeth[6] and it takes nearly all of my time to take care of him just now.

Love to Sister Gorham [**Elizabeth Gorham**],[7] Bro. Gardener,[8] and all the saints in New Ipswich [New Hampshire].

Your sister in hope.

---

[5] The charge made here is that the first-day Adventist ministers ("shepherds") had rejected the first two angels' messages, which, prior to 1844, had been central to their very identity. As James White expressed it, these Adventists now refused "to acknowledge that the great leading movements in our past experience, such as the proclamation of 1843, the fall of the churches or Babylon, and the midnight cry in 1844, were the work of God, and a perfect fulfilment of his pure word." Instead, they considered these movements "'a mistake,' the 'work of men,' 'mesmerism,' and 'of the Devil.'"

See: "The Third Angel's Message," *Present Truth,* April 1850, p. 65; EGWEnc, s.v. "Three Angels' Messages."

[6] **James Edson White** was 5 months old, born July 28, 1849.

[7] *Identity:* See Lt 5, 1849 (Apr. 21), note 25.

[8] Most likely a variant spelling of "Gardner." See Lt 5, 1849 (Apr. 21) and Lt 8, 1849 (May 29). This person has not been identified.

1850

(Ms 4, 1850)

JANUARY 28, OSWEGO, NEW YORK

"A Copy of E. G. White's Vision, Which She Had at Oswego, N.Y."

This manuscript is published in entirety in Ellen G. White, *Manuscript Releases,* vol. 16, pp. 30-35.

An urgent call for self-sacrifice. Views on conditional immortality and the millennium.

Last Sabbath evening the Lord gave me a view of many things, which I will now try to relate. I saw the people of God—some were dormant and stupid,[1] they were but half awake, and did not realize the time we were living in. I saw that the man with the "dirt brush"[2] had entered, and some were in danger of being swept away. I begged of Jesus to save them—to spare them a little longer, and to lift them up so that they could get a sight of their situation, before it should be forever too late. The angel said destruction is coming like a mighty whirlwind. I begged of the angel to pity, to save those who were attached to their possessions, and were not willing to cut loose from them, and distribute them to speed the messengers on their way to feed the hungry sheep, who were dying for want of spiritual food.

I could hardly bear the sight of the sheep dying for the want of saving, present truth, while some who professed to believe the present truth, were holding on to their property, and were letting them die, by withholding the necessary means to carry forward the work of God. As it was held up before me the sight was too painful, and I begged of the angel to take it away, and remove the painful sight from me. I saw that when the cause of God called for their property, they were sorrowful; as the young man was who had great possessions, and who inquired what he should do to inherit eternal life. I saw that very soon the overflowing scourge would pass over, and sweep their possessions all away; and then it will be too late to sacrifice earthly goods, and

---

[1] In the sense of "lethargic."

[2] "The man with the 'dirt-brush'" refers to a widely published dream William Miller had in 1847. In May 1850 James White republished the dream in *The Present Truth*, with appended footnotes. According to James White, "the man with the 'dirt-brush' represents the clear light of present truth . . . which is now purging the errors away from the remnant."

See: "Brother Miller's Dream," *Present Truth*, May 1850, p. 75. Also published in James White, ed., *Brother Miller's Dream*.

lay up a treasure in heaven.

I then saw the glorious Redeemer, beautiful and lovely. That He left the realms of glory, and came to this dark and lonely world, to give His precious life and die, the Just for the unjust. He bore the cruel mocking, and scourging, and wore the plaited crown of thorns, and sweat great drops of blood, while the burden of the sins of the whole world were upon Him. The angel asked, what for? I saw, I knew it was for us; for our sins He bore all this, that by His precious blood He might redeem us unto God.

Then again was held up before me those who were not willing to sell their possessions,[3] to save one fainting, starving soul; while Jesus stands before the Father pleading His blood, His sufferings and His death, for those souls, and while God's servants were waiting, ready to carry them the saving truth that they might be sealed with the seal of the living God,[4] and yet it was *hard* for some who profess to believe the present truth to even do so little as to hand the messengers God's own money, that He had lent them to be stewards over.

Then the suffering Jesus, His sacrifice, and love so deep as to give His life for them was again held up before me,—and then the lives of those who profess to be His followers: who had this world's goods, and counted it so great a thing to help on the cause of salvation. The angel said, can such enter heaven? Another answered, No, never! never! never! Those who are not interested in His cause here below, can never sing the song of redeeming love above. I saw that the quick work that God was doing on earth would soon be cut short in righteousness; and that the swift messengers must speed on their way. I heard the angel say, Are all messengers? No! no! God's messengers have a message.

I saw that the cause of God had been hindered and dishonored by some going who had no message. Such will have to give an account to God for every dollar they have used in traveling, where it was not their duty to go; for that money might have helped in the cause of God.[5] And for the lack of that very

---

[3] This passage does not necessarily support the interpretation "sell all your property—now." In reporting a vision given a year earlier Ellen White wrote, "God had not required all His people to dispose of their property at the same time, but in a time of need He would teach them . . . when to sell, and how much to sell."

See: Ellen G. White, Ms 3, 1849 (Jan. 18); *idem, A Sketch of the Christian Experience and Views of Ellen G. White,* p. 45. For further comment on this issue, see Ms 3, 1849 (Jan. 18), note 2, and Ms 14, 1850 (Sept.), note 2.

[4] *See:* EGWEnc, s.v. "Seal of God."

[5] This passage highlights the growing problem of "self-appointed" traveling preachers. In part it was a problem of maintaining unity of teaching and doctrine but also the financial problem of unsuitable "messengers" absorbing scarce donations for travel while legitimate preachers were sometimes unable to travel for lack of funds. The whole issue had been raised by Ellen and James White as early as 1848. According to John Loughborough a partial solution was found in 1853 by issuing approved preachers a card "simply stating that they were approved in the work of the gospel ministry . . . signed by two of the leading ministers." A full resolution to the problem would not come until the organization of the early 1860s.

See: Joseph Bates to Brother and Sister Hastings, Aug. 7, 1848; James White to Brother and

means which has been wasted, souls have starved to death, for the want of spiritual food, that might have been given them by God's called and chosen messengers.

The mighty shaking[6] has commenced, and is going on, and all will be shaken out, who are not willing to take a bold and unyielding stand, and sacrifice for God and His cause. The angel said, Think ye He will compel any to sacrifice and give up their possessions? No! no! It must be a freewill offering: it will take all to buy the field. While viewing these things, the burden seemed too heavy to be borne. I felt that I could have given my life, if it could be the means of helping any to see their awful situation.

I saw that professed friends had wounded the cause. Again I was compelled to cry for God to spare His people, some of whom were fainting and dying. Then I saw the judgments of Almighty God were speedily coming. I begged of the angel to speak in his language to the people, —said he, All the thunders and lightnings of Mount Sinai cannot move those who will not be moved by the plain truths in the Word of God; neither would an angel's message move or awake them. I saw that the rebels must and will be purged out. The angel said, Get ready, get ready, get ready.

I saw that the judgments were just upon us, and that the trouble would soon be to this land, and that blood would flow in streams. The angel said it will soon be even to the horses' bridles.[7] That was an awful time.

I saw that we must be willing to go alone, and that we must cut loose from every one that will not walk godly in Christ Jesus. I saw that the unbelief of brother or sister, father or mother, husband, wife or children was no excuse for any, to hinder them from doing their duty. And that those will lose their souls, if they seek to please their unbelieving friends, more than God, and they will be counted unworthy to be partakers of Christ's glory. I saw that Jesus was rejected by His own nation, and if Jesus suffered we must be partakers of His sufferings. Said the angel, *Cut clear, cut clear, cut clear* from everything or anyone that hinders thy progress. I saw that the ties of nature between man and wife, parents and children need not be severed. Still, those who believe God and His truth must obey God even if it displeased their nearest and dearest friend.

I saw that there would be no chance to get ready after Jesus leaves the most holy place, therefore we must get right now, while there is a chance;

Sister Collins, Sept. 8, 1849; J. N. Loughborough, *The Church, Its Organization, Order, and Discipline*, pp. 100, 101. For an overview of early developments toward church organization, see Andrew G. Mustard, *James White and SDA Organization: Historical Development, 1844-1881*, pp. 117-129.

[6] *See:* EGWEnc, s.v. "Shaking."

[7] Rev. 14:20: "And the winepress was trodden without the city, and blood came out of the winepress, even unto the horse bridles, by the space of a thousand and six hundred furlongs."

very soon it will be too late. I saw that God's people must press together and not be too willing to see faults in each other, for where there is union there is strength. I saw that the people of God were generally too dull, too dormant and unbelieving. The angel said, Watch, *watch, watch.* I saw a crown of glory laid up for those who make a covenant with God by sacrifice. I saw that a sacrifice would not increase, but decrease and consume. I was then pointed to him who had defied the armies of Israel, that truth would overcome error, and that light would shine out of darkness.

I was then pointed to the beauty and loveliness of Jesus. Upon His head were crowns, a crown within a crown. His robe was whiter than the whitest white. No language can describe His glory, and His exalted loveliness. All, all who keep the commandments of God, will enter in through the gates into the city and have right to the tree of life and ever be in the presence of that lovely Jesus whose countenance shines brighter than the sun at noon day.

I then saw the Word of God pure and unadulterated, and that we must answer for the way we received the truth proclaimed from that Word. I saw that it had been a hammer to break the flinty heart in pieces, and a fire to consume the dross and tin, that the heart might be pure and holy. I saw that the Apocrypha was the hidden book, and that the wise of these last days should understand it.[8] I saw that the Bible was the standard book, that will judge us at the last day. I saw that heaven would be cheap enough, and that nothing was too dear to sacrifice for Jesus, and that we must give all to enter the kingdom. I heard an angel say, Think ye God will place His seal where there is an idol? No, no.

Then I was pointed to Adam and Eve in the garden of Eden. They partook of the forbidden tree and then the flaming swords were placed around the tree of life, and they were driven out of the garden of Eden, lest they should partake of the tree of life and be immortal sinners. I saw that the tree of life was to perpetuate immortality. I heard the angel say, who of the family of Adam have passed those flaming swords, and partaken of that tree? I heard another angel answer, *Not one* of the family of Adam have passed those flaming swords and partaken of the tree of life, therefore there is not an immortal sinner. The soul that sinneth it shall *die* an everlasting death, a death that lasts *forever,* where there is no *hope* of a resurrection, and then the wrath of God will be appeased.[9]

---

[8] The significance of this obscure but fascinating statement on the Apocrypha has occasioned considerable discussion, primarily regarding what status it might accord the Apocrypha. Ellen White never subsequently commented on the subject except to consistently uphold the primacy of Scripture. For two somewhat different interpretations, see Denis Fortin, "Sixty-six Books—or Eighty-one? Did Ellen White Recommend the Apocrypha?" *Review*, Mar. 28, 2002, p. 9; Ron Graybill, "Under the Triple Eagle. Early Adventist Use of the Apocrypha," *Adventist Heritage,* Winter 1987, pp. 25-32. See also EGWEnc, s.v. "Apocrypha."

[9] *See:* SDAE, s.v. "Immortality."

I then saw the holy city, and that we should rest in the city, through the 1000 years,[10] and reign as kings and priests unto God. Then Jesus will descend upon the Mount of Olives, and the mount will part asunder and become a mighty plain for the Paradise of God to rest upon. The rest of the earth will not be cleansed until the wicked dead are raised and come up around the city at the end of the 1000 years. Then fire will come down from God out of heaven and devour them, burn them up root and branch. Satan is the root, and his children are the branches. Then the same fire that will devour the wicked will purify the earth. I saw that the feet of the wicked would never desecrate the earth made new. All the immortality we now have is by faith in hope of immortality at the appearing of Christ.

January 28, 1850

---

[10] The visions of the millennium presented here and in Ms 14, 1850 (Sept.), constitute the earliest comprehensive vision views of the millennium.

See: Lt 1, 1845 (Dec. 20), note 16, and Lt 2, 1847 (Apr. 21), note 4; EGWEnc, s.v. "Millennium."

1850

(Lt 4, 1850)

[FEBRUARY 18, OSWEGO, NEW YORK][1]

LETTER TO

Philip and Nancy Collins.[2]

Portions of this letter are published in Ellen G. White, *Manuscript Releases,* vol. 1, p. 31; vol. 5, p. 91; vol. 6, p. 339.

News to friends of recent travels, of publishing work, and of their move to Oswego, New York.

Dear Bro. and Sister Collins:

We were very glad to hear from you[3] that you were striving to be overcomers by the blood of the Lamb and the word of your testimony. Be bold in the cause of God. Do not falter. God loves bold soldiers and they will get the victory. Oh how good is the Lord to us! Can we doubt His goodness for a moment? No, no. His watchful care has been over us or we should have fallen out by the way.

We do not want you to feel, Brother Collins, that you cannot write us unless you can send us some money. No, no. Write us. We are just as glad to hear from you as though you sent us ever so much money. The way is now fully open for James to go forward in publishing *The Present Truth.*[4] We love

---

[1] The day, month, and place of writing are derived from the postmark on the letter, which reads "Oswego, N.Y. Feb. 18." The year, 1850, can be inferred in different ways. The fact that the letter is written in Oswego in February and discusses the continued publication of *The Present Truth* points unambiguously to 1850 because *The Present Truth* was published in Oswego only between December 1849 and May 1850.

[2] *Identity*: The letter identifies the addressee as "Phillip [*sic*] Collins, New Bedford, Mass." The name of Philip's wife, Nancy, can be obtained from the 1850 census and other sources.

See: 1850 U.S. Federal Census, "Nancy Collins," Massachusetts, Bristol County, Dartmouth, p. 442.

[3] None of the letters from Philip and Nancy Collins to the Whites has been preserved. Six letters from either James or Ellen White to the Collins family are on file, dating back to 1846.

See: James White to Philip and Nancy Collins: Aug. 26, 1846; Sept. 8, 1849; Jan. 28, 1850; Feb. 18, 1850. Ellen G. White, Lt 7, 1849 (Sept.); Lt 4, 1850 (Feb. 18).

[4] The first issue of *The Present Truth* was published by James White in July 1849. Although financial contributions from readers had at first more than covered costs, by the end of the year the periodical was in debt. Further, his close coworker, Joseph Bates, opposed the whole project; "Brother Bates discouraged me about the paper and I gave it up forever." The turning point that turned James White from his discouragement was Ellen White's vision of January 9, 1850. He wrote on January 10: "Last night we had a wonderful, powerful time here at Brother

you and love to hear from you. We should have written you before but we have had no certain abiding place, but have traveled in rain, snow and blow with the child from place to place.[5] I could not get time to answer any letters and it took all James' time to write for the paper and get out the hymn book.[6] We do not have many idle moments. Now we are settled, I can have more time to write.

Do not let the suggestions of Satan hold you down. Be of good cheer. The Lord is coming to reward His faithful children. Be diligent to make your calling and election sure.

Let us not rest unless we have the abiding witness that our ways please God. Souls are coming out upon the truth all around here. They are those who have not heard the Advent doctrine and some of them are those who went forth to meet the Bridegroom in 1844, but since that time have been deceived by false shepherds until they did not know where they were or what they believed.[7]

Much love to the children and yourselves.

James has gone to the Office.

In haste.

B. C. Stoors. . . . Ellen had the following view in relation to the 'Present Truth.' I [Ellen] saw the paper, and that it was needed. . . . I saw that God did not want James to stop yet; but he must write, write, write, write, and speed the message and let it go."

See: Ellen G. White, *Spiritual Gifts [vol. 2],* p. 116; James White, "The Paper," *Present Truth,* December 1849, p. 47; James White to Leonard Hastings, Jan. 10, 1850; EGWEnc, s.v. "*Present Truth.*"

[5] From the time **James Edson White** was 6 weeks old he had traveled with his parents from place to place in New England and western New York during the autumn and early winter of 1849. In late November or December 1849 they settled in Oswego, New York. "We rented a house in Oswego, and borrowed articles from our brethren, and commenced house-keeping."

See: Ellen G. White, *Spiritual Gifts [vol. 2],* pp. 116-122.

[6] *Hymns, for God's Peculiar People, That Keep the Commandments of God, and the Faith of Jesus,* compiled by James White, was first advertised for sale the following month in the March 1850 issue of *The Present Truth.* It contained the words for 53 hymns and sold for 12 1/2 cents.

See: James White, compiler, *Hymns, for God's Peculiar People;* "Hymns for God's Peculiar People . . . ," *Present Truth,* March 1850, p. 64.

[7] Sabbatarian Adventism in western New York, where the Whites were located at this time, was experiencing remarkable growth. Writing three months earlier, James White enthusiastically reported that "in Western N.Y. the number of Sabbath keepers is increasing fast. There are more than twice the number now than six months ago." Of particular interest here is the observation that some of the new believers "are those who have not heard the Advent doctrine." This indicates a broadening view of the scope of mission as compared to earlier evangelism, which focused on reaching other Adventists who had passed through the Millerite movement.

See: James White to "Brother Bowles," Nov. 8, 1849; introductory article "The 'Shut Door' and Ellen White's Visions"; EGWEnc, s.v. "Shut Door."

1850

(Lt 10, 1850)

MARCH 18, OSWEGO, NEW YORK

LETTER TO

Leonard W. Hastings.[1]

This letter is published in entirety in Ellen G. White, *Manuscript Releases,* vol. 14, pp. 52-54.

A letter of comfort to a close friend, Leonard Hastings, whose wife had just died, aged 42, leaving him alone with six children.

Dear Brother Hastings:

I hardly know what to say to you. The news of your wife's death was to me overwhelming. I could hardly believe it and can hardly believe it now.[2] God gave me a view last Sabbath night which I will write.

I saw God gave Brother Bates [**Joseph Bates**][3] a dream which if he had followed, he would have been with you in your wife's distress; and if Brother Chamberlain [**Ezra L. H. Chamberlain**][4] had not been with him, he would have gone to God alone, and he would have seen by the dream and by the

---

[1] *Identity:* The letter is addressed "Leonard Hastings, New Ipswich, N.H."

[2] Ellen White had a strong friendship with Elvira Hastings. "Especially was the heart of sister Hastings knit with mine, as were David's and Jonathan's," she wrote in her autobiography. "Our union was not marred while she lived."

See: Ellen G. White, *Spiritual Gifts [vol. 2],* p. 111.

[3] *Identity:* Other than the well-known Joseph Bates, several other Bateses are mentioned in the *Review* in the period up to the end of 1852: "Daniel Bates," "W. Bates," "Peter Bates," and "M. R. Bates." Nevertheless, there are indications that Ellen White is referring to Joseph Bates here. The connection between Bates and the Hastingses alluded to in this letter can be confirmed in the existing three personal letters from Joseph Bates to Leonard and Elvira Hastings during the period 1848-1849. It is also clear from James White's correspondence that Joseph Bates had visited the Hastingses in New Ipswich, New Hampshire, during the autumn of 1849. In addition, the connection between Bates and Chamberlain indicated in this letter corresponds well with the movements of Joseph Bates and lay preacher E.L.H. Chamberlain who, during the period 1849-1851, interacted several times on committees and meetings.

See: Search term "Bates," "Hastings," and "Chamberlain" in *Words of the Pioneers;* James White to Leonard and Elvira Hastings, Jan. 3, 1850.

[4] The only Chamberlain mentioned in the early Sabbatarian papers (*The Present Truth, The Advent Review, The Advent Review and Sabbath Herald)* prior to 1852 is E.L.H. Chamberlain, of Middletown, Connecticut. The likelihood that Ellen White was writing to E.L.H. Chamberlain is increased by the fact that she describes him in this letter as a preacher (even though "it was not his duty to travel"), which matches the description in the *Review* of his preaching activities.

See: Search term "Chamberlain" in *Words of the Pioneers.*

drawings of the Spirit that he must come directly to your house when Satan had got your wife in his grasp, and by faith in God would have wrenched her from the power of the enemy. But he leaned upon Brother Chamberlain some for duty and followed his impressions instead of the light God gave him in the dream.

I saw it was for no wrong of yours that she was taken away, but if Brother Bates had come directly to your house, she would have been rescued from the grasp of the enemy.

I saw they did wrong in afflicting the afflicted by reproving you for having the funeral on the Sabbath. I saw they had better been looking at themselves and seeing where they had erred from the path of duty that God had marked out for them to go in.

I saw that she was sealed and would come up at the voice of God and stand upon the earth, and would be with the 144,000. I saw we need not mourn for her; she would rest in the time of trouble,[5] and all that we could mourn for was our loss in being deprived of her company. I saw her death would result in good.

I warn Arabella [**Harriet Arabella Hastings**][6] and the rest of the children to prepare to meet Jesus, and then they will meet their mother again, never more to be parted. O children, will you heed her faithful warning that she gave you while she was with you, and let not all her prayers that she has offered up to God for you, be as water spilt upon the ground? Get ready to meet Jesus and all will be well. Give your hearts to God and do not rest a day unless you know that you love Jesus.[7]

Dear brother, we have prayed to God to gird you up and strengthen you to sustain your loss. God will be with you and uphold you. Only have faith. God has shown me about Brother Chamberlain that it was not his duty to travel. I saw his company was pleasant while he [was] with us, but when he was gone everything was gone. He had not left any truth from the Word of God for the mind to feast upon and had left nothing at all substantial, but everything had gone when he went. I saw he was not one of the messengers.[8]

---

[5] *See:* EGWEnc, s.v. "Seal of God"; "144,000"; "Time of Trouble."

[6] Arabella was about 17 at the time of her mother's death and the oldest of six children. Her full name is given as "Harriet A. Hastings" in her 1854 obituary. Ellen White in her correspondence sometimes referred to her as "Arabella" and sometimes as "Harriet" (cf. Lt 5, 1849 [Apr. 21], and Lt 10, 1850 [Mar. 18], with Lt 7, 1851 [July 27], and Lt 3, 1851 [Aug. 11]). Presumably the middle initial "A" in the obituary stands for "Arabella."

See: Obituary: "Harriet A. Hastings," *Review,* Sept. 5, 1854, p. 31; 1850 U.S. Federal Census, "Harriet A. Hastings," New Hampshire, Hillsborough County, New Ipswich, p. 272.

[7] James White reported that three months later, on June 22, 1850, while on a visit to New Ipswich, New Hampshire, he baptized four of the oldest Hastings children.

See: W. [James White], "Our Tour East," *Advent Review,* August 1850, p. 14; Ellen G. White, *Spiritual Gifts [vol. 2],* pp. 111, 112.

[8] Another vision given in 1852 reinforced the message here discouraging Chamberlain

Dear Brother Hastings, sorrow not as those who have no hope. The grave can hold her but a little while. Hope thou in God and cheer up, dear brother, and you will meet her in a little while. We will not cease to pray for the blessings of God to rest upon your family and you. God will be your sun and your shield. He will stand by you in this your deep affliction and trial. Endure the trial well and you will receive a crown of glory with your companion at the appearing of Jesus. Hold fast truth, and you will be crowned with her with glory, honor, immortality and eternal life.

Give my love to Sister Gorham [**Elizabeth Gorham**][9] and all the saints. Much love to you and your dear children.

---

from assuming responsibilities as a traveling preacher. The case of Chamberlain illustrates the growing problem of "self-appointed" traveling preachers in this early period.

See: Ellen G. White, Lt 4, 1852 (Oct. 25); Ms 4, 1850 (Jan. 28), note 5.

[9] *Identity:* See Lt 5, 1849 (Apr. 21), note 25.

1850

MARCH 1850

"My Dear Brethren and Sisters."

Article published in *The Present Truth,* vol. 1, no. 8, March 1850, p. 64.

1850

APRIL 15, 1850

Date given for an unauthenticated vision. See Appendix A.

1850

APRIL 1850

"To the 'Little Flock.'"

Article published in *The Present Truth,* vol. 1, no. 9, April 1850, pp. 71, 72.

1850

MAY 1850

Message to Eli Curtis.

Article published in *The Present Truth,* vol. 1, no. 10, May 1850, p. 80.

1850

(Ms 5, 1850)

[JULY 29, OSWEGO, NEW YORK][1]

"A Vision the Lord Gave Me in Oswego, July 29, 1850."

Portions of this manuscript are published in Ellen G. White, *Manuscript Releases,* vol. 18, pp. 10-13.

General exhortation; warnings against spiritualism; instruction on rebaptism; the cases of Richard Gorsline and R. R. Chapin.

I saw some in Zion[2] that were languishing; they were dormant and unbelieving. I asked the angel if Zion should languish. Said the angel, She is rising never to fall again. God has stretched out His hand the second time to recover the remnant of His people.[3] I saw some that meet together at the conferences at Oswego [New York] and vicinity were not right. They do not partake of the spirit of the lovely Jesus; they have not vital godliness, and unless they soon partake of the spirit of Jesus and have their hearts sanctified by the truth they profess to believe, they will be purged out of the camp of Israel. I saw there needed to be a searching of heart among them.

Said the angel, Thou art upon the enchanted ground.[4] Dost thou not see it? Awake and arise and put on the strength of the Lord. The powers of darkness are rising. Art thou rising? Is it not getting the victory over thee? I was pointed back to the children of Israel in Egypt. I saw when God worked through Moses before Pharaoh, the magicians came up and said they could do the same, (that they could work the same miracles). I saw the same work was going on now on the earth that the magicians carried on anciently. I saw

---

[1] This is the date and place of the vision according to the title given in the source document. The date and place of this manuscript is not known, but it was probably written in Oswego, New York, within a few days of the vision.

[2] "Zion" here used in metaphorical sense to denote the people of God.

[3] Cf. Isa. 11:11, 12: "And it shall come to pass in that day, that the Lord shall set his hand again the second time to recover the remnant of his people. . . . And he shall . . . gather together the dispersed of Judah from the four corners of the earth."

[4] An allusion to the allegorical "Enchanted Ground" found in John Bunyan's *Pilgrim's Progress.* Of all the dangers awaiting Christian pilgrims on their journey, none are greater than those facing them in the Enchanted Ground, where the very air makes travelers drowsy, inviting a sleep from which there will be no awakening.

See: John Bunyan, *The Pilgrim's Progress,* p. 209.

the signs and mighty wonders of the devil have increased within a few months ten fold and it will still be on the increase and spread.[5] And unless Israel is constantly rising and is growing in grace and in the knowledge of the truth, the powers of darkness will get the victory over them.

I saw we must be daily rising and keep the ascendancy above the powers of darkness. I saw singing to the glory of God often drove the enemy away and shouting would beat him back and give us the victory.[6] I saw there was too little glorifying God, too little childlike simplicity among the remnant. I asked the angel why there was not more faith and power in Israel. Said he, Ye let go of the arm of God too quick. Press your petitions to the throne and hold on by living faith. Believe ye receive the things ye ask for, and ye *shall have them.*

I was then pointed to Elijah. He was subject to like passions as we are, and he prayed earnestly. His faith endured the trial. Seven times he prayed before the Lord, and at last the cloud was seen. I saw we had doubted and wounded Jesus by our unbelief. God's people are rising, said the angel, never to fall again. Be careful said the angel, lest the branches be cut off and others are raised up in their stead. I saw some would bear fruit and work to the glory of God. I saw we must keep close to Jesus and fast and pray if we could not get the victory over the powers of darkness.

I then saw Brother Gorsline [**Richard Gorsline**],[7] that he had wounded and torn the hearts of God's people. I saw he had been stubborn and rebellious,

---

[5] The language of this paragraph seems to be a general reference to spiritualism. The "rappings" in the house of the Fox sisters in Hydesville, near Rochester, New York, had first started on March 31, 1848. See Ellen White's vision of March 24, 1849, for her earliest extant warning against the phenomenon (Ms 1, 1849 [Mar. 24]). It was not until November 1849, however, when the first public demonstrations of spirit contact took place in Corinthian Hall, Rochester, that spiritualism began to sweep the country "like a prairie fire." This would harmonize well with Ellen White's statement here, some eight months later, that "the signs and mighty wonders of the devil have increased within a few months ten fold."

For one account of the rapid spread of spiritualism in 1849 and the early 1850s, see Paul Kurtz, *The Transcendental Temptation,* pp. 322-325.

[6] *See:* Appendix article "Ellen White and Religious Enthusiasm in Early Adventist Experience"; EGWEnc, s.v. "Ecstatic Experiences." See also cautions in the vision of December 25, 1850 (Ms 11, 1850) against "unhealthy and unnecessary" excitement.

[7] *Identity:* Ellen White is probably referring to "R. Gorsline," who is the only "Gorsline" mentioned in the *Review* during the period 1850-1863 for whom a first name is given. James White at a later date records that "Richard Gorsline" left a legacy to the church of $470.87. Census records for 1850 indicate a "Richard Gorsline" living in Oswego, New York, whose age corresponds with that found in Richard Gorsline's obituary in the *Review*. Taken together, these items indicate strongly that Ellen White is referring to Richard Gorsline of Oswego, New York.

See: Search term "Gorsline" in *Words of the Pioneers*; Eld. James White, *An Appeal to the Working Men and Women in the Ranks of Seventh-day Adventists,* p. 52; 1850 U.S. Federal Census, "Richard Gorsline," New York, Oswego, Oswego City, Ward 2, p. 170; obituary: "Richard Gorsline," *Review,* July 19, 1864, p. 63.

and unless he changed his course entirely, the church should disfellowship him, for he has been a dead weight to the church.

Said the angel, Jesus' work is almost finished in the sanctuary. It is no time to be stupid[8] now; a quick work will the Lord do upon the earth, the four angels will soon let go the four winds.[9] Said the angel, Beware how thou treadest enchantment all around thee, East and West, North and South. If Satan can get thee to slumber now, he is sure of his prey. I saw some in Israel had been half starved for food, and when the present truth[10] was presented to them they ate it with thankfulness and gratitude like half-starved children.

Said the angel, Can ye stand in the battle in the day of the Lord? Ye need to be washed and live in newness of life. (Then I saw those whose hands are now engaged in making up the breach and are standing in the gaps[11] that have formally, since '44, broken the commandments of God and have so far followed the Pope as to keep the first day instead of the seventh, would have to go down into the water and be baptized in the faith of the shut door and keeping the commandments of God, and in the faith of Jesus[12] coming to sit on the throne of His father David and to redeem Israel. I also saw those who have been baptized as a door into the professed churches will have to be baptized out of that door again,[13] and into the faith mentioned above, and all who have not been baptized since '44 will have to be baptized before Jesus comes, and some will not gain progress now until that duty is done and then they must live anew unto God and serve him faithfully.)

Said the angel, Will ye sink and let others take the stars to your crown? I told the angel I could not endure to see any in Israel sinking. Thou Advocate,

---

[8] In the sense of "lethargic."

[9] The loosing of the "four winds" (cf. Rev. 7:1) indicates the time when Christ's intercession has ceased, general probation has closed, and a "time of trouble" begins. "I saw that the four angels would hold the four winds until Jesus' work was done in the sanctuary, then the seven last plagues will be poured out" (Ms 2, 1849 [Jan. 17]).

See: EGWEnc, s.v. "Plagues, Seven Last"; "Time of Trouble."

[10] *See:* EGWEnc, s.v. "Present Truth."

[11] An allusion to the theme of restoration and, in particular, the restoration of true Sabbath observance, found in Isaiah 58:12: "Thou shalt be called, The repairer of the breach, The restorer of paths to dwell in." As early as 1846 Sabbatarian Adventists saw their task as that of restoring long-neglected truths, including the Sabbath, before the Second Advent.

See: P. Gerard Damsteegt, *Foundations of the Seventh-day Adventist Message and Mission*, pp. 138, 139, 250-253.

[12] Damsteegt notes that "the phrase 'the Sabbath and the shut door' was frequently used" at this time "to identify the specific theological position of Sabbatarian Adventists." See also his discussion of the integration of Sabbath, shut door, and sanctuary in the visions of Ellen White after 1849.

See: Ibid., pp. 153-155; introductory article "The 'Shut Door' and Ellen White's Visions"; EGWEnc, s.v. "Shut Door."

[13] *See:* EGWEnc, s.v. "Baptism."

save the purchase of Thy blood. What more can we do for Thee? Oh, that we had more to give to the lovely Jesus; more to render to Him for His merciful kindness unto us. We will do anything, we will go anywhere, only lend us strength from the Sanctuary.

The angel said, Some tried too hard to believe; faith is so simple ye look above it. Satan has deceived some and got them to looking at their own unworthiness. I saw they must look away from self to the worthiness of Jesus and throw themselves just as they are, needy and dependent and unworthy, upon His mercy and draw by faith, strength and nourishment from Him.

Said the angel, The desolations of Zion are accomplished. I saw he took away the first and established the second, that is, those who were in the faith would become rebellious and be purged out and others who had not heard the Advent doctrine and rejected it would embrace the truth and take their places.[14]

Said the angel, Will ye lack faith? Climb up; take hold; never let go of the promises of God, for they are sure. Ye have been discouraged too quick.

I begged strength of the angel as I saw I must come back to this world. I covenanted to live unto God. I begged of the angel not to let me feel again the awful anguish of seeing some in Israel sinking. He said strength should be given me to endure all that God should lay upon me.

I then saw Brother Chapin [**Roderick R. Chapin**][15] that he had been rescued from the jaws of the lion as a bird is rescued from the snare of the fowler. I saw God had felt after him while he was in darkness and he had but just escaped with the skin of his teeth and all his work at Hamilton [New York] must be taken back before he can gain progress. I saw he must make square work for eternity. I saw his soul was worth more than ten thousand worlds like this. I did praise and adore God that He had borne with Bro.

---

[14] It is of interest that the affirmation, some paragraphs earlier, of "the faith of the shut door and keeping the commandments of God" is followed by this recognition of accessions to the movement of those "who had not heard the Advent doctrine and rejected it." This highlights the need for careful analysis of how Ellen White and others used the term "shut door."

See: Introductory article "The 'Shut Door' and Ellen White's Visions"; EGWEnc, s.v. "Shut Door."

[15] *Identity:* Although several persons with the surname "Chapin" appear in the *Review* during the 1850s, all seven mentions of "Chapin" for whom first names are given during the period before 1852 are of "R. R. Chapin." Therefore it is likely that this is the person Ellen White is addressing. By 1854 R. R. Chapin had joined the oppositional "Messenger Party" and several of his letters appear in *The Messenger of Truth* signed "R. R. Chapin, Greece, New York." The 1850 census for Greece lists his name as "Roderick Chapin."

See: Search term "Chapin" in *Words of the Pioneers*; Joseph Bates, "From Bro. Bates," *Review*, Aug. 15, 1854, p. 6; R. R. Chapin, "Who Are the Remnant," *The Messenger of Truth*, Oct. 19, 1854, p. 2; 1850 U.S. Federal Census, "Roderick Chapin," New York, Monroe County, Greece, p. 153.

Chapin and finally had stretched out His arm in that dark spot and brought him to the light that he might discover the darkness he had been in.[16]

This is written in haste. Excuse bad writing.

---

[16] There is no indication here or elsewhere of the nature of the "darkness" that R. R. Chapin had been involved in. It may be that Chapin's problems in 1850 were similar to those that led to his break with the movement in 1854, which included the rejection of Ellen White's visions. *See:* EGWEnc, s.v. "*Messenger* Party."

1850

(Ms 5a, 1850)

[JULY, EAST HAMILTON, NEW YORK][1]

"To the Church in Your Place."

This manuscript is published in entirety in Ellen G. White, *Manuscript Releases,* vol. 21, pp. 237, 238.

To the church in East Hamilton, New York, and vicinity: a call to vanquish evil by giving praise and glory to God.

To the church in your place.[2] What God showed me while I was with you.[3] I saw that you had been sinking, growing dormant and unbelieving. I also saw that you have not glorified God, as you should have done, by offering praise. I saw that the powers of darkness had been getting the victory over you.

I was then pointed to Sister Abbey's mother[4] and saw she had never been one of us. I saw her approaching Brother and Sister Abbey and saying "The Lord saith" when He had not spoken, and telling things which she said God had shown her, that she had spun out of her own bowels to get her desires accomplished. I saw she had laid her hand upon everything like the power of God, especially singing and shouting. This troubled the evil spirit in her, and she had laid her hand upon it to stop it.

I saw [that] Satan had worked through her effectually to bind God's children. When one had attempted to make an effort to rise and get the victory, the rest were like loadstones to drag him down. I saw you should rise together, and unitedly get the victory over the powers of darkness and sing

---

[1] This information is based on a handwritten copy of the manuscript, not in Ellen White's hand, which has the following words on the back: "Vision of E. G. White seen at East Hamilton, July 1850." Thus the place and date refer to the receipt of the vision, whereas writing it out presumably occurred shortly thereafter.

[2] I.e., East Hamilton and vicinity. See note 1.

[3] Ellen and James White had visited nearby Hamilton July 20-22, 1850, on their return journey to Oswego, New York, after a 10-week itinerary through New York, several New England states, and Canada East.

See: W. [James White], "Our Tour East," *Advent Review,* August 1850, p. 15.

[4] There appear to have been two Sabbathkeeping Abbey families living in the vicinity of East Hamilton—Alonzo and Diana Abbey in nearby Madison, and **Ira** and **Rhoda Abbey** in Brookfield, only a few miles distant. Whether the "Sister Abbey" Ellen White refers to here is Diana or Rhoda Abbey has not been established with certainty.

See: 1850 U.S. Federal Census, "Alonzo Abbey," New York, Madison County, Madison, p. 53; 1850 U.S. Federal Census, "Ira Abbey," New York, Madison County, Brookfield, p. 83; search term "Abbey" in *Words of the Pioneers.*

and shout to the glory of God.[5]

I saw that we are the only people upon earth from whom God is to get glory, and if we should hold our peace the very stones would cry out, for God must receive glory from some of those who dwell upon the earth. The only company who can praise and honor God, I saw, are those who are keeping the commandments of God and have the faith of Jesus.

Then a kernel of corn was held up before me with the chit gone. The body of the corn I saw was there, but the life was gone. Said the angel, "It can produce no fruit because the life is gone. There is danger of having the form without the power. A theory of faith will not save you; vital godliness you must have, the life and power of religion in the soul."

I saw that Satan had agents to work through, and his angels to operate upon these agents that they might receive strength from Satan to get the victory over God's people and triumph over them. I saw that the powers of darkness are rising constantly, for Satan has come down in great power knowing that his time is short, and I saw that unless you are rising daily, and growing in grace, strength, and knowledge of the truth, the powers of darkness will get the victory over you. If ever there was a time when we should be wide awake in the cause of God it is now; you must keep the ascendancy above the powers of darkness.

Singing, I saw, often drove away the enemy and shouting would beat him back. I saw that pride had crept in among you, and there was not childlike simplicity among you. The fear of man, I saw, must all go.

I saw that the reason you have been in such bondage is that you are under the influence of the spirit of Grandmother,[6] some more and some less, and that you must go down into the water and be baptized and live in newness of life unto God.

You must rebuke every particle of that spirit and come out entirely from it, assert your liberty in the name of the Lord, be free, and stand in the liberty of the sons of God.

I saw that you should take hold of the work of the Lord with as much energy as you would take hold of your daily labor, and serve God heartily as though you loved to serve Him and as though it was your delight. When you get down before God, wrestle with Him until you get the victory and can shout victory over the powers of darkness.

This is the amount of the vision. Some parts of it might have escaped my mind, but I have written all I could remember except the individuals' cases; them I delivered when with you, and you will remember them no doubt. Now

---

[5] See cautions against "unhealthy and unnecessary excitement" in the vision of December 25, 1850 (Ms 11, 1850). See also Appendix article "Ellen White and Religious Enthusiasm in Early Adventist Experience"; EGWEnc, s.v. "Ecstatic Experiences."

[6] Probably a reference to "Sister Abbey's mother" mentioned in the second paragraph.

do, do stand in the liberty. Some of you I feel are free, and I hope if you are not all free, that you will rise now and lift up your heads and rejoice in God.

Praise the Lord, dear children, as much as you please, for praise is comely for the upright. You have enough to praise Him for; He has redeemed you by His most precious blood, and is soon to save you with an everlasting salvation. Finally, Brethren, be at peace among yourselves.

Hiram Edson

1850

(Lt 8, 1850)

AUGUST 4, CENTERPORT, NEW YORK

LETTER TO

Harriet Arabella Hastings.[1]

This letter is published in entirety in Ellen G. White, *Manuscript Releases,* vol. 19, pp. 129-132.

Letter to 17-year-old Arabella Hastings, eldest of six children whose mother had recently died. It contains news, accounts of several visions, and encouragement to the bereaved family.

Dear Sister Arabella:

This is the first opportunity I have had to write you since we left you. We have been traveling just as fast as we could go since we left your place. We have not allowed ourselves time to rest or hardly time to sleep. We have felt that the King's business required haste, that what we did must be done quickly. God gave us a victorious time on our journey. The truth triumphed. I will not write the particulars of our journey for you will have it in the paper.[2]

The Lord showed me that he, James [**James Springer White**], must take the testimonies that the leading Adventists published in 1844 and republish them and make *them* ashamed.[3] He is now doing that work.[4] Then the Lord

---

[1] The letter is addressed "Harriet A. Hastings, New Ipswich, N.H." Presumably the initial "A" stands for "Arabella." Ellen White in her letters sometimes refers to her as "Arabella" and sometimes as "Harriet" (cf. Lt 5, 1849 [Apr. 21], and Lt 10, 1850 [Mar. 18], with Lt 7, 1851 [July 27], and Lt 3, 1851 [Aug. 11]).

[2] James White reported on "Our Tour East" in *The Advent Review* of August 1850. During their 10-week itinerary starting from Oswego, New York, on May 15, the Whites had traveled some 1,500 miles (2,400 kilometers) through Maine, Massachusetts, New Hampshire, Vermont, and Canada East. Somewhere during the second half of June they had visited the Hastings family in New Ipswich, New Hampshire. Ellen White's pleasure at the results of the trip are matched in the words of James in a letter to a friend: "I saw tenfold more accomplished than I looked for in Vt. and C.E."

See: W. [James White], "Our Tour East," *Advent Review,* August 1850, pp. 14, 15; James White to Leonard Hastings, July 21, 1850; Ellen G. White, *Life Sketches,* pp. 132, 133. For further reading on this visit and the expansion of Adventism in Canada, see Denis Fortin, *Adventism in Quebec,* esp. pp. 61, 62.

[3] The date of this vision is not known, but James White had mentioned it in a letter already two weeks earlier, on July 21, 1850.

See: James White to Leonard Hastings, July 21, 1850.

[4] During August, September, and November of 1850 James White published several issues

showed me we must go east again. Last Monday evening while at Brother Lillis's [**Henry Lillis, Jr.**][5] (Brethren Rhodes [**Samuel W. Rhodes**], Lillis, Edson [**Hiram Edson**] and Harris [**William Harris**] present) I was greatly distressed for some in Israel. The burden was heavy. The brethren prayed the Lord to roll off the burden, and I was taken off in vision, a little of which I will write you.[6]

I saw the powers of darkness were rising. Satan has come down in great power, knowing that his time is short. Said the angel, as he pointed to Israel, "Art thou rising? Thou art upon the enchanted ground.[7] Dost thou not see it? Awake and arise and put on the strength of the Lord." I was pointed back to the children of Israel in Egypt. I saw when God worked through Moses before Pharaoh the magicians came up and said they could do the same. I saw the same work was now going on in the world and among the professed churches similar to the work of the magicians anciently. I saw the power of the magicians has increased tenfold, within a few months, and it will still be on the increase and spread, and unless Israel is rising and increasing in power and strength and is growing in grace and in the knowledge of the truth, the powers of darkness will get the victory over them.[8] I saw we must be

---

of *The Advent Review*. It contained mostly reprints of articles by prominent Millerite leaders such as William Miller and J. B. Cook written in 1844 and 1845 supporting the prophetic significance of October 22, 1844. Articles on the Sabbath and sanctuary by Cook and O.R.L. Crosier also were included. The overall effect was to demonstrate that in several ways leading Millerites had departed from the faith they had held in the mid-1840s.

See: Advent Review, August-November 1850; *Advent Review [Extra],* September 1850.

[5] *Identity:* It is very likely that Ellen White is here speaking of Henry Lillis, Jr., of Oswego, New York. There are two indications that this is the case. First, it is clear that "Brother Lillis" lived in Oswego, since we know that Ellen White was in Oswego on that "Monday evening" (i.e., July 29, 1850—see Ms 5, 1850). Second, we are told that the meeting took place in the Lillis home. There is some evidence that Henry Lillis's home was used for meetings.

See: O.R.L. Crosier, "Brief Tour: Oswego-Auburn-Seneca Falls-Geneva," *Advent Harbinger and Bible Advocate,* Aug. 16, 185, p. 70; [James White], "The Cause Wounded," *Review,* Aug. 19, 1851, p. 11.

[6] For Ellen White's first account of this vision, see Ms 5, 1850, headed "A Vision the Lord Gave Me in Oswego, July 29, 1850."

[7] An allusion to the allegorical "Enchanted Ground" found in John Bunyan's *Pilgrim's Progress.* Of all the dangers awaiting Christian pilgrims on their journey, none are greater than those facing them in the Enchanted Ground, where the very air makes travelers drowsy, inviting a sleep from which there will be no awakening.

See: John Bunyan, *The Pilgrim's Progress,* p. 209.

[8] It is likely that in this paragraph Ellen White is referring to the recent and rapid rise of spiritualism. The language is very similar to that of her report of a vision given three weeks later on August 24 (Ms 7, 1850) which makes explicit mention of the "rappings" and of spiritualism. The rappings in the house of the Fox sisters in Hydesville, near Rochester, New York, had first started on March 31, 1848. Ellen White's first extant warning concerning them was her March 24, 1849, vision (see Ms 1, 1849). It was not until November 1849, however, when the first public demonstration of spirit contact took place in Corinthian Hall, Rochester, that spiritualism began to sweep the country "like a prairie fire." This would harmonize well with Ellen White's statement here that "the power of the magicians has increased tenfold, within a

constantly rising and keep the ascendency above the powers of darkness. I saw singing to the glory of God often drove the enemy, and shouting would beat him back and give us the victory.[9] I saw there was too little glorifying God in Israel and too little child-like simplicity.

I asked the angel why there was not more power in Israel. Said he, "Ye let go of the promises of God too quick. Press your petitions to the throne, and hold on by faith. Believe ye receive the things ye ask for, and ye *shall have* them." I was then pointed to Elijah. He was subject to like passions as we are, and he prayed earnestly. His faith endured the trial. Seven times he prayed before the Lord and at last the cloud was seen. I saw we had doubted and wounded the lovely Jesus by unbelief. I saw enchantment was all around us, and if Satan could get us to slumber he was sure of his prey. Said the angel, "Have faith in God." I saw some tried too hard to believe. Faith is so simple, ye look above it. Satan tried to deceive some of the honest children and had got them looking to self to find worthiness there. I saw they must look away from self to the worthiness of Jesus and throw themselves, just as dependent and unworthy as they are, upon His mercy and draw by faith strength and nourishment from Him.

Dear sister, I have not forgotten you, although I have not written you. I have often thought of you and prayed for you and the rest of the children that you and their faith fail not. Do not mingle with the world; keep separate from them. If you mingle with them you will surely lose strength. Seek to live near to God and to hold sweet communion with Him. Be diligent to make your calling and election sure. I believe God loves you and will save you if you hold fast whereunto you have attained. Everything and everyone is coming to naught but those who have this truth in them, the commandments of God and the faith of Jesus. Remember, sister, if you would come off victorious you must overcome by the blood of the Lamb and the *word* of your *testimony.* We are in a glorious cause that will triumph and that will never come to naught. Eternal life we are striving for. It is not for any riches or honor in this world, but it is for a home in glory, an enduring substance the *beauty* of which will *never wear* away and its glory will *never vanish.* Remember the Master of the house became poor, that we through His poverty might be made rich. We must be willing to be despised and trodden under foot here. We are soon to be exalted to a home in glory, a treasure in the heavens. Praise the Lord, we

---

few months."

For one account of the rapid spread of spiritualism in 1849 and the early 1850s, see Paul Kurtz, *The Transcendental Temptation: A Critique of Religion and the Paranormal,* pp. 322-325.

[9] See cautions against "unhealthy and unnecessary" excitement in the vision of December 25, 1850 (Ms 11, 1850). See also Appendix article "Ellen White and Religious Enthusiasm in Early Adventist Experience"; EGWEnc, s.v. "Ecstatic Experiences."

will go through and behold Him whom our souls admire. Press, press, dear sister, to the mark of the prize. Have faith in God. Endure trials; be patient in tribulations. Pray, pray much; keep the victory above the powers of darkness.

Much love to your dear father and to your sisters and brother. Tell them to be faithful to serve God. I have often prayed for them. Tell them to pray much that their sins may be confessed upon the head of the scapegoat and borne away into the land of forgetfulness. A little longer and Jesus' work will be finished in the Sanctuary. Kiss the babe for me. Tell Charles to be a good little boy that he may meet his mother at the appearing of Jesus.[10] My little one [**James Edson White**] is with me; he knew me when I got home. I had been gone from him two months. He first looked at me, then flung his little arms around my neck. He is now very feeble, but we have prayed for him. He will be healed, I believe.[11]

In love.

---

[10] *See:* Note 1 above on Arabella Hastings' family.

[11] Edson, who had turned 1 year old just a week earlier, had been looked after by **Clarissa M. Bonfoey** at the home of Ira Abbey in Brookfield, New York, during his parents' long absence. His sickness mentioned here turned into a full-blown crisis within the next few days (see Lt 12, 1850 [Aug. 15]).

See: Ellen G. White, *Spiritual Gifts [vol. 2],* pp. 127, 132; 1850 U.S. Federal Census, "Ira Abbey," New York, Madison County, Brookfield, p. 11.

1850

(Lt 12, 1850)

AUGUST 15,[1] CENTERPORT, NEW YORK

LETTER TO

Stockbridge Howland and Louisa M. Howland.[2]

This letter is published in entirety in Ellen G. White, *Manuscript Releases,* vol. 15, pp. 207-209.

News to close friends of the dramatic healing of her baby Edson and of her husband.

Dear Bro. and Sister Howland,

I send this vision to you for you to read to the church in Topsham [Maine].

Brother Rhodes [**Samuel W. Rhodes**][3] came here last Tuesday which is just one week ago today.[4] We were glad to see him. He has just got out a new chart. It is larger than any chart I ever saw; it is very clear. We like his chart much.[5]

---

[1] This date is found in a handwritten copy of Ellen White's letter. There is a discrepancy between this date, August 15, which fell on a Thursday in 1850, and the statement made in the opening of the letter that it was written on a Tuesday. It may be that the original letter was written on Tuesday, August 13, but that the copyist misread the 13 for a 15. It might also be that the letter was started on Tuesday, August 13, but not completed until August 15. Either way the exact date of writing is not critical. There are several strong indications that the letter was written in the first half of August 1850.

[2] The reference to Topsham in the opening sentence leaves little doubt that the letter is addressed to Stockbridge and Louisa M. Howland, of Topsham, Maine. There are several other Howlands mentioned in the *Review* in this period. One of them, Frances H. Howland, was the daughter of Stockbridge and Louisa; the other, F. T. Howland, was from Rhode Island. The Whites corresponded frequently with Stockbridge and Louisa in particular since their young son Henry lived with them during this period.

See: Search term "Howland" in *Words of the Pioneers.*

[3] *Identity:* "Brother Rhodes" is described in this letter as being on his way to Michigan. A week or so later "S. W. Rhodes" writes to *The Advent Review* of his travels and lectures in Jackson and North Plains, Michigan. Clearly this is a reference to the prominent itinerant preacher Samuel W. Rhodes.

See: S. W. Rhodes, "Extracts of Letters," *Advent Review,* September 1850, p. 48.

[4] *See:* Note 1.

[5] The reference here is to charts showing prophetic symbols from Daniel and Revelation together with time calculations. In a vision given later the same year Ellen White was instructed that a chart should be published and that it would be an effective means for "souls to come to the knowledge of the truth." It is possible that the chart which was subsequently published in January 1851 was modeled on Rhodes's chart, which had pleased the Whites so much in August.

My babe [**James Edson**] had been very sick for about a week. We had prayed for him and he was some better and we thought he would recover. Tuesday, P.M., James [**James Springer White**] and myself went to Port Byron [New York] with Brother Rhodes. He was to take a canal boat and go on his way to Michigan. It seemed as though we could hardly let him go. We knew not why we felt so.

On our way home it seemed to me that Satan had stepped in and was troubling Edson. We found it even so; we found the child at the point of death. James took his horse and carriage and started to overtake Bro. Rhodes. He went five miles [eight kilometers], overtook him and brought him back. That night they prayed for Edson and he has come up very fast since. Satan wanted to hinder the work of the Lord, so he afflicted the child, but he was beaten back by faith in God and His name shall have the glory.[6]

When Satan found he could not take the life of the child, he tempted me that God had left me or the child would have been healed when we first prayed for him. I sank under this temptation in despair and was so until last Sabbath evening. My heart seemed within me like lead, but God delivered me that eve and Satan's power was broken.

The next he got hold of was Clarissa [**Clarissa M. Bonfoey**].[7] She was sunken and discouraged. At the same time James was taken with the cholera morbus. He failed very fast until yesterday, P.M. Then he made a request for us to pray for him. Bro. Harris [**William Harris**][8] was gone to his work so that it only left Sister Harris [**Lydia Harris**],[9] Clarissa, and Sarah [**Sarah B. Harmon**][10] and myself. We all felt unworthy to engage in the work, but we felt that the work of the Lord was hindered by his lying on a sick bed, and

---

See: Ellen G. White, Lt 26, 1850 (Nov. 1); "The Chart," *Review,* January 1851, p. 38.

[6] For more details on the healing of Edson and James, see Ellen G. White, *Spiritual Gifts [vol. 2],* pp. 136-140.

[7] Clarissa Bonfoey's connection with the White family went back to 1848, when she looked after their baby Henry for some weeks during their travels. It appears that after June 1849 she assisted in their household on a more permanent basis.

See: Ellen G. White, *Spiritual Gifts [vol. 2],* pp. 96, 113; obituary: "Clarissa M. Bonfoey," *Review*, June 12, 1856, p. 55.

[8] *Identity:* There are several indications in this letter that Ellen and James White are staying at the house of "Bro. Harris" in Centerport, a hamlet just outside the village of Port Byron, Cayuga County, New York. This is no doubt the "William Harris" whose name appears in the *Review* under the address "Port Byron." Port Byron, a mile or so from Centerport, had a post office and would therefore be used as the postal address.

See: Wm. Harris, "From Bro. Harris," *Review,* Nov. 8, 1853, p. 142; *idem,* "From Bro. Harris," *Review,* Feb. 5, 1857, p. 110; William Harris, "From Bro. Harris," *Review,* Sept. 10, 1857, p. 151; obituary: "Wm. Harris," *Review,* Apr. 22, 1873, p. 151.

[9] 1850 U.S. Federal Census, "Lydia Harris," New York, Cayuga County, Mentz, p. 97.

[10] In her published account Ellen White explains that this was her sister **Sarah B. Harmon** (later Belden).

See: Ellen G. White, *Spiritual Gifts [vol. 2],* p. 138.

we knew unless God should deliver him he could not get well. He had a high fever. He had the cramp take him in his hips and extend down to his feet. His stomach was much strained by vomiting. We knew something must be done. I anointed his head and stomach and bowels in the name of the Lord, then we took hold of faith for him. Our united prayers went up to God and the answer came. Sister Harris and Clarissa were set entirely free and they prayed God with a loud voice. The Spirit caused Clarissa to laugh aloud.[11] James was healed every whit; the great distress he had had in his head was every whit removed and he looked as though he had got the holy anointing. The fever and all pain left him and he ate and was strengthened. He walked out upon his faith, harnessed his horse and he and I went to Port Byron, one mile and a half [two kilometers] and back.[12] He gained strength very fast. He is quite strong today. Praise the good Lord.

When Satan found his power was completely broken upon him, he went to the child again. He waked us crying at the top of his voice. He seemed to have the colic and we went up to the chamber, anointed his stomach with oil and prayed over him, rebuked Satan and he had to flee. We heard no more from him till morning. He is quite well today but rather weak. We feel quite free from his (Satan's) power today. He has made a desperate struggle to get some of us, but we have driven him back.

The Lord showed me some weeks ago that as James would begin to republish what the leaders had written in 1844, upon the truth,[13] Satan would try to hinder us; but we must struggle for the victory and go on. It has been just so. He knows this work will hurt his cause and save some jewels. That is why he rages so, but he is driven back.

---

[11] *See:* Appendix article "Ellen White and Religious Enthusiasm in Early Adventist Experience"; EGWEnc, s.v. "Ecstatic Experiences."

[12] For the purpose of collecting the proof sheets for *The Advent Review,* first published in August 1850.

See: Ellen G. White, *Spiritual Gifts [vol. 2],* p. 139.

[13] During August, September, and November of 1850 James White published several issues of *The Advent Review*. It mostly contained reprints of articles by prominent Millerite leaders such as William Miller and J. B. Cook, written in 1844 and 1845, supporting the salvific significance of October 22, 1844. Articles on the Sabbath and sanctuary by Cook and O.R.L. Crosier also were included. The overall effect was to demonstrate that in several ways leading Millerites had departed from the faith they had held in the mid-1840s.

See: Advent Review, August–November 1850; *Advent Review [Extra],* September 1850.

176

Copied Nov. 34

Aug 15. 1850.

Dear Bro. and Sister Howland:

I send this vision to you for you to read to the church in Topsham. Bro. Rhodes came here last Tuesday which is just one week ago today. We were glad to see him. He has just got out a new chart; it is larger than any chart I ever saw. it is very clear, we liked his chart much. My babe had been very sick for about a week, we had prayed for him and he was some better & we thought he would recover. Tuesday P. M. James and myself went to Port Byron with Bro. Rhodes, he was to take a canal boat and go on his way to Michigan. it seemed as though we could hardly let him go. we knew not why we felt so. On our way home it seemed to me that Satan had stepped in and was troubling Edson. we found it even so, we found the child at the point of death. James took his horse and carriage & started to overtake Bro. Rhodes. He went 5 miles overtook him and brought him back, that night they prayed for Edson and he has come up very fast since. Satan wanted to hinder the work of the Lord so he afflicted the child but he was beaten back by faith in God and his name shall have the glory. When Satan found he could not take the life of the child he tempted me that God had left me or the child would have been healed

Copy of an Ellen White letter to Stockbridge and Louisa Howland (Aug. 15, 1850 [Lt 12, 1850]), the original of which is not extant. Copied in Record Book, No. 1, by Jessie F. Waggoner in the 1880s.

The Howland home in Topsham, Maine, where the Whites lived in 1847-1848.

Stockbridge Howland and his wife, Louisa

1850

(Ms 6, 1850)

[AUGUST 22], N.P.[1]

A Dream.

This manuscript is published in entirety in Ellen G. White, *Manuscript Releases,* vol. 16, pp. 171, 172.

A dream with vivid symbolism of judgment and deliverance.

A dream the Lord gave me August 22. I dreamed of being in a wagon with Bro. Rhodes [**Samuel W. Rhodes**][2] and James [**James Springer White**] and we were to pass a bridge covered with water. As we passed over the bridge I was much frightened for the water came into the body of the wagon and it seemed that we were sinking. I had my babe[3] with me and I was so frightened I almost let him fall into the water. Brother Rhodes assured me a number of times that there was no danger and that we must necessarily pass through the water over the bridge.

After we had passed safely through the water, my eyes were attracted to something strange in the air. I saw angels marching through the air singing with solemn, clear voices. "For the great day of his wrath is come and who shall be able to stand?"[4] Their voices rang through the air. They had mantles upon their shoulders that reached to their feet. Brother Rhodes began to shout with a loud voice and said, And shall I see Him whom my soul loveth?[5]

James was counting the angels and I stood trembling with fear. My life came up before [me] and looked so full of wrongs. I could not see how I should be able to stand. Just then Satan came where I was and said to me, You are lost; you are now my property, [you] will go with me to the dark regions. My feelings I cannot describe; to be separated from the Jesus I had loved and

---

[1] The manuscript begins with the words "A dream the Lord gave me August 22." Although we are not told the year that the dream was given, this can be deduced from a second account of the dream, written by Ellen White a week or so later. On September 1, 1850 (Lt 14, 1850), she described the same dream in almost the same language, adding the information that she had the dream "about one week ago." From these circumstances we can conclude that this account was probably written shortly after the vision of August 22, 1850.

[2] *Identity:* No doubt Samuel W. Rhodes. No other "Bro. Rhodes" is mentioned in the *Review* in the early 1850s.

[3] **James Edson White**, Ellen's youngest child, was about 13 months old at the time of writing.

[4] Rev. 6:17.

[5] S. of Sol. 3:1-4.

to take up my abode with those that I abhorred looked dreadful to me. At the same time I felt unworthy to be with the lovely Jesus.

While in this dreadful perplexity one of the angels came where I was and said to Satan, She is not your property for she has been redeemed unto God by the precious blood of Jesus. She is the purchase of His blood. Satan fled. My feelings changed. My soul was overflowing with gratitude and thankfulness to God. I saw the saints as light fell and was reflected from the face of Jesus. Their faces would light up as they rose to meet the angels.

Many I saw sleeping. I said as I saw those poor souls, they have heard of Jesus' coming and that great day of God's wrath just upon them, but as time went on a little longer than they expected it would, they have lost their interest. Stupidity[6] has crept over them and now they slumber never to awake. They ought to have watched and then they would have seen the angels. This dream has made quite an impression upon my mind.

[6] In the sense of "lethargy."

1850

(Ms 7, 1850)

[AUGUST 24, CENTERPORT, NEW YORK][1]

"A Vision the Lord Gave Me at Brother Harris's [William Harris],"[2] August 24, 1850.

See also Ms 7a, 1850. Portions of this manuscript are published in Ellen G. White, *Manuscript Releases,* vol. 6, pp. 250, 251; vol. 8, p. 220; Arthur L. White, *Ellen G. White: The Early Years,* pp. 183, 184.

Vision of Satan's attempts to hinder the work of God through sickness and affliction and through the deceptions of spiritualism.

I saw the cruel power of Satan that has afflicted us of late and bound us to keep the truth from coming out in the paper,[3] that meant to have taken the life of little Edson [**James Edson White**], but our united prayer drove him back and weakened his powers; and when James [**James Springer White**] and myself went to Port Byron [New York] with Brother Rhodes [**Samuel W. Rhodes**],[4] Satan stepped in, because some of the strength of faith was gone,

---

[1] The heading of this manuscript tells us that the vision of which this is an account was given "at the house of Brother Harris" on "August 24, 1850." That Brother Harris lived in Centerport, New York, is argued in note 2 below. Presumably this account of the vision was written in Centerport shortly after August 24, 1850.

[2] *Identity*: In her published account of the dramatic events mentioned in the opening paragraphs, Ellen White adds the information that they stayed during this period with "Bro. Harris" at Centerport [New York]. This was no doubt the "William Harris" whose name appears in the *Review* under the address "Port Byron" [New York]. Port Byron, a mile or less from Centerport, had a post office and would therefore be used as the postal address for Centerport.

See: Ellen G. White, *Spiritual Gifts [vol. 2],* p. 136; Wm. Harris, "From Bro. Harris," *Review,* Nov. 8, 1853, p. 142; *idem,* "From Bro. Harris," *Review,* Feb. 5, 1857, p. 110; William Harris, "From Bro. Harris," *Review,* Sept. 10, 1857, p. 151.

[3] "The paper" mentioned here and farther on in the letter refers to *The Advent Review.* Several issues were published in August, September, and November 1850. It mostly contained reprints of articles by prominent Millerite leaders such as William Miller and J. B. Cook, written in 1844 and 1845, supporting the prophetic significance of 1844. Articles on the Sabbath and sanctuary by Cook and O.R.L. Crosier also were included. The overall effect was to demonstrate that in several ways leading Millerites had departed from the faith they had held in the mid-1840s.

See: Advent Review, August-November 1850; *Advent Review [Extra],* September 1850.

[4] *Identity:* In another account of the events related here Ellen White adds the information that "Brother Rhodes" was on his way to Michigan and had stopped in Centerport in order to meet the Whites. A week later "S. W. Rhodes" wrote to the editor of *The Advent Review* about

to take the life of the child; when we came back he was at the point of death.

I saw our acting out faith and sending for Brother Rhodes after he had started on his journey saved the life of the child, for God heard the prayers of Brother Rhodes and healed Edson.[5]

I saw the child was not afflicted because I held him dear, as an idol, but Satan wanted to sadden our hearts and cause the nominal Adventists[6] to triumph and say, Where is their God, and to hinder the work of God in papers coming out.

When Satan saw his power was broken upon the child, he laid hold of James and afflicted his body, and he would have afflicted him unto death but God put bounds to his power and would not suffer it. The angels of God were hovering over us, and thus far could the enemy go and no farther. I saw his affliction had been the means of drawing us nearer to God to feel our dependence upon Him, and He heard our prayers for James although we were weak, and answered them, and the balm of Gilead was applied and the sick was made whole, and others who had been bound and oppressed were set free and James was raised up so that he could go on with the paper.

Then I saw it was the work of the enemy as we were going from Oswego [New York] to Volney [New York] to destroy us on the way by our being thrown from the wagon. I saw the angels of Satan triumphed as they were carrying out their purposes, but I saw the angels of God were around, and, as we fell, their arms were put beneath us that we might not be injured. I saw the hands of one of the angels were busy at work and wrought for us or we should have been destroyed by Satan. I saw had we gone back to Oswego, we should have pleased the enemy; our going on gave us the perfect victory.

I saw these efforts of Satan were to hinder the paper from coming out, for the lines that were being published were written in the Spirit of God, and would rejoice the hearts of the trusting ones. Satan knew it would hurt his cause because it would be seen by these testimonies that most of the Advent people once believed as we do that there was a shut door in '44,[7] and to have the plain, clean truth come out in the paper would cause many to decide for

---

his travels and lectures in Michigan. It is therefore reasonable to conclude that the reference here is to the prominent itinerant preacher Samuel W. Rhodes. An additional argument is that the only "Rhodes" mentioned in the *Review* during this period is Samuel W. Rhodes.

See: Ellen G. White, Lt 12, 1850 (Aug. 15); S. W. Rhodes, "Extracts of Letters," *Advent Review,* August 1850, p. 48; search term "Rhodes" in *Words of the Pioneers.*

[5] For a full account of the healing of Edson and James in early August 1850, see Ellen G. White, *Spiritual Gifts [vol. 2],* pp. 136-140; *idem,* Lt 12, 1850 (Aug. 15).

[6] The expression "nominal Adventists," or some variant thereof, was commonly used by early Sabbathkeeping Adventist writers to indicate those Adventist groups coming out of the Millerite movement that rejected the Sabbath, the prophetic significance of October 22, 1844, and the continuing gift of prophecy in the church.

[7] *See:* Introductory article "The 'Shut Door' and Ellen White's Visions"; EGWEnc, s.v. "Shut Door."

the truth and to take a firm and unyielding stand for God and His truth. I saw that the paper would strengthen the things that remain and would help build up God's people in the most holy faith.

I saw that Satan had entered the dwelling of Bro. Harris to take the life of some one of us, but God had through Jesus given us the victory, perfect and entire. Said the angel, Gird it about thee; buckle on every piece of the armor, but above all take the shield, for the shield of faith guards the heart, the very life, from the darts of the enemy.

I saw Satan would work more powerfully now than ever he has before. He knows that his time is short and that the sealing of the saints[8] will place them beyond his power, and he will now work in every way that he can and will try his every insinuation to get the saints off from their guard and get them asleep upon the present truth or doubting it so as to prevent their being sealed with the seal of the living God; and that Satan will ere long come almost in human shape and that his angels were all around them seeking some way that they might devour them. But I saw that God had His angels and they were hovering around the saints and their wings were wafting over them to keep off the unhallowed influence and to protect them from the power of Satan and his angels.

I saw that God wanted His people to be separated from the world, for wicked persons were the lawful prey of the enemy and he would work through them in every way to perplex and destroy the saints, and if we were obliged to be in company with the wicked persons we must pray and watch every moment lest we should partake of their spirit, for they corrupted the atmosphere where they were and their very breath was darkness, and that the wicked would wax worse and worse, and we must cut loose from them and be free and free indeed, and God does not want His people to mingle with the wicked more than they are obliged to.

I saw that the rapping was the power of the devil.[9] Some of it was directly from him and some indirectly, but it all proceeded from Satan. It was his

---

[8] *See:* EGWEnc, s.v. "Seal of God."

[9] Warnings against spiritualism and predictions of its spread can be found in the visions of Ellen White as early as March 1849 when she saw that "the mysterious knocking in N. Y." would increase and spread. This was a mere 12 months after the first rappings in the house of the Fox sisters in Hydesville, New York, and well before the first public demonstrations of spirit contact in November 1849, which launched the movement to spectacular popularity. Ellen White and other writers subsequently commented on the accurate fulfillment of these predictions.

See: Ellen G. White, Ms 1, 1849 (Mar. 24); Lt 5, 1849 (Apr. 21); *idem, Supplement to the Christian Experience and Views of Ellen G. White*, pp. 4-7; Herbert E. Douglass, *Messenger of the Lord,* p. 161; Rene Noorbergen, *Ellen G. White: Prophet of Destiny,* pp. 140-154; Roger W. Coon, *The Great Visions of Ellen G. White,* vol. 1, pp. 49-61; Herbert E. Douglass, *Dramatic Prophecies of Ellen White,* pp. 23-44.

work that he accomplished in different ways and the nominal churches[10] and world were so covered up in gross darkness that they thought and held forth that it was the power of God.[11] Said the angel, Should not a people seek unto their God, for the living to the dead? Should the living go to the dead for knowledge? For the dead know not anything. For the living God, do ye go to [the] dead? They have departed from the living God to converse with the dead who know not anything.

I saw it would soon be considered blasphemy to speak against the rapping and it would spread more and more, and Satan's power would increase and some of his devoted followers would have power to work miracles, and to bring fire from heaven and they would claim to accomplish all the miracles that Jesus did when He was upon earth, by the power of spiritualism and mesmerism. I saw that time was soon to come in the future [when] we should have to keep hold of the strong arm of Jehovah, for I saw all these great signs and mighty wonders of the devil were to deceive God's people and to overthrow them, and our minds must be stayed upon God, and we must not fear the wicked, but be bold and valiant for the truth.

Could our eyes be opened, we should see forms of wicked angels around us, trying to invent some new and effectual way to annoy and destroy us, and we should also see angels of God guarding us from their power, for I saw that God's watchful eye was over Israel and that He would protect and save them if they would put their trust in Him, and when the enemy should come in like a flood, the Spirit of the Lord would lift up a standard against him.

I saw we must buckle on the whole armor and take the shield of faith and we should be enabled to stand and the fiery darts of the enemy could not move us, and should be mighty and terrible as an army with banners. I saw we are on the enchanted ground[12] and we must watch lest we should fall asleep. Said the angel, *Remember,* beware of the *enchanted ground.*

---

[10] The term "nominal churches" was often used by early SDA writers to indicate Protestant and Roman Catholic churches that had experienced a moral fall through their rejection of the message of an imminent Second Coming.

See: P. Gerard Damsteegt, *Foundations of the Seventh-day Adventist Message and Mission,* pp. 179-192.

[11] In a study of nineteenth-century Spiritualism R. Laurence Moore notes that "many believers in the Spiritualist phenomena made a large point of calling themselves 'Christian Spiritualists.' . . . Without question many of those who attended Spiritualist Sunday meetings in the nineteenth century belonged to other churches," albeit mainly theologically "liberal" churches, such as Quakers, Unitarians, and Universalists.

See: R. Laurence Moore, "Spiritualism," in Edwin S. Gaustad, ed., *The Rise of Adventism: Religion and Society in Mid-Nineteenth Century America,* pp. 82, 83.

[12] An allusion to the allegorical "Enchanted Ground" found in John Bunyan's *Pilgrim's Progress.* Of all the dangers awaiting Christian pilgrims on their journey, none are greater than those facing them in the Enchanted Ground, where the very air makes travelers drowsy, inviting a sleep from which there will be no awakening.

See: John Bunyan, *The Pilgrim's Progress,* p. 209.

I then saw Brother Edson [**Hiram Edson**][13] that he must gird on the whole armor and stand in readiness to go, for a journey was before him,[14] and that souls needed help and that Jesus' work was almost finished in the Sanctuary, and that we must work while the day lasts, and when Satan comes up with his power to oppress us we must have faith in God and beat him back, and if we could not get the victory, we should fast and pray and we should surely get the victory and triumph over Satan.

I saw that Bro. and Sister Edson would have to move soon from the place where they now live, for there was enmity enough in the hearts of the wicked there to take their lives, for they hated them for the truths they believed and have advocated, for it condemned them, and a number of times the wicked had it in their hearts to take the lives of Brother and Sister Edson [**Esther Edson**];[15] but God had defeated the wicked, and guarded their lives. I saw the Lord wanted Sister Edson to be free before He leaves the sanctuary. I saw that their children had perplexed and troubled them, for they had none of God's grace to assist them to resist the devil and to overcome their evil tempers and dispositions; therefore they were lawful prey of the enemy and he could work through them as he chose to accomplish his purposes.

And as the hearts of the saints are the temples for the indwelling of the Holy Ghost, so when their hearts are temples for Satan's spirit and all evil to dwell in they would act worse and worse, for they could not help acting out what was in their hearts. I saw Ophelia [**Viah Ophelia Edson**][16] had

---

[13] *Identity:* In part "Bro. Edson" can be identified by the mention further on in the letter of his daughter "Ophelia." We know from census and other records that Hiram Edson, of Port Gibson, New York, had a daughter named Viah Ophelia, aged about 6 in 1850. Another reason for concluding that Hiram Edson is referred to here is that there appears to have been no other Sabbatarian Adventist family by the name "Edson" appearing at this time in the *Review.*

See: 1860 U.S. Federal Census, "Hiram Edson," New York, Oswego County, Palermo, p. 857; "Family Record" in Edson family Bible (DF 588, EGWE-GC); search word "Edson" in *Words of the Pioneers.*

[14] Whether or not a literal journey is meant, this passage suggests that Edson was being commissioned for a greater evangelistic task. Available reports in the *Review* indicate that Edson participated in several lengthy preaching itineraries in 1851. Most of January and early February he traveled and preached with George Holt, probably in New York State. In July and August he traveled for six weeks with J. N. Andrews in New York and Pennsylvania, and in November and December he accompanied Joseph Bates in Canada West.

See: Geo. W. Holt, in *Review,* February 1851, p. 48; Hiram Edson, in *Review*, February 1851, p. 48; *idem,* "Letters," Sept. 2, 1851, p. 24; Joseph Bates, "From Bro. Bates," *Review,* Jan. 13, 1852, p. 80.

[15] At the time of writing the Edsons were living in Port Gibson, where Hiram Edson had farmed for many years. They moved from Port Gibson to Port Byron, New York, some time between February and July 1851, as is evidenced by the addresses Edson gives in his letters to the *Review* and other circumstantial evidence.

See: Hiram Edson, "Letter From Bro. Edson," *Review,* March 1851, p. 51; *idem,* "Letters," Sept. 2, 1851, p. 24.

[16] *See:* Note 13 above.

partaken of the spirit of the wicked children, but if her parents watched over her carefully and would keep her from the influence of the wicked and would have strong and living faith for her, their faith would save her and the grace of God would operate upon her heart and she would go with them into the kingdom.

1850

(Ms 7a, 1850)

[AUGUST 24, CENTERPORT, NEW YORK][1]

"A Vision the Lord Gave Me at the House of Brother Harris [William Harris],"[2] August 24, 1850.

Variant of Ms 7, 1850. Portions of this manuscript are published in Ellen G. White, *Manuscript Releases*, vol. 7, p. 318.

Vision of Satan's attempts to hinder the work of God through sickness and affliction and through the deceptions of spiritualism.

I saw the cruel power of Satan that had afflicted us of late, and bound us to keep the truth from coming out in the paper.[3] I saw he meant to have taken the life of little Edson [**James Edson White**], but our united faith drove him back, and weakened his power. And as James [**James Springer White**] and myself went to Port Byron [New York] with Bro. Rhodes [**Samuel W. Rhodes**],[4] Satan stepped in because some of the strength of faith was gone, to take the life of the child and when we came back he was at the point of death, where no human power could save him. I saw our acting out faith and sending for Bro. Rhodes after he had started on his journey saved the life of the child. For God heard the prayers of Bro. Rhodes and saved the life of the child.[5]

I saw the child was not afflicted because I held him dear as an idol, but to sadden our hearts, and to cause the nominal Adventists[6] to triumph and to say where is their God, and to hinder the work of God in preventing the papers coming out.

When Satan saw his power was broken on the child, he laid hold of James

---

[1] The headings of this manuscript and its variant, Ms 7, 1850, inform us that the vision of which this is an account was given "at the house of Brother Harris" on "August 24, 1850." That Brother Harris lived in Centerport, New York, is argued in Ms 7, 1850 (Aug. 24), note 2. Presumably this account of the vision was written in Centerport shortly after August 24, 1850. This copy is accompanied by a note from J. N. Loughborough that reads: "Copied Nov. 8, 1914, from an original printed sheet of which the paper had become rotten with age."

[2] *Identity*: See Ms 7, 1850 (Aug. 24), note 2.

[3] "The paper" mentioned here and farther on in the letter refers to *The Advent Review*. *See: ibid.*, note 3.

[4] *Identity:* See *ibid.*, note 4.

[5] For a full account of the healing of Edson and James in early August 1850, see Ellen G. White, *Spiritual Gifts [vol. 2]*, pp. 136-140; *idem*, Lt 12, 1850 (Aug. 15).

[6] On the expression "nominal Adventists," see Ms 7, 1850 (Aug. 24), note 6.

and afflicted his body. And he would have afflicted him unto death but God put bounds to his power and would not suffer it. The angels of God were hovering and thus far the enemy could go, and no farther. I saw his affliction had been the means of drawing us nearer to God to feel our dependence upon Him. God heard our prayers for James although we were weak, and answered them and the balm of Gilead was applied. The sick [were] made whole and others who had been bound and oppressed He set free, and James was raised up so he could go on with the paper.

Then I saw it was the work of the enemy as we were going from Oswego [New York] to Volney [New York] to destroy us on the way by our being thrown from the wagon. I saw the angels of Satan triumphed as they were carrying out their purpose, but I saw that the angels of God were around to protect us. As we fell their arms were put beneath us that we should not be injured. I saw that the hand of one angel was busy at work and wrought for us or we should have been destroyed by Satan. I saw had we gone back to Oswego we should have pleased the enemy, our going on gave us the perfect victory over him.

All these efforts of Satan I saw were to hinder the papers coming out, for the lines that were being published were written in the Spirit of God and would rejoice the hearts of the trusting ones. And Satan knew it would hurt his cause because it would be seen by these testimonies *that most of the advent people once believed as we do that the door was shut in '44.*[7] And to have the plain clear truth come out in the paper would cause many to come out in the truth and take an unyielding stand for the truth. I saw that the paper would strengthen the things that remain and would help build up God's people in the most holy faith.

I saw Satan had entered the home of Brother Harris to take the life of some one of us but God had through Jesus given us the perfect, entire victory. Said the angel, Gird it about thee, buckle on every piece of the armor, and above all take the shield of faith, for the shield of faith guards the heart, the very seat of life, from the darts of the enemy.

I saw that Satan will work more powerfully now than ever before, for he knows that his time is short and that *the sealing of the saints*[8] *will soon be over.* And he will now work in every way, and try every insinuation to get the saints off their guard, and get them to [fall] asleep upon present truth, or doubting it, so as to *prevent their being sealed* with the seal of the living God. I saw that Satan would now come in almost human shape and that his angels were all around seeking some way that they might devour them. But I saw that God and His angels were hovering around the saints and their wings were wafting

---

[7] *See:* Introductory article "The 'Shut Door' and Ellen White's Visions"; EGWEnc, s.v. "Shut Door."

[8] *See:* EGWEnc, s.v. "Seal of God."

over them to keep off the unhallowed influence and to protect them from the power of Satan and his angels.

I saw that God wanted His people to be separate from the wicked, for every wicked person was the lawful prey of the enemy and he would work through them in every way to perplex and destroy the saints. If we were obliged to be in company with a wicked person we must pray, pray, pray, and watch every movement lest we partake of their spirit, for they corrupted the atmosphere where they were, and their breath was darkness. I saw the wicked would wax worse and worse and that we must cut loose from them and be free, free indeed. I saw that God did not want His people to mingle with the wicked.

I saw the rapping spirit was the power of the devil.[9] Some of it was directly from him, and some indirectly, but it all proceeded from Satan. It was his work that he accomplished in different ways. And the nominal church[10] and the world were so covered up in gross darkness that they thought and held forth that it was the power of God.[11] Said the angel, Should not a people seek unto their God, for the living to the dead? Should the living go to the dead for knowledge? The dead know not anything. For the living God do ye go to the dead to inquire? They have departed from the living God to converse with the dead that know not anything.

I saw it would be considered blasphemy to speak against the rapping. And it would spread more and more, and Satan's power would increase, and some of his devoted followers would have power to work miracles and to bring down fire from heaven. I saw they would account for all the miracles that Jesus did when He was upon the earth, by the rapping and mesmerism. I saw that time was soon to come, and we should have to keep hold of the arm of Jehovah. For I saw that all these signs and mighty wonders of the devil were to deceive God's children and overthrow them. I saw that our minds must be stayed upon God and we must not fear the face of the wicked but be bold and valiant for the truth.

Could our eyes be opened we should see forms of wicked angels around us trying to invent some new way to annoy and destroy us. And we should also see the angels of God guarding us from their power. I saw God's watchful eye was over Israel and He would protect and save them if they would trust in Him. And when the enemy should come in like a flood the Spirit of the Lord would lift up a standard against him.

I saw we must buckle on the whole armor and take the shield of faith and we should be enabled to stand, [and] all the fiery darts [of] Satan could not move us. We should be mighty and terrible as an army with banners. I saw we

---

[9] *See:* Ms 7, 1850 (Aug. 24), note 9.
[10] On the term "nominal churches," see *ibid.*, note 10.
[11] *See: Ibid.*, note 11.

were on the enchanted ground,[12] and we must watch lest we fall asleep. Said the angel, Remember the enchanted ground.

I then saw Sister S. Peckham [**Sophronia Peckham**][13] that she would have to break loose from her husband, for he has no part nor lot with the saints. I saw he had sapped her strength, and that he had a fire of her kindling, that she would talk the truth with him and try to impress him with it. He would appear to have a love for the truth and a little feeling. I saw all his care was to get this world, and to lay up a treasure upon the earth. I saw she must look to Jesus and draw strength and grace from Him or she would fall right upon the borders of Canaan. I saw she had been losing her life and strength of late, for the weight of her husband has dragged her down, and the company of the wicked has opened a wide door for the devil to hit her with his darts. I saw she must shake off these shackles and go free or she will fall. I saw that the time had come when though Noah, Daniel, and Job were in the land they could not save son or daughter, husband, or any one but their own souls by their own righteousness.

In love and sorrow.

---

[12] *See: Ibid.*, note 12.

[13] *Identity:* The *Review* carried a letter from "S. Peckham" in 1852 with the address "Volney, N.Y." According to census records there were several Peckhams in Volney in 1850, but only one wife with an S initial, namely Sophronia Peckham, married to Job B. Peckham. This identification is fairly certain because on May 18, 1859, Ellen White mentions receiving news from "Sophrona Peckham giving an account of her husband's death." According to tombstone evidence Job B. Peckham had died two months earlier, on March 19, 1859. (Both spellings of her first name ["Sophronia" and "Sophrona"] appear in the sources.)

See: S. Peckham, "From Sister Peckham," *Review,* June 10, 1852, p. 23; 1850 U.S. Federal Census, "Job B. Peckham," New York, Oswego County, Volney, p. 351; Ellen G. White, Ms 6, 1859 (May 18 entry); "Peckham, Job B.," RootsWeb, *Mt. Pleasant Western Cemetery, Volney, Oswego Co., N.Y.,* 2000, www.rootsweb.ancestry.com/~nyoswego/cemeteries/mtpleasntwestvol4.html (Oct. 20, 2011).

1850

AUGUST 24, 1850

Date given for an unauthenticated vision. See Appendix A.

1850

(Lt 14, 1850)

SEPTEMBER 1, PORT BYRON, NEW YORK

LETTER TO

Prudence M. Bates.[1]

Portions of this letter are published in Ellen G. White, *Manuscript Releases,* vol. 7, pp. 351, 352; vol. 8, pp. 221, 222.

Account of Satan's efforts to hinder publication of The Advent Review *together with an impressive dream of judgment and deliverance.*

Dear Sister Bates:

We received your letter dated August 26, last night. We were very glad to hear from you. We have been waiting some time to hear from you. We have not received your letter in answer to mine.[2] Perhaps you sent it to Centerport

---

[1] *Identity:* No doubt Prudence M. Bates, wife of **Joseph Bates**. One ground for this inference is Ellen White's mention of a letter sent by Sister Bates that Ellen had not yet received (by Sept. 1). Although that letter itself is not extant, we know from a "letters received" notice in *The Advent Review* that the Whites subsequently received a letter from "P. M. Bates" sometime after Sept. 2, 1850. Added confirmation is provided by the torn address panel for this letter on which the words "Mrs. Joseph B. . . ." are found together with the first three letters of the address "Fai . . ." suggesting Fairhaven, Massachusetts, home of Joseph Bates.

The title "Sister" Bates is of interest. This is the earliest extant indication that Prudence Bates had become a Sabbathkeeper. About two months later James White remarked that for years Joseph Bates had kept the Sabbath alone but that "now she [Sister Bates] and her husband are walking in all the commandments and ordinances of the Lord."

See: "Letters received since September 2," *Advent Review,* September 1850, p. 64; 1850 U.S. Federal Census, "Joseph Bates," Massachusetts, Bristol County, Fairhaven, p. 209; "Conferences," *Advent Review,* November 1850, p. 72.

[2] None of the letters mentioned in the opening of this letter are in the White Estate archives.

[New York]; if you did, it went to another Centerport about 70 miles [112 kilometers] from here.[3] There is no post office where we live. Our post office address is Port Byron, one half mile [.8 kilometers] from this place. Did you send it in my name at Port Byron; if you did, it is now in the office and we can get it on the morrow. Please write us if you sent it to Centerport and we will send there for it.

We are all quite well here now. Praise the Lord. We are free. We have had a victorious time here this morn. Satan thought to have got some victory over us, but he has been driven back by faith in God.

Sister Clarissa Bonfoey [**Clarissa M. Bonfoey**][4] was oppressed by the enemy. Her body was afflicted. Our united prayers went up to God and healing power came down. Brother Edson [**Hiram Edson**][5] (who has been with us 8 days) laid hands upon her in the name of the Lord, and she was made whole and gave glory to God with a loud voice. The enemy has tried hard to take some of our lives here of late. One after another of us has been afflicted almost unto death. Had it not have been for the balm in Gilead and the Physician there, we must have perished.

The Lord shewed me some weeks before we came to this place, that we must gird on the whole armor, for we were to have a great conflict with the enemy while we were getting out the paper,[6] for he knew the paper would hurt his cause and would be the means of strengthening the things that remain and would cause souls that were undecided to take a decided stand for God and His truth. Satan meant to hinder the work of the paper by causing sickness and distress in our company, but we laid hold of the sure promises of God. We anointed with oil in the name of the Lord and prayed over the sick and they were healed.[7]

---

[3] No other "Centerport" is found within that kind of distance. Possibly there is confusion here with the town of Centerville, New York, about 90 miles (145 kilometers) from Centerport.

[4] Clarissa Bonfoey's connection with the White family went back to 1848, when she looked after their son Henry for some weeks during their travels. It appears that after June 1849 she assisted in their household on a more permanent basis.

See: Ellen G. White, *Spiritual Gifts [vol. 2],* pp. 96, 113; obituary: "Clarissa M. Bonfoey," *Review,* June 12, 1856, p. 55.

[5] Up until mid-1851 there appears to have been no other "Bro. Edson" among Sabbatarian Adventists than Hiram Edson, of Port Gibson, New York, as evidenced by occurrences of that name in the periodicals of that period.

See: Search term "Edson" in *Words of the Pioneers.*

[6] "The paper" mentioned here and farther on in the letter refers to *The Advent Review.* Several issues were published in August, September, and November 1850. It contained mostly reprints of articles by prominent Millerite leaders such as William Miller and J. B. Cook written in 1844 and 1845 supporting the prophetic significance of 1844. Articles on the Sabbath and sanctuary by Cook and O.R.L. Crosier also were included. The overall effect was to demonstrate that in several ways leading Millerites had departed from the faith they had held in the mid-1840s.

See: Advent Review, August–November 1850; *Advent Review [Extra],* September 1850.

[7] For a full account of these healings, see Ellen G. White, *Spiritual Gifts [vol. 2],* pp. 136-140.

Oh, what battles we have had to fight with the enemy since we commenced to get out the paper. We have had to *pray, pray, pray,* and have *faith, faith, faith,* and that is all the way we have been enabled to live. I know you will rejoice with me when I tell you we have the perfect entire victory over the powers of darkness. We triumphed in God today for we have just had a rich full draught from the well of Bethlehem.

I will now write you a dream which I had about one week ago.[8] I dreamed of being with Bro. Rhodes [**Samuel W. Rhodes**][9] and James [**James Springer White**] in a wagon. We were to pass a bridge covered with water. While passing it, I was much frightened, for the water came into the body of the wagon. I had my babe in my arms. I came near letting him fall into the water through fright. Brother Rhodes assured me a number of times that there was no danger and that we must necessarily pass through that water that covered the bridge. After we had passed over the bridge through the water, my eyes were fixed upon something in the air that looked very strange to me. I saw angels marching through the air. They had light mantles on their shoulders that reached to their feet. And they were singing in solemn clear voices, *For the great day of His wrath has come and who shall be able to stand*. Their voices rung all through the air.

Brother Rhodes began to shout with a loud voice, "And shall I see Him whom my soul loveth?" James was counting the angels, and I stood trembling with fear lest I should not be *able* to *stand*. My mind ran back to my past life. I could see in it many wrongs and I could see no way that I could be saved. Just then Satan came where I was and said to me, "You are now my property. You are lost and you will go with me to the dark regions."

My feelings I cannot describe to you. I was filled with anguish unutterable. I knew that Jesus was all my joy and to be separated from Him was more than I could endure. And at the same time, I felt unworthy to be with the lovely Jesus. While I was thus in awful perplexity, one of the angels that was marching through the air, came where I was and said to Satan, "She is not your property. She has been redeemed unto God by the precious blood of Jesus. She is the purchase of His blood and He will save her." Then the enemy fled and my heart was filled to overflowing with thankfulness and praise to God. I saw the saints, that their garments would change and they would receive the mantle and their faces would light up as they would meet the angels in the air.

I looked around and saw some sleeping. Oh, how I felt as I saw some who now profess to be with us asleep as I saw them. I said, "Poor souls. They have

---

8 *See*: Ellen White's dream of August 22, 1850, as originally recorded in Ms 6, 1850

9 *Identity:* No doubt Samuel W. Rhodes. No other "Bro. Rhodes" is mentioned in the *Review* in the early 1850s.

See: Search term "Rhodes" in *Words of the Pioneers.*

heard of Jesus' coming and that the day of His wrath was very soon to come, but as time went on a little longer than they expected it would, they have lost their interest. Stupidity has crept over them and now they slumber never to awake again. They ought to have watched and then they would have seen the angels." This dream has made a great impression on my mind. I hope it will cause me to double my diligence and to make my calling and election sure.

If ever there was need of watching, it is now. Satan's host is arrayed against us and we must have the whole armor buckled tight about us or the darts of the enemy will hit us. Above all, we must take the shield of faith whereby we shall be able to quench the fiery darts of the enemy. Satan has great power and we must have *living, abiding* faith in God or the powers of darkness will get the ascendency over us and Satan will triumph. We will be free and we must be free in order to glorify God.

Joseph Bates and his wife, Prudence. Joseph Bates photo courtesy of the Center for Adventist Research.

1850

(Ms 14, 1850)

SEPTEMBER,[1] SUTTON, VERMONT

A Vision the Lord Gave Me at Sutton, Vermont.

This manuscript is published in entirety in Ellen G. White, *Manuscript Releases,* vol. 12, pp. 246-252. See also *The Present Truth*, November 1850, pp. 86, 87.

Some weaknesses in the teaching and practice of Joseph Bates; On the sequence of earth's final events.

A vision the Lord gave me at Sutton, Vermont, September 1850.

I saw the loveliness of Jesus and the love that the angels have for one another. Said the angel, Can ye not behold their love? Follow it. Just so, God's people must love one another. Rather let blame fall on thyself than on a brother.

I was then pointed back to western New York and saw that Bro. Bates [**Joseph Bates**][2] did not give the message—"Sell that ye have and give alms"—in its clear light. It caused some to follow for the loaves and fishes,[3] and now they are ready to be purged out. Falsehoods have been in their mouths. I saw that Bro. Bates's holding up "sell that ye have &c." in a wrong light had caused those who had been coveting others' property to take lenity[4] from it and to rejoice and triumph, and had also caused those who had property to hold on to it.[5] Those who had been coveting were zealous to attend conference with

---

[1] The Whites attended a conference in Sutton, Vermont, September 26-29. The exact date of the vision is not known; it may have been prior to, during, or after the conference.

See: "Conferences," *Advent Review,* November 1850, p. 72.

[2] *Identity:* Although several persons with the surname "Bates" appear in the *Review* in the period up to 1853, only Joseph Bates fits this document's general description of a writer, preacher, close associate of James White, etc. More specifically, "Brother Bates's" radical views on selling property (note 5) and his writing for non-Sabbatarian Adventist papers (note 13) identify him as Joseph Bates.

See: Search term "Bates" in *Words of the Pioneers.*

[3] In a parallel account Ellen White elaborates on this thought: "I saw that the object of selling was not to give to those who are able to labor and support themselves; but to spread the truth. It is a sin to support and indulge those who are able to labor, in idleness."

See: E. G. White, "Dear Brethren and Sisters," *Present Truth,* November 1850, p. 86.

[4] "Lenity" is probably used here in its now-obsolete sense of a "lenitive," i.e., something capable of easing pain or discomfort. The meaning of this passage would then be that some of the poorer members took comfort from—indeed, rejoiced in—Bates's radical demand that wealthier members should sell their properties, for they expected that some of the proceeds would be used to alleviate their poverty.

[5] The situation described in this paragraph had been touched upon by James White some

their families, not to glorify God, but for the loaves and the fishes. They had better remained at home and worked with their hands to supply the wants of their families and to have something to give to sustain the cause of truth.

I saw that Bro. Bates erred again in praying for the sick before unbelievers. I saw if any among us were sick and called for the elders of the church to pray over them we should follow the example of Jesus. He went into an inner chamber, and we should go into a room by ourselves separate entirely from unbelievers, and then the atmosphere would not be polluted by them. By faith we could take hold on God and draw down the blessing. I saw that God's cause was dishonored and reproached in W. New York at the general conference by praying for the sick in the midst of unbelievers.

I also saw that Bro. Bates erred in attending the washing of saints' feet and the communion among unbelievers. It only caused reproach to come on the cause of God. I saw that the example of Jesus should be followed. He took His disciples away alone, separate from the wicked, and first washed their feet, and then gave them to eat of the broken bread to represent His broken body and gave them to drink of the juice of the vine to represent His spilled blood.[6]

I saw that Bro. Bates and all the shepherds should be careful in these things, and move understandingly, and follow the example of Jesus in these things. I saw that a Judas might be among us from time to time, that would

---

months earlier. In November 1849 he complained of "some fiery spirits" in western New York "whose principal message was 'Sell that ye have and give alms.'" The influx of means brought about by such appeals had not always been used wisely. Two months later White wrote of "means . . . squandered away, and worse than lost in W. New York." Ellen White's vision given here places some responsibility for this state of affairs on Joseph Bates. Bates's radical interpretation of Christ's instruction can be seen in a tract published in January 1849. He cites the revolutions taking place in Europe as portents of the time of trouble and urges members to sell their properties and not to delay with the hope that prices would rise. Ellen White, also writing in January 1849, had a considerably more qualified message. "I saw that God had not required all of His people to dispose of their property at the same time, but in a time of need He would teach them . . . when to sell and how much to sell."

See: James White to Bro. Howland, in Ellen G. White, *Spiritual Gifts [vol. 2]*, p. 119; James White to Leonard Hastings, Jan. 10, 1850; Joseph Bates, *A Seal of the Living God*, pp. 68, 69; Ellen G. White, "To Those Who Are Receiving the Seal of the Living God," (broadside, Jan. 31, 1849).

[6] The position taken here needs to be seen in the context of the times. The bitter disputes of 1845 over the rite of foot washing had pitted the majority of Adventists against this, as it seemed to them "fanatical practice." When Sabbatarian Adventists subsequently continued to practice foot washing, the opprobrium of other Adventist bodies was clear. Joseph Bates wrote in 1848 of Sabbatarians as "very despised," and that they were given derogatory names, such as "'door-shutters,' 'mystery folks,' 'Jewdeizers' [*sic*], 'feet washers,' 'deluded fanatics,' etc." Adding to the controversy was the question of foot washing between the sexes. In this context the instruction to avoid causing unnecessary "reproach" by practicing foot washing with nonmembers present can be understood.

See: Joseph Bates, *A Vindication of the Seventh-day Sabbath,* p. 6; Donald D. Reiber, "An Investigation Into the Development of Feet-Washing Among Advent Believers From 1844 to 1860"; George R. Knight, *Millennial Fever,* pp. 251, 252, 271.

appear to be with us, but they would eat and drink to their own damnation,[7] but God would make them manifest quickly, and they would be purged out from among Israel.

I saw that the above named errors of Bro. Bates, and others more dangerous, brought confusion and had destroyed James's [**James Springer White**] confidence in Bro. Bates; I saw that James at first had godly jealousy for the truth, then other jealousy crept in until he was jealous of most every move Bro. Bates would make.[8] These wrongs I saw must be taken out of the way.

Then I saw Bro. Bates. Said the angel, Be not quick to receive error, nor too slow to receive the truth. I saw that the women of Rev. 14:4 meant the churches and that we were bid to "come out of her" that we be not defiled, partake of her sins, and receive of her plagues. I saw that Bro. Bates had not applied Rev. 14:4 correctly, and his error had caused confusion.[9] Then I saw that after Jesus leaves the sanctuary the plagues will be poured out. Said the angel, It is the wrath of God and the Lamb that causes the destruction or death of the wicked.

I saw that at the voice of God the saints will be mighty and terrible as an army with banners, but they will not then execute the judgment written. But after they are changed in a moment, in the twinkling of an eye, and are caught up with the sleeping saints, and receive their harps, crowns, &c, and enter the city, Jesus and the saints sit in judgment, the books are opened, the book of life and the book of death. The book of life contains the good deeds of the saints, and the book of death contains the evil deeds of the wicked. These books were compared with the statute book—the Bible—and according to that they were judged. The saints in unison with Jesus passed their judgment upon the wicked dead. Behold ye, said the angel, the saints sit in unison with Jesus and mete out to each of the wicked according to the deeds done in the body, and it is set off against their names what they must receive at the

---

[7] 1 Cor. 11:29: "For he that eateth and drinketh unworthily, eateth and drinketh damnation to himself, not discerning the Lord's body."

[8] Scarcity of sources prevents any adequate insight into the personal relationship between James White and Joseph Bates during this period. However, one sign of discord can be found in Bates's opposition to White's publication of *The Present Truth,* which had driven White to despair at the end of 1849. Another sign is White's complaint in a letter that Bates's radical call for members to sell their properties had led to money being "squandered away, and worse than lost." Despite this criticism White continues the letter on a conciliatory note. "I do not doubt for a moment Brother Bates' good will and kindness toward us. Still he does not see everything correctly at one glance." In a chapter entitled "Patriarchs in Conflict and the Transfer of Leadership," Joseph Bates's biographer George R. Knight surveys a range of theological and policy issues on which Bates and White differed, mainly in the years before 1851.

See: James White to Leonard Hastings, Jan. 10, 1850; Lt 4, 1850 (Feb. 18), note 4; George R. Knight, *Joseph Bates,* pp. 152-171.

[9] Exactly how Bates differed with his colleagues on the interpretation of Revelation 14:4 is not clear from Bates's published comment on this text.

execution of the judgment. This I saw was the work of the saints with Jesus through the 1000 years.[10]

At the end of the 1000 [years] Jesus, with the holy angels and all the saints, leave the city, and while He is descending with them the wicked dead are raised, and then the very men that pierced Him will see Him afar off in all His glory, and all the holy angels and the saints with Him. They will see the prints of the nails in His hands and in His feet, and where they thrust the spear into His side, and they will wail because of Him. I saw that the prints of the nails and of the spear were His glory.[11]

Then it is that Jesus stands upon the Mount of Olives and the Mount parts asunder and becomes a plain, and the city comes down from God out of heaven and settles on the plain. Then Satan imbues the wicked that have been raised, with his spirit, and he flatters them that the army in the city is small and that his army is large and that they can overcome them and take the city.

While Satan is rallying his army the saints are in the city beholding the beauty and glory of the paradise of God. Jesus was at their head leading them. All at once the lovely Jesus was gone from our company, but soon we heard His lovely voice saying, Come ye blessed of my Father, inherit the kingdom prepared for you from the foundation of the world.

We gathered about Jesus and just as He closed the gates of the city the curse from God was pronounced upon the wicked. The gates are shut. Then the saints use their wings and fly to the top of the wall of the city. Jesus is also with them. His crown looked brilliant and glorious. It was a crown within a crown, seven in number. The crowns of the saints were of the purest gold, and were decked with stars, and shone like the sun, as they moved all together to the top of the city. Their faces shone with glory, for they were in the express image of Jesus.

Then the wicked saw what they had lost. And fire was breathed from God upon them and consumed them. Then was the execution of the judgment. The wicked received according as the saints in unison with Jesus had meted out to them through the 1000 years. The same fire from God that consumed

---

[10] Ellen White's vision of the judgment and last-time events was given at Sutton, Vermont, possibly during the conference held September 26-29, 1850. According to the account given in *The Present Truth,* there was significant disagreement among the conference participants "relative to the Judgment, etc." Earlier that same month James White had again taken a strong stand against Joseph Bates's views on the subject. The account continues, however, that "before we left the place of meeting our trials were all removed. Errors were confessed, and perfect union, as sweet as heaven, was felt among us all." It may be that the instruction Ellen White received in vision, as outlined in this section of the manuscript, was instrumental in helping to bring about agreement.

See: "Conferences," *Advent Review,* November 1850, p. 72; "The Day of Judgment," *Advent Review,* September 1850, pp. 49-51; George R. Knight, *A Search for Identity,* pp. 80, 81; EGWEnc, s.v., "Judgment, God's."

[11] *See:* EGWEnc, s.v. "Eschatology."

the wicked purified the whole earth. The mountains melted with fervent heat, the atmosphere also, and all the stubble was consumed. Then our inheritance opened before us glorious and beautiful. Then we inherited the whole earth made new. We shouted with a loud voice, Glory Alleluia.

Then I saw that God had not given to Bro. Bates the gift of discernment; but his gift was to talk the Word. None had a gift like his. He could talk to a small company when there was not more than two present, as well as to a large company. This gift is greatly needed in the church. I saw that he had prepared the way in many places for the Lord to speak through visions. The angel then pointed to Bro. Bates and said, Be careful how thou treadest, lest the flock be torn. Draw near to God. Thou hast been in danger. Can ye not see it? That must be healed every whit. This people must be humble.

I begged of Jesus to forbid that there should be any discord among the shepherds, for then the flock would be scattered as sheep without a shepherd. I prayed Jesus to encircle them now in His lovely arms. I saw that the disunion between the shepherds had affected the flock. Then I saw that in the scattering time[12] when paper after paper was dying, Bro. Bates wrote for them until the last, and now in the gathering time when precious souls that have been hid beneath the rubbish and have not had the privilege of hearing the truth, need light from different ones, his testimony has been withheld.[13] I saw that if ever the saints could be benefited by comforting words and the truth made clear in the paper, it is now in the gathering. God wants the papers to cease in the scattering time, but now the truth should be sung, preached, prayed, and published. Then I saw we must drink deep, deep from the water of the fountain. Said the angel, Ye must reflect the lovely image of Jesus more and more. I saw that we were almost home, to rest in the city 1000 years. Said the angel, Ye must love one another as Jesus hath loved you.

I saw that Bro. Bates's heart must be open, ready to yield up a dear point when the clear light shines. I saw that we must be more like Jesus. Everything in heaven is in perfect order, and the events of the judgment will come in

---

[12] *See:* EGWEnc, s.v. "'Scattering' and 'Gathering' Times."

[13] Joseph Bates's contributions to "dying" Adventist papers may be illustrated by two letters with substantial theological content that he had had submitted to S. S. Snow's *Jubilee Standard* during its brief existence of four months during 1845. By contrast, Bates had written nothing for *The Present Truth* or *The Advent Review* until September 1850. Part of the reason for his reticence to contribute articles may well have been his objection, in principle, to the publishing of periodicals, an objection that had brought deep discouragement to James White. However, the admonition to Bates found in this vision of September 1850 appears to have given him a strong impetus to write. When the new periodical, the *Second Advent Review and Sabbath Herald,* began publication two months later, Bates became not only a frequent contributor of substantial articles but also a member of the publishing committee.

See: Joseph Bates, "Letter From Bro. Joseph Bates," *Jubilee Standard,* May 29, 1845, p. 90; *idem,* "Letter From Bro. Bates," *Jubilee Standard,* June 12, 1845, p. 110; George R. Knight, *Joseph Bates,* pp. 162-166.

perfect order. Then I saw James and Bro. Bates. Said the angel, Press together, press together, press together, press together, ye shepherds, lest the sheep be scattered.[14] Love one another as I have loved you. Swim, swim, swim, plunge deep, deep, deep in the ocean of God's love. Come into a nearness with God. I saw that we must overcome perfectly and get the victory over the powers of darkness.

I saw that Bro. Bates with the other shepherds should consult those in whom they have reason to have confidence, and who have been in all the messages, and are firm in all the present truth, and have not wavered upon it, before they receive and advocate any new point of importance which they think the Bible sustains. Then I saw that all the shepherds would be perfectly *united,* and *that* union the church would feel and the shepherds would be strong, and each one would know just what work the other was doing, and thereby they could hold up each other's hands, and the church would be benefited, and then there would be but little danger of any of the shepherds' receiving dangerous error with which to divide the precious flock.

---

[14] The evidence, as assessed by George Knight, is that the two men did indeed come to "press together." After 1850 their differences were "relatively minor." "The two men would sustain a generally supportive relationship with each other between 1851 and 1872, when Bates died."

See: George R. Knight, *Joseph Bates,* pp. 168, 169.

1850

(Ms 15, 1850)

[OCTOBER 23, DORCHESTER, MASSACHUSETTS][1]

"A Vision Given on October 23, 1850."

Portions of this manuscript are published in Ellen G. White, *Manuscript Releases,* vol. 6, p. 249. See also *The Present Truth,* November 1850, pp. 86, 87.

Importance of publishing a periodical; need for prophetic chart; end-time prophecies; errors of Clorinda Minor.

A vision the Lord gave me October 23, 1850, at the house of Bro. Nichols [**Otis Nichols**][2] in Dorchester, Mass. I saw that we must redouble our efforts now in this gathering time.[3] I saw it was a shame for us to refer to the scattering time for examples to govern us now in the gathering time, for if God does no more for us now than He did then, we never shall be gathered. In the scattering Israel were torn and smitten, but now God will heal and bind them up.

I saw that God had stretched out His hand the second time to recover the remnant of His people.[4] They are those who have been covered up beneath the rubbish since 1844.[5] I saw that efforts to spread the truth should now be

---

[1] The place and date of the vision are given in the first line of the letter. It was probably written up shortly after the vision since an abbreviated account using similar phrases is found in the November issue of *The Present Truth.* No Ellen White handwritten original is known to exist. This copy derives from Hiram Edson's papers. See Appendix A for comments on an unauthenticated copy of this vision.

See: E. G. White, "Dear Brethren and Sisters," *Present Truth,* November 1850, pp. 86, 87.

[2] *Identity:* Only Otis Nichols fits the description given here.

See: Search term "Nichols" in *Words of the Pioneers.*

[3] Using the language of Ezekiel 34, post-Disappointment Adventists had described the divisions within Adventism following 1844 as the "scattering time" (see second paragraph). By 1849, however, Sabbatarian Adventism had developed a cogent theological platform and was beginning to experience strong membership growth. The new situation was described as the "gathering time."

See: EGWEnc, s.v. "'Scattering' and 'Gathering' Times."

[4] Cf. Isa. 11:11, 12.

[5] An allusion to a widely published dream William Miller had in 1847. Central to the dream were jewels covered in dust and rubbish. A man with a "dirt-brush" entered the room, and brushed away the rubbish, restoring the brilliance of the precious stones. James White published the vision in *The Present Truth* in 1850. According to White's interpretation, the dust and rubbish represent the "darkness and error" that had covered "the clear light of . . . the third angel's message." Ellen White here uses the metaphor to refer to those who accepted the Advent call in 1844 but who had since then been misled by various post-1844 theories. In this situation God was graciously calling these Adventists a "second time" out of error to the light of the third angel's message.

made, such as were put forth in 1843 and '44. In the scattering, efforts made to spread the truth had but little effect—accomplished little or nothing—but now in the gathering time when God has set His hand to gather His people, efforts to spread the truth will have their designed effect, and all should be zealous and united in the work.

I saw that a paper was needed and that all should be interested in it. I saw that the burden of the paper was laid on James, and that it is as important to publish the truth as to preach it. I saw that James should not be discouraged if all did not feel the interest in the paper that he did. I saw that Bro. Bates had not the interest in the paper that he should have, and that his lack of interest had discouraged James.[6] I saw that James should set his face as a flint, and go forward. I saw the flock looking for the paper, and were ready like hungry children to eat the truth published in it.

I saw that the truth should be made plain on tables,[7] that the earth and the fullness thereof is the Lord's, and that necessary means should not be spared to make it plain. I saw that the angels' messages, made plain, would have effect. I saw that the old chart was directed by the Lord, and that not a peg of it should be altered without inspiration. I saw that the figures on the chart were as God wanted them, and that His hand was over and hid a mistake in some of the figures so that none could see it until His hand was removed.[8]

See: "Brother Miller's Dream," *Present Truth,* May 1850, p. 75. Also published in James White, ed., *Brother Miller's Dream.*

[6] James White later observed that Bates had "refused for one year to write for our little paper, because to publish a paper was to do as others had done who had backslidden." In December 1849 Bates had written to White forcefully expressing his opposition to the publication of a periodical, a letter which had brought James deep discouragement. Despite Ellen White's vision of January 1850 supporting the paper, it appears that Bates's opposition continued till the autumn of 1850, as evidenced by this manuscript.

George R. Knight surveys this disagreement between White and Bates in *Joseph Bates,* pp. 162-166. See also Ellen G. White, Ms 14, 1850 (Sept.).

[7] In another account of the vision, written one week later, Ellen White clarifies the intent of this passage. "God shewed me the necessity of getting out a chart. I saw it was needed and that the truth made plain upon tables would effect much." The reference here is to a chart showing prophetic symbols from Daniel and Revelation together with time calculations. The expression "plain on tables" was taken from Habakkuk 2:2, 3 and had been applied by the Millerites earlier to their use of prophetic charts. The summons for Sabbatarian Adventists to publish a chart was quickly acted upon. Three months later 300 copies of a prophetic chart prepared by Otis Nichols were ready for distribution.

See: Ellen G. White, Lt 26, 1850 (Nov. 1); "The Chart," *Review,* January 1851, p. 38. For a general historical overview of the production of the first chart, see Arthur L. White, *Ellen G. White: The Early Years,* pp. 184, 185.

[8] A parallel account substitutes "1843 chart" for "old chart." This chart, widely used by the Millerites, displayed calculations that the Second Advent would take place in 1843, not recognizing the computational error involved. The assertion here that God's "hand was over and hid a mistake in some of the figures" has been the occasion of much discussion and debate. On the one hand are those who, like D. M. Canright, exclaim, "God helped them make the mistake!" and who make this a reason to reject the authenticity of the visions. Others, such as

I saw that the two-horned beast[9] had a dragon mouth, and that his power was in his head, and that the decree would go out of his mouth. Then I saw the mother of harlots, that the mother was not the daughters, but separate and distinct from them.[10] She has had her day, and it is past, and her daughters, Protestant sects, were next to come on the stage and act out the same mind that the mother had when she persecuted the saints. I saw that as the mother has been declining in power the daughters have been growing, and soon they will exercise the power once manifested by the mother.

F. D. Nichol, point to biblical examples in which God conceals truth from people for a while for purposes of testing. Thus, God concealed the true nature of His purposes from Abraham for some time when he was commanded to take his son to Mount Moriah. This was the position taken by Ellen White. In 1858 she wrote, "I saw that God was in the proclamation of the time in 1843. It was His design to arouse the people, and bring them to a testing point."

See: D. M. Canright, *Seventh-Day Adventism Renounced,* p. 68; Ellen G. White, *Spiritual Gifts [vol. 1],* p. 133; Francis D. Nichol, *Ellen G. White and Her Critics,* pp. 342-344.

[9] Not until some months later, in May 1851, did a Sabbatarian scholar (J. N. Andrews) first propose that the United States of America be identified with the "two-horned" beast of Revelation 13.

See: J. N. Andrews, "Thoughts on Revelation XIII and XIV," *Review,* May 19, 1851, pp. 82-84. For the development of early Sabbatarian interpretation of the two-horned beast, see P. Gerard Damsteegt, *Foundations of the Seventh-day Adventist Message and Mission,* pp. 196-203.

[10] In the main, this exposition of Revelation 17 follows earlier Millerite thinking that after 1843 increasingly identified "Babylon . . . mother of harlots" with the Roman Catholic Church and her offspring harlots as the apostate Protestant churches. The general identification of "Babylon" with Roman Catholicism had a much longer past, reflecting a common position among Protestant scholars going back to the Reformation.

More specifically, this passage may have been directed against the position taken by James White during the 1850s, which tended to downplay the Roman Catholic identity of "Babylon" in Revelation 17. As pointed out by Damsteegt, White seems to have taken his cue for the identification of "Babylon" in Revelation 17 from his understanding of "Babylon" in the second angel's message of Revelation 14. He insisted that since Millerites had not been called out of the Catholic Church in 1843-1844, but out of the Protestant "nominal" churches, "Babylon" did not include the Catholic Church. Turning to "Babylon" in Revelation 17, in an 1851 article, while paying lip service to the Roman Catholic "Mother" and Protestant "harlots" schema of the Millerites, James White sought to conflate the two, seeing them instead as "a family of harlots". . . "symbolical of all the churches." The assertion in Ms 15 that "the mother . . . [is] not the daughters, but separate and distinct from them" seems to be a rejection of this approach. Though James White's article in December 1851 cited above was published after the vision recorded in Ms 15, 1850, yet he may well have held the opinions expressed there earlier.

See: James White, "Come out of Babylon!" *Review,* Dec. 9, 1851, p. 58; P. Gerard Damsteegt, *Foundations of the Seventh-day Adventist Message and Mission,* p. 179, note 99. For Millerite and early Sabbatarian interpretations of "Babylon," see further P. Gerard Damsteegt, *Foundations of the Seventh-day Adventist Message and Mission,* pp. 46-48, 179-184; Alberto R. Timm, *The Sanctuary and the Three Angels' Messages,* pp. 44-47, 81-83, 182-187; Reinder Bruinsma, *Seventh-day Adventist Attitudes Toward Roman Catholicism 1844-1965,* pp. 42-45, 62, 63, 89. For a general history of prophetic interpretation, see LeRoy Edwin Froom, *The Prophetic Faith of Our Fathers* (see especially vol. 2, pp. 528-532; vol. 3, pp. 252, 253, 744; and vol. 4, pp. 392-401 for summaries of non-Millerite Protestant interpretations of "Babylon"). *See also:* EGWEnc, s.v. "Babylon in Eschatology."

I saw that the nominal churches and nominal Adventists,[11] like Judas, would betray us to the Catholics, to obtain their influence to come against the saints. The saints will be an obscure people, but little known to the Catholics, but the church and nominal Adventists will know of our faith and customs, and will betray the saints and report them to the Catholics as those who disregard the institution of the pope—that is, they keep the Sabbath and disregard Sunday.

Then the Catholics bid the Protestants to go forward and issue a decree that all who will not observe the first day of the week instead of the seventh shall be slain,[12] and the Catholics, whose numbers are large, will stand by the Protestants. The Catholics will give their power to the image of the beast, and then Protestants will work as their mother worked before them to destroy the saints. But before their decrees bring forth or bear fruit, the saints will be delivered by the voice of God.

Then I saw that Jesus' work in the sanctuary[13] was almost *finished, almost finished,* and after His work there is finished He will come to the door of the tabernacle, or door of the first apartment, and confess the sins of Israel upon the head of the scapegoat.[14] Then He will put on the garments of vengeance. Then the plagues[15] come upon the wicked, and they do not come until Jesus puts on the garments of vengeance and takes His seat upon the great white cloud. Then, while the plagues are falling, the scapegoat is being led away. He makes a mighty struggle to escape, but he is held fast by the hand that bears him away. If he should effect his escape, Israel would be destroyed (or slain). I saw that it would take time to bear him away into the land of forgetfulness after the sins were put upon his head.

---

[11] The term "nominal church" or "nominal churches" was often used by early Sabbathkeeping Adventist writers to indicate Protestant and Roman Catholic churches that had experienced a moral fall through their rejection of the message of an imminent Second Coming. The expression "nominal Adventists," or some variant thereof, was commonly used to indicate Adventist bodies coming out of the Millerite movement that rejected the Sabbath, the prophetic significance of October 22, 1844, and the continuing gift of prophecy in the church.

See: P. Gerard Damsteegt, *Foundations of the Seventh-day Adventist Message and Mission,* pp. 179-192.

[12] Based on Revelation 13, these predictions of a future persecution of those refusing to honor Sunday as a day of worship affirmed earlier studies dating back to 1847 and the work of Joseph Bates. Despite the dire predictions made here and elsewhere in Ellen White's writings about the future actions of fallen Christendom, she made a clear distinction between these churches as institutions and the individuals belonging to them. Thus her more complete comments affirm that "in the churches which constitute Babylon, the great body of Christ's true followers are still to be found" and that "there are now true Christians in every church, not excepting the Roman Catholic communion . . . ."

See: Joseph Bates, *The Seventh Day Sabbath: A Perpetual Sign* (1847), p. 59; Ellen G. White, *The Great Controversy,* pp. 390, 449.

[13] *See:* EGWEnc, s.v. "Doctrine of the Sanctuary."

[14] *See:* SDAE, s.v. "Scapegoat."

[15] *See: Ibid.*, s.v. "Plagues, Seven Last."

Jesus clothes Himself with the garments of vengeance and takes His place upon the great white cloud[16] before the plagues are poured out. The great white cloud, I saw, was not in the holy place but entirely separate from the holy and most holy, entirely separate from the sanctuary.

As Jesus passed through the holy place, or first apartment, to the door to confess the sins of Israel on the scapegoat, an angel said, This apartment is called the sanctuary. Then the angel repeated these words and said this is the time spoken of, and he saw that there was no man and wondered that there was no intercessor; we had no mediator between God and man and the plagues could be withheld no longer, for Jesus had ceased to plead for Israel, and they were covered with the covering of Almighty God and lived in His sight, and those who were not covered felt the plagues, for they had nothing to shelter them.

I saw that there was a cherub sitting on either end of the mercy seat with their wings spread over the ark. There also stood two angels, one by either end of the ark, with their wings spread out on high and touching each other, while their other wings reached to each side of the apartment. I saw that the wings of the angels did not reach above the Father, for that would bring Him too low. I saw that the Father was in the midst above the cherubims, and His glory is shed down upon the ark, and the train of His glory fills the temple.

Then I saw the "daily," that the Lord gave the correct view of it to those who gave the first angel's message. When union existed before 1844, nearly all were united on the correct view of the "daily," but since, in the confusion, other views have been embraced and darkness has followed.[17] I saw that God

---

[16] Rev. 14:14, 15.

[17] In a parallel account of this vision, published a few weeks later, Ellen White gives a fuller report of this section of the vision: "Then I saw in relation to the 'daily,' that the word 'sacrifice' was supplied by man's wisdom, and does not belong to the text; and that the Lord gave the correct view of it to those who gave the judgment hour cry. When union existed, before 1844, nearly all were united on the correct view of the 'daily'; but since 1844, in the confusion, other views have been embraced, and darkness and confusion has followed." This expanded passage suggests that "the correct view" was that "the word 'sacrifice' was supplied by man's wisdom."

The issue here relates to the activities of the "little horn" power of Daniel 8 by which "the daily sacrifice was taken away, and the place of his sanctuary was cast down" (verse 11). Millerite expositors had opposed the interpretation held by some that the reference here was to Antiochus Epiphanes, who violated the Temple at Jerusalem and stopped Temple sacrifices for a period of about three years in the second century B. C. A common Millerite counterargument was that the word "sacrifice" was not in the original text, but was supplied by the KJV translators.

Ellen White's vision confirms the Millerite view that the word "sacrifice" was supplied "by man's wisdom." But the vision goes on to lament the fact that "since 1844, in the confusion, other views have been embraced." Julia Neuffer points out that among those "other views" was the position among emerging Literalist ("age-to-come") Adventists in the late 1840s and early 1850s that "daily sacrifice" was a reference to the future restoration of Jewish Temple rites in Jerusalem.

In the early twentieth century, considerable controversy arose among church leaders as to whether this passage confirmed the "old" view of "the daily" against the "new" view being argued by Prescott, Daniells, and others.

had not made a test of time since 1844, and that time never again will be a test.[18]

Then I had a view of Sister Minor [Clorinda S. Minor][19] and others with her, that their visions were not true, that God had not spoken by them. I saw that if we are to go to Jerusalem, then the truth should not be made plain upon tables, for our minds should be turned towards Jerusalem and our means should be reserved to get the saints to Jerusalem. I saw that the faults and errors of Sister Minor and those with her in past time had not been confessed.[20] This is the reason why they have been left to run into great errors. I saw that Bro. Bates must be careful and be willing to receive light that comes in other ways besides through visions. I saw that he was too slow to receive light from his brethren.

See: E. G. White, "Dear Brothers and Sisters," *Present Truth,* November 1850, p. 87; Julia Neuffer, "The Gathering of Israel," p. 12. On the controversy over the "old" versus "new" views of "the daily," see Arthur L. White, *Ellen G. White: The Later Elmshaven Years,* pp. 246-261.

[18] For details of the flurry of time-setting among a few Sabbatarian Adventists in 1850 and 1851, see Lt 8, 1851 (Nov. 12), note 8.

[19] Clorinda Minor, former Millerite writer and speaker, adopted a strong Literalist position in the later 1840s and 1850s, actively supporting the emigration of Jews to Palestine and their conversion to Christianity, in preparation for the Second Advent. After a preliminary trip to Palestine in 1849, Mrs. Minor returned to the United States in the spring of 1850 to promote and raise funds for a group of farmer-settlers to go to Palestine to further their Literalist agenda. This is the background for the warnings found in Ellen White's vision, given later the same year.

See: Moshe Davis, *America and the Holy Land,* p. 173; Barbara Kreiger with Shalom Goldman, *Divine Expectations, an American Woman in 19th-Century Palestine*; Julia Neuffer, "The Gathering of Israel," pp. 12, 13; SDAE, s.v. "Clorinda S. Minor."

[20] Clorinda Minor was somewhat tainted by her connection to the Gorgas fanaticism of October 1844. Accepting R. C. Gorgas's vision predicting that the Second Advent would take place at 3:00 a.m. on October 22, 1844, she joined in leading an exodus of Millerites out of Philadelphia to await the Advent. Ellen White vividly described a very uncomfortable meeting with Clorinda Minor in 1845, who was portrayed as leaning toward a "spiritual view of Christ's coming." These may be among the "faults and errors of Sister Minor" that Ellen White alludes to here.

Ellen G. White, *Spiritual Gifts [vol. 2],* pp. 72-74; George R. Knight, *Millennial Fever,* pp. 211, 212; Francis D. Nichol, *The Midnight Cry,* pp. 321-334.

1850

OCTOBER 23, 1850

Date given for an unauthenticated vision. See Appendix A.

1850

(Lt 26, 1850)

NOVEMBER 1, PARIS, MAINE

LETTER TO

Reuben and Belinda Loveland.[1]

This letter is published in entirety in Ellen G. White, *Manuscript Releases,* vol. 15, pp. 210-213.

Letter to personal friends with news and spiritual encouragement.

Dear Brother and Sister Loveland:

We received your very kind letter here at Paris [Maine] yesterday, enclosing the ten, for which we thank you.[2]

We are all enjoying quite good health and have had some sweet seasons of late. How good it is to have a God that we can go to, and tell our wants to Him; and He like a tender parent supplies our wants, and in sickness He is our Physician and will undertake our case and heal us every whit. Should we not rejoice and glorify our God?

Since we last wrote you[3] we have been to Fairhaven [Massachusetts]

---

[1] Most likely the recipients of this letter are Reuben and Belinda Loveland, of Johnson, Vermont. There appear to have been no other Lovelands among Sabbatarian Adventists in this period. Up to the end of 1852 all nine references to "Loveland" in the *Review* are prefixed "Reuben" or "R" or "B." Confirming the identity is another letter to "Brother and Sister Loveland" from Ellen White written some weeks later, on December 13, 1850, in which she specifically locates them in Johnson ("Are you free in Johnson?") and goes on to send "love to your eldest daughter" and "much love to the one at home." This greeting is very similar to that of the present letter, which sends "much love to your daughter who is not at home" and "love to the next oldest." As seen in note 11 below, the eldest daughter of Reuben and Belinda had in fact married and left home by this date.

See: Search term "Loveland" in *Words of the Pioneers;* Ellen G. White, Lt 30, 1850 (Dec. 13); 1850 U.S. Federal Census, "Reuben Loveland," Vermont, Lamoille County, Johnson, p. 64.

[2] This letter is not in the White Estate archives. According to one source, the Lovelands became Sabbathkeepers in 1850, so their acquaintance with the Whites was quite recent. Their first meeting could well have been four months earlier when Ellen and James White attended a conference in Johnson (July 6, 7, 1850). The enclosed $10 is part of a pattern of generous giving by the Lovelands. Mrs. Loveland's obituary states that she and her husband "sacrificed their home farm for the advancement of the message, and moved onto a back lot."

See: W. [James White], "Our Tour East," *Advent Review,* August 1850, p. 15; obituary: "Belinda Loveland," *Review,* Mar. 22, 1906, p. 23; Belinda Loveland, "From Sister Loveland," *Review,* June 11, 1857, p. 46.

[3] This letter is not in the White Estate archives.

to attend a conference there. Brother Bates was present. We had quite an interesting meeting. James baptized two.[4] Both were filled with the Holy Spirit.

Monday we returned to Dorchester [Massachusetts] where our dear Brother Nichols [**Otis Nichols**][5] and family live. There in the night God gave me a very interesting vision, the most of which you will see in the paper.[6] God shewed me the necessity of getting out a chart.[7] I saw it was needed and that the truth made plain upon tables[8] would effect much and would cause souls to come to the knowledge of the truth.

Thursday we left Dorchester for Topsham, Maine. Friday, Brother Howland's [**Stockbridge Howland**][9] family and my little boy [**Henry Nichols White**] went with us to Gorham [Maine] to spend the Sabbath with our parents [**Robert** and **Eunice Harmon**]. Found them strong in the faith. We had a good season with them. We parted with them Sunday sorrowful, because we were obliged to part, but rejoicing that we were of one faith and that soon we should meet, if faithful, never more to part.

You write of trials. We should be glad to know what they are that we may understand your cases and may know how to sympathize with you. We love you and your little band and should love to see you much, but do not expect to at present. We shall stay here at Paris some little time. James is now getting out a paper here. It is an excellent place to get out the paper.

Now do write and tell me if there is anything in your place that prevents your rising. God wants His people to rise and get the victory over the powers of darkness.[10] Be free and free indeed, the fountain is full and free. Let us

---

[4] Held October 19-20, 1850. *See*: "Conferences," *Advent Review,* November 1850, p. 72.

[5] *Identity:* The Dorchester address clearly identifies "Brother Nichols" as Otis Nichols.
See: Search term "Nichols" in *Words of the Pioneers.*

[6] Ellen G. White, "Dear Brethren and Sisters," *Present Truth,* November 1850, pp. 86, 87.

[7] Reference to charts showing prophetic symbols from Daniel and Revelation together with time calculations. The statement here should not be understood as meaning that no prophetic charts had been made or used by Sabbatarian Adventist preachers prior to this. Two months earlier, in August 1850, Ellen White had mentioned a chart made by Samuel W. Rhodes. However, the vision of October 1850 reported here seems to have led directly to the first publication of a prophetic chart. Prepared by Otis Nichols, an edition of 300 copies was ready for distribution by January 1851.

See: Ellen G. White, Lt 12, 1850 (Aug. 15); "The Chart," *Review,* January 1851, p. 38. For a general historical overview of the production of the first chart, see Arthur L. White, *Ellen G. White: The Early Years,* pp. 184, 185.

[8] The expression "plain upon tables" was taken from Habakkuk 2:2, 3 and had been applied earlier by Millerites to their use of prophetic charts.

See: Ellen G. White, *The Great Controversy,* p. 392.

[9] *Identity:* The mention of Ellen White's "little boy" in connection with "Brother Howland" leaves no doubt that Stockbridge Howland, in whose home Henry White stayed in early infancy, is referred to here.

[10] This may be an allusion to the problems facing the young movement in Vermont. According to James White, writing three months earlier, some Adventists (not Sabbatarians)

drink and do not let the enemy prevent us from drawing sap and nourishment from Jesus, the living vine. Let us not rest unless we know that our lives are hid with Christ in God. We must have daily the full assurance that we are accepted of Him. If we have, all is well. We then can come to a throne of grace with holy boldness and draw strength and glory from the sanctuary and be triumphant in God. I do long for the mind that was in Christ. Day after day I discover my unlikeness to the meek and lovely Jesus. I want His fashioning hand to be laid upon me, for I would reflect the lovely image of Jesus.

At times I feel the power of God even in my flesh and yet I am not satisfied. I want to plunge deeper and deeper in the ocean of God's love and be wholly swallowed up in Him. Be strong in God. Do not sink. My vision comes up before me and the words of the angel even now seem to ring in my ears, "Get ready, get ready, get ready. Time is almost finished, almost finished, almost finished. Cry, cry, for the arm of the Lord to be revealed, for the arm of the Lord to be revealed. Time is almost finished. What you do, ye must do quickly!"

Much love to all of your dear band. Much love to your daughter who is not at home.[11] Tell her she will have to wade through deep waters, but God is with her and He will strengthen and uphold her, and though she passes through deep waters they will not overflow her.

Love to the next oldest.[12] (I cannot remember the names of either.) Tell her for me that she has a part to act in the cause of God, and if she would be saved she must overcome by the blood of the Lamb and the word of her testimony. Tell her not to hold back and get barrenness to her soul, but take a part in your little social meetings and she will get great strength to her soul and will not be a clog in the meetings. Tell her to be strong and faint not by the way.

Much love to dear Brother and Sister Heath.[13] I should love to see them

---

were spreading "corrupt views" in Johnson and other places in Vermont about the necessity of a celibate lifestyle. Ellen White described a meeting in Johnson with "two females" from this faction, "with white linen dresses to represent the righteousness of the saints," and tells of the dramatic exit of "these fanatics" as "the power of God filled the room."

See: Ellen G. White, *Spiritual Gifts [vol. 2],* pp. 131, 132; W. [James White], "Our Tour East," *Advent Review,* August 1850, p. 15.

[11] Anne D. Loveland, aged 18, had married Orange Bailey sometime before the summer of 1850 and lived on a neighboring farm.

See: 1850 U.S. Federal Census, "Orange Bailey," Vermont, Lamoille County, Johnson, p. 64; obituary: "Ann D. Bailey," *Review,* Oct. 16, 1856, p. 191.

[12] Florinda Loveland, aged 16. *See*: Obituary: "Florinda Loveland," *Review,* Dec. 27, 1855, p. 103.

[13] No firm identification has been made. Several persons by the surname "Heath" are found in the *Review* in the early 1850s, but none identified as coming from Johnson, Vermont, or vicinity. However, one of Reuben Loveland's neighbors in Johnson in 1850 is "Joseph W. Heath." Perhaps he is the "J. W. Heath" mentioned in the *Review* for January 1851, and the person, together with his wife, referred to here.

much, and talk over the glorious hope that we have and of soon coming into possession of a far more and exceeding eternal weight of glory. Tell them to be valiant for the truth and keep up good courage and all of your little band. It is as the garden of Eden before us and a desolate wilderness behind us. Tell them to press, press their way to the Kingdom.

James [**James Springer White**] would write some but he is now writing at the same table for the paper. He sends love to Brother and Sister Loveland and your children and all of the band. I have written this in great haste.

In hope of the speedy redemption at the voice of [God].

Write Often!!!
E. G. White

We have received an excellent letter from Brother Rhodes [**Samuel W. Rhodes**].[14] He is valiant for the truth and God has been making him mighty. Many souls have been brought into the truth through his labors. Today we received an excellent letter from Brother Bates [**Joseph Bates**].[15] He is still in Fairhaven [Massachusetts].

See: 1850 U.S. Federal Census, "Reuben Loveland," "Joseph W. Heath," Vermont, Lamoille County, Johnson, p. 64; "Letters Received Since Dec. 24," *Review,* January 1851, p. 31.

[14] This letter is not in the White Estate archives. The only "Rhodes" appearing in the *Review* of the early and mid-1850s was the traveling preacher Samuel W. Rhodes.

See: Search term "Rhodes" in *Words of the Pioneers.*

[15] *Identity:* The Fairhaven location of Bates identifies him as Joseph Bates.

See: Search term "Bates" in *Words of the Pioneers.*

1850

(Lt 28, 1850)

NOVEMBER [27],[1] PARIS, MAINE

LETTER TO

the Church in Brother Leonard W. Hastings'[2] House.

This letter is published in entirety in Ellen G. White, *Manuscript Releases,* vol. 16, pp. 206-209.

News to family friends of the Whites' move to Paris, Maine, recent conferences attended, death of Sister Foey, etc.

To the Church in Bro. Hastings' house,

Dear Friends:

I have neglected writing you for some time. I will now give my reasons. First, I had no time to write for weeks after I received Sister Arabella's [**Harriet A. Hastings**][3] kind and welcome letter,[4] or I should have complied with her request to have answered it within two weeks. I liked the letter very much. We were all interested in the letter and hope my delay will not prevent you from answering this as soon as you read it and I will not wait so long next time.

James' [**James Springer White**] and my health is quite good now. Our home is in Paris [Maine] at Brother Andrews' [**Edward Andrews**][5] within a few steps of the post office and printing office. We shall stay here some little time.[6]

---

[1] The handwritten original bears the date of November 7, which may have been when Ellen White began the letter. The date, November 27, is inferred from the later statement in the letter, "Nov. 20, one week ago . . ."

[2] *Identity:* The letter is addressed "Leonard Hastings, New Ipswich, N.H."

[3] Arabella's identity is hinted at by her association in these opening lines with "Bro. Hastings' house." Arabella was the oldest of the Hastings children, about 17 years old. Her name is given as "Harriet A. Hastings" in her obituary. Ellen White sometimes referred to her as "Arabella" and sometimes as "Harriet" (cf. Lt 5, 1849 [Apr. 21], and Lt 10, 1850 [Mar. 18], with Lt 7, 1851 [July 27], and Lt 3, 1851 [Aug. 11]). Presumably the middle initial stands for "Arabella."

See: Obituary: "Harriet A. Hastings," *Review,* Sept. 5, 1854, p. 31.

[4] This letter is not in the White Estate archives.

[5] *Identity*: In a letter to E. P. Butler in 1861 James White goes into some detail about the rent and other payments made to Edward Andrews while the Whites boarded with the Andrews in 1850/1851.

See: James White to E. P. Butler, Dec. 12, 1861.

[6] The Whites arrived in Paris at the end of October 1850 and moved to Saratoga Springs, New York, in August 1851.

See: Ellen G. White, Lt 26, 1850 (Nov. 1); James White to "Brethren in Jackson," Aug.

This is a very kind family, yet quite poor.[7] Everything here is free as far as they have. We do not think it right to be any expense to them while here.[8] I want to see you all very much and dear Sister Gorham [**Elizabeth Gorham**].[9]

Our conference at Topsham[10] [Maine] was one of deep interest. Twenty-eight were present; all took part in the meeting.

Sunday the power of God came upon us like a mighty rushing wind. All arose upon their feet and praised God with a loud voice; it was something as it was when the foundation of the house of God was laid. The voice of weeping could not be told from the voice of shouting.[11] It was a triumphant time; all were strengthened and refreshed. I never witnessed such a powerful time before.

Our next Conference was in Fairhaven [Massachusetts]. Brother Bates and wife [**Joseph** and **Prudence M. Bates**][12] were present. It was quite a good meeting. On our return to Brother Nichols' [**Otis Nichols**],[13] the Lord gave me a vision and shewed me that the truth must be made plain upon tables[14]

4, 1851.

[7] Edward Andrews's occupation is listed as "labourer" in the 1850 census. Charles Stevens, a contemporary, speaks of "a small wooden house occupied jointly by Brother and Sister White and Edward Andrews and family."

See: 1850 U.S. Federal Census, "Edward Andrews," Maine, Oxford County, Paris, p. 190; Charles F. Stevens, [memory statement], n.d., Center for Adventist Research, Andrews University.

[8] Subsequently the Whites paid "$1.00 per week for board . . . and two-fifths of the rent of the whole house."

See: James White to E. P. Butler, Dec. 12, 1861.

[9] *Identity:* See Lt 5, 1849 (Apr. 21), note 25.

[10] The sequence of events mentioned in this section can all be dated thanks to James White's report in the *Review* and Ellen White's letter of November 1: Conference at Topsham—Oct. 12-13; conference at Fairhaven—Oct. 19-20; vision at "Brother Nichols'"—Oct. 21, 1850.

See: "Conferences," *Advent Review,* November 1850, p. 72; Ellen G. White, Lt 26, 1850 (Nov. 1).

[11] A few weeks later, in a vision received on December 24, Ellen White received cautions against "unhealthy and unnecessary excitement" (Ms 11, 1850). *See also*: Appendix article "Ellen White and Religious Enthusiasm in Early Adventist Experience"; EGWEnc, s.v. "Ecstatic Experiences."

[12] The special mention of Joseph Bates's wife may be of significance. In his published account of this Fairhaven conference, James White added that for years Prudence Bates had rejected the Sabbath and Joseph had kept it alone. But "now she and her husband are walking in all the commandments and ordinances of the Lord."

See: "Conferences," *Advent Review,* November 1850, p. 72.

[13] *Identity:* In an earlier parallel account, Ellen White adds the information that they had traveled to Dorchester, "where our dear Brother Nichols and family live." The reference here is clearly to Otis Nichols, of Dorchester, Massachusetts.

See: Ellen G. White, Lt 26, 1850 (Nov. 1); search term "Otis Nichols" in *Words of the Pioneers.*

[14] A reference to prophetic charts. In a letter citing the same vision, written a few weeks earlier, Ellen White wrote, "God shewed me the necessity of getting out a chart. I saw it was needed and that the truth made plain upon tables would . . . cause souls to come to the knowledge of the truth." The expression "plain upon tables" was taken from Habakkuk 2:2, 3 and had been applied by Millerites earlier to their use of prophetic charts.

See: Ellen G. White, Lt 26, 1850 (Nov. 1); *idem, The Great Controversy,* p. 392.

and it would cause many to decide for the truth by the three angels' message with the two former being made plain upon tables.

I also saw it was as necessary for the paper to be published as for the messengers to go, for the messengers need a paper to carry with them, containing present truth to put in the hands of those that hear, and then the truth would not fade from the mind, and that the paper would go where the messengers could not go. Other things I saw which will appear in the paper.[15] How do you all get along? Are you all striving for eternal life? I want to see you very, very much[16] and think I shall before long. Now is the preparation time and I hope we shall all make sure work for eternity. Time looks very short and what we do we must do quickly.

Nov. 20, one week ago, Brother Henry Nichols [**Henry O. Nichols**][17] and self went to Topsham. We had just risen from the dinner table Thursday, when one of Bro. Foey's [John Green Foy][18] children came in and said their mother was insensible. We hastened over the river one mile [1.6 kilometers] and found our dear Sister Foey dying. My distress was great as I found she did not know me. She continued long in great distress until between three and four o'clock and then breathed her last. She has left a husband and three children to mourn her loss.

Friday morning, Brother Henry came to Paris for James to shave him to attend the funeral. We had a very solemn interesting time. The Lord did not

---

[15] Ellen G. White, "Dear Brethren and Sisters," *Present Truth,* November 1850, p. 87.

[16] Ellen White showed added concern for the Hastings family, especially the children, after the death of Mrs. Elvira Hastings in February 1850. The Whites subsequently visited the bereaved family in June 1850, at which time the four eldest children were baptized by James White.

See: Ellen G. White, Lt 10, 1850 (Mar. 18); W. [James White], "Our Tour East," *Advent Review,* August 1850, p. 14.

[17] *Identity:* Son of Otis Nichols of Dorchester, Massachusetts. According to one source, Henry Nichols "assisted" in the "editorial work" in Paris.

See: Charles F. Stevens [memory statement].

[18] *Identity:* Surprisingly there is no trace of the name "Foey" in the *Review.* Neither is there any person by that name in all the state of Maine in the 1850 census. The probability therefore is that there is a spelling discrepancy here. It is likely that Ellen White is referring to John Green Foy, of Brunswick, Maine. Brunswick is just across the Androscoggin River from Topsham, which corresponds with Ellen White's account that they "hastened over the river one mile [1.6 kilometers]" from Topsham. Ellen White later in life reminisced about "Brother Foy and his family of Brunswick" who had "accepted the Sabbath truth" together with the Stockbridge Howland family of nearby Topsham "a few years" after 1844. According to John Foy's obituary in 1861, his wife had died earlier, leaving him with six children. The fact of his wife's prior death fits well with Ellen White's account. The only discrepancy is that Ellen White in this letter gives the number of the Foy children as three, whereas the obituary and the 1850 census mention six children. On balance, however, the evidence in favor of the proposed identity seems to outweigh the discrepancy over the number of children.

See: Search terms "Foey" and "Foy" in *Words of the Pioneers*; Ellen G. White, Ms 86, 1903 (Aug. 9); obituary: "John G. Foy," *Review,* Feb. 26, 1861, p. 119; 1850 U.S. Federal Census, "John B. [*sic*] Foy," "Dorcas Foy," Maine, Cumberland County, Brunswick, p. 231.

leave us but let His Spirit rest upon us. Sister Foey's last days were decidedly her most spiritual and best days. Brother Foey has this to console him, that she died a Christian. He bears up well. God gives him grace to endure the affliction. Oh, how good it is to have a hope in God that will sustain in all scenes of trial and affliction. Praise God for a hope, a good hope. What would you, any of you, give for your hope?

Hold fast the faith. Be strong in God and lean upon His everlasting arm. It will never fail you but will bear you up under every affliction. I hope you will all grow stronger and stronger in the truth. Do not falter but press your way to the kingdom.

One week ago, last Sabbath, we had a very interesting meeting. Brother Hewit[19] from Dead River [Maine] was there. He came with a message to the effect that the destruction of the wicked and the sleep of the dead was an abomination within a shut door that a woman Jezebel, a prophetess, had brought in, and he believed that I was that woman, Jezebel.[20]

We told him of some of his errors in the past, that the 1335 days were ended[21] and numerous errors of his. It had but little effect. His darkness

---

[19] *Identity:* It is possible that "Brother Hewit" was the "Oren Hewitt" (or Hewett), of Dead River, Maine, who sent several letters to first-day Adventist papers during the latter 1840s. Whether there is any connection between that Oren Hewitt and the "Oren Hewett" of New York State mentioned in the *Review* in the early 1850s cannot be established on the basis of present evidence.

See: "Brother Oren Hewett Writes From Dead River," *Advent Herald,* May 8, 1847, p. 111; "Bro. Oren Hewet, Dead River, Me.," *Bible Advocate,* Apr. 24, 1847, p. 111; obituary: "Oren Hewett," *Review,* May 1, 1855, p. 222; search terms "Oren Hewett" and "O. Hewett" in *Words of the Pioneers.*

[20] An allusion to "that woman Jezebel, which calleth herself a prophetess" (Rev. 2:20).

[21] A reference to the 1335-day prophecy of Daniel 12:12. The united position of Sabbatarian expositors during this and subsequent stages was that the 1335 day/year period had ended in 1843/1844. Ellen White's statement here, however, if taken on its own, is rather ambiguous and could be taken as denying that the 1335 days had ended (and affirming that its fulfillment was still future). Some have cited this Ellen White letter to support the idea of a future literal 1335-day period just preceding the Second Advent. Such an interpretation of the vision, however, runs counter to Ellen White's caution given just one month earlier "that God had not made a test of time since 1844, and that time never again will be a test" (Ms 15, 1850 [Oct. 23]). Therefore the alternative reading of the passage seems preferable, viz.: "We told him . . . that the 1335 days were ended." This reading is confirmed if, in fact, "Brother Hewitt" is Oren Hewett, of Dead River, Maine (see note 19 above). Oren Hewett (Hewitt) wrote several supportive letters to *The Bible Advocate* in 1847, an Adventist paper that repeatedly set new times for the Second Advent, times often held to coincide with the ending of the 1335 days/years (see, e.g., Blakeslee, Wilcox, and Bates below). It would therefore be understandable for Hewett, coming from *The Bible Advocate* background, to see the 1335 days stretching beyond 1844, and for Ellen White and the Sabbatarians to oppose him on this point.

See: Ellen G. White, Ms 15, 1850 (Oct. 23); E. S. Blakeslee, "Time of the Advent," *Bible Advocate,* Sept. 2, 1847, p. 34; L. Wilcox, "Brother L. Wilcox's Letter—Concluded," *Bible Advocate,* Apr. 13, 1848, p. 58; Joseph Bates, *A Vindication of the Seventh-day Sabbath,* pp. 51, 52. For a general survey and critique of a futurist interpretation of this vision and of the 1335 days of Daniel 12, see Alberto R. Timm, "The 1,290 and 1,335 Days of Daniel 12."

was felt upon the meeting and it dragged.

I felt that I must say a few words. In the name of Jesus, I got up and in about five minutes the meeting changed. Every one felt it at the same instant. Every countenance was lighted up. The presence of God filled the place. Brother Hewit dropped upon his knees and began to cry and pray. I was taken off in vision and saw much that I cannot write. It had a great effect on Bro. Hewit. He confessed it was of God and was humbled in the dust. He has been writing ever since that meeting and is now writing from the same table renouncing all his errors that he has advanced. I believe God is bringing him up and he is calculated to do good, if God moves through him.

Much love to Dear Sister Gorham. Tell her to be strong. God is with her and He will not leave her. Much love to you all. I hope the children will not get sleepy, but will be interested in the truth and be diligent to make their calling and election sure. Write, be sure and write, and do not do as I have done. I love you, all of you. Write.

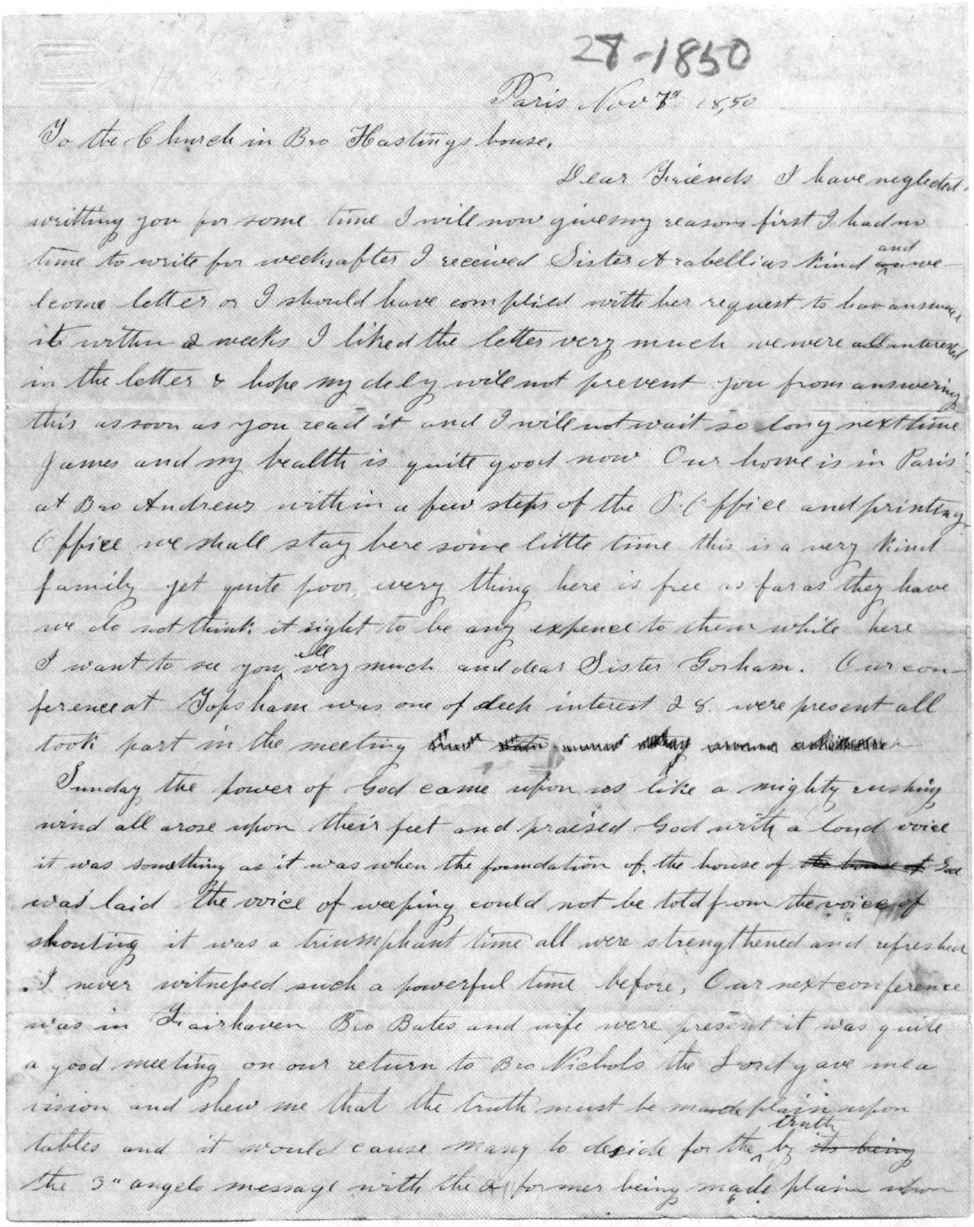

28-1850

Paris Nov 7th 1850

To the Church in Bro Hastings house,

Dear Friends I have neglected writting you for some time I will now give my reasons first I had no time to write for weeks after I received Sister Arabellias kind and welcome letter or I should have complied with her request to have answered it within 2 weeks I liked the letter very much we were all interested in the letter & hope my dely will not prevent you from answering this as soon as you read it and I will not wait so long next time James and my health is quite good now Our home is in Paris at Bro Andrews within a few steps of the P Office and printing Office we shall stay here some little time this is a very kind family yet quite poor, every thing here is free as far as they have we do not think it right to be any expence to them while here I want to see you all very much and dear Sister Gorham. Our conference at Topsham was one of deep interest 28 were present all took part in the meeting ~~[illegible]~~ Sunday the power of God came upon us like a mighty rushing wind all arose upon their feet and praised God with a loud voice it was something as it was when the foundation of the house of ~~[illegible]~~ God was laid the voice of weeping could not be told from the voice of shouting it was a triumphant time all were strengthened and refreshed. I never witnessed such a powerful time before, Our next conference was in Fairhaven Bro Bates and wife were present it was quite a good meeting on our return to Bro Nichols the Lord gave me a vision and shew me that the truth must be made plain upon tables and it would cause many to decide for the truth by ~~its being~~ the 3d angels message with the 2 former being made plain upon

Ellen White's letter to the "Church in Bro. Hastings' House," November 7, 1850 (Lt 28, 1850), with a closing note by James White

tables I also saw it was as necessary for the paper to be published as for the messengers to go, for the messengers needs a paper to carry with them containing present truth to put in the hands of those that hear, and then the truth would not fade from the mind, And that the paper would go where the messengers could not go, Other things I saw which will appear in the paper, How do you all get along are you all striving for eternal life, I want to see you very, very much and think I shall before long. Now is the preparation time and I hope we shall all make shure work for eternity time looks very short and what we do we must do quickly.

Nov 20" one week ago Bro Henry Nichols & self went to Topsham we had just arose frome the dinner table Thursday when one of Bro Foxeys children came in and said their Mother was insenceable we hastened over the river one mile and found our dear Sister Foxey dying my distress was great as I found she did not know me she continued along in great distress untill between 3 and 4 O clock and then breathed her last she has left a husband and 3 children to mourn her loss Friday Morn Br Henry came to Paris for James to have him to attend the funeral we had a very solemn interesting time the Lord did not leave us but let his spirit rest upon us Sister Foxeys last days was decidedly her most spiritual and best days. Bro Foxey has this to console him that she died a christian he bears up well, God gives him grace to endure the affliction O how good it is to have a hope in God that will sustain in all scens of trial & affliction prais God for a hope a good hope what would you any of you give for your hope? Hold fast the faith be strong in God and lean upon his everlasting arm it will never fail you but

will bear you up under every affliction. I hope you will all grow
stronger & stronger in the truth do not falter but press your
way to the kingdom. One week ago last Sabbath
we had a very interesting meeting Bro Hewit from dead
river was their he came with a message to the band that
the destruction of the wicked and the sleep of the dead was
an abomination within a shut door that that a woman
Jezebel a prophetess had brought in and he believed
that I was that woman Jezebel. we told him of some
of his errors in the past that the 1335 days were ended
and numerous errors of his it had but little effect
his darkness was felt upon the meeting and it drag-
ged I felt that I must say a few words in the name
of Jesus I got up and in about 5 minutes the meeting
changed every one felt it at the same instant every coun-
tenance was lighted up the presence of God filled the
place Bro Hewit dropped upon his knees & began to
cry and pray I was taken off in vision & saw much
that I cannot write it had a great effect upon Bro
Hewit he confessed it was of God & was humbled in
the dust, he has been writting ever since that meeting
& is now writting from the same table renouncing all
his errors that he has advanced I believe God is bringing
him up & he is calculated to do good if God moves throu
him. much love to Dear Sister Gorham tell her to
be strong God is with her and he will not leave her
much love to you all I hope the children will not get sleepy
but will be interested in the truth, & be dilligent to make
their calling an election shure. write be shure & write & do
not do as I have done I love you all do you write, E. G. White.

My Dear Bro. Hastings, and all your dear children,
I have not forgotten you by any means. Once I had but
few friends, then I could often write long letters; but now
I have so many that I have time to write but seldom.
We are all well, and there is a good prospect here of doing
printing very cheap and well. I have sent you Present
Truth No. 11 and shall send you Advent Review No. 1 tomor
row. I shall enlarge the paper and send it out often.
The truth is gaining ground Praise the Lord. I wish
to be affectionately remembered to all ~~you~~ who love the
truth. I want the children to write.
Love to all who love the truth— James White.

Leonard Hastings,
New Ipswich
N. H.

1850

NOVEMBER 1850

"Dear Brethren and Sisters."

Article published in *The Present Truth,* vol. 1, no. 11, November 1850, pp. 86, 87.

1850

(Lt 31, 1850)

[DECEMBER],[1] PARIS, MAINE

LETTER TO

Mary Nichols.

Previously unpublished.

Powerful revival at Paris, Maine, conference November 1850.

[From a letter of **Mary Nichols** to Sister Collins [**Nancy Collins**],[2] December 12, 1850.]

We have received a good letter from Sister Ellen [Ellen G. White]. She is in Paris, Maine.[3] She writes, "The conference there[4] was one of deep interest. Some who had been in great error confessed their errors, and came out clear

---

[1] The date is inferred from Ellen White's account in the letter of a conference held in Paris, Maine, either November 16-17 or 23-24, 1850 (see notes below). Her letter would therefore have been written in late November or early December, but well before Mary Nichols's letter of December 12, 1850.

[2] *Identity:* Probably Nancy Collins, of Dartmouth, Massachusetts, wife of **Philip Collins**. No other Collins family appears in the *Review* until 1853.

See: Search term "Collins" in *Words of the Pioneers.*

[3] The Whites had moved to Paris, Maine, at the end of October 1850.

See: Ellen G. White, Lt 26, 1850 (Nov. 1).

[4] Even though the wording here is ambiguous, another account by Ellen White of the same conference places it in Paris. According to the *Review* the conference took place either November 16-17 or 23-24, 1850.

See: Ellen G. White, Lt 30, 1850 (Dec. 13); A. S. Stevens, "Letter From Sister A. S. Stevens," *Review,* December 1850, p. 16; [announcement], *Present Truth,* November 1850, p. 88.

in the truth. The Spirit of the Lord fell upon a young sister present. She went to several of the children, wept over them, and asked them if they would go to heaven with her, repeating it several times, 'Will you go with me? I am going to the Kingdom, will you go with me?' One of them fell upon his knees on the floor, and cried out, 'I will, I will.' And such a scene followed as cannot be described—all fell upon their knees, some were crying for mercy, others for a closer walk with God, and some for salvation, full and free. It seemed as though Jesus Himself entered the room, and I could see Him standing at the hearts of the children, and had been waiting for entrance, until His locks were wet with the dew of night; and their hearts were so filled with pride and unbelief, that there was no room for the lovely Jesus. But at last victory was given unto us, and darkness and unbelief fled away; and some were shouting and praising God."[5]

---

[5] *See:* Appendix article "Ellen White and Religious Enthusiasm in Early Adventist Experience"; EGWEnc, s.v. "Ecstatic Experiences."

1850

(Lt 30, 1850)

DECEMBER 13, PARIS, MAINE

LETTER TO

Reuben and Belinda Loveland.[1]

Portions of this letter are published in Ellen G. White, *Manuscript Releases,* vol. 1, pp. 31, 32; vol. 4, p. 270; vol. 5, p. 226; vol. 6, p. 252; vol. 8, p. 223; vol. 9, pp. 98, 99.

A letter to personal friends containing news and spiritual encouragement.

Dear Brother and Sister Loveland:

We have waited some time for an answer to our last,[2] but as none comes we write again, fearing you have not received it. We are all quite well in body and tolerable free in mind. We have trials, I assure you, with all the people of God and we have made up our minds for them, but let come what will we are determined to tread the narrow, thorny pathway.

Our last conference[3] was one of deep interest. Two were dug from beneath the rubbish. The present truth was presented in its clear light and it found way [to] the hearts of the erring. Before the meeting closed all were upon their knees, some were crying for mercy that had been cold hearted and indifferent, others were begging for a closer walk with God and for salvation. It was a powerful time as I ever witnessed; the slaying power of God was in our midst.

---

[1] *Identity:* The information given in the third paragraph that the Lovelands live in Johnson or vicinity makes it clear that this letter is addressed to Reuben and Belinda Loveland of Johnson, Vermont. The inference is strengthened by the fact that all nine references to "Loveland" in the *Review* before 1853 are prefixed "Reuben" or "R." or "B."

See: 1850 U.S. Federal Census, "Reuben Loveland," Vermont, Lamoille County, Johnson, p. 64; search term "Loveland" in *Words of the Pioneers.*

[2] This is probably a reference to Ellen White's letter to the Lovelands of November 1, 1850 (Lt 26, 1850).

[3] A notice in the November 1850 issue of *The Present Truth* announced "a conference of the brethren at Paris, Me., Nov. 16, to hold over the first day." That this Paris conference is the one Ellen White alludes to becomes very clear when one examines a letter she wrote to Mary Nichols sometime before December 12 describing a Paris conference in very similar language:

- "All fell upon their knees, some were crying for mercy, others for a closer walk with God, and some for salvation" (Lt 31 to Mary Nichols).
- "All were upon their knees, some were crying for mercy . . . , others were begging for a closer walk with God and for salvation" (Lt 30 to the Lovelands).

See: [No title], *Present Truth,* November 1850, p. 88; Ellen G. White, Lt 31, 1850 (Dec.).

Shouts of victory filled the dwelling.[4] The saints here seem to be rising and growing in grace and the knowledge of the truth.

Are you free in Johnson [Vermont]? Does God manifest Himself to you? Are the dead weights shaken off? You, of course, have nothing to do with Terry;[5] do not have him in your house. There is something about that man, *black*, that he did not confess at the conference.[6] He is unclean, unholy in the sight of God, and if you have him in your house you will be unclean because he is a dead body. The power of Satan is very great and Terry will make a complete agent for Satan to work through to destroy you all. He may appear to break down and be humble but it is forever too late for him. God shewed me at the conference that the last ray of light was taken from him and that He would visit him with His judgments. Cut loose entirely from every dead weight and every fornicator.

Oh, what a time this is! Oh, how carefully do we need to walk before God! Time is almost finished. Oh, do, do be free. Make one mighty struggle for victory and you will have it. I warn all of you to ply the oar and every one row his own boat up stream. The wind and tide is against us. Multitudes are going downstream, and we, if we enter the port of glory, must press our way through the multitudes and row for our life (eternal life) up stream. Will we row? One cannot row another's boat. We must strive for heaven with all our might. Every one has a part to act and something to do in the cause of God. None of you should keep silent in your meetings. Surely every one who has tasted of the powers of the world to come can say something in honor of the lovely Jesus. Eternal life we are striving for. Shall we get discouraged? No, no. The riches of Eden are before us and we must pass through the strait if we would enter the wide. Let us double our diligence to make our calling and election sure. Victory, victory, will be ours if we endure a little longer.

I do beg and pray to be more like Jesus that I may reflect His lovely image. More and more I long to be filled with all the fullness of God. It is our privilege to rejoice in a whole Saviour, One that saves us from all sin. We will

---

[4] On ecstatic phenomena in early Adventist worship, see Appendix article "Ellen White and Religious Enthusiasm in Early Adventist Experience" and EGWEnc, s.v. "Ecstatic Experiences." Arthur L. White sees the tide turning against "emotionalism" in Adventist worship after Ellen White's vision of December 24, 1850, which contained cautions concerning ecstatic exercises.

See: Arthur L. White, *Ellen G. White: The Early Years,* pp. 195, 200-203.

[5] This is the only mention of "Terry" in Ellen White's writings. No identification has been made.

[6] The two most recent conferences in Vermont attended by the Whites were held in Johnson (July 6, 7, 1850) and Sutton (Sept. 26-29, 1850). Although not specifically mentioning "Terry," Ellen White writes of a confrontation with certain "fanatical spirits" at the Johnson conference.

See: W. [James White], "Our Tour East," *Advent Review,* August 1850, p. 15; "Conferences," *Advent Review,* November 1850, p. 72; Ellen G. White, *Spiritual Gifts [vol. 2],* pp. 131, 132.

not rest unless we know the length and breadth, height and depth of perfect love. I expect you are buffeted by the enemy. Do not yield one inch to him. Let faith be in lively exercise. Let it enter within the second veil and take hold upon the most excellent glory.

Dear Brother Rhodes [**Samuel W. Rhodes**][7] was with us in our last conference.[8] It was good to see his face once more and cheering to hear him talk the plain cutting truth of God from the Bible. How plain our position is: We know that we have the truth. Brother Rhodes has now gone in company with Brother John Andrews [**John Nevins Andrews**] to the eastern part of the State to hunt up the scattered sheep.[9] We have received two letters from them.[10] God is at work and is bringing souls from the rubbish[11] to the clear light of truth. We have received cheering letters from different places. God is with Israel.

I had the privilege of being with my oldest boy [**Henry Nichols White**] two weeks.[12] He is a lovely-dispositioned boy. He became so attached to his mother it was hard to be separated from him; but as our time is all employed in writing and folding and wrapping papers, I am denied the privilege of having his company. My other little one [**James Edson White**] is many hundred miles from me.[13] Sometimes Satan tempts me to complain and think

---

[7] *Identity:* Only Samuel W. Rhodes fits the description of an itinerant preacher surnamed "Rhodes" in 1850.

[8] The announcement in *The Present Truth* of "a conference of the brethren at Paris, Me., Nov. 16" adds, "We hope that Bro. Rhodes will meet with us."

See: [No title], *Present Truth,* November 1850, p. 88.

[9] The *Review* of January 1851 notes that "Brn. Rhodes and Andrews returned from Eastern Maine Dec. 31. They found a good number . . . who joyfully received the truth."

See: [No title], *Review,* January 1851, p. 31.

[10] These letters are not in the White Estate archives.

[11] An allusion to a widely publicized dream William Miller had in 1847. Central to the dream were jewels covered in dust and rubbish. A man with a "dirt-brush" entered the room, and brushed away the rubbish, restoring the brilliance of the precious stones. James White published the vision in *The Present Truth* in 1850. According to White's interpretation, the dust and rubbish represent the "darkness and error" that had covered "the clear light of . . . the third angel's message."

See: "Brother Miller's Dream," *Present Truth,* May 1850, p. 75. Also published in James White, ed., *Brother Miller's Dream.*

[12] Henry Nichols White, now aged 3, had lived with the family of Stockbridge Howland in Topsham, Maine, since he was 1 year old. During this travel itinerary in the autumn of 1850 Ellen and James White had the opportunity to meet Henry during the conference in Topsham, October 12-13. After a visit to Fairhaven, Massachusetts, the following weekend, Ellen White returned to Topsham and spent some time with Henry, among other things taking him to Gorham, Maine, to visit his grandparents.

See: Arthur L. White, *Ellen G. White: The Early Years,* pp. 135, 136, 283; "Conferences," *Advent Review,* November 1850, p. 72; Ellen G. White, Lt 26, 1850 (Nov. 1).

[13] James Edson White, 1 year old, was looked after at this time by Clarissa Bonfoey, probably at the home of Ira and Rhoda Abbey in Brookfield, New York. In August 1851 Edson and Clarissa rejoined the White family in Saratoga Springs, New York.

See: Ellen G. White, *Spiritual Gifts [vol. 2],* pp. 143, 152.

my lot is a hard one, but I will not harbor this temptation. I should not want to live unless I could live to do some good to others. I want all self to die. I have this consolation that God is pleased with my sacrifice, that of offering up my children to Him. Do pray for me. I need much grace to perform my duty faithfully and deliver the straight messages that God lays upon me to deliver.

I wish I could see you. I have much I should love to say to you [but] I cannot write much. Love to your eldest daughter.[14] Tell her to be of good courage and hope in God and His arm will hold her up and protect her from the tempter's power. Oh, tell her to have faith and rejoice in God. Much love to the one at home.[15] Tell her to look to Jesus and take up her cross, for unless she bears the cross she cannot wear the crown. Love to all the dear saints. Tell them to walk carefully before God; tread in the footsteps of Jesus.

When I wrote you last I was bound in spirit. I had no liberty. I could not tell the reason I was [not] free before I commenced to write. Perhaps I ought not to have written.

I hear, by the by, that Mrs. Foster has gone to live with her husband.[16] Was she right? James and self felt that she was wrong. He told me that he could have no communion with her, neither could I; but I told him she must be good, for you had perfect confidence in her. I felt that she was in the way when Brother Rhodes was healed.[17] Do, do rid yourselves of every hindrance and go free. God wants you to be free. We love you and hope you come off victorious. Heaven is cheap enough. Look away from this dark, dark earth to the riches of Eden.

I have got a glimpse of what God is preparing for His children and it has spoiled this world for me. Everything here looks desolate and dreary. The glorious charms of heaven attract my soul above. Oh, what could we poor mortals do without a God? We do not deserve the least of His notice. What can it be that the high and lofty One, He who taketh up the isles as a very little thing, and the nations before Him are as but a drop in the bucket; yet He condescends to us who are as the small dust of the balance. Yes, even the hairs of our head are numbered. Oh, let us humble ourselves before the mighty God of Jacob. Thanks be to God for His goodness to such poor worms. I do love Jesus. He is my all and in all. I do love Him with my whole

---

[14] Anne D., age 18, married to Orange Bailey.

See: 1850 U.S. Federal Census, "Orange Bailey," Vermont, Lamoille County, Johnson, p. 64; obituary: "Ann D. Bailey," *Review,* Oct. 16, 1856, p. 191.

[15] Florinda Loveland, aged 16. *See*: Obituary: "Florinda Loveland," *Review,* Dec. 27, 1855, p. 103.

[16] There is insufficient information in this letter or in other available materials from the 1850s to be certain about the identity of "Mrs. Foster" or to explain more fully the nature of her domestic problems.

[17] No further information about the healing of S. W. Rhodes during this period has been found in the writings of Ellen White or in early publications.

soul, and my very being cries out after the living God. Stem the current a little longer. Press your way to the kingdom.

James sends love to you all that love God in sincerity and truth. He joins with me in the above. Pray for me.

In much love.

E. G. White

Be sure and, just as soon as you get this, write us all the particulars, how you are. Do not forget to answer this immediately.

1850

(Ms 10, 1850)

DECEMBER 24, PARIS, MAINE

Utterances in Vision.[1]

Portions of this manuscript are published in Arthur L. White, *Ellen G. White: The Early Years,* p. 201.

Utterances in vision, December 24, 1850.

Great and holy. Walk carefully before Him. High and lifted up. Everything in perfect order. Know what thou doest. Must be so. Move in order, move in order. A meaning to everything. Yea how perfect, how beautiful, how lovely, is this order.

Let them go, let them go.[2] Souls are coming to the knowledge of the truth. The burden not on him alone (Bro. White).[3] Look ye, let them go. They have not moved in God at all times.[4] Encourage it not, for it will tend to destruction. There has been a stretching beyond. Look beyond the mortal. God will teach by His Word and Spirit.

Hast thou had compassion? God suffered him to go where none had confidence in him. God loves him still, make him to hope and all will be well (H.S.G.).[5] She must make thorough work (S.C.).[6] Oh, how mighty, how

---

[1] On December 25, 1850, Ellen White wrote an account of a vision she had received "last evening" while "united in prayer" with others in Paris, Maine (see Ms 11, 1850). Interestingly, one of those present the previous evening had recorded the actual words spoken by Ellen White while in vision, as found in this document (Ms 10, 1850). This provides a rare opportunity to compare the vision utterances with Ellen White's written account of the same vision. A comparison shows that while the two are clearly related, as shown by common expressions, most of the factual content of the written account could not have been deduced from a reading of the vision utterances by themselves. Examples of this are given in the notes that follow. More generally it can be said that this comparison of Ms 10 and Ms 11, 1850, gives reason for readers to be cautious in trying to interpret other transcriptions of vision utterances for which there do not exist corresponding vision accounts by Ellen White

[2] Only by reading the vision account in Ms 11, 1850, do we discover that "them" refers to the papers published by James White.

[3] Ms 11, 1850, reveals that the subject is James White. "I saw that James had not borne the burden alone but that the angels of God had assisted and had oversight of the paper." (The words "Bro. White" placed in brackets are not in the original but were inserted later by an editor.)

[4] From Ms 11, 1850, we learn that "they" refers to the members of the Fairhaven, Massachusetts, band.

[5] "H.S.G." is a later editorial insertion. Only the vision account identifies the subject of these statements as "Bro. Gurney," i.e., **Heman S. Gurney**, of whom it is said in Ms 11, 1850, that "God loved him still" and that "all would be well."

[6] "She" is identified only in Ms 11, 1850, as Sally Chase. (The "S.C." is an editorial

glorious would Israel be if they would go according to the Word of God. Hast thou thought all was unadulterated? How liable is the enemy to work there? Does He frown upon His people, because they are jealous with a godly jealousy? What then? Truth, truth, present truth, the Word of God. Hold it before them. How beautiful to hold the Word of God. Thy ways are past finding out. He never erred in wisdom.

Strive to lift the mind from self. Strive to let it dwell on *high* and *lofty* things. They need help. Souls who are honest need their prejudices torn away. What will stand the present position? Have that the whole burden of the message. First, second and third angels' messages. They must yield. The force of it how mighty; it is the mighty truth.

Oh, we thank Thee that we have received the truth.

A poor, despised company, but how honored of God. Should one tarry that has the message? Fly, fly. Buckle the armor on.[7] Do we expect to be free? Fight the good fight of faith. The Laodiceans will make a struggle. Will they [obtain] the victory? One will chase a thousand and two put ten thousand to flight. Coming to conclusions. They know not where they are. Lost in the fog. Terrible fear shall take hold of them. Anguish of spirit will seize them. Dare they admit that the door is shut? They said it was of the devil, a sin against the Holy Ghost. To admit it is against their own life. They shall die the death. Look ye at the pattern. Follow Him, meek and lowly. Shut your eyes to everything but the truth.

---

insertion.)

[7] According to Ms 11, 1850, "Bro. Bates" is being addressed here—"he must buckle on the armor," etc.

1850

(Ms 11, 1850)

DECEMBER 25, PARIS, MAINE

Vision at Paris, Maine.

This manuscript is published in entirety in Ellen G. White, *Manuscript Releases,* vol. 13, pp. 299-302.

A vision concerning the situation in Fairhaven, Massachusetts, and beyond, urging order in worship and cautioning against "unhealthy and unnecessary excitement."

We were united in praying last evening for the Spirit of the Lord to fall upon us. God heard our earnest cries. I was taken off in vision. I saw how great and holy God was. Said the angel, "Walk carefully before Him, for He is high and lifted up and the train of His glory fills the temple." I saw that everything in heaven was in perfect order. Said the angel, "Look ye; Christ is the head; move in order, move in order. Have a meaning to everything." Said the angel, "Behold ye, and know how perfect, how beautiful the order in heaven; follow it."

Then I saw that the papers[1] would go and that it would be the means of bringing souls to a knowledge of the truth. I saw that James had not borne the burden alone but that the angels of God had assisted and had oversight of the paper.

Then the angel pointed to Fairhaven [Massachusetts], and said, Ye have not moved in God at all times.[2] There has been a stretching beyond the movings of God, and [ye] have moved in self. I saw that the mind should be taken from mortals and be raised to God.

I saw that the exercises were in great danger of being adulterated,[3] and

---

[1] At the time of writing, December 1850, the first issue of the *Second Advent Review and Sabbath Herald* was published in Paris, Maine. It replaced *The Present Truth* and *The Advent Review,* which ceased publication in November 1850.

See: SDAE, s.v. *"Adventist Review."*

[2] The problems and tensions found in the Fairhaven, Massachusetts, company at this time are alluded to in contemporary published reports. According to the August 1850 *Advent Review*, "the brethren" were "in a tried state. . . . Some, who had wounded the precious cause in Fairhaven, have been 'purged out from among them' as 'rebels.'"

See: W. [James White], "Our Tour East," *Advent Review,* August 1850, p. 14.

[3] The cautions given in this vision regarding ecstatic manifestations ("exercises") are seen by Ellen White's biographer and grandson Arthur L. White as a turning point for the young

their former opinion and knowledge governing in a measure their exercise, therefore implicit confidence could not be placed in these exercises, but if any one was lost to everything around him, and he should be in the state that Paul was in, whether in the body or out of the body, he could not tell,[4] and God communicate to him through His angels, there would be then no danger of a mistake.

I saw that we should strive at all times to be free from unhealthy and unnecessary excitement. I saw that there was great danger of leaving the Word of God and resting down and trusting in exercises. I saw that God had moved by His Spirit upon your company in some of their exercises and their promptings; but I saw danger ahead.

Then I saw Bro. Gurney [**Heman S. Gurney**],[5] that there was hope for him, that God loved him still, and that before he left Fairhaven he was not humble as he should be, and did not feel his wrong, and He suffered him to take a course that would cause nearly all to let him drop. I saw that he had suffered intensely on account of his former course,[6] and he was much humbled. He must be made to hope and all would be well.

Then I saw a faint hope for Sally Chase.[7] I saw that the course that had been taken toward her by disfellowshipping her had been right, for her jealous, evil surmising, and self breaking out every little while was enough to drag down and oppress a whole meeting. Yet I saw she loved the truth and cause better than anything else, although she had often wounded it and caused it

---

movement. "The Word of God was elevated, and visions were pointed out as safe guidance, but ecstatic experiences could have questionable backgrounds and be misleading."

See: Arthur L. White, *Ellen G. White: The Early Years,* p. 203; James Michael Wilson, "Enthusiasm and Charismatic Manifestations in Sabbatarian Adventism." *See also:* Appendix article "Ellen White and Religious Enthusiasm in Early Adventist Experience"; EGWEnc, s.v. "Ecstatic Experiences."

[4] 2 Cor. 12:1-4.

[5] *Identity:* The only "Gurney" appearing in the *Review* before December 1852 is "[Heman] S. Gurney," of Fairhaven, Massachusetts.

See: Search term "Gurney" in *Words of the Pioneers.*

[6] It is possible that the "wrong" course taken by Heman Gurney is that mentioned by James White in a letter written the previous year. White there speaks disapprovingly of an "intimacy" between a certain "Delia" and "Brother Gurney." "The stand that Brother Gurney has taken the past three years in trying to hold up Delia has encouraged her to continue in the way to ruin."

See: James White to "Bro. and Sister Collins," Sept. 8, 1849.

[7] *Identity:* Although there is no mention of a "Sally Chase" from Fairhaven, Massachusetts, in the *Review* from this period, it does contain a number of references to a "Sarah Chase" from 1851 to her death in 1878. According to her obituary Sarah Chase came from Fairhaven and had "embraced the present truth in its early days under the labors of Eld. Joseph Bates." Since "Sally" is often used as a diminutive form of "Sarah" it may be that Ellen White is referring to Sarah Chase.

See: Search term "Chase" in *Words of the Pioneers;* obituary: "Sarah Chase," *Review,* June 13, 1878, p. 191.

to be reproached. I saw she must take thorough work speedily, and confess humbly her errors and wrongs to the children of God, and then she could be healed. I saw that the church in Fairhaven should not fellowship her unless she makes an entire reformation.

I saw that the burden of the message now was the truth. The Word of God should be strictly followed and held up to the people of God. And it would be beautiful and lovely if God's people would be brought into a strait [place], to see the workings of God through exercises of visions. But I saw in our conference meeting, some laid out the work that God was to give exercises, and rebels were to be purged out in the meeting. Then the honest, conscientious ones began to tremble. I am afraid [that] I shall be purged out, and they take their minds from Jesus, and fix them upon themselves and others, and the meeting leaves them lower than it found them. I saw that we must try to lift our minds above self and have them dwell upon God, the high and lofty One.

Then I saw souls that were needy. They were honest and they needed the prejudice torn from them that they have received from their leaders, and then they can receive the truth. I saw the burden of the message should be the first, second, and third angels' messages,[8] and those who had any hope in God would yield to the force of that truth. How mighty and glorious it looked to me. Oh, what a privilege is ours, that of being among the children of God and believing the mighty truth—a poor, despised company, but how honored of God.

I saw if Israel moved steadily along, going according to Bible order, they would be as terrible as an army with banners.[9] Said the angel, Should any tarry that have the truth and can give an explanation of it from the Word of God? No, no! They must go quickly.

Then I saw Bro. Bates [**Joseph Bates**], that he must buckle on the armor. Said the angel, Dost thou expect to be free from trials? Fight the good fight of faith. The angel of God will go before thee, and some souls will be benefited and receive the truth.

Then I saw Laodiceans.[10] They will make a mighty effort. Will they get the victory? One who has the truth will chase a thousand, and two will put ten thousand to flight. They are coming to conclusions that bring them into

---

[8] *See:* EGWEnc, s.v. "Three Angels' Messages."

[9] S. of Sol. 6:4: "Thou art beautiful, O my love, as Tirzah, comely as Jerusalem, terrible as an army with banners."

[10] Prior to 1856 Sabbatarian Adventists identified their movement with the Philadelphia church of Revelation 3:1-6. The mainstream Adventists who rejected the validity of the seventh-month movement and the Sabbath were seen as symbolized by the lukewarm Laodicean church of Revelation 3:14-21.

See: P. Gerard Damsteegt, *Foundations of the Seventh-day Adventist Message and Mission*, pp. 147, 148; [James White], "The Seven Churches," *Review,* Oct. 16, 1856, p. 189.

close quarters, and they cannot tell where they be themselves, for they are lost in the foggy, terrible fear that takes hold of them. Anguish of spirit will seize them. Dare they admit that the door is shut? The sin against the Holy Ghost was to ascribe to Satan what belongs to God or what the Holy Ghost has done.[11] They said the shut door was of the devil and now admit it is against their own lives. They shall die the death. Look ye at the pattern. Follow Him, for He is meek and lowly in heart. Shut your eyes to everything but the present, saving truth.

---

[11] The power and revival that had attended the preaching of 1844 (the "seventh-month movement" leading up to October 22, 1844) subsequently became a divisive issue. Some mainstream ("Albany") Adventists ascribed the power of the 1844 movement to "mesmerism" and worse. As James White noted in 1850, some "who took an active part in the seventh month cry, have since pronounced that movement the work of the Devil." But, he warned, "attributing the work of Christ and the Holy Ghost to the Devil, was in the days of our Saviour, blasphemy, and it is blasphemy now."

See: "Brother Miller's Dream," *Present Truth,* May 1850, p. 74, also published in James White, ed., *Brother Miller's Dream*; introductory article "The 'Shut Door' and Ellen White's Visions"; EGWEnc, s.v. "Shut Door."

1851

(Lt 6, 1851)

APRIL 1, PARIS, MAINE

LETTER TO

Reuben and Belinda Loveland.[1]

Portions of this letter are published in Ellen G. White, *Selected Messages,* book 3, p. 63; *idem, Manuscript Releases,* vol. 6, p. 252.

Belinda Loveland questions the source of Ellen White's vision regarding Nelson Hollis. The influence of Hollis's accusations against James White causes crushing discouragement for the Whites.

Dear Brother and Sister Loveland:

We have just returned from a visit to Topsham [Maine] and Gorham [Maine]. On our return we found a number of letters, and among them was one from you. Many things in your letter I do not understand. You speak of your telling me concerning Brother Hollis [**Nelson A. Hollis**].[2] I cannot remember that you told me anything about [him]. I know that if you told me anything it affected me not or I could now remember it. But, dear sister, what if you had said ever so much? Would that affect the visions that God gives me? If so, then the visions are nothing.[3]

God has shown me the true state of Brother Hollis. I know from the vision that his influence has been bad and against us.[4] How could Brother Hollis say

---

[1] *Identity:* This letter is addressed "Reuben Loveland, Johnson, Vt." For "Belinda" as his wife's name, see, for example, 1860 U.S. Federal Census, "Belinda Loveland" and "Reuben Loveland," Vermont, Lamoille County, Johnson, p. 819.

[2] *Identity:* The only "Hollis" mentioned in the *Review* throughout the 1850s and early 1860s is Nelson A. Hollis. This identity is confirmed by Ellen White in *Spiritual Gifts,* where, in narrating what appear to be the same events, she refers to "N. A. H."

See: Search term "Hollis" in *Words of the Pioneers*; Ellen G. White, *Spiritual Gifts [vol. 2],* pp. 145, 146.

[3] The issue raised here and in the fifth paragraph concern the genuineness of Ellen White's vision. Had the vision been "influenced" by what Belinda Loveland told Ellen White concerning the Hollis case? The question of whether Ellen White had prior knowledge of matters shown her in vision was seen by some as of central importance. But she makes the point in this letter that even if she had had prior information about Hollis, "would that affect the vision that God gives me? . . . My opinion has nothing to do with what God has shown me in vision."

See also: Lt 3, 1847 (July 13), note 7.

[4] In what way had Hollis's influence "been bad and against us"? In a parallel account in *Spiritual Gifts* Ellen White says of "N. A. H." (Nelson A. Hollis) that he was the "instigator"

that he had not said anything about it anywhere else when he told Brother Bates,[5] Brother Rhodes, and Andrews, and they did not know but [what] we were wrong from what he said, and came to the conference with that feeling? Since I have had the vision, I have seen Brother Bates and he told us that he reproved Brother Hollis for his feelings towards James. He told Brother Bates the same that he told Brother Heath. This looks dark in Brother Hollis. How could he say he came on purpose to the Conference[6] to confess, when Brother Rhodes asked him on his way to Waterbury [Vermont] if he did not think that he had wrong feelings toward James? He said, No, that he could meet him, and not feel condemned or as though he had done wrong. I cannot repeat it word for word, but that was the amount of it, and more that I cannot repeat, that makes things look very crooked in him.

Brother Rhodes was astonished when he read the same in a letter from Brother Barrows, and you write the same that he went on purpose to confess. Brother Rhodes says it is the darkest thing he has seen in Brother Hollis. Poor soul, he is entirely deceived by the devil.

Our spirits were completely crushed after the conference. James was about to return home in that state of things. I was taken very sick. The burden seemed as though it would crush me. God, in answer to prayer, healed me and showed me Brother Hollis was wrong and also showed me just what he had been about and that James must stop a while longer in Vermont.

What you or any one else has said is nothing at all. God has taken the matter in hand and Brother Hollis knows not what manner of spirit he is of. God has shown Brother Hollis's case in vision and unless he soon becomes as a little child and breaks in pieces before God, he will be left to himself. What you have said, Sister Loveland, influenced me not at all. My opinion has nothing to do with what God has shown me in vision. But enough of this.

We have received letters from some that we have never before heard from. There is a great call for publications. The work of the Lord is moving onward. We had consecrated ourselves anew to God, soul, bodies, and spirit to do His work. Oh, that we may do it faithfully; time is very, very short. What we do must be done quickly and we must be very humble or God will not use us in His cause.

---

of accusations that "Bro. White was making money" and "had too good a horse." James White had as a result "sunk beneath his trials."

See: Ellen G. White, *Spiritual Gifts [vol. 2]*, pp. 145-147.

[5] The names Bates, Rhodes, Andrews, Heath, and Barrows appearing in these two paragraphs do not play central roles in the narrative, so no attempt is made here to annotate them.

[6] The reference to Waterbury makes it likely that the conference in Waterbury, Vermont, January 18, 19, 1851, is intended.

See: [Notice], *Review*, January 1851, p. 31; W. [James White], "Our Visit to Vermont," *Review*, February 1851, p. 45.

I am satisfied that we have lived too far from God. We must take hold upon His strength and then He will bless us. We have lived beneath our privilege. There is a fulness in Jesus. I feel my own unworthiness and I know that I deserve not the mercy and blessings of God. I have had severe trials of late. Pray for us.

Much love to your husband, yourself, and children and all who love God in deed and in truth.

In haste.

1851

APRIL 7

"Eli Curtis."

Article published in *Second Advent Review and Sabbath Herald,* vol. 1, no. 8, Apr. 7, 1851, p. 64.

1851

APRIL 27, PARIS, MAINE

Date given for an unauthenticated vision. See Appendix A.

1851

(Ms 5, 1851)

MAY 18, PARIS, MAINE

Opposition to the Sabbath.

Portions of this manuscript are published in Ellen G. White, *Manuscript Releases,* vol. 6, pp. 168-172. See also Ellen G. White, *Early Writings,* pp. 68, 69.

> *Vision regarding opposition to the Sabbath, spiritual needs of the band in Paris, Maine, and Satan's attempts to hinder the work of James White.*

I will now write you[1] the vision that the Lord gave me May 14. I saw the great goodness of God to us, that while we have been passing through the deep waters they have not overwhelmed us. I saw the beauty and loveliness of Jesus, and it seemed as though I could never bear to be parted from His lovely

---

[1] The last paragraph of the letter identifies "you" as "Bro. Rhodes."

presence. Then I saw a light coming from the excellent glory that encircled the Father. It approached nearer and nearer unto me. I began to tremble, my body shook like a leaf; it seemed to me if that light came close to me I should be dissolved or struck out of existence, but the light passed me. Then could I realize what a terrible[2] God we have to do with, and that we must be so holy that we can live in His sight.

Then I saw how little some realized the holiness of God, and what they must be in order to live in His sight, through the time of trouble. I begged of Jesus to make those who were believing His appearing like Himself.

Then I saw how the blind guides were trying to make souls as blind as themselves, and they knew not what was coming upon them. I saw that they were exalting themselves against God and His truth, and as the truth triumphs, souls who have believed these teachers to be men of God and have looked to them, inquire of these teachers what it means, for they are troubled. And these teachers, with the object of getting rid of the law of God or the seventh-day Sabbath, will answer them thereto. I saw that there was no honesty in them in taking their position against the Sabbath of the Lord God. All they wanted was to get around the Sabbath of the Lord, and keep some other day than the one sanctified and set apart by Jehovah.

For (the angel said) they are not subject to the law of God, neither indeed can be, and if they are driven off of one position they will take an opposite one, (but equally as weak as the first). I saw that there was no strength in their arguments.

I saw that God's people were coming into the unity of the faith, and those that believe that the seventh day is the Sabbath, are united in their views and understanding of the Bible truths in all important points, and that they believe and speak the same things. But those who oppose the seventh-day Sabbath are cut up and divided; there are hardly two agreed.[3] One comes forward in opposition to the Sabbath commandment and declares it to be thus and so, and at the conclusion calls it settled; then a second comes up and tears the first down, and declares it to be some other way. But they will not have

---

[2] In the sense of "awe-inspiring" (as in Ex. 34:10, Ps. 99:3, Joel 2:31, KJV).

[3] Several articles opposing the Sabbath had appeared in the *Advent Herald* and *Advent Harbinger* during the spring of 1851 before Ellen White received this vision. Earlier, in 1847-1848, the *Bible Advocate* had run a major series of letters and articles debating the Sabbath issue. The point made here about contradictory arguments being used against the Sabbath can be illustrated from the writings of Joseph Turner. He had argued in the autumn of 1847 that Sunday is in actual fact the seventh day and therefore the true Sabbath of the commandment. By the following May, Turner had abandoned this position, arguing instead that for the Christian the law is abolished.

See: "Repairing the Breach," *Review,* June 2, 1851, p. 95, for a contemporary survey of articles opposing the Sabbath in the non-sabbatarian Adventist press. Merlin Burt provides an extensive analysis of the Sabbatarian debate of 1847-1848 in "Sabbatarian Adventism From 1844 to 1849," pp. 326-352.

it, any of them, that the seventh day is the Sabbath, and they do not agree among themselves, but are blind and dishonest and are standing out against the Sabbath commandment. They want to silence the flock, therefore they get up something to silence them and lull them to sleep upon these truths which condemn them and cut them off. Their followers read their Bibles so little that error could be easily made by these blind leaders to appear like truth, and the followers receive it as such, not looking any higher than their leaders, and they, having a disposition to get rid of the fourth commandment, love these errors and love to have it so.

Then I saw those at Milton [New York], that they need help, and that they had called loud for it, and we should not disregard their call, for souls could be benefited there, and that we must go and visit them. They were looking to the visions and were anxious to know more about them.[4] Then I saw that Bro. John [**John Nevins Andrews**][5] must stay but a short time in Paris[6] [Maine], that he must go and write. And I saw that one could not always bring out clear light upon every point in a subject, as two could who understood the same subject, and that John should watch carefully and if he could make any other point in the subject of the parable, or any other subject, clearer, it was his duty to do so. Then I saw that this band must have steady, living faith, more faith, and draw down the blessings from God. I saw that faith had been but little

---

[4] Three months earlier traveling preacher **George W. Holt** had visited former Millerites in the West Milton–Ballston Spa area of New York with the result that some "embraced the truth in full." Possibly in response to Ellen White's vision on May 14, recorded in this manuscript, a "general conference" was arranged for the weekend of June 27-29, 1851, at which several prominent preachers, including the Whites, spoke. In July Ellen White wrote from Ballston Spa that "there is quite a company in this vicinity who are out in all the truth." Apparently a number of the new Sabbathkeepers in the West Milton–Ballston Spa area had doubts about the visions of Ellen White. She wrote on July 21, "The visions trouble many. They [know] not what to make of them." The issue was no doubt particularly pressing since the Whites settled in Ballston Spa after the conference and later in nearby Saratoga Springs, so that the one having the visions was living right among them. It may well have been in part to meet the many questions being raised that Ellen White's first book was published in August (*A Sketch of the Christian Experience and Views of Ellen G. White*) containing biographical material and a selection of her most prominent visions.

See: Geo. W. Holt, "From Bro. Holt," *Review,* March 1851, p. 56; Horace Cushman, "Conferences," *Review,* May 19, 1851, p. 88; Ellen G. White, Lt 7, 1851 (July 27); Lt 4, 1851 (July 21); *idem, A Sketch of the Christian Experience and Views of Ellen G. White.*

[5] *Identity:* The information given here that "Bro. John" is staying in Paris and is a writer clearly identifies him as John Nevins Andrews. Although only 21 at the time and living with his parents in Paris, Maine, J. N. Andrews had already published several weighty articles in *The Present Truth* and *Review* and was a member of the *Review* publishing committee from its inception in November 1850.

[6] According to notices in the *Review,* J. N. Andrews left Paris during the summer of 1851 and followed the *Review* office to Saratoga Springs and Rochester, New York, not to return to his parents' home for any period of time until his health failed in 1855.

See: [Notice], *Review,* Sept. 2, 1851, p. 24; [Notice], *Review,* Mar. 23, 1852, p. 112; "The Office," *Review,* Feb. 20, 1855, p. 182.

in exercise among the band, and that they must get ready, for the clouds are gathering and will soon burst upon us.[7]

I saw that this world was rocked in the cradle of security so that communications might not be cut off from place to place, and that messengers might have full time to carry the message to the children of God, that they receive it and be sealed with the seal of the living God,[8] and be prepared to pass through the time of trouble[9] such as never was. I saw that it must be a time of peace in order for the servants of God to do their work for souls.

Then I was shown concerning the wicked who now die and are happy. I saw in their sickness and death if they should once realize their awful condition they would die in such agony of mind, and would make such appeals, as would frighten some to profess the truth that *did not* love it, that never could be saved and go through the time of trouble, and others would be deranged. And again, if they felt their lost condition it would show that Satan had not power enough over them to blind their minds so they could not feel their own condition. I saw that the wicked were Satan's lawful prey, and that they were completely deceived by him, therefore now is the time when there are no bands in the death of the wicked.

Then I saw that we must work fast while the days last. I begged God to let His messengers go and work fast for the salvation of souls. I saw that God was willing to give us great blessings, if we would only have faith, and when we went out among the people we must go in the name of the Lord, for without Him we can do nothing.

Then again I saw the goodness of God to us in giving us a baptism of His Spirit before we had waded through the deep waters. I saw how busy Satan had been. He saw that the nominals[10] could not overthrow us, so he began to put prejudices in the minds of our dearest brethren, so as to hinder the work and overthrow James, and also to cause the faith in the visions to be destroyed. But he failed in his endeavors, and then he attacked his body, but by faith James [**James Springer White**] was wrenched from his grasp and placed in the hands of the Great Physician who applied the balm and set

---

[7] More details concerning the problematic state of the Paris, Maine, band are given by Ellen White in Lt 3, 1851 (Aug. 11). Ron Graybill traces the at-times-troubled history of two prominent Sabbatarian families in Paris, the Andrewses and the Stevenses, from the 1840s to the early 1860s, in "The Family Man," in Harry Leonard, ed., *J. N. Andrews: The Man and the Mission,* pp. 16-19, 25-28.

[8] *See:* EGWEnc, s.v "Seal of God."

[9] *See:* EGWEnc, s.v. "Time of Trouble."

[10] The expression "nominal Adventists" or some variant thereof was commonly used by early Sabbatarian Adventists to refer to those Adventist bodies coming out of the Millerite movement that rejected the Sabbath, the prophetic significance of 1844, and the continuing gift of prophecy in the church.

See: P. Gerard Damsteegt, *Foundations of the Seventh-day Adventist Message and Mission,* pp. 179-192.

him free.[11] I saw that Satan's darts were hurled at us more than at others so as to destroy the confidence of God's children in the visions, and to get James down so as to stop his work on the paper.

I saw that each one of us must labor for the salvation of souls, that we all can do something. I saw that this band should not rest unless they had the abiding witness that their ways pleased God. I saw that they had not seen their true state, and I prayed the angel to unfold it to them, that they might see themselves as God sees them.

I saw that there was a lack of their studying their Bibles as they should, but let their minds run upon other things, and reading that did not profit. I saw that the Bible was the statute book that was to judge us in the last days, and that it should be studied much and carefully to know whether our lives will compare with the Word of God. I saw that if any should lose their love for the Word of God, that they should not rest but pray very earnestly for God to baptize them with His Spirit into an understanding of His Word, that they may love it better than anything else.

I also saw something concerning you, that you had no wrong intentions in your heart when you said what you did at Bro. N's, but that you were under a wrong influence,[12] and that Satan was striving with all his power to get you to give up in discouragement now, and get you looking to yourself. I saw that you must not give way to him one moment, but look to your compassionate, tender High Priest, for He loves you. We love you, Bro. Rhodes [**Samuel W. Rhodes**].[13] Do not sink down. Press against the temptations of Satan.

---

[11] The events alluded to here may well refer to the experiences in January of the same year when James White had been falsely accused at the Waterbury, Vermont, conference of misappropriating funds, an experience that subsequently caused him to sink "beneath his trials. He was so weak he could not get to the printing office without staggering."

See: Ellen G. White, *Spiritual Gifts [vol. 2]*, p. 147; *idem*, Lt 6, 1851 (Apr. 1).

[12] No information has been found bearing on this incident.

[13] *Identity:* No doubt referring to Samuel W. Rhodes. The only "Rhodes" mentioned in the *Review* before 1857 is Samuel W. Rhodes.

See: Search term "Rhodes" in *Words of the Pioneers.*

1851

(Lt 10, 1851)

[MAY 18, 19,[1] PARIS, MAINE[2]]

LETTER TO
Samuel W. Rhodes.[3]

Previously unpublished.

Brief letter of greetings and news to accompany a longer vision account (Ms 5, 1851).

Dear Brother Rhodes:

I have written this vision to you[4] so if you see any one in danger through any wrong that God has shown me in others or generally, that you may read them what I have seen. John [**John Nevins Andrews**][5] will go from here in a few days.

---

[1] The date of writing is not given. However, in the nineteenth-century record book that preserves this letter, it immediately follows on the same page as a vision account ends (Ms 5, 1851), thus suggesting that the two items are related. As indicated in the notes below, the contents of Lt 10, 1851 (May 18) suggest that it is a kind of add-on to Ms 5, 1851, and that it is written on the same day as Ms 5, Sunday, May 18, 1851, with a postscript added the following day, Monday, May 19, 1851.

[2] The place of writing is not given in the original source. However, it is known that the Whites were in Paris, Maine, on May 18-19, 1851 (see note 1).

See: Ellen G. White, Ms 5, 1851 (May 18).

[3] *Identity:* No doubt referring to the itinerant preacher Samuel W. Rhodes, the only "Rhodes" mentioned in the *Review* prior to 1857.

See: Search term "Rhodes" in *Words of the Pioneers.*

[4] As mentioned in note 1, the physical contiguousness of this letter with Ms 5, 1851, suggests that the two documents are related. In Ms 5, dated May 18, 1851, Ellen White gives a general account to Rhodes of her vision on May 14. It appears that Lt 10 is an addendum to the vision account in which Ellen White personally addresses Samuel Rhodes, asking him to relate her vision to others, where that would be profitable.

[5] *Identity:* In the vision account (Ms 5, 1851) to which this letter appears to be the sequel Ellen White also speaks of "Bro. John," of Paris, Maine. Reasons are given there (note 5) for identifying "John" with John Nevins Andrews. Ellen White was instructed that Andrews should not stay long with his parents in Paris but "must go and write." This instruction correlates well with the report given here (Lt 10) that "John will go from here in a few days." From notices in the *Review* we know that J. N. Andrews left Paris by June 1851, not to return to his parental home for any length of time until his health failed in 1855.

See: Joseph Bates, "Letters," *Review,* Aug. 5, 1851, p. 6; [Notice], *Review,* Sept. 2, 1851, p. 24; [Notice], *Review,* Mar. 23, 1852, p. 112; "The Office," *Review,* Feb. 20, 1855, p. 182. For details of Andrews's travels as reported in the *Review,* see search term "Andrews" in *Words of the Pioneers.*

We have good victory in our prayer seasons. God often meets with us, and blesses us, and we feel to triumph in the God of our salvation. Satan has been making mighty efforts to overthrow us, but God has been holding us up, praise His dear name. We are determined to hold the victory, and come off conquerors.

One week ago last Sabbath we went up to Bro. Davis's [**Charles** and **Harriet Davis**][6]—Brother John, James, and self. They were glad to see us, and they are strong in all the present truth. He feels very thankful that God has brought him out; he says that he has enjoyed perfect love since the conference at Brother Stevens' [**Cyprian Stevens**][7] when you were here. She is good. May the Lord uphold them.

I must close, for I have many letters to write today.[8] Much love to all who love God.

In much love, in haste.

E. G. White

Monday morning.[9]

We were called up last night by Sister Andrews. Bro. A. [**Sarah L.** and **Edward Andrews**][10] was very, very sick. He was in excruciating pain all through his body, so that he groaned, wrung, and twisted. We anointed him with oil when he had confessed, of his own accord, that he had encouraged the company of the wicked too much, and mingled with them too much. She confessed the same. We had quite a powerful time, the pain was removed from Bro. A. and he praised God aloud.

---

[6] *Identity:* The only Sabbathkeeping Davis family in the vicinity of Paris, Maine, during the 1850s was that of Charles and Harriet Davis, living in nearby Woodstock.

See: Obituary, "Charles Davis," *Review*, June 17, 1884, p. 399; 1850 U.S. Federal Census, "Charles Davis," Maine, Oxford County, Woodstock, p. 203; 1860 U.S. Federal Census, Maine, Oxford County, Woodstock, p. 753; search term "Davis" in *Words of the Pioneers.*

[7] *Identity:* The conference is identified as having taken place "here," i.e., in Paris, Maine. The only Sabbathkeeping Stevens family known to live in Paris during this period is that of Cyprian and Almira Stevens. According to a notice in the *Review,* Samuel Rhodes was invited to speak at a conference held in Paris six months earlier, on November 16, 1850. It is probable that this is the conference referred to here.

See: [Notice about Paris conference], *Present Truth,* November 1850, p. 88; search term "Stevens" in *Words of the Pioneers.*

[8] Of these, only Lt 10, 1851, and Ms 5, 1851 (May 18), are found in the White Estate archives.

[9] *See:* Notes 1 and 4 above.

[10] *Identity:* While living in Paris, Maine, from late 1850 to the summer of 1851, the Whites boarded at the house of Edward and Sarah Andrews, parents of J. N. Andrews.

See: James White to E. P. Butler, Dec. 12, 1861.

1851

(Ms 9, 1851)

1851,[1] PARIS, MAINE

Testimony to Believers at Paris, Maine.

This manuscript is published in entirety in S. T. Belden, G. W. Amadon, and William Hall, *To Brother J. N. Andrews and Sister H. N. Smith* (PH016), pp. 31, 32.

Counsel and reproof for the families of Edward Andrews and Cyprian Stevens.

I was shown that there had been but little carefulness to follow the pattern. I was shown that there was a link between Brethren Andrews' and Stevens' families [**Edward Andrews** and **Cyprian Stevens**][2] that would have to be broken. This link did not tend to make them strengthen each other in the most holy faith, or to cause one another to grow in grace, but it did tend, if they were wrong, to make them build one another up in that wrong and hide each other's faults that needed to be brought out and got rid of in order to have the approbation of God and His free, strengthening Spirit among them. This attachment that bound one to the other was not formed because each family was so holy and reflected the image of Jesus so fully.[3]

---

[1] The original writing bears a dateline of "Paris, 1851." The vision would have been received no later than June 1851, as the Whites had left Paris by that time en route to New York State.

[2] *Identity:* The mention of the unhealthy "link" between the Andrews and Stevens families letter and their doubts about the visions, finds an echo in a later letter in which Ellen White writes of the Andrews and Stevens families of Paris who "strengthened each other's hands in sympathizing and linking together," and who "despised the visions." The reference must be to the families of Edward Andrews and Cyprian Stevens, who lived in Paris, Maine, until the mid-1850s.

See: Ellen G. White, Lt 8, 1860 (June 11).

[3] Further details regarding the nature of the "link" between the two families are given by Ellen White in later documents. During the period October 1850 to June 1851 when the Whites lived in Paris, Ellen had conveyed certain reproofs for members of the families, given in vision. James had reiterated and upheld the reproofs. The two families did not react positively, but reinforced each other's resentment. Nine years later, in 1860, their negative sentiments were unchanged. In the words of Ellen White: "When in Paris you strengthened each other's hands in sympathizing and linking together. . . . There was not deep searching of heart to confess wrongs and make thorough work by the two families. The same feelings exist with them now. They have despised reproof, despised the visions." By the early 1860s, however, several members of the two families showed a change of heart. Letters of apology and confession are on file, including one from Pauline Stevens, who writes, "I can now see that our folks and Sr. Andrews did very wrong in talking over our grievances together."

See: Ellen G. White, Lt 8, 1860 (June 11); P. R. Stevens to Ellen G. White, Jan. 27, 1862; Ron Graybill, "The Family Man," in Harry Leonard, ed., *J. N. Andrews: The Man and the*

If you stood more separate and had an eye single to the glory of God, you would be much stronger and God would be honored much more. I saw that you did not love Jesus as well as you loved each other, and you were more zealous to please each other than you were to please Jesus who died for you. I saw that if you studied more daily to glorify God and to have the abiding witness that your ways please Him, you would be strong and valiant in the truth and would carry a holy influence with you.

I saw that you have a knowledge of the truth and a form of godliness, but the power has been lacking. You have not had faith in God as you should have had, and when you have obtained the victory it has lasted you but a short time. I saw that we must have victory every day and come up steadily. I saw that our keeping house has discovered selfishness in your families,[4] and I saw that there has not been true faith in the visions—that some have doubted them and still have not true faith in them and if they remained where they were they would doubt them still more. I was shown the danger of doubting the visions. Had you believed the visions in time back, you would not have been left to go into the error you did.[5] I saw that we must have vital godliness and heart holiness if we would be covered with the covering of Almighty God.

Mission, pp. 16-18.

[4] When Ellen and James White first went to Paris, Maine, they boarded with the Edward Andrews family, but after some time they "undertook to keep house to prevent utter starvation" as James expressed it. Apparently the Andrews and Stevens families were less than helpful in assisting the Whites in setting up their own household. Years later Pauline Stevens, daughter of Cyprian Stevens, expressed her regrets to Ellen White: "I should have been willing to let you have things to have assisted you in keeping house such as armchairs, looking glass . . ."

See: James White to E. P. Butler, Dec. 12, 1861; P. R. Stevens to Ellen G. White, Jan. 27, 1862.

[5] Ellen White writes elsewhere of the Andrews and Stevens families that "for years . . . [they had been] held in error, fanaticism and darkness." While few details are known, Ellen White later recalled that Edward Andrews was at one time deeply involved in "no-work" fanaticism. "There is nothing that would have brought Brother Andrews out of his idea that they must not work, and that they would be supported by the outside people." Andrews's sister-in-law, Persis Sibley Andrews Black, made a similar observation in a diary entry in March 1846 concerning "brother Edward [Andrews], who—poor deluded man—with his family still believe in the speedy coming of Christ . . . [and] have done no labor for more than two years and have lived in constant expectation that every day the world wo'd be consumed by fire."

Marian Crawford (née Stowell), a member of the band of Sabbathkeepers in Paris in the 1840s recalled, in a letter written in 1908 to W. C. White, that Cyprian Stevens for a time practiced religious creeping. "One time at South Paris," she wrote, "Cyprian Stevens got down in front of the stage coach full of passengers. It frightened the horses so it nearly upset the coach. The driver handed the lines to a man that sat beside him, jumped down with his whip, and gave Bro. Stevens the full benefit of it. One eye was badly swollen and his whole face was bruised as well as his body."

See: Ellen G. White, Lt. 8, 1860 (June 11); Ms 131a, 1906; Diary of Persis Sibley Andrews Black, as in Ron Graybill, "The Family Man," p. 17; M. S. Crawford, to W. C. White, c. Oct. 9, 1908, "Extracts From Letter of M. S. Crawford to W. C. White."

1851

(Ms 1, 1851)

JUNE 21,[1] [CAMDEN, NEW YORK]

Time Setting.

This manuscript compares to what is published in *Second Advent Review and Sabbath Herald . . . Extra,* vol. 2, no. 1, July 21, 1851, p. [4].

Warning against those predicting the Second Advent in the autumn of 1851. The third angel's message "needs not time to strengthen it."

The Lord showed me that the message must go, and that it must never be hung on time, for time never will be a test again. I saw that some were getting a false excitement arising from preaching time;[2] that the third angel's message can stand on its own foundation, and that it needs not time to strengthen it, and that it will go in mighty power and do its work, and will be cut short in righteousness.

I saw that some were making everything bend to the time of this next fall, that is, making their calculations and disposing of their property in reference to that time. I saw that this was wrong, for this reason: instead of their going to God daily, and earnestly desiring to know their present duty, they looked ahead and made their calculations as though they knew the work would end this fall, without inquiring their duty of God daily.

E. G. White

---

[1] The source of this document is a copy made by "A. A. D." on "June 29, 1851." The copy has been given the heading "Copy of a Vision the Lord Gave Sister White, June 21, 1851, at Camden, N.Y." This manuscript, therefore, would have been written sometime between June 21 and 29, 1851.

[2] This warning to Sabbatarian Adventists against setting a definite time for the Second Advent is an amplification of the brief caution contained in Ellen White's vision some months earlier, on October 23, 1850. In a way, these warnings are quite surprising since Sabbatarians had eschewed time setting and had often made the point that it was the non-Sabbatarian Adventists who had set time after time in the years following 1844. In 1850-1851, however, a brief flurry of time-setting broke out among some Sabbatarians, mostly in Vermont and New Hampshire. Joseph Bates appears to have been the prime mover, having published a pamphlet sometime during 1850 arguing briefly (and almost incidentally) for the Second Advent in the autumn of 1851. His ideas, however, were never given any support in the *Review;* indeed, James White wrote against them in the summer of 1851. This, together with the warnings in the visions (both of which were published in the *Review*), weakened the movement well before the predicted time.

See: Ellen G. White, Ms 15, 1850 (Oct. 23); Joseph Bates, *An Explanation of the Typical and Anti-Typical Sanctuary,* pp. 10, 11; "Our Present Work," *Review,* Aug. 19, 1851, p. 13. For an overview of the 1851 time-setting episode, see Arthur L. White, *Ellen G. White: The Early Years,* pp. 207-210.

[As later edited by E. G. White. Date of editing unknown.]

Copy of a Vision the Lord Gave Sister White, June 21, 1851, at Camden, N.Y.

The Lord has instructed me that the message must go, and that it must not hang on time, for time never will be a test again. I saw that some were getting up a false excitement from preaching time; the third angel's message can stand on its own foundation, and it needs not time to strengthen it, and that it will go in mighty power and do its work and will be cut short in righteousness.

I saw that the First Day Adventists are setting the time[3] and some of our own people were making everything bend to this next fall—that is—making their calculations and disposing of their property in reference to that time, and some of our people are in error here. I saw that this was wrong for this reason: instead of their going to God daily and earnestly, desiring to know their present duty, they looked ahead and made their calculations as though they knew the work would end this fall, without inquiring their duty of God daily.

[3] For a contemporary survey of non-Sabbatarian Adventist time-setting, see Joseph Bates, "Midnight Cry in the Past," *Review*, December 1850, p. 23. P. Gerard Damsteegt provides a detailed analysis in "Early Adventist Timesettings and Their Implications for Today," *Journal of the Adventist Theological Society* 4, no. 1 (Spring 1993): 151-168; Alberto R. Timm, *The Sanctuary and the Three Angels' Messages*, pp. 53 (note 9), 156 (note 139).

1851

(Ms 2, 1851)

JUNE 23, CAMDEN, NEW YORK

Testimony Regarding the Company at Camden, N.Y.

Previously unpublished.

Vision concerning lack of sympathy for Almira Preston among Camden, New York, members.

The Lord shewed me the company in Camden [New York]. I saw that Sister Almira Preston [**Almira Preston**] was a child of God and that the band had been very wrong and had not stood in the light of God's countenance. I saw that the destiny of a soul should never hang on *dreams or impressions,* that these two things have governed the band much.

I saw that Sister A. Preston was in the midst of perfect darkness, none to help or encourage her. Her being in the midst of wicked influences had weakened and discouraged her. When she came among the brethren, then was the time for [them] to strengthen her, and pray for her, and call down the blessings of God upon her, and to try in every [way] that they could to encourage her. But instead of that, they had pushed her off into the jaws of the lion because she did not appear to be as strong as others. I saw that God loved her and frowned upon the course of the band; that if God bore no more with them than they had borne of some of their numbers He would long since have withdrawn His mercy from them and left them wholly to themselves.[1]

---

[1] Further details on the relationship between Almira Preston and the company in Camden, New York, can be found in a parallel account in *Spiritual Gifts* in which Ellen White tells of a certain "Sr. E. P." of Camden. There are clear similarities in the two accounts that indicate that "E. P." is in fact Almira Preston:

Ms 2, 1851: "I saw that Sister Almira Preston was a child of God and that the band had been very wrong and had not stood in the light of God's countenance. I saw that the destiny of a soul should never hang on dreams or impressions, that these two things have governed the band much."

Spiritual Gifts [vol. 2], p. 150: "I . . . saw that some of the church had been disfellowshipped without sufficient cause, through the influence of dreams and impressions. I was shown that Sr. E. P. was a child of God, and they had no cause for rejecting her."

The reasons Ellen White uses "E. P." instead of "A. P." in *Spiritual Gifts* can be accounted for by the fact that she uses variant spellings: "Almira" and "Elmira." The former spelling is found in Ms 2, 1851, and the latter in Ms 2a, 1851 (June 23), a variant of Ms 2.

Assuming that the "E. P." of *Spiritual Gifts* is in fact Almira Preston, we get further interesting detail there, including the information that her husband "had bound her with cords so tightly as to much bruise her" to prevent her coming to the meeting at which the Whites were present. Also included in this account is the reaction of the Camden company to Ellen

(Ms 2, 1851) June 23, 1851

I saw that if Sister A. Preston would be humble and hold this faith before God, that would keep her, and among all her trials bring her off victorious.[2]

White's vision of their unfair treatment of Almira Preston: "I related the vision given me for the church, and those who had acted a part in casting her off confessed to her heartily. It was an affecting time. Many wept aloud."

See: Ellen G. White, *Spiritual Gifts [vol. 2]*, pp. 150, 151; *idem*, Ms 2a, 1851 (June 23).

[2] The record of the *Review* is that Almira Preston, despite moving to an area in Illinois isolated from other believers, remained a loyal and enthusiastic member until her death in 1888.

See: Search term "Preston" in *Words of the Pioneers;* obituary: "Almira Preston," *Review*, July 17, 1888, p. 463.

1851
(Ms 2a, 1851)

JUNE 23, CAMDEN, N.Y.

Testimony Regarding the Company at Camden, N.Y. (Variant of Ms 2, 1851.)

Previously unpublished.

Vision concerning a lack of sympathy for Elmira Preston and Brother and Sister Prior among the Camden, New York, members.

The Lord showed me the company in Camden [New York]. I saw that Sister Elmira[1] Preston [**Almira Preston**] was a child of God, and that the band had been very wrong and had not stood in the light of God's countenance. I saw that the destiny of a soul should never hang on *dreams* or *impressions,* [and] that these two things have governed the band much.

I saw that Sister E. Preston was in the midst of perfect darkness [with] none to help or encourage her, and [that] her being in the midst of wicked influences had weakened and discouraged her. When she came among them, then was the time for the brethren to strengthen and pray for her and to call down the blessings of God upon her, and to try in every way that they could to encourage her. But instead of that they had pushed her off into the jaws of the lion because she did not appear to be as strong as others.

I saw that God loved her and frowned upon the course of the band. [I saw] that if God bore no more with them than they had borne of some of their number, He would long since have withdrawn His mercy from them and left them wholly to themselves.[2] I saw that if Sister E. Preston would be humble and hold fast her faith before God, that would keep her, and among all her trials bring her off victorious.[3]

I then saw Brother and Sister Prior [**Edward** and **Georgianna Prior**],[4]

---

[1] A variant spelling of "Almira" found in Ms 2, 1851 (June 23).

[2] For further details on the relationship between Elmira Preston and the company in Camden, New York, see Ms 2, 1851 (June 23), note 1.

[3] The record of the *Review* is that Almira Preston, despite moving to an area in Illinois isolated from other believers, remained a loyal and enthusiastic member until her death in 1888.

See: Search term "Preston" in *Words of the Pioneers;* obituary: "Almira Preston," *Review,* July 17, 1888, p. 463.

[4] *Identity:* The 1850 U.S. Federal Census lists only one Prior family in Camden, New York—that of Edward and Georgianna Prior, together with five children. They lived close to another Sabbathkeeper, Chandler B. Preston (brother-in-law of Almira Preston).

See: 1850 U.S. Federal Census: "Edward Prior," New York, Oneida County, Camden, p.

that God had not left them. Their brethren cutting them off had driven them to distraction and despair, and they had yielded the Sabbath on this ground [and felt] that it would be of no value for them to keep it, for all their endeavors to get into the kingdom would be useless.

I was pointed back and saw that Brother and Sister Prior had been wrong, that bitter words had often passed between them, and that they must get the victory over every wrong word and action and be united with each other, bear with each other, and try to help each other along to the kingdom; then they could have strength. I saw that they must be very humble before the Lord and pray much to Him for grace. When they felt wrong they must not *talk* but go to God and pray for strength and grace to overcome.

I saw that they had suffered much bodily and mentally since the band cut them off. I saw [that] unless the band were more careful and strengthened the weak among them, God would give them to feel, as they have caused others to feel, what it is to be lost or left of God, without a hope. I saw [that] if the band had done wrong willfully, God would have withdrawn His Spirit from them. I saw that they had erred greatly in judgment and had not stood in the light of God. If they had, they would not have moved so wrongly, for it was an awful thing to reject one of *God's* children.

In love.

486; obituary: "John S. Preston," *Review,* Oct. 30, 1879, p. 151.

1851

[CIRCA JUNE 24-26], N.P.

EXTRACT FROM NONEXTANT LETTER TO

Stockbridge and Louisa M. Howland.

Quoted in Ellen G. White, *Spiritual Gifts [vol. 2],* pp. 149-151.

1851

JUNE 29, CAMDEN, NEW YORK

Date given for an unauthenticated vision. See Appendix A.

1851

(Lt 4, 1851)

JULY 21, BALLSTON SPA, NEW YORK

LETTER TO

Abram A. Dodge and Caroline Dodge.[1]

This letter is published in entirety in Ellen G. White, *Manuscript Releases,* vol. 5, pp. 99-101.

Plans for publishing in Saratoga Springs, New York, and for the publication of Ellen White's first book.

Dear Brother and Sister Dodge:

I now sit down to address you a few lines. The reason I have not written

---

[1] *Identity:* Until 1856 the only persons surnamed "Dodge" in the *Review* were Abram A. Dodge with his wife, Caroline Dodge, of Jackson, Michigan; and H. W. Dodge, of Stoddard,

before is [that] my time has been improved. I have been writing out the visions for publication and expected them to be out sooner and then you could have them in print;[2] but as the first paper is delayed[3] and you will be anxious to learn something of our calculations, I will wait no longer.

After you left us we began to enquire of the Lord what He would have us to do, or where we should publish, and it was shown me in vision that James [**James Springer White**] must lay his hand to the work and strive to open the way, and if the way should bend before him, he must remain; but if it was shut up and did not open, we must go elsewhere.[4] James has been doing as God showed me he must do, and the way has opened before him so that the first paper will be off today, and will be folded and in the office tomorrow morning. He does his publishing at Saratoga, nine miles [14 kilometers] from here. We have not yet got a house. We shall get one as soon as possible near the Springs where it will be only a few miles from the printing office. We expect our friends this week from Maine,[5] and in about three weeks shall be entirely settled, if not before.

New Hampshire. There are some rather clear indications that Ellen White is addressing the Dodges from Michigan. First, James White's letter of August 4, 1851, seems to associate Brother Dodge with "the brethren in Jackson." Second, Ellen White seems to indicate that she had met "Brother and Sister Dodge" at a conference in Camden. Just one month earlier (June 20-22) the Whites attended a conference in Camden, New York, to which several persons from Jackson, Michigan, had come. There is no mention of any delegates from New Hampshire. The fact that Ellen White requests the Dodges to greet "those dear friends I saw at Camden" makes it possible that she is referring to the Jackson delegation.

See: Search term "Dodge" in *Words of the Pioneers;* James White to "Brethren in Jackson," Aug. 4, 1851; "Our Tour to This State," *Review Extra,* July 21, 1851, pp. [3, 4].

[2] Ellen White's first book, a pamphlet of 64 pages containing an account of major visions together with a brief autobiographical account, was published the following month, August 1851. This is the "pamphlet" mentioned in the fourth paragraph.

See: Ellen G. White, *A Sketch of the Christian Experience and Views of Ellen G. White.*

[3] The first issue of the *Review* to be published in Saratoga Springs, New York, was the *Extra,* printed on July 21, 1851, the same day Ellen White wrote this letter. In the *Extra* James White outlined plans for moving publication of the paper from Paris, Maine, to Saratoga Springs.

See: "The Review and Herald," *Review Extra,* July 21, 1851, p. [3].

[4] By this time it had become clear to the Whites that they would not return to Paris, Maine, to continue publishing there. On August 11 Ellen White wrote, "The Lord showed me about four or five weeks ago that we must not go to Paris again, that they had not appreciated our labors there."

See: Ellen G. White, Lt 3, 1851 (Aug. 11). For an account of the troubled relationship between the Whites and the company in Paris, see Gerald Wheeler, *James White,* pp. 62, 63, 101-109.

[5] The identity of "our friends . . . from Maine" is given in the parallel *Spiritual Gifts* account: "We then rented a house [in Saratoga Springs], and sent for Bro. and Sr. Belden, and Sr. Bonfoey who was then in Maine taking care of little Edson." "Sr. Belden" was at the time of writing still **Sarah B. Harmon**, Ellen White's sister. She was married to **Stephen Belden** two weeks later, on August 5. Stephen Belden subsequently worked for 11 years as a printer and in the business office of the *Review.* **Clarissa Bonfoey** brought the Whites' son, Edson, now

After we parted with you and came to Brother Thompson's [**Jesse Thompson**],[6] we felt a great interest for this family, especially the children; and Tuesday morning we felt agony of soul for them. We felt that God must work for them, and our earnest, united prayers ascended within the second veil;[7] we claimed the promises for them, and for the first time their voices were heard in prayer. They had a good time that morn, and now they generally pray morning and evening. God is at work for them; praise His holy name.[8]

There is a stir all around here since the conference reports are being carried. (Evil, of course.) Some are anxious to hear for themselves and will come to the meetings. The visions trouble many. They [know] not what to make of them. We shall have the visions published in pamphlet form and if all the particulars are not published in the pamphlet, that I saw at Brother Cushman's, [**Horace Cushman**][9] and if you desire it, I can write it off for you. As it was coming out so soon in the pamphlet, I thought that you would not wish me to write them all off for you. We now think that you can have the book in about four weeks. You must write us upon the reception of this. Do not delay. We want much to hear from you. My health has been quite poor for a short time; the heat affects me, and I have had a very distressing turn of losing my breath. I am weak still, but better than I have been. James's health is the same as when you saw him. We are longing to be delivered from this body of suffering, and put on a glorious immortality.

---

almost 2, but their older son Henry, soon to turn 4, stayed with the Howlands in Maine for another two years, until the autumn of 1853.

See: Ellen G. White, *Spiritual Gifts [vol. 2],* p. 152; Gerald Wheeler, *James White,* p. 66; John Nevins Andrews et al., *Defense of Elder James White and Wife,* p. 34.

[6] *Identity:* Several sources mention a Jesse Thompson living two miles (three kilometers) from Ballston Spa, New York, where this letter is written. See, for example, Jesse Thompson, "Smiting," *Review,* Aug. 5, 1851, p. 8.

[7] The imagery used here refers to the veil separating the two apartments of the sanctuary. As Ellen White explains elsewhere, "the priest in the holy place, directing his prayer by faith to the mercy-seat ["within the second veil"], . . . represents the people of God directing their prayers to Christ before the mercy-seat in the heavenly sanctuary."

See: Ellen G. White, *The Spirit of Prophecy,* vol. 1, p. 274; Siegfried H. Horn, ed., *The Seventh-day Adventist Bible Dictionary,* s.v. "Veil."

[8] Ellen G. White's letter written one week later, July 27, 1851 (Lt 7, 1851), provides further details of the experience of Jesse Thompson's children.

[9] Almost certainly Ellen White is referring to either Horace Cushman, of Milton, New York; or George P. Cushman, of Tunbridge, Vermont, since these are the only two Cushmans (together with Horace Cushman's family) mentioned in the *Review* during this period. The choice between the two is helped by the information given in this letter that Ellen White had a vision at "Brother Cushman's." While there is no mention of the Whites ever visiting George Cushman in Vermont, they had met Horace Cushman just three weeks earlier at the West Milton, New York, conference that was "held at the house of Bro. Horace Cushman." It is, therefore, almost certain that Horace Cushman is referred to here.

See: Search term "Cushman" in *Words of the Pioneers;* [Notice re conference at West Milton], *Review,* Sept. 16, 1851, p. 32; "Our Tour to This State," *Review,* July 21, 1851, pp. [3, 4].

Be strong in the Lord, dear friends. Hold fast whereunto you have attained. Much love to those dear friends I saw at Camden [New York], and all the saints that I have not seen. Tell them to exercise strong and living faith in God, and be united strongly with each other, and not be easily tried. Where there is union, there is strength. Be firm and valiant for God and His cause. I should love to see you all, and perhaps we may before Jesus comes. The truth is triumphing, and will still triumph, more and more. Be sure and write us, all of you, and we will try to answer your letters.

Your sister in much love and great haste.

1851

JULY 21

"Experience and Views." "Dear Brethren."

Articles published in *Second Advent Review and Sabbath Herald . . . Extra,* vol. 2, no. 1, July 21, 1851, pp. [1-4].

1851

(Lt 7, 1851)

JULY 27, BALLSTON SPA, SARATOGA COUNTY, NEW YORK

LETTER TO

Leonard W. Hastings and Harriet Arabella Hastings.[1]

Portions of this letter are published in Ellen G. White, *Manuscript Releases,* vol. 6, p. 253; vol. 8, pp. 339, 340.

Mainly news to friends regarding the Whites' impending move to Saratoga Springs, New York; plans for publishing the visions; and the imminent arrival of son Edson and Ellen's sister Sarah.

Dear Brother Hastings and Sister Harriet:

We received a letter a few days ago from you which you sent to Paris

---

[1] *Identity:* That the "Brother Hastings" addressed is Leonard W. Hastings of New Ipswich, New Hampshire, is shown, among other ways, by the greetings to "Sister Gorham." Other letters from Ellen White that are clearly written to the Leonard Hastings family also include greetings to "Sister Gorham." (See, e.g., Lt 5, 1849 [Apr. 21], and Lt 10, 1850 [Mar. 18].) The identity of "Sister Harriet" is suggested in this opening greeting by her association with "Brother Hastings." Harriet Arabella was the oldest of the Hastings children, about 18 years old. Apparently, after her mother's death one year earlier, Harriet had assumed major responsibility for the younger children; therefore Ellen White chooses to address the letter to the father and the eldest daughter.

See: Obituary, "Harriet A. Hastings," *Review,* Sept. 5, 1854, p. 31; 1850 U.S. Federal Census, "Leonard Hastings," New Hampshire, Hillsborough County, New Ipswich, p. 272.

[Maine] and they sent it here.[2] You speak of Sister Gorham [**Elizabeth Gorham**][3] and want advice. We cannot see how there can be any wrong in her boarding that man providing that she will not have to work so hard and will not have to cook for him on the Sabbath. I have conversed with James about it and with some others. They see it just as I do. We do not think that God will condemn Sister Gorham in the least.

We should love to see you all but do not expect to have the privilege. Here we are in the State of New York. We make our home at Brother Thompson's [**Jesse Thompson**][4] (at whose table we are now writing). He and his wife are wholehearted in the truth. They have four daughters with them in the faith. Their ages are 24, 22, 20, and 12. They are good-hearted girls and are trying to serve God. Their voices were never heard in prayer until after the Milton [New York] conference.[5] We had a powerful season of prayer and the burden of their cases was rolled upon me. I pled the promises of God for them, and could not give it up, and finally their voices were raised in prayer to God. It was a sweet season. God has commenced to work for this family and our prayer is that it may be carried on to His own glory.

Brother Thompson used to be a Christian minister. He preached twenty years before he embraced the second advent doctrine. He is quite powerful when the Spirit of God rests upon him. James is busily engaged writing for the paper.

We get our publishing done about nine miles [14 kilometers] from here, to Saratoga Springs [New York]. We have been trying to get a house at the Springs but so many are flocking there from quarters of the world to drink the Spring water that rent is very high, and after we should pay a great amount of rent we should have to take up with just what we could get. As soon as cold weather comes the fat and lazy will go from the Springs and we can get cheaper and better rent.

There is quite a company in this vicinity who are out in all the truth; and

---

[2] The Whites were based in Paris, Maine, from October 1850 to the following June, when they traveled to New York State, settling first in Ballston Spa for a few weeks, and then, more permanently, in nearby Saratoga Springs. For a survey of the Whites' travels during 1851, see Arthur L. White, *Ellen G. White: The Early Years,* pp. 205-226.

[3] *Identity:* See Lt 5, 1849 (Apr. 21), note 25.

[4] *Identity:* The fact that "Brother Thompson" lives in or near Ballston Spa, that earlier he was a Millerite preacher, and the information given about his family provide useful clues to his identity. The *Review* of this period has several mentions of a Jesse Thompson of Ballston Spa, New York. George W. Holt writes, from nearby West Milton in early 1851, of meeting "Elder Thompson, an old preacher, and one of the first in the Advent, who traveled much with Bro. Miller . . . [who] has, with his wife, embraced the third angel's message."

See: Jesse Thompson, "Smiting," *Review,* Aug. 5, 1851, p. 8; S. W. Rhodes, "Conference," *Review,* Mar. 2, 1852, p. 104; Geo. W. Holt, "Letter From Bro. Holt," *Review,* March 1851, p. 56.

[5] A conference was held in West Milton, New York, near Ballston Spa, June 27-29, 1851.

See: Horace Cushman, "Conferences," *Review,* May 19, 1851, p. 88.

then there are others who are not fully established. T. M. Preble[6] has been around here and has injured some but our prayer to God is that He would palsy the influence that he has had, and that He would let the clear light upon His truth shine out, so as to establish the wavering. My health had been quite poor for a few days but I am now better. I have been writing out the visions that God has of late given me that will benefit His children and we shall have all the visions published in a pamphlet in a few weeks.[7] Were it not for this, I would write the visions to you, had I time. I suppose you have got the last paper by this time.[8] The next paper will contain many good letters, I trust.

James enjoys quite good health for him. Our friends from Maine have not yet arrived. We expect them every day. We need their help.[9] We should love to see you all very much. Will you not write to us, and tell us all how you get along? We feel interested for you. We have not forgotten you although we have been silent so long. May the Lord bless and strengthen you. We love you and will never cease to pray for you. Remember me to Sister Gorham. Tell her not to be bound and oppressed by the enemy but keep up good courage. Our warfare is almost over.

Much love to all your children. Tell them to be watchful and press their way to the kingdom. They must be sufferers with Jesus if they would be partakers with Him of His glory. Gaze upon the lovely Jesus until you reflect His lovely image. Pray for us, all of you that love God, and do not neglect to write to us. James sends love to you both and all the children and Sister Gorham.

In love and great haste.

---

[6] T. M. Preble had played a major role in promoting Sabbatarianism among Adventists soon after 1844. Yet by 1847 he had reversed his position and thereafter used his influence and pen against the Sabbath.

See: SDAE, s.v. "Thomas M. Preble."

[7] *A Sketch of the Christian Experience and Views of Ellen G. White,* containing a selection of prominent visions and a short biographical account, was published the following month, in August 1851.

[8] One week earlier a special "Extra" edition of the *Review* had been published at Saratoga Springs containing several major visions of Ellen White, together with other materials.

See: Review Extra, July 21, 1851.

[9] According to the account given in *Spiritual Gifts,* the Whites "sent for Bro. and Sr. Belden, and Sr. Bonfoey who was then in Maine taking care of little Edson." "Sr. Belden" was Ellen White's sister, but at the time of writing was still **Sarah B. Harmon**. She was married to **Stephen Belden** some days later, on August 5. Stephen Belden subsequently worked for 11 years as a printer and in the business office of the *Review*. **Clarissa Bonfoey** brought the Whites' son Edson, now almost 2, but their older son Henry, soon to turn 4, stayed with the Howlands in Maine for another two years, until the autumn of 1853.

See: Ellen G. White, *Spiritual Gifts [vol. 2],* p. 152.

1851

(Lt 3, 1851)

AUGUST 11,[1] SARATOGA SPRINGS, NEW YORK

LETTER TO

Harriet Arabella Hastings.[2]

Portions of this letter are published in Ellen G. White, *Selected Messages*, book 3, pp. 260, 261; *idem*, *Last Day Events*, pp. 286, 287.

Beginnings of publishing in Saratoga Springs, New York; vision on the importance of the Sabbath; problems in the Paris, Maine, band.

Dear Sister Harriet:

I sit down by candle light to address you a few lines. We are all quite well and smart today. We have just been moving and are not settled yet. Last Tuesday we moved to Saratoga Springs [New York],[3] and the same day that we moved No. 1, Volume 2 of the paper came off[4] and we folded and wrapt them. Not having a table to wrap and fold on, we took a fireboard and put it on an old sink and made that answer; and by sitting up very late we got the papers into the mail next morn.

Yesterday, which was Sabbath, we had a sweet, glorious time. The Lord

---

[1] The original letter bears the dateline of August 11, which was a Monday, but it is evident from the second paragraph that the letter was begun on Sunday, August 10.

[2] *Identity:* There are several indications in this letter that Harriet A. Hastings, daughter of **Leonard Hastings**, of New Ipswich, New Hampshire, is being addressed. Most specific are the lines "We received the four dollars that your father sent. One dollar was to go for the visions. I believe three for the paper." The following issue of the *Review* (Aug. 19, 1851) listed among the "Receipts" "Leonard Hastings, $3" and, under the heading "Receipts for the Pamphlet 'Experience and Views'" "Leonard Hastings, $1." The pamphlet "Experience and Views," it should be noted, consisted for the most part of a reprint of earlier visions. Confirming evidence that Harriet Hastings is being addressed is found in the closing greeting, "Much love to all the children and your father," without any mention of the mother. Elvira Hastings had died 18 months earlier, leaving her husband and six children.

See: "Receipts," *Review,* Aug. 19, 1851, p. 16; W. [James White], "Our Tour East," *Advent Review,* August 1850, p. 14; 1850 U.S. Federal Census, "Leonard Hastings," New Hampshire, Hillsborough County, New Ipswich, p. 272.

[3] After spending several weeks in nearby Ballston Spa at the home of Jesse Thompson.

See: "Our Tour to This State," *Review Extra,* July 21, 1851, p. [3, 4]; Ellen G. White, *Spiritual Gifts [vol. 2],* p. 152.

[4] Volume 1 had been published in Paris, Maine, the last issue coming out on June 9, 1851. Publication had been suspended for some weeks during the summer because of the Whites' travels.

met with us and the glory of God was shed upon us and were made to rejoice and glorify God for His exceeding goodness unto us. I had a deep plunge in the ocean of God's love. It seemed that the angels of God were hovering all around. The love of God was shed abroad in my heart, my whole being was ravished with the glory of God and I was taken off in vision. I saw the exceeding loveliness and glory of Jesus. His countenance was brighter than the sun at noonday. His robe was whiter than the whitest white.

How can I, dear Sister, describe to you the glories of heaven, and the lovely angels singing and playing upon their harps of ten strings? Dear Sister, is not heaven cheap enough?

I saw that we sensed and realized but little of the importance of the Sabbath, to what we yet should realize and know of its importance and glory. I saw we knew not what it was yet to ride upon the high places of the earth and to be fed with the heritage of Jacob. But when the refreshing and latter rain shall come from the presence of the Lord, and the glory of His power, we shall know what it is to be fed with the heritage of Jacob and ride upon the high places of the earth. Then shall we see the Sabbath more in its importance and glory. But [we] shall not see it in all its glory and importance until the covenant of peace is made with us at the voice of God, and the pearly gates of the New Jerusalem are thrown open and swing back on their glittering hinges, and the glad and joyful voice of the lovely Jesus is heard, richer than any music that ever fell on mortal ear, bidding us to enter, that we had a perfect right in the city, for we had kept the *commandments* of God, and heaven, sweet heaven is our home, for we have kept the commandments of God.[5]

Dear Sister, after I came out of vision this world looked desolate to me, the views that God has given me have spoiled this world for me. Nothing here looks lovely. I rejoice with you that you have turned your back upon the world and are laying up for yourself a treasure in heaven, an enduring substance. Praise the Lord.

Monday morn. You speak about going to Paris [Maine] and about our coming there again, and you meeting us in Boston [Massachusetts]. The Lord

---

[5] For a complementary perspective, compare this statement with the following parallel passage found in Ellen White's first vision, "Jesus . . . laid hold of the pearly gate, swung it back on its glittering hinges, and said to us, 'You have washed your robes in My blood, stood stiffly for My truth, enter in.' We all marched in and felt we had a perfect right in the city" (*Early Writings,* p. 17).

The formulation in Lt 3, 1851, which focuses on the commandments of God, is clearly an amplification of Revelation 22:14: "Blessed are they that do his commandments, that they may have right to the tree of life, and may enter in through the gates into the city" (KJV). Clearly, an understanding of the teaching of the early visions on salvation and its grounds cannot be based on isolated statements but requires an integrated analysis of all relevant passages. For two recent book-length treatments, see Woodrow W. Whidden II, *Ellen White on Salvation,* and Gunnar Pedersen, "The Soteriology of Ellen G. White Compared With the Lutheran Formula of Concord."

showed me about four or five weeks ago that we must not go to Paris again, that they had not appreciated our labors there, and that they would yet desire to see some of the servants of God in Paris. I saw that they had not heeded the visions that God has given them, and unless they did heed them they would pass through awful trials and judgments.

I saw that Brother Stevens' [**Cyprian Stevens**][6] and Andrews' [**Edward Andrews**][7] families would have to die a greater death to this world than they ever yet have died. It is impossible for me to describe to you their present state. Their letters that they write you may appear to be spiritual and interesting, but they are in a dark place. They think a great deal too much of their appearance, and are proud and are much more devoted to *themselves* than they are to God.[8]

Do not go to Paris. If you go anywhere go to Topsham, Maine, to Brother Howland's [**Stockbridge Howland**],[9] the one that has the charge of my little boy Henry [**Henry Nichols White**]. You would meet a hearty reception from them, and Frances and Rebekah you could but love. Frances is 23, Rebekah is 16. It would not cost so much to go from Boston to Topsham as it would to go from Boston to Paris. You would be disappointed greatly if you should go to Paris. You had much better remain where you are. I write this to you in confidence, that you may know just how things stand in Paris.

You ask[10] respecting the ages of Brother Thompson's [**Jesse Thompson**][11] family. Betsey the eldest is 24, Sally, the next is 22, Nancy is 20, Mary is 12. They are very interesting girls and believe that we have the truth, and are willing to do all they can to help the cause.

Brother Cushman [**Horace Cushman**][12] has four daughters. Two have

---

[6] *Identity:* See note 8.

[7] *Identity:* See note 8.

[8] The resentment of the Cyprian Stevens and Edward Andrews families of Paris against the leadership of the Whites and their skepticism of the visions throughout the 1850s is surveyed by Ronald Graybill in "The Family Man," in Harry Leonard, ed., *J. N. Andrews: The Man and the Mission,* pp. 16-19, 25-28. For more detail, see references given in notes to Lt 8, 1860 (June 11).

[9] *Identity:* "Bro. S. Howland and family, of Topsham, Me.," writes Ellen White in 1860, "for the period of five years had the care of my Henry."

See: Ellen G. White, *Spiritual Gifts [vol. 2],* p. iii.

[10] The White Estate archives contain none of the letters of the Howland family to the Whites from this period.

[11] *Identity:* In a letter to Harriet A. Howland and her father written two weeks earlier from nearby Ballston Spa, Ellen White told of a "Brother Thompson" (identified as Jesse Thompson—see Lt 7, 1851 [July 27], note 4) with whom they were staying. The Thompson daughters, she wrote, were ages 24, 22, 20, and 12. It is apparent that in this letter (Lt 3, 1851) Ellen White is referring to the same Jesse Thompson family, because the identical ages of the daughters are given again.

[12] *Identity:* The only Cushmans mentioned in the *Review* during this period were Horace Cushman (and his family), of West Milton, New York, and George P. Cushman, of Tunbridge, Vermont. Since Ellen White seems to be describing members living in her vicinity in this letter, it is reasonable to suppose that she is referring to Horace Cushman, of nearby West Milton.

been married and have children, but are now at home, their husbands being so opposed that they could not live with them, and they brought both of their wives to Brother Cushman's, and their children. They are very interesting women. The two youngest are 20 and 17. Margaret is 20, Anna is 17, I believe. Then he has another daughter married in the faith, and one son married and one unmarried. They are good children.

Sister Thompson [**Maria Thompson**][13] reminds me of your mother; she looks much like her. Much love to Sister Gorham [**Elizabeth Gorham**].[14] Tell her to trust wholly in God. He will take care of her. We received the two dollars she sent but are afraid she sent too much for her limited means. We received the four dollars that your father sent. One dollar was to go for the visions. I believe three for the paper. If this is not correct, please inform us.

Much love to all the children and your father. Write us soon.

In love.

This is confirmed by the facts she gives regarding the names and ages of the children, which correspond well with information found in the 1840 and 1850 censuses.

See: 1840 U.S. Federal Census, "Horace Cushman," New York, Saratoga County, Milton, p. 85; 1850 U.S. Federal Census, "Horrace [*sic*] Cushman," New York, Saratoga County, Milton, p. 341; search term "Cushman" in *Words of the Pioneers.*

[13] *Identity:* See 1850 U.S. Federal Census, "Mariah [*sic*] Thompson," New York, Saratoga, Ballston, p. 538.

[14] *Identity:* It can be assumed that "Sister Gorham" lived near Harriet Hastings, of New Ipswich, since Harriet is being asked to give greetings from Ellen White. Elizabeth Gorham, of the nearby town of Mason, is the most likely candidate. See note 25 in Lt 5, 1849 (Apr. 21), for a fuller rationale.

A SKETCH

OF THE

CHRISTIAN EXPERIENCE

AND

VIEWS

OF

ELLEN G. WHITE.

SARATOGA SPRINGS, N. Y.
PUBLISHED BY JAMES WHITE.
1851.

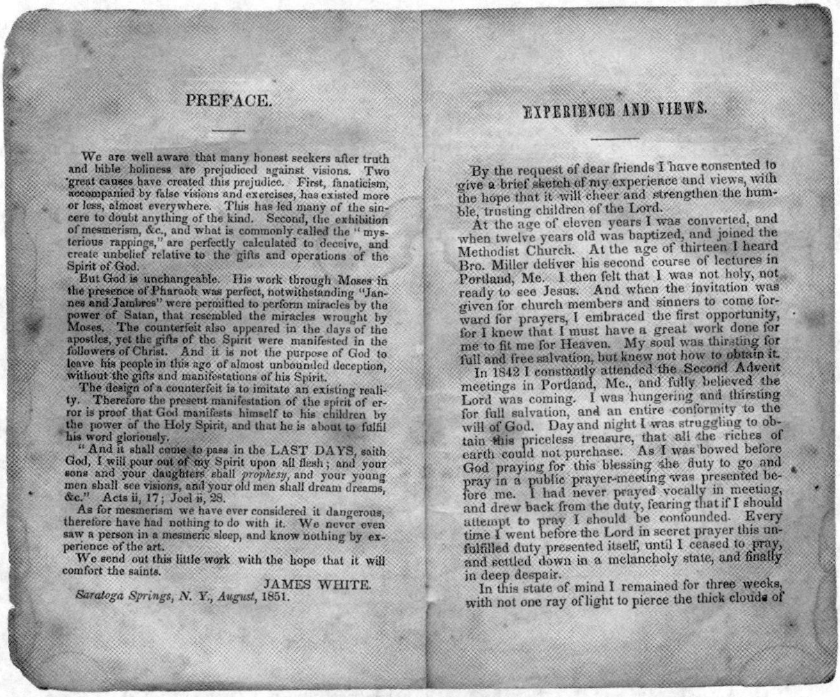

PREFACE.

We are well aware that many honest seekers after truth and bible holiness are prejudiced against visions. Two great causes have created this prejudice. First, fanaticism, accompanied by false visions and exercises, has existed more or less, almost everywhere. This has led many of the sincere to doubt anything of the kind. Second, the exhibition of mesmerism, &c., and what is commonly called the "mysterious rappings," are perfectly calculated to deceive, and create unbelief relative to the gifts and operations of the Spirit of God.

But God is unchangeable. His work through Moses in the presence of Pharaoh was perfect, notwithstanding "Jannes and Jambres" were permitted to perform miracles by the power of Satan, that resembled the miracles wrought by Moses. The counterfeit also appeared in the days of the apostles, yet the gifts of the Spirit were manifested in the followers of Christ. And it is not the purpose of God to leave his people in this age of almost unbounded deception, without the gifts and manifestations of his Spirit.

The design of a counterfeit is to imitate an existing reality. Therefore the present manifestation of the spirit of error is proof that God manifests himself to his children by the power of the Holy Spirit, and that he is about to fulfil his word gloriously.

"And it shall come to pass in the LAST DAYS, saith God, I will pour out of my Spirit upon all flesh; and your sons and your daughters shall *prophesy*, and your young men shall see visions, and your old men shall dream dreams, &c." Acts ii, 17; Joel ii, 28.

As for mesmerism we have ever considered it dangerous, therefore have had nothing to do with it. We never even saw a person in a mesmeric sleep, and know nothing by experience of the art.

We send out this little work with the hope that it will comfort the saints.

JAMES WHITE.

Saratoga Springs, N. Y., August, 1851.

EXPERIENCE AND VIEWS.

By the request of dear friends I have consented to give a brief sketch of my experience and views, with the hope that it will cheer and strengthen the humble, trusting children of the Lord.

At the age of eleven years I was converted, and when twelve years old was baptized, and joined the Methodist Church. At the age of thirteen I heard Bro. Miller deliver his second course of lectures in Portland, Me. I then felt that I was not holy, not ready to see Jesus. And when the invitation was given for church members and sinners to come forward for prayers, I embraced the first opportunity, for I knew that I must have a great work done for me to fit me for Heaven. My soul was thirsting for full and free salvation, but knew not how to obtain it.

In 1842 I constantly attended the Second Advent meetings in Portland, Me., and fully believed the Lord was coming. I was hungering and thirsting for full salvation, and an entire conformity to the will of God. Day and night I was struggling to obtain this priceless treasure, that all the riches of earth could not purchase. As I was bowed before God praying for this blessing the duty to go and pray in a public prayer-meeting was presented before me. I had never prayed vocally in meeting, and drew back from the duty, fearing that if I should attempt to pray I should be confounded. Every time I went before the Lord in secret prayer this unfulfilled duty presented itself, until I ceased to pray, and settled down in a melancholy state, and finally in deep despair.

In this state of mind I remained for three weeks, with not one ray of light to pierce the thick clouds of

Ellen White's first book, published in 1851, described her conversion and earliest visions. 64 pp. Now found in Early Writings, *pp. 11-78. Courtesy of James R. Nix.*

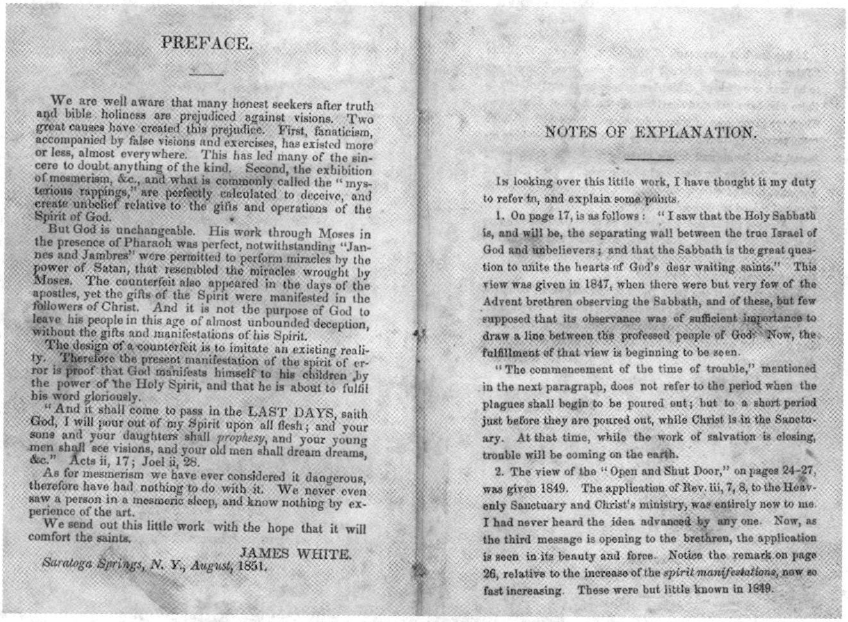

PREFACE.

We are well aware that many honest seekers after truth and bible holiness are prejudiced against visions. Two great causes have created this prejudice. First, fanaticism, accompanied by false visions and exercises, has existed more or less, almost everywhere. This has led many of the sincere to doubt anything of the kind. Second, the exhibition of mesmerism, &c., and what is commonly called the "mysterious rappings," are perfectly calculated to deceive, and create unbelief relative to the gifts and operations of the Spirit of God.

But God is unchangeable. His work through Moses in the presence of Pharaoh was perfect, notwithstanding "Jannes and Jambres" were permitted to perform miracles by the power of Satan, that resembled the miracles wrought by Moses. The counterfeit also appeared in the days of the apostles, yet the gifts of the Spirit were manifested in the followers of Christ. And it is not the purpose of God to leave his people in this age of almost unbounded deception, without the gifts and manifestations of his Spirit.

The design of a counterfeit is to imitate an existing reality. Therefore the present manifestation of the spirit of error is proof that God manifests himself to his children by the power of the Holy Spirit, and that he is about to fulfil his word gloriously.

"And it shall come to pass in the LAST DAYS, saith God, I will pour out of my Spirit upon all flesh; and your sons and your daughters shall *prophesy*, and your young men shall see visions, and your old men shall dream dreams, &c." Acts ii, 17; Joel ii, 28.

As for mesmerism we have ever considered it dangerous, therefore have had nothing to do with it. We never even saw a person in a mesmeric sleep, and know nothing by experience of the art.

We send out this little work with the hope that it will comfort the saints.

JAMES WHITE.

Saratoga Springs, N. Y., August, 1851.

NOTES OF EXPLANATION.

In looking over this little work, I have thought it my duty to refer to, and explain some points.

1. On page 17, is as follows: "I saw that the Holy Sabbath is, and will be, the separating wall between the true Israel of God and unbelievers; and that the Sabbath is the great question to unite the hearts of God's dear waiting saints." This view was given in 1847, when there were but very few of the Advent brethren observing the Sabbath, and of these, but few supposed that its observance was of sufficient importance to draw a line between the professed people of God. Now, the fulfillment of that view is beginning to be seen.

"The commencement of the time of trouble," mentioned in the next paragraph, does not refer to the period when the plagues shall begin to be poured out; but to a short period just before they are poured out, while Christ is in the Sanctuary. At that time, while the work of salvation is closing, trouble will be coming on the earth.

2. The view of the "Open and Shut Door," on pages 24-27, was given 1849. The application of Rev. iii, 7, 8, to the Heavenly Sanctuary and Christ's ministry, was entirely new to me. I had never heard the idea advanced by any one. Now, as the third message is opening to the brethren, the application is seen in its beauty and force. Notice the remark on page 26, relative to the increase of the *spirit manifestations*, now so fast increasing. These were but little known in 1849.

Ellen White added two pages of explanatory notes to her first book in March 1853. See Early Writings, *pp. 45, 85, 86.*

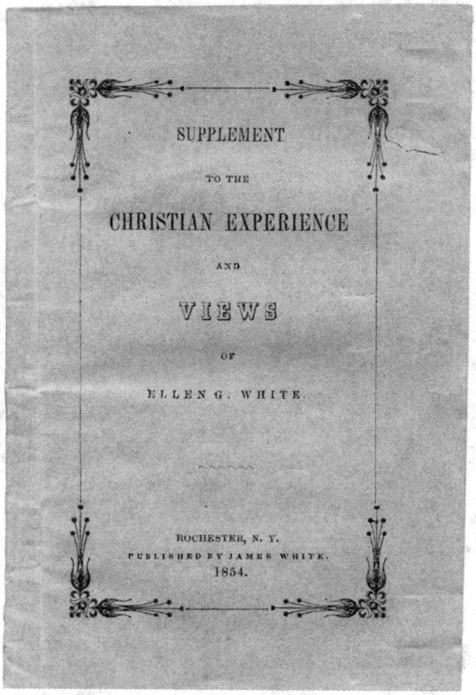

SUPPLEMENT

TO THE

CHRISTIAN EXPERIENCE

AND

VIEWS

OF

ELLEN G. WHITE.

ROCHESTER, N. Y.

PUBLISHED BY JAMES WHITE.

1854.

A 48-page supplement was announced in the January 10, 1854, Review and Herald. *Now found in* Early Writings, *pp. 85-127.*

1851

AUGUST

PUBLICATION OF

A Sketch of the Christian Experience and Views of Ellen G. White, Saratoga Springs, N.Y.

Published by James White. 64 pp.

1851

(Lt 1, 1851)

OCTOBER 19, SARATOGA SPRINGS, NEW YORK

LETTER TO

Chandler B. Preston and Eliza Ann Preston.[1]

Portions of this letter are published in Ellen G. White, *Manuscript Releases,* vol. 5, pp. 226, 227; vol. 8, pp. 223, 224.

Letter of personal encouragement to friends in Camden, New York.

Dear Brother and Sister Preston:

We received a letter a few days since from Brethren [Ira] Abbey[2] and [William] Hyatt.

---

[1] *Identity:* The earliest issues of the *Review*, up to November 1852, mention only one Preston (apart from one "Jenet Preston"), viz., a Chandler B. Preston living in Camden, New York. The strongest indication that this is the same Preston family is the greeting sent toward the end of the letter "to you both and Jennetta and Gilbert." Evidence from the 1850 U.S. Federal Census reveals a "Janett" and a "Gilbert" listed in Chandler Preston's household, aged 14 and 8, respectively. Despite the variation in spelling, this is telling evidence. Further confirmation is found in the fact that several of the names of persons Ellen White asks the Prestons to greet are found among Adventists in or around Camden at this time. This includes the names Prior (see Ms 2a, 1851 [June 23]), Abbey (*Review,* Dec. 9, 1851, p. 64), and Almira ("Almiry") Preston (Ms 2, 1851 [June 23]).

See: 1850 U.S. Federal Census, "Chandler B. Preston," New York, Oneida County, Camden, p. 243; search term "Preston" in *Words of the Pioneers.*

[2] *Identity:* Bracketed unbolded first names or surnames in this letter derive from later

The letter stated that the little band in your vicinity[3] were rising; it also stated that Brother William Wakefield wanted the paper. We have sent the papers to him, all the while James has never erased his name from our list. If he has not received the papers it must be in the office now, [for] he has sent his paper regularly ever since last winter to McConnellsville, [near] Vienna, N.Y. Brn. should not be so heedless whom we send the papers to as to let them lie in the office.

Our meeting yesterday was interesting; especially in the evening the Spirit of God settled upon us like the dew upon the mown grass, and our hearts were made joyful in God. We feel the need of being fully prepared and fitted to stand in the battle in the day of the Lord. We are doing up work for eternity, and may the Lord help us that we may have it done and well done, that we may receive the refreshing and latter rain that is soon to come from God upon all those who are zealous of *good works.*

It becomes us to search our hearts carefully and have every wrong purged away from us that we may be pure and holy and stand in the clear light of God where we can shed a holy influence. We love you as we ever have;[4] should be pleased to hear from you but much more pleased to see you. I hope and pray that the enemy may make no more inroads. Strive hard to preserve union among you. Where there is union there is strength, and God will work among you, by you, and through you, if you will only strive to be wholly consecrated to God and be at peace among yourselves,[5] and each one strive with all their might to keep the victory over *self* and over every besetment, every wrong word and action.

We do not think that we shall be able to attend the conference at Camden [New York],[6] or, I might say, it is impossible for us to attend it unless we give

---

editorial insertions penciled on the original handwritten letter. Since the following names play only an ancillary role in the letter, no attempt has been made to establish or verify their full identities: Abbey, Hyatt, Wakefield, Curtis, Waters, Prior, Lucinda. Some of these names have been annotated elsewhere in this volume, but it should not be assumed that the same individuals are signified each time, since the same surname or first name will often be carried by several church members.

[3] Presumably the Camden, New York, area (see note 1).

[4] The friendship of the Prestons and the Whites no doubt went back to the two visits the Whites made to Camden in 1850 and to the Camden conference in June of 1851, which was held in the Prestons' house.

See: "The State of the Cause," *Present Truth,* May 1850, p. 80; Ellen G. White, *Spiritual Gifts [vol. 2],* pp. 133, 134; "Conferences," *Review,* May 19, 1851, p. 88.

[5] James White reported in the May 1850 issue of *Present Truth* that the Camden band had "been scattered and torn by spiritualism, and other errors; but God is uniting and healing them. . . . Gospel order is being restored by the church in this vicinity."

See: "The State of the Cause," *Present Truth,* May 1850, p. 80.

[6] The Whites did in fact attend the conference in Camden, which started on December 25, 1851.

See: "Our Tour West," *Review,* Feb. 3, 1852, p. 86.

up the paper entirely. We shall start next Thursday for the east to be gone three weeks,[7] and the paper must be delayed. The flock of God need the paper and must have it. Aunt Rachel [Cushing][8] sends her love to you both and Jennetta and Gilbert [Preston][9]and Sister [Nelson] Curtis. Tell Sister Curtis for me to keep up good courage, to hope in God. He will not leave nor forsake her. Sister Clarissa [**Clarissa M. Bonfoey**] is better than she has been for months.[10] Aunt Rachel's health is good; the spring water does her good. Sarah and Stephen [**Stephen** and **Sarah Belden**] enjoy health. The spring water agrees with us all but Clarissa. Edson [**James Edson White**] is smart[11] and well; he talks very plain. James's [**James Springer White**] health is quite good for him. We are striving for eternal life[12] and we know that heaven will be cheap enough if we have to go through suffering and afflictions to get there.

Much love to Sister Almiry Preston [**Almira Preston**] and Bro. and Sister Prior, Brother and Sister [Elmer] Waters, Brother Alonzo [Abbey] and wife, and Brother Ira and wife, and Brother Hyatt, and accept much yourselves. Love to your children. Tell them to be faithful and of good courage.

In love.

We have some good times; we love to have Aunt Rachel with us. She is of our company and we could not part with her anyway.

Much love to Lucinda [Abbey] and all the children.

---

[7] The itinerary took the Whites to four conferences in Massachusetts, New Hampshire, and Vermont (Oct. 23-Nov. 18).

See: "Our Tour East," *Review*, Nov. 25, 1851, p. 52.

[8] *Identity:* The title "Aunt" suggests that Rachel might be related to James or Ellen or perhaps to the Prestons, to whom the letter is written. An effort has been made to identify "Aunt Rachel," but without success. The bracketed earlier editorial suggestion that her surname was "Cushing" has been investigated, but without finding any relationship to the Whites or the Prestons.

[9] *See:* Note 1.

[10] Ellen White concludes the letter with news of the health of her family—James and her son Edson, aged 2. Probably living in the same house were Clarissa Bonfoey, who had assisted in the White household since 1849, and Ellen's sister Sarah, newly married to Stephen Belden.

[11] In the sense of "vivacious."

[12] *See:* Lt 3, 1851 (Aug. 11), note 5.

1851

(Lt 8, 1851)

NOVEMBER 12,[1] WATERBURY, VERMONT

LETTER TO
Stockbridge and Louisa M. Howland.[2]

Portions of this letter are published in Ellen G. White, *Manuscript Releases,* vol. 3, pp. 242-245, 401-403; vol. 5, pp. 239, 240; vol. 6, pp. 118, 253; vol. 8, pp. 225-227; Arthur L. White, *Ellen G. White: The Early Years,* pp. 219-222.

Struggles over time-setting and mistrust of the visions at conferences in New Hampshire and Vermont, autumn 1851.

Dear Brother and Sister Howland:

Here we are at Brother Butler's [**Ezra Pitt Butler**].[3] Oh, how changed everything is here. God has wrought for us mightily; praise His holy name. At Washington [New Hampshire][4] the Lord took the rule of the meeting Himself. Stephen Smith [**Stephen Smith**] and Brother Butler were present. There were about 75 present, all in the faith. Brother Stephen Smith was filled with a wrong spirit. He and J. Hart [**Josiah Hart**][5] had filled the minds of many with prejudice against us. False reports had been circulated, and the band had been sinking and had lost the power of the third angel's message.[6] They were sickly, but knew not the cause. The reason was that there was an

---

[1] Although this letter was started on November 12 in Waterbury, Vermont, it was not finished till some days later. This is clear from the fact that it relates events after November 12, including the situation when the Whites returned home to Saratoga Springs, New York, on November 18.

See: "Our Tour East," *Review,* Nov. 25, 1851, p. 52.

[2] *Identity:* The fond greetings to "my little Henry" at the end of the letter unmistakably identifies the recipients as Stockbridge and Louisa M. Howland, of Topsham, Maine. The Howlands provided a home for Henry White for five years (1848-1853).

See: Ellen G. White, *Spiritual Gifts [vol. 2],* p. iii; 1860 U.S. Federal Census, "Stockbridge Howland," Maine, Sagahadoc County, Topsham, p. 433.

[3] *Identity:* The only Butler of Waterbury, Vermont, mentioned in the *Review* during this period is Ezra Pitt Butler.

See: Search term "Butler" in *Words of the Pioneers.*

[4] In this letter Ellen White recounts some experiences of a four-week journey to attend conferences in Massachusetts, New Hampshire, and Vermont, October 23-November 18, 1851. For details of the itinerary, see "Our Tour East," *Review,* Nov. 25, 1851, p. 52, and Arthur L. White, *Ellen G. White: The Early Years,* pp. 216-223.

[5] The full name, Josiah Hart, is given later in the letter.

[6] *See*: EGWEnc, s.v. "Three Angels' Messages."

accursed thing in the camp, and by the assistance of God we were trying to get it out of the camp.[7]

Brother Butler was dark. The time had passed and left those who believed in it very low and dark, and the influence of those who believed the time has been very distracting.[8] Brother Holt [**George W. Holt**][9] talked on the gifts of the Spirit. S. Smith did not confess his wrongs at all; such a self-confident person, who felt so perfectly whole, we have seldom seen. God wrought for us; there was a mighty breaking down before God.

You remember I was not very well when we parted.[10] I continued to grow feeble and all day Sabbath was very weak, not able to sit up; in the eve I fainted quite away. The brethren prayed over me and I was healed and taken off in vision. I had a deep plunge in the glory, and the state of things in Washington was revealed to me, which I declared plainly to them. The vision had a powerful effect. All acknowledged their faith in the visions except Brother Butler and S. Smith.

We all felt it duty to act, and, by a unanimous vote of the brethren, S. Smith was disfellowshipped by the church until he should forever lay down

---

[7] An allusion to the sin of Achan, who, against God's express command, secretly hid booty taken at the conquest of Jericho. Military defeat followed the Israelites until Achan's sin was exposed and dealt with. The "accursed thing" had to be rooted out of the camp of Israel before God's blessing could be restored. See Joshua 6; 7.

[8] Several persons mentioned in this letter, including E. P. Butler, had been caught up in the minority time-setting movement that expected the Second Advent in October 1851. Sabbatarian Adventists in general had eschewed time-setting and had often made the point that it was the other Adventist bodies that had repeatedly set times for the Advent in the years following 1844. In 1849, however, Hiram Edson had published a pamphlet predicting the Second Advent in 1850. Little is known of the influence of that pamphlet. Of more consequence was a brief flurry of time-setting in 1850-1851 that broke out among some Sabbatarians, mostly in Vermont and New Hampshire. Joseph Bates appears to have been the prime mover, having published a pamphlet sometime during 1850 arguing briefly (and almost incidentally) for the Second Advent in the autumn of 1851. His ideas, however, were never given any support in the *Review;* indeed, James White wrote against them in the summer of 1851. This, together with the warnings in the visions (both of which were published in the *Review*), weakened the movement well before the anticipated time. Those who persisted in holding to the 1851 theory tended to be skeptical of the visions that contradicted their ideas, as can be seen in the events of this letter.

See: Hiram Edson, *The Time of the End;* Joseph Bates, *An Explanation of the Typical and Anti-Typical Sanctuary,* pp. 10, 11; "Our Present Work," *Review,* Aug. 19, 1851, p. 13. For an overview of the 1851 time-setting episode, see Arthur L. White, *Ellen G. White: The Early Years,* pp. 207-210; Alberto R. Timm, *The Sanctuary and the Three Angels' Messages,* pp. 68, 69; EGWEnc, s.v. "Time Setting."

[9] *Identity:* The *Review* had earlier announced that "Bro. G. W. Holt" would come to the Washington, New Hampshire, conference. Holt was one of the "preaching brethren" who spoke at the various conferences attended by the Whites on this journey.

See: "Conferences," *Review,* Oct. 21, 1851, p. 48; "Our Tour East," *Review,* Nov. 25, 1851, p. 52.

[10] The Howlands had met Ellen and James White three weeks earlier at the West Medford, Massachusetts, conference (Oct. 24-27, 1851).

See: James White to "Dear Brethren in Christ," *Review,* Nov. 11, 1851.

his erroneous views.[11] His wife then broke down and said she knew that her husband was not right. The work of God went right on in the meeting. Sunday eve, after we had disfellowshipped Brother Smith (in the afternoon), we had a glorious season. Many confessed that they had been prejudiced against us by different individuals such as S. Smith and J. Hart, but they praised God that they had seen us and were convinced that the visions were of God. The brethren and sisters generally arose and expressed their opinions and feelings; it was a good time. Monday forenoon we held another meeting and it was the best meeting of the whole; sweet union and love prevailed in the meeting. We then sang the farewell hymn and with sad yet joyful hearts parted—sad that we must part with those we love so well and had taken such sweet counsel with; but joyful that our hearts had been strengthened and comforted together, that the clear light of truth had shone upon us, and that we were soon to meet to part no more, where no discord or disunion reigns.

Just as the meeting closed, Sister Meade [**Sarah Phelps Mead**],[12] who had been afflicted with a slow fever, requested us to pray for her. We went into a room by ourselves, Brethren Holt, Wheeler, Stowell, James [**James Springer White**] and self. After I had anointed her with oil we prayed over her and she was healed every whit and fell prostrate by the power of God. That night we got into a rowboat and went on to the pond about one mile [1.6 kilometers] to Brother Mead's [**Stephen Newell Mead**].[13] His sister was there with a very sick child. We anointed it with oil and prayed over it, and God heard our prayers. Then the two Brother Meads rowed us back again in the night, and the next day we went to Claremont [New Hampshire] and took the [railroad] cars for Royalton [Vermont].

Tuesday, the same eve, the conference commenced.[14] Brother Butler was at that meeting, also Brother Josiah Hart who was so strong on the time,

---

[11] Stephen Smith had a fitful relationship with Sabbatarian Adventists in the 1850s, being disfellowshipped and then taken back at least twice. Toward the end of the 1850s he "finally" left the movement but returned under remarkable circumstances in 1885.

See: Arthur L. White, *Ellen G. White: The Early Years,* pp. 490-492; EGWEnc, s.v. "Stephen Smith."

[12] *Identity:* See note 13 below.

[13] *Identity:* Probably S. Newell Mead, of Washington, New Hampshire, who, according to his obituary, first became a Sabbathkeeper one year earlier, "in the fall of 1850." He married Sarah Phelps in 1849. Newell's sister, Sarah, married William Farnsworth, among the earliest of the Sabbatarian Adventists in the Washington group.

See: Obituary: "S. Newell Mead," *Review,* Mar. 13, 1888, p. 175; obituary: "Sarah Phelps Mead," *Review,* Apr. 14, 1921, p. 22; *History of Washington, New Hampshire, From 1768 to 1886,* pp. 397, 398, 535; 1860 U.S. Federal Census, "Newell Mead," New Hampshire, Sullivan, Washington, p. 1135.

[14] The conference took place at Royalton, Vermont, and was announced to begin "Nov. 4th . . . and hold about two days."

See: "Our Tour East," *Review,* Nov. 25, 1851, p. 52; "Conferences," *Review,* Oct. 21, 1851, p. 48.

and after it passed by, got a substitute, "the age to come,"[15] and was carrying that about. Such confusion and distraction has followed the time, and fighting against the visions! They had also lost the power of the third angel's message, and some of them were in complete darkness. Brother Hart was stiff and unyielding enough. I got up and told him what God had shown me concerning him. Brother Butler began to break away and come into the clear light. Thursday we seemed to have gone about as far as we could, and to have done all we could, yet there was much more to be done in order for things to be set just right.

In the morn we all seemed to have an agonizing cry for God to work like Himself, a wonder-working God. Our prayers were answered. The power of God came down; it was a good season; angels were hovering over us. I was taken off in vision and saw just the state of things there, and just the state that Brother Baker[16] was in, and Brethren Hart and Butler. I got up and told the vision. It had quite a powerful effect. Brother Hart began to give way a little and break down, but still he did not confess much. Brother Butler came almost out there at Bethel.

I had some straight messages to bear to different individuals, which had their effect. When we parted, we parted in love, and union prevailed among nearly all.

Thursday afternoon we left Royalton and took the cars for Waterbury [Vermont]. We changed cars at Northfield [Vermont], and as we stepped from the cars met Brother Baker; he came with us to Waterbury. Found Brethren Loveland[17] and Lindsay waiting for us at the depot. We went about two miles [three kilometers] to Brother Butler's, stopped there a few hours for refreshment, and went eight miles [13 kilometers] in the eve toward Johnson [Vermont] and stopped with Sister Benson that night, and the next day went on to Johnson, the place appointed for the conference. Some had already arrived to attend the meeting. I did not expect Brother and Sister Butler that night, for we parted with Brother Butler the day before about noon and he had to drive 50 or 60 miles [80 to 96 kilometers] to reach home and then prepare to come 25 miles [40 kilometers] farther to Johnson. But he had got so waked up he could not stop on the way, but drove until one o'clock the next morn before he got home. He was anxious to get his wife to Johnson. She

---

[15] *See:* EGWEnc, s.v. "Adventist Denominations."

[16] The likelihood is that "Brother Baker" is Joseph Baker, of Lebanon, New Hampshire, since the only Bakers appearing in the *Review* up to December 1852 are Joseph Baker and S. E. (Sarah E.) Baker. This inference is confirmed by the information given in the letter that "Brother Baker" was being called to preach, since we know that Joseph Baker preached widely throughout New England and New York State in the early 1850s.

See: Search term "Baker" in *Words of the Pioneers.*

[17] The following surnames in this letter, which receive only brief mention, have not been fully identified: Loveland, Lindsay, Benson.

was not right; had been a strong believer in the time and had felt very wrong toward James and Brother Holt because they struck against the time. But about three o'clock two wagon loads came from Brother Butler's—Brethren Hart and Baker in one wagon, and Brother Butler, his wife and sister, in the other wagon.

The meeting that eve was deeply interesting. There were about 73 present. Brother Baker spoke, and spoke quite well, about the time and his disappointment; yet he did not view things in their true light. He was much discouraged and sunken. After he sat down, a man by the name of Walker[18] arose, who had very lately embraced the truth and thought and acted as though he knew *it all.* He said he expected the brethren were expecting a confession from him because he was so strenuous upon the time, but said he had nothing to confess and he did not think Brother Baker had. He was not sure but something did take place, that Jesus did leave the Most Holy the time they said He would. He was happy, these were the happiest days of his life. He went on in this strain, with such a wild spirit, that all were disgusted with him. The Spirit of God came upon James, and he arose and rebuked him in the name of the Lord. His mouth was closed in a moment; he could not say *anything* more, but sat down and did not say anything through the meeting. He was rebuked by God. This was a great help to the meeting and a great help to Brother Baker.

I got up and told them what God had shown me about some trying to get a substitute after the time passed; some would get Jesus upon the great white cloud,[19] others would be looking to old Jerusalem, or as they called it, the age-to-come.[20] I asked Brother Walker where he would be or what would

---

[18] *Identity:* This could well be William Walker, of Morristown, Vermont. Six months later a notice appeared in the *Review* that "the brethren in [Vermont] . . . are not in fellowship with William Walker . . . of Morristown, and that the course pursued by him is a subject of grief to the church."

See: [Notice], *Review,* May 6, 1852, p. 8.

[19] A reference to Revelation 14:14: "And I looked, and behold a white cloud, and upon the cloud one sat like unto the Son of man, having on his head a golden crown, and in his hand a sharp sickle." The setting is the end of probation, of Jesus having left the sanctuary and about to execute judgment.

[20] Ellen White's warning here against "looking to Old Jerusalem" and "age-to-come" should be seen against the background of the strong emergence of these views among some non-Sabbatarian Adventists in 1850 and 1851, especially as championed in the *Advent Harbinger.* Basic to these views was the reign of Christ on earth during the 1,000 years, the continuance of probation during the millennium, and the conversion and restoration of Jerusalem to the Jews. Some months earlier Clorinda Minor in her book *Meshullam! Or, Tidings From Jerusalem* had issued an appeal for Adventists to emigrate to Jerusalem in order to work for the conversion and development of Jews living in the area. Evidently age-to-come teachings held an appeal even to a few Sabbathkeepers, hence the admonishment given here.

See: Julia Neuffer, "The Gathering of Israel"; SDAE, s.v. "*Messenger* Party"; David Tallmadge Arthur, "'Come Out of Babylon,'" pp. 224-227; George R. Knight, *Millennial Fever,* pp. 288, 289.

be his state if Jesus had now left the Most Holy and His work for the saints was all done and he in the state he then was? I talked plainly. The Lord helped me. I showed them how the messengers that had been toiling in the scattering time had labored to get the truth before them, how much they had suffered, and now when God's cause was prospering, they embrace the third angel's message and enter into the labors of the chosen messengers of God and lift up their heel against them. But I am making my story too long.

Sabbath day the brethren lectured. James talked twice from the Word, Brother Holt once. It was a very interesting time. Truth never looked so plain and clear. One hundred were present. It was a precious time, praise the Lord.

Sunday Brother Holt lectured in the forenoon and James in the afternoon. In the morning meeting before Brother Holt commenced to lecture, Sister Butler [**Sarah Butler**], who came to the meeting and was obliged to keep [to] her bed nearly all the while, confessed in the meeting that she had been wrong. Then Brother Butler talked very well; there was a confession made all around with weeping. Then I got up and told my vision about Brethren Baker and Hart and others. I never had it in a more clear manner. I told Brother Baker [that] his going to the churches to proclaim the third angel's message was all wrong, that he had to tame down that message or he could not have got into the churches, and that he had been taking the children's bread and giving it to dogs.[21] I told him just how his case was shown to me, and also told them all that the messengers of God should be perfectly united in their views of Bible truth and should consult with each other and should not advance any new view until they first went to the messengers and examined those views with the Bible, and if they were correct let all the messengers spread them, and if they were error lay them to one side. Then the gospel seed would be sown in union and raised in strength; and all the messengers, East and West, North and South, would be telling the same story.

After I got through talking it was time for the lecture to commence, so none made any remarks. In the afternoon after James talked, Brother Baker arose; none knew what he was about to say. He told them that every word of the vision related in the forenoon concerning him, was truth, just exactly as it was. (I saw in vision that Brother Baker had not had any bitter feelings towards us like some others.) He referred to this in particular; he knew it to be just so. "Well now," says he, "you will say, What is Brother Baker going to do with the visions? I will tell you. It is high time for me to decide there is no half way work about this business; the visions are *all* of God or there are none of them of God. Well, say you, what is Brother Baker going to do? *Believe the visions.* I see that they are inseparably connected with the third

---

[21] An allusion to Matthew 15:26: "But he answered and said, It is not meet to take the children's bread, and to cast it to dogs."

angel's message and if I give up the visions I must give up the third angel's message; and if I give up the third angel's message I give up that we have had the first and second; and if I give up that we have had the first, second, and third angels' messages, I give up the Word of God, my Christian experience, and am an infidel at once."

I never witnessed such a melting, weeping time before. Bro. Butler had taken his stand the day before and told the brethren and sisters in public where to find him, on the side of the visions. "I believe them to be of God, am a full believer in the visions, so you may know where to find me." Others expressed their belief, and hearty confessions were made by Brother Hart and others. Never did I witness such a powerful time.

Monday morn we had another meeting; the power of God rested upon us. I was taken off in vision and saw many things. I saw that Brother Baker must not sink down, that God had a work for him to do, not to feed the dogs but the starving sheep. "Feed the sheep, feed the sheep," said my accompanying angel. It was a melting, weeping time when I related the vision. Brother Baker was comforted and made strong.

We parted with the brethren and sisters while sweet love and union prevailed among all. Sister Butler, who came to the meeting so sick, went home quite well and much strengthened. Six wagon loads of us left Johnson and came to Sister Benson's 20 miles [32 kilometers], took some refreshment and then went on to Brother Butler's. Brethren Baker and Hart were with us.

Brother Baker had not slept any for two or three nights, troubled with disease of the heart. He said he must go home and be sick some days but we got a spirit of prayer for him and the Lord heard us pray. Brother Baker was healed and he glorified God with a loud voice; he had a baptism of the Holy Ghost. We parted with him and Brother Hart rejoicing, triumphant in God.

One thing I have not mentioned. Brother Baker has come into the salutation[22] and washing the saints' feet which he never believed in before. We stopped (Brethren Holt, Wheeler, James, and self) a few days and wrote. Wednesday Brethren Holt and Wheeler went to Vergennes, Vt. to inform them that we should be there Sabbath and Sunday. Brother Butler carried us to Vergennes Thursday, 44 miles [71 kilometers]. Sabbath day it was very stormy but we went

---

[22] The "salutation," or "holy kiss," was practiced by early Sabbathkeeping Adventists. Ellen White supported the practice on the basis of Paul's instruction in 1 Thessalonians 5:26, but warned against its misuse. Improperly practiced, the holy kiss had the potential of causing public scandal and charges of fanaticism, as had happened in 1845-1846. The majority of Adventist bodies rejected both foot washing and the holy kiss.

See: SDAE, s.v. "Foot Washing"; Ellen G. White, *Supplement to the Christian Experience and Views of Ellen G. White,* p. 38; Joseph Bates, *A Vindication of the Seventh-day Sabbath,* p. 71; George R. Knight, *Millennial Fever,* pp. 251, 252.

three miles [five kilometers] to Brother Evarts' [**Elon Everts**];[23] there were but few [who] could attend that meeting on account of the storm. Brother Evarts is a blessed brother, but has been in the "age to come" all over and he said he could not give it up. When we were there he was in a very dark place.

Henry Allen lived about one mile [1.6 kilometers] from Brother Evarts.' He held such a strong mixture of views that if followed out would lead to spiritualism [of] the worst kind, such as spiritual wifery.[24]

Sabbath eve I had a great burden such as I have borne before. I saw that Brother Evarts must give up his "age to come," that he had lost the power of the third angel's message, and I saw that the accursed thing must be put out of the camp or Israel would be sickly. That accursed thing was such views as I have mentioned that Henry Allen held. He was not at the meeting at Brother Evarts,' being sick.

After I had the vision and told it, Brother Evarts began to confess and break down before God. He gave up his "age to come" and felt the necessity of keeping the minds of all on the third angel's message. I had as solemn a view at that time as I ever had in my life.

The next day we went to Henry Allen's and God gave me a cutting message for him, and I dared not daub [it] with untempered mortar. Never did I have such a cutting message for any one before. He did not break down. We withdrew all fellowship from him until he should give up his spiritual union views and get right.[25] We left the brethren and sisters there in a much better state than we found them. I must close.

Edson [**James Edson White**] is well and smart.[26] Clarissa [**Clarissa M.**

---

[23] *Identity:* Very likely "Brother Evarts" is Elon Everts who lived in New Haven, a few miles from Vergennes. (The variation in spelling is probably not significant.)

See: Search term "Everts" in *Words of the Pioneers.*

[24] "Spiritualism" in this context seems to refer to the belief in a spiritual rather than a literal Second Coming. A faction of Adventists rejected the central Millerite teaching of the literal Second Advent and instead held that Christ had come spiritually to believers in 1844. This spiritualized interpretation of the Second Advent led, in a few extreme cases, to the practice of "spiritual wifery." Millerite historian David Arthur suggests the following logic behind the practice: "This practice was based on the scriptural idea that in the kingdom of heaven there would be no marrying or giving in marriage. Since these were persons who believed that they were immortal and had entered the kingdom, it followed that they were now in their spiritual state. They also took Christ's statement concerning hating and forsaking the family in order to follow Him as a literal command. The former idea led to 'spiritual' couples or to a 'spiritual matrimony without sexual connexion.'"

See: David Tallmadge Arthur, "'Come Out of Babylon,'" p. 121. See also George R. Knight, *Millennial Fever,* pp. 252, 253.

[25] Two years later the following notice appeared in the *Review:* "The brethren in the vicinity of New Haven have suffered severe trials in times past in consequence of the course pursued by Henry Allen. . . . Allen now teaches the no-Sabbath heresy."

See: "Eastern Tour," *Review,* Nov. 15, 1853, p. 149.

[26] This closing paragraph contains news of the family: Edson, age 2. Clarissa Bonfoey, who had helped in the White household since 1849; Ellen's sister Sarah Belden and brother-in-law Stephen Belden. By this time Anna (Annie) R. Smith, sister of future *Review* editor Uriah

Bonfoey] is well. I have not seen Sarah [**Sarah B. Belden**] yet. She is seven miles [11 kilometers] from here visiting the brethren and sisters. Stephen [**Stephen Belden**] has just gone to see her. James is well and Aunt Rachel; I also. Anna Smith [Annie R. Smith] is with us. She is just the help we need. She takes right hold with James and helps him much. We can leave her now to get off the papers and can go out more among the flock. Henry [**Henry Nichols White**], Edson says thank you for his Bible and box of candy. He is much pleased with them. James, Clarissa, Annie, Aunt Rachel and self send love to you all, especially my little Henry. Hope he will be good.

In love,

E. G. White

I would here say our healths failed a number of times on our journey. It seemed as though we could not go through the meeting. But we would go away alone with a few brethren and sisters and pray together, and God heard and answered and when we returned home we were better than when we left home.

E. W.

Eliza Willard[27] has come out strong in all the truth. Deborah Dunham has also come into the truth. Her sister has been so troubled, and Brother Day's girl, that they have broken down before God, given their hearts to Him and have been baptized. The work of God is going on, praise His name, we will rejoice in Him.

E. W.

Give our love to all of the church. You see I have written you a long letter. You must do the same to me. After you read this please to copy it off for Mother [**Eunice Harmon**] in plain hand writing. It will save my writing another letter. Do write it to her as soon as you can, and answer this after you copy it off for her. I want to hear from you very much. Do write. Tell Henry to be very good and love the Lord.

In great haste and much love.

Smith, had joined the *Review* team as editorial assistant, a post she filled for the next three years. The identity of "Aunt Rachel" has not been determined.

[27] No positive identifications have been made of Eliza Willard, Deborah Dunham, or Brother Day's daughter.

1851

(Lt 5, 1851)

DECEMBER 14, SARATOGA SPRINGS, NEW YORK

LETTER TO

Robert Barnes.[1]

Portions of this letter are published in Ellen G. White, *Manuscript Releases,* vol. 8, p. 225; Arthur L. White, *Ellen G. White: The Early Years,* p. 224.

Vision against the use of tobacco.

Dear Brother Barnes:

I received a few lines from Bro. Hewett [**Oren Hewett**].[2] He wishes me to write whether I have seen in vision it is wrong to use tobacco.

I have seen in vision that tobacco was a filthy weed, and that it must be laid aside or given up.[3] Said my accompanying angel, "If it is an *idol* it is high time it was given up, and unless it is given up the frown of God will be upon the one that uses it and he cannot be sealed with the seal of the living God.[4] If it is used as a medicine,[5] Go to God, He is the great Physician and those that

---

[1] *Identity:* A useful indication of Barnes's identity is the greeting toward the end of the letter, "Much love to Brother and Sister Flanders," the implication being that they live in the same vicinity. An examination of notices appearing in the *Review* from this period reveals a Robert Barnes and an S. W. Flanders, both living in Canaan, Maine. Thus it is reasonable to suppose that Ellen White is addressing Robert Barnes.

See: "Appointments," *Review,* May 27, 1852, p. 16; "Agents," *Review,* Jan. 6, 1853, p. 136.

[2] *Identity:* This letter is not in the White Estate archives. However, the receipt of a letter from "O. Hewett" is recorded in the "Letters Received" section of the *Review,* December 9, 1851. The name "O. Hewett" ("Oren Hewett") appears frequently in the *Review* from 1850 until his death in Rochester, New York, in 1855.

See: Search term "Hewett" in *Words of the Pioneers.*

[3] The date of the vision or visions referred to here is not given. According to James White, writing many years later, the earliest vision given Ellen White against tobacco was in the autumn of 1848. No contemporary account of that vision has been preserved. The 1848 date, however, is confirmed by Joseph Bates in January 1849. Of this "idle and sinful habit," he writes, "God has shown several times by visions that He disapprobates it in every way."

See: EGWEnc, s.v. "Tobacco"; James White, "Western Tour," *Review,* Nov. 8, 1870, p. 165; Joseph Bates, *A Seal of the Living God,* p. 67. For broader analyses of the part played by Ellen White's visions in the emerging health consciousness of Sabbatarian Adventists, see P. Gerard Damsteegt, *Foundations of the Seventh-day Adventist Message and Mission,* pp. 221-241; Herbert E. Douglass, *Messenger of the Lord,* pp. 278-309.

[4] *See:* EGWEnc, s.v. "Seal of God."

[5] Inhaling tobacco smoke, according to folklore dating back to Indian traditions, was an

use the filthy weed for medicine greatly dishonor God." There is a "balm in Gilead"; there is a "physician there." "Be ye clean that bear the vessels of the Lord." "Be ye clean that bear the vessels of the Lord."

I saw that Christ will have a church without *spot* or *wrinkle* or *any such thing* to present to His Father, and as He leads us through the pearly gates of the New Jerusalem, or the golden city, Jesus will look upon His redeemed children and see of the travail of His soul and be *satisfied*. Glory be to God; that will be a great salvation, purchased for us by our lovely Saviour. If we are followers of the lovely Jesus, our Pattern, we are safe. He denied Himself. He was a man of *sorrows* and acquainted with *grief.* If we are made partakers with Him of His glory, we must be partakers with Him of His sufferings. And after Jesus has done so much for us, will anyone be undecided whether to deny himself of the filthy weed for His sake?

We must be *perfect Christians,* deny ourselves all the way along, tread the narrow, thorny pathway that our Jesus trod, and then if we are final overcomers, heaven, sweet heaven, will be cheap enough.

Those who have been in the habit of using tobacco will have a struggle to leave it off, but they must not be discouraged. If they cannot overcome by praying to God themselves, let them be as humble as Brother Rhodes [**Samuel W. Rhodes**][6] was. When he was leaving off using tobacco he called for the brethren to pray for him and we did. He was cured and has desired none since. Go to God, dear brother, wrestle with Him and you can overcome; pray in faith, nothing doubting. Jesus will be touched with the brother's infirmities. We are all as well as usual here. Be of good courage, Brother Barnes. "Be humble, be little, be meek, and be low, for Jesus our Saviour was abundantly so."

Much love to Brother and Sister Flanders. I hope they will be overcomers and push the battle to the gate. Love to your wife, and all that love God.

James [**James Springer White**] is very busy writing for the paper.[7] Night before last the papers came off about eight o'clock at night. We sat up and wrapped and folded them, all about three bushels, so as to get them in the office the next morn. We did not retire to rest until past one o'clock A.M. I must close.

In love.

---

effective treatment against coughs, bronchitis, asthma, etc. It is possible that Oren Hewett, who was "wasting with consumption" for several years before his death in 1855, was smoking to treat his cough, or considering doing so, and had written to Ellen White for counsel on the matter.

See: David Armstrong and Elizabeth Metzger Armstrong, *The Great American Medicine Show,* p. 14; obituary: "Oren Hewett," *Review,* May 1, 1855, p. 222.

[6] *Identity:* No doubt Samuel W. Rhodes. No other Rhodes is mentioned in the *Review* in the early 1850s.

See: Search term "Rhodes" in *Words of the Pioneers.*

[7] I.e., the *Review.*

1851
(Lt 9, 1851)

DECEMBER 21, SARATOGA SPRINGS, NEW YORK

LETTER TO
Abram A. Dodge and Caroline Elizabeth Dodge.[1]

Portions of this letter are published in Ellen G. White, *Reflecting Christ,* p. 350; *idem, Manuscript Releases,* vol. 2, p. 248; vol. 6, p. 253; vol. 8, p. 228.

Personal testimony to God's goodness despite trials and difficulties. Encouragement for friends in Michigan and some news.

Dear Brother and Sister Dodge:

I have a few moments leisure and will spend them in writing to you. My health has been quite poor for a short time back, but am much better today. At times James and self feel almost worn out. It is seldom we retire before eleven or twelve o'clock at night;[2] we have no idle moments. Were it not for the strength we daily receive from God, we should sink.

Praise the Lord that we have a compassionate, tender High Priest that can be touched with the feelings of our infirmities. We do not expect rest here, No, no. The way to Heaven is a cross-bearing way; the road is straight and narrow, but we will go forward with cheerfulness knowing that the King of glory once trod this way before us. We will not complain of the roughness of the way, but will be meek followers of Jesus, treading in His footsteps. He was a man of sorrows and acquainted with grief. He for our sakes became poor that we through His poverty might be made rich. We will rejoice in tribulation and keep in mind the recompense of reward, the *far more,* the *exceeding* and *eternal weight of glory.*

We will not have a murmuring thought because we have trials. God's dear children always had them, and every trial well endured here will only make us rich in glory. I crave the suffering part. I would not go to heaven without

---

[1] *Identity:* Until 1856 the only persons surnamed "Dodge" in the *Review* were Abram A. Dodge with his wife, Caroline Dodge, of Jackson, Michigan; and H. W. Dodge, of Stoddard, New Hampshire. Since the Dodges of Lt 9 are clearly located in Jackson, Michigan (see greetings toward the end of the letter), it is very likely that Ellen White is addressing Abram and Caroline Dodge.

See: Search term "Dodge" in *Words of the Pioneers.*

[2] "Night before last," Ellen White wrote one week earlier, "we sat up and wrapped and folded [the *Review*]" "until past one o'clock A.M." (Lt 5, 1851 [Dec. 14]).

suffering if I could, and see Jesus who suffered so much for us to purchase for us so rich an inheritance; and to see the martyrs who laid down their lives for the truth, and the sake of Jesus. No, no. Let me be perfected through sufferings. I long to be a partaker with Christ of His sufferings, for if I am, I know I shall be partaker with Him of His glory.

Jesus is our pattern. Let us study to have our lives as near like Christ's as possible. My soul cries out after the living God. My very being longs after Him. Oh, for to reflect His lovely image perfectly! Oh, for to be wholly consecrated to Him! Oh, how hard it is for dear self to die. We can rejoice in a whole Saviour; One that saves us from all sin. We can be shut in with God where we can daily say, "I live yet not I, for Jesus Christ liveth in me to will and do of His own good pleasure." Glory be to God. I know that my life is hid with Christ in God. The curtain has been lifted, I have seen the rich reward laid up for the saints. I have had a taste of the joys of the world to come, and it has spoiled this world for me. My affections, my interests, hopes, my all is in heaven. I long to see the King in His beauty, Him whom my soul loveth. Heaven, sweet heaven. "I long to be there; and the thought that 'tis near, makes me almost impatient for Christ to appear."[3] Praise the Lord for a good hope through Jesus Christ of immortality and eternal life.

Let us have faith, living faith in God, and love one another as God has loved us. We are very apt to see faults in others, and are not so quick to discover our own faults. If it were the daily study of each of us to show ourselves approved unto God, and should [we] seek earnestly to glorify God, and not have our own will and not please ourselves, I know we should be strong and flourish in the vine. The refreshing is coming from the presence of the Lord. Let us set our hearts in order, that the truth of God may live in us; that it may purify us, ready to receive the latter rain.

The voice of the angel seems to ring in my ears tonight so loud and clear, *Get ready, get ready, get ready,* lest ye be weighed in the balance and found wanting.

Christ will have a church to present to His Father without *spot* or *wrinkle* or *any such thing,* and as He leads us through the pearly gates of the golden city, He will look upon the purchase of His blood, His redeemed children, and *see* the travail of His soul and be *satisfied.* I long to see the lovely Jesus whose countenance lights up the glorious city; Him whom angels adore, and as they bow, cast their glittering crowns before Him, and then touch their golden harps and fill heaven with their rich music, of songs to the Lamb.

The language of my soul is, "Though dark are the waters, and rough is the wave, if Jesus permits the wild surges, I'll brave. For that heavenly music

---

[3] Lines taken from the hymn "I Long to Be There," first published among Sabbathkeeping Adventists by James White in *Hymns for Second Advent Believers,* 1852. For more on the publication history of this hymn, see James R. Nix, *Early Advent Singing.*

hath ravished me so, I'll join in the chorus, I'll go, let me go."[4] My soul is on wing for glory.

Dear Brother and Sister, I have not forgotten the seasons we had together at Milton [New York] Conference.[5] May the Lord strengthen and bring you through every trial, that you may come off victorious. We are to overcome by the blood of the Lamb and the word of our testimony. Let us walk carefully before the Lord and press to the mark of the prize.

Next Tuesday or Wednesday we start on our way for the Camden [New York] Conference. If Jesus only comes up to the feast (and I believe He will), we shall have a glorious meeting. I know if we are as humble as we ought to be, and realize from whence our strength cometh, and have faith, living faith, God will work mightily for us, and His stately steppings will be seen among us.

James [**James Springer White**] is very busy correcting proof sheet. Sister Annie Smith [Annie Rebekah Smith] is assisting him,[6] and that gives me a little time to write. I have written this evening after the Sabbath by candlelight, with aching eyes, so you must excuse poor writing. Be of good courage. Do not let anything sink you down and discourage you. Remember we are almost home. Much love to all the brethren and sisters in Michigan, especially those that I have seen and am acquainted with. Tell them to be of good cheer. "To be little, be humble, be meek, and be low; for Jesus our Saviour was abundantly so." Oh, let us be meek followers of the Lamb.

Dear Brother and Sister, do write us; we should love to hear from you and the brethren and sisters in Jackson [Michigan]. James and self send love to you and all that love Jesus.

In haste and love.

---

[4] Lines from the hymn "What Heavenly Music," included in James White's first hymnal, *Hymns for God's Peculiar People,* 1849. For more on the publication history of this hymn, see James R. Nix, *Early Advent Singing.*

[5] Abram Dodge, with his bride of just a few months, had made the lengthy journey together with other believers from Jackson, Michigan, to attend the conference in Camden, New York, June 20-22, 1851. It is not certain whether they also attended the West Milton, New York, conference the following weekend. There was subsequently a second conference advertised for West Milton, three months later, September 19-21, 1851. Hence when Ellen White writes of her meeting with the Dodges at the "Milton Conference," it is not clear which Milton conference she is referring to.

See: Obituary: "Caroline Smith Dodge," *Review,* Sept. 23, 1915, p. 21; "Our Tour to This State," *Review Extra,* July 21, 1851, p. [3]; [Notices], *Review,* Sept. 2, 1851, p. 24.

[6] Annie Rebekah Smith, 23-year-old sister of future *Review* editor Uriah Smith, had recently joined the *Review* team as editorial assistant. In a letter written one month earlier Ellen White expressed her feelings about Annie Smith: "She is just the help we need. She takes right hold with James and helps him much. We can leave her now to get off the papers and can go out more among the flock."

See: Ellen G. White, Lt 8, 1851 (Nov. 12).

1852

(Ms 2, 1852)

MARCH 14, BALLSTON, NEW YORK

"Extracts From Sister White's Vision at the General Conference in Ballston, New York."[1]

Previously unpublished.

Preparing for earth's final events. Utterances while in vision and explanations given after coming out of vision.

"If the sins do not go beforehand to judgment, they will never go. Thy people (repeated four times) not ready (three times). In that time one sin uncovered will crush the soul. Heaven will give no answer. That time will try men's souls. Confusion will take place and their desire will not be accomplished.[2] Can ye not see?—subjects of grace in that time of trouble[3] one, or once sealed,[4] sealed for heaven. Get ready! Get ready! Get ready! Get *ready*. Almost finished.

"Look ye! Light all the way that is given must be acted upon. If that light is rejected, then stupidity will increase. Look ye! The ark of God can abide. The Most Holy is above the ark. Why cannot that ark abide there?[5] The heart

---

[1] The Ballston conference, held March 12-15, 1852, is best known for the decision made to move the publication of the *Review* from Saratoga Springs to Rochester, New York. Ms 2, 1852, is a third-party account of Ellen White's vision, of which a parallel copy is dated March 18 (see notes on Ms 1, 1852 [Mar. 18]). It is in two parts. The first, in quotation marks, records her purported utterances while in vision, and the second contains certain explanations she made after coming out of vision. The identity of the third-party recorder is not known.

Caution needs to be exercised in reading and interpreting this text. In addition to being written by a third person and thereby increasing the potential for inaccuracies, the intermittent, discontinuous character of Ellen White's utterances while in vision means that there is often insufficient context available to make the meaning of individual statements clear or to understand the overall structure of the vision. The same caution should be applied to the brief summary of Ellen White's "explanations" found in the second part of the manuscript. The brevity of these comments clouds their meaning.

See: "The Conference," *Review,* Mar. 23, 1852, p. 108.

[2] For comment on these opening statements, see notes on the "explanations" in the second part of the manuscript.

[3] *See:* EGWEnc, s.v. "Time of Trouble."

[4] *See:* EGWEnc, s.v. "Seal of God."

[5] An allusion to the ark of the ancient Hebrew sanctuary, a symbol of God's presence in the camp of the Israelites. Compare the language used here with the following passage in a document written two years later: "A death-like stupor has hung upon the people of God. The reason is, the ark is not with them, for the holy commandments have been broken, and God has taken it away in His anger" (Ms 1, 1854 [Feb. 12]).

is not right with God. Ye I behold (repeated). Those that have that excellent reward sacrifice to obtain it. How afraid to die that they may live. Die to self, it is the hardest thing. Can ye not see that the people of God will be one when that unity prevails? Then will ye see His stately steppings[6] even among you. The angels of God will behold it.

"The sword cannot touch them. Can ye not see that prayers are going up from that company? His ear is heavy.[7] That fountain is open for Judah and Jerusalem to wash in.[8] Think ye that they can cover up the least sin and yet get in where the angels are? That sanctuary a great High Priest. Israel is not right. Why? Oh, why are ye not in love to plunge—bring them up, get ready (four times). He is coming. Unless you get ready, others will go in before you. Suffer them not to blind their eyes to their own destruction. Help the children to get ready. The four angels[9] holding for Israel to get ready. Will the angels wait? No, look ye! Can ye not see? Not ready, something to be done. Self! Self! O Jesus, pity and forgive thine erring children."

After she came out of vision some things were more fully explained. Respecting that time [which] will try men's souls, confusion will take place and their desire will not be accomplished.

That desire was with the people to dethrone their kings, but it would not be accomplished, for kings would reign until Christ begins to reign. Said she, I saw away off there in Europe just as things were moving to accomplish their desires, there would appear to be a slacking up once or twice. This would serve to harden the hearts of the wicked, but the work would not settle down, only appear to; for the minds of the rulers were as intent in sustaining themselves, as were the minds of the people to get the ascendancy.[10] I saw that

---

[6] For a sense of Ellen White's use of "His stately steppings," compare with the following passage: "The Lord walks among men by His providences; but His stately steppings are not heard, His presence is not discerned, His hand is not recognized."

See: Ellen G. White, "Meetings at South Lancaster, Mass.," *Review,* Mar. 5, 1889, p. 146.

[7] "Behold, the Lord's hand is not shortened, that it cannot save; neither his ear heavy, that it cannot hear" (Isa. 59:1).

[8] "In that day there shall be a fountain opened to the house of David and to the inhabitants of Jerusalem for sin and for uncleanness" (Zech. 13:1).

[9] *See:* EGWEnc, s.v. "Seal of God"; "Time of Trouble."

[10] Adventist pioneer ministers disagreed on how this passage should be understood. This is not surprising, given its intermittent and almost cryptic character. J. N. Loughborough wrote in 1916 that Ellen White was referring in part to the revolutions that swept through central Europe in 1848 but that died down within a short space of time. "There was," he wrote, "one slacking up after the revolution of 1848. In the present war, beginning in 1914, is manifest on a still larger scale the determination to overthrow kings and rulers. . . . The testimony seems to indicate a second slacking up before the final conflict of the nations shall come." Alonzo T. Jones, on the other hand, speaking before the General Conference session in 1893, interpreted these statements in terms of future persecution by state-church alliances in Europe and America.

See: J. N. Loughborough, *Questions on the Sealing Message* (1916), p. 12, as in *Words of the Pioneers;* A. T. Jones, "The Third Angel's Message–No. 24," *General Conference Daily*

each party ruled and rulers were stretching their thoughts intensely on this work before them. The sins of Israel must go to judgment beforehand. Every sin must be confessed at the sanctuary.[11] Then the work will move; it must be done now ("now" probably referred to some present). The remnant in the time of trouble will cry, "My God, my God, why hast Thou forsaken me?"[12]

The latter rain[13] is coming on those that are pure. None receive the latter rain but those that did all they could. Christ would help us. All could be overcomers by the grace of God through the blood of Christ. When the four angels let go,[14] Christ would set up His kingdom.

Bulletin, Mar. 26, 1893, p. 518.

[11] Based on 1 Timothy 5:24: "Some men's sins are open beforehand, going before to judgment; and some men they follow after." The reading given this text here is that those who confess their sins now will be clear in the coming judgment while the unrepentant will then face their unconfessed sins. "I warn all who profess the name of Christ to closely examine themselves and make full and thorough confession of all their wrongs, that they may go beforehand to judgment, and that the recording angel may write pardon opposite their names" (Ellen G. White, *Testimonies for the Church,* vol. 1, p. 263).

[12] "In the time of trouble, if the people of God had unconfessed sins to appear before them while tortured with fear and anguish, they would be overwhelmed; despair would cut off their faith, and they could not have confidence to plead with God for deliverance. But while they have a deep sense of their unworthiness, they have no concealed wrongs to reveal. Their sins have gone beforehand to judgment, and have been blotted out" (Ellen G. White, *The Great Controversy,* p. 620).

[13] *See:* EGWEnc, s.v. "Latter Rain."

[14] For early interpretations of the four angels of Revelation 7:1-3, see notes under Ms 1, 1848 (Nov. 18, 19).

1852

(Ms 1, 1852)

MARCH 18, N.P.[1]

The Nations. Remarks in Vision.[2]

This manuscript is published in entirety in Ellen G. White, *Spalding and Magan's Unpublished Manuscript Testimonies of Ellen G. White,* pp. 2a, 3.

Preparing for earth's final events. Utterances while in vision and explanations given after coming out of vision.

Thou wouldest not want him to step out if thou knewest thy situation. That desire was to disenthrone these kings, but that could not be, for kings must reign till Christ began to reign.

I saw in Europe just as things were moving to accomplish their desires, there would seemingly be slacking up once or twice, thus the hearts of the wicked world would be relieved and hardened, but the work would not settle down (only seem to), for the minds of kings and rulers were intent upon overthrowing each other, and the minds of the people to get the ascendancy.[3]

---

[1] This date differs from that of a parallel account of the vision—Ms 2, 1852—which is headed "Extracts From Sister White's Vision at the General Conference in Ballston, New York, March 14, 1852." There is no necessary discrepancy. Most probably March 14 was the date of the vision and March 18 the date when the account was formally written up or copied.

[2] This is a third-party account of Ellen White's vision of March 14, 1852. A. T. Jones claimed in 1893 that a certain "O. Hewitt" was present when Ellen White received the vision and had "secured" a copy. (This was most likely **Oren Hewett**, despite the variant spelling, the only person with that initial and surname in the *Review* from this period.) This may or may not mean that Hewett was the scribe. According to J. N. Loughborough, the manuscript was "found among Brother Bates's papers, after his death," which raises the possibility that it was Joseph Bates who recorded the vision. One typed copy of this manuscript, dated May 3, 1903, bears Ellen White's handwritten interlinear comments (inserted in this text between the < > symbols), indicating her acceptance of the contents. Whether she also wrote her own report of the vision is not known.

A study of the parallel account of the March 14 vision in Ms 2, 1852, suggests that at least part of the Ms 1 text consists of Ellen White's explanations of her vision to the gathered assembly after coming *out* of vision rather than her utterances while *in* vision. In either case it is necessary to observe certain precautions in interpreting the text. Not only is it written by another person, but its intermittent, discontinuous character means that there is often insufficient context available to make the meaning of individual statements clear or to understand the overall structure of the vision.

See: A. T. Jones, "The Third Angel's Messsage–No. 24," *General Conference Daily Bulletin,* Mar. 26, 1893, p. 518; J. N. Loughborough, *Questions on the Sealing Message* (1916), p. 12, as in *Words of the Pioneers.*

[3] *See:* Ms 2, 1852 (Mar. 14), note 10.

I saw that all minds were intensely looking and stretching their thoughts on the impending crisis before them.

The sins of Israel must go to judgment beforehand.[4] Every sin must be confessed at the sanctuary, then the work will move. It must be done now. The remnant in the time of trouble[5] will cry, My God! my God! why hast Thou forsaken me?[6]

The latter rain[7] is coming on those that are pure—all then will receive it as formerly.

When the four angels let go,[8] Christ will set up His kingdom.

(None receive the latter rain but those who do all they can) <to water others with truth, eternal truth.> Christ would help us. All could be overcomers by the grace of God through the blood of Jesus. All heaven is interested in the work. Angels are interested.

Think ye that He will bring His hand to Himself until He has accomplished the object for which He stretched it out? Yea, more bitter hatred against those that keep the law than against the Catholics.[9]

Truth, the truth, let it shine. Hold them by the side of truth. What are they rich in? They seek falsehood, deception, and cunning. Behold! where is their strength? Is it in the truth? A mere knowledge of the truth will never save.

How long then, angel of God, before the message will go with a loud voice?[10] Other things to be accomplished. They must make themselves more vile. If Jesus should make His appearance in their midst, they would despise Him. They advocate their errors for a while, until the people get disgusted with it, then they add another.[11] Nights upon their beds, horror gets hold of

---

[4] Based on 1 Timothy 5:24. See Ms 2, 1852 (Mar. 14), note 11.

[5] *See:* EGWEnc, s.v. "Time of Trouble."

[6] *See:* Ms 2, 1852 (Mar. 14), note 12.

[7] *See:* EGWEnc, s.v. "Latter Rain."

[8] For early interpretations of the four angels of Revelation 7:1-3 see notes on Ms 1, 1848 (Nov. 18, 19); EGWEnc, s.v. "Seal of God."

[9] Sydney E. Ahlstrom, in his authoritative study *A Religious History of the American People,* considers the first half of the nineteenth century to be "the most violent period of religious discord" in American history, a period when "a bitter and secretive form of anti-Catholic nativism reached the very threshold of national power."

See: Sydney E. Ahlstrom, *A Religious History of the American People,* p. 555.

[10] *See:* EGWEnc, s.v. "Loud Cry."

[11] It is possible that this is an allusion to the condition of the popular churches whose "errors" would continue to accumulate before earth's final events. Prior to 1852 Sabbatarian Adventists had thought of the "fall" of the churches as a *past* event, culminating in 1844 with the second angel's message of Revelation 14 and the call to leave the churches of "Babylon." In June 1852, however, James White first published a broader view of continuing deterioration in the churches after 1844, leading to a *future* and final warning to come out of Babylon, a view that was to become the dominant one among Seventh-day Adventists. It may be that this vision, given a few months earlier, in March 1852, provided the impetus for James White's seminal article.

them. Can ye not see it? Live unto God. He has gotten them safe in the snare. The honest are getting disgusted. Satan works at the very ones that do him the most harm. God can make them a host against their enemies.

Ye give up too quick. Ye let go too soon that Arm! The arm of God is mighty. Satan works in different ways to steal the mind off from God. Victory, victory, we must have it over every wrong. A solemn sinking into God. Get ready. Set thine house in order. <These words were spoken in vision.>

See: [James White], "Babylon," *Review,* June 24, 1852, p. 9. For a survey of early developments in the understanding of the second angel's message, see P. Gerard Damsteegt, *Foundations of the Seventh-day Adventist Message and Mission,* pp. 179-192.

1852

APRIL 16, ROCHESTER, NEW YORK

EXTRACTS FROM A NONEXTANT LETTER TO

Stockbridge and Louisa M. Howland.

Published in Ellen G. White, *Spiritual Gifts [vol. 2],* pp. 160, 161.

1852

(Lt 2, 1852)

JUNE 2, ROCHESTER, NEW YORK

LETTER TO

Brethren and Sisters in Jackson.

This letter is published in entirety in Ellen G. White, *Manuscript Releases,* vol. 17, pp. 341-343.

An appeal for unity and humility in the Jackson, Michigan, company in face of fault-finding and internal dissension.

To the Brethren and Sisters in Jackson [Michigan]:

A few nights since, the Lord gave me a vision and showed me the state of things in the West. I saw it was dark, dark, dark, and that laborers were needed there. I saw that Brother Bowles [**John C. Bowles**][1] had got out of his place and thought he had a great work to do when he had not. I also saw that he thought his work was of a great deal more importance than it really was. I saw that some fanciful views had been pressed by Brother Bowles that were

---

[1] *Identity:* One clue to Bowles's identity is the fact that he presumably lives in or near Jackson, since the letter is addressed "To the Brethren and Sisters of Jackson." The *Review* has a number of references to a "J. C. Bowles," of Jackson, Michigan, in the early 1850s. Further, no "Bowles" other than "J. C. Bowles" (or Brother Bowles) is found in the *Review* during the 1850s. The 1850 U.S. Federal Census gives his full name as "John C. Bowles."

See: 1850 U.S. Federal Census, "John C. Bowles," Michigan, Jackson County, Jackson, p. 335; search term "Bowles" in *Words of the Pioneers.*

of no special importance until some who would have received the truth have been pushed off.[2]

I was pointed back and saw [that] when the trouble arose in Jackson much of it was caused by not following the Bible rule. There was too much talking over a brother's or a sister's faults among the band or church, and the brother that was thought to be wrong kept in ignorance that any trial was existing in the minds of others concerning him, until his (considered) faults had been talked over and over by nearly all the church, and he felt the coldness of his brothers and sisters and knew not the cause until it broke out all of a sudden, and he [was] made aware of what has been going on. Then the confidence that he has previously had in his brethren is shaken, his love for them has begun to be weakened, and a breach is made at once in the band that was previously united.[3]

All this trouble can be saved if each one of the brethren and sisters are frank and open-hearted, and when they feel any brother errs, go to him and tell him your trials and fears; tell him in love, and perhaps he can make things that you have not understood plain, so that you will be relieved.

I saw there had been too much noticing little things in Jackson, that did not accord with your minds on such and such things. If Satan can get your minds off of the important work in the last days, upon little things that gender strife, his object is accomplished. All he wants is to weaken and overthrow you. I saw in the trial you had at Jackson [that] Brother Bowles saw many things in their true light, but he moved unadvisedly. He had no intention of moving wrong, but he did not look at things on every side and consider sufficiently what was the wisest course to take, but moved too much on the impulse of the moment, and then I saw all things in confusion. I saw that Brother Bowles had not that meek and childlike spirit that he ought to have. He is too much lifted up and exalted, and he must humble himself or God

---

[2] John C. Bowles had engaged in lay preaching as far afield as Wisconsin, and appears to have been a leading figure in the Jackson company. No information is available concerning Bowles's reaction to the reproof and admonition found in this letter or to a similar reproof a year later (June 2, 1853).

See: Search term "Bowles" in *Words of the Pioneers;* Ellen G. White, Ms 1, 1853 (June 2).

[3] The band of Sabbathkeeping Adventists at Jackson was the first to be established in the state of Michigan, in 1849. A number of positive reports and letters had been published in the *Review* showing the commitment of the Jackson members. Nevertheless by the summer of 1852 problems of internal dissension and gossiping as indicated in this letter were surfacing. Joseph Bates admitted publicly in the *Review* that the band in Jackson had "been wading through manifold trials, and buffetings of the Enemy." The testimony and appeal of Ellen White's June 2 letter appears to have contributed to a reconciliation among the members. Bates reports that at a conference held in Jackson three weeks after her letter was sent "God in answer to prayer . . . endowed His children with grace, which caused love and unity to prevail throughout the church."

See: Brian E. Strayer, "Early Advent Waymarks in Jackson, Michigan: Parts I & II"; Joseph Bates, "Jackson, Mich., Conference," *Review,* July 8, 1852, p. 40.

will humble him. I saw that Brother Case [**Hiram S. Case**][4] had been doing what he could, but he had not moved judiciously at all times, and had given the enemies of the truth some cause to reproach him and those who believed the truth. It was impossible for him to reach some. His testimony would do them no good. But I saw that God had worked for Brother Case because he had received the admonitions and advice of his brethren and had acted upon it, and if he was humble, God would work for him still. But he must be very careful before unbelievers how he speaks, lest he give the enemies of the truth cause to reproach Israel.[5]

Dear brethren and sisters, keep self humble and in all things follow the Bible rule. Satan knows he cannot make us doubt the truth. The arguments of our enemies are powerless and effect nothing against the truth. Satan knows that his only way now is to try to separate very near friends and thereby weaken the children of God. United you'll stand. Divided you'll fall. Oh, press together; grieve not the angels of God who are watching over you. Let them not bear the tidings upward that you are disunited, each one pulling apart. Remember, now is the time that God is gathering His people into the unity of the faith. Will you not be co-workers with God, and press together?

I beg of you to each one of you humble yourselves before God. Let your brother's faults alone; go to God and beg of Him not to show you your brother's heart but your own heart and your own wrongs, and when each one of you humble yourself before God, let self die. There will be no trouble. You can but love one another and be united by strong cords of love and fellowship. Finally, be at peace among yourselves, and may the God of peace sanctify you

---

[4] *Identity:* As with the Brother Bowles mentioned at the beginning of the letter, "Brother Case" presumably lived in or near Jackson, since the letter is addressed "To the Brethren and Sisters of Jackson." Further, the description here given of Case suggests that he is a preacher. H. S. Case from Michigan fits this specification. He receives frequent mention in the *Review* as a traveling preacher in the period 1851-1853. The question is whether he lived in Jackson, Michigan, at the time of this letter, i.e., June 1852. According to the 1850 census and early reports in *The Present Truth* and *The Advent Review,* H. S. Case lived in North Plains, Ionia County, some 60 or 70 miles [97-113 kilometers] north of Jackson. There is, however, evidence that he had moved to Jackson by or before 1852. Notices in the *Review* from February and May 1852 speak of Brother "Case, from Jackson Mich." and of "H. S. Case [who] writes from Jackson." Taken together, there seems little doubt that Ellen White is writing of Hiram S. Case.

See: Search term "Case" in *Words of the Pioneers;* 1850 U.S. Federal Census, "Hiram Case," Michigan, Ionia County, Lyons, p. 312; Bowman R. Brown, "From Bro. Brown," *Review,* May 6, 1852, p. 6.

[5] Hiram S. Case, a former Millerite lecturer, had become a Sabbathkeeper in 1850. For a couple of years he traveled and preached widely in Michigan, Ohio, Illinois, and Wisconsin. This letter from Ellen White provides the first recorded intimation of problems in his ministry. Despite the appeal made to Case in this letter and the hopes expressed that he would change his course, the problems had grown into a full-scale crisis by the following summer, as revealed in a June 1853 document. By 1854 he had broken with the movement and cofounded the opposition *Messenger* Party.

See: Ellen G. White, Ms 1, 1853 (June 2); EGWEnc, s.v. "*Messenger* Party."

wholly, and preserve you blameless unto His appearing and kingdom. I would say I have written this to the church because it is public affairs.

Brother Bates [**Joseph Bates**][6] is with us. He is coming to see you West. His duty is there for present. I never saw him as free as now. God is with him. James sends much love to all the church. Accept the same from me. Please write as soon as possible.

[6] *Identity:* The information in the next sentence that Brother Bates "is coming to see you" provides clear evidence that Joseph Bates is being referred to. The following issue of the *Review*, published on June 10, announces that Joseph Bates would be attending a conference in Jackson, Michigan, starting June 25.

See: Joseph Bates, "Appointments," *Review,* June 10, 1852, p. 24.

1852

JUNE 10

"To the Brethren and Sisters."

Article published in *The Advent Review, and Sabbath Herald,* vol. 3, no. 3, June 10, 1852, p. 21.

1852

AUGUST, ROCHESTER, NEW YORK

"Dear Young Friends."

Article published in *The Youth's Instructor,* vol. 1, no. 1, August 1852, pp. 6, 7.

1852

(Ms 4, 1852)

SEPTEMBER,[1] WASHINGTON, NEW HAMPSHIRE

Extract Regarding the Latter Rain.

This manuscript is published in entirety in Ellen G. White, *Spalding and Magan's Unpublished Manuscript Testimonies of Ellen G. White,* p. 4.

Vision concerning some believers in Washington, New Hampshire, who were putting the coming of the Lord "too far off" and becoming worldly.

---

[1] The earliest copy of this manuscript is headed "Washington, N.H., Sept., 1852." The vision itself can with fair certainty be dated September 10, 1852 (see note 2 below).

(Ms 4, 1852) September 1852

You are getting the coming of the Lord too far off.[2] I saw the latter rain[3] was coming *as* suddenly *as* the midnight cry,[4] and with *ten times the power.*

---

[2] It would appear that only a short fragment of Ellen White's vision is given here and that James White provides a fuller report of the vision a few weeks later in the *Review*. In the October 14 issue James tells of his and Ellen's visit to Washington, New Hampshire, during the weekend of September 10-12, 1852. Ellen, he reports, received a vision the first evening. (James, as was sometimes his custom, used a more circuitous expression: "The Lord showed His willingness to bless His people assembled, by graciously pouring out His Spirit the first evening.") He then gave what appears to be a summary of some of the highlights of the vision. Significantly, he began with the words "there was evidently a lack of active faith on the part of some of the brethren. *Some had put the coming of the Lord too far off,* and were getting worldly" (italics supplied). The similarity here with the opening sentence of Ms 4—"you are getting the coming of the Lord too far off"—seems too striking to be a coincidence. Added to the fact that the date and place of the manuscript (September 1852, Washington, New Hampshire) correspond with James White's report, it seems clear that Ms 4 and James White are speaking of the same vision. James's summary runs into five paragraphs centering on the self-deception of many who "think that a theory of the truth will save them, while they lack many things that constitute a Christian."

See: James White, "Eastern Tour," *Review*, Oct. 14, 1852, p. 96.

[3] *See:* EGWEnc, s.v. "Latter Rain."

[4] *See:* EGWEnc, s.v. "Midnight Cry."

1852

(Lt 4, 1852)

OCTOBER 25, ROCHESTER, NEW YORK

LETTER TO

Dear Friends.

Portions of this letter are published in Ellen G. White, *Manuscript Releases,* vol. 6, pp. 253, 254.

Problem of self-appointed, poorly qualified preachers; need for following biblical principles in dealing with church discipline.

Dear Friends:

The Lord gave me a vision while in Dorchester [Massachusetts][1] concerning things in Boston [Massachusetts] and vicinity. I saw concerning the commencement of the distraction in Boston and vicinity, that if God's order had been observed by the church and each had understood his place and kept in it, the trouble would not have occurred,[2] and the church would now be in a healthy state. But some have run before they have been sent, and confusion has followed.

I saw the conference at Fairhaven [Massachusetts] last March, that it was an important one[3] and in an important time. Souls were getting waked up to the truth, their expectations were raised and were not realized, and it was worse than if they had had no meeting, for they were farther from the truth when the meeting closed than when it began.

I saw that Brother Chamberlain [**Ezra L. H. Chamberlain**][4] was not in

---

[1] In a letter written some three weeks earlier, on September 30, James White wrote of a vision that "Ellen had . . . this morning." His summary of the main points of that vision makes it clear that it was the same vision here described by Ellen White.

See: James White to "Dear Brother," Sept. 30, 1852.

[2] Details follow further on of accusations raised against Sr. Temple of Boston.

[3] The Fairhaven conference was advertised for the weekend of February 27-29, 1852, "and longer if thought best." Among the business carried out at the conference was the appointment of local agents for the *Review*. Full confidence was expressed for "Bro. White in the management of the paper."

See: O. Davis, "Conferences," *Review,* Feb. 3, 1852, p. 88; "The Fairhaven Conference," *Review,* Mar. 23, 1852, p. 108.

[4] *Identity:* A report in the *Review* on the Fairhaven conference provides first name initials of several leading figures who were present: "Brn. F. Wheeler, O. Davis, H. S. Gurney, E.L.H. Chamberlain, J. C. Day, and O. Nichols."

See: "The Fairhaven Conference," *Review,* Mar. 23, 1852, p. 108.

the way of his duty when he went to Fairhaven, Portland [Maine], Topsham [Maine], Paris [Maine], etc. I saw that he encouraged others to attend the meeting at Fairhaven whose duty it was to remain at home,[5] and if these individuals had not gone, God would have sent sufficient laborers that were humble, and that He would have worked through them, the cause would have progressed, and souls would have embraced the truth. But the cause was wounded by the reason of some moving out of their place, and taking a work on them that God had never laid on them.

I saw that individuals when they returned from Fairhaven, did not return right, and Bro. Chamberlain encouraged the church meeting that was held in Boston,[6] encouraged Brother Chase[7] to bring his troubles before the church, when neither Brother Chamberlain or the church had anything to do with it, until the Bible rule had been strictly followed[8] by Brother Chase, and instead of bringing out Sister Temple's [**Elizabeth Temple**][9] faults before the church, it ought to have been brought to her, and have given her [a] chance to have answered for herself, and to have cleared herself if she could.[10]

I saw that Brother and Sister Chase did very wrong in listening to the

---

[5] A main focus of this vision was the problem of unsuitable and "self-sent" traveling preachers who absorbed scarce donated funds for their travels while well-qualified preachers were sometimes unable to travel for lack of funds. In the case of E.L.H. Chamberlain, "God has shown me," Ellen White wrote two years earlier, "that it was not his duty to travel. . . . I saw that he was not one of the messengers." According to James White's summary of this vision, Brethren Ralph and Chase also belonged to those preachers who were "clogs" at the Fairhaven conference.

See: Ellen G. White, Ms 4, 1850 (Jan. 28); James White to "Dear Brother," Sept. 30, 1852.

[6] The exact date of the Boston church meeting is not known, but from the description given here appears to have been held in early March 1852.

[7] *Identity:* A number of persons bearing the surname "Chase" appear in the *Review* in the 1850s. A positive identification of which of these is the "Brother Chase" of this letter can hardly be made. There does, however, seem to be the suggestion both in this letter and in James White's account that Bro. Chase is a preacher. The only Chase in the *Review* from this period explicitly described as a preacher is David Chase, of Fairhaven/Acushnet, Massachusetts. No positive identification, however, can be made here.

See: Search term "Chase" in *Words of the Pioneers;* James White to "Dear Brother," Sept. 30, 1852.

[8] *See:* Matt. 18:15-17.

[9] *Identity:* The *Review* in 1853 mentions a "Sr. E. Temple of Boston, Mass." This may be the "Sister Temple" referred to, since Sr. Temple is closely tied to Boston in this passage. The full name "Elizabeth Temple" is given in her obituary.

See: "Appointments," *Review,* May 26, 1853, p. 8; obituary: "Elizabeth Temple," *Review,* Feb. 24, 1885, p. 127.

[10] The specific charges made against Elizabeth Temple by Brother Chase are not known. Mrs. Temple's standing with the Boston group does not appear to have suffered any longstanding damage. Some months later the *Review* informed its readers that "meetings will be held every Sabbath" at the home of "Sr. E. Temple of Boston."

See: "Appointments," *Review,* May 26, 1853, p. 8.

reports of that wicked girl of Sister Gorham's[11] that God hated her cruel disobedience to her mother and her rebellion to Him. I saw that it was the work of Satan to bring trouble into the camp by wicked children, and their stories never should be listened to and encouraged, and confidence put in them. When they talk against a child of God, they must be silenced at once, and their testimony should never be received or preferred before the testimony of one who has professed the truth of God, and has been united with the body. I saw that when Brother Chase brought these things out in meeting, he did not profess the meek spirit of Jesus, but was agitated by a wrong spirit. I saw that it was the same with Sister Chase. I saw that Brother Chamberlain possessed a flattering spirit, and by flattering Brother and Sister Chase he has injured them much, and he has also injured others in the same way, by praising them up and making a great deal of them.

I saw that God's messengers did not go with smooth words, but they always bear a plain testimony, even if they are as meek as the beloved disciple; yet they should deal plainly and not flatter even their best friends. I saw if Brother Chamberlain had denied himself in times past when he has been out, and had encouraged his wife and helped her to meetings nearby where she could have got strength, it would have been much more pleasing to God. But he thought too much of his own self-gratification.

I saw that Brother Chamberlain has been sinking, and the Spirit of God would be entirely taken from him unless he moves more to the glory of God, and less to please himself. I saw that he had too good an opinion of himself, was not as humble before God as he ought to be, when he has made so many crooked moves. I saw that it had weighed too much with him what others said. Brother Day [**John C. Day**][12] has not had the right judgment and has encouraged Brother Chamberlain and others to travel, and, if they should go [it] would only be a curse to the cause,[13] and would ruin their own souls.

I saw that if Brother Chamberlain had more of an eye single to the glory of

---

[11] *Identity:* It is tempting to conclude that Ellen White is referring here to a daughter of Elizabeth Gorham's who is repeatedly mentioned by her in correspondence between 1848 and 1851. But **Elizabeth Gorham** lived in Mason, New Hampshire, some 50 miles [80 kilometers] from Boston, the scene of the action in this letter. For a discussion of the identity of "Sister Gorham," see Lt 5, 1849 (Apr. 21), note 25.

[12] *Identity:* Although there are a number of Adventists with the surname "Day" in the 1850s, there are certain indications that John C. Day is being referred to here. Most telling is the fact that "J. C. Day" was a leading figure at the Fairhaven conference, as reported in the *Review*, and Lt 4 seems to be describing the character and actions of the leaders participating in the Fairhaven and Boston meetings.

See: "The Fairhaven Conference," *Review*, Mar. 23, 1852, p. 108; search term "Day" in *Words of the Pioneers*.

[13] James White, commenting on this part of the vision, agrees with vigor: "I see means consecrated to God worse than thrown away in being given to such men as Brethren Chamberlain, Lothrop, and I think means given to Brother Day has hurt him."

See: James White to "Dear Brother," Sept. 30, 1852.

God, and cared less for the good opinion of his brethren, he would not make so many crooked moves. I saw in the case of trial in Boston, he should not have made up his mind so readily, not gone to the unexperienced to consult with them, but he should have gone to those who had taken a straightforward course. He should have consulted Brother Nichols [**Otis Nichols**][14] before giving his opinion that the trouble must be settled, and that there must be a church meeting to settle it. There has been too much moving at random without the counsel and strength of God.

I saw that Brother Day had too much confidence in himself, and did not lean upon the strong arm of God enough. I saw that he has been mistaken and thought that God had a greater work for him to do than He had ever laid upon him, and that there was more importance attached to his labors than there really was. I saw that he had used too much means and traveled too extensively. I saw that Brother Day went to Conn. when God did not send him,[15] and he did not have right judgment, for two dead bodies that had nearly corrupted the whole church before they were separated from it he had tried to unite again with the living. I saw that God was not in the move at all, and that Conn. was in an awful dark place on account of the crooked moves and errors of some there.

I saw that Brother and Sister Chase had looked on Sister Temple as an ungodly woman, and had not given up that idea or those wrong feelings yet. They had accused her falsely and had used deception in her case. I saw that Brother and Sister Chase had a proud heart that had not yet been fully subdued by grace.

I saw Brother Lothrop [**Howard Lothrop**],[16] that he also had traveled too

---

[14] *Identity:* Otis Nichols, a leading Sabbatarian figure living in Dorchester, just outside Boston, would have been well informed about the problems relating to Elizabeth Temple in Boston. In addition, the *Review* reports that "O. Nichols" attended the Fairhaven conference, and Lt 4 seems to be an analysis of various Sabbatarian leaders at that meeting in February/March 1852.

See: Otis Nichols, "The Fairhaven Conference," *Review,* Mar. 23, 1852, p. 108.

[15] No mention of J. C. Day's trip to Connecticut has been found; however, there are scattered reports of Day attending meetings in Leverett, Massachusetts, and Washington, New Hampshire, during the previous 12 months, as well as the meetings in Fairhaven and Boston mentioned in this letter.

See: G. W. Holt, "From Bro. Holt," *Review,* Mar. 2, 1852, p. 102; (writer unknown), "To the Dear Disciples of Jesus in Dartmouth," Nov. 7, 1851.

[16] *Identity:* With one or two exceptions, only H. (Howard) and E. (Edward) Lothrop appear in the *Review* during this period. Of these, only Howard Lothrop fits the description here of a preacher who "had traveled too extensively." While there is no record of Edward preaching, Howard was active in Canada East as well as undertaking an extensive preaching tour of Vermont, Massachusetts, and Rhode Island some months earlier. The identity of Howard Lothrop as this "Brother Lothrop" seems certain.

See: Howard Lothrop, "From Bro. Lothrop," Mar. 2, 1852, p. 102; search term "Lothrop" in *Words of the Pioneers.*

extensively and was too self-sufficient. I saw that souls who wanted the truth would come into meeting to hear, and repeatedly Brother Lothrop would get up and talk until he would talk the Spirit all away from the meeting. These souls would leave disgusted with the truth, when, if the right course had been taken and Brother Lothrop had not moved in his own strength, the unbelievers would have been convinced that power and strength were with Israel, and they would have decided to have gone with the humble few.

I saw that Brother Lothrop would have to be more humble before God where he can receive the admonitions of his brethren, and would have to give up his *impressions* and *feelings*.[17] He has been led by them altogether too much, and he . . . [The remainder is missing.]

---

[17] This is the earliest negative report of Howard Lothrop's preaching style and his independent attitude toward his colleagues. James White recalled in 1861 that "at almost every meeting we met him [we] had good cause to reprove him for his fanaticism; [and] that he afterwards went in full fury with the *Messenger* spirits against us and the *Review*."

See: James White, "Organization," *Review*, Aug. 27, 1861, p. 100.

1852

OCTOBER, ROCHESTER, NEW YORK

"Beauties of the New Earth."

Article published in *The Youth's Instructor,* vol. 1, no. 2, October 1852, pp. 12, 13.

1852

NOVEMBER, ROCHESTER, NEW YORK

"Dear Young Friends."

Article published in *The Youth's Instructor,* vol. 1, no. 3, December 1852, pp. 20-22.

1853

FEBRUARY 17

"To the Saints Scattered Abroad."

Article published in *The Advent Review, and Sabbath Herald,* vol. 3, no. 20, February 17, 1853, pp. 155, 156.

1853

FEBRUARY

"Keep the Sabbath Holy."

Article published in *The Youth's Instructor,* vol. 1, no. 5, February 1853, p. 37.

1853

(Ms 2, 1853)

MARCH 1, N.P.

The Character That God Requires in His Ministers.

Portions of this manuscript are published in Ellen G. White, *Early Writings,* p. 103.

The character that God requires in His ministers. Warning against the use of tobacco and an appeal for personal cleanliness.

I saw how holy a minister of Christ should be, how pure in conversation and actions. He should ever bear in mind that he is handling words of inspiration, words of a holy God. He must bear in mind that the flock is entrusted to his care, and he is to bear their cases to Jesus and plead for them as Jesus pleads for us to the Father.

I was pointed back to the children of Israel anciently, and saw how pure and holy ministers of the sanctuary had to be because they were brought by their work into a close connection with God. They that minister must be holy, pure, and without blemish, or God would destroy them.

I saw that God had not changed. He was just as holy and pure, just as particular as ever He was. He changeth not. Those who profess to be the ministers of Jesus should be men of experience and deep piety, and then at all times and in all places they can shed a holy influence and be a blessing to the cause, and not a curse.[1]

---

[1] This first section of the manuscript, dealing with the moral requirements of ministers, was incorporated into a section headed "Gospel Order" when it was published some months later, with a few modifications, in *Supplement to the Christian Experience and Views of Ellen G. White.* The drive by the Whites for a basic measure of church order in the early 1850s tended to concentrate on the problem of "self-sent" unauthorized preachers who lacked the skills and/or moral qualities needed to represent the young movement properly. James White echoed the sentiments of this passage in a series of articles in December 1853, also entitled "Gospel Order": "He who enters upon the work

I saw the brethren using tobacco, tea, etc., [and that it] was a needless expense, and had a bad effect upon the cause; that tobacco defiled the children of God, and they must lay it aside, never to touch it again; that God did not require His servants to help to sustain anyone that used this filthy weed.

I saw that God wanted His children to be clean and holy. I was pointed back to the children of Israel, and saw the commands of God to wash their clothes and in all things to be clean and neat, lest the Lord should pass by and see their uncleanness. I saw that if ever there was a people that should be clean and tidy it is those who are believing that they are soon to be made immortal and are to dwell with holy angels and with a holy God.[2]

I saw that God had not changed in this thing, but wanted His children now to be as particular and careful as the children of Israel were; and if there were persons among us that were not clean and tidy, after giving admonition after admonition and they did not mend their ways, the church must disfellowship them because His frown would be upon the camp.[3]

---

of the gospel ministry, must be called of God, a man of experience, a holy man of God."

See: Ellen G. White, *Supplement to the Christian Experience and Views of Ellen G. White,* pp. 21, 22; "Gospel Order," *Review,* Dec. 13, 1853, p. 180. For a detailed study of the development of Seventh-day Adventist organization in the early decades, see Andrew Gordon Mustard, *James White and SDA Organization.*

[2] Although a comprehensive program of health reform was not given Ellen White until 1863, some aspects were shown earlier, such as the strictures against tobacco and an appeal for personal hygiene found in this vision. According to James White, the earliest vision given Ellen White against tobacco, tea, and coffee was in the autumn of 1848, although no contemporary account of that vision has been preserved.

See: James White, "Western Tour," *Review,* Nov. 8, 1870, p. 165; EGWEnc, s.v. "Tobacco." For surveys of the development of health reform among Seventh-day Adventists, see Herbert E. Douglass, *Messenger of the Lord,* pp. 278-298; P. Gerard Damsteegt, *Foundations of the Seventh-day Adventist Message and Mission,* pp. 221-241; Dores Eugene Robinson, *The Story of Our Health Message.*

[3] Two years later (1855), in her first published statement on the need for cleanliness and tidiness among members, Ellen White highlighted the seriousness of this issue for a movement struggling to advance in a hostile environment: "It is a dishonor to God, and a stain upon His cause . . . [to] go with slack, untidy habits uncorrected. . . . The world is watching for their [Sabbatarians'] faults, they despise God's children, and to give them occasion to reproach the religion of Christ is a sin in the sight of God."

Stern, prophetic warnings of the type given here, of unholy conduct bringing the "frown" and disapprobation of God on individuals and assemblies, are frequent in the writings of Ellen White. Balancing such statements, however, is the insistence on the loving benevolence of God that ever seeks to draw the sinner to Himself. "All heaven is interested in your salvation," she writes to young people in 1852. "God has given His only beloved Son to die for your transgressions, angels are watching over you, and are trying to turn your attention to God, to seek your soul's salvation."

See: Ellen G. White, "To the Church," *Review,* June 12, 1855, p. 246; *idem,* "Dear Young Friends," *Youth's Instructor,* December 1852. Andrew Mustard discusses the question of church discipline in the setting of a wider study of the nascent development of order and organization among Sabbatarian Adventists in the 1850s in *James White and SDA Organization,* pp. 122, 123. See also SDAE, s.v. "Church Discipline."

1852

MARCH

"Notes of Explanation"

Added to Ellen G. White, *A Sketch of the Christian Experience and Views of Ellen G. White,* pp. 1, 2.

1852

APRIL 14

"Dear Brethren and Sisters."

Article published in *The Advent Review, and Sabbath Herald,* vol. 3, no. 24, April 14, 1853, p. 192.

1853

(Lt 10, 1853)

[MAY,[1] ROCHESTER, NEW YORK]

LETTER TO

Mary S. Chase.

Portions of this letter are published in Ellen G. White, *Spiritual Gifts [vol. 2],* pp. 174-178; James White, *A Brief Account of the Last Sickness and Death of Nathaniel White, Who Died May 6th, 1853,* pp. 8-10.

The final hours of Nathaniel White, James White's brother.

---

[1] No place or date is given for this letter. Most likely, however, it was written in Rochester, New York, shortly after the funeral of Nathaniel White, who died there on May 6, 1853, but before the Whites set out on their journey to Michigan two weeks later, on May 20.

See: [James White], *A Brief Account of the Last Sickness and Death of Nathaniel White,* p. 3; *idem,* "Western Tour," *Review,* June 9, 1853, p. 12.

"I know I love God and He loves me," said he [**Nathaniel White**].[2] "There is much more I wish to say but have not strength."[3]

It was with a strong effort he said as much as he did. Before he commenced talking, James [**James Springer White**] assisted him to rise from the bed, according to his wish, and sit in the rocking chair. He was so exhausted it was some minutes before he could speak. James told him not to be in a hurry, but take all the time he wanted. The windows in his room had to be lowered at the top and raised at the bottom, for him to have air in order to speak more freely.

After he had said what he wished to, we united in prayer with him. It was a sweet season. He manifested great interest while we were praying, responding to our prayer, saying, "Amen," and "Praise the Lord; glory to God. I will praise Him, for He is worthy to be praised. His name is Jesus, and He will save us from our sins."

He prayed with us, but was unable to sit up. James told him he could lie on the bed just as well. So he prayed lying upon the bed. He prayed earnestly and in faith. He did not ask to get well, but for a full consecration to God's will, to be baptized with His Spirit, and purified by His blood. Said he, "Thou hast forgiven me all my sins, and blotted them out from Thy remembrance. Thou hast sanctified me to Thyself. And I will honor Thee as long as I have breath."

His eyes were very bright. His face shone, and he looked very happy. He said the room seemed light and he loved us all. After we arose from our knees, he said, "Anna [**Anna White**],[4] I love you. Come here." She went to his bedside and he embraced her. He seemed to be very joyful and said, "I am happy. The Lord has blessed me." James and Anna participated in his joy and happiness. It was a weeping, rejoicing time for us all. Nathaniel was triumphant in God through the day, although he was very sick. He said he

---

[2] *Identity:* Large extracts from this letter are incorporated in James White's tract *A Brief Account.* Nathaniel White, James White's brother, died at age 22 of tuberculosis. He had come to live with Ellen and James six months earlier in poor health, hoping to recover and to assist at the *Review* office.

[3] The abrupt start to the letter indicates that the beginning is missing. Fortunately we know something about the content of the missing section. James White, in a tract published in memory of Nathaniel White, quoted extensively from Ellen's letter, including some 30 lines preceding the point where Lt 10 begins. In those lines Ellen White recorded events during the last few days of Nathaniel's life, whereas the part of her letter found in Lt 10 dealt exclusively with events on May 6, 1853, the day of his death. Lt 10 is addressed to the family of Nathaniel White. The closing paragraphs indicate that the letter was initially sent to Nathaniel's sister, Mary Chase, with instructions that she then forward it to her parents and her sister Elizabeth to read.

See: [James White], *A Brief Account,* pp. 8-10.

[4] *Identity:* Anna White, sister of Nathaniel and James White, had come, together with Nathaniel, from Maine to Rochester, New York, to live with the Whites six months earlier, in November 1852. Naturally Anna was present at the bedside of Nathaniel during his last hours.

wished someone to be with him to lift him that day. He said he wanted them with him every moment. His wish was granted. I did not attend to anything else that day, but sat in his room and entertained him by reading the Bible and conversing with him. And then Stephen Belden [**Stephen Belden**], my brother-in-law,[5] who loved Nathaniel dearly, and Nathaniel loved him for his piety and devotion, was at home and did not go to the office but stood ready to move and lift Nathaniel at any moment. And although he was so weak, yet he seemed happy. As I read the Bible to him, he would say, "How appropriate that is, how beautiful. I must remember that."

At one time that day Anna and I were sitting with him. He spoke out and said, "I don't think my lungs are affected any, it is my stomach." And just before he had told us his right lung did not afford him any breath and his left was clogging with phlegm. He ever seemed anxious to conceal his true situation from us and to make us think he was in a better situation than he was. When he said nothing was the matter with his lungs, I looked at Anna, and she at me, in astonishment. Neither of us spoke. Anna soon left the room. I then said, "Nathaniel, you are very sick. You may die in two hours, and unless God interposes, you cannot live two days."

He said very calmly, "Oh, not so soon as that, I guess." He immediately arose from the bed, sat in the rocking chair and commenced talking. He went back to the time when he was converted,[6] told how much he enjoyed his experience, how afraid he was of sinning, and then when he began to forget God and lose the blessing, and then how high his hopes were raised; he meant to be a man in the world, to get an education and fill some high station.

And then he told how his hopes had died as affliction's hand pressed heavily upon him, how hard it was for him to give up his expectations. He was unreconciled to this sickness. He said he felt that he could not have it so. He would be well, he would not yield to it, he would shake it off.

Then he spoke of the time when he was at Boston [Massachusetts], how feeble he was, how hard he tried to bear up, and sometimes he suffered so in mind he was afraid he would be crazy. And often when his labor was finished and he went to his boarding place and to his room, which was up three flights of stairs, his limbs would become so weak and his head so dizzy he would be obliged to hold on to the railing of the stairs to keep from falling backward. And his heart would beat so violently he would have

---

[5] Stephen Belden had married Ellen White's sister Sarah B. Harmon in 1851, the same year that he started to work in the *Review* office. Apparently the Beldens, together with other *Review* staff, boarded with the Whites in Rochester at this time.

[6] According to James White, "[Nathaniel] gave his young heart to the Lord, at the age of ten years, and was soundly converted."

See: [James White], *A Brief Account,* p. 3.

to sit down and rest before he could go any farther. After he rested a little, he would go on again. Often he was obliged to lie upon the bed with his clothes on until he was rested. He said his feelings at such times were almost desperate. He would almost speak aloud, "I will not give up to it, I will shake this off. I will be a man. I will be well. I will be somebody and let my friends know I am somebody."

He said he murmured against God and thought it was cruel that he could not have strength.

Then he spoke of his coming to Rochester [New York], how trying it was to have us wait upon him, and how galling was the idea that he was dependent. He said, "It seemed to me that the kindness, the brotherly kindness of you all, was more than I could bear. It seemed as though it would kill me, and I have thought I wanted to get well to pay you for all this."

He then spoke of his embracing the Sabbath. Said he, "At first I was not willing to acknowledge the light I saw. I wished to conceal it, but the blessing of God was withheld from me until I acknowledged the Sabbath. Then I felt confidence toward God." Said he, "I love the Sabbath now, it is precious to me." Said he, "I now feel reconciled to my sickness. I know that it is the only thing that will save me. I praise the Lord if He can save me through affliction. I know, yes, I know, it is the only thing that will save me and bring me right." Said he, "I have been impatient sometimes through my sickness, but for some weeks I have been getting the victory. I know, Ellen, that I am the Lord's and He is mine. I love Him and He loves me. For three weeks I have enjoyed sweet communion with God in secret prayer. I have often felt His sweet Spirit, and felt as though I could shout at the top of my voice and praise God."

Said he, "My trust is in God today, and I will trust in Him if my breath stops today." His face lighted up as he praised the Lord for His goodness.

He said much that I cannot now write. He seemed to be tired after he had ceased talking, and wished to lie down. I called Stephen, who assisted him on the bed. He rested awhile until his dinner was brought in and he was helped up. [He] sat in the rocking chair and ate his dinner as though it tasted good. He ate unusually heartily, and then wished to ride out.

We felt afraid to have him go, and tried to persuade him not to, but he was set about it. He felt that he *must* go. Said he, "I will lie down and rest me while Stephen is getting ready." We told him we were fearful the wind was too strong, and the day before he had raised much blood. But he insisted upon going. Said he, "Stephen can lift me from the bed, and hold me up in his arms while you put on my coat and cap, and then he can put me in the carriage, and it need not tire me at all."

Anna was afraid to ride out with him that day. So I put on my bonnet and shawl and got his coat and hat. The horse was harnessed at the door. Stephen lifted him from the bed, and while he sat upon the side of the bed we put on his rubbers and were putting on his coat, got one arm into one sleeve and about to put in the other arm when we noticed a flush come over his face from his forehead to his chin. He looked up, while a painful smile came over his face, and said, "I shall have to give it up, I guess. I find I shall have to trust in God a little longer. But I hate dreadfully to give it up. Now, if I had been sitting in the chair, I could have gone, but it makes me weak to lie on the bed."

He sat a few minutes and said, "I have a good mind to get up and run and give one leap and go into that carriage and ride."

I sat with him through the afternoon. He talked perfectly calm about different things. Said he, "I have been wondering what made my feet so hot. I have my rubbers on." I came to look, and asked him if I should take them off. He said, "Yes." I sat upon the floor and took one foot in my lap and took off one of his rubbers and then the other. This I did so that I should not wrench his body any. He looked at me and smiled. That was the last little act I did for dear Nathaniel.

In the course of the afternoon he would speak often of his disappointment because he could not ride out. About five o'clock P. M. he sent for me, as I had just stepped out of his room. He said he wished us to pray with him, for he was some pressed for breath. A number of us went into his room and prayed for him and he prayed for himself. We were half an hour upon our knees. When we arose, he said he was some better. At our usual supper time we prepared poor Nathaniel's supper, and Anna carried it in to him and wanted to sit with him. But he wished her to go out and eat with the rest of the family. I said, "I will sit with Nathaniel." Brother Stephen Belden was in the room, and he said he would like to have Stephen sit with him. Stephen lifted him from the bed and sat him in the rocking chair. Said Stephen, "Will you eat now?" "Well," said Nathaniel, "it is hardly my supper time." But he cast his eyes upon the watch that hung up before him, and said, "Yes, it is, but I am not hungry. I ate a hearty dinner."

In a few minutes he said he felt faint and did not know but [what] he was going to die. Stephen said, "Oh, I guess not." He sent for us, and we all went into his room. I had not had time to taste anything before I was called. As soon as I entered the room, I knew that he was dying. For a moment he seemed to be troubled. I said, "Nathaniel, dear, trust in God; He loves you, and you love Him. Trust right in Him as a child trusts in its parents. Don't be troubled. The Lord will not leave you." Said he, "Yes, yes."

We prayed, and he responded, "Amen, praise the Lord." As I saw he was going, I put my hand upon his forehead and commended him to God and prayed that he might have an easy passage, and that the light of God would shine around him. He turned his large bright eyes upon us and smiled. He did not seem to suffer pain, but breathed shorter and shorter, rocking in his chair, until about three minutes before he died. He did not groan once or struggle or move a muscle of his face or limbs, but breathed shorter and shorter until he fell asleep.

This was a house of mourning indeed. Sabbath and first-day I was in a high fever. I could not shed a tear. I felt as though my heart would burst. I was not able to shed a tear until the funeral. When they were about to screw on the coffin lid and we were taking our last look at him before he was carried out of the house, then I found relief in tears.

As soon as we came from the place of his burial, or the vault we laid him in,[7] I fainted quite away. Poor Anna felt his death as keenly as one could feel it, but we begged of her to be calm or she would sink beneath it. She heeded what we had to say as much as she could and tried to restrain her feelings and govern them for our sake and the sake of her health.[8]

Dear Sister Mary [**Mary S. Chase**],[9] I did not think of writing only three pages when I commenced, but I knew not where to stop. You must excuse all mistakes, for I have written in great haste. We love dear Anna very much. I know of no difference of feeling between her and my own natural sisters. Our hearts are knit together. Anna is a sweet, good girl.

After you read this please send it to your parents [**John** and **Betsey White**] for them and Sister Elizabeth [**Elizabeth ("Lizzie") W. Tenney**][10] to read, and then if you wish it I will see that you have it again. We shall come to Palmyra [Maine] when we go East, and I then hope to have the privilege of seeing you.[11] And we can tell you more about dear Nathaniel than I can write.

My husband's health is improving some. Please write to me. I should be

---

[7] After the funeral, writes James White, we "followed our dear brother to Mount Hope Cemetery, where he was placed in a vault, to remain ten days, that he might be seen if any relatives should come to Rochester during that time. When the time had expired, my family . . . went to Mount Hope, and saw him placed in the silent grave."

See: [James White], *A Brief Account,* p. 5.

[8] Described as "very feeble" when she arrived in Rochester in November 1852, Anna White, like her brother, succumbed to tuberculosis 18 months later, in November 1854, age 25.

See: Obituary: "Anna White," *Review,* Dec. 12, 1854, p. 135.

[9] *Identity:* See note 3 above. Ellen White was fond of her sister-in-law, Mary Chase. "Our hearts," she wrote at one point, "run together like two drops of water" (Lt 2, 1855 [Aug.]).

[10] *Identity:* See note 3 above. James White's sister, who was married to Thomas B. Tenney and living in St. Albans, Maine, a few miles from her parents in Palmyra.

[11] The visit took place late September to early October 1853. "From Topsham we went to Palmyra, where our parents reside. Our visit with them, also the families of two sisters in the same county, were most agreeable, and we trust beneficial."

See: James White, "Eastern Tour," *Review,* Nov. 1, 1853, p. 133.

much pleased to hear from you. James sends his love. Receive the same from your unworthy sister.

E. G. White.

Please remember me to your parents and Lizzie. I have not forgotten them, but often think of our short visit to Palmyra with pleasure.[12]

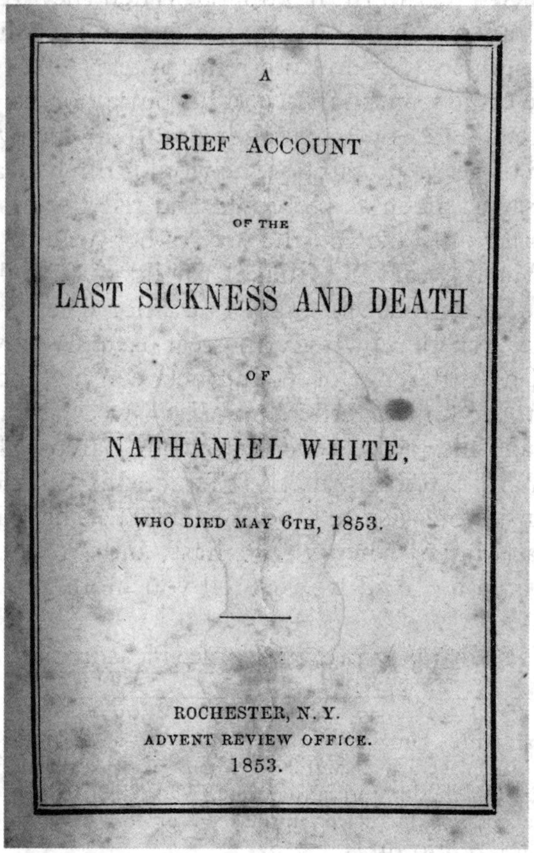

A

BRIEF ACCOUNT

OF THE

LAST SICKNESS AND DEATH

OF

NATHANIEL WHITE,

WHO DIED MAY 6TH, 1853.

ROCHESTER, N. Y.
ADVENT REVIEW OFFICE.
1853.

12-page tract describing the death of James White's brother, Nathaniel. Courtesy of the Center for Adventist Research.

---

[12] The previous September James and Ellen White "had a very pleasant visit with our aged parents in Palmyra. . . .We also spent a few happy hours with Bro. and Sr. Tenney of Albans. With Sr. T. (a sister in the flesh) and her husband, we wept in view of God's tender mercies in sparing us to meet again. These were the happiest hours of our life. Time could never erase the impress made upon our feelings as we bid each other a hearty farewell in the Lord, and as we left them upon the door-rock, weeping."

See: "Eastern Tour," *Review*, Oct. 14, 1852, p. 96.

1853

(Lt 2, 1853)

MAY 26, PLYMOUTH, MICHIGAN

LETTER TO

Anna White.[1]

Portions of this letter are published in Arthur L. White, *Ellen G. White: The Early Years,* p. 274.

News of Ellen and James White's first journey to Michigan.

Dear Sister Anna:

I now sit down to fulfill my promise to you and write a few lines, knowing you will feel anxious to hear how we bear our journey.[2]

At Mill Grove [New York] James and self were in a very poor state of health. Tuesday we were undecided whether to return to Rochester [New York] or continue our journey. James was hardly able to sit up, his throat troubled him much, and his food distressed him. I was afraid some, how it would turn with him, but we prayed for him and the Lord gave us to feel that we must start and trust in Him.[3]

We took the [railroad] cars about four o'clock P.M. for Buffalo [New York]. The boat did not start until half past nine in the evening from Buffalo. We waited in the boat from five till half past nine. It was a very nice boat, the air was sweet and there was every convenience on the boat. We took a stateroom where instead of finding narrow berths we found a nice large bed for both of us, made up clean, and a neat looking glass in the room, a large Testament like Sarah's [**Sarah B. Belden**][4] with the Psalms in the back.

---

[1] *Identity:* The context of the letter, especially the last paragraph ("remember us to each member of the family"), suggests that Anna is a member of, or very close to, the White family. Ellen White recounted that during this period "the Office hands boarded with us, and our family numbered from fifteen to twenty." The only "Anna" among this group was Anna White, sister of James White, who had come to live with the Whites in Rochester some months earlier, in November 1852; hence it is likely that this is the person addressed.

See: Ellen G. White, *Spiritual Gifts [vol. 2],* p. 191; [James White], *A Brief Account of the Last Sickness and Death of Nathaniel White,* p. 3.

[2] The Whites had left Rochester, New York, for their first visit to Michigan a few days earlier, on May 20.

See: James White, "Western Tour," *Review,* June 9, 1853, p. 12.

[3] Additional details on the crisis facing the Whites in Mill Grove are given in Ellen G. White, *Spiritual Gifts [vol. 2],* pp. 179-181.

[4] *Identity:* Given the family setting of this letter, this is no doubt a reference to Ellen White's

There was a washbowl, soap, towel, and by turning a faucet we could bring water in the bowl. We felt almost at home. We prayed together before retiring and committed ourselves to the watchful care of Him who never slumbers or sleeps, and we felt assured that He would keep us from all accident and harm.

Some through fear sat up through the night. We paid nothing extra for our meals which we took on board the boat, or for our stateroom.

We slept sweetly through the night. James felt much better than he expected to. He began to feel better directly after leaving Mill Grove, and he has been growing better ever since.

Wednesday morn it was pleasant but the wind blew and the boat rocked considerable; some were seasick but we went into our room and lay down. We slept sweetly for one hour and a half; we did not get up until about noon.

They had plenty on the table that we could eat and not hurt us, which was quite fortunate for us; we thanked the Lord in our heart for the food although we did not do it vocally. There were a great number of crying children on the boat; they were cross and ill-tempered. I thought of my little Edson [**James Edson White**] and felt thankful he was not like them. We tried to keep our hearts uplifted to God for strength, especially that James might be strengthened.

The boat landed us at Detroit [Michigan] about half past three o'clock P.M. There were six hundred on board. We were obliged to wait in Detroit until six P.M. We then took the cars for Wayne [Michigan]—distance 18 miles [29 kilometers]. We arrived at Wayne about seven, and found Brother Lyon [**Henry Lyon**][5] waiting for us at the depot with a good team. We had been some troubled about the distance we were to ride in the night air, but Brother Lyon came prepared with nice buffalo robes and we did not feel chilly at all. We rode 12 miles [19 kilometers] and arrived at Brother Lyon's about ten o'clock. Brother and Sister Cornell [**Merritt E.** and **Angeline M. A. Cornell**][6] are here; they are solid and good.

This is a most beautiful place surrounded with fruit trees. I should love to have you here today, but should not know what to do with you tomorrow. We shall have to ride 30 miles [48 kilometers] and part of the way it is a very rough road.

I am of good courage but not very well in body. We believe the Lord

---

sister Sarah, whose husband, Stephen Belden, had worked at the *Review* office since 1851.

[5] *Identity:* The address line at the top of the letter together with travel information given in the text locates "Brother Lyon" in Plymouth, Michigan. The only "Brother Lyon" living in Plymouth, Michigan, mentioned in the *Review* during this period is Henry Lyon.

See: Search term "Lyon" in *Words of the Pioneers.*

[6] *Identity:* The only Cornells mentioned in the *Review* as living in Plymouth, Michigan, during this period were the traveling preacher Merritt E. Cornell and his wife, Angeline M. A. Cornell.

See: Search term "Cornell" in *Words of the Pioneers.*

will give us strength. The enemy made a powerful effort to keep us from Michigan,[7] but he has not succeeded as yet. Oh, that God would give us strength from the sanctuary. We shall plead for it until it comes, it must come, we cannot labor without it. It will come from God, we believe, and [we] mean to walk out by faith. The promise will not fail us, it will be verified.[8]

You must pray for us. I never saw the necessity of living near to God as now. We must keep our mind stayed upon Him and feel our entire dependence, and watch and pray lest we enter into temptation. We must exercise faith continually and act it out. We can have full and free salvation. You know what it is, dear Anna; don't settle down short of this. The storehouse is full and free, don't let us go hungry here, when there is enough and to spare.

Anna, have faith, have faith in God. It seems to me that the faith of the family is rather weak; they must come up. Remember us to each member of the family. I shall write them before long. How are Sarah and Clara [**Clarissa M. Bonfoey**]?[9] Is their health good for them? We want to hear from you all. James sends much love to Anna and the rest of the family.

In much love.

---

[7] Referring, no doubt, to the serious health problems described at the beginning of the letter.

[8] In a letter written to her parents shortly after returning from the Michigan journey Ellen White noted that "my husband in the strength of God endured the journey and his labor well. His strength did not entirely fail him but once. He was unable to preach at Bedford."

See: Ellen G. White letter of June 23, 1853, to parents in Gorham, Maine, as in Ellen G. White, *Spiritual Gift [vol. 2]*, p. 182.

[9] *Identity:* Again, given the fact that this is a letter to family members at home, this is no doubt a reference to Clarissa Bonfoey, who had assisted in the White household for several years. Ellen White occasionally referred to her as "Clara" (see Lt 1, 1856 [July 15], and Lt 6, 1856 [c. 1856]).

1853

(Ms 1, 1853)

JUNE 2, JACKSON, MICHIGAN

A Vision Given at Jackson, Michigan, June 2, 1853.

Portions of this manuscript are published in Ellen G. White, *Manuscript Releases,* vol. 13, pp. 359, 360.

Some negative aspects of Samuel W. Rhodes's influence on leaders and members of the Jackson, Michigan, company.

I was first shown that when Brother Rhodes [**Samuel W. Rhodes**][1] first came to Michigan[2] many things he did not see in their true light, and he would have been a much more effective laborer if he had possessed more of a calm, meek, forbearing spirit. But his hasty, overbearing spirit was much against him. Many more would have embraced the truth if he had not possessed such a spirit of severity.[3] Some that witnessed his labors would say: "Well, it is just as we have been told, Those that teach the Sabbath have a bad spirit." And they decided that the message was not of the Lord.

I also saw that Brother Rhodes had a hurried, excitable spirit, and that it had a great effect on the brethren at Jackson [Michigan]. From what God had shown through vision in favor of Brother Rhodes, the brethren put the utmost confidence in him, as though he would not err. The wrong impressions were given concerning the brethren's property, as though it was a burden to them, and they must get it off their hands as soon as possible or it would crush them, and they must lay up their treasure in heaven, &c.[4] Brethren Bowles [**John**

---

[1] *Identity:* The description given in this letter of "Brother Rhodes"—a preacher, visiting Michigan on more than one occasion, designing a prophetic chart, etc.—makes it very clear that Samuel W. Rhodes is being referred to. Further, no other "Rhodes" is mentioned in the *Review* in the early 1850s.

See: Search term "Rhodes" in *Words of the Pioneers.* On the prophetic chart designed by S. W. Rhodes, see Ellen G. White, Lt 12, 1850 (Aug. 15).

[2] Samuel Rhodes's first preaching trip to Michigan took place in August 1850.

See: S. W. Rhodes, "Extracts From Letters," *Advent Review,* September 1850, p. 48.

[3] This is the earliest extant testimony of reproof for Samuel Rhodes, who in the early and mid-1850s was one of the young movement's most active and traveled preachers. His negative traits here pointed out—an overbearing spirit, severity and harshness—clearly remained with him, because Ellen White returned to this same problem time and time again in the 1850s and 1860s. See, for example, Ms 6, 1854 (Feb. 19); Lt 8, 1857 (July 19); Lt 16, 1859 (Oct. 28); Lt 5a, 1861 (Apr. 5); Lt 4, 1870 (Mar. 23).

[4] This was not the first time that the emerging movement had been embarrassed by radical interpretations of Christ's words "Sell that ye have and give alms." As early as 1849 James White had complained of "some fiery spirits" in western New York "whose principal message

C. Bowles][5] and Case [**Hiram S. Case**][6] thought they must do as Brother Rhodes did, and carry out the hasty, harsh, severe spirit; for he was in union with the brethren, and he must be right, and it was safe to do as he did.

I saw that the brethren that had property had the greatest confidence in Brother Rhodes, and they commenced to sacrifice their property, and handed it out without having the true object set before them (the suffering cause), and they handed out freely, too much and too often. I saw that the teachers should have stood in a place to correct these errors, and exerted a good influence in the church. Money was made to be of little or no consequence, the sooner disposed of the better, and Brethren Holt [**George W. Holt**][7] and Rhodes set a bad example to those who had property (and those who had not, also) by accepting large donations, and not giving the least caution to those who had means, to not use it too freely and carelessly. And by accepting such a large amount of means without questioning whether God had given them [i.e., the donors] light to bestow so largely, [they] sanctioned the brethren giving too freely and bountifully—those who gave not being particular to enquire into the necessity of the case whether there was actual need or not, and finding out how it was bestowed or disposed of.

Those who had means were thrown into great darkness and perplexity, and Brother Case was hurt by too much means being put into his hands. He did not study economy but lived extravagantly, in his travels laid out money here and there, to no effect, spread a wrong influence by his being so flush

---

was 'Sell that ye have and give alms.'" Funds brought in by such appeals had often been used unwisely. White protested about "means . . . squandered away, and worse than lost in W. New York."

See: James White to Stockbridge Howland, in Ellen G. White, *Spiritual Gifts [vol. 2],* p. 119; James White to Leonard Hastings, Jan. 10, 1850.

[5] *Identity:* The only "Brother Bowles" mentioned in the *Review* during the 1850s is the preacher J. C. Bowles, of Jackson, Michigan, who fits the description given here. His first name, John, is given in the 1850 census.

See: Search term "Bowles" in *Words of the Pioneers;* 1850 U.S. Federal Census, "John C. Bowles," Michigan, Jackson County, Jackson, p. 420.

[6] *Identity:* This letter contains some very specific information about Brother Case, especially his involvement in the Abigail Palmer affair and the reproof given to him for using "the Lord's money" extravagantly while on his preaching itineraries. On the latter issue there is a letter of confession some weeks later in the *Review* from H. S. Case in which he regrets not seeing "the importance of a careful use of means that has been put into my hands. I have done wrong in using the Lord's money as I should not have done." There can be no doubt that H. S. Case is referred to in this letter.

See: H. S. Case, "From Bro. Case," *Review,* Aug. 28, 1853, p. 64; Lt 2, 1852 (June 2), notes 4, 5.

[7] *Identity:* Brother Holt is here coupled with itinerant evangelists Samuel W. Rhodes and Hiram S. Case as having accepted large donations and spending too freely in the course of their travels. The implication is that Brother Holt is also a traveling preacher. Ellen White is no doubt referring to George W. Holt, the only itinerant preacher by that surname among Sabbatarian Adventists in the early 1850s.

See: Search term "Holt" in *Words of the Pioneers.*

with the Lord's money, and would say, to others and in his own heart, to himself, there is means enough in Jackson, more than can be used up before Jesus comes.[8] And some were very much hurt by such a course, and came into the truth wrong, and not realizing that it was God's money that they were using, and not feeling the worth of that means.

And I saw that these poor souls who have just embraced the third angel's message, and have had such an example set before them, will have much to learn, to deny self and suffer for Christ's sake. They will have to learn to give up their ease and cease studying their convenience and comfort, but bear in mind the worth of souls, and if they feel the "woe" upon them, they will not be for making great preparations and fixings outwardly to travel in ease and comfort. And those who have no calling have been encouraged into the field.[9] And those who do not travel at all have been affected by these things, to not feel the need of economizing, denying themselves and putting into the treasury of God. They would feel and say there are enough others who have means enough, they will give for the paper[10]—I need not do anything—the paper will be supported without my help.

I saw that Brother Case knew not what trials and sufferings and privations were, and he has not heeded the vision given concerning following the desires of the eyes as he should, and has erred many times since in the same way. I saw that there had been a careless, profligate use of the Lord's money, by Brother Case, and he has not got rid of this error yet, nor seen it in its true light—has much to learn yet, and others have been affected by these things somewhat, by some of the messengers not setting the right example, or casting the right influence. I saw that these things must be understood in their true light, and

---

[8] An article by J. B. Bezzo in the *Messenger of Truth* provides some rare insights into the ministry of Hiram Case and his break with the Sabbatarian Adventists. It gives a glimpse into the financial support provided by Jackson members to Hiram Case and his family. Thus, in 1853 "Bro. Drew told Bro. Case that if he wo'd move to his place, he would furnish him with a cow, house to live in, and would help support his family while he was carrying the third angel's message." It appears from Bezzo's article that the Jackson church had accepted financial responsibility for the Case family, an arrangement that was very unusual if not unique during the early 1850s, when most traveling preachers received only irregular financial support from the various companies they visited. Bezzo's article is, in the main, critical of the level of support provided for Hiram Case and family. Bezzo wrote in 1854 after both he and Case had joined the opposition *Messenger* Party.

See: J. B. Bezzo, "H. S. Case," *Messenger of Truth,* Nov. 2, 1854, pp. [2-4].

[9] The problem of self-appointed preachers using up scarce donations in their travels continued to afflict the fledgling movement during the years before organization took place in the early 1860s. A *Review* article in 1852 reminded "those who have means" that they should not "bestow it upon every one who may profess to be called of God to preach. . . . They should first be satisfied that they are called of God to teach, before they give them means to travel."

See: "The Faith of Jesus," *Review,* Aug. 19, 1852, p. 61. See also Ms 4, 1850 (Jan. 28), note 5.

[10] I.e., the *Review.*

these evils which have grown out of false teachings must be corrected, and right impressions be cast.

I saw an oppressive spirit exercised by some of the brethren toward others. Brother Bowles has partaken largely of this oppressive exalted spirit. So, also, have Brethren Case and Russell [**Charles P. Russell**],[11] drunk deeply of it. Some others have been affected with it. The little leaven has almost leavened the whole lump, and in order for sweet union and harmony to be in the church this unholy leaven must be entirely purged from it. I saw that it was impossible for the church to love one another as Christ has loved them, until they give up that their opinion is better than their brethren's. They must have a spirit of humility, and be more ready to see their own faults, than their brethren's, and say less about their brethren's faults.

I saw that there had been no trusting in God by Brother Case; for if he was at any time a little perplexed or brought into a strait, instead of crying to God, and trusting in Him, he had murmured against those who had the means, and then when the brethren did help it was not prized. There was an ungrateful, unthankful feeling like this: it was no more than they ought to do—the means was the Lord's &c. This feeling, I saw, was all wrong and hid God's face from those who had it, and this spirit and feeling which is so cruel must be seen and confessed, and put entirely aside or it could not be blotted out, and the same evils will again occur, and the ark of God be stayed[12] as it has been for many months.

I saw that the dreams of Brother Miller,[13] in Oswego [New York], were a device of the enemy, and Brother Rhodes was captivated with them, listened to them, followed them, for a time, and made much of them. I then saw that his hasty visit to Michigan, and right back in a few days, spending so much means, cast a wrong influence as though means was very plenty, at his command, and was all wrong. If it had been right God would not have

---

[11] *Identity:* Further information helping to identify Brother Russell is given toward the end of the letter where Hiram S. Case and Russell are connected with the incident involving Sr. Palmer's indiscretion. In a parallel account by Ellen White in *Spiritual Gifts*, Case and Russell are identified simply as "C. and R." The outcome of the Palmer incident, as Ellen White described it, was that "C. and R. . . . began to fight against my testimony, and here commenced what is called the 'Messenger' party." It is well known from several primary sources that Hiram Case and C. P. Russell were cofounders of the breakaway *Messenger* Party. Census records for 1850 list a Charles P. Russell living in Jackson, Michigan.

See: EGWEnc, s.v. "*Messenger* Party"; Ellen G. White, *Spiritual Gifts [vol. 2]*, pp. 181, 182; 1850 U.S. Federal Census, "Charles P. Russell," Michigan, Jackson County, Jackson, p. 672.

[12] An allusion to the ark of the ancient Hebrew sanctuary, a symbol of God's presence in the camp of the Israelites. Compare the language used here with the following passage in a document written some months later: "A death-like stupor has hung upon the people of God. The reason is, the ark is not with them, for the holy commandments have been broken, and God has taken it away in His anger" (Ms 1, 1854 [Feb. 12]).

[13] *Identity:* The identity of "Brother Miller," of Oswego, has not been established.

suffered him to come to Michigan in darkness, but would have enlightened his mind as to the true situation of the church. Wisdom would have been given him to have moved right, and checked wrong influences and upheld the right. But I saw almost every move made by Brother Rhodes while in Michigan the second time from the East, was all wrong. The church was not benefited, and the frown of God[14] was not removed from the church but remained there still. Some were thrown into great trial, others were exalted, and Brother Rhodes had something of a spirit of lording it over God's heritage. Rebukes were given by Brother Rhodes which came not from God, but which were in himself, and God had nothing to do with it. Brother Bowles and Case had the same spirit and they followed Brother Rhodes, and lorded it over God's heritage.

And those who had means were thrown into a great darkness and perplexity, not daring to question into any move of Brother Rhodes, or inquire into anything on account of being rebuked or repulsed by Brother Rhodes's severity, and they were thrown into a state of fear, afraid to speak out things that they had seen and known. And these things must be confessed and taken out of the way before Brother Rhodes can be free, and move in the wisdom of God.[15] He will fall into the snare of the enemy, and be left to make wrong moves. He cannot make straight paths for his feet until he takes up the wrongs behind him. I saw that Brother Rhodes had exercised this severe spirit in other places, and others have been influenced in the same manner, partaking of the same spirit.

I saw that this feeling that the messenger's course must not be questioned, and that their judgment and understanding is correct in almost everything, and that they must be exalted above the brethren, is all wrong. There has been a lording it over God's heritage. I saw that those who profess to be teachers, should be patterns of piety, meekness, and great humility, possessing a loving, kind spirit, winning souls to Jesus and the truth of the Bible.

---

[14] On God's displeasure and "frown," see Ms 2, 1853 (Mar. 1), note 3.

[15] Seven weeks after this vision was given, on July 23, 1853, Samuel Rhodes wrote a confession, in the manner of the times, that was published in the *Review*. "I see some things . . . which call for a confession on my part, which indeed is humiliating but shall be freely and frankly made. . . . I have not at all times possessed enough of the mind of Christ and have been left to a hurried, overbearing, oppressive spirit, and to deal out rebukes sometimes that were not dictated by the Spirit of the Lord." It cannot be established with certainty that this "confession" was a direct response to Ellen White's vision of June 2, although it seems likely. This was the first of several confessions from Rhodes appearing in the *Review* over the next decade.

See: S. W. Rhodes, "Letter From Bro. Rhodes," *Review,* Aug. 11, 1853, p. 55; "From Bro. Rhodes," *Review,* Jan. 8, 1857, p. 78; "Resignation," *Review,* Dec. 18, 1860, p. 40; "From Bro. Rhodes," *Review,* Jan. 22, 1861, p. 78; "From Bro. Rhodes," *Review,* Apr. 9, 1861, p. 167; "From Bro. Rhodes," *Review,* May 6, 1862, p. 182; "Communication From Br. Rhodes," *Review,* Dec. 3, 1867, p. 395.

I saw sensitive feelings of the messengers fearing lest others will think they are wrong. I saw that there was great backwardness in some of confessing their faults, fearing lest the confidence of the brethren in them will be destroyed. All these feelings, I saw, must be overcome and given up before the church can be in a healthy state. I saw that those who profess to be servants of the living God, to lead souls to Christ, must be willing to be servants of all, instead of being exalted above the brethren, and they must possess a kind, courteous spirit.

I saw that Brother Rhodes must break in pieces before God, and confess many things that he has done wrong. I saw an evading confession by Brother Rhodes, and excusing over all mismoves instead of coming out frankly and honestly and with childlike simplicity take all wrongs out of the way. I saw that Brother Rhodes had labored and labored to show that he was not wrong. I saw that if Brother Rhodes has moved ever so honestly yet if he has been wrong or done wrong, and afterwards evidence comes that he has done wrong, he must cease to confer with flesh and blood, and must confess his errors with meekness and humility.

Errors and wrongs must be confessed thoroughly, and honesty cannot stand as an excuse for not confessing, and by confessing it would not lessen the confidence of the church in the messenger that has erred, but would set a sweet, childlike example to the church, and a spirit of confession would be encouraged in the church, and sweet union would be the result. Humility, I saw, was lacking in Brother Rhodes.

I saw that Brother Bowles's going West was all wrong[16] and grew out of the wrong action and influence in the church by Brother Rhodes. I saw that death, death, followed Brother Bowles. He was lifted up and exalted by the devil, thinking he was something when he was nothing. I saw that he had not seen his mismoves and his exalted feelings, and his being so puffed up by the enemy, thinking that he was doing a great work when some souls were pushed off where it seemed as though there was no possibility of reaching them.[17]

---

[16] According to scattered mentions in the *Review* John Bowles and Hiram Case preached in Illinois and Wisconsin during the autumn of 1851 and the spring of 1852.

See: H. S. Case, "Conference in Illinois," *Review,* Sept. 16, 1851, p. 32; Wm. B. Putnam, "From Bro. Putnam," *Review,* Mar. 31, 1853, p. 183.

[17] Although he shows a definite bias against Bowles and therefore must be read with caution, J. B. Bezzo gives an unflattering picture of John Bowles. Among other episodes Bezzo writes of a meeting held near Saline, Michigan, where "brother Bowles . . . arose and made some remarks, from which Sr. Kellogg got the idea that her children were lost. It had such an effect upon her mind that she became almost distracted; brother K. entertained fears that she would go crazy."

The reproof given to John Bowles in this letter is very similar to that which he had received one year earlier, in June 1852. There is no indication that Bowles had changed his ways, and this may account for the stronger tone of this second letter. This is the last mention of John Bowles in the Ellen White letters and manuscripts. Three months later, in September 1853, he died "after a short illness, of the typhus fever."

See: J. B. Bezzo, "H. S. Case," *Messenger of Truth,* Nov. 2, 1854, p. [2]; J. Whitmore,

I saw that Brother Rhodes would yet have to see and feel that he has exercised an oppressive, overbearing spirit towards his brethren and sisters, and had felt a kind of a spirit of lording it over God's heritage. All these things, I saw, must be confessed and taken out of the way. I saw that they must strive to quicken their memory and not be too willing to forget.

I saw that the wrongs of the church and messengers must be seen and confessed before the grievous wound could be healed.[18] Troubles have been in Jackson, and they would seem at times to be healed but it has been slightly. The pestilent matter has been left deep and unobserved, to burst out again and make it almost incurable. The wound has been healed slightly, and has not been probed to the bottom yet.

I saw that Brethren Case and Rhodes have nominally admitted and acknowledged the visions but have not followed them out, but have resisted the conclusion that the visions would bring them to if they fully believed, and the effect that the Lord meant that it should have upon them, and His design in giving the vision had many times failed by these brethren closing the eyes, evading the point &c. I saw that Brother Case had followed the desires of his eyes of late.

I saw the chart-making business was all wrong. It originated with Brother Rhodes and was followed out by Brother Case. Means have been spent in making charts and forming uncouth, disgusting images to represent angels and the glorious Jesus. Such things, I saw, were displeasing to God. I saw that God was in the publishment of the chart by Brother Nichols [**Otis Nichols**].[19] I saw that there was a prophecy of this chart in the Bible,[20] and if this chart is designed for God's people, if it [is] sufficient for one it is for another, and if one needed a new chart painted on a larger scale, all needed it just as much.

I saw that it was a restless, uneasy, unsatisfied, ungrateful feeling in

---

"From Bro. Whitmore," *Review*, Oct. 4, 1853, p. 103; Ellen G. White, Lt 2, 1852 (June 2).

[18] Of the four "messengers" reproved in this manuscript, the confessions of Hiram Case and Samuel Rhodes appeared in the *Review* within a few weeks. To make confession publicly in the columns of the *Review* was not uncommon in the 1850s and 1860s.

See: H. S. Case, "From Bro. Case," *Review*, Aug. 28, 1853, p. 64; S. W. Rhodes, "Letter From Bro. Rhodes," *Review*, Aug. 11, 1853, p. 55.

[19] The "charts" depicted prophetic symbols from Daniel and Revelation together with time calculations. In October 1850 Ellen White had received instruction in vision that a prophetic chart should be published. During the next few months Otis Nichols supervised the publication of a chart that was advertised for distribution and sale in January 1851. "We are much pleased with the arrangement of the Chart," wrote James White, ". . . and we are satisfied that it will be a great help to those who teach the present truth."

See: Ellen G. White, Lt 26, 1850 (Nov. 1); "The Chart," *Review*, January 1851, p. 38. For general historical overview of the production of the first chart, see Arthur L. White, *Ellen G. White: The Early Years*, pp. 184, 185.

[20] Probably a reference to Habakkuk 2:2, 3. In 1850 Ellen White wrote that "God shewed me the necessity of getting out a chart. I saw it was needed and that the truth made plain upon tables . . . would cause souls to come to the knowledge of the truth." The expression

Brother Case that desired another chart. I saw that these painted charts had a bad effect upon the congregation. It caused a light, chaffy spirit of ridicule to be in the meeting.[21]

I saw that the charts ordered by God struck the mind favorably, even without an explanation. There is something light, lovely, and heavenly in the representation of the angels on the charts. The mind is almost imperceptibly led to God and heaven. But the other charts that have been gotten up disgusted the mind, and caused the mind to dwell more on earth than heaven. Images representing angels look more like fiends than beings of heaven. I saw that the charts had for days and weeks occupied Brother Case's mind when he should have been seeking heavenly wisdom from God, and should have been growing in graces of the Spirit and the knowledge of the truth.

I saw that if the means that have been wasted in getting out charts had been spent in getting out the truth clearly before the brethren, in publishing tracts &c., it would have done much good and saved souls. I saw that the chart-making business has spread like the fever.

I saw that Sr. Palmer [**Abigail Palmer**][22] had been proud and exalted, and had been worldly-minded, that she had not possessed right feelings and a right spirit towards unbelievers. There was a feeling of hatred in her heart toward them, and words were spoken concerning them which should never have been said, and God had been grieved and Jesus wounded by these things. I saw that the Christian should have noble feelings, and all the scorn and derision of unbelievers should not move them, and cause a disturbed feeling to arise in their hearts, and anything like retaliation should never be felt or resorted to by Christians. I saw that Sr. Palmer must get very humble and low before God, and humble herself greatly before Him, and make haste to get right before God, lest His sweet Spirit be entirely grieved away.

I then was pointed again to Sr. Palmer. Said the angel, It does not belong there. Words were spoken but not the ones that were said that she spake. I saw words spoken that were wrong, that should not have been spoken, and which in no way could glorify God; but which were the fruits of the risings of self.

"plain upon tables" was taken from Habakkuk 2:2, 3 and had been applied by Millerites earlier to their use of prophetic charts.

See: Ellen G. White, Lt 26, 1850 (Nov. 1); *idem, The Great Controversy,* p. 392.

[21] Hiram Case's interest in painting prophetic charts that were subsequently less than well received by others is documented by J. B. Bezzo. During a tour of Ohio in 1851, wrote Bezzo, "Case got up a new chart. He was gone about six weeks, and when he returned, the brethren had a trial with him about the chart. He confessed his wrong, and asked their forgiveness."

See: J. B. Bezzo, "H. S. Case," *Messenger of Truth,* Nov. 2, 1854, p. [3].

[22] *Identity:* The Jackson, Michigan, setting of this letter makes it relatively easy to identify "Sr. Palmer." There is frequent mention in the *Review,* from 1851 onward, of a "D. R. Palmer," of Jackson. No doubt Ellen White is here referring to his wife, Abigail.

See: Search term "Palmer" in *Words of the Pioneers;* 1860 U.S. Federal Census, "Dan R. Palmer," Michigan, Jackson County, Jackson, Ward 4, p. 134.

But the words which were considered the most sinful she did not speak.[23]

I also saw that the testimony of a child should never be received against the testimony of a child of God, unless other persons of experience in the things of God and to be relied on, should hear and witness the same. Great carefulness should be used on this point. I saw trouble between the two families before this circumstance happened, or was brought up, which caused the one to be willing, yes, too willing, to see the faults of the other, and Bro. Case's daughter had indulged in very wrong feelings toward Sr. Palmer, and she was willing to make it appear worse than it was. I saw that it was a great lack of judgment crediting her testimony and pressing it upon others to do so. I saw that there has been a thrusting with side and shoulder by Brethren Case [and] Russell.[24] Brother Bowles has possessed the same spirit, and has formerly done it much, and oppressed the children of God, and hard, harsh, bitter, cutting words have proceeded from his mouth. He must search after these things, and take them all away, confess them, lest they appear before him when there is no mediator to stand between an offended God and guilty man—when there is no atoning blood to wash away the stain of sin.

I saw that the weakness of [the] Jackson Band was known all through Jackson; also, in other places, many had been weakened and burdened by Brother Case spreading or introducing the trials of [the] Jackson Band to almost every place he went. This, I saw, was all wrong and God was displeased with such a course. I then saw that we should never intimate our trials in any way to the wicked. I saw that Satan had laughed as he saw those who professed to have wisdom from God, and believing they were having the last message of mercy to the world, should make the wicked acquainted with their troubles and trials, and let them in to see the weakness of the Band. I was pointed back to the time when Hezekiah led the enemies into the house of God, and

---

[23] Further details of the incident mentioned here are given by Ellen White in *Spiritual Gifts* and by John Loughborough, who was an eyewitness to some of the events. Central to the episode was an angry outburst by Abigail Palmer of the Jackson, Michigan, band, aimed at a non-Adventist neighbor. Witnessing the scene was 17-year-old Savilla, daughter of Hiram Case, who claimed (according to Loughborough) that the offensive word "bitch" had been used. Hiram Case and Charles Russell insisted that Abigail Palmer should confess, but she denied using the vile epithet. The Jackson group became divided on the issue. Sometime thereafter, in early June 1853, the Whites visited Jackson, and Ellen was given the vision that is here reported. Abigail subsequently admitted to having used the word "witch" rather than "bitch."

See: Ellen G. White, *Spiritual Gifts [vol. 2]*, pp. 181, 182; J. N. Loughborough, "Some Individual Experience," in *The Great Second Advent Movement*, 1992 reprint ed., pp. 558-560; J. Morrill, "From Sister Morrill," *Messenger of Truth*, Nov. 30, 1854, p. [4].

[24] Little is said here about the reactions of Case and Russell to Ellen White's vision. But according to the parallel account given in *Spiritual Gifts*, they totally rejected the part of the vision that denied that Mrs. Palmer had used the offensive term. They went further and "began to fight against my testimony, and here commenced what is called the 'Messenger' party."

See: Ellen G. White, *Spiritual Gifts [vol. 2]*, pp. 181, 182; EGWEnc, s.v. "*Messenger* Party."

shewed them the sacred, secret things there, the vessels of gold &c., of the temple, which was a heinous sin in the sight of God, and He pronounced a heavy curse upon them.[25]

I saw that it was a shame to those who are teachers to set such an example to the flock. I saw that great dishonor was brought upon the cause of God by letting the wicked (who are abhorred of God and who had such a wicked, ungodly spirit that there was nothing that was too hard for them to say or any suffering too severe for them to inflict upon the saints if it was in their power) know their weakness, even so much as to come to them for testimony. If they had been left to do this, decide the case of the church on such testimony, God would leave forever those who did it, in perfect darkness, unfit to have to do with the holy cause of God. I saw that we had nothing to do with the wicked, that the affairs of the church should be kept in the church. That we have no confessions to make to the wicked, unless we have done them a personal injury. I saw that Brother Case's course had most effectually destroyed the confidence of the church in his judgment, also his influence in Jackson was gone. My feelings were intense as I saw these things. I saw that Brethren Case, Russell, and Bowles had all erred in their feelings toward the wicked; they have felt a spirit of hatred in their hearts towards them which was displeasing to a holy God.

I saw that Brother Case has not known yet what wants and trials are in regard to means since he embraced the third angel's message; therefore he has not, neither his wife or daughter, felt thankful and grateful to God for opening the hearts of His children to bestow donations upon them. I was pointed back to the time *where* and how the third angel's message found Brother Case. Said the angel: Look back and remember what God and the truth have done for thee; do not forget it. I saw that the brethren had done for and treated Brother Case as parents would treat their children, and there was but little thankfulness or gratitude in return. I saw that they had not prized the help and assistance of their brethren. There has been a lack of humility in the family.

I saw that Brother Case's daughter did not mean to lie about Sr. Palmer, but she thought she heard her say something much as she told, and she was willing to have it look worse than it was, and as bad as possible. I saw that she must get rid of her pride and get humble before God, with her father and mother, and confess heartily to God and the church.

I saw that Brother Russell had been exalted in his own eyes. He has been humble in times past, and enjoyed pure religion; but he has got to have a great work done for him before he will again understand the movings of the Spirit of God and flourish in the Lord.

---

[25] Cf. 2 Kings 20:12-18.

I saw Brother Case has indulged in wrong feelings, and talked it over and over, at home and abroad, and all the family partook of a jealous, wrong spirit, when even if others had been wrong, it was no excuse for them to sin. I saw that Brother Case loved his ease too well, and indulged himself altogether too much. He knew not what it was to suffer for the truth's sake. He has not learnt yet half that he will have to learn.

I saw that Brother Russell has had a hard, oppressive spirit and Brother Case's daughter has indulged in very wrong feelings and her parents have not checked it by example or reproof, but encouraged it by example. I saw that a great work must be done for Brother Case or he would be laid aside as unfit to carry the truth of God to others, and unfit to be an example to the flock; for if he remains as he is, his influence will be as it has been, death, death, death.[26]

I saw that the Lord had been displeased with some of the brethren for following the desires of their eyes, and getting costly Bibles when a cheaper Bible contained all the words of God, and answers the same purpose. I saw money had been wasted in this thing to gratify a selfish feeling. I saw that the messengers must be examples to the flock, and every cent and dollar that has been misspent would have to be rendered an account for in the day of judgment.

I saw that the understanding that Brother Bowles got of the trial some time back was nearly right; but it was not a revelation he had but his understanding was convinced, and then it was he moved all wrong, and threw everything into confusion.

---

[26] Eventually, some months later, Hiram Case was "laid aside." There is some uncertainty as to the date when Case was dismissed from the ministry. According to J. B. Bezzo, it was at a meeting held in Sylvan, Michigan, in January 1854 that "it was decided that Bro. Case should not carry the message." The *Review*, however, says the decision was made at a conference in Jackson, Michigan, on February 17, 1854. Bezzo adds that Case was disfellowshipped "a short time after this [Sylvan] meeting" at a meeting held in Jackson.

See: J. B. Bezzo, "H. S. Case," *Messenger of Truth,* Nov. 2, 1854, p. [4]; Ed., "H. S. Case," *Review,* Apr. 18, 1854, p. 102.

THE MESSENGER OF TRUTH.

"PROVE ALL THINGS—HOLD FAST THAT WHICH IS GOOD."

VOLUME 1. JACKSON, MICHIGAN, FIFTH-DAY, NOV. 30, 1854. NUMBER 5.

THE MESSENGER OF TRUTH
WILL BE PUBLISHED SEMI-MONTHLY, AS LONG AS THE CAUSE OF GOD DEMANDS IT.

PUBLISHING COMMITTEE:
W. J. LUSK, H. S. CASE,
C. P. RUSSELL, J. B. BEZZO.
H. DREW, ERASTUS CLARK.

TERMS.—Gratis, except the reader desires to give something towards its publication.

ALL communications, orders and remittances for "THE MESSENGER OF TRUTH," should be directed to C. P. RUSSELL, Jackson, Michigan.

POETRY.

For the Messenger of Truth.

To all the brethren far and near,
Let this unvarnished truth appear—
We only wish to state the fact,
To show how some professors act.
It is proclaimed from east to west,
The visions are not made a test;
But when we come to case in hand,
We see just how the visions stand.
I cannot say I ever could
Believe those visions came from God;
The visions came from E. G. White,
With contradictions dark as night;
Altho' some people think them pure,
And think her sayings all are sure,
So they will take them for their guide,
And in her words they still confide.
I wish to state what I have seen,
And you will know just what I mean;
The visionites may do their best
To show they were not made a test.
When gospel order came along,
And with it faith in visions strong,
Some leading members of the band
Took gospel order all in hand;
They met their Brethren as they should—
Alas! but not to do them good—
They made the matter worse and worse,
Till all were blighted with a curse;
They said a deacon must be made,
If gospel order was obeyed;
They chose to have a vision lover,
So they elected brother Glover.
Besides, he is an agent here,
And anti-visionists must clear,
If they should undertake to speak,
Or for investigation seek,
Out gospel order straight would come—
"Now shut your mouth, or else go home."
So here we see what visions do,
When faith in them is carried through;
They bind the poor bewildered soul
To wander under their control,
And move according to their teaching,
And stop good ministers from preaching,
And when we come to the conclusion,
Instead of order, make confusion.
We wish to state what we have heard,
And try to get it word for word,
When they were used for brother Case,
They read those visions to his face;
They told him he was much to blame,
And sister White had seen the same,
They read the visions o'er and o'er,
Which mentioned all his crimes, and more—
Some said they feared he'd lose his soul
If he did not confess the whole.
They told him he must bow and break,
He soon began to fear and quake;
His soul was filled with shame and grief,
His friends then prayed for his relief.
He owned the visions were a test,
And felt his soul had now been blest.
Our brother Case once had a call
To go and preach the truth to all;
But soon the Jackson band, and others,
Whom he once tho't were christian brothers,
Contrived a plan to turn him out
Because those visions he would doubt.
They brought up charges, new and old,
And came upon him brave and bold,
And silenced him, and shut his mouth
From preaching east, west, north or south.
When Case's trial had begun,
The visions told him what he'd done.
He said "the visions truly teach
That I am not the man to preach—
I hope the brethren will forgive,
And pray for me and let me live."
And since that time I've heard him say,
He thought there was no other way
For him to have his crimes forgiven,
That he might be prepared for Heaven.
"I thought the Jackson brethren came
To crush me down and hurt my name;
I find they prove to be my friends,
I promise now to make amends."
All join in prayer with one accord,
To render thanks, and ask the Lord
To let his spirit fill the place,
And bless beloved brother Case.
The meeting then continued on
Till morning light began to dawn.
A gospel preacher came from home—
As far as Sylvan he had come—
And when he got within the door
He met with opposition sore;
That *vision* woman had a view,
That he had nothing more to do;
He had no message from the Lord,
To go and preach his holy word;
So home he went, and left the field
To her vain visions, he must yield.
The Lord forgive him, (if he will,)
For foolishness and sitting still.
Beware, my friends, I say beware,
Lest you are taken in this snare,
And thus deceived by her design,
And led away from truth divine.
Our brother Case is now set free
To preach where e'er his call may be.
It is a fearful thing to mock,
Or to become a stumbling block,
While we profess to serve the Lord,
And trust in Christ for our reward.
We hope that all who love the cause,
Will go with us and keep God's laws,
And not be led astray by this,
Nor do, or say, or think amiss.
If any one is disaffected
Because the visions are rejected,
And thinks this story is unpleasant,
Let them inquire of others present;
If they will not relate the same,
Then tell me where I am to blame.
If this is not sufficient proof,
Let all these verses stand aloof,
And I can take up other cases,
And write more lines to fill their places.

FROM A BROTHER.

The Visions.

In our first No. I endeavored to show some of the confusion existing in the visions of E. G. White. As I have since then examined them more closely, and have seen some of them as published elsewhere besides in her 'Experience and Views,' I wish to say a few words more about them.

On p 10, she says, 'Soon we heard the voice of God like many waters, which gave us the day and hour of Jesus' coming.' Then *after* God had spoken the time, and the saints knew and understood his voice, had the Holy Ghost poured on them, were sealed and united, had written in their foreheads 'God, New Jerusalem, and a glorious star containing Jesus' new name,' 'stretched forth the hand in the name of the Lord, and the wicked fell helpless to the ground,' they saw Jesus coming on the white cloud, and all 'Gathered paleness' and 'Cried out who shall be able to stand.'

Some of our brethren who contend for the truthfulness of the visions, refer to Jer. xxx. 6 as proof that this portion of the visions is true. We will read a few 'verses of this chapter. 4th verse 'And 'these are the words that the Lord spake 'concerning Israel, and concerning Judah. '5. For thus saith the Lord; We have heard 'a voice of trembling, of fear, and not of 'peace. 6. Ask ye now, and see whether 'a man doth travail with child? wherefore 'do I see every man with his hands on 'his loins, as a woman in travail, and all 'faces are turned into paleness? Alas! 'for that day is great, so that none is like 'it: it is even the time of Jacob's trouble, 'but he shall be delivered out of it.'

Now, these verses show that all faces are turned into paleness in the time of Jacob's trouble; *before* he is delivered out of it. The question now arises, when is Jacob delivered out of his trouble?—James White, in a pamphlet entitled '*A Word to the Little Flock*,' published by Joseph Bates of Fair Haven Mass. 1847, 'page 10, says, 'In the last closing strife 'with the Image Beast, when a decree goes 'forth that as many as will not worship the 'image of the beast shall be killed; the 'saints will cry day and night, and be de'livered by the voice of God.' Those who believe Ellen's visions, will of course take them as evidence. On page 20 of her 'work, she says, 'A decree went forth to 'slay the saints, which caused them to 'cry day and night for deliverance.—'This was the time of Jacob's trouble.—'Then all the saints cried out with an'guish of spirit, and were delivered by the 'voice of God. Then the 144,000 tri'umphed. Their faces were lighted up 'with the glory of God.'

Here, by taking it for granted that the visions are true, we have two points established. 1st, Jeremiah shows us that all faces are turned into paleness in the time of Jacob's trouble *before* he is delivered out of it, and secondly, the visions tell us that he is delivered by the voice of God. Now, when does she say the voice of God is heard? Is it *before* Jesus is seen on the white cloud, or *after* it? On pages 17, 18 she says, 'In the time of trouble, we 'all fled from the cities and villages, but 'were pursued by the wicked, who entered 'the houses of the saints with the sword. 'They raised the sword to kill us, but it 'broke, and fell as powerless as a straw. 'Then we all cried day and night for deliv'erance, and the cry came up before God. 'The sun came up and the moon stood still. 'The streams ceased to flow. Dark heavy 'clouds came up, and clashed against each 'other. But there was one clear place of 'settled glory, from whence came the '*voice of God* like many waters, which 'shook the heavens, and the earth. The 'sky opened and shut, and was in commo'tion. The mountains shook like a reed 'in the wind, and cast out ragged rocks 'all around. The sea boiled like a pot, 'and cast out stones upon the land. And 'as God spake the day and hour of Jesus' 'coming, and delivered the everlasting 'covenant to his people, he spake one sen'tence, and then paused, while the words 'were rolling through the earth. The 'Israel of God stood with their eyes fixed 'upwards, listening to the words as they 'came from the mouth of Jehovah, and 'rolled through the earth like peals of 'loudest thunder, It was awfully solemn. 'At the end of every sentence, the saints 'shouted, Glory! Hallelujah! Their coun'tenances were lighted up with the glory of God; and they shone with the glory 'as Moses' face did when he came down 'from Sinai. The wicked could not look 'on them for the glory. And when the 'never-ending blessing was pronounced 'on those who had honored God, in keep'ing his Sabbath holy, there was a 'mighty shout of victory over the Beast, 'and over his Image. Then commenced 'the Jubilee, when the land should rest. 'I saw the pious slave rise in triumph 'and victory; and shake off the chains 'that bound him, while his wicked master 'was in confusion, and knew not what to 'do; for the wicked could not understand 'the words of the voice of God. Soon 'appeared the great white cloud. It 'looked more lovely than ever before.—'On it sat the Son of Man.'

It is plain to be seen that in this vision she has the events at the coming of Christ, to occur in the following order: First, The time of trouble, (the time that all faces are turned into paleness, Jer. xxx, 6, 7,) the wicked pursuing the saints with the sword, and the saints crying day and night for deliverance. Second, The voice of God like many waters that shook the heavens and the earth, and gave the day and hour of Jesus' coming. Third, The saints shouting at the end of every sentence. and their countenances being lighted up. Fourth, The never-ending blessing being pronounced. Fifth, The shout of victory, and the commencement of the jubilee when the land should rest; and seventh, The Son of Man on the great white cloud.

Now let the reader turn back a little and again read the quotation taken from p. 20, of her book where she sees, first, The decree to slay the saints and their crying day and night which is the time of Jacob's trouble, and second, their being delivered by the voice of God, and triumphing. This agrees with the former deducement. Now turn to p. 10, 11, and read the order in which she *there* presents those events: "Soon we heard 'the voice of God like many waters, 'which gave us the day and hour of Jesus' 'coming. The living saints, 144,000, in 'number, knew and understood the voice, 'while the wicked thought it was thunder 'and an earthquake. When God spake the 'time, he poured on us the Holy Ghost, 'and our faces began to light up and shine 'with the glory of God as Moses' did 'when he came down from Mount Sinai.

"The 144,000 were all sealed and per'fectly united. On their foreheads was 'written, God, New Jerusalem, and a 'glorious star containing Jesus' new 'name. At our happy, holy state, the 'wicked were enraged, and would rush 'violently up to lay hands on us to thrust 'us in prison, when we would stretch 'forth the hand in the name of the Lord, 'and the wicked would fall helpless to 'the ground. Then it was that the syna'gogue of satan knew that God had loved 'us who could wash one another's feet, 'and salute the holy brethren with a holy 'kiss, and they worshiped at our feet.—'Soon our eyes were drawn to the East, 'for a small black cloud had appeared 'about half as large as a man's hand, 'which we all knew was the sign of the 'Son of Man. We all in solemn silence 'gazed on the cloud as it drew nearer, 'and it became lighter, glorious, and still 'more glorious, till it was a great white 'cloud. The bottom appeared like fire, 'a rainbow was over it, around the cloud 'were ten thousand angels singing a 'most lovely song. And on it sat the 'Son of Man, on his head were crowns, 'his hair was white and curly and lay on 'his shoulders. His feet had the appear'ance of fire, in his right hand was a 'sharp sickle, in his left a silver trumpet. 'His eyes were as a flame of fire, which 'searched his children through and 'through. Then all faces gathered pale'ness, (the time of Jacob's trouble, Jer. 'xxx, 6, 7,) and those whom God had re'jected gathered blackness. Then we all 'cried out, who shall be able to stand?"

Here the order of events is, first the voice of God, (which, according to page 20 of her book, delivers the saints in the time of Jacob's trouble when all faces gather paleness, Jer. XXX, 6, 7,) giving the day and hour of Jesus' coming, the pouring of the Holy Ghost on the saints, their faces shining with the glory of God, and their being sealed.—Second, The wicked rushing up to thrust the saints in prison, (which, according to page 17, was the time they all cried day and night for deliverance and the cry came up before God, and p. 20 they were delivered by the voice of God, which had already been heard,) and falling helpless to the ground. Third, The synagogue of satan worshipping at the Saints' feet. Fourth, The appearance of the little black cloud and the Son of Man, and fifth, All faces gathering paleness; which, according to Jeremiah, was in the time of Jacob's trouble; out of which, according to her visions, the saints "were delivered by the voice of God," which she represented to have been heard some time before Jesus appeared on the white cloud.

It is certainly painful in the extreme, to think that men of mind and talent will follow after such fables as this. O, foolish brethren, who hath bewitched you that ye should contend for the truthfulness of such a mass of confusion as those visions are, because you "do not deny the gifts of the Holy Spirit?"

(TO BE CONTINUED.)

Letter from Bro. Barringer.

[illegible]MITTEE:—As there are quite a number who are giving in their testimony to the ill treatment they have received from professed brethren, I deem it my duty to give in my testimony also, as such doings were to be a striking sign of the times, just previous to the end.

I find that since our great disappointment in '43 and '44, there has existed a severe strife and unscriptural contention among the Advent believers in general. And having experienced these evils, in this place, I have become a peculiar lover of gospel order, and whatever truths God has provided for us in our time of disappointment. I have been denied as fair a treatment in many respects, as has been given me by worldlings. I have been accused of evil conduct, in the way of inuendos, and mysterious and disgusting proceedings until I began to regard myself somewhat guilty of their accusations, so thick and fast did the temptations and accusations come upon me. I do not attempt to justify myself from all blame, but after I have confessed to persons of faults resulting from my previous imperfect schooling in gospel truths, church order, &c., I have obtained no satisfaction to speak of.—The obvious reason appears to be this.—I had obtained certain views from the bible respecting the third proclamation, and this led me in direct conflict with those who desire to have the pre-eminence in the church. All my attempts to have personal difficulties settled, after this, was regarded as only an attempt to supplant them. In fact, I had no real faults against any person living, until after I had obtained these views,—all previous difficulties were regarded by me only as misunderstandings common to this imperfect state. I found, however, that the truths for the times required me to regard my injuries as the result of an evil disposed heart of my persecutors.—I then commenced to deal with them as such, but I was treated as one who had gone out from them, and was not to be heard, as a brother. It is true, I have been treated with some *formal* respect by those who were so firmly committed to gospel order, &c., that they had not the conscience to disregard the claims of church order altogether. I am aware these faults are modified by the evil nature of the times somewhat, but I must believe, notwithstanding this, that covetousness and malice have mainly actuated them in many respects.

Various have been the excuses advanced in justification of their course.—A prominent one of which has been that I was insane. This defence, Elder Himes has resorted to, little realizing the mental anguish it has caused me. To be treated on the right hand and on the left, as a deranged man, and that, too, independent of my knowledge of the facts in the case, is trying in the extreme. After having thus robbed me both spiritually and temporally, and failing to substantiate their reckless course, they have begun to treat me as of no consequence whatever. As the libertine who has forced his victim to shame, leaves them to perish in neglect, so they have stained and paralized me with their venom, and would now bury me before I am dead.—No, I am not dead yet, and hope to live to declare yet the works of the Lord.

I am a firm believer in the destruction of the wicked, and for this belief mainly I have been treated as above described, from the principal leaders in the *Advent Herald* party.

And I now wish to say, that I wish to unite with no party henceforth who secretly disfellowship me for some vital error, (by them considered,) held by me, while they openly profess fellowship.—Especially do I wish no union with any party who deprive me of freedom of speech and free discussion, whether this Popish opposition be manifested by visionites, dreams, or by the Pope himself, or his subordinate officers. Spiritual slavery is the life of Popery, and bible freedom the only safety from it.

I have had but little association with the so called "commandment keepers," but so far as my experience goes, I find the spirit of Popery or covetousness quite extensively prevailing among the *Advent Review* party. I have reason to believe some of that party wish to hear what further light might be given respecting the third message, but the leaders have witheld it. It is time that the true remnant—those who have been cast out on the pretence that God would thereby be glorified—had some medium of defence.

People at the present time, aided by satan and their own [illegible], can easily work themselves up into mental consolation independent of the bible. Instead of a christian departure from evil and a bible confession of faults, they choose the less humiliating way of reasoning themselves out of their duty; and satan is ever ready to confirm them in the transgression. But I have learned to place no confidence in those who will not consent to be governed by the bible, as our highest light.

Yours, in the christian warfare,
H. BARRINGER.

Troy, N. Y., Nov. 11, 1854.

From Bro. Bushman.

A few thoughts from one cast out by brethren; notwithstanding the words of our Saviour, Luke, xxii, 3, 4, Mat. xviii, 21, 22, Mark, xi, 25, 26, "And when ye stand praying, forgive, if ye have aught against any; that your Father also which is in heaven may forgive you your trespasses. But if ye do not forgive, neither will your Father which is in heaven forgive your trespasses." O let us be careful that we be not of those classes that our Saviour in Mat. xxiii, 1, 3, speaks of. They that forgive not an erring brother, but treat him scornfully, are dictated by a different revelation from that which our Great Master in heaven has given us. Now to the revelation of our Saviour; hear ye Him. "For I testify unto every man that heareth the words of the prophecy of this book, if any man shall add unto these things, God shall add unto him the plagues that are written in this book." Hear the wise man, Prov. xxx, 5, "Every word of God is pure; he is a shield unto them that trust in Him," (not in the arm of mortal man,) 6th verse, "add thou not unto his words lest he reprove thee and thou be found a liar." And again; Deut. iv, 2, "Ye shall not add unto the word which I command you, neither shall ye diminish aught from it."

The word of God ought to be the rule of faith and action of every bible christian; for "All scripture is given by inspiration of God, and is profitable for doctrine, for reproof, for correction, for instruction in righteousness, that the man of God may be perfect, thoroughly furnished unto all good works"—2d Tim. iii, 16, 17. My Father in heaven, enable us to understand thy word that we may know thy will of us in all things, that we may be found of thee at thine appearing without spot and blameless, is the daily prayer of your unworthy brother in tribulation and patience. JOHN BUSHMAN.

Tekonsha, Mich., Nov. 6, 1854.

Opposition paper, The Messenger of Truth, *launched by C. P. Russell and H. S. Case. Original dimensions (H x W): 20 x 13.5 in. (51 x 34 cm.). Courtesy of the State Library of Pennsylvania.*

MESSENGER OF TRUTH

BUY THE TRUTH, AND SELL IT NOT.

JACKSON, FIFTH-DAY, NOV. 30, 1854.

RECEIPTS.—F. Rinney, L. Fitch, Wm. Clark, E. Bugbee, E. Peirce, J. Teff, H. H. Nottingham, each $1,00.

W. Munroe, R. R. Chapin, each $2,00.

Stephen Munroe, $5,00. B. Clark, Sophia Munroe, J. Smith, each $0,50.

Conference.

There will be a conference in the township of Waterloo, in what is called the Tamarack School House, near brother Eli Bugbee's, to commence on Sixth-day evening, Dec. 29th, and hold over Sabbath and First-day.

We would earnestly solicit a general attendance of the brethren far and near.

Dear brethren, come and meet with us; come in the Spirit, praying for Heaven's blessing to crown our meeting. Will Br'n E. Clark and A. F. Sarvis meet with us if possible?

Those who come on the cars, will want to take the *mail train* on the M. C. R. R., and stop at Francisville; when there, inquire for Hiram Drew.

IRA WYMAN.
H. S. CASE.

☞ We are obliged to omit a number of good letters, in consequence of not having those we desired at the commencement of the paper.

A Dark Piece of Work.

Through the kindness of the Lord, we have been put in possession of a printed circular letter, purporting to be copied from a letter written by Bro. A. L. Burwell, to Bro. Ira Wyman. This circular was enfolded in the *Review and Herald*, and sent without any date attached to it, to the *visionite* brethren in Mich., for (as circumstances clearly show,) the sole purpose of injuring the character of Bro. Wyman here in Michigan.

We will copy the letter just as it appears in the printed circular, then state the circumstances attending it, and compare it with the original letter which Bro. Wyman received from Bro. Barwell, in order to get before the minds of the brethren scattered abroad, the iniquitous work that is now being carried on by J. White at Roch'r. The following is the circular:

COPIED FROM A LETTER FROM A. L. BURWELL TO IRA WYMAN.

"I received your letter 18th July, desiring my decision whether I consider you worthy of the 'horse.' You say that 'wo me if I preach not the last message of mercy to poor mortal man,' and 'Man says wo me if I preach;' which [illegible] Brother, can you expect me to aid in an independent or opposing train to be put in operation, even if it is [illegible], it is propelled with a 'wo me.' If it [illegible] in union and harmony, fellowship and countenance of our faithful, self-sacrificing, Beloved Brethren and Sisters? Can you expect that I will willingly aid in a division of the Church of Christ? No, my brother, I know full well that a 'house' (church) divided against itself, it cannot stand.'

Now the position that you occupy is, that the Brn. have charges preferred against you, and you do not afford the requisite satisfaction to insure their fellowship and approbation in your preaching the present truth.

Here are some of the reasons which you require of me to render, if I say give up the horse. You say that you 'shall not give up the horse, without a line direct from me.' I must say to you that the order the Br'n. Bates, Cottrell, White and others, have presented to you for 'the horse,' I presume was not a forgery; for the Br'n, Gardner, Everts and myself have sent such an order to said Br'n., to present to you.—I must say, that you have rolled the responsibility on me that will array me in direct opposition to my former Brethren, or that I individually must say, give up the horse. I must say that painful circumstances, some of which are referred to, demand that I should say, that I wish you to give up the horse to some of the foresaid mentioned brethren, when they present said order. Now, dear Brother, I understand that you say that if you give up the horse, that you shall claim $25,00, because you have been to said expense in doctoring and medicine for the horse. I think that I shall speak the mind of my brethren, also my own, when I say it is astonishing to make such a demand, and also you say that the horse is worth $45,00 more than when [illegible].—I must think the demand unjust; but if you demand it, give up the horse, and if the horse will sell for $25,00 over the $50,00, her cost, then when she is disposed of you shall have it. And, rather, although I judge it unjust, if your claim $25,00 whether the horse will fetch any over $50,00, you shall have it when the horse is sold, if you will give her up.

In Feb. 1852, Bro. Everts told Brother Wyman that he (Bro. W.) must have a horse, and accordingly made an effort to purchase one for him, but failed. Br. Burwell had one which he valued at $80. Br'n Everts and Gardner, each agreed to pay him $10, and he let Bro. W. have the horse, thus himself giving $10. Br. W. found it would not answer his turn, and returned it. Bro. Everts had one that he valued at about $80; Bro. Gardner went to purchase it for Br'n Sperry and Wyman to travel with. Bro. Everts wanted the horse to be all the time employed in the cause, and proposed to let it go for $20, less, upon the condition that when Bro. Sperry did not go with it, Br. W. should take it. Soon after this horse was purchased, Bro Gardner sold one of his, so that when Bro. S. was not using his one, he (Bro. G.) wanted to use it on his farm. When he was thus using it, Bro. W. did not feel free to ask for it, and therefore was obliged to stay at home, or go by public conveyance to carry the message.

The following fall, when J. White held his first conference in St. Lawrence Co., N. Y., Bro. Wyman went and told Bro. Everts his circumstances in regard to being obliged to stay at home for the want of a horse. Bro. E. then mentioned the conditions upon which he had let the horse go, which were as stated above; and then told him he must have a horse, so that he could feel free to go when he pleased.

Bro. Burwell had one which he bought at administrator's sale for $39. It was an injured animal, and he told Bro. W. to take it and use it what he could. He took it and went to doctoring it, and it commenced improving, and continued to improve all winter. However, he was frequently obliged to leave it on the road, (it being unable to travel) and go by public conveyance to meet his appointments. The next spring, as he was talking of moving to N. Y., Br'n Everts, Gardner and Burwell held a consultation about purchasing a horse for him to have to carry the message with. They wanted to know if the one which he had thro' the winter would answer his purpose.—He told them it would, if it did not grow any worse, or words to that effect. Bro. Gardner spoke and said he could not help any towards buying it, for he had all he could do to support Bro. Sperry (his son-in-law.) After this, Bro. Burwell told Bro. W. the horse was his (Bro. W.'s,) and what *he* (Bro. B.) gave, was for his (Bro. W.'s) own personal benefit. The horse was then valued at $50, and Bro. B. told Bro. W. that Bro. Gardner had as great a burden as he could bear, without assisting in purchasing the horse.—Therefore, the understanding was, that the horse was given by Br'n Burwell and Everts. When Bro. W. was about taking it away to N. Y., Bro. B. told him he thought he would not be apt to keep it long, for undoubtedly he would soon have a chance to trade it for a stouter one; he also said he never expected to see it again. When Bro. W. and family were about to leave Vt., Sr. Burwell requested them to write all the particulars about their circumstances &c., which they agreed to do.

Bro. W. in a private letter, stated that since they had been in N. Y., his family had been obliged to eat bran bread; and that too, through the influence of James White; because he (Bro. Wyman,) had sympathy for those who rejected the visions; and that he should leave that place, if he had to sell his horse to get means to [illegible] the first door that opened; even if it were to go back to Vt., or to Panton.

Last May, at the conference at Barre, J. White stated that he had a copy of this letter, which was [illegible] (through stealth,) by J. N. Andrews, and sent to him; and accompanying the copy, an order from Br'n Burwell, Gardner and Everts, for the horse. He did not, however, read the order. He also stated that what Bro. W. had written about his family being so destitute was false; for Bro. Andrews had written to inquire about it, and the brethren at Clarkson said it was not so. Bro. Wyman told him he could prove his statements to be correct, for he had put his watch into the hands of the brethren to be sold, so as to get something to live upon; otherwise, he should have to go to the Poor House. Furthermore, Sr. Heath had told the brethren, his family was destitute of provisions of every kind. At this meeting, Bro. W. made an humble confession, yet J. White alone, withdrew the hand of fellowship from him, and then went right to Rochester and told some of the brethren he had made an humble confession, and was coming right along with them. Immediately after the conference at Rochester last June, Br'n Bates, Cottrell and Pond came to Brother Wyman with what they called an order from Br'n Burwell, Gardner and Everts for the horse.

They read it, but did not let him read it. After they read it, they told him they had withdrawn the hand of fellowship from him, and they were going to publish him in the *Review*. Bro. Wyman told them he did not choose to comply with the order, for he was not certain that it came from farther east than Rochester. The alleged order mentioned that if the horse was not in a salable condition, some of the brethren must take it and get it in salable order, and then sell it and give J. White the avails of it to use.

In order to get a better understanding of the matter, it seems necessary to go back and show some of the correspondence which took place between Bro. Wyman and others after he left Vt. I will begin with a letter from Sr. Burwell to Bro. W., dated Panton, Oct. 15th, 1853.

"DEAR BROTHER WYMAN:—It is with feelings such as I never before experienced, that I now attempt to answer your kind letter, which I received two weeks ago to night. I need not tell you we were glad to hear from you, and more especially to hear what the Lord had done for you in raising you to health, and preparing you to be one to sound the last note of warning the world will ever hear; and O, may the good Lord still work for you and give you health and strength to proclaim this last message with a *loud voice*. It seems as though the Lord had been fitting you up to bear the trials (if they may be so called,) you probably have been called to pass through before this time.—Think it not strange concerning what has taken place; you would not, did you know the cause perhaps. I think one great trouble was, some one heard that preparations were being made for your removal back to Panton. That they could not bear; now, what *shall* be done? At the Stowe meeting, they said something must be done. They voted in a Committee to write to you, just as they used to do at the old Baptist church meetings. But I will go no farther, for I could not describe it. The Lord forbid there ever should be another such a meeting of those who profess to believe in the third angel's message.

I suppose you have read an account of it in the paper; brother White did not get it far out of the way, in saying there was a great lack of the Spirit *there*. The meeting commenced Friday afternoon, no preaching till Sunday. The Spirit seemed to be lacking in the ministers as well as the people.* * Now Brother Wyman, what do you think of what has been done, and how do you feel about it? If you have done any thing worthy of death, I hope you will not refuse to die. If you have done *any thing* wrong, I hope the Lord will show it to you, and you will confess it. I think if we have a conscience void of offence toward God and man, we need not fear, though man may say all manner of evil against us. * * I will not attempt to give you a description of what has taken place since you were here. We have had trial upon trial, and sometimes feel as though we could not take another step. * * We were disappointed in hearing that you were not coming here. * * Dear Bro. Wyman, suffer me to give you a word of advice;—to be faithful; don't let any thing prevent you from doing your whole duty. The Lord wants faithful laborers in his vineyard, and I do believe he has called you to be one of them. * * You say you think of coming to Vermont; don't let any thing prevent your coming if you are able; we want to see you very much.

These extracts show that when Bro. W. left Vt., he had warm hearted friends, who believed the Lord had called him to preach, and who would have been glad to have him return to Vt. But *some one* did *not* want him to move back; and I think I shall not get it far out of the way was the one who had the strongest objections to his returning. He had influenced the br'n in N. Y. against him, and *now* he wanted to prohibit his returning to his former brethren. [illegible] as Sr. [illegible] says, they concluded "*Something must be done.*" Accordingly Ellen must have a vision, in which she pretended to see that Bro. Wyman "Dwelt too much upon exciting themes;" that "The influence he had left had been to have the flock look to their feelings and impressions, and think they could not have a meeting or blessing without shouting or a noise;" that he "Had dwelt too much upon the affairs of Europe and raised excitement." He had "Fed those who live on excitement too much;" had "Lacked judgment in traveling, had followed his impressions and feelings and *told others* the Lord showed him this, and that, the Lord guided him here and there, when it was only his *impressions* and *feelings* he had followed." He had "Traveled in many places and spent a great deal of means and effected nothing," his "Moving to Orangeport caused great trial to some there, and considerable expense." "And now after all the expense and trial you've caused in Orangeport and Norfolk, for you to be uneasy and dissatisfied with your situation and do as I saw you wished to do, and would do with any of the Br'n favoring it, move back to Vt., in Panton or in other places, would dishonor God, and wound his cause."

Here was where the "Shoe pinched," Sr. Burwell got it pretty straight when she said, "I think the trouble was, some one had heard that preparations were being made for your removal back to Panton. That they could not bear."

How easy for Ellen to frame a host of complaints against him, similar to that which lay so heavily upon their minds, and then wind up with *it*, and say it wo'd "Dishonor God," for him to "*Move back to Vt., in Panton.*" The next thing to look at, will be a letter of admonition, which was as Sr. Burwell says, 'Fixed up at that (the Stowe) meeting. I would be glad to give the whole letter, but I have only room for a few extracts. Some of the paragraphs are as follows. 'We must in brief, but in love and deep anxiety, state to you, that inasmuch as you have repeatedly been counseled, and even very strictly admonished, respecting your lack of judiciousness in your movements,' &c.

'We are informed that your injudicious course has been, and is a deep grief to our most candid humble brethren; they feel that the cause among the bands from such a course, suffers, and the manner of your ministry, in dwelling upon doctrines, although drawn from the Bible, (viz: the political aspects of Europe, &c.,) which are excitable, not so much to profit, as to feed and awaken curiosity, and divert and absorb the mind in that which does not that permanent good they are in famishing need of. * * * We beg and entreat of you dear Brother, to listen to the admonitions of your brethren, to refrain from useless extravagances (probably living on bran bread,) in the future, and also from wrong selections of subjects to present for food, to the famishing saints. * * We must remind you that before you embraced the present truth, griefs were preferred against your injudiciousness,' &c."

Here they had to go back to *before* he embraced the present truth, to pick up something against him. "As to the means or channels of our information, we would say it is not of an isolated way, but of a general, or too general report, till the Lord in mercy has repeatedly shown it to dear Sister White." "Barrows, Butler and Everts, Committee."

This admonition was dated Sept. 11th, 1853, but was not rec'd by Bro. Wyman until Feb. 1854. Sr. Burwell in a letter to him dated Jan. 29th, 1854, says, 'I beg of you dear Brother, to look up, to trust alone in that arm that is able to deliver. * * I have no doubt but that the Lord has called you to sound this last message of mercy to the world, and he does not want you bound down under the cruel power of the enemy, or by any other means. * * And now Bro Wyman. I feel as though it was your duty and privilege to go right out into the field, and labor for God. * * Have you never received the report that was fixed up at that (the Stowe) meeting for you? I do not understand it. If you have not received it, I think it is time there was something done about it. If those who prepared that report, concluded not to send it to you, is there not a confession due from them? I think there is; it is required of *one* to confess his faults as much as another. God is no respecter of persons. * * Brother Wyman, I entreat of you, not to let anything that has been done, or that man can do, deprive you from doing your duty. Paul says, I. Cor. iv, 3, with him it is a very small thing to be judged of man's judgment. * * I believe the time is near at hand, when God will bring to light the hidden things of darkness. * * Brother Gardner is confined to his room with a lame foot and ankle. About six weeks ago, he was drawing wood, and his foot got under the [illegible] Last night he called on Bro. Buck, Charles (Bro. Sperry) and the rest of the family to pray for him. The work was not done, although he thinks it has commenced to amend. I know if things were right here it might be done in one minute, as well as in six weeks' time.'

Bro. Wyman, in a letter to Bro. and Sr. Burwell dated Barre, July, 1854, says: "My health is good, and has been the most of the time since last fall, when God, for Christ's sake, forgave me all my sins, according to the promise of James v. 'And if he have committed sins, they shall be forgiven *him*.' When I called on the brethren to pray for me, and when the Lord raised me up, I knew it, and it was almost beyond the expectation of the brethren. God raised me up, then all my past sins were forgiven. If God did not forgive me my sins, why did he raise me up?" "You may have the impression that I do not believe in the third angel's message.' I never felt stronger in the present truth, than I do now. My heart is fixed, O God, my heart is fixed in thee." "I received a letter of admonition from those brethren that were appointed to address me, last February, although it was dated Sept. 11th. I felt thankful for the kind spirit by which it was written, and I was astonished when I read the letter. I was surprised not to find a charge that the 400 brethren (a statement that J. White made,) or that the committee had against me. Somebody had reported to the 400 brethren that I had traveled too extensively, and had spent too much means, in traveling, &c. Now, that went from Rochester to Vt., and from Vt. back to western New York. The address says that it is reports. Then reports say that I have '*Frequently*' been admonished.' If the report is true, then it must have been when I was asleep; for I do not remember but once when I was admonished, (is *once, frequently?*) then James White did it in a meeting, and did it in that way that grieved, or drove the spirit of God out of the house; and if it had not been on the Sabbath, it would have driven the brethren and sisters out, and would have driven them home. Some got started to leave as it was, and put on their coats to go. They said Bro. White had not the spirit of Christ. Then to wind up, '*Our dear Sr. White has repeatedly seen you in vision.*' When the address was written to me, I had no knowledge of her ever seeing me but twice, and in the *second* vision, she condemned me for what she justified me in the first vision. I have the visions with E. G's. name attached to them. Is *twice* '*Repeatedly*?' And last, former reproofs have not by me been regarded. How can I regard a reproof, until I know what the reproof is? Justify my course in one vision, and see that it was right for me to do so and so, then have another, and condemn me for doing so and so. Oh, what confusion. Then there came a report from Vt., that I have been circulating stories about Bro. White's window shades and carpets, &c. That also went from Rochester to Vt. That report is absolutely false; it is what others have done, and have felt grieved about, and what *others* have said, has been laid to me. When the brethren and sisters would tell me about those shades and carpets, I have told them again, and again, that I never took notice of what they had on the floor, or up to the windows. I have told James and Ellen that I never did. I challenge them or any other individual, to prove that I have reported such stories. It is false, and *absolutely* false. Such proceedings are enough to make angels weep, and devils blush. Why do they have to tell such stories? *Why* Ellen had a vision, and I had been murmuring against James, and the sin is counted greater than those that sinned or murmured against Moses and Aaron. E. G's. name attached to it. Thus we have our antitypical Moses; S. S. Snow, of New York city, is Elijah the Prophet, now we have Moses the Prophet. Moses led the first house of Israel, and James leads the second house of Israel. Oh, shame on such folly."—

On the 20th of Nov. 1853, a note of admonition to Bro. Wyman was written by Br'n Arnold, Orton and Lamson, from which I take the following extract:

"After the brethren had commenced this morning, there was a deep struggle in prayer, for the Lord to teach in this matter, and he heard the groans and saw the tears of his sighing ones, and gave Sister White a view of things, as he saw fit, which we herewith enclose. From this teaching of the Lord, you will discover that your course," &c. This vision then is all they relied on for evidence. Now let them talk about the visions not being a rule of action. See what this vision says, relative to Bro. Chapin.—"I saw that Bro. Chapin thought that he was capable of carrying the message, and thought that he was a messenger. Some of his brethren thought he was, but said the angel, 'God says he is not. He that does not see as man seeth, has not chosen [illegible]'

"I saw that the unjust surmisings and insinuations had more effect and influence, than to have talked out boldly. I saw that God had heard and marked it well, that Br'n Wyman and Chapin would meet again what they have said." "I was pointed back by the angel, to the murmurings of Aaron and Mariam. They said 'Hath the Lord spoken alone by Moses? Hath he not spoken also by us?' And the curse of God was upon them for it, and their sin was marked, although it was not half as great as the cruel work that has been going on by these brethren." "And it did not become those who have but recently embraced the third angel's message, to act the part of Bro. Wyman." I should have been very glad to have given the whole of this long *selfish vision*, but my space will not admit.

From the circumstances and correspondence I have here presented, it is plain to be seen that Bro Wyman left Vt., in good standing; and that through the jealousy of J. White, (Ellen's first vision about him plainly discloses it,) because he had sympathy for those who were disaffected toward the visions, and because he had success in preaching, where *he* (J. W.) had not, he has been hunted and tracked wherever he has went, until they have finally succeeded (as they supposed) in getting him out of their way; and to wind all up, after all their charges against him, they are dependant upon this *vain selfish vision* for evidence. And now, that he has come to Mich., James has taken a dark underhanded measure to injure him here. In the first place, if he has any thing substantial against Bro. Wyman, why not come out like an honest man and make his statements in the *Review*? Is he the servant of Christ?—Was Christ ever guilty of such intrigue as this?—See what he says; John xviii, 20, 'I spake openly to the world; * * In secret have I said nothing.' Again; why did he not give the date of the letter?—This itself ought to be sufficient to convince every person that is not a dupe, that it was thrown out as an underhanded insinuation that the order referred to in the 'Letter,' had been presented to Bro. Wyman, after he had received the 'Letter;' which in fact was not the case, for the letter was not received by Bro. Wyman until only a few days before he started for Mich., and the order was not bro't to him. And even if the order had been brought to him after he had received the letter, how much justice is there in requir-

1853

JUNE 23, N.P.

EXTRACTS FROM A NONEXTANT LETTER TO

Robert and Eunice Harmon.

Published in Ellen G. White, *Spiritual Gifts [vol. 2],* pp. 182, 183.

1853

(Lt 3, 1853)

JUNE 29, ROCHESTER, NEW YORK

LETTER TO

the Church in Jackson [Michigan].

Portions of this letter are published in Arthur L. White, *Ellen G. White: The Early Years,* p. 281.

An appeal to members and leaders in Jackson, Michigan, for wholehearted reformation in the face of serious problems and divisions in the band.

To the church in Jackson [Michigan]:

Dear Brethren and Sisters:

My mind has been exercised about writing this evening something to Jackson.

We arrived here at home safe last Tuesday[1] and found our family as well as usual, and what was best of all, enjoying the sweet presence and blessing of God. We had a sweet, melting time at our meeting Tuesday eve.

Dear Brethren and Sisters, I know that you have trials to pass through, and after what has recently occurred you may have a scene of trial to go through. But you must be decided, dear brethren, and God will help you.

---

[1] The Whites had recently come back from their first trip to Michigan, having left their home in Rochester, New York, on May 20 and returned on June 21, 1853.

I tried to write out the vision to the church in a careful manner, and get it before the brethren in its true light.[2] I hope none of the church will stop short of a thorough work.

God has taken hold of the work in Jackson and designs to let the brethren have a sight of themselves, that they may seek meekness, seek righteousness, that they may be hid when the fierce anger of the Lord shall come. In the fear of God I would say search, brethren, search, dig deep; get all the pestilent matter stirred up, and have it purged away that God may smile upon you in love and compassion again.

God has wrought for you in Jackson, and after what God has done to set the church right, any [who] doubt His work, or do not receive the teachings of God, who has "pled with you face to face" through the weak clay, I fear for them. God can do no more for them than He has done, and you must not have communion with them, but separate them from your company.[3] It is

---

[2] Ellen White here begins a discussion of the state of the Sabbatarian Adventists in Jackson, Michigan. Although she had received a vision relating to the Jackson band one year earlier (June 1852) the vision mentioned here is clearly of more recent origin. When the Whites visited Jackson a few weeks earlier, they had found the group deeply divided over accusations that **Abigail Palmer** had spoken offensively to a nonmember, with **Hiram Case** and **Charles Russell** being foremost among the accusers. According to one account, "these two men had succeeded in dividing the church so that they then held no public meetings." While there, on June 2, Ellen White was instructed in vision not only concerning the Palmer case but also about other problems within the Jackson band and with several of its leading members. The vision mentioned here is no doubt the June 2 vision as recorded in Ms 1, 1853.

See: Ellen G. White, Lt 2, 1852 (June 2); *idem,* Ms 1, 1853 (June 2); "The Advent Harbinger," *Review,* July 4, 1854, p. 173.

[3] Which members of the Jackson company were subsequently disfellowshipped or broke away? It is well known that Hiram Case and Charles Russell, both of whom were reproved in the June 2 vision, were disfellowshipped and subsequently formed the opposition *Messenger* Party. Russell apparently was excluded from fellowship within a matter of weeks, but for Hiram Case separation was a drawn-out process. For one thing, Ellen White made a special appeal to Case some weeks after the vision in this letter of June 29. "Dear Brother Case, make thorough work. Dig deep and confess from the bottom." For a while Case responded positively. In August he even made public confession in a letter to the *Review* editor. "I have done wrong in using the Lord's money as I should not. . . . I do deeply regret, and humbly ask the forgiveness of all my brethren and sisters." However, events subsequently took a turn for the worse, and on February 17, 1854, leading Michigan brethren decided that "we no longer consider him [Case] qualified to travel and teach the third angel's message." (According to J. B. Bezzo, that decision had already been made in Sylvan, Michigan, in January 1854, with fellowship being withdrawn from Case "a short time after.")

Apart from Case and Russell there were other casualties. The incident involving the alleged offensive language of Abigail Palmer continued to fester in the Jackson band even after Ellen White was shown in vision on June 2, 1853, that Mrs. Palmer did not use the epithet she was accused of using (see Ms 1, 1853). Savilla Case, 17-year-old daughter of Hiram Case, who had originated the accusation, at first acknowledged the truth of the vision but subsequently retracted her confession, insisting that the vision "was false" (see Morrill). What had begun in 1853 as a disagreement over church discipline soon developed into a full-scale division among the members over the authority of Ellen White's visions. The exact extent of the revolt in Jackson against the visions is not known, but several names (in addition to Case and Russell)

the only way you can live, and the only course you can take to wipe away the stain and reproach that has been brought upon the church in Jackson. Do not daub with untempered mortar[4] or heal the hurt of the daughter of My people slightly crying peace, peace, when there is no peace.[5]

Some have been in an awful state in Jackson and would have remained in that dreadful state had not the Lord taken hold of the work and shown them it was not peace, that they did not understand themselves and must die, die to self, and be Christians (Christlike) in every sense of the word; in malice, children, but in understanding, men. Do not let the enemy take advantage of you in Jackson, as some in other places have let him do. I went into Conn. [Connecticut], found them in a sad state. Their wrongs were shown in vision. Some received it, others rose up in rebellion and said they did not believe the vision. Their children were in a sad state but were much affected by the visions and would have got right but their parents stood in their way. The Lord took His Spirit from these parents and they went their own ways and were filled with their own doings. Weeks and months passed by, judgment after judgment followed them, until they repented, and deeply repented their slighting [of] God's teachings, and confessed heartily their wrongs and errors.

We believe that the Lord forgave them, but their children, their poor children, never could be reached afterwards. They cared nothing for God or His truth. Their parents had taught them the lesson of rebellion and how sure and true [they] had followed their example. Most of these children went on in sin and wickedness, and now some of them of more than two families have gone on in the depths of iniquity until some are excluded even from the family circle.[6]

Now, Brethren, look at these parents who heeded not the admonition of God for themselves and children. God wanted to save them and their children; they rejected the teachings of God, and while they were rejecting light from Heaven their children became hardened and lost, without God and without

---

are mentioned in the *Messenger of Truth,* including "Sr. Eliza Smith," "Sr. Knight," and "Sister Morrill." In nearby Sylvan, Michigan, 19 members in a joint letter to the *Messenger of Truth* declared that they had "no confidence in the visions of E. G. White" and were withdrawing from the fellowship of the Sylvan band.

See: "The Advent Harbinger," *Review,* July 4, 1854, p. 173; H. S. Case, "From Bro. Case," *Review,* Aug. 18, 1853, p. 64; "H. S. Case," *Review,* Apr. 18, 1854, p. 102; James White, "Western Tour," *Review,* May 23, 1854, p. 142; J. B. Bezzo, "H. S. Case," *Messenger of Truth,* Nov. 2, 1854, p. [4]; "Forgive One Another," *Messenger of Truth,* Oct. 19, 1854, pp. [1, 2]; J. Morrill, "From Sister Morrill," *Messenger of Truth,* Nov. 30, 1854, p. [4]; "Withdrawal of Fellowship," *Messenger of Truth,* Nov. 30, 1854, p. [4].

[4] An expression found in Ezekiel 13:10-16 that carries the connotation of whitewashing an unsound structure in order to make it appear sound.

[5] Words taken from Jeremiah 6:14 referring to religious leaders who glossed over the sins of the people, lulling them into a false sense of security.

[6] Which Connecticut families and children are referred to here has not been determined.

hope in the world. What kind of an account will those parents have to render to God for children committed to their trust? How will they feel in the time of trouble as they see their children withering beneath the plagues of God unmixed with mercy?

Now I beg of you in Jackson to act like Christians; take hold of the work of your children in earnest. What kind of an example has been set [for] the children in the late trials in Jackson? A tattling, faultfinding spirit has been encouraged in the children; also a hard, bitter spirit.[7] Parents, beware. You must render a strict account to God for the children committed to your trust. Oh, encourage in your children a kind courteous spirit. If they complain of a brother or sister, listen not to them but check it at once.

Again, I would say to our brethren, make straight work, be decided, have no fellowship with the unfruitful works of darkness. I hope thorough confessions will be made, and the church must not receive anything but thorough, heartfelt confessions.[8] Those who think so much of dear self that they cannot see their faults and confess them fully, God wants you to separate from them.

The Lord showed me in vision He was at work for the last time to settle things in Jackson, and those who rejected the light from Heaven and the means God had taken to set them right, He would leave to themselves; He had called upon them for the last time. They have been crooked, crooked, crooked, and yet exalted in their own eyes, thinking they were almost without fault, when they were wrong, in darkness and unbelief.

May God pity you in Jackson, for I fear for some they are so shut up in themselves and in darkness and the deception of the devil, that they will continue until Jesus leaves the sanctuary and they are weighed in the balance and found wanting. Brethren, if ever you moved decidedly in Jackson, move now, for the sake of the cause of God, for the sake of your precious children, move; have a thorough reformation in Jackson. All of you get as low as you possibly can, confess and confess until all the reproach is wiped away and you are a sweet, united band of brethren. I love you. I love you all, but I must clear my garments from the blood of souls. I shall meet in the judgment what I have told you that God has shown me, and then if I have daubed with untempered mortar, if I have clipped the truth, where will be my excuse?

---

[7] Although not mentioned by name, Savilla Case is no doubt referred to here in particular. She had brought the original report claiming to have heard Mrs. Palmer's insulting language, a claim that brought in its train bitter infighting among Jackson members.

[8] Besides the confession of Hiram Case mentioned above, **Samuel Rhodes** also published his confession, in the August 11, 1853, issue of the *Review*. A traveling preacher, Rhodes had had a harmful influence on the Jackson group that had been indicated in the June 2, 1853, vision. In his *Review* confession Rhodes regretted his "overbearing, oppressive spirit" and lack of humility, which had caused him to "wound the cause of the dear Lord and Saviour, which cause I most ardently love."

See: S. W. Rhodes, "Letter From Bro. Rhodes," *Review*, Aug. 11, 1853, p. 55.

Oh, brethren, if you all turn in less than a week to be my enemies, I still will lift up my voice and declare to you faithfully what God has shown me. I cannot, I dare not, hold my peace. The curse of God will rest upon me if I do.

Dear Brother Case [**Hiram S. Case**],[9] make thorough work. Dig deep and confess from the bottom and then the bars will be put up behind you and you will not be so likely to go astray again.[10] What shall I say more, dear friends? Make straight paths for your feet lest that which is lame be turned out of the way. Do be humble, be watchful, prayerful; in understanding, men, but in malice, children.

Look at the troubled, confused state you have been in and then acknowledge the teaching of God, which He has given to set you right. I have written this in great haste by lamp light. Excuse all mistakes.

In love, from your sister.

---

[9] *Identity:* Several letters and manuscripts from Ellen White written during the summer of 1853 refer to problems in the Jackson company in which "Brother Case" featured prominently. Having established "Brother Case" to be Hiram S. Case in the first of these documents (Ms 1, 1853 [June 2], note 6), we can assume that this is the same Case referred to in the others.

[10] *See:* Note 3 above for his reaction to this admonition.

1853

(Lt 4, 1853)

JUNE 30, ROCHESTER, NEW YORK

LETTER TO

Alfred B. and Adaline Pearsall.[1]

Previously unpublished.

In response to a query on parenting.

Dear Brother and Sister Pearsall:

We received your letter yesterday.[2] I hardly know how to answer it. Parents have a sacred duty to perform to their children, which many neglect, but they will yet mourn their sad neglect.[3] Great care should be taken by parents to study the disposition of their children, and it is also necessary to be very kind and affectionate to their children, and thereby gain their affections, and make them love you. It is not the wisest course to be very severe but it is always best to be decided and unyielding, and when we tell a child anything, never let them tease you out of it. Be very careful of this.

July 5, 1853

You see I commenced your letter some days ago but have not had time to

---

[1] It is safe to conclude that the addressees are Alfred B. Pearsall and his wife, Adaline, of Grand Rapids, Michigan. During the period 1852-1858 no other Pearsalls are mentioned in the *Review*.

See: 1850 U.S. Federal Census, "A. B. Pearsoll" [*sic*], Michigan, Kent County, Grand Rapids, p. 373. For full name "Alfred B. Pearsall" see 1880 U.S. Federal Census, "Alfred B. Pearsall," Michigan, Calhoun County, Battle Creek, p. 63; search term "Pearsall" in *Words of the Pioneers.*

[2] This letter is not in the White Estate archives.

[3] It is interesting to note that the *Review*, dated June 23, 1853, had carried an article by A. A. Dodge entitled "Admonition to Parents." Dodge's emphasis, in the manner of the times, centered on the liberal use of "the rod." The same draconian approach had characterized an article on the same topic by Elias Goodwin the previous year, in 1852. Ellen White's vision on this issue, briefly related here, provides a much more nuanced approach to child discipline, a corrective to the severity of Dodge and Goodwin.

See: A. A. Dodge, "Admonition to Parents," *Review,* June 23, 1853, pp. 21-23; Elias Goodwin, "Duty of Parents to Their Children," *Review,* Aug. 5, 1852, p. 53.

finish it. Last Sabbath I was taken off in vision and was shown many things,[4] some of which I have not [time] to write.

I saw something about the government of children, that parents were standing in the place of God to their children and that parents must be united in their efforts to save their children, and must take hold of the Word in good earnest and while they may be corrected for their faults, ever encourage their well-doing and pray with them and for them.

---

[4] Various parts of this vision of "last Sabbath" (July 2, 1853) are related in Lt 5, 1853 (July 5), Ms 3, 1853 (July 2), and Ms 4, 1853 (July 2). Ellen White writes that her original account of the vision of July 2 "covers 24 pages" (Lt 5, 1853 [July 5]).

1853

(Ms 3, 1853)

JULY 2, ROCHESTER, NEW YORK

Vision for Commandment Keepers.[1]

This manuscript is published in entirety in Ellen G. White, *Manuscript Releases,* vol. 5, pp. 424-426.

On the importance of personally testifying to the power of God; attending the meetings of those "in error"; the need for the Review *to be published more frequently; the dangers of attributing the power of the 1844 message to the devil.*

I saw that there was a great necessity of more energy being manifested by the commandment keepers in their meetings, and out of their meetings. I saw that all should have something to say for God, and by so doing they would be blest, for a book of remembrance is kept of those who do not forsake the assembling of themselves together.[2] The remnant are to overcome by the blood of the Lamb and the word of their testimony.

I saw that some expected to overcome alone by the blood of the Lamb, without making any special effort of their own. I saw that God had been merciful in giving us the power of speech. He has given us tongue and utterance; and we are accountable to Him for it, and we should glorify God with our mouths, speaking in favor of Him and His truth. We should overcome by the word of our testimony through the blood of the Lamb.

I saw that they did not come together to sit still, and look at each other. But those were remembered of God who came together to honor and glorify Him, to speak of His glory and talk of His power. Such ones would be remembered, and blessings from God would rest upon them and they would

---

[1] Three days later Ellen White gave more information about the extent of this vision. "Last Sabbath" [July 2] "I was taken off in vision and saw many things of great interest to us. I have scribbled off the vision. It covers 24 pages." Although the full 24-page account has not been preserved, this manuscript, as well as Ms 4, 1853, and Lt 5, 1853, relates parts of the vision. Six months later, in January 1854, selections from these letters and manuscripts were published in *Supplement to the Christian Experience and Views of Ellen G. White.*

See: Ellen G. White, Lt 5, 1853 (July 5); *idem, Supplement to the Christian Experience and Views of Ellen G. White,* pp. 14, 34, 35, 38, 45 (*Early Writings,* pp. 95, 96, 114, 115, 117, 118, 124, 125).

[2] Cf. Mal. 3:16: "Then they that feared the Lord spake often one to another: and the Lord hearkened, and heard it, and a book of remembrance was written before him for them that feared the Lord, and that thought upon his name."

be refreshed. If all moved as I saw they should, no precious time would run to waste. No reproofs would be needed, or called for, about long prayers and testimonies, for all the time would be occupied by short, sweet, testimonies and prayers that were to the point.

Ask, believe, and receive. There is too much mocking God, too much praying that is no praying and that wearies angels and that displeases God. Too many vain, unmeaning petitions.

First I saw that we were to feel needy, then ask God for the very things we need, and believe that He gives them to us, even while we ask. I then saw if we took this course our faith would grow, all would be edified, the weak would be made strong and encouraged, the discouraged and desponding made to look up and believe that God is a rewarder of all those who diligently seek Him.

I saw that the strong hand of the enemy is set against the work of God,[3] and the help and strength of everyone who loves the cause of truth should be enlisted and great interest manifested by them to uphold the hands of those who advocate the truth and to take a course to shut out the enemy and weaken his power. All should stand as one united in this work, every energy of the soul should be awake, for what is done should be done quickly.

I then saw the third angel. Said my accompanying angel, "Fearful is his word, awful is his mission. He is the angel that is to select the wheat from the tares, and seal or bind the wheat for the heavenly garner."[4] These things should engage the whole mind, the whole attention.

Again I was shown the necessity of those who believe we are having the last message of mercy being separate from those who are daily receiving or imbibing new error. I saw that neither young or old should attend the assemblies of those who are in error and darkness. Said the angel, "Let the mind cease to dwell on things of no profit."[5]

I saw that Satan and those who published error are very busy and energetic

---

[3] The "strong hand of the enemy" no doubt included the major opposition from mainstream Adventism that was being experienced by Sabbatarian Adventists at this time. A casual survey of the *Review* in the early 1850s reveals, for example, scores of references to anti-Sabbatarian articles in the *Advent Harbinger*, edited by Joseph Marsh.

See: Search term "Harbinger" in *Words of the Pioneers.*

[4] A similar passage published by Ellen White a few months later reads: "The third angel is binding them (sealing them) in bundles for the heavenly garner." The general thought here is that the Sabbath, or "sealing message," of the third angel will at some future time separate God's people from the disobedient, the wheat from the tares, with eternal consequences.

See: Ellen G. White, *Supplement to the Christian Experience and Views of Ellen G. White,* p. 7 (*Early Writings,* p. 89); EGWEnc, s.v. "Seal of God"; "Three Angels' Messages."

[5] Ellen White included this passage and elaborated on it a few months later in her *Supplement to the Christian Experience and Views of Ellen G. White.*

See: Ellen G. White, *Supplement to the Christian Experience and Views of Ellen G. White,* pp. 45, 46 (*Early Writings,* pp. 124, 125).

to get their views before the minds of others, and that it was not as it should be, that the only paper owned and approved of God should come out so seldom.[6] I saw that the last day signs should be brought out and shown clear, for the spiritual manifestations of the devil were on the increase.

I saw that all must be united and have their sympathies with the paper, and with those who have the burden and labor upon them. I saw the Lord would not have or suffer anyone to have charge of the paper unless He qualified them for the work and fitted them for the station. . . . [Ellipses in original.]

I saw that many who enjoyed the truth of the first and second angels' messages and felt the power and glory of the messages, have since rejected the light that came from heaven, called it of the devil,[7] and there was more hope of sinners than of such. Many who know nothing of the first two messages, saw not their effects and their glory, that have not hardened their hearts, will be brought to the light of truth. As they see one precious link of the chain, they could understand and see the whole chain and joyfully acknowledge the first and second messages. But those who have called the power of the Holy Ghost that attended these messages of the devil, and will not hear the third, are those who will be shut out.[8]

---

[6] The *Review* at this time was generally published semimonthly, but the idea of publishing it weekly had been discussed in its columns several times during the previous two years. No decision had been taken because of the financial implications and because, as R. F. Cottrell pointed out, there was the question of whether a sufficient number of quality articles would be submitted to sustain a weekly. It seems that the confirmation provided by this vision of July 2, 1853, caused James White, as editor, to decide to go weekly. A few days later, in the July 7, 1853, *Review* he declared: "we are fully satisfied that the time has come when it [the *Review*] should be issued [weekly]. . . .We shall probably be able to commence about the first of August, if our readers send the means to commence with."

See: "The Review Weekly," *Review,* July 7, 1853, p. 32. For examples of the discussion over having a weekly edition, see: "The Paper," *Review,* June 9, 1851, p. 104; "The Review and Herald," *Review,* Mar. 2, 1852, p. 104; R. F. Cottrell, "A Weekly Paper," *Review,* July 7, 1853, p. 29.

[7] Despite the great vitality and power that attended Millerite preaching of the first and second angels' messages in 1844, Millerite leader George Storrs shocked his colleagues when, within a few weeks of the disappointment of October 22, 1844, he denied that the power of the movement should be attributed to the Holy Spirit, ascribing it instead to "mere human influence, which I call Mesmerism." Others subsequently went further down this line of thought. According to James White, some "who took an active part in the seventh-month cry have since pronounced the movement the work of the Devil."

See: Geo. Storrs, "Confession," *The Midnight Cry,* Nov. 14, 1844, p. 157; [James White], "Brother Miller's Dream," *Present Truth,* May 1850, p. 74.

[8] *See:* Introductory article "The 'Shut Door' and Ellen White's Visions"; EGWEnc, s.v. "Shut Door."

1853
(Ms 4, 1853)

JULY 2, ROCHESTER, NEW YORK

Extract From a Vision Given at Rochester, July 2, 1853.[1]

Previously unpublished.

On public evangelism: benefits of working two and two; need to enter new areas.

I saw that it was now time for the brethren to move out wherever there was an opening and God would go before them and would open the hearts of some to hear. New places must be entered, and when new places are entered, it would be well to go two and two so as to hold up the hands of each other, whenever they can consistently and not neglect other places.[2] I saw that the brethren must not go over and over through the same field of labor, but must be hunting out souls in new places, setting the truth before those who are not now enlightened as to our present position.[3]

---

[1] According to her account written a few days later, it took Ellen White 24 pages to record the vision she received on Sabbath, July 2, 1853, of which this fragment is a small part. "Last Sabbath the power of God settled upon me. I was taken off in vision and saw many things of great interest to us. I have scribbled off the vision. It covers 24 pages" (Lt 5, 1853 [July 5]). Although the full account has not been preserved, this manuscript, in addition to Ms 3, 1853, and Lt 5, 1853, relates parts of the vision, also published some months later in *Supplement to the Christian Experience and Views of Ellen G. White.*

See: Ellen G. White, Lt 5, 1853 (July 5); Ms 3, 1853 (July 2); *idem, Supplement to the Christian Experience and Views of Ellen G. White,* pp. 22, 23 (*Early Writings,* p. 104).

[2] The practice of ministers going out two by two in public evangelism was sometimes followed before this time, but with the beginnings of tent evangelism the following summer (1854) it seemed to become the rule that it should not be a solo effort but involve two or more ministers. From the 1880s and onward Ellen White frequently urged those engaging in public evangelism, including colporteurs, to work in teams of two, with the motivation given that this was the method of Christ. "Calling the twelve about Him, Jesus bade them go out two and two. . . . None were sent forth alone. . . . In our own time evangelistic work would be far more successful if this example were more closely followed" (*The Desire of Ages,* p. 350).

See: Search terms "tent meeting," "tent meetings," in *Words of the Pioneers;* Ellen G. White, *The Desire of Ages,* p. 350. For extracts from Ellen G. White's writings recommending team evangelism, see section "Advantages of Two and Two," in Ellen G. White, *Evangelism,* pp. 72-74.

[3] A conspicuous example of following this instruction can be seen in the shift of focus of evangelism from East to West starting in the mid-1850s. James White expressed the principle behind this shift in 1857: "We have labored in the East and in the West, and speak the things we know. And no consideration whatever, excepting a sense of positive duty, could induce us at

288 DEWEY'S ROCHESTER

Whidden, John N. student, University, b. 49 High
Whipple, Daniel S. boiler maker, h. 70 Joiner
Whipple, Amisella Mrs. h. Hickory
Whipple, Ralph Mrs. b. 93 S. Fitzhugh
Whitaker, John, joiner, h. 43 Asylum
Whitbeck, Jacob, physician, 121 North
Whitbeck, John F. physician & surgeon, office and h. N. St. Paul
Whitbeck, Orrin, teamster, b. 88 Exchange
Whitbeck, Orrin L. teamster, b. 8 Summit Park
Whitbeck, Silas E. teamster, b. 8 Summit Park
Whitbeck, Volkert, clerk, 120 State, b. Frank cor. Brown
Whitbeck, Wm. Farmer, h. 8 Summit Park
Whitcker, Hiram Rev. h. 19 Jones
White, Amos, shoe cutter, 114 Buffalo, h. 40 High
White, A. A. clairvoyant physician, 262 State
White, Benedict, pottery and h. German
White, Charles W. shoemaker, h. 241 Exchange
White, David, boarding house, 122 Main
White, Edward F. clerk, Holmes' forwarding house, b. 24 Kent
White, Edward, shoemaker, b. Centre Hotel
White, Francis, clerk, 53 Main, b. 1 Atwater
White, Francis E. clerk, Main, b. North American Hotel
White, George, app. 8 Exchange, b. 29 Adams
White, Henry E. attorney, 32 Smith's Arcade
White, Hiram C. h. 13 South
White, James, h. 109 Monroe
White, James, laborer, h. Grape cor. Campbell
White, James, carriage maker, h. 49 Adams
White, James, laborer, h. rear 13 Monroe
White, John, h. Prospect cor. Clifton
White, John, machinist, S. Water, h. Monroe
White, John, carman, b. 1 Mortimer
White, John W. printer, Advertiser office, h. 18 Greig
White, Ficholas, soap maker, h. Wilder n. Grape
White, Peter, porter, Eagle Hotel, h. Vincent Park n. River
White, S. George, jeweller, 8 Exchange, b. 29 Adams
White, Seth, blacksmith, b. 10 Delavan
White, William, laborer, b. Furnace
White, William, wagon maker, 87 Main
White, William A. brakeman, B. & R. R. R. b. 100 State
White, Colvin Mary, boarding house, 109 State
White, Jane, domestic, Commercial Hotel
Whitehair, Sovreign, color maker, Weddle's factory, h. Summer Alley
Whitehead, Robert W. wine & liquor dealer, 92 State, h. 30 Platt
Whitehouse, John, music teacher, h. Jefferson
Whitehouse, Thomas, painter, 176 State, h. 5 Ambrose
Whiting, John H. piano forte tuner, b. 12 Mill
Whiting, Samuel, whitewasher, h. 7½ Adams
Whiting, William, book keeper, Kremlin Saloon, Exchange

Rochester, New York, City Directory (1853-1854), listing James White's home address on Monroe Street. Courtesy of the Reynolds Library, Rochester, New York.

---

present to labor on the gospel-hardened shores of New England, while so much can be done in the wide West."

See: [James White], "Moving West," *Review,* May 7, 1857, p. 5.

1853

(Lt 5, 1853)

JULY 5, ROCHESTER, NEW YORK

LETTER TO

Abram A. and Caroline Dodge.[1]

Portions of this letter are published in Arthur L. White, *Ellen G. White: The Early Years*, p. 282.

An appeal for decisive reform in the Jackson, Michigan, company, especially in the area of financial stewardship.

Dear Brother and Sister Dodge:

I have but a few moments to write, so must be brief. We are prospering in the Lord and are of good courage. For a time after we arrived here James's health was very poor,[2] his lungs were much affected, but we had some powerful seasons of prayer for him and the Lord in mercy has drawn near and condescended to answer our petitions. He is much better than he has been, and is of good courage.

Last Sabbath the power of God settled upon me. I was taken off in vision and saw many things of great interest to us. I have scribbled off the vision. It covers 24 pages,[3] many things were explained to us which we did not understand and which were necessary for us to know. I saw that we must have the truth got out oftener—that the only paper in the land owned and

---

[1] *Identity:* Until 1856 the only persons surnamed "Dodge" in the *Review* were Abram A. Dodge with his wife, Caroline Dodge, of Jackson, Michigan; and H. W. Dodge, of Stoddard, New Hampshire. There is clear evidence in this letter that Ellen White is addressing Abram and Caroline Dodge, since she speaks plainly of "you in Jackson" and mentions other persons from the Jackson company by name.

See: Search term "Dodge" in *Words of the Pioneers.*

[2] The Whites had returned two weeks earlier, on June 21, from a one-month tour of Michigan, their first visit to that state. According to Ellen's account in *Spiritual Gifts,* on their return James "was troubled with aching head and cold feet. He could sleep but little."

See: James White, [Notice], *Review,* June 23, 1853, p. 24; Ellen G. White, *Spiritual Gifts [vol. 2],* p. 183.

[3] Although the full 24-page account of the July 2 vision has not been preserved, this letter, and also Manuscripts 3 and 4, 1853, relate parts of the vision. Six months later, in January 1854, these parts were included in *Supplement to the Christian Experience and Views of Ellen G. White.*

See: Ellen G. White, Ms 3, 1853 (July 2); Ms 4, 1853 (July 2); *idem, Supplement to the Christian Experience and Views of Ellen G. White,* pp. 14, 22, 23, 35, 38, 45 (*Early Writings,* pp. 95, 96, 114, 115, 117, 118, 124, 125).

approved of God should come out oftener than once in two weeks, while papers that are full of error come out weekly and some oftener than that.[4] I saw that the way was opening for us to extend our labors. I saw something about things west.

I saw that there has been a cruel denying of the power of God by some in Jackson [Michigan]. The course of Brother Russell [**Charles P. Russell**][5] and a few connected with him is very dark, and if he pursues such a course still he must be cut off from the fellowship of the saints. He has had such a good opinion of himself that it looks impossible that God should show that he was wrong; and he has been closing his eyes to himself and doubting what God has shown concerning him. He is deceived and is suffering himself to be deceived, and I greatly fear will be given up to his own ways to be filled with his own doings.[6]

Dear Brn., you must move united and shoulder to shoulder if you would have the error and mismoves, which have eaten in the church like the canker, removed and a healthy influence exerted in the church. I saw that God had taken hold to assist you in Jackson[7] and now you must take hold and help

---

[4] The idea of publishing the *Review* weekly rather than twice monthly had been raised in its columns several times during the previous two years and had been generally well received. No decision had been taken because of the financial implications and, as R. F. Cottrell pointed out, there was the question of whether sufficient quality articles would be submitted to sustain a weekly. It seems that the confirmation provided by this July 2 vision caused James White, as editor, to decide to go weekly. A few days later, in the July 7, 1853, *Review,* James White declared: "we are fully satisfied that the time has come when it [the *Review*] should be issued [weekly]. . . . We shall probably be able to commence about the first of August, if our readers send the means to commence with."

See: "The Review Weekly," *Review,* July 7, 1853, p. 32. For examples of the discussion over having a weekly edition, see: "The Paper," *Review,* June 9, 1851, p. 104; "The Review and Herald," *Review,* Mar. 2, 1852, p. 104; R. F. Cottrell, "A Weekly Paper," *Review,* July 7, 1853, p. 29.

[5] *Identity:* The indications given here of a "Brother Russell" who is implicated in the problems at Jackson and who faces possible disfellowshipping leave little doubt that Charles P. Russell is being referred to. According to early sources, C. P. Russell was disfellowshipped some weeks later.

See: "The Advent Harbinger," *Review,* July 4, 1854, p. 173; A. N. Seymour, "The Shut Door Sabbatarians," *Advent Harbinger,* June 3, 1854, p. 395.

[6] Ellen White had alluded to problems with Charles P. Russell, one of the leading members of the Jackson group, already one year earlier (Lt 2, 1852 [June 2]). By June 1853 Russell was deeply involved in an imbroglio involving Abigail Palmer in which he showed great severity. A vision given Ellen White June 2, 1853, rebuked Russell for his harshness, a rebuke that he refused to accept. The worsening situation led some weeks later to his separation from the Sabbatarian Adventists.

See: EGWEnc, s.v. "*Messenger* Party"; Ellen G. White, Lt 2, 1852 (June 2); Ms 1, 1853 (June 2). For a survey of the Palmer case, see Arthur L. White, *Ellen G. White: The Early Years,* pp. 276, 277; also J. N. Loughborough, *Rise and Progress of the Seventh-day Adventists,* pp. 188-190.

[7] Probably a reference to the reproofs and appeals to the Jackson band contained in Ellen White's visions of May 1852 (Lt 2, 1852 [June 2]) and June 1853 (Ms 1, 1853 [June 2]).

yourselves in the fear of God and work diligently to wipe away the reproach that has been brought upon the cause by the unwise moves of some. Those who are on the Lord's side will be with you and those on the side of Baal and confusion will be against you. God is sifting you with a sieve and if there is any among you that rebel, God will separate him from you that you may move on. I saw that things in Jackson had not been held up in their wrong light. Oh, no, but if Brn. in Jackson could see these things as God sees them and could see how His frown has been upon Jackson for these wrongs, they would ever feel a grateful thankfulness to God that He had not taken His Spirit utterly from them and left them in darkness and error. I mean those who have been in the wrong who have brought sorrow and mental anguish on all the church. I saw that it had been the work of the enemy through false teaching to cause the Brn. to be in haste to dispose of their means, and not leaving them free to act, leaving them for God to teach, to direct, and guide by the operation of the Spirit upon the heart when they shall sell, and how much, and when to give and how much.[8]

The messengers, some of them, have taken this burden upon themselves when they had no authority for so doing. Instead of those who have means looking to their Brn. for direction, they must look to God, for they are His stewards and God knows just how much means will be wanted and when. But men know not and Satan has worked to help the means away from the true object, and when the time has come when publishments must come out more frequently, there are means that have been wasted[9] which will be needed, and the lack is felt. God's ways are not as our ways, nor His thoughts as our thoughts. Those who have means often have been made to feel that they were stewards of men instead of stewards of God, and have looked to men for light and teaching instead of God. These evil, I saw, must be remedied.

But I must be in haste. We have not forgotten your kindness to us. We

---

These visions pointed out weaknesses and internal dissension in the group, as well as problems relating to its leaders.

[8] The question of the propriety of Jackson members' selling their property to support traveling preachers had become an important concern by 1853, and was central to Ellen White's vision of June 2, 1853. As early as 1849 Ellen White had reproved **Joseph Bates** for advising members to sell their property immediately, even at a loss, to support the work. In the June 2 vision a prominent preacher, **Samuel W. Rhodes**, was admonished for giving similar extreme counsel. "Wrong impressions were given [by Rhodes] concerning the brethren's property, as though it was a burden to them, and they must get it off their hands as soon as possible."

See: Ms 14, 1850 (Sept.), note 5; Ellen G. White, Ms 1, 1853 (June 2).

[9] While not mentioning specific names here, the June 2 vision, one month earlier, had in particular reproved a leading Jackson member and traveling preacher for wasteful spending. **Hiram Case** had "lived extravagantly, in his travels laid out money here and there . . . [saying] to others and in his own heart, to himself, there is means enough in Jackson, more than can be used up before Jesus comes." Waste of that kind would make it more difficult to meet pressing financial needs such as financing a weekly edition of the *Review* (i.e., the "publishments").

See: Ellen G. White, Ms 1, 1853 (June 2).

remember the kindness of Bro. Smith's[10] family with gratitude; thank them for me. Brother Dodge, I remember your kind attentions and the interest you manifested for us.[11] You all seem very near to me. Give my love to each member of the family and to the Brn. and sisters. Tell them to be faithful, and have no communion with the unfaithful works of darkness.

Bro. Dodge, look up, be of good cheer, the Lord is our God. We shall be overcomers in a little while.

E. G. White

[Variant copy of vision:]

I saw that it had been the work of the enemy through false teachings to cause brethren to be in haste to dispose of their means, and not leaving them free to act, not leaving them for God to teach, direct, and guide by the operations of His Spirit upon the heart, when they shall sell, and how much, and when to give and how much. The messengers, some of them, have taken this upon themselves when they had no authority for so doing. Instead of those having means looking to their brethren for direction, they must look to God, for they are His stewards and God knows just how much means will be wanted, when and where; but men know not, and the enemy has worked to keep the means away from the true object. And when the time has come that the work of God is to be more extensive, when publications, tracts, and papers must come out more frequently, means that have been wasted and carelessly disposed of will be needed, and the lack will be felt. God could rain down money from heaven, but it is not His plan. Everything is arranged here

---

[10] *Identity:* The difficulty in identifying "Bro. Smith's family" of Jackson lies in the fact that several different Smiths from that vicinity and during that period are mentioned in printed sources. Apart from the well-known Cyrenius Smith family (including his wife, Louisa, and son William) there are references to "E. Smith," "L. Smith," and "Eliza Smith" in Jackson. Ellen White mentions a Smith family in Jackson in four letters written between July and December 1853 in a way that suggests that in all four she is referring to the same family. The only hint as to its full identity is found in the December letter. "Tell Sister C. Smith I thank her for her present. Much love to her and all that family." This may well be a reference to Sister Cyrenius Smith and gives some reason for identifying "Bro. Smith" here as **Cyrenius Smith**.

See: A. N. Seymour, "The Shut Door Sabbatarians," *Advent Harbinger*, June 3, 1854, p. 395; [C. P. Russell], "Forgive One Another," *Messenger of Truth,* Oct. 19, 1854, pp. [1, 2]; search terms "Smith," and "Jackson" in *Words of the Pioneers;* Ellen G. White, Lt 6, 1853 (Aug. 3); Lt 7, 1853 (Aug. 24); Lt 9, 1853 (Dec. 5).

[11] No doubt Ellen White is here referring to her recent visit, with James to Michigan and to Jackson in particular, where they would have met the Dodge family. James White later wrote appreciatively of "Bro. A. A. Dodge, who kindly took us from place to place" during their travels in Michigan.

See: "Western Tour," *Review,* July 7, 1853, p. 28.

on earth so as to move like clockwork in the cause of God, and when this is thrown out of order the cause must suffer in consequence. And the one who has caused the jargon[12] must suffer loss, if he enters the kingdom of God. I saw that God's ways are not our ways, nor His thoughts as our thoughts. Those who have means often have been made to feel that they were stewards of men instead of stewards of God, and have looked to men for light and teaching instead of God. These evils I saw must be remedied.

Cyrenius Smith and his wife, Louisa. Courtesy of the Center for Adventist Research.

[12] "Jargon" used here perhaps in the sense of "confusion."

1853

(Ms 5, 1853)

JULY, N.P.

Extract From a Vision Regarding James White.

Previously unpublished.

James White's depression, summer 1853.

I saw that James [**James Springer White**] has been sinking since he returned home. He looked on the dark side too much, looked at appearances too much, and did not trust so fully in God as he should.[1] I saw that God's ways are not as our ways, that He works in a mysterious way His wonders to perform; that although James was worn from his journey, yet God had upheld him on the journey, and he was better when he returned than when he went to Michigan,[2] and had he remained at home his health would have sunk beneath sickness, and now at the present time he would have been more feeble than he now is. I saw that he must have faith and look up. I saw that the Lord had raised him up help so that he could have a change of mental labor, and talk the truth.[3] I saw that trials caused by some affected James's courage and health, and he had looked at it as though the Lord had dealt hard with him, when He was dealing in mercy and compassion.

---

[1] The setting of this manuscript fragment is the weeks following the Whites' return from their first journey to Michigan on June 21, 1853. James White's "sinking" feelings and tendency to look on "the dark side" led him to write some uncharacteristically self-pitying lines to "Brother Abraham" on July 31: "This moment most of my whole frame is in pain—worn out—while others go in ease, free from care. . . . I sometimes fear I shall murmur and be lost. Oh, that God would work, I will be reconciled. . . . If I die, don't weep for me but for those whose course has worn me out."

See: James White to Abram Dodge, July 31, 1853.

[2] For a poignant account by Ellen White of James's precarious state of health at the start of their trip to Michigan, see *Spiritual Gifts [vol. 2],* pp. 179, 180.

[3] By the summer of 1853 the Review publishing house employed a staff of 15. The most recent recruit had been **Uriah Smith**, who had joined the staff some weeks earlier on May 3, 1853, and who would rise to the position of resident editor before the end of 1855. His sister, Annie R. Smith, had joined the staff already in 1851. "She is just the help we need," wrote Ellen White. "She takes right hold with James and helps him much. We can leave her now to get off the papers and can go out more among the flock."

See: Eugene F. Durand, *Yours in the Blessed Hope, Uriah Smith,* p. 24; J. N. Loughborough, *The Great Second Advent Movement*, p. 320; Ellen G. White, Lt 8, 1851 (Nov. 12).

1853

(Lt 6, 1853)

AUGUST 3, ROCHESTER, NEW YORK

LETTER TO

Abram A. and Caroline Dodge.[1]

Portions of this letter are published in Ellen G. White, *Manuscript Releases,* vol. 7, p. 351.

A letter containing family news and encouragement to friends in Jackson, Michigan, where the believers face a difficult church disciplinary situation.

Dear Brother and Sister Dodge:

We received your kind letter[2] and were glad you wrote to us so particular as you did. I should have answered it before but have not had time. I have now written 26 pages since Sabbath. It is now Wednesday morning. I have quite a number of letters yet to write this week.[3]

We are all quite well in body, and free in mind. James's health has been poor but we are holding on to the arm of God for him. Will you not make him a special subject of prayer? God will hear you pray. I believe He has answered our prayers in a measure; but James must realize more of the divine blessing or he will not stay with us long to carry forward the work of God. Don't forget his case.[4] My health is quite good. We have some most blessed seasons around the family altar. God does manifest Himself unto us. Praise His blessed name.

---

[1] *Identity:* Until 1856 the only persons surnamed "Dodge" in the *Review* were Abram A. Dodge with his wife, Caroline Dodge, of Jackson, Michigan; and H. W. Dodge, of Stoddard, New Hampshire. There are several clear indications that Ellen White is here addressing Abram and Caroline from Jackson. Most specific is the report of church disciplinary action in relation to "Brother Case" and "Brother Russell." Both of these names are linked to the Abigail Palmer crisis in the Jackson band in June 1853. In addition, Ellen White asks the Dodges to greet Palmer and Smith, both well-known surnames among the Jackson members.

See: Search term "Dodge" in *Words of the Pioneers;* J. N. Loughborough, "Some Individual Experience," in *The Great Second Advent Movement,* 1992 reprint ed., pp. 558, 559; Brian E. Strayer, "Early Advent Waymarks in Jackson, Michigan: Parts I & II," p. 4.

[2] This letter is not in the White Estate archives. It is likely that it was in reply to a letter from Ellen White written one month earlier, on July 5, 1853 (Lt 5, 1853).

[3] None of which have been preserved.

[4] James White, writing a few days earlier, also to Abram Dodge, is more explicit: "My difficulties are in my back between my shoulders, shoulder blades, breast, and lungs, and very nervous."

See: James White to Abram Dodge, July 31, 1853.

I had a vision a few weeks ago which I will try to send to you if I can possibly get time to write it before I go East. I will send it to Brother Palmer [**Dan R. Palmer**][5] if I do.

I am sorry to hear some have to be disfellowshipped for not moving with the church. I am sorry for them, and sincerely pity them. May the Lord save them from ruin.[6] Poor Brother Case [**Hiram S. Case**],[7] and poor Brother Drew [**Hiram Drew**].[8] I hardly know who to sympathize with the most. You must watch over Brother Drew; don't let him be deceived as to Brother Case's true state. But be careful of one thing: do not be cast down yourselves. Remember, you must not sink down if you would have any influence over others. You must keep free, believe in God, and act out your faith. Pray much to God and He will strengthen you.

---

[5] *Identity:* The Jackson, Michigan, setting of this letter suggests that Ellen White is referring to Dan R. Palmer. There is frequent mention in the *Review,* from 1851 onward, of a "D. R. Palmer," of Jackson, with no mention of any other "Brother Palmer" in Jackson.

See: Search term "Palmer" in *Words of the Pioneers.*

[6] Of the three persons mentioned in this paragraph and the one following, Charles Russell was probably disfellowshipped late summer 1853 and Hiram Case sometime before May 1854. Hiram Drew was disfellowshipped sometime during the winter of 1853/1854.

There were several problematic aspects to Case and Russell's relation to the Sabbatarian Adventists. But the precipitating factor that subsequently led to their expulsion seems to have been their concerted and public campaign against the visions after they were reproved in a vision in June 1853 for their severity against Mrs. Palmer. Russell later claimed that he was disfellowshipped "because I do not believe the visions," and his supporters, such as A. N. Seymour, alleged that "the Sabbatarians made the visions of Ellen White a test of fellowship." Yet the records suggest that Case and Russell did much more than simply disbelieve the visions; they launched a divisive campaign against the visions and against the leadership of James White. A *Review* editorial later maintained that "the vision [of June 1853] was not made a test of fellowship. These men were disfellowshipped on account of their unchristian conduct."

See: "The Advent Harbinger," *Review,* July 4, 1854, p. 173; A. N. Seymour, "The Shut Door Sabbatarians," *Advent Harbinger,* June 3, 1854, p. 395; J. N. Loughborough, *Rise and Progress of the Seventh-day Adventists,* pp. 188-190; J. B. Bezzo, "Test of Fellowship," *Messenger of Truth,* Oct. 19, 1854, pp. [2, 3]. For the views of those who defended Case, Russell, and Drew against all charges made against them, see J. B. Bezzo, "Test of Fellowship," *Messenger of Truth,* Oct. 19, 1854, pp. [2, 3]; *idem,* "H. S. Case," *Messenger of Truth,* Nov. 2, 1854, pp. [2-4]; A. N. Seymour, "The Shut Door Sabbatarians," *Advent Harbinger,* June 3, 1854, p. 395.

[7] *Identity:* The Jackson setting and church disciplinary context leave no doubt that Hiram S. Case is being referred to. He was finally disfellowshipped sometime between January and May 1854.

See: James White, "Western Tour," *Review,* May 23, 1854, p. 142. For further details, see Lt 3, 1853 (June 29), note 3.

[8] *Identity:* Clues to the identity of "Brother Drew" are found in the remark about his being disfellowshipped, in the way his name is coupled with those of Case and Russell, and in his location in the Jackson area. All three specifications fit well with Hiram Drew, a Sabbatarian Adventist from Jackson County who was disfellowshipped from the band in Sylvan, Michigan (15 miles [24 kilometers] from Jackson), some months later. Drew subsequently joined Case and Russell in the breakaway *Messenger* Party.

See: EGWEnc, s.v. "*Messenger* Party"; J. B. Bezzo, "Test of Fellowship," *Messenger of Truth,* Oct. 19, 1854, pp. [2, 3].

I have scarcely any hopes of Brother Russell [**Charles P. Russell**].[9] He has stood out against light and has had such an unbounded good opinion of himself. I fear he will never get a look into his own heart; he is completely blinded as to his situation. But I would say to the church, be free, move carefully, trusting wholly in God. We have not forgotten you, but often think of you and your kindness to us. We should be very glad to see you again.[10] Much love to Brother and Sister Palmer; hope they will go forward with courage and energy. Tell them to be faithful. I meant to have written them before now; but this is as busy a house as you ever saw. We have meetings here on the Sabbath, and there is so much folding to do, and stitching, sewing, &c. it keeps us every moment employed.[11] But we are pleasantly situated away from the bustle and confusion in the midst of the city; a yard around the house for Edson to run in, and some fruit trees. But our fruit is almost an entire failure. We shall not have over 20 peaches, and apples but very few, no apricots; a few quinces and grapes we shall have; but we are disappointed as to fruit. But we thank the Lord for what He has blessed us with; we will not complain. If faithful we shall soon eat of the fruit of the tree of life and drink of its healing waters.

I love you all; my heart is united with yours. Be of good courage and endure toil and trial a little longer and we shall see the King in His beauty. Much love to Brother Smith's[12] family. We love them and want to see them; tell

---

[9] *Identity:* As with H. S. Case (note 7 above), the Jackson setting and church disciplinary context clearly indicate that Charles P. Russell is the person referred to. Early records seem to indicate that Russell was disfellowshipped sometime during the summer of 1853 (see note 6 above).

[10] Ellen and James White had paid their first visit to the Jackson members two months earlier, June 2-5, 1853.

[11] The Whites, together with the *Review* staff, had moved to a large house on Mount Hope Road on the outskirts of Rochester, New York, in April 1852, which served as living quarters as well as printing office. Some months later office space for printing the *Review* was rented downtown, but this letter suggests that certain tasks such as folding, stitching, and sewing were still carried out at the house.

For circumstances leading to the move to Rochester, see Arthur L. White, *Ellen G. White: The Early Years,* pp. 229-231.

[12] *Identity:* The difficulty in identifying "Bro. Smith's family," of Jackson, lies in the fact that several different Smiths from that vicinity and during that period are mentioned in printed sources. Apart from the well-known Cyrenius Smith family (including his wife, Louisa, and son William) there are references to "E. Smith," "L. Smith," and "Eliza Smith" in Jackson. Ellen White mentions a Smith family in Jackson in four letters written between July and December 1853 in a way that suggests that in all four she is referring to the same family. The only hint as to its full identity is found in the December letter. "Tell Sister C. Smith I thank her for her present. Much love to her and all that family." This may well be a reference to Sister Cyrenius Smith and gives some reason for identifying "Bro. Smith" here as Cyrenius Smith.

See: A. N. Seymour, "The Shut Door Sabbatarians," *Advent Harbinger,* June 3, 1854, p. 395; "Forgive One Another," *Messenger of Truth,* Oct. 19, 1854, pp. [1, 2]; search terms "Smith" and "Jackson" in *Words of the Pioneers;* Ellen G. White, Lt 6, 1853 (Aug. 3); Lt 7, 1853 (Aug. 24); Lt 9, 1853 (Dec. 5).

them to write us, we want to hear from them often. We have been expecting a letter from Brother Rhodes [**Samuel W. Rhodes**][13] for some time, have received none as yet since the conference. How it will turn with him I cannot tell. Perhaps he will receive it, and it may be he will sink down beneath it.[14]

Pray for us.

In love.

---

[13] No doubt Samuel W. Rhodes. No other Rhodes is found in the *Review* in the early 1850s. *See:* Search term "Rhodes" in *Words of the Pioneers.*

[14] In a vision given two months earlier, on June 2, Samuel W. Rhodes's "overbearing spirit" and severity had been pointed out together with the harmful effect this had had on the congregations he visited. In addition he was reproved for his extreme teaching that members with lands and houses should sell as soon as possible in order to support the young movement. It seems that in these closing lines Ellen White is wondering how Rhodes had reacted to this testimony of reproof. Would he "receive it" positively, or would he, like Case and Russell, "sink down" and reject the testimony? James White, writing a few days earlier, on July 31, also to the Dodges, hoped that "Brother Rhodes will make straight work confessing. . . . He has only admitted the vision to me." The August 11 issue of the *Review* did in fact carry a public confession from Rhodes. "I see some things . . . which call for a confession on my part, which indeed is humiliating but shall be freely and frankly made. . . . I have not at all times possessed enough of the mind of Christ and have been left to a hurried, overbearing, oppressive spirit, and to deal out rebukes sometimes that were not dictated by the Spirit of the Lord." Some months later (Dec. 28) James wrote that "Brother Rhodes . . . is trying to get right."

See: Ellen G. White, Ms 1, 1853 (June 2); James White to Abram Dodge, July 31, 1853; S. W. Rhodes, "Letter From Bro. Rhodes," *Review,* Aug. 11, 1853, p. 55; James White to Abram Dodge, Dec. 28, 1853.

1853

AUGUST, ROCHESTER, NEW YORK

"Dear Brethren and Sisters."

Article published in *The Advent Review, and Sabbath Herald,* vol. 4, no. 7, August 11, 1853, p. 53.

1853

(Lt 7, 1853)

AUGUST 24, ROCHESTER, NEW YORK

LETTER TO

Cyrenius and Louisa Smith.[1]

Portions of this letter are published in Arthur L. White, *Ellen G. White: The Early Years,* p. 282.

Family news to friends in Jackson, Michigan.

Dear Brother and Sister Smith:

We received the box of things Monday; it came all safe. Thank you for your kindness and generosity. The carpet is very nice, almost too nice to lay down

---

[1] *Identity:* Even though the letter reveals that "Brother and Sister Smith" live in the Jackson, Michigan, area, it is still difficult to identify them since there are several Smiths from that vicinity during that period as mentioned in printed sources. Apart from the well-known Cyrenius Smith family (including his wife, Louisa, and son William), there are references to "E. Smith," "L. Smith," and "Eliza Smith" in Jackson. Ellen White mentions a Smith family in Jackson in four letters written between July and December 1853 in a way that suggests that in all four she is referring to the same family. The only hint as to their full identity is found in the December letter. "Tell Sister C. Smith I thank her for her present. Much love to her and all that family." This may well be a reference to Sister Cyrenius Smith and gives some reason for identifying "Bro. Smith" here as Cyrenius Smith. The notes that follow will proceed on the assumption that Cyrenius and Louisa Smith are the addressees.

See: A. N. Seymour, "The Shut Door Sabbatarians," *Advent Harbinger,* June 3, 1854, p. 395; [C. P. Russell,] "Forgive One Another," *Messenger of Truth,* Oct. 19, 1854, pp. [1, 2]; search terms "Smith" and "Jackson" in *Words of the Pioneers;* Ellen G. White, Lt 6, 1853 (Aug. 3); Lt 7, 1853 (Aug. 24); Lt 9, 1853 (Dec. 5).

upon the floor of a chamber. Thank you for the labor you have bestowed upon the carpet, skirt, and gloves. Accept our united thanks for your remembrance of us. Tell little Sis,[2] Eddy [**James Edson White,** aged 4] likes his walnuts very much.[3] Thank Sister Palmer [**Abigail Palmer**][4] and Sister Dickinson [**Celesta B. Dickinson**][5] for their remembrance of me.

We felt very sorry to hear of Brother Palmer's [**Dan R. Palmer**][6] illness. I hope he is much better. May the Lord spare him to help on His cause and glorify His name.

James [**James Springer White**] has had some discouraged feelings of late, is much better now body and soul.[7] Luman [**Luman V. Masten**][8] is coughing again; his lungs are affected, but the Lord is our physician; we shall hold on to His almighty arm. His labors are much needed in the office. He has overdone often. Stephen Belden [**Stephen T. Belden**] and Fletcher Byington [**John Fletcher Byington**] do not return from the office until 10, 12, 2 or 3 o'clock. They have labored uncommonly hard of late, and God has strengthened them,

---

[2] This person has not been identified.

[3] According to J. N. Loughborough, Cyrenius Smith, of Jackson, had earlier demonstrated his generosity in selling his farm to aid "in the prosecution of the work of the message." Adventist historian Brian Strayer has noted the exceptional generosity of the Jackson members. The carpet mentioned here would have been a welcome addition to the large but sparsely furnished house in which not only the Whites lived but also some of the *Review* staff. Ellen White recounts that in all "our family numbered from fifteen to twenty" during the Rochester period.

See: J. N. Loughborough, *The Great Second Advent Movement,* p. 285; Brian E. Strayer, "Early Advent Waymarks in Jackson, Michigan: Parts I & II"; Ellen G. White, *Spiritual Gifts [vol. 2],* pp. 191, 160, 161.

[4] *Identity:* The only Palmer of Jackson, Michigan, mentioned in the *Review* during the 1850s is Dan R. Palmer. His wife's name was Abigail.

See: Search term "Palmer" in *Words of the Pioneers;* 1860 U.S. Federal Census, "Dan R. Palmer," Michigan, Jackson County, Jackson, Ward 4, p. 134.

[5] *Identity:* Although there were a number of Dickinsons mentioned in the *Reviews* of the 1850s, the only one associated with Jackson, Michigan, was Preston Dickinson, whose wife's name was Celesta B.

See: Search term "Dickinson and Jackson" in *Words of the Pioneers;* obituary: "Celesta B. Dickinson," *Review,* July 20, 1869, p. 31.

[6] *Identity:* See on "Sister Palmer" in note 4.

[7] For descriptions of James White's health problems during the summer of 1853, see Ellen G. White, *Spiritual Gifts [vol. 2],* pp. 183, 184; Lt 6, 1853 (Aug. 3); Ms 5, 1853 (July); James White to Abram Dodge, July 31, 1853.

[8] *Identity:* Luman is here connected with "the office" and mentioned together with Stephen Belden and Fletcher Byington, who also assisted in publishing the *Review.* There is reason for identifying Luman with a "Bro. L. V. Masten," who is mentioned in the paper as being "foreman" of the printing operation and who "died of Consumption, in this city [Rochester], . . . March 1st, 1854 . . . aged about 25 years." His full name is never given in the *Review,* but years later Ellen White wrote "we buried Luman, foreman of the office, with consumption." The references to his coughing and his lungs in this letter confirm this identification.

See: "The Pamphlet," *Review,* Oct. 14, 1852, p. 91; obituary: "Bro. L. V. Masten," *Review,* Mar. 14, 1854, p. 63; Ellen G. White, Lt 95, 1886 (Feb. 16).

or they must have broken down. The Lord blessed us abundantly last Tuesday eve; our hearts were made glad and to rejoice in God. Praise His holy name.

We start on our journey East in one week from today.[9] I can write but little, as I have much to do. The paper comes off today. My little Edson's health is much better than it has been. We feel determined to have unshaken confidence in God. Our hearts cry out after the living God. My soul is not satisfied. I long to see the King in His beauty and be made like Him.

Dear friends, how thankful we should be that we have a hope in God, that our treasure is on high. We will praise Him, we will honor Him, for He is high and lifted up and greatly to be praised.

Please to remember me to all that I am acquainted with. I love them in Jackson [Michigan].[10] Much love to your dear family. Thank Sister Caroline for writing and Sister Dickinson. James thanks you for what you have sent. May the Lord reward you is our prayer.

I am not quite as well as usual; am filling with water; have bloated more or less since I returned from Michigan.[11] My trust is in God. He will strengthen me, and rebuke disease. I have written some of my vision and directed it to Brother Palmer.[12] You will have seen it, I think, before this reaches you. The gloves and skirt fit well.

From your unworthy sister.

---

[9] A two-month journey from which the Whites returned in early November 1853.
See: James White, "Note to Brother Waggoner," *Review,* Nov. 8, 1853, p. 144.

[10] Ellen and James White had visited the believers in Jackson three months earlier at the beginning of June 1853. It was the Whites' first visit to Michigan.
See: "Western Tour," *Review,* June 23, 1853, p. 21.

[11] The Whites had returned to Rochester, New York, on June 21, 1853.
See: James White, [Notice], *Review,* June 23, 1853, p. 24.

[12] This letter is not in the White Estate archives.

1853

(Lt 11, 1853)

DECEMBER 3, N.P.

LETTER TO

Brother Pierce.[1]

Portions of this letter are published in Arthur L. White, *Ellen G. White: The Early Years,* p. 404.

Multiple issues: unauthorized preachers; overcautious preachers; use of medicinal herbs; tobacco; defining "faith of Jesus"; prayer for the sick.

Dear Brother Pierce:

I have tried to write the vision that I had at Stowe [Vermont],[2] but have been very feeble, and after I wrote the vision[3] found my nerves were so weak I could not answer your questions. By writing too steadily and getting very weary, and then taking cold, I have been suffering for nearly a week with nervous toothache and ague in the face. My pain increased every day until I was unable to do anything. My sufferings were great. Last night at family prayer we took hold of the arm of God and carried my case to the great Physician and pleaded and wrestled with Him until He applied the balm and my aching head was relieved and my tired nerves were quieted, and we had a rejoicing time. All were abundantly blessed and triumphed in God.[4]

---

[1] *Identity:* Although this letter provides no firm information to determine which "Brother Pierce," out of several possibilities, is being addressed, its references to events and personalities associated with the State of Vermont suggest the name of **Stephen Pierce**, of Roxbury, Vermont.

See: Search term "Pierce" in *Words of the Pioneers.*

[2] Ellen and James White had attended a conference in Stowe, Vermont, three months earlier at the beginning of September 1853. J. N. Loughborough cites witness testimony that Ellen White received a vision on this occasion.

See: James White, "Appointments," *Review,* Aug. 11, 1853, p. 56; *idem,* "Eastern Tour," *Review,* Oct. 4, 1853, p. 104; J. N. Loughborough, *The Great Second Advent Movement,* p. 207.

[3] This account of the 1853 Stowe vision has not been located in the writings of Ellen White. Our only certain knowledge of the contents of the vision is found in the short abstracts in this letter.

[4] More severe illness, however, followed Ellen White during the winter and spring of 1853/1854. "For months [I] have been unable to do anything," she wrote in April 1854, citing "constant pain in my heart for months" and a swelling on an eyelid that had obliged her "to give up writing entirely for a time."

See: Ellen G. White, *Spiritual Gifts [vol. 2],* pp. 184-188; *idem,* Lt 2, 1854 (Apr. 11).

But this is not answering your letter. First you inquire, "What so dreadful is among Sabbathkeepers?" Will not the vision answer this question? I think it will. God's people coming right up to the judgment not ready, unprepared, and not setting a good example but standing in the way of sinners; and God showed me that there was something dreadful in this as well as other things that the vision points out.

About some being too fast and some too slow, I saw that some have run into the field to labor before they were sent, and traveled extensively.[5] I might mention individual cases. Brother Lothrop [**Howard Lothrop**][6] is one that was shown me. His influence has been bad in many places. He has thought too much of himself, when he had but little judgment.[7] Towle [**John R. Towle**] and Eastman [Ezra Eastman][8] were others whom God had never sent, and who were only a curse to the cause. Others were shown me

---

[5] The problem of "self-sent" unauthorized preachers who lacked the skills, knowledge, or moral qualities needed to represent the movement properly is mentioned frequently during these early years. James White echoed the sentiments of this passage in a series of articles the same month entitled "Gospel Order." "He who enters upon the work of the gospel ministry must be called of God, a man of experience."

See: "Gospel Order," *Review,* Dec. 13, 1853, p. 180. For a detailed study of steps taken to license ministers and wider aspects of church organization, see Andrew Gordon Mustard, *James White and SDA Organization.*

[6] *Identity:* The only Lothrop mentioned in the *Review* from this period who is identified as a preacher is Howard Lothrop, of Eaton, Canada East. In 1852 and 1853 Lothrop reported in letters to the *Review* of his preaching itineraries, the most extensive of which took him from Canada through Vermont and Massachusetts to Rhode Island and back to Canada in the winter of 1851-1852.

See: Howard Lothrop, "From Bro. Lothrop," *Review,* Mar. 2, 1852, p. 102; search term "Lothrop" in *Words of the Pioneers.*owH.

[7] One year earlier, in October 1852, Ellen White had written of Howard Lothrop that he "had traveled too extensively and was too self-sufficient. . . . Repeatedly Brother Lothrop would get up and talk until he would talk the Spirit all away from the meeting." Lothrop subsequently broke away from the Sabbatarian Adventists and, according to James White, "went in full fury with the *Messenger* spirits against us and the *Review.*"

See: Ellen G. White, Lt 4, 1852 (Oct. 25); James White, "Organization," *Review,* Aug. 27, 1861, p. 100.

[8] *Identity:* "Towle and Eastman," of whom we are told that they were preachers "whom God had never sent," are no doubt the J. R. Towle and Ezra Eastman, who had been upbraided some weeks earlier at a conference in Vermont. "The brethren felt it their duty," it was reported in the *Review*, "to express their opinion relative to Ezra Eastman and J. R. Towle, who profess to observe the Sabbath, and teach the present truth. . . . All were agreed . . . that they do not consider them proper persons to teach the present truth." This is the only mention of "Ezra Eastman" in the *Review* during the 1850s. Nothing is known for certain about him other than what is found in this notice. However, more clues as to J. R. Towle's full identity are available. Of particular significance is Towle's mention in the *Review* that his father-in-law's name was Joseph Brooks and the fact that several of his letters were written from Canaan, New Hampshire. Genealogical sources chronicle the marriage of "J. R. Towle" to "Mary M. Brooks" in Canaan, New Hampshire, in 1834, and amplify "J. R." to "John R."

See: James White, "Appointments," *Review,* Oct. 25, 1853, p. 128; "Eastern Tour," *Review*, Nov. 15, 1853, pp. 148, 149; search term "Towle" in *Words of the Pioneers.*

who felt in a hurry to go out and talk the truth to others who had not yet learned it themselves.

Every individual case I saw is not now clear to my mind. But I saw that Brethren Baker [**Joseph Baker**],[9] Everts [**Elon Everts**], and Butler [**Ezra Pitt Butler**][10] were too cautious, moved too slowly. There was not that kind, courteous feeling cherished by some of the brethren that there ought to be. There is too much severity used when it is not timely or when the mind is not prepared for it. Some reprove unwisely and others are too backward, and let things go on that God is displeased with, and not rebuke or reprove them. I did see that Brother Hart[11] had pressed the abstinence of herbs in case of sickness too far. I saw that it was right to use herbs that are beneficial for the use of man, but the poisonous herbs—tobacco, etc.—it was not right to use, because it was injuring and breaking down the constitution, weakening the system, ruining the nerves, and clogging and destroying the mind and reasoning powers which God has given us to serve Him with, that with the mind we may serve the law of God and adore and honor our Creator. I saw that others had erred in the same way, but the particular individuals I did not see or cannot recollect of seeing.[12]

Again you inquire what the faith of Jesus is. I have seen that the brethren and sisters have not understood the faith of Jesus in its true light. They have taught that it is healing the sick, etc. It is not healing the sick, merely, but it is *all* the teachings of Jesus in the New Testament.[13] "The commandments of

---

[9] *Identity:* The context indicates that Baker, Everts, and Butler were preachers. The only Baker in the early 1850s identified as a preacher is Joseph Baker, of Lebanon, New Hampshire. The additional information given that he has been "too cautious, moved too slowly" is confirmed in available sources. Although an active preacher in 1851 and 1852, by 1853 little is reported of his activities. By October 1853 James White expressed regret that "our dear Bro. Baker has been in the field but little." After 1854 Baker dropped out of the workforce.

See: James White, "Eastern Tour," *Review,* Oct. 4, 1853, p. 104; search term "Baker" in *Words of the Pioneers.*

[10] *Identity:* In the early 1850s the only persons named Everts and Butler and identified as preachers in the *Review* were Elon Everts, of Vergennes, Vermont, and E. P. Butler, of Waterbury, Vermont.

See: Search terms "Everts" and "Butler" in *Words of the Pioneers.*

[11] *Identity:* Insufficient information is available to determine which of several possible Harts is referred to here.

[12] In addition to "Brother Hart" Ellen White might have mentioned **Luman Masten**, who had taken a similarly uncompromising stand two months earlier in a letter to the *Review.* Speaking of medicinal "roots and herbs" Masten exclaimed, "Let such as have no faith use them!" The more moderate approach to herbal remedies indicated in this vision of December 1853 had apparently been the practice of the Whites all along. In 1848, for example, they "had used simple herbs" when their baby Henry was sick, although "they had no effect."

See: Ellen G. White, *Spiritual Gifts [vol. 2],* p. 104. For an earlier statement by Ellen White against the use of tobacco, see Lt 5, 1851 (Dec. 14). Her earliest vision concerning tobacco was given in 1848, according to James White ("Western Tour," *Review,* Nov. 8, 1870, p. 165).

[13] The discussion here concerns the interpretation of the expression "the faith of Jesus" appearing in the message of the third angel in Revelation 14:12: "Here is the patience of the

God and the faith of Jesus." I saw that it was the whole New Testament which relates to Jesus.

It is impossible for me to write out all that I have seen about the elders of the church in reference to visions. I know not that I have anything special about it.

You inquire if we should pray for none that are sick except those in the third angel's message, or pray for all that shall make application, etc. James 5[:14, 15] is our rule to follow. "Is any sick *among you*? Let them call," etc. It is those that are among us. God has shown me those who keep God's commandments [are] to have nothing to do in praying for the sick of those who are daily trampling them underfoot, unless it is in some special case where souls are convicted of the truth and are decided to move out upon it. The partition wall between commandment keepers and those who trample them underfoot should be kept up.[14]

Your next question: The elders referred to in James [5:14] are not merely those who have been ordained, but aged persons, those also who have experience and judgment in the things of God—those whose lives are circumspect and who . . . [Remainder missing.]

---

saints: here are they that keep the commandments of God, and the faith of Jesus." As Gerard Damsteegt has outlined it in his study of early Seventh-day Adventist theological development, there were varying understandings of "the faith of Jesus" in the 1850s, including the idea mentioned here that it refers to the healing of the sick.

See: P. Gerard Damsteegt, *Foundations of the Seventh-day Adventist Message and Mission,* p. 194.

[14] Throughout her writings Ellen White appeals to the principles found in James 5:14-16 when praying for the sick. Prayer for healing is not to be undertaken lightly or indiscriminately but in the context of faith, confession of sin, and the sincere purpose of the sick person to live in accordance with the will of God. The will of God encompasses both the moral law and the laws of health. Prayer will not benefit the one who is *willfully* transgressing God's commandments. Ellen White draws out this distinction in her response to Pierce's inquiry. That this does not mean that prayers for healing should be undertaken only for Seventh-day Adventist members is clearly illustrated elsewhere in Ellen White's personal example and teaching. See, for example, the encouragement she gives to nurses and doctors at Seventh-day Adventist medical institutions to pray with, and give spiritual counsel to, patients not of that faith or even of any faith, again within the guidelines given in James 5.

For a fuller discussion of these principles by Ellen White, see *Counsels on Health,* pp. 373, 374, *Medical Ministry,* pp. 246-248, *The Ministry of Healing,* pp. 144, 145, 225-233, and *Prayer,* pp. 225-237.

1853

(Lt 9, 1853)

DECEMBER 5, ROCHESTER, NEW YORK

LETTER TO

Sister Kellogg.[1]

Portions of this letter are published in Ellen G. White, *Early Writings,* pp. 115-117; *idem, Manuscript Releases,* vol. 5, pp. 205, 240, 241; vol. 6, pp. 22, 23.

A vision regarding the rite of foot washing, together with encouragement for members to testify publicly in meeting of God's goodness. Personal news.

Dear Sister Kellogg:

We received your very kind letter in due time,[2] and designed answering it before, but have been quite sick. Took cold in my face and head, and suffered much with the teethache, and ague in my face. I tried to continue my writing which weakened my nerves, and it seemed at times I should be distracted. I suffered for about one week, nothing seemed to give me relief. Last Thursday eve, the family bore my case to the great Physician and I tried to have faith for myself and was immediately healed. The glory of the Lord shone about us, and we all rejoiced and triumphed in God for His unbounded goodness to us. All in the room were blest and shouted the praise of God.

Dear Sister, I have much that I might write you, but have so much to write to different individuals. But I will give you a sketch of the vision I had at our last conference.[3]

At our last conference I was shown in vision the backwardness of some in our meetings. Some held back because they had nothing new to say and

---

[1] *Identity:* There are a number of Kelloggs mentioned in the *Review* of the 1850s, but few indications in this letter to decide which one is being addressed here. The greetings to "Sister C. Smith" at the end probably places "Sister Kellogg" in Jackson, Michigan, where Cyrenius Smith and two Kellogg families resided in December 1853. There is no clue in this letter, however, to whether "Sister Kellogg" was wife of Leander Kellogg or of **John Preston Kellogg**, both living in Jackson.

See: Search terms "Kellogg," "Jackson," and "Smith" in *Words of the Pioneers.*

[2] This letter is not in the White Estate archives.

[3] The most recent conference attended by the Whites, according to *Review* records, was in New Haven, Vermont, October 28-29, 1853, near the end of their 10-week eastern itinerary.

See: "Conference at Rochester," *Review,* July 7, 1853, p. 32; [James White], "Eastern Tour," *Review,* Nov. 15, 1853, p. 148.

must repeat the same story. I saw that pride was at the bottom of this. That God and angels witnessed the testimonies that were borne and God was well pleased and glorified by the testimonies of all His humble children. I saw that God and His angels admired simplicity and humility.

I saw that God had been displeased and angels grieved that heirs of God and joint heirs with Jesus, should suffer precious time to run to waste while the saints sit still, saying nothing in favor of God and the truth. I saw that if the brethren and sisters were in the place they had ought to be in, they would not be at a loss to find something to say in honor of Jesus who hung upon Calvary's cross for their sins. If they would cherish more of a realizing sense of the condescension of God in giving His only beloved Son to die a sacrifice for our sins and transgressions, and the sufferings and anguish of Jesus to make a way of escape for guilty man, that he might receive pardon and live, they would be more ready to magnify and extol Jesus. They could not hold their peace, but with thankfulness and gratitude would talk of His glory and tell of His power, and blessings from God would rest upon them for so doing. Even if the same story was repeated, God was glorified by it. The angel of God showed me *those* who rest not day nor night crying Holy, Holy, Lord God Almighty. Continual repetition, said the angel, yet God is glorified by it. And although we tell the same story over and over it honors God, and shows that we are [not] unmindful of Him, or His goodness and mercies to us.

I saw the nominal churches[4] had fallen, coldness and death reigned in their midst. God gave them His word to humble them, if they had followed His teachings. But they got above the work, it was too humbling for them to repeat the same simple story, when they met together. They tried to get something new and great, and studied how they could please men, and have their words exact to their ear, and God's Spirit left them, for instead of praying and talking to God, they prayed and talked to man.

I saw that when we followed in the humble way, we should have the movings of the Spirit of God, and there would be no jargon.[5] All would be in sweet harmony and we should not be in danger, if we followed the humble channel of truth depending wholly upon God, of the evil angels taking possession of us and affecting us at all. It is when we get above the Spirit of God, moving in our own strength, that the angels of God cease watching over us, and we are left to the buffetings of Satan.

---

[4] The term "nominal churches" was often used by early Adventist writers to describe the Protestant and Roman Catholic churches that had experienced a moral fall through their rejection of the message of an imminent Second Coming.

See: P. Gerard Damsteegt, *Foundations of the Seventh-day Adventist Message and Mission,* pp. 179-192.

[5] "Jargon" used here perhaps in the sense of "confusion."

I saw that duties were laid upon us in God's Word to be performed to keep us humble and separate from the world, and from backsliding like the nominal churches. Washing feet and the Lord's supper should be more frequently practiced by us.[6] Jesus set us the example and told us to do as He had done to us. I saw that the example of Christ should be as exactly followed as possible. Yet brethren and sisters have not always moved as judiciously as they should in washing feet, and confusion has been caused. I saw that the messengers of God must be careful how they introduce this duty. I saw that no example was given us in God's Word for the brethren to wash the sisters' feet, but there was an example of the sisters washing their brethren's feet.[7] Mary washed the Saviour's feet with her tears and wiped them with the hairs

---

[6] For the transition from a sporadic observance of the ordinances in the 1840s and 1850s toward a quarterly observance in the 1860s and beyond, see Roger H. Ferris, "The Ordinances of Foot-Washing and the Lord's Supper in the Seventh-day Adventist Denomination," pp. 28, 29, 42, 46.

[7] Should this passage on intergender foot washing be taken as implying that it was common practice among Sabbatarian Adventists in the early 1850s for men to wash the feet of women and vice versa? Does the passage constitute instruction radically curtailing such practices? There are only a handful of reports in the *Review*, during this period, of the foot-washing ceremony being observed, and none of them describe how it was carried out. It seems unlikely, however, that mixed gender washing, particularly men washing the feet of women, was a common feature. Such a practice was considered scandalous and had raised a hue and cry in both the secular and religious press during 1845-1846, when some Millerite factions had adopted "promiscuous" (i.e., mixed) foot washing. It seems more than likely that if mixed gender washing had been a common feature of Sabbatarian Adventism in the early 1850s it would have been highlighted by critics of the movement. Although no comprehensive study has been done of early critics of the Sabbatarian Adventists, random reading of this literature has not uncovered accusations of such practice.

An alternative interpretation of this passage is that Ellen White is primarily addressing those who argued that foot washing per se was an unbiblical practice. According to one such argument, as set out here by B. Mathewson in 1858, "in Christ Jesus 'there is neither *male* nor *female*. . . .Where is one example where Christ ever separated the sexes for worship or the performance of an ordinance?" Hence, he argues, "there can be no impropriety for the sexes to engage . . . promiscuously . . . in the ordinance of the Lord's supper." And yet, as "all must see," such a mixed service "would have an appearance of evil" and "be a great source of scandal to the church." The inescapable conclusion is that Christ never intended foot washing as a general ordinance. To this kind of argument James White responded some years later, in 1859: "We reply that confining ourselves strictly to the example set us in the sacred record involves no breach of propriety. We have the examples of females washing the feet of males, but not vice versa." James White's counterargument clearly echoed the position found in this 1853 letter by Ellen White.

For a history of the ordinance of foot washing among Seventh-day Adventists, see Roger H. Ferris, "The Ordinances of Foot Washing and the Lord's Supper in the Seventh-day Adventist Denomination." For examples of contemporary critics of foot washing as an ordinance, see B. Mathewson, "Some Reasons for Not Practicing Feet Washing as a Religious Ordinance," *The World's Crisis,* Sept. 8, 1858, p. 4; L. H. Chase, "Feet-Washing," *Advent Harbinger,* Sept. 24, 1853, pp. 114, 115. James White's response to Mathewson is found in "Feet-Washing," *Review,* Feb. 24, 1859, p. 108. For reactions to mixed gender foot washing in 1845-1846, see George R. Knight, *Millennial Fever,* pp. 251, 252, and David Tallmadge Arthur, "'Come Out of Babylon,'" pp. 116-119; EGWEnc, s.v. "Lord's Supper."

of her head. Also the widow who is mentioned. If she have lodged strangers, if she have washed the saints' feet. I saw that God had moved upon the sisters to wash the brethren's feet and it was according to the gospel order and would glorify God when He laid this cross upon them and it would humble the one that performed it. All, I saw, should move in this thing understandingly and not make the washing of feet a tedious ceremony.

Dear Sister, it is almost dark [and] I can write but a few words more. Hope you and your dear children are prospering in the Lord. Tell them to live humble, close to the bleeding side of Jesus; tell them to pray much and subdue all pride and selfishness and live wholly for God. Much love to them and your husband and self. We received your donation, thank you for it. Will try to use it to the glory of God. Husband did not know but that the money might be credited to the paper; did not know but some like Brother Case [**Hiram S. Case**][8] might say that money had been sent in that had been made no account of. I did not know as all understood that any present sent to me was not credited in the paper. How do you understand it? Tell Sister C. Smith[9] I thank her for her present. Much love to her and all that family; also all the brethren and sisters. Pray for us. We are quite well except Luman [**Luman V. Masten**].[10] We are believing for him.

E. G. White

Tell the brethren and sisters to write us and for the *Instructor*. That little

---

[8] *Identity:* The concern expressed here that "Brother Case" might accuse the Whites of misappropriation of funds is a clear indication that Hiram S. Case is referred to. Hiram Case, cofounder of the *Messenger* Party, had earlier accused James White of speculation in connection with the selling of Bibles in Michigan.

See: James White, "Western Tour," *Review,* May 23, 1854, p. 142; EGWEnc, s.v. "Messenger Party." For a view of the speculation charges from the point of view of a *Messenger* Party member, see J. B. Bezzo, "H. S. Case," *Messenger of Truth,* Nov. 2, 1854, pp. [2-4]. For further *Messenger* Party allegations that James White was misappropriating donations for the *Review,* see C. P. Russell, "From Bro. Russell," *Messenger of Truth,* Nov. 2, 1854, p. [2]. This letter provoked a robust response from J. N. Andrews, R. F. Cottrell, and U. Smith in "Malicious Insinuation," *Review,* Nov. 21, 1854, p. 117.

[9] *Identity:* See note 1. The name of **Cyrenius Smith**'s wife was Louisa.

See: Obituary: "Louisa Smith," *Review,* Jan. 10, 1882, p. 30.

[10] *Identity:* No doubt the same Luman of whom Ellen White wrote some three months earlier that he "is coughing again; his lungs are affected." She added that Luman worked in the *Review* office. Years later, writing of the Rochester, New York, period, she recalled that "we buried Luman, foreman of the office, with consumption." Doubtless Ellen White was here referring to "L. V. Masten" (as he was always referred to in the *Review*), foreman of the printing operation, who died of consumption a few months later, on March 1, 1854, "aged about 25 years."

See: Ellen G. White, Lt 7, 1853 (Aug. 24); Lt 95, 1886 (Feb. 16); obituary: "Bro. L. V. Masten," *Review,* Mar. 14, 1854, p. 63; "The Pamphlet," *Review,* Oct. 14, 1852, p. 91.

paper will come out soon if the friends send in matter. Tell all to be interested and write for the *Instructor* if they want it.[11] Write us often.

In love.

[11] Launched in August 1852 as a monthly paper for children and youth, the *Youth's Instructor* seems to have been faltering at the time of this letter, with no issue published since August 1853. This might explain the plea for articles to be submitted.

See: SDAE, s.v. *"The Youth's Instructor."*

1853

DECEMBER 16, ROCHESTER, NEW YORK

"Exhortation to the Young."

Article published in *The Youth's Instructor,* vol. 2, no. 1, January 1854, pp. 5, 6.

1854

JANUARY

PUBLICATION OF

Supplement to the Christian Experience and Views of Ellen G. White, Rochester, N.Y.

Published by James White. 48 pp.

1854

(Ms 1, 1854)

FEBRUARY 12, BROOKFIELD, NEW YORK

Reproof for Adultery and Neglect of Children.

Portions of this manuscript are published in Ellen G. White, *Child Guidance,* p. 540; *idem, Manuscript Releases,* vol. 1, pp. 33, 34; vol. 6, pp. 217-219; vol. 7, p. 1; Arthur L. White, *Ellen G. White: The Early Years,* pp. 290-292. See Ms 3, 1854 (Feb. 12), for a parallel account.

Reproof for adultery and neglect of children in Caughdenoy and Roosevelt, New York.

I saw the situation of many in our meeting at Oswego [New York].[1] They were in the way of the work of God, especially at [Caughdenoy, New York].[2] God's frown[3] was upon them, and some at [Roosevelt, New York]. The ax has not been laid at the root of the tree. Those who have indulged in the wicked passions of the heart have been fellowshipped. If God had made Brother [Ross][4] [**Alexander Ross**][5] overseer of the flock, he would have seen the corruption of the people. The ax has not been laid at the root of the tree. God will not look upon sin now any sooner than He did anciently when Israel sinned. Sins have not been held forth in their sinful character, but have been made to appear as though sins have been lightly regarded by God.

I saw the seventh commandment had been broken by some who are now held in fellowship by the church; and in consequence God's frown is upon the church. This sin is awful in these last days, and the church has brought God's frown and curse upon them by regarding this sin so lightly. I saw that it was an enormous sin, and that there have not been as vigilant efforts made as there should have been, to satisfy the displeasure of God and remove His frown, by taking a straightforward course with the offender. An awfully corrupting influence has been shed over the young. The young see how lightly this sin is regarded, and those committing this horrid sin, on confessing they have done wrong and are sorry, are restored to all the privileges of the house of God, and held in the embrace and full fellowship of the church, hence it has been thought a small sin to break the seventh commandment.

This course has removed the ark of God from the camp.[6] If there were no other sin to remove the ark from the camp, this would be sufficient to do it. Those who commit this sin should be suspended from the church and

---

[1] The Whites had held meetings in Oswego the previous weekend, February 4-5, as part of a two-week New York tour that also included Brookfield and Lincklaen.

See: "Appointments," *Review,* Jan. 31, 1854, p. 16; "The Meetings," *Review,* Mar. 14, 1854, p. 61.

[2] The place name is left blank in the source document, but in the parallel account (Ms 3, 1854) the name Caughdenoy is supplied. The same applies to the name Roosevelt in the next sentence.

[3] On God's displeasure and "frown," see Ms 2, 1853 (Mar. 1), note 3.

[4] The name "Ross" is left blank in the source document, but is found in the parallel account (Ms 3, 1854).

[5] *Identity:* The initial difficulty in identifying "Brother Ross" is that there were at least two Ross brothers (Alexander and Manley) who were members of the Caughdenoy/Roosevelt group throughout the 1850s and beyond. Further information given in this letter, however, makes it likely that Alexander Ross is being referred to. "Brother Ross" is described as an "overseer" in the local group, albeit not fulfilling that role very well. Alexander fits this description, filling a number of leadership roles, such as local preacher, organizer of tent meetings and conferences and *Review* agent, whereas there is no mention of Manley Ross leading out.

See: Search term "Ross" in *Words of the Pioneers;* Ellen G. White, "The Cause in New York," *Testimony to the Church* (1872) (PH159), p. 81.

[6] An allusion to the ark and of the ancient Israelite tabernacle, a symbol of God's presence and leading (Num. 10:33-36).

not have the fellowship and privileges of the house of God. Said the angel, "This is not the sin of ignorance." It is a known sin, and will receive the awful visitation of God, whether committed by old or young. Never was this sin regarded by God to be so sinful as at present, because God is purifying to Himself a peculiar people zealous of good works.

Some professing the present truth can see and hear all the blazing truth for these last days calculated to arouse Israel and, with all this light, can sin with a high hand, give way to all the loose passion of the carnal heart, gratify their animal propensities, disgrace the cause of God, then confess they have sinned and are sorry. And the church receives them and says Amen to their prayers and exhortations which are a stink in the nostrils of God and causes His wrath to come upon the camp. He will not dwell in their assemblies. Those who move on thus heedlessly plastering over these sins will be left to their own ways, to be filled with their own doings. Those who anciently committed these sins were taken without the camp and stoned to death. Temporal and eternal death was their doom; and because the penalty of stoning to death is abolished, this sin is indulged in beyond measure, and thought to be a small offense.

I saw another individual who was very wrong in the sight of God and had transgressed God's commandment and had dishonored his parents. Guile had been found in his mouth; he had taken the name of God in vain, and had desecrated the house where the saints had assembled to worship God, by giving way to passions of an unsubdued heart, and yet he has been held up and approbated by Brother ——— and daubed with untempered mortar.[7] Also, his own relatives and M.[8] have covered the sins of others. The ax has not been laid at the root of the tree. Wicked feelings that God abhors have been fostered, Satan has been well pleased, and laughed because grace was not sufficient to overcome the natural infirmities, but that evil passions and the rising of self would be indulged in by those who profess to be Christians—Christ-like.

They have indulged in all the passions of the carnal or natural heart, been far from God, far from the truth, have been impatient, fretful, faultfinding, and the church has called it a small thing, and he has been exalted in his own eyes. God's Spirit has been withdrawn from him, and he knew it not. He has not been willing to bear reproof, but has been ready to rise up in heart and justify self, was rich and increased in goods, had a whole spirit, would get angry, and all this has been nourished and fostered by some of the church.

If those who have been in the church for weeks and months have not learned the straitness of the way, and what it is to be Christians, and cannot

---

[7] An expression found in Ezekiel 13:10-16 that carries the connotation of whitewashing an unsound structure in order to make it appear sound.

[8] The identity of the individuals mentioned in this passage is unknown.

hear all the straight truths of the Word of God, it were better that they were cut off from Israel. It is too late in the day to feed with milk. If souls a month or two old in the truth, who are about to enter the time of trouble[9] such as never was, cannot hear all the straight truth, or endure the strong meat of the straitness of the way, how will they stand in the day of battle? Truths that we have been years learning must be learned in a few months by those who now embrace the Third Angel's Message.[10] We had to search and wait the opening of truth, receiving a ray of light here and a ray there, laboring and pleading for God to reveal truth to us. But now the truth is plain; its rays are brought together. The blazing light of truth, when it is presented as it should be, can be now seen and brought to bear upon the heart.

There is no need of milk after souls are convinced of the truth. As soon as the conviction of truth is yielded to and the heart willing, the truth should have its effect; the truth will work like leaven, and purify and purge away the passions of the natural heart. It is a disgrace for those who have been in the truth for years to talk of feeding souls who have been months in the truth, upon milk. It shows they know little of the leadings of the Spirit of the Lord, and realize not the time we are living in. Those who embrace the truth now will have to step fast. There will have to be a breaking up of heart before the Lord, a rending of heart, and not the garment.[11]

Those who have healed the hurt of the daughter of my people slightly[12] must humble themselves greatly before God, and it may be His wrath will be turned away from Israel and He will march through their midst again in power. Said the angel, "Fearful is the work of the third angel, and awful is his mission. He is to select the wheat from the tares, and bind or seal the wheat for the heavenly garner."

I was then pointed to [Brother Ross],[13] of whom the angel said, "Ye have not been a co-worker with the Third Angel. Ye have not separated the vile from the precious." I then saw that death, death had reigned in your midst. I was then shown that Elizabeth[14] did not die having her work all done. As life was held up before her, she failed of a triumphant victory. The hearts of many who prayed for her to be raised up were not right in the sight of God. Some who professed to lose their strength were not exercised by the Spirit of

---

[9] *See:* EGWEnc, s.v. "Time of Trouble."

[10] *See:* EGWEnc, s.v. "Three Angels' Messages."

[11] A reference to the Jewish custom of rending one's garments as a sign of great grief (e.g., Joel 2:13).

[12] An expression taken from Jeremiah 6:14 referring to prophets and priests who glossed over the people's sins, thereby lulling them into a false sense of security.

[13] The name "Ross" is left blank in the source document, but is found in the parallel account (Ms 3, 1854).

[14] The identity of this person is not known, neither are any further details of the events described here available.

God. Many shouted when it was no shouting. A soul was going into the grave unapprised of it, but she will be saved. Others will have to bear the sin of her not being a triumphant overcomer. She was not accountable for the lack.[15] All impatience or fretfulness should have been corrected by those who watched over her, that she might be reconciled to live or die.

The next thing shown me was the sins of parents in neglecting their children.[16] I saw they would have an awful account to give. They have fostered and cherished the evil tempers of their children until God's frown was upon them and their children. They have forgotten that which was written in the Holy Word, "He that spareth the rod hateth his son," and the children are left to come up instead of being brought up or trained up. The poor little children are thought not to know or understand the meaning of a correction at the age of eight, nine, or ten months, and they begin to show stubbornness very young, and it is cherished and nourished by its parents till their evil passions grow with their growth and strengthen with their strength.

The house of God is desecrated, the Sabbath violated by Sabbath believers' children. They run about the house, play, talk, and manifest their evil tempers in the very meetings where the saints have met together to glorify God and worship Him in the beauty of holiness. The place that should be holy, and where a holy stillness reigns, and where perfect order, neatness, and humility should exist is made to be a perfect Babylon, and a place where confusion, disorder, and untidiness reigns. These things shut out God from our assemblies, and cause His wrath to be kindled that He will not be pleased to go out with the armies of Israel to battle against our enemies. He would not give the victory in [the] Oswego meeting.[17] The enemies of our faith triumphed. God was displeased. God's anger is kindled that His house should be made like Babylon.

Parents, I saw, stood in the place of God to their children, and they will have to render an awful account whether they have been faithful to the little few that have been committed to their trust. I saw that you were rearing children

---

[15] The case of Elizabeth and her fellow church members finds a prominent parallel in Ellen White's portrayal of William Miller's last years. Although in his prime Miller "was firm and undaunted," yet in his final years before his death in 1849 "leading men . . . [were] watching lest he should embrace the third angel's message." "At length Wm. Miller raised his voice against the light from heaven." Yet "he was not as accountable as those who kept him from the truth. They are responsible, and the sin rests upon them." Miller, she concludes, "will come forth at the sound of the last trump."

See: Ellen G. White, *Spiritual Gifts [vol. 1],* pp. 132, 167, 168.

[16] In the parallel account (Ms 3, 1854), Ellen White refers in particular to the parents in Caughdenoy as guilty of this neglect.

[17] No doubt referring to the meetings in Oswego the previous week, attended by the Whites. In a later report James White hints at some of the problems that attended that meeting and the "low state of the church." "The day was spent in plain, close remarks relative to what constitutes a Christian, and our present duty."

See: "Oswego Meeting," *Review*, Feb. 14, 1854, p. 28.

to be cut down by the destroying angel[18] unless you speedily turn square about and be faithful to your children. Think you that God can cover or hide iniquity in children and preserve them whom He hates? No, never. God hates unruly children[19] who manifest passion and evil tempers, etc. He cannot save them

---

[18] An allusion to the tenth plague in Egypt and/or Ezekiel's vision of judgment in Ezekiel 9. In an expanded version of this passage appearing in print some months later Ellen White includes both of these events. "The destroying angel is soon to go forth again, not to destroy the first-born alone, but 'to slay utterly old and young, both men, women and little children' who have not the mark."

See: Ellen G. White, "Duty of Parents to Their Children," *Review,* Sept. 19, 1854, pp. 45, 46.

[19] When Ellen White edited this statement for publication in the *Review* seven months later, she rephrased it to read that God "cannot love unruly children who manifest passion." This statement, together with the warning to her 5-year-old son in 1860 that "wicked, naughty children God does not love" (Lt 3, 1860 [Mar. 14]), have been the subject of considerable discussion. Critics have asked, "How could someone who claimed to receive heavenly visions be so terribly wrong about the character of God?" Others, while agreeing that these early statements do not seem to express accurately God's loving attitude, have argued that Ellen White grew in her perception of God's character, and that this is evidenced in her later writings.

It is difficult to reconcile this thesis of a harsh "early" Ellen White with the very different picture of her that is revealed in many other statements from her pen during the same period that deal with God's attitude toward wayward children. All the following extracts are taken from Ellen White articles published in the 1850s in the *Youth's Instructor,* a paper for children and youth:

1. "Dear young friends, your case is not now hopeless. Jesus so loved you that He died for your sins" (January 1854, p. 6).
2. "He knows your weakness, and is ready to have compassion upon you, although you may have sinned much against Him" (May 1854, p. 38).
3. "Oh, what love! what unbounded love and condescension the Son of God manifested for us. He died to give life to those who were His enemies!" (January 1854, p. 5).
4. "All heaven is interested in your salvation. God has given His only beloved Son to die for your transgression, angels are watching over you, and are trying to turn your attention to God, to seek your soul's salvation" (December 1852, p. 20).

Statements such as these portray the love of God in the sense of His benevolence, His intense desire for the well-being of sinful, rebellious children and youth. However, another standard dictionary definition of "love" (in its verbal form) is "to be pleased with" something or somebody. Clearly God does not take pleasure in children or any persons when they engage in evil, wicked acts. This aspect of God's disfavor is expressed in Scripture in such passages as Psalm 11:5: "The Lord tests the righteous, but the wicked and the one who loves violence His soul hates" (NKJV). This would seem to be the most likely sense of the terms "hate" and "love" used by Ellen White when she writes that God does not love wicked, naughty children. The same thought, expressed differently, is found in the following appeal to a young person: "How can you rest, knowing that Jesus does not smile upon you . . . , because you reject offered mercy, and sin against Him every hour?" (*Youth's Instructor,* January 1854, p. 5).

Understood in this light, Ellen White's language here (and in Lt 3, 1860) is misconstrued if it is made to conflict with her other statements from the same period affirming God's love for erring youth. But the risk of miscommunicating this fundamental truth underscores Ellen White's later admonition to parents to articulate clearly the distinction between God's displeasure with the rebellious and His merciful love that seeks to bring such ones to Himself:

> [Jesus] would have [the fathers and mothers] teach their children that God loves them, that their natures may be changed, and brought into harmony with God. Do not teach your children that God does not love them when they do wrong; teach them that He loves

in the time of trouble. They will be eternally lost through parents' neglect.[20] Their blood will be upon their parents. How can parents be saved with the blood of their children upon them, when they might have saved their children? God says, "I know Abraham, that he will command his household after him."

Parents, it is your duty to have your children under perfect subjection, having all their passions and evil tempers perfectly subdued. I saw that if they were carried to the house of God, they should be made to know where they were, that they were not at home, but where God met with His people, and they should be kept quiet from all play and running about, and then God will deign to meet with His people.

The truth, I saw, had but little effect. When it was talked, there seemed to be no power in it to stir the depth of the soul. A death-like stupor has hung upon the people of God. The reason is, the ark is not with them, for the holy commandments have been broken, and God has taken it away in His anger.

Parents, correct your children; commence while young, while impressions can be easily made and their evil tempers subdued, before passions take deep root and are strengthened with their strength.

I then saw a lack of cleanliness among Sabbathkeepers. I saw that God would have a clean and holy people, a people [in whom] He can delight. I saw that the camp must be cleansed or the Lord would pass by and see the uncleanness of the children of Israel and would not go forth with their armies to battle, but would turn from them in displeasure and our enemies would triumph over us, and we left weak in shame and disgrace. I saw that God would not acknowledge an untidy and unclean person as a Christian. His frown was upon such. Our souls, bodies, and spirits are to be presented blameless by Jesus to His Father, and unless we are clean in person and pure in heart, we cannot be presented blameless to God.[21]

---

them so that it grieves His tender Spirit to see them in transgression, because He knows they are doing injury to their souls. Do not terrify your children by telling them of the wrath of God, but rather seek to impress them with His unspeakable love and goodness, and thus let the glory of the Lord be revealed before them.—*Signs of the Times,* Feb. 15, 1892, p. 231.

For additional viewpoints on this issue, see Herbert E. Douglass, *Messenger of the Lord,* pp. 59, 60; Alden Thompson, *Escape From the Flames,* pp. 146-149; Jerry Moon, *W. C. White and Ellen G. White,* pp. 36-41.

[20] The question of the destiny of children who die before reaching "the age of accountability" has been an unsettled issue among Christians. It receives only passing mention in the writings of Ellen White, perhaps the most substantial treatment being in *Selected Messages,* book 3, pp. 313-315. No major analyses of Ellen White's position on infant salvation have been published. For partial studies, see Alberto R. Timm, in *Revistra do Ancião* (Brazil), October-December 2006, p. 7; Edwin Harry Zackrison, "Seventh-day Adventists and Original Sin," pp. 247, 248, 366-371; Woodrow W. Whidden II, "The Soteriology of Ellen G. White," pp. 130-132; Jairyong Lee, "Faith and Works in Ellen G. White's Doctrine of the Last Judgment," pp. 328-330.

[21] *See:* Ms 2, 1853 (Mar. 1), note 3.

I saw that the houses of the saints should be kept tidy and neat from dirt and filth and all uncleanness. I saw that the house of God had been desecrated by the carelessness of parents, with their children, and by the untidiness and uncleanness there. I saw that these things should meet with an open rebuke, and if there was not a change immediately in some that profess the truth, in these things, they should be put out of the camp.

I then saw the corruption of these last days. Some of those who profess the present truth are corrupt, and the same sins exist now that existed before the destruction of the old world. The world is almost ripe for destruction. Correct your children in love, not in passion. Do all your part, and God will do His. God despises our prayers for our children until we have done all on our part to save them. God corrects His children when they go astray from Him, and parents should correct their children when they disobey them. Correct their tempers. Above everything take care of them on the Sabbath. You may as well violate the Sabbath yourselves as to let your children do it. If you suffer your children to play upon the Sabbath,[22] God looks upon you as Sabbath breakers, or commandment breakers.[23] Your children should be made to mind you. Your word should be their law. Parents, take hold of this work, for the destroying angel is soon to pass around and slay utterly both old and young, men, women, and little children. Oh, do not be found wanting when weighed in the balance.

I saw then that they were eating and drinking, marrying and giving in marriage. I saw that the hearts of the young were now filled with the thoughts of getting married. Some of them became disobedient to their parents, got wanton, and many without consent of their parents or the church of God,

---

[22] Even children can be taught the concept of Sabbath holiness. In an article written for children and young people in 1853 Ellen White appealed to them through the words of Isaiah to turn "from doing thy pleasure on my holy day; and call the sabbath a delight, . . . not doing thine own ways, nor finding thine own pleasure" (Isa. 58:13). "Dear children," she urged, "are you as careful as you should be in keeping the Sabbath?"

Beyond the avoidance of behavior disruptive to the spirit of the Sabbath, Ellen White elsewhere encouraged parents to make Sabbath "the most interesting day of the week" for their children, adding, "How can children receive a more correct knowledge of God, and their minds be better impressed, than in spending a portion of their time out of doors, not in play, but in company with their parents?"

See: Ellen G. White, "Keep the Sabbath Holy," *Youth's Instructor,* February 1853, p. 37; *idem,* "How Shall We Keep the Sabbath?" *Testimonies for the Church,* vol. 2, pp. 582-585. For Ellen White's general counsel on children and the Sabbath, see *Child Guidance,* pp. 527-537.

[23] Ellen White may be referring not only to the general principle of parental responsibility but also to the specific demands of the fourth commandment, which holds the head of a household responsible to see that sons, daughters, employees, and even guests be given Sabbath privileges. James White made this specific point two years later: "God's law requires that all who remain in our dwellings should join in observing the rest of the holy Sabbath. We may endeavor to keep the Sabbath, yet if our children are left to break it, the sin will fall on us."

See: J. W. [James White], "Nor Thy Stranger That Is Within Thy Gates," *Review,* Dec. 11, 1856, p. 45.

and not having God in all their thoughts, and not inquiring whether it was His will or pleasure or not, do not marry to glorify God, but to glorify their loose passions and their depraved lusts. Such sins as this brought destruction upon the old world, and destroyed those who would not have God in all their thoughts. Awful sins of these last days are to bring the unmingled fury of God upon the world.

I then saw the appetite must be denied, that rich food should not be prepared, and that which is lavished upon the appetite should be put in the treasury of the Lord. It would tell there, and those who denied themselves would lay up a reward in heaven. Pride and idols must be laid aside. I saw rich food destroyed the health of the bodies and was ruining the constitution, was destroying the mind, and was a great waste of means.[24]

I saw some who were sickly among the saints, made themselves [so] by indulging the appetite. If we wish good health we must take special care of the health God has given us, deny the unhealthy appetite, eat more coarse food with little grease. Then you can consistently ask God's blessing upon such food as is congenial with your natures. We must pray as did Solomon for food convenient for us, and act accordingly, and God will bless us. Some Sabbathkeepers make a god of their bellies, waste their means in getting rich food. Such I saw, if saved at all, would know what pinching is unless they deny their appetites and eat to the glory of God. There are but few who eat to the glory of God.

---

[24] In addition to the emphasis here on avoiding "rich food," earlier visions had instructed against the use of tobacco, tea, and coffee. To the motivation given for avoiding such items, that they were destructive of health and were a waste of money that "should be put in the treasury of the Lord," was added the concept of the connection between spirituality and physical health. The conviction that health reform was an integral part of the third angel's message developed after Ellen White's comprehensive health reform vision of 1863.

For surveys of the development of health reform among Seventh-day Adventists and its theological implications, see P. Gerard Damsteegt, *Foundations of the Seventh-day Adventist Message and Mission,* pp. 221-241, and Herbert E. Douglass, *Messenger of the Lord,* pp. 278-298.

1854

(Ms 3, 1854)

FEBRUARY 12, BROOKFIELD, NEW YORK

Testimony for Churches in New York State.

Portions of this manuscript are published in Ellen G. White, *Testimonies on Sexual Behavior, Adultery, and Divorce,* pp. 247-249; *idem, Selected Messages,* book 3, pp. 257, 273-275; *idem, Manuscript Releases,* vol. 5, pp. 230, 231; vol. 7, p. 368-370; vol. 9, pp. 321-323. See Ms 1, 1854 (Feb. 12), for a parallel account.

Reproof for adultery and neglect of children in Caughdenoy and Roosevelt, New York.

The Lord gave us labor of spirit last First day, and while we were engaged in earnest prayer I was taken off in vision and saw the state of some of the professed Israel of God. I saw the situation of many at our meeting in Oswego [New York].[1] I saw that they were standing in the way of the work of God, especially those at Caughdenoy [New York]. I saw that God's frown[2] was upon them, also upon some in Roosevelt [New York].

Said the angel, "The axe has not been laid at the root of the tree." Those who have indulged in the wicked passions of the heart have been fellowshipped. If God had made Brother Ross [**Alexander Ross**][3] an overseer of the flock, he would have seen the evil and corruption among the people. The axe has not been laid at the root of the tree. God has not altered nor changed. He is a jealous God, and will not look upon sin now with any more allowance than He did among ancient Israel. Sin is sin. Sins have not been held forth in their sinfulness, but it has been made to appear as though sins have been lightly regarded by God.

I saw that the seventh commandment has been violated by some who are now held in fellowship by the church. This has brought God's frown upon them. This sin is awful in these last days, but the church has brought God's frown and curse upon it by regarding the sin so lightly. I saw it was an enormous sin, and there have not been as vigilant efforts made as there should have been to satisfy the displeasure of God and remove His frown by taking a strict, thorough course with the offender. It has had an awful, corrupting influence upon the young. They see how lightly the sin of breaking the seventh

---

[1] *See:* Parallel account, Ms 1, 1854 (Feb. 12), note 1.
[2] On God's displeasure and "frown," see Ms 2, 1853 (Mar. 1), note 3.
[3] *Identity:* See Ms 1, 1854, note 5.

commandment is regarded, and the one who commits this horrid sin thinks that all he has to do is to confess that he was wrong and is sorry, and he is then to have all the privileges of the house of God and be held in embrace or fellowship of the church.

They have thought it was not so great a sin, but have lightly esteemed the breaking [of] the seventh commandment. This has been sufficient to remove the ark of God from the camp,[4] if there were no other sins to cause the ark to be taken away and weaken Israel.

Those who break the seventh commandment should be suspended from the church and not have its fellowship or the privileges of the house of God.[5]

Said the angel, "This is not a sin of ignorance. It is a knowing sin and will receive the awful visitation of God, whether he who commits it be old or young."

Never was this sin regarded by God as being so exceedingly sinful as at the present time. Why? Because God is purifying unto Himself a peculiar people, zealous of good works. It is at the very time when God is purifying this peculiar people unto Himself that [unsanctified] individuals step in among us. Notwithstanding the straight truths they have heard, the terrors of the Word of God set before them, and all the blazing truth for these last days calculated to arouse Israel—they sin with a high hand, give way to all the loose passions of the carnal heart, gratify their animal propensities, disgrace the cause of God, and then confess they have sinned and are sorry! And the church receives them and says "Amen" to their prayers and exhortations, which are a stink in the nostrils of God and cause His wrath to come upon the camp. He will not dwell in their assemblies. Those who move on thus heedlessly, plastering over these sins, will be left to their own ways, to be filled with their own doings.

Those who anciently committed these sins were taken without the camp and stoned to death. Temporal and eternal death was their doom; and because the penalty of stoning to death is abolished, this sin is indulged in beyond measure, and is thought to be a small offense.

I saw three men. One of them was not a Sabbathkeeper but was opposed to the law of God. I saw that he was one who had a false spirit and exercised spiritual magnetism[6] and called it the Spirit of God. The other man seemed to

---

[4] An allusion to the ark and of the ancient Israelite tabernacle, a symbol of God's presence and leading (Num. 10:33-36).

[5] This instruction to disfellowship members committing adultery does not mean that there is no place for the restoration of these members. See, for example, Ellen G. White, *Testimonies on Sexual Behavior, Adultery, and Divorce,* pp. 253-267; Elbio Pereyra, "Marriage, Divorce, and Remarriage in the Writings of Ellen G. White."

[6] As the context makes clear, Ellen White is speaking of mesmerism, or, as it was later called, hypnotism. The terms "spiritual magnetism," "animal magnetism," and "mesmerism" are found in her early work, with "hypnotism" being introduced by the turn of the century.

me to be with him or in his company and somewhat united with him, and he partook of the same spirit, but he was a professed Sabbathkeeper. I saw that the truth of God had not purified his heart or he would not possess a false spirit and be using this false spirit, calling it the power of God.

The men above mentioned I have never seen except in vision, except the third man, who I saw was Brother Thompson.[7] He was exercised with the same evil spirit or spiritual magnetism and, like the other two, would impart it to others or affect others with it. I saw that Brother Thompson had formerly been affected with spiritualism[8] and never had had it eradicated from him. The third angel's message had not purified the man, and he would have to have a great work done for him or he could never enter heaven.

I was then pointed to a company. It seemed to be a family, with others present. I saw them bowed. Two of these men were present. I was particularly pointed by the angel who accompanies me while in vision, to Brother Thompson. I saw him walking the room and then raising his arms and putting them down like a person making mesmeric passes, and the one he was near commenced to sink away beneath the power which he felt and

---

The terms "animal magnetism" and "mesmerism" were used interchangeably in the literature of the late eighteenth and ninteenth centuries. Widespread public interest in mesmerism in North America had been awakened by the public demonstrations of Charles Poyen de Saint Sauveur in 1836. By the 1840s hundreds of lecturers, including a number of clergy, toured the country inducing mesmeric trances in front of fascinated audiences. Like "Brother Thompson" (see note 7 below), some associated the hypnotic trance with religious phenomena. La Roy Sunderland, a Methodist clergyman, emphasized the similarities between hypnotically induced trances and the swooning, prostration, and visionary experiences of early-nineteenth-century Methodist revival meetings.

See: EGWEnc, s.v. "Hypnotism"; Ann Taves, *Fits, Trances, & Visions,* pp. 132-148.

[7] *Identity:* Several Thompsons are mentioned in the *Review* during the 1850s, so the identity of "Brother Thompson" in this manuscript is not straightforward. One wonders if Ellen White is referring to Jesse Thompson, of Ballston Spa, New York, of whom she had written in 1851. However, there is no intimation in the 1851 documents or in references to Jesse Thompson in the *Review* that he was involved in the kind of problems brought up here. He is given only positive mentions—a generous contributor, conferences held in his house, etc. But there is one indication that Jesse Thompson may have reached a crisis in his relation to the Sabbatarian Adventists by early 1854. This is the fact that after fairly frequent references to Thompson in the *Review* between 1851 and 1853, nothing is heard of him after February 7, 1854 (very close to the February 12, 1854, date of the manuscript), nor does his obituary appear in the *Review* in 1858. Hence there is a possibility that Ellen White is referring to Jesse Thompson in this passage.

See: Dave Bixby, "Briggs Cemetery, Town of Ballston," n.d., http://saratoganygenweb.com/brigscem.htm (Sept. 13, 2011); Ellen G. White, Lt 3, 1851 (Aug. 11), Lt 7, 1851 (July 27); search term "Thompson" in *Words of the Pioneers.*

[8] Thompson's involvement in both mesmerism and spiritualism was not unusual. As historian Ann Taves has noted of this period: "Spiritualists frequently were involved with mesmerism, either as mesmerizers or as mesmeric subjects, before and after becoming Spiritualists." The basic hypothesis uniting the two practices was that the hypnotic trance "could provide access to the spirit realm."

See: Ann Taves, *Fits, Trances, & Visions,* pp. 168, 166.

which was called the power of God. I was pointed to others and saw them wilting beneath the same power. I saw that the family there had but just tasted of the third angel's message. A good work had just been wrought for them in bringing them to God and His truth, and although they felt the power of spiritual magnetism that night and its effects since, God would not lay the sin[9] to their charge, for they were innocent, being inexperienced. I saw that they had much to learn, and if they were humble God would lead them along and teach them His will and the present truth and what they must be in order to be saved and reign with Christ in glory.

I saw how this spirit or power will leave the individual, after the power has passed off. Instead of their having more strength from God than they had before they felt this power, and more grace to overcome every wrong word or action, instead of being spiritually minded and having their minds fixed upon heaven and heavenly things, it was the reverse of this. Those who have been exercised by this false spirit have a depressed, sunken, empty, void, unsatisfied, stupid[10] feeling. They will feel a lack of the grace of God, be in danger of speaking impatiently and from the impulse of the moment, feel that they have lost all their religion, though they hardly know how.

I saw that when the blessing of God rested upon any one, it will not cause him to lose the use of his arms so that he cannot control them, or cause the arms to shake, jerk, etc.

[Page in original handwritten manuscript missing.]

Truths that we have been years learning, those who now embrace the third angel's message will have to learn in a few months.[11] We had to search and wait the opening of truth and receive a ray of light here and a ray there, and labor and beg for God to reveal truth to us. But now the truth is plain; its rays are brought together. The blazing light of truth can now be seen at once,

---

[9] "As for mesmerism," wrote James White in 1851, "we have ever considered it dangerous, therefore have nothing to do with it." Ellen White, in her first extended comment on mesmerism in 1862, wrote that "Satan uses these very things [phrenology and magnetism] to destroy virtue and lay the foundation of Spiritualism."

See: Ellen G. White, *A Sketch of the Christian Experience and Views of Ellen G. White,* p. 2; *idem,* "Phrenology, Psychology, Mesmerism, and Spiritualism," *Review,* Feb. 18, 1862, pp. 94, 95.

[10] In the sense of "lethargic."

[11] The focus here on the shortness of time is a recurring theme in the visions. Some critics later charged Ellen White with being a false prophet. In 1883 she responded, "Am I accused of falsehood because time has continued longer than my testimony seemed to indicate?" Citing New Testament warnings such as "the time is short" (1 Cor. 7:29) and Christ's words "behold, I come quickly" (Rev. 22:7), she concluded that "the angels of God in their messages to men represent time as very short. Thus it has always been presented to me. It is true that time has continued longer than we expected in the early days of this message. . . . But has the word of the Lord failed? Never! It should be remembered that the promises and threatenings of God are alike conditional."

See: Ellen G. White, *Selected Messages,* book 1, p. 67.

and when it is presented as it should be it is brought to bear upon the heart at once. There is no need of milk for any soul, after he is convinced of truth. As soon as the conviction of truth is yielded to and the heart is willing to let the truth have its effect, it will begin to work like leaven. It will purify and purge away the passions of a natural heart.

It is a disgrace for those who have been in the truth for years to talk of feeding souls who have been months in the truth, upon milk. It shows that they know but little of the leadings of the Spirit of God and realize not the time that we are living in. Those who embrace the truth now will have to step fast. And there will have to be a breaking of heart before the Lord, a rending of the heart and not the garments.[12] A thorough work will have to go on in the hearts of those who have been thus at fault, and those who healed the hurt of the daughter of My people slightly[13] will have to humble themselves greatly before God. It may be His wrath will be turned away from Israel and He will march through their midst again in power.

Said the angel, "Fearful is the work of the third angel; awful is his mission. He is to select the wheat from the tares and bind or seal the wheat for the heavenly garner."

I was pointed to Brother Ross. Said the angel, "Ye have not been a co-worker with the third angel. Ye have not separated the vile from the precious."

Then I saw that death had reigned in your midst. I was shown the one that died,[14] that she died without a perfect readiness. Life was held before her and she had not a triumphant victory. The hearts of many who prayed for her to be raised up were not right with God. Some appeared to lose their strength or be exercised. It was not the Spirit of God. Many shouted, but it was no time for shouting. A soul was going into the grave unapprised of it, but she will be saved. Others will have to bear the sin of her not being a triumphant overcomer.[15] She was not accountable for it. Whenever an impatient word was spoken, or whenever there was any impatience or fretfulness manifested, it was the duty of those she was with to tell her her critical situation, and the danger of manifesting anything like unreconciliation, impatience, etc. It was their duty to show her that she must be reconciled to the will of God and prepare for her last change, and that if she was not reconciled to God's will she was not prepared to be raised up or to die.

The next thing that was shown me was the great sin of parents neglecting

---

[12] A reference to the Jewish custom of rending one's garments as a sign of great grief (e.g., Joel 2:13).

[13] An expression taken from Jeremiah 6:14 that refers to prophets and priests who glossed over the people's sins, thereby lulling them into a false sense of security.

[14] In the parallel account of this manuscript (Ms 1, 1854) Ellen White reveals that it was "Elizabeth" who had died. Elizabeth's full identity is not known, neither have any further details about the incident related here been found.

[15] *See:* Ms 1, 1854, note 15.

their children. I saw that they would have an awful account to give in Caughdenoy. They had fostered and cherished the evil tempers of their children until God's frown was upon them and their children. They have forgotten that which is written in the Holy Word, "He that spareth his rod hateth his son," and the children are left to come up instead of being brought up or trained up. The poor little children are thought not to know or understand a correction at eight, nine, or ten months old. They begin to show stubbornness very young, and it is cherished and nourished by their parents until these evil passions grow with their growth, and strengthen with their strength.

The house of God is desecrated and the Sabbath violated by Sabbath believers' children. They run about the house, play, talk, and manifest their evil tempers in the very meetings where the saints have met together to glorify God and to worship Him in the beauty of holiness. The place that should be holy, where a holy stillness should reign, and where there should be perfect order, neatness, and humility, is made to be a perfect Babylon and a place where confusion, disorder, and untidiness reign. This is enough to shut out God from our assemblies and cause His wrath to be kindled, that He will not be pleased to go out with the armies of Israel to battle against our enemies.

God would not give the victory in the Oswego meeting.[16] The enemies of our faith triumphed. God was displeased. His anger is kindled that His house should be made like Babylon.

Parents, I saw, stood in the place of God to their children and they will have to render an awful account whether they have been faithful to the little few that were committed to their trust.

I saw that you were rearing children to be cut down by the destroying angel[17] unless you speedily turn square about and be faithful to your children. Think you God can cover or hide iniquity and preserve children whom He hates? No, never. God hates unruly children[18] who manifest passion, evil tempers, etc. He cannot save them in the time of trouble. They will be eternally lost.[19] Parents, negligent, unfaithful parents, their blood will be upon you, and can you expect to be saved in the day of God's fierce anger with the blood of your children upon you,—children who might have been saved had you acted as faithful parents should? God said of Abraham, "I know him, that he will command his children and his household after him," and He gave him the name of being the father of the faithful.

Parents, it is your duty to have your children under perfect subjection, having all their passions and evil tempers perfectly subdued. I saw that if they were carried to the house of God, they should be made to know where they

---

[16] *See:* Ms 1, 1854, note 17.
[17] *See:* Ms 1, 1854, note 18.
[18] *See:* Ms 1, 1854, note 19.
[19] *See:* Ms 1, 1854, note 20.

are, that they are not at home but where God meets with His people. They should be kept quiet, from all play and running about, then God will deign to meet with His people.

The truth, I saw, had had but little effect. When it was talked, there seemed to be no power to stir up the depth of the soul. A deathlike stupor has hung upon the professed people of God, and the reason is that the ark is not with them, for its holy commandments have been violated, and God has taken it away in His anger.

Parents, correct your children. Commence while they are young, when impressions can be made early and their evil temper subdued before it takes deep root and is strengthened with their strength. Correct your children in love. Do not correct them in passion or let them have their way until even you yourself are angry and then punish them. Correct your children, and then after you have done your duty, carry them to God and ask God to help you. Tell Him you have done your part, and then plead with Him to do His part, that you cannot do. Beg of Him to temper their dispositions, to make them mild and gentle by His Holy Spirit. God will hear you pray. He will love to answer your prayers. But He despises your prayers while you neglect your duty to your children and then pray Him to do the work for them. God corrects us when we go astray from Him, and you are bound to correct your children when they disobey you and show passion and an evil temper.[20]

Above everything, take care of your children upon the Sabbath. Do not let them violate it, for you may just as well violate it yourself as to let your children do it. When you suffer your children to play upon the Sabbath, God looks upon you as a commandment breaker. You transgress His Sabbath.[21]

Your children should be made to mind you. Your word should be their law. Parents, take hold of this work, for the destroying angel is soon to pass around and slay utterly both old and young—men, women, and little children. He will spare only those upon whom is the mark. Oh, do not be weighed in the balances and found wanting!

I then saw a lack of cleanliness among Sabbathkeepers and some at Caughdenoy. I saw that God was purifying unto Himself a peculiar people. He will have a clean and a holy people, a people in whom He can delight. I saw that the camp must be cleansed, or God would pass by and see the uncleanness of Israel and would not go forth with their armies to battle. He would turn from them in displeasure, and our enemies would triumph over us and we be left weak, in shame and disgrace.[22]

I saw that God would not acknowledge an untidy, unclean person as a

---

[20] For a representative selection of Ellen White's writings on the subject of child discipline, see *Child Guidance*, pp. 233-290.

[21] *See:* Ms 1, 1854, notes 22, 23.

[22] *See:* Ms 2, 1853 (Mar. 1), note 3.

Christian. His frown was upon such. Our souls, bodies, and spirits are to be presented blameless by Jesus to His Father, and unless we are clean in person, and pure, we cannot be presented blameless to God.

I saw that the houses of the saints should be kept tidy and neat, free from dirt and filth and all uncleanness. I saw that the house of God had been desecrated by the carelessness of parents with their children and by the untidiness and uncleanness there. I saw that these things should meet with an open rebuke, and if there was not an immediate change in some that profess the truth in these things they should be put out of the camp.

I then saw the corruptions of these last days. Even some of those who profess the truth are corrupt and the same sins exist now that existed before the destruction of the old world by a flood. The world is almost ripe now for destruction, as it was then. I saw that when they were eating and drinking, marrying and being given in marriage, the flood came and took them all away.

I saw that the hearts of the young are now filled with the thought of getting married. Some of them become disobedient to their parents, become wanton, and marry without the counsel of their parents or the church of God. Not having God in all their thoughts, not inquiring whether it is according to His will or pleasure or not, they do not marry to glorify God but to gratify their loose passions and their depraved lusts. Such sins as these brought the flood upon the old world, and destroyed those sinners who would not bear God in their thoughts. Awful sins of these last days are to bring the unmingled fury of God upon the world.

I then saw that the appetite must be denied, that rich food should not be prepared, and that which is spent upon the appetite should be put into the treasury of God.[23] It would tell there and those that denied themselves would lay up a reward in heaven. I saw that God was purifying His people.

Pride and idols must be laid aside. I saw that rich food was destroying the health of bodies, was ruining constitutions, destroying minds, and was a great waste of means.

I saw that many were sickly among the remnant, who have made themselves so by indulging their appetites. If we wish good health, we must take special care of the health that God has given us, deny the unhealthy appetite, eat less fine food, eat coarse food free from grease. Then as you sit at the table to eat you can from the heart ask God's blessing upon the food and can derive strength from coarse, wholesome food. God will be pleased to graciously bless it and it will be a benefit to the receiver.

I saw that we should pray as Solomon did—"Feed me with food convenient for me," (Prov. 30:8)—and as we make the prayer, act it out. Get food that

---

[23] *See:* Ms 1, 1854, note 24.

is plain and that is essential to health, free from grease. Such food will be convenient for us.

There are some Sabbathkeepers who make a god of their bellies. They waste their means in obtaining rich food. Such, I saw, if saved at all will know what pinching want is unless they deny their appetites and eat to the glory of God. There are but few who eat to the glory of God. How can those who have cake and piecrust filled with grease ask God's blessing upon it and then eat with an eye single to God's glory? We are commanded to do all to the glory of God. We must eat and drink to His glory.

I then saw that Brother Ross had not taken the right ground concerning the little affairs of his brethren. [Original page torn, last five lines unreadable.]

1854

(Ms 6, 1854)

FEBRUARY 19, LINCKLAEN, NEW YORK[1]

Courtesy and Kindness.

Previously unpublished.

Influence of Samuel W. Rhodes on believers in Lincklaen, New York; traits required of ministers.

The Lord showed me in vision last evening the state of things in Lincklaen [New York] and vicinity.

I was shown the shortness of time,[2] and the importance of all realizing it and feeling the worth of souls for whom Christ died. I was shown the low state of the brethren; the ark of God was gone out of the camp.[3] I was shown that a right influence had not been exerted by Bro. Rhodes [**Samuel W. Rhodes**];[4] a good example has not been set, and darkness and weakness has been the consequence. I saw that Bro. R. had possessed an overbearing spirit in this vicinity,[5] and has often

---

[1] The Whites visited the believers in Lincklaen, New York, on February 18 and 19, 1854, as part of a three-week itinerary in New York State, returning home to Rochester on February 21.

See: James White, "Appointments," *Review,* Jan. 24, 1854, p. 8; *idem,* "At Home," *Review,* Feb. 28, 1854, p. 48.

[2] On the shortness of time, see Ms 3, 1854 (Feb. 12), note 11.

[3] An allusion to the ark of the ancient Hebrew sanctuary, a symbol of God's presence in the camp of the Israelites. Compare the language used here with the following passage in Ms 1, 1854 (Feb. 12): "A death-like stupor has hung upon the people of God. The reason is, the ark is not with them, for the holy commandments have been broken, and God has taken it away in His anger."

[4] *Identity:* For several reasons it seems clear that Samuel W. Rhodes is being referred to: his inclusion among "the lecturing brethren," the reproof for his severity, and his influence on the Lincklaen group. S. W. Rhodes, a well-known traveling preacher in the 1850s, had, according to *Review* accounts, made at least five visits to the Lincklaen believers prior to this. Regarding his severity, see note 5, below.

See: Bro. Rhodes, "Extracts of Letters," *Review,* Aug. 19, 1851, p. 16; "Conference at Bath, N. Y.," *Review,* Sept. 16, 1851, p. 32; E. A. Poole, "From Bro. Poole," *Review,* July 8, 1852, p. 39; G. W. Holt, S. W. Rhodes, "Appointments," *Review,* Aug. 19, 1852, p. 64; Samuel W. Rhodes, "Appointments," *Review,* Jan. 6, 1853, p. 136.

[5] Eight months earlier, on June 2, 1853, Rhodes's harshness and overbearing manner had been the focus of Ms 1, 1853 (June 2). He apparently accepted the reproof, as evidenced by a letter to the *Review* some weeks later in which he confessed to an "overbearing, oppressive spirit." Little seemed to have changed in the long run, however, since Ellen White returned to Rhodes's problems in this area in several letters written in the 1850s and 1860s. See, for example Lt 8, 1857 (July 19); Lt 16, 1859 (Oct. 28); Lt 5a, 1861 (Apr. 5); Lt 4, 1870 (Mar. 23). For Rhodes's letter of confession in 1853, see S. W. Rhodes, "Letter From Bro. Rhodes," *Review,* Aug. 11, 1853, p. 55.

hurt the oil and wine,[6] has misjudged individuals, and has laid burdens upon them that did not belong to them. I saw that this has been done in the case of Brother and Sister Poole [**Ezra A.** and **Sally Marilla Poole**].[7] Brother R. has spoken from the impulse of the moment or from impatient, fitful feelings which has caused a *deep,* deep wound that has never been healed with suitable confessions and a free acknowledgment of wrongs without qualifications and justifying self.

I saw that the lecturing brethren should above all others possess a kind, courteous spirit. They must bear and forbear and lay by a hasty, fitful, uneasy spirit, and for the sake of precious souls must bear to be opposed with a bitter spirit, and not retaliate. But if the messenger of God lets self rise and bears down upon the opposer with an impatient spirit, it is just what the opposer wants. He goes away with all the natural, irritable feelings of his heart awake, saying as he goes, I am as well off as he is. He is no better off than I am. I know he has not the Spirit of God. He is not a Christian.

But if the servants of the Most High should possess a meek, forbearing spirit, and for the sake of the souls of others if they have no hope of the opposer, suffer their abuse with patience, keep the heart uplifted to God, praying for strength, He would let angels of God strengthen them, and arrows of conviction would be fastened in the hearts of unbelievers. God would be glorified, and others would take knowledge of them that they have been with Jesus. I saw that Brother Rhodes should not cut so much with his words, but hold forth the truth and let that cut them, and even exercise wisdom in this. Do not bring the most denouncing truths from God's Word to bear upon the opposers, for it will only irritate and stir up their wrath.

I was pointed to Jesus. He knew what was in man's heart. He took upon Himself man's nature, yet He was the beloved of the Father, the Son of the Most High God. The hearts of all men, and the result and effect of every word He spoke He knew perfectly. And man, frail man, must not feel that he is authorized to speak with that authority, and rebuke in such a cutting manner and with that assurance, that the Son of man did. Weak, failing man knows not the effect of what he says. By being severe and rebuking in a sharp manner, [he may] drive souls from the truth and close their ears from ever listening to it, and they may be lost in consequence of some mismoves of the messengers, whose mission was to save souls. Who can tell the worth of a soul

---

[6] An expression borrowed from Revelation 6:6.

[7] *Identity:* The only "Poole" mentioned in the *Review* before 1858 is "Bro. E. A. Poole." His address is given as Lincklaen, New York. The address matches the opening line of this manuscript, which places the persons and events "in Lincklaen and vicinity." His first name, Ezra, and the name of his wife can be found in census sources.

See: Search term "Poole" in *Words of the Pioneers;* 1860 U.S. Federal Census, "Ezra A. Poole," New York, Chenango County, Lincklaen, p. 215; 1880 U.S. Federal Census, "Ezra A. Poole," New York, Chenango County, Lincklaen, p. 148A.

for whom Christ died? Christ pitied the fallen race of men and consented to give up the glory He had with the Father, and took upon Himself man's nature, that He might sympathize with them in their woes, and then to die an ignominious death upon the cross to redeem them to His Father. He suffered every indignity, slight, and scorn without a retaliating look or word, when He could have had legions of angels to assist Him had He asked His Father.

Said the angel, Follow His example in these things and ye will adorn your profession. Servants of God are ye, coworkers with Jesus and the third angel. Do ye possess a gathering spirit? I saw that Brother Rhodes has not possessed the meek spirit of Jesus as he should, and unbelievers even in this place have been borne down upon, and testimonies have been borne them which God did not dictate and which wounded the precious cause of God. I saw that Brother Rhodes' influence upon this band has not been good, but has injured some, and this is one cause of the church being in so low a state. I saw that some have carried out the example set them by Brother Rhodes, especially two of the brothers Swan[8] and a sister connected with them. Others have been influenced, but the ones mentioned above have greatly erred; they have given way to excitable, fitful feelings, and have, like Brother Rhodes, possessed an overbearing spirit.

I saw that the course taken toward Mr. Crandall[9] was not right. Wisdom was not used, and great injury it has done some that he was connected with. Satan has taken advantage of and separated them from the people of God through the mismoves of the brethren and through Brother Rhodes' lack of wisdom. The effect should have been studied, and the church must be willing to suffer something to save the souls of those he is connected with and over whom his influence extends. Although he may burden the meeting, bear it; call upon God for additional strength, and God will hear and will impart it.

I saw that every one that professes the truth, wherein they have manifested an overbearing spirit should take it away and leave the blood of his soul upon his own head. He may take advantage of the brethren's confessions. If he does, he will have that sin to bear, and the brethren will be clear. I saw that Mr.

---

[8] *Identity:* Samuel Swan (1821-1881), a member of the Lincklaen group, had four sons in their 20s and early 30s, all living locally at the time of the 1850 census. Three of them are known to have joined the Sabbatarian movement, Samuel Prentice in 1850, Charles D. possibly at the same time, and Julius Augustus in the early 1880s. Nothing is known of William W. Swan's relationship to the church.

See: Roger Swan, "The Swan Family: Descendants of Samuel Swan and Harriet Smith," November 2002, http://rootsweb.com/~nychenan/swan-ged.htm (07/20/2005); obituary: "Samuel P. Swan," *Review*, Aug. 2, 1881, p. 94; obituary: "Julius A. Swan," *Review*, Mar. 20, 1913, p. 286; obituary: "Charles D. Swan," *Review*, Feb. 25, 1873, p. 87.

[9] *Identity:* The identity of "Mr. Crandall" has not been established.

Crandall was not right, and that he never has been fully in the angel's message. He was living in open violation of the fourth commandment, "Remember the Sabbath day . . . stranger that is within thy gates." I saw that God could not approbate him while transgressing this commandment. I also saw he not only transgressed it openly [himself, but] by suffering labor to be done by his son, his manservant, and maid servant.

1854

(Lt 1, 1854)

MARCH 10, ROCHESTER, NEW YORK

LETTER TO

Harriet Newall Stevens.[1]

Portions of this letter are published in Ellen G. White, *Manuscript Releases,* vol. 5, p. 436.

Letter to a close acquaintance containing mostly family news.

Dear Sister Harriet:

I have just received a letter from you.[2] We were glad to hear from you, but my health is so very poor [I] can write but a few lines now. I have been almost entirely confined to my room since we returned [from] our last three weeks' journey in this state.[3] Was unable to sit up but a few hours in the day most of the time on the journey, have done nothing like work for six weeks. Disease of the heart is making rapid progress upon me, and unless I soon regain some strength of body and soul to rise above my fearful and threatening disease, I cannot continue long. You may inquire, Has Sister White given up to die? I answer, No. I still hope because others wish me to, and my faith is increasing that the enemy will not be permitted to triumph over me. But I have been sorely afflicted and have been brought very near death's door.[4]

---

[1] *Identity:* The reference in the last paragraph of the letter to a submission from Harriet to the *Instructor* provides specific evidence for identifying the addressee as Harriet Newall Stevens (later Smith). Harriet's "An Address to the Youth" was published in *The Youth's Instructor* in April 1854, which dovetails nicely with Ellen White's mention in this March 10 letter that Harriet's submission had been received. Ellen White became well acquainted with Harriet Stevens and her family of Paris, Maine, during the period October 1850 to summer 1851, when the Whites were based in Paris. Harriet Stevens had literary ability, with several poems, articles, and letters published in the *Review* and *Youth's Instructor.* At least one of Harriet's poems was set to music and printed in early Adventist hymnals. She subsequently assisted periodically at the *Review* office in Rochester, New York, and Battle Creek, Michigan.

See: H. N. Stevens, "An Address to the Young," *Youth's Instructor,* April 1854, pp. 29, 30; obituary: "Harriet N. Stevens Smith," *Review,* Mar. 30, 1911, p. 23.

[2] This letter is not in the White Estate archives.

[3] James and Ellen White had arrived back in Rochester on February 21, 1854, after a three-week journey in central New York.

See: "At Home," *Review,* Feb. 28, 1854, p. 48. Arthur L. White provides a summary of the highlights of this tour in *Ellen G. White: The Early Years,* pp. 289-292.

[4] For a fuller autobiographical account of Ellen White's sickness during these months and her remarkable healing, see Ellen G. White, *Spiritual Gifts [vol. 2],* pp. 184-188.

We had a special meeting appointed to devote to the special purpose of presenting Brother J. N. Andrews' [**John Nevins Andrews**] case to the throne of grace, pleading with God to rebuke disease upon him and restore him to health, that Israel may not be led to mourn his loss. Sorrow upon sorrow will come upon us if he is removed from us.[5]

We also have covenanted to pray three times a day and make Brother John's case a special subject of prayer; also to strive to cultivate deep piety in our own hearts that we may grow strong in faith and be prepared for the events which are just before us, *the time of trouble.*

Thank you for your kind letter. Do not wait for me to write and answer every letter, for I am too feeble to write much. My sickness has been very discouraging and wearing. I will try to keep you apprised of my state of health. You need not think because we do not write often that we do not wish to hear from you. Our time is occupied and we are even pressed. But poor me—[I] am punished with sitting and lying, doing nothing.

You must excuse all bad writing for I am writing on a trunk in my lap. Anna [**Anna White**][6] was glad of the communication for the *Instructor.* Be of good cheer. Much love to each of the children. In much love.

---

[5] News of J. N. Andrews's illness would naturally be of concern to Harriet Stevens. Both had been members of the Sabbatarian band in Paris, Maine, from its beginning until Andrews left Paris in 1851. Since then he had been based in Saratoga Springs and Rochester, together with the Whites. Notices regarding J. N. Andrews's failing health started to appear in the *Review* in March 1854. By February 1855 James White described Andrews as "feeble" and "broken down at the age of 25." Andrews then returned to his parents' home in Paris, Maine, "to labor with his hands, hoping to regain his health and sustain himself."

See: [Notice], *Review,* Mar. 7, 1854, p. 56; "The Office," *Review,* Feb. 20, 1855, p. 182.

[6] *Identity:* Anna White, sister of James White, edited *The Youth's Instructor* for some months in 1854, before her death in November of the same year.

See: Obituary: "Anna White," *Review,* Dec. 12, 1854, p. 135; EGWEnc, s.v. "*The Youth's Instructor.*"

1854

(Lt 2, 1854)

APRIL 11, ROCHESTER, NEW YORK

LETTER TO

Brother and Sister Pierce.[1]

Previously unpublished.

An account of Ellen White's serious illness during the winter of 1853-1854 and of her remarkable healing.

Dear Brother and Sister Pierce:

We received your letter in due time[2] and as you make inquiry concerning my health, I would say it has been very poor all winter. For months [I] have been unable to do anything. The swelling upon my eye commenced to grow directly after we returned from visiting the East.[3] It is upon my upper eyelid. It has increased in size and has troubled me so much [I] have been obliged to give up writing entirely for a time. My whole eye was very painful, especially the ball.

But this has not been all my difficulty. I have been troubled with disease of the heart for years but of late this disease has made rapid progress upon me. I have had constant pain in my heart for months. We have all been alarmed as we have been aware of the progress of disease. A few weeks since I had an alarming attack of paralysis. My left arm, tongue and head were numb and then extreme coldness followed.

---

[1] *Identity:* A number of Pierces are mentioned in the *Review* during the early 1850s. Unfortunately this letter provides little firm basis for determining which Pierce couple is being addressed. The first sentence suggests that the Whites had recently received a letter from Br. and Sr. Pierce. This might refer to a letter written on March 30 by "Alvarer Pierce" to James White, which was published in the *Review* on April 18. No other recent letter from a Pierce is found in the *Review.* On the other hand, Alvarer (or Alvarez, as it is spelled in subsequent mentions) Pierce states in his letter that he had known of the Sabbath for only "eight or ten weeks," so it seems unlikely that he would be acquainted with Ellen White's ill health that he inquires about. No firm conclusions regarding the identity of the Pierces seem to be justified, given the scarce and conflicting evidence.

See: Search term "Pierce" in *Words of the Pioneers;* Alvarer Pierce, "From Bro. Pierce," *Review,* Apr. 18, 1854, pp. 102, 103.

[2] *See:* Note 1, above.

[3] A journey of more than two months with appointments in Vermont, Massachusetts, Maine, and New Hampshire, returning to Rochester, New York, in early November 1853.

See: Ellen G. White, Lt 7, 1853 (Aug. 24); James White, "Note to Brother Waggoner," *Review,* Nov. 8, 1853, p. 144.

I sent for my husband, not knowing but that in a short time I should be silent in death. We tried to look to the Lord. I grew weak very fast, was almost blind. That night we had a little meeting and I presented my case as a special subject of prayer. I told them I was satisfied that my work upon earth was done unless there was a speedy deliverance wrought for me. We prayed for the Spirit of God to indict our petitions. The sweet Spirit of God did rest upon me, the pain in my head was rebuked and my soul was abundantly blessed, and I could not refrain from weeping and praising God. My soul was filled with love and gratitude for His unbounded goodness to unworthy me.

The next day the pain in my heart continued, but I was free in the Lord; my peace was like a river. That night I again requested the prayers of those present, and for the first time in my life was anointed with oil. I felt less of the Spirit than before, when prayed for, but I believed in the sure promises of God, that they would be verified, that God would give me strength to still be of some use in His service. I felt no change that night but rested well and awoke with the praise of God upon my lips, and the pain gone from my heart. The Lord has done for me that which no physician upon earth could do. It is about three weeks since I was healed and my heart remains free from pain. I believe that the Lord will remove the swelling from my eye, and give me strength to do His will.[4]

We feel the necessity of drawing near to God, of having our every motive and action governed by His Spirit.

Dear Brother, as a spirit of irreverence is very common it should be reproved at all times. Those who are [as] ignorant as you speak of concerning this being a sin, should always be reproved before they are rebuked publicly. Those who are so thoughtless as to continue to get off their guard after being reproved, and knowing the mind of the body of the church concerning this irreverence, should be rebuked publicly, for this sin has brought the frown of God upon us.

Your donation [of] $5 was gratefully received. Thank you for your interest [in] my welfare concerning being healed of disease of heart. Much love to all that love God. Pray for us that God would give husband and self health to labor for Him.

In much love.

---

[4] For additional details of Ellen White's illness and remarkable recovery during this period, see Ellen G. White, *Spiritual Gifts [vol. 2]*, pp. 184-188.

1854

(Ms 4, 1854)

APRIL, ROCHESTER, NEW YORK

Testimony.

This manuscript is published in S. T. Belden, G. W. Amadon, and William Hall, *To Brother J. N. Andrews and Sister H. N. Smith* (PH016), pp. 32, 33.

Opposition to the visions and the leadership of James White as a reason for moving the Review office from Rochester, New York.

I saw that with some there has not been a receiving of what God has shown. It has been doubted. It has borne but with a feather's weight. I saw that straight testimonies must be borne, and they have not been received. I then saw that the church must be united, and if they could not endure straight testimonies when they were needed and we were bound, we must move the office and go where we could bear them.[1] I saw that we neither of us had done our duty. There has been a holding back, a shunning to declare the whole counsel of God. I saw that God wanted us to be free, that if we did not follow the movings of His Spirit and bear the testimonies He gave

---

[1] By April 1854, the date of this manuscript, opposition to the visions of Ellen White among a small minority of Sabbatarian Adventists was developing and would soon result in the formation of the breakaway *Messenger* Party. However, the focus of this vision seems to be not on external challenges but on opposition from within, specifically in the Rochester area, where the "office" was located from 1852 to 1855. Ellen White later specified certain names: "Brn. Lamson, Orton, and Andrews, and the Stevens family," who "felt justified to array themselves against us." That **J. N. Andrews** is mentioned is, perhaps, surprising, given his later stature in the church. Still in his early 20s he had already made his mark as a scholar, writer, and itinerant preacher. Andrews, however, tended to undermine the Whites by siding with those who were admonished. As he later confessed, "sympathy for my immediate friends when reproved for their wrongs has been one great cause of leading me into the dark." The mention of "the Stevens family" is no doubt a reference to **Harriet N. Stevens**, a young woman of literary bent from Paris, Maine, who joined the *Review* staff in 1854 or 1855. Writing to Harriet some years later, in 1860, Ellen White asserted that "the visions" "do not bear a feather's weight on your mind" and that she had shown the same attitude while employed in Rochester. Further, if someone was admonished or reproved by the Whites, "you sympathize with him, confide in him," thus undermining their leadership. Significantly, both J. N. Andrews and Harriet Stevens came from Paris, Maine, where the parents of both maintained a skeptical attitude toward the visions throughout the 1850s.

See: Ellen G. White, Lt 7, 1860 (June); *idem, Testimony to the Church at Battle Creek* (1872) (PH123), pp. 72, 73; J. N. Andrews to Brother White, Feb. 2, 1862; Ron Graybill, "The Family Man," in Harry Leonard, ed., *J. N. Andrews: The Man and the Mission,* pp. 24-28; Gerald Wheeler, *James White,* pp. 101-109.

us,[2] He would leave us in bondage and then our health and strength would fail, and worse than all this, the bondage would be felt on the people, and if there is not freedom and liberty here, we must move where there would be freedom and where the testimonies given us of God would be received. I saw that some had doubted what God had taught, therefore it could not have weight with them or serve to move them. I saw this, and begged of God to use another instrument, to send by one whom they would receive, or to fit up the frail instrument that the church might be convinced. Said the angel, God has chosen His own way, that through the simple means He has ordained that light should be given, and if it is not received God will give them up to their own ways to be filled with their own doing.

---

[2] The specific inclusion of James White here brings out the fact that Ellen is speaking of opposition not only to her visions but also to the work of James. In a letter written in 1860 she wrote very frankly about the situation created by "the straight testimony and reproofs given by Brother White" through the years. Looking back to their time in Paris, Maine, 1850-1851, she acknowledged that "the feelings then were that James was censorious and severe" and that similar feelings had been held by some during the years in Rochester, New York (1852-1855). However, Ellen White held that the reproofs given in Paris "were no more than the case deserved." Moreover, "when they were reproved, instead of carefully searching their own heart and confessing their ways, self rose right up [and they said], 'It can't be so.'" She recognized that "Brother White is not perfect. In the ardor of his feelings he may speak too strongly," but pled that those affected discuss the matter with him personally rather than spread rancor among others.

See: Ellen G. White, Lt 8, 1860 (June 11).

1854

APRIL

"He Will Come Again."

Article published in *The Youth's Instructor,* vol. 2, no. 4, April 1854, pp. 28, 29.

1854

MAY, ROCHESTER, NEW YORK

"To the Young."

Article published in *The Youth's Instructor,* vol. 2, no. 5, May 1854, pp. 37, 38.

1854

(Ms 5, 1854)

[JUNE, SYLVAN, MICHIGAN] [1]

Portion of Vision Given at Sylvan, Michigan, June 1854.

Portions of this manuscript are published in Ellen G. White, *Manuscript Releases,* vol. 5, pp. 205, 206.

Proper discipline of children as it relates to their salvation.

I saw the great responsibility of parents to their children, and they must not neglect their solemn duty. Parents, you stand in the place of God to your children, and you must not suffer them to manifest cruel tempers or passions;

[1] The words "Portion of Vision Given at Sylvan, Mich., June 1854" appear on the earliest typed copy. Unfortunately, no handwritten source for this document has been found. Nevertheless, the amount of detail given in this heading—the location as well as month of the vision—suggests that this information has its origins in the earliest sources.

their temper must be subdued, their will broken,[2] or parents will have to render an account of the neglect of their duties to their children. God cannot cover sin and wickedness. Children are the lawful prey of the enemy because they are not subjects of grace, have not experienced the cleansing blood of Jesus.[3] The evil angels can work through these children, and some parents are careless, and suffer them to work with but little restraint. Parents have much to do in this matter, and by subduing or correcting their children can lessen the power of the evil angels upon them and after they have done this duty, they can then bring their children to God, and in the name of Jesus claim His blessing upon them. But God is dishonored and insulted when parents bring their children to Him unsubdued and unconverted, with all their evil tempers and passions, and ask Him to work for them. Parents, you must first do your duty; then go to God and ask Him to do His part, and He will hear you. Correct your children and subdue them, then God will be entreated of you.

I was shown the children of Israel in Egypt when the destroying angel was to pass through the land he was to destroy all the firstborn of man and beast. Israel was commanded to gather their children and families into their houses with them and then mark their door posts with the blood that the destroying angel might pass by the dwellings of Israel; and if they failed to go through this process there was no difference made between them and the Egyptians.

The destroying angel is soon to go forth again, not to destroy the firstborn only, but to slay utterly old and young, both men and women and little children who have not the mark. Parents, the Lord has shown me that if you wish to save your children, separate them from the world, keep them from other wicked children.[4] Subdue their tempers and evil passions; teach them to obey you; then they can more easily obey the commandments of God. After you have done your duty, carry your children to God and plead His blessing upon them, and He that said, "Suffer little children to come unto Me and forbid them not" will be ready to listen to your prayers for them, and the seal or mark of the believing parents will cover the children if they are brought

---

[2] In this context, the "will" that Ellen White says must be broken appears to be the perverse will, the determination to let "cruel tempers or passions" have sway, resulting in "sin and wickedness." Elsewhere her counsels *against* breaking the will warn of an undue, dictatorial control that destroys the child's individuality (*Child Guidance,* pp. 210, 211; *Education,* pp. 288, 289; *Review,* July 8, 1902).

[3] A reference to children who have not yet reached the stage where they can personally understand and experience conversion ("age of accountability").

[4] The analogy between the separation of believers' children from "the world" and the separation of ancient Israelites from the Egyptians at the time of the tenth plague is clarified by Ellen White in 3SG 224: "In order to escape the great judgment of God which He was to bring upon the Egyptians, the token of blood must be seen upon their houses. And they were required to separate themselves and their children from the Egyptians, and gather them into their own houses, for if any of the Israelites were found in the houses of the Egyptians, they would fall by the hand of the destroying angel."

up right.[5] If parents neglect their duty, and leave their children to indulge in wicked, evil passions, the destroying angel will cut them down, and you parents will have an awful account to give for the neglect of your children. You who have not done your duty, now awake and redeem the time. It is but short, but you can work faithfully and can do much for your children. God corrects us when we err and go astray from Him, and you should correct your children when they do wrong. It will be for their happiness here and hereafter.

---

[5] This passage appears to deal with the destiny of children below the age of accountability. Just as protection was afforded the firstborn children of believing Israelites during the tenth plague, so in the future final crisis the "mark of the believing parents will cover the children if they are brought up aright." The parallel is brought out clearly in Manuscript 26, 1885 (Oct. 22): Asked whether "the little children of . . . believing parents would be saved," Ellen White responded, "The faith of the believing parents covers the children, as when God sent His judgments upon the first-born of the Egyptians."

The question of the destiny of children who die before reaching "the age of accountability" has been an unsettled issue among Christians. It receives only passing mention in the writings of Ellen White, perhaps the most substantial treatment being in *Selected Messages,* book 3, pp. 313-315. No major analyses of Ellen White's position on infant salvation have been published. For partial studies, see Alberto R. Timm, in *Revistra do Ancião* (Brazil), October-December 2006, p. 7; Edwin Harry Zackrison, "Seventh-day Adventists and Original Sin," pp. 247, 248, 366-371; Woodrow W. Whidden II, "The Soteriology of Ellen G. White," pp. 130-132; Jairyong Lee, "Faith and Works in Ellen G. White's Doctrine of the Last Judgment," pp. 328-330.

1854

(Ms 7, 1854)

[CIRCA JUNE],[1] N.P.

A Vision Concerning the Children of the Jackson [Michigan] Church.

Previously unpublished.

Proper discipline of children as it relates to their salvation.

I saw that the destroying angel was to slay utterly old and young, men and women, and little children. I then saw that if the Advent parents would have their children saved in the time of trouble from the destroying sword they must take care of them now.[2] They must subdue their passions and correct their wrongs faithfully and with vigilance, [and] suffer not a wrong in them for a moment. I saw that the parents, many of them who believe the present truth, will see their children cut down before their eyes because they have been so tender of their children. They have not used the rod as they should,[3] and their evil propensities have been indulged, and God cannot save them because He cannot cover iniquity.[4] I saw that the parents stood in the place of God to their children. God had intrusted them to the parents' care and they

---

[1] The original/earliest copy bears no date, but the content of this manuscript is very similar to that of Ms 5, 1854 (June). There are also some verbal parallels. It is likely, therefore, that the two accounts describe the same vision. According to a heading at the top of Ms 5, the vision was "given at Sylvan, Mich., June 1854." (See Ms 5, 1854, note 1, regarding the integrity of this heading.)

[2] An allusion to the tenth plague in Egypt and Ezekiel's vision of judgment in Ezekiel 9. In an expanded version of this passage appearing in print some months later Ellen White cited both sources. "The destroying angel is soon to go forth again, not to destroy the first-born alone, but 'to slay utterly old and young, both men, women and little children' who have not the mark."

See: Ellen G. White, "Duty of Parents to Their Children," *Review,* Sept. 19, 1854, pp. 45, 46.

[3] This instruction taken in isolation may suggest that severity in child discipline is being called for. That this is not the case is seen in other documents from the same period. Thus in 1853 Ellen White advised that "it is not the wisest course to be very severe," recommending that "great care should be taken by parents to study the disposition of their children . . . to be very kind and affectionate to their children." Her article on child discipline published in 1854 urges parents to "correct your children in love. Do not let them have their own way until you get angry, and then punish them."

See: Ellen G. White, Lt 4, 1853 (June 30); *idem,* "Duty of Parents to Their Children," *Review,* Sept. 19, 1854, pp. 45, 46. For selected extracts from Ellen White's writings on child discipline, see *Child Guidance,* pp. 223-290.

[4] *See:* Ms 5, 1854, note 5.

would have to render an account if they had been unfaithful of their trust.

I saw that every time the parents suffered their children to go unpunished after they had manifested anger or given way to their evil tempers, the sin was set down to the parents' account and they would have to answer for it, for the parents are generally much more to blame than the children, who are wicked and wrong because the parents neglect their duty. I saw that parents must arouse themselves on this point and do their duty.

I saw that parents trust to the Lord that which God has enjoined upon them. Often they ask God to bless their children, when they stand directly in their children's way. They must first do their duty to their children—correct their tempers, their disobedience and wrongs, and then pray with them and for them for God to do His part and change the heart and bless the children, because they have done what they could do for them.

1854

(Lt 3, 1854)

JULY 12, ROCHESTER, NEW YORK

LETTER TO

Alfred B. and Adaline Pearsall.[1]

This letter is published in entirety in Ellen G. White, *Manuscript Releases,* vol. 7, p. 208.

A warning to a prominent layman against improper familiarity with female church members.

Dear Brother and Sister Pearsall:

In the vision at Grand Rapids [Michigan] I was shown something of your case. I saw that Brother Pearsall had not abstained from all appearance of evil, had been too familiar with the sisters, and had not always behaved with discretion and comeliness with his own wife in the presence of others. These things have brought a reproach upon the cause.[2] Dear Brother Pearsall, you have been indiscreet in practicing the salutation[3] and have made but

---

[1] *Identity:* It can safely be concluded that the addressees are Alfred B. Pearsall and his wife, Adaline Pearsall, partly because during the period 1852 to 1858 no other Pearsalls are mentioned in the *Review*. In addition there is the fact that Alfred and Adaline Pearsall lived in Grand Rapids and the opening sentence assumes that the Pearsalls were acquainted in some way with "the vision at Grand Rapids." In fact, the Whites had attended tent meetings in their hometown less than one month earlier, June 16-18, 1854, and Ellen White had had a vision there. "On the evening of June 18," writes John Loughborough, who accompanied the Whites, "Sr. White had a vision at the house of Bro. Fitch. The vision was full of instruction, reproof, and counsel, for the church present."

See: 1850 U.S. Federal Census, "A. B. Pearsoll" [*sic*], Michigan, Kent County, Grand Rapids, p. 373. For full name, "Alfred B. Pearsall," see 1880 U.S. Federal Census, "Alfred B. Pearsall," Michigan, Calhoun County, Battle Creek, p. 63; search term "Pearsall" in *Words of the Pioneers;* J. N. Loughborough, "Recollections of the Past—No. 11," *Review,* Feb. 24, 1885, p. 122.

[2] Judging by frequent mentions in the *Review,* A. B. Pearsall was a prominent layman in the Grand Rapids church, a liberal donor to church causes and an agent for the *Review* in his area. His prominence added to the "reproach upon the cause" that his indiscretions were bringing.

See: "Receipts," *Review,* July 22, 1852, p. 48; "Agents," *Review,* Feb. 3, 1853, p. 152; "To Correspondents," *Review,* Aug. 4, 1853, p. 48.

[3] The "salutation," or "holy kiss," was practiced by early Sabbatarian Adventists. Ellen White supported the practice on the basis of Paul's instruction in 1 Thessalonians 5:26 but warned against its misuse. Improperly practiced, the holy kiss had the potential of causing public scandal and charges of fanaticism, as had happened when it was practiced among some Millerites in 1845-1846.

little difference as to the time and place, whether you were surrounded by unbelievers or not, and had been ready to practice it too frequently, and no good but evil has resulted from it.

I saw that you had dwelt too much upon little things, nonessentials; had entered too largely into others' business and affairs, and were too precise to bring them to your views and ideas, and the result has been bad. You have been too severe upon others, noticed their faults too much and dwelt upon them, have dwelt too much on articles of dress &c., &c. I saw that you had done very wrong, and been exceedingly unguarded in taking sisters upon your knees. God's Word does not allow it, and you have no right to do it, and you have sinned in so doing. I saw that you could not be too careful and reserved with the sisters. No married man has any right to sit another woman upon his knee, or allow it in a woman, but his own wife. You must be more judicious, more guarded, and watch your . . . [The remainder is missing.]

See: SDAE, s.v. "Foot Washing"; Ellen G. White, *Supplement to the Christian Experience and Views of Ellen G. White*, p. 38; Joseph Bates, *A Vindication of the Seventh-day Sabbath*, p. 71; George R. Knight, *Millennial Fever*, pp. 251, 252.

1854

(Lt 7, 1854)

[JULY, ROCHESTER, NEW YORK][1]

LETTER TO

John Norton and Mary Walker Loughborough.[2]

Portions of this letter are published in Ellen G. White, *Manuscript Releases,* vol. 7, pp. 259, 352.

News of the serious sickness of two members of the White household: Anna White and Clarissa Bonfoey.

Dear Brother John and Sister Mary:

I have written off the vision for you as soon as I could.[3]

---

[1] This letter was apparently written in 1854, after the return of the Whites from their second visit to Michigan. The incidents mentioned in this letter clearly parallel those found in the *Spiritual Gifts* account, which can be firmly dated 1854. Concerning the exact date of Lt 7 we are helped by Ellen White's information that James White had left for "tent meetings" in Vermont on the day of her writing. From the *Review* we learn that the Vermont tent meetings started on July 21, 1854, so presumably James would have left Rochester, New York, some days prior to that. Lt 7 would not have been written earlier than July 12, since Ellen mentions a letter she has sent to "Brother Pearsall," and a letter to Pearsall of that date is found in the White Estate archives.

See: Ellen G. White, *Spiritual Gifts [vol. 2],* p. 191; "Vermont Tent," *Review,* Aug. 15, 1854, p. 4; Ellen G. White, Lt 3, 1854 (July 12).

[2] *Identity:* It is safe to assume that Ellen White is here addressing John and Mary Loughborough, the best known John and Mary couple of this period. There is supporting evidence for this position, in particular the postscript that places John and Mary in or near Jackson. That corresponds well with the fact that John Loughborough made Jackson, Michigan, his base during the summer of 1854 while engaging in tent evangelism in various places in that state. Less tangible is the hint in the opening sentences that the Whites had recently met John and Mary. Here again we know that the two families had met as recently as the previous month at the tent meeting in Grand Rapids, Michigan, June 16-18, and had attended other meetings together in May.

See: Search term "Loughborough" in *Words of the Pioneers;* J. N. Loughborough, "Recollections of the Past—No. 11," *Review,* Feb. 24, 1885, p. 122.

[3] Which vision is referred to here? The language suggests that the vision was recent and that the Loughboroughs were well acquainted with it. John Loughborough had in fact either witnessed or been close by during two of Ellen White's recent visions, in Sylvan, Michigan, on May 13 and in Grand Rapids, Michigan, on June 18. The likelihood is that Ellen White is referring to the Grand Rapids vision since she speaks further on of having sent a copy of the vision to "Brother Pearsall." The White Estate archives do in fact contain a letter to "Brother and Sister Pearsall" dated just before this letter—July 12, 1854—the opening line of which reads "in the vision at Grand Rapids I was shown something of your case." As to the contents of the June 18 vision little is known besides the fragment dealing with Brother Pearsall and

I came home from Michigan as you will know expecting to get rest, but we did not get home until Friday, the very day the conference commenced.[4] That day our house was crowded and was so all through the conference. As soon as the conference closed Clarissa[5] [**Clarissa M. Bonfoey**] was taken sick with fever and ague, and when we returned from the West we found that Anna [**Anna White**] had greatly changed. Consumption has marked her for his victim, and to all human appearance in a few months she will be laid by Nathaniel's [**Nathaniel White**][6] side. We have had a serious time. I found Clarissa and Anna could not eat, had no appetite, and our family did not understand providing for the sick. The conference brought so much labor upon the family they had all they could do, and I was obliged to keep on my feet day after day to wait upon the sick until my feet at night would be blistered, and it was impossible for me to rest I was so exhausted.

Clarissa was very low and two or three times a day we labored in prayer to have the power of the enemy rebuked upon Clarissa. The anxiety of my mind was very great, it has been wrought up to the highest pitch.

Sister Seely[7] lives the next house to us, and there was Brother Rhodes [**Samuel W. Rhodes**][8] sick with fever and ague, and a few days since Brother

---

John Loughborough's summary: "This vision was full of instruction, reproof, and counsel, for the church present, and also encouragement of success for the tent enterprise."

See: J. N. Loughborough, "Recollections of the Past—No. 10," *Review,* Jan. 27, 1885, p. 57; *idem,* "Recollections of the Past—No. 11," *Review*, Feb. 24, 1885, p. 122; Ellen G. White, Lt 3, 1854 (July 12).

[4] The Whites returned to Rochester on Friday, June 23, 1854, after a seven-week journey through Michigan, Ohio, and Wisconsin. The day of their return coincided with the opening day of a major conference held June 23-26 in Rochester.

See: J. N. Andrews, Uriah Smith, "Rochester Conference," *Review,* July 4, 1854, p. 173; Western Tour," *Review,* July 4, 1854, p. 172.

[5] *Identity:* In a parallel account given in *Spiritual Gifts* the surname Bonfoey is given. "After the labor of the conference was over, Sr. Bonfoey was taken down with the fever and ague." Clarissa Bonfoey had assisted in the White household for a number of years, but there are several references to her sicknesses and frail health. She died two years later at age 35.

See: Ellen G. White, *Spiritual Gifts [vol. 2],* p. 191.

[6] *Identity:* Anna White and her brother Nathaniel, siblings of James White, came to live with the Whites in Rochester in November 1852. Already in poor health on arrival, Nathaniel died of tuberculosis six months later, in May 1853, "in the 22nd year of his age." Anna, also described as "very feeble" on arrival, died of the same illness in November 1854, age 25.

See: [James White], *A Brief Account of the Last Sickness and Death of Nathaniel White,* p. 3; obituary: "Anna White," *Review,* Dec. 12, 1854, p. 135.

[7] *Identity:* Probably Laura Seeley (also spelled Seely), wife of **David Seeley**. Laura Seeley's obituary in 1860 describes her as "the very first" in Rochester "to receive the third [angel's message] and come out on the Sabbath of the Lord," so she would presumably have been there when this letter was written six years earlier, in 1854.

See: Obituary: "Laura Seely," *Review,* June 5, 1860, p. 23.

[8] *Identity:* In a letter to the *Review* some months later S. W. Rhodes tells of "the ague and fever with which I was so severely attacked last June at Rochester [which] stayed fast by me . . . until Aug. 29th." This corresponds well with Ellen White's description in this letter of "Brother Rhodes" as being "sick with fever and ague [chills]" in Rochester, and confirms his full identity.

John Andrews [**John N. Andrews**] was taken down with the fever and ague. He had two or three days [of] chills here,[9] but he has now gone to Brother Orton's [**Jonathan T. Orton**].[10]

Anna and Clarissa have been very, very sick. The power of the enemy was broken upon Clarissa about two weeks since, yet her chills continued until yesterday. She and Anna have been unable to labor at all. My sewing has laid almost entirely still. I have been disheartened and nearly discouraged to have so many sick around. I have to have a care in this family that I ought not to have, yet I have felt thankful that my health is so good, but I am getting worn out.[11]

This morning we anointed Anna and prayed for her, just before James left for Vt.[12] Anna has neglected her own case, seemed to be rather stupid to her own condition, until we have feared much it was too late for her. Our trust now is in God, but Anna to all appearance is marked for the grave. We have had some faith that God will have compassion and save her to labor for Him. She has had no faith for herself, but now is aroused some to take hold of God. The above is my excuse for not writing before. I am not going to get down or get discouraged, but do pray for me. I need your prayers. We are trying to hold on to faith. James has gone to Vt. to attend the tent meetings there. I felt that it was his duty to go. I would request the brethren and sisters to remember us in their prayers. Write us often. You must not expect an answer, this is the last letter I can write you for it wearies me much. I have written and sent the vision to Brother Fitch and one to Brother Pearsall [**Alfred B. Pearsall**], also

---

See: S. W. Rhodes, "From Bro. Rhodes," *Review,* Nov. 7, 1854, p. 102.

[9] Notices regarding J. N. Andrews's failing health started to appear in the *Review* in March 1854. In November or December 1854 the Whites took him into their own home, giving him "the best room in the house." By February 1855 James White described Andrews as "broken down at the age of 25." Sometime in May 1855, still not restored, Andrews left Rochester to help on his father's farm in Paris, Maine, hoping to regain his health.

See: "To Correspondents," *Review,* Mar. 7, 1854, p. 56; James White to "Dear Brother," Feb. 9, 1855; "The Office," *Review,* Feb. 20, 1855, p. 182; "Business," *Review,* May 29, 1855, p. 240.

[10] *Identity:* The only Ortons known to live in Rochester during this time are Jonathan T. Orton and his wife, Caroline. They lived very close to the Whites' house at 109 Monroe Street.

See: Search term "Orton" in *Words of the Pioneers;* Jon K. Clayburn, ed., *Rochester's Adventist Heritage,* p. 50.

[11] Ellen White's pregnancy undoubtedly contributed to her tiredness. Her third son, William Clarence, would be born in another five or six weeks, on August 29, 1854.

See: James White to "Brother and Sister Smith," Aug. 29, 1854.

[12] This paragraph adds the detail that James White left to attend tent meetings in Vermont. On July 21, 1854, the first tent meetings to be held in Vermont opened in Waitsfield, with James White present. Allowing a few days to reach his destination, we can assume that White left Rochester in mid-July, which also gives us the approximate date of the letter, since it was written on the day of his departure.

See: J. N. Loughborough, *Rise and Progress of the Seventh-day Adventists,* p. 203; "Vermont Tent," *Review*, Aug. 15, 1854, p. 4.

one to Brother and Sister Brooks and the band in Bedford. I have attempted to write the vision to Brother Frisbie [**Joseph Birchard Frisbie**], but had no liberty to write.[13]

Much love to all.

E. G. White

I meant to have written Brother Smith's family but am too tired. They must excuse me now. I will say that I was very sorry that I did not know when the box of books went to Jackson so that your things did not go, Mary, nor the manuscript. I meant to have sent about Luman, and the frame of the purse Brother Dodge [**Abram A. Dodge**] spoke of. I was sorry but James did not think to speak to me about it till it was mailed and in the wagon.

I would say I spoke of quilts when I was West but I hope none will trouble themselves or rob themselves to send [to] me. We have enough to reach around and if we have a smaller family next spring can do without any more. I spoke about having some strips of carpet woven. I have been thinking we might do without them very well, especially if we reduce our family. So don't trouble about them.

I received a letter from Sister Kellogg.[14] Thank her for writing. It does not tire me too much. Will write her soon.

Much love to each member of Brother Smith's family, also to Bro. and Sister. Their great kindness will never be forgotten by me.[15]

---

[13] Of the four letters mentioned here, only the letter to Brother Pearsall has survived. *See:* Ellen G. White, Lt 3, 1854 (July 12).

[14] This letter is not in the White Estate archives.

[15] The greetings to various members in Jackson no doubt reflect the generosity and hospitality the Whites had received from the Jackson members on several occasions in 1853 and 1854 during their travels in Michigan.

1854

(Lt 8, 1854)

[CIRCA JULY],[1] N.P.

LETTER TO

Brethren and Sisters at Bedford [Michigan].[2]

This letter (previously designated as Lt 14, 1861) is published in entirety in Ellen G. White, *Manuscript Releases,* vol. 21, pp. 364-366.

The weaknesses of Seley Hungerford. An appeal to Bedford members for a spirit of self-denial that they may "sacrifice something for God and His cause."

Dear Brethren and Sisters at Bedford [Michigan]:

While at Grand Rapids I saw the cases of some. I was first shown the case of Brother Hungerford [**Sealey Hungerford**][3]—that he was far from God. He

---

[1] No place or date is given in the earliest copies of this letter. As explained in note 3 below, there is strong census evidence for dating this letter in the 1850s, and other reasons for placing it in the mid-1850s. Even more specifically, a good case can be made for a June/July 1854 date. At this time Ellen White mentioned that she had written to "the band in Bedford" to relate a vision (Lt 7, 1854 [July]). This vision, as argued earlier (Lt 7, 1854, note 3), was given in Grand Rapids, Michigan, on June 18. This matches the circumstances of Lt 8 exactly: a vision received at Grand Rapids sent to Bedford. It therefore seems likely that the vision mentioned in Lt 7 is the same as that in Lt 8 and that both letters were written sometime between June 18 and mid-July 1854. The place of writing is not certain. The Whites arrived back in Rochester, New York, from their journey to Michigan, Ohio, and Wisconsin on June 23, 1854.

See: J. N. Andrews, Uriah Smith, "Rochester Conference," *Review,* July 4, 1854, p. 173; "Western Tour," *Review,* July 4, 1854, p. 172.

[2] "Bedford" is a fairly common town name in the United States. However, a survey of mentions of believers in "Bedford" in the *Review* of the 1850s and early 1860s reveals that they all refer to Bedford in Michigan. The mention of Grand Rapids confirms the Michigan setting. A further question arises in that there are two Bedfords in Michigan; Bedford, Calhoun County, and Bedford, Monroe County. It is evident from a perusal of the *Review* that there was a group of Sabbatarian Adventists in Bedford, Calhoun County, from the early 1850s, but there is no mention of any group in Bedford, Monroe County.

See: Search term "Bedford" in *Words of the Pioneers.*

[3] *Identity:* Identification is quite certain since the only Hungerford family living in Bedford, Calhoun County, at the time of any of the censuses taken during the nineteenth century was that of Seley P. and Mary Ann Hungerford and their children. They are listed for that township in 1850 but not in 1860 or in subsequent censuses. By 1860 Mary had died, and Seley had moved from Bedford. Further, both "S. P." and "Mary Hungerford of Bedford, Mich." are active Sabbatarians in the mid-1850s, being mentioned in the *Review* during the period 1854-1857 in the form of receipts for moneys paid and in an obituary for Mary (Ann), who died in 1857, aged 42. There seems little reason to doubt that Ellen White is describing the case of

realized but little what it was to be a true Christian, a follower of Christ. I saw that religion did not consist in making a noise, but that Brother Hungerford was in the habit of going into meeting and praying long and loud, and after the meeting closed his heat and excitement were gone, and then he was light and trifling; that he seemed to have no foundation, no heartwork—did not show the fruits of a Christian. His conduct out of meeting was such as God abhors. He was too familiar with the sisters, his life was not at all in accordance with his profession, and every day he gave his profession the lie.

He is a reproach to the cause, and it would be better if he had never embraced the third angel's message than to take the course he does—appear to be full of zeal in meeting and when you look for the fruits out of meeting they are not to be found. I saw that he was too dilatory. Much of his time that he should spend in laboring with his hands to support his family and to help the cause was idled away. I saw that he would have to give an account for his strength and time that he has idled away. He is just as accountable for his time and strength as those who have property are accountable for what God has given them. God has given strength to Brother H and he has made a bad use of it. He has not spent it to the glory of God but has felt satisfied and easy if he could go a distance to meeting and idle away his time there when it were much better for him if he was at home laboring with his hands, for he would be no benefit in meeting.

Brother H's heart is far from God. His imprudent conduct has brought a reproach upon the cause that will not be easily wiped away. To be a Christian is to be Christlike, and the habit Brother H has of shouting is no evidence that he is a Christian, for his shouting is regarded by God as no shouting. Half of the time he himself knows not what he is shouting at.

There is also a great lack of neatness and order. God wants His children in these last days to be neat and clean. His commands to the children of Israel were definite in regard to cleanliness. God has not changed or altered. He wants His children in these last days to be clean and holy and have no guile found in their mouth. God will not own a filthy person as a Christian. There is no place for such in heaven, for all is neatness and order there.[4]

I saw that some in Bedford were at fault, did not realize how precious their time was, and that they must be diligent and faithful in the things of this world, or God would not trust them with the true riches. I saw that all did not realize that their time, their strength, was the Lord's, that it was not their own. If they did realize this they would be more diligent, not to add

---

Seley P. Hungerford, and that this letter is written in the 1850s, probably in the middle of the decade.

See: 1850 U.S. Federal Census, "Seley P. Hungerford," Michigan, Calhoun County, Bedford, p. 98; search term "Hungerford" in *Words of the Pioneers.*

[4] See Ms 2, 1853 (Mar. 1), note 3.

land to land and building to building, but to obtain all they could by using the strength God has given them for His precious cause, and then they will receive their reward hereafter.

I saw that there was not that spirit of sacrifice in Bedford that there should be; that some were not careful enough to study, when they decided to attend meetings, whether they were going to gratify themselves or to glorify God. Those who know the truth and are established in it should deprive themselves of privileges in order to assist other souls who are hungry and starving for present truth in other places. There is too much of a spirit and feeling like this: that those who are diligent in their affairs at home, and deprive themselves of the privileges of attending meeting abroad were worldly-minded, when the truth of the matter was they were making a sacrifice of their inclinations and desires, and with their hands were laboring to obtain something for the necessity of God's servants. All these things were noticed of God.

It is not the will of God for His children to be engrossed in cares and get worldly-minded. No, no; and they will never do this if the suffering cause is ever before them. They must die to self. God is not displeased, but approbates His children getting together every Sabbath and listening to the testimonies of each other. Neither does He frown upon their going once a year, or perhaps oftener, to a distance to meeting. But when souls have had a feast—and a rich one—hearing from God's Word of His precious truth, then is the time for them to improve upon what they have heard. Instead of going again and again to hear more, let them ponder over and over what they hear. Many will have to render an account for privileges they have had in attending meeting and hearing the truth they have made no improvement upon.

I saw that it was necessary that all should have the true object rest before them, and then they should be diligent in business, fervent in spirit, serving the Lord. They must remember what Jesus has suffered and sacrificed for them, and they must be watching for an opportunity that they may sacrifice something for God and His cause—watch and see how they can be the means of doing others good. There is too much of a feeling like this: My time is my own; but it is not so. It is not your own. You are bought with a price, and are soldiers, and you must be ever at your post, wherever it is, at home or abroad. Idleness and slothfulness God abhors. Ease and love of self-gratification must be overcome and all must have a spirit of sacrifice.

Those who are in the habit of indulging in passion and of being impatient will have to overcome it. They will, and must be, perfectly subdued by grace or they can never enter heaven. Jesus is the example that is set before us. He endured all the slight and indignity that could be heaped upon Him, yet He opened not His mouth. He that could have had a legion of angels to assist Him had He asked His Father, was the meek Lamb and was spit upon, crowned with a crown of thorns and stretched on Calvary's cross, there to die an ignominious death for our sins. O, it behooved Christ to suffer all this to make a way of escape for lost man! He was the innocent Sufferer, and shall we dare to complain of any sacrifice we have made or can make? Shall we murmur who shall suffer something for our own sins? O, no let us crave the suffering part.

Brethren and sisters in Bedford, learn to suffer more. Learn to deny yourselves more. There is need of it. Die to self. Do not love your ease too much. Have energy in your daily labors and energy in the cause of God. Your reward is not here. Jesus has purchased for us an immortal inheritance and for that we can endure anything. O what love, what wondrous love has been manifested us by the Beloved of the Father! O, do not, any of you, neglect the preparation necessary, and finally be weighed in the balances and found wanting!

1854

JULY 25

"To the Young."

Article published in *The Advent Review, and Sabbath Herald,* vol. 5, no. 25, July 25, 1854, p. 197.

1854

SEPTEMBER 19

"Duty of Parents to Their Children."

Article published in *The Advent Review, and Sabbath Herald,* vol. 6, no. 6, September 19, 1854, pp. 45, 46.

1854

(Lt 5, 1854)

DECEMBER 16, ROCHESTER, NEW YORK

LETTER TO

Brethren and Sisters.[1]

Portions of this letter are published in Ellen G. White, *Manuscript Releases,* vol. 6, p. 297; vol. 7, pp. 259, 260.

News of James White's sickness and the death of his sister Anna.

---

[1] The familiar tone of the letter and the assumption that the receivers are well acquainted with Ellen White's children and Anna and Nathaniel White suggests that the letter may be addressed to James's or Ellen's family or close friends in Maine. However, there is insufficient information in this letter to justify secure conclusions.

(Lt 5, 1854) December 16, 1854

Dear Brethren and Sisters:

I have been wanting to write you for some time but a multitude of cares has hindered me. I have not forgotten your kindness to us, No, no. But we have passed through trials and suffering.

Dear Anna [**Anna White**][2] sleeps in Jesus. For weeks before she died she was entirely helpless and had to be lifted from six to nine times a day, and for months she could not walk without help. Oh, it has been a fearful scene of suffering we have passed through. Anna died a hard death. Oh, how my mind has suffered. My feelings have been intense. Nathaniel [**Nathaniel White**][3] lies low in the grave. Anna sleeps in Jesus.

I have been very fearful, yes greatly alarmed, that the disease that has preyed upon Nathaniel and Anna is preying upon James [**James Springer White**].[4] He has been afflicted in the same way and unless he is speedily relieved he will go in the same way. We have prayed and wrestled with God, and are still holding on to His promises. We have set apart noon in this family for a season of prayer especially for James. We believe God will work for him. Pray for him especially.

Henry's [**Henry Nichols White,** aged 7] health is good. Edson [**James Edson White,** aged 5] is not very well. Baby [**William Clarence White,** born August 29, 1854] seems to be in perfect health. He is a great fat boy. Is three months and a half old and he weighs 17 pounds [7.7 kilograms]. He is good natured, seldom cries, is very playful and active. He has but one fault; that is, he is afraid of singing.[5] My health is quite good for me. But James, poor James, I think he must leave the work sometimes and have quiet rest. I fear at times his life will fall a sacrifice to his incessant labors.[6] I ask again your

---

[2] *Identity:* Anna White, James White's sister, who had lived with the Whites in Rochester, New York, for the previous two years. Already in poor health on arrival, she had died of tuberculosis two weeks earlier on November 30, 1854, age 25.

See: Obituary: "Anna White," *Review,* Dec. 12, 1854, p. 135. Ellen White gives further detail on the last days of Anna White in Ellen G. White, *Spiritual Gifts [vol. 2],* pp. 193, 194.

[3] *Identity:* Nathaniel White, brother of Anna White and James White, had died the previous year, on May 6, 1853, also in the Whites' home in Rochester.

See: [James White], *A Brief Account of the Last Sickness and Death of Nathaniel White.*

[4] "After Anna's death, my husband's health became very poor. He was troubled with cough and soreness of lungs. . . . He seemed to be fast following Nathaniel and Anna to a consumptive's grave."

See: Ellen G. White, *Spiritual Gifts [vol. 2],* pp. 194, 195.

[5] Ellen White's relationship with her sons and their early training is discussed in Jerry Moon, *W. C. White and Ellen G. White,* pp. 34-54; George R. Knight, *Walking With Ellen White,* pp. 79-90.

[6] Some weeks later, seemingly at the end of his tether, James White expressed some of the pressures he and Ellen were under: "The care of a large family, and of the *Review, Instructor,* and Tracts, has fallen principally on us. In this time we have traveled and labored in the churches about one third of the time. This amount of care and labor, together with protracted sickness

prayers. I do want to see you very much. I have about as much as I can do to take care of my three children. You have seen Henry, well Edson has more life and roughery than Henry, so you must know my hands are full.

January 9, 1855. You see the above has been written for some time before I finished it. I made a visit to Mill Grove [New York], and have but just returned. We are as well as usual. Baby weighs 19 pounds [8.6 kilograms], is a fat, healthy boy, perfectly good-natured, seldom cries. My health is quite good except a trouble of bloating which makes me feel unpleasant. I weigh 150 pounds [68 kilograms]. I am very grateful to the friends for their donations to me. I will try to use it just right, knowing it is the Lord's money. You thought of sending a box of dried fruit; it would come very acceptably. Can you get some spikenard? [You] need not preserve it in sugar; send it dry. James ate a part of that you sent to poor Anna and thought it did him good. Many of our friends recommend a constant use of it to James as very healing and useful for the lungs.[7] John Thomas[8] and James need to use it freely.

I want to see you very much. Oh, shall I have the privilege?

---

and deaths in our family, has brought us very near the grave. In this prostrated condition we have been saddened with pecuniary embarrassment, and the unreasonableness of "false brethren." Our usual hours of confinement to our business in past time have been from 14 to 18 out of the 24. This has well nigh ruined our health."

See: "The Office," *Review,* Feb. 20, 1855, p. 182. For a survey of the problems facing James White at this time, see Arthur L. White, *Ellen G. White: The Early Years,* pp. 301, 302, 304-310, 316-318.

[7] American spikenard was a traditional frontier remedy in the old Northwest. According to John Caruso, "The prescription for pneumonia was the same as that of any cough: large quantities of a syrup consisting principally of spikenard and elecampane."

That Ellen White is seeking for an herbal remedy for James's sickness (in addition to the daily prayer sessions mentioned earlier in the letter) may seem anomalous given the many accounts of faith healings among Sabbatarian Adventists from the earliest days of the movement. Clearly, however, the Whites were not averse to the use of natural remedies, as the following extracts illustrate. "We gave remedies with no success" (*Life Sketches,* p. 243). "My child grew feeble. We had used simple herbs, but they had no effect" (*Life Sketches,* p. 253). "I suffered for about one week, nothing seemed to give me relief" (Lt 9, 1853 [Dec. 5]).

There are indications that the use of natural remedies was a contentious issue among some Adventists in the 1850s. Speaking of "roots and herbs," L. V. Masten exclaimed in the *Review,* "Let such as have *no faith* use them! I am fully persuaded that God is well pleased to hear prayer for the sick." On the other hand, D. Hewitt approved of the use of "harmless roots and vegetables" as remedies while warning against the "many kinds of medicine now in use, [which are] deleterious and poison."

A vision received by Ellen White in 1853 sanctioned the use of "beneficial" herbs: "I did see that Brother Hart had pressed the abstinence of herbs in case of sickness too far. I saw that it was right to use herbs that are beneficial for the use of men, but the poisonous herbs—tobacco, etc.—it was not right to use, because it was injuring and breaking down the constitution" (Lt 11, 1853 [Dec. 3]).

See: John Anthony Caruso, *The Great Lakes Frontier,* p. 331; James White and Ellen G. White, *Life Sketches* (1880), pp. 243, 253; L. V. Masten, "Faith," *Review,* Oct. 4, 1853, p. 101; D. Hewitt, "Faith and Medicine," *Review,* Oct. 9, 1856, p. 182.

[8] This person has not been identified.

James says ask them if they can get some spikenard and send me. Much love to all the dear children of God.

From your unworthy sister.

John Loughborough and his wife, Mary. Courtesy of the Center for Adventist Research.

1854

(Lt 6, 1854)

1854 WINTER,[1] N.P.

LETTER TO

Mary J. Loughborough.[2]

Portions of this letter are published in Ellen G. White, *Manuscript Releases,* vol. 10, p. 20.

An appeal to Mary Loughborough to be fully supportive of her husband in his traveling ministry.

Dear Sister Loughborough:

The Lord shewed me that the field of your husband's labors was west, that his work was not east. I saw that the hungry sheep west must be fed and that Brother John would have trials to pass through and much to bear from opposers. When he shall have finished his errands that the Lord has sent him on and shall return home for rest and sympathy, you must be prepared to sympathize with him, and to comfort him and hold up his hands. He must not come home to be burdened and to hold up your hands, but you must be prepared to hold up his hands by kind, sympathizing words, and by your prayers.[3]

---

[1] No place or date is given at the head of this letter, but at the end are found the words "Winter 1854." Even though this is probably an editorial insertion, the handwriting suggests that its origin is close to the period. There is additional internal evidence that this letter was written before the Loughboroughs moved west from Rochester, New York, to Iowa in 1856. As is seen in subsequent letters from Ellen White to Mary Loughborough (see note 4 below), after their move Mary suffered for several years from being separated from relatives and friends in the Rochester area. In this letter (Lt 6), however, it seems quite clear that Mary was still living among her loved ones in Rochester, hence it was written prior to their 1856 move west.

[2] *Identity:* The only Loughboroughs mentioned in the *Review* during the 1850s are John N. Loughborough, a prominent minister and writer who is very frequently referred to, and his brother William K. Loughborough, who receives only occasional mention in this period. Since this letter indicates that "John" is the husband of "Sister Lougborough" it is clear that the addressee is Mary J. Loughborough.

See: Search term "Loughborough" in *Words of the Pioneers.*

[3] There are indications in this and subsequent letters to Mary Loughborough that she found it hard to be married to an itinerant preacher, especially in the early years. Mary Walker and John Loughborough had married in 1851, both aged about 19. The following year John, already a part-time preacher for the "First-day Adventists," as he called them, became a Sabbatarian Adventist and started full-time preaching and traveling. The year 1853 must have been particularly trying for Mary. Leaving Mary at home in Rochester, New York, early that year, John embarked on a two-month itinerary with Hiram Edson through western New York

I saw that his heart often suffered many pangs, that if you had been careful of your words and yielding, he would not have felt. I saw that you have not realized your duty to your husband. He has and does still fondly love you, but there has not been that tenderness on your part towards him and for him that there should be. Often things have been said which would barrow up the soul, and cause him deep sorrow; often you have talked for the sake of talking, which wounded your husband and caused him sorrow and distress. I saw that you had not loved as he has loved, your affections have been too much divided.

Your friends have taken too much of your sympathy. There has not been boldness enough on your part when you have been with them, there has been a shunning or shrinking from letting them know that the interest of your husband, and yourself, was in heaven, and not on the earth.

You have sought to please your friends altogether too much, and if you would have eternal life you must cut loose from relatives and acquaintances and not seek to please them but have your eye single to the glory of God, and serve Him with your *whole heart.*[4]

This will not wean you from your husband at all, but will draw you closer to him, and cause you to leave father, mother, sisters and brothers and friends and cleave to your husband, and love him better than anyone on earth, and make his wishes your wishes. And you can live in harmony and happiness.

I saw that you had often teased and fretted him until he would speak impatiently to you. This I saw on both sides was all wrong. God has given the man the preference; he is the head and the wife is to obey the husband, and the husband is not to be bitter against the wife, but love her as his own body.[5] Dear Sister, I saw that you were not half given up to God, not half consecrated to Him. Your will was not swallowed up in the will of God. And you must get ready, fitted and prepared for Christ's coming, or you will come short,

---

and Pennsylvania. He then returned to Rochester for a few weeks before setting off again on a five-month journey through Ohio, Michigan, Illinois, and Wisconsin, coming back at the end of September. Ellen White's letter suggests that Mary was not fully prepared for this kind of sacrifice, a theme to which she returns in later letters.

For an accessible account of J. N. Loughborough's life adapted from primary sources, giving the biographical details listed above, see Adriel Chilson, ed., *Miracles in My Life.*

[4] In addition to the problem of John Loughborough's long absences from home, mentioned above, Ellen White is probably referring to the problem of Mary's strong ties to friends and relatives in the Rochester area, which made her unwilling to move westward, where John's work lay (see opening sentence of letter). The Loughboroughs finally moved west to Iowa in 1856 and the following year to Michigan, but Mary continued to pine for Rochester. In a strong appeal to Mary in 1858 Ellen admonished her friend, "You must die to Rochester." Ellen further reminded Mary that when she married John, she knew about "his wandering life. You chose him, a messenger of God."

See: Adriel Chilson, ed., *Miracles in My Life,* pp. 45, 50; Ellen G. White, Lt 1, 1858 (Mar. 3).

[5] Extracted from Ephesians 5:23-28.

be weighed in the balance and found wanting. You must be more devoted to God, more in earnest about your soul's salvation and your eternal interest. I saw that if you would labor with your husband for God, you would not lose your reward. That is, labor to have him free and not lay a feather in his way but cheer, encourage, and hold him up by your prayers. God will notice it and will reward you.

In love.

1855

(Ms 3, 1855)

MAY 5,[1] [BATTLE CREEK, MICHIGAN][2]

Fragments.

Portions of this manuscript are published in Arthur L. White, *Ellen G. White: The Early Years,* p. 318.

Prospects of recovery for James White. Future of publishing house.

I then inquired if James [**James Springer White**] would be spared or would be removed before the time of trouble.[3] Said the angel, What is that to thee?[4] Follow Jesus, follow the opening providence of God. Have unwavering faith in His promises. Walk by faith and not by sight.

In regard to the office and what our duty is in regard to it, had no light,[5]

---

[1] It is often the case with manuscripts relating the content of visions that the date assigned is the date of the vision, not the date of committing it to writing, which usually followed shortly after. This may be the case with this manuscript also, since James White reports elsewhere that Ellen had a public vision in Battle Creek on May 5, 1855.

See: James White, "Meetings at Battle Creek," *Review,* May 15, 1855, p. 228.

[2] According to James White's report, Ellen and he were in Battle Creek, Michigan, on Sabbath, May 5, 1855, the date given to this manuscript.

See: Ibid.

[3] Ellen White's question probably reflects her anxiety concerning James's state of health throughout most of 1855. After his sister Anna White, who lived in the White home, died of tuberculosis in November 1854, Ellen was "greatly alarmed, that the disease that has preyed upon Nathaniel and Anna is preying upon James" (Lt 5, 1854 [Dec. 16]). Although he gained some relief during the spring of 1855, his condition again worsened, and Ellen White later confessed that for months prior to their move to Battle Creek in November 1855 she "greatly feared" that her children "might be left without a father's care."

See: Ellen G. White, Lt 5, 1854 (Dec. 16); *idem,* "Communication From Sister White," *Review,* Jan. 10, 1856, p. 118; *idem, Spiritual Gifts [vol. 2],* pp. 194-198; EGWEnc, s.v. "Time of Trouble."

[4] An allusion to John 21:22, 23.

[5] The future of the publishing house ("the office") had been under intense discussion for several months. In the February 20, 1855, issue of the *Review* James White had publicly issued a cry for help, citing overwork, poor health, and lack of financial support as reasons that fundamental changes had to be made. One of the options considered to ease the situation was relocation. During the week prior to the May 5 vision the Whites had consulted with members in Battle Creek, Michigan, about locating the publishing house in their town. James White felt that "the climate, water, prices of rent, fuel, provisions etc. seem favorable to the location," but he was not ready to make a decision yet. Ellen White's statement that she had "no light" probably refers to this relocation issue. The question was decided only in late August 1855, after James White had investigated the relative advantages of locating in Vermont.

See: "The Office," *Review,* Feb. 20, 1855, p. 182; James White, "Meetings at Battle Creek," *Review,* May 15, 1855, p. 228. For a survey of events leading to the move to Battle

but was sighted to other visions that God had given.[6] Look at them carefully; lose not sight of the opening providences of God; carefully regard all His teachings and obey them. I saw that no longer should those connected with the office bear the burdens they have borne.[7] They must, they must, be free in mind and then their health will improve. There has been none to help them bear their burdens, but if faint or discouraged the comfort they had was to see others in the same state.

Creek, see Gerald Wheeler, *James White,* pp. 81-83.

[6] An example of an earlier vision dealing with possible relocation of the press was Ms 4, 1854, written in April 1854: "I then saw that the church must be united, and if they could not endure straight testimonies when they were needed and we were bound, we must move the office and go where we could bear them."

[7] Willing sacrifice had been a central motif for the 15 or so persons working at the publishing house. "Those who . . . joined us in this enterprise," James White noted, "toiled for no more than food and clothing. Their deprivations at times, and their toils were not small." Ellen White provides further insights in an 1853 letter: "Luman is coughing again; his lungs are affected. . . . He has overdone often. Stephen Belden and Fletcher Byington do not return from the office until 10, 12, 2 or 3 o'clock. They have labored uncommonly hard of late, and God has strengthened them, or they must have broken down." Luman Masten subsequently died of tuberculosis (1854, age about 25), as did two other colleagues, Anna White (1854, age 26) and Annie Smith (1855, age 27). Conditions of employment did improve after the move to Battle Creek in November 1855. According to the February 21, 1856, edition of the *Review,* "those who labor in connection with the *Review,* receive moderate wages."

See: "The Office," *Review,* Feb. 20, 1855, p. 182; Ellen G. White, Lt 7, 1853 (Aug. 24); "The Church at Battle Creek: To the Churches and Brethren Scattered Abroad," *Review,* Feb. 21, 1856, p. 168; Gerald Wheeler, *James White,* pp. 77, 78.

1855

JUNE 12

"To the Church."

Article published in *The Advent Review, and Sabbath Herald,* vol. 6, no. 31, June 12, 1855, p. 246.

1855

(Lt 1, 1855)

AUGUST 26, TOPSHAM, MAINE

LETTER TO

John Nevins Andrews.[1]

Portions of this letter are published in Ellen G. White, *Manuscript Releases,* vol. 9, pp. 313, 314.

Concerning the wisdom of J. N. Andrews' plans to marry Angeline Stevens.

Dear Brother John:

There were two things in the vision given me at Paris [Maine][2] that I could not remember. Some things were perfectly lost to me while with you, or hid from me so that I could not speak them.[3] While writing the other parts

---

[1] *Identity:* That Ellen White is addressing John Nevins Andrews is evident primarily by the focus on an impending marriage to "Angeline." J. N. Andrews married Angeline S. Stevens the following year, on October 29, 1856.

See: Ron Graybill, "The Family Man," in Harry Leonard, ed., *J. N. Andrews: The Man and the Mission,* p. 21.

[2] Ellen and James White had left Paris, Maine, three days earlier after spending nine days there (Aug. 14-23, 1854). While in Paris, Ellen received a vision, probably on August 22, concerning James's overwork and consequent ill health. Whether this August 22 vision also included the J. N. Andrews instruction given here or whether it was given in a separate vision during Ellen's visit to Paris is not known. For evidence that the Whites spent August 14-23 in Paris, see Ms 2, 1855 (Aug. 26), note 2, and Lt 2, 1855 (Aug.). On the August 22 vision, see James White to "Dear Brother ("Private"), [c. Aug. 24,] 1855, and Ms 2, 1855 (Aug. 26).

[3] J. N. Andrews, because of continuing health problems, had moved back to his parents'

of the vision these things have unfolded to my mind.

I told you that I saw you could not glorify God by taking the step you have contemplated, as you have glorified Him in your past life. Instead of having less care while engaged in the great work, as you approach the time of trouble your care will be doubled, your anxiety increased. In no way are you bettering your situation. Instead of marrying one that can take care of, and nurse you, it is just the opposite. I saw that in this thing your eye has not been single to the glory of God and the advancement of His cause. Since your return home you have been losing spiritual strength and energy. You have not, while engaged in this matter, grown in grace.

I will now write the part hid from me while with you. I saw that you could do no better now than to marry Angeline [**Angeline S. Stevens**]; that after you have gone thus far it would be wronging Angeline to have it stop here. The best course you can now take is to move on, get married, and do what you can in the cause of God. Annie's disappointment cost her her life.[4]

---

home in Paris by May 1855. Ellen White was thus able to meet him in person during this visit to Paris.

See: "The Office," *Review,* Feb. 20, 1855, p. 182; "Business," *Review,* May 29, 1855, p. 240.

[4] *Identity:* Ronald Graybill has argued convincingly that Ellen White is here referring to Annie Rebekah Smith, gifted poet and writer. Annie Smith came to Saratoga Springs, New York, in 1851 to assist James White with the *Review* as copy editor and moved with the publishing office to Rochester, New York, when it relocated there in 1852. Seen in their context, the words "Annie's disappointment" imply unrequited love, and Graybill argues that Annie Smith, possibly through a misunderstanding, thought that Andrews had a serious romantic interest in her, hopes that were subsequently dashed. Graybill endeavors to show that Annie's disappointed hopes left their trace in some of her poems and hymns.

Certainly J. N. Andrews would have been in frequent contact with Annie Smith during her time at the *Review*. Throughout this period, in between extended preaching tours, Andrews lived in the vicinity of the *Review* office, first at Saratoga Springs and then in Rochester. While at Rochester, Andrews boarded for months at a time with the Whites, as did a number of *Review* staff, including Annie Smith.

Annie Smith also fits the description of Lt 1 in the fact of her tragic death from tuberculosis one month earlier, on July 26, 1855, at age 27. The assertion "Annie's disappointment cost her her life" may appear a very severe indictment against J. N. Andrews. Graybill suggests a milder interpretation: "It was probably justified even from a medical standpoint, since depression makes one so much more vulnerable to disease and since there was plenty of disease lurking in that house on Mount Hope Avenue [the White residence in Rochester]. James White's brother Nathaniel and sister Anna had already died of tuberculosis in those crowded quarters."

Although far less likely, there is a possibility that Ellen White is, in fact, referring to **Anna White**, sister of James White, rather than to Annie Smith. She calls Anna White "Annie" in at least two places in her writings. Anna White and her brother **Nathaniel White** came to live with the Whites in Rochester in 1852. Described as "very feeble" when she arrived, Anna became a Sabbathkeeper soon thereafter, her health improved, and by 1854 she had been given the editorship of *The Youth's Instructor*. However, illness set in again, and she succumbed to tuberculosis in November 1854, at age 25. J. N. Andrews conducted her funeral service.

See: Ron Graybill, "The Life and Love of Annie Smith," *Adventist Heritage* 2 (Summer 1975): 14-23; "Letters," *Review,* Sept. 2, 1851, p. 24; "Conferences," *Review,* Mar. 23, 1852, p. 112; J. N. Andrews et al, *Defense of Eld. James White and Wife,* p. 20; James White to E. P.

I saw that you were injudicious in her case, and it all grew out of a mistaken view you had of James [**James Springer White**]. You thought that he was harsh and impatient toward Paris friends, and you stepped right in between Annie and us; sympathized with her in everything. Your interest manifested for her was undue and uncalled for, and showed that you had a great lack of confidence in us.[5]

I saw that the impression upon the minds of friends in Paris is now and has been, yourself not excepted, that we made too much of the trials there; that they were not so faulty as we thought. This is not so. The things there have been shown in vision in their true light, and have not been exaggerated at all. Nothing have we held and nothing do we hold towards friends in Paris. No, no. I only relate the vision which refers to things that trouble or difficulties grew out of.[6]

I saw that now it would be better for you both to marry, but God had not designed it so. But the best course now, with the least evil results, is to go forward.

You shall have the rest of the vision about different things. Will write you when I have time.[7]

E. G. White

Please read and return this to me at Rochester [New York], and I will send the whole together.

Butler, Dec. 12, 1861; Ron Graybill, "The Family Man," p. 20; Ellen G. White, Lt 95, 1886 (Feb. 16); Ms 89, 1899 (June 19); obituary: "Anna White," *Review*, Dec. 12, 1854, p. 135.

[5] The criticism in this paragraph and the next, that J. N. Andrews had unwisely sympathized with those who had been admonished and rebuked by the visions, is a recurring theme in subsequent letters from Ellen White to Andrews.

See: Ellen G. White, Lt 8, 1860 (June 11); Lt 11, 1862 (Nov. 9).

[6] References in Ellen White's writings to resentment against the Whites by the Andrews and Stevens families of Paris, Maine, go back to 1851. The two families had not taken well to the leadership of the Whites during their stay in Paris in 1850-1851, in particular resenting the rebukes received through Ellen White's visions and from James White. For the next decade several members of the two families gave faint recognition to the visions and were critical of the leadership of James White. Even J. N. Andrews took part to some degree in this negative spirit.

See: Ellen G. White, Ms 9, 1851 (1851), and Lt 8, 1860 (June 11). For surveys of the relationship of the Andrews and Stevens families to the Whites, see Gerald Wheeler, *James White,* pp. 101-109; Ron Graybill, "The Family Man," pp. 16-18.

[7] This letter, if written, is not in the White Estate archives.

1855

(Ms 2, 1855)

AUGUST 26, [TOPSHAM, MAINE][1]

Vision at Paris, Maine.

Portions of this manuscript are published in S. T. Belden, G. W. Amadon, and William Hall, *To Brother J. N. Andrews and Sister H. N. Smith* (PH016), pp. 33-35; Arthur L. White, *Messenger to the Remnant*, p. 40.

Call for James White to cut down on his overwork, which was endangering his life.

I saw while at Paris [Maine][2] that James's [**James Springer White**] health has been in a critical situation; that his anxiety of mind has been too much for him. When the present truth was first published, he had to put forth double energies and labor with but little encouragement, and from the first he has taken burdens upon him that were too much for his strength. The burdens were not equally borne. While he took much responsibility, some were not willing to take any, and those who shunned taking responsibilities and burdens did not realize his burdens and were not as interested in the cause as they should have been. There was a lack. James felt it and laid his shoulder under burdens that were too heavy.

He has thought he could deny himself of many things that were actually necessary to health and God would sustain him; that he could labor days without any rest. The labor has not only been days but nights too.[3] He has looked upon things in their wrong light; he has violated the laws of nature, and his health has suffered in consequence.

---

[1] No place of writing is given in the original. That the manuscript is written in Topsham is inferred from the fact that Ellen White wrote a letter on the same day, August 26, 1855, from "Topsham, Maine" (Lt 1, 1855).

[2] The vision can be dated to sometime between August 14 and August 23, 1855, when the Whites visited Paris, Maine, in the course of their 11-week tour to the East. A careful reading of James White's letter headed "Private" suggests that the vision took place on August 22, 1855.

See: Ellen G. White, Lt 2, 1855 (Aug.); James White to Abram A. Dodge, Aug. 20, 1855; *idem,* to "Dear Brother," Aug. 24, 1855; *idem,* to "Dear Brother" ("Private"), [c. Aug. 24,] 1855.

[3] James White's distress had come to a head some months earlier. In the February 20, 1855, issue of the *Review* he expressed himself forcefully: "The care of a large family, and of the *Review, Instructor*, and Tracts, has fallen principally on us. In this time we have traveled and labored in the churches about one third of the time. This amount of care and labor, together with protracted sickness and deaths in our family, has brought us very near the grave. . . . Our usual hours of confinement to our business in past time have been from 14 to 18 out of the 24."

See: "The Office," *Review*, Feb. 20, 1855, p. 182.

I saw by these extra efforts more souls would be saved, but it is these efforts that have undermined the constitution and taken away his strength. Regardless of his own interest and health, he has labored with interest for others and it has not been appreciated. His reward from many has been dissatisfaction, evil surmising, and jealousy. Those who should have helped him bear the burdens were a burden themselves by their unwise course. By care and incessant labor and overwhelming anxiety has the work gone on until now the present truth is clear, its evidence by the candid undoubted, and it is easy work now to carry on the paper to what it was a few years ago. The truth is now made so plain that all can see it and embrace it if they will, but it needed much labor to get it out clear as it is, and such hard labor will never have to be performed again to make the truth clear.[4]

I was pointed back to Paris[5] when we were there and Brethren Andrews [**John Nevins Andrews**] and Rhodes [**Samuel W. Rhodes**][6] went to Vermont. James was all awake to the interest of the cause and the interest of Brethren Andrews and Rhodes that they should go comfortable, and neglected his own health.[7] He had been closely confined through the winter, his health and strength run down by lack of nourishing food[8] and by constant labor.

---

[4] For more detail on the difficulties and challenges faced by James White in establishing his publishing work, see biographies by Gerald Wheeler and Virgil Robinson. Gerald Wheeler, *James White;* Virgil Robinson, *James White.*

[5] Which of James White's many journeys is being described in this paragraph and the next? We are told that it was undertaken while the Whites were living in Paris (October 1850–June 1851), that James made sure that Andrews and Rhodes on their trip to Vermont traveled comfortably while he traveled uncomfortably, exposed to the cold, with resulting long-term consequences to his health. This sounds very much like James and Ellen's journey to New Hampshire and Vermont in January 1851, described by Ellen at some length in her autobiographical account *Spiritual Gifts.* The notes that follow confirm that this is the case.

See: Ellen G. White, *Spiritual Gifts [vol. 2],* pp. 144-147.

[6] *Identity:* Notices in the *Review* make clear that "Brethren Andrews and Rhodes" were traveling preachers who had traveled together in eastern Maine during December 1850 and in New Hampshire, Vermont, and Canada East in January 1851. The only traveling preachers in that period with those surnames were John Nevins Andrews and Samuel W. Rhodes.

See: [Notice] *Review,* January 1851, p. 31; J. N. Andrews, "Conference at Melbourne, C. E.," *Review,* January 1851, p. 38; search terms "Andrews" and "Rhodes" in *Words of the Pioneers.*

[7] According to the *Spiritual Gifts* account and notices in the *Review,* the Whites lent their horse to Rhodes and Andrews in early January 1851 so that they could travel independently and in relative comfort on their preaching itinerary to Vermont and Canada East. This left the Whites without personal transport for their journey to New Hampshire and Vermont, also in January, and having to arrange transportation on an ad hoc basis as they went along. One of the low points of their trip was the three-day sleigh journey to Waterbury, Vermont. "There were three of us in an open sleigh, without a buffalo skin or even a horse-blanket to protect us from the cold."

See: Ellen G. White, *Spiritual Gifts [vol. 2],* p. 145.

[8] James White later recalled that while boarding with the Andrews family in Paris, during the winter of 1850-1851, "I seldom ate anything beside potatoes and salt with a few spoonfuls of milk on them and corn bread."

[He] required the greatest care and [needed] to journey comfortably, but he neglected his own health and trusted to get along any way and journeyed most uncomfortably and inconveniently, thinking if he sacrificed for others, God would take care of his health. He disregarded the laws of health, did not study his ease or comfort and was exposed to colds to save expense and help others; and the effects of colds taken upon that journey, and then the trials connected with the journey, have never yet been got rid of. The constitution became run down, disease fastened itself upon the lungs and its effects are still visible.

After all this evidence that his brethren had of his interest in the cause, many looked over it all and the very ones he had helped were jealous and fault-finding; and in Brother Butler's [**Ezra Pitt Butler**][9] house where he labored under many difficulties and had to wade through evil feelings of jealousy and unbelief, it cost him much. He labored far beyond his strength, and through other's wrong courses, he was left alone with but little, if any, sympathy. His friends were his enemies. Although they did not all realize it, it was so.[10]

These trials have done their work; but although all even now do not realize or understand the sufferings of mind caused by those trials, God has noticed them. Not one sorrowful pang will be passed by unnoticed. Disease has been making progress upon him,[11] but God has answered prayer in his behalf and done that for him that no medicine could do. I saw the efforts made for the recovery of health were right, but God's power above all,[12] said the angel. I

See: James White to E. P. Butler, Dec. 12, 1861.

[9] *Identity:* Until February 1853 the only "Butler" mentioned in the *Review* was Ezra P. Butler, of Waterbury, Vermont. That Ellen White is referring to E. P. Butler is confirmed by the fact that the Whites visited Waterbury in the course of the January 1851 journey here described.

See: Search term "Butler" in *Words of the Pioneers.*

[10] This is a comment on the Whites' visit to Waterbury (E. P. Butler residence), scheduled for January 18, 19, 1851. The parallel account in *Spiritual Gifts* throws further light on the "jealousy" and "fault-finding" found there. "Satan had tempted some of the brethren that we had too good a horse" and "jealousy was aroused that Bro. White was making money." "Our spirits were crushed," writes Ellen, "to receive such treatment from our brethren."

See: Ellen G. White, *Spiritual Gifts [vol. 2],* pp. 145, 146.

[11] During the winter of 1854-1855 Ellen White expressed the fear that James was contracting tuberculosis, the same disease that had recently taken the lives of his brother Nathaniel and sister Anna. Although James gained some relief during the spring of 1855, his condition again worsened, and Ellen later confessed that for months prior to their move to Battle Creek in November 1855 she "greatly feared" that her children might be left "without a father's care."

See: Ibid., pp. 194-198; *idem,* "Communication From Sister White," *Review,* Jan. 10, 1856, p. 118.

[12] The Whites clearly did not agree with members such as L. V. Masten, who rejected any medical intervention at all—even natural remedies—and wrote, "Let such as have no faith use them!" James White, feeling better for a time in the spring of 1855, attributed some of his improvement to various remedies. "Faith in God, cold water compresses, and bathing, Hough's syrups, rest, or, rather, usual hours of labor, walking, running, horse-back riding etc., are slowly raising me. I feel confident that God approves a portion at least of these remedies."

saw that medicine could not cure him. God's power had sustained him and by still looking to the stronghold, he would obtain strength. I saw that he must lay aside his anxiety and care, for God is willing he should be relieved from such wearing labor and have rest in a measure[13] and attend more to the cultivation of the minds of our children; try to fit them for heaven, explain in an easy way to them, and in an understanding manner, the way of salvation.

I saw also that more time should be spent in devotion and care for our own souls; that our duty would not be as we travel to enter into individual trials and the burdens would not be laid upon us as they have been; that such mental trials and sufferings endured for others' wrongs would be too much for his now broken-down health. God is lifting these burdens from us and James has not understood it; has feared he was displeasing God and that was why he did not feel the burdens, but in mercy God has been relieving from these burdens. He could now take all the anxiety and care upon him, labor with all his might and last a short time and go down to the grave; or he can now be relieved while he has some strength left, improve and last longer and his voice can be heard and he can have influence yet and do good.

See: James White to Abram A. Dodge, Mar. 11, 1855; L. V. Masten, "Faith," *Review,* Oct. 4, 1853, p. 101.

[13] With the move a few months later of the publishing house from Rochester, New York, to Battle Creek, Michigan, James White obtained some measure of relief. While White remained overall manager of the publishing work, Uriah Smith was appointed resident editor, and financial responsibility was vested in a publishing committee rather than being the personal responsibility of James White as before. In addition, with the move to Battle Creek, the Whites no longer had to run a lodging house for *Review* workers, as they had done in Rochester. Ellen White sums up the positive changes in *Spiritual Gifts:* "From the time we moved to Battle Creek, the Lord began to turn our captivity."

See: Ellen G. White, *Spiritual Gifts [vol. 2],* p. 203. For surveys of improvements for the Whites with the move to Battle Creek, see Arthur L. White, *Ellen G. White: The Early Years,* pp. 320, 321; Gerald Wheeler, *James White,* pp. 86, 87.

1855
(Lt 2, 1855)

AUGUST,[1] PARIS, MAINE

LETTER TO
Harriet Newall Stevens.[2]
Previously unpublished.

A visit to James White's parents and two sisters in Maine.

Dear Sister Harriet:

Here I am at your old home in the girls' chamber.[3] I presume you have spent many hours here. Well, it is a pleasant place, a pleasant house. Everything seems pleasant except the sickness of Angeline [**Angeline S. Stevens**] and Paulina [Paulina R. Stevens],[4] poor children are truly afflicted.

Since we wrote you last[5] a few things may have transpired that will be interesting. Will write just as it has been. Left Palmyra [Maine] Sabbath morn,[6] sick and disheartened, for Hartland [Maine].[7] Father [**John White**] seemed too much worried and troubled about his work to be hardly at all interested in

---

[1] No year is given, but the sequence of events related in this letter matches what is reported by James White for their visit to Maine in 1855. According to the *Review* report, the Whites visited Palmyra, then traveled to Hartland for Sabbath meetings, and on to East Pittsfield for further meetings on Sunday.

See: James White, "Visit to Maine," *Review*, Sept. 4, 1855, p. 36.

[2] *Identity:* Major clues to Harriet's identity are that she had lived in Paris (first and last paragraphs) and that she has two sisters named Angeline and Paulina (which is the likeliest interpretation of the first paragraph). These particulars exactly fit Harriet Stevens, daughter of **Cyprian** and **Almira Stevens**, of Paris, Maine. Ellen White was closely acquainted with Harriet Stevens, who had left Paris the year before to assist James White at the publishing house in Rochester, New York. Now that Ellen was visiting Harriet's house in Maine, it was natural for her to write a friendly letter to Harriet, back home in Rochester.

See: 1850 U.S. Federal Census, "Harriet Stevens," Maine, Oxford County, Paris, p. 194.

[3] The Whites' visit to Paris, Maine, was in mid-August 1855, toward the end of an 11-week journey through New York, Vermont, Massachusetts, and Maine, which had started in mid-June and ended back in Rochester, New York, on August 30, 1855.

See: "At Home," *Review*, Sept. 4, 1855, p. 36.

[4] *See:* Note 2.

[5] The most recent letter from Ellen White to Harriet Stevens that is still extant is Lt 1, 1854, written March 10, 1854, more than a year earlier, but would not fit into the short-term time scale suggested here. The letter referred to here is not in the White Estate archives.

[6] Aug. 11, 1855. See "Visit to Maine," *Review*, Sept. 4, 1855, p. 36.

[7] The three towns mentioned in these opening paragraphs—Palmyra (the parental home of James White), Hartland, and Pittsfield—are within about 10 miles (16 kilometers) of each other.

the things of God. This grieved us much. He had given up almost his anxiety and concern upon the Sabbath question and concluded Sunday would do for him, that as he was situated, the Lord would not require him to keep a new Sabbath and he could not work upon Sunday if he did, and he had about made up his mind to settle down in Palmyra.

James [**James Springer White**] was burdened and distressed beyond measure on the way to Hartland. He wept like a child. I pitied him. He said he wanted to help his folks, but they would not be helped. Mother [**Betsey White**] did not feel as Father did. She longed to keep the Sabbath. She believed it with all her heart.[8]

At Hartland had a good meeting. All there were very glad to see us. There is a band in Pittsfield [Maine] lately been raised up. First rate people, I should judge; some of them were present.

James had quite a free time and the church was much comforted. Took supper with Brother and Sister Flanders [**Samuel W.** and **Elizabeth M. Flanders**].[9] They seem good. She is quite feeble. I do not think she can stay with us long. She seems to love the truth much. James was much distressed that night. Could not seem to get liberty. I was quite sick, but was relieved in answer to prayer.

Sunday, rose with sick headache, but go we must. Had an appointment to Pittsfield in the afternoon, about 12 miles [19 kilometers] distant. We rode in company with Abram and wife.[10] They have three children, quite smart, nice children. We stopped on the way to Brother Burton's [**Samuel G. Burton**],[11] a poor Brother with nine children. Was so sick, had to lie down and in about an hour arose, refreshed, took dinner with them. They had molasses to sweeten

---

[8] John White was a longstanding member and deacon in the Christian Connection denomination. According to his obituary, John White had since 1842 "cherished faith in the leading points of the Advent doctrine," without, apparently, leaving the Christian Connection. Despite the efforts of Ellen and James, he did not become a Sabbathkeeper until some years later (see note 15 below).

See: "The Venerable Dead," *Review,* July 18, 1871, p. 36.

[9] *Identity:* Although there are several individuals named Flanders mentioned in the *Review* during the 1850s, the only ones located in the Hartland–Pittsfield area of Maine, through which the Whites were traveling, were Samuel W. and Elizabeth M. Flanders, of Canaan, about eight miles (13 kilometers) from Hartland.

See: Search term "Flanders" in *Words of the Pioneers.*

[10] These persons have not been identified.

[11] *Identity:* Very likely "Brother Burton" is S. G. Burton of Pittsfield, Maine, the only Burton mentioned in the *Review* during the 1850s. Since he is located in Pittsfield, the very area through which the Whites were traveling, the identity is confirmed. That "S. G." stands for "Samuel G." is given in census information.

See: Search term "Burton" in *Words of the Pioneers;* 1840 U.S. Federal Census, "Samuel G. Burton," Maine, Somerset County, Pittsfield, p. 210; 1850 U.S. Federal Census, "Samuel P. [*sic*] Burton," Maine, Somerset County, Pittsfield, p. 93; 1860 U.S. Federal Census, "Simon [*sic*] G. Burton," Maine, Somerset County, Mayfield, p. 0; 1870 U.S. Federal Census, "Samuel G. Burton," Maine, Somerset County, Mayfield, p. 238.

our drink with. They are real good people. After dinner we prepared to start again when our father's old [horse] "Dianna" acted bad, threw herself down, etc., but we got along without much difficulty. Was some frightened though. At a schoolhouse our meeting was held. It was well filled. Lothrope [**Howard Lothrop**][12] and wife were present. They acted as though they were trying to pray James down, also self, but did not do much. He has been trying to make a division between Pittsfield and Hartland band, has had some success and the evidence is quite certain that he has sent for the *Messenger* paper, that wicked, vile paper, and distributed it everywhere broadcast. I think he is one of their kind, and the sooner we are rid of them the better. As soon as meeting was done, out they went before we had hardly time to look up. Did not even speak to us.

I think the children will not be left in darkness. They will see these things and know of what spirit he is of.

After meeting closed we went to the house [of] one of the brethren. They made us stop to supper, molasses again for drink. There we met a Scotch girl from the highlands of Scotland. She is a Sabbathkeeper. Talks much like Jane [**Jane ("Jenny") Fraser**].[13]

We drove to Father's that night, found Mary Chase [**Mary S. Chase**][14] had come there from Fairfield [Maine]. It was a glad meeting. She is a dear good sister. Our hearts run together like two drops of water. That night we talked the truth out as it is and then James prayed and prayed out all his feelings. There was a whole sermon in that prayer. Every word had weight to it and I knew it was reaching the heart. Father was deeply moved. Next morn the same spirit came upon me and I could not hold my peace. The Lord helped to pour

---

[12] *Identity:* Ellen White's association of Mr. Lothrop with the "*Messenger* paper," which was published by the breakaway *Messenger* Party, provides a useful indication of his identity. James White later recalled an "Eld. Lothrop" who had joined "in full fury with the Messenger spirits against us and the *Review*." Since both "Lothrope" and "Lothrop" are associated with the *Messenger* Party, it seems likely that they are one and the same person, despite the divergence in spelling. James White provides the further information that Lothrop was a preacher and that the Whites had met him in Canada East. This points to Howard Lothrop, from Eaton, Canada East, as the person in question. There are several reports in the *Review* of Howard Lothrop's preaching activities during the early 1850s, and James White mentions meeting with "Brother and Sister Lothrop of Eaton" while in Canada East in 1850.

See: [James White], "Organization," *Review*, Aug. 27, 1861, p. 100; W. [James White], "Our Tour East," *Advent Review*, August 1850, p. 15; search term "Howard Lothrop" in *Words of the Pioneers;* EGWEnc, s.v. "*Messenger* Party."

[13] *Identity:* Probably Jane Fraser, who assisted in the White household. According to the 1860 census she originally came from Scotland.

See: 1860 U.S. Federal Census, "Jane Frazer," Michigan, Calhoun County, Battle Creek, p. 224.

[14] Older sister of James White, married to Daniel Chase in Fairfield, some 20 miles (32 kilometers) from Palmyra.

See: 1850 U.S. Federal Census, "Mary Chase," Maine, Somerset County, Fairfield, p. 133.

out my feelings. Oh, how much there was in these words to me, "For what is a man profited, if he shall gain the whole world and lose his own soul? or what shall a man give in exchange for his soul?" (Matt. 16:26)—the soul, the soul for whom Christ died, who can realize the worth of the soul. Oh, what is the approbation of the world? What are its scoffs or frowns when our soul's interest is at stake?

A change, a wonderful change took place in Father's feelings in one day. His mind is settled. He will move just as soon as he can.[15] He was tenderhearted, subdued, all the rest of the while we were there, and Father's dignity was most all gone. Lizzie Tenney [**Elizabeth Tenney**][16] and her husband came to see us in the rain, Monday. Lizzie is lame. Lamed her ankle by a misstep. Both of these seemed very kind and put themselves out to be obliging and kind. I helped Mother all the time I was there. Did up the dishes nearly every time occasion required.

Tuesday, Father and Mary helped us to the depot about six miles [nine kilometers]. We parted with the tenderest of feelings. And on, on, we came in the [railroad] cars. The old stage brought us to Paris Hill [Maine]. Changed there for a single wagon and soon we were to your own home. Just before we got here saw Frances, Rebekah, and Angeline[17] coming out of a house. They had just entered it but took their leave rather unceremoniously, I guess, and hastened home. We were glad enough to see them.

---

[15] James White reported a few weeks later in the *Review* that his parents "desire to see a more fertile soil, and to spend the rest of their days in a milder climate, free from the cares of the old farm home." They did eventually settle in Battle Creek, Michigan, to be with James and Ellen. The exact date of their move is not known, but according to later reminiscences of James White his father spent his last "twelve years at Battle Creek, Michigan, where he died July 5, 1871," thus locating the move to about 1859. Certain entries in Ellen White's diary for 1859 support this date (Ms 5, 1859 [Jan. 28 and Mar. 20]). The statement "He will move just as soon as he can" might also, given the context of the letter, refer to John White's intent to keep the Sabbath in the future. There is some disagreement in the sources as to when John and Betsey White actually began to keep the Sabbath. James White, in *Life Sketches,* claims 1856, but in his father's obituary he gives the year as 1860. The earliest contemporary reference to their observance of the Sabbath is found in Lt 31, 1859 (Feb. 21).

See: "Visit to Maine," *Review,* Sept. 4, 1855, p. 36; James White, *Life Sketches* (1880), p. 9; "The Venerable Dead," *Review,* July 18, 1871, p. 36; Martha Byington, 1857 diary; Ellen G. White, Lt 31, 1859 (Feb. 21), note 4.

[16] Older sister of James White married to Thomas B. Tenney, a farmer living in St. Albans, Maine, about five miles (eight kilometers) from Palmyra.

See: 1860 U.S. Federal Census, "Thomas B. Tenney," Maine, Somerset County, St. Albans, p. 160.

[17] Harriet Stevens had three sisters listed in the 1850 census: Angeline S., Paulina R., and Frances J. It seems very likely that Ellen White is here referring to these sisters. The identity of "Rebekah" is uncertain.

See: Note 2 above; 1850 U.S. Federal Census, Maine, Oxford County, Paris, p. 194.

1855

OCTOBER

"Watch and Pray."

Article published in *The Youth's Instructor*, vol. 3, no. 10, October 1855, p. 81.

1855

DECEMBER

Publication of *Testimony for the Church*, [No. 1],

Battle Creek, Michigan. Published by *Advent Review* Office. 16 pp.

1855

(Ms 1, 1855)

[CIRCA 1855],[1] N.P.

Fragments.

Portions of this manuscript are published in Ellen G. White, *The Adventist Home*, p. 177; *idem, Manuscript Releases,* vol. 6, p. 297; vol. 9, pp. 196, 197.

> *Three fragments: cautions on church discipline; protecting the family; James White's leadership of the publishing work.*

---

[1] The original carries no information as to date or place of writing. The three fragments that comprise this manuscript appear in close proximity to each other in an old record book, giving some reason to assume that they are of approximately the same date. An earlier editor has dated the documents "circa 1855." There is some internal evidence to support that approximate date, especially in the third fragment dealing with James White's illness and publishing work (see discussion in note 5). The mention of "the Conference at Sylvan" in the first paragraph is not as useful a clue to the date as may first appear, since Ellen White attended meetings in Sylvan, Michigan, in 1853, 1854, and 1855. Taking all things into consideration, it seems best to stay with the broad "circa 1855" judgment of the earlier editor.

At the Conference at Sylvan[2] [Michigan] I saw the necessity of the messengers' dwelling on the preparation more than they have done. Souls are not prepared for what is coming on the earth, and unless they speedily get ready they will be weighed in the balance and found wanting. I saw that Bro. Cranson [**Samuel T. Cranson**][3] had moved too fast in some cases, that there had not been that patience and forbearance with individuals that there ought to have been. Others of the brethren had moved too fast.[4]

I saw that great caution should be used and the church will have to bear some with individuals who do not always understand the movings of the Spirit of God, and always have some errors. And if these individuals were disfellowshipped they would be brought more closely in connection with an unholy influence and the possibility of saving them be lost. But if they were still retained in the fellowship of the church, they will be where the church can have some influence over them and may by moving judiciously and carefully

---

On the respective dates of the Sylvan conferences, *see:* "Western Tour," *Review,* July 7, 1853, p. 28; James White, "Western Tour," *Review,* May 23, 1854, p. 142; James White, "Cause in Michigan," *Review,* May 29, 1855, p. 236.

[2] *See:* Note 1 above.

[3] *Identity:* From the description given in this passage it is clear that "Bro. Cranson" is a preacher ("messenger") that likely is based in Michigan. The only person mentioned in the *Review* during this period who matches this description is Samuel T. Cranson, of Tompkins, Michigan, a lay preacher during the years 1853-1855. Cranson was present at the 1854 Sylvan Conference.

See: Search term "Cranson" in *Words of the Pioneers;* James White, "Western Tour," *Review,* May 23, 1854, p. 142.

[4] The discussion that follows, cautioning S. T. Cranson and other leaders against haste in disfellowshipping members, can be seen in the context of the call for "Gospel Order" in the *Review* from James and Ellen White in 1853-1854. For years Sabbathkeeping Adventists had struggled with the problem of self-appointed preachers propagating beliefs at variance with those of the main body and with members who were far out of line. The problem became more urgent with the rapid growth of membership in the early 1850s and the beginnings of a schismatic movement (the *Messenger* Party) in 1853. It was to address this pressing issue that James White published his landmark "Gospel Order" series in December 1853, urging greater measures to promote unity. Ellen White, who had addressed the matter on a number of earlier occasions, included a major article entitled "Gospel Order" in her *Supplement to the Christian Experience and Views of Ellen G. White,* published the following month (January 1854).

The problem with Cranson and others was, according to this manuscript, that they were overzealous in implementing gospel order, particularly in the area of disfellowshipping deviant members. James White made the same point in a more general way in June 1854: "The brethren in Michigan" he wrote, "have taken hold of the subject of Gospel Order in good earnest. This is a subject of the greatest importance . . . but in this matter there must not only be great frankness, and plain dealing with those who do not come up to the gospel rule, but the graces of meekness and patience will be much needed."

See: "Gospel Order," *Review,* Dec. 6, 1853, p. 173; Dec. 13, 1853, p. 180; Dec. 20, 1853, pp. 188-190; Dec. 27, 1853, pp. 196, 197; Ellen G. White, *Supplement to the Christian Experience and Views,* pp. 15-23 (*Early Writings,* pp. 97-104); EGWEnc, s.v. "*Messenger* Party." For general studies on the development of organization in the Seventh-day Adventist Church during the early decades, see Andrew Gordon Mustard, *James White and SDA Organization;* George R. Knight, *Organizing to Beat the Devil,* pp. 15-96.

win them to all the truth, which will discover to them their errors, and cause them to yield them up and be fully united to the church.

I saw that the messengers and the church must have compassion with some, making a difference. Now the messengers of God must seek wisdom and know how to treat each individual case. All must not be treated alike. By close examination it will be seen that individual cases differ. Some are to be borne with longer than others, but if one is living in disobedience to the commandments of God, the church must act and must separate them from them. And for other sins it will often be necessary to disfellowship souls if they continue in their sins; yet great care should be used and great patience and forbearance exercised.

I saw that Brother Cranson had tried to do right and just as well as he knew how, yet he has failed at times. I saw that judgment and caution must be used. The messengers must all move out unitedly and with decision and energy; yet they must have meekness and patience and in love for souls fulfill their duty. They must all go among the people with the power and Spirit of God with them, and must have energy that will arouse the stupid and those who are off their watch and cause them to awake and get ready. Prepare! Prepare! should be sounded in the ears of the people, for the great day of God's wrath is coming, and who shall be able to stand! And while messengers cry to God to prepare and get ready, they must be awake and have energy themselves and let it tell to all that hear them that they are standing between the living and the dead. Preachers and people who believe the third angel's message should set a holy, lively example. Their conversation and actions should show that they are looking for the appearing of the great God and our Saviour Jesus Christ.

There is a sacred circle around every family which should be preserved. No other one has any right in that sacred circle. The husband and wife should be all to each other. The wife should have no secrets to keep from her husband, and let others know, and the husband should have no secrets to keep from his wife to relate to others. The heart of his wife should be the grave for the faults of the husband, and the heart of the husband the grave for his wife's faults. Never should either party indulge in a joke at the expense of the other's feelings. Never should either the husband or wife in sport or in any other manner complain of each other to others, for in frequently indulging in this foolish, and what may seem perfectly harmless, joking, it will end in trial with each other and perhaps estrangement. I have been shown that there should be a sacred shield around every family.

I saw that God had qualified him who had to stand at the head of the publishing for his station, and if he did not fill his place, God would remove him from it. God had the oversight of the work. I saw that this was an important place.[5] I saw that it was God who had rebuked the disease that was on James when nature had resisted it as long as it was possible and could do no more, and disease had fastened upon him and when Satan was exulting that he had his prey and that he would lay him in the grave, then God's hand interposed and He put bands around James and strengthened him to fill the place He had put him in.

---

[5] Two ways of reading this fragment suggest themselves: (1) that the first two sentences refer to **Uriah Smith** and the remainder of the section refers to James White, or (2) that the whole fragment deals only with James White.

In November 1855 Uriah Smith had taken over the position of chief editor, a post previously occupied by James White. Two months later Ellen White related details of "my last vision" to Smith: "I saw that no station on earth is more important than [the one that] those occupy that are at the head of the paper, and write for it. . . . God has placed you there. It is an important work" (Lt 8, 1856 [Jan. 21]). The parallels between these sentences and the content and wording of Ms 1, 1855, are interesting and suggest the possibility that Uriah Smith is under discussion. The phrase "if he did not fill his place, God would remove him from it" suggests that Smith at some point had considered giving up his post. Ellen White confirms that this was the case in Lt 6, 1857 (Oct. 8): "I saw that the Lord had called you to occupy the place you are now in, and God has not released you. God has not selected or designed Brother Waggoner for the office to occupy your place. . . . I saw if you break away from that office, your happiness and peace ends."

It is also possible, perhaps more probable, that the whole passage deals with James White. White had been discouraged to the point of giving up publication of the *Review* on more than one occasion, but his experience during the winter of 1854-1855 fits the description of this passage particularly well. After his sister Anna White died of tuberculosis, in November 1854, James became seriously sick with symptoms similar to those of Anna. "I have been very fearful," wrote Ellen White, "that the disease that has preyed upon Nathaniel and Anna is preying upon James. He has been afflicted in the same way and unless he is speedily relieved he will go in the same way." In his discouragement over ill health and financial problems and the inordinate workload required to keep the publishing work progressing, James announced in the *Review* in February 1855 that there would have to be "a complete change in many respects . . . even if we leave the Office entirely." James White's health did gradually improve over the spring and summer of 1855. It is quite possible that this manuscript fragment dates from this time, noting James's ill health, gradual improvement, and inclination to be released from his publishing responsibilities, but above all appealing to James to rise above these challenges and continue "to stand at the head of the publishing" work. The only discordant note in this interpretation is that in some ways James did stand down from his publishing leadership some months later, in November 1855, when Uriah Smith took over as resident editor and various committees took over financial and managerial tasks, responsibilities previously held by James. Was James then disobedient to the call to continue to "stand at the head of the publishing"? It appears not, because James White, despite some responsibilities devolving on others in 1855, continued to hold overall responsibility for the publishing work even after that.

See: Ellen G. White, Lt 8, 1856 (Jan. 21); *idem,* Lt 6, 1857 (Oct. 8); *idem,* Lt 5, 1854 (Dec. 16); [James White], "The Office," *Review,* Feb. 20, 1855, p. 182. For a survey of administrative changes at the *Review* in November 1855, see Gerald Wheeler, *James White,* pp. 86, 87.

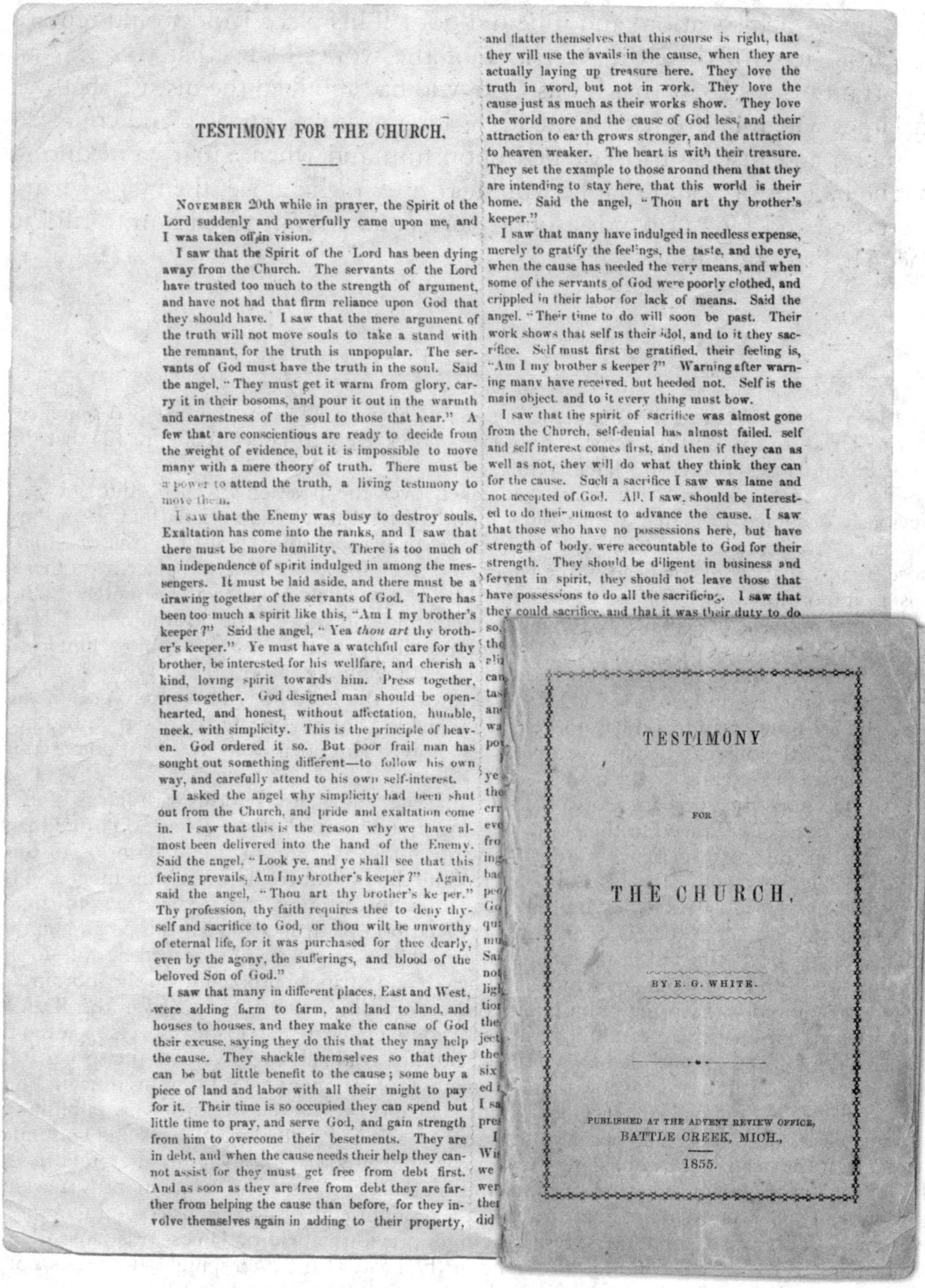

TESTIMONY FOR THE CHURCH.

NOVEMBER 20th while in prayer, the Spirit of the Lord suddenly and powerfully came upon me, and I was taken off in vision.

I saw that the Spirit of the Lord has been dying away from the Church. The servants of the Lord have trusted too much to the strength of argument, and have not had that firm reliance upon God that they should have. I saw that the mere argument of the truth will not move souls to take a stand with the remnant, for the truth is unpopular. The servants of God must have the truth in the soul. Said the angel, "They must get it warm from glory, carry it in their bosoms, and pour it out in the warmth and earnestness of the soul to those that hear." A few that are conscientious are ready to decide from the weight of evidence, but it is impossible to move many with a mere theory of truth. There must be a power to attend the truth, a living testimony to move them.

I saw that the Enemy was busy to destroy souls. Exaltation has come into the ranks, and I saw that there must be more humility. There is too much of an independence of spirit indulged in among the messengers. It must be laid aside, and there must be a drawing together of the servants of God. There has been too much a spirit like this, "Am I my brother's keeper?" Said the angel, "Yea *thou art* thy brother's keeper." Ye must have a watchful care for thy brother, be interested for his wellfare, and cherish a kind, loving spirit towards him. Press together, press together. God designed man should be open-hearted, and honest, without affectation, humble, meek, with simplicity. This is the principle of heaven. God ordered it so. But poor frail man has sought out something different—to follow his own way, and carefully attend to his own self-interest.

I asked the angel why simplicity had been shut out from the Church, and pride and exaltation come in. I saw that this is the reason why we have almost been delivered into the hand of the Enemy. Said the angel, "Look ye, and ye shall see that this feeling prevails, Am I my brother's keeper?" Again, said the angel, "Thou art thy brother's keeper." Thy profession, thy faith requires thee to deny thyself and sacrifice to God, or thou wilt be unworthy of eternal life, for it was purchased for thee dearly, even by the agony, the sufferings, and blood of the beloved Son of God."

I saw that many in different places, East and West, were adding farm to farm, and land to land, and houses to houses, and they make the cause of God their excuse, saying they do this that they may help the cause. They shackle themselves so that they can be but little benefit to the cause; some buy a piece of land and labor with all their might to pay for it. Their time is so occupied they can spend but little time to pray, and serve God, and gain strength from him to overcome their besetments. They are in debt, and when the cause needs their help they cannot assist for they must get free from debt first. And as soon as they are free from debt they are farther from helping the cause than before, for they involve themselves again in adding to their property, and flatter themselves that this course is right, that they will use the avails in the cause, when they are actually laying up treasure here. They love the truth in word, but not in work. They love the cause just as much as their works show. They love the world more and the cause of God less, and their attraction to earth grows stronger, and the attraction to heaven weaker. The heart is with their treasure. They set the example to those around them that they are intending to stay here, that this world is their home. Said the angel, "Thou art thy brother's keeper."

I saw that many have indulged in needless expense, merely to gratify the feelings, the taste, and the eye, when the cause has needed the very means, and when some of the servants of God were poorly clothed, and crippled in their labor for lack of means. Said the angel. "Their time to do will soon be past. Their work shows that self is their idol, and to it they sacrifice. Self must first be gratified, their feeling is, "Am I my brother's keeper?" Warning after warning many have received, but heeded not. Self is the main object, and to it every thing must bow.

I saw that the spirit of sacrifice was almost gone from the Church, self-denial has almost failed. self and self interest comes first, and then if they can as well as not, they will do what they think they can for the cause. Such a sacrifice I saw was lame and not accepted of God. All, I saw, should be interested to do their utmost to advance the cause. I saw that those who have no possessions here, but have strength of body, were accountable to God for their strength. They should be diligent in business and fervent in spirit, they should not leave those that have possessions to do all the sacrificing. I saw that they could sacrifice, and that it was their duty to do so,

TESTIMONY

FOR

THE CHURCH.

BY E. G. WHITE.

PUBLISHED AT THE ADVENT REVIEW OFFICE,
BATTLE CREEK, MICH.,
1855.

Ellen White's first "Testimony for the Church" was initially published in broadside format. Original dimensions: 10.75 x 15 in. (27 x 38 cm.). It was printed shortly thereafter along with additional material in a 16-page pamphlet. Now found in Testimonies for the Church, *vol. 1, pp. 113-126.*

1856

(Lt 9, 1856)

JANUARY 1, BATTLE CREEK, MICHIGAN

LETTER TO

Elsie Philomela Below.[1]

Portions of this letter are published in Arthur L. White, *Ellen G. White: The Early Years,* pp. 332-334; Ellen G. White, *In Heavenly Places,* p. 352; *idem, Manuscript Releases,* vol. 3, p. 225; vol. 7, p. 231.

Letter, to E. P. Below, a close friend, containing news of family events since the Whites moved to Battle Creek some weeks earlier. Also includes a strong testimony to God's goodness.

Dear Sister Below:

We received your kind and welcome letter in due time, containing three dollars, one from Sister Boyers [**Mary Boyer**],[2] and two from yourself. Thank you for your donation.

We have been meaning to write you for some time, but have had many visions to write to individual cases, and have scarcely got through yet.

My health is quite good except a lame ankle. In coming from Sarah's

---

[1] *Identity*: This letter does not reveal the address of "Sister Below," but gives the surnames of a number of believers who clearly live in the same vicinity, including Boyer and Cottrell. Mill Grove in New York State matches these criteria well. Perhaps the clearest evidence of this is the "Letter From the Church at Mill Grove, N.Y . . . ," which was published in the *Review* in December 1855 and is jointly signed by, among others, several Cottrells, two Boyerses, and, significantly, by "E. P. Below."

Elsie Below was a close friend of the Whites, living in Mill Grove. "You have been a mother to us," wrote James White to Mrs. Below some months later. Details are not known except that after the Whites' third son, William, was born in August 1854, Elsie traveled from Mill Grove to Rochester, New York, to assist Ellen for a time. After Elsie Below's second husband died in 1855, the Whites urged her to move to Battle Creek, Michigan. "We want you near us," James urged.

See: R. F. Cottrell and others, "Letter From the Church at Mill Grove, N.Y., to Elder J. M. Stephenson," *Review,* Dec. 18, 1855, p. 93; obituary, "Elsie P. Below," *Review,* Dec. 10, 1889, p. 782; James White to "Dear Sister," Nov. 4, 1856; Ellen G. White, Ms 23, 1889 (Diary, Nov. 12, 1889).

[2] A letter to the *Review* published just two weeks earlier was signed by 13 members of the Mill Grove group. Among them are Mary and Elijah Boyer. No doubt these are the Boyers mentioned in two places in Lt 9.

See: R. F. C. [R. F. Cottrell], "Letter From the Church at Mill Grove, N.Y., to Elder J. M. Stephenson," *Review,* Dec. 18, 1855, p. 93.

[**Sarah B. Belden**][3] to our house, I slipped and fell, wrenching my foot backwards and putting my ankle out of joint. In rising it flew back again, but the bone of my left limb is injured, split, and I am a cripple for the present, cannot bear a pound's weight upon it. It is more than a week since I was hurt. I can hobble around a little with crutches, but I will not murmur or complain. It was a merciful Providence that saved me from breaking my limb in two places. When I think how my limb twisted and then the whole weight of my body fell upon it, I know that the angels of God must have protected me or I should be suffering with distress from a broken limb.

Jenny [**Jane Fraser**] and Clarissa [**Clarissa Bonfoey**][4] are quite well; Clarissa has not been as well as she is now for eight years. Jenny is much better than she has been since before she had the ague. The children are quite rugged. Edson [**James Edson White**, age 6], you know, has been generally poorly but he is coming up; is quite tough. James [**James Springer White**] enjoys better health than he has for some time back. We praise the Lord for this. For weeks past the Lord has been good and gracious to us, and I long to be more devoted to Him. We have lived at too great a distance from God, and that is why we have had so little strength. We must draw nearer to God.

This world is too dark for me, it is not my home. Jesus said He would go away and prepare mansions for us, that where He is there we may be also. We shall ever dwell with and enjoy the light of His precious countenance. My heart leaps with joy at the cheering prospect. We are almost home. Heaven, sweet heaven, it is our eternal home. I am glad every moment that Jesus lives, and because He lives we shall live also. My soul says, Praise the Lord. There is a fullness in Jesus, a supply for each, for all, and why should we die for bread or starve in foreign lands?

I hunger, I thirst, for salvation, for entire conformity to the will of God. We have a good hope through Jesus. It is sure and steadfast and entereth into that within the veil. It yields us consolation in affliction, it gives us joy amid anguish, disperses the gloom around us and causes us to look through it all to immortality and eternal life. It is just what we need. We cannot part with it. Earthly treasures are no inducement to us, for while we have this hope it reaches clear above the treasures of earth that are passing away and takes hold of the immortal inheritance, the treasures that are durable, incorruptible, undefiled, and that fade not away. This hope we will cherish. We will cling closer and closer to it. It will live when everything else dies.

---

[3] *Identity:* Although there can be no certainty, it is probable that the reference here is to Ellen White's sister Sarah B. Belden, whose husband, Stephen T. Belden, was employed as printer at the office of the *Review and Herald*. The Beldens had moved with the Whites to Battle Creek in connection with the removal of the *Review* office and plant from Rochester late in 1855.

[4] *Identity:* This mention of "Jenny and Clarissa," coming as it does in the section of the letter dealing with family news, can refer only to Jane ("Jenny") Fraser and Clarissa Bonfoey.

Our mortal bodies may die, and be laid away in the grave. Yet the blessed hope lives on until the resurrection, when the voice of Jesus calls forth the sleeping dust. We shall then enjoy the fullness of the blessed, glorious hope. We know in whom we have believed. We have not run in vain, neither labored in vain. A rich, a glorious reward is before us; it is the prize for which we run, and if we persevere with courage we shall surely obtain it.

I cannot express my gratitude to God for what He has done and is still doing for us. For weeks our peace has been like a river.[5] The heavenly dew has distilled upon us morning, noon, and night, and our souls triumph in God. It is easy believing, easy praying. We love God, and yet our souls pant for living water. There is salvation for us, and why do we stay away from the fountain? Why not come and drink that our souls may be refreshed, invigorated, and may flourish in God? Why do we cling so closely to earth? There is something better than earth for us to talk about and think of. We can be in a heavenly frame of mind. Oh, let us dwell upon Jesus' lovely, spotless character, and by beholding we shall become changed to the same image. Be of good courage. Have faith in God.

We should love to hear from you and Sister Cottrell and of the children as often as possible. I designed writing Sister Cottrell a letter with this but James has other writing I must do, so she must excuse me. Much love to Brother and Sister Cottrell[6] and their children, Willard[7] and his wife. Tell them to go on. The crown is before us. Put all the armor on; like valiant soldiers, stand. Much love to Mary and Frank.[8]

---

[5] Since the move from Rochester to Battle Creek two months earlier the Whites had experienced several positive changes. James White had been relieved of sole fiscal and editorial responsibility for the publishing work by the establishment of a publishing committee and with the appointment of Uriah Smith as resident editor for the *Review*. Second, an action had been taken at a general conference in November expressing regret for past neglect of the visions of Ellen White and a determination to restore them to their rightful place. Third, and not least significant, with the move to Battle Creek the Whites no longer had to operate a boarding house for the publishing workers, as they had done in Rochester. It all amounted to significant relief. As Ellen White summed it up in *Spiritual Gifts*: "From the time we moved to Battle Creek, the Lord began to turn our captivity."

See: Ellen G. White, *Spiritual Gifts [vol. 2]*, p. 203. For a survey of events surrounding the move to Battle Creek, see Arthur L. White, *Ellen G. White: The Early Years,* pp. 316-322.

[6] *Identity:* The difficulty in identifying "Brother and Sister Cottrell," of Mill Grove, New York, is that there were at least three Cottrell families associated with the church in Mill Grove at the time this letter was written: **Roswell Fenner** and **Catherine (née Harvey) Cottrell**; **John Harvey** and **Maryette Cottrell**; Solomon Gates and Prudence Cottrell. It is unlikely that Solomon and Prudence are referred to in this warm greeting, since Ellen White writes a few years later (Ms 3, 1861 [c. 1861]) that "Solomon's wife was always bitter against the gifts."

See: Search term "Cottrell" in *Words of the Pioneers*.

[7] This person has not been identified.

[8] Most probably Elsie Below's two children, still at home: Frank, about 18, and Mary, about 13.

See: "John C. Below" in the 1850 U.S. Federal Census, New York, Erie County, Newstead,

I hope Frank is attending to his eternal interest, and is preparing for the judgment. Tell him I want to meet him in heaven. Tell Mary to be faithful, to watch and pray. That is the life of the Christian. Love to Brother and Sister Boyers and their children. I want to see you all, Brother Harvey [**John Harvey Cottrell**][9] and family and all the saints—I cannot number all. Pray for us.

We are going to ride about 13 miles [21 kilometers] today in the country. The brethren think we ought to have a little house put up. We pay now $1.50 per week for rent, and have scarcely any conveniences at that. Have to go a great distance for water; have no good shed for our wood. We put a few boards up at our own expense just to cover our wood. We shall make a beginning; cannot tell how we shall succeed.[10] May the Lord guide us in all our undertakings is my prayer.

Do write to us. You are very near our hearts. What a nice piece Brother Roswell [**Roswell Fenner Cottrell**][11] wrote! It hit the nail on the head; it will do much good.

In love.

---

p. 214; "Elsa P. Below," 1860 U.S. Federal Census, Michigan, Calhoun County, Michigan, p. 224.

[9] *Identity:* Most probably John Harvey Cottrell. The 13 signatories of the "Letter From the Church at Mill Grove, N.Y., to Elder J. M. Stephenson," published in December 1855, include "John H. Cottrell," whose full name was John Harvey Cottrell. There is evidence that John Harvey was addressed by his middle name, Harvey. There are examples of this usage in the writings of both Ellen White and John Loughborough. It may well be that "Harvey" was used rather than "John" in order to distinguish him from his father, John Cottrell.

See: R. F. C. [R. F. Cottrell], "Letter From the Church at Mill Grove, N.Y., to Elder J. M. Stephenson," *Review,* Dec. 18, 1855, p. 93; Roy F. Cottrell, "A Brief Sketch of Cottrell Family History," (1965), pp. 6, 13; Ellen G. White, Ms 3, 1861 (c. 1861); J. N. Loughborough, "Recollections of the Past—No. 3," *Review,* Feb. 12, 1884, p. 107.

[10] For the first year the Whites rented a cottage on Van Buren Street. The weekly rent of $1.50 can be compared to James White's weekly wages of $4.09 at the *Review*. By the autumn of 1856, with the help of friends, a small house was built on Wood Street where the Whites lived until 1863.

See: Gerald Wheeler, *James White,* pp. 87-92.

[11] *Identity:* Clues to the identity of "Brother Roswell" include the fact that he probably lived in or near Mill Grove, and had recently written an item for the *Review*. Only Roswell Fenner Cottrell seems to fit this description. Two weeks earlier a letter from Cottrell, openly supportive of Ellen White's visions, had been published in the *Review*, breaking a long trend of silence in the *Review* on the visions. "If the visions are not of God, they will surely come to nought. . . . But we have not been able to discover anything in them which conflicts with the commandments of God."

See: R. F. C. [R. F. Cottrell], "Letter From the Church at Mill Grove, N.Y., to Elder J. M. Stephenson," *Review,* Dec. 18, 1855, p. 93.

1856

JANUARY 10

"Communication From Sister White."

Article published in *Advent Review, and Sabbath Herald,* vol. 7, no. 15, January 10, 1856, p. 118.

1856

(Lt 8, 1856)

JANUARY 21, BATTLE CREEK, MICHIGAN

LETTER TO

Harriet Newall Stevens.[1]

Previously unpublished.

Concern for negative influence of Harriet Stevens on Uriah Smith, Roxanna Bacheller, and Harriet Hastings.

Dear Sister Harriet:

I received your letter in due time[2] but have not known what to write you. When your letters arrived, father and mother were far from us at Iowa to visit my only brother.[3] Knew not how to have you direct the things until mother could tell me.

---

[1] *Identity:* Harriet's close relationship to Uriah, her stay in Rochester, and her relationship to Roxana are the chief features of this letter, which help to identify her as Harriet Newall Stevens. Harriet married Uriah Smith the following year, 1857, and had worked in the office of the *Review and Herald* in Rochester, New York, together with Roxanna Bacheller in 1854 and 1855.

See: Obituary: "Harriet Smith," *Review,* Mar. 30, 1911, p. 23; obituary: "Roxanna Cornell," *Review,* Dec. 10, 1895, p. 799.

[2] This letter is not in the White Estate archives.

[3] In a rare letter to Ellen White from her mother written six weeks earlier, Eunice Gould Harmon tells of her visit with her husband to their son **John B. Harmon**, living in Bellevue Town, Iowa. Despite John's efforts to make his parents comfortable, Eunice had no wish to stay for long. She declared: "the far West fever will never move me!" Ellen's only other brother, Robert, had died three years earlier on February 5, 1853.

See: Eunice Harmon to Ellen White, Dec. 10, [1855]; obituary: "He Sleeps in Jesus,"

I am now a cripple. Fell four weeks ago today, laming myself. I injured my ankle bone considerably. I am confined to my crutches, but have reason to praise God that my limb is not broken. I know that the care of the angels was over me, or I should now be suffering with a broken limb.

There are some things I have seen in vision concerning you [that] I must write. I wrote it to Uriah [**Uriah Smith**][4] and will send you a copy.[5]

Dear Brother Uriah, in my last vision I saw particularly the position you occupy, that it was pleasing to God for you to stand as you do in regard to the paper,[6] that the Lord would strengthen and uphold you if you walked carefully before Him, and He would make you an instrument of good to His children. In order to grow every day in grace and overcome the temptations of Satan, you must have the help of God and you can shed a holy influence.

I saw some things that were a detriment to you or a hindrance. I was shown the communication from Harriet to you was like so many clogs to you. They lack the savor. If Harriet was baptized with the Spirit of God, if she was devoted to Him, then her letters would have a good influence, and if she enjoyed salvation, her letters would breathe it. Harriet has a good talent, but the sweet, humble, devoted, childlike spirit is lacking, and without this all that talent is no more than the talent of any of the world. She lacks consecration. She lacks religion. God will not accept the thoughts of her mind unless they run in the channel of salvation, purified and refined by His Spirit.

Unless there is a work done for Harriet, she cannot be saved. A form will be of no advantage to her. If Harriet would spend a portion of her time in praying to God that she spends in writing letters, it would be much more for her benefit and the benefit of others. I saw that multitudinous letters void of the Spirit of God, sent abroad, are a curse to God's cause and a curse [to] the one that writes them.

I saw that God had a higher, holier calling and work for you. That you should not spend your precious time in answering such letters. I saw that no station on earth is more important than [the one that] those occupy that are

---

Review, Apr. 14, 1853, p. 192.

[4] *Identity:* See note 1 above.

[5] Harriet Stevens, 23, from Paris, Maine, had spent up to a year during 1854/1855 assisting at the publishing house in Rochester, New York. During this time a relationship developed between Uriah Smith and Harriet that eventually led to their marriage two years later. Although Harriet was a person of literary talent, the visions of Ellen White pointed to her lack of spiritual "consecration." Perhaps in part for this reason Harriet did not continue her employment at the Review for more than a year after the press was moved to Battle Creek, Michigan, in November 1855. The contents of the vision recounted in Lt 8 would act as a caution to Uriah as he contemplated a continuing relationship with Harriet.

[6] Uriah Smith had been appointed resident editor of the *Review* just a few weeks earlier, in November 1855, at age 23.

See: Joseph Bates, Uriah Smith, "Business Proceedings at the Conference at Battle Creek, Mich.," *Review*, Dec. 4, 1855, p. 76.

at the head of the paper, and write for it, and expressly who have to do with it. God has placed you there. It is an important work. Brother Uriah, you must be consecrated to God in order to fill your place and exert a holy influence. I knew not at first what to do with the vision but concluded to send it [to] you, Uriah, and also to Harriet.

Here is a vision written to Roxana [**Roxanna Bacheller**].[7]

Dear Sister Roxana. My mind is burdened and distressed. After the vision that was given me for you and Harriet, while you were at Rochester [New York], I begged and prayed that it might have its designed effect upon you and Harriet, but could see no effect of a change. In the last vision given me here at Battle Creek [Michigan], I saw that there had been no change. There had [been] no more consecration or devotion. I saw that the attachment manifested there in Rochester between your mother,[8] Harriet, and yourself was a curse to you all. This few bundling together to the neglect of others meets the frown of God instead of His approbation. It is acting out the foolish affection manifested by the world for each other. It is not sanctified by God. It does not advance His glory.

The work of serving God is an individual work and if this was fully realized by you and others of the young, and you would watch strictly over pride and correct wrongs in each other—pride, self-exaltation and a selfish spirit—God would be better pleased. But now the young have joined hands to take the thoughts and affection from Jesus and center them upon each other. They unite in frivolity and pride, and this misapplied affection is only a curse. It should first center in God, be tried, purified and refined by Him, then it will lead to a holy yearning of soul for others that are on the background, not to bundle together but to bring them near to the cross that the same love that animates and strengthens the heart of one may be felt by all.

The inquiry will be made, What shall I do to be saved? It is not sinners alone that should make this inquiry, but if those that have named the name of Christ could get sight of their own hearts, their love to be like the world, the vanity and pride lurking in the heart, the cry would be raised, What shall *I* do to be saved?

I saw that you were not the same Roxana now that you were before Harriet came to Rochester. The hope that you possess is not a saving hope. It cannot

---

[7] *Identity:* The letter identifies Roxana as coming from Vermont, with "Warren and your mother" and that she had been employed at "the office" at Rochester. The reference is clearly to Roxanna Bacheller, who came from Panton, Vermont, together with her mother and brother in 1852, and worked at the *Review and Herald* office in Rochester, New York. "Roxana" is also spelled "Roxanna" in other sources, e.g., *Spiritual Gifts [vol. 2],* p. 304 and obituary: "Roxanna Cornell," *Review*, Dec. 10, 1895, p. 799.

[8] Cynthia Bacheller, 1814-1883.

See: Obituary: "Cynthia Bacheller," *Review,* Jan. 15, 1884, p. 47; obituary: "Roxanna Cornell," *Review,* Dec. 10, 1895, p. 799.

save you unless you let it purify you and you act it out. I was pointed back to last summer. I saw that your heart was not in the work of God. It was not knit with God's cause, but only as far as you received full compensation for your labor, so far was your interest. A selfish feeling possessed you to take from the treasury of God, by receiving pay more than your labor deserved, more than you actually earned. You did not realize that you were laboring in the cause of God and you were not willing to make extra efforts unless it was for your own self-advantage. God notices this. Such a principle is not pleasing to Him. Often in the office stories and other things have occupied your time; and your interest that should be fully in the work was not there.

The gratitude that should fill your heart for the merciful dealings of God in bringing you from Vermont, and Warren [**John Warren Bacheller**] and your mother, all of you, being together and the way being opened before you to obtain a living, and the good health He has blessed you all with, has not called forth from you humility and gratitude. I saw that if God removed these blessings from you now, trials will arise that you have not anticipated that will bring anguish of soul [to] all. All of you, each one of you, have possessed selfishness and feelings of independence that did not become you.

The union between you and Harriet was all wrong. Her influence has had a tendency to lead your mind directly from God, from your eternal interest. Your mind has been upon story books too much, and your reading these books together fills the mind with things not pertaining to your eternal interest. [In] vain reading and shutting the Spirit of God from you, you have lost your humility and have thought more of your appearance. Oh, you had better been studying your own hearts, how you should show yourselves approved unto God.

Harriet, I have now written both visions, and I would ask you if you have not been reproved for these very things before in vision, and how could you set the example that you did to Roxana and read with her. Roxana is not the girl she was. Vanity fills her heart, and she has no appearance of a Christian about her.

Last Sabbath she made a good move, came forward to the anxious seat for prayers. May the Lord have mercy upon the fatherless and widow is my earnest prayer.

Sister Harriet, do you remember the vision about Brother Hastings' [**Leonard Hastings**] family and the influence of your letters upon them, and your influence upon Arabella [**Harriet Arabella Hastings**]?[9] It led her from

---

[9] *Identity:* The close association in this passage between Arabella and the Hastings family and the information regarding Arabella's early death clearly identify her as Arabella Hastings, who died at age 21 in 1854 and who was the oldest daughter of Leonard and Elmira Hastings. Ellen White in her correspondence sometimes referred to her as "Arabella" and sometimes as "Harriet" (cf. Lt. 5, 1849 [Apr. 21], and Lt 10, 1850 [Mar. 18], with Lt 7, 1851 [July 27], and

God and she never, until her sickness, possessed the spirit [that] she should, after her wanderings. It was easier for her to wander than to return from these wanderings. I have seen in vision she was afflicted and her life was the forfeit.[10]

Lt 3, 1851 [Aug. 11]). In Arabella's 1854 obituary her name is given as "Harriet A. Hastings." Presumably the middle initial stands for "Arabella."

See: Obituary: "Harriet A. Hastings," *Review,* Sept. 5, 1854, p. 31.

[10] Arabella Hastings died on August 1, 1854, while on an extended visit to Harriet Stevens in Paris, Maine.

See: Obituary: "Harriet A. Hastings," *Review,* Sept. 5, 1854, p. 31.

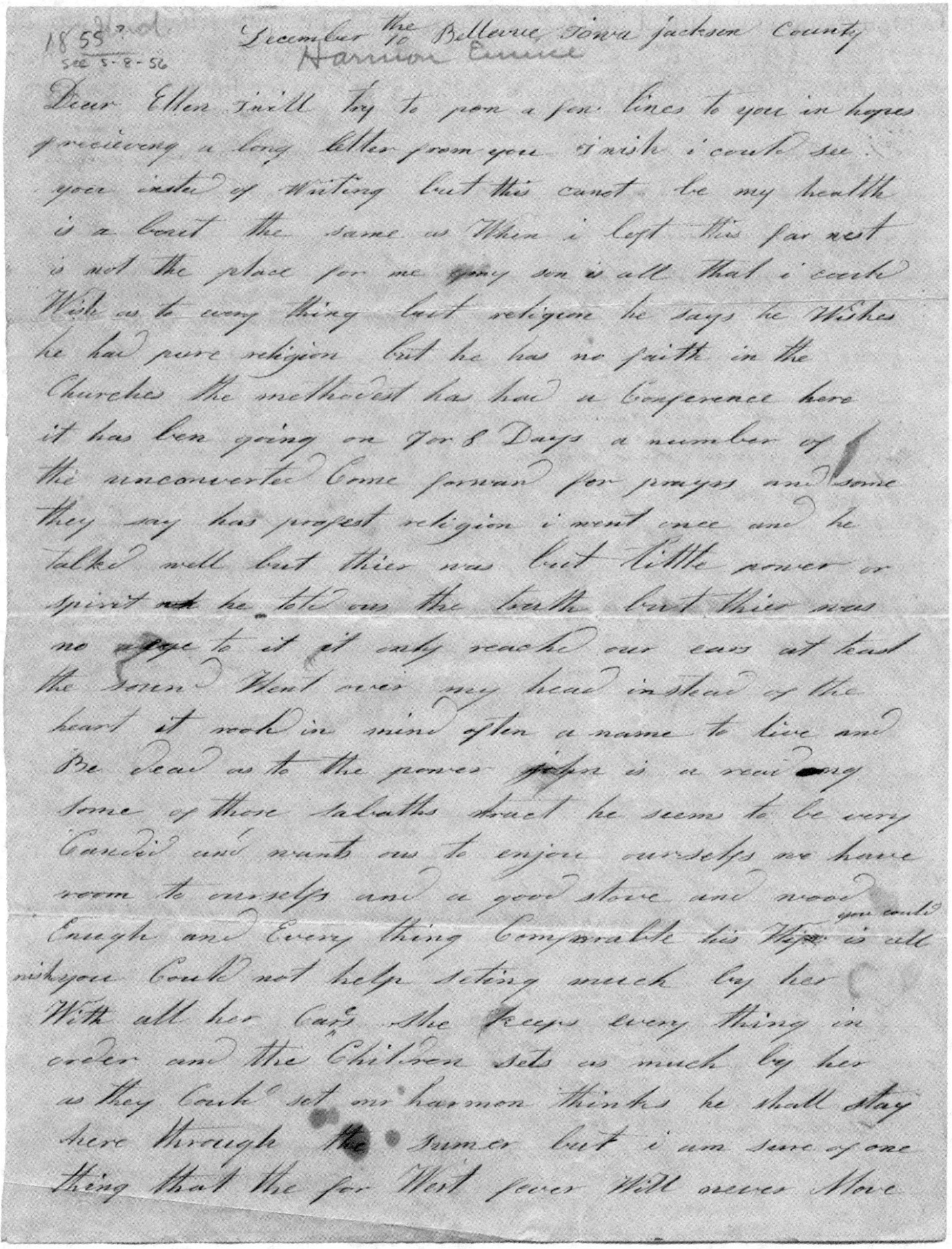
1855 2nd
see 5-8-56

December the 10 Bellevue Iowa jackson County
Harmon Eunice

Dear Ellen i will try to pen a few lines to you in hopes
of recieving a long letter from you i wish i could see
you insted of writing but this canot be my health
is a bout the same as when i left this far west
is not the place for me my son is all that i could
wish as to every thing but religion he says he wishes
he had pure religion but he has no faith in the
Churches the methodist has had a Conference here
it has ben going on 7 or 8 Days a number of
the unconverted Come forward for prayrs and some
they say has profest religion i went once and he
talked well but thier was but little power or
spirit he told us the truth but thier was
no [illegible] to it it only reached our ears at least
the sound went over my head instead of the
heart it put in mind often a name to live and
Be dead as to the power [illegible] is a reading
some of those sabbaths tract he seems to be very
Candid and wants us to enjoy ourselves we have
room to ourselves and a good stove and wood
Enough and Every thing Comfarable his wife is all you could
wish you Could not help seting much by her
With all her Cars she keeps every thing in
order and the Children sets as much by her
as they Could set mr harmon thinks he shall stay
here through the sumer but i am sure of one
thing that the far West fever will never Move

Letter to Ellen White from her mother, Eunice Harmon, December 10, 1855

me have you heard any thing from Carline
i canot assertain the place of her residence i fear
all is not White or she would let me know
I have not heard from main but i received
a few lines from Melisa While at your house
If any Comes i wish you Would send them
i want to hear a bout you all do send

the Wether at present
is very Mild

Farwell Dear Ellen and
all the rest

your brother and companion
sends much love to you all
he is perusing the advent paper
and seems to like them they want me to stay
as long as possible mr harmon thinks if
he he keeps this way he shall go a little out
of town but i am unsettled
i shall return back in first of spring

those pocket hankerchiefs
you gave me before i went
to main i keept them very
Carful and When i got
here i had not so much as
one if i left them i wish
you would take care of
them until i return
and mr harmons black
hankerchief the one that
was roberts he left it
I think more then i
should of a new one

i had them all the
morning before i
started that is all i
can remember

because you can ask sarah
but i do not think that
i left them thier

From Eunice D. F. 325

1856

(Lt 2a, 1856)

January 24, Battle Creek, Michigan

Letter to

Brother and Sister Loveland.[1]

Portions of this letter are published in Arthur L. White, *Ellen G. White: The Early Years,* pp. 335, 336; Ellen G. White, *Reflecting Christ,* p. 351; *idem, Manuscript Releases,* vol. 10, p. 21.

> *Letter of encouragement to a couple who are distressed, probably because of the strident opposition of the breakaway* Messenger *Party in the mid-1850s.*

Dear Brother and Sister Loveland:

We received a letter from Sister Loveland. It was a sad letter, and we felt bad about things in your place.[2]

But, dear sister, you must not sink down discouraged. The faint-hearted will be made strong; the desponding will be made to hope. God has a tender care for His people. His ear is open unto their cry. I have no fears for God's cause. He will take care of His own cause. Our duty is to fill our lot and place, live low, humble at the foot of the cross, and live faithful, holy lives before Him. While we do this we shall not be ashamed, but our souls will confide in God with holy boldness.

God has released us from burdens; He has set us free. Ever since the

---

[1] *Identity:* There is very little factual information in this letter bearing on the identity of "Brother and Sister Loveland," so it is probably best to leave that issue open. It is true that Ellen White wrote three letters to **Reuben** and **Belinda Loveland** in 1850 and 1851, but that will not in itself carry the inference that she is now addressing the same couple. The *Review* from this period lists about 10 persons with the Loveland surname.

See: Ellen G. White, Lt. 26, 1850 (Nov. 1); Lt 30, 1850 (Dec. 13); Lt 6, 1851 (Apr. 1); search term "Loveland" in *Words of the Pioneers.*

[2] The letter from Sister Loveland is not in the White Estate archives, hence there can be no certainty as to the cause of her sadness and discouragement. Ellen White's response, however, contains significant clues. Interestingly, most of the paragraph beginning "Dear Sister, our enemies may triumph," and the last three paragraphs are also found in Chapter 28 of *Spiritual Gifts,* volume 2, in the context of the challenges in dealing with the opposition *Messenger* Party. Key expressions such as "a corrupt people" who have "separated from the people of God" appear in both places. There is a likelihood, therefore, that much of Sister Loveland's concern relates to the activities of the *Messenger* Party, possibly in her own locality.

Ellen G. White, *Spiritual Gifts [vol. 2],* pp. 195, 196, 200-202; EGWEnc, s.v. "*Messenger* Party."

conference[3] we have been rising. Our meetings have increased in interest every Sabbath. I have been trying with all my heart to shake off the shackles that bound me. And for weeks and months I can say I have been free, and free indeed, and again I have a testimony for the children of God. I am determined to work out what God works in. Salvation I prize above everything else. My eternal interest engrosses my whole attention.

God has wrought for us in a remarkable manner since the conference. My husband has been much afflicted. Incessant labor has nearly carried him to the grave.[4] But our prayers have ascended to God morning, noon, and night for his restoration. All medicine has been entirely laid aside, and we have brought him in the arms of our faith to our skillful Physician. We have been heard and answered. An entire change has been wrought for him. The disease has left his lungs and made its appearance upon his thighs and limbs in the shape of large red blotches, and we believe, without a doubt, if he is careful of the health God has given him, his strength will increase and he will be able to overcome the disease that has fastened upon him.

Dear Sister, it would be impossible for me to go into a recital of the sufferings I have passed through, the anxiety, and the dread thought that I should be left a widow, my dear children without a father's care. The scene has changed. God's hand has mercifully been reached down to our rescue. My husband enjoys good health, and my children are rugged. They never enjoyed so good health before. Little Willie [**William Clarence White**] is healthy and very pleasant.

I never took so much comfort with my family as now. Our family has always been so large. But now we only number eight[5] and I can enjoy the

---

[3] Ellen White is evidently writing of the general conference held at Battle Creek, Michigan, just two months earlier in late November 1855. The buoyant language used in this letter to describe that conference is very similar to that found in her letter published in the *Review* on January 10, 1856. Two significant actions taken at the November conference had a direct and personal bearing on the Whites. First, James White was relieved of sole fiscal and editorial responsibility for the publishing work by the establishment of a publishing committee, and by the appointment of Uriah Smith as resident editor for the *Review*. Second, action was taken expressing regret for past neglect of the visions of Ellen White and a determination expressed to give them their rightful place in the mission of the church.

See: E. G. White, "Communication From Sister White," *Review,* Jan. 10, 1856, p. 118. For general account of the November 1855 Battle Creek conference, see Arthur L. White, *Ellen G. White: The Early Years,* pp. 319-330.

[4] For more details on James White's afflictions during this period, see Ellen G. White, *Spiritual Gifts [vol. 2],* pp. 194-199.

[5] While still in Rochester, New York, prior to the move to Battle Creek in 1855, "the Office hands boarded with us, and our family numbered from fifteen to twenty." With the move to Battle Creek the Whites no longer had to run a boardinghouse. Apart from James, Ellen, and their three children, the "family" of eight mentioned here would include **Jane Fraser** and/or **Clarissa M. Bonfoey**, who helped in the White household, and possibly Ellen's parents. The remainder of this letter parallels extracts from a letter Ellen White wrote to Louisa Howland, published in *Spiritual Gifts [vol. 2],* pp. 199-202. The original letter is not extant.

company of my children, they can be more under my own watchcare, and I can better train them in the right way. All of us are united for the blessing of God, and morning, noon, and night His sweet blessing distills upon us like the dew, making our hearts glad and strengthening us to fill our place and glorify our Redeemer.

Dear Sister, our enemies may triumph. They may speak lying words, and their slandering tongue frame slander, deceit, guile; yet will we not be moved. We know in whom we believe. We have not run in vain, neither labored in vain. Jesus knows us, dear sister. A reckoning day is coming and all will be judged according to the deeds that are done in the body. My eye is fixed upon the mark of the prize, and in the strength of God I will make my way straight through here.

It is true the world is dark. Opposition may wax strong. The trifler and scorner may grow bolder and harder in his iniquity. Yet, for all this, we will not be moved. We have not run as uncertain. No, no. My heart is fixed, trusting in God. We have a whole Saviour. We can rejoice in His rich fulness. I long to be more devoted to God, more consecrated to Him. This world is too dark for me. Jesus said He would go away and prepare mansions for us, that where He is we may be also. Praise God for this. My heart leaps with joy at the cheering prospect.

Religion is made to dwell too much in an iron case. Pure religion and undefiled leads us to a childlike simplicity. We want to pray and talk with humility, having a single eye to the glory of God.[6] There has been too much of a form of godliness without the power. The outpouring of the Spirit of God will lead to a grateful acknowledgement of the same; and while we feel and realize the wondrous love of God, we shall not hold our peace, we shall sacrifice to God with the voice of thanksgiving and make melody to Him with our hearts and voices. Let us plant our feet upon the Rock of ages and then we will have abiding support and consolation. Our soul will repose in God with unshaken confidence.

Why do we so seldom visit the fountain when it is full and free? Our souls often need to drink at the fountain in order to be refreshed and flourish in the Lord. Salvation we must have. Without vital godliness our religion is vain. A form will be of no advantage to us. We must have the deep workings of the Spirit of God. My whole soul is interested in this last message of mercy to be given to the world. We are to be purified and refined under this message.

Dear sister, do not be discouraged. God is sifting His people. He will have a clean and holy people. We cannot read the heart of man. God has not placed in man a window, that we can look into his heart and see what is

---

See: *Ibid.*, p. 191. For information on the composition of the White household as of January 1, 1856, see Lt 9, 1856 (Jan. 1) and Lt 4, 1856 (Dec. 24), note 1.

[6] Cf. Matt. 6:22.

there, but He has opened ways to keep the church pure and clean. A people has arisen, a corrupt people that could not live with the people of God. All their evil passions must be gratified. They had a suitable time to repent if they would, and overcome their wrongs, but no. Self was too dear to die. They nourished it and it grew strong, and they separated from the peculiar, self-denying people of God.[7]

I thank God for this way that has been opened to save the church from the frown and wrath of God that must have come upon them if these corrupt individuals had remained with them. Every honest one that may be deceived by this people will have the light in regard to them if every angel has to leave glory to visit them and enlighten their minds. We have nothing to fear in this matter. As we near the judgment, all will manifest their true character and it will be made plain to what company they belong.

The sieve is going, and let us not say, Stay Thy hand, O God. We know not the heart of man. If God causes the feelings of the heart to be manifested and gives you sight of what is in the heart by the words of the mouth (by the fulness of the heart the mouth speaketh), let it not afflict your soul too much, although your hopes may be cruelly disappointed. But the church must be purged, and will be. "Fret not thyself because of evildoers." [Ps. 37:1.] God reigns; let the people tremble.

---

[7] *See:* Note 2 above.

1856

[CIRCA JANUARY 24]

LETTER

Extracts From Nonextant Letter to Louisa Howland.

Quoted in Ellen G. White, *Spiritual Gifts [vol. 2]*, pp. 199-202.

1856

JANUARY

"The New Year."

Article published in *The Youth's Instructor*, vol. 4, no. 1, January 1856, p. 5.

1856

(Lt 10, 1856)

[CIRCA JANUARY],[1] N.P.

LETTER TO

David Henry Lamson.[2]

Previously unpublished.

---

[1] The original/earliest copy bears no place or date of writing. However, there are strong indications that this letter was written some time after the conference held in Battle Creek, Michigan, November 1855, as argued in note 5 below. Exactly how long after the conference is not known, but its similarities with Lt 2a, 1856, written on January 24, 1856, suggest that it was written about the same time, i.e., about January 1856.

[2] *Identity:* In 1953 Mary E. Lamson donated this letter to the White Estate archives with the explanation that "the enclosed is a letter written by Mrs. E. G. White to my father, David H. Lamson, enclosed with a letter written to him by George Amadon."

See: Mary E. Lamson to E. G. White Estate, Nov. 8, 1953.

(Lt 10, 1856) circa January 1856

Encouragement and concern for 21-year-old David Lamson, whose faith may have been waning.

Dear Brother:

George [**George Washington Amadon**][3] has requested me to write a few lines in his letter. All are at meeting and so I will improve a few moments now.

Let me inquire, brother, How are you? Does the present truth look as precious to you as it used to? Or have you lost your first love and has your interest decreased? As you are separated from those of like precious faith, the need of double watchfulness and prayer I suppose you realize.[4] David, you have enjoyed the sweet salvation of God. Do you enjoy this now? Are you awake to the charms of the present truth? Do you see new beauty and glory in His Word? Is Jesus your own dear Saviour, your buckler and shield, your front guard and rereward? Is His praise in your heart and upon your lips? If it is not, awake, awake, stir thyself; arouse the drowsy energies of your soul. Christ is coming—precious *news!* It is always new. We rejoice in it. It cheers us in gloom and darkness. *Almost home! Precious sound!* Our home here is a sorrowful one but Jesus has gone to prepare for us a holy and happy home, and sorrow will never be known there.

The Lord has wrought for us in a signal manner. He has heard prayer for my husband and myself. We have often visited the throne of grace. We have earnestly wrestled with God for healing power. Morning, noon, and night we have felt the sweet blessing of God. It has distilled upon us like the dew. We have known here what sweet victory and salvation was since the conference. Our meetings here increase in interest every Sabbath.[5] I sincerely wish you

---

[3] *Identity:* See note 2.

[4] Little is known about David Lamson's earliest contacts with Sabbatarian Adventism except that he witnessed Ellen White in vision on June 26, 1854, in Rochester, New York. Several of his cousins were baptized in 1853 in nearby Clarkson, New York, and it is possible that David also was baptized on that occasion, although the *Review* account does not include names. When he was about 20 years old (c. 1855) he left New York and moved to Walton Township in Michigan, where he is listed in the 1860 census as "farmer." This move, it seems, is the occasion for Ellen White's concern for young David Lamson, that he had moved to an area with few, if any, persons of his faith around.

See: J. N. Loughborough, *The Great Second Advent Movement,* pp. 207, 208; *idem,* "Clarkson Meeting," *Review,* Sept. 27, 1853, p. 96; obituary: "David Henry Lamson," *Review,* Oct. 26, 1897, p. 687; 1860 U.S. Federal Census, "David H. Lamson," Michigan, Eaton County, Walton, p. 70.

[5] The events alluded to in this paragraph and the language she uses to describe them sound very similar to Ellen White's accounts elsewhere of the conference held at Battle Creek on November 16-19, 1855, and of events before and after the conference. The literary parallels are too striking to be coincidental.

See: "The Conference," *Review,* Dec. 4, 1855, p. 75. Note parallels in content between Lt 10, 1856 (Jan.), Lt 2a, 1856 (Jan. 24), and Ellen White's account of the 1855 Battle Creek

could attend meeting with us here upon the Sabbath.[6] The windows of heaven are often opened and blessings from God are poured upon us. We feel deeply our weakness, our own unworthiness, but the lovingkindness of God to so unworthy a creature as myself has not changed. His love often warms my heart and calls forth from me grateful acknowledgments of the same. I will not hold my peace. The praise of God is in my heart and upon my lips.

Dear brother, do not yield one particle of the truth. Stand stiffly for the truth and then the truth will make you free. There is a rich fullness in Jesus, a supply for each, for all. Oh come, David, come to salvation's Fountain and drink, that your soul may revive and flourish.

Oh, why do we die for bread or starve in a foreign land? Our Father's house has rich supplies, and bounteous are His hands. Jesus is precious. Let us live close to His bleeding side, and let us not shrink at trials. If you think you have many trials, I would say, Remember Calvary. Remember the King of glory in the garden sweating as it were great drops of blood. Next, see Him condemned, mocked at, spit upon, and then hung upon Calvary's cross, the nails driven through His tender hands and feet. Hear Him cry in the agony of His soul, "My God, My God, why hast Thou forsaken Me?" All this untold agony, all this unrealized suffering was for you and me, for our sins, and if we have trials let us remember Him that endured the contradiction of sinners against Himself. Oh, for the deep movings of the Spirit of God! I want to earnestly covet the purifying trials that will make me richer in glory.

Please write me just how you prosper. We all feel interested for you.

In love.

---

conference in *Spiritual Gifts [vol. 2]*, pp. 199-203.

[6] Since David Lamson lived only about 20 miles (32 kilometers) from Battle Creek, in Walton, Eaton County, Michigan, it would not be difficult for him to attend Sabbath services in Battle Creek, at least occasionally.

See: Obituary: "Elizabeth Louise Lamson," *Review*, Aug. 19, 1926, p. 22; 1860 U.S. Federal Census, "David H. Lamson," Michigan, Eaton County, Walton, p. 70.

1856

FEBRUARY

"Thankfulness, and the True Object of Our Affections."

Article published in *The Youth's Instructor,* vol. 4, no. 2, February 1856, p. 13.

1856

FEBRUARY 21

"Extracts."

Article published in *Advent Review, and Sabbath Herald,* vol. 7, no. 21, February 21, 1856, pp. 166, 167.

1856

MARCH

"Watch and Pray."

Article published in *The Youth's Instructor,* vol. 4, no. 3, March 1856, p. 21. (Reprint of October 1855 article.)

1856

APRIL, BATTLE CREEK, MICHIGAN

LETTER TO

Charles and Rachel Ann Sperry.

The correct date of this letter (previously misdated to 1861) was discovered too late in preparing this volume to insert the letter here. See pp. 772-775.

1856

(Ms 2, 1856)

[CIRCA MAY 27],[1] N.P.

Testimony for David Arnold,[2] Alexander Ross,[3] and others.

Previously unpublished.

David Arnold's discursive, formal preaching and extreme position

---

[1] No date or place of the vision described is given in the earliest copy of this manuscript. The contents are not readily datable except in very general terms. Until recently editors had assigned it the date "circa 1861." However, an examination of the correspondence from this period reveals a letter by Amanda Westcott that provides a more precise date. Writing on July 16, 1856, she describes a vision given Ellen White during "the conference at Battle Creek" that matches the vision account in Ms 2 very closely, even to the wording. Thus, according to Amanda Westcott, Ellen White saw "that Bro. Arnold and Bro. Hart had been too exacting about the note James published in the *Review*." Ellen White's account in Ms 2 reads almost identically: "I saw that Brethren Hart and Arnold had been too exacting about the matter of the note James published in the paper." This and other parallels seem too close to be coincidental. The vision, wrote Westcott, took place during "the conference at Battle Creek." The context suggests that the conference had taken place recently. The most recent conference at Battle Creek, Michigan, prior to her letter took place May 23-27, 1856. There are several reasons for concluding that the Ms 2 vision was given at that time. Among these is the fact that David Arnold, whose case is described in Ms 2, writes in the *Review* of his attendance at the May 1856 "general conference" in Battle Creek where "the Lord . . . manifested through one of the gifts of the Holy Spirit my condition." The details given in the Westcott letter and in a later report by Ellen White (*Testimonies for the Church,* vol. 1, p. 127) indicate that the Ms 2 vision was probably given on the last day of the conference, May 27, 1856.

See: Amanda Westcott to M. Crawford, July 16, 1856; J. W. [James White], "The Conference," *Review,* June 12, 1856, p. 52; David Arnold, "From Bro. Arnold," *Review,* Apr. 23, 1857, p. 199.

[2] *Identity:* There are several reasons for identifying Brother Arnold with David Arnold of Oswego County, New York. Particularly telling is the statement in the last paragraph that "Brethren Hart and Arnold had been too exacting about the matter of the note James published in the paper." We know from other sources that both David Arnold and a Brother Hart had taken issue with the Whites on whether the visions should be a test of fellowship. Arnold believed they should be and had reacted negatively to James White's article "A Test" the previous autumn in the *Review* (Oct. 16, 1855), in which White insisted that "the visions are not a test." Arnold subsequently debated the issue in a letter to Ellen White and also submitted his viewpoints to James White for publication in the *Review.* White, however, "declined publishing it," as Arnold pointed out in a letter to M. Crawford on February 3, 1856. In the same letter David Arnold notes that "Bro. Hart is a strong one on the visions" and had also "labored hard and long last summer" with James White "to convince him that they [the visions] were a test."

See: J. W. [James White], "A Test," *Review,* Oct. 16, 1855, pp. 61, 62; D. Arnold to M. Crawford, Feb. 3, 1856.

[3] *Identity:* A clear indication that Alexander Ross is referred to here is found in the third paragraph, where Ellen White "saw that Brother Ross's dreams and impressions had not

on the visions of Ellen White. Need for sensitivity in dealing with the mistakes of Alexander Ross. Call for experience of "free and full salvation" in the congregations of Arnold and Ross.

I saw in vision concerning Brethren Arnold [**David Arnold**], and Ross [**Alexander Ross**], and others.

I saw that there was a wrong. There were difficulties in Oswego County [New York]. I saw that Brother Arnold had not understood what manner of spirit he was of, and he came to the conference[4] with another spirit. It was not the Spirit of Jesus. I saw that since he was ordained, set apart by the brethren,[5] he has taken an exalted position that God had never assigned him, a position that it was impossible for him to rightly fill to the glory of God. Exaltation and self-esteem has led astray and perverted his judgment, and a deathly influence, instead of a saving influence, has been the consequence. I saw that this influence had injured Brother Ross.[6]

I saw that Brother Arnold had reasoned away and made of none effect what God had shown in vision in regard to Brother Ross.[7] Brother Arnold has not seen as God seeth in regard to Brother Ross. I saw that Brother Ross's dreams and impressions had not been from the true Source.[8] He has been, and still is, exalted, and has a large share of self-esteem. This will too surely prove his ruin unless it is seen and there is a breaking down before God.

I saw that Brother Ross and Brother Arnold have built themselves up upon Brother Rhodes's [**Samuel W. Rhodes**][9] past errors or what they think are

---

been from the true Source." One year later "Alex Ross," of Caughdenoy (Oswego County), confessed in the *Review* to his "unwisely giving heed to peculiar impressions and dreams, which I am fully persuaded are not from the right source."

See: Alex Ross, "From Bro. Ross," *Review,* Apr. 9, 1857, p. 182. See also note 1.

[4] Probably a reference to the "general conference" held in Battle Creek May 23-27, 1856, i.e., the conference at which Ellen White had the vision here recounted. David Arnold later confirmed that he attended that conference.

See: J. W. [James White], "The Conference," *Review,* June 12, 1856, p. 52; David Arnold, "From Bro. Arnold," *Review,* Apr. 23, 1857, p. 199.

[5] David Arnold, together with Hiram Edson, had been ordained six months earlier, "to act as Elders in the church."

See: J. N. Loughborough, "Oswego Conference," *Review,* Dec. 27, 1855, p. 101.

[6] David Arnold, from Volney (near Fulton), New York, lived only seven or eight miles (12 kilometers) from Alexander Ross in Caughdenoy.

[7] The only earlier mention of Alexander Ross still preserved is found in a vision given two years earlier, in February 1854, which focused on his failure as leader to deal firmly with some serious moral lapses in his congregation. Ellen White may be referring to that vision here or to another one, the record of which has been lost.

See: Ellen G. White, Ms 1, 1854 (Feb. 12).

[8] *See:* Note 3 above.

[9] *Identity:* No doubt Samuel W. Rhodes. No other Rhodes is found in the *Review* in the early 1850s.

See: Search term "Rhodes" in *Words of the Pioneers.*

his wrongs. They have both pushed and crowded Brother Rhodes, when God had been healing the past wrongs and errors in judgment that he has made formerly, and God has been fitting him up to work for Him in His cause.[10]

I saw that it was a weakness with Brother Arnold, his reasoning as much as he does. There is no religion or Jesus in it. It destroys the life of religion and encourages a formality that discourages and disheartens the people of God, and destroys the interest of meetings. This reasoning has grieved away God's Spirit, for I saw that God hates this reasoning that he has indulged in. I saw that this reasoning has mystified and fogged up the plainest facts and made them to be another thing. It has affected others; souls have felt with cringing its influence.

I saw that the case of Brother Ross must be handled carefully, yet decidedly and with firmness. Possessing the Spirit of Jesus, show him his true state. I saw that humble confessions from him were due his brethren who have been oppressed by him.[11]

I saw that in considering the wrongs of Brother Ross there had been feelings that were not free from self on his brethren's part. A feeling would rise in their hearts unlike the humble Pattern. However wrong Brother Ross may have been, his brethren could not be justified in having a single feeling or using a single word that was wrong.

Many of those in union with Brother Ross know but little of the things of God. I saw that a great work must be done for Brother Ross, and not only for him but for many in that section of country. Free and full salvation from God is scarcely felt; daily communion with God and consecration to Him is a rare thing. Said the angel, "Oh, how far from the bleeding side of Jesus! When at His feet strife and contention cease."

I saw that Brother Arnold's course had affected many. Amanda[12] has been drinking down the same spirit, the same feelings and ideas, and she is in danger of being led astray and discouraged and perplexed. I saw that Sister Arnold did not possess that feeling and spirit that God approbates; an humble spirit she does not possess. She has had too much of a complaining spirit. She talks more than is for her own spiritual good or the spiritual good of others or for the glory of God.

I saw that Brethren Hart and Arnold had been too exacting about the

---

[10] Samuel W. Rhodes, a prominent itinerant preacher in the early and mid-1850s, had frequently visited the various groups in Oswego county and vicinity. Rhodes had been reproved in 1853 and 1854 for his "overbearing spirit," harshness, and severity.

See: Ellen G. White, Ms 1, 1853 (June 2); *idem,* Ms 6, 1854 (Feb. 19).

[11] *See:* Note 3 above.

[12] *Identity:* This may be Amanda Westcott, who lived with the Arnold family from 1856 to the time of her death in 1870.

See: Obituary: "Amanda Westcott," *Review,* Mar. 7, 1871, p. 95.

matter of the note James published in the paper.[13] These two have made nearly all the difficulty about this matter. Others would have had but little trouble had not these brethren stirred it up. I saw that God had especially guided His servants in their judgment and counsel concerning Brother Arnold's case, and then in addition set to His seal that it was right by the descent of His Holy Spirit in answer to the united, earnest cries of His children. I saw that there were one or two that did not see or feel the case of Brother Arnold as it stood in the sight of God, but these had not the right judgment.

---

[13] *See:* Note 2 above.

1856

MAY

"The Lord Is Good."

Article published in *The Youth's Instructor*, vol. 4, no. 5, May 1856, pp. 37, 38.

1856

JUNE

"Search the Scriptures."

Article published in *The Youth's Instructor*, vol. 4, no. 6, June 1856, p. 44.

1856

(Lt 1, 1856)

JULY 15, BATTLE CREEK, MICHIGAN

LETTER TO

Stockbridge and Louisa M. Howland.[1]

Portions of this letter are published in Arthur L. White, *Ellen G. White: The Early Years*, pp. 341, 342.

Letter from Battle Creek, Michigan, to close friends, Stockbridge and Louisa Howland, of Topsham, Maine, containing news of travel,

---

[1] *Identity*: The reference to Topsham at the close of the letter together with the personal tone and the confidence expressed that the Howlands could take good care of Ellen White's infant boy clearly indicate that the letter is addressed to Stockbridge and Louisa M. Howland, of Topsham, Maine. The Howlands had earlier provided a home for Henry White, infant son of James and Ellen White, for five years.

See: Ellen G. White, *Spiritual Gifts [vol. 2]*, p. iii; 1860 U.S. Federal Census, "Stockbridge Howland," Maine, Sagadahoc County, Topsham Township, p. 443.

preaching and family. Letter ends with an appeal to the Howlands to move to Battle Creek.

Dear Bro. and Sister Howland:

No doubt you are wondering why Sister White does not write you, but cares, sickness, and journeying have hindered me. We returned last week from a journey of two weeks. We had a weary journey, but the Lord strengthened us. We started for our journey intending to remain four days at Hastings [Michigan][2] and then return home, but Sunday as we were going to the Court House, my husband to preach Sister Hutchinson's [**Amanda Hutchinson**][3] funeral sermon, two Brn. met us and said they had come for us 16 miles [25 kilometers] on foot to get us to go to Bowne [Michigan], that some were anxious to be baptized, and as they had only heard one (Bro. Frisbie [**Joseph Birchard Frisbie**])[4] they wanted a new gift. They went to the Court House and the Lord gave my husband strength and liberty to talk the truth. After [the] meeting closed these two brethren then walked home from that afternoon meeting 16 miles. All their errand was to get us to go to that people. We sent an appointment for that place, then went on our way to Grand Rapids, from Grand Rapids to Bowne. Our meeting on the Sabbath was well filled, although it was in the midst of the hay harvest. We both had liberty.

Perhaps you will have an interest to hear about these Brn. more particularly. They are only a few months in the message, they numbered 17, two strong in the faith. A physician and wife, very smart people, moved away, but before we left there were two more embraced the truth, making their number good. These brethren never heard but one man talk the truth, and they had read our publications, been convinced, and within three months 17 Sabbathkeepers were raised up.

They are substantial souls; some of them, or all, used tobacco. One Bro.

---

[2] "Providence permitting, Bro. & Sr. White will hold meetings with the Brethren in Hastings, Sabbath and First-day, June 28th and 29th."

See: "Appointment," *Review,* June 26, 1856, p. 72.

[3] *Identity*: James White, reporting on the same trip, states that "Sister Hutchinson . . . fell asleep April 8th." An obituary appearing in the *Review* gives April 8, 1856, as the death date of Amanda Hutchinson (c. 1800-1856), noting that "she has left an aged companion [Elisha] and four children to mourn her untimely loss."

See: J. W. [James White], "Our Late Visit," *Review,* July 24, 1856, p. 92; 1850 U.S. Federal Census, "Amanda Hutchinson," Michigan, Barry County, Hastings, p. 106; obituary: "Amanda Hutchinson," *Review,* June 19, 1856, p. 63.

[4] *Identity*: "Bro. J. B. Frisbie writes from Bowne, Kent Co., Mich., March 17th, 1856:—I am now lecturing to crowds in the town of Bowne, 14 miles [22 kilometers] north of Hastings, where they have never heard a lecture before."

See: J. B. Frisbie, "Extracts From Letters," *Review,* Mar. 27, 1856, p. 206.

had just bought two pounds [.9 kilograms]; he read the piece in the *Review*,[5] he laid aside his tobacco, and has tasted none since. This ought to shame those who profess the third angel's message, and have professed it for years, yet need to be often exhorted about their tobacco. A number of these Brn. have left off the use of tobacco, and another [also] that has just been converted out from the world from being a profane man to the third angel's message.

Sabbath noon four were led down into the water and baptized. One sister came to be baptized, a beautiful woman, intelligent, [who] had been a school teacher for years. But for three years [she] has been a cripple, has wheels to her chair and goes round the room on these wheels and does her work in this way. James and her husband carried her into the water and there she was baptized. Not one went in so calm, and was so sweetly blest as that sister.

Sunday two decided for the truth, and three more are thoroughly convinced. Their heart is with us, and we think they will start from that meeting to take a stand for the whole truth, notwithstanding husbands and fathers [who] stand in the way. The two that decided while we were there slept not all night. They were counting the cost and decided, come life or death, to sell all to buy the field. They were hungry souls for the truth and it was good to try to encourage them. But I must write upon something else.

When we returned home found my little Willie [**William Clarence White**, age 22 months] sick with sore mouth and canker; he is better now but the summer complaint troubles him some. Henry [**Henry Nichols White**, age 8] is quite a large boy, does a great many errands, is a smart boy. Edson [**James Edson White**, age 6] is a smart boy making good progress in reading. Henry says he sent you a letter. I would like to have seen it and corrected it some. Poor Clara [**Clarissa M. Bonfoey**],[6] yet not poor, sleeps in the cold grave; her loss we deeply feel; it can never be made up; it was so sudden, too. That tumor broke within and she mortified immediately. My children need her care. How can I go at all? It seems to me I must be confined at home constantly. Oh, do move out here and then I will leave my baby with you; the best little fellow you ever saw, and when I go [I] can feel easy about him.[7] Why don't you come? Can't you come? There is work enough here and it is nearly one half higher than in Topsham [Maine]. It does seem that I must have you here.[8] My

---

[5] In the previous few months the *Review* had carried two major anti-tobacco articles in addition to minor notices.

See: J. N. A. [John N. Andrews], "The use of tobacco a sin against God," *Review,* Apr. 10, 1856, p. 5; J. M. McLellan, "Idolatry," *Review,* June 12, 1856, pp. 49, 50.

[6] *Identity:* Clarissa M. Bonfoey, housekeeper in the White home, died a few weeks earlier, on May 30, 1856, at age 35. In her writings Ellen White occasionally calls Clarissa "Clara."

See: Obituary: "Clarissa M. Bonfoey," *Review,* June 12, 1856, p. 55; Ellen G. White, *Spiritual Gifts [vol. 2],* pp. 208, 209.

[7] *See:* Note 1 above.

[8] See note 1 on the close bond between the Howlands and the Whites. The Howlands did

health is better than it has been. My husband enjoys better health. Do write me. Why keep silent so long?

Love to all.

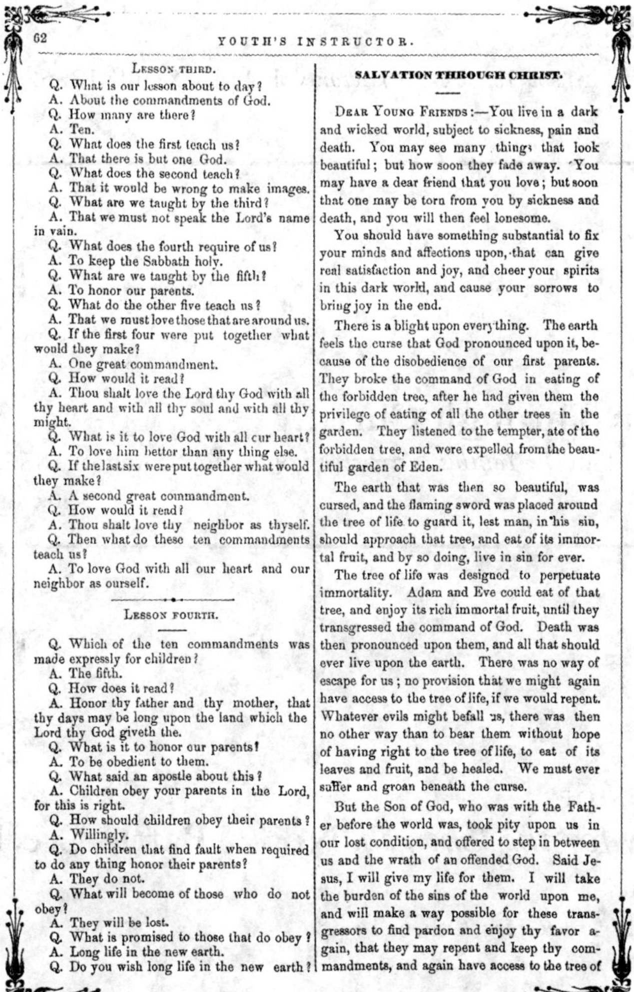

62 YOUTH'S INSTRUCTOR.

LESSON THIRD.

Q. What is our lesson about to day?
A. About the commandments of God.
Q. How many are there?
A. Ten.
Q. What does the first teach us?
A. That there is but one God.
Q. What does the second teach?
A. That it would be wrong to make images.
Q. What are we taught by the third?
A. That we must not speak the Lord's name in vain.
Q. What does the fourth require of us?
A. To keep the Sabbath holy.
Q. What are we taught by the fifth?
A. To honor our parents.
Q. What do the other five teach us?
A. That we must love those that are around us.
Q. If the first four were put together what would they make?
A. One great commandment.
Q. How would it read?
A. Thou shalt love the Lord thy God with all thy heart and with all thy soul and with all thy might.
Q. What is it to love God with all our heart?
A. To love him better than any thing else.
Q. If the last six were put together what would they make?
A. A second great commandment.
Q. How would it read?
A. Thou shalt love thy neighbor as thyself.
Q. Then what do these ten commandments teach us?
A. To love God with all our heart and our neighbor as ourself.

LESSON FOURTH.

Q. Which of the ten commandments was made expressly for children?
A. The fifth.
Q. How does it read?
A. Honor thy father and thy mother, that thy days may be long upon the land which the Lord thy God giveth the.
Q. What is it to honor our parents?
A. To be obedient to them.
Q. What said an apostle about this?
A. Children obey your parents in the Lord, for this is right.
Q. How should children obey their parents?
A. Willingly.
Q. Do children that find fault when required to do any thing honor their parents?
A. They do not.
Q. What will become of those who do not obey?
A. They will be lost.
Q. What is promised to those that do obey?
A. Long life in the new earth.
Q. Do you wish long life in the new earth?

SALVATION THROUGH CHRIST.

DEAR YOUNG FRIENDS:—You live in a dark and wicked world, subject to sickness, pain and death. You may see many things that look beautiful; but how soon they fade away. You may have a dear friend that you love; but soon that one may be torn from you by sickness and death, and you will then feel lonesome.

You should have something substantial to fix your minds and affections upon, that can give real satisfaction and joy, and cheer your spirits in this dark world, and cause your sorrows to bring joy in the end.

There is a blight upon every thing. The earth feels the curse that God pronounced upon it, because of the disobedience of our first parents. They broke the command of God in eating of the forbidden tree, after he had given them the privilege of eating of all the other trees in the garden. They listened to the tempter, ate of the forbidden tree, and were expelled from the beautiful garden of Eden.

The earth that was then so beautiful, was cursed, and the flaming sword was placed around the tree of life to guard it, lest man, in his sin, should approach that tree, and eat of its immortal fruit, and by so doing, live in sin for ever.

The tree of life was designed to perpetuate immortality. Adam and Eve could eat of that tree, and enjoy its rich immortal fruit, until they transgressed the command of God. Death was then pronounced upon them, and all that should ever live upon the earth. There was no way of escape for us; no provision that we might again have access to the tree of life, if we would repent. Whatever evils might befall us, there was then no other way than to bear them without hope of having right to the tree of life, to eat of its leaves and fruit, and be healed. We must ever suffer and groan beneath the curse.

But the Son of God, who was with the Father before the world was, took pity upon us in our lost condition, and offered to step in between us and the wrath of an offended God. Said Jesus, I will give my life for them. I will take the burden of the sins of the world upon me, and will make a way possible for these transgressors to find pardon and enjoy thy favor again, that they may repent and keep thy commandments, and again have access to the tree of

31

Ellen White's article "Salvation Through Christ" in The Youth's Instructor, *August 1856.*
Original dimensions: 9.75 x 6.5 in. (25 x 16 cm.).

---

eventually move to Battle Creek, but not until 15 years later, in 1871.

See: Obituary: "Stockbridge Howland," *Review*, Apr. 17, 1883, p. 254.

1856

JULY

"Jesus Says."

Article published in *The Youth's Instructor*, vol. 4, no. 7, July 1856, p. 52.

1856

AUGUST

"Salvation Through Christ."

Article published in *The Youth's Instructor*, vol. 4, no. 8, August 1856, pp. 62, 63.

1856

AUGUST

PUBLICATION OF

Testimony for the Church, No. 2, Battle Creek, Michigan.

Published by *Advent Review* Office. 16 pp.

1856

(Ms 1, 1856)

DECEMBER 9,[1] ROUND GROVE, ILLINOIS

Vision Given at Round Grove, Illinois.

Portions of this manuscript are published in Ellen G. White, *Testimonies for the Church,* vol. 1, pp. 149-153.

> *A lament over the decline in spirituality among many Adventists who had migrated to the West in the midfifties, coupled with an appeal to "be zealous and repent."*

I was shown in vision some things concerning the brethren and sisters at Round Grove [Illinois]. I saw that God had warned those that had moved from the East to the West. He had shown them their duty,—that it must not be their object to get rich; but to do good to souls, to live out their faith and tell to those around them that this world was not their home. The warning was sufficient if it had been heeded; but there was no considering of what God had shown, but rushed on and on, become drunk with the spirit of the world.[2]

"Look back" said the angel, "and weigh all that God has shown in regard to those moving from the East to the West." Have ye obeyed it? I saw that ye had gone entirely contrary to God's teachings, purchased largely, and instead

---

[1] An early heading to this manuscript reads, "Vision Given at Round Grove, Dec. 9th," with no year given. We know, however, from other sources, that Ellen and James White were in Round Grove, Illinois, for several weeks during November-December 1856.

See: E. Everts, J. Hart, "Conference," *Review,* Nov. 27, 1856, p. 32; "To Friends in the West," *Review,* Nov. 6, 1856, p. 8.

[2] Soon after arriving in Round Grove, in late November 1856, Ellen White noted that "there is quite a settlement of Sabbathkeepers here, from Vermont, New York and Michigan." With the opening up of new lands in the West, Adventists were part of a national movement westwards. The journey that Ellen and James White undertook in November and December of 1856 to western Illinois and Iowa was especially directed to those believers who had recently moved there from the East. This manuscript, reporting on a vision given while at Round Grove, expresses general disappointment at the spiritual state of the Adventist settlers, and their preoccupation with material pursuits, especially so in view of earlier warnings. In her first "Testimony for the Church," published one year earlier, Ellen White had written: "I was shown some coming from the East to the West. I saw that it should not be the object of those who leave the East for the West, to get rich, but to win souls to the truth. . . . If God has called you West, He has a work, an exalted work, for you to do."

See: Ellen G. White, *Spiritual Gifts [vol. 2],* p. 214; James White, "Western Tour," *Review,* Jan. 15, 1857, p. 84; Ellen G. White, *Testimonies for the Church,* vol. 1, p. 118; Arthur L. White, *Ellen G. White: The Early Years,* pp. 345-349.

of your works saying to those around you that ye are seeking a better country, it has plainly declared that here was your home and treasure.[3] Your works have denied your faith, nor is this all,—the love that should exist between brethren is gone. "Am I my brother's keeper," has been manifest. A selfish, covetous spirit has been in the hearts of the brethren. Instead of looking out for the interest of thy brother, and caring for him, it has been entirely contrary. In deal there has been manifested a selfish spirit,—a close spirit that God despises. The people of God that make so high a profession and that number themselves among the peculiar people of God, saying by this profession [that] they are zealous of good works, should have a noble, generous disposition, and should ever manifest a disposition to favor their brethren instead of their own selves, and should give their brethren the best chance. Generosity begets generosity, selfishness begets selfishness.

I saw that through the past summer, the prevailing spirit has been to grasp as much of this world as they possibly could. I saw that the commandments of God have not been kept. With the mind we serve the law of God, and the mind has been serving the world; and while the mind was all occupied with things of earth, and serving themselves, they could not serve the law of God. The Sabbath has not been kept; the work of six days has been carried into the seventh. One hour, and even more, has often been taken off from the commandment—an hour of holy time from the holy Sabbath.

I saw that some of the Sabbathkeepers who say to the world they are looking for Jesus' coming, and that they believe we are having the last message of mercy, yet give way to the natural feelings and barter and trade, and are a proverb among unbelievers, for their keenness in trade,—sharp and always getting the best end of a bargain.[4] Better lose a little and exert a holier, happier influence, and show that this world is not their god.

I saw that brethren should feel interested for each other, especially should those who are blessed with health have a kind regard and care for those that have not good health, and should favor them. They should remember the lesson taught by Jesus of the good Samaritan. Here has been one that has had a generous heart, but in the wise providence of God he has been cruelly torn in pieces, and unable to bear or surmount obstacles. His nerves have received

---

[3] Although this manuscript addresses the situation of the whole band of believers at Round Grove, little is known of the circumstances of individuals, the extent of their real estate holdings, etc. One exception is that of **Elon Everts** and his family. Ellen White writes of their struggles with materialism, as does Elon Everts himself in letters to the *Review*. The Everts family had moved west to Illinois in 1855 and had, as Ellen White describes it, purchased "large attractive lands, thus plainly declaring by their works that this world was their home."

See: Ellen G. White, "A Warning," *Review*, Apr. 15, 1858, p. 174.

[4] In the case of **Elon Everts**, his business practice "was so close and snug in deal, it really carried him beyond the bounds of strict truth and honesty."

See: Ibid.

a shock from which he will never recover. Yet he erred in judgment, purchased too largely. Still his brethren should have especially looked to and pitied and sympathized, and lent him a helping hand. But no, and when he is crippled and afflicted, his brethren have oppressed, and have not favored him. If all had kindly looked to, and aided him a little, they would not have felt it and they would have supplied his lack, comforted and cheered his heart, and had a sweet satisfaction and reward of well-doing in their own souls. [They would have] comforted and strengthened an afflicted brother, and would have done as they would have wished to be done by, were they crippled like he.[5] God has noticed these things.

Said Jesus, Love one another as I have loved you. How much? Why, His love cannot be told. He left the glory that He had with the Father before the world was, and was wounded for our transgressions, bruised for our iniquities, the chastisement of our peace was upon Him, and with His stripes we are healed. He bore every indignity and scorn patiently. Behold His agony in the garden when He prayed that the cup might pass from Him, His hands and feet wounded,—all this for guilty, lost man. And Jesus says, Love as I have loved you. How much? Well, enough to give your life for a brother. But has it come to this, that self must be gratified, the Word of God neglected? The world is their god—they serve it and the love of God has departed.

If ye love the world, the love of the Father is not in you. The Word of God has been neglected; in that are the warnings to God's people and in it are their dangers pointed out. But [they have had so many] cares and perplexities [that] they have hardly allowed themselves time to pray. There has been a mere empty form without the power of salvation. Jesus prayed, and Oh, how earnest I saw were His prayers, and yet He was the beloved Son of God. If Jesus manifested so much earnestness, so much energy and agonizing, how much more need those whom He has called to be heirs of salvation, dependent upon God for all their strength, to have their whole souls stirred to wrestle with God, and cry, "I will not let Thee go except Thou bless me." But I saw hearts here had been overcharged with surfeiting and drunkenness and the cares of this life, and God and His Word have been neglected.

I saw that it was easier for a camel to go through the eye of a needle than for a rich man to enter the kingdom. Also, says Jesus, "Lay not up for yourselves treasures upon earth, where moth and rust doth corrupt, and where thieves break through and steal; but lay up for yourselves treasures in heaven, where neither moth nor rust doth corrupt, and where thieves do not break through and steal; for where your treasure is, there will your heart be also." Matt. 6:19-21.

I saw it would have been better if there had been no attempts to preach the

---

[5] The identity of the person described in this paragraph is not known.

truth, for all their works denied their faith; and the last thing before attending the meeting was this world. It was carried even to the house of God, planning upon earthly things. It was world, world, until standing up to talk, and as soon as teaching the people was ended, it was world again. No time to meditate upon the truth,—no time to labor, wrestle and pray for salvation.[6] I saw that it would have been better if they had stayed at home, for minds have been waked up to the subject and no power and force is brought to bear upon them, and the interest dies down. Many cannot be reached again. When the truth is presented, it should be in the power and spirit; bring them to the point to decide—show them the importance—it is life or death. With becoming zeal, pull souls out of the fire. But, Oh, the withering, blighting influence that has been cast! Men waiting for their Lord, and yet possessing large and attractive lands. The farms have preached louder, yes, much louder than words can, that this world is their home. The evil day is put off; peace and safety reign. Oh, the withering, blighting influence! God hates such worldly-mindedness. "Cut loose, cut loose," were the words of the angel.

I was shown that all should have an eye single to the glory of God, yet those who have possessions have been too willing to excuse themselves on account [of] their wives and children. But I saw God would not be trifled with. When He speaks He must be obeyed. If wives or children stand in the way and hold back, they should say as Jesus said to Peter, Get behind me Satan, why tempt ye me to withhold from God what justly belongs to Him, and ruin my own soul? Have an eye single to the glory of God—don't look to wives or children, yet treat them tenderly and then shape your course for God's glory.[7]

I saw that many would have to learn what it is to be a Christian—that it

---

[6] **Josiah Hart** and **Elon Everts,** both preachers in and around Round Grove, were evidently convicted by the testimony of this vision. In a letter published in the *Review* three weeks later, on January 1, 1857, Hart testified, "I am now fully convinced that my course since I moved west . . . has gone to show that my affections were placed on the earth." Everts confessed in the same issue "with shame and regret, that my worldly mindedness and conduct has made me a citizen of this world." He pledged to place "my lands, my entire earthly substance, on the altar anew." Whether Everts acted on this pledge is discussed in note 7.

See: J. Hart, "Communication From Bro. Hart," *Review,* Jan. 1, 1857, p. 72; E. Everts, "Communication From Bro. Everts," *Review,* Jan. 1, 1857, p. 72.

[7] The case of **Elon Everts** is particularly apropos here. According to Ellen White's analysis in her article "A Warning," Everts had gone west in 1855 "with one intention, his wife with another." When he was convicted to sell some of his holdings "to advance the cause of God," his wife and daughter "easily persuaded" him not to go ahead. "Three times she [Elon's wife, Maria] was reproved by vision," but without relenting. After Maria died in 1856, Elon's daughter, Matilda, continued to "plead" with her father not to sell, and he acceded to her wishes. Subsequently, when Elon died in 1858 he "left his large property to his daughter" and "nothing was bestowed upon the cause of God."

See: Ellen G. White, "A Warning," *Review,* Apr. 15, 1858, p. 174; *idem, Spiritual Gifts [vol. 2],* p. 215.

is not in name, but it is having the mind of Christ, submitting to the will of God in all things. Especially [will] the young who have never known what privations or hardships are, who have a set will, and do not bend that will to the glory of God, [have a great work to do]. They go along very smoothly until that will is crossed, and then they have no control over themselves. They have not the will of God before them. They do not study how they can best glorify God, or advance His cause, or do good to others; but it is self, self, how can it be gratified? Such religion is not worth a straw. Those that possess it will be weighed in the balance and found wanting.

The true Christian will love to wait and watch for the teachings of God and the leadings of His Spirit. But religion with many is merely a form—vital godliness is gone. Many dare to say, I will do this, or that, or I will not do this, and so the fear of offending God is scarcely thought of. Those thus described, I saw, could not enter heaven. They may flatter themselves that they shall be saved, but God has no pleasure in them—their lives do not please Him. They are an annoyance to Him,—their prayers are an offense unto Him.

I saw that God now calls them to be zealous and repent; He kindly and faithfully admonishes them to buy gold, white raiment, and eyesalve that they may be rich. They can choose either to partake largely of salvation, be zealous, or be spued out of the mouth of God as disgusting, be rejected, and be thrust from Him.[8]

I saw that God would not bear always. He is of tender pity, but His Spirit will be grieved away for the last time. Mercy's sweet voice will be no more heard—its last precious notes will have died away and the described will be left to their own ways to be filled with their own doings.

I saw that those who profess to be looking for the coming of the Lord should not have a close, penurious spirit. I saw that some of those that have been called to talk the truth, to save souls as they that must give an account, have wasted much precious time for the sake of saving a little, when their time was worth a great deal more than that gained by them. It displeased God. This close dealing He hates. It is right that economy should be used, but it has been stretched into meanness without any goodly

---

[8] The extracts here from Revelation 3:15-19, the message to the Laodiceans, are significant. Just two months earlier an article entitled "The Seven Churches" by James White in the *Review* had signaled a major shift in the self-understanding of the emerging Sabbatarian Adventist movement. Prior to that the lukewarm Laodicean church was seen as applying to those Adventists coming out of the 1844 experience who had rejected the third angel's message, often called "nominal Adventists." In his article of October 16, James White had now boldly identified Sabbatarian Adventists with Laodicea and called them to repentance for their lukewarmness. It was a message that seemed particularly apt in describing the situation of many Adventist settlers in the West.

See: J. W. [James White], "The Seven Churches," *Review,* Oct. 16, 1856, pp. 189, 192; P. Gerard Damsteegt, *Foundations of the Seventh-day Adventist Message and Mission,* pp. 244-248; EGWEnc, s.v. "Laodicean Message."

object, only to already add to their treasure which will shortly eat their flesh like fire, unless they as faithful stewards make a right disposition of their Lord's goods.

John Andrews and his wife, Angeline. Courtesy of the Center for Adventist Research.

1856

(Lt 4, 1856)

DECEMBER 24, VOLNEY, IOWA

LETTER TO

Friends at Home.[1]

Portions of this letter are published in Arthur L. White, *Ellen G. White: The Early Years,* pp. 347, 348.

The rigors of a 200-mile [322-kilometer] midwinter journey by open sleigh to Waukon, Iowa. Ellen White's concerns about the welfare of her children at home.

Dear friends at home:

Here we are 14 miles [22 kilometers] this side of Waukon [Iowa].[2] We are all quite well. Have had rather a tedious time getting thus far. Yesterday for miles there was no track. Our horses had to plough through snow, very deep, but on we came. Oh, such fare as we have had on this journey. Last Monday we could get no decent food and tasted not a morsel, with the exception of a small apple, from morn until night. We have most of the time kept very comfortable, but it is the bitterest cold weather we ever experienced.

We introduce our faith at every hotel we enter, and have some two or three invitations to hold meetings on our return. One landlord was the first class of society. A man of sense and influence told us our entertainment should cost us nothing if we would hold meetings there. There seems to be an interest awakened at every place we stop. We think we shall have some meetings in this place next First day.

Well, how are my dear children? Jenny [**Jane Fraser**],[3] keep little Willie

---

[1] *Identity:* This would include Ellen White's three children and her housekeeper, all mentioned in the letter. There may well have been more persons living in the White home at this time. One month later Ellen White mentions in a letter that "our family" "number eight." The remaining two persons were probably Ellen's parents, **Robert** and **Eunice Harmon**. There are indications that the Harmons had moved to Battle Creek by the end of 1855 (see Lt 8, 1856 [Jan. 21]).

See: Ellen White to "Brother and Sister Loveland," Lt 2a, 1856 (Jan. 24).

[2] Ellen and James White together with Elon Everts and Josiah Hart had started their journey by sleigh about two weeks earlier from Round Grove, Illinois. Although the journey was less than 200 miles (322 kilometers), they had been held up along the way by deep snowdrifts.

For an account of the purpose and results of this very significant mission to Waukon, *see:* Arthur L. White, *Ellen G. White: The Early Years,* pp. 345-349; Ellen G. White, *Spiritual Gifts [vol. 2],* pp. 217-22; J. W. [James White], "Western Tour," *Review,* Jan. 15, 1857, p. 84.

[3] *Identity:* Jane ("Jenny") Fraser and Clarissa M. Bonfoey had worked together in the White

[**William Clarence White**, age 2] quite close at home this bitter cold weather. Don't let my children expose themselves. Watch their clothing. Don't let them be warm and sweating in the house and when they go out dress them very warm. Keep their stockings patched up warm. Have each of the children learn every day a lesson. Encourage them to learn every way you can.

Have had some bad dreams about little Willie. Oh, how thankful shall I be to see home, sweet home, again and my dear little boys, Henry [**Henry Nichols White**, age 9], Edson [**James Edson White**, age 7] and Willie.

Children, be good and love the Lord and as Jenny wishes you to mind what she tells you, as you would your mother. Be kind to each other, loving, yielding and don't be foolish and unsteady. Be sober, read the precious Word of God. Children, be thankful for your comfortable home. We often suffer with cold, [and] cannot keep warm [even] sitting before the stove. Their houses are so cold and your mother suffers with cold in her head and teeth all the time. Wear two dresses all the time.

Right about here there seems to be a better class of people and better houses than back, but last night we slept in an unfinished chamber, the pipe running through the top of the house, and it was entirely open, a large space, big enough for a couple of cats to jump out of.

Had a long time, the brethren did, with a Presbyterian minister, dignified enough, I assure you. He had no evidence for First day and if Uriah[4] [**Uriah Smith**] had been here he would have laughed in his sleeve.

Pray for us. We are near the scene of conflict. I say pray for us, for God to open the way for our return, or we may be blocked in and remain all winter.[5] Pray for the Lord to give us success.

In love.

---

household until the untimely death of Clarissa Bonfoey in May 1856. After that, for several years, Jane Fraser appears to have had chief responsibility for the household and for the children during the absences of Ellen and James White. In letters to her children Ellen White frequently appeals to them to "mind Jenny," to "make Jenny happy," etc. While she almost always referred to Jane as "Jenny," there are one or two instances in Ellen White's letters in which she uses "Jane."

See: Ellen G. White, Lt 3, 1861 (Mar. 18); Lt 10, 1859 (Sept.); Lt 12, 1857 (Jan. 30).

[4] *Identity:* No doubt **Uriah Smith**, newly appointed resident editor of the *Review*. During the previous 12 months he had frequently written on various aspects of the Sabbath.

See: Review: Dec. 11, 1855, p. 84; Dec. 18, 1855, p. 92; Feb. 7, 1856, p. 48; Feb. 14, 1856, p. 156; Feb. 28, 1856, p. 172; June 19, 1856, p. 60; June 26, 1856, p. 68; Aug. 7, 1856, p. 108; Sept. 25, 1856, p. 164; Nov. 13, 1856, p. 12.

[5] The Whites' return journey from Waukon to Battle Creek, Michigan, at the beginning of January, was not without incident. The second part of the trip, from Galena, Illinois, to Battle Creek, was undertaken by train. "When we were about nine miles [14 kilometers] from Battle Creek," recounts Ellen White, "the drive wheels ran off the track, and we went several rods with them off. If the small wheels had run off the track, we must have been plunged down an embankment of six feet [2 meters]. We had to wait there five hours in so short a distance of home."

See: Ellen G. White, Lt 12, 1857 (Jan. 30).

1856

DECEMBER 24, VOLNEY, IOWA

LETTER TO

Henry Nichols White, James Edson White, and William Clarence White.

Original letter is not extant. Published in Ellen G. White, *An Appeal to the Youth,* pp. 40-44. [Mistakenly dated 1857 in publication.]

1856

(Lt 6, 1856)

[CIRCA 1856],[1] N.P.

LETTER TO

Merritt E. Cornell, Dan R. Palmer, and John Preston Kellogg.[2]

Portions of this letter are published in Ellen G. White, *Manuscript Releases,* vol. 5, p. 237.

---

[1] This letter is undated, but there is sufficient internal evidence to give an approximate date. The mention of tent meetings indicates that it cannot be dated earlier than 1854, when such meetings were first held by Sabbatarian Adventists. On the other hand, the implication in the last paragraph that the *Messenger* Party (see EGWEnc) is still active suggests a date no later than about 1858, by which time, according to James White, the party had dissolved. Another feature of the document implies that it was written no later than 1856. Much of the focus is on the relationships between certain members of the Jackson group, including a tense standoff between J. P. Kellogg and Dan R. Palmer, described in the last paragraphs. However, from other sources it is known that while Palmer stayed on in Jackson, Kellogg moved from Jackson to Battle Creek, Michigan, in 1856.

See: J. W. [James White], "A Sketch of the Rise and Progress of the Present Truth," *Review,* Jan. 14, 1858, p. 77; J. N. Loughborough, *Rise and Progress of the Seventh-day Adventists,* pp. 199, 200, 202, 203.

[2] *Identities:* The primary clue to the identity of "Cornell" as Merritt E. Cornell is the mention of his wife's name, Angeline, later in the letter. Likewise "Kellogg" is identified as John Preston Kellogg by the reference to his son's name, Smith. The fact that this letter describes the strained relationship between J. P. Kellogg of Jackson, Michigan and "Bro. Palmer" suggests that the person referred to is Dan R. Palmer, also of the Jackson, Michigan, group.

Counsel to Merritt E. Cornell on his insensitive criticism of J. P. Kellogg and to Angeline Cornell on her attempts to control her husband's traveling ministry.

To Brethren Cornell, Palmer, and Kellogg:

I was pointed back to the church meeting held at Battle Creek [Michigan] at the time when Brother and Sister Cornell's case was investigated.[3] I saw that the work commenced well for Brother and Sister Cornell, but it did not go deep enough. The brethren were so rejoiced that Brother and Sister Cornell see where they erred that they did not continue their faithful warning and reproof, and our brother and sister did not continue to reach to the bottom and overcome every wrong. The enemy stepped right in, and Brother Cornell hardly felt satisfied with the course pursued by the brethren when his case was investigated.

He began to feel jealous of Brother Smith.[4] Hard feelings crept in and he felt a repulsive feeling towards him. I saw these feelings were all wrong. I saw Brother Kellogg conversing with Brother Cornell and he was open-hearted and faithfully told him his feelings. They separated, and Brother Cornell kept turning the matter over and over in his mind. Satan made every word mean a great deal. Jealousy put a bad construction upon his motives, and from that time the work of the enemy was fully commenced to separate these brethren.

And Brother Cornell began to push Brother Kellogg. He looked back to last summer, and every word or expression was magnified and made the most of. I saw that when the conference was appointed here at Battle Creek, Brethren Kellogg and Palmer should have come, but they did not. They lost much [they] might have had, and had they attended the conference the existing trouble would have been saved.

I then saw Brother Waggoner [**Joseph Harvey Waggoner**] did not move right in coming so hastily back to Jackson[5] [Michigan]. The blame rested

---

See: Obituary: "Angeline M. A. Cornell," *Review*, Jan. 7, 1902, p. 14; 1850 U.S. Federal Census, "John Kellogg," Michigan, Livingston County, Tyrone Township, p. 885; "Business Proceedings of the Conference at Battle Creek, May 26th, 1856," *Review*, May 29, 1856, p. 44; search terms "Palmer" and "Jackson" in *Words of the Pioneers*.

[3] The seventh paragraph implies that the charges investigated in Battle Creek concerned Angeline Cornell's negative influence on her husband's traveling ministry. Unfortunately no other sources have been found that throw further light on the date or purpose of this Battle Creek meeting.

[4] *Identity:* There is insufficient information in this short mention of "Brother Smith" to indicate which Smith is being referred to.

[5] *Identity:* The only "Waggoner" in the fledgling movement during this period is Joseph Harvey Waggoner, so there is no difficulty in identification. On the other hand, the event referred to in this paragraph, the hasty return to Jackson, has not been located in either correspondence or published sources.

wholly upon himself, but as he was in difficulty Brethren Palmer and Kellogg should have made the best of it and taken hold to relieve his pressing necessity and not wait for particular feelings to guide them. Necessity is necessity and it must, if possible, find immediate relief.

I saw that Brother Kellogg had been observing for some time that the cause of God did not rise and progress. I saw that he had looked at Sister Angeline [**Angeline M. A. Cornell**][6] and considered that she was burdening her husband. I saw that when Brother Cornell felt like going to a place to labor and she did not feel reconciled to it, it was hard for her to cheerfully submit to her husband. She thought her feelings must be regarded. She had strong, willful feelings about the matter. She had a way of her own about it, and at such times, if her wishes were not yielded to, she often had a nervous fit. All this was caused by unsubdued temper, and at such times Brother Cornell would be in doubt whether he had pursued the right course in being decided and moving according to the dictates of his own conscience, or whether he had not better have yielded to her wishes more, on account of her poor health.

His sympathies were awake at once and he has yielded his sense of duty altogether too much, and it has only fed this willful, unsubdued spirit. It is these things that are a great reason for her poor health. The only way for Angeline to get the victory over this is to govern herself and submit to God, consecrate herself to God, yield up her will and her stubborn spirit, and then these nervous fits would not occur. These things hinder the work of God and throw Brother Cornell into a state of anxiety and care, cripple his usefulness, and mar the work of God.[7]

These things have caused Brother Kellogg to lose confidence in Angeline, and he knew that Brother Cornell had been influenced by these things. Angeline had affected him and he looked back to the investigation at Battle Creek where the work commenced well and honestly and correctly, but did not go as thorough and deep as it ought to have gone. His confidence in Brother and Sister Cornell was shaken.

Brother Kellogg had tried to be a faithful and true steward and administer as God had prospered him.[8] He saw no fruit of scarcely anything he had done,

---

See: Search term "Waggoner" in *Words of the Pioneers.*

[6] *Identity:* Angeline M. A. Cornell, wife of Merritt E. Cornell. See note 2.

[7] That Angeline Cornell was sometimes more of a hindrance than a help to her husband's traveling ministry appears to have been a continuing problem. See, for example, Ellen White's admonitions and appeals to Angeline in Lt 10, 1863 (Nov. 28), and Lt 11, 1865 (c. 1865).

[8] According to J. N. Loughborough, within a year or two of becoming a Sabbathkeeper in 1852, J. P. Kellogg sold his farm "worth about $3,500, for the sole purpose of having means to use in advancing the work." Kellogg, with others, subsequently lent without interest or gave generously for constructing the *Review* building in Battle Creek in 1855 and for purchasing the first tent to be used for Adventist public evangelism in 1854.

See: J. N. Loughborough, *Rise and Progress of the Seventh-day Adventists,* pp. 198-204.

and settled it in his mind that he would be doubly assured that the objects of his charity should be worthy before he would impart his means to them. He became discouraged. Unbelief came in, and when Brother Palmer went to Brother Kellogg burdened,[9] Brother Kellogg was tried. It did not look right to him. He looked at his own poor health, and almost every one of his family that could help him were invalids. He looked at his son, who had very nearly lost his life by traveling with the tent and enduring so much exposure,[10] and he looked at Brother Palmer's family in almost perfect health; he compared the plain manner of his wife's and children's clothes to the different course Sister Palmer [**Abigail Palmer**][11] had taken in dressing herself and children, and he felt that he was misjudged.

He could not see that he had lost the spirit of sacrifice. He gave way to his feelings, and the temptation of the enemy came in. He yielded, was hasty. He saw this afterwards, was convinced he manifested wrong feelings, and confessed it.

The proposition of Brethren Palmer and Kellogg was correct, to let this difference of opinion drop. This would have been just right. If Brother Cornell had been standing in the counsel of God, how easy could he have been peacemaker and fulfil one duty of his calling. How easy then for the breach to be healed. It should have been Brother Cornell's study, How can I help the cause of God and prevent an open rupture here? One Holy Ghost meeting would have healed the wound; but instead of healing the difficulty, Brother Cornell made a wide breach.

Then instead of the Lord's working, Brother Cornell began to work. He was not then God's instrument, but going at his own bidding. And, instead of feeling Who is sufficient for these things? and with prayer and tears going to Brother Kellogg, and like a child entreating him as a father, he felt sufficient for the work. He had a self-dignity and an exalted spirit and he pushed the matter through to cut off one that was more experienced in the cause of God than himself. He was blind to his own weakness, blind to his own heart, and the sweet, melting Spirit of God was not with him.

As Brother Kellogg was pursued in this matter, he hardly knew what to

---

[9] Dan R. Palmer, like J. P. Kellogg, had been very generous in his support of the Sabbatarian movement.

See: Brian E. Strayer, "Early Adventist Waymarks in Jackson, Michigan," pp. 14-16.

[10] John Loughborough recalls that he was present on the occasion in 1854 when J. P. Kellogg not only volunteered to pay a large share for the purchase of a large tent for evangelism in Michigan but also proposed that one of his sons, **Albert Kellogg,** about 18 years old, should accompany the tent as "tent master." Therefore it is most probable that it was Albert Kellogg who "nearly lost his life."

See: J. N. Loughborough, *The Great Second Advent Movement,* p. 562.

[11] *Identity:* See 1860 U.S. Federal Census, "Abigail Palmer," Michigan, Jackson County, Jackson, Ward 4, p. 134.

make of it. He was astonished, and he gave way to his feelings and manifested a wrong spirit. I saw the work against Brother Kellogg was cruel. He had been desponding, had lost his faith and looked upon the dark side too much, and had distrusted God. But his brethren could have come in and comforted him and encouraged him and he would have overcome these feelings and when God should call upon him to aid His children he would have cheerfully assisted.

I saw that the burden that has been upon him has been almost too much for him. His children have lain near his heart and their eternal interest has been his main study, while others—who have neglected the spiritual interest of their children—are not prepared to sympathize with him in his anguish of spirit if he saw his children going astray and losing their interest in the truth. The course of his son Smith [**Smith Moses Kellogg**][12] has almost crushed him,[13] and while his heart has been sore stricken his comforters have been like Job's. The brethren could have soothed him in his anguish, but instead of this the iron entered their hearts and he has been thrust with side and shoulder.

I saw the course of Brother Dickinson's [**Preston** and **Celesta B. Dickinson**][14] family in regard to Smith was most cruel and unnatural. The advice for children to disregard the special wishes of their parents—this cannot be too highly censured. I saw if God had not had a kind regard for Brother Kellogg in this time of severe trial, his mind would have strained; but God's hand has been beneath him.

I saw that Brother Cornell had not counseled with his aged brethren as he should have done; he was too independent. Those who have brought up a family and, like Abram, have commanded them after themselves, are almost always better prepared to judge in matters of the church than young preachers. Some of the preachers have got out of their place. They have felt perfectly qualified in church matters when their own hearts were not right. I

---

[12] *Identity:* Obituary: "Smith M. Kellogg," *Review,* Feb. 9, 1928, p. 22.

[13] Exactly what Smith Moses Kellogg had done to cause his parents grief is not stated, but Ellen White returns to this subject several years later in a letter written "circa 1861." She states there that Smith's marriage to Maria S. Dickinson (in 1858) upset the parents, but even before that "his former course has caused his parents many heartaches and much anxiety and distress."

Ellen White, Lt 15, 1861 (c. 1861); obituary: "Smith M. Kellogg," *Review,* Feb. 9, 1928, p. 22.

[14] *Identity:* Several Dickinsons appear in the columns of the *Review* in the 1850s, the question being which Dickinson is referred to in this letter. The general impression given from this passage is that the Dickinson family and Smith Kellogg live in the same vicinity. It is therefore probable that Ellen White is referring to the family of Preston and Celesta B. Dickinson, longtime residents of Jackson, Michigan, including the three years or so in the mid-1850s, when John Preston Kellogg and family lived in Jackson.

See: Obituary: "Preston Dickinson," *Review,* May 12, 1868, p. 350; 1850 U.S. Federal Census, "Preston Dickinson," Michigan, Jackson County, Jackson Township, p. 654; E. Green, "From Bro. Green," *Review,* Oct. 7, 1858, p. 159; Richard W. Schwarz, *John Harvey Kellogg, M.D.,* pp. 16, 17.

saw that Brother Cornell must die to self-dignity and must get rid of jealousy, for it is cruel as the grave.

Said the angel, "God's children are as the apple of His eye, and when you touch them to hurt them you touch the apple of God's eye." Said the angel, "The oil and the wine have been hurt. Hurt not the oil and the wine." Said the angel, "Rebuke not an elder, but entreat him as a father." This, I saw, did not mean preachers, but aged men, those that are fathers in experience. This has been overlooked in Brother Kellogg's case.[15] He has been treated more like a disobedient child than a father.

I saw that with great trembling should the young preachers receive an accusation against their fellow laborers and the old hoary-headed fathers of the church. I saw there was not that weeping spirit and meek spirit among the preachers there should be. I saw that all that was required of Brother Cornell was to break all down before God, have a humble, childlike spirit, and then will he plant himself firmly in the hearts of his brethren. I saw you must be careful how you stretch out your hand to bring rebels into the camp, lest the Lord destroy you and them together. If God has honest ones among the *Messenger* Party that have left us, they will find enough to do to come all the way back, confessing humbly their wicked course. We must not meet them halfway.[16] Let them make thorough work themselves, then shall we know that God has wrought for them.

In love.

---

[15] In 1856 Merritt Cornell was 29 and apparently had no children (see Lt 10, 1863 [Nov. 28], to Angeline Cornell: "you have only yourself and husband to care for"). J. P. Kellogg, on the other hand, was 49 and the father of 12 children (eventually 16, although not all survived).

See: Obituary: "Merritt E. Cornell," *Review,* Jan. 23, 1894, p. 63; obituary, "J. P. Kellogg," *Review,* May 31, 1881, p. 350.

[16] At least part of the concern expressed here appears to be that scarce time and resources should not be diverted trying to debate with and reclaim those who had decided to join the *Messenger* Party. The Sabbatarian movement had more pressing priorities, as argued by Ellen White in 1855: "Christ is coming, and the great work of the last message of mercy is of too much importance for us to leave it and come down to answer such falsehoods, misrepresentations, and slanders, as the *Messenger* party have fed upon."

See: Ellen G. White, *Testimonies for the Church,* vol. 1, p. 123; EGWEnc, s.v. "*Messenger* Party."

1857

(Lt 1, 1857)

JANUARY 28, BATTLE CREEK, MICHIGAN

LETTER TO
Anthony L. and Achsah Burwell.[1]
Previously unpublished.

An appeal to bereaved parents to turn from their materialism and set a godly example to their only remaining child.

Dear Brother and Sister Burwell:

In the vision given at this place I was shown something concerning you. I saw that it was easier for a camel to go through the eye of a needle than for a rich man to enter the kingdom of heaven. God has been merciful to you. He has in mercy spared you one child; and if you both pursue a right course, there is some prospect of her being influenced by the truth and being saved in the kingdom. But I saw that unless you were willing to make a sacrifice for this and prize her salvation and your own enough to act out your faith, cut loose from the world, and act like men waiting for their Lord, there is no prospect, none at all. Your course will influence her. Show her by acting out your faith that you really believe the message, "Be zealous . . . and repent."

When you really [believe] this message the effect upon you will be to separate from the world, live out your faith, sell that you have, give alms, and lay up for yourselves a treasure in the heavens. God has come very near unto you when you were at a great distance from Him. He took two idols from you that you might draw near unto Him and that God alone might be exalted and reign supreme in your heart, and that your eye might be single to His glory. These children were snatched away to save you and her.[2]

---

[1] *Identity:* The letter informs us that God "has in mercy spared you one child" and that her name is Anna. This information clearly identifies the addressees as Anthony L. Burwell and Achsah Burwell, of Parma, Michigan. Two of their three children died in 1856, leaving only Anna Lucretia King (née Burwell), age 12.

See: A. Burwell, "From Sr. Burwell," *Review,* Jan. 1, 1857, p. 71; obituary: "Anthony L. Burwell," *Review,* Jan. 28, 1873, p. 55; obituary: "Achsah Burwell," *Review*, June 8, 1886, p. 366; 1850 U.S. Federal Census, "Anthony L. Burwell," Vermont, Addison County, Panton Township, p. 262; obituary, "Mrs. Anna Lucretia King, née Burwell," *Review,* Mar. 5, 1931, p. 28.

[2] Whereas the language used here suggests that the death of the two children was the direct action of God, in other places Ellen White describes death and suffering as the works of Satan. "Satan, the author of sin and all its results, had led men to look upon disease and death as

Brother, you love this world, especially Brother Burwell. You realize not how much your heart is set upon and glued to this world and how little you are willing to sacrifice for the better and heavenly country. If you prize the precious pearl of exceeding value highly enough to sell all that you have to purchase it, I saw that you could have it. Unless you prize it enough for this, it is not yours, neither can you have it.

Dear Brother, I dare not hold my peace. I must deal faithfully and truly with you. From what God has shown me, I fear your property will shut you out of heaven, because you love it, whether you realize it or not, better than anything else.[3] A terrible calamity came upon you, yet it has not had the effect that God designed it should, to wean you from the world. Your possessions are still dear to you, are of worth, great worth, so much so that it looks to you to be a great thing to sacrifice anything even for your own soul's sake. Every idol, brother and sister, is not yet sacrificed with you, and if there is one idol left, whatever that idol be, it will shut you out of heaven.

I saw that you were in a hard place to serve God and should not let anything stand in the way—property, friends, or anything—of seeking counsel of God and placing yourselves in a situation to benefit your own souls. Let everlasting life be the object ever before you. The world is nothing, and less than nothing. Your possessions are a snare to you and I fear you will be taken in the snare and it will be impossible to escape. Make haste to get ready, for the days of

---

proceeding from God. . . . [However] the history of Job had shown that suffering is inflicted by Satan, and is overruled by God for purposes of mercy." These are not necessarily contradictory positions. Parallels can be drawn from Scripture where "by figure God is frequently said to do that which He permits or does not prevent."

Elaborating on this point in 1883, Ellen White wrote that she "was shown that the judgments of God would not come directly out from the Lord upon them [those refusing His merciful warnings], but in this way: They place themselves beyond His protection. He warns, corrects, reproves, and points out the only path of safety; then if those who have been the objects of His special care will follow their own course independent of the Spirit of God, after repeated warnings, if they choose their own way, then He does not commission His angels to prevent Satan's decided attacks upon them."

See: Ellen G. White, *The Desire of Ages,* p. 471; Francis D. Nichol, ed., *The Seventh-day Adventist Bible Commentary,* vol. 4, p. 662; Ellen G. White, Lt 14, 1883 (Aug. 8).

[3] The Burwells migrated from Vermont to Michigan in 1856. The value of their property, according to census information, doubled from a respectable $3,000 in 1850 to $6,000 in 1860, with a further $1,500 in "personal estate." Anthony Burwell died in 1873. Already by 1855 Ellen White had published a general admonition to those who, like the Burwells. were moving to better economic opportunities in the West. "I saw that it should not be the object of those who leave the East for the West to get rich, but to win souls to the truth." More published and unpublished testimony in the same vein had followed.

See: Ellen G. White, Lt 2, 1857 (Oct. 21); 1850 U.S. Federal Census, "Anthony L. Burwell," Vermont, Addison County, Panton, p. 262; 1860 U.S. Federal Census, "Anthony Burwell," Michigan, Jackson County, Parma, p. 19; 1870 U.S. Federal Census, "Anthony Burwell," Michigan, Jackson County, Sandstone, p. 11; obituary: "Anthony L. Burwell," *Review,* Jan. 28, 1873, p. 55; Ellen G. White, *Testimonies for the Church,* vol. 1, p. 118.

preparation are few. Tear away the rubbish from the door of your heart and open the door and let the Saviour in.

I saw that if you expect Anna [**Anna Lucretia King** (née **Burwell**)][4] to be saved you must do more on your own part, make more decided efforts than you ever yet have made. One thing I saw you had erred in, that is in the company you suffer to be in your dwelling. Whatever sacrifice you should have to make for this should be cheerfully done. Have only those with you or in your dwelling that are clean and holy. Encourage none to be with you except those whose influence is saving. Whatever the consequences may be, this step should be taken. Have all clean in your dwelling. Then you may expect that the Lord will bless your efforts. But for years past it has been impossible to save your children while there was so little effort made to have all about them such that God could come into your dwelling. Have not those with you that love not God and that God hates. Take hold of the work in earnest, be in haste to get ready. Oh, make every effort for the salvation of your daughter! You have never realized the danger of having those around you whose influence was not good, but deathly. You must with decision have a pure, clean company around you. Anna's salvation depends upon the course you pursue.

---

[4] *Identity:* See note 1.

1857

(Lt 12, 1857)

JANUARY 30,[1] BATTLE CREEK, MICHIGAN

LETTER TO

Harriet Newall Stevens.[2]

Previously unpublished.

> *Letter to Harriet Stevens urging her to seek God's guidance on whether to rejoin the staff at the* Review *publishing office in Battle Creek, Michigan.*

Dear Sister Harriet:

We received a letter from Bro. John [**John Nevins Andrews**][3] yesterday. Enclosed was a line from you. We were glad to hear from you once more. The letter was dated the 5th.[4] We received it the 29th.

---

[1] The original/earliest copy reads "1856," but the contents indicate that it should read 1857.

[2] *Identity:* There can be little doubt that the "Harriet" being addressed is Harriet Newall Stevens, soon to marry *Review* editor Uriah Smith. Two paragraphs of the letter are devoted to the possibility of "Harriet" joining the *Review* staff, provided she is personally convinced that this would be God's will for her. Some weeks later, in the spring of 1857, Harriet Stevens moved to Battle Creek, Michigan, and rejoined the *Review* staff (with whom she had previously worked in 1854-1855).

Confirming this identity, the first paragraph indicates that "Harriet" wrote her letter from Waukon, Iowa (see notes 3 and 4 below), and it is known from other sources that Harriet Stevens was living in Waukon during this period. The Cyprian Stevens family had moved to Waukon in the spring of 1856. Whether Harriet moved at the same time as the family is unclear, but the evidence is strong that she was there when the Whites visited Waukon in December 1856. In a passage in *Spiritual Gifts [vol. 2]* Ellen White describes striking charismatic phenomena at an evening meeting at Waukon in December 1856. "The power of God fell upon the company," she wrote, and "I was prostrated by the power of God. Sister H. N. S. fell from her chair helpless. It seemed to be an awful, yet glorious place. I had no strength for two hours, but seemed to be wrapped in the glory of God." There can be little doubt that "H. N. S." refers to Harriet Newall Stevens.

See: Obituary, "Harriet N. Stevens Smith," *Review,* Mar. 30, 1911, p. 23; Ellen G. White, *Spiritual Gifts [vol. 2],* p. 220.

[3] *Identity:* The identity of "Bro. John" becomes clear at the end of the letter, where he is associated with Angeline. John Nevins Andrews had married **Angeline Stevens** three months earlier, in October 1856. Other indications that J. N. Andrews is referred to include the date of "John's" letter (see note 4) and the mention of his ill health (see note 15).

See: Ron Graybill, "The Family Man," in Harry Leonard, ed., *J. N. Andrews: The Man and the Mission,* p. 21.

[4] A letter signed "J. N. Andrews, Waukon, Iowa, Jan. 5th, 1857," appears in the *Review* for

James is quite well for him. I am not as well as when I was with you. I had been traveling so long in the open air, that when bought into a right warm home, I dropped and fainted like a bird. There was no strength in me for more than a week and have felt drooping and weak ever since my return.[5]

Our conference[6] was quite a good one, but there were all kinds. Many came from a distance, and some of them, their hearts were not right but they were crooked. Some the Lord wrought for and set free. The next Sabbath after this, Brother and Sister Gurney [**Heman S. Gurney** and **Ann Eliza Gurney**][7] came to Battle Creek [Michigan]. We had an excellent meeting with them. Brother Gurney seems as good as ever, his testimony went well last Sabbath.

Oh, how thankful was I to get home once more. When we were about nine miles [14 kilometers] from Battle Creek, the drive wheels ran off the track, and we went several rods with them off. If the small wheels had run off the track, we must have been plunged down an embankment of six feet [two meters]. We had to wait there five hours in so short a distance of home. The passengers were all of them hungry, except ourselves. We had three pounds [1.4 kilograms] of crackers. We divided round among them. They had tasted nothing, many of them, since the night before.

We found our children very well. Willie [**William Clarence White**, age 2] is a fat, healthy, little fellow, and clings closer than ever to his mother. Jane's [**Jane Fraser**][8] health is better than it ever has been since she lived with us.

Feb. 5, 1857. This may be the letter "dated the 5th" mentioned here, but it is addressed to the editor, "Bro. Smith," so it may be that Andrews had sent several letters on that date, including one, no longer extant, to the Whites.

See: J. N. Andrews, "Note From Bro. Andrews," *Review,* Feb. 5, 1857, p. 108.

[5] A reference to the Whites' recent six-week journey to Illinois and Waukon, Iowa, part of it exposed in open sleds. They had returned a few weeks since, in early January 1857. For an account of the purpose and results of this very significant mission to Waukon, see Arthur L. White, *Ellen G. White: The Early Years,* pp. 345-349; Ellen G. White, *Spiritual Gifts [vol. 2],* pp. 217-222; J. W. [James White], "Western Tour," *Review,* Jan. 15, 1857, pp. 84, 85.

[6] Ellen White is probably referring to a meeting at the "House of Prayer" in Battle Creek advertised in the *Review* for January 17, 1857.

See: James White, "Next Sabbath," *Review,* Jan. 15, 1857, p. 88.

[7] *Identity:* All references to "Gurney" in the *Review* during the 1850s appear to be to the family of Heman S. Gurney and his wife, Ann Eliza Gurney. This makes it almost certain that they are the persons referred to here. The timing of their visit to Battle Creek confirms the identity. The Gurneys had moved from Massachusetts to Jackson, Michigan, just two or three months earlier. Having been acquainted with the Whites since the midforties, it is not surprising that they took an early opportunity to visit them in nearby Battle Creek after the Whites returned from their journey to Iowa.

See: Search term "Gurney" in *Words of the Pioneers;* "Business," *Review,* Nov. 13, 1856, p. 16; Arthur Whitefield Spalding, *Origin and History,* vol. 1, p. 402.

[8] *Identity:* Jane ("Jenny") Fraser and Clarissa M. Bonfoey had worked together in the White household until the untimely death of Clarissa Bonfoey in May 1856. After that, for several years, Jane Fraser appears to have had chief responsibility for the household and for the children during the absences of Ellen and James White. In letters to her children Ellen White frequently appeals to them to "mind Jenny," to "make Jenny happy," etc. While almost always

She does the washings and all the housework, and she enjoys peace of mind. Never saw Jane in so good a place.

We have felt desirous of attending the conferences appointed in the Eastern states, but we see no good way open for our children. Their eternal interest is a great weight and burden to me. Oh, will the Lord save my children, my poor children? I have no evidence [that] if Henry [**Henry Nichols White**, age 9] or Edson [**James Edson White**, age 7] should now die that they would come up in the first resurrection. I carry a burdened heart for them all the time. Oh, that salvation may come to this home, and from the eldest to the youngest, may be heard the song of praise.[9]

The message to the Laodicean church affects every way, in every sense and every where.[10] The church here is rising. God is working for us. We feel the necessity of working with energy. This message to the church calls for more than common efforts, on our own part. A deep interest in our own cases should we feel. We should afflict our souls on our own account, turn our eyes within and mourn and pray and beg for our salvation.

Harriet, my mind is just the same as it was when with you. "The Lord has need of thee" means something. Enquire and find out what it means. There is need of help in the Office; and Harriet, go to God, find out His will concerning you, expect that the Lord will teach you; consecrate yourself wholly to God. Don't rest down, but rise, rise, live on the plan of addition. "Add to your faith virtue; and to virtue knowledge; and to knowledge, temperance; and to temperance patience; and to patience godliness; and to godliness brotherly kindness; and to brotherly kindness charity. For if these things be in you and abound, they make you that ye shall neither be barren nor unfruitful in the knowledge of our Lord Jesus Christ." 2 Peter 1:5-8.

The burden of this matter rests with you. God will surely give you the burden of this matter if He calls you to fill so important a place. There is a

---

referring to Jane as "Jenny," there are one or two instances in Ellen White's letters where she uses "Jane."

See: Ellen G. White, Lt 10, 1859 (Sept.); Lt 2, 1855 (Aug.).

[9] "Children of eight, ten, or twelve years are old enough to be addressed on the subject of personal religion. . . . Very young children may have correct views of their state as sinners and of the way of salvation through Christ" (Ellen G. White, *Testimonies for the Church,* vol. 1, p. 400).

[10] A radically new understanding of the message to the Laodicean church of Revelation 3:15-19 had been signaled just three months earlier, in October 1856, in an article by James White. Prior to then the lukewarm Laodicean church had been seen as applying to those Adventists who rejected the Sabbath, often called "nominal Adventists." In his article of October 16, 1856, James White had instead boldly identified Sabbatarian Adventists with Laodicea and called them to repentance for their lukewarmness. This new message had led to repentance and revival.

See: J. W. [James White], "The Seven Churches," *Review,* Oct. 16, 1856, pp. 189, 192; P. Gerard Damsteegt, *Foundations of the Seventh-day Adventist Message and Mission,* pp. 244-248; Ellen G. White, *Spiritual Gifts [vol. 2],* pp. 222-230; EGWEnc, s.v. "Laodicean Message."

way open any time that you feel that it is your duty to come. Help is needed and God forbid that we shall choose that help, but let the Lord choose for us, then all will be right.

Harriet, write me just how you feel. Write me as to a sister. We feel interested for you, and would love to have you here; but we want you to know for yourself that you are moving [in] the counsel of God. Then you can with confidence believe that He has called you to fill the important place, will be near to you to strengthen you, to lend you grace and power to keep yourself in His love, and a sweet satisfaction you will have every day knowing He has called you to the work.[11] He will sustain you, and if you try to keep yourself, He will let you have His approbation and the light of His countenance. Write for the *Instructor*, Harriet.[12]

Dear Sister, we think of you all. Would love to see you more than we have ever wished to see you before. We have not forgotten the time or place where Jesus walked through our midst like a mighty terrible one.[13]

Give my love to all the people of God. Our hearts are knit with you. Oh, how I should love to see Sister Mary [**Mary J. Loughborough**], Sister Orton [**Caroline Orton**], Drucilla [Drusilla Orton], and Brother Orton [**Jonathan T. Orton**][14] and all, and Brother John. Oh, that God [may] work

---

[11] Note that there is no outright invitation in these paragraphs for Harriet Stevens to join the *Review* staff. Harriet's earlier stint at the *Review* during 1854/1855 in Rochester, New York, had not been without friction. Ellen White later recalled Harriet's unhappiness with the leadership of the Whites, particularly when reproofs were given. However, Harriet seemed to have undergone a very positive change of attitude a few weeks earlier during the visit of the Whites to the believers in Waukon.

See: Ellen G. White, Lt 8, 1860 (June 11); *idem, Spiritual Gifts [vol. 2],* pp. 220, 221.

[12] Harriet Stevens had earlier contributed several articles for the *Youth's Instructor* and a poem for the *Review*. See, for example: H. N. Stevens, "The Sabbath," *Review,* January 1851, p. 25; "Influence of Worldly Reading," *Youth's Instructor,* January 1854, pp. 1, 2; "An Address to the Young," *Youth's Instructor,* April 1854, pp. 29, 30.

[13] Probably a reference to the charismatic events that attended meetings held in Waukon one month earlier, at the end of December 1856, at which Harriet Stevens was also present. Ellen White describes this occasion in similar terms: "I saw that if they would . . . confess their wrongs, Jesus would walk through our midst in power. . . . Sr. L. began to confess in a clear, decided manner. . . . As she confessed, the flood-gates of heaven seemed suddenly opened, I was prostrated by the power of God. Sr. H. N. S. [Harriet Newall Stevens] fell from her chair helpless. It seemed to be an awful, yet glorious place. I had no strength for two hours, but seemed to be wrapped in the glory of God."

See: Ellen G. White, *Spiritual Gifts [vol. 2],* p. 220.

[14] *Identities:* Establishing the identity of the persons mentioned in the last two paragraphs is helped by the fact that Harriet Stevens is asked to greet them, i.e., they all live in or around Waukon (see notes 2 and 4 above). Given that premise, the probability is that "Sister Mary" refers to Ellen White's friend Mary J. Loughborough. Together with her husband, **John Norton Loughborough**, she had moved to Waukon in November 1856. John Loughborough, however, had left Waukon in early January 1857, and hence is not greeted together with Mary in this letter.

As to the Orton family, there is a letter in the *Review* signed "J. T. Orton, Waukon, Iowa, Jan. 1857" and containing a comment on the visit of the Whites. Jonathan T. and Caroline Orton's daughter was Drusilla.

for him mightily in restoring him to health.[15] May we not expect it? May we not pray and believe for it? I do hope that Angeline [**Angeline Stevens**][16] and John may fully consecrate themselves that He may do a great work for them. Do let us hear from you often. Write, write. Our hearts are knit together.

Much love to your parents, brothers and sisters. Love to Sister Andrews [**Sarah L. Andrews**], and Brother Andrews [**Edward Andrews**] and William [**William P. Andrews**].[17] I hope he will love God with all his heart that he may at last eat of the leaves of the tree of life, that are for the healing of the nations. Tell him there will be no lame ones there.[18] All will be health.

See: J. N. Loughborough, *Rise and Progress of the Seventh-day Adventists,* p. 208; J. T. Orton, "From Bro. Orton," *Review,* Feb. 12, 1857, p. 118; "Jonathan Orton," 1850 U.S. Federal Census, New York, Monroe County, Rochester, Ward 7, p. 317.

15 J. N. Andrews, because of intense overwork during the early 1850s, had lost his health and been forced to abandon his extensive traveling ministry already by May 1855, after which he lived with his parents in Paris, Maine, and, later, near Waukon. His continued health problems at the time of this letter are indicated in a note from Andrews to the *Review* editor, published February 5, 1857: "Allow me to say to many friends who have written to me, that the condition of my head has rendered it impossible for me to write in reply. I hope that it will not always be thus."

See: "The Office," *Review,* Feb. 20, 1855, p. 182; "Business," *Review,* May 29, 1855, p. 240; J. N. Andrews, "Note from Bro. Andrews," *Review,* Feb. 5, 1857, p. 108.

16 *Identity:* See note 3 above.

17 *Identities:* Edward and Sarah L. Andrews moved to Waukon in 1855, together with their two sons, William P. and John Nevins Andrews.

See: Edward Andrews, "Extracts of Letters," *Review,* Jan. 17, 1856, p. 127; obituary, "William P. Andrews," *Review,* Aug. 8, 1878, p. 55.

18 James White wrote in 1855 regarding J. N. Andrews, "His only brother is a cripple."

See: James White to "Dear Brother," Feb. 9, 1855.

1857

APRIL

PUBLICATION OF

Testimony for the Church, No. 3, Battle Creek, Michigan.

Published by *Advent Review* Office. 16 pp.

1857

(Ms 1, 1857)

JUNE, VERMONT

Lack of Appreciation of the Ministry.

Portions of this manuscript are published in Ellen G. White, *Last Day Events*, pp. 234, 235.

> *Lack of appreciation of the ministry. Call for local churches to take responsibility for their own spiritual welfare and to release their ministers for more productive work in unentered areas.*

I was shown some things concerning the preaching brethren.[1] I saw their energies and strength were exhausted in laboring for a church that does not generally appreciate their labors. I saw that it would be better for the church to be thrown upon their own effort for a time. I saw they must be laborers. I saw that the principal part of Bro. Hutchins' [**Alfred S. Hutchins**] and Bro. Sperry's [**Charles W. Sperry**][2] labor has been to keep the church together. They have taken the burden of the church upon themselves, to dig around it, labor and labor for them until the church would, after the brethren had gotten

---

[1] The exact date of this vision is not known. The only vision from June 1857 mentioned in the sources is that of June 21, received while the Whites were in Buck's Bridge, New York. *See:* J. W. [James White], "Eastern Tour," *Review,* July 16, 1857, p. 88.

[2] *Identities:* The fact that Hutchins and Sperry are "preaching brethren" (first line) makes it fairly certain that Ellen White is referring to Alfred S. Hutchins and Charles W. Sperry. These two preachers often worked together. Between 1853 and 1861 there are a dozen or so reports of their teaming up to give lecture series in Vermont, Canada, and New York. There is also

a little victory, enjoy it, but make scarcely any effort for it themselves. [Then] in a few weeks [they] are sleepy and need the same effort made for them again. They tire and exhaust the strength of the worn-out servants of God.[3] Again the servants of God plow through and get a little victory, [only] to be lost as easily as before. But when, with their own faith and wrestling with God, they obtain the victory, then it is lasting. They know then how much it costs, and they will preserve their consecration. I saw that so much of the efforts of these brethren should not be spent upon a world-loving and sleepy church. I saw that those who have not yet embraced the truth are anxious to hear, and these brethren should go where, at the present time, they can accomplish the most good[4] with their feeble strength.

The church must arise. They do not half heed the message to the Laodicean church.[5] There are those in the church who love this world better than they love Jesus. They love their treasures here better than they love heaven or eternal life, and with their earthly treasure they will perish. The True Witness now speaks to a lukewarm church, Be zealous and repent; but they scarcely hear or heed the message. A few are afflicting their souls. A few are heeding the counsel of the True Witness. Unless the church speedily arouses they will go into darkness, be ensnared and overcome by the enemy.

---

some evidence that A. S. Hutchins and C. W. Sperry fit the description given in this paragraph of being "worn-out servants" and of "feeble strength." See note 3 for details.

See: Search terms "Hutchins" and "Sperry" in *Words of the Pioneers.*

[3] When the Whites visited A. S. Hutchins and his wife in Vermont on June 9, 1857, they noted that they looked "pale, care-worn and much wasted in flesh and strength." The Whites feared that "a lukewarm, worldly church had suffered them to bear burdens grievious to be borne" and that they had been "borne down by laboring in unnecessary trials in the church." C. W. Sperry also sounded worn out in a letter to the *Review* editor three months earlier, where he spoke of his "incessant labor and poor health."

See: J. W. [James White], "Eastern Tour," *Review,* June 25, 1857, p. 61; C. W. Sperry, "From Bro. Sperry," *Review,* Mar. 19, 1857, p. 158.

[4] At the end of May or early June 1857, a "Tent Committee" requested that Hutchins and Sperry leave their familiar but less fruitful areas of Vermont and vicinity and "go West," to new states more open to the Sabbatarian message. Already by the end of July the Hutchins and Sperry families had moved to Michigan.

See: E. L. Barr, "Tent Meetings in New England," *Review,* June 11, 1857, p. 48; A. S. Hutchins, "From Bro. Hutchins," *Review,* July 30, 1857, p. 101.

[5] A radically new understanding of the message to the Laodicean church of Revelation 3:15-19 had been signaled just nine months earlier, in October 1856, in an article by James White. Prior to that the lukewarm Laodicean church had been seen as applying to those Adventists who rejected the Sabbath, often called "nominal Adventists." In his article of October 16, 1856, James White had instead boldly identified Sabbatarian Adventists with Laodicea and called them to repentance for their lukewarmness. At first this new message had led to repentance and revival but Ellen White later noted that after some months many members had "lost the effect of the message," hence the reproof and appeal found in this June 1857 manuscript.

See: J. W. [James White], "The Seven Churches," *Review,* Oct. 16, 1856, pp. 189, 192; P. Gerard Damsteegt, *Foundations of the Seventh-day Adventist Message and Mission,* pp. 244-248; Ellen G. White, *Spiritual Gifts [vol. 2],* p. 224; EGWEnc, s.v. "Laodicean Message."

I saw we are in the investigative judgment.[6] Soon judgment will be pronounced on our works and our actions which are passing in review before God. A solemn, awful period! Who realize this great work? I saw that those who do not now appreciate, study, and dearly prize the Word of God, spoken by His servants, will have cause to mourn bitterly hereafter.

I saw that the Lord in judgment will, at the close of time, walk through the earth; the fearful plagues will begin to fall. Then those who have despised God's Word, those who have lightly esteemed it, shall wander from sea to sea, and from the north even to the east; they shall run to and fro to seek the Word of the Lord and shall not find it. A famine is in the land for hearing the Word.[7] The ministers of God will have done their last work, offered their last prayers, shed their last bitter tear for a rebellious church and an ungodly people. Their last solemn warning has been given.

Oh, then how quickly would houses and lands, dollars that have been miserly hoarded and cherished and tightly grasped, be given for some consolation by those who have professed the truth and have not lived it out, for the way of salvation to be explained or to hear a hopeful word, or a prayer, or an exhortation from their ministers. But no, they must hunger and thirst on in vain; their thirst will never be quenched, no consolation can they get; their cases are decided and eternally fixed. It is a fearful, awful time. There can much be done now to bring in those jewels who are hid beneath the rubbish, who will highly prize the truth as it falls from the lips of God's servants.

I was shown that many of the church have at this time of peril more care for their farm and their cattle than they have for the servants of God, or the truth which they preach; their labors are so common among them that the laborers are not considered worthy of their hire. His strength must be exhausted, his life embittered by scarcely a well day, must spend and be spent, and yet the church asleep as to these things.

But I saw that God was not asleep. Said the angel, "Jesus says, 'I know thy works'; yes, selfish, professed Sabbathkeepers. God knows thy works. Ye covetous, world-loving Sabbathkeepers," said the angel, "God knows thy works." I saw that every privation the servants of God have endured are all written in the book, every tear is bottled up. Every pang of agony they have endured is recorded in the book. "I know thy works," says the True Witness.

---

[6] This is the earliest known use by Ellen White of the term "investigative judgment." The term, if not the concept itself, was new among Sabbatarian Adventists, having first appeared six months earlier in the *Review* in presentations by Elon Everts and James White.

See: E. Everts, "Communication From Bro. Everts," *Review,* Jan. 1, 1857, p. 72; J. W. [James White], "The Judgment," *Review,* Jan. 29, 1857, p. 100. For a brief survey of the developing understanding of the pre-Advent or investigative judgment up to 1857, see Paul A. Gordon, *The Sanctuary, 1844, and the Pioneers;* SDAE, s.v. "Investigative Judgment"; EGWEnc, s.v. "Investigative Judgment."

[7] Cf. Amos 8:11, 12.

All that has been done to help the servants of God is all recorded; all of it is written in the book. All the selfish withholding from God's servants are all written in the book. "All thy deeds," said the angel, "are passing in review before God."

I saw that the church now must afflict their souls. They must labor, they must agonize or go down. I saw it was best to leave the churches to work for themselves now, that they may feel their weakness while there is a chance for them to zealously repent and buy gold, white raiment, and eye salve, the treasures they must possess if they would have eternal life.

1857

(Lt 14, 1857)

JULY 12, BATTLE CREEK, MICHIGAN

LETTER TO

Elon Everts.[1]

Portions of this letter are published in Ellen G. White, *Manuscript Releases,* vol. 6, p. 130.

Admonition to an Adventist preacher to sell a portion of his large farms and "lay up treasure in heaven." Instructions regarding tent meetings.

Dear Brother Everts:

I was shown while at Lancaster, Mass.,[2] that the work of God was progressing in the West, and that you must be narrowing down your large farms. Do not talk your faith. *Sell that ye have and give alms,* says the angel. Not moving fast enough, said the angel. Cut loose, cut loose from your treasures here; lay up a treasure in heaven.[3]

---

[1] *Identity:* The "Brother Everts" addressed is, among other things, associated in this letter with the expanding work in the "West," owning "large farms," and working "with the tent." There can be no doubt that Ellen White is writing to Elon Everts, preacher from Vermont, who moved west to Round Grove, Illinois, in late 1855, where he purchased "large attractive lands." In the summer of 1857 Elon Everts lectured at tent meetings in Wisconsin and Illinois. A further reason for determining that "Brother Everts" is Elon Everts is that the *Review* mentions no other Evertses during this period.

See: "Business," *Review,* Dec. 4, 1855, p. 80; J. N. Loughborough, J. Hart, E. Everts, "Tent Meetings," *Review,* May 28, 1857, p. 32; Ellen G. White, "A Warning," *Review,* Apr. 15, 1858, p. 174; search term "Everts" in *Words of the Pioneers.*

[2] Very likely a reference to Ellen and James White's visit to tent meetings in Lancaster, Massachusetts, six weeks earlier, at the end of May 1857.

See: J. W. [James White], "Eastern Tour," *Review,* May 28, 1857, p. 36; *idem,* "Eastern Tour," *Review,* June 25, 1857, p. 61; E. L. Barr, "From Bro. Barr," *Review,* Aug. 13, 1857, p. 118.

[3] The radical challenge Ellen White here gives to Elon Everts would not be new to him. Already by the end of 1855, about the same time the Everts family moved out to Illinois from Vermont, she had issued a general warning and an appeal to the growing numbers of Adventists moving westward. There was a real danger of their becoming engrossed in the material pursuits of buying and developing lands to the neglect of their spiritual mission. Articles sounding the same warning in the *Review* had followed, reinforced by the Laodicean message which was beginning to be preached in 1856 (see "Laodicean Message" in EGWEnc). Although Everts himself felt convicted to give some of his assets for evangelistic work, his wife and daughter apparently were implacably opposed. Of Everts's wife, Maria, Ellen White reveals that "three times she was reproved by vision" on this issue, but without relenting. After Maria died in November 1856, Everts's daughter, Matilda, continued to oppose her father's plans, and when

I saw that as you go with the tent, be not in haste to take it down after there is an interest awakened; remain until they decide; bring them to the point to decide; press upon them the necessity of decision. I have seen that there is too much haste in moving the tent from place to place, and staying long enough in a place.[4]

I have seen that the work would spread and increase in Illinois, Wisconsin, Iowa, and Minnesota. The Lord is moving upon the people, and the servants of God should keep pace with the opening providence of God and with the work of the third angel's message.

Tell Brother John [**John Norton Loughborough**],[5] [that] before we left this state for the East, I sent a letter to Mary [**Mary J. Loughborough**] and there was something in it I wished you to see, so I sent it to you. There were two dollars in it, a little present I sent her. Did you receive it?

In love.

---

he himself died two years later "nothing was bestowed upon the cause of God," with the whole estate passing to the daughter.

See: Ellen G. White, *Testimonies for the Church,* vol. 1, p. 118; E. Everts, "Communication From Bro. Everts," *Review,* Jan. 1, 1857, p. 72; Ellen G. White, "A Warning," *Review,* Apr. 15, 1858, p. 174; *idem, Spiritual Gifts [vol. 2],* p. 215.

[4] In memoirs written in the 1880s John Loughborough recalls that during the summer of 1855 the New York tent was pitched 14 times in eight towns with meetings mostly held for only two or three days on each occasion. He goes on to add that "before the summer's campaign closed, Sr. White told that us [*sic*] she had been shown that we would see greater results from our tent-meetings if we visited a less number of places with our tents, and continued our efforts longer in each place." The earliest published comment by Ellen White on this issue is from 1857.

See: J. N. Loughborough, "Recollections of the Past—No. 13," *Review,* Mar. 24, 1885, p. 186; Ellen G. White, *Testimonies for the Church,* vol. 1, p. 148.

[5] *Identity:* During the summer of 1857, when this letter was written, Elon Everts was engaged in tent meetings with John Loughborough and Josiah Hart in Wisconsin and Illinois. It therefore seems likely that the "Bro. John" he is asked to convey the message to is John Loughborough and that "Mary" is his wife, Mary Loughborough.

See: J. N. Loughborough, J. Hart, E. Everts, "Tent Meetings," *Review,* May 20, 1857, p. 32.

1857

(Lt 8, 1857)

JULY 19,[1] BATTLE CREEK, MICHIGAN

LETTER TO

Samuel W. Rhodes.[2]

Previously unpublished.

S. W. Rhodes temperamentally unsuited to oversee meetings dealing with church discipline.

Dear Brother Rhodes:

I have written to Brother Edson [**Hiram Edson**][3] the general part of a vision for the church in New York, given me at Ulysses, Pennsylvania.[4]

---

[1] The original/earliest copy of this letter gives the month and day but not the year. That the year is 1857 can be inferred from the correspondence between this vision and the vision entitled "Love One Another," published in November 1857 in *Testimony for the Church,* No. 4. Both accounts state that the vision was given in Ulysses, Pennsylvania, and both deal with the issue of church trials in New York, with the church in Roosevelt, New York, given special mention. It is very likely that the two accounts refer to the same vision, although to different parts of it (see note 4 below). The published account is useful in that it gives the full date of the Ulysses vision, July 6, 1857, from which we conclude that Lt 8 is also written in 1857.

See: Ellen G. White, *Testimony for the Church,* No. 4, pp. 13-18 (*Testimonies for the Church,* vol. 1, pp. 164-168).

[2] *Identity:* "Brother Rhodes" is portrayed in this letter as a leader, working in New York (Roosevelt mentioned in particular) and with a tendency to severity in his relations to church members. There can be little doubt that Samuel W. Rhodes is being addressed, an itinerant preacher who was reproved by Ellen White for his harshness and severity on several occasions during the 1850s and beyond. Moreover, reports in the *Review* indicate that S. W. Rhodes's work was centered in New York during that period. On S. W. Rhodes's severity, see, for example, Ms 1, 1853 (June 2); Ms 6, 1854 (Feb. 19); Lt 16, 1859 (Oct. 28); Lt 5a, 1861 (Apr. 5). For his travels during 1857, see search term "Rhodes" in *Words of the Pioneers.*

[3] *Identity:* Like S. W. Rhodes, the implication is that Edson is a church leader of some kind, based in New York. Even though several Edsons appear in the *Review* during the 1850s, only Hiram Edson is from New York and an active preacher.

See: Search term "Edson" in *Words of the Pioneers.*

[4] No doubt the vision given at Ulysses, Pennsylvania, two weeks earlier on July 6, 1857, as mentioned in Ms 2, 1857 (July 24). The "general part" of that vision is recorded in Ms 2, 1857, and deals with the problems of church trials in New York, whereas this letter to S. W. Rhodes deals with the sensitive matter of Rhodes's own part in encouraging those trials and with the involvement of certain other named individuals. The letter to Edson that Ellen White had written (prior to July 19), giving a "general account" of the vision of July 6, is not in the White Estate archives. It was, however, probably close in content or identical to the account found in Ms 2, 1857, which bears the date July 24. Some months later, in November 1857, it was published (see note 1 above).

I was shown that the church took advantage of a vision that was given to reprove you, and did wrong, felt hard to you. Then the vision that was given to reprove the church you took advantage of, and have listened to the church trials altogether too much.[5] You have encouraged them by listening to this one and that one's report. You have not had tender pity, have been too severe.[6] I saw that your temperament was a hurried one, and the Lord would not lay it on you generally to settle church trials (thank God). You have too strong feelings, are not patient enough. God has a kind care for you but you have erred in having so many church trials.[7] I saw that the Lord had given Brother Edson good judgment in regard to matters in the church.[8] He has not filled his place.

I saw that you move too strongly, make up your mind that things are so, and then move hurriedly, not studying the effect of these things afterward. Upon those things you must reform. You can comfort and strengthen the church with the gift God has given you, but you must move more patiently, throw off so much perplexity that you have. Your anxiety to see the church where they ought to be, has led you to try too hard to get them there. It has had the wrong effect in many cases. You have failed often.

You have manifested selfish feelings in connection with Brother Treadwell [**William Treadwell**][9] against another. That brother is not right, but more had been laid to his charge than belongs there, and this is the way with many

---

[5] Exactly which visions are referred to here is not known. By the time this letter was written we know of two documents (Ms 1, 1853 [June 2], and Ms 6, 1854 [Feb. 19]) that contain reproof for S. W. Rhodes, and a variety of documents, published and unpublished, containing admonition to the churches on different issues.

[6] Although S. W. Rhodes was an effective, hardworking traveling minister, he struggled with a harsh, overbearing temperament. A series of letters from Ellen White to Rhodes stretching over many years appealed to him on this issue, warning him of the dire influence of his severity on others. Rhodes, to his credit, several times confessed his weaknesses in the pages of the *Review*.

See: Note 2 above; S. W. Rhodes, "Letter From Bro. Rhodes," *Review*, Aug. 11, 1853, p. 55; "From Bro. Rhodes," *Review*, Jan. 8, 1857, p. 78; "Resignation," *Review*, Dec. 18, 1860, p. 40; "From Bro. Rhodes," *Review*, Jan. 22, 1861, p. 78; "From Bro. Rhodes," *Review*, Apr. 9, 1861, p. 167; "From Bro. Rhodes," *Review*, May 6, 1862, p. 182; "Communication From Br. Rhodes," *Review*, Dec. 3, 1867, p. 395.

[7] Amanda Westcott, in a letter to a friend, gives a somewhat unflattering description of Rhodes's management of a church trial in Roosevelt: "Last Friday they met at Bro. Chapel's for trial, Bro. Rhodes being chief man among them. They staid [*sic*] there all day talking, but doing little or no good."

See: Amanda Westcott to Mrs. Crawford, July 16, 1856.

[8] *See:* Note 13 below.

[9] *Identity:* That "Brother Treadwell" is William Treadwell is inferred from the fact that no other Treadwell is mentioned in the *Review* throughout this period. In addition, his address is given (in 1858) as "Gilbert's Mills, N.Y.," which is just a few miles from Roosevelt, a town that is the focus of events in this letter.

See: Search term "Treadwell" in *Words of the Pioneers;* Wm. Treadwell, "From Bro. Treadwell," *Review*, Apr. 1, 1858, p. 158.

of the church trials. It gives the jealous, the selfish, opportunity to carry out these evil propensities.[10] All these evils must be corrected.

Nearly every one I saw in Roosevelt [New York] has been wrong. Brother T. Finch [**Truman P. Finch**][11] was not right. When he left he had the same faultfinding spirit. Brother Chapel [**Levi R. Chapel**][12] has not been free from it. I saw that there needed to be a thorough reformation all through that section. The professed people of God have disgraced themselves in the eyes of the world by these trials[13] that they never would have had if their hearts had been right in the sight of God. Hatred has caused many of these trials, but the poor souls knew it not.

In love.

---

[10] Little is known of the details of the church trials in which Treadwell, Finch, and Chapel were involved.

[11] *Identity:* The only "T. Finch" appearing in the *Review* during this period is Truman P. Finch, living in Roosevelt until sometime in 1857, when he moved to Michigan. This corresponds well with Ellen White's locating of Finch in Roosevelt and with her words "when he left. . ."

See: Search term "Finch" in *Words of the Pioneers;* "Business Items," *Review,* Apr. 16, 1857, p. 192.

[12] *Identity:* Although there are several Chapels in the *Review* during this period, L. R. Chapel is the likely person referred to here, since he lived in Palermo, New York, a town near Roosevelt.

See: Search term "Chapel" in *Words of the Pioneers.*

[13] The problems of infighting and excessive church trials among members at Roosevelt continued despite Ellen White's appeals in July 1857. Two years later she noted that the same problems continued to "cleave to some like the leprosy" in that church. There seems to have been some improvement, however, at least in the eyes of James White, who reported from a conference held in Roosevelt in 1859 that "the brethren are recovering from their low state. . . . A rash, hasty, fitful spirit has had a blighting influence in Central New York, but it is being removed under the judicious labors of Brn. Wheeler and Edson." It appears that the "good judgment" of Hiram Edson, mentioned earlier in this letter to Rhodes, may have played a part by 1859 towards restoring better relationships among the members.

See: Ellen G. White, Lt 17, 1859 (Oct. 28); J. W. [James White], "Roosevelt, N. Y., Conference," *Review,* Sept. 15, 1859, p. 132.

1857
(Ms 2, 1857)
JULY 24, N.P.

Testimony for the Church in Central New York.[1]

Portions of this manuscript are published in Ellen G. White, *Testimonies for the Church,* vol. 1, pp. 164-168.

The misuse of church discipline: causes and cures.

Vision given at Ulysses, Pennsylvania, July 6, 1857.[2]

I have seen in regard to the state of the cause in New York. I have seen that there have been so many church trials[3] that God had not the least to do with, that the church have lost their strength and they know not how to regain it. The love for one another has been gone; a faultfinding, accusing spirit has prevailed. It has been considered a virtue to hunt up everything about one another that looked wrong and make it appear fully as bad as it was. The bowels of compassion that yearn in love and pity towards brethren have been all dried up by faultfinding, picking at everything bearing the appearance of wrong, until the noble feelings of the soul are withered. The mind should be elevated to dwell upon eternal scenes, heaven, its treasures, its glories, and should take sweet and holy satisfaction in the truths of the Bible and searching up the precious promises that His Word affords to comfort and lift up the mind from trifles to weighty, eternal things.

But, oh, how different has the mind been employed! Picking at straws![4]

---

[1] A slightly edited version of this manuscript published a few months later, in November 1857, specifies that the vision "relates to things as they have existed in Roosevelt, N. Y., and Oswego Co., in particular, also to other places in that State."

See: Ellen G. White, *Testimony for the Church,* No. 4, p. 13.

[2] Ulysses, Pennsylvania, was the last stop by the Whites on an eight-week tour through New York, Massachusetts, Maine, and Vermont, returning home to Battle Creek, Michigan, on July 9, 1857. The vision in Ulysses was given one week following the Whites' visit to Parish, in Oswego County, New York, where the problem of excessive church trials had overshadowed the weekend meetings. "It has been accusations and church trials, over and over, until many seem to have forgotten how to worship God in spirit and in truth," wrote James White.

See: J. W. [James White], "Eastern Tour," *Review,* July 16, 1857, p. 88.

[3] Meetings of a local congregation called to consider questions of church discipline.

[4] Writing some months earlier, Ellen White noted that some members were "watching for every fault" in others. "A person's dress, bonnet, or apron, takes their attention. . . . All the religion a few poor souls have consists in watching the garments and acts of others, and finding fault with them." Some indication of the amount of time expended on church trials is found in this comment by Amanda Westcott in an 1856 letter: "Last Friday they met at Bro. Chapel's for trial, Bro. Rhodes being chief among them. They staid [*sic*] there all day talking, but doing

Church meetings, as they have been held, have been a living curse to New York. These manufactured trials have given free liberty to evil surmisings. Jealousy has been fed. Hatred has existed, but they know it not. A wrong idea has been in the minds of the brethren to reprove without love, hold others to your idea of what is right, and spare not, but bear down with crushing weight.

I saw that many in New York have had so much care for their brethren, to keep them straight, that they have neglected their own hearts. They are so fearful that their brethren will not be zealous and repent [that] they forget that they have wrongs that must be righted,[5] and with their hearts unsanctified they try to right their brethren. Now the only way the church in New York can arise is to attend to their own individual cases, and each set his own heart in order. If sin is plain upon a brother, breathe it not to another, but with love for the brother's soul, with a heart full of compassion, with bowels of mercies, tell him the wrong, then leave it upon the brother and God. You have discharged your duty. You are not to pass sentence.

You have made it too light an affair to rein up a brother, condemn him, and hold him under condemnation. There has been a zeal of God but not according to knowledge. If all set their own hearts in order, when they meet together their testimony would be ready to come from a full soul, and the people around that believe not the truth would be moved. The witness of the Spirit would tell to their hearts that you are the children of God. Our love for each other should be visible to all. It will tell. It will have influence.

I saw that there is a way for the church in New York to arise. Individually take hold of the work in earnest; be zealous and repent. And after all wrongs are righted that you have knowledge of, then believe God accepts. Go not mourning, but take God at His word; seek Him diligently, and believe that He

---

little or no good." This passage, with its focus on trivial church trials, did not mean that there was no place for proper church discipline. See, for example, Lt 3, 1853 (June 29).

See: Ellen G. White, *Testimonies for the Church,* vol. 1, p. 145; Amanda Westcott to Mrs. Crawford, July 16, 1856.

[5] The expression "be zealous and repent" is taken from the message to the Laodiceans in Revelation 3:19: "As many as I love, I rebuke and chasten: be zealous therefore, and repent." The implication here is that some members were misusing the Laodicean message to focus on the shortcomings of other members rather than letting it speak to their own faults. Ellen White, writing elsewhere of the situation during this period, says of the "the message to the Laodiceans" that "some thought others were not as zealous in repenting as they should be, and instead of taking care of their own souls' interest, they began . . . to reprove and bear down upon their brethren." Since Sabbatarian Adventists had only begun to apply the Laodicean message to their own movement less than a year earlier, it is quite possible that the rash of church trials plaguing the movement as described in Ms 2, 1857 (July 24), was at least partly a result of those who were misusing it.

See: Ellen G. White, Lt 17, 1859 (Oct. 28). For surveys of the developing understanding of the "Laodicean message," see P. Gerard Damsteegt, *Foundations of the Seventh-day Adventist Message and Mission,* pp. 244-248; Felix A. Lorenz, "A Study of Early Adventist Interpretations of the Laodicean Message"; EGWEnc, s.v. "Laodicean Message."

receives you. A part of the work is to believe. He is faithful that has promised. Climb up by faith.

I saw that in New York they can arise as well as in other places, and they can drink of the salvation of God. They can move understandingly, and each one have an experience for himself in this message of the True Witness to the Laodicean church. The church feel that they are down, but know not how to arise. The intention of some may be ever so good [and] they may confess; yet I saw they were watched with suspicion and so they were made an offender for a word, until they have no liberty, no salvation. They dare not act out the simple feelings of the heart, because they are watched. Everything is stiff and unnatural. It is God's pleasure that His people should fear Him, and have confidence before each other.

I saw that many had taken advantage of what God had shown about the sins and wrongs of those in New York. They had taken the extreme meaning of what had been shown in vision, and then confessed it until it has had the tendency to weaken the faith in what God has shown, and also to discourage and dishearten the church.[6] I was also shown that with delicate and tender compassion should brother deal with brother. Delicately should he deal with feeling. And I saw that it is the greatest work that ever yet was done, and the nicest point to touch the wrongs of another. With the deepest humility should a brother do this, considering his own weakness, lest he should also be tempted.

I have seen the great sacrifice Jesus made to redeem man. He did not consider His own life too dear to sacrifice. "Love one another as I have loved you," He said. Ask yourself the question, Do you feel, when a brother errs, you could give your life to save him from that error, and that danger? It places him in [danger] of losing his soul. If you feel thus, you can approach him and affect his heart. You are just the one to visit that brother. But it is a fearful truth that many who profess to be brethren are not willing to sacrifice their opinions or judgment to save a brother. There is but little love for one another. A selfish spirit has been manifested.

Discouragement has come upon the church. They have been loving the world, loving their farms, cattle, etc. Now Jesus calls them to cut loose, to lay up treasures in heaven, buy gold, white raiment, and eyesalve—precious treasures that will obtain for the possessor an inheritance in the kingdom of God.

The people of God must move understandingly. They must know that

---

[6] A clearer idea of what is meant here is found in Lt 8, 1857, written five days earlier, in which Ellen White gives more details of the same vision. Some church members in New York, she recounts, knowing that traveling preacher **Samuel W. Rhodes** had been reproved in the visions for his severity and harshness, had taken the opportunity to scold Rhodes personally and reinforce the reproof.

every known sin is confessed; then it is their privilege and duty to believe that Jesus accepts them. They must not wait for others to plow through the darkness, obtain the victory, then enjoy it. Such enjoyment will last no longer than [until] the meeting closes. There must be a serving God from principle instead of feeling. Morning and night obtain a victory for yourselves in your own family. Let not your daily labor hinder this. Take time to pray, and believe as you pray that God hears you. Have faith mixed with your prayers and it will be effectual. You may not at all times feel the immediate answer, but then it is your faith is tried. You are proved to see whether you will trust God, whether you have living, abiding faith. "Faithful is he that calleth you, who also will do it." 1 Thess. 5:24.

Walk the narrow plank of faith, trust all on the promises of God. Trust God in darkness; that is the time to have faith. But you often let feeling govern you. You look at yourselves when you do not feel comforted by the Spirit of God. You do not trust enough in Jesus, precious Jesus. You do not make His worthiness to be all, all, as you should. The very best you can do will not make you merit the favor of God. It is Jesus' worthiness that will save us; His blood cleanses us. Do what you can on your part. Be zealous and repent, then believe.

Confound not faith and feeling together. They are distinct. Faith is ours to exercise. This faith we must exercise. Believe, believe. Let your faith take hold of the blessing and if your faith takes hold of it, it is yours by faith. Your feelings have nothing to do with this faith. When faith brings the blessing to your heart, then you rejoice in the blessing. It is no more faith but feeling. The feeling has swallowed up the faith.

The people must steadily arise and come out from their darkness and let their light shine. They are standing right in the way of the work of God. They must let the message of the third angel[7] do its work upon their hearts, clear the rubbish away from the door and open the door and let the Saviour in. God is dishonored by your long, faithless prayers and exhortations—confessing, but no reforming. I saw you must look away from the unworthiness of self and exalt Jesus. Talk of light, of heaven, and you will have light. Talk darkness and you will have darkness.[8]

I saw that Brother Edson [**Hiram Edson**][9] has not taken his place in the

---

[7] *See:* EGWEnc, s.v. "Three Angels' Messages."

[8] Regrettably, despite the appeal and counsel of this testimony, problems continued in Roosevelt. Two years later, in 1859, Ellen White noted that similar problems continued to "cleave to some like the leprosy" in that church. She appealed to the members to "print on your heart and memory the testimony given at Ulysses," i.e., the counsels found in this manuscript. *See:* Ellen G. White, Lt 17, 1859 (Oct. 28).

[9] *Identity:* The intent of this final passage concerning "Brother Edson" is clarified in Ellen White's earlier letter to S. W. Rhodes in which she reports on the same vision. She there contrasts Rhodes's severe, impatient handling of church trials with Edson's "good judgment."

church. He has kept back for fear of getting out of his place. I saw that Brother Edson has good judgment in matters of the church. It needs collected, patient, persevering men to judge in matters of the church. A hurried spirit must not decide. Brother Edson must take his place.

The clear implication is that Edson, like S. W. Rhodes, is a church leader. This information, in addition to the New York setting of the letter, leaves little doubt that Ellen White is referring to Hiram Edson, of Martville, New York, and not to another member with the same surname.

See: Ellen G. White, Lt 8, 1857 (July 19); search term "Edson" in *Words of the Pioneers.*

1857

(Lt 3, 1857)

OCTOBER 8,[1] BATTLE CREEK, MICHIGAN

LETTER TO

Uriah Smith and Harriet Newall Smith.[2]

This letter is published in entirety in S. T. Belden, G. W. Amadon, and William Hall, *To Brother J. N. Andrews and Sister H. N. Smith* (PH016), pp. 28-30.

Letter to recently married Uriah and Harriet Smith, offering advice and urging them to fully consecrated service.

Dear Brother Uriah and Sister Harriet:

While at Monterey[3] [Michigan] I was shown that all did not realize the importance of the work in the office.[4] It was repeated to me what has been so often shown, that there must be a drawing near to God, a consecration to Him, that there has not been. I saw that you should not let your interest for each other in the least draw you from the work of God. That holy, sacred work to you both should be the first and greatest, and more dear than anything else besides, and your interest and care should not be for each other, nor in the least interfere with your work in the office.[5] There is danger of this and it has been somewhat so now,—wrapped up too much in each other, and the glory of God not in view as it should have been.

I saw that you could have the salvation of God if you seek earnestly

---

[1] As Ellen White was not in Battle Creek but in Monterey on October 8, 1857, the most reasonable conclusion seems to be that "October 8, 1857" was the date when the vision recounted in this letter was received, not the date when the letter was written. According to the detailed report appearing in the *Review* Ellen White was in Monterey, Michigan, on October 8 and received a vision there at an evening meeting. She probably wrote the letter some time later, after her return to Battle Creek.

See: J. W. [James White], "Report of Meetings!" *Review*, Oct. 22, 1857, p. 196.

[2] *Identity:* The facts given in the letter, that "Uriah" and "Harriet" are recently married and that "Uriah" holds a leading position in "the paper," positively identify the couple as Uriah Smith, chief editor of the *Review*, and Harriet N. Smith, who had married four months earlier, in June 1857.

See: Obituary: "Harriet N. Smith," *Review*, Mar. 30, 1911, p. 23.

[3] *See:* Note 1 above.

[4] The Review and Herald office, located in Battle Creek.

[5] Both Uriah and Harriet were employed at the *Review*. Harriet, a person of literary talent, had earlier worked at the *Review* during the period 1854-1855. She rejoined the staff in the spring of 1857, shortly before her marriage.

See: Obituary: "Harriet N. Smith," *Review*, Mar. 30, 1911, p. 23.

enough for it. I did not see that God was displeased with your marriage.[6] By consecrating all to God, seeking the Spirit and power of God, your united efforts could better glorify God than you could separately; but there is danger of your living to each other, and if there is not an entire interest and entire care for the paper the Lord will remove you and have some one that their whole interest is swallowed up in the work.

God wants that the only paper in the land bearing His solemn truth should come out right. A lack of the Spirit of God, or interest, is felt in the paper. If the salvation of God is with the one that writes for the paper, the same spirit will be felt by the reader.

A piece written in the Spirit of God, angels approbate and impresses the same upon the reader. But a piece written when the writer is not living wholly for the glory of God, not wholly devoted to Him, angels feel the lack in sadness. They turn away and do not impress the reader with it because God and His Spirit are not in it. The words are good, but it lacks the warm influence of the Spirit of God.

I saw that there must not be a shunning of burdens. You must reprove wrong when you see it,—those in the office.[7]

I saw you were feeling discouraged, Uriah. I saw that you should overcome when you are discouraged.[8] You can do nothing aright. With energy and courage, take hold of the salvation of God. You can have His assisting grace, but you must wrestle for it.

I saw that there was a feeling among the hands of the office [that was] too selfish. There must be a sacrificing spirit with every one. Their interest must be [in] the paper, that everything be just right about it, that there be no errors about it. I saw God was not pleased with the hands in the office. They are not enjoying the salvation of God and they have but a faint realizing sense of the time in which we live and what God requires of them.

---

[6] The vision is somewhat ambivalent about the recent marriage of Harriet and Uriah. The marriage is portrayed as having potential for good, but also for harm to the work of God. Harriet's marriage was not insignificant—she was marrying the *Review* editor, a key thought leader of the Sabbatarian movement. Harriet, unfortunately, had a problematic background, having for many years shown little confidence in the leadership of the Whites or in the visions. She seemed to have undergone a change of heart during the Whites' visit to Waukon 10 months earlier, but at this stage it was an open question which direction she would take in the future and what influence her opinions would have on Uriah. See Lt 7, 1860 (June), for details of Harriet Stevens's earlier problems with the Whites and the visions.

[7] Described by his biographer, Eugene Durand, as a "gentle man," Smith may have found this a particularly uncongenial task. The matter of correcting negligent workers at the office had developed into a major crisis by 1860, with Harriet, Uriah, and others rising up against James White whenever he cautioned or reproved workers.

See: Eugene F. Durand, *Yours in the Blessed Hope, Uriah Smith,* p. 35; Ellen G. White, Lt 7, 1860 (June).

[8] In Lt 6, 1857 (Oct. 8), there is the strong suggestion that Uriah Smith had been discouraged to the point of contemplating resigning from his post.

I saw that there should be a willingness to suffer some loss of time if their help is needed to hasten off the paper, in any little aid they can render; but their feeling has been, they cannot leave their particular part of the work. There must be a spirit of consecration and self-denial in the office, and the greatest lack is the Spirit of God or salvation. There must be a change in that office, a reformation, then the blessings of God will rest upon those in the office. A care, I saw, should rest with weight upon every one, especially yourself, that the paper be free from error or mistakes. God is displeased with His work being marred with so much imperfection.

Uriah Smith and his wife, Harriet. Courtesy of the Center for Adventist Research.

1857

(Lt 6, 1857)

[OCTOBER 8, BATTLE CREEK, MICHIGAN][1]

LETTER TO

Uriah Smith.[2]

This letter is published in entirety in S. T. Belden, G. W. Amadon, and William Hall, *To Brother J. N. Andrews and Sister H. N. Smith* (PH016), pp. 25-28.

> *Advice and encouragement to Uriah Smith, who has considered resigning from his post as* Review *editor. An appeal to Harriet Smith to be a help, not a hindrance, to her husband.*

Dear Brother Uriah:

While at Monterey[3] [Michigan], we had a most powerful meeting. The Spirit of the Lord rested upon me. I was shown in vision many things; was shown the straitness of the way, the necessity of each understanding their own heart, the danger of deceiving themselves as to their true state and be found wanting. I saw again the state of things in the office.[4] The cloud still hangs over it; all is not right there.

I saw that the Lord had called you to occupy the place you are now in, and God has not released you. God has not selected or designed Brother Waggoner [**Joseph Harvey Waggoner**][5] for the office to occupy your place;

---

[1] The original gives no date or place of writing. The main clue to its date is its similarity to Lt 3, 1857 (Oct. 8). Both letters recount a vision given at "Monterey," both deal with the state of affairs at the Review and Herald office in Battle Creek, both address Uriah and Harriet Smith, and both make mention of the discouragement of the *Review* editor, Uriah Smith. It seems quite probable that both letters are partial descriptions of the same Monterey, Michigan, vision given on October 8, 1857. The same Monterey vision also included counsel for Sylsbre B. Rumery (Lt 9, 1857 [Oct.]) and a general call for sacrificial giving (see Ellen G. White, *Testimonies for the Church,* vol. 1, pp. 170-178 and *Spiritual Gifts [vol. 2],* pp. 239-250). As with Lt 3 we do not know the actual date of writing of Lt 6. Its content suggests that it might be the letter of "reproof" Ellen White later reported sending to the Smiths sometime in 1858 (see Lt 7, 1860 [June]). If so, this letter could have been written some months after the vision.

[2] *Identity:* The references in this letter to "Brother Uriah" as editor, closely related to "Harriet" and "James," positively identity him as Uriah Smith, resident editor of the *Review*, married to Harriet and closely associated at the *Review* office with James White.

[3] *See:* Note 1.

[4] The Review and Herald publishing office.

[5] *Identity:* Before becoming a Sabbatarian Adventist, Joseph Harvey Waggoner had edited the *Sauk County Democrat* in Baraboo, Wisconsin, and since 1855 he had been a corresponding

there are serious objections to this. The Lord has laid upon James [**James Springer White**] the duty of traveling a portion of the time and He calls you to throw your whole soul into the work, be devoted to God, devoted to the work. Let your influence tell in the meeting, tell in the office, and your own soul will flourish, and a saving, gathering influence will be shed around.

Dear Brother, the Lord will help your lack. But I saw there has been expected more of you than they ought to expect, and that that is not in you. It is not in you to take all that care, burden and responsibility that some others do. If you had been able to bear responsibility and care, you could fully fill the place as an editor, and the care and responsibility would not be laid upon James.[6]

I saw that there has been feeling that James was too sensitive, too strong feeling; but I saw that someone must have the care and feel, and feel strongly too, and move decidedly in the office.[7] There is danger of some expecting too much of you, and there is danger of your expecting too little.

I saw that James and Brother Waggoner erred in not freely talking their fears to you. You were deceived as to their feeling and acted under a mistaken idea of things, and you and Harriet [**Harriet Newall Smith**] were wrong in moving in such haste, without first getting a thorough understanding of the matter. Your action in the matter displeased God. You made a wrong move in introducing the matter where it should not be mentioned, when your past experience was sufficient to teach you the effect that a great fire is kindled by a little matter.[8]

I saw if you break away from that office, your happiness and peace ends. But where you lack now, it is supplied.

God has not released James from the office. He has the care, responsibility and burden, and God has not released you from your place. I saw like two brothers, true yoke-fellows should you labor together, your interest one. You

---

editor for the *Review*. No doubt it was J. H. Waggoner, with his editorial experience, that Uriah Smith had in mind as his possible replacement.

See: Harry Ellsworth Cole, *A Standard History of Sauk County, Wisconsin,* vol. 1, p. 443; search term "Waggoner" *Words of the Pioneers.*

[6] Although James White had been relieved of many of his earlier editing and publishing responsibilities by the reorganization of 1855, he remained sole legal owner of the Review and Herald publishing house and was some sort of general manager, without officially carrying that title. As such he would have to fill in for any shortcomings in the work of the newly appointed resident editor, Uriah Smith.

For surveys of the organization of the publishing work during the 1850s, *see:* SDAE, s.v "Publishing Department"; Richard W. Schwarz and Floyd Greenleaf, *Light Bearers,* pp. 81, 82.

[7] In a memorial tribute to James White in 1881 Uriah Smith speaks of "one of the strongest traits in his [James White's] character, which was his pre-eminent love for the cause in which he was engaged. To that he subordinated all else; for that he was willing to renounce home and friends."

See: U. Smith, *In Memoriam,* pp. 34, 35.

[8] No further information has been found relating to the incident alluded to here.

have shut up too much the interest to yourself; together should you labor, unitedly together should your hearts be knit so close that Satan cannot get a wedge between you. United together can your interest tell, both working together in union. Your interest should not be divided. God is not pleased with this.[9] You have no separate interest in that office in the sight of God. Your work is one, your interest one, and here you have been too close, not as united as you should be.

I saw that the Lord has seen fit to bring Harriet in a place where she can work for the Lord and help you,[10] and I saw she must be on her watch to help when it is needed, to speak a word in season when it is needed, a word right and not on the wrong side. She must bear in mind that she can help, and must be very cautious not to hinder. She will have trials and if they are borne well, she will not lose the reward. The Lord's eye is upon every doing; His eye sees every influence.

Harriet, I saw that where you could hinder more than help is here. Let your mind be affected by any wrong influence, Uriah is affected by the same. You have watched John's [**John Nevins Andrews**][11] opinions and views, and they have had more effect and influence with you than is due, and then the door is open for your views or understanding to affect Uriah. Here is a door open for the enemy to work and you both must be on your guard. Satan will get in if he can. John is not standing in the light.[12]

---

[9] Whether this call for unity between Uriah Smith and James White was heeded is not known, but three years later the problem had resurfaced. "Uriah and James," wrote Ellen White in June 1860, "were shown me a distance apart from each other, not united. Darkness was in the office."

See: Lt 7, 1860 (June). For an analysis of the Smith-White relationship, see Eugene F. Durand, *Yours in the Blessed Hope, Uriah Smith,* chap. 18.

[10] Harriet Smith, a person of literary talent, had earlier worked at the *Review* during the period 1854-1855. She rejoined the staff in the spring of 1857, shortly before her marriage.

See: Obituary: "Harriet N. Smith," *Review,* Mar. 30, 1911, p. 23.

[11] *Identity:* The mutual interplay of negative influence between Harriet, Uriah, and "John" mentioned here is described in considerable detail in Lts 7 and 8, 1860. Lt 8, addressed to John Nevins Andrews, mentions the impact of his opinions on Harriet Smith (his sister-in-law) throughout the 1850s. "I saw that you have not taken a decided position in regard to the past, and your position influences Harriet and Uriah much." It seems very likely, therefore, that the "John" of Lt 6, 1857, is John Nevins Andrews. (See also note 12 below.)

[12] Although J. N. Andrews had made an outstanding contribution to the Sabbatarian movement in the early 1850s in terms of his preaching and scholarly writing, his attitude toward the visions and the leadership of James White was ambivalent for many years, until about 1860. Andrews later explained that during this period, while he had no "feelings of enmity" toward the Whites, he "lacked to some extent that living faith in the visions" (1862). Ellen White attributed some of Andrews's problems to the negative influence of his own family and that of the Cyprian Stevens family, all of whom had a long history of skepticism toward the visions and of resentment toward James White's robust leadership style. The fact that both Uriah Smith and J. N. Andrews married into the Cyprian Stevens family led to a situation in which these prominent leaders were to some extent influenced by their respective wives against James White and against the visions. Judging by the tone of Lt 6, Harriet (Stevens) Smith,

I have seen that you could have the blessing of God resting upon you, could live in the hearts of the people of God. You must with confidence and courage go forward, have faith in God, draw strength from Jesus. Unitedly you can serve Him, unitedly obtain the victory, and unitedly share the reward.

I saw that great was your privilege. You can enjoy sweet union with God, with childlike confidence can you rely upon Him. And Harriet, you can by occupying a right position, living in the counsel of God, help Uriah more than any other one and more than you think you can.

Never act or talk on the doubtful side, but let the weight of your words and acts be to strengthen faith, to dispel doubts. You have not realized for years the responsibility that rests upon you. God has given you a taste of eternal joys to lead you on, to reach out, to hope, to elevate and bring you closer to Himself. God requires you to look to these manifestations of His grace and love. These abundant blessings were for some special object. When much is given, much will be required. If your influence is governed by the Spirit of God, you can do much. If it is not sanctified by the Spirit of God, it will tell much on the wrong side.

You have felt too much that it was but a little matter or but little consequence what you may say or do. Take heed. There is more importance attached to these things than you have thought of. The grace of God can sanctify and purify your judgment, and together can you labor for the interest of God's cause.

---

recently married to Uriah, had not at the time of writing (1857) adopted a strongly critical stance toward the Whites, but this became very evident by 1860, as revealed in the detailed account of Lt 7, 1860.

See: J. N. Andrews to "Brother White," Feb. 2, 1862; *idem,* "Confession," *Review,* Dec. 17, 1861, p. 22; Ellen G. White, Lt 7, 1860 (June); Ron Graybill, "The Family Man," in Harry Leonard, ed., *J. N. Andrews: The Man and the Mission,* pp. 14-41.

1857

(Lt 9, 1857)

[OCTOBER][1] N.P.

LETTER TO
Sylsbre R. Rumery.[2]

Previously unpublished.

An appeal to Sylsbre Rumery, a man of considerable means and a "love of money," to act more generously toward Victor Jones, a poor fellow member of the Monterey, Michigan, church.

Given in Monterey.[3]

Dear Brother Rumery:

You remember the vision given last Thursday eve.[4] In that vision I saw the

---

[1] *See:* Note 3.

[2] *Identity:* There are indications in the letter that "Brother Rumery" is a man of means who lives in or near Monterey. The only church member who fits this description is Sylsbre Rumery, of Monterey, Michigan. His real estate value is listed in the 1860 census at a comfortable $4,000 and in 1870 at an impressive $20,000. Rumery was also a man of influence, holding several civic offices at various times in the township of Monterey, including treasurer and highway commissioner.

See: 1860 U.S. Federal Census: "Sylsbre Rumery," Michigan, Allegan County, Monterey, p. 144; 1870 U.S. Federal Census: "Sylsbre Rumery," Michigan, Allegan County, Monterey, p. 266; *History of Allegan and Barry Counties, Michigan,* p. 288.

[3] The original/earliest copy bears no date. However, the words "Given in Monterey" appear at the top of the letter in Ellen White's handwriting, no doubt referring to the vision "given last Thursday eve." Only one vision given to Ellen White in Monterey on a Thursday evening is known, viz., that of Thursday, October 8, 1857. As the first line indicates, this account of the vision was written some days later.

See: J. W. [James White], "Report of Meetings!" *Review,* Oct. 22, 1857, pp. 196, 197.

[4] On Thursday evening, October 8, 1857, as reported by James White in the *Review,* a meeting was held in Monterey "in the school-house near Bro. George Lay's. . . . Mrs. White arose and spoke with much freedom. The place was filled with the Spirit of the Lord. Some rejoiced, others wept. . . . When seated, Mrs. W. began to praise the Lord, and continued rising higher and higher in perfect triumph in the Lord, till her voice changed, and the deep, clear shouts of Glory! Hallelujah! thrilled every heart. She was in vision." Sylsbre Rumery, it appears, was present on this occasion. The Monterey vision contained specific instruction for several individuals: Sylsbre Rumery (Lt 9, 1857 [Oct.]), Anthony Burwell (Lt 2, 1857 [Oct. 21]), and Uriah and Harriet Smith (Lt 3, Lt 6, 1857 [Oct. 8]). Counsel of a more general nature was published the following month in the *Review* and also in *Testimony* No. 4.

See: J. W. [James White], "Report of Meetings!" *Review,* Oct. 22, 1857, p. 196; E. G. W.,

case of Brother Victor Jones [**Victor V. Jones**]. I saw that the Lord loved him but he had had reasons for discouragement.[5] He possessed a noble, generous disposition. He looked for and expected to find the same disposition in his brethren, but was disappointed. They said by their profession we are pilgrims and strangers, yet their heart and treasure were here.

Brother Rumery, you could in many little acts have eased Brother Jones's burden, and never felt it; but for years you have loved money better than religion, better than God, and it is like taking out the right eye, cutting off the right arm, to part with this money. You do not realize it, but it is your god. You cannot appreciate the worth of the soul until you die to this world, and overcome your love of money. God is displeased with, and looks with a frown[6] upon, your close dealing with your brethren, making a little something out of them, taking advantage of them when you can. God hates such things, and every single instance wherein you are guilty is written in the book and will stand against you unless you humbly repent of it and reform.

I saw that instead of inquiring into Brother Jones's wants, feeling a kindly sympathy for him, you have coldly shut up the bowels of compassion toward him. He expected when you embraced the present truth[7] it would work a reformation in you in these things. He was disappointed and his hands were weakened and fell without strength at his side. He felt and said, "It is no use," "It is no use. I can't live religion. I can't keep the truth." He has stumbled over your selfishness, your love of the world, but God has pitied and reached out a helping hand. His propensities are strong habits that would ruin his family and himself, and he will have a constant war to subdue this dreadful appetite and overcome it. His brethren can help him if they will. You can help him and favor him and love him—not in word merely, but in deed, in action—and

---

"He Went Away Sorrowful, for He Had Great Possessions," *Review,* Nov. 26, 1857, pp. 18, 19; Ellen G. White, *Testimonies for the Church,* vol. 1, pp. 170-178.

[5] In his report of the Monterey meeting James White mentions a "poor, discouraged brother" who also witnessed Ellen White in vision on October 8. Partly because of "neglect by his wealthy brethren . . . [he] was returning to strong habits." Although he does not give his name, the description makes it reasonably certain that James White is speaking of Victor Jones. Ellen White's vision included "a most touching and encouraging message" for Jones, such that he "raised his head. . . and he and his good wife are again happy in hope." The 1860 census listed the value of Victor Jones's real estate at a paltry $100 compared to Rumery's $4,000. Apart from his poverty Jones had other "reasons for discouragement," including a "propensity" for strong drink and a wealthy Adventist neighbor, George T. Lay, who showed too much interest in Jones's wife.

See: J. W. [James White], "Report of Meetings!" *Review,* Oct. 22, 1857, p. 196; 1860 U.S. Federal Census: "Victor Jones," Michigan, Allegan County, Monterey, p. 142; **George T. Lay**; Ellen G. White, Ms 2, 1863 (June 6).

[6] On God's displeasure and "frown," see Ms 2, 1853 (Mar. 1), note 3.

[7] Rumery was a recent convert, having "embraced the views of Seventh-day Adventists" in 1857, "under the labors of Eld. Joseph Bates."

See: Obituary: "Sylsbre Rumery," *Review,* Dec. 2, 1884, p. 766.

bind to your heart with strong Christian cords an erring, burdened brother. Brother Rumery, you have felt, "Am I my brother's keeper?" Said the angel, "Thou art thy brother's keeper, and in a degree responsible for his soul." Jesus died for you. Said the angel: "Love one another as I have loved you." How much? Enough to give your life for a brother. Said Jesus, "Can ye drink of the cup? Can ye be baptized with the baptism?" "Love one another as I have loved you." Will you for this world's goods suffer him to stumble over your close dealing—your close, covetous dealing—to perdition? That brother that stumbles thus will be required at your hand.

God calls for noble-hearted men, and the love of the world has eaten out this nobleness that shows forth in them the image of their Maker. Now God designs the truth to purify, to purge from you this love of the world. It must do it or your case is hopeless. You have not dealt generously and truly with Brother Jones. You let the love of money crowd out all the noble principles of the soul. Every noble, generous act is written in the book; every neglect of a brother, every selfish advantage taken of a brother, is written in the book.

Dear brother, in the vision God has given me as it has unfolded to my mind I have felt distressed, distressed. I have many fears that you will never get the world out of your heart.[8] You will have to work faster and more in earnest than you yet have done. May the Lord open your eyes to yourself. May you see that the greatest share of your heart is occupied with the world.

I saw that at present God does not call for the houses His people need to live in,[9] that there was no need of these at present. But if those who have an abundance here do not hear His voice and cut loose from the world and sacrifice for God, He will pass them by and call to those who are willing to do anything for Jesus, to sell even their homes to meet the wants of the cause.

---

[8] Ellen White's description of Rumery in 1859 and 1860 indicate that he did make serious efforts at reform, but in the long run there appears to have been little change to his basic materialistic bent. "This world is his god," Ellen White wrote in 1869, "he has not heeded the warning given him years ago." According to his obituary written in 1884, Rumery "made no profession of religion at the time of his death, yet he cherished a love for the truth held by this people."

See: Ellen G. White, Ms 5, 1859 (diary entries for Jan. 11, 12); Ms 4, 1860 (c. 1860); Ms 16, 1868 (diary entries May 8, 9); *idem, Testimony for the Churches at Allegan and Monterey* (1869) (PH099), pp. 29-41; obituary: "Sylsbre Rumery," *Review*, Dec. 2, 1884, p. 766.

[9] Although the visions of Ellen White had through the years consistently called members to financial sacrifice, they had also opposed extreme interpretations of what such sacrifice might entail. When Joseph Bates in 1849 urged members to sell their properties without delay, Ellen White responded that "God had not required all of His people to dispose of their property at the same time, but in a time of need He would teach them . . . when to sell and how much to sell." Similarly, in 1857 in the wake of the Laodicean call for revival "a few taught that the brethren must sell all out before they could be free." Thus Ellen White's statement here is a call for moderation in the face of the extremism of a few, while still calling for sacrificial giving by all members.

See: Ellen G. White, Ms 14, 1850 (Sept.), note 5; *idem, Spiritual Gifts [vol. 2],* p. 223.

God will have a freewill offering and those who give must esteem it a privilege to do so. It is not God's design for a few to be eased and others burdened. There must be a greater willingness to do each his part as God has prospered him. I was shown that those who are poor, and have the least of this world's goods, see the wants of the cause, [and] divide and divide to meet the wants of the cause, while the able and wealthy do not do so.

One dollar is held more tightly by you than ten are by the day laborer. It will be hard for you to see this. Oh, the deceitfulness of riches! The more the possessor has the less does he see the wants of the cause and the more difficult it is to hear the voice of Jesus when it calls for his means. He is sorrowful.

Brother Rumery, it is very hard for you to deny self and take an upright, generous, noble course that all who see you can know that a reformation is wrought in you by the truth. This change is looked for in you. You must cut loose, cut loose from the world. You can have this world if you pursue the same course you have pursued, but you cannot have heaven nor its treasure. Choose ye whom ye will serve, God or Mammon. The time has come for you to choose. Dear Brother Rumery, I came to your house purposely to tell you the vision but my heart sank within me. I knew my weakness and knew I should feel the deepest distress for you while relating it to you, and I was afraid I should not have strength to do it, and should mar the work. Now brother, I am afflicted and distressed for you, and when at your house was so burdened I could not stay. I send this communication to you with much trembling. I fear from what I have seen that your efforts will be too weak. You will make no change. Oh, will you get ready for Jesus' coming? I kept the vision from every one, even my husband, but I must speak plainly to you. You must have a thorough work done for you or you will fail of heaven. Said the angel, "It is easier for a camel to go through a needle's eye, than for a rich man to enter the kingdom of God." Luke 18:25.

In trial.

1857

(Lt 2, 1857)

OCTOBER 21,[1] BATTLE CREEK, MICHIGAN

LETTER TO

Anthony L. Burwell.[2]

Portions of this letter are published in Arthur L. White, *Ellen G. White: The Early Years,* p. 363.

An appeal to Anthony Burwell who loves "earthly treasure better than the truth."

Dear Brother Burwell:

While at Monterey [Michigan] your case was shown me in vision.[3] I saw that you were too sleepy for your own eternal interest, and that of your family. You have not made the effort you should to break loose from the world. Your grasp is fast upon it, and its treasure looks good and precious to you.[4] I viewed

---

[1] Only "Oct. 21" is given in the original/earliest copy, not the year. However, there is a strong case for assigning it to 1857 since Ellen White's description of a vision given her in Monterey in the last paragraphs closely matches the contents of a vision she received in Monterey, Michigan, on October 8, 1857 (Ellen G. White, *Testimonies for the Church,* vol. 1, pp. 170-178). Moreover, the first half of the letter, dealing with Anthony Burwell's situation, is very similar to the warnings and appeals found in Ellen White's letter to Burwell some months earlier, on January 28, 1857 (Lt 1, 1857).

[2] *Identity:* The identity of "Brother Burwell" can be established by the similarity of the content of this letter with that written to Anthony L. Burwell and his wife in January of the same year. Both letters warn Burwell of his ingrained materialism. Both letters also speak of death among his children and that only Anna remains. This combined information clearly matches the situation of Anthony L. Burwell, of Parma, Michigan, two of whose children died in 1856, leaving only Anna Lucretia Burwell.

See: A. Burwell, "From Sr. Burwell," *Review,* Jan. 1, 1857, p. 71; obituary: "Anthony L. Burwell," *Review,* Jan. 28, 1873, p. 55; obituary: "Achsah Burwell," *Review,* June 8, 1886, p. 366; 1850 U.S. Federal Census, "Anthony L. Burwell," Vermont, Addison County, Panton, p. 262.

[3] Judging by the contents of this letter, Ellen White is referring to a vision received in Monterey, Michigan, on October 8, 1857, barely two weeks earlier. Part of that vision, a general exhortation to liberality on the part of wealthier members, was published the following month, November 1857. It would appear that the same vision also contained this specific appeal to Anthony Burwell which Ellen White chose to convey in a private letter.

See: Ellen G. White, *Testimonies for the Church,* vol. 1, pp. 170-178; "*Testimony to the Church,* No. 4," *Review,* Nov. 12, 1857, p. 5.

[4] According to U.S. census records, the Burwells' property value increased dramatically between 1850 and 1860.

See: Lt 1, 1857 (Jan. 28), note 3.

you in a fearful, critical situation. You do not yet possess the spirit of sacrifice, and I greatly fear you never will. God, I saw, had tried to save you. Fearfully, terribly has He approached you, taken the fruit of your own body from you without hope. All this was to cut you loose from the world, save you, your wife, and Anna [**Anna Lucretia King** (née **Burwell**)].[5]

When you were here in the spring, I saw that your house should be freed, that it had been polluted by a wrong influence. You know fully what was seen. Have you followed the light?[6] I saw, Brother Burwell, you should dig down deep; try your motives. Many, or most, of them are purely selfish. A more thorough work must be accomplished for you or you are ruined.

Anna is in the broad road to hell. Oh, such disobedience, such unloveliness toward her dear mother! I dare not write it, and wish not to think about it. A fearful record of it is kept in the book. Anna will meet it again. All the heartache that she causes her mother is noticed of God. She is forming a character, but not for heaven.

Unless the hand of God is turned aside by your deep humility and humble walk, there is more anguish in store for you. God has given you a bitter cup to drink that it might purify you and wean you from this world. The object is not gained. You love this world, love your earthly treasure better than the truth. If you had followed the light God had given you, and gone earnestly and zealously about the work, things would be entirely different in your family.

I fear, from what God has shown me, you are so little acquainted with your own heart you will not see the evils there and subdue them, but they will increase. Your besetments hold the victory, and the grace of God finds no room in your heart. The love of the world finds a large place in your heart. You have no idea of sacrificing for the cause of God. A sacrifice does not increase, but decreases.

I was shown in vision at Monterey that God was calling upon those who have this world's goods to sacrifice of their substance.[7] A few have listened to

---

[5] *Identity:* During 1856 the Burwells lost their only son, Charles, age 18, and oldest daughter, Francis, age 20. Only Anna Lucretia Burwell remained, age 13 at the time of the writing of this letter.

See: A. Burwell, "From Sr. Burwell," *Review,* Jan. 1, 1857, p. 71; 1850 U.S. Federal Census, "Anthony L. Burwell," Vermont, Addison County, Panton Township, p. 262; obituary: "Anna Lucretia King, née Burwell," *Review,* Mar. 5, 1931, p. 28.

[6] Whether the reference here is to the vision Ellen White reported to the Burwells in her letter of January 28, 1857, or whether there was a subsequent vision is not clear. In her January letter she had written, "One thing I saw you had erred in, that is in the company you suffer to be in your dwelling. . . . Have only those with you or in your dwelling that are clean and holy." Her special concern appeared to be that their daughter should have a positive home environment. It seems that this is the matter which is being raised again in this October letter.

See: Ellen G. White, Lt 1, 1857 (Jan. 28).

[7] A more detailed account of the vision published a few weeks later makes certain qualifications. Thus, "I saw that at present God does not call for the houses His people need to live in, unless expensive houses are exchanged for cheaper ones." In another instance Ellen

the call, but many will go away sorrowful like the young man who came to Jesus to know what he should do to inherit eternal life. At the answer of Jesus, "Go and sell that thou hast," he was sorrowful, for he had great possessions.

This is like the faith of many of the Sabbathkeepers. They submit to keep the Sabbath, to go along with this unpopular people. They can dwell upon the truth; but when Jesus says, Sacrifice for the truth, sell that thou hast, lay up treasure in heaven, they are sorrowful. Their idol has been touched. Oh, this earthly treasure is more dear to them than eternal life. They would be highly pleased if they could have both, but as they cannot, they cling more closely to the earthly treasure and care not whether they lay up treasure in heaven or not. They will perish with their earthly treasure.

I saw that God was testing those that have possessions here to see how much they love this truth. He will soon pass by them if they heed not His voice. He will call those that are willing. The day laborer will bear the burden cheerfully. I saw they were the richest men. They can hand out ten dollars to the cause of God easier than the wealthy one dollar. Such are truly rich. I saw you must work, work in earnest, for your time [to] do [so] will soon be past.

White complains of some who took this message to the extreme in 1857: "A few taught that the brethren must sell all out before they could be free."

See: Ellen G. White, *Testimonies for the Church,* vol. 1, p. 177; *idem, Spiritual Gifts [vol. 2],* p. 223.

1857

OCTOBER

"Jesus Calls."

Published in *The Youth's Instructor,* vol. 5, no. 10, October 1857, p. 76.

1857

(Lt 5, 1857)

NOVEMBER 22, BATTLE CREEK, MICHIGAN

LETTER TO

Elon Everts.[1]

Previously unpublished.

Mary Loughborough's struggles with homesickness. "Worldly-mindedness among the brethren in Round Grove."

Dear Brother Everts:

The Lord has wrought for us since you left. After the conference[2] my mind was very much depressed. Discouragement pressed heavily upon me.

---

[1] *Identity:* Little is said directly about "Brother Everts" in this letter that might help to identify him, but it is implied that he has recently attended a conference at which Ellen White was present, is well acquainted with John and Mary Loughborough, and possibly lives in the area of Round Grove. This scenario matches the circumstances of Elon Everts well, having moved to Round Grove, Illinois, two years earlier (note 7), worked with John Loughborough in tent evangelism during the summer of 1857, and attended a conference with the Whites at Battle Creek two weeks earlier (note 2). For Everts's association with Loughborough in 1857, see J. N. Loughborough, "Sketches of the Past—Nos. 101, 104," *Pacific Union Recorder,* Aug. 4, 1910, p. 7 and Sept. 1, 1910, p. 1.

[2] The implication seems to be that Ellen White is speaking of a recent conference, and that Elon Everts had been present. The most recent conference attended by Ellen White was the "General Conference" held at Battle Creek, Michigan, two weeks earlier, November 6-9, 1857. In his announcement of the forthcoming conference in the *Review* some weeks earlier, James White had specifically invited "Brn. Andrews, Loughborough, and Everts from the West" to attend.

See: James White, "General Conference in Battle Creek," Oct. 22, 1857, p. 200; Joseph Bates, Uriah Smith, "Business Proceedings of the General Conference, of Nov. 6th, 1857," *Review,* Nov. 12, 1857, p. 4.

Last Friday night John [**John Norton Loughborough**] and Mary [**Mary J. Loughborough**][3] came here. At our prayer season my discouragement was so great it seemed to me I could not pray. But at last, in the agony of my soul, I cried unto God, and the light of heaven shone upon me. I was made free and to rejoice in God.

I was soon taken off in vision and was shown some things concerning Mary and John; that it was not Mary's duty to go East; that God would not prosper her if she went.[4] That God was willing to receive her and bless her again, but her will must die; she must yield to the will of God. Mary was affected.[5] We are willing to do anything for these poor children.

I saw that there was too much worldly-mindedness among the brethren in Round Grove [Illinois]. They get involved purchasing lands, and any effort made to raise means, to use it as it is needed in the cause of God, they eagerly seize it, so that there is no means left to sustain the servants of God, and the laborer for God is not considered worthy of his hire.[6] There will have to be a change among the brethren in Round Grove. They are eaten up with

---

[3] *Identities:* There are strong indications in the letter identifying "John" and "Mary" as John N. and Mary J. Loughborough. For one thing they are said to have visited Ellen White in Battle Creek, Michigan, "last Friday night," i.e., November 20. Such a visit by the Loughboroughs would be entirely plausible given the fact that they had moved from Iowa some weeks earlier, reaching Battle Creek "the first of November" 1857. More significant, the appeal to Mary for full consecration to God and the warning against her going "East" closely match the content of Ellen White's letter to Mary Loughborough written three months later (see note 4).

See: J. N. Loughborough, "Sketches of the Past—No. 106," *Pacific Union Recorder,* Oct. 6, 1910, p. 1; Ellen G. White, Lt 1, 1858 (Mar. 3).

[4] What Ellen White means by her warning to Mary Loughborough about going "East" is clarified in a letter to Mary three months later: "It was God's will that you should not go to Rochester last fall." The heart of the matter was Mary's longing to live near her friends and relatives in the Rochester, New York, area. Having just spent a year in Waukon, Iowa, with her husband gone most of the time, Mary had seemed determined to move back to Rochester, even though John's ministerial talents were needed primarily in the Midwest.

See: Ellen G. White, Lt 1, 1858 (Mar. 3).

[5] Records indicate that Mary Loughborough struggled with herself over these issues, with varying degrees of success, especially in the early years of her marriage. In 1854 Ellen White appealed to Mary to "cut loose from relatives and acquaintances and . . . have your eye single to the glory of God." In December 1856 Mary "confessed her past lack of consecration, and gave herself anew to the Lord, and could say to her husband, Go forth in the name of the Lord to do his work." Yet this letter, November 22, 1857, and that of March 1858 indicate that Mary at times still struggled to reconcile herself with John's itinerant work and with a desire to return to Rochester.

See: Ellen G. White, Lt 6, 1854 (winter); Lt 1, 1858 (Mar. 3); J. W. [James White], "Western Tour," *Review,* Jan 15, 1857, p. 84.

[6] John Loughborough recalled that for his evangelistic work in Round Grove and vicinity during the period January-April 1857 the members awarded him his "board and lodging, a buffalo robe overcoat, and ten dollars in money." He added, laconically, "ministerial work was not a source of great financial gain."

See: J. N. Loughborough, "Sketches of the Past—No. 104," *Pacific Union Recorder,* Sept. 1, 1910, p. 1.

the spirit of the world. They must begin to live out their faith, and die to the world. The third angel's message is not lived out; it is talked, but not acted upon.[7]

There must be a separation from the world, an acting out of their faith.

Other things I will write soon to individuals. I was shown the case of George Butler [**George Ide Butler**]. He has been misjudged and wronged by some in Round Grove. They have limited the Holy One of Israel. It is nothing strange that God should turn the infidel unto Him, and in the future they need not marvel if the conversion of infidels should be multiplied. I saw that the Lord had mercifully extended His mercy to George Butler and opened unto him His Word, that he could see its beauty and harmony, and be led to love and worship its Author.[8]

E. G. White

Dear Brother Everts: Mary is coming round right. We are going to settle them to housekeeping if it is possible. This church can help some; but there have been so many objects of charity here that I hardly dare mention another case, for most of them are poor, have snug work[9] to get along themselves. Last night I learned one brother, a French brother, was entirely destitute, and his family had lived on potatoes for two weeks. They must be helped. It is our

---

[7] A vision given one year earlier, in December 1856, had also highlighted the materialism and declining spirituality of some of the Round Grove members. Elon Everts, to whom this letter is addressed, a farmer and traveling minister, had migrated to Round Grove from Vermont in 1855. Some months earlier, in July 1857, Ellen White had admonished Everts, "you must be narrowing down your large farms. . . . Cut loose, cut loose from your treasures here; lay up a treasure in heaven." The testimonies to Everts and the Round Grove members were part of a larger appeal to the increasing numbers of Sabbatarian Adventists who were migrating from the Eastern states to the Midwest in the mid-1850s. As early as 1855 Ellen White had appealed to those moving westward not to become engrossed in the material pursuits of buying and developing lands to the neglect of their spiritual mission.

See: Ellen G. White, *Testimonies for the Church,* vol. 1, p. 118; Ms 1, 1856 (Dec. 9); Lt 14, 1857 (c. 1857).

[8] George Ide Butler, later to become a long-serving General Conference president for the Seventh-day Adventists, was in his youth a skeptic despite being brought up by Millerite parents who later became Sabbathkeepers. Why the group at Round Grove, in particular, had "misjudged and wronged" George Butler is not clear. In 1855, while still an unbeliever, George Butler had visited Round Grove with the apparent intention of courting Lentha Lockwood, one of the band. Whether this circumstance had turned some of the believers in Round Grove against Butler or whether it was just a general skepticism about the genuineness of his conversion the following year is a matter for speculation.

See: Emmett K. Vande Vere, *Rugged Heart: The Story of George I. Butler,* pp. 15, 16; M. C. Wilcox and W. C. White, "George Ide Butler: A Sketch of His Life," *Review,* Aug. 29, 1918, p. 14.

[9] "Snug work"—an archaic expression implying just enough to get by.

book-binder. I guess you remember him.[10]

Brother Everts, if you have some carpeting you can spare, please send it on. They will have to have one, to save work.

If we can only get them fixed in Battle Creek, an important move is made toward making Brother John free.[11]

If Sister Stone,[12] or any of the rest of the sisters, have sheets or pillowcases that they can send on to Mary, it would be a help. Every little will help. Please interest others for them, and send what you can for them by Brother Holden. There will be much we shall have to do that others cannot do.

In love.

---

[10] Possibly John M. Daigneau, a French Canadian, who with his wife, Vitaline, had recently become Sabbathkeepers. They lived not far from the Whites' home in Battle Creek.

See: EGWEnc, s.v. "John M. Daigneau."

[11] The hopes of the Whites seemed to be that if the Loughboroughs could be helped to establish a home in Battle Creek, Mary would have less reason to pine for Rochester. Not mentioned in these last paragraphs is the fact that about this time James White did some private fund-raising and was able to buy a small house for the Loughboroughs in Battle Creek. John Loughborough explains the details in later reminiscences. "Brother White found opportunity to obtain a lot and cottage for the writer for four hundred dollars. Aside from about one hundred and fifty dollars that I paid, he raised the money from willing brethren who could invest twenty-five dollars each."

See: J. N. Loughborough, "Sketches of the Past—No. 105," *Pacific Union Recorder,* Sept. 8, 1910, p. 2.

[12] There is insufficient data available to identify "Sister Stone" or "Brother Holden" with any degree of certainty.

1857

NOVEMBER 26

"'He Went Away Sorrowful, for He Had Great Possessions.'"

Published in *Advent Review, and Sabbath Herald,* vol. 11, no. 3, November 26, 1857, pp. 18, 19.

1857

NOVEMBER

"'It's Natural.'"

Published in *The Youth's Instructor,* vol. 5, no. 11, November 1857, p. 84.

1857

NOVEMBER

PUBLICATION OF

Testimony for the Church, No. 4, Battle Creek, Michigan.

Published by Steam Press of the *Review and Herald* Office. 39 pp.

1857

DECEMBER 31

"The Future."

Published in *Advent Review, and Sabbath Herald,* vol. 11, no. 8, December 31, 1857, p. 59.

1857

(Lt 15, 1857)

[CIRCA 1857],[1] N.P.

LETTER TO

Stephen Pierce.[2]

This letter is published in entirety in Ellen G. White, *Manuscript Releases,* vol. 18, pp. 248-253.

---

[1] The original/earliest copy of this letter is undated, but internal evidence places it sometime between 1856 and 1859. The clearest indication that it cannot have been written before 1856 is found toward the end of the letter, where Sabbatarian Adventists are identified with the Laodicean church of Revelation 3:14-21. An article by James White entitled "The Seven Churches" in October 1856 had signaled a major theological shift. Prior to that the lukewarm Laodicean church of Revelation was seen as symbolizing those Adventist bodies that rejected the Sabbath, but in his article James White boldly identified Sabbatarian Adventists with Laodicea and called on them to repent for their lukewarmness. For this reason this letter can hardly be dated earlier than October 1856. Neither can it have been written later than February 22, 1859, the death date of Amanda Phillips, who appears to be the "Sister Phillips" addressed several times in the letter.

The more specific suggestion "circa 1857" as the date for this letter builds on the comment in the second-to-last paragraph that Stephen Pierce had not contributed enough to the *Review*, of which he was a corresponding editor. "You have been silent too much. . . . In the paper you could speak to hundreds. . . . Your talent, Bro. P., has been almost buried up." It seems likely that the sparseness of his articles were the occasion for James White's publicly expressed consternation in December 1856: "Some of our Corresponding Editors have well done; but where are Brn. Pierce and Andrews? The inquiry goes round the church, '*Why Don't THEY write?*'"

See: J. W. [James White], "The Seven Churches," *Review,* Oct. 16, 1856, p. 189; P. Gerard Damsteegt, *Foundations of the Seventh-day Adventist Message and Mission,* pp. 244-248; obituary: "Amanda Phillips," *Review,* Mar. 24, 1859, p. 143; J. W. [James White], "Why Don't They Write?" *Review,* Dec. 11, 1856, p. 48.

[2] *Identity:* A number of Pierces are mentioned in the *Review* during the 1850s, but there

A call for Stephen Pierce and Daniel Phillips to expand their vision and employ their preaching talents to the full.

Dear Brother Pierce:

Duty compels me to write a few lines. The Lord has shown me of late some things in vision which I feel duty to write you. I saw that all was not right with you, that you are in a place where your influence can tell but little; you are in too narrow a compass. I saw that Brn. Pierce and Phillips [**Daniel C.** and **Amanda Phillips**][3] can be of use in the cause of God. Both their gifts are needed where they have not yet been, where their gifts are new and can affect more.[4] The King's business is important, and requires haste. Jesus is coming, and there is no time to dally. With energy and zeal souls must be pulled out of the fire.

The past was opened before me. I was shown that there was a lingering of that spirit that Bennet and Libby had[5] that has not been sufficiently shaken off

---

are certain clues in this letter that help to single out the one being addressed. This Pierce appears to come from Vermont, he is a preacher, and he has written for the *Review* (albeit not enough). The only Pierce who fulfills these specifications during this period is Stephen Pierce, of Roxbury, Vermont. See notes below for further evidence to support this identification.

See: Search term "Pierce" in *Words of the Pioneers.*

[3] *Identity:* This letter informs us that "Brother and Sister Phillips" come from Vermont and that "Bro. Phillips's gift of exhortation is needed." Daniel C. Phillips and his wife, Amanda, of Roxbury, Vermont, seem to be the couple that most clearly fulfill these criteria. Of Daniel C. Phillips it is said in his obituary that "hundreds among our brethren . . . listened to his stirring testimonies." The *Review* carried a number of reports, especially from 1857 to 1858, of the evangelistic travels of a "Brother Phillips," of Vermont.

See: Obituary: "D. C. Phillips," *Review,* July 11, 1882, p. 446; search term "Phillips" in *Words of the Pioneers.*

[4] Up to the mid-1850s both Stephen Pierce and Daniel Phillips had tended to restrict their preaching to their home state of Vermont with occasional forays a little further afield. As concerns Phillips, his participation in tent meetings in Michigan and Illinois during the autumn and winter of 1857 may be attributed to Ellen White's challenge in this letter for him to enter new fields. (Whether this was the case depends on the exact date of the letter.) Viewing the paths subsequently taken by Stephen Pierce and Daniel Phillips after being challenged in this letter to greater efforts, it is clear that Pierce's response was the more positive of the two. He served in the 1860s as president of the Vermont and Minnesota conferences. Phillips, after some effective ministry in the 1850s, became involved in several compromising situations that lessened his usefulness, as evidenced in letters to him from Ellen White in the early 1860s.

See: A. S. Hutchins, "Tent Meeting in Colchester, Ills." *Review*, Oct. 15, 1857, p. 188; J. N. Loughborough, "Tent Meetings at Lyndon and White Rock, Ills." *Review*, Oct. 15, 1857, p. 189; "Appointments," *Review,* Oct. 22, 1857, p. 200; John Byington, "Meetings at Gun Lake, Mich.," *Review,* Feb. 4, 1858, p. 104; J. H. Waggoner, "Appointments," *Review,* Feb. 11, 1858, p. 112. For details on Phillips's problems in the 1860s, see Ellen G. White, Lt 2, 1862 (Jan. 20); Lt 4, 1864 (Jan. 12); Lt 4a, 1864 (Jan.); Lt 4b, 1864 (Dec. 23).

[5] In August 1850 James White reported in *The Advent Review* that "the brethren in Johnson and in other places in Vermont, have suffered greatly from the corrupt views and teachings of J. G. Bennett, John Libby, Noah Bailey, and others of the same stamp." As to the nature of their

by Bro. and Sr. Phillips, and as long as this spirit, the last of it, is not shaken off, it tells, and it has its influence. It is foreign to the Spirit of God. I saw that the spirit that both Bennet and Libby possessed while Bro. and Sr. Phillips were in union with them, was an unclean spirit and an unholy spirit, and Bro. and Sr. O. have not as yet realized and admitted and shaken it off. The spirit moved strongly on the feelings, and these feelings, many of them, are yet cherished as sacred, as [indited by] the Holy Ghost. But many times when it was upon Bro. and Sr. Phillips, they knew not what spirit they were of.

At the time these men were professing so much of the Holy Ghost, especially Bennet, his life was corrupt, his heart vile. I was shown that a great many have been entirely thrown off their balance by not understanding the spirit that some of these [seemingly] very good and professedly holy men possessed. [They believe] that they have felt the influence of and received great blessings through the influence of their prayers and apparent faith. It has stumbled many an honest soul, and here they have grounded and made shipwreck of faith. They trusted to feeling, to an influence or power that was brought to bear upon their feelings.

I saw that many, very many, had been truly converted through the influence of persons who were living in open violation of the commandments of God, their lives vile and corrupt. Others, I saw, were very sick. A case was held up before me of one of my relatives, a Methodist minister; 80 miles [129 kilometers] he was sent for, to pray for a sick sister who sent for him, in compliance with the teaching of James. He went and prayed in earnest, and she prayed; she believed the minister to be a man of God, a man of faith. Physicians had given her up to die of consumption. She was healed immediately. She arose and prepared supper, a thing she had not done for ten years. Now, the minister was vile, his life was corrupt, and yet here was a great work. He took the glory all to himself.

Then again the scene mentioned above passed before me. I saw [that] the woman was a true disciple of Christ; her faith was that she should be healed. I saw their prayers: one was misty, dark, fell downward. The other prayer was mixed with light or specks which looked to me like diamonds, and arose

---

"corrupt views," these included a preoccupation with a celibate lifestyle, focusing on texts such as 1 Corinthians 7:29 ("they that have wives be as though they had none").

The Whites had visited Johnson, Vermont, some weeks before the article was published. Ellen White later described their meeting on that occasion with "Libbey and Bailey, and two females, with white dresses to represent the righteousness of the saints," and recounted the dramatic exit of "these fanatics" as "the power of God filled the room." It is possible that "J. G. Bennett" mentioned in the above article is the same Bennet that Ellen White met in Claremont, New Hampshire, in 1845 and described as "darkness and iniquity covered up with a pious garb."

See: W. [James White], "Our Tour East," *Review,* August 1850, pp. 14, 15; Ellen G. White, *Spiritual Gifts [vol. 2],* pp. 131, 132, 46-48; James White and Ellen G. White, *Life Sketches* (1880), pp. 206-209.

upward to Jesus and He sent it up to His Father like sweet incense, and a beam of light was immediately sent to the afflicted [one], and she revived and strengthened under the influence.

Said the angel, God will gather every particle of true, sincere faith; like diamonds shall they be gathered up and will surely bring a return or answer; and God will separate the precious from the vile. Although He bears long with the hypocrite and sinner, yet he will be searched out. Though he may flourish with the honest a while like the green bay tree, yet the time will come when his folly will be made manifest and he be brought to confusion.

Said the angel, Shall He leave the poor, suffering saints who are deceived, destitute entirely of His Spirit? Oh, no! I saw He would win and woo them, that if they cleave to Him and if they would listen to His voice, He would say to them, This is the way; walk ye in it.

But I saw there is great danger always of those who are brought so close, so near this unclean spirit as you have been, Bro. and Sr. Phillips. I saw that God would separate the precious from the vile. There would be truth or something from God to call for a decision. The corrupt have no disposition to receive that call for a decision, but are separated from the precious by the precious receiving this truth by the others neglected. Here is the separation made. God will work in mysterious ways to save the true, honest ones. I saw the great danger of those who have been connected with this spirit [of] setting down this or that as the power of God, and, knowing [thinking] this to be His power, they yield this or that [and] they give up their whole Christian experience.

I saw, Bro. and Sr. Phillips, this was your case, and the only safe course for you was to shake off entirely that spirit, [get] out from it entirely. Call it a deception you were under, as it really was, and then feast upon the truth, the present truth. I saw there is among you a spirit of linking up with a few, making everything of this one or that one that has any leading out to pray for the sick; and others who do not engage in it as zealously as you, are of but little account or have but little influence.

Oh, I saw that this was not all of the requirements of Jesus, and those who pray for the sick are not all who have the faith of Jesus.[6] The faith of Jesus takes in the whole life and divine character of Christ. I saw that you are too

---

[6] The discussion here concerns the interpretation of the expression "the faith of Jesus" appearing in the message of the third angel in Revelation 14:12: "Here is the patience of the saints; here are they that keep the commandments of God, and the faith of Jesus." As Gerard Damsteegt has outlined in his study of early Seventh-day Adventist theological development, there were varying understandings of "the faith of Jesus" in the 1850s, including the idea, apparently held by the Phillipses, that the expression referred exclusively to the healing of the sick.

See: P. Gerard Damsteegt, *Foundations of the Seventh-day Adventist Message and Mission,* p. 194.

exclusive; also Bro. Pierce. You are leaning too much on Sister Phillips. Sr. P. has too much confidence in herself, and you have too much confidence in her judgment, in her feelings. God is willing to teach Bro. Pierce his duty that he may know it for himself. You all go too much by feeling. I saw Bro. Pierce would often try to talk the truth; if he did not have that liberty and success, that freedom he anticipated, he settled down [thinking] that God did not call him to that work. Now, if it had not been for this, Bro. Pierce might have been more useful than he has been.

All, every one of God's called and chosen servants, have had just such times, and if they had followed their feelings, would have given up that that was not the work God had given them to do. But the servants of God will always have obstacles to surmount. But do not yield up readily; keep trying, and plow your way through the darkness. Look away to Jesus, depend on Him entirely.

You follow feelings too much, and if you feel clouds come over you, you let it influence you too much. Feeling is as unsafe a guide as you can follow. You make altogether too much of a happy flight of feeling or a shouting time. These times will come, but they are not always an undoubted evidence that we are right. You have made too much of these seasons, and in some of them there has been a fanatical spirit not in accordance with the spirit of truth. I saw that there was a more useful place for your gifts to be occupied where they can move and stir souls.

Now is the time for God's people not to be in a corner, not where they have been over and over, but where their gifts are new. Bro. Phillips's gift of exhortation is needed. God calls for it. He calls Bro. and Sr. P. to shake themselves from the last and least particle of that spirit that is mentioned above, for it is against the Spirit of God. God is about to work for His people; and great work is being done.

I saw that this call to the Laodicean church will affect souls. A becoming zeal is called for by God on our part. We must repent, throw away our whole feelings, feel our destitution, buy gold that we may be rich, eye salve that we may see, white raiment that we may be clothed.[7] Sr. P., I saw that you had a too high opinion of your own judgment, too much exalted. Bro. Pierce has listened and looked up to you as though your judgment was unerring.

Just so long as you are all so closely shut in with yourselves, your usefulness is comparatively nothing. Your linking together is too close for your own good. Said the angel, Each one strike out on your own individual responsibility as to each other, yet relying wholly upon God for victory. Look away from each other; measure not yourselves by yourselves. Jesus is the pattern; look to Him as the example, not to each other. Lean wholly upon God.

---

[7] *See:* Note 1 above on Laodicea.

Bro. Pierce, you have been silent too much; too much shut up with yourself. In the paper you could speak to hundreds, but you have a few of you contented yourselves together. Your talent, Bro. P., has been almost buried up; it must be brought into use. But you have so little confidence in your own success that if you do not have that freedom that you expect, you sink down and give it up. Arouse, arouse; let not feelings guide you, but a sense of your duty, a sense of the truth, the important truth. Let that influence you and move. Bro. Pierce, your gift is needed.

Bro. Phillips, your gift is needed in exhortation. I saw there had been considerable feeling with you and others in Vt. about the brethren coming West. You have not felt right about the matter. I saw that the great work would be West. Many fields have not yet been visited that should be. It is true that many of those that have moved have not answered the design of God. God directed them to go, but not to do as they have done. After they were West, they should have lived out their faith; but they have acted like drunken men.[8] But God is working for them. They see their sin and error and are laying their possession upon the altar, and preparing to labor for God.

In love.

---

[8] In the mid-1850s a considerable number of believers from New England migrated to what is now called the "Midwest." This resulted, at least temporarily, in dwindling numbers in some New England congregations, and in some cases resentment from those left behind. As one man expressed it: "When the Lord called those dear brethren from Vt., to the West, many were sorely afflicted like myself, and felt as though we were left desolate and forsaken." *Review* editorials, on the other hand, saw the westward movement much more positively, as an opportunity for rapid evangelical growth: "We would say that those in the East, who have toiled year after year to pull a very few souls out of the fire, that the same efforts in the West, or even here in Michigan, would convert twenty to the truth, where you have seen one conversion. . . . No consideration whatever, excepting a sense of positive duty, could induce us at present to labor on the gospel-hardened shores of New England, while so much can be done in the wide West." Meanwhile it was also recognized that some Adventist settlers had moved west mainly out of an expectation of economic gain, and were experiencing spiritual decline.

See: E. L. Barr, "From Bro. Barr," *Review,* Aug. 13, 1857, p. 118; J. W. [James White], "Moving West," *Review,* May 7, 1857, p. 5.

1858

MARCH 2, GREEN SPRING[S], OHIO

LETTER TO

Henry Nichols White and James Edson White.

Original letter is not extant. Published in Ellen G. White, *An Appeal to the Youth,* pp. 42-44.

1858

(Lt 1, 1858)

MARCH 3, GREEN SPRINGS, OHIO[1]

LETTER TO

Mary J. Loughborough.[2]

This letter is published in entirety in Ellen G. White, *Manuscript Releases,* vol. 21, pp. 252-257.

> *An appeal to Mary Loughborough to be willing to sacrifice frequent contact with her husband, relatives, and friends for the sake of her husband's call to a traveling ministry.*

Dear Sister Mary:

We are now at Brother Sharp's [**William D. Sharp**].[3] They have recently

---

[1] This was the first stop for the Whites on a three-week journey to Ohio taking in conferences in Green Springs (Feb. 26-28, 1858), Gilboa (Mar. 6, 7) and Lovett's Grove (Mar. 13, 14). *See:* J. W. [James White], "Meetings in Ohio," *Review,* Mar. 25, 1858, p. 149.

[2] *Identity:* There are numerous indications in this letter that "Sister Mary" is Mary J. Loughborough. These include her marriage to John, a traveling minister, being "pleasantly situated, with a home of your own," and her penchant for Rochester. This corresponds well with Mary Loughborough's marriage to John Loughborough, by this time a prominent itinerant preacher, the fact that the Loughboroughs had recently obtained a house in Battle Creek, Michigan, and that Mary had spent most of her married life in Rochester, New York. For an accessible and detailed account of J. N. Loughborough's life edited from primary sources, giving the biographical details listed above, see Adriel Chilson, ed., *Miracles in My Life: Autobiography of Adventist Pioneer J. N. Loughborough.*

[3] *Identity:* "Brother Sharp" evidently lives in or near Green Springs, Ohio, and has "recently

embraced the truth. Seem to be first-rate people. We have suffered in mind considerably since we have been here. I have felt deep agony of soul. I have looked back at a few past months and as I realize how little I have imitated Jesus' self-sacrificing, devoted life, I am led almost to despair. As I examine the life of our Saviour, the great sacrifice He has made for us, and then be led through His sufferings and anguish, my heart melts within me. Oh, what suffering and agony, endured to save lost and fallen man! And this salvation is extended to us freely if we will accept it, if we will suffer with Christ, deny ourselves for His sake.

Dear Mary, last Monday I was shown in vision some things that bear with weight upon my mind. I was led through the life of Christ to see His meek, self-denying life. This great sacrifice was to obtain for us a great salvation. And if we obtain this great salvation it must be by our making a sacrifice on our part. As Jesus sacrificed for us, we must sacrifice for Jesus. As He denied Himself for us, we must deny ourselves for Jesus. As He endured privation and suffering for us, so we must endure privation and suffering for Jesus. As He was tempted of Satan, as He was buffeted by Satan forty days then left for a season and angels ministered unto Him, so we shall be buffeted by Satan for a season; and if we resist him these seasons will be followed by grace and strength from God imparted unto us by His angels.

As Jesus endured agony and often was in lonely prayer and in agony of spirit, pleading with His Father, so we, if we are truly Christ's followers, will often feel agony of soul and will pour out our earnest prayer to our Father; we shall groan in spirit after God. But these seasons when the soul is enshrouded in darkness will not drive the true Christian from God. I was shown that the disciples of Christ, without an exception, are not their own. Jesus has bought them with a dear sacrifice, His own blood. He claims them. Their time, their strength, are His. Their will, their mind, are subject to His will. Their will is yielded, given up. They wait and watch for the will and counsel of God to be manifested concerning them.

I saw that the will is either submitted to Jesus for Him to govern and lead, or the person retains or sets up his or her own will, not willing to submit to Jesus against his own peculiar desires or will. Then Satan steps in and he molds this will to his own pleasure. Christ or Satan has the government of the will, and we are the subjects of one or the other. I was pointed to Christ. Although

---

embraced the truth." The person most likely corresponding to this description is William D. Sharp. According to his obituary in the *Review* he had moved to Ohio from Connecticut, married in 1851 "at Greenspring, Ohio," and had "accepted the third angel's message in 1858." William Sharp is listed in the 1850 and 1870 censuses of Green Creek township (of which the village of Green Springs is a part), and his place of origin is given as Connecticut.

See: Obituary: "William D. Sharp," *Review,* Jan. 5, 1911, p. 23; 1850 U.S. Federal Census, "William Sharp," Ohio, Sandusky County, Green Creek, p. 884 (443); 1870 U.S. Federal Census, "Wm. D. Sharp," Ohio, Sandusky County, Green Creek, p. 123.

He was tempted of the devil forty days, yet His will was submitted to the will of His Father and He yielded not, although He was tempted in every way by Satan—stronger than any of His disciples have ever been tempted. His will was not yielded to the will of the enemy for a moment.

Now, dear Mary, it is possible for your will to be subject to the will of God. Unless you do yield your will to God, choose His way, His pleasure, His will, instead of your own, I saw that you were none of His. He will not own you, He will not accept you. He leaves you for Satan to take possession of the will that you would not yield to Him, and Satan will mold this will as he pleases. I was shown that the plan of salvation was laid out, and God will not change or deviate in His plan to save any one.

God has made one great condescension to save erring, lost man: He yielded His dearly Beloved from His bosom, to suffer indignity, scorn and hate, to die an ignominious death upon the cross. If any one will be His disciple now he must live a self-denying life. His will must die. The plan of salvation is laid. Now man must condescend, now man must yield. His life must be a continual yielding. God does not deviate or change from His plan at all, to save any. The great condescension has been made. Now it all lies with man, whether he will accept the plan God has laid down, whether he will yield his will to the will of God. God does not change now to accommodate man. He is left now to choose life or death. If he chooses life, he chooses the cross, the suffering, self-denying life of Christ, and he must not go murmuring along at the ruggedness of the way.

The life of Christ and His sacrifice, the Innocent suffering for the guilty, should forever still the least murmur or complaint. It should be accounted a privilege to suffer for Christ and thus glory in the cross of Christ. I saw that He is honored by the lives of those who eagerly lay hold of salvation, those who consider it a privilege to suffer for Jesus.

Mary, dear Mary, I have seen that God's providence has placed John [**John Norton Loughborough**][4] and you where you are. God has been working for you both that you, Mary, may be left without excuse.[5] That time has come.

---

[4] *Identity:* See note 2.

[5] Just 15 months earlier the Loughboroughs had been in a bleak situation, in Waukon, Iowa. Discouragement had led John Loughborough off course from his earlier wholehearted devotion to evangelism. Despite considerable talent as a preacher, by December 1856 Loughborough was low in funds and fully engaged in carpentry, in order to make a living. The visit of the Whites to Waukon in that same month was a decisive turning point for him. "It was on this occasion that I laid up my carpenter tools for good," he writes, and returned to full-time evangelism. The Whites, recognizing Loughbough's strengths and the leading role he could play in the movement, were anxious to settle him and his wife in Battle Creek, the headquarters of the movement. James White had raised funds to buy them a house, and Ellen had solicited bedding and other household essentials for them from friends. From this point of view the situation of the Loughboroughs had been turned around and the potential of a bright future of service lay ahead.

Now it is for you to come up, to eagerly grasp the merits of Christ's blood, lay hold of the plan of salvation, submit your will to the will of God, choose to suffer with Christ or choose your own will, your own way, travel the way of the transgressor and lose eternal life, lose heaven. You can serve God if you will. You can devote yourself to Him and redeem the time.

Mary, dear Mary, if you remain a little longer in your present state I fear that God will not pity, He will not bear always. Mary, I fear for you greatly. I was shown that God lays out the work for John. He must perform it. Just as long as he remains a servant of God he must go at His bidding. God does not lay out His work to gratify the will or pleasure of any. If John should follow as you would wish, follow your will, your pleasure, he is no longer a servant of Jesus Christ; for your will is unsanctified, not subject to God's will. Fearful have been the responsibilities you have been willing to take upon yourself. Only let your will be gratified and you would risk the consequences.

Dear Mary, I saw that you were a slave, yes, a slave, to your own unsubdued will. You are in complete bondage. It holds control and cruel power over you. I saw that your *will*, your *set will*, must die—or your hopes of eternal life; both cannot live at the same time. I was shown that the Lord will lay out the work for John, and you must leave *all* to follow Jesus. Then, Mary, will you realize the blessing of God. Then can you say, The yoke of Christ is easy, His burden light.

I was pointed back and saw some of those that professed to be John's best friends have been frowned upon by God for their close, snug[6] dealing to one of His chosen servants. Verily, they will have their reward. John has been moved this way and that in doubt and perplexity, but God has wrested him out of the hand of those that would have his labors for nought, those that have been willing to add additional burdens to those that God has laid upon him, those that would be unmoved if they saw him working with his hands;[7] and the Lord in His wise and merciful providence provided him a place of rest, a field of labor where many will appreciate and be benefited by his labor.

Mary, your will has often pulled John one way, when God directed him in another. You have operated in opposition to the will and way of God. I saw all these years that your life has been linked with John you could have been a coworker with John, laying up for yourself a reward. But for the sake

---

See: J. N. Loughborough, *Rise and Progress of the Seventh-day Adventists,* p. 211; J. N. Loughborough, "Sketches of the Past—No. 105," *Pacific Union Recorder,* Sept. 8, 1910, p. 2; Ellen G. White, Lt 5, 1857 (Nov. 22).

[6] In the sense of "deceptive."

[7] The reference here seems to be to John Loughborough's coming to Waukon in October 1856 and having to work at carpentry to support his family. Loughborough says that J. N. Andrews (who had already been in Waukon for a year) "invited" him to come to Iowa. Whether Ellen White has Andrews in mind as one of those "that would have his labors for nought" is difficult to tell.

See: J. N. Loughborough, "Sketches of the Past—No. 101," *Pacific Union Recorder,* Aug. 4, 1910, p. 7.

of gratifying a special desire or will of your own, you have murdered your way along,[8] making yourself miserable by your lack of consecration and often embittering John's life and making him miserable.[9]

You can make John happy that he ever saw you and that you ever linked your life with his wandering life. You chose him, a messenger of God. You knew his calling.[10] I saw your life was an unpleasant one before you chose John. You can make him regret his connection by your following your own way and pleasure. John is mortal. He has loved you, Mary; do not drive him to regret his choice. God's eye is upon every movement, every act. You can redeem the time and make a straight work for eternity. Yield your will to the will of Christ and all will be well. Think not the way of salvation is a hard way. Look, look at the life of Christ. What suffering endured for man!

Mary, you must die to Rochester [New York].[11] It will only be to the injury of yourself and others in your present state to visit Rochester. God has been reaching down His hand to save you. It was God's will that you should not go to Rochester last fall; it would have proved your ruin. John would have been driven from the field to laboring with his hands. God would not have it so. He laid out the work for John, to save you both. I saw that you can never have the light of God's countenance until you acknowledge the hand of God in all this. He has wrought for you, but you have shut your eyes to His work. If you humbly submit to God, then will it please God to have you visit Rochester, for you can glorify God. I saw that John must fix his eye upon his captain, Jesus, follow the counsel of God, whether it meets your will or not. He must be steadfast. His course must be fixed, but with the greatest tenderness and care should he deal with Mary, never wounding with words, but yet be decided.

---

[8] An archaic expression with the sense of "acted wretchedly."

[9] The insights given here into John Loughborough's difficult home situation may explain some of the "discouragement" that he confesses to having had in the autumn of 1856 that led him to migrate to Iowa, apparently without the endorsement of the Whites. Although in his memoirs Loughborough cites financial reasons for his discouragement, pressure from his wife may also have played a part.

See: Ibid.

[10] The Loughboroughs married in 1851 and did not become Sabbathkeeping Adventists until the following year. However, John had been preaching for the "First-day Adventists," as he called them, since 1849 (three weeks before his seventeenth birthday), and was an established lay preacher by the time they married two years later.

See: Adriel Chilson, ed., *Miracles in My Life,* pp. 11-17.

[11] Even though the Loughboroughs were comfortably situated in their own house in Battle Creek, Mary apparently longed to be near friends and relatives in Rochester, New York. After leaving Waukon a few months earlier, in October 1857, Mary had seemed determined to move back to Rochester, whatever the consequences for John and his work. Ellen White's vision of November 1857, showing that "it was not Mary's duty to go East," appeared for a while to have made Mary resigned to settling down in Battle Creek, but by March 1858, the date of this letter, she was struggling over the same issue again.

See: Ellen G. White, Lt 6, 1854 (winter); Lt 5, 1857 (Nov. 22).

Mary, dear Mary, do consecrate yourself to God; then can you be happy; then can His Spirit rest upon you. Mary, I feel the deepest interest for you. I love you. I know that your happiness depends upon the course of your action. And unless it is entirely different in many respects than it has been, you cannot have life, have salvation. I have written this letter sadly, discouragingly. My heart aches while I write. Gladly would I write encouragingly if I had it to write. I was in hopes that God would never give me another message for you.[12] I fear the use you will make of it, and it will prove a savor of death unto death.[13] Mary, I have felt agony of soul. I have cried in agony for above an hour.

Mary, your only happiness is in submitting to God. Will you submit to Him? Will you yield to the claims of salvation? If you get right before God, it will be His will to have John labor some in Rochester; but if you go there with John, your heart not right in the sight of God, your influence would not be saving. The enemies of God and the truth would exult, John's soul would be weighed down in anguish, and it would be of no avail for him to labor. If you are united in the work of God, trusting in Him, your will in subjection to God's will, then acknowledge the leading of God and His will concerning you, and you will gain a victory not to be easily lost.

The time has come when God must be glorified by a humble acknowledgment that His way and will is to be preferred to your own way and will, and your unconsecrated will yielded. The time has come now when you can establish yourself in the hearts of the brethren and sisters, when you can form a character. All have felt to pity and sympathize with you on account of your situation. Now the Lord has safely and happily delivered you. You are pleasantly situated, with a home of your own. You are without an excuse. God does not require John to place himself under embarrassment and trial and want for the sake of gratifying an unconsecrated desire or will that, if followed, will lead to certain death.

I saw that John must be free and follow his conviction of right. He has been tossed about, not knowing which way to go or what to do. God has chosen for him a place, situated you both comfortably, and his mind now is at rest, and God will lead him in a straight path, and he must follow. You have no friends or relatives that are too dear to sacrifice or leave for God, to obey or follow Him. If you love them more than Jesus, you are not worthy of Him,

---

[12] Two earlier letters on the theme of Mary's lack of total commitment, one from 1854 and one from 1857, have been preserved.

See: Ellen G. White, Lt 6, 1854 (winter); Lt 5, 1857 (Nov. 22).

[13] A reference to 2 Corinthians 2:15, 16: "For we are . . . a sweet savour of Christ, in them that are saved, and in them that perish: To the one we are the savour of death unto death; and to the other the savour of life unto life." Mary can either accept the appeal and it will be to her a "savour of life," or she can reject it and it will become a "savour of death."

and will have no part with Jesus. Here is a sacrifice to make right here. The heart will govern the mind. Have your heart right and consecrated and there will be no trouble with your will. I speak plainly. I look upon you as in the greatest danger. I want to save you. I beg of you to submit to God. There is no more required of you than is required of every Christian. Will you obey the requirements? Will you submit to God?

Mary, I will ever be your true friend. I will love you. I will do all in my power for you; but to encourage you to do wrong, I never shall. John, I saw that James [**James Springer White**] and you, as ministers of Jesus Christ, must watch your words, and your minds must dwell upon the truth.[14] Whoever you are with, don't talk at random. Let your words be solemn. The day of the Lord is at hand. I was pointed to the life of John the Baptist.[15] His life was without pleasure. It was sorrowful and self-denying. He proclaimed Christ's advent and then could not see and enjoy the power manifested by Christ. He knew that when Jesus should fully establish Himself as a Teacher he must die. He was cruelly beheaded. I saw that the least disciple that followed Jesus, witnessed His miracles, heard the comforting words that fell from His lips, was greater than John the Baptist; that is, more exalted and honored, had more pleasure in his life.

We are proclaiming Christ's second advent. Our walk should be sober; our conversation upon Jesus, upon the truth; and we should glory in the cross of Christ.

I have written in great haste. Have not time to look over and correct mistakes. Reserve no copy, so you must preserve this for me again.

In love.

---

[14] The last few lines are addressed to John Loughborough. Since moving to Battle Creek in November 1857, John Loughborough had gone out to preach with James White on a number of weekends in towns such as Monterey, Otsego, Jackson, and Hillsdale, all within a 50-mile (80-kilometer) radius of Battle Creek. They also had plans to conduct a series of conferences in New York State during the spring (which never materialized, because of lack of funds).

See: J. N. Loughborough, James White, "Appointments," *Review,* Nov. 19, 1857, p. 16; *idem,* "Appointments," Dec. 17, 1857, p. 48; "Appointments," *Review*, Jan. 28, 1858, p. 96; J. N. Loughborough, "Conferences in New York," *Review,* Apr. 1, 1858, p. 160.

[15] In *Spiritual Gifts [vol. 1],* pp. 29, 30, Ellen White reused the next few lines in writing on the life of John the Baptist. Her description of John's "sorrowful" life has been contrasted by some with later statements that speak of the joy he experienced in his life mission. Such statements should be viewed as complementary. Although John's life was without the pleasures associated with the "enjoyments and luxuries of life," and he was denied the privilege of sharing in Christ's miraculous ministry, Ellen White recognized that true joy is not constrained by one's circumstances. She brought both perspectives together when she wrote, "Aside from the joy that John found in his mission, his life had been one of sorrow" (*The Desire of Ages,* pp. 101, 220).

1858

(Lt 2, 1858)

[CIRCA MARCH 1858],[1] N.P.

LETTER TO

Azmon Woodruff.[2]

This letter is published in entirety in Ellen G. White, *Manuscript Releases,* vol. 21, pp. 258, 259.

Problems of "wrangling and strife" in churches of Oswego County, New York.

Dear Brother Woodruff:

I have seen things on the very points you have mentioned in your letter[3] and at the time I had the vision for those in New York.[4] I saw a few individual cases. I saw especially the cases of Brother Chapel and wife [**Levi R.** and **Eliza Chapel**],[5] Brother Treadwell [**Wiliam Treadwell**],[6] Manley Ross [**Manley T.**

---

[1] The original/earliest copy gives no date or place of writing. The letter must, however, have been written after the vision at Green Springs, Ohio (see par. 3), that, as argued in note 8, was received on March 1, 1858. Exactly how long after that date this letter was written is not known, but the context suggests a short time span, hence "circa March 1858."

[2] *Identity:* Helping to identify "Brother Woodruff" is the information given that he was living in Oswego County, New York. The only Woodruff appearing in the *Review* during this period who lived in Oswego County was Azmon (or Azmond) Woodruff, of Palermo, New York.

See: 1860 U.S. Federal Census, "Azmon Woodruff," New York, Oswego County, Palermo, p. 831; search term "Woodruff" in *Words of the Pioneers.*

[3] This letter is not in the White Estate archives.

[4] This vision, as evident from the next two paragraphs, was received before the Green Springs, Ohio, vision of March 1, 1858 (see note 8). The vision that best matches the description found here is that given on July 6, 1857 (Lt 8, 1857 [July 19]) "for the church in New York," that focused on the believers in Roosevelt, Oswego County. It specifically mentioned Brethren Treadwell, Finch, and Chapel, all of whom also feature in this letter.

[5] *Identity:* The strong suggestion in this letter that Brother Chapel was living in Oswego County, New York, provides useful evidence of his identity. Among the several Chapels mentioned in the *Review* from this time, only L. R. Chapel had an Oswego County address. His wife's name was found in census records.

See: 1850 U.S. Federal Census, "Levi R. Chapel," New York, Oswego County, Palermo, p. 33; search term "Chapel" in *Words of the Pioneers.*

[6] *Identity:* Without doubt, "Brother Treadwell" is William Treadwell, for no other Treadwell is mentioned in the *Review* throughout this period. William Treadwell's address is there given as "Gilbert's Mills, N.Y.," which further confirms his identity, since Gilbert's Mills is in Oswego County, the focus of this letter.

See: Search term "Treadwell" in *Words of the Pioneers.*

Ross], also Truman Finch [**Truman P. Finch**], who were the active ones in this matter. They have erred in feeling as they have felt, and the influence I saw was deathly.

When in Ohio[7] I saw again the wretched state of things in New York. Satan was standing right in your midst, his evil angels exulting that through his temptations—exalting some and tempting others to be very strenuous, professing zeal for the truth and crowding your brethren, thrusting with side and with shoulder, bringing a reproach upon the truth, making yourself a stink to the places around you—you make the truth disgusting, make it an abhorrence. You are as a people accountable to God for the wretched influence cast against the truth.

I saw that Brother Chapel and wife, Brother Treadwell and others with them, have not seen themselves. They must see their wrong course in being so exacting and watching their brethren to magnify their wrongs. Their own hearts must have a work; self must die with them, and they must possess more of a spirit to live and let live. I saw while at Green Springs, Ohio,[8] that the evil angels had much to do with the brethren in Oswego County [New York]. I saw that the holy angels had one after another left you, grieved, displeased, and disgusted with your wrangling and strife.[9] There is the vision I wrote after the meeting. I will copy it:

"I saw that the cause of God had been cursed in Oswego County by wrangling and strife. Some will have to unlearn almost all they have been learning for years, for it has been strife, debate, and to smite with a fist of wickedness. I saw that some have placed themselves in a position to watch others, when God has not placed them on the watchtower at all. They have

---

[7] *See:* Note 8.

[8] The only known visit by Ellen White to Green Springs, Ohio, during the 1850s or 1860s, took place February 26-March 3, 1858. While there she received a vision on March 1. No earlier copy is extant for the portion copied in the remainder of this letter.

See: James White, "Appointments," *Review,* Feb. 18, 1858, p. 120; Ellen G. White, Lt 1, 1858 (Mar. 3).

[9] The problem of "wrangling and strife" among members in Oswego County, was not a new one. The Roosevelt church in particular seems to have been implicated. In July 1856 Amanda Westcott wrote of internal dissension in Roosevelt, a full-day church "trial," and the division of the church into two factions. Union seems to have been restored only after intervention from "Bro. Sperry of Vt." One year later conditions appear to have deteriorated. Ellen White writes of faultfinding (with special mention of Finch and Chapel) and numerous church trials in Roosevelt through which "the professed people of God have disgraced themselves in the eyes of the world" (Lt 8, 1857 [July 19]). Ironically, the "Laodicean" call to the churches "be zealous . . . and repent" (Rev. 3:19) that had gone out in the late autumn of 1856 seems in certain cases to have led to an increase in dissension and church trials. The problem was that some members had interpreted the Laodicean message as a call to watch for faults among fellow members rather than to repent of their own shortcomings.

See: Amanda Westcott to Mrs. Crawford, July 16, 1856; Ellen G. White, Lt 8, 1857 (July 19); Lt 17, 1859 (Oct. 28); EGWEnc, s.v. "Laodicean Message."

climbed up there themselves and must come down. Some have noticed little things in the house, in dress, the manners, and have reproved and ordered about this, that, and the other. It only hurts their influence and places the individual beyond the reach of their help.

"It is the duty of preachers to talk the truth, but when they come down from the work to reprove for little things, to bend the individual to see as they see, to feel as they feel, they take upon them the work that belongs to the Spirit of God. I saw that all have something to learn, an experience to obtain for themselves, and if the servants of God stand ready to reprove for all these little things, they will try to please the servants of God and yet they have not learned by their own convictions that these things are wrong.[10] Their experience depends upon the one that reproved them. They look to and depend upon him to have an experience for them. Their trust and dependence is taken from God.

"That is why they are so weak in New York. They fear the servants of God and one another. Their experience grows out of this fear and they do not form a religious character for themselves. They do not have an individual, independent experience. They learn to look to man instead of to God and are bent this way and that way, but are not steadfast, strong in a living experience they have obtained for themselves.

"Something must be done for the individual by the Lord. They must learn to look to God for duty, not to their minister or brethren, and when an individual strives to bend his brethren to his own peculiar notions or ideas of things, he takes that upon him which God has not laid upon him. Minds are differently constituted; they cannot run in the same channel of ideas or impressions. I saw that it was notions and ideas that some think others must be brought to, that has destroyed spirituality and independent experience in New York. There is a depending upon one another for light and blessing. They have not learned to look to God for duty and counsel in this thing. Do you say in New York, man is made to lose his identity and is made a mere thing to be moved by another's mind, another's experience? God will surely judge for these things."

---

[10] One of the preachers probably alluded to here is **Samuel W. Rhodes**, who had worked extensively among the Oswego churches. "Many have depended on you to have an experience for them," Ellen White wrote to Rhodes in 1859, "because you have told them what they *must* do, and what they *must* not do. . . . You have . . . descended to little particulars, and entered into family matters that in no way concerned you."

See: Ellen G. White, Lt 16, 1859 (Oct. 28).

1858

APRIL 15

"A Warning."

Published in *Advent Review, and Sabbath Herald,* vol. 11, no. 22, April 15, 1858, p. 174.

1858

APRIL

"Bereavement."

Published in *The Youth's Instructor,* vol. 6, no. 4, April 1858, p. 29.

1858

SEPTEMBER

PUBLICATION OF

Spiritual Gifts [vol. 1], Battle Creek, Michigan.

Published by Steam Press of the *Review and Herald* Office. 219 pp.

1858

OCTOBER 21, MANNSVILLE, NEW YORK

LETTER TO

Brother and Sister ———.

Nonextant letter published in Ellen G. White, *Testimony for the Church,* No. 5 (Battle Creek, Mich.: Steam Press of the *Review and Herald* Office, 1859), pp. 26-32. [Ellen G. White, *Testimonies for the Church,* vol. 1, pp. 204-209.]

1858

(Ms 2, 1858)

DECEMBER 27,[1] BATTLE CREEK, MICHIGAN

Testimony Regarding the Work in Vermont, New Hampshire, and Massachusetts.

This manuscript is published in entirety in Ellen G. White, *Manuscript Releases,* vol. 21, pp. 373-377.

Oppositional elements in Massachusetts and New Hampshire: The cases of J. C. Day, S. N. Haskell, and Stephen Smith.

---

[1] The original/earliest copy gives only "December 27," omitting the year. References to the decline of the *Messenger* Party (see EGWEnc) indicate that this manuscript was probably written in the period 1857-1860. A more precise date seems to be promised in the opening statement that the testimony here recorded was "shown in vision while at Mansville, New York." The Whites visited Mannsville (the usual spelling) three times during this period—in 1857, 1858, and 1861. However, the records mention a vision only on the occasion of the 1858 meeting. Strengthening the case for 1858 is the fact that the 1858 vision, as published in *Testimonies for the Church,* vol. 1, pp. 204-209, shows some similarities to parts of this manuscript. The notes that follow assume an 1858 date.

For mentions of the three visits to Mannsville, see James White, J. N. Loughborough, "Appointments," *Review,* Sept. 30, 1858, p. 152; J. W. [James White], "Eastern Tour," *Review,* Dec. 1, 1859, p. 12; J. N. Loughborough, Isaac Sanborn, "Appointments," *Review,* July 16, 1861, p. 56. For accounts of Ellen White's vision at Mannsville in 1858, see Ellen G. White, *Testimonies for the Church,* vol. 1, pp. 204-209; J. N. Loughborough, *The Great Second Advent Movement,* p. 337.

I was shown in vision while at Mansville, New York,[2] the state of things in the east, especially in the states Vermont, New Hampshire, and Massachusetts. I saw that the course of J. C. Day [**John C. Day**], while among the Messenger advocates,[3] was cruel, crooked, and wicked; that people were composed of dissatisfied ones who would not bear reproof,[4] but considered their judgment better than that of their brethren who had an experience in the truth and the cause of God. These unruly spirits came together and united together to work or fight against those whom God had raised up to stand in defense of His truth. Satan and his angels were at war with them, fighting against them, and these people were co-workers with Satan and the evil angels. Falsehoods and lies would be formed by Satan's children, and this people loved them and eagerly reported them to others. J. C. Day was one of these; if he did not make the lies, he loved them.

I saw the angels of God grieved and they followed their commission to mark every falsehood, every thrust, every stain put upon the defenders of God's truth. Every bitter feeling, every feeling of hate, they were to record, for they would meet it again. I saw J. C. Day strengthening the hands of wicked men, trying to tear away the confidence of God's people in us and in the visions.[5]

---

[2] James and Ellen White visited Mannsville, New York, for a few days starting October 19, 1858, in the course of a two-month itinerary through Ohio, New York, and several New England states. "The Lord has seen fit in His goodness to give me a vision at this place," Ellen White noted on October 21, 1858. According to J. N. Loughborough, who accompanied the Whites, the vision was given before a "large assembly."

See: James White, J. N. Loughborough, "Appointments," *Review,* Sept. 30, 1858, p. 152; Ellen G. White, *Testimonies for the Church,* vol. 1, pp. 204-209; J. N. Loughborough, *The Great Second Advent Movement,* p. 337.

[3] John C. Day had joined the Sabbatarian Adventists in 1851 but defected to the breakaway *Messenger* Party in 1854 or 1855. By October 1856, however, he had returned to the Sabbatarian Adventists and written a contrite letter to the *Review* asking "forgiveness . . . of the entire church."

See: John C. Day, "Letter From Bro. Day," *Review,* Oct. 9, 1856, p. 184.

[4] The best known examples of persons who "would not bear reproof" were **Hiram Case** and **Charles P. Russell**, founders of the *Messenger* Party. J. C. Day may also have held a grudge against the visions, dating back to 1852. In 1852 J. C. Day had been actively discouraged by the Whites from continuing his traveling ministry which he had apparently engaged in since accepting the Sabbath in 1851. In vision Ellen White "saw that he [Day] has been mistaken and thought God had a greater work for him to do than He had ever laid upon him." It is possible that Day was offended by this vision and that this was one reason for his subsequent defection.

While it is true that anti-White, anti-vision sentiments were prominent in the *Messenger* Party, these did not constitute its entire platform. Other significant theological differences also emerged. Thus the "Age-to-Come" view of the judgment and millennium, which differed fundamentally from the eschatology of Sabbatarian Adventists, became an important plank of the *Messenger* Party after the accession of J. M. Stephenson and D. P. Hall in 1855 or 1856.

See: EGWEnc, s.v. "*Messenger* Party"; SDAE, s.v. "*Messenger* Party"; John C. Day, "Letter From Bro. Day," *Review,* Oct. 9, 1856, p. 184; Ellen G. White, Lt 4, 1852 (Oct. 25).

[5] Day later professed himself "sorry from my heart . . . for many things I have written for the 'Messenger,' especially those pieces in which I have written anything against Bro. or Sr.

Then I was shown that as the Messenger people could not make their rebellious feelings and spirit do the work they wished it should—get down the *Review*—they ceased, in a measure, from their work.[6] Some gave up the Sabbath, others changed their evil course and fully united with God's people. Others did not see the wickedness of their course and never made thorough work or repented heartily of their evil work. Pardon was written against the names of those who made thorough work, but if they again fall into a like snare and pursue an evil course, all their past evil is remembered against them.

Some, I saw, seemed to others to make thorough work. But that God who reads the heart knew that the seeds of rebellion were within them, and by their names was written, "Unstable souls, who wrest the truth to their own destruction."

I saw that J. C. Day had never realized that he had been a close co-worker with Satan and his evil angels. If he had realized this, he would not have fallen into such a snare. I saw while attending the meeting at Lancaster, [Massachusetts,][7] that if J. C. Day made thorough work he could still be of some use to fill in here and there; but God would never suffer him to take charge of His flock or to travel from place to place, to any extent, to talk the truth. If he lived a life of repentance from that time until Jesus comes, he could not undo the evil he had done.

While at Mansville I saw that in no way should the least charge of the flock rest upon J. C. Day, for he had weakened himself by his former course

---

White." (The "Messenger" refers to *The Messenger of Truth,* a paper issued by the *Messenger* Party.)

See: John C. Day, "Letter From Bro. Day," *Review,* Oct. 9, 1856, p. 184.

[6] The *"Messenger of Truth"* ceased publication in 1857 or 1858. One of the objectives of this publication was to bring down and supersede the *Review*, a goal which editor C. P. Russell thought could be achieved in three months after the start of publication in 1854. James White reported in January 1858 that "not one of the eighteen messengers" that the *Messenger* Party "once boasted . . . is now bearing a public testimony, and there is not one place of regular meeting to our knowledge among them east or west."

See: C. P. Russell, "From Bro. Russell," *The Messenger of Truth,* Nov. 2, 1854, n. p.; J. N. Andrews, R. F. Cottrell, U. Smith, "Malicious Insinuation," *Review,* Nov. 21, 1854, p. 117; J. W. [James White], "A Sketch of the Rise and Progress of the Present Truth," *Review,* Jan. 14, 1858, p. 77; J. N. Loughborough, *Rise and Progress of Seventh-day Adventists,* p. 217.

[7] The only meetings known to have been attended by the Whites up to this time in "Lancaster" were the tent meetings held in Lancaster, Massachusetts, 18 months earlier, in May 1857. James White noted that Ellen White had received a vision during these meetings. "The Spirit of the Lord came down upon us on Sabbath afternoon, and the Lord there pled with his people, as it were, face to face." It is also of interest to note that J. C. Day lived in Lancaster and would most probably have met the Whites on this occasion. This is hinted at in James White's observation that he and Ellen had met "with those who had said forgive us for our alienations from the cause, and who repeated the same in tears."

See: O. Nichols, "Change of Appointment," *Review,* May 14, 1857, p. 16; J. W. [James White], "Eastern Tour," *Review,* May 28, 1857, p. 36; search terms "J. C. Day" and "John C. Day" in *Words of the Pioneers.*

in co-working with the evil angels, and he was weak and subject to their suggestions and evil power. The only chance for his salvation now was to live a life of repentance and be subject to the church and not confide in his own judgment or opinion. I saw that a rebellious spirit has been within him, and when he could find a willing ear how quickly would suspicion, jealousy, doubt, and an evil, lying report be poured into that ear.[8] Oh, the evil course! Death has marked his track!

I saw that if J. C. Day and others who have been connected with him, could have drawn off a company with them, how quickly would it have been done; and there would have been a class worse than the former disaffected ones to work their work of death. But they find these things will not go, and they settle back wishing to be again in union with the church and ready at a fit opportunity to rebel again.

I then saw **Stephen Haskell** [**Stephen N. Haskell**] and wife [**Mary E. Haskell**]. Said the angel, "He is not sound in the faith. Mark them that cause division among you. An undercurrent is at work. They are coworkers with the evil angels and know it not. Confusion and a deathly [word missing] mark their track." I saw that the views that Stephen Haskell and his wife have advocated concerning mortifying the flesh[9] are all erroneous and will lead to deadly evils and the destruction of souls, and instead of increasing moral purity will hasten and strengthen moral pollution. Said the angel, "God reads the heart." I saw that S. Haskell has tried to make it appear that he was in union with the church when it was not the case. He has scattered evil, error, and division every place he has entered, and this has been in a sly undercurrent that has been at work to destroy confidence in the visions and in those who have the charge of the work at Battle Creek.[10]

---

[8] J. C. Day's instability can be seen in that after returning to the Sabbatarian Adventists in 1856 he again defected in the early 1860s, this time to join the offshoot movement of Gilbert Cranmer in Michigan, a forerunner to the Church of God (7th Day). In 1864 Day expressed his opposition to Ellen White's visions in Cranmer's paper *Hope of Israel,* classing himself with "those who have been cast off because they have dared to express their doubts as to the inspiration of E. G. White's visions."

See: Richard C. Nickels, *A History of the Seventh Day Church of God,* p. 44.

[9] Although S. N. Haskell later provided many years of distinguished leadership to the church, the comments made here indicate that the early years after his adoption of the Sabbath in 1853 or 1854 were problematic. The matter of the Haskells' advocacy of "mortifying the flesh" seems at least in part to be related to denying themselves "wholesome food" (see two paragraphs on) as a religious duty. No further details are given here but Ellen White elaborates on this theme in a letter to "Brother and Sister A" published in 1859 (*Testimonies for the Church,* vol. 1, pp. 204-209). Some have argued that "Brother and Sister A" are in fact the Haskells.

See: EGWEnc, s.v. "Stephen N. Haskell."

[10] Some years later S. N. Haskell in a published statement confessed that "after I first embraced the present truth, and heard of Bro. and Sr. White . . . my mind became very much prejudiced against them, especially against Bro. White. . . . I was prepared to look upon every move of his with suspicion and jealousy." Haskell attributed his negativity to the Whites to the

These things are all marked by God. S. Haskell and his wife have strengthened the hands of Stephen Smith [**Stephen Smith**][11] in his rebellion, and have strengthened the hands of other disaffected ones, and have affected some conscientious souls who were constantly fearful that they should not do everything they could to deny self. They have drunk down his errors that he has talked to them, and these errors have been scattered here and there all around where he has traveled; coworker with the evil angels.

I saw that as God gave His beloved sleep, so He was willing they should have nourishing, strengthening food, and I saw that if S. Haskell and his wife were baptized with the third angel's message they would see enough precious, saving truth to dwell upon, and they would not have time to dwell upon error, dangerous error, and scatter it among God's people. I saw that if God has important truth He will give it to His people, not to two or three solitary individuals and leave all the rest of His people in darkness. The third angel is leading out a people and fitting them for translation. They are to be purified through the truth.

Some, I saw, had made crosses for themselves and killing duties to break down their will over. But I saw that there were crosses and duties enough in God's Word to slay every individual without getting new duties or tests. I saw that a time of trouble was before us, when stern necessity will compel the people of God to live on bread and water; but I saw that God did not require His people to live so now.

God commands that all whom He has not especially called to labor in word and doctrine should labor with their hands [doing] the thing that is good, and supply their own necessities, and have wherewith to bestow upon others. And I saw that it was the will of God that they should eat wholesome food to strengthen the system or the temple of God. But in the time of trouble none will labor with their hands. Their sufferings will be mental, and God will provide food for them.

---

fact that he had become "acquainted with those who were their enemies." Included among these acquaintances was probably J. C. Day, described earlier. J. C. Day and S. N. Haskell would have had ample opportunity to meet as they both lived in Worcester County, Massachusetts, during the latter 1850s.

Concerning Haskell's lack of union with the Battle Creek leadership, he later recalled how, in the late 1850s, "I preached, organized churches and Sabbath Schools, ordained elders . . . but I was not even licensed. Did not know it was necessary to have a license to preach." Haskell's reconciliation with the Whites and Battle Creek can be traced in the letters he sent to the *Review* between November 1859 and June 1863, that, though worded generally, seem to reflect his own situation. In 1862, for the first time, he writes positively of the value of "the gift of prophecy, in correcting wrongs," and in 1863 he speaks of "the folly of steering through these last-day perils on an independent train," adding that "many of us here in the East have much to learn."

See: John Nevins Andrews et al., *Defense of Elder James White and Wife,* p. 33; S. N. Haskell to W. W. Prescott, Aug. 23, 1907, in Ella M. Robinson, *S. N. Haskell Man of Action,* p. 26; S. N. Haskell, "Self," *Review,* Nov. 10, 1859, p. 198; *idem,* "From Bro. Haskell," *Review,* Aug. 19, 1862, p. 95; *idem,* "From Bro. Haskell," *Review,* June 23, 1863, p. 31.

[11] *See*: Notes 14, 15.

I saw that God also enjoined cleanliness upon His ancient Israel, and God is no less particular now than He was then. He enjoins upon His people in the latter day strict cleanliness of body and clothing and purity of mind, of thoughts, and of words, for He is to translate them to heaven.[12]

I saw that if Stephen Haskell had spent his time in laboring with his hands, which he has spent in traveling, it would have been much more pleasing to God.[13] I saw that he had done much more hurt than two or three to follow after him could undo, because evil grows of itself, and when once it has taken root it thrives; but good has to be continually nourished and cherished in order to live. Evil is like weeds in a garden that need no nourishing but will grow rank. Unless the precious plants are constantly cherished and dug about, the weeds rise higher than the precious plants, shut out the sun from them, and they grow sickly and die.

I saw that those who sow error cannot root it up in years. They may perhaps change their course of action, but never can they bend or change the minds of those whom they have influenced in the wrong. Their errors are growing in the minds of others, and if Jesus is so merciful as to blot out the transgressions of those who have sown this seed, and save them, they will suffer loss; they can but save their own souls. Their course has wounded the cause of God and brought shame upon the name of Jesus, and this is not easily wiped away. It lives in the minds of many.

I saw the course Stephen Smith [**Stephen Smith**] has pursued. He has been a co-worker with the evil angels. I saw that he was first a co-worker with the evil angels when he went into the "spiritual second advent,"[14] and then many other errors were received by him. The enemy has had easier access to him. Repeatedly has he joined the enemy's ranks and strengthened the hands

---

[12] *See:* Ms 2, 1853 (Mar. 1), note 3.

[13] Haskell had preached on a part-time lay basis both before and after becoming a Sabbathkeeper in the early 1850s. His occupation in the 1860 census is listed as master roofer. Haskell's "traveling" ministry, mentioned here, was probably minor or unreported since the *Review* contains little mention of such travels during the 1850s.

See: 1860 U.S. Federal Census, "Stephen Haskell," Massachusetts, Worcester County, Worcester, Ward 7, p. 143; search term "S. N. Haskell" in *Words of the Pioneers;* EGWEnc, s.v. "Stephen Haskell."

[14] Following the "Great Disappointment" of October 22, 1844, when the Second Advent did not literally take place, a minority of Millerites took the position that Christ had come on that date, but "spiritually." Some of these so-called spiritualizers adopted bizarre practices, but it was a short-lived phenomenon that had dissipated by 1846 or 1847. We know little about Stephen Smith before he became a Sabbathkeeper about 1850. However, a letter from Smith to the *Voice of Truth* paper in 1845 shows that he was active in the Millerite movement. Ellen White's statement here together with some mentions in the *Review* indicate that he subsequently became a "spiritualizer" for a period during the latter 1840s.

See: George R. Knight, *Millennial Fever,* pp. 245-263; David Tallmadge Arthur, "'Come Out of Babylon,'" pp. 108-112; Stephen Smith, "Boat Delusion," *Voice of Truth,* Apr. 9, 1845, p. 13; James White, "Eastern Tour," *Review,* Nov. 8, 1853, p. 140.

of the wicked. Every time he has fallen he has grown weaker and was more easily again a subject to the temptations and power of the evil angels.

I saw that he had taken a dreadful course against the defenders of God's truth. While he was in the "new time"[15] he ranted on, railed out against the truth and God's chosen servants. Bitter and cruel were his words. He spent his substance in the enemy's ranks and was a co-worker with the evil angels.

As that excitement dies down, again he begins to reflect upon the truth, and finally the truth melts him. He feels his wayward course some, and knows he is liable to fall again. He is not yet converted to the truth. He feels the need of help. As God shows his case in vision his unsubdued feelings arise. Oh, then if there is a faithful, experienced friend near, he can help him so that he will be enabled to see the way God is working and the humble course he must take. But an independent, self-sufficient spirit comes over him.

Evil angels are tugging at his heartstrings, and J. C. Day and others help them. They whisper their suspicions and surmisings together. Evil reports are related by them both. They strengthen each other's hands, they love the lies they have heard, and as they journey to the Sutton, [Vermont,] Conference[16] such conversation as they have together, such evil communications! Angels heard it all, witnessed all, and it is written, to be met by them again. When they came to the Sutton meeting they were no more prepared to work for God than while they were in sympathy with the Messenger [Party]. The seeds of rebellion have sprung up within them and are now yielding a flourishing crop. Evil angels exulted over them: Satan triumphed. I saw other individuals also engaged in this work and affected by the spirit of death and Satan that has been at work.

I saw that these individuals would never be entrusted with the care of the flock. If they can occupy a humble position, labor with their hands and take care of their own souls and live a life of repentance till Jesus comes, they will do all that God requires of them; and if they seek meekness, seek righteousness, it may be they may be hid in the day of the Lord's fierce anger. I saw the cruel, wicked words Stephen Smith has spoken in his self-sufficient, reckless manner. Said the angel, "God will not be trifled with. Will God select such changeable, wavering ones to lead His flock? Never, never."

---

[15] No doubt a reference to Stephen Smith's earlier support for 1854 as the date of the Second Advent. Although consistently resisted and refuted in the *Review*, the 1854 date was championed with some success by a non-Sabbatarian Adventist paper, the *World's Crisis.* David Arthur, a Millerite scholar, calls the 1854 movement "the most formidable time movement since 1844."

See: Stephen Smith, "Returning to the Ranks," *Review,* Feb. 19, 1857, p. 126; O. Nichols, "New Time Theory," *Review,* Mar. 14, 1854, p. 59; Uriah Smith, "The Sanctuary," *Review,* Apr. 4, 1854, pp. 85, 86; David Tallmadge Arthur, "'Come Out of Babylon,'" p. 283.

[16] There is no way of determining which of several conferences in Sutton, Vermont, is being referred to here. The most recent had been held one year earlier, December 18-21, 1857.

See: E. L. Barr, "Appointments," *Review,* Dec. 3, 1857, p. 32.

God's wisdom is unsearchable, and He will not entrust the care of precious souls to those who are subject to erroneous evil influences. God will entrust His flock only to those who have depth of experience, substantial souls of excellent judgment, who can see evil as it hangs over the flock instead of being the first to plunge into it.

I saw the individuals mentioned in this letter were looking to Battle Creek and were jealous and suspicious of the work there and were exciting prejudice in others' minds about the individuals there who have charge of the work. They would put their hands in to mold the work there. I saw that the Captain of the Lord's Host has charge of the work there and that He watches over the individuals to whom this work is entrusted. And the Lord's Captain needs not the interference of any of these individuals who are like the waves of the sea, tossed to and fro, subject to the influence of the evil angels.

All heaven is interested in the important work at Battle Creek. Satan and his evil angels are arrayed against it, and men who will be co-workers with these evil angels are to be no judges about the work there.

1858
(Ms 3, 1858)

[CIRCA 1858],[1] N.P.

Testimony for John and Mary Loughborough.

Portions of this manuscript are published in Ellen G. White, *Manuscript Releases,* vol. 10, p. 281.

Mary Loughborough's struggles with homesickness and loneliness; a call for complete commitment to God's will.

I was shown the case of Brother and Sister Loughborough. I saw that Sister Mary [**Mary J. Loughborough**] had stood in Brother John's [**John Norton Loughborough**] way; that she had not been consecrated to God; that she understood but little of what it was to deny herself for Christ's sake; that instead of studying her own ease, inclinations, and wishes, she should lie passive in the hands of God, and study His holy will, and instead of following out her own will, be ready to inquire, What wouldst Thou have me to do, Lord?

I saw that for some time past, Sister Mary has had a rebellious spirit, has been self-willed; that her will had not yet been broken; that that will was her idol, and that idol would shut her out of heaven unless speedily sacrificed. I saw that she did not bring the coming of the Lord as near as she should, and that her mind, instead of being at Rochester [New York],[2] should be all swallowed up in the work of God, and she should be seeking opportunities to help her husband, to hold up his hands, and to labor wherever there was an opportunity.

---

[1] The original/earliest copy gives no place or date of writing. The primary clue to the date is the emphasis in this manuscript on Mary Loughborough's intense desire to move back to Rochester, New York, to enjoy the company of friends and relatives. Having spent the early years of her married life in Rochester, Mary did not adjust well when the family moved to distant Waukon, Iowa, in November 1856. After a difficult year in Waukon, with John away most of the time, Mary seemed determined to move back to Rochester, giving little heed to the need of the church for John's labors in the Midwest. She eventually became reconciled to not returning to New York through the testimony of Ellen White's visions of November 1857 (Lt 5, 1857 [Nov. 22]) and March 1858 (Lt 1, 1858 [Mar. 3]), appealing to Mary to be less self-centered and to "die to Rochester." The crisis passed, and the Loughboroughs settled in Battle Creek, Michigan, for the next decade until Mary's death in 1867. Since there is no mention of Mary pining for Rochester after 1858, this undated manuscript seems best to fit into the period of 1857-1858.

[2] Several letters from Ellen White document Mary Loughborough's difficulty in reconciling herself to the long absences of her traveling preacher-husband and her wish to return to friends and relatives in Rochester, where she had lived most of her married life (Lt 6, 1854 [winter]; Lt 5, 1857 [Nov. 22]; Lt 1, 1858 [Mar. 3]).

I saw that Sister Mary had murmured against God and against her husband. Satan was constantly harassing her mind about going to Rochester. I saw that when God called Brother John to Rochester, then it would be time enough for her to think of going, but it was all a snare of Satan for her to feel that she must go to Rochester. I saw that God had nothing for Mary to do in Rochester, and she had nothing in God's Word that would bear her out in going there. All her desires to go arose from wrong feelings. I saw that she gave herself up to weak, childish feelings. She had made efforts to overcome herself and her wishes, but they were altogether too weak and feeble. She must have determination in this matter, decision, and not be tossed to and fro, and be so changeable.[3] It is high time that her childish feelings were put away, and as God had favored her with a kind husband, one whom He has chosen to labor for Him and sound the last note of warning, she should feel a grateful feeling instead of murmuring, and should submit to his wishes, not so reluctantly, not so sadly, but with cheerfulness.

I saw that Brother John has been too lenient. If Sister Mary yields to such childish feelings as she has in times past, Brother John must be as decided as he would be with a child. But it should not be so. Mary should be a companion for John, one with whom he can consult and advise, and she should be the tender, affectionate wife, to watch over him, to study to ease his burden instead of adding to it, to study to help him instead of hindering, that she, with him, may share in the reward and be the means of doing good here and making others happy.

I saw that Satan had tried to put jealous thoughts into Mary's mind—that there was a lack of love on John's part to her. But it is not so. The lack of love is on Sister Mary's side. There is a lack of love on her part. I saw that this discontented, homesick feeling which Sister Mary indulges in is all of the enemy, and binds a heavy weight upon the spirits of John. When he goes into meeting he often has to labor through this oppression upon his spirits, when he is trying to present the truth to hundreds, and when the decision of souls for life or death would result from that meeting. And I saw that unless Sister Mary stood out of Brother John's way, God would move her out of the way, for He has already been trifled with, and the tender Spirit grieved almost entirely away.

I saw that God had given her sufficient warning three times before, but

---

[3] Mary Loughborough's best known declaration of reconciliation to John's itinerant ministry was made in December 1856 in Waukon, Iowa. In a meeting that was later reported by James White in the *Review*, Mary "confessed her past lack of consecration, and gave herself anew to the Lord, and could say to her husband, Go forth in the name of the Lord to do his work." Yet within a year her commitment had wavered as is seen in Ellen White's letters to her in November 1857 and March 1858.

See: J. W. [James White], "Western Tour," *Review,* Jan. 15, 1857, p. 84; Ellen G. White, Lt 5, 1857 (Nov. 22); Lt 1, 1858 (Mar. 3).

these warnings had been but little regarded.[4] Again He had warned, and unless Sister Mary moves speedily from the critical situation she is in, it will be forever too late, for God will not bear always. He will give her up to her unsubdued, unsanctified will, to follow her own ways and be filled with them, and finally to be weighed in the balances and found wanting.

I saw that Brother John must go forward and be decided, and serve God for himself, if he had to separate from Mary and go to heaven alone. God would pity him, angels would pity him and would strengthen him to endure; and if he took a straightforward course, and put his whole confidence in God, He would make him a triumphant overcomer.

I saw that God had wrought for Sister Mary, and that she could save her own soul and be a help to others. God did make her a help to her husband when she first went West.[5] Her efforts were accepted of God. But the ever-busy enemy was not firmly and decidedly resisted and she was taken in the snare. The enemy knew that there was no way that Brother John could be affected and his spirit depressed like having Sister Mary differing from him, and then seeing her weeping around, unreconciled to God's will, unprepared for Christ's coming, and taking a course to effectually ruin her own soul. These things were like a lead weight upon his spirit. I saw that instead of this Sister Mary should stand in a place to hold up the hands of her husband, and by cheerful looks, words, and actions cheer his spirits; she should be ready to pray with and for him, and then with him she will share the reward.

I saw that Mary had limited the Holy One of Israel. The Lord saith, My grace is sufficient for you. Sister Mary says, No, Lord, it is not. I have tried my best to overcome and cannot. Satan stands laughing because grace is not sufficient to overcome the natural infirmities. I saw that Sister Mary could overcome. I saw that all of Sister Mary's inclinations and will and wishes must bend to the cause of God, and instead of Sister Mary's saying, I will do this and that, she should say, If the Lord will, I will do this and that.

I saw that Sister Mary must be consecrated to God, must take hold of the work in earnest, redeem the time and make a strong effort to subdue her will, die to self, and be determined to be contented and not make herself, as well as those around her, perfectly miserable. A thick, heavy cloud, I saw, had hung over her, and the evil angels had access to her to tempt and annoy her, and

---

[4] *See:* Note 2.

[5] Mary Loughborough's first journey west with her husband was to Ohio in November 1853. They intended to stay there only a few weeks, but their work was so fruitful that their visit was extended to May 1854. John then continued to Michigan and spent the summer in tent evangelism. It is probable that Mary also accompanied him to Michigan.

See: J. N. Loughborough, "Sketches of the Past—No. 91," *Pacific Union Recorder,* Mar. 10, 1910, p. 2; *idem,* "Sketches of the Past—No. 96," *Pacific Union Recorder,* Apr. 28, 1910, p. 1; Adriel Chilson, ed., *Miracles in My Life,* p. 37.

unless she had more of a fixed, settled determination she would certainly be overcome and lose her soul.

I saw that Mary must be sober and be a living example to those around her; she must have her words and actions tell for God, and shed a holy influence around her. She must not measure herself by others. Christ is her Pattern and Example, and by following Him she will partake of His divine character, but if she leans on any arm of flesh, and makes man an example, she will surely come short. Any other one's course will be no excuse for Mary, for Christ is the Pattern to be followed.

He was a Man of sorrows and acquainted with grief. He bore the slight and indignity of man and opened not His mouth. He was hung on Calvary's cross to make a way of escape for lost man; and shall we sinners for whom Christ died and made such a sacrifice complain or think anything that we may suffer hard? To look at the matter in its true light, shall we think that we sacrifice anything? Oh, what is our sacrifice? We change bad for good, evil and sin for righteousness, death for life. Says Jesus, My yoke is easy and My burden is light. We believe it, Lord, therefore will we bear it without a murmur or complaint. God will accept no half-hearted work in this matter. We must make a whole sacrifice, die to self, have our wills and desires sanctified.

Mary, I saw that your will must be swallowed up in the will of God. You must have a fixed determination to yield your wishes and desires, and must be willing to suffer anything and everything for the cause of God, instead of for your pleasure. You must think of the suffering cause and perishing souls, and must remember that Christ is soon coming and we are to be judged according to the deeds done in the body. Heaven is worth everything. Mary has not realized the worth of her own soul, has been careless, and has hardly thought or realized that God read her very thoughts, and that all these unreconciled, wilful feelings were known to God. I saw that it was time that Sister Mary was alarmed about her own salvation; that unless she was diligent now she could not redeem the time.

I saw that Brother John must keep humble, must watch, and must live very near to God. He has a vigilant foe to contend with who is ever watching for an opportunity to weaken him. His darts are flying thick and fast.

1859

(Ms 2, 1859)

JANUARY 1, [BATTLE CREEK, MICHIGAN][1]

Diary.[2]

Portions of this manuscript are published in Ellen G. White Estate, *"I'd Like to Ask Sister White . . . ,"* p. 26.

Diary entry for Sabbath, January 1, 1859: baptism and Communion service.

January 1. The commencement of another year. My husband went down into the water and buried seven with Christ in baptism; two of them were but children.[3] One prayed earnestly in the water to be kept unspotted from the world. As Jesus was raised from the dead so the candidates were raised up out of the water. May they live a new life unto God. Will they be enabled to crucify self and imitate the self-denying life of Jesus?

In the eve the church followed the example of their divine Lord. Said Jesus on the night that He was betrayed, "If I then, your Lord and Master, have washed your feet; ye also ought to wash one another's feet. For I have given you an example, that ye should do as I have done to you. . . . If ye know these things, happy are ye if ye do them." [John 13:14-17.]

I was greatly blessed while engaged in washing the feet of my dear mother. It seemed to me to be the last time I should have the privilege.[4] I felt called out to cry earnestly unto God that those weary feet might run in the way of God's commandments, travel the whole length of the Christian road, and after her weary pilgrimage is ended, lay off her armor at the feet of her Redeemer, and finally stand upon the Mount Zion and walk the streets of gold. We wept together and that season will be long

---

[1] See Jan. 1 entry, Ms. 5, 1859.

[2] The Ellen G. White Estate has in its archives the small, bound, commercial diary for 1859 that Ellen White used during that year. The record for January 1 in that diary (see Ms 5, 1859) is a condensed version of what appears below. The question arises, Why did Ellen White write two versions of the January 1 entry? One possible answer is that on January 1, 1859, she had not yet bought the diary and so wrote that day's record elsewhere. Subsequently, wanting to transfer the material into her diary, but finding it too voluminous for the small space allotted, she was forced to condense it.

[3] On the identity of the two children, see Jan. 1 entry, Ms 5, 1859.

[4] Ellen White expressed the same worry some weeks later: "Cut and made some caps for Mother. It may be the last time I shall have the privilege of making caps for her head" (Ms 5, 1859 [Feb. 8 entry]). In fact, **Eunice Harmon** lived another five years.

See: Obituary: "Eunice Harmon," *Review*, Jan. 26, 1864, p. 71.

remembered.

A holy solemnity pervaded the congregation. The place seemed awful and solemn on account of the presence of the Lord. After we had followed the example of our Lord in washing feet, we partook of the communion. It was an impressive scene as we called to mind the sufferings of our dear Saviour for our sins. Our hearts were deeply melted, and overflowed with gratitude and love to Him who had paid such a dear price to ransom us from the power of Satan and hopeless misery.

Ellen White's earliest known diary, 1859. Original dimensions: 5 x 3.25 in. (13 x 8 cm.).

1859

(Ms 5, 1859)

JANUARY 1–MARCH 31

Diary,[1] January to March.

Portions of this manuscript are published in Ellen G. White, *Selected Messages,* book 2, p. 337; book 3, pp. 261, 262; *idem, Welfare Ministry,* pp. 322-325; *idem, Manuscript Releases,* vol. 3, pp. 136-142; vol. 4, p. 437; vol. 7, pp. 216, 217; Arthur L. White, *Ellen G. White: The Early Years,* pp. 396-400.

[Battle Creek, Michigan] Sabbath, January 1

It is the commencement of the new year. The Lord gave James [**James Springer White**] liberty Sabbath afternoon in preaching upon the necessary preparation for baptism and to partake of the Lord's supper. There was much feeling in the congregation. At intermission, all repaired to the water, where seven followed their Lord in baptism. It was a powerful season and of the deepest interest. Two little sisters about eleven years old were baptized.[2] One, Cornelia C.,[3] prayed in the water to be kept unspotted from the world.

In the eve the church followed the example of their Lord and washed one another's feet, and then partook of the Lord's supper. There was rejoicing and weeping in that house. The place was awful, and yet glorious, on account of the presence of the Lord.

---

[1] Probably this is Ellen White's first regular diary. If there are earlier diaries, they have not been preserved. Arthur L. White argues plausibly that Ellen White was motivated to start a diary by the difficulties she experienced in writing her first major autobiographical work (*Spiritual Gifts* [vol. 2]), which was started in 1858 and published in 1860. In the foreword to that book she admits having "labored under great disadvantages, as I have had to depend in many instances, on memory, having kept no journal till within a few years." It may well be that in order to forestall such problems in the future she started keeping a diary in 1859.

See: Arthur L. White, *Ellen G. White: The Early Years,* p. 394; Ellen G. White, *Spiritual Gifts [vol. 2],* p. iii.

[2] *Identities:* According to James White's report in the *Review,* among those baptized on this occasion were "two little girls . . . the eldest daughter of widow sister Cranson, and the youngest daughter of brother and sister C. Smith." The eldest daughter of **Mary Cranson**, a member of the Battle Creek group, was **Lucretia Cranson**, about 12 years old. The only "C. Smith" among the members at this time was **Cyrenius Smith** whose youngest daughter Mary Lettece Smith was 11.

See: 1850 U.S. Federal Census, "Lucinda [*sic*] Cranson," Michigan, Jackson County, Spring Port, p. 296; 1860 U.S. Federal Census, "Lucretia Cranson," Michigan, Calhoun County, Battle Creek, p. 23; obituary: "Mary Abbey," *Review,* Aug. 18, 1921, p. 22.

[3] This person has not been identified.

[Battle Creek] Sunday, January 2

Sister Augusta Bognes[4] was sent for to assist me to prepare for another journey.[5] Made a coat for Edson [**James Edson White**]. He will accompany us. We tried to comfort Augusta. She is cast down and discouraged; health poor, and no one to depend on. She has laid aside her armor and shield of faith. May the Lord strengthen the weak hands and confirm the feeble knees. Gave Sister Irving [**Catherine Irving**][6] a warm cloak and dress and a few other things to make over for her.[7]

[Battle Creek] Monday, January 3

Went to the office; called in at Brother Loughborough's [**John Norton Loughborough**][8] and at my sister's.[9] Wrote seven pages to Doctor Naramore [**John Naramore**],[10] then took dinner at my sister's. Had a good interview with

---

[4] This person has not been identified.

[5] Ellen White left a few days later, on January 7, for a journey of almost three weeks and 210 miles (338 kilometers) through western Michigan. Accompanying her were her son Edson (age 9), J. N. Loughborough, his wife Mary, and their daughter Teresa, 11 months old. (See entries for Jan 8, 18, 19.)

See: J. N. Loughborough, "Diary," entry for Jan. 26, 1859.

[6] *Identity:* Further diary entries provide clues as to the identity of "Sister Irving." She had a daughter, Agnes, age 17, and a husband who was on his deathbed (Jan. 6, Mar. 10, Apr. 23). According to further information published in *The Good Samaritan,* she lived "about ten miles [16 kilometers] from Battle Creek." All this points to Catherine Irving, listed in the 1860 census as living in Ross township, Michigan, a few miles from Battle Creek. According to the census, there was an Agnes, age 18, in the household, but no male adult. The name of Catherine's dying husband can be found in a *Review* obituary, which reported that William Irving, "of Ross, Mich.," died on June 4, 1859, "of consumption."

See: E. G. W. [Ellen G. White], "From My Diary," *The Good Samaritan,* December 1859, p. 5; 1860 U.S. Federal Census, "Catherine Irving," Michigan, Kalamazoo County, Ross, p. 25; obituary: "William Irving," *Review,* June 9, 1859, p. 23.

[7] Descriptions of the desperate plight of the Irving family are found under entries for Jan. 6 and Mar. 10.

[8] *Identity:* J. N. Loughborough and his wife, Mary Jane, had moved to Battle Creek in 1857 and lived within about 100 yards (91 meters) of the Whites.

See: J. N. Loughborough, "Sketches of the Past—No. 106," *Pacific Union Recorder*, Oct. 6, 1910, p. 1; Glenn Davis and Jean Davis, "Notebook, Vol. 1," deposited at Historic Adventist Village, Battle Creek, Michigan (section on J. N. Loughborough).

[9] Ellen White's sister **Sarah B. Belden**. Cf. diary entry for Mar. 1: "Called to see Sister Sarah and Mother." Sarah's husband, **Stephen Belden**, worked as printer at the *Review and Herald.* The Beldens had moved to Battle Creek in 1855 in conjunction with the relocation of the *Review* office from Rochester, New York.

[10] *Identity:* The February 3, 1859, issue of the *Review* mentions "Bro. and sister Naramore of Rochester, who have lately embraced the truth." Other letters and receipts from 1859 and early 1860 add the title "Dr." and the initial "J." The 1860 census gives the full name "John Naramore"—a dentist living in Rochester, New York. None of the 10 letters mentioned under January 3 and January 4 are in the White Estate archives except the letter to Bro. Hastings (see Lt 1a, 1859 [Jan. 4]).

See: Search term "Naramore" in *Words of the Pioneers;* 1860 U.S. Federal Census, "John Naramore," New York, Monroe County, Rochester, Ward 7, p. 335; J. N. Loughborough,

my father and mother.[11] Went to the office again after dinner, and wrote four pages to Brother Orton's [**Jonathan T. Orton**][12] family; also wrote four pages to Brother Howland's [**Stockbridge Howland**] family, and wrote to Sister Ashley [**Melora A. Ashley**] and Brother Collins' [**Philip Collins**] family. Paid Widow Cranson [**Mary Jane Cranson**][13] $1.00 for making a couple of shirts. Paid Sister Bognes $1.00 for making a coat. She was unwilling to take it, but I felt it duty to hand it to her. She is poor and sickly. May the Lord pity and care for her. Said Jesus, The poor ye have always with you. May the Lord rid us of selfishness and help us to care for others' woes and relieve them.

[Battle Creek] Tuesday, January 4

Went to the office. Wrote a number of letters to different ones who were acquainted with our experience. Wished them to call up the events and write them to us.[14] Wrote to Brother Hastings [**Leonard W. Hastings**] of New Ipswich, N.H., Brother Collins [**Philip Collins**] of Dartmouth, Mass., Noah Lunt [**Noah Norton Lunt**] of Portland, Me., and Brother Nichols [**Otis Nichols**][15] of Dorchester, Mass. Wrote a vision given me for Brother Bates.

"Sketches of the Past—No. 114," *Pacific Union Recorder,* Aug. 17, 1911, p. 1.

[11] **Robert** and **Eunice Harmon** had moved to Battle Creek from Maine by 1856, possibly late 1855 (see Lt 8, 1856 [Jan. 21]). Extant records indicate that they were somewhat unsettled, at times living with the Whites (daughter Ellen), at times with the Beldens (daughter Sarah) or in other temporary accommodation. Also recorded are two or three lengthy visits they made to their son John B. Harmon, who lived in Illinois. It appears that the Harmons were staying with their son in Illinois when Eunice Harmon died in 1864.

See: Ellen G. White, Lt 8, 1856 (Jan. 21); Ms 5, 1859 (Mar. 29 entry); Ms 7, 1859 (July 26 entry); Lt 11, 1860 (Oct. 22); Lt 6a, 1861 (July 26); Lt 27, 1861 (June 19); Lt 29, 1861 (Nov. 13); James White to "Dear Sister," Nov. 4, 1856; 1860 U.S. Federal Census, "Jn. B. Harman," Illinois, Greene County, Between the Creeks, p. 184; Eunice Harmon to "Ellen," Dec. 10 (1855?); obituary: "Eunice Harmon," *Review,* Jan. 26, 1864, p. 71.

[12] *Identity:* Cf. Mar. 30 entry, where Ellen White mentions writing a letter to "Brother J. T. Orton." Elsewhere during 1859 she refers to "Drusilla" and "Alva" in connection with "Brother Orton" (Lt 3, 1859) which clearly connects "Brother Orton" with Jonathan T. Orton, of Rochester, New York, who had two children by that name. (For identities of other addressees listed in the entries of January 3 and January 4, see note 15.)

See: 1850 U.S. Federal Census, "Jonathan Orton," "Drusilla Orton," "Alva Orton," New York, Monroe County, Rochester, Ward 7, p. 317.

[13] *Identity:* An obituary notice in the *Review* the following year reports the death of "Mary Jane Cranson (widow)" who "fell asleep in Jesus at Battle Creek, Mich., Aug. 27, 1860 . . . aged thirty-five years."

See: Obituary: "Mary Jane Cranson," *Review,* Sept. 18, 1860, p. 143.

[14] This is another indication that Ellen White was gathering materials to write her first major autobiographical work (*Spiritual Gifts [vol. 2]*), which was published the following year (see note 1 above).

[15] *Identities:* The fact that Ellen White provides the addresses of Brethren Hastings, Collins, Lunt, and Nichols helps to establish their full identity. That these individuals "were acquainted with our experience" and could provide information for her planned autobiographical book, makes the identity certain. All of them were pioneers of the Sabbatarian Adventist movement going back to the 1840s. It is likely that the letters written the previous day to "Brother

[See also Lt 1a, 1859, written on this date.]

[Battle Creek] Wednesday, January 5

Thought of remaining at home to prepare for my journey. At noon James said they needed help at the office. I went down to help them. There was a difficulty in the press. No papers to fold. All waiting for work. While waiting I wrote to Brother Benedict's [**Joseph Perry Benedict**][16] family. While [I was] busily engaged in writing, Sister McClemule[17] came in. I must leave to talk with her. Jenny [**Jane Fraser**],[18] Mother, and Willie [**William Clarence White**] came next. Showed them the press. Jenny and Mother spent the afternoon with Sister Smith.[19] While [I was] folding, Sister Cornell [**Cornelia A. Cornell**][20] came in and wished me to go down street to get some things

---

Howland," "Sister Ashley," and "Brother Collins" had a similar purpose since all three surnames are those of pioneers from the 1840s—Stockbridge Howland, Melora A. Ashley, and Philip Collins.

[16] *Identity:* This is the first of several mentions of "Brother" and "Sister" Benedict and their "daughters" in the 1859 diary. Some of these make it quite clear that the Benedicts lived in Battle Creek. Fortunately, the 1860 census has only one Benedict household in Battle Creek, that of Joseph (age 55), Milly (age 50), Diantha (age 26), Betsy (age 15), and Benjamin (age 53). That these are the Sabbatarian Benedicts Ellen White is addressing is confirmed by J. N. Loughborough, who makes mention of a "Sr. Diantha Benedict," apparently living in the Battle Creek area, in his diary for 1859 (the title "Sr." indicating her Sabbatarian faith). This letter is not in the White Estate archives.

See: 1860 U.S. Federal Census, "Joseph Benedict," Michigan, Calhoun, Battle Creek, p. 53; J. N. Loughborough, "Diary," entry for Jan. 4, 1859.

[17] This person has not been identified.

[18] *Identity:* The family context presented here, especially the presence of 4-year-old William, strongly suggests that "Jenny" is Jane Fraser, who for several years had helped in the White household.

[19] Two unrelated families with the name Smith are known to belong to the Battle Creek group at this time—**Harriet** and **Uriah Smith** and **Louisa** and **Cyrenius Smith**. It is uncertain whether Harriet or Louisa is referred to here, but it is more likely Harriet, who assisted at the Review office.

See: Search terms "Smith" and "Battle Creek" in *Words of the Pioneers.*

[20] *Identity:* Three **Cornell** brothers, **Merritt E.**, **Myron J.**, and **James**, with their families, were members of the Battle Creek Adventist community at various times from the 1850s and onward. However, at the time of writing, i.e., January 1859, two of these families were not living in Battle Creek. Merritt E. spent the winter of 1858-1859 preaching in Ohio. It is known from several sources that his wife, Angeline, usually accompanied Merritt on his preaching tours. They had no children. James Cornell, a shoemaker, although listed in the 1860 census as living in Battle Creek, was apparently working in Monterey, Michigan, at this time, because Ellen White notes in her diary that on Jan. 16, 1859, eleven days later, she "took dinner at Brother James Cornell's" in Monterey. Ellen White is most probably referring to Cornelia, wife of Myron Cornell, in this diary entry.

See: J. W. [James White], [notice re. M. E. Cornell], *Review,* Sept. 30, 1858, p. 152; Ellen G. White, Lt 10, 1863 (Nov. 28); Ms 5, 1859 (Jan. 16 entry); obituary: "Angeline M. A. Cornell," *Review,* Jan. 7, 1902, p. 14; 1860 U.S. Federal Census, "James Cornell," Michigan, Calhoun County, Battle Creek, p. 25. For lists of early Battle Creek church members, see EGWEnc, s.v. "Battle Creek Tabernacle."

for Roxanna.[21] Walked down, got the things, returned to Brother Smith's for supper, then home with Jenny, Mother, James, Edson, and Willie. Found Father very cheerful at home.

[See also Lt 13, 1859, written on this date.]

[Battle Creek] Thursday, January 6

Made a cap and a vest for Edson. At night am very weary. Gave Agnes [**Agnes Irving**][22] a half-worn dress paramatta[23] for her mother. They are poor. The husband and father is sick. Their crops have failed. They have breadstuff to buy and nothing to buy with. Agnes is their main support.[24] She is only seventeen. There are four children now at home. They must suffer unless the church interest themselves in their behalf. May the Lord have mercy upon the needy, and put it into His children's hearts to dispense to them with a liberal hand.[25]

[Otsego, Michigan] Friday, January 7

Went to Otsego[26] to Brother Leighton's [**George Leighton**].[27] It was a cold drive, yet we kept quite comfortable. Slept well that night.

[Otsego] Sabbath, January 8

It is the holy Sabbath. May we honor and glorify God today.

We went with Brother Leighton in his sleigh to Otsego, four miles [six

---

[21] *Identity:* This might be **Roxanna Cornell**, wife of James Cornell and sister-in-law to Cornelia Cornell. It is possible that Cornelia, knowing Ellen White planned to visit Monterey within the next week or so, requested Ellen to take "some things" to her sister-in-law.

[22] *Identity:* See note in Jan. 2 entry.

[23] A lightweight fabric made of cotton or silk and wool.

[24] Agnes Irving worked in the White home from January to May 1859 for "nine shillings a week" ($1.12), leaving just before her father died in early June.

See: Ellen G. White, Ms 5, 1859 (Mar. 10 entry); Ms 6, 1859 (May 24 entry); obituary: "William Irving," *Review,* June 9, 1859, p. 23.

[25] For further details of the response of the White family to the Irvings' plight, see entries under March 10, 15, 17, 29. The desperate situation of the Irvings seems also, in part, to have caused James White to launch *The Good Samaritan* paper later that year. The second issue, published in December 1859, contained among other items an appeal by Ellen White on behalf of the Irvings. In the following issue, February 1860, several sums of money were receipted "for Sister I. of No. 2," and a report was given of funds that had been dispersed to "Sr. Widow Irving."

See: "Receipts," *The Good Samaritan,* February 1860, p. 12; Harriet N. Smith, Ann J. Kellogg, Huldah Godsmark, "Widow Cranson," *The Good Samaritan,* February 1860, p. 12.

[26] Here begins the account of the three-week journey, with John Loughborough at the reins. In a diary entry Loughborough noted that they left Battle Creek at 9:00 a.m. and arrived in Otsego, some 30 miles (48 kilometers) away, "a little before 6."

See: J. N. Loughborough, "Diary," entry for Jan. 7, 1859.

[27] *Identity:* The only "Leightons" identified in the *Review* as living in Otsego, Michigan, during this period are George Leighton and his family.

See: Search term "Leighton" in *Words of the Pioneers.*

kilometers]. It was very cold; could hardly keep comfortable. Found the meetinghouse not very warm. All were so cold. Must take time to get warm. Brother Loughborough preached upon the judgment. Then I said a few words. Not very free. Then the church readily gave in their testimonies. Many of those who were Cranmer's [Gilbert Cranmer][28] followers were present.[29] They wished to know why there should be a division. They said the house of God was not divided; that as God was with us so He was with them, that Cranmer preached the same as Brother Loughborough preached.[30] They sang a great deal, and we felt that it was time for us to speak. I said a few words, then John explained who had made the division. They seemed displeased. We felt freer.[31]

[Otsego] Sunday, January 9

Rested well last night, but feel a depression of spirits this morning. It is very cold today. Word has been brought to us that the Baptist meetinghouse has been locked up to keep us out. They do not hold meetings there themselves, neither will they let us enter.

---

[28] *Identity:* The fact that "Cranmer" is connected in this passage with "division" among the believers and that his followers are found in Otsego suffice to identify him as Gilbert Cranmer, who had separated from the Sabbatarian Adventists in 1858, the beginnings of what later became the Church of God (7th Day). A conference held in Battle Creek in May 1858 had warned that "G. Cranmer has been preaching views contrary to the present truth," and a letter, some months later, from Otsego church members reported that Cranmer had "drawn off with him eight of the [Otsego] church . . . all of the men being tobacco eaters."

See: Joseph Bates, Uriah Smith, "Business Proceedings of the Conference of May 21st, 1858," *Review,* May 27, 1858, p. 13; George Leighton, Rocksilda Leighton, "Testimony," *Review,* Sept. 9, 1858, p. 132. For biographical information on Gilbert Cranmer, see Robert Coulter, *Story of the Church of God (Seventh Day), passim;* Gilbert Cranmer, *Autobiography of Gilbert Cranmer, as Told to M. A. Branch* (n.d.); Richard C. Nickels, *A History of the Seventh Day Church of God, passim;* SDAE, s.v. "Marion Party."

[29] J. N. Loughborough notes in his diary that he "spoke to about 30, some of them Cranmerites."

See: J. N. Loughborough, "Diary," entry for Jan. 8, 1859.

[30] Gilbert Cranmer taught the seventh-day Sabbath and the Second Advent and in that sense "preached the same as Brother Loughborough preached." There were differences, however. The following year, in conversation with Joseph Bates, Cranmer asserted that "we . . . believe and teach the same as the Battle Creek church, except the visions of Mrs. White, and a part of the midnight cry, and some of the work in the Sanctuary." According to Cranmer's later memoirs his antipathy to the visions was a leading factor in his secession. "I made up my mind I would not belong to a church that was ruled by a woman any longer." J. N. Loughborough maintained that it was Cranmer's unwillingness to give up tobacco and reform his domestic life, as called for in Ellen White's vision one year earlier, that caused him to break away.

See: Joseph Bates, "Letter From Bro. Bates," *Review,* Jan 26, 1860, p. 76; Richard C. Nickels, *A History of the Seventh Day Church of God,* pp. 36, 37; J. N. Loughborough, *Rise and Progress of the Seventh-day Adventists,* p. 216; *idem,* "Recollections of the Past—No. 17," *Review,* Feb. 1, 1887, p. 74.

[31] "The Lord gave me victory over my enemies," Loughborough jotted down in his diary. "They tried to rage but facts were told by Sr. White and me."

See: J. N. Loughborough, "Diary," entry for Jan. 8, 1859.

We held meetings in Brother Russell's [**Lester Russell**][32] house. The room was filled. A number of new ones were out to hear. John had much freedom. There was deep feeling in the meeting both forenoon and afternoon. The saints were strengthened. I had freedom in exhorting the people. Some wept aloud. Brother Hatten's [**Lewis Hadden**] brother and his wife[33] were present. They are not in present truth. They know not God. They seemed deeply affected. That meeting will be long remembered. Cranmer's followers were present. The Lord gave us liberty and His salvation. We closed the meeting with the victory.

[Allegan, Michigan] Monday, January 10

Left Brother Leighton's Monday afternoon for Allegan. Was heartily received by Dr. Lay's [**Horatio S. Lay**] family. Sister Lay [**Julia M. Lay**][34] seems free. Had a pleasant interview with the family. The Lord met with us at our season of prayer, yet my spirits are somewhat depressed.

[Monterey, Michigan][35] *Tuesday, January 11*

Went to Brother Rumery's [**Sylsbre R. Rumery**].[36] Was well received.

---

[32] *Identity:* The only Russell mentioned in the *Review,* said to live in Otsego, is Lester Russell. The 1860 census confirms this identity, because the only Russell family listed for Otsego is that of Lester Russell.

See: Search term "Russell" and "Otsego" in *Words of the Pioneers;* 1860 U.S. Federal Census, "Lester Russell," Michigan, Allegan County, Otsego, p. 54.

[33] *Identity:* The name "Hatten" does not appear in the *Review* for this period, nor in the 1861 list of Otsego church members, nor is there any "Hatten" living in Otsego, according to the 1860 census. However, the similar-sounding name "Hadden" is found in all three sources, so it is likely that this is simply a spelling error by Ellen White. As to the identities of "Brother Hatten" and his brother and wife, some help can be found in the register of Otsego church members of 1861. This lists "Lewis Hadden" with some of his family, and also "Hettie M. Hadden," who was married to George Hadden. No proof that Lewis and George Hadden were brothers has been found, but it seems likely, since both came to Michigan from Putnam County, New York, and both married daughters of Jeremiah Travis, of Putnam County. That "Brother Hatten" is Lewis and his brother and wife are George and Hettie, who are interested but not yet members, is inferred from the fact that there is no mention of Hettie in the *Review* before 1860, whereas Lewis ("L. Hadden") is found already in 1857. George, it appears, never joined the Adventists.

See: "Book of Records of the Seventh-day Advent Church in Otsego"; William Richard Cutter, *Genealogical and Family History of Southern New York and the Hudson River Valley,* vol. 3, p. 889; search term "Hadden" in *Words of the Pioneers.*

[34] *Identities:* The 1861 register of church members in Allegan lists only two persons with the surname "Lay," Horatio S. and Julia M. Lay. Moreover, Horatio Lay, according to church and local records, was a medical doctor in Allegan at the time of Ellen White's diary entry, and so is undoubtedly the "Dr. Lay" that she refers to.

See: "Allegan SDA Church: 1863-1976"; *History of Allegan and Barry Counties, Michigan,* p. 158; search term "H. S. Lay" in *Words of the Pioneers;* obituary: "Dr. Horatio S. Lay," *Review,* Mar. 13, 1900, p. 176.

[35] The names that follow are from Monterey, so even though it is not explicitly stated, Ellen White and her party must have traveled from Allegan to Monterey on this day.

[36] *Identity:* The *Review* mentions three Rumerys from this period: "S. Rumery," of Monterey,

His brother's wife was visiting with them. I never saw them in so good a state of mind as at this time. The Lord has been working for them. They feel more the spirit of present truth than I ever saw them have before.[37] In the evening, Brother George Lay [**George T. Lay**], his wife, and Sister Jones [**Elizabeth Jones**][38] came. We had a very interesting interview, relating some of the interesting incidents of our eastern journey. We had a season of prayer before we parted. Brother Rumery prayed like a little child. Seemed to feel much for his children. The Spirit of the Lord was with us, and we felt that our interview was profitable.

[Monterey] Wednesday, January 12

Wednesday morn had a solemn season of prayer. Brother Rumery felt deeply. He again pled with God in great simplicity for his children. May the Lord answer the father's prayers and give him his children to go with him. There is an improvement in the children. They obey more readily and the oldest boy seems more steady.[39]

I went to Brother Thompson's.[40] Was gladly received, yet did not enjoy the visit; was unwell. Brother Kenyon[41] has gone to Allegan. After supper I went

---

"J. Rumery," and "B. J. Rumery." Monterey church board minutes, census records, and other sources show three members of the same family—Sylsbre Rumery, married to Betsie J., and one of their sons named Jeremiah.

See: "Records of the Seventh-day Adventist Church, Monterey, Michigan [1860-1880]"; 1850 U.S. Federal Census, "Silsbury Rumery," Michigan, Allegan County, Monterey, p. 35.

[37] Two years earlier the situation had been quite different. In October 1857 Ellen White wrote to Sylsbre Rumery: "You have loved money better than religion, better than God," and taken advantage of fellow church brethren in sharp business deals.

See: Ellen G. White, Lt 9, 1857 (Oct.).

[38] *Identity:* J. N. Loughborough's diary entry for January 11 reads: "In the evening Bro. George Lay & wife & Sister V. Jones visited here." This is most likely referring to Elizabeth, the wife of Victory Jones. The Jones and Lay families appear to have been neighbors, according to the 1860 census.

See: J. N. Loughborough, "Diary," entry for Jan. 11, 1859; "Records of the Seventh-day Adventist Church, Monterey, Michigan [1860-1880]"; 1860 U.S. Federal Census, "Victor Jones" and "George Lay," Michigan, Allegan County, Monterey, p. 142.

[39] Sylsbre's three oldest children were baptized in 1862. The "oldest boy," Jeremiah L., later served as an elder in the Monterey church, assisted in tent meetings, and led in colporteur work in Michigan. Sylsbre left the church, but his wife "continued faithful to God" until her death.

See: "Records of the Seventh-day Adventist Church, Monterey, Michigan [1860-1880]"; W. H. Littlejohn, "Michigan," *Review,* Jan. 16, 1883, p. 43; J. N. Brant, "Northern Michigan Canvassers," *Review,* June 10, 1890, p. 366; obituary: "Sylsbre Rumery," *Review,* Dec. 2, 1884, p. 766; obituary: "Betsie Lay Rumery," *Review,* June 15, 1916, p. 22.

[40] This person has not been identified.

[41] *Identity:* Several Kenyon families were associated with the Monterey group at this time. Most mentioned in the *Review* and in Monterey church minutes were Harvey and Amy P. Kenyon and Harmon M. and Sarah M. Kenyon. Harmon later became a well-known minister. Which "Brother Kenyon" is referred to in this diary entry cannot be determined.

See: "Records of the Seventh-day Adventist Church, Monterey, Michigan [1860-1880]"; search terms "Kenyon" and "Monterey" in *Words of the Pioneers.*

to Brother Day's [**John S. Day**].[42] Had quite a good visit, yet do not feel in a visiting mood. My spirits are depressed. The snow is leaving us. Brother Day proposed to go to Otsego for our wagon, and save John the journey.[43]

[Monterey] Thursday, January 13

Brother Day carried out his proposal. He started for Allegan. We rode with him as far as Brother Oren Jones' [**Orrin B. Jones**].[44] We intended visiting them today. Found Sister Jones' mother and sister there, and we drove on to Brother Leander's [**Leander M. Jones**].[45] Brother Leander had gone hunting. Their little one is not well.

[Monterey] Friday, January 14

Expected James. A letter came that he is not coming because Brother Andrews was expected.[46] The church are all disappointed, for Brother Fisher's [**John Fisher**][47] case has been a great trial, and they intended to take up his case and enter into an examination of things which have transpired. But now we know not what to do. May the Lord direct and give wisdom. He alone

---

[42] Monterey church records from the period 1860-1862 mention only one person with the surname "Day"—John S. Day.

See: "Records of the Seventh-day Adventist Church, Monterey, Michigan [1860-1880]."

[43] Changeable weather complicated their travel. Having left Battle Creek on Friday, January 7, with horses and wagon, they found it advisable on Monday to switch to a sleigh and leave the wagon behind in Otsego. However, in this entry, two days later, Ellen White notes that "the snow is leaving us," necessitating a long backtrack of some 15 miles (24 kilometers) to Otsego to retrieve their wagon.

See: J. N. Loughborough, "Diary," entries for Jan. 7-13, 1859.

[44] The spelling favored in several other sources is "Orrin."

See: Obituary: "Orrin B. Jones," *Review,* Aug. 28, 1883, p. 559; 1870 U.S. Federal Census, "Orrin B. Jones," Michigan, Allegan County, Allegan, p. 46; "Orrin B. Jones," *Record of Deaths, Allegan Co., Michigan,* vol. 2, p. 15, no. 579.

[45] Leander Jones and Orrin ("Oren") Jones were brothers.

See: Record of Deaths, Allegan Co., Michigan, vol. 2, p. 15, no. 579, "Orrin B. Jones," d. Aug. 20, 1883, and vol. 3, p. 14, no. 22, "Leander M. Jones," d. Jan 16, 1902. In both entries the parents are given as "Davis Jones and Betsey."

[46] The *Review* had already announced that James White would be in Monterey that weekend. James White, it seems, received very short notice of J. N. Andrews's stop in Battle Creek on his way from Iowa to Rochester, New York, and decided to give his visit priority. During his stay in Battle Creek, Andrews was co-opted to participate in an important meeting on "Systematic Benevolence" on January 16, and together with J. B. Frisbie and James White to write up a report on this subject "founded upon the declarations of holy Scripture."

See: L. M. Jones et al., "Appointments," *Review,* Jan. 6, 1859, p. 56; J. W. [James White], [no title], *Review,* Jan. 27, 1859, p. 80; J. W. [James White], "Systematic Benevolence," *Review,* Feb. 3, 1859, p. 84.

[47] *Identity:* A few weeks later, on February 17, 1859, the *Review* reported that "the churches at Allegan and Monterey have recently been caused to bleed in consequence of the course of Elder John Fisher, for whom they have cheerfully done much, hoping for something from him in return better than ingratitude and rebellion."

See: James White, "The French Mission," *Review,* Feb. 17, 1859, p. 104.

can straighten things here. Brother Jones returns—no success.[48] There was meeting in the evening. The house was nearly filled. John preached upon, "Whom he did foreknow, he also did predestinate." He had freedom. I then said a little upon the necessity of having decision of character, that the half-hearted and indifferent would be left behind. Those who choose eternal life will show it in their lives, and will at last obtain it.

[Monterey] Sabbath, January 15

The ground is again covered with snow. Brother John preached upon the inheritance of the saints, giving the election doctrine a rub. [49] The house was crowded. All listened with the greatest attention. In the afternoon I tried to talk a little. May the Lord bless my weak efforts to the good of some precious soul.

In the eve there was a church meeting to investigate Father Fisher's [**John Fisher**] case. He broke down a little. Made some confession, and was put upon probation, not to be acknowledged as a messenger but as a learner[50] of the third angel's message. His heart is not in unison with us. He is far out of the way. The church is destined still to have trials with him.[51]

[Monterey] Sunday, January 16

Am quite sick. Went to the meeting. Was so sick I was obliged to return home to Brother Leander's. John preached on the Sanctuary. Had a free time. Took dinner at Brother James Cornell's [**James Cornell**].[52] Brother Leighton was there and three Sister Fosters,[53] and Sister McDonald[54] was present. I felt

---

[48] Leander Jones's hunting expedition was clearly not for sport but out of dire necessity. Two weeks later Ellen White "sent Sister Leander Jones some things for her children, and Jenny sent her her best bonnet." She added, "May the Lord enable us to see the wants of the poor and give us a ready and willing heart to supply them" (Feb. 3 diary entry).

[49] Loughborough later reported that there was one person in the Monterey congregation "whose heart had been touched with the truth . . . [yet was] on the point of rejecting the whole truth because it did not agree with the doctrine in which he had been traditionated from his youth; namely unconditional election."

See: J. N. Loughborough, "Meetings in Otsego, Monterey and Wright, Mich.," *Review,* Feb. 3, 1859, p. 85.

[50] Assigning John Fisher "learner" status had some justification. Formerly a Baptist minister, Fisher had become a Sabbathkeeper just 10 months earlier, in March 1858. Yet within a few months the *Review* was already carrying reports of his public preaching.

See: M. E. Cornell, "Meetings at Stony Creek, Mich.," *Review,* Apr. 8, 1858, p. 165; Joseph Bates, Uriah Smith, "The Conference," *Review,* May 27, 1858, p. 13; John Fisher to "Bro. Smith," *Review,* Aug. 12, 1858, p. 102.

[51] Exactly why Fisher was in conflict with the Monterey church is not known. However, the Jan. 17 entry indicates that among those issues was his rejection of the visions of Ellen White.

[52] *Identity:* See notes on Jan. 5 entry.

[53] No Fosters have been found among the Monterey group during this period, although there were some in nearby Allegan.

See: "Allegan SDA Church: 1863-1976"; search term "Foster" in *Words of the Pioneers.*

[54] This person has not been identified.

so miserable I could not converse. In the afternoon I went to Brother George Lay's. Met Brother Rumery there. It was snowing fast. Had quite a pleasant interview in the eve. But Oh, why am I so depressed, why so cast down and homesick? Have I departed from God, that I am thus left in darkness? Oh, restore unto me the joys of Thy salvation; then shall my lips praise Thee and my heart rejoice.

[Monterey] Monday, January 17

Felt better this morn. We remained at Brother George Lay's through the day. We feel lonesome and sad. There is but little to cheer the spirits or make the heart glad. The case of Father Fisher lies heavily upon us all. Brother Inman [**Eldad Inman**][55] from Wayland [Michigan] is here. It seems to me he has too much of the minister about him; he is given too much to talk; prays lengthy, and exhorts lengthy. Father Fisher read to him a long piece he had written against the visions. Brother Inman leaves us for his home.

[Grand Rapids, Michigan] Tuesday, January 18

Brother Lay harnessed his horses to a sleigh and took Mary [**Mary Jane Loughborough**],[56] Edson, and myself over the log way and over the bad going ten miles [16 kilometers] to the plank road.[57] The road is very bad and rough. John followed us with the horses and wagon. We feel very thankful for the easy conveyance over the bad road. Sister Lay went with her husband for the ride. After we struck the plank, we had a good road all the way to Grand Rapids. Tarried with Brother James Cramer [**James I. Cramer**] over night. Had a good visit with them. Brother Cramer is a cripple—caused by a fall from a building. I am so weary and lame through riding I cannot move without suffering pain.

---

[55] *Identity:* The information that Brother Inman was from Wayland is very useful since there is a letter in the *Review* just two months earlier signed "Eldad Inman. Wayland, Mich."

See: Eldad Inman to "Bro. Smith," *Review,* Nov. 25, 1858, p. 7.

[56] *Identity:* See notes on entries for Jan. 2 and 3.

[57] Charles Dickens, who traveled in America in the 1840s, described his experience with log roads, also called "corduroy roads": "A great portion of the way was over what is called a corduroy road, which is made by throwing trunks of trees into a marsh, and leaving them to settle there. The very slightest of the jolts with which the ponderous carriage fell from log to log was enough, it seemed, to have dislocated all the bones in the human body."

Plank roads, on the other hand, gave a much smoother ride, and were popular in mid-nineteenth-century America. Costing $1,000 to $2,000 per mile to construct and expensive to maintain, plank roads were owned by private corporations, which charged tolls for their use. John Loughborough noted in the accounts section of his diary that he paid 45 cents "toll" on this day, no doubt for travel on the plank road to Grand Rapids.

See: Charles Dickens, *Pictures From Italy. American Notes,* pp. 378, 379. For an informative description of early American roads, see Eric Sloane, *Our Vanishing Landscape,* pp. 57-70.

[Wright] Wednesday, January 19

Have slept but little through the night. A little daughter was born to add to Brother and Sister Cramer's responsibilities. The mother and child are comfortable.

In the afternoon we went to Wright. Brother Cramer, the elder [**Christopher G. Cramer**],[58] took a seat in our carriage to pilot us. He is acquainted with the road. It is a good road. Have no milk for Teresa [Teresa C. Loughborough].[59] She cries. Oh, that we may be as earnest for the bread of life as she is for temporal food! She will not be satisfied. May our earnest cries go up to God for His salvation. About dark arrived at Brother Root's [**Ephraim Henry Root**]. They welcomed us heartily. It is a good home with plenty of house room. Sister Root [**Hezzy Root**][60] is in feeble health. There was a meeting in the evening. We were too weary to go. John and Brother Cramer went. Had a good meeting.

[Wright] Thursday, January 20

Rested well through the past night. Feel lonesome today. It is dark and rainy. This is an excellent family. In the afternoon, Brethren Frisbie [**Joseph Birchard Frisbie**] and Rhodes [**Samuel W. Rhodes**][61] came. Brother Frisbie

---

[58] *Identity:* A Brother "C. G. Cramer," from Grand Rapids, Michigan, is mentioned in the *Review* in 1857. The 1850 census for Grand Rapids reveals a "Christopher Cramer," age 42 and head of a household that included "James Cramer," age 19. That "Christopher Cramer" and "James Cramer" are the Cramers mentioned in this narrative can be confirmed by comparing date and place information in their respective obituaries with that in the 1850 census entry. That they are father and son is suggested by the expression "the elder" used of Christopher. The 1850 census tells us that Christopher was head of a household that included James but does not specify that James was son to Christopher.

See: C. G. Cramer to "Bro. Smith," *Review,* Mar. 26, 1857, p. 165; Joseph Bates, Uriah Smith, "Business Proceedings of the General Conference of Nov. 6th, 1857, *Review,* Nov. 12, 1857, p. 4; 1850 U.S. Federal Census, "Christopher Cramer," Michigan, Kent County, Grand Rapids, p. 178; obituary: "Christopher G. Cramer," *Review,* July 15, 1873, p. 39; obituary: "James I. Cramer," *Review,* Sept. 3, 1914, p. 23.

[59] See note on Jan. 2 entry and obituary: "Teresa C. Loughborough," *Review,* Jan. 12, 1860, p. 63.

[60] *Identity:* The only Roots living in Wright, Michigan, mentioned in the *Review* for this period are Ephraim H. and Hezzy Root with family.

See: Search terms "Root" and "Wright" in *Words of the Pioneers.*

[61] *Identities:* As is made clear in the Jan. 23 entry, Frisbie was a preacher, and must therefore be J. B. Frisbie, the only preacher with that surname in this period. The previous summer Frisbie and Samuel W. Rhodes had preached together in Wright and other parts of western Michigan. In July 1858 it was reported in the *Review* that Rhodes had baptized 38 persons at Wright. This suggests that he would have an interest in being present at the conference in Wright taking place in January 1859 and that he is the Brother "Rhodes" Ellen White refers to here.

See: J. B. Frisbie, S. W. Rhodes, "Meetings in Northern Mich.," *Review,* July 15, 1858, p. 72; *idem,* "From Brn. Rhodes and Frisbie," *Review,* Sept. 2, 1858, p. 126.

informs us that my husband will not come.[62] Am very sorry. Our labors should be together.

[Wright] Friday, January 21

Feel a little more cheerful in spirits. Meeting commenced today. The house was well filled.[63] They came from Caledonia, Rome, Vergennes, Ionia [all in Michigan].

Sabbath drawing on. Had a lengthy meeting in the afternoon and none in the evening. Many testimonies were given in. Many of them lacked the Spirit. I spoke a little; feel deeply my unworthiness.

I have felt so homesick on the journey. I fear that I have not been willing to sacrifice the company of my husband and children to do others good. I desire a willingness to make a whole sacrifice and crucify every selfish feeling. I feel a lack of the Spirit of God. Have had a weeping time before the Lord. And again while attempting to bear testimony in meeting, my heart was full. I could not refrain from weeping.

[Wright] Sabbath, January 22

This morning I have been pleading and wrestling with God. I have a gleam of light but this cannot satisfy me. I must know that my way pleases God. Went to the meeting with a heavy heart. Am much depressed in spirit.[64] I fear my work has hindered me from communing with God as much as I should. There were about three hundred present—a very attentive congregation. Deep interest was manifested. Brother John Loughborough had freedom in talking. He dwelt on the inheritance of the saints. The same subject was continued in the afternoon. His tongue is like the pen of a ready writer. The people of God seem hungry for the bread of life. They eagerly devour every word that is spoken. I try to exhort; have not much liberty. Something holds me. Oh, that [five illegible words] that confine me, and bear a testimony that will reach the heart. Meeting closed at five o'clock. No meeting in the evening. Quite a number tarry at Brother Root's. Their prayers lack faith and energy; are dry and formal. And I am enveloped in clouds and am much discouraged. Oh,

---

[62] James White, who had originally intended to join his wife and the Loughboroughs during this weekend's conference at Wright and the previous weekend's meetings, was in the end unable to attend. See notes under Jan. 14 above.

See: J. B. Frisbie, "Appointments," *Review*, Jan. 13, 1859, p. 64.

[63] Loughborough adds, "About 200 Sabbath-keepers came together to this conference, nearly 100 of whom have embraced the truth within the past year in Wright and vicinity." The conference was held in "the new meeting-house which is in process of erection."

See: J. N. Loughborough, "Meetings in Otsego, Monterey, and Wright, Mich.," *Review*, Feb. 3, 1859, p. 85.

[64] Loughborough, likewise, was depressed. "I felt sad till about 11 o'clock," he wrote in his diary for this Sabbath.

See: J. N. Loughborough, "Diary," entry for Jan. 22.

that I might come to the feet of Jesus and tell Him all my wants! I shall claim the promises of God through all my unworthiness. He will appear for me and set me free. My soul thirsteth for God. I long for His salvation.

[Wright] Sunday, January 23

Meeting commenced at half past eight and the house was well filled. It was a prayer and conference meeting. The exhortations and prayers were more spirited. No time was lost. Two or three arose at once to speak. One sister arose three times and could not speak. Others would arise and she sat down. At length she gave it up. The conference meeting ended. Brother Loughborough gave an interesting discourse which would tend to wean the hearts of the people of God from earth, turn their attention from their trials, and cause them to work for the things which are unseen, which are eternal. There was a short intermission. Brother Loughborough again gave an interesting, appropriate discourse. I then followed in exhortation. Had freedom and victory, speaking of the life and sufferings of Christ and of His coming the second time, the Life-Giver to raise the dead and change the living.

In the evening Brother Frisbie preached upon the Sabbath. He did not have his usual liberty. Brother Loughborough said a few words and I followed, saying a few words, that none of us were compelled to receive salvation but we could receive it if we would. We could choose life or death. Many desire life but do not choose it. They love the world, its fashion, its pleasure, and they plainly show they have not chosen eternal life. Their treasure is here. This world is their home. The lives of those who choose life and salvation will be marked with their choice. Their conduct will say plainly that they are seeking a better country, even a heavenly, a city that hath foundations, whose builder and maker is God. Our meetings closed this night.

[Grand Rapids, Michigan] Monday, January 24

We rode to Grand Rapids to Brother Cramer's, the elder. Many have stopped on their way home—a large company for whom to get dinner, but it passed off very agreeably. In the eve I went up to young Brother Cramer's; had some conversation with them and then a season of prayer. I felt called out to pray for the elder Brother Cramer, who is deeply afflicted with ill health and lameness. Had some freedom in prayer. I believe he will be speedily strengthened to glorify God. We feel that our evening's interview was profitable.

[Caledonia, Michigan] Tuesday, January 25

It looks like a storm. I feel rather cast down. My teeth troubled me through the night. We rode 14 miles [22 kilometers] to Brother Hardy's [**William J.**

Hardy].[65] Brother Cramer did not give us the right directions, and we went four miles [six kilometers] out of our way. Did not arrive at Brother Hardy's until dinner time. It was snowing fast. We were heartily welcomed by the family. A good dinner was soon in readiness for us, of which we thankfully partook. This is a colored family. Although the house is poor and old, everything is arranged with neatness and exact order. The children are well behaved, intelligent, and interesting. May I yet have a better acquaintance with this dear family. The meeting is four miles [six kilometers] beyond Brother Hardy's. They accompanied us to the meeting. It was held in a private house. Brother Loughborough talked for thirty minutes on the gift of the Spirit of God. Then I spoke of neatness and order.

[Battle Creek, Michigan] Wednesday, January 26

Rested but little the past night. Brother Gerald [**Lyman Gerould**][66] is poor, yet with a warm heart. He welcomed us to his humble house and provided for us as well as he could.

It is a beautiful day. We feared we should be obliged to ride in a storm, but we have a very good road and everything seems favorable. We are homeward bound today and expect before night to meet husband and children. At noon took a dry luncheon at an old hotel, while the horses were feeding.[67] Joyfully,

---

[65] *Identity:* Although there are several Hardys mentioned in the *Review* during this period, the one referred to here is almost certainly William J. Hardy. According to the diary kept by J. N. Loughborough on this trip, "Bro. Hardy" lived in or near the township of Caledonia, Kent County. In a letter to the *Review* in 1858, William J. Hardy tells of worshipping with "the Sabbath-keepers in Caledonia," although he apparently lived in the adjoining township of Gaines. Additional confirmation is provided by Ellen White's observation that the Hardys were "a colored family." The 1860 census lists "Wm. J. Hardy" as "mulatto."

See: J. N. Loughborough, "Diary," entry for Jan. 25; Wm. J. Hardy, "From Bro. Hardy," *Review*, Apr. 29, 1858, p. 191; 1860 U.S. Federal Census, "Wm. J. Hardy," Michigan, Kent County, Gaines, p. 94.

[66] *Identity:* J. N. Loughborough informs us in his diary entry for Jan. 25 that the traveling party came to Caledonia on that day. The problem is that there is no mention in census records nor in the *Review* of any "Brother Gerald" living in Caledonia township during this period. Loughborough says that they stayed with "Br. Geruld." Three months later, on passing through Caledonia again, Ellen White wrote in her diary of staying the night at "Brother Gerould's." She may be using alternate spellings for the same person. There is some evidence of this ambivalence found when comparing Lt 12, 1861 (Dec.), with Ms 3, 1863 (July 22). In both cases she addresses various persons in the Caledonia church, including a "Brother Gerould" in Lt 12 and a "Brother Gerald" in Ms 3. Yet the counsel given to both of them is so similar that there seems little doubt she is addressing the same person. The spelling "Gerould" is preferred in this study since that is the use consistently adopted in the *Review*.

See: J. N. Loughborough, "Diary," entry for Jan. 25; Ellen G. White, Ms. 6, 1859, entry for Apr. 28; search terms "Gerald" and "Gerould" in *Words of the Pioneers;* 1850 U.S. Federal Census, "Lyman Jerrald," Michigan, Kent County, Gaines, p. 255; 1860 U.S. Federal Census, "Lyman Jerrold," Michigan, Kent County, Caledonia, p. 152.

[67] Loughborough added that they drove from 5:30 a.m. to 5:30 p.m., with time out for eating and feeding the horses, on this final day of the journey.

we again met our family. Little Willie seems overjoyed to meet us again. Poor child, he has been very sick in my absence. Is now better but looks miserable. My husband has been sick, but the Lord has preserved their lives. With gratitude to God I take my place in my family again. There is no place to be so dearly prized as home.

[Battle Creek] Thursday, January 27

Rested but little the past night. Was so thankful and happy to meet my family again and to be in the society of my husband and children [that] I could not sleep. Have a headache through the day.

[Battle Creek] Friday, January 28

Had the privilege of sitting at the table with my husband's father and mother[68] and my father and mother. We enjoyed the interview much.

[Battle Creek] Saturday, January 29

Have spent a very restless night. My lungs are very sore. Every breath causes me pain. Cannot attend meeting today.

At noon Sister Kelsey [**Eunice Rebecca Kelsey**][69] came up to take dinner with us.

[Battle Creek] Wednesday, February 2

My lungs trouble me very much.

[Battle Creek] Thursday, February 3

Very sick all day with sick headache. Henry Pierce [**Henry Harlow Pierce**],[70] from Monterey, was at our house. Sent Sister Leander Jones [**Harriet**

See: J. N. Loughborough, "Diary," entry for Jan. 26.

[68] **John** and **Betsey White** had visited Battle Creek two years earlier, according to Martha Byington's diary for November 30, 1857. However, this time they came with the intention to stay. Within a couple of months of this diary entry they had moved into their own house just across the street from Ellen and James (see diary entry for Mar. 20 below). For discussions of the date of John and Betsey White's arrival in Battle Creek, see Lt 2, 1855 (Aug.), note 15, and EGWEnc, s.v. "'Deacon' John White." Regarding Ellen White's parents, see under Jan. 3 diary entry above.

See: Martha Byington, 1857 diary.

[69] *Identity:* Presumably this is the same "Sister Kelsey" described in the Mar. 2 diary entry as a "widow" living 13 miles (21 kilometers) from Battle Creek. Eunice Kelsey, an active Adventist, fits this description very well, having lost her husband 18 months earlier and living in Leroy Township, which lies some miles south of Battle Creek. Her younger daughter, Mary Ellen, married Ellen and James White's son William Clarence in 1876.

See: obituary: "A.P.H. Kelsey," *Review,* Aug. 13, 1857, p. 119; 1860 U.S. Federal Census, "Eunice Kelsey," Michigan, Calhoun County, Leroy, p. 226; obituary: "Eunice Rebecca Kelsey," *Review,* June 21, 1906, p. 23.

[70] *Identity:* A letter in the *Review* from "Henry H. Pierce, Monterey, Mich.," dated July 13, 1857, gives the middle initial, and H. H. Pierce's obituary provides the full middle name.

Jones][71] some things for her children, and Jenny sent her her best bonnet. May the Lord enable us to see the wants of the poor and give us a ready and willing heart to supply them.[72]

[Battle Creek] Friday, February 4

Health poor. Went to the stores with Brother Bates and Augusta Bognes.[73] They purchased a coat for Brother Bates [**Joseph Bates**].[74]

[Battle Creek] Saturday, February 5

Attended meeting all day. James preached twice. Had freedom. His text was, "This generation shall not pass, until all these things be fulfilled." In the afternoon I had a free time as I bore testimony. Brethren Carmen [**John Frost Carman**] and Street [**Sherman A. Street**][75] tarried with us all night. They urge us strongly to come to their place.

[Battle Creek] Sunday, February 6

Visited my mother;[76] obtained some facts in my experience.[77]

See: Henry H. Pierce, "From Bro. Pierce," *Review,* July 30, pp. 102, 103; obituary: "Henry Harlow Pierce," *Review,* Nov. 12, 1901, p. 14.

[71] *Identity:* See notes under Jan. 13, 14 above; **Leander M. Jones**.

[72] *See:* Note under Jan. 14 above. Leander and Harriet Jones lived in Monterey. The implication is that Ellen White was sending these gifts in care of Henry Pierce, who was returning to Monterey.

[73] This person has not been identified.

[74] *Identity:* Apparently the coat was a gift from the church members in Monterey and Allegan. In an undated letter addressed "to the church in Monterey and Allegan," Joseph Bates wrote, "I am very much obliged to you for the twelve dollars you sent Sr. Augusta Bouges to buy me a coat. I needed one about this time, about as much as any garment." Events mentioned in the letter indicate that it was written in February 1859, even though earlier editors have dated it "cir. 1852." The generosity of the Monterey members did not stop here. The following year, 1860, a house was built in Monterey for the Bateses. Extant church minutes indicate that the house was financed in whole or in part by Monterey members.

See: Joseph Bates, "To the Church in Monterey and Allegan" (n.d.); *History of Allegan and Barry Counties, Michigan,* p. 286; "Records of the Seventh-day Adventist Church, Monterey, Michigan [1860-1880]," monthly meeting minutes for Oct. 7, 1860, Jan. 6, 1861, Jan. 5, 1862.

[75] *Identities:* Brethren "Carmen" and "Street" urged the Whites "strongly to come to their place." There is no mention in the *Review* of a "Carmen" and a "Street" living close to each other; in fact, the surname "Carmen" does not appear at all during this period. However, there are several references to a "J. F. Carman" and an "S. A. Street," both from West Windsor, Eaton County, Michigan, about 35 miles (56 kilometers) east of Battle Creek. This provides almost certain evidence for the identities of these two persons and indicates that Ellen White is using the alternative spelling "Carmen" for "Carman." The full names of both are found in sources specified below.

See: Search terms "Carmen," "Carman," and "Street" in *Words of the Pioneers;* obituary: "John Frost Carman," *Review,* May 10, 1923, p. 22; obituary: "Sarah Jane Street," *Review,* Mar. 25, 1915, p. 22.

[76] *See:* Notes for Jan. 3 entry.

[77] Probably for purposes of the autobiography Ellen White was preparing. See notes under Jan. 1 and Jan. 4 above.

[Battle Creek] Monday, February 7

Sent a letter to my sister Mary [**Mary Plummer Foss**] and one to Jane Seaman.[78] Visited my mother in the afternoon; made her a cap. Had a conversation with **Robert Holland**[79] in the evening. Sarah's [**Sarah B. Belden**][80] hired girl was sick.

[Battle Creek] Tuesday, February 8

Wrote a letter to Sister Drusilla Lampson [**Drusilla Lamson**][81] and Sister **Mary Chase**.[82] In the afternoon visited Sister Lyon [**Deborah Lyon**],[83] in

---

[78] *Identity:* Little more than her location can be known for sure about the "Jane Seaman" of this diary entry. The few available sources locate her either in Rochester, New York, or in nearby Clarkson. It could well be that Ellen White is writing to an acquaintance from her Rochester years in the early 1850s. Questions remaining unanswered include whether "Jane Seaman" was, in fact, the "Sarah Jane Seaman," of whom more is known; whether she was the wife of "E. R. Seaman," an active layman from Rochester; and whether she was born "Sarah Jane Loughborough," a cousin of J. N. Loughborough. The letters to Mary Foss and Jane Seaman are not in the White Estate archives.

See: Angeline Stevens Andrews, "Diary" entries for Feb. 23, 24, 1862; search term "Seaman" in *Review and Herald* online collection, www.adventistarchives.org; obituary: "Sarah Jane Seaman," *Review,* July 27, 1869, p. 39.

[79] *Identity:* Evidence supports identifying this Robert Holland as the one who conducted the short-lived first school for Sabbatarian Adventist children in Battle Creek, in 1856 or 1857. Frequent receipts appear in the *Review* from 1854 onward for a "R. Holland," with the full name "Robert Holland" given in 1868, together with address in Napoleon, Michigan. Although his occupation in the 1870 census is given as "pedlar," the fact that the 1860 census lists him as "School Teacher" confirms his identity.

See: W. C. White, "Memories and Records," p. 1; E. M. Cadwallader, *A History of Seventh-day Adventist Education,* p. 6; search term "Holland" in *Words of the Pioneers;* "Receipts," *Review,* June 18, 1867, p. 16; 1870 U.S. Federal Census, "Holland, Robert," Michigan, Jackson County, Napoleon, p. 22; 1860 U.S. Federal Census, "Robert Holland," Michigan, Kent County, Caledonia, p. 157.

[80] *See:* Notes for Jan. 3 entry.

[81] Drusilla Lamson, about 28 years old and living just outside Rochester, New York, was a daughter of **Jonathan T.** and **Caroline Orton**. Ellen White knew Drusilla well from the years the Whites spent in Rochester (1852-1855), where the Ortons were prominent members of the Sabbatarian group. The spelling "Lamson" rather than "Lampson" is found in the *Review* and most other sources.

See: 1860 U.S. Federal Census, "Drusilla Lampson," New York, Monroe County, Gates, p. 173; 1850 U.S. Federal Census, "Drusilla Orton," New York, Monroe County, Rochester Ward 7, p. 317; search term "Orton" in *Words of the Pioneers.*

[82] Ellen White's sister-in-law, married to Daniel Chase, of Fairfield, Maine. The letters to Drusilla Lampson and Mary Chase are not in the White Estate archives.

[83] The most frequently mentioned Lyon family in Battle Creek during this period is that of Henry and Deborah Lyon. Both in their 60s, they had moved to Battle Creek in 1853. Ellen White might also be referring to Mary H. Lyon, unmarried and in her 30s, also a member of the Battle Creek group. However, in other correspondence Ellen White refers to Mary Lyon not as "Sister Lyon" but as "Sister Mary" (Lt 19, 1861 [Oct. 13], and Lt 14, 1862 [Jan. 13]) or "Sister Mary Lyon" (Lt 2, 1862 [Jan. 20]). The likelihood, therefore, is that "Sister Lyon" is Deborah Lyon.

See: Search term "Lyon" in *Words of the Pioneers;* [notice re address of Henry Lyon], *Review,* Dec. 27, 1853, p. 200; obituary: "Henry Lyon," *Review,* May 28, 1872, p. 191;

company with Mother White [**Betsey White**][84] and Sister Ballou.[85] Had quite a pleasant interview. Cut and made some caps for Mother. It may be the last time I shall have the privilege of making caps for her head,[86] but my prayer is that she may wear a crown of glory in the kingdom of heaven. Brother Den[87] has been thrown down and beaten by drunken men. Two men interfered. Brother Den complained of the men. They were shut up last night. They have their trial today. The same men struck my husband three times with a whip. Did not hurt him. The world is growing worse and worse. My prayer is, O Lord, gather not my soul with sinners, nor my life with bloody men.

[Battle Creek] Wednesday, February 9

Had a good season of family prayer. My soul hungers and thirsts for salvation and holiness of heart. My anxiety is great for my children. I was led out to cry earnestly to God for them that they may be subjects of His grace and heirs of salvation. Wrote my twin sister[88] a letter, also one to my sister Mary and one to Brother and Sister Folsom [**Paul** and **Margaret Folsom**].[89]

[Battle Creek] Thursday, February 10

Am not well. In the forenoon Sister Harriet Smith [**Harriet N. Smith**][90] visited us. In the afternoon Sister Kellogg [**Ann Janette Kellogg**][91] came and,

---

obituary: "Deborah Lyon," *Review,* Mar. 10, 1874, p. 103; 1860 U.S. Federal Census, "Mary H. Lyon," Michigan, Calhoun County, Battle Creek, p. 122.

[84] *See:* Notes on Jan. 28 entry.

[85] The identity of this person has not been established. The only Adventist Ballou family known from this period is **James M.** and **Hulda Ballou**, living in Jefferson County, New York. It is possible, of course, that Hulda Ballou was visiting Battle Creek at this time.

See: Search term "Ballou" in *Words of the Pioneers.*

[86] Ellen's mother, **Eunice Harmon**, died almost five years later, aged 77.

See: Obituary: "Eunice Harmon," *Review,* Jan. 26, 1864, p. 71.

[87] This person has not been identified.

[88] *Identity:* Ellen White's twin sister, **Elizabeth N.** ("Lizzie"), married to **Reuben M. Bangs** and living in Gorham, Maine. Elizabeth Bangs never became a Sabbathkeeper, but the two sisters had a warm relationship. Some of their correspondence, covering several decades, has been preserved in the White Estate archives. None of the letters written on this date are in the White Estate archives.

[89] *Identity:* The only "Folsom" mentioned in the *Review* before 1864 is Paul Folsom, living near Boston, Massachusetts. The name of his wife is found in census records. It could be that the Ellen White's main purpose in writing this letter was to request from the Folsoms details for her forthcoming autobiography. Paul Folsom, to whom published references go back to 1851, was a leading figure among Sabbatarian Adventists in Massachusetts. For years regular Sabbath services and conferences had been held at the Folsom home in Somerville, just north of Boston. There are several references to visits by Ellen and James White to their home.

See: Search term "Folsom" in *Review and Herald* online collection, www.adventistarchives.org; 1860 U.S. Federal Census, "Margaret Folsom," Massachusetts, Middlesex County, Somerville, p. 76; Ellen G. White, Lt 9, 1859 (Sept. 6), Ms 7, 1859 (diary entries Sept. 5, 19).

[90] Wife of *Review* editor **Uriah Smith**.

[91] *Identity:* This is most likely Ann Janette Kellogg, second wife of John Preston Kellogg,

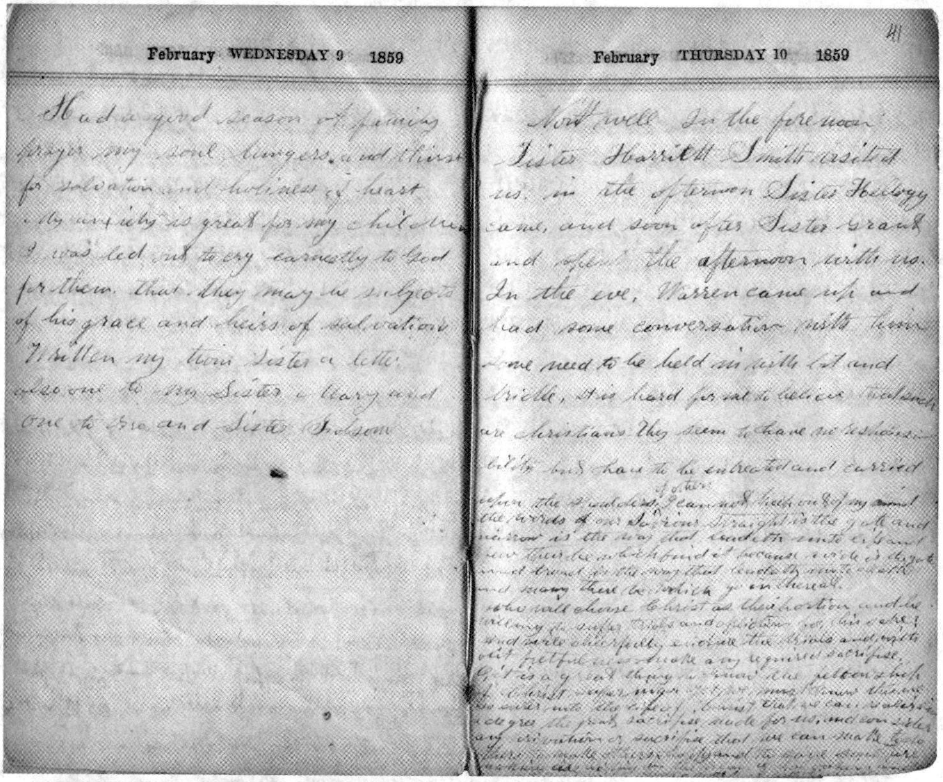

February WEDNESDAY 9 1859

Had a good season of family prayer my soul hungers and thirsts for salvation and holiness of heart. My anxiety is great for my children. I was led out to cry earnestly to God for them that they may be subjects of his grace and heirs of salvation. Written my twin sister a letter, also one to my sister Mary and one to Bro and Sister Folsom.

41

February THURSDAY 10 1859

Not well. In the forenoon Sister Harriett Smith visited us. In the afternoon Sister Kellogg came, and soon after Sister Grant and spent the afternoon with us. In the eve, Warren came up and had some conversation with him. Some need to be held in with bit and bridle. It is hard for me to believe that such are Christians. They seem to have no responsibility but have to be entreated and carried upon the shoulders of others. I cannot keep out of my mind the words of our Saviour: Straight is the gate and narrow is the way that leadeth unto life and few there be which find it because wide is the gate and broad is the way that leadeth unto death and many there be which go in thereat. Who will choose Christ as their portion and be willing to suffer trials and affliction for his sake, and while cheerfully endure the trials and [illegible] without fretfulness make any required sacrifice. O it is a great thing to know the fellowship of Christ sufferings. Yet we must know this, we [illegible] enter into the life of Christ that we can realize in a degree the great sacrifice made for us, and consider any deprivation or sacrifice that we can make to [illegible] others to make others happy and to save souls [illegible]

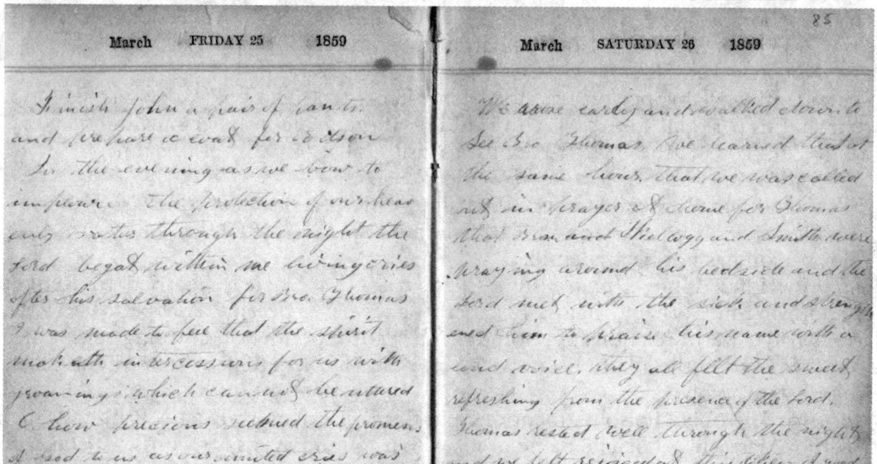

March FRIDAY 25 1859

Finish John a pair of pants and we have a coat for Edson. In the evening as we bow to implore the protection of our heavenly Father through the night the Lord begat within me living cries after his salvation for Bro. Thomas. I was made to feel that the spirit maketh intercessions for us with groanings which cannot be uttered. O how precious seemed the promises of God to us as our united cries was sent up for the restoration of our afflicted brother. Our trembling faith grasped the strong promises of God, and we felt like agonizing like the importunate widow until our petitions should be answered and our dear Bro. restored to health again.

85

March SATURDAY 26 1859

We arose early and walked down to see Bro. Thomas. We learned that at the same hour that we was called out in prayer at home for Thomas that Bros. and Kellogg and Smith were praying around his bedside and the Lord met with the sick and strengthened him to praise his name with a loud voice. They all felt the sweet refreshing from the presence of the Lord. Thomas rested well through the night and we felt rejoiced at this token of good from the Lord. We had a praying season for our dear brother. The [Lord] met with and blessed him and us again and he praised the Lord for his great goodness. At half past one o'clock there was united with the Office met again to pray for Thomas recovery. The Lord gave us a measure of freedom.

Ellen White's diary entries from February and March 1859

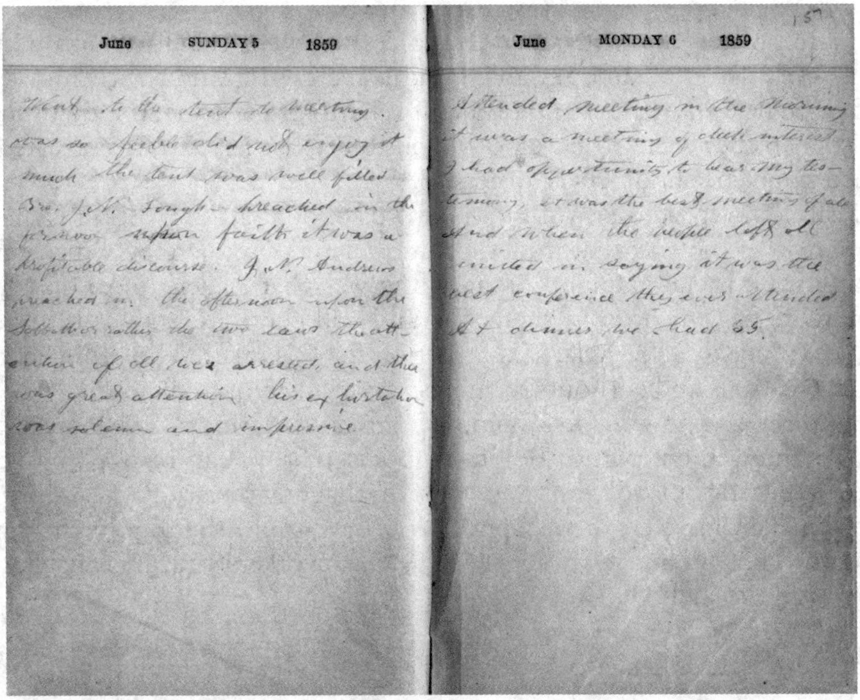

June SUNDAY 5 1859

Went to the tent to meeting. was so feeble did not enjoy it much the tent was well filled Bro. J.N. Loughborough preached in the forenoon upon faith it was a profitable discourse. J.N. Andrews preached in the afternoon upon the Sabbath rather the two laws the attention of all was arrested and there was great attention his exhortation was solemn and impressive

June MONDAY 6 1859

Attended meeting in the morning it was a meeting of deep interest I had opportunity to bear my testimony, it was the best meeting of all And when the people left all united in saying it was the best conference they ever attended At dinner we had 55.

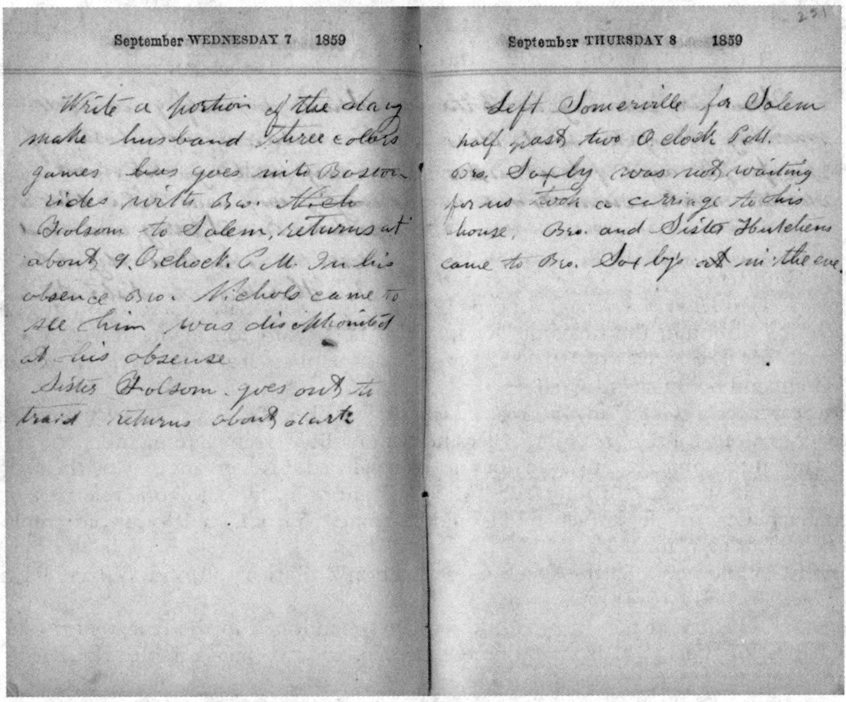

September WEDNESDAY 7 1859

Write a portion of the day make husband three collars James bus goes into Boston rides with Bro. Nichols Folsom to Salem, returns at about 9 O clock P.M. In his absence Bro. Nichols came to see him, was disappointed at his absense Sister Folsom goes out to trade returns about dark

September THURSDAY 8 1859

Left Somerville for Salem half past two O clock P.M. Bro. Sofly was not waiting for us took a carriage to his house, Bro. and Sister Hutchens came to Bro. Soflys at in the eve.

Ellen White's diary entries from June and September 1859

soon after, Sister Grant [**Nancy Grant**],[92] and spent the afternoon with us. In the eve Warren[93] came up and I had some conversation with him. Some need to be held in with bit and bridle. It is hard for me to believe that such are Christians. They seem to have no responsibility but have to be entreated and carried upon the shoulders of others.

I cannot keep out of my mind the words of our Saviour, "Strait is the gate and narrow is the way that leadeth unto life, and few there be which find it; because wide is the gate and broad is the way that leadeth unto death, and many there be which go in thereat." Who will choose Christ as his portion and be willing to suffer trial and affliction for His sake? Who will cheerfully endure the trials and without fretfulness make any required sacrifice? Oh, it is a great thing to know the fellowship of Christ's sufferings; yet we must know this. We must so enter into the life of Christ that we can realize in a degree the great sacrifice made for us and consider that any privation or sacrifice that we can make to make others happy and to save souls is aiding in the plan of salvation. Thus we are coworkers with God, coworkers with His angels.

[Battle Creek] Friday, February 11

Am not well. Unable to write. Keep my chamber nearly all day.

[Battle Creek] Sabbath, February 12

Sabbath attended meeting all day. Brethren Charles Jones [**Charles Jones**] and Henry Pierce [**Henry Harlow Pierce**][94] were present. My husband preached in the forenoon, How shall a young man cleanse his ways? etc. It

---

a prominent Sabbatarian Adventist who had moved to Battle Creek in 1856. J. P. Kellogg's oldest daughter, Julia, age 21, as well as Louisa, wife of his oldest son, Merritt G., were also members of the Battle Creek church, so technically speaking they might also have been referred to as "Sister Kellogg." However, it seems more likely that the title "Sister Kellogg" would be reserved for Ann Janette, the most senior of them.

See: Timothy Hopkins, *The Kelloggs in the Old World and the New*, vol. 1, p. 636; Richard W. Schwarz, *John Harvey Kellogg, M.D.*, p. 17; EGWEnc, s.v. "Battle Creek Congregation."

[92] *Identity:* Although the surname "Grant" was fairly common in the *Review* during the 1850s and early 1860s, lists of Battle Creek church members from this period mention only Nancy Grant and her husband, Walter.

See: Search term "Grant" in *Words of the Pioneers;* EGWEnc, s.v. "Battle Creek Congregation."

[93] *Identity:* Both John Warren Bacheller and Samuel B. Warren were members of the Battle Creek group at this time. Ellen White does not normally address persons only by their surname, without any title such as "Brother" or "Mr." It is more likely that she is referring to **John Warren Bacheller**, usually known by his middle name "Warren," a 19-year-old employed at the Review printing plant.

See: EGWEnc, s.v. "Battle Creek Congregation"; obituary: "John Warren Bacheller," *Review*, Oct. 25, 1917, p. 18.

[94] *Identity:* "Henry Pierce, from Monterey" was mentioned in the diary entry of Feb. 3. Since Charles Jones also was from Monterey, perhaps the two men came to the Battle Creek meeting together.

See: Obituary: "Charles Jones," *Review*, Mar. 24, 1904, p. 23.

seemed to be a right and proper subject, appropriate for the people. In the afternoon we had a conference meeting. It was a profitable time. The presence of the Lord was with us. Free testimonies were borne and all who have recently professed the truth bore their testimony. Agnes [**Agnes Irving**][95] spoke. I never heard her before. Brother Jones and Brother Pierce tarried with us over the night.

[Battle Creek] Sunday, February 13

Have some little freedom in writing. My carpet was brought home today, and Sister Byington [**Catherine Byington**][96] offers to give me the weaving of it. It is very kind in her. Do not know as I ought to accept it.

[Battle Creek] Sabbath, February 19

The Lord was with us in meeting.

[Battle Creek] Monday, February 21

Sent a letter of eight pages to Dr. Naramore [**John Naramore**][97] and a couple of pages to Brother Orton [**Jonathan T. Orton**].[98]

[See also Lt 31, 1859, written on this date.]

[Battle Creek] Sabbath, February 26

Had a good meeting. There was preaching in the forenoon and prayer and conference in the eve. It is encouraging to see those who have lately embraced the truth so ready to bear their testimony. May the Lord build them up in the most holy faith and strengthen them to run the whole length of the Christian road that they may obtain an everlasting victory, a rich and glorious reward.

My lungs are very painful. Every breath causes me distress. In the eve Brother and Sister Godsmark [**Richard** and **Huldah Jane Godsmark**][99]

---

[95] *Identity:* 17-year-old Agnes Irving (see Jan. 6 and Mar. 10 entries). Agnes was baptized three months later (see Ms 6, 1859 [Apr. 23 entry]).

[96] *Identity:* A clue as to the identity of "Sister Byington" is found in Ellen White's diary entry for Apr. 16 (Ms 6, 1859), where the family of "Brother Byington" is said to be located in or near Ceresco, Michigan, a few miles from Battle Creek. The *Review* published numerous letters from John and/or Catherine Byington signed "Ceresco, Michigan." They had moved from New York to Ceresco (actually to the adjacent township of Newton; Ceresco was probably the postal address) in 1858. One might question whether this "Sister Byington" refers to the wife of John and Catherine's son, **John Fletcher Byington**, or maybe to their adult daughter, **Martha**. In her diaries, however, Ellen White tended to refer to younger members of an extended family by their first names, thus, in this case, reserving the title "Sister Byington" for the mother.

See: Search terms "Byington" and "Ceresco" in *Words of the Pioneers;* 1860 U.S. Federal Census, "Catherine Byington," Michigan, Calhoun County, Newton, p. 244.

[97] *Identity:* See under Jan. 3 above. This letter is not in the White Estate archives.

[98] *Identity:* See under Jan. 3 above. This letter is not in the White Estate archives.

[99] *Identity:* As is made clear in the diary entries for March 23 and 24, the Godsmarks lived

visited us to spend the night with us. I suffered so much pain I could not sit up. Unwillingly I retired. I was disappointed; had hoped to enjoy the society of these Christian friends. I passed through considerable suffering before sleeping.

[Battle Creek] Monday, February 28

Mary Loughborough came here; stopped with us to dinner. Her baby was sick.[100] In the afternoon went in to Sister Ratel's [**Marguerite Ratelle**].[101] Had a pleasant interview. Her babe had on an old, torn, white dress—the best he has except one that she keeps to put on him when she goes out with him. She speaks of her children that died two years since.[102] She does not wish them alive again. The family are all poor. The oldest girl much prizes a Bible

---

locally. The 1860 census lists only two Godsmark households in all of Michigan, that headed by John Godsmark and that headed by his brother Richard Godsmark, both living in Bedford Township, a few miles north of Battle Creek. There is no mention of John Godsmark or any of his household in the *Review* or other current Adventist sources, whereas these contain many mentions of "R. Godsmark," "Richard Godsmark," and "Sr. H. Godsmark." By elimination, therefore, we are left with the conclusion that Ellen White is referring to Richard and Huldah Godsmark, of Bedford.

See: 1860 U.S. Federal Census, "John Godsmark," Michigan, Calhoun County, Bedford, p. 116; 1860 U.S. Federal Census, "Richard Godsmark," Michigan, Calhoun County, Bedford, p. 118; search term "Godsmark" in *Words of the Pioneers;* Mark Bovee, "Richard Godsmark: A Man of God Who Left His Mark in the Battle Creek Area."

[100] Teresa C. Loughborough died the following January of "lung fever, which terminated in consumption"; she was less than 2 years old. J. N. Loughborough's diary for 1859 contains a number of references to Teresa's health.

See: Obituary: "Teresa C. Loughborough," *Review,* Jan. 12, 1860, p. 63; J. N. Loughborough, "Diary," entries for Sept. 20, 30; Oct. 8, 11; Dec. 27, 31.

[101] *Identity:* The name "Ratel" (or "Ratelle," as in the June 22 diary entry) does not appear in Adventist sources. However, census records from Battle Creek and vicinity list the family of Joseph and Marguerite Ratelle from 1860 onward (with various spellings). Persuasive evidence that Marguerite is the "Sister Ratel(le)" Ellen White writes of is found in a newspaper interview given by Marguerite Ratelle on her ninetieth birthday in which she tells of moving to Battle Creek about 1854 and how "she knew Elder James White . . . and Mrs. Ellen G. White, the prophetess, well, they living neighbor to her." The article adds that "their friendship was a pleasant one despite their religious differences, Mrs. Ratelle being a Baptist."

See: 1860 U.S. Federal Census, "Margret Rotell [*sic*]," Michigan, Calhoun County, Emmett, p. 152; 1870 U.S. Federal Census, "Margaret Ritell [*sic*]," Michigan, Barry County, Johnstown, p. 194; 1880 U.S. Federal Census, "Margret Rattell [*sic*]," Michigan, Calhoun County, Battle Creek, p. 50; 1900 U.S. Federal Census, "Margaret Ratelle," Michigan, Calhoun County, Battle Creek Ward 3, p. 165; "In Battle Creek Over 63 Years: Mrs. Marguerite Ratelle, Who is 90, Recalls Early Day Experiences," newspaper account, Oct. 2, 1919, in Ross Coller Collection, Willard Library, Battle Creek, Michigan; "Mrs. Chapman, B. C. Resident 82 Years, Dies," Mar. 12, 1937, in Ross Coller Collection, Willard Library, Battle Creek, Michigan; obituary: "Mrs. Elmira Chapman," *Lake Union Herald,* Mar. 30, 1937, p. 10.

[102] "Seven children were born" to the Ratelles, according to a newspaper account, "but only three lived to man and womanhood." The "babe" mentioned in this entry is Joseph E. Ratell, born in 1858, who died some months later, in July 1859.

See: "In Battle Creek Over 63 Years: Mrs. Marguerite Ratelle, Who is 90, Recalls Early Day Experiences"; on Joseph E., see burial records in Oakhill Cemetery, Battle Creek, Michigan.

I gave her. She reads out of it to her parents.[103] Sister R's health is very poor. Has spit blood. I fear she will not fill her place in her family long.[104] She tries to do right. Her husband is a poor, wicked, passionate man and she has great trials. May the Lord sustain her. She begs us to pray for her that she may do right at all times.

[Battle Creek] Tuesday, March 1

Walked to the office. Called to see Sister Sarah and Mother. Sarah gave me a little dress and two aprons for Sister Ratel's babe. I then called on Sister Aurora Lockwood [**Aurora B. Lockwood**].[105] Had a pleasant interview with her. She is a choice sister, beloved of God and highly respected of all the church.

I rode down to the city and purchased a few things. Bought a little dress for Sister Ratel's babe. Came to the office, assisted them a little there and then came home to dinner. Sent the little articles to Sister Ratel. Mary Loughborough sends her another dress, so she will do very well now. Oh, that all knew the sweetness of giving to the poor, of helping do others good and making others happy! The Lord opened my heart to do all in my power to relieve those around me. Give me to feel my brother's woe!

[Battle Creek] Wednesday, March 2

Unwell all day. Tried to write a little. Sister Kelsey and her son called on us. Sister Kelsey [**Eunice Rebecca Kelsey**][106] seems sad. She brought wheat to sell and it is musty. Cannot dispose of it. She needs means to use.[107] We prepared her a warm meal and had her sit down and partake of it before starting for

---

[103] The oldest daughter, Elmira E., almost 11 at the time, became a lifelong Seventh-day Adventist.

See: 1860 U.S. Federal Census, "Elmira Rotell [*sic*]," Michigan, Calhoun County, Emmett, p. 152; obituary: "Mrs. Elmira Chapman," *Lake Union Herald,* Mar. 30, 1937, p. 10.

[104] Marguerite Ratelle overcame her health problems and died at 94.

See: "Aged Resident Dies in Indiana: Mrs. Margarette Ratelle, 94, Receives Call," newspaper article, Jan. 24, 1923, in Ross Coller Collection, Willard Library, Battle Creek, Michigan.

[105] Sister of George I. Butler, who later served as General Conference president. Originally from Vermont, later living in Illinois, 32-year-old Aurora, and her husband, **Ransom G. Lockwood**, had recently moved to Battle Creek, where Aurora was employed at the Review publishing office.

See: Obituary: "Aurora Butler Lockwood," *Review,* Jan. 28, 1902, p. 15; Josiah Hart, "Business of Round Grove Conference," *Review,* Mar. 18, 1858, p. 141; John Nevins Andrews et al., *Defense of Elder James White and Wife,* p. 61.

[106] *See:* Jan. 29 notes.

[107] The situation described reflects the difficulties facing Eunice Kelsey, recently widowed with four children, and apparently trying to run a farm with the aid of her oldest son, aged about 16. (See Jan. 29 entry above.)

See: 1860 U.S. Federal Census, "Eunice Kelsey," Michigan, Calhoun, Leroy, p. 226.

the 13-mile [21-kilometer] ride home. It is chilly weather. I lent her a cloak; feared she would suffer. I feel the deepest sympathy for this devoted widow. She has been a kind friend to us and in time of need has assisted us liberally.[108] May the Lord abundantly bless the widow and be her God and husband, and be a God to the fatherless. I look upon my kind husband and see that God has dealt very mercifully with me in sparing to me my husband and dear children. Oh, my heart shall always be grateful for His rich mercy and loving kindness.

[Battle Creek] Thursday, March 3

My health is very poor. Am troubled with severe cramp in my side. Have some fear as to the result. I cannot stand straight, and walk with much pain and difficulty. Intended visiting the brother Dan [?] John.[109] It is impossible to go. I feel a strange weakness. Gain some strength by taking a little tomato wine.[110]

[Battle Creek] Friday, March 4

I have a strong desire to get nearer to God. My heart pants after God, the living God. My time is employed in sewing. Made two caps for my boys. In the eve, at the commencement of the Sabbath, we assembled at Brother T. Meade's [**Thomas B. Mead**] to pray for him, that God would heal him of his disease. He is fast going down, and unless God in mercy raises him, he will go down into the grave. We had unusual freedom in prayer for Thomas.[111] I was

---

[108] The frequent contributions of the Kelseys to various church needs are attested to in the receipt columns of the *Review.*

See: Search term "A.P.H. Kelsey" in *Words of the Pioneers.*

[109] The handwritten original is unclear, with some indication that the word "Dan" (or "Den") has been crossed out, leaving just the name "John." If this is the case, the reference may be to John N. Andrews, who arrived in Battle Creek on March 3 en route to Rochester, and that Ellen White was not well enough to meet him. The following day, March 4, however, Andrews had dinner with the Whites. (See entries for Mar. 3 and 4.)

[110] Medicinal use of "tomato wine" in the nineteenth century is chronicled by Andrew F. Smith. "Recipes for tomato wine were published beginning in the 1840s. J. P. Nichols' recipe . . . was basically tomato juice with sugar. Nichols considered it medicinal . . . 'far better and much safer for a tonic, or other medicinal uses, than the wines generally sold as Port Wines, etc. for such purposes. It is peculiarly adapted to some diseases and states of the system, and is particularly recommended for derangements of the liver.'"

It should be noted that of the five mentions in her 1859 diary of Ellen White taking wine or giving it to others, in four cases the context makes it clear that it was for medicinal use (Ms 5, 1859 [Mar. 3, 10], Ms 6, 1859 [Apr. 15, May 7]). When Ellen White on April 13 simply stated that she "sent her [Sister Fults] a bottle of wine," it can be safely assumed that this was also for a medicinal purpose.

See: Andrew F. Smith, *The Tomato in America,* p. 190; James White, "A Little Grape Wine," *Review,* Mar. 17, 1868, p. 220; EGWEnc, s.v. "Beverages."

[111] Thomas Mead, who had earlier worked at the Review and Herald press, died of tuberculosis two years later, at age 33.

See: Obituary: "Thomas B. Mead," *Review,* Aug. 27, 1861, p. 103.

abundantly blessed. How precious the name of Jesus sounded to me. Brother John Andrews came to this city last night. We have met today and he took dinner with us. Has related particulars concerning his visit at R. We listened with great interest.[112]

[Battle Creek] Sabbath, March 5

Did not attend meeting today. My husband was sick. Have remained with him to wait upon him. The Lord met with us and blessed us this morn. I had unusual liberty in prayer. Brother John Andrews preached twice today. He spent the eve and night with us. We enjoyed the visit much.

[Battle Creek] Sunday, March 6

Had an interview with Martha Byington [**Martha Dormer Amadon** (née **Byington**)].[113] Cut out a dress. We were perplexed; took it all to pieces and made it over. Spent the afternoon with [Mary] Loughborough; attended meeting in the eve. Had quite a free, interesting meeting. After it was time to close, the subject of voting was considered and dwelt upon. James first talked, then Brother Andrews talked, and it was thought by them best to give their influence in favor of right and against wrong. They think it right to vote in favor of temperance men being in office in our city, instead of—by their silence—running the risk of having men of non-temperance put in office. Brother Hewitt [**David Hewitt**][114] told his experience of a few days, and is

---

[112] When J. N. Andrews left for Rochester six weeks earlier (see notes under Jan. 14), James White described his trip as "an important mission." Andrews later reported that he had done further research on the history of the Sabbath while in Rochester and that he would "soon forward" a manuscript to the *Review*. No doubt his research was done at the Rochester Theological Seminary library, which at this time had a collection of some 7,000 volumes, much of it in the area of church history. Some months later, in September 1859, Andrews' 96-page pamphlet *History of the Sabbath and First Day of the Week . . .*" was published, priced at 10 cents. This was expanded to a 340-page book by the same title in 1861.

See: J. W. [James White], [notice], *Review*, Jan. 27, 1859, p. 80; J. N. Andrews, "My Visit East," *Review*, Apr. 28, 1859, p. 181; George Ripley and Charles A. Dana, ed., *The New American Cyclopaedia: A Popular Dictionary of General Knowledge*, s.v. "Rochester"; "History of the Sabbath," *Review*, Oct. 22, 1861, p. 168; "New Works," *Review*, Sept. 1, 1859, p. 120.

[113] *Identity:* Martha Dormer Byington, daughter of **John Byington**, first General Conference president. This is one of several references showing that Martha Byington worked in the White home, at least sporadically, prior to her marriage to George W. Amadon in 1860. The earliest of these is a notation in her diary dated Sept. 4, 1857: "Arrived at Bro. White's in BC," followed by "Began teaching White boys," dated Nov. 12, 1857.

See: Obituary: "Martha D. Amadon," *Review*, Feb. 4, 1937, p. 21; Martha Byington, 1857 diary, notes on back cover; Ellen G. White, *An Appeal to the Youth*, p. 43.

[114] The identity of "Brother Hewitt" is not at first obvious, since a number of Sabbatarians with that surname lived in various places during this period. The same holds for the names Hart, Lyon, and Kellogg, mentioned in the following lines. However, the likelihood is that most of the men listed lived in Battle Creek or vicinity. This conclusion is based on the fact that the "meeting" that they attended was not advertised or reported in the *Review*, which no doubt it would have been if it had been held with representation from a wider area. If, then, the field

settled that it is right to cast his vote. Brother Hart talked well. Brother Lyon [**Henry Lyon**] opposed. No other objected to voting, but Brother Kellogg [**John Preston Kellogg**] begins to feel that it is right. Pleasant feelings exist among all the brethren. Oh, that they may all act in the fear of God. Men of intemperance have been in the office today, in a flattering manner expressing their approbation of the course of Sabbathkeepers in not voting, and expressing hope that they will stick to their course and, like the Quakers, not cast their vote. Satan and his evil angels are busy at this time and he has a work upon the earth. May Satan be disappointed, is my prayer.[115]

[Battle Creek] Monday, March 7

It is rainy today. It looks very gloomy without, but if the Sun of righteousness shines in my heart all is well and no outward appearance and gloom can make me sad. Today the votes are cast for town officers.

[Battle Creek] Tuesday, March 8

It is a day when infirmities are striving for the victory. I suffer much pain in my left shoulder and lung. My spirits are depressed. Brother John Andrews leaves today. He came up to visit us in the eve. Had a pleasant interview. I got together a few things for him to take home. Send Angeline [**Angeline**

---

is narrowed to the Battle Creek area, most likely the men referred to are David Hewitt, Henry Lyon, and John Preston Kellogg. No "Brother Hart" can be found living in the Battle Creek area during this time, so it remains uncertain whether the visitor was Asa Hart, of Ingham County, Michigan; A. G. Hart, from Iowa; P. Hart, from Connecticut; or some other Hart.

See: Search terms "Hewitt," "Hart," "Lyon," and "Kellogg," in *Words of the Pioneers;* EGWEnc, s.v. "Battle Creek Congregation."

[115] This report showing that leading Sabbatarian Adventists, including Ellen White, favored participation in the 1859 Battle Creek local election, is noteworthy. Although having strong views on moral issues such as slavery and temperance, most Adventists had until now rejected the path of political activism to achieve changes in society. "We declare our neutrality in politics," Uriah Smith had asserted before the 1856 presidential election, "and refuse to take part in a contest so exciting as the one which is now agitating this nation." The transition from such an apolitical stance to a more activist, albeit a selective and cautious activist, stance in the years that followed is traced in the studies by Syme, Gordon, Butler, and Morgan listed below. They also offer differing perspectives on the influence of premillenialism, views on the role of America in prophecy, and other factors in shaping Seventh-day Adventist perspectives on political involvement.

See: "Politics," *Review,* Sept. 11, 1856, p. 152; Eric Douglas Syme, *A History of SDA Church-State Relations in the United States;* Paul A. Gordon, "The Right to Vote—Shall I Exercise It?" *Review,* Sept. 18, 1980, pp. 4-7, and Sept. 25, 1980, pp. 11-13; Jonathan M. Butler, "Adventism and the American Experience," in Edwin S. Gaustad, ed., *The Rise of Adventism,* pp. 173-206; Douglas Morgan, *Adventism and the American Republic.* Further details on the political struggle over temperance in the Battle Creek election of 1859 are given by Yvonne D. Anderson, "The Bible, the Bottle, and the Ballot: Seventh-day Adventist Political Activism 1850-1900," *Adventist Heritage,* August 1982, pp. 39-41.

Andrews][116] a new calico dress, nine shillings [$1.12],[117] and a stout pair of calfskin shoes. Father gives the making of the shoes and the making of a pair of boots for Brother John Andrews. I send the little boy a nice little flannel shirt and yarn to knit him a pair of stockings. I send Sister, or Mother, Andrews [**Sarah L. Andrews**] a nice large cape, well wadded, for her to wear. I made a bag to put them in, of towel cloth. Wrote three small pages to Sister Mary Chase.[118] In it wrote recipe obtained from John's.[119]

[Battle Creek] Wednesday, March 9

I suffer so much pain in my shoulder, lung, and my whole side, I can write but little. Wrote six small pages to Sarah Whipple [**Sarah B. Whipple**].[120]

I visited my mother. Made her a black cap. In the eve Sister Mary Meade [**Mary Jane Mead**][121] came in for husband and self to visit them and encourage Thomas. He is much cast down. His lungs trouble him much. James talked

---

[116] *Identity:* The setting here is John Andrews's imminent return home to Iowa and Ellen White's presents to his wife, Angeline, infant son, Charles Melville, and mother, Sarah L. According to the 1860 census, John Andrews and his family lived on the same farm as his parents, Sarah and Edward, in Allamakee County.

See: 1860 U.S. Federal Census, "Edward Andrews," Iowa, Allamakee, Waukon, p. 186.

[117] Although after the American Revolution the old colonial currency of pounds, shillings, and pence was replaced by dollars and cents, through force of habit many people continued to think in terms of the old currency. To accommodate such traditionalist thinking, retail prices and wages were often expressed in shillings and pence well into the nineteenth century although actual payment would be made in American currency (or with certain foreign coins that remained legal tender until 1857). The "exchange rate" applied to such transactions in Michigan, New York, and Ohio was set at eight shillings to the dollar, or 12.5 cents to the shilling. (Rather confusingly for the traveler, different exchange rates were employed in other states.) Thus when Ellen White wrote here of giving "nine shillings" and on March 10 of paying "nine shillings a week" in wages, this would translate into one dollar and 12.5 cents.

See: Robert E. Wright, *Hamilton Unbound: Finance and the Creation of the American Republic,* p. 99; Daniel Adams, *Arithmetic,* p. 221.

[118] *See:* Feb. 8 entry. This letter is not in the White Estate archives.

[119] This person has not been identified.

[120] This letter to Sarah Whipple is not in the White Estate archives. One point of contact between Sarah, her husband, **John G. Whipple**, and the Whites at this time was their common concern for **Michael B. Czechowski**, the Polish ex-Catholic priest-turned-Sabbatarian Adventist preacher, who had recently started evangelistic work among French Canadians living in the vicinity of the Whipples in northern New York, close to the Canadian border. A few months earlier James White had appealed for contributions to the impoverished Czechowski family and specifically commended "Brn. Taylor and Whipple" for having "done much for him." Later in 1859 Ellen White gave donated clothing to Sarah Whipple to be forwarded to Czechowski.

See: James White, "Bro. M. B. Czechowski," *Review,* Dec. 30, 1858, p. 48; E. G. W. [Ellen G. White], "Articles of Clothing," *The Good Samaritan,* December 1859, p. 8; search terms "J. G. Whipple" and "Sarah B. Whipple" in *Words of the Pioneers.* For a survey of M. B. Czechowski's evangelism in New York 1858-1861, see Rajmund L. Dabrowski, "The Sojourn of M. B. Czechowski on the American Continent," in *Michael Belina Czechowski 1818-1876,* pp. 106-116.

[121] Wife of **Thomas B. Mead** (cf. Mar. 4 entry).

encouragingly, then we had a season of prayer. The Lord met with them and all are much encouraged.

[Battle Creek] Thursday, March 10

Walked to the city and back. Was very weary. Purchased John F.[122] a pair of pants. In the afternoon Sister Irving [**Catherine Irving**] came in. She looked sad and appeared to be chilled. Agnes [**Agnes Irving**][123] was much affected, as she noticed a little reluctance on the part of her mother to tell her how sick father was. She burst into tears and cried out in an earnest manner, "Ma, tell me how Pa is?" She had feared that he was dead. Her mother, deeply affected, told her he was failing slowly. Oh, what a scene I witnessed! The mother compelled to come to the daughter for her hard-earned wages to support a dying husband and father and four children. The mother's feelings—entirely overcome as she feels her necessity and her reluctance to take all her daughter's wages.

For ten weeks the daughter has lived with us and we have paid her nine shillings [$1.12] a week. All but one dollar of this she has handed to her mother. Her clothes are poor, yet she does not appropriate any means to her own use. She forgets herself in her self-sacrifice and devotion to her parents. It was as affecting a scene as I have ever witnessed. The reluctance of the mother to accept, through necessity, the wages—all the wages—of a daughter, and the willingness and freedom of the daughter to have all go to her poor afflicted parents.

The mother and daughter wept, and we wept. We aided them some. Paid half toward a pair of boots for a little brother—one dollar. I paid one dollar fifty for a pair of shoes for the mother. Husband gave her one dollar in money. Henry [**Henry Nichols White**, age 11] gave her ten cents, Edson [**James Edson White**, age 9] ten cents, and little Willie [**William Clarence White**, age 4] ten. Husband gave her five dollars more to buy a few luxuries for the sick one. We parted with considerable half-worn clothing to make over. We put up one pint [.5 liters] of rich grape wine[124] and another pint of currant for the sick one, and sent a little handful of dried apples for the sick one's table.

[Battle Creek] Friday, March 11

It has been dark and stormy all day. It has rained and blown very hard.

---

[122] This could well be **John Quincy Foy**, a 16-year-old from Maine who had come two years earlier to learn the printing trade at the Review and Herald Press. The 1860 census lists "John Q. Foy" as living with the Whites, which could explain why Ellen White is buying clothing for him.

See: 1860 U.S. Federal Census, "John Q. Foy," Michigan, Calhoun County, Battle Creek, p. 6.

[123] *See:* Jan. 2 and Jan. 6 entries above, and variant in E. G. W. [Ellen G. White], "From My Diary," *The Good Samaritan,* December 1859, p. 5.

[124] *See:* Note under entry for Mar. 3.

Husband has been preparing for a garden. Rather early spring. Large holes are prepared in the earth for the pieplant.[125]

[Battle Creek] Sabbath, March 12

Not able to attend meeting.

[Battle Creek] Tuesday, March 15

Went to the office. Wrote two letters: one to J. Clark [**Joseph Clarke**],[126] Portage [Ohio], three pages of foolscap; one to Paul Folsom [**Paul Folsom**],[127] six pages of note paper.

Sister Decker[128] sends in ten dollars to James [**James Springer White**] and Uriah [**Uriah Smith**] to apply where it is most needed. Applied two dollars to Sister Irving. William[129] handed me one dollar to dispose of for her.

[Battle Creek] Wednesday, March 16

Wrote a letter of six pages to Sister Decker.

[Battle Creek] Thursday, March 17

George [**George Washington Amadon**],[130] Agnes, and myself visited Brother Irving [**William Irving**].[131]

[Battle Creek] Friday, March 18

Finished the arrangement of letters to the office.

---

[125] Garden rhubarb.

[126] *Identity:* There are a number of persons with the names "Clark" or "Clarke" mentioned in the *Review* during this period, but the only ones said to live in Portage, Ohio, are Joseph Clarke and his wife, Sarah. The letters written by Ellen White to Joseph Clarke and Paul Folsom are not in the White Estate archives.

See: Search terms "Clark" and "Clarke" in *Words of the Pioneers.*

[127] *See:* Feb. 9 entry.

[128] *Identity:* Which "Sister Decker" this was cannot be determined. During this period Rachel Decker, of Iowa; Adelia M. Decker, of New York; Emma E. Decker; and Elizabeth S. Decker were mentioned in the *Review.* The letter and Ellen White's reply the next day are not in the White Estate archives.

See: Search term "Decker" in *Words of the Pioneers.*

[129] This person has not been identified.

[130] *Identity:* The information given here that "George" accompanied Ellen White to visit "Brother Irving" on March 17 finds its parallel in J. N. Loughborough's diary entry for that day. On March 17 Loughborough writes, "George and Sr. White at Bro Irvings to-day." A month earlier, on Feb. 10, Loughborough again referred to "George": "George paid me $5.00." It is clear that Loughborough is referring to George W. Amadon, because in the accounts section of his 1859 diary it is revealed that "George Amadon" was boarding with the Loughboroughs "at 1.50 pr week," with an entry for Feb. 10 reading "George paid cash $5.00." Ellen White expanded on this date's entry in *The Good Samaritan,* December 1859, pp. 5, 6.

See: J. N. Loughborough, "Diary," entry for Mar. 17.

[131] *Identity:* See Jan. 2 entry.

[Battle Creek] Sabbath, March 19

Attended meeting in the forenoon. Brother Loughborough preached with great liberty upon the sleep of the dead and the inheritance of the saints. Tarried at home in the afternoon. Read to my children, wrote a letter to Brother Newton and wife,[132] encouraging them in spiritual things. In the evening attended meeting for communion and washing feet. Was not as free as I wished to be on such occasions. My teeth troubled me. Returned home before meeting closed.

[Battle Creek] Sunday, March 20

My health is very poor. Father and Mother are moving over their things today.[133] Mary Ann, Brother Irving's daughter, just returned from visiting her parents. They are somewhat anxious to get near the village of Battle Creek.[134] Brother Thomas Meade came to our house. Stopped with us until his things were moved. I was surprised to see how fast he has run down. He is very weak. We must trust in God. If we look at appearances we should think his case hopeless, for he seems marked for the grave. Mary, his wife, took dinner with us. She is very worn and tired from moving,[135] and then her husband's weak state depresses her spirits. May the Lord spare Thomas to his family and to the church, is our earnest prayer. The arm of flesh cannot save him. The Lord is mighty to save. In Him we trust. We believe we shall not trust in vain.

[Battle Creek] Monday, March 21

I suffer considerably in body, yet went down street to assist in buying Father and Mother things to keep house with. Returned home for dinner

---

[132] *Identities:* Which "Newton" this was of several Sabbatarians by this name cannot be determined. The letter is not in the White Estate archives.

See: Search term "Newton" in *Words of the Pioneers.*

[133] Ellen White often used the expression "Father and Mother" to refer to James White's parents, **John** and **Betsey White**. When referring to her own parents, the Harmons, Ellen most often (though not always) used the form "my father," etc. In this case there is clear evidence that Ellen is writing of John and Betsey White because of references in this entry and in the March 21 and March 24 entries to "Father and Mother" relocating. Property records confirm that James and Ellen White sold property to John White on March 22, 1859.

See: Deed, Calhoun County, Michigan, liber 46, p. 164, Mar. 22, 1859, recorded June 29, 1859.

[134] The Irving farm was in Ross Township, Kalamazoo County, about 10 miles (16 kilometers) northwest of Battle Creek.

See: 1850 U.S. Federal Census, "William Irvin," Michigan, Kalamazoo County, Ross, p. 300.

[135] Although the exact date is not known, the Meads moved to Waukon, Iowa, in 1859. James White raised funds to enable them to buy a small house there. It is probable that the move mentioned in this diary entry relates to the Meads' transfer to Iowa. The earliest mention of the Meads in Iowa is found in an entry in Ellen White's diary, Oct. 21, 1859 (Ms 8, 1859). For James White's fund-raising on behalf of Thomas Mead, see J. W. [James White], "Brother Mead," *The Good Samaritan,* December 1859, p. 6; John Nevins Andrews et al., *Defense of Elder James White and Wife,* p. 18.

and finished the trading in the afternoon. I suffer much from weariness. Brother and Sister Grant [**Walter** and **Nancy Grant**][136] came up with things for Brother Irving's family. I have a sick headache. Was obliged to retire.

[Battle Creek] Wednesday, March 23

Visited Brother Godsmark's [**Richard Godsmark**] and met with a hearty reception. Had a prayer meeting in the eve, at the stated time of their prayer meeting. We had quite a refreshing season, although there were but a few.

[Battle Creek] Thursday, March 24

Arose early. Assisted my husband and Brother Richard [Richard Godsmark] in taking up a currant bush to plant in our garden. Sister Hulda [**Huldah Jane Godsmark**] rode down to Battle Creek with us. Brother Richard and Orvilla[137] came on after with a load. We arrived at home two hours before they came. They took dinner with us. It is a cold, blustery day. Brother Richard and wife will suffer unless they are warmly clothed. I lend them cloak, mittens, and necktie to protect them. The weather is very changeable, but in the new earth there are no chilling winds, no disagreeable changes. The atmosphere is ever right and healthy. Father and Mother are contented in their new home. May the Lord give them peace of mind and continual refreshing from His divine presence.

[Battle Creek] Friday, March 25

Finished John[138] a pair of pants, and prepare a coat for Edson. In the evening, as we bow to implore the protection of our heavenly Father through the night, the Lord begat within me living cries after His salvation for Brother Thomas. I was made to feel that the Spirit maketh intercession for us with groanings which cannot be uttered. Oh, how precious seemed the promises of God to us as our united cries were sent up for the restoration of our afflicted brother. Our trembling faith grasped the strong promises of God and we felt like agonizing like the importunate widow until our petition should be answered and our dear brother restored to health again.

[Battle Creek] Sabbath, March 26

We arose early and walked down to see Brother Thomas. We learned

---

[136] *See:* Feb. 10 entry.

[137] *Identities:* The context of the entries for March 23 and 24 appears to be an overnight visit by the Whites to their friends Richard and Huldah Godsmark, living on a farm about seven miles (11 kilometers) from Battle Creek in Bedford Township. The identity of "Orvilla" is likely Arvilla M. Lane, age 21, daughter of Huldah Godsmark, from her first marriage, and still living at home.

See: 1860 U.S. Federal Census, "Orvilla M. Lane," Michigan, Calhoun County, Bedford, p. 118; Linda Andrews Alger, "The Lane-Godsmark Family," pp. 6, 7.

[138] *See:* Mar. 10 entry.

that at the same hour that we were called out in prayer at home for Thomas that Brethren Kellogg [**John Preston Kellogg**] and Smith[139] were praying around his bedside, and the Lord met with the sick and strengthened him to praise His name with a loud voice. They all felt the sweet refreshing from the presence of the Lord. Thomas rested well through the night and we felt rejoiced at this token of good from the Lord. We had a praying season for our dear brother. The Lord met with and blessed him and us again and he praised the Lord for His great goodness. At half past one o'clock those connected with the office met together to pray for Thomas's recovery. The Lord gave us a measure of freedom.

[Battle Creek] Sunday, March 27

Went to the office today to cover books. Sent out the things sent in for Brother Irving's [family].

[Battle Creek] Monday, March 28

Covered, or made, a mattress for the lounge. Very weary. In the eve folded and prepared different signatures[140] for different books.

[Battle Creek] Tuesday, March 29

Quite unwell. Was obliged to rest in the forenoon. In the afternoon wrote three letters and had an interview with my father, which causes me much sadness of heart. They are going east. Father is a second child, but knows it not.[141] In the eve, stitched one hundred books. While we were engaged at family prayer Brother Carmen [**John Frost Carman**][142] came. Went out to Brother Irving's. Returned in the eve. Brother Irving is a little more comfortable.

[Battle Creek] Wednesday, March 30

Set out the raspberry bush. Went to Mr. Manchester's [Elias C. Manchester][143] for strawberry plants. Got some currant bushes. Brother

---

[139] *Identities:* Although John Preston Kellogg had grown sons who also were members of the Battle Creek congregation, it is more likely that the title "Brother Kellogg" would be reserved for John Preston. As to the identity of "Smith," this was no doubt either **Uriah Smith** or **Cyrenius Smith**, both members of the Battle Creek group.

See: EGWEnc, s.v. "Battle Creek Congregation."

[140] The first steps in binding a book.

[141] "Second child" probably means "second childhood." Apparently her father, in his old age, was beginning to lose his reasoning faculties. As for "going east" there is no record of the Harmons moving east at this time. Instead they traveled west to Illinois in July to spend time with their son, John B. Harmon (Ms 7, 1859 [diary entries July 22, 26]). None of the three letters written on this date are in the White Estate archives.

[142] *See:* Feb. 5 entry.

[143] According to the 1860 census, the only "Manchester" family in Battle Creek was that of Elias C. Manchester, a prosperous merchant. The property on which the Whites built their

Carmen left this morn. Brother John Farnsworth [**John P. Farnsworth**][144] went with him. Thomas is no worse, but slowly improving. Praise the Lord for this manifestations of His loving kindness. We can truly say with the Psalmist, "This poor man cried and the Lord heard him." [Ps. 34:6.] I also cried unto the Lord and He heard my prayer. Therefore, I will praise the Lord as long as I live.

Sent off three letters—one to Brother Nichols [**Otis Nichols**][145] and one to Brother Howland, [**Stockbridge Howland**] having one enclosed to Brother Foey [**John G. Foy**],[146] and one to Brother J. T. Orton [**Jonathan T. Orton**].

[Battle Creek] Thursday, March 31

Planted a patch of strawberries. Sent a letter of twelve pages of note paper to my sister.

---

house in 1856 had earlier belonged to E. C. Manchester, who sold it in 1855 to Cyrenius Smith,who, in turn, sold it to James White in 1856.

See: 1860 U.S. Federal Census, "Elias C. Manchester," Michigan, Calhoun County, Battle Creek, p. 11; H. B. Peirce, *History of Calhoun County, Michigan,* pp. 99, 100; Glenn Davis and Jean Davis, "Notebook, Vol. 1," deposited at Historic Adventist Village, Battle Creek, Michigan, (section on Ellen and James White).

144 *Identity:* It is likely that "Brother John Farnsworth" is the same "John Farnsworth" listed in the 1860 Battle Creek census, partly because his census entry is next to that of John Fletcher Byington, Adventist printer at the Review and Herald press, indicating that they were near neighbors. According to the census John Farnsworth was born in New Hampshire and was 26 years old. This raises the probability that "John Farnsworth" is, in fact, John P. Farnsworth, son of William Farnsworth, of Washington, New Hampshire, sometimes loosely considered "the first Seventh-day Adventist." The only problem is the stated age, "26." John P. Farnsworth was, in fact, 25 years old when the census was taken in June 1860. This discrepancy, however, is not serious, given the anomalies often found in census records.

See: 1860 U.S. Federal Census, "John Farnsworth," Michigan, Calhoun County, Battle Creek, p. 27; SDAE, s. v. "Farnsworth, William"; obituary: "John P. Farnsworth," *Review,* Jan. 16, 1919, p. 31.

145 *Identities:* For Nichols, see Jan. 4. For Howland and Orton, see Jan. 3. None of the letters mentioned under Mar. 30 or 31 are in the White Estate archives.

146 *Identity:* The name "Foey" first appears in Lt 28, 1850 (Nov. 27). It is argued there in a note that "Foey" is a misspelling of "Foy" and that Ellen White is probably referring to John Green Foy, living in Brunswick, Maine, just across the Androscoggin River from Topsham, Maine, where fellow member Stockbridge Howland lived. It is likely that Ellen White is referring to the same J. G. Foy in this diary entry, given that she is enclosing his letter with her letter to Stockbridge Howland, of Topsham, suggesting that Howland lived close to "Foey" and could personally deliver the letter to him. Ellen White would have had occasion to write to J. G. Foy, since it appears that his 16-year-old son, **John Quincy Foy**, lived, or had lived, with the Whites in Battle Creek (see Mar. 10 above).

1859
(Ms 6, 1859)

APRIL 1–JUNE 30

Diary, April to June.

Portions of this manuscript are published in Ellen G. White, *Selected Messages,* book 3, pp. 262, 263; *idem, Welfare Ministry,* p. 325; *idem, Manuscript Releases,* vol. 3, pp. 142, 143; vol. 5, p. 218; vol. 7, pp. 217, 218; Arthur L. White, *Ellen G. White: The Early Years,* pp. 404-406.

[Jackson, Michigan] Friday, April 1

Went with our team 50 miles [80 kilometers] to Jackson [Michigan].[1] Enjoyed the ride. It is a beautiful day.

We see something which teaches us a lesson in almost everything around us. As we journeyed along we met a smooth, clever-looking dog; as he trotted along, we noticed a large, fierce, savage-looking dog standing by the roadside looking very fierce, waiting the coming of the clever-looking animal, ready to pounce upon him. We thought we would watch the result. Soon the little dog that was trotting along noticed his fierce companion and slacked his pace. He seemed to understand the nature of his enemy and he dared not run by, but in a most humble manner crawled along upon the ground. Thus he continued to crouch and crawl until he had come up to the fierce-looking dog, who immediately pounced upon him. The dog would not battle but rolled upon the ground in a begging manner. The big dog could not fight alone. He left the clever, pleading animal, who was still afraid of irritating him. So he walked along slowly, acting as though he wished to run but did not dare to. At length he increased his pace a little until he was sure he could outrun the other big dog; then he ran along as fast as he could go, looking back to see if the other followed. If human beings would only manifest such humility under injustice as this dumb creature, how many unhappy quarrels might be saved.

---

[1] This trip to Jackson was part of a larger plan by the Whites to visit the churches in Michigan on a more systematic basis. "During the warm season," James White explained in the *Review* on March 31, "[we] propose visiting a number of our churches [in Michigan] about once in three months, and being out somewhere nearly every Sabbath." Visits to six Michigan churches followed in the next two or three months in accordance with the plan, but Ellen's health deteriorated during the early summer, and by July James had to cancel the ambitious schedule. "We cannot at present [continue]. Our team became unfit for use [and] Mrs. W. has not been able to journey."

See: James White, "Quarterly Meetings," *Review,* Mar. 31, p. 152; *idem,* "Conferences in Michigan," *Review,* July 14, 1859, p. 64.

[Jackson] Sabbath, April 2

Brother Meade's[2] family came to the meeting. Also Brother Burwell and wife [**Anthony L.** and **Achsah Burwell**],[3] and a near neighbor who has recently commenced to keep the Sabbath. May the Lord enable them, Brother and Sister Gregory [**John** and **Esther C. Gregory**],[4] to persevere. They seem good. The meeting was profitable.

Nothing of particular interest occurs. In the even attend to the ordinances.[5] My mind was particularly depressed. A horror of great darkness settled upon me. James felt it, also Brother Palmer. We commenced to follow the example of our dear Saviour to wash one another's feet. While in this act the dark clouds parted and revealed to us again our Saviour. James and Brother Palmer [**Dan R. Palmer**][6] were also set free. Our mourning is turned to rejoicing. We feel a peace of mind which is ever desirable to be felt by the Christian.

---

[2] *Identity:* This may be a reference to the family of **Thomas B. Mead** of Battle Creek ("50 miles [80 kilometers]" distant), mentioned in the diary a few weeks earlier (see Mar. 4, 9, 20). No members surnamed "Mead[e]" are known to have lived in Jackson or its vicinity at this time.

See: Search terms "Meade" and "Mead" in *Words of the Pioneers.*

[3] *Identity:* Anthony and Achsah Burwell lived in Parma, close to Jackson. No other Burwells appear in the *Review* from this period.

See: Obituary: "Anthony L. Burwell," *Review,* Jan. 28, 1873, p. 55; 1860 U.S. Federal Census, "Ashash [*sic*] Burwell," Michigan, Jackson County, Parma, p. 19; search term "Burwell" in *Words of the Pioneers.*

[4] *Identity:* "Brother and Sister Gregory" lived in the same neighborhood as the Burwells, i.e., in Parma, and "recently commenced to keep the Sabbath." This matches the situation of John and Esther Gregory. According to Esther's obituary, published three years later, she and her family lived in Parma, and her husband had "some three years since . . . commenced keeping the Sabbath of the Lord." Her husband's name was obtained from the 1860 census.

See: Obituary: "Esther C. Gregory," *Review,* Apr. 29, 1862, p. 175; 1860 U.S. Federal Census, "Jno Gregory," Michigan, Jackson County, Parma, p. 21.

[5] The fact that church ordinances were "attended to" in Jackson on this occasion was probably in response to a letter of complaint that had appeared in the *Review* just a few days earlier. In his letter J. Whitmore noted that the Jackson members "have not had the ordinances of the Lord's house administered to us in a long time, only once I believe in three or four years." This was not an unusual situation. When Ellen and James White visited the believers in Wright and Caledonia, Michigan, a few weeks later, in each case it was the first time the members had participated in these rites. (See May 2 and May 4 entries below.)

For the transition from a sporadic observance of the ordinances in the 1840s and 1850s toward a quarterly observance in the 1860s and beyond, see Roger H. Ferris, "The Ordinances of Foot-Washing and the Lord's Supper in the Seventh-day Adventist Denomination."

See also: J. Whitmore, "Extracts From Letters," *Review,* Mar. 31, 1859, p. 151.

[6] *Identity:* Although the *Review* during this period mentions several persons with the name "Palmer," only "D. R." Palmer (Dan R.) and his wife (Abigail) are identified as living in Jackson, Michigan. Dan Palmer, according to historian A. W. Spalding, was the first Adventist in Michigan to accept the Sabbath message, in 1849.

See: Search term "Palmer" in *Words of the Pioneers;* Arthur Whitefield Spalding, *Origin and History of Seventh-day Adventists,* vol. 1, p. 251.

[Jackson] Sunday, April 3

Stayed at Jackson today. Visited Brother Gurney [**Heman S. Gurney**].[7]

[Battle Creek] Monday, April 4

It is cold and windy, yet we returned home. Took dinner at Brother Burwell's. They gave us six dozen eggs, three chickens, and a few dried apples. Brother Burwell handed me one dollar for Brother Irving's family, and Sister Palmer [**Abigail Palmer**] handed me $1.25 for [supplying] Agnes [**Agnes Irving**][8] a dress.

[Battle Creek] Wednesday, April 6

Finished covering the lounge. Sister Frisbie [**Delphia Jane Frisbie**][9] called upon me. She has been unwell. Is better today. We urged her to stop for supper. She consented. Sent the children a little cake. Louisa Bovee [**Louisa C. Bovee**][10] called in. Promised to call on her tomorrow afternoon a few hours. I have never yet visited her.

[Battle Creek] Thursday, April 7

Spent my time, two-thirds of the day, writing to Brother and Sister Church.[11] Wrote six pages and [a] half of note paper. In the afternoon visited Louisa Bovee for the first time. Had a profitable interview. After supper had a season of prayer. Felt something of the blessing of God while entreating His mercy and strength. I am opposed to afternoon visiting and chit-chat upon this, that, and the other thing, which imparts no spiritual strength to either party, the visitor or the receiver.

[Battle Creek] Friday, April 8

Made my husband a neck stock.[12] Set out strawberry plants. Went down

---

[7] *Identity:* See Lt 12, 1857 (Jan. 30).

[8] *Identity:* See Jan. 2 and 6 entries (Ms 5, 1859).

[9] *Identity:* For her husband, J. B. Frisbee, see Jan. 20 diary entry above (Ms 5, 1859). The full name of his wife, Delphia Jane, was obtained from her obituary and other sources.

See: Obituary: "Delphia Jane Frisbie," *Review,* Feb. 6, 1908, p. 31.

[10] Louisa C. Bovee, 22, married to shoemaker **Seymour C. Bovee**.

[11] These individuals have not been identified.

[12] Although the earliest extant photograph of the White family, dated about 1857, shows James wearing some type of neckstock, later photographs show no evidence of decorative neckwear. In his 1865 compendium *Health: or How to Live* James White included an article by Dr. R. T. Trall that was hostile to any kind of neckwear on health grounds. "The common neck-stock or cravat is one of the worst articles known: by confining and heating the throat, it predisposes to colds, rheumatism, quincy, bronchitis, etc." However, the evidence, photographic or otherwise, is too scanty to come to any reliable conclusions as to whether James White avoided cravats, etc., on principle.

See: R. T. Trall, "Dr. Trall on Clothing," in James White, ed., *Health: Or How to Live,* sec. 5, p. 3; Ron D. Graybill, "Heirloom: Leaves From Ellen White's Family Album," *Adventist Heritage,* Spring 1982, p. 6.

into the city with Agnes [Irving] to purchase some necessary articles of dress for Agnes.

[Convis, Michigan] Sabbath, April 9

Rose early and rode about 12 miles [19 kilometers] to Convis to meet with the saints there. The ride was refreshing. Called at Brother Brackett's [**Ezra Brackett**].[13] They accompanied us to the place of meeting, about two miles [3 kilometers] distant from his house. A little company of Sabbathkeepers were collected in a large, commodious schoolhouse. James had great freedom speaking to the people. I said a few words. Meeting held until about two o'clock. Nearly all bore testimony to the truth. After the meeting closed, a woman came to meeting; thought it was to be in the afternoon. She had walked a mile [1.6 kilometers]. She read the notice in the paper but did not read carefully enough to find out the time of meeting; therefore lost it all. After supper, as the hours of holy time were closing, we had a refreshing season of prayer. James talked with the children before bowing to pray.

[Convis] Sunday, April 10

It is very rainy. Think it impossible to get to the meeting today. We will do what good we can in Brother Brackett's family. Sister Smith [**Laura Smith**], her husband [**William Smith**][14] and daughter came half a mile [.8 kilometers] to see us. Had some conversation upon the Sabbath. Brother Smith is convinced that the seventh day is the Sabbath, but the cross stands in his way. He fears his children.[15] Oh, that the Lord would strengthen him to keep all

---

[13] *Identity:* The only Brackett family in Convis according to the 1860 census was that of Ezra and Mary Brackett. Both "Mary Brackett" of Convis and "E. Brackett" are mentioned in the *Review* from this period. Mary Brackett had begun to keep the Sabbath about two years earlier. Ezra had followed about a year later.

See: 1860 U.S. Federal Census, "Ezra Brackett," Michigan, Calhoun County, Convis, p. 184; search term "Brackett" in *Words of the Pioneers;* obituary: "Mary D. Brackett," *Review,* Mar. 7, 1882, p. 158.

[14] *Identities:* The list of charter members of the Convis Seventh-day Adventist Church, organized in January 1861, includes only one Smith family, "William Smith and wife." The name of his wife, Laura, was obtained from census and obituary sources.

See: H. B. Peirce, *History of Calhoun County, Michigan,* p. 154; 1870 U.S. Federal Census, "Laura Smith," Michigan, Calhoun County, Convis, p. 8; obituary: "Laura Smith," *Review,* June 25, 1872, p. 15.

[15] Nevertheless, two years later when the Convis church was organized, William Smith was listed among its charter members. As to his children, his daughter Mary "kept the Sabbath with her parents" before her untimely death in 1860, age 17. William Smith's younger son, Stephen, also seems to have seriously considered joining the movement. "I saw that angels of God were seeking to attract . . . [Stephen] to the truth," Ellen White wrote in 1865. "He was turning partly away saying, 'Not yet. I cannot yet yield to the restraint of life religion imposes.'"

See: H. B. Peirce, *History of Calhoun County, Michigan,* p. 154; obituary: "Mary Smith," *Review,* Apr. 26, 1860, p. 183; Ellen G. White, Ms 4, 1865 (c. 1865).

His precepts and give him courage to acknowledge the truth, letting the Lord take care of the results. We feel that the day has been spent profitably.

[Battle Creek] Monday, April 11

Spent most of the day making a garden for my children. Feel willing to make home as pleasant for them as I can, that home may be the pleasantest place of any to them.

[Battle Creek] Tuesday, April 12

Continued to make garden. Went down to Sister Benedict's [**Millie Benedict**][16] for some plants. My heart is called out in sympathy for them. I know they are poor and Brother Benedict is very feeble; unable to work.[17] The mother and the daughters are in feeble health. May the Lord pity them and may He live in the hearts of the church, is my prayer.

[Battle Creek] Wednesday, April 13

Went down to Sister Fults'[?].[18] Sent her a bottle of wine.[19] She gave me some plants for my children. Obtained some sage roots; divided with her.

[Battle Creek] Thursday, April 14

Very windy; keep close indoors today.

[See also Lt 18, 1859, written on this date.]

[Battle Creek] Friday, April 15

Write extracts of a letter to Doctor Naramore [**John Naramore**].[20] Send Sister Benedict a present of $1.30, for favors received of them. Put up Brother Benedict one pint of currant wine and one pint of grape [wine].[21] May the Lord bless the afflicted is my prayer. My heart aches for the needy.

[Ceresco, Michigan] Sabbath, April 16

Rode seven miles [11 kilometers] to Ceresco, to attend a meeting with the brethren. The meeting was comforting to the church. The Lord met with us and we were all refreshed. Praise His dear name. After meeting closed, took

---

[16] *See:* Jan. 5 entry (Ms 5, 1859).

[17] *See:* Apr. 15 entry and biographical sketch of **Joseph Perry Benedict**.

[18] This person has not been identified.

[19] *See:* Mar. 3 entry (Ms 5, 1859).

[20] *Identity:* See Jan. 3 entry (Ms 5, 1859). For the text of the extracts from the letter to John Naramore, see Lt 18, 1859 (Apr. 14). An edited version of the extracts, without personal references to Dr. Naramore, was published in the *Review* two weeks later.

See: E. G. W. [Ellen G. White], "The Sinner's Trials," *Review*, Apr. 28, 1859, pp. 181, 182.

[21] *See:* Mar. 3 entry (Ms 5, 1859).

supper with Brother Hide's[22] family. Then rode to Brother Byington's [**John Byington**][23] and to Glover's [**Charles S. Glover**].[24] Had a good interview with them. Sabbath afternoon engaged in prayer for Martha [**Martha Dormer Amadon** (née **Byington**)][25] whom we found much reduced with fever and ague [chills]. The Lord truly met with us. Martha was blessed and strengthened. James was powerfully moved upon by the Spirit of the Lord. Brother Byington appeared cold and unfeeling. His heart is too much wrapped up in the things of this world.[26] In the eve engaged in prayer at Brother Glover's. The Lord gave us a sweet peaceful season. Brother Glover prayed so sweetly; his heart all melted by the sweet influence of the Spirit of God. Sister Glover's health is not good.

---

[22] *Identity:* This mention of a "Hide" family living in or near Ceresco should be compared with J. N. Loughborough's diary account, also from 1859, in which he visits a "Bro. Hyde" while in Ceresco. It is likely that Loughborough is referring to the same family and that he has the correct spelling. One possibility is that Ellen White is referring to Margaret S. and John Hyde, of the adjacent township of Newton, where John Byington and Charles Glover, also mentioned in this entry, lived. The obituary for Margaret Hyde in 1891 establishes that she and her husband had lived in Newton Township since the 1840s, and implies that their connection with Sabbathkeeping Adventists went back to the very early period. The name "Margaret Hyde" appears among *Review* receipts in 1862 but without giving her address.

See: J. N. Loughborough, "Diary," entries for Jan. 27, 29, Feb. 13; search terms "Hide" and "Hyde" in *Words of the Pioneers;* obituary, "Margaret S. Hyde," *Review,* Jan. 6, 1891, p. 15.

[23] See Feb. 13 entry (Ms 5, 1859).

[24] *Identity:* According to the 1860 census, the only Glover family in Calhoun county was that of Charles S. Glover. It further indicates that Charles S. Glover was one of the neighbors of John Byington, leaving little doubt about the identity of the "Brother Glover" and his family.

See: 1860 U.S. Federal Census, "Charles Glover," "John Byington," Michigan, Calhoun County, Newton, p. 244.

[25] *Identity:* Of the three families mentioned in this entry, the only family member named "Martha" in the 1860 census is 25-year-old Martha Byington. This identity is confirmed by the reference in this entry to Martha's serious illness and the prayers that were offered on her behalf. Two months later, on June 21, Ellen White wrote to John Byington and reminded him that "God had been very merciful to you. God has heard the earnest prayers put up in Martha's behalf, and spared her life when she was marked for the grave."

See: 1860 U.S. Federal Census, "John Hyde," Michigan, Calhoun County, Newton, p. 237; "Charles Glover," "John Byington," p. 244; Ellen G. White, Lt 2, 1859 (June 21).

[26] Other sources provide some explanation for Byington's "cold and unfeeling" mood. Six months earlier, at the request of James White, the Byingtons had sold their long-term home in Buck's Bridge, New York, and moved to the Battle Creek area. The move involved financial loss, which caused John Byington to descend into a state of "gloom and unbelief" (Lt 28, 1859). Although Byington had previously been an active itinerant preacher, for about a year from the summer of 1858 there is no record of his filling any preaching appointments. Finally, in July 1859, after receiving challenging letters from Ellen White, he resumed his evangelistic work. "He looked happier than I had seen him for months," Ellen noted in her diary on July 12, 1859. "Says after a week he is going out to labor for the Lord." In 1863 Byington would be elected the first president of the newly organized General Conference.

See: Obituary: "John Byington," *Review,* Jan. 25, 1887, pp. 57, 58; Ellen G. White, Lt 28, 1859 (June/July); Lt 2, 1859 (June 21); Ms 7, 1859 (July 12 entry); search term "Byington" in *Words of the Pioneers.*

[Battle Creek] Sunday, April 17

Again visited Brother Byington. Had a good, sociable time with the family, but Brother Byington is cold and cloudy. His heart is all on this world. The Lord pity and bless him. My husband is afflicted with an ulcered tooth. It was snowing. Cleared off. At noon concluded to venture to the meeting. There were but few out. Husband talked in pain. We then rode home seven miles [11 kilometers].

[Battle Creek] Monday, April 18

Husband's tooth still very painful. My heart troubles me much. A collection of water around it. Am much pressed for breath. Received a number of excellent letters. One from Mary Chase [**Mary S. Chase**].[27] Husband received one from John White [**John W. White**].[28] I received one from Emily Brissee [**Emily C. Brazee**].[29] I have long wanted to hear from Emily. She still holds on to the truth.[30] Her husband is converted; keeps the Sabbath with her. Received a letter from Brother Orton [**Jonathan T. Orton**].[31]

[Battle Creek] Tuesday, April 19

My heart still troubles me. There seems to be a heavy weight upon it. In the eve Brother Hilliard [**Aaron H. Hilliard**][32] came with his wife and seven children. We are glad to see them and we keep them over night.

---

[27] *See:* Feb. 8 entry (Ms 5, 1859).

[28] *Identity:* In other documents, Ellen White consistently uses the name "John White" to refer to her brother-in-law, John W. White, a Methodist clergyman living in Ohio at this time. Ellen's father-in-law was also a "John White," but she normally addressed him as "Father White" or just "Father." In addition, he was living in Battle Creek at the time and would therefore have no need to send a letter to James White.

See: Ellen G. White, Lt 25, 1871 (July); Lt 9, 1881 (Oct. 20); Lt 59, 1884 (Sept. 11); Lt 61, 1884 (Nov. 27).

[29] Both spellings, "Brizzee" and "Brazee," are found in the *Review*. Emily Brazee lived in New York State and had known Ellen White at least since 1852, possibly from the late 1840s. See biographical sketch.

[30] While living in New Bedford, Massachusetts, Emily Brazee's mother had started keeping the Sabbath in the 1840s through the efforts of Joseph Bates. It is possible that Emily Brazee also had taken the same step at that time. See biographical sketch.

[31] *Identity:* See Jan. 3 entry (Ms 5, 1859).

[32] *Identity:* Aaron H. Hilliard's obituary notes that he moved from "Northern New York" to Michigan "in the spring of 1859." In the May 19, 1859, *Review* James White adds the information that "Bro. A. Hilliard and wife from N. Y. have joined" the church in Otsego, Michigan. Clearly it is Aaron Hilliard and family who stayed overnight with the Whites en route to Otsego, as described in the April 19 and 20 diary entries. The Hilliards are best known in Adventist history for the fact that it was in their home that Ellen White received her groundbreaking health vision in 1863.

See: Obituary: "Aaron H. Hilliard," *Review* Sept. 2, 1875, p. 71; J. W. [James White], "Report From Bro. White," *Review,* May 19, 1859, p. 204; Richard W. Schwarz and Floyd Greenleaf, *Light Bearers,* pp. 104, 105.

[Battle Creek] Wednesday, April 20

Brother Hilliard's family left for their new home at Otsego. May the Lord counsel them, is my prayer. Mary Loughborough [**Mary J. Loughborough**] and Carrie Carpenter [**Caroline Carpenter**][33] were here in the afternoon. Visited my mother, but am pressed for breath.

[Battle Creek] Thursday, April 21

Worked on a rug. Wrote a letter to Daniel Bourdeau [**Daniel T. Bourdeau**].[34] This morn there was a feeling of sympathy among certain of the flock for Brother Benedict's family. We have contributed a mite for their relief—about seven dollars. Purchased them different things to eat, and carried it to them. Brother and Sister Benedict visited us all day. Had a very interesting and pleasant interview. My mother came to see me, which was a great comfort to me.

[Battle Creek] Friday, April 22

Suffer for breath.

[Battle Creek] Sabbath, April 23

Sister Brackett [**Mary Brackett**],[35] Sister Lane [**Sarah Lane**][36] and her daughter, Sister Scott [**Mary A. Scott**],[37] and Sister Smith came from Convis

---

[33] J. N. Loughborough's accounts for 1859 show that 20-year-old Carrie Carpenter worked in the Loughborough home at this time. Since she was paid only $1.00 per week, she probably also lodged there.

See: J. N. Loughborough, "Diary."

[34] A 24-year-old French Canadian living in Vermont, Daniel T. Bourdeau had become a Sabbathkeeper about two years earlier. He was well known to the Whites since he had subsequently spent considerable time in Battle Creek translating tracts and other publications into French. He then returned to northern Vermont and at the time of this letter was a traveling preacher, mostly reaching out to the French-speaking population on both sides of the Canadian border. This letter is not in the White Estate archives.

See: James White, "The Present Truth in French," *Review*, Dec. 24, 1857, p. 56; D. T. Bourdeau, "Letters," Aug. 5, 1858, p. 94; search term "D. T. Bourdeau" in *Words of the Pioneers*.

[35] *See:* Apr. 9 entry above.

[36] *Identity:* "Sister Lane" is said to come from Convis. The 1861 list of charter members for the Convis, Michigan, church includes "Thomas Lane and wife" and "Mrs. Sarah Lane," and it seems unclear at first which of the two women is being referred to in this diary entry. Ellen White, however, adds the information that "Sister Lane" has a daughter. Of the two, only Sarah Lane had a daughter, Caroline, age 18. Thomas and Maria Lane, who married in 1856, had only one son, Charles, age 1. It therefore seems fairly certain that Sarah Lane is indicated here.

See: H. B. Peirce, *History of Calhoun County, Michigan*, pp. 154, 155; 1850 U.S. Federal Census, "Sarah Lane," Michigan, Calhoun County, Convis, p. 179; 1860 U.S. Federal Census, "Thomas Lane," Michigan, Calhoun County, Convis, p. 180.

[37] *Identity:* A few weeks later a Mary Scott from Convis wrote to the *Review* telling of her baptism on April 23 in Battle Creek, thus in every detail matching the information given on "Sister Scott" in Ellen White's diary. There are good reasons for concluding that this Mary

to the meeting at Battle Creek. They took dinner at our house. Meeting was interesting through the day. Brother Waggoner preached in the forenoon. His discourse was appropriate. At intermission four were baptized—Sisters Hide, Scott, and Agnes Irving, and Brother Pratt.[38] Our afternoon meeting was very interesting. My husband never had greater liberty. The Lord's Spirit was in the meeting. The Lord gave me freedom in exhortation. In the eve the ordinances of the Lord's house were attended to. It was a solemn, interesting occasion. I was unable to attend, being much exhausted.

[Battle Creek] Sunday, April 24

Brother Palmer [**Dan R. Palmer**][39] and Brother Glover [**Charles S. Glover**] tarried with us last night.

For self, $2.00; for J. Foey,[40] 81c; for Henry and Edson, $1.50; for James White, $1.42; for boys, 60c.

[Battle Creek] Monday, April 25

Went to the office in the morning. Stayed through the day. Prepared an article for the *Review*, and wrote a short piece for the *Instructor*;[41] read proof. Took dinner at Brother Cyrenius Smith's [**Cyrenius Smith**]. Had a pleasant little visit. Returned home quite tired.

[Battle Creek] Tuesday, April 26

Worked hard all day on a dress to wear through the mud. Brother Benedict tried to borrow money to discharge a debt. Was unable to let him have it for that object, for necessity was in the Office.

Scott is Mary A. Scott, whose obituary appears in the *Review* of Jan. 19, 1905. Among other things, the obituary informs us that Mary A. Scott "accepted present truth . . . forty-six years ago" which coincides with the April 1859 date for her baptism recorded in the diary.

See: Mary Scott, "From Sister Scott," *Review,* May 19, 1859, p. 207; obituary: "Mary A. Scott," *Review,* Jan. 19, 1905, p. 23.

[38] The identity of this person has not been established.

[39] *See:* Apr. 2 entry.

[40] Given that this seems to be a list of expenditures for White family members, "J. Foey" might well refer to 16-year-old **John Quincy Foy**, who apparently was living with the Whites at this time and is listed among the family members in the 1860 census (see Ms 5, 1859 [Mar. 30 entry]). For earlier evidence of Ellen White spelling "Foy" as "Foey," see notes under Lt 28, 1850 (Nov. 27), and Ms 5, 1859 (Mar. 30 entry).

[41] The *Review* article referred to must have been "The Sinner's Trials," published a few days later on April 28, the last Ellen White article to appear in the *Review* during 1859. "The Sinner's Trials" was an edited version of Ellen White's letter to Dr. Naramore two weeks earlier (see under Apr. 15 above). As to the "short piece for the *Instructor*" Ellen White submitted items for both the April and May 1859 issues of the *Youth's Instructor*.

See: E. G. W. [Ellen G. White], "The Sinner's Trials," *Review,* Apr. 28, 1859, pp. 181, 182; E. G. White, "Little Ellen," *Youth's Instructor,* April 1859, p. 32; Ellen G. White, "Be Lovely," *Youth's Instructor,* May 1859, p. 36.

[Battle Creek] Wednesday, April 27

Agnes [Irving] left for home today.[42] Visited Mrs. Fults. Had a pleasant, friendly interview. She trembles as she sees the binding force of the law of God, yet she does not venture to obey. She is a strong-minded woman but keenly feels that her husband's opposition will destroy the peace and harmony of the family. I pointed her up to God. There is One who has greater claims upon her than her husband, and Him above all should she fear to displease. She must follow the dictates of her own conscience, even if she has foes in her own household. She admits this, yet lacks strength from God to break away from old friends and associates to form new ones. May the Lord strengthen this trembling child to follow in the humble, self-denying path that Jesus has traveled.

[Caledonia, Michigan] Thursday, April 28

Up quite early and started on our journey. Roads are very bad. Traveled 50 miles [80 kilometers]. Were greatly exhausted when we reached Brother Gerould's [**Lyman Gerould**][43] at night. Rested well through the night.

[Wright] Friday, April 29

Again we started on [our] journey to Grand Rapids. Roads bad until we gained the plank.[44] Took dinner at old Brother Cramer's [**Christopher G. Cramer**][45] and continued our journey to Wright. Roads bad. Bridge swept away at Berlin. We are obliged to ford the stream; water up to the wagon box. It was hard, dangerous, climbing the bank on the other side of the stream. No accident befell us, which ought to call gratitude from our hearts. Arrived at Brother Root's [**Ephraim Henry Root**] about six o'clock. Sister Root [**Hezzy Root**][46] has a babe one week old. She is very smart. Sits up the most of the time.

[Wright] Sabbath, April 30

Attended meeting today. About 200 present. It was a good meeting. Husband preached upon the law of God in connection with baptism. A Mr. Palmer[47] arose to ask a question which appeared to be merely to bring himself into notoriety and throw confusion, but no notice was taken of him. The meeting progressed. I exhorted a little,[48] then others followed with their sweet testimonies.

---

[42] Agnes Irving's father had only a few weeks to live at this point. Doubtless his serious illness caused her to go home for two weeks, even though the wages she earned for working in the White home were desperately needed by her family (see Ms 5, 1859 [Mar. 10 entry]).

[43] *Identity:* See Jan. 26 entry (Ms 5, 1859).

[44] That is, the plank road. See Jan. 18 entry (Ms 5, 1859).

[45] *Identity:* See Jan. 19 entry (Ms 5, 1859).

[46] *Identities:* See Jan. 19 entry (Ms 5, 1859).

[47] This person has not been identified.

[48] One of those present, M. M. Elmondorph, tells a little of the content of this exhortation.

[Wright] Sunday, May 1

A good congregation. The Lord met with us in the afternoon and eve. The fore part of the day we were not idle. We called on Brother Tubbs [**Ira B. Tubbs**].[49] Spent a few hours in profitable conversation; then left to call on Brother and Sister Ferguson [**Justus** and **Lucretia Ferguson**].[50] They live in a splendid house. Have no children, and all things looked rather dreary and desolate. Yet we had a profitable season of conversation and prayer before parting with them. We next went to Brother McPherson's [**Samuel A. McPherson**].[51] We were heartily received and we enjoyed the interview with them much. They are open-hearted, sound people. This brother is also wealthy, but has it all in lands,[52] for he cannot use much.

[Wright] Monday, May 2

We met together again to break bread and wash the saints' feet. It had never been practiced by them,[53] but husband set the example to the men and I to the

---

"My heart beat in unison with the testimony of Sister White, as in her exhortation she tried to point us forward to the near coming of the Saviour, and the beauties of the earth made new."

See: M. M. Elmondorph, "From Sister Elmondorph," *Review,* July 7, 1859, p. 54.

[49] *Identity:* Five males between 18 and 40 years of age with the surname "Tubbs" are listed in the 1860 census for Wright, Michigan. Four of them, probably all five, were sons of Ira Tubbs, age 60, also living in Wright. Ira and his wife, Hannah, had become Sabbatarian Adventists in 1857, but it is unclear which if any of the grown sons had joined the movement by 1859 at the time of Ellen White's visit. However, even if one or more of the sons had joined, it seems likely that Ellen White would reserve the title "Brother Tubbs" for the father, Ira.

See: 1850 U.S. Federal Census, "Ira Tubbs," Michigan, Ottawa County, Wright, p. 16; 1860 U.S. Federal Census, "Philander Tubbs," Sylvester Tubbs," "Ira Tubbs," Michigan, Ottawa County, Wright, pp. 118, 122.

[50] *Identity:* The information given that "Brother and Sister Ferguson" lived in or near Wright and that they had no children suggests that Ellen White is referring to Justus and Lucretia Ferguson. According to Justus Ferguson's *Review* obituary, he lived in Wright from about 1850 to his death in 1878, and the 1860 census affirms that the couple had no children, or at least none living at home at this time.

See: Obituary: "Justus Ferguson," Feb. 7, 1878, p. 47; 1860 U.S. Federal Census, "Justen Furgeson," Michigan, Ottawa County, Wright, p. 122.

[51] *Identity:* The only McPhersons living in Wright Township according to the 1860 census were Samuel A.; his wife, Polly; and their children. The *Review* confirms that there was a Brother "S. A. McPherson" living in Wright during this period (more precisely in the village of Berlin, located within Wright township). He had started keeping the Sabbath a year earlier, in the spring of 1858.

See: 1860 U.S. Federal Census, "Samuel McFerson," Michigan, Ottawa County, Wright, p. 121; S. A. McPherson, *Review,* "Extracts From Letters," Apr. 7, 1859, p. 159.

[52] The 1860 and 1870 censuses list the value of Samuel McPherson's real estate at $4,000, although he may have had additional undeclared real estate assets.

See: 1860 U.S. Federal Census, "Samuel McFerson," Michigan, Ottawa County, Wright, p. 121; 1870 U.S. Federal Census, "Samuel McPherson," Michigan, Ottawa County, Polkton, p. 14.

[53] James White adds, in his account, that it was "Monday at 9 A. M." when they met "to attend to the ordinances of the Lord's supper and washing of feet." Roger Ferris in his study of Sabbatarian observance of the Communion service in the 1850s notes that it was "often

sisters, then all heartily engaged in it. It was an interesting occasion. The solemnity of the place made it still more profitable. There was weeping and rejoicing, humbling before God altogether. It was a season long to be remembered.[54] Husband never talked more interestingly and appropriately than when breaking the bread, and sobs and groans were heard from the congregation.

[Caledonia, Michigan] Tuesday, May 3

Rode to Caledonia.

[Caledonia] Wednesday, May 4

Attended the ordinances in the afternoon. It is the first time they have ever attended to this exercise. It was a solemn, interesting season.

[Allegan, Michigan][55] *Thursday, May 5*

Started on our way to Monterey. We are both weary and worn.[56]

[Monterey, Michigan] Friday, May 6

Rode from Dr. Lay's [**Horatio S. Lay**][57] to Monterey. Stopped at Brother Day's [**John S. Day**].[58]

---

celebrated in the evening" and surmises that this was because of a "sincere desire to emulate . . . in every detail" the Passover as it was practiced by Christ and in the Old Testament. The Whites do not appear to have prioritized such thinking, at least not in Wright, where they had spent three days, or in Caledonia two days later, where the ceremony was observed "in the afternoon" (see May 4 entry). On the observation that the ordinances "had never been practiced by them," see under Apr. 2 above.

See: J. W. [James White], "Report From Bro. White," *Review,* May 12, 1859, p. 197; Roger H. Ferris, "The Ordinances of Foot Washing and the Lord's Supper in the Seventh-day Adventist Denomination," p. 22.

[54] Martin Cole, who was present, later wrote to the *Review*: "It was the first time that I ever had the privilege of taking part in that spirit-humbling and pride-annihilating ordinance, even the washing of feet. There it seemed that every evil desire and bad wish was cleansed from each heart, and nothing but pure love abounded."

See: Martin V. Cole, "From Bro. Cole," *Review,* July 7, 1859, p. 55.

[55] By combining the information given under May 5 and 6 with James White's account, it appears that on May 5 the Whites reached Allegan, where they stayed overnight with Dr. Lay.

See: J. W. [James White], "Report From Bro. White," *Review,* May 19, 1859, p. 204.

[56] At this point in the journey, James White notes, they had driven their team "about 120 miles [193 kilometers], much of the way over desperate roads" since setting out from Battle Creek the previous Thursday. Muddy roads appear to have been the greatest obstacle to travel. On this day they came across "some natives stuck in the mud" on the road ahead. "The Indian and squaw got out and waded through the water and mud, and their famishing team drew out their papooses." It was then the turn of the Whites to pass the muddy stretch. "We sat in the carriage, and between hope and fear watched the desperate struggles of our team, who soon took us to the dry land."

See: J. W. [James White], "Report From Bro. White," *Review,* May 12, 1859, p. 197; *idem,* "Report From Bro. White," *Review,* May 19, 1859, p. 204.

[57] *Identity:* See Jan. 10, 1859 (Ms 5, 1859).

[58] *Identity:* See Jan. 12, 1859 (Ms 5, 1859).

[Monterey] Sabbath, May 7

In great weakness attended the meeting. Could not remain. Obliged to leave and lie down until dinner time. They got me wine and raw egg,[59] which revived my strength some. Took a wet sheet pack.[60]

[Otsego, Michigan] Sunday, May 8

Rode to Otsego.[61]

Monday, May 9

Looks like rain, yet we prepared to return home.

Tuesday, May 10

Very weary and sick.

---

[59] Commonly recommended medication for general debility at the time. Thus "A Treatise on the Practice of Medicine" (1858 edition) advises that "Should the failing strength require further support . . . sometimes it becomes necessary to have recourse to the most stimulating food, as essence of beef . . . milk-punch, egg and wine, etc." James White gives more detail in 1868 regarding Ellen's occasional use of this mixture. "During the past year, Mrs. W. has, at three or four times, had feelings of great debility and faintness in the morning. . . . To prevent distressing fainting at these times, she, immediately after rising, has taken an egg in a little pure, domestic, grape wine, perhaps a spoonful at a time. . . . During the past year, she may have used one pint of wine." In later years, as methods for preserving wine/grape juice from fermentation became available, Ellen White still recommended the egg-wine mixture under certain circumstances, but this time with unfermented wine. Thus she advised Dr. Kress in 1901, severely ill with pernicious anemia: "Get eggs of healthy fowls. . . . Drop them uncooked into the best unfermented wine you can find. This will supply that which is necessary to your system."

See: George B. Wood, *A Treatise on the Practice of Medicine,* vol. 1, p. 239; James White, "A Little Grape Wine," *Review,* Mar. 17, 1868, p. 220; Ellen G. White, Lt 37, 1901 (May 29); note under Mar. 3 entry (Ms 5, 1859).

[60] Through the years the Whites had experimented with a range of simple remedies when illness struck. Prayer and faith in God were never thought of as excluding the use of such remedies. Ellen White's use of "a wet sheet pack" as described here is one of probably only two or three mentions of the Whites using water therapy in the 1850s. In 1855 James tried to cure his cough and painful throat and lungs through "faith in God, cold water compresses, and bathing, Hough's syrups, rest, . . . walking, running, horse-back riding etc." Although water treatment ("hydropathy") was experiencing a good deal of popularity in antebellum America, the Whites seem to have been more cautious than convinced of its value at this stage, but willing to try it. The 1860s were to see a radical change in their attitude.

See the following Ellen White documents with accompanying notes: Lt 8, 1849 (May 29); Lt 11, 1853 (Dec. 3); Lt 5, 1854 (Dec. 16); Ms 2, 1855 (Aug. 26). Also: James White to "Bro. Abram," Mar. 11, 1855; EGWEnc, s.v. "Hydrotherapy." For a summary of the early history of hydropathy in the United States, see Ruth C. Engs, *Clean Living Movements: American Cycles of Health Reform,* pp. 95-98.

[61] In Otsego James White spoke to "a large congregation assembled in the tavern dance hall." "We declined occupying the fiddler's stand," reported White, "and took the middle of the floor, with the people all around us."

See: J. W. [James White], "Report From Bro. White," *Review,* May 19, 1859, p. 204.

[Battle Creek] Friday, May 13

My heart troubles me much.

[Battle Creek] Sabbath, May 14

Attended meeting in the forenoon. Brother Loughborough preached. It was an appropriate discourse. It enlightened my mind some concerning the message to the Laodiceans.[62] Light seemed to break into my mind that since the message to the Laodiceans has gone forth the delay that we are now in is to develop character, to bring out what is in the heart, and separate the precious from the vile.[63] The lukewarm are being spued out of the mouth of God. Oh, what came over me as I looked over the congregation and saw the sisters with their ruffles on, their bonnets covered with bows and ribbons. If this is the index to the heart, oh what pride dwells in those hearts! The sign is truly hung out. My soul is distressed and burdened. I could not forbear weeping. They profess to be working for Jesus to change their vile bodies and fashion them like unto His most glorious body, and yet what pride they manifest! May the Lord have mercy, is my prayer.

---

[62] J. N. Loughborough notes in his diary for May 14 that on this Sabbath morning "I spoke with much freedom from the 1st Ps. 'Pay thy vows unto the Lord.'" It is likely that the article "Vows," by Lougborough, appearing a few weeks later (June 16) in the *Review,* is a transcript or summary of his May 14 sermon, since it is prefaced by the same text from Psalm 1 and the content closely follows Ellen White's description given in this diary entry.

See: J. N. Loughborough, "Diary," entry for May 14; J. N. L. [J. N. Loughborough], "Vows," *Review,* June 16, 1859, p. 29; EGWEnc, s.v. "Laodicean Message."

[63] Ellen White is no doubt meditating on the following line of reasoning in Loughborough's sermon concerning the reason for the "delay," as it later appeared in his *Review* article. "When the Laodicean message was given [late 1856], we thought surely the message of the third angel would soon go forth with a loud cry. All that were not zealous the Lord will spue out of his mouth...More than two years have passed since that message was first given. . . . We supposed the spueing out was immediately to come; but character must first be developed... God is weighing his people."

Loughborough was not the first to raise the question of the why the Laodicean message, given more than two years earlier, had not led to greater reform among members. In December 1858 M. E. Cornell reminded *Review* readers of "the hope [that] was entertained that this message would prepare the people for the latter rain" and asked pointedly, "Why is it not done?" Loughborough's suggested explanation found its confirmation in Ellen White's vision of June 9 (see June 4 entry below) as published in *Testimony for the Church,* No. 5, a week or two later. "God will prove His people. Jesus bears patiently with them, and does not spew them out of His mouth in a moment. . . . If the message had been of as short duration as many of us supposed, there would have been no time for them to develop character. . . . [God] gives them time for the excitement to wear off, and then proves them to see if they will obey the counsel of the True Witness."

See: J. N. L. [J. N. Loughborough], "Vows," *Review,* June 16, 1859, p. 29; M. E. Cornell, "The Laodicean Message," *Review,* Dec. 16, 1858, p. 32; Ellen G. White, *Testimonies for the Church,* vol. 1, pp. 186, 187; EGWEnc, s.v. "Loud Cry" and "Laodicean Message."

[Battle Creek] Sunday, May 15

Agnes Irving commenced work again.[64] Attended meeting in the evening. Said a few things upon dress.

[Battle Creek] Monday, May 16

Health poor. Pressed for breath. Have had strange symptoms. My tongue has grown numb.

[Battle Creek] Tuesday, May 17

Went down to the city. Purchased a dress. Laid out for self, $2.75.

[Battle Creek] Wednesday, May 18

Mother came to visit me. She appeared to be in better spirits than usual. Received two letters from Sophrona Peckham [**Sophronia Peckham**], giving an account of her husband's death. He had only five days' illness. She writes that he embraced the Sabbath before his sickness. She has hopes in his death.[65] A letter from Sister Lizzie [**Elizabeth N. Bangs**], my twin, giving an account of my niece's[66] sickness. She is not expected to recover. My mother took her when but one year and a half old, and brought her up until she was sixteen. Brother Frisbie [**Joseph Birchard Frisbie**] has a dispatch that his father [**Elihu Frisbie**] was killed the day before at ten o'clock.[67] He

---

[64] *See:* Apr. 27 entry above.

[65] Sophronia's husband, **Job B. Peckham**, of Volney, New York, had died on March 19, age 35. Nine years earlier, in 1850, Ellen White had warned Sophronia that Job's whole focus "was to get this world" and that "he had sapped her [spiritual] strength." (Both spellings of her first name ["Sophronia" and "Sophrona"] appear in the sources.)

See: 1850 U.S. Federal Census, "Job B. Peckham," New York, Oswego County, Volney, p. 351; "Peckham, Job B.," RootsWeb, *Mt. Pleasant Western Cemetery, Volney, N. Y.* (n.d.), June 24, 2003, www.rootsweb.com/~nyoswego/cemeteries/mtpleasntwestvol4.html; Ellen G. White, Ms 7a, 1850 (Aug. 24).

[66] *Identity:* The identity of this niece is uncertain. Although speculative, what little evidence there is suggests that Ellen White is referring to her sister **Harriet McCann**'s daughter, Melissa Tapley. According to the description given, this niece had stayed in the Harmon home for some 14 years. This could explain why the 1850 census lists a girl named "Melissa," age 11, living in the home of Robert and Eunice Harmon even though they were both listed as 66 years old and had no daughter by that name. Adding some weight to this proposal is the fact that the birth year for this Melissa would be about 1839, which matches the year of birth of Melissa Tapley, also 1839 according to the genealogist Artemas C. Harmon. Detracting somewhat from this line of reasoning is the opinion that the niece was "not expected to recover." Melissa Tapley confounded such predictions by living at least into her 70s, as attested by the 1910 census. However, she does seem to have had continued poor health. Ellen White noted in 1886 that Melissa "has no health, but is liable to die any time."

See: 1850 U.S. Federal Census, "Robert Harmon," Maine, Cumberland County, Gorham, p. 291; Artemas C. Harmon, ed., *The Harmon Genealogy,* p. 79; 1910 U.S. Federal Census, "Mellissa C. Tapley," Maine, York County, Saco, p. 13A; Ellen G. White, Lt 95, 1886 (Feb. 16).

[67] *Identity:* According to the obituary appearing on June 9, "Bro. E. Frisbie of Battle Creek,

was brought home on the [railroad] cars at noon.

[Battle Creek] Thursday, May 19

Miserable in health and depressed in spirits. My husband attended the funeral of old Brother Frisbie today, then he left Battle Creek to go in the cars to Allegan to attend his appointment.[68] Oh, how desolate my heart feels! A strange sadness is upon me. I am so lonely, so distressed! Such a gloom rests upon everything. It seems that a heavy stone is placed upon my heart. O God, do not forsake me in my weakness and misery.

I sometimes think that my work is done, and feelings come over me that I am of no use, can do no good; and then it seems as though it would be a sweet relief to rest in the grave. Everywhere I look there is a lack of vital godliness, and my whole heart is sick. I shun company. It seems so hollow and heartless, no God or heaven in it. Oh, how I desire solitude! I love to be alone. My disposition has been trusting, confiding, but I have seen so many false hearts and friends, a mistrust and disgust has fallen upon me. I seem to have no power to break it.

[Battle Creek] Friday, May 20

Have felt deeply today for my dear children. Prayed with them and for them. They may soon be left without a mother's care. Disease is bearing me down. My heavenly Father alone knows my almost constant pain. I have found some relief in prayer today. It did seem that the Lord heard me and would pity me. I am sorry I feel so deeply and am so sensitive. But few can enter into or understand my feelings or trials. But God knows all. He is acquainted with the whole burdened heart. May the Lord be pleased to revive my courage, and lift up my desponding heart and water it with the dew of heaven, that it may flourish again. Have cut out Johnny[69] and Willie each a pair of pants from three yards [three meters] of cloth. Have pieced Willie's considerably.

---

the aged father of Eld. Joseph B. Frisbie, was killed on the 17th ult." He was thrown from a wagon when the team became frightened, "one of the hind wheels . . . striking his head immediately back of his right ear, and causing almost instant death." In *History of Washtenaw County, Michigan,* E. Frisbie's first name is given as "Elihu" (p. 754) or "Elisha" (p. 778). Federal and Michigan census records tend to support "Elihu."

See: Obituary: "Bro. E. Frisbie," *Review,* June 9, 1859, p. 23; *History of Washtenaw County, Michigan,* pp. 754, 778.

[68] According to J. N. Loughborough's diary, James White did not leave for Allegan but went in the opposite direction to Jackson and on to Hillsdale. It seems that Loughborough is right on this point, since the *Review* had advertised "a Conference in Hillsdale, Mich., May 21st and 22nd," adding that "Bro. and sister White design to be present." The reason Ellen White did not accompany James on this trip as advertised was, no doubt, that she was "miserable in health and depressed in spirits," as she put it.

See: J. N. Loughborough, "Diary," entries for May 19, 21; "Conference at Hillsdale," *Review,* May 12, 1859, p. 200.

[69] This may be **John Quincy Foy**. See Mar. 10 entry (Ms 5, 1859).

[Battle Creek] Sabbath, May 21

Not able to go to meeting in the forenoon. Unable to sit up. Felt unable to attend in the afternoon, but resolved to go. Suffered much pain in my side while sitting. Brother Frisbie preached: "In such an hour as ye think not, the Son of Man cometh." After he sat down, Brother Bates [**Joseph Bates**][70] talked well. Then I said a little about living up to our profession, having our dress correspond to our profession. I felt a solemn sense of what we should be who profess to be waiting for translation. The meeting was profitable.

[Battle Creek] Sunday, May 22

Feel a little better in body. In the afternoon Brother [**Ransom G. Lockwood**] and Sister Lockwood [**Aurora Lockwood**][71] visited me, also Sister Cornell [**Cornelia A. Cornell**][72] and Sister Lyon [**Deborah Lyon**].[73] Had a very pleasant interview.

[Battle Creek] Monday, May 23

My mother came to visit me. She seems quite cheerful. At noon my husband came unexpectedly. I was very glad to see him. My prayers have been for him, morning and night, that God would be with him and return him to us again in safety.

[Battle Creek] Tuesday, May 24

Agnes [Irving] left for her home today.[74] Wrote two short letters, one to Sophrona Peckham [**Sophronia Peckham**] and one to my brother J. B. Harmon [**John B. Harmon**]. He intends visiting us.[75] Walked down to the office. Was much exhausted by the walk.

[Battle Creek] Wednesday, May 25

Feel very languid. Oh, why is it that such gloom rests upon everything? Why can I not rise above this depression of spirit?

[Battle Creek] Sabbath, May 28

Attended meeting all day. Felt pressed in spirit to bear a straight testimony upon pride, love of fashion. God is separating His people from the world. He is purifying them unto Himself, and those who will not heed reproof, who

---

[70] *Identity:* See Feb. 4 entry (Ms 5, 1859).

[71] *Identities:* See Mar. 1 entry (Ms 5, 1859).

[72] *Identity:* See Jan. 5 entry (Ms 5, 1859).

[73] *Identity:* See Feb. 8 entry (Ms 5, 1859).

[74] Her father, seriously ill, died on June 4. See Jan. 6 entry (Ms 5, 1859).

[75] "I have not seen [him] for twenty years," Ellen noted in her diary when John Harmon and his wife arrived in Battle Creek on July 22 (Ms 7, 1859 [July 22 entry]). These letters are not in the White Estate archives.

choose to possess their own way, to manifest the evil passions of the heart, will be left behind. God will have a pure and a holy, self-denying, cross-bearing people. The message to the Laodiceans looks clearer to me. I see God will not do His work of spewing out until character is developed, His professed people proved, tested, and tried. Now God is proving His people to see if they will obey Him. "Be zealous . . . and repent." If they will not, He will spew them out of His mouth. There are some among us of whom God will soon say, "Their sins shall not be cleansed with sacrifice or offering forever." Like the house of Eli, a heavy curse will rest upon them.[76]

[Battle Creek] Thursday, June 2

A company came from Moscow [Michigan]. They tarried with us over night.[77] We were very glad to see them. I am suffering with pain in my side and great depression of spirits.

[Battle Creek] Friday, June 3

A number came from Monterey and stopped with us. Am sorry that I cannot enjoy their company. I have no health and my mind is completely depressed.

[Battle Creek] Sabbath, June 4

Was very sick and much discouraged.[78] Unable to attend meeting. All report that it was the best meeting they ever attended.[79]

---

[76] Cf. with meditation on the Laodicean message in May 14 entry.

[77] A "General Conference" to be held in Battle Creek had been advertised for the weekend June 2 to 6 with a "general invitation . . . extended to all, east, west, north and south, to attend." The delegations from Moscow and Monterey stayed in the White home, and explains why the Whites had 35 persons for dinner on June 6. General instructions given to members coming from out of town were that "our sleeping rooms will be given up to females," whereas "the brethren will have the next best chance in our barns, in the Tent, or on unoccupied floors in our houses."

See: James White, "General Conference," *Review,* May 19, 1859, p. 8.

[78] Ellen White sums up her sickness and depression endured during this period in the pamphlet *Testimony for the Church,* No. 5, published shortly after June 16. "Disease seemed to make continual progress upon me, and I thought that I must lie down in the grave. I had no desire to live, therefore I could not take hold of faith and pray for my recovery." The crisis came one night when "I fainted at midnight. Brethren Andrews and Loughborough were sent for, and earnest petitions were offered to God in my behalf. The depression, the heavy weight was lifted from my aching heart, and I was taken off in vision." Ellen White's biographer, Arthur White, surmises that the vision was received on June 4, but it was more likely on June 9 when J. N. Loughborough records in his diary, "at 10 p.m. I was called to go and pray for Sister White. She had a vision of 12 minutes." The disparity between "midnight" and "10 p.m." seems within the margin of human error given the circumstances.

See: Ellen G. White, *Testimonies for the Church,* vol. 1, p. 185; E. G. W. [Ellen G. White], "Testimony for the Church No. 5," *Review,* June 16, 1859, p. 32; Arthur L. White, *Ellen G. White: The Early Years,* p. 407; J. N. Loughborough, "Diary," entry for June 9.

[79] For a summary report of the conference meetings and business proceedings, see "The Conference," *Review,* June 9, 1859, p. 20, and Joseph Bates, Uriah Smith, "Business Pro-

[Battle Creek] Sunday, June 5

Went to the tent for meeting. Was so feeble did not enjoy it much. The tent was well filled. Brother J. N. Loughborough preached in the forenoon on faith. It was a profitable discourse. J. N. Andrews preached in the afternoon upon the Sabbath, or rather the two laws. The attention of all was arrested and there was great attention. His exhortation was solemn and impressive.

[Battle Creek] Monday, June 6

Attended meeting in the morning. It was a meeting of deep interest. I had opportunity to bear my testimony. It was the best meeting of all, and when the people left, all united in saying it was the best conference they ever attended. At dinner we had thirty-five.

[Battle Creek] Tuesday, June 7

We were all much worn out.

[Battle Creek] Sunday, June 12

Sister Diantha [**Diantha Wilkinson** (née **Benedict**)][80] came to help me sew.[81] Her visit she thought was a benefit to her.

[Battle Creek] Tuesday, June 14

Diantha helped them fold at the Office.

[Battle Creek] Wednesday, June 15

Diantha went home early in the afternoon. Brother Andrews, Uriah [**Uriah Smith**], and Harriet [**Harriet Smith**][82] were visiting there.

Thursday, June 16

We rose early and rode to Brother and Sister Benedict's.

Friday, June 17

Diantha left early to do a little job for herself. Brother Day [**John S. Day**][83] came.

---

ceedings of the General Conference of June 3-6, 1859," *Review,* June 9, 1859, p. 21.

[80] *Identity:* See comments on the identity of "Brother Benedict" under Jan. 5 entry (Ms 5, 1859).

[81] Two months earlier in her diary Ellen White sympathized with the Benedict family: "They are poor and Brother Benedict is very feeble; unable to work" (Apr. 12). It seems that the work provided for daughter Diantha (June 12-17 entries) and Mrs. Millie Benedict (Lt 10 and Lt 15, 1860 [Oct. 12 and Nov. 21]) was one of the ways the Whites tried to help the family.

[82] *Identities:* The only "Uriah" from this period of Sabbatarian history is Uriah Smith. The coupling of "Uriah" with "Harriet" makes certain that the reference is to Uriah's wife, Harriet.

[83] *Identity:* See under Jan. 12 (Ms 5, 1859).

Sabbath, June 18

We went to the tent meeting at Marshall.[84] After the meeting closed, rode to Brother Glover's [**Charles S. Glover**][85] at Ceresco.

Sunday, June 19

Could not go to the tent meeting on account of rain. Took dinner at Brother Byington's [**John Byington**]. Then Martha [**Martha Dormer Amadon** (née **Byington**)][86] accompanied me to the Creek.[87]

[Battle Creek] Monday, June 20

Was very sick all day.

[Battle Creek] Tuesday, June 21

Was a little better.

[See also Lt 2, 1859, written on this date.]

[Battle Creek] Wednesday, June 22

Very unwell, yet Martha and self visited Sister Daigneau[88] and Sister Ratelle [**Marguerite Ratelle**].[89] It was a profitable visit. They wished to get supper; we would not allow it. We do not believe in going to visit and taking up all the time preparing something to eat. We conversed upon our religious experience, then had a sweet, interesting season of prayer. We believe the Lord will go with Sister Ratelle as she moves in the country.

---

[84] J. N. Loughborough and J. N. Andrews held a series of public meetings, June 16-July 3, in Marshall, Michigan, about 12 miles (19 kilometers) from Battle Creek.

See: J. N. Andrews, J. N. Loughborough, "Tent Meeting at Marshall," *Review,* Aug. 11, 1859, p. 93.

[85] *Identity:* See Apr. 16 entry.

[86] *Identities:* See Apr. 16 entry.

[87] I.e., Battle Creek.

[88] *Identity:* The reference here, quite likely, is to Vitaline M. Daigneau, a French Canadian Sabbatarian who lived just a few dozen yards (meters) from the Whites until the mid-1860s. This inference is strengthened by the coupling of "Sister Ratel" with "Sister Daigneau," since Marguerite Ratelle and Vitaline Daigneau were sisters as well as fellow believers. Detracting somewhat from any firm conclusion is the possibility that Ellen White is instead alluding to Vitaline Daigneau's mother-in-law, Domatile Daigneau, who also lived close by. In Lt 10, 1861 (Oct. 18), Ellen White indicates that Domatile had been an Adventist (a "sister") at an earlier period, but it is not clear whether this was the case in 1859 when Ellen White visited "Sister Daigneau."

For a comprehensive collection of local government, local press, as well as Adventist sources related to the Daigneau and Ratelle families, see Glenn Davis and Jean Davis, "Notebook, Vol. 1" (section on Daigneau). See also 1860 U.S. Federal Census, "Vitaline Daigneau," "Domatile Daigneau," Michigan, Calhoun County, Battle Creek, pp. 5, 6.

[89] *Identity:* See Feb. 28 entry (Ms 5, 1859).

[Battle Creek] Thursday, June 30

Sister Cranson [**Mary Jane Cranson**][90] made me quite a long visit. We had a familiar conversation upon her situation. She is to be pitied. We helped her do some things.[91]

[See also Lt 28, 1859, written circa June/July 1859.]

[90] *Identity:* See Jan. 3 entry (Ms 5, 1859).

[91] Mary Cranson's health had declined since her husband's death of tuberculosis in 1855. Within a few months after this diary entry, she was so "feeble" that she was "unable to do her housework" and care for her children. *The Good Samaritan* reported in February 1860 that the Battle Creek church had supported Mrs. Cranson with $3 per week since August 1859. She died a few months later, leaving three orphaned children.

See: Harriet N. Smith, Ann J. Kellogg, Huldah Godsmark, "Widow Cranson," *The Good Samaritan,* February 1860, p. 12.

1859
(Ms 7, 1859)

JULY 1–SEPTEMBER 30

Diary, July to September.

Portions of this manuscript are published in Ellen G. White, *Manuscript Releases,* vol. 3, p. 143.

[Battle Creek, Michigan] Friday, July 1

Jenny and self walked down to the city. It was a tiresome walk.

[Battle Creek] Sabbath, July 2

Had sinking turns. Suffered much all through the day.

[Battle Creek] Sunday, July 3

I was very weak.

[Battle Creek] Monday, July 4

Wrote nearly all day—important matter.

[Battle Creek] Tuesday, July 5

Was very weak in body.

[Battle Creek] Wednesday, July 6

Rode down to the city with Mary Loughborough [**Mary J. Loughborough**] and my husband. Took our bonnets from the milliner.

[Battle Creek] Thursday, July 7

Went down to Brother and Sister Smith's [**Cyrenius** and **Louisa Smith**].[1] Had some conversation with them upon a vision I had. Feel bad that they do not realize their state as it is.

[Battle Creek] Friday, July 8

We had much to do today. Dried half a bushel of cherries.

---

[1] *Identity:* For the identity of "Brother and Sister Smith," see Lt 32, 1859 (July 9), notes 1 and 2. It seems fairly certain that the "conversation" and "vision" here referred to are described in Lt 32, 1859, written to the Smiths two days later, regarding their lack of concern for the needs of a widow and a poverty-stricken minister.

See: Ellen G. White, Lt 32, 1859 (July 9); Ms 4, 1859 (c. July).

[Battle Creek] Sabbath, July 9

Had a strange sinking turn. Unable to attend meeting. Wrote to Brother and Sister Smith.[2]

[Battle Creek] Sunday, July 10

Wrote a number of letters to Sisters Harris, Abbey, Lowry, Churchill.

[Battle Creek] Monday, July 11

Went to the office. Arranged James' and my letters. Took dinner at Fletcher's [**John Fletcher Byington**].[3] Indians pitched their tents in Manchester Oaks.

[Battle Creek] Tuesday, July 12

Rode down street. Traded some. Spent the rest of the day in writing. Met Brother Byington [**John Byington**][4] at Fletcher's. He looked happier than I had seen him for months. Says after a week he is going out to labor for the Lord, and expects to be absent six months. Thank the Lord for this.[5]

[Battle Creek] Friday, July 22

My brother [**John B. Harmon**] that I have not seen for twenty years came from Illinois with his wife [**Lucy J. Harmon**][6] to visit us.

My brother leaves tonight at twelve o'clock. My father and mother accompany him.

[Battle Creek] Wednesday, July 27

It seems very lonely today: Brother and Father and Mother gone. Perhaps we shall never meet them again.[7] This makes me sad.

---

[2] On the letter written to the Smiths, see note 1 above (July 7 entry). None of the letters mentioned under July 10 are in the White Estate archives.

[3] *Identity:* The surname "Fletcher" has not been found among Adventists in Battle Creek during this period. Very likely Ellen White is speaking of John Fletcher Byington, a printer at the Review and Herald press. She always addressed him by his middle name, no doubt to distinguish him from his father, **John Byington**, for whom she also tended to reserve the basic title "Brother Byington." Note the diary entry for the following day, July 12: "Met Brother Byington at Fletcher's," alluding to the fact that John Byington was visiting the house of his son, John Fletcher Byington.

See: Search term "Fletcher" in *Words of the Pioneers.* For Ellen White's use of "Fletcher Byington" or "Fletcher," see Lt 7, 1853 (Aug. 24); Lt 28, 1859 (June/July); Lt 7, 1860 (June); Lt 174, 1906 (June 7); Ms 5, 1861 (c. 1861).

[4] *Identity:* See under July 11.

[5] John Byington, a traveling preacher, had for some time given up his vocation because of discouragement. See under Apr. 16 (Ms 6, 1859) for background.

[6] *Identities:* See Artemas C. Harmon, ed., *The Harmon Genealogy,* p. 79; 1860 U.S. Federal Census, "Lucy J. Harman," Illinois, Greene County, Between the Creeks, p. 184.

[7] By mid-November, at the latest, however, Robert (and probably Eunice) was back in Michigan.

Went down street to purchase material to use in Brother Czechowski's [**Michael B. Czechowski**][8] family. The merchant was kind enough to send her a dress.

[Battle Creek] Thursday, July 28

Went to the Office; assisted my husband.

[Battle Creek] Sabbath, July 30

Mother White [**Betsey White**][9] is quite ill with dysentery. Took her to our own house to nurse her up. Husband preached twice today. The truth was set forth in a clear, powerful manner. His text was, "Preach the Word."

[Battle Creek] Tuesday, August 2

Brethren J. N. Andrews and J. N. Loughborough came from the tent meeting.[10]

[Battle Creek] Thursday, August 4

Mother is now able to go to her home again.

[Jackson, Michigan] Wednesday, August 17

Left Battle Creek for Jackson on our eastern journey.[11] Arrived at Jackson

---

See: Ms 8, 1859 (Nov. 16 entry).

[8] The uncommon name and the fact that Ellen White was assisting the family with clothing suffice to identify this person as Michael B. Czechowski. A former Catholic priest from Poland, Czechowski suffered persecution after becoming a Protestant and eventually moved to America. For some time he preached for the Baptists in northern New York. In 1857 he became a Sabbathkeeper and the following year returned to New York to preach his newfound faith full-time. James and Ellen White engaged themselves in raising funds for the support of the poverty-stricken Czechowski family. Appeals were made for donations in the *Review* and *The Good Samaritan*. In addition, Ellen White collected items of clothing for the Czechowskis as seen in this diary entry and the December 1859 issue of *The Good Samaritan*.

See: James White, "To the benevolent," *Review,* Apr. 15, 1858, p. 176; James White, J. P. Kellogg, Cyrenius Smith, "Missionary report," *The Good Samaritan,* December 1859, p. 8; E. G. W. [Ellen G. White], "Articles of Clothing," *The Good Samaritan,* December 1859, p. 8. For a survey of M. B. Czechowski's work in New York 1858-1861, see Rajmund L. Dabrowski, "The Sojourn of M. B. Czechowski on the American Continent," in Rajmund L. Dabrowski and B. B. Beach, ed., *Michael Belina Czechowski 1818-1876,* pp. 106-116.

[9] *Identity: The Jewett Family of America: Year Book of 1912-1913,* p. 81; 1860 U.S. Federal Census, "Betsey White," Michigan, Calhoun County, Battle Creek, p. 6.

[10] Andrews and Loughborough had just completed two weeks of tent meetings in Centerville, St. Joseph County, Michigan. "I breakfasted at Bro. White's," Loughborough notes in his diary on this first day after his return to Battle Creek.

See: J. N. Andrews, J. N. Loughborough, "Tent Meeting at Centerville, Mich.," *Review,* Aug. 25, 1859, p. 108; J. N. Loughborough, "Diary," entry for Aug. 2.

[11] This journey East was originally planned to take six or seven weeks, but was extended while en route. The Whites returned to Battle Creek three months later, on November 21, having traveled in excess of 2,000 miles (3,220 kilometers).

about two o'clock p.m. Found Brother Palmer's [**Dan R. Palmer**][12] family well. Had a praying season that eve. Felt like wrestling earnestly with God for the spirit of labor, and we had an assurance that our prayers would be answered.

[Carlton, New York] Thursday, August 18

Awoke a little past two A.M. Took the [railroad] cars at four. Feel very miserable. Rode all day. Oh, what an exhibition of hoops![13] What pride and fashion! Surely hoops cannot be convenient in the cars. Our journey on the cars ended about six p.m.[14] Found Brother Buckland [**Curtis P. Buckland**][15] and Cottrell [**Roswell F. Cottrell**][16] waiting with covered carriages. We had a very easy conveyance to Brother Buckland's, about five miles [eight kilometers].

[Carlton] Sabbath, August 20[17]

They are coming in to the meetings. One hundred in the forenoon, above two hundred in the afternoon.[18] Brother White preached forenoon and

---

See: J. W. [James White], "Eastern Tour," *Review,* Sept. 29, 1859, p. 148; J. W. [James White], "At Home," *Review,* Dec. 8, 1859, p. 20.

[12] *Identity:* See Apr. 2 entry (Ms 6, 1859).

[13] The hoop skirt was a women's undergarment designed to give a fashionable belled-out shape to the outer skirt through a series of circular supports.

[14] They left the train at Albion, New York (cf. Aug. 22 entry and notice in *Review*). James White felt exhilarated after covering more than 300 miles (483 kilometers) in one day: "It seemed hardly possible that we had left . . . Jackson, Mich., only sixteen hours before. We were hurried over the roads, through the dust, and from one train to another, with such speed that we seemed to forget headaches, and other ills."

See: "Appointments," *Review,* Aug. 18, 1859, p. 104; J. W. [James White], "Eastern Tour," *Review,* Sept. 1, 1859, p. 116.

[15] *Identity:* The tent meeting held on "Brother Buckland's" farm described in the following entries is clearly the same meeting recounted in Curtis P. Buckland's obituary many years later: "In 1859 another tent meeting was held on his farm by Bro. and sister White." Buckland lived in Carlton, New York.

See: Obituary: "Curtis P. Buckland," *Review,* Feb. 3, 1891, p. 79.

[16] *Identity:* The next day's diary entry states that "Brother Cottrell," along with James White, preached at the Carlton meetings. Prior announcements in the *Review* indicate that it was "Bro. R. F. Cottrell" who organized the weekend gathering.

See: "Appointments," *Review,* Aug. 4, 1859, p. 88.

[17] In her diary Ellen White mistakenly placed this entry in the space for Friday, August 19, and the Sunday, August 21, entry in the Saturday, August 20, space. That the meetings described in these entries actually took place on August 20 and 21 is apparent, in part, from the dates announced beforehand in the *Review* and from retrospective reports by R. F. Cottrell and James White.

See: "Appointments," *Review,* Aug. 4, 1859, p. 88; R. F. C. [R. F. Cottrell], "Tent Meeting and Conference in Western New York," *Review,* Sept. 1, 1859, p. 120; J. W., "Eastern Tour," *Review,* Sept. 1, 1859, p. 116.

[18] James White felt that "the number present was small compared with such meetings in Michigan and some other parts of the country." About "two-thirds of the congregation" were nonmembers, "people in the vicinity."

afternoon. Brother Cottrell in the evening. Have meeting in the evening.

[Carlton] Sunday, August 21

Large congregation. Good attention. Tent full. Some women with their rich silks and satins sit upon the ground just inside of the curtain. I preached from this text, "Preach the Word."[19]

[Rochester, New York] Monday, August 22

Left Brother Buckland's for Albion. There took the cars for Rochester. Found Brother Orton [**Jonathan T. Orton**][20] waiting for us, and he took us to his home in his carriage.

[Rochester] Tuesday, August 23

Tarried with Brother Orton through the day. Traded in Rochester. Laura Seeley [**Laura Seeley**][21] came to Brother Orton's. Poor afflicted soul!

[Roosevelt, New York] Wednesday, August 24

Left Rochester for Syracuse. There took the Omnibus[22] for Central Square. Hired a conveyance for Roosevelt. Made our stopping place and home at Brother Sprague's.[23]

[Roosevelt] Thursday, August 25

Wrote to Brother Peabody [**William Peabody**].[24] Was very weary.

See: J. W. [James White], "Eastern Tour," *Review,* Sept. 1, 1859, p. 116.

[19] On Ellen White as speaker and preacher, see R. Edward Turner, *Proclaiming the Word,* pp. 8-35; Horace John Shaw, "A Rhetorical Analysis of the Speaking of Mrs. Ellen G. White"; EGWEnc, s.v. "Preaching."

[20] The only male "Orton" from Rochester, New York, mentioned in the *Review* during this period is "J. T. Orton." More complete name details come from census and other records.

See: Search term "Orton" in *Words of the Pioneers;* 1850 U.S. Federal Census, "Jonathan Orton," New York, Monroe County, Rochester, Ward 7, p. 317.

[21] *Identity:* That Ellen White is referring to Laura Seely (also spelled Seeley) is very likely since she was a Sabbathkeeper living in Rochester and also because of the description "poor afflicted soul." When she died of "paralysis" the following May, age 38, it was recorded that "her sufferings were great for many months before her death."

See: Search terms "Seely" and "Seeley" in *Words of the Pioneers;* obituary: "Laura Seely," *Review,* June 6, 1860, p. 23.

[22] Name given to an enlarged version of the traditional horse-drawn stagecoach carrying upward of 20 passengers on fixed routes at set fares.

See: Philip Steadman and Gerrylynn K. Roberts, *American Cities and Technology,* p. 31.

[23] The identity of this person has not been established.

[24] *Identity:* Within the space of two weeks Ellen White wrote three letters to a "Brother Peabody." One of these, written September 2, 1859, has survived and provides useful clues as to his identity. First, she describes Peabody as a man of "considerable means" and encourages him to donate more "to advance the cause of present truth." Second, he is in his "old age," with his head "already white." This description matches well that of church member William

[Roosevelt] Friday, August 26

They are coming in to the meeting. Brother and Sister Wheeler [**Frederick** and **Lydia Wheeler**][25] are here. I am sick today. Had a meeting in the eve at the commencement of the Sabbath. It was a good meeting. Husband preached. There was a conference meeting appointed for the morning. I had opportunity to talk.

[Roosevelt] Sabbath, August 27

They have a neat little meetinghouse.[26] It was filled and crowded and many could not get in at all. In the afternoon they were obliged to give it up to the women and infirm and aged men. They drew up the wagons to the windows and the men filled them full.[27] I had freedom in preaching.

[Roosevelt] Sunday, August 28

The meeting was held in the tent.

[Volney, New York] Monday, August 29

Left Roosevelt for Volney. Rode in a lumber wagon. It was very wearisome.

[Volney] Tuesday, August 30

Had a meeting in the schoolhouse. Bore my testimony after my husband preached.

Peabody, of Scottsville, New York. The value of his real estate is listed at a very sizable $15,000 in the 1850 census, and his generous and frequent donations to the Advent movement are attested to in the receipts sections of the *Review*. Furthermore, William Peabody was 68 years old, which could justify the view that he was of "old age."

See: Ellen G. White, Ms 7, 1859 (entries for Aug. 25, Sept. 6); Lt 4, 1859 (Sept. 2); 1850 U.S. Federal Census, "Wm Peabody," New York, Monroe, Wheatland, p. 245; obituary: "William Peabody," *Review,* Jan. 22, 1867, p. 82; search term "Peabody" in *Words of the Pioneers.*

[25] *Identity:* There is little doubt that Frederick and Lydia Wheeler are referred to here. Although Frederick Wheeler is best known as the minister who pioneered Sabbatarian Adventism in New Hampshire in the 1840s, he subsequently moved to New York State in 1857 and was given special responsibility for central New York, including the Roosevelt church in Oswego County. Frederick Wheeler, living in nearby West Monroe, New York, frequently helped organize conferences and meetings at Roosevelt during this period.

See: Saml. W. Rhodes, R. F. Cottrell, "Conference at Roosevelt, N.Y.," *Review,* Mar. 19, 1857, p. 157; search term "F. Wheeler," in *Words of the Pioneers.*

[26] The Roosevelt meetinghouse had been completed earlier the same summer and dedicated during the weekend of June 17-19, 1859.

See: "Appointments," *Review,* June 2, 1859, p. 16.

[27] A large tent had been pitched next to the meetinghouse, but because of rainy, chilly weather, it had been decided to hold Sabbath meetings in the meetinghouse, despite the overcrowding. Next day, the weather being fine, the tent was used and filled to capacity. James White estimated that "probably there were present eight or nine hundred persons."

See: J. W. [James White], "Roosevelt, N.Y., Conference," *Review,* Sept. 15, 1859, p. 132.

[Springfield, Massachusetts] Wednesday, August 31

Left Volney for Fulton, about five miles [eight kilometers] away. There took the cars for Syracuse [New York] and changed cars for Utica and again to Albany and tarried at Springfield over night; lodging and breakfast cost $2.00.

[Kensington, Connecticut] Thursday, September 1

We again took the cars for Berlin, Connecticut. Arrived at Brother Belden's [**Albert Belden**][28] before noon. They received us gladly.

[See also Lt 3, 1859, written on this date.]

[Kensington] Friday, September 2

Brother Sperry [**Charles W. Sperry**][29] came from Vermont to consult James about meeting in Vermont. Great confusion about appointment.[30] Brother Andrew Graham [**Andrew Graham**] came to take us to visit his people. We did not enjoy the visit much. We were so perplexed to know how to correct the appointment. Took dinner with Brother Bruce Graham [**Bruce Graham**]. Then went to William Graham's [**William Henry Graham**].[31] His wife is sick, confined to her bed. We had a praying season with her and left for Brother Belden's.

[See also Lt 4, 1859, written on this date.]

---

[28] *Identity:* Albert Belden lived in Kensington village, which was included in the territory of Berlin township. Although other Beldens are listed in the *Review* from this period, the only one said to be located in Berlin/Kensington is Albert Belden. Albert Belden and his wife, Hannah, had known the Whites since 1848, when the first of what are known as the "Sabbath and Sanctuary Conferences" was held in their home in Rocky Hill, Connecticut. Later, during the summer of 1849, the Whites lived in the Belden home. It was while there that Edson White was born and that James White started publishing *The Present Truth.* Their son, Stephen Belden, married Ellen White's older sister, Sarah Harmon.

See: Search term "Belden" in *Words of the Pioneers;* Arthur L. White, *Ellen G. White: The Early Years,* pp. 161-169.

[29] *Identity:* The more than 200 mentions of "Sperry" in the *Review* during the 1850s refer almost exclusively either to Charles W. Sperry; his wife, Rachel Ann; or his young son J. Byron. Charles Sperry was a leading preacher in Vermont, fitting the description given here of "Brother Sperry" as coming from Vermont and consulting with James White about the preaching schedule of the Whites in that state.

See: Search term "Sperry" in *Words of the Pioneers.*

[30] The tours undertaken by the Whites were normally planned and advertised well in advance, but on this tour they made major itinerary changes while en route. James White's original plan for the tour, made in August, makes no mention of visiting Vermont, but it was added to the published itinerary after some weeks. Under these changing circumstances it is understandable that misunderstandings of this kind could take place.

See: James White, "Appointments," Aug. 4, 1859, p. 88; James White, "Appointments," Sept. 15, 1859, p. 136.

[31] The three Grahams, Andrew, Bruce, and William Henry, are listed in the 1860 census for Berlin, Connecticut. Census details strongly suggest that they are brothers, as does Ellen White's letter to "Brethren Graham" (Lt 7, 1859 [Sept. 24]). See biographical sketch of each for references.

[Kensington][32] *Sabbath, September 3*

Quite a number have collected together. Dear precious souls are among them who have endured many hardships, suffered affliction and anguish. Sister Chamberlain [**Mary Ann Chamberlain**][33] is dressed in deep mourning. We call up the severe afflictions she has suffered. Buried a child, a noble boy named Joseph, about four years old. Buried her husband with that dreadful disease, smallpox. Then buried a daughter, a young woman grown. Gave birth soon after to a pair of twins; at an early age buried one; another son died in Michigan. Her son Joseph, a sweet, interesting boy of eight years, was drowned. Jane, a young woman grown, died of consumption.[34] Her afflicted heart was comforted by hearing the words spoken. She was greatly strengthened.

[Somerville, Massachusetts] Monday, September 5

Left Connecticut for Springfield [Massachusetts] on our way to Boston [Massachusetts]. Arrived at Boston; took a hack[35] for Hay Market Square. Then took the horse railroad for Somerville. Arrived at Brother Folsom's about dark. Were received heartily by Brother and Sister Folsom [**Paul** and **Margaret Folsom**].[36]

---

[32] In his report for the *Review* James White stated that meetings on September 3 and 4 took place in Kensington, Connecticut.

See: J. W. [James White], "Eastern Tour," *Review,* Sept. 29, 1859, p. 148.

[33] *Identity:* The details about deaths in her family (see next note) match the experience of Mary Ann Chamberlain so closely that there can be no doubt about her identity. The Chamberlains lived in Middletown, Connecticut, about 10 miles (16 kilometers) from the meetings being held at Kensington. Having been closely acquainted with the Whites since 1848, naturally Mary Ann wanted to attend these meetings.

[34] Of the deaths in Mary Ann Chamberlain's family mentioned in this entry, several can be confirmed from other sources:

Her husband, **E.L.H. Chamberlain**, "died of the small pox, in Middletown, Conn., Nov. 18th, 1855" (*Review,* Jan. 24, 1856).

Two months later, January 26, 1856, a stepdaughter, Frances Rogers Chamberlain, died, age 20 (*Sizer Genealogy*).

On March 14, twins were born to Mary Ann, one of which, Ada, died after less than three months (*Sizer Genealogy*).

On November 10, 1857, a stepson, William Card Chamberlain, died, age 18 (*Sizer Genealogy*).

A son, Joseph Gurney, drowned June 10, 1859, age 10. (*Sizer Genealogy*).

See: Obituary: "E.L.H. Chamberlain," *Review,* Jan. 24, 1856, p. 134; Lillian Hubbard Holch, ed., *Sizer Genealogy,* pp. 205, 206, 208.

[35] A shortened term for "hackney"—a horse-drawn carriage.

[36] *Identity:* A letter to the *Review* editor dated October 8, 1858, is signed "Paul Folsom, Somerville, Mass." Further, the only Folsom mentioned in the *Review* before 1864 is Paul Folsom. His wife's name, Margaret, appears in census records. Paul Folsom, to whom published references go back to 1851, was a leading figure among Sabbatarian Adventists in Massachusetts. For years regular Sabbath services and conferences had been held at the Folsom home in Somerville, just north of Boston. Several references report visits to their home by Ellen and James White.

[Somerville] Tuesday, September 6

Found myself quite well this morn. Spent a portion of the day writing.[37] Wrote home to Henry [age 12], Jenny [**Jane Fraser**],[38] and Willie [age 5]. Wrote to Topsham [Maine], Brother Sperry,[39] and sent a letter to Brother Peabody, to Brother J. B. Harmon [**John B. Harmon**],[40] and to Sister Sarah Belden [**Sarah B. Belden**].[41]

[Somerville] Wednesday, September 7

Wrote a portion of the day. Made husband three collars. James went into Boston. Rode with Brother Folsom to Salem [Massachusetts]. Returned about 9 o'clock p.m. In his absence, Brother Nichols [**Otis Nichols**][42] came

---

See: P. Folsom, "From Bro. Folsom," *Review,* Oct. 21, 1858, p. 175; search term "Folsom" in *Review and Herald* online collection, www.adventistarchives.org; 1860 U.S. Federal Census, "Margaret Folsom," Massachusetts, Middlesex County, Somerville, p. 76; Ellen G. White, Lt 9, 1859 (Sept. 6); Ms 7, 1859 (Sept. 5 entry).

[37] Of the eight letters mentioned in this entry, only the letter to Henry is definitely known to be preserved in the White Estate archives (Lt 5, 1859 [Sept. 6]). The letter to Willie is most probably Lt 9, 1859—sometimes dated September 26, 1859. The original handwritten draft, however, has a line through the number "2," probably indicating an intention to cross it out, in which case the date is September 6.

[38] *Identity:* In an undated Ellen White letter to her son Willie, apparently written the same month, she admonishes him to eat the candy she sent "only when Jenny thinks it is best," and in a letter on September 15 she appeals to Willie to "mind Jenny and try to please her." According to the 1860 census "Jane Frazer" lived in the White household; "housework" was listed as her occupation. Thus, when Ellen White states that she is writing "home to Henry, Jenny, and Willie" it is fairly clear that she is writing to Jane Frazer (usually spelled "Fraser"). According to W. C. White, Jane Fraser had joined the White household as cook sometime before 1855 while the Whites were living in Rochester, New York. She appears to have stayed with them until at least 1861 and to have had responsibility for the children when the Whites were traveling.

See: Ellen G. White, Lt 10, 1859 (Sept.); Lt 6, 1859 (Sept. 15); Lt 26, 1861 (May 4); 1860 U.S. Federal Census, "Jane Frazer," Michigan, Calhoun County, Battle Creek, p. 224; William C. White, "Sketches and Memories of James and Ellen G. White: XIV Beginnings in Rochester," *Review,* June 13, 1935, p. 9.

[39] These two letters may have been related to the conferences that the Whites were to attend in Topsham on September 24, 25, and the meetings in Vermont scheduled for October 8-16, which had been arranged with Charles Sperry some days earlier (see Sept. 2 entry above).

See: James White, "Appointments," *Review,* Sept. 22, 1859, p. 144.

[40] Ellen White's older brother, living in Illinois. It is probable that Ellen's parents were at this time staying with John Harmon and his wife (see July 22, 26, 27 above).

[41] Ellen White's sister, living in Battle Creek.

[42] *Identity:* The September 14 entry gives more detail: "Go to Brother Nichols' to visit them. The girls are absent from home. Henry was at home." This corresponds to the family situation of Otis Nichols of Dorchester, just south of Boston. According to the 1860 census and other records, Otis Nichols had two daughters (Mary E. and Anna) and one son, **Henry Otis Nichols**, living at home. Otis Nichols, a well-to-do farmer and active layman, had been a mainstay of support for Ellen White as early as 1845 when Ellen (then Harmon) stayed with the Nichols family for several months.

See: 1860 U.S. Federal Census, "Otis Nichols," Massachusetts, Norfolk County, Dorchester, p. 228.

to see him. Was disappointed at his absence. Sister Folsom went out to trade. Returned about dark.

[Salem, Massachusetts] Thursday, September 8

Left Somerville for Salem at half past two o'clock p.m. Brother Saxby [**William L. Saxby**][43] was not waiting for us. Took a carriage to his house. Brother and Sister Hutchins [**Alfred S.** and **Esther M. Hutchins**][44] came to Brother Saxby's in the eve.

[Salem] Friday, September 9

Some are coming in to the meeting. May the Lord bless His people and fit us up to do the work committed to us.

[Salem] Sabbath, September 10

More brethren out than we had expected to see. The meeting was held in the Lyceum Hall. It is strangely constructed, the seats arising from the platform. Every row of seats is one step higher or ascending. The pulpit or stand is raised only one step. A great many can be convened.[45] Our meeting Sabbath was profitable and interesting. James preached on baptism and that sin is the transgression of the law. I said a few words. Others gave in their exhortation. At two o'clock p.m. James preached again with liberty upon the unity of the church. I then talked upon the necessity of living out our profession and

---

[43] *Identity:* A short note that appeared two weeks earlier in the *Review* is helpful in identifying "Brother Saxby": "W. L. Saxby: Bro. White will see you on his eastern tour, in regard to press." The only W. L. Saxby mentioned in the *Review* is William L. Saxby, who lived in Massachusetts during this period. It is most probable, therefore, that the Whites stayed with William L. Saxby and his wife, Euphemia, during their stay in Salem, Massachusetts. The only minor difficulty with this conclusion is that there is no record of W. L. Saxby living in Salem. Records place the Saxbys in Springfield, Massachusetts, until 1857, then in Worcester of the same state, and finally in Vermont by 1860. Nevertheless it is likely that the Saxbys lived in Salem before moving to Vermont in 1860.

See: "Business Notes," *Review,* Aug. 25, 1859, p. 112; search term "Saxby" in *Words of the Pioneers;* 1860 U.S. Federal Census, "William L. Saxby," Vermont, Franklin County, Enosburgh, p. 43.

[44] *Identity:* In a letter to the *Review* written three weeks later, itinerant preacher "A. S. Hutchins" reports, "We left Maine to meet Bro. and Sr. White in Salem, Mass., where we were happy to meet them again." In a letter written a few days later Ellen White reported how "James and Brother Hutchins took their places in the center of the platform" and that "Brother Hutchins talked quite freely" on the Sabbath (Lt 8, 1859 [Sept. 15]).

See: A. S. Hutchins, "Report From Bro. Hutchins," *Review,* Oct. 6, 1859, p. 157.

[45] The Lyceum Hall in Salem, Massachusetts, had been built in 1831. It "could accommodate 700 patrons in amphitheater-style seating and was decorated with images of Cicero, Demosthenes, and other great orators of bygone days." The hall received lasting fame in 1877 when Alexander Graham Bell used it for his first public demonstration of the telephone.

See: Salem, Massachusetts: The City Guide, *Salem Tales: Of Lectures and Lyceums* (n.d.), Nov. 13, 2006, www.salemweb.com/tales/lyceum.shtml.

enduring temptation. No public meeting. In Brother S's [**William L. Saxby**] house for the church. James talked at length upon our acting in union to place ourselves in a position to hold property legally. Passed off with profit.[46]

[Salem] Sunday, September 11

Prayer meeting in the morn. The church bore their testimony. Were quite free. As the people were collecting together, I exhorted the people. James preached in the morning, "Preach the Word," etc. In the afternoon finished the discourse. He was very clear. Many thought it was the most forcible discourse on the Sabbath they ever heard. The sofa was placed on the platform, on one side of the stand, and Sister Hutchins and self took our seats upon it. At the close of the afternoon discourse I again bore my testimony. Had some liberty. In the eve James preached again; dwelt upon the Lawgiver; was quite clear and free. There were about 175 present.[47] Again I exhorted the people. Was free. The Lord gave me free utterance and when the series of meetings closed we felt we had done what we could. After the meeting closed, had some conversation with Sister Dana;[48] related the wonderful dealings of God with me in past time.

[Somerville, Massachusetts] Monday, September 12

My rest was much broken last night, yet I felt quite well this morn. We assembled for prayers. Husband talked before engaging in prayer upon the necessity of being kind, courteous, pitiful, of being of tender compassion to one another. Remarks were appropriate and instructive. James and Brother Nichols prayed. It was a sweet, precious season. We shall go to Somerville. Brother Saxby took his covered easy carriage and we rode 16 miles [25 kilometers] to Somerville. Sister Saxby accompanied us. It was a pleasant ride.

---

[46] Although the wording is unclear, it appears that this discourse on church ownership was not part of the weekend public meetings but for church members only in William Saxby's house. Until 1861 the Review and Herald publishing house was legally owned solely by James White, with all the risks attendant on such individual ownership. As stated here James clearly favored legal incorporation for the publishing house and other church buildings so that the church, not individuals, would be the corporate owner. The Whites sought to persuade church members during this autumn 1859 tour of the wisdom of "holding church property legally" and reported later that they had "found no real objections in the minds of the brethren." During the early months of 1860 the issue was openly debated in the columns of the *Review,* with vigorous opposition to incorporation from some quarters.

See: J. W. [James White], "Making Us a Name," *Review,* Apr. 26, 1860, pp. 180-182. For a survey of the development of this and other organizational issues, see Andrew Gordon Mustard, *James White and SDA Organization;* Gerald Wheeler, *James White: Innovator and Overcomer,* pp. 113-142; George R. Knight, *Organizing to Beat the Devil.*

[47] James White was disappointed by the turnout at these public meetings. "The people were well notified by hand-bills, and notice in the leading Journals; but few came out."

See: J. W. [James White], "Eastern Tour," *Review,* Sept. 29, 1859, p. 148.

[48] This person has not been identified.

[Somerville] Tuesday, September 13

Go into Boston to trade.[49]

[Dorchester, Massachusetts] Wednesday, September 14

Go into Boston again to trade. Go to Brother Nichols' to visit them. The girls are absent from home. Henry [**Henry Otis Nichols**][50] was at home. Amelia Hastings [**Sarah Amelia Hastings**][51] went with us.

[Dartmouth, Massachusetts][52] *Thursday, September 15*

Brother Nichols took us with his conveyance into Boston to take the cars. We are at Brother Ashley's.[53] Are quite well. This seems to be a good home for us.

[See also Lts 6 and 8, 1859, and *An Appeal to the Youth,* pp. 65, 66, for letters written on this date.]

[Dartmouth] Friday, September 16

Early in the morn we walked to Sister Collins' [**Nancy Collins**],[54] one

---

[49] "Bought some remnants—drilling, bed ticking, 27 yards [24 meters] factory cloth, two pieces, fine and course, woolen cloth for pants, cloth for my boys, remnants of merino shawls, etc." (Lt 8, 1859 [Sept. 15]).

[50] *See:* Sept. 7 entry above.

[51] *Identity:* Amelia Hastings lived with the Folsom family in Somerville, where the Whites had spent several nights. According to the 1860 census taken the following summer, Amelia Hastings assisted the Folsoms in their confectionary business. It is probable that Amelia Hastings was a daughter of well-known Sabbatarian pioneer **Leonard W. Hastings**, of New Ipswich, New Hampshire. Evidence for this is found in Ellen White's Lt 1a, 1859 (Jan. 4) and an 1858 letter from Joseph Bates, both of which mention an "Amelia" within the Leonard Hastings family context. The 1850 census lists a "Sarah A." in the Hastings household. The details of these sources support the conclusion that her full name was Sarah Amelia Hastings.

See: 1860 U.S. Federal Census, "Amelia Hastings," Massachusetts, Middlesex County, Somerville, p. 77; Joseph Bates to "Dear Sr. Emma," Apr. 25, 1858; 1850 U.S. Federal Census, "Leonard Hastings," New Hampshire, Hillsborough County, New Ipswich, p. 272.

[52] On September 15, 1859, Ellen White wrote to Jenny Fraser, "Here we are at Dartmouth in the house of Brother Ashley" (Lt 8, 1859).

[53] *Identity:* James White reported in 1853 that "three brethren by the name of Ashly [*sic*], also their wives . . . had joined the Sabbathkeepers" in Dartmouth, Massachusetts. According to local church records, probably dating from 1861, and from the *Review,* their names were Richard C. Ashley, George L. Ashley, and Jarvis T. Ashley. Which of the three brothers is referred to here is not known.

See: James White, "Eastern Tour," *Review,* Nov. 1, 1853, p. 133; Dartmouth, Massachusetts, "Copy of Sheet From Dartmouth New Bedford Church Clerk's Record"; search terms "Ashley" and "Ashly" in *Words of the Pioneers.*

[54] *Identity:* The facts given here that Sister Collins' husband had died (recently, it seems), and that she had a son Gilbert, who was healed in response to prayer at age 12, unmistakably reveal that Ellen White is referring to Nancy Collins, of Dartmouth, Massachusetts. Her husband, Philip, had died just three months earlier, and her son had been dramatically healed in 1849, as related by Ellen White in *Spiritual Gifts.* (Ellen White's account in *Spiritual Gifts* gives the son's age as "thirteen.")

See: Obituary: "Philip Collins," *Review,* June 23, 1859, p. 39; Ellen G. White, *Spiritual Gifts [vol. 2],* pp. 108, 109.

mile [1.6 kilometers]. It seemed like home to get in their big kitchen again; but one we miss, who was well and active when we were here before. Brother Collins has sickened and died and has been borne away to the silent grave. His loss is deeply felt, not only by his family, but by all the church. This family only numbers two, the mother and her son. They love the truth. I call to mind the time when Gilbert was a boy of twelve years, was not expected to live, but we offered earnest prayer to God in his behalf. As we raised him from the bed in my arms, the great drops of perspiration stood on his brow. The Lord answered our prayer. He was restored to health; his hearing was restored.

[Dartmouth] Sabbath, September 17

It is rainy today. We fear some will be hindered from coming to meeting, but the Lord doeth all things well. The rain will result to His glory.

But few came out, but husband had good liberty in speaking.[55]

[Portland, Maine] Monday, September 19

Left Brother Ashley's for Somerville. Arrived at Boston; found Brother Philipps[56] waiting for us. He drove us into Boston. There we traded some. Then called at Brother Hale's,[57] of Charleston [Charlestown, Massachusetts]. Purchased shoes, then went on to Brother Folsom's. Took dinner with them, and at three took the cars at Boston for Portland and Brunswick [Maine]. As we arrived at Portland, we ascertained that the last train of cars had been taken off. We were disappointed. Took a carriage for Brother Lunt's [**Noah Norton Lunt**].[58] Tarried

---

[55] James White adds, "Our meetings were very small, but very good. Three decided to keep the Sabbath."

See: J. W. [James White], "Eastern Tour," *Review,* Oct. 13, 1859, p. 164.

[56] This person has not been identified.

[57] *Identity:* No "Brother Hale" living in Charlestown is mentioned in the *Review* or other church sources. However, the 1860 census lists an "Apollus Hale" in Charlestown who was a "shoe dealer." Ellen White's diary entry seems to suggest that they bought shoes from Brother Hale, in which case she may well be referring to Apollus (or Apollos, as his name is spelled elsewhere) Hale. One question that remains unanswered is whether this Apollos Hale of Charlestown is identical with the prominent Millerite preacher and writer of the same name. According to Millerite-Adventist historian Isaac C. Wellcome, Apollos Hale was obliged "after a time," for health reasons, "to abandon constant preaching and devote himself to secular business." There is some additional circumstantial evidence available, but further sources are needed to come to a definite conclusion regarding the identity of Apollos Hale of Charlestown.

See: Search term "Hale" in *Words of the Pioneers;* 1860 U.S. Federal Census, "Apollus Hale," Massachusetts, Middlesex County, Charlestown, p. 347; Isaac C. Wellcome, *History of the Second Advent Message and Mission,* p. 236; SDAE, s. v. "Apollos Hale."

[58] *Identity:* The name "N. N. Lunt," of Portland, Maine, appears frequently in the *Review* during this period. His full name appears in his obituary. Noah Lunt, a joiner living in Portland, Ellen White's native town, had personally known Ellen and her family since 1843.

See: Search term "Lunt" in *Words of the Pioneers;* obituary: "Noah Norton Lunt," *Review,* Jan. 28, 1902, p. 63.

with them overnight. Brother Lobdel [**Edward Lobdell**][59] came in, in the eve. This hindrance cost us $1.50.

[En route to Topsham, Maine] Tuesday, September 20

In morn took a carriage for cars. When we arrived at the Brunswick depot did not find a carriage there. I am waiting while my husband is gone to speak for a carriage.

[See also *An Appeal to the Youth,* pp. 47-49, for letters written to Henry, Edson, and Willie (2), on this date.]

[Sabbath, September 24]

[See Lt 7, 1859; Lt 20, 1859; Lt 21, 1859; Ms 1, 1859; and Ms 1a, 1859, all written on or about this date. See also Lt 10, 1859, written circa late September 1859.]

---

[59] *Identity:* There is no mention of a "Lobdel" in early sources, but there is frequent mention of an "Edward Lobdell," of Portland, Maine, no doubt the person referred to here. Edward Lobdell, a brick mason, age 42, who had been a Sabbathkeeper for about two years at this point, subsequently served as elder of the Portland church.

See: Search terms "Lobdel" and "Lobdell" in *Words of the Pioneers.*

1859

(Ms 8, 1859)

OCTOBER 10–NOVEMBER 20

Diary, October to November.

Portions of this manuscript are published in Ellen G. White, *Manuscript Releases,* vol. 3, pp. 144, 145; vol. 7, p. 218.

[Tuesday, October 4]

[See Lt 19, 1859, and *An Appeal to the Youth,* pp. 50, 51, written on this date.]

[Roxbury, Vermont][1] *Monday, October 10*

We were awake quite early. Brother Pierce [**Stephen Pierce**][2] came for us quite early. Was obliged to shut myself up to write. The brethren are scattering to their homes. We rode to Brother Pierce's, three miles [five kilometers]. Climbed a mountain half a mile [.8 kilometers] high. The house is full of company, but had no time to visit. Shut myself in the chamber to write.

[See also Lt 22, 1859, written on this date.]

[Roxbury] Tuesday, October 11

Left Brother Pierce's for Brother Grant's [**Harrison Grant**].[3] Took dinner at Brother Grant's. Brother Howard [**Daniel Howard**] waited for us to pack and then took us to his house. It was climb, climb the mountain. They have a very pleasant place on the top of the mountain. There is a level space and excellent tilling land. They are at some distance from neighbors. Sister Howard

---

[1] There is a gap in Ellen White's diary between September 20 and October 10. During this period the Whites continued their three-month itinerary, attending conferences in Topsham, Maine, Washington, New Hampshire, and Roxbury, Vermont. The Roxbury meetings had ended the day before, but Ellen and James stayed on in the Roxbury area for a few more days, leaving for northern Vermont on October 12.

See: James White, "Appointments," Sept. 22, 1859, p. 144.

[2] *Identity:* According to this entry "Brother Pierce" lived in the vicinity of Roxbury. The parallel account in Lt 30, 1859 (Oct. 12), adds the information that he had "talked with great freedom and power" during the weekend meetings. Stephen Pierce, a Vermont preacher, fits both these specifications. He is mentioned in the *Review* as an active preacher living in Roxbury during this period.

See: J. A. and M. A. Spofford, "From Bro. & Sr. Spofford," *Review,* May 20, 1858, p. 7; search term "Pierce" in *Words of the Pioneers;* SDAE, s.v. "Stephen Pierce."

[3] *Identity:* Although there are a number of Sabbathkeepers with the surname "Grant" mentioned in the *Review* during this period, only Harrison Grant is said to live in Roxbury, Vermont. Harrison Grant, age 38, later became president of the Minnesota Conference.

See: Harrison Grant, "To the Churches in Vt.," *Review,* Aug. 5, 1862, p. 80.

[**Clarissa Howard**][4] is afflicted with asthma. Her husband and children help her do her work.

[En route to Bakersfield, Vermont] Wednesday, October 12

We awoke at three o'clock and arose at four o'clock. Took breakfast at half past four. Attended prayers, then prepared for Brother Howard to take us to Northfield [Vermont]. Left Brother Howard's at five a.m. Rode seven miles [11 kilometers] to Northfield, waited one hour. James sent a draft home and a little book to Willie. We are now on our way to St. Albans[5] [Vermont]. Shall meet Brother Bourdeau [**Augustin Cornelius Bourdeau**][6] there.

[See also Lt 30, 1859, written on this date.]

[Berkshire, Vermont] Friday, October 14

P.M. Left Brother Agustin [Augustin] Bourdeau's. Have been very unwell. It has been very stormy. Feared we must go to the meeting in a storm. The distance is about ten miles [16 kilometers].[7] But the clouds disappeared and we had a pleasant time and started for the meeting. Had a much better time than we feared. Stopped at Brother Martin's [**John Martin**].[8] We are

---

[4] *Identity:* The diary entry for October 12 informs us that "Brother Howard" lived seven miles [11 kilometers] from Northfield, Vermont. The only "Howard" living in the Northfield area according to the 1860 census is the family of Daniel and Clarissa Howard. Further confirmation that Ellen White is referring to Daniel Howard is found in an 1865 *Review* obituary for a "Clarissa Howard" whose husband's name is given as "Daniel Howard." Although Clarissa died in Minnesota, the obituary explains that the Howards had moved to Minnesota 18 months earlier from Vermont.

See: 1860 U.S. Federal Census, "Daniel Howard," Vermont, Washington County, Northfield, p. 220; obituary: "Clarissa Howard," *Review,* Feb. 14, 1865, p. 95.

[5] Lt 30, 1859 (Oct. 12), further relates that the journey from Northfield to St. Albans was made by train. A. C. Bourdeau then took the Whites by carriage 14 miles [22 kilometers] to Bakersfield, Vermont, where they spent the night. The following day, Thursday, they traveled a few miles further to Enosburgh where they stayed overnight at the house of A. C. Bourdeau.

[6] *Identity:* In the October 6, 1859, issue of the *Review,* "A. C. Bourdeau" writes, "If we do not hear from Bro. White before Oct. 11th, we will meet him with a team at St. Albans' depot the day following at 10 a. m." Augustin Bourdeau, 25, had begun preaching in Vermont soon after accepting the Sabbatarian Adventist message three years earlier.

See: A. C. Bourdeau, "Appointments," *Review,* Oct. 6, 1859, p. 160.

[7] Meetings had been advertised for October 15 and 16 in Berkshire, Vermont, about ten miles (16 kilometers) from Enosburgh where the Whites had spent the night (see notes under Oct. 12).

See: James White, "Appointments," Sept. 22, 1859, p. 144.

[8] *Identity:* A comparison of the narrative here with the parallel account found in Lt 30, 1859, makes it clear that the Whites stopped at Brother Martin's house as they were traveling the few miles between Enosburgh and Berkshire, Vermont. Although quite a few Martins are mentioned in the *Review* during this period, the only one for whom a Vermont address is given is in a notice from 1862 concerning "John Martin" of "Berkshire Center, Vt." That John Martin was living in Berkshire at least two years earlier (and thus close to the time of the Whites' 1859 visit) is shown by his appearance on the 1860 census list for Berkshire.

very weary and retire early. Met at Brother Martin's many friends who are dear to us.

[Berkshire] Saturday, October 15

It is snowing very hard. We feel very thankful that we came on our way Friday. Many were coming to the meeting in the storm.[9] We gathered at the meetinghouse—a large, commodious house. Met Brother Daniel Bourdeau [**Daniel T. Bourdeau**][10] on the steps of the meetinghouse. We were glad to meet him. He is very dear to us.[11] James preached in the forenoon and afternoon. I bore my testimony. The Lord gave me liberty and power. The people seemed to feel. A Brother Howlett [**John Howlett**],[12] an old Methodist minister, spoke. He spoke with fervor and intelligence. He was but a babe in the truth, but a big stream of truth poured from his lips and his whole being talked. Brother Stone [**Albert Stone**], Brother Buck [**Harry G. Buck**],[13] and other brethren bore testimony.

[See also Lt 11, 1859, written on this date.]

[Berkshire] Sunday, October 16

The storm is over. We tarried at Brother Martin's. Last eve we had

---

See: Ellen G. White, Lt 30, 1859 (Oct. 12); "Business Notes," *Review,* Mar. 4, 1862, p. 112; 1860 U.S. Federal Census, "John Martin," Vermont, Franklin County, Berkshire, p. 28.

[9] James White reported that "quite a host of whole-hearted brethren from Northern Vermont, Canada, and some from other States" attended the Berkshire meetings.

See: J. W. [James White], "Eastern Tour," *Review,* Nov. 10, 1859, p. 196.

[10] Daniel T. Bourdeau, 23, a brother of Augustin C. Bourdeau, and also an itinerant preacher.

[11] Ellen and James White would have known Daniel Bourdeau well since the summer of 1857, when he had gone to Battle Creek from Vermont "to learn the present truth more perfectly, and to translate some of our works into French."

See: James White, "The Present Truth in French," *Review,* Dec. 24, 1857, p. 56.

[12] *Identity:* Apart from the description of "Brother Howlett" as "an old Methodist minister" and the fact that this meeting took place in Vermont, Ellen White adds in another place that the Howletts came from Canada (Ms 9, 1862 [Nov.]). These clues point with some certainty to John Howlett, who, according to his daughter's obituary, settled in Quebec (Canada East) and was "formerly a Methodist minister."

See: Obituary: "Elizabeth Cross-Clark," *Review,* Sept. 10, 1925, p. 21.

[13] *Identities:* The narrative sequence of this entry—James "preached," Ellen "bore my testimony," an old Methodist minister "spoke," and Brother Stone and Brother Buck "and other brethren bore testimony"—suggests that Stone and Buck might be preachers. James White, in his report, reinforces this impression by listing Stone and Buck together with A. C. and D. T. Bourdeau and M. B. Czechowski, who were well-known ministers: "At Berkshire we met brethren Stone, Buck, Taylor, A. C. and D. T. Bourdeau, and our good Bro. Czechowski. . . . We spoke to them [the audience] twice on the Sabbath, and four times on first-day." The only Stone and Buck that fit this description are Albert Stone and Harry G. Buck, both active evangelists at this time in the region of northern Vermont and northern New York, where this meeting was being held.

See: J. W. [James White], "Eastern Tour," *Review,* Nov. 10, 1859, p. 196; search terms "Stone" and "Buck" in *Words of the Pioneers.*

a conversation with a brother who is in trouble. He has once kept the Sabbath but was so persecuted by his own family he ceased to keep it, yet believed it. Now he feels God has left him. We tried to comfort him. He related to us that when he came to the meeting, his wife told him unless he would promise that he would not keep the Sabbath she would not live with him. He would not promise, and they lodged separately. Poor man, he has been much troubled. His wife's father was very violent. Would strike him. His children joined them. But after his wife's father had made a passionate threat against him, he suddenly fell sick, and he was called from the field to witness his sudden death. It is believed that the Lord removed him in His anger. We tried to comfort the poor, trembling brother. We know not how it will turn with him. He has, as it were, to deal with demons in his own family. Sunday night went with Brother Austin [**Horatio Nelson Austin**].[14]

[Madrid, New York] Tuesday, October 18

Had a blessed season of prayer with Brother and Sister Taylor [**Charles O.** and **Matilda W. Taylor**],[15] and his mother, and Brother and Sister Whipple [**John G.** and **Sarah B. Whipple**],[16] and Czechowski [**Michael Belina Czechowski**].[17] After dinner Brother Taylor took us to the [railroad] cars. We rode from twelve o'clock to five p.m. At Madrid [New York] met Brother Henry Hilliard [**Henry Hilliard**].[18] He took us to his own comfortable home.

---

[14] A number of Austins are mentioned in the *Review* during this period, but the only one clearly identified as living in Berkshire, Vermont, is "Sister C. R. Austin," who wrote frequently to the *Review* from 1854 and onward. Various sources give her full name, Caroline Regina, and that of her husband, Horatio Nelson Austin. The Austins were dairy farmers and had become Sabbathkeepers five years earlier, in 1854.

See: Obituary: "H. N. Austin," *Review,* Jan 21, 1890, p. 47; search terms "Austin" and "Berkshire" in *Review and Herald* online collection, www.adventistarchives.org.

[15] *Identities:* Among the speakers especially invited to this conference was Charles O. Taylor, an ordained minister from Rouses' Point, Clinton County, New York, about 35 miles (56 kilometers) west of Berkshire, Vermont. His wife's name is found in various sources.

See: A. C. Bourdeau, "Appointments," *Review,* Oct. 6, 1859, p. 160; C. W. Sperry, "Communications," *Review,* Mar. 19, 1857, p. 158; obituary: "Chas. O. Taylor," *Review,* Sept. 7, 1905, pp. 19, 20.

[16] *Identity:* Prior to 1863 the only Whipples mentioned in the *Review* appear to be John G. Whipple and his wife, Sarah B. Living in Perry's Mills, New York, within 50 miles (80 kilometers) of the conference being held at Berkshire, Vermont, it is not surprising that they were present at the conference.

See: Search term "Whipple" in *Words of the Pioneers.*

[17] The Taylor, Whipple, and Czechowski families all lived in Clinton County, New York, at this time where Czechowski was preaching to French-speaking people in the Canadian border region. For further information on the three families, see notes under March 9 diary entry (Ms 5, 1859).

[18] A leading church figure in the Madrid-Buck's Bridge area. He was appointed a member of the first New York Conference committee when the conference was organized in 1862.

See: J. N. Andrews, J. M. Aldrich, "Doings of the N.Y. Conference," *Review,* Nov. 4, 1862, p. 182.

A good warm supper was prepared for us. We met warm friends here. We are very weary but can rest.

[Madrid] Wednesday, October 19

It is cold and stormy. We sent to the village to get some cotton flannel to make us comfortable. Brother Haskell, his wife and daughter [**Lewis** and **Salina Haskell** and Jane Haskell], Sister Claflin [**Nancy Claflin**], and Sister Matthews came in from Norfolk[19] on their way to attend the meeting. We took dinner together and then all together we started for the little meetinghouse at Bucksbridge [Buck's Bridge]. We were somewhat disappointed. The house is well filled.[20] Brother W[hite] had liberty and with earnest, comforting, strengthening words, cheered the little company. I had freedom talking of faith, showing the difference between faith and feeling. After the meeting closed, we returned home and sewed some. Am so unwell I cannot eat.

[Madrid] Thursday, October 20

Finds us at Brother Hilliard's.

[Mannsville, New York] Friday, October 21

We rose at about four a.m. It was cold and snowy. We took a luncheon and started out in a storm for Madrid depot. Waited one hour for cars. Then took the cars for Potsdam [New York] depot. Waited there one hour for the cars. While waiting a little boy was brought in who was afflicted with inflammation of the eyes. He bore his affliction very patiently. His eyes were screened with a shade and a thick, lined veil. They were taking him to the doctor's in Rochester to get aid.

We journeyed about 25 miles [40 kilometers] and the engine pump broke down, and we were obliged to wait two hours before starting again. By this delay we failed to make connection at Watertown [New York] and were obliged

---

[19] *Identities:* Both the names "Haskell" and "Claflin" from Norfolk, New York, appear in the *Review* during this period (Lewis Haskell and Nancy Claflin). There is no mention of a "sister Matthews" from Norfolk, however, so she remains unidentified. The names of Lewis Haskell's wife and daughter are taken from the 1860 census.

See: Search terms "Haskell," "Claflin," "Matthews," and "Norfolk" in *Review and Herald* online collection, www.adventistarchives.org; 1860 U.S. Federal Census, "Jane Haskell," New York, St. Lawrence County, Norfolk, p. 21.

[20] The building was small, about 20 x 30 feet (6 x 9 meters). It had been erected in 1855, and Adventist historian A. W. Spalding considered it "probably" the first church to be built by Sabbatarian Adventists. In recent years, however, Brian Strayer has pointed to a letter by Joseph Bates in the *Review* that indicates that a church had been built in Jackson, Michigan, a year earlier, in 1854.

See: Arthur Whitefield Spalding, *Origin and History of Seventh-day Adventists,* vol. 1, pp. 222, 403; Brian E. Strayer, "Early Adventist Waymarks in Jackson, Michigan," pp. 12, 13; *idem,* "The First Church Built by Sabbathkeeping Adventists," *Adventist Review,* Mar. 2, 1989, p. 25; Joseph Bates, "From Bro. Bates," *Review,* Apr. 25, 1854, p. 111.

to wait in the depot eight hours. This was a great disappointment to us, for we should be out over the Sabbath; but others were also disappointed. There was one woman and her two brothers who were filled with grief. Their mother was dying; letters had been sent them, but were not received. Oh, what a world of sorrow, disappointment, and affliction we are living in!

While waiting in the depot we became acquainted with a couple directly from Waukon [Iowa]. They bring sad news from Brother Thomas Meade [**Thomas B. Mead**]. They give a sad report of him; he is failing fast.[21]

Sabbath commenced. We tried to call our thoughts from the things around us to sacred things. We took the cars at about eight and rode 25 miles [40 kilometers], and within two miles [3 kilometers] of the depot Brother Ballou [**James Madison Ballou**][22] met us on the cars. They have been worried about us, fearing we could not come. He stepped on the cars, rode out two miles, and then found us and went back again. There was Brother Miles [**Alonzo Miles**][23] waiting for us to take us to his house.

[Mannsville] Sabbath, October 22

It is pleasant weather. We had a season of prayer. Brother and Sister Miles once joined the Messenger [Party], and turned from us and sought to injure

---

[21] Thomas Meade, 32, died of tuberculosis in July 1861. He had earlier been an employee at the Review and Herald press. The Whites had raised funds to help his family. For details, see notes under Mar. 20 diary entry (Ms 5, 1859).

[22] *Identity:* The only "Ballou" appearing in the *Review* from this period is a "J. M. Ballou," so the initial question is whether any person by that name lived in Mannsville or vicinity, where he met the Whites. The 1850 census does have a "James M. Ballou" listed in the nearby township of Boylston. Depending on where in Boylston James Ballou lived, it could have been as close as three or four miles (five kilometers) from Mannsville. The likelihood, therefore, is that Ellen White is referring to James M. Ballou. His full name is given in his obituary.

See: Search term "Ballou" in *Words of the Pioneers;* 1850 U.S. Federal Census, "James M. Ballou," New York, Oswego County, Boylston, p. 8; obituary: "James Madison Ballou," *Review,* June 12, 1888, p. 383.

[23] *Identity:* "Brother Miles" clearly lives in Mannsville, New York, or vicinity, since that is where the weekend meetings were being held. According to the 1860 census, both Alonzo Miles and Randolph Miles with their families lived in the Ellisburg township, in which Mannsville is located. The information given in the October 22 entry that "Brother and Sister Miles once joined the Messenger [Party]" strongly suggests that the "Brother Miles" Ellen White is referring to is Alonzo Miles. Five years earlier Alonzo Miles (then living in Illinois) had written a rather brusque letter to the *Review* saying that he had received the *Messenger* Party paper, *Messenger of Truth,* and asked whether, as it claimed, the visions of Ellen White were becoming a test of fellowship among Sabbathkeepers. After that nothing is heard of Alonzo Miles in the *Review*—no letters or subscription receipts—until 1860 when a subscription is again receipted, suggesting that he had returned to the "Battle Creek" Sabbatarians. There is no evidence that Randolph Miles, probably Alonzo's brother, ever defected to the *Messenger* Party.

See: 1860 U.S. Federal Census, "Alonzo Miles," New York, Jefferson County, Ellisburg, p. 46; 1860 U.S. Federal Census, "R. Miles," New York, Jefferson County, Ellisburg, p. 83; A. Miles, "From Bro. Miles," *Review,* Dec. 5, 1854, pp. 125, 126; search term "Miles" in *Words of the Pioneers.*

us, but now they sob out their repentant prayers and beg God to forgive them.[24] Brother Miles took us to the meeting. The new house[25] was filled. Some were obliged to stand in the entry. The Lord blessed us with liberty and freedom. James preached with freedom and I had freedom in exhortation. Our meeting was free all day. At noon we ate our luncheon at Brother Wilcox's [**Henry H. Wilcox**][26]; took supper at Brother Miles'. After Sabbath quite a number came in to spend the evening.

[Mannsville] Sunday, October 23

Again we repaired to the meetinghouse. The house was crowded again. Brother White preached with freedom; I followed with exhortation. The Lord gave me perfect freedom. The Spirit rested upon us. One aged sister gave vent to her feelings by shouting praise to God. Brethren Chase [**Lewis Chase**][27] and Bailey also opened their mouths and glorified God. In the eve Brother White was free again and our meeting closed with victory. We tarried that night at Brother Janks'.[28] He and family have embraced the truth since we were last there.

[Friday, October 28]

[See Lts 16 and 17, 1859, written on this date.]

[Sunday, October 30]

[See *An Appeal to the Youth,* pp. 53-56, for a letter to Henry and Edson White, written on this date.]

---

[24] *See:* Note under Oct. 21 above.

[25] One year earlier, when the Whites visited Mannsville, the meetings had been held "in the commodious kitchen of Mr. Ballou."

See: J. N. Loughborough, *The Great Second Advent Movement,* p. 336.

[26] *Identity:* References to a number of persons with the surname "Wilcox" appear in the *Review* during this period, but only "H. H. Wilcox" lived in or near Mannsville, New York. Census records from 1850 and 1860 confirm that Henry H. Wilcox lived near Mannsville.

See: H. H. Wilcox, "Communications," *Review,* Dec. 25, 1856, p. 63; H. H. Wilcox, "From Bro. Wilcox," *Review,* June 24, 1862, p. 30; 1850 U.S. Federal Census, "Henry H. Wilcox," New York, Oswego County, Boylston, p. 190; 1860 U.S. Federal Census, "H. H. Wilcox," New York, Jefferson County, Ellisburg, p. 34.

[27] *Identity:* The only "Chase" staying in the Mannsville area during the 1850s and mentioned in church sources is Lewis Chase, who lived in the adjoining township of Sandy Creek. Lewis Chase was a Methodist minister in the 1840s. His affiliation with Sabbatarian Adventists seems to have lasted only through the 1850s.

See: Lewis Chase, "Extracts of Letters," *Review,* Apr. 3, 1855, p. 208; search term "Chase" in *Review and Herald* online collection, www.adventistarchives.org; Glenn F. Thibault, "Thibault and Chase of New England and NY," November 2004, RootsWeb, Dec. 18, 2006, http://worldconnect.genealogy.rootsweb.com; 1860 U.S. Federal Census, "Lewis Chase," New York, Oswego County, Boylston, p. 41.

[28] The identities of Brother Bailey and Brother Janks have not been established.

[Wright, Michigan] Sabbath, November 12[29]

It is stormy. We left Brother McPherson's [**Samuel A. McPherson**][30] for Brother Root's [**Ephraim Henry Root**].[31] Arranged ourselves for meeting. The meetinghouse was well filled.[32] Brother John Loughborough preached in the forenoon, James in the afternoon. I followed in exhortation. Had freedom, speaking upon faith.

[Wright] Sunday, November 13

The storm continues. We went to the meetinghouse. Brother Loughborough preached in the forenoon. Brother White in the afternoon. I followed in exhortation. Was free.

[Grand Rapids, Michigan] Monday, November 14

We rode to Grand Rapids, 14 miles [22 kilometers]. The road is very rough and it is tedious to ride.[33] Arrived at Grand Rapids about noon. Brethren Rumery, Day, Lay, Gray, Jones,[34] and Loughborough are in company with us. A refreshing dinner was prepared for us; after dinner we visited Sister Cramer [**Sarah A. Cramer**]. In the eve the brethren all came to Brother Cramer's,[35] and had a good, profitable interview and a free season of prayer. It is stormy.

---

[29] During the three-week break in the diary, the Whites had held meetings in Brookfield, New York, and in Lapeer and North Plains, Michigan. J. N. Loughborough had joined the Whites in Lapeer in early November and shared in the preaching during the remainder of the Whites' itinerary until their return to Battle Creek on November 21.

See: James White, "Appointments," *Review,* Sept. 15, 1859, p. 136.

[30] *Identity:* See note for diary entry May 1, 1859 (Ms 6, 1859).

[31] *Identity:* See Jan. 19 entry (Ms 5, 1859).

[32] According to James White's report, "storm and mud hindered many from attending" the conference at Wright, "yet the house was well filled." He also noted that "more than one hundred have been immersed since the work commenced in Wright less than two years ago."

See: J. W. [James White], "Eastern Tour," *Review,* Dec. 8, 1859, p. 20.

[33] J. N. Loughborough adds that it took them four and a half hours to accomplish these 14 miles (22 kilometers).

See: J. N. Loughborough, "Diary," entry for Nov. 14.

[34] Why these five men accompanied the Whites and Loughborough at this point of the journey is not clear, neither can their identity be fully established. Apart from Brother "Gray," however, all these names are found in the Monterey church records, and it was toward Monterey that the White party was headed. Earlier in the year Ellen White had twice visited Monterey and mentioned each of these names in her diary, identified in the notes as **Sylsbre R. Rumery**, **John S. Day**, **George T. Lay**, and (possibly) **Victor Jones**.

See: "Records of the Seventh-day Adventist Church, Monterey, Michigan [1860-1880]"; Ellen G. White, Ms 5, 1859, note on Jan. 11, 12.

[35] *Identities:* See notes under Jan. 18 and 19 diary entries (Ms 5, 1859) regarding the James I. Cramer and Christopher G. Cramer families, both belonging to the Grand Rapids band at this time. Christopher Cramer appears to have been a widower, according to the 1860 census, so "Sister Cramer" would be Sarah, wife of James Cramer. Whether Christopher or James Cramer is the "Brother Cramer" with whom the group met in the evening has not been determined.

[Monterey, Michigan] Tuesday, November 15

It is a beautiful day. We rose early and took our breakfast. Had a season of prayer and then started on our weary journey. The going is very rough. We broke one of the traces[36] and were delayed a while. Changed carriages, and about noon tarried to rest the horses. Then took a little luncheon, and in one hour were on our way again to Monterey. The plank road is very rough, but for ten miles [16 kilometers] the road is very bad.[37] Log ways, mud holes, and yet on we go, singing, "The road may be rough, but it cannot be long,"[38] etc. As we came up to Brother G. Lay's [**George T. Lay**] he stopped us and urged us to go in. We complied with his request and tarried with him over night.

[Monterey] Wednesday, November 16

We rose weary, lame, and sick. The journey was too much for us. Yet we wrote much of the day, and there we met my father, whom we have not seen for three months.[39] Toward night we rode to Brother Day's [**John S. Day**].[40] Tarried there over night.

[Monterey] Thursday, November 17

Took breakfast at Brother Day's, and took dinner at Brother H. Pierce's

---

[36] The straps, chains, or ropes by which a carriage is drawn by horses.

[37] J. N. Loughborough's diary entries clarify the intent of this somewhat imprecise statement. It appears that the Whites first traveled south from Grand Rapids on the plank road toward Kalamazoo for about 14 miles (22 kilometers), after which, however, they had to turn off the plank and drive the last ten miles (16 kilometers) to Monterey on a really poor road. The Grand Rapids-Kalamazoo plank road had been built in the mid-1850s and had no doubt deteriorated in time, thus making it a "very rough ride" for the Whites in 1859. Mark Twain is said to have quipped after traveling this same plank road that he would have enjoyed the trip had not "some unconscionable scoundrel" "now and then dropped a plank across it."

See: J. N. Loughborough, "Diary," entry for Nov. 15, compare Jan. 18; Ellen G. White, Ms 5, 1859 (Jan. 18 entry); Will Dunbar and George S. May, *Michigan: A History of the Wolverine State,* p. 271. On plank roads see also notes under Jan. 18 above (Ms 5, 1859).

[38] Originally from a poem by Henry Francis Lyte that opens with the line "My rest is in heaven; my rest is not here." One verse reads:

"A scrip on my back, and a staff in my hand,
I march on in haste through an enemy's land;
The road may be rough, but it cannot be long,
And I'll smooth it with hope, and I'll cheer it with song!"

First published in a volume of Lyte's religious poetry in 1833, by midcentury the poem was set to music and included in a variety of hymnals.

See: John Julian, ed., *A Dictionary of Hymnology,* s.v. "Lyte, Henry Francis"; Thomas Dowell, *Farewell to the Outward Bound,* p. 15.

[39] Four months earlier, on July 27, **Robert** and **Eunice Harmon** had left Battle Creek together with their son **John B. Harmon** for an extended visit to his home in Illinois. At the time Ellen White feared that "perhaps we shall never meet them again." However, as is seen in this diary entry, Robert Harmon (and probably also Eunice) was back in Michigan within a few months. Why Robert Harmon was visiting Monterey at this point is not known.

See: Ellen G. White, Ms 7, 1859 (July 27 entry).

[40] *Identity:* See under Jan. 12, 1859, entry (Ms 5, 1859).

[**Henry Harlow Pierce**].[41] We then looked over Brother Bates' [**Joseph Bates**] house.[42] Returned to Brother Day's and found Sister McClellan there. She has sold out and come to buy in Monterey. She will take one of two places, either Brother Leander Jones' [**Leander M. Jones**] or Brother H. Pierce's.

[Monterey] Friday, November 18

Rose languid and weary. Took breakfast at Brother Orrin Jones' [**Orrin B. Jones**].[43] Left soon after prayers, for Brother Day's. James and self took a wet sheet pack.[44] I wrote until near noon. Took dinner at Brother Day's; just before the commencement of the Sabbath we went to Brother Leander's; tarry with them tonight.

[Monterey] Sabbath, November 19

Brother Loughborough preached. A large congregation assembled at the Monterey meetinghouse. The house was full—crowded. Our earnest prayer this morn has been, Give us the living testimony; let us feel the burden of Thy work, the weight of Thy cause, the worth of souls. Then will Thy people be renewed and strengthened, and those not right, those not in union with Thy church, will be reproved, corrected.

Brother White preached in the p.m. on the work, the success of the three messages. He was clear and free in his discourse. The Lord gave me liberty in speaking and referring to the travail of Elijah. Elisha would follow the man of God. Elijah said, "Go back, Elisha;" but, "No," said he, "as the Lord liveth and as thy soul liveth I will not leave thee." He would see the end of the matter. He followed on and he saw the fiery chariot and the glory and the mantle of Elijah fall upon Elisha. So those who will follow on with the people of God, suffer trials with them, press on with them, when the mighty angel descends from heaven, clothed with the panoply of heaven and gives strength to the third angel, the power of the message is felt by them. The heavenly showers fall on them. The latter rain drops in their vessels.

---

[41] *Identity:* See under Feb. 3, 1859, entry (Ms 5, 1859).

[42] Probably Joseph Bates had not yet moved into the house. Perhaps it was still unfinished. According to the *History of Allegan and Barry Counties* it was in 1860 that Bates "located at Monterey as pastor of the little flock." This date is confirmed by letters from Bates to the *Review* that are signed "Monterey, Michigan" from March 1860 onward. Joseph Bates was in no financial position to build a house. Minutes of the Monterey church from 1860 and 1861 reveal that at least part of the financial burden was borne by local church members.

See: History of Allegan and Barry Counties, Michigan, p. 286; search term "Bates" in *Words of the Pioneers;* "Records of the Seventh-day Adventist Church, Monterey, Michigan [1860-1880]," Oct. 7, 1860, Jan. 6, 1861.

[43] *Identity:* See notes under Jan 13 above (Ms 5, 1859).

[44] *See:* Note under May 7 above (Ms 6, 1859).

[Otsego, Michigan][45] *Sunday, November 20*

It is pleasant today, and there was a large gathering at the meetinghouse. They could not all get into the house. Brother John prayed. Brother White preached, finishing his subject upon the Messages. After he closed there was five minutes' intermission. The house was so crowded it was very uncomfortable.[46] Brother Loughborough is now preaching from the parable concerning a man going into a far country to receive to himself a kingdom, and return, etc. Many are standing, for they can find no seats.

---

[45] J. N. Loughborough, who was accompanying the Whites, added in his diary that after these meetings they left Monterey in the afternoon of November 20 and spent the night at Aaron Hilliard's house (in Otsego).

See: J. N. Loughborough, "Diary," entries for Nov. 20 and 21, 1859.

[46] The overcrowding caused James White to suggest that the Monterey members build a larger meetinghouse even though the present one was only 2 years old. A larger church edifice was constructed in 1862. At its dedication the building was so crowded that the floor gave way and sank eight inches.

See: J. W. [James White], "Eastern Tour," *Review,* Dec. 8, 1859, p. 20; J. W. [James White], "Meetings at Monterey," *Review,* Sept. 3, 1857, p. 144; U. S. [Uriah Smith], "Michigan Annual Conference," *Review,* Oct. 14, 1862, p. 156.

1859

(Lt 1a, 1859)

JANUARY 4, BATTLE CREEK, MICHIGAN

LETTER TO

Leonard W. Hastings, Sarah Amelia Hastings, and Emma A. Hastings.[1]

Previously unpublished.

Letter requesting the Hastings family to submit material for Ellen White's autobiography.

Dear Brother Hastings, Amelia, and Emma:

I sit down to write a few lines and make a request of you to sit down together and talk over what you have witnessed of our experience. If there is anything of importance you can think of, write it all out, especially the events of our first visit to your place.

The Lord's healing Sister Hastings [**Elvira Hastings**],[2] and the work done for the little one, please write all the particulars. This will help us much, for we are about to get out a book upon my experience.[3] Brother Nichols

---

[1] *Identities:* In her diary entry for January 4, 1859, Ellen White noted that she "wrote to Brother Hastings of New Ipswich, N.H," doubtless a reference to this letter. Having given the address of "Brother Hastings," it is safe to conclude that she is addressing Leonard W. Hastings, of New Ipswich, New Hampshire, the only person who fits the description. The style of the greeting and letter that follows suggests that "Amelia" and "Emma" are family members. At the time of writing, Leonard Hastings' wife and oldest daughter had died. Two females remained in the family whose names are given as "Sarah A." and "Emma A." in the 1850 census, aged about 20 and 18, respectively. In the greeting "Emma" corresponds with the "Emma A." of the census, but "Amelia" is more difficult to account for. Most likely the "A." of "Sarah A." stands for Amelia, and she was known by her middle name. Strengthening this conclusion is a letter by Joseph Bates written in 1858 in which he also lists "Emma" and "Amelia" among the Hastings family members.

See: Ellen G. White, Ms 5, 1859 (Jan. 4 entry); 1850 U.S. Federal Census, "Leonard Hastings," New Hampshire, Hillsborough County, New Ipswich, p. 273; Joseph Bates to Emma Hastings, Apr. 25, 1858.

[2] *Identity:* See Elvira Hastings, "An Unfinished Letter . . . ," *Review,* August 1850, p. 15.

[3] Ellen White's first major autobiographical account, *My Christian Experience* . . . , was published the following year, 1860. It included a testimony by Leonard Hastings of how his wife, Elvira, and infant son Frederick, were healed following the prayer of Ellen and James White during their first visit to the Hastings family in 1849.

See: Ellen G. White, *Spiritual Gifts [vol. 2],* pp. 112, 113; obituary: "Frederick Hastings," *Review,* June 6, 1918, p. 21.

(Lt 1a, 1859) January 4, 1859

[**Otis Nichols**][4] has promised to write out the particular events that occurred under his observation. If this testimony comes from others, it will have effect, much more, than if we should write it ourselves. May the Lord help you in this matter.

In love,

Ellen G. White

Write it all out, and send on as soon as possible.

---

[4] *Identity:* As with Leonard Hastings (see note above), Ellen White requests "Brother Nichols" to write down memories from the early pioneer days that could be incorporated into her autobiography. Subsequently in her book *My Christian Experience* . . . Ellen White includes a number of incidents involving Nichols from the mid-1840s and also includes a quotation from Nichols's own account. She also adds that "Brother Nichols" is "O. Nichols," from Dorchester, Massachusetts. The *Review* and other sources confirm that only Otis Nichols matches this initial and address.

See: Ellen G. White, *Spiritual Gifts [vol. 2],* pp. 68, 77-79; "Statement by Otis Nichols" (DF 105, EGWE-GC); search term "Nichols" in *Words of the Pioneers.*

1859

(Lt 13, 1859)

JANUARY 5, BATTLE CREEK, MICHIGAN

LETTER TO

Friends [Joseph Perry Benedict family].[1]

Portions of this letter are published in Ellen G. White, *Manuscript Releases,* vol. 5, p. 291.

Admonition to the family members of Joseph P. Benedict for their low confidence in decisions made by the local church.

Dear Friends:

While in Rochester, N.Y., there were some things shown me concerning individuals at Battle Creek.[2] I saw that all was not right with you. There is not that solemnity and watchfulness in your family which becomes those who are looking for their Lord.

I saw that the third angel is leading out a people and fitting them for translation. They are to be purified through obeying the truth. I saw that a work must be done in your family before God can be well pleased with you. You are not right. Your ways are not pleasing to God. God is leading out a people and all heaven is interested to unite this people together and draw them away from the world. I saw that you possess a dissatisfied feeling with the church and your sympathy runs out after those that it should not.

Instead of pressing with the church and having confidence in the church,

---

[1] *Identity:* Although the original copy does not identify these "Friends," the initial assumption would be that Ellen White is addressing the family of Joseph Perry Benedict, of Battle Creek. According to her diary (Ms 5, 1859), she "wrote to Brother Benedict's family" on January 5, with no mention of other letters written that day. This assumption is strengthened by the close parallel between the admonitions found in this letter and those specifically directed to members of the Joseph Benedict family in 1862 (see note in third paragraph). By 1859 Joseph Benedict was chronically ill and unable to work. James and Ellen White tried to help the poverty-stricken family with gifts of food and money and by occasionally employing Joseph's wife, Millie, and daughter Diantha (see **Diantha Wilkinson** [née **Benedict**]) in their home or at the Review office (see Mss 5 and 6, 1859 [entries for Jan. 5 and June 12]).

[2] Three months earlier, in October 1858, Ellen and James White, together with the Loughboroughs, had attended a "general conference" in Rochester, New York, in the course of a tour of the Eastern states. J. N. Loughborough mentions that Ellen White was given a vision in Rochester.

See: J. T. Orton, "Appointment for Western New York," *Review,* Sept. 23, 1858, p. 144; J. N. Loughborough, *Rise and Progress of the Seventh-day Adventists,* p. 220.

you have too much confidence in your opinion and judgment. If there is a disaffected one who complains of the church, you too often sympathize with him, and instead of checking the complainer, receive what he says and get up a tried, dissatisfied feeling and speak of the wrongs (as you consider them) of the church. If any case of dissatisfaction arises you take the wrong side and unite with the complainer.[3] Here you show your lack of confidence in the church, and this course causes the church to lose confidence in you. You feel like drawing off from the church, and the church feels it and they lose confidence in you.

You are not willing to confide in the judgment of the church, but prefer to rely upon your own judgment and opinion. This is wrong. If all in the church should take this course, the utmost confusion would reign in the church. When you take a humble position, and are willing to be counseled, advised, and corrected by those of sound judgment and experience in the church, then the church will feel it, will know it, and you will be united with them. Your hearts will be one, your experience one, and a healthy, wholesome influence will be felt in your family.

When you are baptized with the third angel's message, the soul-purifying truth for this time will make a separation between you and the world that you have never yet experienced. You will see then those who are wrong in their true character, and your sympathy will be more fully with God's peculiar people whom He is purifying unto Himself.

Please excuse this hastily written line. Overlook the poor writing. Different ones have broken in upon me. Have written a few lines at a time.

In love.

---

[3] It appears that even after this admonition some members of the Benedict family continued to "unite with the complainer" against decisions of the local church. Three years later, in 1862, Ellen White pointed out that the problem still persisted with the mother and eldest daughter. "If one is sharply reproved and censured for his wrong course . . . Sister Benedict and Diantha would attach the highest importance to the feelings of such. . . . It is made of greater account than all the moves and actions of the church."

See: Ellen G. White, Ms 6, 1862 (c. 1862).

1859

(Lt 31, 1859)

FEBRUARY 21, BATTLE CREEK, MICHIGAN

LETTER TO

Stephen and Almira Pierce.[1]

Previously unpublished.

Letter requesting Stephen and Almira Pierce to submit material for Ellen White's autobiography.

Dear Brother and Sister Pierce:

I can write but a few lines, and will come right to the point. I am getting out a book and relating a little of my experience. If you could give me a little [of] the particulars of your wife's state when she was despairing, and when she attended the Wolcott meeting, please give fully the effect of the vision upon her—the influence of them.[2]

We are all as well as usual now. The Lord has wrought for us. Father and Mother White are living with us.[3] They have embraced the

---

[1] *Identities:* The identities of "Brother and Sister Pierce" are readily available since Ellen White in this letter requests them to write an account of their experiences for inclusion in her autobiography (see note below), an account that in its published form was signed "Stephen Pierce" and "Almira Pierce." Stephen and Almira Pierce, both of Vermont, began to keep the Sabbath in 1852. Stephen Pierce played an important part in the development of the church in Vermont, both as preacher and, in the early 1860s, as president of the Vermont Conference.

See: Ellen G. White, *Spiritual Gifts [vol. 2],* pp. 168-171.

[2] In preparing her first autobiographical volume, *My Christian Experience . . .*, published the following year, Ellen White requested a number of persons with whom she had interacted, especially in the earlier years of the Sabbatarian movement, to submit written accounts of these experiences (e.g., Ms 5, 1859 [Jan. 4]). The allusion here to Almira Pierce "when she was despairing" goes back to 1852 when the Whites first met Almira and Stephen Pierce at meetings in Wolcott and Panton, Vermont. Almira had for many years been subject to severe and prolonged depression. However, at the Panton conference Ellen White "was taken off in vision" and received "a comforting message . . . for Sr. Pierce" that brought about very positive and lasting changes. The Pierces provided a detailed account of these experiences, and Ellen White included them in her autobiography.

See: Ibid.

[3] The exact date that **John** and **Betsey White** moved to Battle Creek is not known. The chronological information provided in retrospect by James White in *Life Sketches* (1880) and in a eulogy after his parents' death (1871) is not entirely consistent. However, if we take at face value his statement that John White spent the last 12 years of his life in Battle Creek, the date of John White's move to Battle Creek would be about 1859. As early as January 28, 1859, Ellen

Sabbath[4] and are coming right along into all the present truth. The Lord has truly wrought for us, and we will praise His dear name.

The church here seem to be rising. I feel more anxious desire for holiness and an entire conformity to the will of God than ever before. I want my ways right in the sight of God.

Dear Sister Pierce, you must not be discouraged. Trust in God. His watchful eye is over you; His ear is ever open to your cry. If the clouds envelope [*sic*] you, don't be discouraged. Call to mind the lovingkindness of God, and then believe He will not leave you to sink. His own strong arm will be reached down and lift your head above the cloud and reveal to you His own lovely face and fill you with earnest desire for His image to be reflected in you.

Don't distrust God for a moment. His lovingkindness changeth not. The very weakest saint can glorify God. Gird about you every piece of the armor and fight manfully the battle of the Lord.

Much love to all your family. Your dear children—I hope they are subjects of grace and are striving for an imperishable crown.

In much love.

White mentions with evident satisfaction that she "had the privilege of sitting at the table with my husband's father and mother and my father and mother."

See: James White and Ellen G. White, *Life Sketches* (1880), p. 9; "The Venerable Dead," *Review,* July 18, 1871, p. 36; Ellen G. White, Ms 5, 1859 (Jan. 28 entry).

[4] This is the earliest reference to John and Betsey White's keeping the Sabbath. In later accounts James White dates their Sabbathkeeping to 1860, but this 1859 report is preferable, being contemporary. John and Betsey had struggled with the Sabbath issue for years. In 1855, for example, Ellen White, on a visit to Palmyra, Maine, described how Betsey "longed to keep the Sabbath," whereas John wavered. As Adventist historian James R. Nix has pointed out, even after John White became a Sabbatarian he "concurrently, for the next several years . . . continued to be a member of the Christian Church in Marshall, Michigan."

See: James White and Ellen G. White, *Life Sketches* (1880), p. 11; James R. Nix, "John and Betsey (Jewett) White."

1859

(Lt 18, 1859)

APRIL 14, [BATTLE CREEK, MICHIGAN][1]

LETTER TO

John Naramore.[2]

Portions of this letter are published in Ellen G. White, *Our High Calling,* pp. 9, 201; *idem, Manuscript Releases,* vol. 21, p. 248; *idem,* in *Advent Review, and Sabbath Herald,* vol. 13, no. 23, April 28, 1859, pp. 181, 182.

Extract of letter written to Doct. N., dated April 14, 1859.[3]

We often think those who serve God have many more trials than the unbeliever, and that the path marked out for them to travel in is rugged, and they must deny themselves of many pleasures in order to travel it.

Last Sabbath I was led to compare the life of the sinner with the life of the righteous. The sinner does not desire or care to please God, therefore can have no pleasing sense of His approbation. But does the sinner enjoy his worldly pleasure and enjoyment unalloyed? Oh, no. There are times when the sinner is fearfully troubled. He fears God but does not love Him.

Are the wicked free from disappointment, perplexity, earthly losses, poverty, and distress? Many of them suffer a lingering sickness, yet have no

---

[1] According to her diary Ellen White spent April 14, 1859, at home in Battle Creek (Ms 6, 1859).

[2] *Identity:* Earlier editors identified "Doct. N." with "Doctor Naramore." A scan of *Review* receipts during the 1850s reveals fewer than a dozen persons whose names are prefixed "Dr." and only one whose surname begins with N—"Dr. J. Naramore." More telling, perhaps, is the fact that Ellen White mentions writing letters to "Doctor Naramore" on three occasions around this time, on January 3, February 21, and April 15, 1859 (Ms 5, 1859; Ms 6, 1859). According to the *Review,* "J. Naramore" lived in Rochester, New York, and the only Doctor Naramore listed in the 1860 census for Rochester was John Naramore, a dentist.

See: 1860 U.S. Federal Census, "John Naramore," New York, Monroe County, Rochester Ward 10, p. 335; J. N. Loughborough, "Sketches of the Past—No. 114," *Pacific Union Recorder,* Aug. 17, 1911, p. 1.

[3] It would appear that Ellen White wrote her letter to John Naramore on April 14 and then, before sending it, decided to copy a long extract (that which appears in this document) for eventual publication. Although the letter was written on April 14, it seems that she did not finish copying the extract until the next day. In her diary for April 15 she notes, "Write extracts of a letter to Doctor Naramore." After some editing, probably done on April 25 (See Ms 6, 1859 [Apr. 25 entry]) the extract was published in the April 28, 1859, issue of the *Review* under the title "The Sinner's Trials."

See: E. G. W. [Ellen G. White], "The Sinner's Trials," *Review,* Apr. 28, 1859, pp. 181, 182.

strong and mighty One to lean upon, no strengthening grace from a higher power to support them in their weakness. They lean upon their own strength. They obtain no consolation by looking forward to the future, but a fearful uncertainty torments them; and thus they close their eyes in death, not finding any pleasure in looking forward to the resurrection morn, for they have no cheering hope that they shall have part in the first resurrection. This is the end of the life of pleasure of the sinner.

The Christian is subject to sickness, disappointment, poverty, reproach and distress. Yet amid all this he loves God, he chooses to do His will, and prizes nothing so highly as His approbation. In the conflicting trials and changing scenes of this life, he knows that there is One who knows it all, One who will bend His ear low to the cry of the sorrowful and distressed, One who can sympathize with every sorrow and soothe the keen anguish of every heart. He has invited the sorrowing one to come to Him for consolation. "Come unto me, all ye that labor and are heavy laden, and I will give you rest." [Matt. 11:28.]

Amid all his affliction, the Christian has strong consolation. And if God permits him to suffer a lingering, distressing sickness before he closes his eyes in death, he can with cheerfulness bear it all. While he communes with his Redeemer you often see his countenance radiant with joy, while he contemplates the future with heavenly satisfaction. A short rest in the grave, and then the Lifegiver will break the fetters of the tomb, release the captive, and bring him from his dusty bed immortal, never more to know pain, sorrow, or death. Oh, what a hope is the Christian's! Let this hope of the Christian be mine. Let it be yours. Hope, and we will ask no more.

Many speak of the life of the Christian taking away from us pleasures and worldly enjoyments. I say it takes away nothing worth saving. Is there perplexity, poverty, and distress endured by the Christian? Oh, yes, this is expected in this life. But is the sinner, of whom we speak as enjoying the pleasures of this world, free from these ills of life? Do we not often see them in deep perplexity and trouble? Do we not often notice the pale cheek, the racking cough, indicating consumption? Are they not subject to burning fevers and contagious disease? How often do we hear their complaints of meeting with heavy losses of worldly goods! But these troubles are overlooked.[4]

Christians sometimes think they have a hard time and that it is a condescension in them to lay hold of unpopular truth and profess to be Christ's

---

[4] Since we do not have the whole of Ellen White's letter to John Naramore, but only these extracts, it is difficult to know whether they address Naramore's personal spiritual struggle. Little is known about his association with Sabbathkeeping Adventists, but it probably lasted for only about a year. There is a flurry of mentions of John and Eliza Naramore in the *Review* during 1859, but silence after March 1860.

See: Search term "Naramore" in *Words of the Pioneers.*

followers, that the road seems hard and that they have many sacrifices to make, when in reality they make no sacrifice at all. If in reality they are adopted into the family of God, what sacrifice have they made? Their following Christ may have broken some friendship with their world-loving relatives, but look at the exchange—their names written in the Lamb's book of life, elevated, yes greatly exalted, to be partakers of salvation, heirs of God and joint heirs with Jesus Christ to an imperishable inheritance. Shall we call it a sacrifice on our part to yield error for truth, darkness for light, sin for righteousness, a perishable name and inheritance upon earth for honors that are lasting, and a treasure undefiled that fadeth not away?

Even in this life, the Christian has One upon whom to lean for support, who will help him bear all his trials. Yet the sinner has to bear his trials alone. He goes down into the grave suffering remorse under darkness, bound by Satan, for he is his lawful prey.

It does seem to me that if there is any one who should be continually grateful, it is the follower of Christ. If there is any one who enjoys real happiness, even in this life, it is the faithful Christian. We will rejoice in Jesus Christ. We will live in the light of His countenance.

May the Lord ever give us a lively sense of the great sacrifice that has been made for us, and then present before us the inheritance purchased for us by that dear sacrifice; and may our vision be clear to dwell upon and appreciate the reward and excellent glory prepared for the faithful.

If we appreciate or have any sense of how dearly our salvation was purchased, anything which we may call sacrifice will sink away into insignificance.

1859

APRIL 28

"The Sinner's Trials."

Published in *Advent Review, and Sabbath Herald,* vol. 13, no. 23, April 28, 1859, pp. 181, 182.

1859

APRIL

"Little Ellen."

Published in *The Youth's Instructor,* vol. 7, no. 4, April 1859, p. 32.

1859

MAY

"Be Lovely."

Published in *The Youth's Instructor,* vol. 7, no. 5, May 1859, p. 36.

1859

(Lt 2, 1859)

JUNE 21, BATTLE CREEK, MICHIGAN

LETTER TO

John Byington.[1]

Portions of this letter are published in Ellen G. White, *Manuscript Releases,* vol. 5, p. 290.

Admonition to John Byington, who was losing the spirit of sacrifice and drawing back from his calling as a preacher.

Dear Brother Byington:

The matter for my book is now off my mind. It is in type.[2]

There were some things shown me in regard to you. I saw that the candle of the Lord does not shine about you. He is displeased with you. I was shown that your object in coming to Michigan[3] was good. It was well for you to come. But you have failed in your purposes, and that which should be to you of the greatest importance has come in secondary. Your interest has come first, and the work of God, or things of eternal interest, secondary.[4] I saw that in your vicinity there was an interest awakened; hearts could have been reached. But your energies were exhausted in your own interest, for your own advantage,

---

[1] *Identity:* There is considerable evidence in this letter that "Brother Byington" is the itinerant preacher John Byington, at this time living in Newton township, near Battle Creek. The information given that "Brother Byington" had moved to Michigan, was going through struggles with materialism, and was shying away from evangelistic work, and that "Martha" was healed of her sickness, all relate to recent events in John Byington's life, as shown in the notes below.

[2] A few days earlier Ellen White had placed the following notice in the *Review:* "*Testimony for the Church No. 5* . . . I am preparing a Tract which will probably be ready as soon as orders can reach me. . . . I want all the friends of the cause to have it, pay, or no pay. Those who choose, may send ten cts. a copy."

See: E. G. W. [Ellen G. White], [notice], *Review,* June 16, 1859, p. 32.

[3] Eight months earlier, in October 1858, at the request of James White, John Byington and family had moved from their home in Buck's Bridge, New York, to the Battle Creek area.

See: Obituary: "John Byington," *Review,* Jan. 25, 1887, p. 57.

[4] Farther on in this letter Ellen White expands on this thought: "You love this world, and your heart is altogether too much wrapped up in the things you possess." Similarly, on a visit to John Byington two months earlier she found him "cold and unfeeling," being "too much wrapped up in the things of this world." Part of the problem seems to have been that the move from New York to Michigan had involved financial loss. This caused Byington to descend into a state of "gloom and unbelief."

See: Ellen G. White, Ms 6, 1859 (Apr. 16 entry); Lt 28, 1859 (June/July).

and your labor spent in God's work was a lame sacrifice and unacceptable to Him. There was an opportunity for you to have made a sacrifice, to put into the hands of others to do what you have done, even if things had not exactly suited you, and been at considerable more cost.

Your commission has not run out. Your time is not yours. God does not wait in His work for you to study your convenience or wait your time.[5] Angels of God were prepared to trouble hearts, and through the instruments of God's choosing lay the truth before unbelievers. But the instrument was not ready to do his part, to throw his whole energies into the work, and be a mouthpiece for God. The angels in their work wait not for anyone's convenience, but pass on to do their work, fulfill their mission, and move on other hearts.

Responsibilities are on you that you little realize, and your love of this world leads you astray from your duty. You study your interest, and how you can save a little means, when you should be studying what is your best course to save your fellow man. Satan takes advantage of your carefulness and caution and leads it to be exercised in the wrong way. Nothing exists, in reality, to cast gloom upon your soul; but you dwell upon the dark side, talk doubts and unbelief, which is death to your own soul and has a deadly influence upon others. You dishonor God. You grieve His angels by your unbelief. Your influence is not saving.

There must be an entire change in you in these things. You love this world, and your heart is altogether too much wrapped up in the things you possess. Your commission is not a matter to be laid aside at your will. Your heavenly Father claims your time and obedience, without any murmuring or complaining or unwillingness on your part.

I was pointed back to about one year ago. Your feelings then concerning the purchase of a house for Brother Bates [**Joseph Bates**][6] were prompted by the enemy. Selfishness lay at the bottom of it. And since then you have not been closely united to James.[7] There has been a pulling off. You have felt

---

[5] Although Byington was previously an active itinerant preacher, for about a year from the summer of 1858 there is no record of his filling any preaching appointments. Finally, in July 1859, after receiving this challenging letter (and probably also Lt 28, 1859 [June/July]), Byington resumed his evangelistic work. "He looked happier than I had seen him for months," Ellen White noted in her diary on July 12, 1859. "Says after a week he is going out to labor for the Lord."

See: Ellen G. White, Ms 7, 1859 (July 12).

[6] *Identity:* Circumstances described in the following note leave little doubt that Ellen White has Joseph Bates in mind.

[7] This may be a reference to the house built for Joseph and Prudence Bates in Monterey, Michigan, which was at least partly financed by donations from local church members (see Ms 8, 1859 [note on Nov. 17 entry]). This interpretation is not entirely without problems because the evidence suggests that the Bates did not move into the Monterey house until early 1860 (see above citation), which seems to conflict with Ellen White's statement that the problem arose "about one year ago," i.e., in 1858. Another possibility would be that James White had made a house available to the Bates in 1858 before the move to Monterey in 1860. This may or may not be related to Joseph Bates's later testimony that "at one time" James White "furnished

wrong. I was shown that when you gave yourself up wholly to the work of God, then your love for this world was much weakened.

I saw that God had been very merciful to you. God has heard the earnest prayers put up in Martha's [**Martha Dormer Amadon** (née **Byington**)][8] behalf, and spared her life when she was marked for the grave.[9] And when your own life was in danger, God was merciful to you. Disease was upon you, but as you ventured out in the name of the Lord, angels were hovering around you and Satan was disappointed of his prey. God is angry with you. After He has given you such merciful tokens for good, you have murmured against God. You have not realized this, but it is so.

If you had but a very little of this world's possessions it would be better for your eternal interest. That which you have is a great trouble to you.

I saw that you are standing in your own light and in the way of the salvation of your children. God has given them a heart to love the people of God. They see the consistency that there is in the truth, and the work for them now is to identify themselves with God's people. Here is the cross. God cannot come into your dwelling and set things in order there. You stand right in the way of the work of God.

---

me with a house for my family for fourteen months, for which he refused to receive rent."

John Byington was clearly unhappy and felt that James White's leadership had been compromised by what he considered a display of unjust favoritism toward Joseph Bates. In response to this charge Ellen White responded in another letter to Byington: "God's ways are equal. He does not require one to sacrifice everything and another to make no sacrifice at all." In terms of sacrifice, as Joseph Bates's biographer George R. Knight describes it, Bates had been living "on the financial edge" while carrying on a full-time itinerant ministry ever since the mid-1840s, when he donated his life savings of $8,000 to $10,000 dollars to the cause of preaching the Millerite message. It should also be noted that Bates later willed the house that had been given him in Monterey to the Seventh-day Adventist Publishing Association.

See: John Nevins Andrews et al., *Defense of Elder James White and Wife,* p. 24; George R. Knight, *Joseph Bates,* pp. 184, 169; Ellen G. White, Lt 28, 1859 (June/July).

[8] *Identity:* That the reference is to John Byington's daughter Martha is suggested partly by the intimation of family in the wording of this paragraph, and partly by confirmation from Ellen White's diary that Martha Byington had recently been seriously sick but healed in response to prayer (see note below).

[9] Probably a reference to the situation two months earlier, when the Whites had prayed for Martha, the 25-year-old daughter of John and Catherine Byington, who was "much reduced with fever and ague." In response, writes Ellen White in her diary, "the Lord truly met with us. Martha was blessed and strengthened."

See: Ellen G. White, Ms 6, 1859 (Apr. 16 entry).

John Byington and his wife, Caroline

Daughter, Martha, and son, John F. Courtesy of the Center for Adventist Research.

1859

JUNE

PUBLICATION OF

Testimony for the Church, No. 5, Battle Creek, Michigan.

Published by Steam Press of the *Review and Herald* Office. 32 pp.

1859

(Lt 28, 1859)

[CIRCA JUNE/JULY],[1] BATTLE CREEK, MICHIGAN

LETTER TO

John Byington.[2]

Portions of this letter are published in Arthur L. White, *Ellen G. White: Messenger to the Remnant*, p. 110; *idem, Ellen G. White: The Progressive Years*, p. 98.

> *Admonition to John Byington, who was losing the spirit of sacrifice. The need for vigorous leadership that ventures all—"life, health, strength, time, everything."*

Dear Brother Byington:

James did not let me see the letter you wrote. He meant to conceal it from me, but by accident he let drop a word which caused me to closely inquire into its meaning. To satisfy me he told me as well as he could remember what was in the letter. Brother Byington, I felt grieved.

---

[1] The original letter is undated, but see note below regarding Ellen White's earlier letter referred to in the second paragraph.

[2] *Identity:* Certain clues in this letter help reveal "Brother Byington's" identity. Among them, Ellen White has recently written to him, he has moved from New York, he has no young children, he resented the fact that Joseph Bates was given a house. As seen in the notes below, these experiences belong to John Byington, preacher and future General Conference president. See also notes on identification of "Brother Byington" in Lt 2, 1859 (June 21), a letter that is clearly related to this one.

In my letter to you I felt deeply.[3] I was very cautious that not a word I should say should wound, but that the facts should be related as simply as possible, and they cut. I knew if you realized the matter as it was shown me you would nearly despair, and with strong cries and humble repentance you would seek the forgiveness and favor of God.

You speak of my publishing you. The only answer I can make is, If God should say, Hold up Brother Byington's case and warn others lest they fall into a like snare and through love of this world yield their sacred obligations to God and the truth, you might see your case then published; and I would lift up my voice as a trumpet and cry, "Beware, beware. Love not the world, neither the things that are in the world, for if any man love the world, the love of the Father is not in him."[4]

God is no respecter of persons. He does not bow to man's pride or shape His course to fit man's convenience. He is high and lifted up, and man must bow and yield continually to His will, and shape his course in accordance with the will and mind of God. If any one stands in the way of the work of God, He will lift him out of the way in His own good time, and as He does this it will not be done to suit the pride of the individual, but to speak a loud and effectual warning to others.

This world is in your heart, and to it you have sacrificed your noble calling which, if followed out, would elevate you above the world and fix your grasp upon immortal treasures.

---

[3] It is very likely that Ellen White is referring to her recent letter of June 21, 1859 (Lt 2, 1859). It contained reproof for John Byington's "love of this world," which had led him to disengage from active ministry. In particular he had been discouraged by financial losses incurred during his move from New York to Michigan in late 1858, and by envy when James White arranged for Joseph Bates to be given a house. Byington's response to her letter of reproof apparently was quite negative, as judged by the previous paragraph. This letter (Lt 28, 1859), responding to Byington's negative reaction, refers again to the specific themes of the June 21 letter—the move from New York, John Bates's house, etc.—thus suggesting that it was written fairly soon after June 21. A comparison with Ellen White's diary would seem to indicate that this second letter to Byington had its intended effect. In an entry on July 12 she reported that Byington "looked happier than I had seen him for months. Says after a week he is going out to labor for the Lord, and expects to be absent six months. Thank the Lord for this." Thus this letter, it can be assumed, was written sometime before July 12, 1859.

See: Ellen G. White, Ms 7, 1859 (July 12 entry).

[4] John Byington was clearly apprehensive about having his moral failings published. It may be that he felt rebuked by the recently published *Testimony for the Church,* No. 5, even though it did not specifically mention his name. In the first section of the pamphlet Ellen White pressed home the theme that "the greatest sin which now exists in the church is covetousness. God frowns upon His professed people for their selfishness" (*Testimonies for the Church,* vol. 1, p. 194). Although many of the visions pertaining to individuals were published in the *Testimonies* series through the years, Ellen White in general removed personal names from these accounts. In the earliest *Testimony* pamphlets, often only the initial of the person's surname was used. For a discussion of Ellen White's publication of personal names in 1861, see Arthur L. White, *Ellen G. White: The Early Years,* pp. 432-437.

God forbid that I should dishonor Him by crying, Peace, peace, when there is no peace. We have not a temporal millennium in which to do this last closing work. May the Lord arouse me and breathe upon me His Spirit, and give me energy and zeal to do all in my power to save souls.

I saw, Brother Byington, that the greatest cause or reason that has led you to doubt its being duty for you to leave New York was temporal things. You had an income there that you do not have where you are, and if you do for the cause, you have to sacrifice.[5] As yet you have not known what it is to sacrifice. I was shown this:

Who gave you what you have? Who gave you strength and judgment to acquire it, that with it you might do good, aid in His work, and advance His glory? I saw that the finger of God could quickly touch you, and like Job you [could] be stripped of everything.

I saw that Satan was leading your mind to look upon the dark side, to encourage doubts and unbelief and to live under a cloud. In reality you have nothing existing around you to be the least excuse for your keeping your mind in gloom and unbelief. You have not a family of little children dependent upon you,[6] and you are free from cares that many are perplexed with. God is displeased with you. If you were even brought down to be a common day laborer, having nothing upon which to depend, there would be no excuse for such sadness, such murmuring and gloom. You would not in that case have half the anxiety and trouble you do now, and you would be in no worse position than many of God's servants.

God is not partial. His ways are equal. I wish the curtain could be lifted and you could see your condition as it is. I was shown that your feelings have been wrong towards James. Since that house was purchased for Brother Bates to live in, you have been sinking. You have given way to the enemy and looked with suspicion upon James' motives concerning that matter. You ought to have been foremost in the matter, and cheerfully, gladly helped in getting a home for him, instead of having the least trial in the matter. God's ways are

---

[5] Eight or nine months earlier, in October 1858, at the request of James White, John Byington and family had moved from their farm in Buck's Bridge, New York, where they had lived for 25 years, to the Battle Creek area. The move, Ellen White indicates here, had entailed financial loss, though details are not known. One possible indication of loss is found in comparing the value of Byington's real estate in 1850—a comfortable $4,000—with that in 1860, after the move to Michigan, when it was down to $1,600.

See: Obituary: "John Byington," *Review,* Jan. 25, 1887, p. 57; John and Catherine Byington, "Note to Sister Rice," *Review,* May 19, 1859, p. 206; 1850 U.S. Federal Census, "John Byington," New York, St. Lawrence County, Potsdam, p. 39; 1860 U.S. Federal Census, "John Byington," Michigan, Calhoun County, Newton, p. 244.

[6] At the time of writing Byington was 60 years old and his youngest child, William, about 18.

See: Obituary: "John Byington," *Review,* Jan. 25, 1887, p. 57; 1860 U.S. Federal Census, "William W. Byington," Michigan, Calhoun County, Newton, p. 244.

equal. He does not require one to sacrifice everything and another to make no sacrifice at all.[7]

God's eye is upon all these things. He reads the motives of all, and it is written in the book. God suffered you to be tested to discover to you that selfishness existed in your heart. You have let this matter pass along with a bitter root springing up in your heart to trouble you. The enemy has managed to keep you in a constant hurry that you may have no time to devote to God. All the best of your energy and strength has been spent in your own service.

I was then shown that God will reward those who will bear responsibility and with energy push His work forward and stand in the forefront of the battle. God will have those who will venture something in His work. But there are those who will not fill the place that God would be pleased to have them fill.

I saw that God had chosen James to fill an important place, and has made him His agent to forward His work. I was pointed back to the commencement of the work and was shown that God thrust him out that he might obtain an experience to fill the place He designed for him to occupy as one to manage in His cause, to forward the work, to take responsibilities, and to risk something on the success of this message. God would be pleased if others would also feel the same interest and move with the same energy. But they will not venture.

There are those who have excellent ability and judgment, and exercise it in the things of this world. The children of this world are wiser in their generation than the children of light. I saw that when the children of this world are adopted into the family and service of God, they do not generally turn their judgment and wisdom to a good account in spiritual matters. They exercise good judgment in temporal things but get the impression that God's cause will take care of itself. That judgment and wisdom lent them of God for a high and noble purpose is perverted, put to a wrong use. God is displeased that those who have so much energy and zeal in worldly matters have but little weight or responsibility of His work and manifest but little energy in His cause. They will not venture or risk much, for they lack strong and active faith in the success of this message.

I was shown that Brother Byington, Brother Fletcher [**John Fletcher Byington**], and Brother Smith [**Uriah Smith**][8] have looked with suspicion

---

[7] The house "purchased for Brother Bates" may refer to the house in Monterey, Michigan, to which Joseph and Prudence Bates moved in early 1860, or it may refer to an earlier house that James White provided for them. Ellen White responded to Byington's resentment at what he considered James's favoritism toward Bates with reference to Bates's record of self-sacrifice.

See: Ellen G. White, Lt 2, 1859 (June 21), note 7; Ms 8, 1859 (Nov. 17 entry).

[8] *Identities:* Ellen White, describing the same, but deteriorating, situation the next summer, warned that "James . . . is watched . . . by those in the office, especially you [Harriet Smith], Uriah, and Fletcher." The parallel with this statement makes it clear that "Brother Smith" is Uriah Smith. The 1860 statement also associates "Fletcher" with the "Office," indicating

and distrust upon James because he ventured out to do so much. They shook their heads doubtfully, thought he was going too far, moving too fast. I saw that if these should have their will and their way how the work should move, how it should progress, it would not move at all.[9] Their fears and doubts and lack of energy would cause the work to stand still. The spirit with which they move in the work would be scattered through the body, and feeling would have much to do in governing the work. At times the pulse would beat quick and strong, and then again the feelings would change and the pulse beat slowly and feebly, so it could scarcely be perceived that they moved at all. I saw that those who are not willing to help bear the heavy burdens should not hinder and cast on their own weight to add additional burdens and to clog the work.

I saw that it was a sacrifice for Fletcher and Martha [**Martha Louisa Byington**][10] to care kindly for Thomas[11] as they did. They will not lose their reward, for he is precious in the sight of God, and every kind and generous act to that suffering disciple is remembered in heaven. It is written in the book, and the different ones whose interest, sympathy, and faith was aroused for him have not labored in vain. Every such golden privilege improved will prove for their own advantage in the end.

I saw that there has been a watching to see if there was not a failure in the management of the work, and if it does not come out as expected, some take

---

that the reference is to John Fletcher Byington, who had worked at the Review and Herald press since 1853. Ellen White commonly referred to him by his second name, no doubt to distinguish him from his father, John Byington.

See: Ellen G. White, Lt 7, 1860 (June); Lt 7, 1853 (Aug. 24); Ms 5, 1861 (c. 1861); Lt 174, 1906 (June 7).

[9] The focus of the letter here widens to include John Byington's son, Fletcher Byington, and Uriah Smith, both on the staff at the Review and Herald "Office." Their poor relationship with James White as manager of the office included their "suspicion and distrust" of James and, some paragraphs later, their "satisfaction . . . in watching and finding fault" with James. By the following summer the situation had deteriorated to the point where James White severed his connection with the office for a time and an ad hoc "General Council" had to convene in June 1860 to deal with the crisis. The council published a pamphlet that included the report that Uriah Smith, among others, had apologized and made "very humble acknowledgements." For a discussion on the involvement of Harriet Smith (wife of Uriah) in these troubles, see Letters 7 and 8, 1860 (June; June 11). Both Gerald Wheeler and Eugene Durand include sections in their respective biographies of White and Smith on the occasionally turbulent relationships between Uriah Smith and James White.

See: S. T. Belden, G. W. Amadon, and William Hall, *To Brother J. N. Andrews and Sister H. N. Smith* (PH016), p. 2 (prefatory remarks); Eugene F. Durand, *Yours in the Blessed Hope, Uriah Smith*, pp. 271-280; Gerald Wheeler, *James White*, pp. 103, 104, 176-182.

[10] *Identity:* It is assumed here that "Fletcher and Martha" are John Fletcher Byington and his wife, Martha Louisa.

[11] *Identity:* The description of "Thomas" as a "suffering disciple" who received care and help from others makes it probable that this is **Thomas B. Mead**, a former worker at the Review and Herald press. Living in the vicinity of Battle Creek, he was debilitated by tuberculosis and unable to work.

advantage of it and make as much of it as possible. God has been displeased with these things.

I was pointed back to Moses and saw where God placed him. He occupied a prominent position. Aaron and Miriam murmured against Moses and talked with each other upon the matter. They were jealous of Moses, thought he took too much upon himself. God's anger was kindled against them. I saw that God was displeased with those who do not take the burden themselves and then stand ready to murmur at the one upon whom He lays the heavy burden. I saw that if others would come up and bear the burden he [James] has borne for years, and venture all—life, health, strength, time, everything—to push this work ahead, trusting alone to the success of this message, then God would release him from heavy responsibilities and burdens. But as yet God has made him His agent to stir up to zealous action, and I saw that His blessing has rested upon every essential move that has been made to advance His work, and steadily has the work progressed and one difficulty after another has been surmounted. It is because God's hand was in the work.

I saw that some do not realize that selfishness is at the bottom of their murmuring. God's humble instrument moves too fast for their faith, and his venturing out as he has done has reproved their slow, unbelieving pace. And there has been satisfaction taken in watching and finding fault. Hints have been thrown out, doubts expressed, which have had their influence. They were at fault in this. Their faith was not strong enough to keep pace with him. Had they the strong faith and self denial that they should have, those who have the ability and means might do a great deal in stirring up the people of God, and if they would venture out and risk something it would inspire faith in the hearts of the remnant, and there would be activity and zeal in pushing forward this great work. I was shown that the work was not left in the hands of James or any other one upon earth.[12] Angels of God have charge of the work; they counsel and direct the people through chosen agents, and thus the work moves forward.

I was shown that God in His own wise providence raised James above dependence and want, that his testimony and influence might not be crippled by the galling sense of dependence.[13] God wants to use him as His instrument

---

[12] The portrayal of James White's leadership position given in this passage and elsewhere in the letter carefully avoids conferring upon him some kind of permanent preeminent position in the church. When G. I. Butler in 1873 tried to steer the General Conference toward giving James White special status and preeminence he (White) successfully counteracted the attempt. Andrew Mustard traces the issue of leadership authority during this period in *James White and SDA Organization,* pp. 175-178.

[13] As J. N. Andrews and others noted a few years later: "When Eld. White, in 1848, began the business of publishing, in Middletown, Conn., he did it without any capital at all, and almost without friends. . . . He was dependent upon a few friends in quite humble circumstances for a shelter and for the necessities of life." During the early 1850s, while in Rochester, New

to speak with freedom, independent of man, and in His Spirit raise his voice and with his example call upon the people of God to arouse and with energy to assist with their influence, ability, and judgment and substance in moving forward this great work. And any that wish to be convinced can be, that it is not selfishness or that he may be advantaged himself that he pursues the course he has, but that his object and aim is to advance the work of God which is dearer to him than life. I saw that God will have a voice to tell in the Office and in His cause.

I saw that it is easier for those who look on to complain and find fault than to suggest and lead in a better course. It is very easy and cheap to suggest doubts and fears, but it is not so readily undertaken to tell what shall be done. I was pointed back and saw that amid all the hatred and devices of Satan God had spared the life of James, although Satan has pressed him sore to take away his life. God has wrenched him from the enemy's power and raised him up to still act for Him, to walk out on his faith, to be a succorer to the needy and to strengthen and uphold His servants that He has called into the field. I saw that God had stayed him on the right hand and on the left, that he should not go to extremes, and He has inspired confidence in the hearts of the remnant generally to confide in his integrity and judgment. This has not been the work of man, but the marks of God's hand are seen in it all. His work will go forward. God will choose simple instruments to carry forward this great work, but they only carry out the mind and will of the great Master at the head of the work.

York "he lived in a hired house . . . [that] was furnished with the plainest articles of second-hand furniture. The food of his family was of the least expensive character." After the move to Michigan in 1855, James White's personal financial situation began to improve.

See: J. N. Andrews et al., *Defense of Elder James White and Wife,* pp. 2, 3. For a recent analysis of James White's sources of personal income, see Gerald Wheeler, *James White,* pp. 72, 81, 147-153.

1859
(Lt 32, 1859)

JULY [9],[1] BATTLE CREEK, MICHIGAN

LETTER TO

Cyrenius Smith and Louisa Smith.[2]

Previously unpublished.

On the lack of care by Cyrenius and Louisa Smith for the plight of the Michael B. Czechowski and Mary J. Cranson families.

Dear Brother and Sister Smith:

Since having the conversation with you last Thursday I have been burdened. A heavy weight is upon my spirits, and I have felt strongly convicted that I was wrong in trying to explain the vision I sent you. That is not the work God lays upon me. It is to give to others what He has given to me, and then, if they cannot see everything in the vision, let them humble themselves before God, search their own hearts, try their motives, plead and agonize with Him until they can see. This I have seen in times past was the right way. I have departed from it and am sorry.[3]

---

[1] The original is dated only "July," without day or year. However, this letter is closely related to Ms 4, 1859, as shown by several parallel, almost identical, passages, indicating that it was written about the same time as Ms 4, i.e., about July 1859 (see Ms 4, 1859 [c. July], note 1). There is additional evidence that this letter was, in fact, written on July 9, 1859. Ellen White referred to a conversation she had with Cyrenius and Louisa Smith "last Thursday" about a vision that the Smiths had been reluctant to accept. Ellen White's diary from Thursday, July 7, 1859, confirms that on that day she "went down to Brother and Sister Smith's. Had some conversation with them upon a vision I had. Feel bad that they do not realize their state as it is." This is followed two days later, on July 9, with the brief diary notation, "Wrote to Brother and Sister Smith."

See: Ellen G. White, Ms 7, 1859 (entries for July 7 and 9).

[2] *Identity:* In this letter Ellen White writes that "Brother and Sister Smith" "live near" Mary Cranson who lived in Battle Creek at this time. As far as is known there were two Smith families in the Battle Creek church in 1859, the family of Uriah and Harriet Smith and that of Cyrenius and Louisa Smith. That Ellen White is not writing to Uriah and Harriet is evident since she writes of children, and they had no children at this juncture.

See: 1860 U.S. Federal Census, "Mary J. Cranson," Michigan, Calhoun County, Battle Creek, p. 23. For lists of members of the Battle Creek congregation in the 1850s, see EGWEnc, s.v. "Battle Creek Congregation."

[3] "The Lord has said to me: 'Bear the testimonies. Your work is not to settle difficulties; your work is to reprove, and to present the righteousness of Christ.'"

See: Ellen G. White, *The Writing and Sending out of the Testimonies to the Church* (PH116), p. 8.

In this last vision I was shown that if you had fully believed and acted upon the vision given before, there would have been no necessity for this last one. But the first vision has not been heeded.[4] It had not that effect upon you that God designed it should. I am strongly convicted that I have explained much of the force of the vision away, and it has not accomplished what God designed it should. It is the last time I shall undertake such business. It is a serious matter to lesson the effect of the vision in the least. We are doing up work for eternity, and I must meet what God has committed to me. If I have not discharged my duty faithfully, mine will be a sad fate.

I know from the conversation we had that you do not understand yourselves in the light in which you were shown me. Things which were plainly presented before me you could not understand. It is my duty to put the matter in as clear a light as possible before you, and the work of making you believe it belongs to another. It is not my work, and I shall never again be drawn into it.

I know you do not see this matter as it is. I saw that there was selfishness in many things in you both, that must be corrected.[5] Since I saw you I have dwelt considerably upon what I have seen, and the clearer the vision comes to my mind the more convinced I am that you are certainly blinded about yourselves. In regard to Brother Czechowski [**Michael Belina Czechowski**],[6] selfishness was in both your hearts.[7] I am not mistaken in this matter. Perhaps

---

[4] The "first vision" mentioned here is not found in the White Estate files. As to the failure of the Smiths to heed the earlier vision, there is some evidence that they continued for some time in their disregard of Ellen White's testimonies. By the following year, 1860, a full crisis of confidence in the visions had developed among several leaders associated with the Review and Herald publishing office, among them, Cyrenius Smith, who served on the publishing committee of the *Review*. A council set up to investigate the matter found that Smith had "occupied an extremely faithless position in regard to the visions." Apparently he had a change of heart, for it was reported that "at this Council very humble acknowledgements were made by Brn. J. H. Waggoner and Uriah Smith, and also by Bro. Cyrenius Smith."

See: S. T. Belden, G. W. Amadon, and Wm. Hall, *To Brother J. N. Andrews and Sister H. N. Smith* (PH016), 1860, p. 2.

[5] As can be seen in what follows, the "selfishness" of Louisa and Cyrenius Smith was evident in their uncaring attitude toward the needs of the Czechowski and Cranson families. Paradoxically, the Cyrenius Smith family is mainly remembered by Adventist historians for their earlier generosity toward the fledgling church. In 1852, according to J. N. Loughborough, the Smiths sold their farm in order to free up cash to use for church projects. In 1855 when funds were needed to erect a building to house the Review and Herald press in Battle Creek, Michigan, Smith joined with others to lend $300 toward the project.

See: J. N. Loughborough, "Uncle Elkins and His Nephews," *Review,* Jan. 12, 1897, p. 18.

[6] *Identity:* There is only one Adventist Czechowski family from this period, viz., that of Michael Belina Czechowski, a former Franciscan monk, priest, and militant Polish nationalist, who converted to Sabbatarian Adventism in 1857.

See: Search term "Czechowski" in *Words of the Pioneers*.

[7] Czechowski's conversion in 1857, fluency in French, and keen desire to preach, soon led to plans for him to evangelize full-time among the French-speaking populations of northern New York and Canada East. Beginning in 1858 James White appealed to *Review* readers to make the new venture possible by providing financial support to Czechowski's poverty-stricken

you do not see it so, but God regards it so. Dig deep, I beseech of you. I have not the least personal feeling in this matter. I dare not say peace, peace, when there is no peace.

I have seen that Sister Cranson [**Mary Jane Cranson**][8] has not received from you that heartfelt sympathy that her case required.[9] You have not made her case your own. You have seen and felt deeply the wrongs in her children but have not half felt the wrongs in your own. Her heart has been desolate and lonely, her loss is a living loss. But few have had any just sense of her loneliness and discouragement. I saw that a difference should be made between her, a widow, and others who are differently situated. Her husband wore out his life and died at his post. He had perfect confidence that if his wife and his children could live near you, your influence would be saving, and your sympathy and care would partly make up the loss they would sustain. You have failed in some things. A heavy responsibility rested upon you in this matter. It has not been borne as it ought to have been.

I saw that God has His eye upon the widow and fatherless. Sister Cranson has often distrusted God, her faith has been weak, she has had too much pride, but if many who now see her lack were placed in her condition, they would not do half so well as she has done. I saw that widows whose husbands have devoted their strength to God and have fallen in their work should be regarded in a different light than even other widows. A duty rests upon the church in this matter, and great care should be taken to help strengthen the widow in her affliction.

---

wife and children. It seems that Louisa and Cyrenius Smith were less than enthusiastic about helping the Czechowski family.

[8] *Identity:* For the identity of "Sister Cranson" and background to her situation, see Ms 4, 1859 (c. July), note 2.

[9] For notes on the remainder of this letter, see the last section of Ms 4, 1859 (c. July).

1859

(Ms 4, 1859)

[CIRCA JULY 1859],[1] N.P.

The Case of Sister Cranson.

Previously unpublished.

Lack of sympathy and care by Battle Creek church for widow Mary Jane Cranson.

I was shown the case of Sister Cranson [**Mary Jane Cranson**].[2] I saw that she has not received that heartfelt sympathy that her case required. There are those who have not made her case their own.[3] Some have seen the wrongs in her children and have not been as tender and careful of her feelings in the

---

[1] This manuscript, although undated, contains some indications of its date. As Ellen White described the situation, Mary Cranson, having become a widow, moved to Battle Creek, Michigan, hoping for some "sympathy and care" from church members. The church in Battle Creek, however, had "not felt the obligations belonging to them," and the main thrust of the manuscript is to impress upon the church that help should be extended to deserving widows. It is likely that the decision of the church in Battle Creek to support Mrs. Cranson with a weekly stipend, starting in August 1859 (see note 2 below), was in response to Ellen White's appeal in this manuscript, hence it is likely that this manuscript was written shortly before August 1859. Parallels with Lt 32, 1859 (July 9), further support assigning the date of "circa July 1859" (see Lt 32, 1859, note 1).

[2] **Samuel T. Cranson**, a Sabbatarian preacher, died in 1855 at age 33, leaving his wife, Mary, with three children aged about 8, 6, and 4. In accordance with her husband's plans, Mary subsequently moved from Jackson County to Battle Creek, hoping for moral and perhaps material support from the congregation at the church's headquarters. Like her husband, Mary Cranson contracted tuberculosis and by August 1859 was so weakened that she was unable to look after her household and children. She was also impoverished. The Battle Creek church stepped in and voted to support her with $3 per week. The following summer, James White organized additional fund raising for the Cranson family through the *Review*. Mary Jane Cranson died August 27, 1860, aged 35.

See: Obituary, "Samuel T. Cranson," *Review,* May 1, 1855, p. 222; obituary: "Mary Jane Cranson," *Review,* Sept. 18, 1860, p. 143; 1860 U.S. Federal Census, "Mary J. Cranson," Michigan, Calhoun County, Battle Creek, p. 23; Harriet N. Smith et al., "Widow Cranson," *The Good Samaritan*, February 1860, p. 12; Joseph Bates and S. B. Whitney, "Business Meeting," *Review,* July 3, 1860, p. 56.

[3] Among those in Battle Creek who had been less than helpful to Mrs. Cranson were **Cyrenius** and **Louisa Smith**. Using the same words as found here, Ellen White challenged the Smiths in another letter: "I have seen that Sister Cranson has not received from you that heartfelt sympathy that her case required. You have not made her case your own." As was often the case with other visions she received, Ellen White would write separate letters to individuals pointed out in the vision and then write a general description, without mentioning specific names, to the local church concerned.

See: Ellen G. White, Lt 32, 1859 (July 9).

matter as they should have been, while at the same time those who have been more favorably situated have not half realized, and corrected as they should, their own children's wrongs. Her widowed heart has had many solitary, desolate, agonizing hours that others have known nothing about. Many times she has cast herself away in her loneliness and been strongly tempted to make some hasty move which would have ruined her. Her loss is a living loss. But few have had any just sense of her discouragement and loneliness.

I saw that there should be a difference made with the widow and others who are differently situated. It has troubled her, and lessened her confidence in her brethren, because those who have labored for her required so high wages. It looked heartless to her. She should not have laid out her means in building. The matter should have been overruled by strong counsel and advice. The means used in that addition should have been saved to supply her with life's necessities.

Her husband wore out his life in trying to save souls, doing his Master's business. He was self-denying, self-sacrificing, beloved of God. He died at his post.[4] He had perfect confidence that if his wife and children could live near the brethren their influence would be saving, and their sympathy and care would partly make up for the loss they would sustain. She made a sacrifice in getting to Battle Creek.[5] It has been well that she came. It has been a blessing to her, kept her from a greater evil; but it has not been half the blessing it might have proved if all had that interest and care for her that they should have felt.

I saw that God has His eye upon the widows and fatherless. The church has not felt the obligations belonging to them. Sister Cranson has often distrusted God. Her faith has been weak. She has had too much fear of dependence, too much pride. But if some others, who now see her lack, were placed in her condition they would not do half as well as she has done.

I saw that widows should ever be cared for, especially those whose husbands have devoted their strength to God and have fallen while engaged in His work. They should be regarded in a different light than even other widows, and duty rests upon the church and upon each individual in this matter, and great care should be taken to help strengthen and comfort the widows in their affliction.

---

[4] A former Methodist minister, **Samuel T. Cranson**, of Tompkins, Michigan, became a Sabbathkeeping Adventist in 1853 and began to preach for that movement within a few months. The *Review* carried notices of his preaching activities in Michigan for the next two years until his untimely death in 1855.

[5] According to the 1860 census, Mary Cranson's family lived close to several prominent church members in Battle Creek, such as Uriah Smith, Cyrenius Smith, and Abram A. Dodge.

See: 1860 U.S. Federal Census, "Mary J. Cranson," Uriah Smith," "Cyrenius Smith," "A. A. Dodge," Michigan, Calhoun County, Battle Creek, pp. 23, 24.

1859

(Lt 3, 1859)

SEPTEMBER 1, BERLIN, CONNECTICUT

LETTER TO
Robert and Eunice Harmon.

Previously unpublished.

Description of meetings and travels in western New York, August 1859.

Dear Parents:

Here we are journeying again.[1] We have attended two conferences and are about to engage in the third. In less than two weeks my husband has preached ten times. He is somewhat weary; but today is Thursday and he will rest today and tomorrow, and then engage in labor again.

Our first conference was at Carlton, N.Y.[2] We had never been in that part of the country before. The friends there received us heartily, and every arrangement was made for our convenience and comfort. The [railroad] cars stopped at Albion [New York], five miles [eight kilometers] from Brother Buckland's [**Curtis P. Buckland**][3] in Carlton. He was at the depot waiting for us with a fine span of horses and easy carryall.[4] We had been riding all day[5]—took breakfast at half-past three A.M. at Jackson [Michigan]—and we were very weary. But we enjoyed a bath of cold water which refreshed us much before retiring. We slept well and had Friday to rest.

---

[1] The Whites had started their "eastern journey" two weeks earlier, on August 17, 1859. Although originally intended to take six or seven weeks, the trip was extended while en route, and ended up taking three months.

See: J. W. [James White], "Eastern Tour," *Review*, Sept. 29, 1859, p. 148; J. W. [James White], "At Home," *Review*, Dec. 8, 1859, p. 15.

[2] Held over the weekend, August 19-21, 1859.

See: James White, "Appointments," *Review*, Aug. 4, 1859, p. 88.

[3] *Identity:* Curtis P. Buckland's obituary mentions the fact that he had moved to Carlton in 1858 and that "in 1859 . . . [a] tent-meeting was held on his farm by Bro. and Sister White."

See: Obituary: "Curtis P. Buckland," *Review*, Feb. 3, 1891, p. 79.

[4] A light covered horse-drawn carriage. The adjective "easy" suggests that this "carryall" was comfortable.

[5] James White felt exhilarated after covering more than 300 miles (483 kilometers) in one day: "It seemed hardly possible that we had left . . . Jackson, Mich., only sixteen hours before. We were hurried over the roads, through the dust, and from one train to another, with such speed that we seemed to forget headaches and other ills."

See: J. W. [James White], "Eastern Tour," *Review*, Sept. 1, 1859, p. 116.

Meeting commenced Friday evening. Brother Lampson's[6] family were present, also Brother Orton [and his] wife, [**Jonathan T.** and **Caroline Orton**][7] Drusilla [**Drusilla Lamson**], Alva [**Alva Orton**], and Bradley Lampson [**Joseph Bradley Lamson**],[8] Brother Lindsay [**John M. Lindsay**],[9] wife and children, and a large company from Mill Grove [New York], Brother and Sister Crage [**Stephen B.** and **Miranda B. Craig**],[10] and Brother and Sister Smith,[11] the last two living in Parma [New York]. Many from different places were present. I mention those whom I think you are acquainted with.

Sabbath forenoon there were about one hundred present, and in the afternoon also. Sunday the tent was crowded full and quite a number of females dressed in their rich silks and satins sat upon the grass at the edge of the tent. Many came out from curiosity to hear the woman talk. Husband had perfect freedom in talking to the people. The Lord strengthened me to talk five times.

The people would not be satisfied until I had spoken. We expect that meeting will result in much good. Many were convinced of the truth of our

---

[6] *Identity:* A distinction is made in this statement between "Brother Lampson's family" and "Bradley Lampson [Joseph Bradley Lamson]." "Brother Lampson" probably refers to the father of Bradley, Jonathan Lamson, who was an active member living near Clarkson, about 20 miles (32 kilometers) from Carlton, where the conference was being held. (The discrepancy in spelling between "Lamson" and "Lampson" is understandable and not significant.)

See: Search term "Lamson" in *Words of the Pioneers;* 1850 U.S. Federal Census, "Jonathan Lamson," New York, Monroe County, Clarkson, p. 155.

[7] *Identity:* Among several indications that "Brother Orton" is Jonathan T. Orton, of Rochester, New York, is the fact that "Drusilla" and "Alva," the names of two of Jonathan Orton's children, follow directly after.

See: 1850 U.S. Federal Census, "Jonathan Orton," "Drusilla Orton," "Alva Orton," New York, Monroe County, Rochester, Ward 7, p. 317.

[8] *Identity:* There is some evidence that Joseph Bradley Lamson (or "J. B. Lamson," as he was known in the *Review)* also went by his middle name. Thus, Ellen White reported in the *Review* that she and James stayed with "J. B. Lamson" in December 1865 while J. N. Loughborough, referring to the same event, says they were entertained at "the home of Mr. Bradly [*sic*] Lamson."

See: Ellen G. White, "Our Late Experience," *Review*, Feb. 27, 1866, p. 98; J. N. Loughborough, *Rise and Progress of the Seventh-day Adventists,* p. 269.

[9] *Identity:* The only members with the name "Lindsay" in the vicinity of Carlton at this time were the family of John and Eliza Lindsay, living near Olcott, about 30 miles (48 kilometers) away. Several of the Lindsay children were baptized in 1859-1860.

See: Search term "Lindsay" in *Words of the Pioneers;* R. F. C. [R. F. Cottrell], "Report From Bro. Cottrell," *Review*, Feb. 3, 1859, p. 85; R. F. C. [R. F. Cottrell], "Report From Bro. Cottrell," *Review*, June 5, 1860, p. 21.

[10] *Identity:* The name "Crage" does not appear in the *Review*. But during this period there was a Sabbathkeeping couple named "Craig," living in Hamlin, about 15 miles (24 kilometers) from the meetings at Carlton. It is likely, therefore, that "Crage" is a misspelling. Stephen and Miranda Craig are the only members with that name living near Carlton at this time.

See: Search term "Craig" in *Words of the Pioneers.*

[11] These persons have not be identified.

position. We never saw a more attentive, interested congregation.[12] They numbered above seven hundred on First Day.[13] Many who came in the morning would not leave until the third (five o'clock) meeting closed. Food was taken from the houses and distributed among the eager listeners to truth. While eating our dinner at the house, we concluded that if Jesus had been present He would have had compassion upon the multitude and provided bread for them by His divine power.

After the close of the afternoon meeting we called the young together and just as they were about to leave for their homes we faithfully exhorted them to make sure work for eternity. We told them that they must each have an individual experience and feel an individual responsibility, that unless they should cease to worship at the shrine of fashion they could not be disciples of the meek and lowly Jesus. It was an affecting time. Parents and children wept aloud, and thus we parted. I felt that my garments were clean from their blood. I had prayed for them and warned them faithfully with many tears. I was free. I felt that I had done my whole duty. They must now form a character for heaven or choose the broad road that leads to death. I want to feel a deep interest for souls and labor to do all I can for their salvation. I know that time is short, and I want to do all I can in the cause of my Master.

We left Carlton Monday morn and went to Rochester [New York]. Visited Brother Orton's family. They waited upon us with their horses and hack[14] around the city where we wished to go. Wednesday we left Rochester for Syracuse [New York].

---

[12] "We felt distressed to leave this people," James White added. "Could the tent remain three or four weeks . . . we have no doubt but a good church would be raised up in the vicinity of Carlton."

See: J. W. [James White], "Eastern Tour," *Review*, Sept. 1, 1859, p. 116.

[13] Sunday.

[14] Carriage for hire. Jonathan Orton was a hackman by trade.

1859

(Lt 4, 1859)

SEPTEMBER 2, [KENSINGTON, CONNECTICUT][1]

LETTER TO

William Peabody.[2]

Previously unpublished.

A stewardship challenge for William Peabody, a man of "considerable means."

Dear Brother Peabody:

I will try to write you what was shown me in vision nearly one year ago. I saw that the truth of God would progress, that there was a great work to do, and that the stewards of God have not moved fast enough. They moved too slow.

Dear Brother, I saw that the Lord wanted your means which He has lent you. He calls for you to use it to advance His cause. I saw that there was but a little time for you to use the means which He has lent you in advancing His work.[3] You must work fast to get your treasure before you into heaven and safely secured there, where thieves cannot steal it or moth corrupt it.

I saw that your business was in an unsettled, perplexing state, and you must begin to square up your business. Get it into a snug compass. Be getting ready to move to the better country, even the heavenly. I saw that you should work as fast as possible to remove the means which God has lent you from the hands of unbelievers and transfer it to the believers, and aid in advancing the last message of mercy ever to be given to the world. I saw that you should be

---

[1] See notes on Ellen White's diary entries for September 1 and 2, 1859 (Ms 7, 1859).

[2] As indicated in this letter, "Brother Peabody" is of advanced age and has "considerable means." Probably this description can fit only William Peabody of Monroe County, New York, 68 years old and worth $10,000 to $15,000 at the time of writing. (See notes below.)

See: Search term "Peabody" in *Words of the Pioneers.*

[3] William Peabody, a relatively wealthy farmer from New York, with real estate worth $15,000 in 1850, had become a Sabbathkeeper in 1853. At the time Ellen White wrote to him he was 68 years old and probably not in the best of health. When he died at 75 it was said that "his death was the result of lingering consumption, under which he had suffered for several years."

See: 1850 U.S. Federal Census, "Wm. Peabody," New York, Monroe County, Wheatland, p. 245; obituary: "William Peabody," *Review,* Jan. 22, 1867, p. 82.

getting things in a close compass, and be preparing for the last great work of the third angel.[4]

I saw that had you been using your means more freely for the cause of God you would have been better off today. I saw that He required much of His servants that they have not performed. And when they become close, selfish, worldly, and covetous, and keep the means which God has lent them, He who has entrusted them this means will reach down His hand to show them how quickly He can scatter and take away what they have. When God's stewards claim the means He has lent them as their own, God often touches what they have and will scatter it. I saw that there was a withholding which tendeth to poverty, and a scattering which increaseth.

In the last vision given me in Michigan, June, 1859,[5] saw that you must have your eyes open to see the wants of the cause and then to freely bestow; that you had but a short time to work and lay up your treasure in heaven. I saw that you would have no reward for assisting or placing your means in the hands of wicked men who despise the truth. Many profess to be your friends because they want a favor of you. Satan and his evil angels work through them to retain your means in his ranks, and exult over their success. Satan works through evil angels—and they work through agents in the form of men—to wrench all the means he can from God's children and place all he can in his own ranks. God's stewards are not always wise. They are more fearful to trust their means to God's keeping than to the keeping of sinful men who are under the control of their master, Satan. I saw that the scenes of this earth's history are fast closing. It will soon all be finished, and what is to be done must be done quickly.

Dear Brother, I have seen that there was a lack among those who have means. They lack faith in the result and success of this message. If they would venture something on the success of this message, it would be more pleasing to God. Their faith would work and their works would preach loudly to unbelievers.

---

[4] Exactly what is intended here is not clear, but it may be counsel for Peabody to sell his land holdings so that he would be in a better position to make donations. A comparison of the 1850 and 1860 censuses indicate that he had made changes in that direction. Whereas in 1850 his land was worth $15,000, in 1860 it was listed at only $2,650, whereas his "personal estate" was valued at $8,500. (The 1850 census did not require information on personal estates.)

See: 1850 U.S. Federal Census, "Wm. Peabody," New York, Monroe County, Wheatland, p. 245; 1860 U.S. Federal Census, "William Peabody," New York, Monroe County, Wheatland, p. 49.

[5] This probably refers to the vision recounted in *Testimonies for the Church,* (vol. 1, pp. 185-195), part of which deals with the stewardship of "brethren . . . who have large possessions" (p. 191). It appears that in this vision Ellen White was shown the case of William Peabody and perhaps other well-to-do members, but the published account was phrased in general terms, omitting individual names. The date of the vision is discussed in Ms 6, 1859 (note on June 4 entry).

I will now write you what I saw concerning God's stewards, those who have considerable means. You were shown me among those whose faith must work, and your means be more freely imparted to advance the cause of present truth. I feel called out to say a few words to you. You are in a responsible place. You have a work to do to impart of your substance to the cause of God.

Dear Brother, inquire carefully, What is my duty? I believe you are willing to do your duty if you know what it is. Many think they are sacrificing but they do not know what it is to sacrifice. A sacrifice decreases, it never increases, but decreases and consumes. I do not know how you can be clear and do your duty without rendering to God the increase of all your substance, and even more than the interest of your means. When you think of touching the principal do you not start back? Do you not shrink? I must speak plainly. I believe that God requires even more of you than the interest. From what God has shown me, you will have to touch the substance, the principal; then you will sacrifice.[6]

If you do not work fast, "The day of the Lord cometh, and thy spoil shall be divided in the midst of thee." [Zech. 14:1.] "Sell that ye have, and give alms; provide yourselves bags which wax not old, a treasure in the heavens that faileth not, where no thief approacheth, neither moth corrupteth. For where your treasure is, there will your heart be also." [Luke 12:33, 34.] It will be much better for you to send your treasure before you into heaven. You should be now using it when the cause can be benefited by it, when the cause of God actually needs it, rather than to wait until a time when the cause is better able to take care of itself. God is constantly raising up men to aid with their substance to advance the truth. This work will go forward. It will be extensive. It is *now* it needs help.

Your life is not secure. Apply your means as you want it while you can. You may live to go through the time of trouble with the remnant, and you may be one of that number who are called blessed. "Blessed are the dead which die in the Lord," etc. Your head is already white. You are ripening up for the great harvest. Act the part faithfully which God assigns you, that at His coming it may be said of you, "Well done, good and faithful servant," etc.

From what I have seen, you should allow yourself in your old age all the necessaries of life's comforts. Nourish your strength. For the sake of saving means, do not in any way expose your health. Take good and faithful care of God's temple. Your health is more to be prized than money. And you should

---

[6] According to figures published in the *Review,* at his death William Peabody left a legacy to the Seventh-day Adventist Publishing Association of $1,035 and another to the Western Health Reform Institute of $1,219.92. He was also a frequent contributor to church causes during his life.

See: "Receipts," *Review,* Oct. 29, 1867, p. 312; search term "Peabody" in *Words of the Pioneers.*

never let means stand in the way of your spiritual interest or hinder your being benefited by assembling with the saints as often as you can, especially in their great gatherings.[7] Your faith will receive strength. Your strength will increase, and the attraction to heaven grow stronger. Your last days should be your happiest and best.

---

[7] On his seventieth birthday William Peabody wrote a letter to the *Review* that included the following sentiments: "I live alone in this village as to keeping the Sabbath. There are none nearer than Rochester. I sometimes go about thirty miles [48 kilometers] to meeting. This is my great enjoyment."

See: Wm. Peabody, "From Bro. Peabody," *Review*, Mar. 12, 1861, p. 134.

1859
(Lt 5, 1859)

SEPTEMBER 6, SOMERVILLE, MASSACHUSETTS

LETTER TO
Henry Nichols White.

Portions of this letter are published in entirety in Ellen G. White, *An Appeal to the Youth*, pp. 44-47.

A letter to her son Henry, age 12.

My dear Son Henry:

I will write you a few lines although I have no news of importance to write.

We received your letter, and were very glad to hear from you.[1] You must write oftener. Send us a letter at Topsham [Maine].[2] Think of everything you have left there and wish us to bring, and we will try to do so.[3]

We hope you are well and happy. Be a good steady boy. If you only fear God and love Him, our happiness will be complete. You can be a noble boy. Love, truthfulness, and honesty—these are sacred treasures. Do not lay them aside for a moment. You may be tempted and often tried, but my dear boy, it is at such a time these lovely treasures shine, and are highly prized. Cling closely to these precious traits, whatever you may be called to suffer. Let truthfulness and honesty ever live in your heart. Never, through fear of punishment, sacrifice these noble traits. The Lord will help you, Henry, to do right. I believe it is your purpose to do right and to please your parents.[4]

You may see little dishonest acts in other boys, but do not think for a moment of imitating them. Learn to despise such things. Do not condescend to mean talk or to mean acts. Shun the company of those who do evil, as you

---

[1] No letters from Henry White to his parents have been preserved.

[2] Two weeks later, on September 20, Ellen White wrote from Topsham, Maine, "My Dear Children: We received your letters to-day" (*An Appeal to the Youth*, p. 47).

[3] From age 1 to 6 (1853) Henry had stayed with the family of Stockbridge Howland in Topsham, Maine. Now 12, he apparently was requesting his parents to bring back some things he had left in Topsham six years earlier.

[4] Ellen White's letters to her young children include a strong element of moral instruction. Being separated from her children during several months of travel in any typical year was one of her greatest trials. Devoted mother that she was, she resorted, while traveling, to parenting her boys via correspondence.

See: Jerry Allen Moon, *W. C. White and Ellen G. White*, pp. 34-41.

would a deadly poison, for they will corrupt everyone who associates with them. Ever have your young mind lifting up, elevated above the low, evil habits of those who have no fear of God before them. You can have correct thoughts, correct ways, and can form a good pure character.

Our dear children are our treasures, and oh, how anxious we are that they should meet the approbation of God. In His strength, you can reform, but never in your own strength. You can give the Lord your heart, and ask Him to forgive your sins, and if you move with sincerity He will accept you and make you white and clean in His own precious blood.

We, your parents, pray much for you that you may be a consistent, true Christian. We know that our Saviour is coming, and will take the good and holy, the honest and pure, to dwell with Him forever in a holy heaven, where all is beauty, harmony, joy, and glory. I want you to remember that Jesus suffered, groaned, and died for you that His blood might cleanse you from sin. But there is a work for you to do, to feel that you are a sinner, lost without the cleansing blood of your Redeemer. You must feel your undone condition without a Saviour. May the Lord clearly open to your young mind the plan of salvation, and lead you to give yourself unreservedly to Jesus as His, to serve Him continually. Come to Him, dear boy, love Him because He first loved you. Love Him for His lovely character, because He loved you well enough to die for you.

Henry, as soon as you were born, we prayed that you might be a Christian boy. We believe that you have felt some of the influence of the Spirit [of God] upon your heart; but we want its sweet influence to abide upon you, and the impressions lasting, your course steady, and you to daily receive grace to resist temptation.

I must close. Love and obey Jenny [**Jane Fraser**]. Do right because you love to. Preserve these letters I write to you, and read them often, and if you should be left without a mother's care, they will be a help to you.[5]

Much love to Father and Mother White [**John** and **Betsey White**].[6] Here is a peppermint for Willie.[7]

From your affectionate mother.

---

[5] For a selection of letters written by Ellen White to her children during this 1859 itinerary, see Ellen G. White, *An Appeal to the Youth,* pp. 45-56, 65, 66; also Lts 9, 6, 10, 1859 (Sept. 6, 15, late Sept.).

[6] Ellen White's parents, **Robert** and **Eunice Harmon**, also lived in Battle Creek during these years, but appear to have been on an extended visit to their son in Iowa at this time (see Ms 8, 1859 [Nov. 16 entry]).

[7] Some have thought that Ellen White here shows favoritism by giving Willie a peppermint but not Henry. However, Willie was only 5 and Henry was 12, so a token of this kind may have been thought more appropriate for the younger boy than the older son.

See: Jerry Allen Moon, *W. C. White and Ellen G. White,* p. 37.

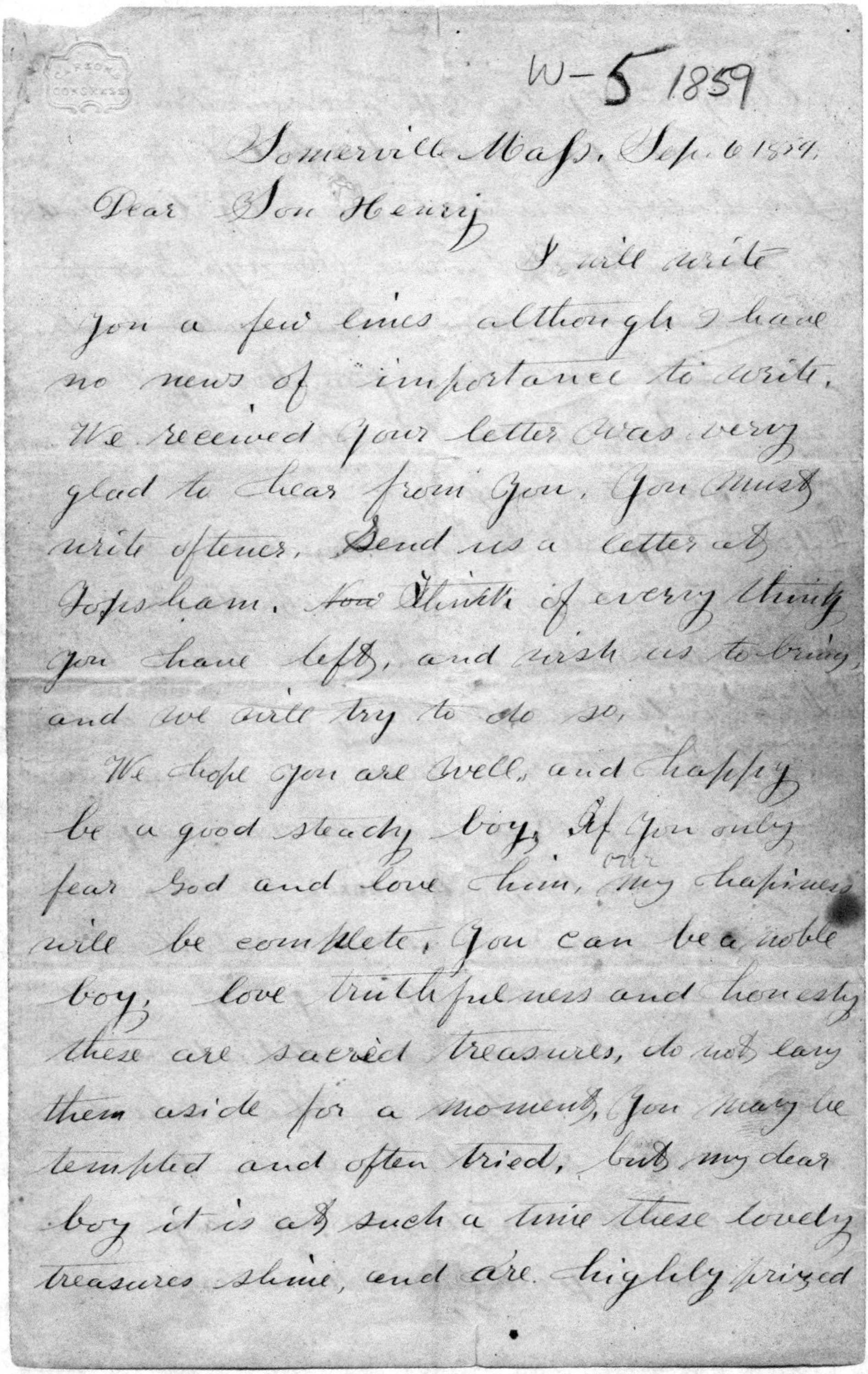

W-5 1859

Somerville Mass. Sep. 6 1859.

Dear Son Henry

I will write you a few lines although I have no news of "importance to write. We received your letter was very glad to hear from you. You must write oftener. Send us a letter at Topsham. ~~Now~~ think of every thing you have left, and wish us to bring, and we will try to do so.

We hope you are well, and happy be a good steady boy. If you only fear God and love him, ~~my~~ our happiness will be complete. You can be a noble boy, love truthfulness and honesty these are sacred treasures, do not lay them aside for a moment, You may be tempted and often tried, but my dear boy it is at such a time these lovely treasures shine, and are highly prized

Ellen White's letter to her son Henry, September 6, 1859 (Lt 5, 1859)

Cling closely to these precious traits, whatever you may be called to suffer. Let truthfulness and honesty ever live in your heart. Never through fear of punishment sacrifise these noble traits. The Lord will help you, Henry, to do right. I believe it is your purpose to do right, and to please your parents.

You may see little ~~mean~~ dishonest acts in other boys, but do not think for a moment of imitating them, ~~but~~ learn to despise such things. Do not condesend to mean talk or to mean acts. Shun the company of those who do evil, as you would a deadly poison; for they will corrupt every one who associates with them. Ever have your young mind lifting up ~~evel~~ elevated above the low evil habits of those who have no fear of God before them. You can have correct thoughts, correct ways, and can form a good pure charecter,

3

Our dear Children are our treasure and O, how anxious we are that they should meet the approbation of God. In His strength you can reform, but never in your own strength. You can give the Lord your heart, and ask him to forgive your sins, and if you move with sincerity he will accept you and make you white and clean in his own precious blood. ———

——— We, your Parents, pray much for you, that you may be a consistant true Christian. We know that our Saviour is coming, and will take the good and holy, the honest and pure to dwell with him forever in a holy heaven, where all is beautiful, harmony, joy, and glory. I want you to remember that Jesus suffered, groaned and died for you that his blood might cleanse you from sin. But there is a work for you to do to feel that you

4

are sinner, lost without the cleansing blood of your Redeemer. You must feel your undone condition without a Saviour. May the Lord clearly open to your young mind the Plan of Salvation and lead you to give yourself unreservedly to Jesus as his, to serve continually. Come to Him dear boy—love Him because he first loved you—Love him for his lovely character. Love Him because he loved you well enough to die for you. Henry, as soon as you was born we prayed that you might be a christian boy. we believe that you have felt some of the influence of the spirit upon your heart; but we want its sweet influence to abide upon you, and the impression be lasting your course be steady, and you daily receive grace to resist temptation.

I must close, love and obey Jenny do right because you love to. Preserve these letters I write to you, and read them often and if you should be left without a mothers care they will be a help to you. From your affectionate Mother,

Much love to G. father and Mother, Willie, Here is a [illegible] for Willie

1859

(Lt 9, 1859)

SEPTEMBER 6,[1] SOMERVILLE, MASSACHUSETTS

LETTER TO

William Clarence White.

Portions of this letter are published in Ellen G. White, *Manuscript Releases,* vol. 3, p. 121.

A letter to her son Willie, age 5.

Dear little Willie:[2]

We are at Brother Folsom's [**Paul Folsom**].[3] You remember, Willie, it is where they make candy.[4] We are trying to get rested up for the meeting next Sabbath.

As we were riding from Springfield [Massachusetts] to Berlin [Connecticut], there were three children in the [railroad] cars. One was a little boy about your age. He was dressed very prettily. I think his hair curled, but although he looked handsome, he was not so, for he did not behave well. He disturbed those who sat near him by his loud, sharp voice, contending and plaguing his sisters until they had no peace. They told him they should tell his mother but he did not seem to care, and he behaved so rudely that we were

---

[1] The handwritten original reads "Sep. 26, 1859," but the number "2" has a line drawn through it, suggesting that it has been crossed out and that "Sep. 6" is intended.

[2] If written on September 6, 1859, this is the earliest extant letter written specifically to Willie from his mother.

[3] *Identity:* Paul Folsom, of Somerville, Massachusetts, gets frequent mention in the *Review* during the 1850s. In the 1860 census his trade is given as "confectioner," which fits well with Ellen White's description: "It is where they make candy." Later in the letter it appears that his wife's name is "Margaret," which also accords with the census records.

See: Search term "Folsom" in *Words of the Pioneers;* 1860 U.S. Federal Census, "Paul Folsom," Massachusetts, Middlesex County, Somerville, p. 76.

[4] There is some evidence that Willie had accompanied his parents the previous year on their tour of the Eastern states, which included a visit to the Folsoms in Somerville. Willie would have been only 4 years old at the time, but Ellen guessed that he would have been impressed enough by the candymakers and the novelty of the streetcars in nearby Boston (par. 6 below) to remember them. That Willie traveled with his parents to Somerville and Boston in 1858 is inferred from the memoirs of J. N. Loughborough, who traveled with them. He recalled an incident involving Willie that happened in October 1858 while they were en route to Massachusetts.

See: J. N. Loughborough, "Sketches of the Past—No. 110," *Pacific Union Recorder,* Jan. 26, 1911, p. 1.

all glad when he got off the cars. I thought then how badly I should feel if my little Willie was so disagreeable.

Now, Willie, that badly-behaved boy with pretty clothes did not make people love him. His pretty face did not make them love him. His behavior made those who had the care of him ashamed of him, and all seemed pleased to get rid of the troublesome boy.

If Willie acts well, if he is gentle, kind, and obedient, father and mother will love him and all good people will love him.[5]

Willie, I must tell you about Margaret's [**Margaret Folsom**][6] cats. She has two cats just alike, just of a bigness. They are just the color of a rat, Maltese color. Sister Folsom takes a piece of meat and holds it up to her shoulder and the kitties will give a spring and climb to the top of her shoulder for the meat and then get down and eat it. These kitties are good, faithful kitties. They catch great big rats. They don't eat them, but bite off their heads and leave them.

Willie, we had a ride in the horse car again.[7] You remember them!

Tell Grandpa and Grandmother[8] that we have not forgotten them. We hope they are well. You must try to make them happy. They love you very much. Do just as Jenny [**Jane Fraser**][9] would have you, my own dear boy.

From your affectionate mother.

Here is a peppermint, Willie.

---

[5] *See:* Lt 5, 1859 (Sept. 6), note 4.

[6] *Identity:* See later in the same paragraph: "Sister Folsom."

[7] Horse-drawn streetcars running on rails were beginning to appear in major American cities in the 1850s. For Boston the launch came in 1856. Carrying upward of 40 passengers, they provided a quieter and more comfortable ride than the old stagecoaches and omnibuses.

See: Chaim M. Rosenberg, *The Great Workshop: Boston's Victorian Age,* p. 20.

[8] Both sets of Willie's grandparents were living in Battle Creek during these years, but since Robert and Eunice Harmon were in Iowa on an extended visit at this time, this reference must be to his paternal grandparents, **John** and **Betsey White**. On the visit of the Harmons to Iowa in 1859, see Ms 8, 1859 (note on Nov. 16 entry)

[9] Jane Fraser had worked in the White household since about 1852, and later had responsibility for the children during Ellen and James White's travels. In W. C. White's later recollections he calls her "my foster mother until I was five years old."

See: W. C. White to Rosetta Perry, Apr. 30, 1928.

1859

(Lt 6, 1859)

SEPTEMBER 15, DARTMOUTH, MASSACHUSETTS

LETTER TO

William Clarence White.

Portions of this letter are published in Ellen G. White, *Manuscript Releases,* vol. 3, p. 120.

A letter to her son Willie, age 5.

Dear little Willie:

Have you received the letters I have written to you?[1]

I will tell you what I saw last Wednesday. The fire companies were out with red caps and red uniforms; the officers had plumes in their caps. Then I saw in an alley, looking out at the firemen, a poor deformed lame man. He was sitting in a little carriage and what do you think was drawing him! It was not a dog or horse, but a goat, harnessed up just like a little horse. I thought, if Willie had seen this it would have pleased him so much. Only think, a goat drawing a wagon with a man in it.

Willie, I am now visiting where there are two little boys, not as large as you are, and two little girl babies. The little boys and girls are cousins.[2] They are very pretty little children. You would love to play with them if you were here.

We hope little Willie is well and happy. We believe you are trying to be a good, sweet little boy. You must try hard to be good. Don't please Satan by giving way to wrong temper, but remember, he that ruleth his spirit is greater than he that taketh a city.[3]

---

[1] Only the letter dated September 6, 1859, has been preserved (Lt 9, 1859).

[2] According to Lt 8, 1859, written the same day, the Whites at this point in their itinerary were staying "in the house of Brother Ashley" in Dartmouth, Massachusetts. James White reported in 1853 that "three brethren by the name of Ashly [*sic*], also their wives . . . had joined the Sabbath-keepers" in Dartmouth. According to local church records, probably dating from 1861, and from the *Review,* their names were Richard C. Ashley, George L. Ashley, and Jarvis T. Ashley. Each had children living at home. Which of the three Ashleys was the "Brother Ashley" with whom the Whites stayed cannot be determined, nor the identity of the children mentioned here.

See: James White, "Eastern Tour," *Review,* Nov. 1, 1853, p. 133; Dartmouth, Massachusetts, "Copy of Sheet From Dartmouth New Bedford Church Clerk's Record"; search terms "Ashley" and "Ashly" in *Words of the Pioneers.*

[3] Jerry Moon, in his analysis of William White's early years, sees impatience as a recurring problem in the young boy, which his mother consequently tried to correct.

How glad we should be to see our dear little Willie again and hear his [sweet] voice. We love you very much, Willie, and want you to be good and pleasant and lovely. Then everyone will love you.

You must tell Grandpa and Grandma[4] that we do not forget them but often think of them and speak of them to our friends. You must try, Willie, to make Grandpa and Grandma happy. Don't grieve them by being noisy and rude, but be quiet and mild, gentle, then they will love you. Mind Jenny [**Jane Fraser**][5] and try to please her. Be a sweet little boy.

From your mother.

See: Jerry Allen Moon, *W. C. White and Ellen G. White,* p. 38.

[4] **John** and **Betsey White** (see note 8 in Lt 9, 1859 [Sept. 6]).

[5] *See:* Note 9 in Lt 9, 1859 (Sept. 6).

1859

(Lt 8, 1859)

SEPTEMBER 15, DARTMOUTH, MASSACHUSETTS

LETTER TO

Jane Fraser.[1]

Previously unpublished.

Letter to her domestic helper, Jane Fraser, describing meetings and travels in Massachusetts, autumn 1859.

Dear Jenny:

Here we are at Dartmouth [Massachusetts] in the house of Brother Ashley.[2,3] We are quite well. My health is good, for me.

I wrote my last letter from Charlestown, Mass.[4] Thursday we rode on the [railroad] cars to Salem [Massachusetts], the place of our next meeting. Made our home at Brother Saxby's [**William L. Saxby**].[5] They were attentive to our

---

[1] *Identity:* The domestic concerns expressed toward the end of this letter ("please get two crocks . . . with good butter," etc.) and the message for Ellen White's son, Henry, indicate that the letter is to Jane Fraser who for a number of years had helped in the White household and who cared for the children in their parents' absence.

[2] *Identity:* James White reported in 1853 that "three brethren by the name of Ashly [*sic*], also their wives . . . had joined the Sabbath-keepers" in Dartmouth, Massachusetts. According to local church records, probably dating from 1861, and from the *Review,* their names were Richard C. Ashley, George L. Ashley, and Jarvis T. Ashley. Which of the three Ashley brothers Ellen White refers to here is not known.

See: James White, "Eastern Tour," *Review,* Nov. 1, 1853, p. 133; Dartmouth, Massachusetts, "Copy of Sheet From Dartmouth New Bedford Church Clerk's Record"; search terms "Ashley" and "Ashly" in *Words of the Pioneers.*

[3] At this point the Whites were about four weeks into a three-month itinerary of New York, Connecticut, Massachusetts, Maine, New Hampshire, and Vermont. For more details of this journey, see Ellen White's diary account (Ms 7, 1859, and Ms 8, 1859).

[4] This might refer to the letter Ellen White "wrote home to . . . Jenny" on September 6, while staying in Somerville, Massachusetts (Ms 7, 1859). The fact that here she says it was written from Charlestown could be explained by the fact that Somerville and Charlestown adjoined each other and had been one town prior to 1842. Whatever the case, this letter to Jenny has not been preserved.

[5] *Identity:* A short note appearing two weeks earlier in the *Review* is helpful in identifying "Brother Saxby": "W. L. Saxby: Bro. White will see you on his eastern tour, in regard to press." The only W. L. Saxby mentioned in the *Review* is William L. Saxby who lived in Massachusetts during this period. It is most probable, therefore, that the Whites stayed with William L. Saxby and his wife, Euphemia, during their stay in Salem, Massachusetts. The only minor difficulty with this solution is that there is no record of W. L. Saxby living in Salem. Records place the Saxbys in Springfield, Massachusetts, until 1857, then in Worcester of the same state, and finally

wants. Brother and Sister Hutchins [**Alfred S.** and **Esther M. Hutchins**][6] came Thursday. Brother Hutchins is quite well. Sister Hutchins is about as usual, but both have good appetites. This is favorable for them. They are in good spirits, enjoying the blessing of God. Brother Nichols [**Otis Nichols**][7] seems as good as ever. He attended our meeting at Salem. The meeting was much better than we had expected.

A large hall—Lyceum Hall—was hired for the meeting. It was rather an odd place for a meeting. It was a very large room. We went up a flight of stairs. The hall was entered by three doors, and from the entrance commenced to descend and continued to descend. Every row of seats was a step lower. We went down into the hall as you go down a pair of stairs. Then there was a platform and upon the platform a stand. This platform was broad.[8]

James and Brother Hutchins took their places in the center of the platform behind the stand, and moved the sofa to one end of the platform. From this platform the seats were ascending unto the entrance of the Hall.

Sabbath our meetings were interesting and profitable. James preached twice. Brother Hutchins talked quite freely. I bore my testimony with some freedom. Sunday, meetings commenced with a conference and prayer meeting. It was a good season. I talked—gave some little description of the sufferings of Christ. There were one hundred twenty-five present. James preached from this text: "Preach the Word." 2 Tim 4:2. He was very clear and free. Those who heard him said they never heard the subject made so plain before. James divided his subject and finished in the afternoon. There were one hundred-

---

in Vermont by 1860. Nevertheless it is likely that the Saxbys lived in Salem before moving to Vermont in 1860.

See: "Business Notes," *Review,* Aug. 25, 1859, p. 112; search term "Saxby" in *Words of the Pioneers;* 1860 U.S. Federal Census, "William L. Saxby," Vermont, Franklin County, Enosburgh, p. 43.

[6] *Identity:* From remarks made further down it is clear that "Brother Hutchins" took part in the preaching during the Salem meetings. Three weeks later itinerant preacher A. S. Hutchins reported in the *Review* how he and his wife had come to Salem and met the Whites. "We left Maine to meet Bro. and Sr. White in Salem, Mass., where we were happy to meet them again."

See: A. S. Hutchins, "Report From Bro. Hutchins," *Review,* Oct. 6, 1859, p. 157.

[7] *Identity:* It seems most likely that either Otis Nichols or his son **Henry O. Nichols** had come from their home in Dorchester, about 15 miles (24 kilometers)] distant, to attend the weekend meetings in Salem. No other male members with the surname "Nichols" living in the Boston area at this time are mentioned in the *Review*. Ellen White always addressed Otis Nichols as "Brother Nichols" and his son as "Henry," so no doubt Otis Nichols is intended here. Earlier the same day Otis Nichols had driven the Whites to the train station in Boston for the trip to Dartmouth.

See: Search term "Nichols" in *Words of the Pioneers;* Ms 7, 1859 (Sept. 15 entry).

[8] The Lyceum Hall in Salem, Massachusetts, had been built in 1831. It "could accommodate 700 patrons in amphitheater-style seating and was decorated with images of Cicero, Demosthenes, and other great orators of bygone days." The hall received lasting fame in 1877 when Alexander Graham Bell used it for his first public demonstration of the telephone.

See: Salem Tales: Of Lectures and Lyceums, www.salemweb.com/tales/lyceum.shtml. Accessed Nov. 13, 2006.

fifty present. James was blessed of the Lord with liberty again. I had some freedom in exhorting at the close of the discourse.

James preached again in the eve. I had freedom, and was strengthened to follow with exhortation. Meetings closed up well. Monday morning we were about to separate, and James spent some little time before morning prayer talking to those present upon having a kind, courteous spirit, being pitiful, etc. We then had a free season of prayer.

And thus we parted. Brother Saxby took us in his easy carriole[9] to Charlestown [Massachusetts]. His wife accompanied us. The next day we went into Boston [Massachusetts] and traded some. Bought some remnants—drilling, bed ticking, 27 yards [24 meters] factory cloth, two pieces, fine and course, woolen cloth for pants, cloth for my boys, remnants of merino shawls, etc. I have ticking enough for three feather ticks. I have done well by you this time in getting you the things you wanted.

Jenny, please get two crocks at Brother Kellogg's[10] and send one to Sister Godsmark's [**Huldah Jane Godsmark**], the other to Sister Byington's [**Catherine Byington**],[11] to pack down with good butter.

Today we are at Sister Collins' [**Nancy Collins**],[12] a good home for weary pilgrims. Last night it was very cold. A heavy frost cut off corn and tomatoes. James saw ice one-eighth of an inch [.3 centimeters] thick.

We are expecting to hear from you all at Topsham [Maine].[13] Hope to hear you are all well, prospering in the Lord. We have not time to write Henry from this place but will write him when we get to Topsham. Hope, dear Henry, you are a good boy and happy in doing right. Jenny, be careful of your strength. Trust in the Lord; forever trust.

---

[9] A light, covered horse-drawn carriage.

[10] Among the Battle Creek members at this time, the only Kelloggs were **John Preston** and **Ann Janette Kellogg** and some of their children. This reference is probably to John Preston or, possibly, to his adult son, **Albert Kellogg**. His other older sons, Merritt Gardner Kellogg and **Smith Moses Kellogg**, were not living in Battle Creek at this time.

See: Search terms "Kellogg" and "Battle Creek" in *Words of the Pioneers;* Timothy Hopkins, *The Kelloggs in the Old World and the New,* vol. 1, p. 636; EGWEnc, s.v. "Battle Creek Congregation."

[11] *Identities:* The Godsmark and Byington families had farms within a few miles of Battle Creek (see respective biographical sketches).

[12] *Identity:* In her diary account Ellen White adds the information that Sister Collins' husband had died and that she had a son, Gilbert, who was healed in response to prayer at age 12 (Ms 7, 1859 [Sept. 16 entry]). These facts unmistakably indicate that Ellen White is referring to Nancy Collins, of Dartmouth, Massachusetts, whose husband, Philip, had died just three months earlier. Her son had been dramatically healed in 1849. Ellen White relates the story in *Spiritual Gifts.* (Her account in *Spiritual Gifts* gives the son's age as "thirteen.")

See: Obituary: "Philip Collins," *Review,* June 23, 1859, p. 39; Ellen G. White, *Spiritual Gifts [vol. 2],* pp. 108, 109.

[13] "My Dear Children," Ellen wrote five days later (Sept. 20), from Topsham, "We received your letters today" (*An Appeal to the Youth,* p. 47).

We went last evening to visit Sister Russell,[14] who is in despair. She will not try to think there is hope for her. She is wasted to a skeleton. We had a very free time praying for her. She rested well that night, which is unusual for her.

I pitied the poor soul, for she has ever tried to be a consistent Christian.

In love.

---

[14] This could be Susan G. Russell, of the Dartmouth church, who died in 1864 of tuberculosis. Her obituary reported that "for the last five years under the power of disease she was somewhat despairing." Susan Russell had been a Sabbathkeeper since 1850.

See: Obituary: Susan G. Russell, *Review,* Jan. 31, 1865, p. 79.

1859

SEPTEMBER 15, DARTMOUTH, MASSACHUSETTS

LETTER TO

Henry Nichols White, James Edson White, and William Clarence White.

Published in Ellen G. White, *An Appeal to the Youth,* pp. 65, 66.

1859

SEPTEMBER 20, TOPSHAM, MAINE

LETTER TO

Henry Nichols White, James Edson White, and William Clarence White.

Published in Ellen G. White, *An Appeal to the Youth,* pp. 47, 48.

1859

SEPTEMBER 20, TOPSHAM, MAINE

LETTER TO

William Clarence White.

Published in Ellen G. White, *An Appeal to the Youth,* pp. 48, 49.

1859

(Lt 7, 1859)

SEPTEMBER 24, TOPSHAM, MAINE

LETTER TO

William Henry, Bruce, and Andrew Graham.[1]

Previously unpublished.

Tragic consequences of a distorted Laodicean message in Connecticut.

Dear Brethren Graham:

Duty compels me to write you a few lines. While my husband is talking to the people I have shut myself in my bedroom to write you.

While at Dartmouth, Mass.,[2] the state of things in Connecticut was shown me in vision and I feel heartsick as I write. I saw that the Lord had not been in the strange work you have had there. Oh, no. An enemy's hand has been working there. I saw that you had run into a fanatical spirit and carried things to great lengths.

I was carried through some of your meetings. Some were burdened, crying out in distress. I heard shrieks, and I saw a pressing of individuals to confess. I saw that a fear came over the church, fearing to speak to this one or the other who had been reproved or held in doubt by these exercises and burdens. It was a cruel work. God's frown[3] is upon it. The enemy meant to carry out his object and drive to utter distraction and confusion.[4]

---

[1] *Identities:* Three weeks earlier, while in Kensington, Connecticut, Ellen White noted in her diary that she had met Andrew, Bruce, and William Graham (Ms 7, 1859 [Sept. 2 entry]). All three are listed in the 1860 census of Berlin Township, in which Kensington is located. Census details strongly suggest that they were brothers. Further, the only Grahams in the *Review* of the 1850s having Connecticut addresses are these three men. One of them, William Graham, was a deacon in the Berlin church for 20 years.

See: 1860 U.S. Federal Census, Bruce Graham and Andrew Graham, Connecticut, Hartford County, Berlin, p. 53; 1860 U.S. Federal Census, "Wm H. Graham," Connecticut, Hartford County, Berlin, p. 34; search term "Graham" in *Words of the Pioneers;* obituary: "William Henry Graham," *Review,* July 2, 1925, p. 22.

[2] The Whites had spent the previous weekend in Dartmouth (Ms 7, 1859 [Sept. 15-17 entries]).

[3] On God's displeasure and "frown," see Ms 2, 1853 (Mar. 1), note 3.

[4] In Lt 19, 1859, written October 4, Ellen White throws more light on the cause of the distressing events in Connecticut described here. An extreme interpretation of the Laodicean message (see EGWEnc) was being urged by some church members and leaders, including the Graham brothers, pressing for speedy confession and reformation among those members who were judged to be delinquent. Those unwilling or unable to comply promptly were thought

I saw the case of Sister Graham [Catharine Graham],[5] your mother. The Lord loves her, yet she has been held off and thrust with side and with shoulder.[6] I saw that she was rather slow to bear her whole weight upon the truth, does not see it in all its importance, yet she will if a right course is pursued towards her. She loves the truth; she sees it is clear, but the state of the church would hold her in uncertainty and doubt and lead her to inquire, Have we not been deceived? The Lord loves Sister Graham, and if she follows on to know the Lord, she will know His goings forth are prepared as the morning.

I was pointed to the case of Brother Landon [**Warren E. Landon**].[7] He has a work to do to overcome lightness, jesting, and joking, which are not convenient for a growth in grace and knowledge of the truth. He must settle into the truth and seek to realize its vital importance. The feelings toward Brother Landon have been wrong. The fear over the church in his case has not been of God. Brother and Sister Landon [**Mary F. Landon**] must be united and have a decision and firmness in the government of their children, restrain and subdue their passions with decision.

I saw the case of Sister Mary North and Brother Wilcox [**Mary S.** and **John Y. Wilcox**].[8] I saw that they have been pressed, crowded, and Mary has been

---

to have been "spued out of the mouth of the Lord" (see Rev. 3:16) and consequently were ostracized by the rest of the group. In Lt 19 Ellen White condemned this "hurried, fanatical spirit," arguing that those behind it should "wait patiently for the Lord to test character and to spue out the lukewarm" rather than taking that "work into their own hands." Essentially, Lt 7 surveys the cases of several Connecticut members who were being pressed to confess or who were thought to be already rejected by God. Ellen White testifies that God had not given up on these persons and, furthermore, that the whole campaign was "cruel work" having "God's frown . . . upon it." See also *Testimonies for the Church,* vol. 1, pp. 186-188, published some months earlier, in which Ellen White warned of various distortions of the Laodicean message.

[5] *Identity:* Two of the Graham brothers, Bruce, 26, and Andrew, 24, were still living at home, according to the 1860 census. The household was headed by "Catharine Graham," age 49.

See: 1860 U.S. Federal Census, "Catharine Graham," Connecticut, Hartford County, Berlin, p. 53.

[6] This expression apparently is borrowed from Ezekiel 34:21.

[7] *Identity:* Out of a number of Landons appearing in receipts and letters to the *Review* during this period the only one explicitly connected to Connecticut is W. E. Landon. Census records show that Warren E. Landon was a blacksmith who worked in various parts of Connecticut during this period and that his wife's name was Mary F. Landon.

See: Search term "Landon" in *Words of the Pioneers;* 1850 U.S. Federal Census, "Warren E. Landon," Connecticut, Hartford County, Farmington, p. 344; 1860 U.S. Federal Census, "Warren Landon," Connecticut, Hartford County, Bristol, p. 45; obituary: "Mary F. Landon," *Review,* Feb. 5, 1884, p. 94.

[8] *Identity:* In 1877 a "John Y. Wilcox" wrote in the *Review* of his "dear wife, Mary S. Wilcox," who had died in Kensington, Connecticut, "aged 51 years." This could be the "Sister Mary North" and "Brother [John] Wilcox" mentioned here if they eventually married despite these disastrous events. (Wilcox's first name is given later in the paragraph.) There is strong evidence that the maiden name of Mary S. Wilcox was Mary S. North. In the 1870 census John Wilcox, age 37, and Mary Wilcox, 47, living in Berlin, Connecticut, have in their household not only two sons but also "Marinda North," age 70. Likely Marinda North was Mary's

crushed. Their attachment was not judicious, and Mary was overanxious; yet the pressing and urging to confess was not of God. Things were confessed that God was not in. They forced their minds to find something and confessed that which God did not require. And then the fear of Sister Mary, the treatment she received—think ye it was pleasing to God? Nay, verily. His eye has noticed it all, His frown is upon it. God loves Sister Mary and will have a care for her. The oil and the wine have been hurt.[9] God has a care for Brother John and will lead him. He must move cautiously. There has been so much confusion in the church that he is in danger of taking false steps, that is, of not considering carefully enough and pondering the path of his feet.

I was shown Sister Lyman,[10] that the Lord has never yet said to His angels, Let her alone.[11] Oh, no. His care is over her still. His eye is upon her. Here again was an impression, an exercise not of God.

Then I saw the case of Brother Moore.[12] He was in darkness, not standing in the light of truth, [not] feeling its weight and importance. Yet God has not left him. It has not yet been said to the angel, Let him alone. God's eye is upon him and He has a message that will take hold of him. But Satan steps in to destroy Brother Moore and drive him off where this message cannot reach him. God was not in that work. The church was not standing in a position where they could move understandingly in his case and carry out the mind of Christ.

Other things I saw; others have felt this same distressed, crowding influence. Exercises and burdens have been carried out that led to fanaticism and confusion. I saw that Brother Barr [**Eli L. Barr**][13] has not been standing

---

mother, who had come to live with her daughter and son-in-law after becoming a widow. Earlier censuses confirm that Marinda North was the mother of Mary Wilcox. The 1850 census shows a family by the name of "North" in Berlin that included Joseph, age 54, Marinda, 51, and Mary, 27. The 1860 census has the same names, Joseph, 65, Marinda, 60, and Mary, 37. Note that the ages of Marinda and Mary fit almost perfectly in all three censuses. Finally, there is evidence that Joseph North was a Sabbathkeeper, as was Mary North. In the *Review* from the 1850s there is notice of a conference to be held "at the house of Bro. Joseph North" in Berlin, and also several mentions of an "M. S. North" (Mary S.[?]).

See: Obituary: "John Y. Wilcox," *Review,* July 15, 1877, p. 15; 1870 U.S. Federal Census, "Wilcox, John," Connecticut, Hartford County, Berlin, p. 21; 1850 U.S. Federal Census, "Joseph North," Connecticut, Hartford County, Berlin, p. 256; 1860 U.S. Federal Census, "Joseph North," Connecticut, Hartford County, Berlin, p. 52; E.L.H. Chamberlain, "Conference in Connecticut," *Review,* Sept. 16, 1851, p. 32; search term "M. S. North" in *Words of the Pioneers.*

[9] An expression borrowed from Revelation 6:6.

[10] *Identity:* This might be Clarissa Lyman, about 75 years old, living in the home of Sabbatarian pioneers **Albert** and **Hannah Belden** in Berlin, Connecticut.

See: 1860 U.S. Federal Census, "Albert Belden," Connecticut, Hartford County, Berlin, p. 52.

[11] Cf. Hosea 4:17: "Ephraim is joined to idols; let him alone."

[12] This person has not been identified.

[13] *Identity:* Further clues to the identity of "Brother Barr" are found in Lt 19, 1859 (Oct. 4),

in the counsel of God. He has had a wrong spirit, has followed impressions and feeling. It has led him astray. I saw that he was more to be blamed in Connecticut than the church there. He, a servant of Jesus Christ, should be ready to correct these wrong influences in the church, but he gave support to them instead of correcting them, and I saw that he had better have been working with his hands than exerting this wrong influence in the church.[14]

In haste.

---

a parallel account describing the same events. He was an itinerant preacher who traveled "among the churches East" and used his influence against the possession of "pictures." Only E. L. Barr fits this description. Throughout the 1850s he traveled and preached widely in the New England states. Moreover, he took strong exception to members spending money on photographs, not only because of the cost but because of "the claims of the second commandment."

See: E. L. Barr, "Conference in Connecticut," *Review,* Mar. 5, 1857, p. 142; search term "Barr" in *Words of the Pioneers.*

[14] A recurring theme in E. L. Barr's letters and reports to the *Review* in the late 1850s is the Laodicean message. An example of the urgency with which he viewed the situation in the churches is seen in this extract from 1858: "Arise! ye that are heartily in the truth . . . and give a testimony that shall ring in the ears of the lukewarm, the self-righteous and the insubordinate ones, and clear your garments from the blood of all men! . . . No hiding nor covering up wrongs now! No half-way work any longer! 'He that being often reproved hardeneth his neck shall suddenly be destroyed and that without remedy.' Prov. xxix, 1."

See: E. L. Barr, "The Cause in the East," *Review,* Aug. 5, 1858, p. 96.

1859

(Ms 1, 1859)

SEPTEMBER 24, TOPSHAM, MAINE

Proof of the Call to the Ministry.

This manuscript is published in entirety in Ellen G. White, *Manuscript Releases,* vol. 21, pp. 13-16.

The ministerial potential of Lewis Bean, D. T. Evans, Stephen Pierce, Daniel C. Phillips, and Hiram Bingham, all from Vermont.

I was shown the state of things in Vermont. Their condition is not pleasing to God. They should have order among them, and have everything done up exact, straight, and square. There is too much leaving things at loose ends, and I saw there has been too much leaving the important truths to dwell on little things. There has been a stiff, unbending spirit with some in Vermont, and a desire to bend others to their ideas or notions.

There has been a moving by feeling, and neglecting the living principles. Dwell on the great principles of our faith, and do not descend to the little particulars. There has been a fault-finding spirit, a watching others that there should not be. I saw that brethren in Vermont must change their course. They must not move from impulse, but from principle.[1]

I was shown the case of the brethren who feel that God has a work for them in the field, Brethren Bean [**Lewis Bean**] and Evans [**D. T. Evans**].[2] If God has called them, the weight and burden of the message will rest in power upon them, and their gift will not be exercised among believers only, but the great burden of their work will be to go out in new fields and raise up a

---

[1] Ellen White expanded on these issues in Ms 1a, 1859 (c. Sept. 24), a parallel account of the vision described here. The repetition that appears in a portion of this manuscript may have resulted from an earlier copyist's conflation of the accounts. As this appears in the earliest handwritten copy of Ms 1, 1859, it is retained here.

[2] *Identities:* The fact that both of these men are from Vermont and have engaged in some preaching makes it easy to identify them. A survey of the *Review* from this period reveals that only Lewis Bean and D. T. Evans fit that description. Lewis Bean's father, Samuel W. Bean, was also a Sabbathkeeper, but there is no hint that he had engaged in any preaching. Lewis Bean worked as a "wheelwright" and "carriage maker" and D. T. Evans was a "shoemaker," but they also undertook lay preaching and, apparently, at this time aspired to full-time public evangelism.

See: Search terms "Bean" and "Evans" in *Words of the Pioneers;* 1850 U.S. Federal Census, "Lewis Bean," Vermont, Caledonia County, Hardwick, p. 195; 1860 U.S. Federal Census, "Lewis Bean," Vermont, Lamoille County, Stowe, p. 264; 1850 U.S. Federal Census, "Derrick T. Evans," Vermont, Orange County, Corinth, p. 152.

company to keep the truth. But I saw that these brethren had not understood their work fully. God has not called them to give themselves unreservedly to the work. Oh, no, they can assist in the work and do errands for the Lord, but they should not feel to throw themselves on the church as messengers or as called and chosen servants of Jesus to travel from place to place, or State to State, to labor and preach.[3] Their time should not be occupied visiting the different churches; they do no good this way in traveling from church to church. The churches generally are just as well off without them. They have a duty to do in case ministers are absent, to baptize or administer the ordinances.[4] It is pleasant to visit the brethren and churches of Sabbathkeepers, but still the church is just as well off without such laborers, unless they have a special message to deliver. These should be careful of their time when they are not on a special errand for God, [and] labor with their hands, [doing] the thing that is good.[5]

Both of these brethren can be of use in their place, but they have thought the Lord has laid more upon them than He has. Brethren in Vermont should be careful and wait until the Lord lays the burden on men before they

---

[3] Reasons that Bean and Evans were unsuited to full-time itinerant ministry are set forth in Lts 20 and 21, 1859 (c. Sept. 24).

[4] It is probable that both Bean and Evans had been ordained as local elders. This statement, therefore, should not be understood as a sanction for unordained laypersons to administer baptism and the Lord's Supper. In 1854, for example, Ellen White had held up the example of the New Testament church, where men were "set apart by the laying on of hands" and then went "forth baptizing . . . and to administer the ordinances of the Lord's house." It seems likely that Ellen White here was simply expressing the judgment that Bean and Evans were qualified for the responsibilities of church elders but not for the wider preaching duties of traveling ministers. A church elder, as his duties were formally described in 1861, "may conduct the meetings of the church, and administer the ordinances of baptism and the Lord's supper in the absence of any higher officer." An elder's authority to baptize would later become more restricted.

See: Ellen G. White, *Supplement to the Christian Experience and Views of Ellen G. White,* p. 19; J. N. Loughborough, Moses Hull, M. E. Cornell, "Conference Address. Organization," *Review,* Oct. 15, 1861, p. 157; George R. Knight, "Early Seventh-day Adventists and Ordination, 1844-1863," in Nancy Vyhmeister, ed., *Women in Ministry: Biblical and Historical Perspectives,* pp. 108, 109.

[5] The trend of thought here seems to be that Bean and Evans should not strain the financial resources of the churches they visited, the practice at the time being that local churches would remunerate visiting preachers for their expenses. Rather, these men should support themselves by their respective trades and make only occasional preaching forays. As to whether Bean and Evans heeded the instruction given them in the years that followed, see notes on Lt 20, 1859 (Bean) and Lt 21, 1859 (Evans), both written circa September 24, 1859. In brief, it may be noted that during the following five years D. T. Evans showed no indication of heeding the testimony. In 1864 Ellen White took the exceptional step of discussing his case in the pamphlet *Testimony for the Church,* No. 10 (*Testimonies for the Church,* vol. 1, pp. 448, 449), although his name appeared only in the first printing. Lewis Bean, on the other hand, followed the counsel more closely. Rather than pursuing a preaching vocation, he served the church for many years as a member of the Vermont Conference executive committee and as conference president for five years.

encourage them to labor. Even if the Lord designs to use individuals, the brethren are in danger of hurrying them along, hurting them by encouraging them too much. They should be left to work their way along, and let God fit them for the work. Let them come along with the deep weight of the work upon them. Some are entirely spoiled by being hurried into the field before the Lord has prepared them for going.[6] Let them endure some hardships and obtain an experience in the work. Those who do not devote their whole time to labor in new fields, and carry the truth, should labor with their hands, and do what they can to supply their own necessities.

I saw that those whom the Holy Spirit and the brethren have set apart to the work will have something to carry, and as they have the burden and weight of the message, they will give unmistakable evidence of their calling. They will not be content merely to travel among the churches, but God will give them the burden to go out in other places where the truth has not been preached, and bring out individuals or a company into the truth. They should not enter into other men's labors and build on other men's foundations.

This evidence will the Lord give His church if He has called men into the field in visiting the different churches. The churches are generally just as well off without these laborers. They have a duty to do, and in case ministers are absent, to baptize or administer the ordinances. I saw that especially Bro. Bean should be careful of his time when he has not a special errand to do for the Lord. He should labor with his hands, [doing] the thing that is good. He can be of use in his place. He has thought the Lord has laid more upon him than He has.

Brethren should be careful and know that the Lord has laid burdens upon men before they encourage them in the field. Even if the Lord is fitting up individuals, the brethren are in danger of hurrying them along and hurting them. They should be left to work their way through and let the Lord fit them for the work. Let them come along with a deep weight of the work upon them, let them endure some hardships, some severe trials, and obtain an experience in the work. Those who are able and are not especially called of God to devote themselves entirely to the work of teaching the truth, should labor with their hands and supply their own necessities.

I saw that those who by the sanction of the brethren and the Holy Spirit are set apart to the work will have something to carry, and as they have the burden and weight of the message, will give unmistakable evidence of their calling. They cannot be content to travel among their brethren, but they will be burdened to go out into new places, and bring out individuals into the

---

[6] Of D. T. Evans Ellen White later wrote, "He has been exalted in his own estimation . . . and has felt that he should be . . . consulted in business matters of the church, when he has not earned a reputation nor proved himself worthy."

See: Ellen G. White, *Testimonies for the Church,* vol. 1, pp. 448, 449.

truth; and if those who have strength, work and preach, it will not require their influence at all, but give them better success. This evidence will God give those whom He has especially called. They will feel such burden for souls, such yearning for others out of the truth, they can but listen to His teachings, and with the Lord with them, they will convince souls.

But some are too easy who think they are called of God; they enter into other men's labors, and build on other men's foundations. Bro. Pierce [**Stephen Pierce**][7] the Lord has blessed and given freedom of speech; he should [not] be handing out his means to help others, but should seek to save his wife care and labor. He should study her convenience and comfort, but should not hand out his means at present. His time is money. His labor is needed in the field, and he must take a different course from what he has.[8]

Bro. Phillips [**Daniel C. Phillips**][9] has the gift of exhortation. He can do good, but he lets feeling govern him too much. He should lift when the work goes hard and he is not called to devote his time, but can fill in here and there. When he is not especially engaged in the work of God, [he] should be economical of his time, should not seek to be eased while others are burdened and have all they can do to get along.[10]

Brother Evans can do errands for God, can interest a congregation, but cannot travel extensively or be a thorough laborer. I was shown the case of Brother Bingham [**Hiram Bingham**].[11] He has a good gift, and can do good, fill in here and there, but his labors can not tell unless he has corresponding

---

[7] The only Vermont preacher surnamed "Pierce" at this time.

See: Search term "Pierce" in *Words of the Pioneers.*

[8] Ellen White had no reservations about the abilities of Stephen Pierce. On hearing him speak two weeks later at a public meeting in Roxbury, Vermont, she commented, "Brother Pierce exhorted and appealed to his townspeople . . . with power." Stephen Pierce proved his worth during the 1850s and 1860s as corresponding editor for the *Review*, speaker, and administrator, serving as president of both the Vermont and Minnesota conferences.

See: Ellen G. White, Lt 30, 1859 (Oct. 12).

[9] *Identity:* Since "Bro. Phillips" came from Vermont and was a preacher, it seems clear that this is Daniel C. Phillips, of Roxbury, Vermont, known for his powerful "exhortations."

See: Obituary: "D. C. Phillips," July 11, 1882, p. 446; Jno. Clarke, "From Bro. Clarke," *Review*, Apr. 1, 1862, p. 143; search term "Phillips" in *Words of the Pioneers.*

[10] Two years earlier Ellen White had been more positive about Daniel Phillips's potential. "I saw that Brn. Pierce and Phillips can be of use in the cause of God. Both their gifts are needed where they have not yet been." However, it appears that certain character deficiencies had become apparent in the intervening time and that these unfitted him for full-time preaching. As to the future, Phillips became involved in various compromising situations in the early 1860s that further curtailed his possibilities for service.

See: Ellen G. White, Lt 15, 1857 (c. 1857); Lt 22, 1859 (Oct. 10).

[11] *Identity:* According to the description given here, "Brother Bingham" is from Vermont (see first paragraph) and apparently does some preaching. The only person that fits this description is Hiram Bingham, from Morristown, Vermont, of whom one or two reports in the *Review* tell of his preaching during the 1850s.

See: H. Bingham, "From Bro. Bingham," *Review*, Feb. 4, 1858, p. 102.

works. He is not careful studying how he can best approach individuals, but broaches the subject abruptly, and injures his influence and the cause he loves. I saw that he should labor at home to set a holy, godly example, be patient, be kind and tender to his relatives and friends, especially his wife and children. His good influence should tell in the neighborhood.[12] He must not have a driving spirit, but a winning one. He can not drive souls into the truth but he can win them much more successfully than he can drive.

[12] The main tenor of the direction given here seems to be that although preaching was not Hiram Bingham's forte there were other ways in which he could serve God. Reports in the *Review* indicate that Bingham chose the latter path in the years that followed. He served on various Vermont Conference committees in the 1860s, transported preachers to various meetings, acted as agent for the *Review* in his town, and gave generously to various branches of church work. Hiram and his wife were also liberal in helping the needy in their own area. At Hiram Bingham's funeral the presiding Baptist minister testified that the Binghams "had done more to relieve the poor, afflicted, and destitute families than any other two persons of his knowledge."

See: Search term "H. Bingham" in *Review and Herald* online collection, www.adventistarchives.org; obituary: "Hiram Bingham," *Review*, Dec. 22, 1874, p. 206.

1859

(Ms 1a, 1859)

[CIRCA SEPTEMBER 24[1]] N.P.

The Cause in Vermont.

Previously unpublished.

Testimony for Vermont ministers: Need for thorough planning of meetings and to preach "the great principles of our faith" rather than "little particulars" of dress and personal behavior. Some current preachers unfitted for full-time, traveling ministry.

I was shown the state of things in Vermont. They should have order among them and have everything done up exact, straight and square. There is too much leaving things at loose ends. There should be order in regard to appointing meetings, and an understanding [of] who is to labor in these meetings.[2] There should be a perfect understanding that the help is sufficient to carry through these meetings in a right way, that the congregation should be held and that interest should exist all through the meeting. I saw that rather than to appoint meetings and the efforts be feeble and the gifts[3] such as not to interest, it would be better not to have such meetings, for the hearers judge the cause and the work to be all of one piece, and decide for error instead of truth.

I was shown that the churches in Vermont have been weakened by leaving the important truth to dwell on little things—to dwell on articles of dress and take notice of little things. There is a faultfinding spirit—neglecting their own soul's interest to keep their brethren and sisters straight. They neglect

---

[1] Although this manuscript is undated, the close verbal parallels between its opening paragraphs and the beginning of Ms 1, 1859, dated September 24, 1859, shows that it comprises a report of the same vision and would presumably have been written out about the same time. The difference between the two documents lies in the fact that Ms 1 goes into personal details that are given only general reference in Ms 1a, no doubt reflecting the fact that the documents were written for different audiences.

[2] A probable case of Vermont preachers "leaving things at loose ends" is found in Ellen White's diary a few weeks earlier. She noted that there was "great confusion" about the upcoming Vermont meetings at which she and James were scheduled to speak.

See: Ellen G. White, Ms 7, 1859 (Sept. 2 entry).

[3] "Gifts" in this case apparently refers to preachers or to their sermons. Cf. the following passage concerning two Vermont preachers: "I saw that Brn. Pierce and Phillips can be of use in the cause of God. Both their gifts are needed . . . where their gifts are new and can affect more."

See: Ellen G. White, Lt 15, 1857 (c. 1857).

the great principles of our faith to descend to little particulars. There has been a stiff, unbending spirit with some in Vermont and a desire to bend others to their ideas of right and to their notions, and they have been tried if other minds did not run in the same channel with their own concerning little things.

Feeling has governed some. They felt bad about this brother or that sister. They had on some article of dress, or there was some article of furniture in their house that you did not feel that they should have. But this does not concern you. Your feelings may be wrong. Dwell upon the important, saving truth, the great principles of our faith and religion, and then leave the brother or sister to the Lord and the angels to convict them of their wrong in dress or furniture or fixings. If they really love God and have extravagance about them, the Lord is just as willing to show them their wrong and convict them of their sin as He is to convict you, or somebody else, or lay a burden on some other one.

Preach the truth, and if the truth is received in the heart it will affect the receiver and purge wrongs from him. Don't be in too great haste. Leave the Spirit of the Lord time to do its work, time to correct wrongs; then the individual has an experience that is worth everything to him. I saw that the brethren in Vermont must not move from impulse but from principle, must not be governed by feeling or impressions, because they are liable to be deceived if they trust here or rely there. They must preach present truth straight, plain, and clear, and not come down from the important things to little things that do not concern them.

There must be a more strict attention paid by all to their own eternal welfare, to cultivate the good seed sown in their own heart, or before they are aware of it, while they are intently watching their brother or sister, poisonous weeds are choking the good seed in their own hearts. And are they then in a situation to remove or correct the wrong in their brethren? Oh, no.

I saw that some, when reproved by the gifts God has placed in the church, immediately commence to retaliate, begin to watch to see if they can't find something in an article of dress in the instrument God uses—the reprover—or in others, to find fault with. They encourage a faultfinding, complaining spirit and bring the displeasure of God upon them more than it was before. They add sin to sin. Instead of putting away their wrong, they hide it or cover it by gratifying their carnal mind in accusing their brother or sister.

I have been shown the case of those brethren who feel that God has called them into His vineyard. If God has called them, the burden and weight of the work will rest upon them; they will feel the burden of the message with power, and they will not exercise their gift so much among believers who have an understanding of the truth but among those in new fields, laboring by every effort, by prayer and holy living and talking the truth, to raise up a company of Sabbathkeepers. They will not run much among the brethren, accomplishing but little.

I saw that some brethren have not fully understood their work. The Lord has not called them to give themselves up wholly or unreservedly to the work of teaching the truth to others. They can assist in the work, do errands for the Lord, but they should not throw themselves wholly on the church as called and chosen servants of Jesus Christ are required to. They are not called to travel extensively from State to State. Their time should not be occupied . . . [remainder missing].[4]

[4] In a parallel account of this vision provided in Ms 1, 1859 (Sept. 24), Ellen White enlarges on the content of the last two paragraphs. She identifies the "brethren" who have misunderstood the extent of their calling as **Lewis Bean**, **D. T. Evans**, **Daniel C. Phillips**, and **Hiram Bingham**. Individual letters to the first three of these persons explaining the vision are found in Lts 20, 21, and 22, 1859 (c. Sept. 24 and Oct. 10).

1859

(Lt 20, 1859)

[CIRCA SEPTEMBER 24],[1] N.P.

LETTER TO

Lewis Bean.[2]

Previously unpublished.

Testimony to Lewis Bean: "You have mistaken your calling—it is not to travel and preach."

Brother B:

I will try to write you what has been shown concerning you. I was shown that if God had called you to devote yourself to His work, when you have not a special errand to do for the Lord, you should labor with your hands the thing that is good. You can be of use in your place. You have thought the Lord had laid more upon you than He has.

---

[1] This date estimate is based on the close verbal parallels between this letter and Ms 1, 1859, written on September 24, 1859. For an example, see note 2 below. Clearly, in both documents Ellen White is reporting the same vision. The only difference is that in Ms 1 she reports on the entire scope of the vision, which involved several persons, whereas in Lt 20 she writes to one of those persons, Lewis Bean, relating that part of the vision that was pertinent to his case. It is reasonable to conclude that the two documents were written about the same time.

[2] *Identity:* The close verbal parallels between the counsel given here to "Brother B" and that given to "Brother Bean" in Ms 1, 1859, make clear that they refer to the same person. The most striking parallel is between the first paragraph in Lt 20 and a passage in Ms 1:

> Lt 20, 1859: "I was shown that if God had called you to devote yourself to His work, when you have not a special errand to do for the Lord, you should labor with your hands the thing that is good. You can be of use in your place. You have thought the Lord had laid more upon you than He has."
>
> Ms 1, 1859: "I saw that especially Bro. Bean should be careful of his time when he has not a special errand to do for the Lord. He should labor with his hands, [doing] the thing that is good. He can be of use in his place. He has thought the Lord has laid more upon him than He has."

The question remains whether "Brother Bean" is Lewis Bean or his father, Samuel W. Bean, both of them Sabbathkeepers at this time. Of "Brother Bean" it is said in this letter that he has done some preaching, albeit not very successfully—"You cannot command attention, you cannot hold a congregation"; more specifically, that he had traveled and preached in Massachusetts. The *Review* carries reports of Lewis Bean's preaching in Massachusetts (July 1858) and Canada (November 1858), but there is no hint in the *Review* or elsewhere that Samuel W. Bean did any preaching.

See: Lewis Bean, "From Bro. Bean," *Review,* Dec. 9, 1858, p. 23; A. S. Hutchins, L. Bean, "New England Conference," *Review,* July 28, 1859, p. 80; search term "Bean" in *Review and Herald* online collection, www.adventistarchives.org.

Brethren should be careful, and know that the Lord has laid the burden upon men before they encourage them into the field. Even if the Lord is fitting up individuals, the brethren are in danger of hurrying them along and hurting them. They should be left to work their way through and let the Lord fit up and qualify men before urging them into the field. If God has called them, they will feel the deep weight of the work upon them. Let them endure hardships, suffer some severe trials, and obtain an experience in the work. Those who are able and are not especially called of God to devote their whole time especially to the work of teaching the truth, should labor with their hands and supply their own necessities.

I have seen that those who, by the sanction of their brethren and the Holy Spirit, are set apart for the work will have something to carry; they will give unmistakable evidence of their calling. Some who think they are called of God are altogether too easy. They enter into other men's labors and build on another man's foundation.

Dear brother, you have mistaken your calling—it is not to travel and preach. You cannot command attention, you cannot hold a congregation. If the Lord had called you to the work of teaching He would have qualified you for the work.[3] It is a great thing to stand between the living and the dead. It is a great thing to feel the burden of souls and to move judiciously and with wisdom as a servant of Jesus Christ should. You have moved too fast and accomplished but little. In the absence of ministers you can move forward to administer baptism if it is necessary, or attend to the ordinances of the Lord's house. You should hold yourself in readiness to advocate the truth whenever you can. This is the duty of everyone who has an understanding of the truth. All should glorify God and seek to save their fellow men in whatever circumstances they are placed.

I saw it was a fact that the brethren, instead of the Lord, were calling men into the gospel field. You have not been called of God to give yourself to the work of teaching the truth. You can do errands for the Lord. There are places and times where and when you can help in the work of God; but this is no

---

[3] Twelve years later, in 1871, Ellen White again wrote of Lewis Bean, "God has not called him especially to minister in word and doctrine." While earning his living as "carriage maker" and merchant Bean served the church in the years after 1859 more in the area of administration than preaching and public evangelism. For many years during the 1860s and 1870s he served on the executive committee of the Vermont Conference, and for five years, from 1870 to 1875, was conference president. Although he held ministerial credentials during most of the 1870s, after he became conference president there is little evidence in the *Review* that he engaged in public evangelism. In 1880 his credentials were not renewed for reasons not fully stated in available sources, and Lewis Bean left Vermont for Michigan, where he died eight years later.

See: Ellen G. White, *Testimonies for the Church,* vol. 2, p. 639; search terms "L. Bean" and "Lewis Bean" in *Review and Herald* online collection, www.adventistarchives.org; 1860 U.S. Federal Census, "Lewis Bean," Vermont, Lamoille County, Stowe, p. 264; SDAE, s. v. "Northern New England Conference"; Ellen G. White, Lt 41, 1880 (Sept. 16).

evidence that God has laid on you the burden of teaching. The Lord did not call you to travel in Massachusetts.[4] Your call to journey there was of no higher authority than your brethren. You cannot get the ears of the people. You are not fitted for the work. And there are others who have been thinking the Lord has a work for them to do to teach the present truth, but they are mistaken in this matter. If they should go, they would be self-made messengers.

[4] *See:* Note 2 above.

1859

(Lt 21, 1859)

[CIRCA SEPTEMBER 24],[1] N.P.

LETTER TO

D. T. Evans.[2]

Previously unpublished.

Weaknesses that unfit D. T. Evans for full-time ministerial work.

Brother E, I was shown in vision you could do errands for the Lord, but it would be of no use for you to travel extensively, for you cannot be a thorough laborer. You have not judgment and wisdom to fill the place that God's servants—who are chosen to teach the present truth and give themselves up wholly to the work—are required to fill. You are not judicious, not careful that your influence and your words tell on the right side. You are not fitted to direct in church matters or to officiate in church trials. Your influence would tend more to draw matters into perplexity than to get out of difficulty. You are not called to travel all the time, or give yourself wholly to the work.[3] You can at times do good in talking the truth where the way opens, but know that the Lord is with you and that He sends you to a place before you go. Every

---

[1] This estimated date is based on the close parallels between this letter and Ms 1, 1859, dated September 24, 1859 (see note 2 below). Clearly, in both documents Ellen White is reporting on the same vision. The only difference is that in Ms 1 she recounts the entire scope of the vision, which involved several persons, whereas in Lt 21 she writes to one of those persons, D. T. Evans, on that part of the vision relevant to him. It is reasonable to conclude that the two documents were written about the same time.

[2] *Identity:* The close parallels between the counsel given here to "Brother E" and that given to "Brother Evans" in Ms 1, 1859, establishes that they refer to the same person. Note this example:

> Ms 1, 1859: "Brother Evans can do errands for God, can interest a congregation, but cannot travel extensively or be a thorough laborer."
>
> Lt 21, 1859: "Brother E, I was shown in vision you could do errands for the Lord, but it would be of no use for you to travel extensively, for you cannot be a thorough laborer."

Ms 1, 1859, reveals that "Brother Evans" lives in Vermont. The only Vermont preacher with that surname during this period is "D. T. Evans," according to the *Review.* His first name appears to have been "Derrick" or "Dimmick," according to the 1850 and subsequent censuses.

See: Search term "Evans" in *Words of the Pioneers;* 1850 U.S. Federal Census, "Derrick T. Evans," Vermont, Orange County, Corinth, p. 152.

[3] Reports in the *Review* from 1857 onward indicate that D. T. Evans sometimes traveled and preached for weeks at a time in Vermont and Canada East. See, for example, Daniel T. Bourdeau, "Letter from Bro. Bourdeau," *Review,* Jan. 27, 1859, p. 77.

one of us is in duty bound to let his influence tell for the truth and advocate it wherever there is an opportunity.

You should not, I saw, give up entirely the idea of laboring with your hands, even if you suffer some inconvenience and unpleasant feelings. You are afraid of your strength. You lack ambition to labor, and should seek God for strength to labor if you lack strength.

There will have to be a great reform with some in Vermont. The idea that many have that the Lord has called them into the vineyard will have to be given up. The enemy is at work in this matter. You have thrown too much burden upon the church.[4] Exercise more,[5] care for your own family, and leave not all that heavy burden for the church while you are eased.[6]

---

[4] This theme is enlarged on in a testimony concerning Evans published five years later: "He has not been a thoroughgoing man in temporal matters, and although he has but a small family, he has needed assistance more or less." He has not been fully "willing to labor with his hands a part of the time to earn means to support his family that they may not be burdensome to the church." In the censuses of this period, Evans's occupation is listed as "shoe maker."

See: Ellen G. White, *Testimonies for the Church,* vol. 1, p. 448, originally published in 1864 in the pamphlet *Testimony for the Church,* No. 10. The first printing of this pamphlet included the name "Brother Evans," but subsequent printings omitted the name. *See also:* 1850 U.S. Federal Census, "Derrick T. Evans," Vermont, Orange County, Corinth, p. 152; 1870 U.S. Federal Census, "Evens [*sic*], Derrick," Vermont, Addison County, Granville, p. 17.

[5] "He has not had a suitable amount of exercise to give tone and strength to his muscles, and for the good of his health."

See: Ellen G. White, *Testimonies for the Church,* vol. 1, p. 448.

[6] To what extent D. T. Evans met the challenge of this testimony is not clear. Apparently there was little change up to 1864, when Ellen White wrote of his case again and pointed out the same problems. This time she took the exceptional step of publishing his name (although only in the first printing of the pamphlet—see note 4 above). Some months after his situation was published the Vermont Conference in session voted, in June 1864, "that Bro. Evans be left under the watchcare of the Executive Committee for them to encourage him to preach in his sphere, only as fast as he complies with the requirements of the last testimony given for his benefit." Not until 1868 was Evans issued a ministerial license again, which he held until 1874. After that there is no further mention in the *Review* of D. T. Evans as a minister. In the 1880 census he is listed as a "farmer" in Nebraska.

See: Ellen G. White, *Testimonies for the Church,* vol. 1, pp. 448, 449; Stephen Pierce, D. T. Bourdeau, "Second Annual Meeting of the Vermont State Conference," *Review,* June 28, 1864, p. 1; search term "Evans" in *Review and Herald* online collection, www.adventistarchives.org; 1880 U.S. Federal Census, "Evans, Dirrick [*sic*] T.," Nebraska, Valley County, Liberty Precinct, p. 14.

1859

(Lt 10, 1859)

[LATE SEPTEMBER],[1] N.P.

LETTER TO

William Clarence White.

Portions of this letter are published in Ellen G. White, *Manuscripts Releases,* vol. 3, pp. 121, 122.

A letter to her son Willie, age 5.

Dear little Willie:

We want to see you very much but it is eight weeks yet before we shall return home—a long time to be away from my children. In the last box we sent to Battle Creek were some little trinkets for you and a little box of candy. You must eat it only when Jenny **[Jane Fraser]**[2] thinks it is best. Eat a very little at a time.

We hope you are a good boy. We believe you are, and that you will make Jenny happy, for you know she will be so lonely when we are to be gone so long. Jenny loves you very much and you must please her. You must not get angry, but remember the Lord could not love you if you should be naughty.[3] Jenny says you are a good boy and this made us feel very glad. I suppose you

---

[1] The similarity in language and tone to other letters from Ellen White to 5-year-old Willie in 1859 (Lt 6 [Sept. 15] and Lt 9, 1859 [Sept. 6]) suggest that it is from the same year, or possibly from 1858 or 1860. An 1860 date can be excluded, however, because the letter was written on a journey that lasted more than eight weeks (see first line), and no such trip was undertaken by her that year. In 1858 the Whites traveled on a lengthy autumn itinerary, but it appears that Willie accompanied them (see note 4 in Lt 9, 1859), so no letters were called for. The autumn journey to the East in 1859 remains the best option. The approximate date "late September" is obtained by counting backwards eight weeks from November 21, the date the Whites returned to Battle Creek.

See: J. W. [James White], "At Home," *Review,* Dec. 8, 1859, p. 20.

[2] *Identity:* See note 9 in Lt 9, 1859 (Sept. 6).

[3] Some commentators see a contradiction between statements such as this and later statements such as "Do not teach your children that God does not love them when they do wrong" (*Signs of the Times,* Feb. 15, 1892). However, they can be harmonized. In the second example Ellen White seems to be speaking about God's love in the sense of His unconditional benevolence. Another standard dictionary definition of "love" is "to be pleased with" something or somebody. Clearly, God does not take pleasure in children or older persons when they engage in evil behavior. This seems the more natural interpretation of "love" when Ellen White urges Willie to remember that "the Lord could not love you if you should be naughty." For a more comprehensive discussion of this issue, together with bibliographical references, see Ms 1, 1854 (Feb. 12), note 19.

visit Grandpa and Grandma[4] every day, and have a good time talking to them.

I must tell you something I saw in the [railroad] cars. A wealthy gentleman took a little box from his pocket and wound it up like a watch. At the top of the box was a glass door, and open flew this little door and a little, tiny bit of a bird, with fine downy feathers popped up, and then forth from the box came a most beautiful song such as canaries sing. And the little feathers would move on the little bird, and it would twirl its pretty little head this way and that, flop its little wings, move its tail and fly about and act just as pretty as though the noise came from its tiny little throat. After the song was sung, down popped the little bird into the box, and down went the cover, and the man put the box into his pocket again. This little bird was artificial, made to look just like a little bird. We asked the man what it cost. He said $200.00 [?]. A great price!

Willie, good-by. Be a good little boy and I will write again soon.

In love. From your mother.

---

[4] **John** and **Betsey White**. (See note 8 in Lt 9, 1859 [Sept. 6].)

1859

(Lt 19, 1859)

OCTOBER 4, NEWPORT, NEW HAMPSHIRE

LETTER TO

Mary Ann Chamberlain.[1]

Previously unpublished.

Extreme interpretations of the Laodicean message by E. L. Barr and others: peremptory exclusion of members and the burning of daguerreotypes.

Dear Sister Chamberlain:

Duty compels me to write you a few lines. About one year ago when we visited the East, things were in great confusion. We were obliged to see things in the utmost confusion, and suffered much in mind on account of this wretched state of things. I was shown in vision while at Clinton [Massachusetts] the cause of this confusion. At the same time I was shown that it would be of no use for Brother Barr [**Eli L. Barr**][2] to travel among the churches East, for he could not do them good; that he had better be laboring in a humble way, working with his hands, than to do this; and that he possessed too much dignity, etc.[3]

---

[1] *Identity:* The name "Chamberlain" appears in quite a large number of the letters and receipts of the *Review* during the 1850s. Very little is said specifically of "Sister Chamberlain" in this letter that could help identify her except that she was involved in the burning of pictures. However, no sources have been found connecting a Chamberlain with such activities. More generally, the letter focuses on the activities and concerns of certain members living in Hartford County, Connecticut, thus implying that "Sister Chamberlain" was acquainted with these persons and probably was living in the same area herself. Two residents of Connecticut, mentioned in the *Review* during the 1850s, are Helen Chamberlain, from Windham County, and Mary Ann Chamberlain, living in Middletown, Hartford County. The latter person is likely the one to whom this letter was written, living, as she did, in the epicenter of the events described. Mary Ann was the widow of **E.L.H. Chamberlain**, pioneer layperson who had invited the Whites to the first of the "Sabbath and Sanctuary Conferences" in Rocky Hill, Connecticut, in 1848.

[2] *Identity:* "Brother Barr," we are told, was a traveling preacher "among the churches East," gave an extreme interpretation of the Laodicean message, and was involved in the burning of pictures. Only E. L. Barr fits this description. For further details, see notes below.

[3] Apart from this brief reference there is no extant record of the Clinton vision. Ellen and James White, together with J. N. Loughborough, had participated in meetings in Clinton, Massachusetts, Nov. 5-7, 1858. Perhaps the following statement in James White's report in the *Review* is an allusion to the vision: "[At] our meeting at Clinton, Mass. . . . the erring were reproved and the distracted and fainting ones were greatly encouraged."

While at Dartmouth, Mass., a few weeks since, again the power of God rested upon me and I was wrapped up in a vision of God's glory. In that vision I was shown the state of things in Connecticut, in Massachusetts, in Maine, and in New York City.[4] My soul was wrung with keen anguish as I saw the state of things. I was shown that the ministers, or those who professed to be servants of God, had caused much of this sad state of things for lack of real spiritual intelligence. Ministers of God should understand their work and their calling. They should not give the least influence to a hurried, fanatical spirit.

I saw that Brother Barr had done this, and when the message to the Laodiceans was given, a hurried fanatical spirit came in and burdens and exercises were had that the Lord was not in. No time was granted individuals to develop character. Angels of God were patiently waiting to weigh moral worth, and to mark the development of character. But some went ahead of the angels and were burdened and exercised because the work was not closed up at once. They did not wait patiently for the Lord to test character and to spue out the lukewarm, but took that work into their own hands; and unless they could see individuals coming up to the point they thought they should reach, they pushed them off.[5] A fear came over them—fear to associate with the ones they thought spued out of the mouth of the Lord. Why did they not read the connection—Rev. 3:18-22? A strange, fearful, excitable, fanatical spirit came in and bore rule.

I saw that if Brother Barr had understood his duty, he would have checked this spirit at once. But he was not standing in the counsel of the Lord. I was pointed to the work in Connecticut. Oh, what a work! The brethren Graham [**William Henry, Bruce**, and **Andrew Graham**][6] were led by a wrong spirit. Those burdens

---

See: J. W. [James White], "Eastern Tour," *Review*, Dec. 30, 1858, p. 45.

[4] The vision given Ellen White while visiting Dartmouth (Sept. 15-18, 1859) is related in Lts 7, 19, 16, and 17, 1859 (Sept. 24, Oct. 4, Oct. 28). The central theme is how the call for repentance in the Laodicean message had been distorted and misapplied in Connecticut (Lts 7, 19) and New York (Lts 16, 17).

[5] In the period after the autumn of 1856, when Sabbatarian Adventists had first begun to apply the Laodicean message (see EGWEnc) of Revelation 3 to their own movement, the call for repentance and wholehearted engagement had been positively received by many members. However, some, instead of pursuing personal reformation, turned their attention to the failings of fellow members. An extreme interpretation of the Laodicean message, condemned in this letter, pressed for speedy confession and reformation among members judged to be delinquent. Those unwilling or unable to promptly comply were thought to have been "spued out of the mouth of the Lord" (see Rev. 3:16) and consequently were ostracized by the rest of the group.

[6] *Identities:* One month earlier, while in Kensington, Connecticut, Ellen White noted in her diary that she had met Andrew, Bruce, and William Graham (Ms 7, 1859 [Sept. 2 entry]). All three are listed in the 1860 census of Berlin Township, in which Kensington is located. Census details strongly suggest that they were brothers. Further, the only Grahams in the *Review* of the 1850s who had Connecticut addresses are these three men. One of them, William Graham, was a deacon in the Berlin church for 20 years.

See: 1860 U.S. Federal Census, "Bruce Graham" and "Andrew Graham," Connecticut, Hartford County, Berlin, p. 53; 1860 U.S. Federal Census, "Wm H. Graham," Connecticut,

and exercises they had were not of the Lord. They were in a deception. Brother Barr encouraged this, and by his words created a fearful excitement when Sister Lyman[7] was set aside by one of these burdens. Brother Barr said, "'He that being often reproved hardeneth his neck shall suddenly be destroyed, and that without remedy.' Who goes next? There may be hope today; tomorrow it is gone."[8]

I was shown Sophronia C.[9] mixed up with these strange exercises; and the burdens and exercises for Mary North and John Wilcox [**Mary S.** and **John Y. Wilcox**][10] were uncalled for. It was not of God. They were made to believe that they had greatly sinned where there was no sin. Their thinking of marriage might have been injudicious; further than this they were not guilty, and the treatment of Mary was cruel in the extreme. God loves Mary and John.

Then the moves Brother Barr made in your place were not actuated by the Lord. It was in his own spirit he came to you. His influence over you and the burning of those pictures[11] and the cases[12] was not right. I was shown that this

---

Hartford County, Berlin, p. 34; search term "Graham" in *Words of the Pioneers;* obituary: "William Henry Graham," *Review,* July 2, 1925, p. 22.

[7] *Identity:* This might be Clarissa Lyman, about 75 years old, living in the home of Sabbatarian pioneers **Albert** and **Hannah Belden** in Berlin, Connecticut.

See: 1860 U.S. Federal Census, "Albert Belden," Connecticut, Hartford County, Berlin, p. 52.

[8] Although this particular statement cannot be traced, the following extract by E. L. Barr, published in the *Review*, illustrates his uncompromising stance. "Arise! ye that are heartily in the truth . . . and give a testimony that shall ring in the ears of the lukewarm, the self-righteous and the insubordinate ones, and clear your garments from the blood of all men! . . . No hiding nor covering up wrongs now! No half-way work any longer! 'He that being often reproved hardeneth his neck shall suddenly be destroyed and that without remedy.' Prov. xxix, 1."

See: E. L. Barr, "The Cause in the East," *Review,* Aug. 5, 1858, p. 96.

[9] It is possible that Sophronia Chamberlain, originally from Maine, is referred to here (not a daughter of Mary Ann Chamberlain, addressee of this letter). About 20 years old at this time, she subsequently married one of the Graham brothers, Andrew Graham, sometime after his first wife died in 1862.

See: 1870 U.S. Federal Census, "Sophronia C. Graham," Michigan, Calhoun County, Battle Creek, p. 21; obituary: "Sophronia Graham," *Review,* July 18, 1871, p. 39.

[10] *Identity:* See note 8 in Lt 7, 1859 (Sept. 24), for evidence of these identifications.

[11] Although not mentioning E. L. Barr by name, James White no doubt had him, among others, in mind when he complained in the next *Review* of those preachers who had "run from place to place on the cars, encouraging a fanatical spirit in burning daguerreotypes &c., worse than wasting their Lord's money, and leaving the brethren in distraction." Originating in France in 1839, daguerreotype photographs achieved their greatest popularity in the United States in the 1840s and 1850s. Prices for a medium-size portrait in the early 1850s ranged from 50 cents to $2, depending on quality. At a time when unskilled labor averaged about $1.00 a day in the Midwest and $1.10 in the Northeast this was a considerable outlay, although more affordable for the middle classes. Part of Barr's criticism was that the daguerreotype craze had led members to use scarce funds that could have been better spent, and on this point both Ellen and James White would no doubt have agreed. Barr's problem, his "fanatical spirit," was to go to extremes and press for the burning of daguerreotypes owned by members.

See: J. W. [James White], "New Fields," *Review,* Oct. 6, 1859, p. 156; Beaumont Newhall, *The Daguerreotype in America,* pp. 11, 63; Robert A. Margo, *Wages and Labor Markets in the United States, 1820-1860,* pp. 67, 68.

[12] Daguerreotypes had glass surfaces and needed the protection of velvet-lined cases.

was a loss that need not to have been. The cases could have been exchanged for something useful. And then again I saw that there was destruction of property that was not your own. It belonged to another. And if you could not conscientiously keep it you should have handed it to the owners and then you would be clear, your duty done, and they could find no reason . . . [remainder missing].

See: Newhall, *The Daguerreotype in America,* p. 11.

1859

OCTOBER 4, NEWPORT, NEW HAMPSHIRE

LETTER TO

Henry Nichols White.

Published in Ellen G. White, *An Appeal to the Youth*, pp. 50, 51.

1859

(Lt 22, 1859)

OCTOBER 10, ROXBURY, VERMONT[1]

LETTER TO

Daniel C. Phillips.[2]

Previously unpublished.

Daniel C. Phillips called only to part-time ministry. His need to be more self-sufficient financially.

Dear Brother P.:

I was shown that you have the gift of exhortation. You can do good, but you let feeling govern you too much. You should lift when the work goes hard.

I was shown that you are not called to devote your whole time to exhortation, but can fill in here and there. When you are not especially engaged in this work of God you should be economical of your time, and should not seek to be eased while others are burdened and have all that they

---

[1] Ellen White's original handwritten letter gives no place or date of writing, but an early copy bears the heading "Roxbury, Vt., October 10, 1859." Moreover, this letter is closely related to the content (and even wording) of Ms 1, 1859, dated September 24, 1859 (see note below), strongly suggesting that both documents were written about the same time.

[2] *Identity:* Although this letter is simply addressed "Dear Brother P." in the original, the early copy mentioned above reads "Dear Brother Phillips." In addition, the close verbal parallels between the counsel given here and that given to "Brother Phillips" in Ms 1, 1859, make it certain that they refer to the same person. See, for example:

Ms 1, 1859: "Bro. Phillips has the gift of exhortation. He can do good, but he lets feeling govern him too much. He should lift when the work goes hard and he is

can do to get along. Your time should be spent to glorify God. It has troubled the minds of many that some are eased while they are burdened.[3]

Those who have property have a duty to do to dispose of their means to God's glory, but the burden does not rest alone upon them. Many of them have acquired their property by hard labor. They used their strength lent them of God, to obtain what they have. Responsibilities rest upon them to dispose of their means in a right manner to honor God. And those who have strength of body should use their time and strength to God's glory, and provide for themselves, and do even more than this. They could bless others by advancing the cause of God with the means earned by the sweat of the brow. They should not live upon the bounty of others, but be diligent in business, fervent in spirit, serving the Lord.

> not called to devote his time, but can fill in here and there. When he is not especially engaged in the work of God, [he] should be economical of his time, should not seek to be eased while others are burdened and have all they can do to get along."
>
> Lt 22, 1859: "You have the gift of exhortation. You can do good, but you let feeling govern you too much. You should lift when the work goes hard. I was shown that you are not called to devote your whole time to exhortation, but can fill in here and there. When you are not especially engaged in this work of God you should be economical of your time, and should not seek to be eased while others are burdened and have all that they can do to get along."

Since Ms 1, 1859, informs us that this "Brother Phillips" came from Vermont, the only clear candidate seems to be Daniel C. Phillips, of Roxbury, Vermont, who traveled with preachers in the 1850s and was known for his powerful "exhortations."

See: Obituary: "D. C. Phillips," *Review,* July 11, 1882, p. 446; Jno. Clarke, "From Bro. Clarke," *Review,* Apr. 1, 1862, p. 143; search term "Phillips" in *Words of the Pioneers.*

[3] In Lt 4, 1864 (Jan. 12), to Phillips, Ellen White is more specific. She recalls the time he assisted in tent meetings, probably those in Illinois during the summer of 1857 (the only tent meetings involving Phillips reported on in the *Review*). "You were not what God required you to be when you went around with the tent. Your love of ease . . . led you to shun responsibilities and shirk the burdens upon others. You were ever seeking to have an easy time." The response of Phillips to this and subsequent visions concerning the direction of his life was not entirely positive. After some effective ministry in the 1850s he became involved in several compromising situations that curtailed his usefulness.

See: Ellen G. White, Lt 2, 1862 (Jan. 20); Lt 4, 1864 (Jan. 12); Lt 4a, 1864 (c. Jan.); Lt 4b, 1864 (Dec. 23).

1859

(Lt 30, 1859)

OCTOBER 12,[1] ENOSBURG, VERMONT

LETTER TO

Friends.[2]

Portions of this letter are published in Ellen G. White, *Manuscript Releases,* vol. 5, p. 231.

News of travels and labors in Vermont to friends at home in Battle Creek.

Dear Friends:

We have just arrived at Brother Saxby's [**John Saxby**],[3] a wealthy, homespun farmer; he is an Englishman, came into this country with nothing, is worth now somewhere about three or eight thousand.

We are very tired. [We] were awake this morn at three o'clock, arose at four, took breakfast half past four and were on our way to Northfield [Vermont] at five o'clock A.M. Brother Howard [**Daniel Howard**][4] carried us with his team seven miles [11 kilometers] to Northfield; took the [railroad] cars for

---

[1] The earliest copy of this letter bears the year 1854, but the copyist undoubtedly mistook a "9" for a "4." The evidence for this, in part, is that James White invariably reported on longer travel itineraries in the *Review*, but he makes no mention of any travels in Vermont during the autumn of 1854. More telling are Ellen White's diary entries for October 10-12, 1859, that match many of the details found in this letter. For example, according to the diary for October 12, the Whites awoke at 3:00, arose at 4:00, ate breakfast at half past 4:00, left at 5:00 for Northfield, driven by Brother Howard, and continued to St. Albans, where Brother Bourdeau would meet them. All of these details are found in this letter.

See: Ellen G. White, Ms 8, 1859 (Oct. 10-12 entries).

[2] The ending of the letter suggests that the letter is directed to members of the White household.

[3] *Identity:* John Saxby, of Bakersfield, Vermont, frequently mentioned in the *Review* during this period. The 1860 census lists his place of origin as England and the value of his real and personal property at $3,871.

See: 1860 U.S. Federal Census, "John Saxby," Vermont, Franklin County, Bakersfield, p. 23; search words "John" or "Jno" "Saxby" in *Words of the Pioneers.*

[4] *Identity:* It can with some certainty be concluded that it was Daniel Howard who drove Ellen and James White the seven miles (11 kilometers) to Northfield. In the 1860 census he is listed under Northfield, Vermont, together with "Clarissa," age 41. About five years later the *Review* carried an obituary for "Clarissa, wife of Bro. Daniel Howard, aged 45 years and 8 months."

See: Obituary: "Clarissa Howard," *Review,* Feb. 14, 1865, p. 95; 1860 U.S. Federal Census, "Daniel Howard," Vermont, Washington County, Northfield, p. 220.

St. Albans [Vermont]. Arrived at that place [at] half past 11 A.M. and found Brother Augustin Bourdeau [**Augustin Cornelius Bourdeau**] and Bro. Saxby waiting with easy teams to take us 14 miles [22 kilometers] to Brother Saxby's. We tarry here tonight, tomorrow we leave for Augustin Bourdeau's, who lives two miles [three kilometers] from this place.[5] Shall tarry there until Friday and then he will take us in his carriage ten miles [16 kilometers] farther to the meeting (to Berkshire) [Vermont].

I will now go back to give you a little history of the meeting.[6] Meetings commenced Friday afternoon. We arrived at Roxbury [Vermont] Thursday noon. Next morn early one of Brother Pierce's [**Stephen Pierce**][7] sons was at the door of Brother Grant [**Harrison Grant**][8] with a team for to take us to his father's. It was climbing a mountain half a mile [.8 kilometers] long. We visited at Brother Pierce's until noon and then went back again to Roxbury about three miles [five kilometers]. Was obliged to shut myself from the company to write.

Sabbath morn it was very stormy. We had a snow storm and there fell above one inch [2.5 centimeters] of snow. Our congregation was quite large, and attention good. Sunday nearly all of Roxbury was out, the large courthouse was filled, and there was the deepest attention and interest. We had a good interview with old friends but so many wanted advice upon this matter and that, and I had so much writing to do to individuals, at the close of the meeting I was more exhausted than I had been to any previous meeting. My head was in a complete whirl.

James had good liberty in preaching. He talked three times Sabbath, and twice Sunday. I followed in exhortation. I had great freedom in talking upon faith, that faith and feeling should not be confounded together. They

---

[5] A. C. Bourdeau lived in Enosburg township, adjoining Bakersfield township, where John Saxby had his farm.

See: SDAE, s.v. "Augustin Cornelius Bourdeau"; 1860 U.S. Federal Census, "A. C. Bordeau [*sic*]," Vermont, Franklin County, Enosburgh, p. 43.

[6] Ellen White is here returning to the events of the previous weekend, with the meetings in Roxbury, Vermont, which had been advertised in the *Review* for Sabbath and Sunday, October 8 and 9.

See: James White, "Appointments," *Review,* Sept. 15, 1859, p. 136.

[7] *Identity:* According to the information given, "Brother Pierce" lives in the vicinity of Roxbury and (further on in the letter) is a powerful speaker. Stephen Pierce fits both of these specifications. He is mentioned in the *Review* as living in Roxbury during this period. He was also a prominent preacher and later church administrator.

See: J. A. and M. A. Spofford, "From Bro. & Sr. Spofford," *Review,* May 20, 1858, p. 7; SDAE, s.v. "Stephen Pierce."

[8] *Identity:* Although there are a number of Sabbathkeepers with the surname "Grant" mentioned in the *Review* during this period, only Harrison Grant is said to live in Roxbury, Vermont.

See: Search term "Grant" in *Words of the Pioneers;* Harrison Grant, "To the Churches in Vt.," *Review,* Aug. 5, 1862, p. 80.

are distinct as the east is from the west. In the darkest hours it is then we should exercise faith, and not suffer our feelings to govern us, but press our faith through the dark clouds to the throne of God and claim the blessing of Heaven. When our faith grasps the blessing then the blessing is ours, for our faith has got hold [of] it, and when our faith brings the blessing down to us—when the dark clouds scatter and divine rays of light from Jesus illumine our darkness—then it is no more faith; it is feeling. The evidence has come and it is feeling that has swallowed up the faith. This view of faith and feeling seemed to enlighten some minds and we had a most powerful conference meeting. Brother Pierce talked with great freedom and power, also Brother Phillips [**Daniel C. Phillips**].[9] Brother Pierce exhorted and appealed to his townspeople and neighbors with power. He appealed to those with whom he had been engaged in business and in civil matters together and entreated them to examine the truth of the Sabbath.

Our meeting ended well, leaving a good influence. Monday we visited Brother Pierce's family but was obliged to write nearly all the time while there.

Tuesday morn we parted with Brother and Sister Hutchins [**Alfred S.** and **Esther M. Hutchins**], Brother and Sister Sperry [**Charles W.** and **Rachel Ann Sperry**][10] and went into Roxbury three miles [five kilometers], took dinner, packed our trunks and then Brother Howard took us up to his house about four miles [six kilometers]; one mile [1.6 kilometers] was up a mountain a mile long. Next morn we awoke at three and took breakfast at four. At five o'clock A.M. Brother Howard helped us to Northfield seven miles [11 kilometers] with his team. Then we took the cars for Enosburg [Vermont] [and] arrived there at 11 o'clock A.M.[11] Found Brother Cornelius Bourdeau

---

[9] *Identity:* An obituary notice in the *Review* reveals a Daniel Phillips living in Roxbury in 1859, so there is some likelihood that Ellen White is writing here of Daniel Phillips. The likelihood is increased by independent evidence that Daniel Phillips used to speak at meetings. (According to census information his middle initial was "C" and there are two or three references in the *Review* to a "D. C. Phillips" who delivered "stirring testimonies" and had a "gift in prayer and exhortation.")

See: Obituary: "Amanda Phillips," *Review,* Mar. 24, 1859, p. 143; 1850 U.S. Federal Census, "Daniel C. Philips," Vermont, Orange County, Randolph, p. 243; "Report of Meetings in Ohio," *Review,* Feb. 25, 1862, p. 101; obituary: "D. C. Phillips," *Review,* July 11, 1882, p. 446.

[10] *Identities:* According to James White's report of this tour, Ellen and he did not just happen to meet two couples with the names Hutchins and Sperry in Roxbury, but "brethren Hutchins and Sperry" were evidently preachers. James White reported that they "tarried after the Conference to hold more meetings in the large town-house." In the *Review,* between 1853 and 1861, there are a dozen or so reports of Alfred S. Hutchins and Charles W. Sperry teaming up together to give lecture series in Vermont, Canada, and New York.

See: J. W. [James White], "Eastern Tour," *Review,* Nov. 10, 1859, p. 196; search terms "Hutchins" and "Sperry" in *Words of the Pioneers;* obituary: "Charles W. Sperry," *Review,* Oct. 1, 1861, p. 143; SDAE, s.v. "Alfred S. Hutchins."

[11] Ellen White here returns to details of their journey from Roxbury on October 12 that she had already related in the opening two paragraphs. On one or two points, such as whether

[**Augustin Cornelius Bourdeau**] waiting for us with two teams. James and self took one, and he the other, and we rode 14 miles [22 kilometers] to Brother Saxby's quite comfortably. But here again we had to climb mountains. In every direction we have yet traveled since we entered Vt. we have had to climb mountains.

Yesterday morn we came to Bro. Bourdeau's. Today we leave for Berkshire, but it rains now and we shall wait until it clears off. Excuse my scribbling, Martha [**Martha Dormer Amadon** (née **Byington**)].[12] Much love to your parents and brothers.[13] I would say Martha, Edson [**James Edson White**] has new stockings somewhere at home in that old chest or in that basket of stockings. Don't let him want for anything.

Write us a long letter at Lapeer[14] [Michigan].

---

they got off the train at St. Albans or Enosburg, the two accounts disagree, and this can be attributed to simple error.

[12] *Identity:* These closing sentences suggest that "Martha" was assisting in the White household. Eighteen months earlier, in March 1858, Ellen, while traveling, had written to her children about "sisters Jenny and Martha" who "care for you, that we may leave home feeling free." "Martha" is almost certainly Martha Dormer Byington, who worked in the White household at least periodically from 1857 until her marriage in 1860. Her diary indicates that she provided private tutoring for the White boys.

See: Ellen G. White, *An Appeal to the Youth,* p. 43; Martha Byington, 1857 diary.

[13] Martha's parents were **John** and **Catherine Byington**, who had moved to Battle Creek in 1858. Her two sisters had died in the early fifties. According to the 1860 census, Martha's brothers Luther (age 21) and William W. (age 19) were still living at home with their parents.

See: 1860 U.S. Federal Census, "John Byington," Michigan, Calhoun County, Newton, p. 244; SDAE, s.v. "John Byington."

[14] According to the schedule of appointments published by James White in the *Review,* the Whites would attend a conference at Lapeer, Michigan, on November 5 and 6.

See: James White, "Appointments," *Review,* Sept. 15, 1859, p. 136.

1859

(Lt 11, 1859)

OCTOBER 15, ENOSBURG, VERMONT

LETTER TO

James Edson White.

This letter is published in entirety in Ellen G. White, *An Appeal to the Youth,* pp. 52, 53.

A letter to her son Edson White, age 10.

My dear Edson:

I have written you a letter of four pages not long ago,[1] but will write you again this afternoon.

The Lord has been very merciful to me on this journey[2] and has given me better health than I have had for one year. I have felt quite lighthearted and at times have felt the sweet peace of God resting upon me.

How is it with you, Eddie? Are you any homesick or do you keep so busy you do not find time to be homesick?[3] I suppose your time is all usefully employed. We do not mean that you shall work all the time. Light work will not hurt you but be healthy exercise for you. We hope you will make some progress in your studies while we are absent.[4]

---

[1] This letter has not been preserved.

[2] At this point the Whites were about two months into a three-month itinerary through New York, Connecticut, Massachusetts, Maine, New Hampshire, and Vermont. For more details of this journey, see Ellen White's diary account in Mss 7 and 8, 1859 (July-Nov.).

[3] As explained in the next paragraph, Edson, for some unknown reason, was temporarily staying with another family. Apparently by the end of October he had moved back home again, as is implied by the fact that Ellen White addresses her letter of October 30 to both Henry and Edson (*An Appeal to the Youth,* pp. 53-56).

[4] John Fletcher Byington had opened a school for Sabbatarian Adventist children in Battle Creek in November 1858. It is possible that Edson was enrolled in this school at the time of writing, especially since James White had given it his recommendation in the *Review*. The uncertainty lies in the fact that Byington's school failed and closed down "after a brief and stormy experience." According to W. C. White, James White "hired a private teacher for his own children, at times, as his finances would permit." One such private teacher had been Martha Byington, who taught "the White boys" beginning in late 1857 (see Ms 5, 1859 [notes under entry for Mar. 6]).

See: W. C. White, "Memories and Records" (DF 256) (Ellen G. White Estate, n.d.), p. 2; James White, "School at Battle Creek," *Review,* Jan. 14, 1858, p. 80; C. Smith, J. P. Kellogg, "A School in Battle Creek," *Review,* Oct. 14, 1858, p. 168. For a history of early school ventures in Battle Creek, see Floyd Greenleaf, *In Passion for the World,* pp. 16-21; Emmett K. Vande Vere, *The Wisdom Seekers,* pp. 11-14; E. M. Cadwallader, *A History of Seventh-day Adventist Education*, pp. 5-8, 21-23.

Be faithful, Eddie, and take a right course, that those who so kindly care for you may love and respect you. I have been so grateful to hear such good news from you—that you were trying to do right and that you had not been wrong or caused the family grief that you are with.

I want to tell you a little circumstance: Yesterday we were with a family where there was a poor, sick, lame boy. He is a cripple for life and never will be able to walk or run like other boys. We inquired into the case and found this poor boy's affliction was caused by his going into a brook of water when he was warm. He has since been a great sufferer. He has a great ugly sore on his hip, which runs all the time, and one limb is drawn up some inches shorter than the other. He is a pale, sickly, feeble little fellow—has been so for five years.

You may sometimes think we are too careful of you and are too particular to keep you out of the river.[5] My dear boy, think of this poor cripple. How easy it is for a young child like you to be a little careless or venturesome and make himself a cripple or invalid for life. I thought, What if this poor boy were mine? What if I should be compelled to see you suffer so? Oh, how my heart would ache that I had not been more careful of you. Eddie, I could but weep as I thought these things. Father and mother love you very much. We instruct you and warn you for your good.

From your affectionate mother.

[5] The Kalamazoo River ran just a few hundred yards from the White home on Wood Street in Battle Creek. Ellen White wrote in 1865 of Edson's "strong desire to go on the river" despite his parents' prohibition. "I think every day it would be nothing strange if my boys should go on the water contrary to our wishes, and one or both of them be drowned in their act of disobedience." Ellen White had reason to be anxious. The previous summer, while the parents were traveling, it had come to light that Edson had not only gone into the river four times but also taken 9-year-old Willie with him. (By then the Whites had moved from Wood Street but still lived close to the Kalamazoo River.)

See: Ellen G. White, Lt 4, 1865 (June 20); Gerald Wheeler, *James White,* pp. 92, 93.

1859

OCTOBER 22, [MANNSVILLE, NEW YORK]

LETTER TO
William Clarence White.

Records indicate a letter may have been written on this date, but no letter is found in the White Estate archives.

1859

(Lt 16, 1859)

OCTOBER 28, HUBBARDSVILLE, NEW YORK[1]

LETTER TO
Samuel W. Rhodes.[2]

Previously unpublished.

Regarding S. W. Rhodes's repeated failure to amend his harshness in handling church affairs.

Dear Brother Rhodes:

Duty compels me to write you a few lines. While at Dartmouth, Massachusetts,[3] I was shown the individual cases of some, and among them of

---

[1] The Whites' visit to Hubbardsville, New York, was part of a three-month tour through several Eastern states: August 17-November 21, 1859.

See: Ellen G. White, Ms 7, 1859 (Aug. 17 entry); J. W. [James White], "At Home," *Review,* Dec. 8, 1859, p. 20.

[2] *Identity:* "Brother Rhodes" is characterized in this letter as a minister, specific mention being made of his work in Roosevelt, Lincklaen, and Lorraine, all in New York. This matches accounts found in the *Review* of the ministry of Samuel W. Rhodes in the 1850s. Further strengthening the identity are the frequent references to his impatience and harshness, a theme that reappears in other letters from Ellen White to S. W. Rhodes.

See: Search term "Rhodes" in *Words of the Pioneers.* On S. W. Rhodes's severity see, for example, Ellen G. White, Ms 1, 1853 (June 2); Ms 6, 1854 (Feb. 19); Lt 16, 1859 (Oct. 28); Lt 5a, 1861 (Apr. 5).

[3] James and Ellen White had visited Dartmouth, Massachusetts, six weeks earlier, on September 17 and 18, 1859.

those who had been laboring in word and doctrine. The course that has been pursued by different ones and the influence that has been exerted among the flock of God were presented before me.

I was shown, dear brother, the course that has been pursued by yourself, and its influence. I was shown that you could not be right until you undo what you have done. What had been shown in your case was again presented before me.[4] I saw that you had covered this up, instead of acting upon it and counteracting the wrong influence you have exerted. I saw that there had been fears in your mind that if the churches were aware of the reproofs you have had, and you should acknowledge you had moved wrongly, that it would destroy your influence, destroy the confidence of the church in you.[5] Here the enemy deceives you, and the wrong influence you have exerted has been, and still is, a stumbling block to many. This stumbling block must be removed by yourself.

I can hold my peace no longer. There are things that must be corrected in the church if they are ever brought into the unity of the faith. You have moved from impulse. You have acted out your feelings and talked hard to different ones, reproving sharply, bearing on individuals with much severity, when there was no occasion for it, except your feelings. You feel strong and act strong—go to extremes.

I was shown that it would be some time before the churches in this state lived down and come out from all the wrong instruction they have received. At Roosevelt [New York] I saw it was cleaving to them like the leprosy, and they will be plunged into darkness and trial until they take an entirely different course.[6]

See: J. W. [James White], "Eastern Tour," *Review,* Oct. 13, 1859, p. 164.

[4] Three earlier visions (1853, 1854, 1857) had called Rhodes to account for his impatient, harsh manner, which had caused considerable damage to the young movement despite his undoubted talents as a preacher. Lt 16, 1859, makes it clear that Rhodes was still struggling with his unfortunate temperament.

See: Ellen G. White, Ms 1, 1853 (June 2); Ms 6, 1854 (Feb. 19); Lt 8, 1857 (July 19).

[5] After the censure and admonishment for Rhodes contained in Ellen White's vision of 1853, Rhodes had made a public confession in the *Review* of some of his failings without, however, acknowledging that the visions had played any part. It was not until 1861-1862 that Rhodes revealed the full story. Rhodes was not alone in trying to keep Ellen White's reproofs secret and in doing little to implement called-for changes. In 1861 she took the exceptional step of publishing the cases of Rhodes and some others in *Testimony for the Church,* No. 6. Her rationale: "I dare not commit them [the reproofs] alone to the individuals to be buried up by them, but shall read what the Lord has seen fit to give me, to those of experience in the church, and if the case demands, bring it before the whole church."

See: Ellen G. White, Ms 1, 1853 (June 2); S. W. Rhodes, "Letter from Bro. Rhodes," *Review,* Aug. 11, 1853, p. 55; *idem,* "From Bro. Rhodes," *Review,* Jan. 22, 1861, p. 78; *idem,* "From Bro. Rhodes," *Review,* May 6, 1862, p. 182; Ellen G. White, *Spiritual Gifts [vol. 2],* p. 293; Arthur L. White, *Ellen G. White: The Early Years,* pp. 434-437.

[6] Two years earlier Ellen White had written to Rhodes concerning the negative influence he was exerting on the churches in central New York, including Roosevelt. His contentious temperament had encouraged a spate of church disciplinary trials whereby "the professed people of God have disgraced themselves in the eyes of the world."

Your course in dictating to individuals is all wrong. It was no part of your work, telling what this one must do, and that one. It is for you to preach the Word and allow your brethren to have consciences, as well as yourself. You have been too forward to mark out the track for others. I was shown the sad state of things in Lincklaen [New York]. Such a state of things need not have been. Your hard speeches and severe reproofs, your decided, unyielding course, have been the means of placing the cause there in almost a hopeless condition.[7] God does not approbate harsh dealing in the church.

Lorraine [New York] was presented before me. Circumstances have come under your observation and you have made quick decisions, accordingly gave your opinion, and counseled when it would have been much better had you remained silent. Your counsel, and the position you took in the cases of Brother Brigham and his wife [**William Henry Brigham** and **Polly A. Brigham**],[8] instead of mending the difficulty, made it worse. He is a quick-tempered, passionate man, but your influence and advice were not correct. Sister Brigham was in fault and was not careful and judicious to carry herself just as she should, and has taken advantage from what you have said to get out of her place. She has not always occupied the position a wife should.

Sister Horr[9] has not been right; she has exercised more authority than she should and had she feared less the influence of her husband and occupied the humble position a wife should, she would have saved herself much trouble and perplexity that she has endured. There has been a great deal of fear of her husband's influence that was all unnecessary. She has done wrong. You have been at fault in deciding for or against individuals by what comes under your observation. There are always two sides to a matter, and many times your influence has been cast all on the wrong side.

Dear Brother, your quick, sharp rebukes, your dictating to individuals, and marking out the course they should follow, has been wrong. Independent, thinking minds will not bear it. And God has not laid that work upon you. You could have had a good influence in this state, but you have killed your own influence by sharp talk, if one differed from you, to pass sentence upon him.

See: Ellen G. White, Lt 8, 1857 (July 19).

[7] Almost five years earlier Ellen White, commenting on "the state of things in Lincklaen," noted that "a right influence had not been exerted by Bro. Rhodes," who "possessed an overbearing spirit . . . and has often . . . misjudged individuals."

See: Ellen G. White, Ms 6, 1854 (Feb. 19).

[8] *Identity:* Out of the dozen or so Brighams mentioned in the *Review* during the 1850s only "Wm. H." is explicitly identified as coming from Lorraine, New York, thus corresponding with Ellen White's description. His full name and that of his wife are given in obituaries.

See: Search term "Brigham" in *Words of the Pioneers;* obituary: "Wm. Henry Brigham," *Review,* May 29, 1866, p. 207; obituary: "William H. Brigham," *Review,* July 10, 1866, p. 47.

[9] This person has not been identified.

The church of God will not bear this; they know it is not the spirit in which the gospel should be carried.

There may be times when we shall be called upon to deal plainly, to rebuke, to reprove with all longsuffering and doctrine. The doctrine must do this sharp work, not *our words,* and there must be *longsuffering.* You must not be impatient and in a great hurry to have one come up exactly where you think he ought to come at once. Leave time for the angels of God to do their work, to move on hearts, to correct wrongs. Let the truth carry on its purifying process. Teach individuals to move from principle, not from feelings or impulse. Allow that others have a conscience as well as you, and let the angels of God convict that conscience, and then the individuals will have an experience that is worth everything to them.

Many have depended on you to have an experience for them, because you have told them what they *must* do, and what they *must* not do. Everyone must have a living experience of his own, an individual experience. "Let brotherly love continue." "Be pitiful, be courteous." Dear brother, it grieves me while I write, but I dare not withhold. You have not acted on what the Lord has shown concerning you. You have not done as you would mark out for others to do in like circumstances. It is your duty to correct the wrong influence you have exerted. You have set the church an example and have noticed little things, and have had many church trials that have proved a curse instead of a blessing. You have not dwelt upon the living principles of our faith but descended to little particulars, and entered into family matters that in no way concerned you. Many that God loved, you have rebuked and reproved in such a manner that they have been driven off and become completely discouraged. Yet God's pitiful eye is over them, and He will yet reach down His arm to receive them.

Those who carry the truth must take a thoughtful, steady course, and their everyday life must be marked with kindness, mercy, compassion, and tenderness. It must not be fitful, impulsive, quick, or retaliating. The servants of Jesus Christ must take such a consistent course that their faith will recommend itself to the understanding of good men, and win unbelievers to the truth.

Servants of God must manifest great wisdom and judgment in dealing with minds. They must remember there are many minds and many differences, and these minds are to be made as one mind. The great principles of our faith are to be brought to harmonize the different minds and make them of one mind and one judgment, but this work cannot be done at once. The ministers of Christ are to do their work, preach the Word, talk the principles, and the angels of God are moving upon these minds constantly to correct evils and bring them into the one channel. You have been in too great a hurry, and have felt too uneasy, nervous, and easily irritated, and this has had a scattering influence. We should all be coworkers together to have a gathering instead of a scattering influence; gather with the angels of God.

Dear Brother, you have not been calm, patient with your brethren. You have not been impartial, but your judgment has often been partial and one-sided. May the Lord help you to purify your soul through obeying the truth. I saw that you have a work to do. Undo what you have done.

Don't smother what the Lord has shown in regard to you. There is scarcely an individual that knows that you have ever been reproved.[10] You have felt afraid to let matters come out as they are. You must change your course, and come into a different position. You have been easily irritated. You have let your tried feelings run away with you. You have destroyed your own influence, and cut and hewed to the right hand and the left and wounded others and your own soul. You have been very set and willful and very unwilling to confess your wrongs in this state. May the Lord open your eyes to see clearly, is my prayer.

---

[10] *See:* Note 5 above.

1859

(Lt 17, 1859)

OCTOBER 28, HUBBARDSVILLE, NEW YORK[1]

LETTER TO
Friends at Roosevelt.
Previously unpublished.

Misunderstanding the intent of the Laodicean message in New York State, particularly in Roosevelt.

Dear Friends at Roosevelt:

I have a duty to do to free my soul in writing you.

While at Dartmouth, Massachusetts, the state of the cause of God in different places was shown me,[2] together with the different influences that have been exerted among the churches. I have been shown that wrong teaching and Satan's taking advantage of different temperaments, have placed things in a very discouraging situation in this state. Oh, the sad, sad work that has been made!

I was shown at Dartmouth that the wrong instruction and influence that have been given in Roosevelt [New York] have not yet been swept away, but cleave to some like the leprosy.[3] I saw that there was no need of the confusion that is there. Satan is unwilling to have wrong corrected in that place. I saw that there have been burdens and exercises there that the Lord did not give.

After the message to the Laodiceans was given, some thought others were not as zealous in repenting as they should be, and instead of taking care of their own souls' interest, they began to be burdened and to reprove and bear down upon their brethren.[4] This was not their work; and while they

---

[1] The Whites' visit to Hubbardsville, New York, was part of a three-month tour through several Eastern states: August 17-November 21, 1859.

See: Ellen G. White, Ms 7, 1859 (Aug. 17 entry); J. W. [James White], "At Home," *Review,* Dec. 8, 1859, p. 20.

[2] James and Ellen White had visited Dartmouth, Massachusetts, six weeks earlier, September 15-18, 1859. Part of the vision, relating to the situation in Roosevelt, New York, is found in this letter. Other parts of the Dartmouth vision dealing with circumstances in Connecticut and other states are found in Letters 7, 19, and 16, 1859 (Sept. 24, Oct. 4, Oct. 28).

See: J. W. [James White], "Eastern Tour," *Review,* Oct. 13, 1859, p. 164.

[3] In a letter to S. W. Rhodes written the same day Ellen White focused on his part in bringing about this sad state of affairs in the Roosevelt church.

See: Ellen G. White, Lt 16, 1859 (Oct. 28).

[4] The situation described in this section had arisen about three years earlier when the call

were thus engaged they got into a worse condition than those whom they were reproving. I saw it was an individual work. "Be zealous and repent." One is not to repent for his brother or sister, but for his own wrongs. Some have looked at and watched others and thought they were not moving fast enough—they did not move just to suit their idea of right—and impressions and burdens followed that God did not dictate. There was a bearing down upon others, binding burdens upon others that they should not bear.

I saw that the Lord had shown sufficient to correct these evils, but with some there was an unwillingness to be corrected, and a tenacious holding on to these burdens and reproofs that the Lord was not in.[5] I saw that individuals were looking back and seeking to straighten out the difficulty and select this impression or that burden to be of God. I saw that they had not wisdom to do this. They are just as liable to cherish an error or a wrong as the right. It was all darkness, their cutting and hewing, attending to others' consciences instead of their own, endeavoring to keep their brethren straight and neglecting their own souls. They will have to yield that experience back there. It is impossible for them to separate the right from the wrong. They should lay it to one side and commence anew. God is just as willing to give them again all the good they had back there. But some have taken the position that if they yielded that experience they should have to give up their whole Christian experience. This does not follow. The Lord has shown them to be wrong, and the safest course for them is to give up that wrong.

The Laodicean message was of God, but you were deceived as to the work accomplished by the message. There was not time given for the angels to do their work, there was not time given for the development of character. The angels of God are waiting for character to be developed and they are weighing moral worth.

I saw that the great care some have had of Brother Ross [**Alexander Ross**][6]

---

to the Laodicean church to be "zealous . . . and repent" (Rev. 3:19) had first begun to be applied by Sabbatarian Adventists to themselves. Revival had followed, as evidenced by many letters and articles on the Laodicean message in the *Review* during 1857. In some churches, however, the call to repent had led to an unhealthy concern over the shortcomings of fellow church members and to a rash of church disciplinary proceedings. Ellen White had addressed the churches of central New York in July 1857 (Ms 2, 1857) on this particular issue.

See: EGWEnc, s.v. "Laodicean Message."

[5] William Treadwell, from Roosevelt, for example, could not see why the Laodicean call should not also include reproving others. "The idea that we have no right to exhort one another . . . I understand to be an unscriptural idea," he argued in the *Review*. "The apostle commands to exhort, admonish and reprove."

See: Wm. Treadwell, "From Bro. Treadwell," *Review,* Apr. 1, 1858, p. 158.

[6] *Identity:* The initial difficulty in identifying "Brother Ross" is that there were at least two Ross brothers (Alexander and Manley) who were members of the Caughdenoy/Roosevelt group throughout the 1850s and beyond. A hint that Ellen White is writing of Alexander and not Manley is found a few lines farther down. "I saw that Brother Ross could do errands for the Lord, but his brethren are so fearful that Brother Ross will get exalted . . ." Ellen White

is uncalled for. They have watched him with jealous care when they should be attending to their own souls. They are not to give account for Brother Ross's sins, but to repent of their own sins and leave Brother Ross to the care of the angels of God. They will convict Brother Ross, and as the great principles of truth are received by Brother Ross, the purifying process will go on and purge away wrongs and convict of error and he will then obtain an experience worth everything to him. But the brethren have acted just as though the salvation of Brother Ross's soul was committed to them, that they must be conscience for him and tell him just what he must do. If he follows this, his experience will be founded in individuals instead of in God.

This is not as God would have it. I saw that Brother Ross could do errands for the Lord, but his brethren are so fearful Brother Ross will get exalted that they exercise an oppressive spirit of bondage. Think ye that God's angels are all asleep? Cannot they convict of wrong? Leave them a chance to do their work, and begin to search diligently your own hearts. Self is not dead yet with many. Correct your own wrongs, and what if Brother Ross does become exalted? You will not have to answer for his wrongs. I have been shown that you have neglected the great principles of our faith, to descend to little particulars, finding fault with others. Begin to work in your own hearts, to set in order your own house.

Brother and Sister Chapel [**Levi R.** and **Jane Eliza Chapel**][7] and Brother and Sister Arnold [**David** and **Lucretia Arnold**][8] have not understood the work of the Laodicean message, and they must search carefully and correct the evil. Others were engaged in the same work in the same spirit but I do not recollect them. You must leave the tangled mass and now dwell upon the great

---

several times uses the expression "do errands for the Lord" to describe lay preachers who are capable of part-time ministry and local leadership but who are not called to travel extensively or to "throw themselves wholly on the church as called and chosen servants of Jesus Christ." The suggestion then is that "Brother Ross" is in some minor position of leadership. This description fits Alexander Ross well. He preached, mostly locally, organized local tent meetings, and served as agent for the *Review*. There is no mention of his brother Manley filling any leadership positions.

See: Search term "Ross" in *Words of the Pioneers*; Ellen G. White, "The Cause in New York," *Testimony to the Church* (1872) (PH159), p. 81; *idem,* Lt 21, 1859 (c. Sept. 24); Ms 1, 1859 (Sept. 24); Ms 1a, 1859 (c. Sept. 24).

[7] Several Chapels are mentioned in the *Review* during this period. Since this letter is addressed to "friends at Roosevelt," the closest match seems to be Levi R. Chapel and his wife, Eliza, who lived in Palermo, just a few miles from Roosevelt.

See: 1860 U.S. Federal Census, "Levi R. Chapel," New York, Oswego County, Palermo, p. 34; search term "Chapel" in *Words of the Pioneers.*

[8] *Identity:* Out of a number of Arnolds listed in the *Review* in the 1850s and early 1860s the only one given an address from Roosevelt or vicinity is David Arnold. David and Lucretia Arnold, who lived in Volney, a few miles from Roosevelt, are probably the couple to which Ellen White is referring.

See: 1860 U.S. Federal Census, "David Arnold," New York, Oswego County, Volney, p. 18; search term "Arnold" in *Words of the Pioneers.*

principles of our faith. Satan has been unwilling that you should understand this matter rightly. The Lord has been showing that things were not right for about two years,[9] and yet you are all in blindness and plunging further and further into difficulty.

At Pennsylvania the state of things in New York was shown me, especially Roosevelt and vicinity.[10] Everything was shown that was needed to correct the evil. But in Ohio again these things were presented before me,[11] and I saw the influence Brother Rhodes [**Samuel W. Rhodes**][12] had exerted, his wrong course, etc., and that it would be some time before its influence would wear away and these wrongs be corrected. I saw that the same spirit existed there at Roosevelt, and was pointed back to where Brother Truman Finch [**Truman P. Finch**] was connected with these things and saw that what he had to do was to correct his wrong course and remove the influence he had cast.[13] And at the same time I saw that the wrong course of the church at Roosevelt had not yet been corrected and confessed. There was a great fear that if confessions of wrongs should be made, it would build up those who were thought to be wrong on the other side, and for fear of this there has been a scrinching, a shrinking from duty, that should have been immediately attended to when the message was given in Ulysses.[14] But some were too generous, gave what was designed for them to their brethren, and have passed on, not making

---

[9] Two years earlier Ellen White had published a vision concerning the "fault-finding, accusing spirit" in "Roosevelt, N. Y., and Oswego Co. in particular." In a letter to S. W. Rhodes, also in 1857, Ellen White named several Roosevelt members, Brethren Treadwell, Finch, and Chapel (in addition to Rhodes), who were deeply involved in this culture of accusation.

See: Ellen G. White, *Testimony for the Church,* No. 4, p. 13 (*Testimonies for the Church,* vol. 1, pp. 164-168); Lt 8, 1857 (July 19).

[10] Ellen White is here probably referring to her vision received at Ulysses, Pennsylvania, in July 1857, which dealt especially with the situation in Roosevelt, New York, as reported in Lt 8, 1857 (July 19), and Ms 2, 1857 (July 24).

[11] While in Green Springs, Ohio, in late February/early March 1858, Ellen White had a vision concerning problems of "wrangling and strife" in Oswego County, New York (which included Roosevelt).

See: Ellen G. White, Lt 2, 1858 (Mar.)

[12] *Identity:* In a letter written to Samuel W. Rhodes on the same day as Lt 17, 1859, Ellen White used almost the same language here used to describe "Brother Rhodes." Writing of his harsh methods, she asserted that "it would be some time before the churches in this state lived down . . . all the wrong instruction they have received." Clearly S. W. Rhodes is the "Brother Rhodes" in this passage. Rhodes's negative influence on churches in Michigan and New York is well documented in several earlier visions of Ellen White.

See: Ellen G. White, Lt 16, 1859 (Oct. 28); Ms 1, 1853 (June 2); Ms 6, 1854 (Feb. 19); Lt 8, 1857 (July 19).

[13] *See:* Ellen G. White, Lt 8, 1857 (July 19), for another reference to Truman Finch's influence on the Roosevelt church.

[14] A reference to Ellen White's vision in Ulysses, Pennsylvania, given two years earlier, containing admonition to the Roosevelt church for their internal dissension and numerous "church trials."

See: Ellen G. White, Ms 2, 1857 (July 24).

thorough work, until they have had less and less disposition to acknowledge their wrong course.

At Dartmouth, Massachusetts, the state of the church in this state was presented before me again,[15] especially the church at Roosevelt and vicinity. They were all tangled up because there was a disposition with some to maintain that God had led them *when He had not.* I saw that the Lord had borne long and patiently with the church there, but the angels are grieved, God's cause wounded and reproached. And I saw that God will not move on many hearts to receive the truth while there is no strength in the church to nourish them. They are standing directly in the way of the work of God, are growing blinder and blinder in mind and more subject to the temptations of Satan. More labor has been spent on the church in Roosevelt than on any other church in the state of New York. They will have to make thorough work and manifest a repentance that needeth not to be repented of, and then the stain will begin to disappear from Roosevelt.

I saw you should print on your heart and memory the testimony given at Ulysses [Pennsylvania]. Confess your own individual wrongs, make no reference to the wrongs of your brethren, and then cry to the Lord earnestly for wisdom. Wait on the Lord and where you do not now see things clearly, you will; light will break in. Gather with the angels of God instead of scattering. Be pitiful; be courteous. Have bowels of compassion for your brethren.

But it has been so different. There has been a blaming, an excusing of self, an accusing spirit against brethren. The third angel[16] is bringing up God's people, elevating them, and fastening their minds and their affections on their eternal interests. A harsh, accusing spirit must be removed from the church before the church can flourish and exert a saving influence.

In haste.

---

[15] *See:* Note 2 above.

[16] *See:* EGWEnc, s.v. "Three Angels' Messages."

1859

OCTOBER 30, BROOKFIELD, NEW YORK

LETTER TO
Henry Nichols White and James Edson White.

Published in Ellen G. White, *An Appeal to the Youth,* pp. 53-56.

1859

DECEMBER

"From My Diary," "At a Business Meeting . . . ," "Friends in Michigan," "Aged Pilgrims," "Money for the Poor and Articles of Clothing."

Published in *The Good Samaritan,* vol. 1, no. 2, December 1859, pp. 5, 6, 8.

1859

(Ms 3, 1859)

1859,[1] N.P.

Vision for James White.

Previously unpublished.

The need for others to share James White's heavy workload in order that he can focus more on "speaking and writing."

I was shown in my last vision that God would have James give himself more to the study of the Word, labor more in word and doctrine, in speaking

[1] The original document bears only the year 1859. This date was confirmed some years later when Ellen White, in 1872, published a slightly edited version of it, together with other

and writing. I was pointed back and saw that we had exhausted our energies in times past. Past anxiety and care had not been in vain. It was needed to bring the cause into a position where it would not languish and sink.[2] Now the cause of God has strength. The tide of opposition is strong against it, but it has sufficient strength to stem this tide.[3] Now such wearing labor, such privations, such agonizing to bring the church up, is not required of us; but James' labors, in connection with mine, are to be spent in different places now and then, not to take the burden of the church—for they must bear their own burden—but to teach them God's Word, the necessity of experimental religion, what it is, and the position they are called upon to occupy. This will be the labor for the church.

And then I saw that the voice must be heard in the great congregation upon points of present truth, in clearness and with decision presenting to the hearers and before the readers of the *Review*,[4] that whosoever will may come and be sanctified through the truth. From what I saw, there must be more consecration on our part, and we must live more in the light of God's countenance. I saw that with his mind exercised more upon Bible truth James would be a better laborer. A little closer application will accustom the mind to dwell upon important truth.

I was shown that God did not lay on us such heavy burdens as we have borne. Talk the truth to the church, show them the necessity of working for themselves. The church has been carried too much.[5] I saw that the reason we

---

documents, in *Testimony for the Church,* No. 21, and prefaced the material with the words "I will now copy from a testimony given in 1859."

See: Ellen G. White, *Testimonies for the Church,* vol. 3, pp. 10, 11.

[2] Throughout the 1850s James White, with the support of Ellen, had been at the forefront of every major new church venture. With his strong leadership and administrative talents he tended to micromanage every aspect of the movement, and this lead to exhaustion. The focus of this vision, that James should shed some of his many tasks and focus on "speaking and writing," was, for a number of reasons, never to become a reality. In 1871, for example, James White was not only reelected General Conference president, but also elected "editor of the *Review* and the *Health Reformer,* president of the Publishing Association, president of the Seventh-day Adventist Benevolent Association, and president of the Missionary Society."

See: Virgil Robinson, *James White,* p. 230.

[3] This "tide of opposition" no doubt included the attempts of the *Messenger* Party (see EGWEnc) to disrupt the Sabbatarian movement led by the Whites during the mid-1850s. By 1858, however, James White reported that not only had the *Messenger* Party challenge faded away, but during the years of conflict paid subscriptions to the *Review* had almost doubled from 1,000 to near 2,000.

See: J. W. [James White], "A Sketch of the Rise and Progress of the Present Truth," *Review,* Jan. 14, 1858, p. 78.

[4] Gerald Wheeler, in his biography of James White, gives White high marks as writer for "careful reasoning and balance. . . . White's articles, tracts, and books have stood the test of time better than many other early Seventh-day Adventist writers. His writings have an authority and sensibility that convinces even the twenty-first-century reader."

See: Gerald Wheeler, *James White,* p. 80.

[5] This theme, that the burdens of church leadership were being disproportionately carried by

were not required to go through hard, distressing places [and] bear heavy burdens, is because the Lord would have our voice tell, and we should be called upon when our help was actually needed. Our influence will be needed to overrule important moves that will be made. Errors occasionally will trouble the church, and our energies must not be exhausted so as to unfit us for the important occasions in which God would have us act a prominent part.

I saw that our efforts have been crippled by the enemy, affecting the church to call forth from us almost double labor to cut our way through, then afterwards follows lassitude and lack of strength. Our efforts have been crippled in this way. I saw that we had a work to do. Sometimes the adversary would resist every effort we might attempt to make, and the condition of the people was not such that God could safely bless them. But I saw that we should go right along and not feel that we are responsible for the result of these different meetings. We do our duty, and if the result is not as we could wish, it should not discourage us and weaken our confidence. At times the power of God will distill upon the people, and the result of our labor be very encouraging. We must take an even course and then in the end we can accomplish much more good.

I saw that we must have system, and plan that we may expend our strength to the best advantage. I saw that care should be used in praying and speaking, that we should not injure the speaking organs but we should command the voice, and by so doing the speaking organs will be preserved from weakness a greater length of time, and will be less liable to disease.[6]

---

the Whites, especially by James White, appears repeatedly in visions from the 1850s and onward. The implication was that some church leaders were not pulling their full weight. Expectations were high that fellow workers would, like James, "venture all—life, health, strength, time, everything—to push this work ahead." Why James White's colleagues in leadership sometimes failed in this respect is not addressed in this manuscript.

See: Ellen G. White, Lt 28, 1859 (June/July). For a selection of Ellen White's visions on this theme from 1855, 1859, 1863, and 1869, see "An Appeal for Burden Bearers," in *Testimonies for the Church,* vol. 3, pp. 9-16.

[6] The need for ministers, in particular, to avoid abusing their vocal cords when speaking in public is a recurring theme in Ellen White's writings. This may well be the earliest instance of such instruction from her pen. For a selection of Ellen White's counsel on the proper care of the vocal organ, see Ellen G. White, *Counsels on Speech and Song,* pp. 193-203.

1859

(Lt 1, 1859)

[CIRCA 1859],[1] N.P.

LETTER TO

T.[2]

Previously unpublished.

The importance of humility and simplicity in prayer.

Dear Brother T:

I was shown your case, that you lacked spirituality and humility. You love the truth; you love to see it triumph, and the cause of God advance. But you fail in your praying and talking. You do not come to God as He loves to have His people come. You should approach God with reverence, like a humble suppliant at His feet, feeling indeed poor, miserable, undeserving the least of His favors.

You use too many flowery words. You reach out beyond your measure. It is more like telling the Lord a story or giving an account of yourself to the Lord, as if He did not know you just as you are, than like humbly asking for His mercy and to pardon your sins. The earnest, simple, broken, penitent prayer is acceptable always to God, and the lofty, wordy prayer is not so much as noticed of Him, for it is disgusting to the ear of the Lord, disgusting to His people. You lack the sweet, meek, broken spirit in your prayers and exhortations.

There must be a thorough change with you or you can be of no help to the people of God. I am instructed that you must take time to pray, time for secret prayer. Your life must be more devoted to God. Examine your heart closely. Try your motives, lest the enemy get the advantage and lead you to think more highly of yourself than you ought to think. You will not have to answer for the sin of covetousness. You love to impart what you have to a suitable object. You love to do your part in aiding the cause of truth. This is regarded of heaven; but with it you must possess meekness, humility, and great carefulness before the Lord, saying, "We give to Thee, Lord, Thine own."

---

[1] This letter is undated, and its content does not contain any clear references to events or other internal evidence by which it may be dated. An early copyist, however, has copied this letter between two other 1859 documents (Ms 2, 1859 [Jan. 1], and Lt 19, 1859 [Oct. 4]), giving some likelihood that it, too, belongs to the same time period.

[2] This person has not been identified.

Fear continually to offend God. Then your influence will be saving. It will tell. It will have an effect upon all with whom you associate. When you pray, ask for the very things you need in a simple, humble, childlike manner. Don't be governed by a flight of feeling, for those who have been governed by this have always been led astray. Dwell upon the living principle; make that the greatest thing. Bear your testimony in the spirit of meekness and simplicity, and it is noticed in heaven. God will make it more effective than much speaking or all the lofty, flowery, unmeaning words that can be arrayed together. Carry out your holy profession in all the walks of life. Have your prayers right to the point, asking just what you need. You want one object before you when you pray, and do not wander from that object, but don't ever be guilty of putting together an array of lofty words as you approach the Great Eternal. Said the angel, A broken heart and contrite spirit God will not despise, but will bend His ear low to the humble, penitent, self-abased child who hardly dares approach God. Such trembling faith will fasten upon the promises securely and will bring gracious returns.

1859

(Lt 15, 1859)

[CIRCA 1859],[1] N.P.

LETTER TO

Brother M and Wife.[2]

Previously unpublished.

An appeal for renewed happiness and mutual respect in a strained marriage.

Dear Brother M and Wife:

Duty compels me to write you a few lines this morn.

While in Rochester, N.Y., I was shown a number of individual cases. Among them your case was shown me. I feel sad as I write. Things were opened before me and I saw the course that you had taken.

Sister M, you are not right. God is displeased with you. You have a bad disposition and oh, how weak are your efforts to overcome it! You have a fretful and stubborn spirit, and I was pointed back and saw that you never yet have subdued this disposition. You never yet have obtained the victory over it.

I saw that you should be grateful that God has given you a good husband, but you have not realized this. You have given way to self, and it has not only injured you and strengthened you in this great evil, but you have fretted at and ruled your husband until his disposition has greatly changed. If you continue as you have, there will be danger of his affections being weaned entirely from you, and he will wish he never saw you. His married life has not been happy. It was in your power to make him happy. You were the object of his choice, but he never looked deep enough into your disposition and inquired, Will she be a help to me in spiritual things? Will she help soothe my careworn spirits? Will she by patient perseverance help me overcome my evil besetments, or by fretfulness and impatience cause these evils to grow upon me, make my home unhappy and discourage me in my Christian walk, and prove a stumbling block in my efforts to obtain the victory over self, and to my overcoming at last and having eternal life?

---

[1] The contents of this letter provide very little help to determine the date of writing, especially since the identities of the addressees are not known. The estimate that it was written "circa 1859" is based on the probability that a copy of this letter originally appeared in a record book together with some letters known to be from 1859.

[2] These persons could not be identified.

I saw, Brother M, that before your marriage you enjoyed religion. But you enjoy but little of it now. You fear your wife's tongue. It is an unruly member and it is often full of deadly evil, for it is set on fire of hell. She makes herself miserable, and you, too. Instead of possessing a cheerful, contented, and happy frame of mind that every Christian should possess, it is fretting, blaming, and groaning. Is God pleased with all this? No, no; His frown is upon it. Brother M, you have felt at times almost like giving up the battle, laying down the weapons of your warfare; but bear up with good courage. Impatience in your wife has begot impatience in you.

Your wife, I saw, did not honor you. She does not consider it a blessing to her and condescension in you to marry her and provide for her a home. This is the case. Thus God looks upon it. You have a better husband, Sister M, than you deserve. But often, before company and alone, you speak disrespectfully to your husband until he has begun to lose his own self respect and to place himself beneath the position that God has qualified him to fill.

Said the angel of God to Brother M, Assert your liberty. "Thou shalt worship the Lord thy God, and him only shalt thou *serve*." [Matt. 4:10.] Sister M, I saw that you have been impatient if your husband did not bow or submit to every wish of yours. You have been exacting and faultfinding. I saw, Brother M, that you should stand at the head of your family. God requires it of you. Keep your spirit free.

Sister M, you are too meddlesome, too free to talk. May the Lord show you yourself, your own heart, and may you with earnestness and zeal make strong efforts for eternal life. You have no time to lose. Your disposition has never been lovely, but now you can overcome if you will make strong efforts to do so and obtain strength from One that is mighty to save. "My grace is sufficient for you." [2 Cor. 12:9.] You must make thorough work or you will be weighed in the balance and found wanting. A thorough reformation must take place with you or you will find no shelter in the day when the fierceness of Jehovah's wrath is poured upon the heads of those who have slighted salvation and made no effort to overcome their carnal hearts. Jesus is your Pattern. Imitate His lovely character, then you will be happy and all around you will feel happy.

Brother M, in the name of my Master, I would say, Go free. Shake off every shackle; break every cord. Possess patience and meekness under all circumstances, however trying it may be to human nature. Heaven, sweet heaven, is worth making any sacrifice or effort for. Elevate yourself; lay hold of God. He loves you yet. Press for the mark of the prize.

1859

(Lt 27, 1859)

[CIRCA 1859],[1] N.P.

EXTRACT OF LETTER TO

William Peabody.[2]

This extract is published in S. T. Belden, G. W. Amadon, and William Hall, *To Brother J. N. Andrews and Sister H. N. Smith* (PH016), pp. 35-38.

To those who murmur at the leadership of James White.[3]

I was shown that God would reward those who will bear responsibilities and with energy push His work forward and stand in the forefront of the battle. God will choose those who will venture something in His work, but there are those who will not fill the place that God would be pleased to have them fill.

I saw that God had chosen James to fill an important place, and has made him His agent to forward His work. I saw that God had made him a burden-bearer from the commencement of his work since 1844. God thrust him out that he should obtain an experience to fill the place He designed for him to occupy, as one to manage in His cause to forward the work. In order to do this he has had to take responsibilities and to risk something on the success of this message.

---

[1] The date of this undated extract of a letter to William Peabody cannot be later than June 1860, when it first appeared in print in pamphlet form. However, it could have been written up to one year earlier when the same material, with only slight verbal differences, appeared in a letter from Ellen White to John Byington that has been dated to June/July 1859 (Lt 28, 1859). Hence, this Peabody letter is assigned to "circa 1859."

See: Ellen G. White, in S. T. Belden, G. W. Amadon, and William Hall, *To Brother J. N. Andrews and Sister H. N. Smith* (PH016), pp. 35-38.

[2] When this letter first appeared in print, in 1860, it was titled "Extract From a Communication to Bro. William Peabody."

See: Ellen G. White, in S. T. Belden, G. W. Amadon, and William Hall, *To Brother J. N. Andrews and Sister H. N. Smith* (PH016), p. 35.

[3] One may wonder why Ellen White sent this vision concerning those who questioned James White's leadership to William Peabody. The same message had been sent as an admonition to John Byington, who clearly was not happy with James White (see note above and Lt 28, 1859). It might be that Peabody also opposed White at this time, although it could well be that Ellen White included this material for other reasons. Since not all of Ellen White's letter has been preserved, which would give more context, no safe conclusion can be drawn. It should be noted, however, that William Peabody, a wealthy New York farmer, was one of the most generous donors to the fledgling Sabbatarian movement, as evidenced by the many receipts listed in the *Review,* including a legacy of more than $2,000 at the time of his death in 1866.

See: Search term "Peabody" in *Review and Herald* online collection, www.adventistarchives.org.

God would be pleased if others would feel the same interest and move with the same energy, but they will not venture. I saw that God was displeased with those who do not take the burden themselves, and then stand ready to murmur at the one upon whom He lays the heavy burden.[4] I saw that if others would come up and bear the burden he has borne for years, and venture all—life, life, health, strength, time, everything—to push this work ahead, trusting alone to the success of this message, then God would relieve him from such heavy responsibilities. God has made him His agent to stir up to zealous action.

I saw that the blessing of the Lord has rested upon every essential move that has been made to advance His cause, and steadily has the work progressed and one difficulty after another been surmounted. It is because God's hand was in the work.

I saw that some do not realize that selfishness is at the bottom of their murmuring. God's humble instrument moves too fast for their faith, and his venturing out as he has done has reproved their slow, unbelieving pace. And there has been satisfaction taken in watching and finding fault. Hints have been thrown out, doubts expressed, which have had their influence. Those responsible were at fault in this. Their faith was not strong enough to keep pace with him. Had they the strong faith and self-denial that they should have, those who have the ability and means might do a great deal in stirring up the people of God, and if they would venture out and risk something in the result and success of this message, it would inspire faith in the hearts of the remnant, and there would be activity and zeal in pushing forward this great work.

I was shown that the work was not left in the hands of James or any other one upon earth.[5] Angels of God have charge of the work, and they counsel and direct the people through chosen agents and thus the work moves forward. I was shown that God in His own wise providence raised James above dependence and want that his testimony and influence might not be crippled by the galling sense of dependence.[6] God will use him as His instrument to

---

[4] In her parallel letter to John Byington, Ellen White names specific individuals who had been involved in the "murmuring" against James White. "I was shown that Brother Byington, Brother Fletcher, and Brother Smith have looked with suspicion and distrust upon James because he ventured out to do so much. They shook their heads doubtfully, thought he was going too far, moving too fast. I saw that if these should have their will and their way how the work should move, how it should progress, it would not move at all."

See: Ellen G. White, Lt 28, 1859 (June/July).

[5] The portrayal of James White's leadership position given in this passage and elsewhere in the letter carefully avoids according him some kind of permanent preeminent position in the church. When G. I. Butler in 1873 tried to steer the General Conference toward giving James White special authority and preeminence, he (White) successfully counteracted the attempt. Andrew Mustard traces the issue of leadership authority during this period in *James White and SDA Organization*, pp. 175-178.

[6] As J. N. Andrews and others noted some years later: "When Eld. White, in 1848, began

speak with freedom, independent of man, and in His strength and Spirit raise his voice, and with his example call upon the people to arouse and with energy to assist with their substance, their influence, ability, and judgment in moving forward this great work. And any that wish to be convinced can be, that it is not from selfishness or to obtain any advantage for himself that he pursues this course. His object is to advance the work of God, which is dearer to him than life.

I saw that God will have a voice to speak in the Office and in His cause. I saw that it was easier for those who look on to complain and find fault than to suggest and lead in a better course. It is very easy and cheap to suggest doubts and fears, but it is not so readily undertaken to tell what shall be done. I was pointed back and saw that amid all the hatred and devices of Satan, God had spared the life of James, although Satan has pressed him sore to take it away.[7] A few years since the Lord wrenched him from the enemy's grasp and from his power, and raised him up still to act for Him, to walk out on his faith, to be a succorer to the needy, and to strengthen and uphold His servants whom He has called into the field. I saw that God had stayed him on the right hand and on the left, that he should not go to extremes, and He has inspired confidence in the hearts of the remnant generally to confide in his integrity and judgment.

This has not been the work of man, but the marks of God's hand are seen in it all. His work will go forward. God will choose simple instruments to carry forward this great work, but they only carry out the mind and will of the great Master at the head of the work.

---

the business of publishing, in Middletown, Conn., he did it without any capital at all, and almost without friends. . . . He was dependent upon a few friends in quite humble circumstances for a shelter and for the necessities of life." During the early 1850s, while in Rochester, New York, "he lived in a hired house . . . [that] was furnished with the plainest articles of second-hand furniture. The food of his family was of the least expensive character." After the move to Michigan in 1855, James White's personal financial situation began to improve.

See: J. N. Andrews et al, *Defense of Elder James White and Wife,* pp. 2, 3. For a recent analysis of his sources of personal income, see Gerald Wheeler, *James White,* pp. 72, 81, 147-153.

[7] Although James White had survived a number of crises, the one that Ellen White described with the most pathos took place during the winter of 1854-1855 and continued through most of 1855. James was, she wrote, "fiercely buffeted by Satan" during this period. She greatly feared that he was fast heading "to a consumptive's grave" and that her "three little boys" would "be left fatherless." "Three times a day we went alone before God . . . in earnest prayer for the recovery of his health. . . . The Lord graciously heard our earnest cries, and my husband began to recover."

See: Ellen G. White, *Spiritual Gifts [vol. 2],* pp. 194-199.

1859

(Ms 9, 1859)

[CIRCA 1859],[1] N.P.

Early Experiences in Meeting Fanaticism.

Portions of this manuscript are published in Ellen G. White, *Spiritual Gifts [vol. 2]*, pp. 49-52.

Meeting fanaticism in Maine during 1845.

[I went] over to their house and there saw Sister T. [Jane B. Turner][2] and bore my testimony to her which was to comfort her poor, sore heart.[3] She was weeping as though her heart would break. She there confirmed the vision which I related to her.[4] We learned from different ones that this one and that one had been set aside. Honest, precious souls had been told that they were rejected of God; that these fanatical persons had flocked to my father's house

---

[1] The first two and last two paragraphs of this manuscript are very close in wording to the corresponding portions of Ellen White's first major autobiographical book published in 1860, *Spiritual Gifts: My Christian Experience, Views and Labors in Connection With the Rise and Progress of the Third Angel's Message*. This suggests that the manuscript is a partial draft of that book. Ellen White announced her intention to write an extended autobiographical account already in March 1858, so this manuscript probably dates from the period 1858-1860.

See: Ellen G. White, *Spiritual Gifts [vol. 2]*, pp. 49-52; Ellen G. White, in *Review*, Mar. 25, 1858, p. 152; Arthur L. White, "Spiritual Gifts, Volume II," *Ministry*, December 1944, pp. 10-12.

[2] Jane B. Turner, wife of Joseph Turner. By 1848 Joseph Turner was based in Hartford, Connecticut, where he edited the *Bible Advocate* and later the *Second Advent Watchman*.

See: 1850 U.S. Federal Census, "Jane B. Turner," Connecticut, Hartford County, Hartford City, p. 434.

[3] During a visit to Claremont, New Hampshire, in the spring of 1845 Ellen Harmon was instructed in vision to return to Maine to "bear testimony" against the "fanatical spirit" of Joseph Turner and John Howell. At a subsequent meeting in Portland, Maine, Joseph Turner was present when Ellen Harmon in vision spoke of Turner's "ungodly course." Turner rejected this part of her testimony, and Ellen Harmon left the meeting "with anguish of spirit." She then went to see Turner's wife, and it is there that the narrative picks up in the first paragraph.

See: Ellen G. White, *Spiritual Gifts [vol. 2]*, p. 49.

[4] Many years later Ellen White gave further details regarding the contents of this vision. It showed Turner "transgressing the commandments, giving attention to other women, and his wife suffering under the great strain." His distraught wife confirmed the vision relating how her husband would sometimes spend "half the night, and sometimes all night" with Sarah Jordan, sister of William Jordan, "giving her visions." Ellen White attributed Sarah's "so-called visions" to Turner's "mesmeric passes." She also related how, sometime later, while in a meeting in Poland, Maine, Turner unsuccessfully tried to "mesmerize" her.

See: EGWEnc, s.v. "Hypnosis and Mesmerism"; Ellen G. White, "Life Sketches" manuscript, pp. 127, 128, EGWE-GC; *idem, Spiritual Gifts [vol. 2]*, p. 38; *idem,* Ms 131, 1906 (Aug. 13).

and made that their stopping place. J. T. [Joseph Turner][5] and J. H. [**John Howell**][6] were leaders in this rank fanaticism. They followed impressions and burdens that led to corruption instead of purity and holiness.

Our parents were disgusted as they saw reason and judgment laid aside by them, and impressions were carried out. They protested against it, and as they could not get rid of this company, they closed their house and left the city for Poland [Maine], where my two married sisters [**Harriet McCann** and **Mary Plummer Foss**][7] were living. This did not suit J. T. and he told me when we arrived at Portland [Maine] that my father was a doomed man. My mother and sisters might be saved, but my father would be lost. The only reason he offered was because he did not give him possession of his house when he left Portland. His denunciations were bitter. We visited Poland, where my parents were, and again from their mouth we heard the fulfillment of the vision given in New Hampshire.[8]

I had been shown that they needed help in Orrington [Maine], and that we must go there, for fanaticism had done its work there also; that fanatical spirits had rushed on without judgment until unbelievers became disgusted with their course. These fanatical ones seemed to think that religion consisted in making a noise, being boisterous, rough, and talking in such a manner as to irritate and cause unbelievers to hate them, and then would rejoice that they suffered persecution.[9] Unbelievers were enraged.

---

[5] In Ms 131, 1906 (Aug. 13), Ellen White related some of these same events using the full name "Joe Turner" or "Joseph Turner."

See: Ellen G. White, Ms 131, 1906 (Aug. 13); *idem,* "Life Sketches" manuscript, pp. 126-128, EGWE-GC.

[6] *Identity:* In Ms 131, 1906 (Aug. 13), Ellen White related some of these same events using the full name "John Howell." Although an Advent Christian minister in later years, John Howell (c. 1820-before 1874) had earlier, in 1845, identified closely with the minority "Bridegroom" Shut Door Adventists. He publicly renounced this position in early 1846. Amid the Adventist theological controversies of the late 1840s and the 1850s, Howell sided with the conditionalists and joined the Advent Christians. Howell's wife, Lucinda S. Howell (later Burdick), was also an active opponent of Ellen White.

See: "John Howell," 1860 U.S. Federal Census, Vermont, Rutland County, Poultney, p. 272; David Tallmadge Arthur, *"Come out of Babylon,"* p. 334; John Howell, "Letter From Bro. Howell," *Voice of Truth,* Jan. 21, 1846, pp. 30, 31; John Howell, "Notices," *Bible Advocate,* Nov. 11, 1847, p. 112; Ellen G. White, *Spiritual Gifts [vol. 2],* pp. 49, 50.

[7] *See:* Artemas C. Harmon, ed., *The Harmon Genealogy,* p. 41; 1850 U.S. Federal Census, "Harriet McCann," Maine, Cumberland County, Poland, p. 34; 1850 U.S. Federal Census, "Mary Foss," Maine, Cumberland County, Poland, p. 46.

[8] *See:* Note 3 above regarding this vision. For a survey of the continued strained relationship between Joseph Turner on the one hand and the Whites and Joseph Bates on the other, see Merlin D. Burt, "Sabbatarian Adventism From 1844 to 1849," pp. 140-146, 151, 348-350.

[9] Some have rejected statements such as these in which Ellen White claims to have campaigned against "fanaticism" of various kinds in 1845. Such claims, it is said, are conscious or unconscious attempts by Ellen White, many years after the events of 1845, to deny her close association, together with James White, with the fanaticism of the period. However, it needs to be remembered that there is contemporary evidence already from the summer of 1845

They could see no consistency in this wild spirit and they made stringent rules that no advent believer should come into town. The innocent here suffered with the guilty. They could not have the privilege of assembling to encourage one another, for even the citizens of the place who were believers were denied this privilege. Sentinels were on the watch to hinder all who should attempt to enter the town.[10] Yet the Lord bade me go. Naturally timid, I would gladly have been excused, but dared not take my own course. My life was not my own.

We first visited Brother S's[11] family in Orrington. They heartily welcomed us to their home and hearts. Every moment was precious to these hungry children and we sat up till a late hour recounting the trials we had passed through and the refreshing seasons we had enjoyed; and we deplored together

---

showing the opposition of James White (by now closely associated with Ellen Harmon) to the fanatical excesses of some Adventists in Maine. In a letter written by James White on August 19, 1845, and published in the *Day-Star,* he regretfully affirms that there is "much ground" for the charges of "fanaticism" and that "many of our best brethren were led away from the truths of the blessed Bible."

See: Ann Taves, *Fits, Trances, and Visions,* pp. 159-161; James White, "Letter From Bro. White," *Day-Star,* Sept. 6, 1845, pp. 17, 18. For later testimonial evidence of Ellen White's opposition to fanatical behaviors and attitudes, see *Spiritual Gifts [vol. 2],* pp. 301, 302; "A Statement Regarding the Charges of Mrs. L. S. Burdick, by Marion C. S. Truesdail," Aug. 17, 1875 (DF 266, EGWE-GC).

[10] At a town meeting in Orrington on June 25, 1845, i.e., about the same period as Ellen Harmon's second visit described in this letter, action was taken to specifically forbid out-of-town Millerites from entering the town. It was "voted that the selectmen prosecute all persons who come into town and are represented as Idle persons, Brawlers and false pretenders going about town and seducing its inhabitants to the same courses of conduct." The designations "Idle persons" and "Brawlers" were common legal terms used against Millerites during this period. The high level of public feeling against visiting Millerites is illustrated by an incident three months earlier, at the end of March 1845, in Atkinson, some 40 miles (64 kilometers) northwest of Orrington. According to newspaper reports "a band of men disguised as Indians . . . forced the doors of a 'Miller' meeting in Atkinson and seized and carried off several persons not supposed to belong to the town and threatened to tar and feather the adventists if they held any more meetings."

See: Orrington town records, June 25, 1845, Article 2, meeting moderated by Justice of the Peace Joseph Doane; "Atrocious Conduct," *Whig and Courier* (Bangor, Maine), Mar. 29, 1845.

[11] Three persons in this manuscript are identified only by what is presumably the first letter of their surnames: Brother S, Brother B, and Brother W. If the names of all Adventists living in Orrington in 1845 were known it might be possible to match the initials with actual individuals, but no such list is known to exist. A newspaper account in the Bangor *Whig and Courier,* Feb. 19, 1845, indicated that there were at least "thirty citizens of Orrington" that had been caught up in the "Miller Excitement," but gave no names. Of greater interest is a notice appearing in several local and out-of-state newspapers on April 28, 1845, and subsequently, reporting that a "Mr. George W. Brown, of Orrington" among other "professors of . . . belief" in "Millerism" had been arrested. It is therefore at least possible that "Brother B's house," which Ellen White visited on this occasion, was that of George W. Brown.

See: "Miller Excitement," *Whig and Courier* (Bangor, Maine), Feb. 19, 1845; "Millerism," *Daily Argus* (Portland, Maine), Apr. 28, 1845; "Millerism," *Eastern Argus* (Portland, Maine), Apr. 28, 1845; "Millerism," *New York Daily Tribune,* May 2, 1845.

the sad state of the cause. I bore a sad and aching heart. It seemed so cruel that the cause of Christ should be injured by injudicious men. Not only were the men injuring their own souls but placing a stigma upon the cause which would not be easily wiped away. Satan was willing to have it so. It suited well his satanic majesty to see the truth mixed with error and then altogether trampled in the dust. He looked with hellish triumph upon the confused, scattered state of God's children.

Next morning as we were in the front room two men entered the door leading into the kitchen. Sister S. as she opened the front room door looked pale and motioned to us. We had no baggage. We put on our bonnets and stepped out of the front door. Just then there was quite a gathering at a meetinghouse near by, for it was fast day. We passed on with the people and were not discovered.

The meetinghouse was in the direction of Brother B's house, where we wished to call. Gladly were we received. We prayed and wept together. Brother B. said we need not fear being troubled in his house, for no one dared to dictate to him about who he should have in his family and who he should not. He had quite a war spirit against the course the citizens were pursuing. He was only partially in union with our people, but a portion of his family were fully with us.

We visited many of the brethren. We were hunted for, but the Lord always directed us out of their way to a place of safety, that, too, without the least effort on our part to conceal ourselves. We were engaged in doing the will of God, going from house to house to visit His tried children.

At one house we found them much afflicted. Their children were sick with measles. We prayed for them and the power of God rested upon us. We passed on to Brother W's and then we rode two miles [three kilometers] farther to visit a family in affliction. Sickness was in their dwelling. We prayed with them and the Lord again met with us and comforted us with His love.

As we rode to the last place we were noticed by several individuals, but we trusted ourselves in the hands of God. Through the earnest entreaty of a few brethren we visited a family that was in great error. A few months before they were standing in the clear light of truth, and we took sweet counsel together. P. K. [Phebe Knapp],[12] a young woman, was with them professing to have visions of God, yet teaching the grossest errors—that the resurrection of the dead had taken place already—and she warned the family she was with not to receive us into their house for we would oppose the truth, referring to the

---

[12] *Identity:* Phebe Knapp (fl. 1845) was one of several female Millerite visionaries who briefly appeared on the scene in 1845. No further information of her subsequent career has been found in Sabbatarian or other Adventist sources.

See: Ellen G. White, Lt 2, 1874 (Aug. 24); Merlin D. Burt, "Sabbatarian Adventism From 1844 to 1849," p. 147.

resurrection being past. She taught numerous other absurd errors.

As the family saw Sister Foss [**Louisa Foss**][13] and myself coming they fastened the door against us. But we opened it, for the door was insecurely fastened. We entered the dwelling in the name of the Lord. Immediately P. K. [Phebe Knapp] fell to the floor in great apparent agony, crying to the family, "You are in danger, danger, danger." I had a few moments of calm conversation with the family. I asked them why they showed me so much coldness. When we last parted with them a few months before, our hearts were one. They had not seen me since, but I was the same; I believed just as I did. I asked who had changed? They had changed and not us. They had been influenced by the spirit of error. I told them they had received error which caused our separation. We loved them, but could have no union with their error.

I then went into the room where P. K. [Phebe Knapp] was groaning and crying out. I bowed in their midst and asked God to hear me, and for His own glory manifest Himself to these poor, deceived souls, and to show them that we had come to do them good, and to convince them of error, and give them evidence that this was a false burden, and rebuke it. P. K.'s burden left her immediately. After exhorting them faithfully and declaring to them their errors, we left them. I was free. I had performed a disagreeable task and the Lord had sustained me.

As Sister Foss and myself walked back we rejoiced in the Lord. The brethren and sisters had not ventured to meet together for some time, but nearly all came together and there was quite a company assembled. It was a time of solemnity, of rejoicing, and weeping. It is impossible to describe such a meeting. There was no noisy shouting, but a solemnity rested upon all. We were suspected of holding a meeting somewhere, and we afterwards learned that persons were sent to Brother W's house to see if we were there, or if there was a meeting. At the time these two men came we were all bowed before God. There was no noise but a peaceful weeping spirit rested upon us. The windows were high so that none of us were noticed from the outside. The men went away satisfied that we were not there.

That night I was shown in vision that our work was done in Orrington, that we must leave by daybreak, for men would come to take us and we should suffer abuse. There was but little sleeping that night, for we wished to speak encouragingly to each other as long as we could, for we knew not when we should meet again on earth. Some did not close their eyes that night, and early the next morning we were on our way. Two brethren took us in a rowboat to

---

[13] *Identity:* In later autobiographical accounts Ellen White wrote of her travels in 1845: "My constant and faithful companion at this time was Sister Louisa Foss, the sister of my brother-in-law." It therefore seems fairly certain that the "Sister Foss" spoken of here is Louisa Foss.

See: James White and Ellen G. White, *Life Sketches* (1880), p. 202.

Camden [Maine], about five miles [eight kilometers].[14] We stepped on board the large steamboat and rode safely over the water to Portland. We received a letter from Brother W. stating that soon after daylight men came to his house for us, and were very angry when they found we had gone. They met the men who had taken us to the steamboat and whipped them, but their testimony was they scarcely felt the stripes.

As I returned to Portland evidence increased of the desolating effects of fanaticism in Maine. J. T. [Joseph Turner] labored to turn my friends and even my relatives against me, and he succeeded in a measure. And what was all this for? It was because I had faithfully told them what had been shown me concerning his fanatical course. And to justify himself he circulated falsehoods to destroy my influence. My lot seemed hard to bear. I sank in discouragement, and my mind wandered for two weeks. My relatives thought I could not live. But the brethren and sisters met together to pray for me. I was sensible to their earnest, effectual prayers. The power of the strong foe was broken, and I was released from his grasp and was immediately taken off in vision.

In this view I saw that the opposition of man and a human influence should never afflict me again. If I felt an influence affecting my testimony I was to cry to God, wherever I should be, for another angel. One was guarding me continually and I should have another to strengthen me when it was necessary, and raise me above the power of any earthly influence.[15] I saw then for the first time the glory of the new earth as follows. [Manuscript ends here. See *Spiritual Gifts (vol. 2),* pp. 52-55, for a description of Ellen White's vision of the new earth.]

---

[14] There appears to be an inaccuracy here. From Orrington to Camden, down the Penobscot River would be closer to 50 miles (80 kilometers), rather than five (eight kilometers). In a later recollection (1874) Ellen White writes of "being taken in a small row boat to Belfast," about 20 miles (32 kilometers) downstream from Orrington. Evidently her memory was not clear on this detail of the journey. Steamboat traffic between Bangor and Portland stopped at several places along the Penobscot River, but it is unclear at which point Ellen Harmon and her companion(s) boarded.

See: Ellen G. White, Lt 2, 1874 (Aug. 24).

[15] Sometime later, while in Poland, Maine, Ellen White was involved in a dramatic confrontation with Joseph Turner. "I remembered the promise which the Lord had given me. . . . I then raised my hands to heaven and earnestly cried, Another angel, Father! another angel!"

See: Ellen G. White, *Spiritual Gifts [vol. 2],* p. 63.

1859

(Ms 10, 1859)

[CIRCA 1859],[1] N.P.

Early Experiences in Meeting Fanaticism.

Portions of this manuscript are published in Ellen G. White, *Spiritual Gifts [vol. 2],* pp. 46-50.

Meeting fanaticism in New Hampshire and Maine during 1845.

[We[2] visited Claremont (New Hampshire), and] inquired for Adventists. We were told that there were two parties, one holding fast their past advent experience, the other had denied it.[3] We stated that we wished to find those who had not denied their past experience, and were directed to Elders B——t [Bennett] and B——s [Billings][4] whom they said believed as we did. They

---

[1] The entire manuscript is very close in wording to the corresponding portions of Ellen White's first major autobiography published in 1860, *Spiritual Gifts: My Christian Experience, Views and Labors in Connection With the Rise and Progress of the Third Angel's Message.* This suggests that the manuscript is a partial draft of that book. Ellen White announced her intention to write an extended autobiographical account already in March 1858, so this manuscript probably dates from the period 1858-1860.

See: Ellen G. White, *Spiritual Gifts [vol. 2],* pp. 49-52; Ellen G. White, in *Review,* Mar. 25, 1858, p. 152; Arthur L. White, "Spiritual Gifts, Volume II," *Ministry,* December 1944, pp. 10-12.

[2] "About this time I was shown that it was my duty to visit our people in New Hampshire. My constant and faithful companion at this time was Sister Louisa Foss. . . .We were also accompanied by Elder Files and his wife, . . . Brother Ralph Haskins and Elder White."

See: James White and Ellen G. White, *Life Sketches* (1880), p. 202.

[3] Within some months of the passing of October 22, 1844, most Adventists had come to deny that the October date had any prophetic significance or that the "seventh month movement," which led up to it, was ordained of God in any special sense. Ellen White's visions, however, supported the minority Adventist position, championed by Joseph Turner and Apollos Hale, that October 22 represented a fulfillment of prophecy, i.e., they were "holding fast their advent experience." For a brief survey of divisions among Adventists in 1845, see George R. Knight, *Millennial Fever and the End of the World,* pp. 236-242.

[4] *Identities:* In the original handwritten draft of this manuscript Ellen White did not provide the full names of these two elders, giving only the first and last letters of their surnames. The same format appears in *Spiritual Gifts [vol. 2],* her earliest full autobiographical account published in 1860. However, in an edited and amplified version of her experiences first published in 1880 (*Life Sketches*), the names of the two elders appear in full as "Elders Bennett and Bellings." Variant spellings, "Bennet" and "Billings," are found in Ellen White's later (1904) memories of these events. The exact identity of the two men is difficult to establish since there were several Millerite Adventists with similar names associated with Claremont, New Hampshire, about the time of Ellen White's visit. Thus, Millerite papers from the mid-1840s feature, among others, "Leonard F. Billings," "A. M. Billings," "John Billings," "J. G. Bennet," and "J. G. Bennett," all said to come from Claremont. There may be some grounds for holding that Ellen White was

had so much to say against these two men that we concluded that they were "persecuted for righteousness' sake." We called on them, and were received and treated kindly; yet a depression came upon me, and I felt that all was not right.

Elder B——t [Bennett] had the appearance of being a very holy man. He spoke upon the subject of faith, and said "that all we had to do was to believe, and what we asked of God would be given." He also had much to say upon charity. Brother White answered, "Blessings are promised on conditions," and quoted John 15:7, "'If ye abide in me, and my words abide in you, ye shall ask what ye will, and it shall be done unto you.' Your theory of faith is empty as a flour barrel with both heads out. True charity is a very delicate personage, never stepping her foot out of the path of Bible truth."

In the afternoon we called at Brother Collier's.[5] We were to have a meeting that night at his house, and supposed they were in union with Elder B——t [Bennett]. We questioned them about him, but could get no information. Said Brother C, "If the Lord has sent you here, you will find them out and tell us."

That evening as I was praying and reaching up by faith to claim the blessing of the Lord, B——t [Bennett] and B——s [Billings] began to groan and cry out, Amen! Amen! and threw their sympathy and influence in with my prayer. Brother White was much distressed. He arose and cried out, "I resist this spirit in the name of the Lord." As I was speaking with freedom they commenced groaning and crying out, Amen! Amen! I had no union with them, for their amens chilled me. Brother White felt their influence upon him again, and arose and in the name of the Lord rebuked their wicked spirit, and they were bound. They could not rise again that night.

After the meeting closed, Brother White said, "Brother Collier, now I can tell you about those two men. They are dealing in a satanic influence and are calling it the Spirit of the Lord." Said Brother C, "I believe that the Lord has sent you. We have called their influence mesmerism,[6] and we do not generally have meetings here because we have no union with their spirit. They

---

referring to J. G. Bennett and A. M. Billings, since the *Advent Herald* in 1844 reported that they preached together as a team: "Bro. J. G. Bennet, of Claremont, N. H . . . is associated with Bro. A. M. Billings . . . [who] are now holding Conferences and Camp-meetings continually."

See: Ellen G. White, *Spiritual Gifts [vol. 2],* pp. 46-48; James White and Ellen G. White, *Life Sketches* (1880), pp. 206-208; Ellen G. White, Ms 46, 1904 (May 18); Leonard F. Billings, "Letter from Bro. L. F. Billings," May 6, 1846, p. 103; John Billings, "Letter from Bro. J. Billings," *Advent Herald,* Mar. 25, 1846, p. 55; Leonard F. Billings, "Letter from Bro. L. F. Billings," May 6, 1846, p. 103. On the teamwork of J. G. Bennett and A. M. Billings, see J. V. Himes, "Conference at East Randolph, Vt.," *Advent Herald and Signs of the Times Reporter,* July 24, 1844, p. 199; "L. F. Billings Writes," *idem,* July 31, 1844, p. 204; "The Saints of God Will Hold a Conference . . . ," *idem,* Aug 7, 1844, p. 8.

[5] This person has not been identified.

[6] *See:* EGWEnc, s.v. "Hypnosis and Mesmerism."

rise above us, manifest much feeling, but they leave an influence darker than Egypt. I never saw them checked or tied up before tonight."

While at family prayer that night the Spirit of the Lord rested upon me and I was taken off in vision. A curtain was lifted, and I was shown the case of these men, and a few others in union with them; that they were practicing deception upon the flock of God while professing to be the chosen holy servants of God. I saw darkness and iniquity covered up with a pious garb over their dark designs and deeds, disclosing iniquities that some had scarcely dreamed of, and that God would rend off that false covering and expose hidden things that some have scarcely thought of.

We returned to Grantham[7] [New Hampshire]. On our way I fell from the wagon and so injured my side that I had to be carried into the house.[8] That night I suffered great pain. Sister Foss [**Louisa Foss**][9] prayed for me, and I united in pleading with God for His blessing and relief from pain. About midnight the blessing of the Lord rested upon me, and those in the house were awakened by hearing my voice while in vision. This was the first time I had a view of the voice of God in connection with the time of trouble.[10] In the same vision I was shown that the cause of God had been wounded in Maine and His children disheartened and scattered by a fanatical spirit, and that J. T. [Joseph Turner] and J. H. [John Howell],[11] whom we had placed confidence in, were scattering the flock, and under a cloak of godliness were casting fear among the trembling, conscientious ones. I saw that we must go and bear our

---

[7] According to the *Life Sketches* (1880) account they were on their way "to Springfield" when the accident happened. Since Grantham lies between Claremont and Springfield, there is no contradiction here.

See: James White and Ellen G. White, *Life Sketches* (1880), p. 213.

[8] *Life Sketches* adds that "the road was very bad. We had to travel over bare ground, and then through snow drifts that still remained. I fell from the wagon . . ."

See: Ibid.

[9] In later autobiographical accounts Ellen White wrote of her travels in 1845: "My constant and faithful companion at this time was Sister Louisa Foss, the sister of my brother-in-law." It therefore seems fairly certain that the "Sister Foss" spoken of here is Louisa Foss, sister of **Samuel Hoyt Foss**.

See: Ibid., p. 202.

[10] In an earlier mention of the "voice of God," published in 1846, Ellen White elaborated further on the place of the "voice of God" (see Rev. 16:17) in the sequence of final events. "About four months since, I had a vision of events, all in the future. . . . I saw the time of trouble, such as never was . . . the time of Jacob's trouble. . . . And I saw famine, pestilence and sword. . . . We cried to God for deliverance day and night. Then we heard *the voice of God* which shook the heavens and earth, and gave the 144,000 the day and hour of God's coming."

See: Ellen G. Harmon, "Letter from Sister Harmon," *Day-Star*, Mar. 15, 1846, p. 7. (Italics supplied.)

[11] In other places Ellen White related some of these events using the full names "Joe" or "Joseph" Turner and "John Howell."

See: Ellen G. White, Ms 131, 1906 (Aug. 13); *idem*, "Life Sketches" manuscript," pp. 126-128, EGWE-GC.

testimony in Maine.[12] I related what I had seen to those present.

We soon returned to Portland [Maine] and found the brethren in great confusion. A meeting was appointed at the house of Sister H. [Elizabeth Haines][13] that I might have an opportunity to relate what had been shown me. While imploring the Lord for strength to discharge this painful duty I was taken off in vision, and in the presence of J. T. [Joseph Turner] was again shown his ungodly course. Those present said I talked it out before him. After I came out of vision he said that I was under a wrong influence, that a part of the vision was right and a part was wrong; that it would take a critical spiritual observer to detect the difference; that this was the same spirit that had always pursued him to crush him, etc.

With anguish of spirit I left the meeting, for I had a message for J. T's wife [Jane B. Turner].[14] I rode to their house and bore my testimony to Sister T, which was to comfort her poor, sore heart. She was weeping as though her heart would break. She confirmed the vision which I related to her.[15] We learned from united testimony that honest, precious souls had been set aside and told that they were rejected of God, and that these fanatical persons had flocked to my father's [**Robert Harmon, Sr.**] house and made that their stopping place. J. T. [Joseph Turner] and J. H. [**John Howell**] were leaders in this rank fanaticism. They followed impressions and burdens which led to corruption instead of purity and holiness.

Our parents were disgusted as they saw reason and judgment laid aside by them. They protested against the hypocrisy they witnessed, and as they could not get rid of this company they closed their house and left the city for

---

[12] See Ms 9, 1859 (c. 1859), note 9, regarding the contention that Ellen White in 1845 was immersed in fanaticism herself and did nothing to oppose it.

[13] In *Life Sketches* (1880) the name "Sister Hanes" is inserted, corrected to "Sister Haines" in the 1888 edition. An explanatory footnote in *Spiritual Gifts* makes it probable that "Sister H." is in fact the same Elizabeth Haines at whose home in Portland Ellen Harmon had her first vision some months earlier.

See: James White and Ellen G. White, *Life Sketches* (1880), p. 213; *idem, Life Sketches* (1888), p. 213; Ellen G. White, *Spiritual Gifts [vol. 2],* p. 302.

[14] Jane B. Turner, wife of Joseph Turner. By 1848 Joseph Turner was based in Hartford, Connecticut, where he edited the *Bible Advocate* and, later, the *Second Advent Watchman.*

See: 1850 U.S. Federal Census, "Jane B. Turner," Connecticut, Hartford County, Hartford City, p. 217.

[15] Many years later Ellen White gave further details regarding the contents of this vision. It showed Turner "transgressing the commandments, giving attention to other women, and his wife suffering under the great strain. . . ." His distraught wife confirmed the vision relating how her husband would sometimes spend "half the night, and sometimes all night" with Sarah Jordan, sister of William Jordan, "giving her visions." Ellen White attributed Sarah's "so-called visions" to Turner's "mesmeric passes." She also related how, sometime later, while in a meeting in Poland, Maine, Turner unsuccessfully tried to "mesmerize" her.

See: EGWEnc, s.v. "Hypnosis and Mesmerism"; Ellen G. White, "Life Sketches" manuscript, pp. 127, 128, EGWE-GC; *idem, Spiritual Gifts [vol. 2],* p. 38; *idem,* Ms 131, 1906 (Aug. 13).

Poland [Maine], where my two married sisters [**Harriet McCann** and **Mary Plummer Foss**][16] were living. This did not suit J. T. [Joseph Turner] and he told me when we arrived at Poland that my father was a doomed man; that my mother [**Eunice Gould Harmon**] and sisters might be saved, but my father would be lost. The only reason he offered was because he did not give him possession of his house. When he left Portland his denunciations were bitter. We visited Poland, where my parents were, and as we listened to the recital of their trials and of incidents which had occurred, the vision given in New Hampshire was confirmed.[17]

---

[16] *See:* Artemas C. Harmon, ed., *The Harmon Genealogy,* p. 41; 1850 U.S. Federal Census, "Harriet McCann," Maine, Cumberland County, Poland, p. 34; 1850 U.S. Federal Census, "Mary Foss," Maine, Cumberland County, Poland, p. 46.

[17] For a survey of the continued strained relationship between Joseph Turner on the one hand and the Whites and Joseph Bates on the other, see Merlin D. Burt, "Sabbatarian Adventism From 1844 to 1849," pp. 140-46, 151, 348-350.

1856

(Lt 11, 1856)

APRIL,[1] BATTLE CREEK, MICHIGAN

LETTER TO

Charles W. Sperry and Rachel Ann Sperry.[2]

Previously unpublished.

Counsel to the Gardners regarding financial sacrifice, especially the necessity of helping to support their daughter and son-in-law, Charles and Rachel Ann Sperry.

Dear Brother and Sister Sperry:

While your parents [Henry Gaines Gardner and Diantha Gardner][3] were here I was shown in vision[4] the following concerning them:

I saw in vision that God was not displeased with your moving west,[5] that

---

[1] The original handwritten letter bears only the month of "April," omitting the year. The year "1861" was added in pencil some time later, probably based on the fact that the Gardners moved west to New York State in 1861. Careful analysis of the letter suggests, however, that the move referred to was a *planned* move west to be with their son in Illinois, not their move to New York in 1861. Diantha Gardner's letter to the *Review* in 1856 clearly refers to this planned move to Illinois. Further confirming the date of 1856 is the stationery used. The watermark on the paper, "Southworth Mfg. Co.," is the same as on two other letters written in 1856, and does not appear on any extant letters from subsequent years, through 1861. The letter closes with a reference to Ellen White's extended illness that closely parallels the account in *Spiritual Gifts [vol. 2]*, pp. 206, 207, identified as occurring in the winter of 1855-1856.

[2] *Identity*: Charles Warren Sperry (1819-1861) and Rachel Ann Sperry (née Gardner) (1831-1863).

See: Ms 1, 1857 (June), note 2.

[3] *Identity*: In 1850 Henry Gaines Gardner (c. 1801-1887) and Diantha Gardner (née Shepherd) (1808-1876), lived in Panton, Addison County, Vermont, where they were active in the Sabbathkeeping group in the area.

See: 1850 U.S. Federal Census, "Henry Gardner," Vermont, Addison County, Panton, p. 8.

[4] The content of this letter, though specifically written for the Gardner family, closely parallels the account of a vision dated 1855, described in *Spiritual Gifts [vol. 2]*, pp. 212-214.

[5] In February 1856 Diantha Gardner wrote, "You have learned no doubt that we expect to go to Ill. in the Spring if the Lord will." The counsel in this letter apparently played a role in changing the family's plans. The Gardners and Sperrys did indeed move from Panton, Vermont, but instead of moving west, they moved east about 18 miles [29 kilometers] to Bristol, Addison County, Vermont, in April of 1857, according to the entries in the 1857 diary of Charles Sperry.

See: Diantha Gardner, "Sister Gardner of Panton, Vt., Writes," *Review*, Feb. 21, 1856, pp. 166, 167; Charles W. Sperry, "Diary" (Berrien Springs, Mich.: Center for Adventist Research,

you could have no influence in Panton [Vermont]. I saw that you must move carefully, have all that you possess upon God's altar, have all your substance there. You have at times thought it was there, but if all had been on God's altar, you would feel more of a spirit of sacrificing. This you have not had. You know but little [of] what it is to sacrifice for God's cause and honor Him with your substance. You have had but few blessings from the poor and needy because their hearts were made glad by your generosity.

I saw that you both naturally loved this world, loved money, and this is, and still will be, a snare to you. You cling to money closely, especially Brother Gardner. I saw that you would have to view these things in altogether a different light before you can be fitted up and prepared for the time of trouble. I saw that in order for you to have health and the blessing of God you must keep the possessions out of your heart, you must get rid of a covetous spirit. You must have your substance where you can use it for God's glory in His cause, as well as to use it for your own self-interest.

I saw that you never have looked at this matter in the true light. I saw that you should not, in going west, let your natural or sympathetic feelings lead you astray. Your son [Samuel H. Gardner][6] is no more precious in the eyes of the Lord because he is your son, than another young man that loves not the truth of God and keeps not His commandments. I saw that you should not link with him but keep entirely separate, and it will save you trouble and perplexity. Yet be patient, treat him kindly, and win him to the truth if you can.

Brother Gardner, you must command your words and actions. Let not your quick, hasty temper run away with you or overcome you. You must be a perfect overcomer. God would be better pleased if you both had more of an open-hearted, generous disposition. Here is where you fail; here is your weak point. You have gained some since you embraced the belief of Christ's coming, but you have not yet come where God wants you to come. You must overcome this lack and be quick to feel and see others' wants.

Deny yourselves, and when you bring a gift to the altar let it be the best of the substance. Reserve not the best for yourself and give the poorest away. God will not accept a lame offering. Present not that that will do you or the receiver no special good. Here is an opportunity for you to deny yourself and sacrifice an offering of the best of your substance, offered heartily, willingly. Upon these things you can improve. God despises an offering given

---

Andrews University), entries for Mar. 23, 1857 and Apr. 21, 1857.

[6] *Identity*: Samuel H. Gardner (1829-1900), son of Henry and Diantha Gardner, had moved west to Ogle County, Illinois, where he had married Esther Heath in 1855 and was becoming a prosperous farmer.

See: "Samuel H. Gardner," in Illinois, Ogle County, Jordan Dodd and Liahona Research, comp., *Illinois Marriages, 1851-1900* [database online] (Provo, Utah: Ancestry.com Operations Inc., 2005).

grudgingly. You must improve on these things if you expect the approbation of God.

I saw that it should not be your object to go west to get rich, but to advance God's cause and His glory. I saw that a solemn responsibility rests upon you. You are God's stewards, handling means that He has lent you. It is not your own. You are not your own. You have been bought with a price.

I saw that Charles [**Charles W. Sperry**] entering your family has been a benefit to you all.[7] It has been a blessing to you. I saw that Charles and Rachel Ann [Sperry] both were beloved of God. I saw that Charles was a precious, chosen vessel and he could do good in the cause of God and should be left free from shackles to devote himself fully to the work of God.

I saw that you could help the cause by freely having a care for them. Do not wait for them to make their wants known, but be quick to see them and supply their lack. They have felt delicate and embarrassed about receiving much from you, and you felt too much as though you were doing considerable. I saw that all that would have to be done for them (if what you have was upon God's altar) could be done with pleasure, as though it were to Jesus, and you would scarcely feel at all what you would do to supply their lack. This is one way in which you can help the cause of God.[8]

You can safely bestow upon them. They are in no way prodigal of their means, and they must be careful lest their frugality should lead them too far, and they go to extremes and be too close, and their example be injurious to others.[9]

All should be careful not to make a god of money. While some have needed a reproof about too free use of means, or extravagant use of it upon themselves, others go to the opposite extreme and are so careful of it as not to use it at all, and the cause of God is not advanced by their means. The means is held to be swept away by God's wrath and does no one good, and they fail of their heavenly treasure, fail of all. God loves to have His children open-hearted, generous, benevolent.

---

[7] According to the 1850 census, Charles and Rachel Ann Sperry were living with her parents, Henry and Diantha Gardner, in Panton, Vermont.

See: 1850 U.S. Federal Census, "Charles W. Sperry," Vermont, Addison County, Panton, p. 8.

[8] Apparently referring to this counsel, Ellen White wrote to Rachel Ann Sperry in 1861: "From what was shown some time ago in vision in regard to the matter—that they [the Gardners] should have a special care of Charles—a duty rested upon them in his case, and their means could not be better applied than in making him comfortable. From the light there given me, there was a fear upon the part of Brother and Sister Gardner that the church would not do all their duty to Brother Sperry, and these feelings have led them not to do for you that which their relationship and God required them to do."

See: Ellen G. White, Lt 8, 1861 (Sept. 26).

[9] In 1861 Ellen White wrote that "Brother Sperry was affected with . . . close economizing."
See: Ibid.

All have an influence. We should be very careful and in no way encourage selfishness, for this God hates. "God loveth a cheerful giver."

As I saw your cases, the angel said, "Cut loose, cut loose. Make decided efforts for thy eternal welfare." I saw you prized money too highly. Then I saw how paltry it was, how soon swept away. But if it was bestowed upon God's cause it would increase and it would be durable riches, safe and sure in heaven. A great work must be done for God's people, for they are getting hold of this world with both hands, and losing their hold of the eternal world. The spirit of sacrifice must revive or some souls will die and it will be those that have and do not.[10]

E. G. W.

Dear Brother and Sister: This is the vision given me for your parents [Henry and Diantha Gardner]. Have copied it as I wrote it then. I have been very, very sick. Was sick when they were here. Had been sick for months before, with difficulty of lungs, every breath caused me pain. When they were here was attacked with brain fever. Gave up my husband and children, expecting to die, but James sent for brethren and sisters to pray for me. I was anointed and prayed for, and was instantly relieved of pain, yet the difficulty from my lungs was not removed.

The morning after I was healed, your mother [Diantha Gardner] was prayed for and blessed and healed. I was taken off in vision and saw the above. My weakness clung to me for weeks. But a few nights since, I dreamed of being in meeting and exhorting all night. In the morning James [**James Springer White**] awoke me thinking I was having a nightmare. I awoke with the forcible impression that I had received strength all through my system.

When I arose and dressed I knew that a wonderful work had been done for me. My throat and lungs were free. I felt like a new being, and the disease has not returned. The angel of God surely touched me in the night, and I was healed. Praise God, praise Him for His wonderful goodness to me. My soul shall triumph in God.[11]

---

[10] A few years later Ellen White commended Henry Gardner for doing "all he could do, and more than he can do in the future," to care for the needs of **John Nevins Andrews**. This suggests that the Gardners responded positively to her appeal.

See: Ellen G. White, Ms 11, 1863 (c. 1863).

[11] For additional details about Ellen White's illness and healing on this occasion, see her account in *Spiritual Gifts [vol. 2]*, pp. 206, 207.

THE JAMES AND ELLEN WHITE FAMILY TREE

The White Family

John White
B: Apr. 12, 1785 (Skowhegan, Maine)
M: c. 1809 (Elizabeth Jewitt)
D: Jul 5, 1871 (Battle Creek, Mich.)

Elizabeth Jewitt
B: Feb. 14, 1788 (Exeter, N.H.)
M: c. 1809 (John White)
D: Jan. 9, 1871 (Battle Creek, Mich.)

Mary Shepherd
B: Jun. 26, 1810 (Palmyra, Maine)
M: (David Chase)
D: Aug. 31, 1889

John Whitney
B: Nov. 2, 1812 (Palmyra, Maine)
M: Jun. 17, 1840 (Anna C. Williams)
D: May 1, 1886 (Ohio)

Samuel Shepard
B: Jan. 2, 1816 (Palmyra, Maine)
M: (1. Harriet Judkins 2. Clarissa Sawyer)
D: Aug. 3, 1890 (unknown)

Elizabeth Jewitt
B: Dec. 16, 1818 (Palmyra, Maine)
M: (Thomas B. Tenney)
D: Sep. 4, 1885

Joseph
B: Jul. 31, 1824 (Palmyra, Maine)
M: never married
D: c. 1828

Benjamin
B: Mar. 31, 1827 (Palmyra, Maine)
M: unknown
D: After 1860

Anna
B: Jan 27, 1829 (Palmyra, Maine)
M: never married
D: Nov 30, 1854 (Rochester, N.Y.)

Nathaniel
B. Jul. 2, 1831 (Palmyra, Maine)
M: never married
D: May 6, 1853 (Rochester, N.Y.)

The Harmon Family

Robert Harmon
B: Feb. 28, 1786 (Standish, Maine)
M: Jul. 4, 1810 (Eunice Gould)
D: Nov. 6, 1866 (Kensington, Conn.)

Eunice Gould
B: 1787 (Portland, Maine)
M: Jul. 4, 1810 (Robert Harmon)
D: 1863 (Greene County, Ill.)

Caroline True
B: Apr. 9, 1812 (Portland, Maine)
M: Jun. 2, 1835 (Mace Richard Clough)
D: Mar. 29, 1883 (Paola, Kans.)

Harriet B.
B: 1813 (Portland, Maine)
M: Aug. 1831 (Samuel McCann)
D: Jan. 21, 1876 (Saco, Maine)

John B.
B: Dec. 29, 1815 (Portland, Maine)
M: (1. Dorcas Gould 2. Abigail Bagby 3. Lucy Bagby)
D: Mar. 6, 1883 (Hardin, Ill.)

Mary Plummer
B: Jul. 21, 1821 (Portland, Maine)
M: Jul. 5, 1842 (Samuel Foss)
D: May 22, 1912 (Auburn, Maine)

Sarah B.
B: Feb. 13, 1823 (Portland, Maine)
M: Aug. 5, 1851 (Stephen Belden)
D: Nov. 25, 1868 (Berlin, Conn.)

Robert F., Jr.
B: Jul. 13, 1825 (Gorham, Maine)
M: never married
D: Feb. 5, 1853 (Gorham, Maine)

Elizabeth N.
B: Nov. 26, 1827 (Gorham, Maine)
M: Apr. 22, 1849 (Reuben M. Bangs)
D: Dec. 21, 1891 (Gorham, Maine)

James Springer White
B: Aug. 4, 1821 (Palmyra, Maine)
M: Aug. 30, 1846 (Ellen Gould Harmon)
D: Aug. 6, 1881 (Battle Creek, Mich.)

Henry Nichols
B: Aug. 26, 1847 (Gorham, Maine)
M: never married
D: Dec. 8, 1863 (Topsham, Maine)

James Edson
B: Jul. 28, 1849 (Rocky Hill, Conn.)
M: 1. Jul. 28, 1870 (Emma L. McDearman)
2. Aug. 3, 1922 (Rebecca Burrill)
D: Jun. 3, 1928 (Otsego, Mich.)

William Clarence
B: Aug. 29, 1854 (Rochester, N.Y.)
M:
D: Sep. 1, 1937 (St. Helena, Calif.)

John Herbert
B: Sep. 20, 1860 (Battle Creek, Mich.)
M: never married
D: Dec. 14, 1860 (Battle Creek, Mich.)

Ellen Gould Harmon
B: Nov. 26, 1827 (Gorham, Maine)
M: Aug. 30, 1846 (James White)
D: July 16, 1915 (St. Helena, Calif.)

Mary Kelsey
B: Apr. 20, 1857
M: Feb. 11, 1876 (William Clarence)
D: Jun. 18, 1890 (Boulder, Colo.)

Ella May
B: Jan. 1, 1882
M: May 1, 1905 (Dores Robinson)
D: May 24, 1977 (Loveland, Colo.)

Mabel Eunice
B: Nov. 1, 1886
M: Sep. 12, 1906 (Wilfred Workman)
D: Apr. 17, 1981 (National City, Calif.)

Ethel May Lacey
B: Sep. 8, 1873
M: May 9, 1895 (William Clarence)
D: Sep. 7, 1969 (Angwin, Calif.)

James Henry
B: Apr. 6, 1896
M: Nov. 15, 1921 (Margaret Rossiter)
D: Apr. 18, 1954 (Sacramento, Calif.)

Herbert Clarence
B: Apr. 6, 1896
M: Jun. 26, 1919 (Anna Johnson)
D: Oct. 22, 1962 (Arlington, Calif.)

Evelyn Grace
B: Jun. 15, 1900
M: Jun. 26, 1919 (John Jacques)
D: Feb. 17, 1995 (St. Helena, Calif.)

Arthur Lacey
B: Oct. 5, 1907
M: Jun. 26, 1925 (Frieda Swingle)
D: Jan. 12, 1991 (St. Helena, Calif.)

Francis Edward
B: Sep. 29, 1913
M: Jul. 12, 1936 (Rachel Rub)
D: May 30, 1992 (Yountville, Calif.)

Marriage dates and death places provided when known.

BIOGRAPHICAL SKETCHES

The following biographical sketches are of persons whose names appear in bold print in Ellen White's letters and manuscripts in this volume. Many of these people have received little or no mention in Seventh-day Adventist histories or encyclopedias, but they are included in this series because Ellen White interacted with them and either wrote to them or mentioned them in the documents included in this volume. Often little is known about them, but learning even a little information about their background can be helpful in understanding Ellen White's interaction with them.

Biographical entries for well-known figures such as James White or Joseph Bates have been abbreviated, since information about their life and work is readily available in standard encyclopedias and histories such as the *Seventh-day Adventist Encyclopedia* (SDAE) or the *Ellen G. White Encyclopedia* (EGWEnc).

The sketches typically begin with brief, general biographical data that includes information about the subjects' relationship to and engagement with the Seventh-day Adventist Church. This is followed by an often lengthier segment that focuses on their relationship to Ellen White, in cases in which such information is known. Each sketch concludes with bibliographical references, which correspond generally to the sequence of the data presented in the sketch. Complete bibliographical references are provided only for sources not included in this volume's bibliography.

Roland Karlman

AMADON, George Washington (1832-1913) and Martha Dormer (1834-1937)

George Amadon was baptized by J. N. Loughborough in 1853. At the time he was working on the Erie Canal driving horses that towed canal boats. Probably in the same year Amadon began employment as typesetter at the Review and Herald office in Rochester, New York, moving to Battle Creek, Michigan, when the office was transferred there in 1855. When the "Review and Herald Publishing Association" was incorporated in 1861, George Amadon was elected vice president. Altogether he worked as a printer at the press for about 50 years, also editing the *Youth's Instructor* (1858-1864 and 1867-1869). Already 70 years old when the Review building burned down in 1902, Amadon did not move to Washington, D.C., when the press was relocated there, but served as visitation pastor in the Battle Creek church during his final years.

Martha Byington, daughter of **John Byington,** first General Conference president, married George Amadon in 1860. In 1853 Martha became the first teacher in a school organized by her father in Buck's Bridge, New York, thought to be the first Seventh-day Adventist school. Later she taught Ellen and James White's sons in Battle Creek for a time, as evidenced by an entry in her diary from 1857. She also did domestic work in the White home prior to her marriage and sporadically thereafter. In 1874 Martha Amadon became the first president of the Dorcas and Benevolent Association, later known as the Dorcas Society.

In later years Ellen White liked to recall how, before he came to the Whites in 1853, George Amadon had been "a mischievous boy working on the towpath with the horses" but had become "one of our main pillars in Battle Creek," whom she regarded "very highly." Judging by available correspondence, relations between the Amadon and White families appear to have been consistently positive, with the exception of a period in the latter 1860s. Several of Ellen White's letters from 1869 outline the antipathy to James White on the part of Martha Amadon, Harriet Smith, and Cornelia Cornell during this period, to the point where "it would have been good news, had you heard my husband was dead." All three women were married to prominent church leaders, who in turn had been influenced by their negative views. Letters from Ellen White to George Amadon in the 1890s and early 1900s show that she placed a great deal of confidence in him, asking him to assist in sensitive matters. This included requesting Amadon to help conciliate in the growing rift between J. H. Kellogg and the church.

See: Obituary: "Martha D. Amadon," *Review,* Feb. 4, 1937, p. 21; obituary: "G. W. Amadon," *Review,* Mar. 20, 1913, p. 279; J. N. Loughborough, "Second Advent Experience—No. 8," *Review,* Aug. 2, 1923, p. 6; SDAE, s.v. "George Washington Amadon," "Martha D. (Byington) Amadon"; Martha Byington, 1857 Diary (Center for Adventist Research, Andrews University), entry for Nov. 12, 1857; Ellen G. White, Ms 83, 1910 (Apr. 16); Ms 78, 1910 (Apr. 2); Lt 13, 1869 (Sept. 24). For a biography of G. W. Amadon, see Milton Raymond Hook, *Flames Over Battle Creek: The Story of George W. Amadon, Review and Herald Printer, Who Shared in the Early Successes and Tragedies of the Seventh-day Adventist Church* (Washington, D.C.: Review and Herald, 1977).

ANDREWS, Edward (1798-1865) and Sarah L. (1803-1899)

Parents of Seventh-day Adventist pioneer **John Nevins Andrews**. A laborer from Paris, Maine, Edward and his wife, Sarah, participated in the Millerite Advent expectation and disappointment of 1844 and became among the earliest Adventist Sabbathkeepers in Maine in 1845. There is some evidence that Edward Andrews was involved in "no work" fanaticism for about two years in the mid-1840s. Ellen and James White boarded in his home for some months from late 1850 to summer 1851. In 1855 the Andrews family moved, with other Adventists, to Waukon, Iowa, where Andrews farmed until his death in 1865. At the age of 80 Sarah Andrews visited her son, J. N. Andrews, in Switzerland, a few months before he died of tuberculosis.

Edward Andrews' relationship to Ellen and James White was strained for many years. As late as 1861 he accused James of cheating him out of $8 in 1850. Together with other members of his family, Andrews cultivated skepticism and opposition to the visions and testimonies of Ellen White. Two years before his death he showed a change of heart and wrote to the Whites "to confess all the wrongs my cruel unbelief has ever heaped on you."

See: Obituary: "Edward Andrews," *Review,* May 2, 1865, p. 175; obituary: "Sarah L. Andrews," *Review,* July 18, 1899, p. 468; 1850 U.S. Federal Census, "Edward Andrews," Maine, Oxford County, Paris, p. 190; Marian C. S. Crawford Stowell in "General Conference Proceedings, Sixth Meeting, Sunday, April 7," *General Conference Bulletin,* Apr. 8, 1901, p. 116; Ron Graybill, "The Family Man," in Harry Leonard, ed., *J. N. Andrews: The Man and the Mission,* pp. 15-19, 26-28; Edward White to "Brother and Sister White," Jan. 25, 1863.

ANDREWS, John Nevins (1829-1883) and Angeline Spaulding (1824-1872)

The first Seventh-day Adventist missionary sent to countries outside North America, J. N. Andrews was a careful biblical scholar and author of the classic *History of the Sabbath.* He was born in Poland, Maine, and died at Basel, Switzerland, at the age of 54. In 1856 he married Angeline S. Stevens. He began to observe the Sabbath in his teens, started his work as a minister at 21 in 1850, and was ordained in 1853. In 1867 he became the third president of the General Conference, a position he held for two years.

In 1874, in company with his children, Charles and Mary (his wife had died in 1872), Andrews sailed from Boston for Liverpool, England, en route to Switzerland. His main achievement in Europe was in starting publishing work in several languages and editing the French monthly paper *Les Signes des Temps.*

In the quality of his biblical and historical research and writing Andrews was unmatched among Adventist writers of his time. He made original contributions in several areas of doctrine, such as the time to begin the Sabbath and in the application of the two-horned beast of Revelation 13 to the United States of America. His groundbreaking classic, *History of the Sabbath,* went through four editions.

For some years both John and Angeline Andrews seem to have had a somewhat ambivalent attitude toward the visions of Ellen White. One likely contributing factor was the influence of their parents on both sides, who for many years were skeptical of the visions, in particular those that involved personal reproof. John tended to express his sympathies to those who were reprimanded, thereby undoing the intended effect. He is said to have insinuated doubts about the genuineness of the visions in the mind of a Michigan minister, J. B. Frisbie, and also to have "unsettled the mind of Henry Nichols in regard to the visions [from which he] . . . never recovered."

Angeline Andrews expressed a change of heart in regard to the visions in letters from 1862. "My heart is pained in view of my past course and the position which I have occupied relative to the visions." As for John, Ellen White later traced his turning point to his presence at the remarkable meetings held during the Whites' visit to Waukon, Iowa, in 1856. "God wrought there in great power. John was convinced that God was in the work." Andrews subsequently became a strong supporter of the ministry of Ellen White, even though at times he failed to heed her testimonies to him. Thus, for example, Andrews ultimately failed to respond to recurring admonitions that he should adopt a more balanced lifestyle.

"Health has been sacrificed by night labor," Ellen White pointed out to him in 1872. "He has robbed himself of rest and sleep." Yet five years later Andrews confessed, "I commence my [editorial] work with the light of the morning and continue it quite late into the night." Also in 1877 Andrews described his unbalanced diet of "baker's bread, graham pudding, potatoes and occasionally a cabbage" and the pronouncement of a physician on examining him during an illness: "This man is almost starved to death."

Although J. N. Andrews' response to Ellen White's testimonies was at times inadequate, yet on a personal level the Whites had the highest regard and respect for the remarkable talents of Andrews and his contributions to the church. He was, in Ellen White's estimation, the "ablest man in all our ranks."

See: SDAE, s.v. "John Nevins Andrews"; obituary: "The Death of Eld. Andrews," *Review,* Oct. 30, 1883, p. 680; obituary: "Death of Sister Andrews," *Review,* Apr. 2, 1872, p. 124; Ellen G. White, Lt 11, 1862 (Nov. 9); Lt 11, 1860 (Oct. 22); Lt 8, 1860 (June 11); *Testimony to the Church at Battle Creek* (Battle Creek, Mich.: Steam Press, 1872), p. 84; J. N. Andrews to "Brother White," June 22, 1877; J. N. Andrews to "Brother White," Feb. 6, 1877; Ellen G. White, Lt 2a, 1878 (Aug. 29); A. S. Andrews to Brother and Sister White, Jan. 30, 1862; Feb. 2, 1862. For detailed studies, see essays in Harry Leonard, ed., *J. N. Andrews: The Man and the Mission.*

ANDREWS, William P. (1838-1878) and Martha (1842-1901)

Younger brother of **John Nevins Andrews**. About 1861 William married Martha A. Butler, granddaughter of **Ezra Pitt Butler** (governor of Vermont, 1826-1828), and sister of **George I. Butler**, later General Conference president. One of their daughters, Edith Andrews, assisted J. N. Andrews at the mission in Switzerland. After William's death, Martha married **Augustin Cornelius Bourdeau**, pioneer minister in New England and Quebec and missionary to Europe.

William Andrews moved with his family to Waukon, Iowa, in 1855 and spent most of the remainder of his years in that state. Other than his ordination as deacon of the Waukon church in 1863 and his appointment to certain church committees, there is little trace of William Andrews in the *Review.* It appears that the only clear reference to him by name in Ellen White's writings was the greeting she sent him in 1857, following her visit to Waukon. She closed with the words "Tell him there will be no lame ones there. All will be health." James White confirmed that William Andrews was "a cripple."

See: Obituary: "William P. Andrews," *Review,* Aug. 8, 1878, p. 55; obituary: "Martha A. Bourdeau," *Review,* Sept. 10, 1901, p. 598; obituary: "Edith Andrews," *Review,* Jan. 26, 1886, p. 59; Isaac Sanborn, "Report From Bro. Sanborn," *Review,* Dec. 8, 1863, p. 13; Ellen G. White, Lt 12, 1857 (Jan. 30); James White to "Dear Brother," Feb. 9, 1855; search term "W. P. Andrews" in *Review and Herald* online collection, www.adventistarchives.org.

ARNOLD, David (1805-1889) and **Lucretia K.** (c. 1812-after 1889)

David Arnold contributed to early Sabbatarian Adventist doctrinal discussions and was the first president of the New York Conference (1862-1863). He joined the Methodist Episcopal Church at 16 and later engaged in the Millerite movement. After the 1844 disappointment, Arnold retained his Adventist beliefs but showed an openness to new ideas outside the more widely held Adventism of Joshua Himes and the *Advent Herald.* In 1848 he hosted an important conference of Sabbatarian Adventists on his farm in Volney, New York, and in 1850 joined the publishing committee of James White's *Advent Review.* From 1849 onward David Arnold contributed a number of significant theological articles to church periodicals. He also served on various New York committees and in 1862-1863 as first president of the newly formed New York Conference.

The earliest mention of David Arnold in a Sabbatarian context is from the 1848 Volney conference. Some 30 or 40 persons were present, including James and Ellen White. It is not certain that Arnold was already a Sabbathkeeper at this time, since the meeting appears, at least in part, to have had an evangelistic purpose. James White reported that "Brother Bates preached the Sabbath to them with strong argument, much boldness and power." Ellen White later recalled that, to her consternation, Arnold strongly urged various heterodox views at the conference. Among them was the idea "that the 1000 years of Revelation xx were in the past," a viewpoint no doubt inspired by recent editorials on the millennium in the *Bible Advocate,* to which Arnold had been a subscriber since its inception in 1846.

Remarkably, Ellen White reported that the "discordant views" of Arnold and others were resolved and "our meeting ended victoriously. Truth gained the victory." According to J. N. Loughborough's later interview with a conference participant, the turning point came when Ellen White, while in public vision, raised a Bible aloft, and turned to and recited a number of Bible passages pertinent to the issues under dispute. David Arnold subsequently held the visions of Ellen White in high regard, even to the point of urging that they be made a test of fellowship, a position that both Ellen and James White rejected and for which Ellen cautioned Arnold.

See: Obituary: "David Arnold," *Review,* July 23, 1889, p. 479; 1880 U.S. Federal Census, "Arnold, Lucretia," New York, Oswego County, Volney, p. 25; SDAE, s.v. "David Arnold"; search terms "D. Arnold" and "David Arnold" in *Review and Herald* online collection, www.adventistarchives.org; James White to Leonard and Elvira Hastings, Aug. 26, 1848; David Arnold to editor, *Bible Advocate,* June 24, 1847, p. 74; J. N. Loughborough, "Recollections of the Past—No. 12," *Review,* Mar. 3, 1885, pp. 137, 138; Ellen G. White, *Spiritual*

Gifts [vol. 2], pp. 97-99; Ms 2, 1856 (May 27). For observations on David Arnold's theological contributions, see, for example, SDAE, s.v. "Sanctuary," "The Daily," and "Spiritism."

ASHLEY, Melora Atwood (née **CRAPO**) (1820-1904) and **Josiah Leonard** (1819-1845)

A follower of William Miller in the early 1840s, living in Dartmouth, Massachusetts, Melora Ashley married Josiah Leonard in 1841 but became a widow in 1845. As early as 1845 or 1846 she became acquainted with Ellen and James White. According to her obituary the Whites "became her intimate friends." Census information indicates that Melora Ashley and her family were neighbors to or lived near **Philip** and **Nancy Collins,** also close friends of the Whites. In 1849 Melora Ashley appears to have been present when the Whites were called to the bed of 13-year-old **Gilbert Collins**, close to death with whooping cough, and to have witnessed his remarkable healing. In 1864, on the advice of the Whites, Mrs. Ashley moved to Battle Creek, Michigan, where she lived her remaining years.

See: Obituary: "Melora A. Ashley," *Review*, Mar. 24, 1904, p. 23; Frederick Adams Virkus and Albert Nelson Marquis, *The Abridged Compendium of American Genealogy: First Families of America. A Genealogical Encyclopedia of the United States* (Chicago: F. A. Virkus & Co., 1926), vol. 2, p. 258; John Nevins Andrews et al., *Defense of Elder James White and Wife,* p. 40; 1850 U.S. Federal Census, "Malora [*sic*] Ashley," Massachusetts, Bristol County, Dartmouth, p. 443; Ellen G. White, *Spiritual Gifts [vol. 2]*, pp. 108, 109, 303.

AUSTIN, Horatio Nelson (1818-1889) and **Caroline R.** (1821-1915)

Church members from Berkshire, Vermont. Horatio Austin was a lifelong resident of Berkshire who, with his wife, became a Sabbathkeeper in 1854. The Austins were dairy farmers and known for their hospitality. "Bro. Austin remarked that his doors were open," reported M. E. Cornell of meetings held in Berkshire in 1862, "that he could keep ten horses, and as many persons as were drawn by them to the place." Ellen and James White stayed with the Austins in 1859 while attending a conference.

Caroline Austin was an active layperson and served for some time during the 1870s as vice president of the Vermont Tract and Missionary Society. A few years after her husband's death, Caroline moved to Battle Creek, Michigan, to live with her daughter Ella, wife of Henry W. Kellogg, who for many years was manager of the Review and Herald Publishing Association. Letters from Ellen White to Henry Kellogg during the 1890s often included greetings to Caroline.

See: Obituary: "H. N. Austin," *Review*, Jan. 21, 1890, p. 47; obituary: "Caroline R. Cummings Austin," *Review*, Mar. 25, 1915, p. 22; "Horatio N. Austin" in *Franklin, Grand Isle Counties, Vermont Business Directory, 1883 [database online]*, ed. Donella K. Ashline, 1999, http://search.ancestry.com (Dec. 4, 2006); M. E. Cornell, "Report From Bro. Cornell," *Review,* Apr. 8, 1862, p. 149; Ellen G. White, Ms 8, 1859 (Oct. 16, 1859, entry);

search terms "C. R. Austin" and "H. N. Austin" in *Review and Herald* online collection, www.adventistarchives.org.

BACHELLER, John Warren (1839-1917) and **Arvilla M.** (1837-1911)

In 1852 James White invited Cynthia Bacheller, a widow from Vermont, together with her two teenage children, Warren and **Roxanna**, to stay with the Whites in Rochester, New York. Warren (known by his middle name) and Roxanna were employed at the Review and Herald publishing office. For Warren Bacheller it was the beginning of his lifework as printer at the Review and Herald, first in Rochester and later in Battle Creek, Michigan, where the press moved in 1855. He married Arvilla Lane in 1862. From 1869 to 1870 he also served as treasurer of the Michigan Conference.

Ellen White had occasion to counsel Warren Bacheller in 1859 about his shortcomings as a worker at the press. In 1872 she noted that he had "been growing cold and careless in regard to your own salvation." However, after the revivals of 1888 and in the years following, she enthused that he had "met with a new conversion." "Brother Warren reveals the blessing of God in his face, for it looks as if the Sun of Righteousness was beaming upon him."

See: Obituary: "John Warren Bacheller," *Review,* Oct. 25, 1917, p. 18; obituary: "Mrs. J. W. Bacheller," *Lake Union Herald,* May 24, 1911, p. 6; Frederick Clifton Pierce, *Batchelder, Batcheller Genealogy* (Chicago: W. B. Conkey, 1898), pp. 577, 578; 1900 U.S. Federal Census, "Arvilla M. Batchelor [*sic*]," Michigan, Calhoun County, Michigan, p. 165A; Wm. C. Gage, "Michigan State Conference: Ninth Annual Session," *Review,* May 25, 1869, p. 173; Ellen G. White, *Testimony to the Church at Battle Creek* (Battle Creek, Mich.: Steam Press, 1872), p. 31; Lt 83, 1889 (Jan. 5); Lt 30, 1890 (Mar. 10).

BACHELLER, Roxanna. See **CORNELL, James** and **Roxanna.**

BAKER, Joseph (c. 1801-after 1873) and **Mary** (c. 1796-1876)

Former Millerite preacher Joseph Baker, a farmer of Lebanon, New Hampshire, became a Sabbathkeeper after being contacted by Joseph Bates in 1850. Soon thereafter he became a sought-after preacher for the Sabbatarian Adventists and traveled widely in New England, New York, and Canada on preaching tours. He also was an able writer and served on the publishing committee of the *Review* for two years. For reasons that may have been connected to failing health, there are no records of Baker's evangelistic work after 1854.

Ellen White's major comment on Joseph Baker appears in a letter written in November 1851. Apparently, together with a minority of other believers in Vermont and New Hampshire, Baker had accepted Joseph Bates's contention that the Second

Advent would take place in October 1851. Ellen White described how, after the passing of that time, Baker was "much discouraged and sunken" while attending a conference in Johnson, Vermont, in November 1851, together with the Whites. Prior to the conference Baker and others had resisted Ellen White's visions, which had opposed the 1851 time setting.

The Johnson conference was a turning point for Baker. "It is high time," he declared, "for me to decide there is no half way work about this business; the visions are all of God, or there are none of them of God. Well, you say, what is Brother Baker going to do? Believe the visions." During the same conference Baker was confirmed in his public ministry as Ellen White saw in vision that "God had a work for him to do, . . . to feed . . . the starving sheep."

See: 1850 U.S. Federal Census, "Joseph Baker," New Hampshire, Grafton, Lebanon, p. 19; obituary: "Mary Baker," *Review,* July 20, 1876, p. 31; [Letter from Joseph Bates], *Present Truth,* November 1850, p. 88; search term "Baker" in *Words of the Pioneers;* Ellen G. White, Lt 8, 1851 (Nov. 12); Arthur L. White, *Ellen G. White: The Early Years,* pp. 207-210.

BALLOU, James Madison (1816-1888) and **Hulda Amelia** (1820-1903)

Born in Vermont, James Ballou came to western New York while a child and married Hulda Hart in 1840 or 1841. Both joined the Millerite movement in the early 1840s. Hulda is said to have become a Sabbathkeeper in 1847. James Ballou is listed in the *Review* as a subscriber and contributor from 1851.

Ballou's obituary relates that "for many years the meetings of the Pulaski [New York] church were held at his house." There is only one extant mention of J. M. Ballou in Ellen White's correspondence. J. N. Loughborough, however, recounts how he visited the Ballou home near Mannsville, New York, in 1858, along with Ellen and James White, and how in answer to prayer Ellen was healed there from a serious inflammation of her face.

See: Obituary: "James Madison Ballou," *Review,* June 12, 1888, p. 383; obituary: "Hulda A. Ballou," New York *Indicator,* July 29, 1903, pp. 3, 4; Adin Ballou, *An Elaborate History and Genealogy of the Ballous in America* (Providence, R.I.: Press of E. L. Freeman & Son, 1888), pp. 1186, 1187; "Receipts," *Review,* Nov. 25, 1851, p. 56; Ellen G. White, Lt 20, 1860 (c. 1860); J. N. Loughborough, *The Great Second Advent Movement,* p. 336.

BANGS, Elizabeth N. (1827-1891) and **Reuben M.** (1820-1893)

Elizabeth ("Lizzie") Bangs was Ellen White's twin sister, born in Gorham, Maine. In 1849 she married Reuben Bangs and settled in Gorham, where they operated a farm for the rest of their lives.

Neither Elizabeth nor Reuben Bangs became Seventh-day Adventists. As teenagers, however, Elizabeth and Ellen had shared their ardor for the Second Advent message of William Miller: "We talked the matter over among ourselves, and decided to earn what money we could, and spend it in buying books and tracts to be distributed gratuitously." In 1845 Elizabeth sometimes accompanied Ellen on her journeys when she related her early visions. For reasons that are not altogether clear, Elizabeth seems to have lost much of her Christian faith in the years that followed, although she strongly denied being an "infidel." Commenting on revival meetings taking place in Gorham in 1885, Elizabeth regretted her religious situation. "I try as hard as any one but as to get the feeling . . . it is impossible. It is a great trial to me but I can't help it. . . . I can't make pretensions that I don't feel." It may be that her problems were due in part to the influence of Reuben. Although of Quaker background, he is said to have been "all against religion . . always picking flaws in religious people."

On a personal level, although Elizabeth and Ellen had relatively little contact during their earlier married years, they corresponded and met fairly often during the last 15 years of Elizabeth's life. This was a difficult period when Elizabeth suffered from illness and "lameness," eventually becoming bedridden for several years before her death. Ellen tried to encourage her sister by visits whenever she came to Maine, by sympathetic letters, presents of money, fruit, books, and subscriptions to the *Review* and *Signs.* In late 1879 or early 1880 Elizabeth came to Battle Creek as a guest of Ellen and James's. For several weeks she took treatments at the Battle Creek Sanitarium. Although Elizabeth did not improve from the treatments, it was a visit that she greatly enjoyed and often reminisced about in later letters.

See: Artemas C. Harmon, ed., *The Harmon Genealogy,* p. 80; Mary Foss to Ellen White, Feb. 26, 1892; Hugh D. McLellan, *History of Gorham, Me.* (Portland: Smith and Sale, 1903), p. 395; Ellen G. White, *Testimonies for the Church,* vol. 1, p. 38; Ellen G. White, Lt 2, 1874 (Aug. 24); Elizabeth Bangs to Ellen White, Oct. 14, 1883, Dec. 30, 1885, Mar. 7, 1880, June 1880; Mary P. Foss to Ellen White, June 19, 1892.

BARNES, Robert (1815-1859) and **Hannah L.** (c. 1824-1856)

Members of the group of Sabbatarian Adventists in Canaan, Maine, in the 1850s, and farmers. On two occasions conferences took place in the Barneses' house, and in 1855 a tent meeting was held at their property, with 500 in attendance. In 1851 Ellen White wrote to Robert Barnes, encouraging him in his struggle to overcome his tobacco habit. Hannah died at age 32 and Robert at 44, having "been afflicted with fits for about thirty years, caused by the bite of a dog."

See: Obituary: "Robert Barnes," *Review,* Aug. 18, 1859, p. 103; obituary: "Hannah L. Barnes," July 10, 1856, p. 86; 1850 U.S. Federal Census, "Robert Barnes," Maine, Somerset County, Hartland, p. 28; search terms "R. Barnes" and "Robert Barnes" in *Words of the Pioneers;* Ellen G. White, Lt 5, 1851 (Dec. 14).

BARR, Eli L. (c. 1813-1864)

Itinerant preacher from Vermont. Of Millerite background, E. L. Barr became a

Sabbathkeeper about 1852 and began preaching soon thereafter. Until 1860 he traveled and preached widely, mostly in the New England states. He died in 1864 after suffering several years from tuberculosis. No records have been found indicating Barr's marital status.

In 1852 Ellen White saw in vision that E. L. Barr was among those preachers "to be depended upon." In 1859, however, he was reproved for his extreme position against the fad for photographs, which he regarded as a violation of the second commandment. Barr also veered toward fanaticism in his interpretation of the Laodicean message. He subsequently publicly acknowledged his mistakes in the *Review* and expressed his "perfect confidence in the gifts of the Spirit, and the testimonies given thereby."

See: Obituary: "E. L. Barr," *Review,* June 14, 1864, p. 23; E. L. Barr, [Letter,] *The Voice of Truth and Glad Tidings,* Mar. 11, 1846, p. 88; [James White], "Eastern Tour," *Review,* Sept. 16, 1852, p. 80; James White to "Dear Brother," Sept. 30, 1852; E. L. Barr, "Conference in Connecticut," *Review,* Mar. 5, 1857, p. 142; E. L. Barr, "From Bro. Barr," *Review,* June 24, 1862, p. 30; Ellen G. White, Lt 19, 1859 (Oct. 4); search term "Barr" in *Words of the Pioneers.*

BARTON, Harriet Augusta (née **STOWELL**) (1833-after 1913) and **Major** (1822-after 1900)

Daughter of **Lewis B.** and **Laura B. Stowell** of Paris, Maine, who in the spring of 1845 were among the first Adventists in that state to adopt the Sabbath. In 1859 Harriet married Major Barton in Warren, Illinois. Barton, born in Rochester, New York, came to Warren in 1853 and operated a livery business, later opening a hotel in the same town in 1873.

Harriet presumably kept the Sabbath with the rest of her family from 1845, and there is a record of her attending a Sabbatarian conference in 1849, at the age of 16. After that, however, no further mention of Harriet or her husband has been found in the *Review* or other denominational sources, nor do their obituaries appear in church papers. It is likely, therefore, that Harriet did not remain with the Seventh-day Adventists.

Harriet Stowell was present at a conference in Topsham, Maine, in 1849 at which Ellen White received a vision. According to an observer who called Harriet by her middle name, Augusta, while "putting the Bible on Augusta Stowell," Ellen White uttered the words "Study it, study it, take it, believe it, walk out on it, the Word of God, faith, the Book of books, the all-seeing eye!" This is the only mention of Harriet Stowell in Ellen White's writings.

See: William Berry Lapham, *History of Paris, Maine, From Its Settlement to 1880,* p. 738; *The History of Jo Daviess County, Illinois, Containing a History of the County—Its Cities, Towns, Etc.* (Chicago: H. F. Kett & Co., 1878), p. 661; obituary: "Marion Stowell Crawford," *Review,* Dec. 18, 1913, p. 1230; Merlin Burt, ". . . Sabbatarian Adventism From 1844 to 1849," pp. 123, 124; 1900 U.S. Federal Census, "Barton Major," Illinois, Jo Daviess County, Warren, p. 202B; Ellen G. White, Ms 5, 1849 (Sept. 23); Joseph Bates to "Brother & Sister Hastings," Sept. 25, 1849.

BATES, Joseph (1792-1872) and **Prudence M.** (1793-1870)

A cofounder and pioneer theologian of the Seventh-day Adventist Church, Joseph Bates came from a background of seafaring and strong engagement in antislavery and health reform. In 1839 he accepted the teachings of William Miller and became a traveling preacher of some prominence in the Millerite movement. In 1845 Bates accepted the seventh-day Sabbath through the writings of T. M. Preble. Subsequently Bates became the leading advocate of the Sabbath among Adventists. His books published in the latter half of the 1840s focused on the eschatological significance of the Sabbath and were formative for the subsequent theological development of the church.

Joseph Bates married Prudence M. Nye in 1818. In his autobiography Bates cited the influence of Prudence among other factors leading to his conversion to Christianity in the mid-1820s. She joined her husband in the Millerite movement of the 1840s but held back when Joseph became a Sabbathkeeper in 1845. Not until five years later, in 1850, did she join the ranks of the Sabbatarian Adventists. "Strong-minded" is how Bates biographer George Knight describes her.

Perhaps the most significant interaction between Ellen White and Joseph Bates was in the theological give-and-take that took place between them during the period, roughly, of 1846 to 1851. Ellen White relates that it was through Joseph Bates that her "attention was first called to the Sabbath" in 1846. Even though at first she rejected his arguments, Ellen and James White were convinced by Bates's first book on the Sabbath, *The Seventh Day Sabbath: A Perpetual Sign,* published in August 1846.

Joseph Bates, in turn, acknowledged indebtedness to the visions of Ellen White as early as April 1847. "I confess," he wrote of the visions, "that I have received light and instruction on many passages that I could not before clearly distinguish." One likely example of such intellectual indebtedness is found in Bates's earliest formulations of the seminal "great controversy" motif in January 1847. Expanding on Revelation 12:17, Bates saw the "remnant . . . made war with . . . for keeping the commandments of God" as a prediction of the persecution of "those who keep God's Sabbath holy."

This was not entirely innovative thinking, however. Already two years earlier, in her first vision, Ellen Harmon described the violent end-time persecution of the saints, although not specifying Sabbathkeeping as grounds for persecution. Bates would not have gained such ideas from current Millerite teaching, which did not anticipate such fierce pre-Advent oppression.

While Ellen White's visions agreed with the main findings of Joseph Bates's biblical interpretations, at times there was tension between the two. For example, as late as 1847 Bates held to the standard Millerite view that the saints would inhabit a renewed earth during the millennium. In contrast, there were indications already in Ellen White's first vision in 1844 that the redeemed would spend the 1,000 years in heaven. Likewise, for a time Bates was convinced that the revolutionary upheavals sweeping through Europe in 1848 were the beginnings of the "time of trouble, such as never was," foretold in Daniel 12:1, while about the same time Ellen White was shown in vision that "the time of trouble, such as never was, had not yet commenced."

See: Obituary: "Joseph Bates," *Review,* Apr. 16, 1872, p. 143; obituary: "Prudy M. Bates," *Review,* Sept. 6, 1870, p. 95; Joseph Bates, *Autobiography of Joseph Bates: With Additional Material From Two Later Editions of the Same Work* (Battle Creek, Mich.: Steam Press, 1868; reprint, Berrien Springs, Mich.: Andrews University Press, 2004), pp. 179-181; George Knight, *Joseph*

Bates: The Real Founder of Seventh-day Adventism, p. 197; Ellen G. White, *Testimonies for the Church,* vol. 1, pp. 75, 76; James White and Ellen G. White, *Life Sketches* (1880 ed.), p. 128; Joseph Bates, "Remarks," in James White, ed., *A Word to the "Little Flock,"* p. 21; Joseph Bates, *The Seventh Day Sabbath: A Perpetual Sign,* 2nd ed., p. 59; Ellen G. White, Lt 1, 1845 (Dec. 20), notes 12, 16; Lt 1, 1846 (Feb. 15), note 11; Lt 1, 1847 (Apr. 7), note 10; Ms 2, 1849 (Jan. 17), note 7.

BEAN, Lewis (1823-1888) and Sophia R. (1823-1911)

President of the Vermont Conference from 1870 to 1875, Lewis Bean and his wife, Sophia, both Vermonters, passed through the Millerite experience and became Sabbathkeepers about 1852. Lewis Bean, a "wheelwright," "carriage maker," and "dry goods merchant," according to censuses of 1850 to 1870, seems to have aspired to a full-time traveling ministry but was advised by Ellen White in 1859, "You have mistaken your calling."

Bean subsequently contributed to the church primarily in the area of administration, serving through the 1860s and 1870s on the Vermont Conference executive committee and as its president from 1870 to 1875. In the 1870s he also held ministerial credentials, but little is reported in the *Review* on this aspect of his work, and his credentials were not renewed after 1879. In a testimony to Sophia Bean, Ellen White urged her to overcome her negative frame of mind by taking heed to the words of Christ, "Come unto me, all ye that labour and are heavy laden, and I will give you rest."

See: Obituary, "Lewis Bean," *Review,* Apr. 24, 1888, p. 271; obituary, "Sophia R. Bean," *Review,* Mar. 30, 1911, p. 23; search terms "Lewis Bean" and "L. Bean" in *Review and Herald* online collection, www.adventistarchives.org; 1850 U.S. Federal Census, "Lewis Bean," Vermont, Caledonia County, Hardwick, p. 195; 1860 U.S. Federal Census, "Lewis Bean," Vermont, Lamoille County, Stowe, p. 264; 1870 U.S. Federal Census, "Lewis Bean," Vermont, Franklin County, Enosburg, p. 24; Ellen G. White, Lt 20, 1859 (c. Sept.); Lt 41, 1880 (Sept. 16); Lt 42, 1880 (Sept. 22); *Testimonies for the Church,* vol. 2, p. 640 ("Sister G").

BELDEN, Albert (1800-1893) and Hannah (c. 1800-1886)

Early church members from Connecticut. Their son, **Stephen T. Belden**, married **Sarah B. Harmon**, a sister of Ellen G. White's. According to *History of Berlin, Connecticut,* Albert Belden, "in the belief that the world was coming to an end in 1843, had disposed of his property, almost giving it away." However, later research by Spalding suggests that the Beldens retained their farm together with one or more houses through the crisis of 1843-1844.

Albert and Hannah Belden are remembered in Adventist history mainly on two accounts. It was in their home in Rocky Hill, Connecticut, that the first of the seminal series of "Sabbath and Sanctuary Conferences" was held in April 1848, a conference attended by James and Ellen White and other leading Sabbatarians. Second, the Beldens invited the Whites to stay in their home during the summer of 1849. While the Whites lived there, their second son, James Edson, was born, and James White embarked on the publication of *Present Truth.* There is no extant correspondence between Ellen White and Albert or Hannah Belden.

See: Obituary: "Albert Belden," *Review,* Nov. 14, 1893, p. 723; obituary: "Hannah

Belden," *Review,* Aug. 24, 1886, p. 542; Catharine M. North, Adolph Burnett Benson, eds., *History of Berlin, Connecticut* (New Haven: Tuttle, Morehouse & Taylor Co., 1916), p. 142; Arthur Whitefield Spalding, *Footprints of the Pioneers* (Washington, D.C.: Review and Herald, 1947), pp. 99-108; Ellen G. White, *Spiritual Gifts [vol. 2],* pp. 91-93, 113-116.

BELDEN, Stephen T. (1829-1906) and (first wife) **Sarah B.** (c. 1823-1868) and (second wife) **Charlotte** (c. 1830-1897?) and (third wife) **Melvina (Lavina)** (c. 1831-1928)

Stephen Belden was a son of Seventh-day Adventist pioneer **Albert Belden** of Connecticut. His first wife, Sarah B. Harmon, was an older sister of Ellen White's. Stephen and Sarah Belden both came from the Millerite movement and began to keep the Sabbath in 1847 and 1848, respectively. They were married by James White in 1851, after which Stephen Belden worked for the Review and Herald publishing house at various locations until 1862 and again for some time during the 1870s.

In 1868, while the Belden family was living in Connecticut, Sarah died of tuberculosis at age 45, leaving five children aged between 6 and 11. Soon thereafter Stephen married Charlotte Alley, who had assisted in the household for a number of years, and in 1871 or 1872 the family moved back to Battle Creek, where Stephen Belden resumed work at the Review and Herald. However, catastrophe struck when Charlotte became insane because of complications following measles. In 1873 the Belden children were taken from Charlotte. "Charlotte is raving over the children's going to Potterville," Ellen White wrote in her diary, adding that she "felt sad and cried . . . [at] the sad state of that family." Apparently by 1877 Charlotte Belden was a patient at the Michigan Asylum for the Insane in Kalamazoo, Michigan. Writing from California, Ellen requested that "someone [go] to Kalamazoo and see if Charlotte Belden is there and her condition." A letter from Stephen Belden in 1879 tells of Charlotte's attempts to leave the asylum. According to another source, she ended her days in the Hospital for the Insane in Middletown, Connecticut, in 1897.

Through the years Ellen and James White provided financial and other practical help to Stephen Belden and his children, as indicated in a number of places in Ellen White's correspondence and diaries. A particularly difficult situation arose sometime in the 1880s when Stephen Belden decided to divorce Charlotte and marry Melvina (Lavina) Devereux. According to William C. White, some church members considered this a serious moral breach and called for church discipline. Ellen White is not known to have commented in writing, although her son William later maintained that she called on people to "let them alone." Regardless of the rights and wrongs of the case, Ellen White continued to be caring and helpful to the Beldens. In the early 1890s she invited them to join her team in Australia. Stephen "does the purchasing for us and helps us in many ways," Ellen related in 1894, impressed with his abilities as "carpenter, blacksmith, agriculturist, etc." In late 1894 the Beldens relocated to Norfolk Island as missionaries. During their closing years there, as they faced illness and economic hardship, Ellen White made arrangements for their financial support.

See: Obituary: "Stephen T. Belden," *Australian Union Conference Record,* Dec. 3, 1906, p. 8; obituary: "Sarah B. Belden," *Review,* Dec. 22, 1868, p. 286; obituary: "Mrs. S. T.

Belden," *Review,* Dec. 13, 1928, p. 22; 1870 U.S. Federal Census, "Charlotte Belden," Connecticut, Hartford County, Berlin, p. 33; 1880 U.S. Federal Census, "Stephen T. Belden" and "Lavina Devereux," Minnesota, Blue Earth County, Mapleton, p. 20; 1880 U.S. Federal Census, "S. T. Belden" and "C. A. Belden," Minnesota, Murray County, Cameron, p. 6; James White, "To the Trustees of the Publishing Association," July 6, 1873; F. E. Belden to W. C. White, Mar. 14, 1937; S. T. Belden to W. C. White, Mar. 5, 1877; W. C. White to W. D. Frazee, Feb. 21, 1927; EGWEnc, s.v. "Stephen T. Belden"; Ellen G. White, Ms 7, 1873 (May 27); Lt 34, 1877 (Nov. 4); Lt 26, 1894 (Nov. 22); Lt 46, 1894 (May 17).

BELOW, Elsie Philomela (1811-1889) and (first husband) **John Gregg** (? -1839) and (second husband) **John C. Below** (c. 1786-1855)

Close friend and, for some years while living in Battle Creek, neighbor to Ellen and James White. Elsie Below began to keep the Sabbath in 1842 through the influence of a Seventh-Day Baptist contact. She joined the Sabbatarian Adventists in 1851, being baptized by Joseph Bates. While living in Mill Grove, New York, Elsie traveled to Rochester, New York, to assist Ellen White after the birth of her third son, William Clarence, in 1854. After the death of Elsie's second husband in 1855, the Whites encouraged her to move to Battle Creek, which she did in 1857. "We want you near us," James White urged. Ellen White spoke at Elsie's funeral in 1889.

See: Obituary: "Elsie P. Below," *Review,* Dec. 10, 1889, p. 782; obituary: "John C. Below," *Review,* May 29, 1855, p. 239; 1860 U.S. Federal Census, "Elsa P. Below," "James White," Michigan, Calhoun County, Battle Creek, p. 6; James White to "Dear Sister," Nov. 4, 1856; Ellen G. White, Ms 23, 1889 (Nov. 12 entry).

BENEDICT, Diantha. See **WILKINSON, Diantha.**

BENEDICT, Joseph Perry (1805-1865) and **Millie** (1810-1882)

Joseph Benedict, a cabinetmaker in his 50s, together with wife, Millie, daughter Diantha [**Diantha Wilkinson (**née **Benedict)**], and possibly other family members, became Sabbatarian Adventists about 1857. At some point in the 1850s the family moved to Battle Creek, Michigan. Ellen White first mentioned the Benedicts in her 1859 diary. "My heart is called out in sympathy for them. I know they are poor and Brother Benedict is very feeble, unable to work."

Ellen and James White tried to help the family in several ways, giving food and money and by occasionally employing Millie and Diantha in their home and at the *Review* office. It is probable that the testimony given in Lt 13, 1859 (Jan. 5), addressed "Dear Friends," was written to the Benedicts. In 1862 Millie and Joseph moved to Wisconsin, where Joseph died three years later.

See: Henry Marvin Benedict, *The Genealogy of the Benedicts in America* (Albany: Joel Munsell, 1870), p. 155; 1860 U.S. Federal Census, "Joseph Benedict," Michigan, Calhoun County, Battle Creek, p. 53; Ellen G. White, Ms 6, 1859 (Apr. 12 entry); Lt 13, 1859 (Jan. 5); obituary: "Millie Benedict," *Review*, Jan. 16, 1883, p. 46; obituary: "Diantha Benedict Wilkinson," *Review*, Feb. 6, 1908, p. 31.

BINGHAM, Hiram (1804-1874) and **Mary** (c. 1809-1882)

Hiram Bingham, who lived out his life in Morristown, Vermont, took part in the Millerite movement of the mid-1840s and became a Sabbathkeeper in 1850 or 1851. His wife, Mary (née Joy), although sympathetic, never joined the Seventh-day Adventist Church. A prosperous farmer, Hiram Bingham gave generously to many branches of church work as well as to needy people in his community. He also shared his administrative talents as a member of various Vermont Conference committees. To a lesser degree Bingham engaged in preaching.

In an 1859 vision Ellen White saw that Hiram Bingham had "a good gift, and can do good, fill in here and there," but was not suited to full-time preaching. Rather, "his good influence should tell in the neighborhood." At Hiram Bingham's funeral, a Baptist minister testified that the Binghams "had done more to relieve the poor, afflicted, and destitute families than any other two persons of his knowledge."

See: Theodore A. Bingham, *The Bingham Family in the United States, Especially of the State of Connecticut* (Easton, Pa.: Bingham Association, 1927), vol. 2, p. 328; obituary: "Hiram Bingham," *Review*, Dec. 22, 1874, p. 206; obituary: "Mrs. Mary Bingham," *Review*, Feb. 27, 1883, p. 143; 1850 U.S. Federal Census, "Mary Bingham," Vermont, Lamoille County, Morristown, p. 170; H. Bingham, "From Bro. Bingham," *Review*, Feb. 4, 1858, p. 102; search term "H. Bingham" in *Review and Herald* online collection, www.adventistarchives.org; Ellen G. White, Ms 1, 1859 (Sept. 24).

BONFOEY, Clarissa M. (c. 1821-1856)

Domestic helper for Ellen and James White, 1848-1856. The few available sources suggest that Clarissa Bonfoey came from the Middletown, Connecticut, area. No mention has been found of a "Clarissa" or "Clara" Bonfoey in official records or genealogies from this period, but it is likely that she was of the line of Bonfoeys who settled in Haddam, Connecticut, near Middletown, during the eighteenth century. Clarissa's first assignment for the Whites was to look after their 10-month-old son, Henry, in Middletown during the summer of 1848 while they traveled to conferences in New York. From 1849 until her untimely death in 1856 at age 35, she seems to have been employed on a more or less permanent basis in the White household as they moved from place to place. She remained single.

Ellen White had a high opinion of Clarissa Bonfoey. "She was a woman of remarkable faith," with "a cheerful and happy disposition, never gloomy, yet not light and trifling." In her letters and autobiographical accounts Ellen described several instances of Clarissa's participation in dramatic faith healings and other charismatic phenomena.

See: Obituary: "Clarissa M. Bonfoey," *Review,* June 12, 1856, p. 55; William Richard Cutter, *Genealogical and Family History of the State of Connecticut* (New York: Lewis Publishing Co., 1911), vol. 4; search term "Bonfoey" in www.ancestry.com (July 28, 2009); Ellen G. White, *Spiritual Gifts [vol. 2],* pp. 96, 113, 138; Ms 147, 1907 (Nov. 12); Lt 14, 1850 (Sept. 1); Lt 123, 1893 (June 21).

BOURDEAU, Augustin Cornelius (1834-1916) and (first wife) **Charlotte** (c. 1836-1883) and (second wife) **Martha** (1842-1901)

A bilingual French Canadian evangelist, Augustin Bourdeau, with his brother, **Daniel Bourdeau,** is best known for pioneering the Seventh-day Adventist message among both English and French communities in Vermont and Quebec.

A. C. Bourdeau was brought up a Baptist in northern Vermont and at a young age preached in the local French immigrant communities. In the early 1850s Augustin married Charlotte Saxby. In 1855 Charlotte's brother, **William L. Saxby**, introduced the Sabbatarian Adventist message to Augustin. By the next summer Augustin began to preach his new faith. For the next quarter century, with few interruptions, he preached and established new churches on both sides of the Canadian border, but in particular in the eastern townships of southern Quebec. Other ministers, including his brother, Daniel Bourdeau, were associated with him in his work in Quebec, but Augustin "stands out as the one who had the most influence in the conversion of members and the establishment of churches." During this period Bourdeau also served as president of the Vermont Conference (1865-1870) and president of the Quebec Conference (1880-1884). From 1884 to 1888 he engaged in evangelism in central Europe. On returning from Europe, he spent his later years of ministry in a number of places in Canada and the United States, often involving work with French-speaking communities.

As early as 1861 Ellen White expressed her respect for the "judgment and experience" of the Bourdeau brothers in their evangelistic endeavors. However, the bulk of her correspondence with A. C. Bourdeau dates from 1886, while he was working in Europe, during a low period in his spiritual experience and effectiveness as a preacher. "Your preaching will do but little good till you are a converted man," she urged. "You live in a past experience instead of having a fresh experience daily. . . . Your discourses are dry and spiritless." Of Martha, Augustin's second wife (sister of **George I. Butler**), Ellen White noted that she was "born with an inheritance of discouragement." In a stirring letter of encouragement written in 1887, Ellen pointed Martha to some verses of Charles Wesley's hymn: "Plenteous grace with Thee is found, Grace to pardon all my sins; Let the healing streams abound. . . ." See also Ellen White's 1883 letter of comfort to Charlotte, who was on her deathbed.

See: Obituary: "Augustin Cornelius Bourdeau," *Review,* Aug. 17, 1916, p. 16; obituary: "Charlotte Bourdeau," *Review,* Dec. 18, 1883, p. 797; obituary: "Martha A. Bourdeau," *Review,* Sept. 10, 1901, p. 598; Denis Fortin, *Adventism in Quebec,* p. 109; search term "A. C. Bordeaux" or "A. C. Bourdeaux" or "A. C. Bourdeau" in *Review and Herald* online collection, www.adventistarchives.org; Ellen G. White, Lt 31, 1861 (c. 1861); Lt 52, 1886 (Nov. 20); Lt 35, 1887 (Feb. 6); Lt 28, 1883 (Sept. 3).

BOURDEAU, Daniel T. (1835-1905) and **Marion Elizabeth** (1842-1929)

A pioneer bilingual evangelist, Daniel Bourdeau was brought up in a French-speaking Baptist community in northern Vermont and converted to Sabbatarian Adventism in 1856 through the agency of his brother, **Augustin C. Bourdeau**, who had converted shortly before. For almost five decades Daniel Bourdeau preached from Massachusetts to California in the United States, and also in Canada and Europe. Of particular note were his pioneering work in Quebec (together with his brother), groundbreaking work in California with John N. Loughborough (1868-1870), and two missionary journeys to Europe (1876-1878 and 1883-1887).

James White said of the Bourdeau brothers in 1857 that they "love and obey the present truth, and they most ardently desire to teach it to the French people." However, for a variety of reasons, for many years the Bourdeau brothers worked mainly with English-speaking communities and only sporadically with French speakers in the United States and Canada. For Daniel Bourdeau the turning point came in December 1872 with the publication of *Testimony for the Church,* No. 22, in which Ellen White called for greater efforts to reach foreign language groups and specifically chided the Bourdeau brothers for their poor response to the need for French books and tracts. Publicly acknowledging these "reproofs and instructions" in a letter to the *Review,* Daniel Bourdeau immediately set about writing and translating, and a few months later, in September 1873, embarked on a challenging mission to reach French-speaking communities in Wisconsin and Illinois. In 1875 Ellen White affirmed his pioneering efforts: "Brother Bourdeau stood nobly amid opposition such as our brethren have no knowledge of." With this encouragement, Daniel Bourdeau's course was set. For the remainder of his life his focus was on evangelism among French-speaking populations in Europe, Canada, and the United States. There were gaps when, for a while, he worked mainly with English speakers, but, as he put it, at such times he felt "like a fish out of water."

Daniel and Marion Bourdeau (née Saxby) had a good personal relationship with Ellen and James White. Daniel later recalled the occasion when, about 1860, on meeting the Whites, "Bro. White flung his arms around me, saying, 'Look unto us as with your father and mother.'" Although Ellen White on many occasions reproved Daniel Bourdeau for specific weaknesses, he still remained to her a "much-respected fellow laborer"—as she addressed him in an 1885 letter. She also had high regard for Marion, who often traveled with Daniel and supported him in his work. "Sister Bourdeau has been a laborer of no little influence . . . a treasure of greater value than finest gold," Ellen exclaimed in 1875 after learning of Marion's work with Daniel in Illinois and Wisconsin. "Would to God," she continued, "we had one hundred women consecrated to the work, going forth as missionaries."

See: Obituary: "Daniel T. Bourdeau," *Review,* July 13, 1905, p. 17; obituary: "Marion Elizabeth Saxby," *Review,* Nov. 14, 1929, p. 29; James White, "The Present Truth in French," *Review,* Dec. 24, 1857, p. 56; Denis Fortin, *Adventism in Quebec,* pp. 101-103; Ellen G. White, *Testimony for the Church,* No. 22 (Battle Creek, Mich.: Steam Press of the Seventh-day Adventist Pub. Assn., 1872), pp. 130, 131; D. T. Bourdeau, "Report From Eld. D. T. Bourdeau," *Review,* Mar. 4, 1873, p. 94; Ellen G. White, Lt 49, 1875 (c. 1875); Lt 7, 1885 (Feb. 10); D. T. Bourdeau to Bro. and Sr. White, Sept. 17, 1879; D. T. Bourdeau to Sr. White, Jan. 12, 1883; search terms "D. T. Bourdeau" and "D. T. Bourdeaux" in *Review and Herald* online collection, www.adventistarchives.org.

BOVEE, Louisa C. (née **LEWIS**) (1836-1876) and **Seymour C.** (1830-1913)

Church members from Michigan. Ellen White's only mention of this family was of Louisa Bovee in her 1859 diary. Louisa had visited Ellen White in Battle Creek on April 6, and Ellen returned the visit the following day. Louisa Bovee was a daughter of Jonah and Caroline Lewis, who were among the earliest Sabbathkeeping Adventists in Battle Creek. Louisa married Seymour Bovee, a shoemaker, sometime in the latter 1850s, and they later settled in Allegan, Michigan. Louisa died at age 40 of "inflammation of the stomach."

See: Obituary: "Seymour Bonee" [*sic*], *Review,* Jan. 1, 1914, p. 21; obituary: "Louisa C. Bovee," *Review,* Oct. 19, 1876, p. 127; Ellen G. White, Ms 6, 1859 (entries for Apr. 6, 7); EGWEnc, s.v. "Battle Creek Congregation."

BOWLES, John C. (c. 1802-1853) and **Phebe** (c. 1808-after 1850)

John Bowles was a preacher from Jackson, Michigan. A former Millerite, he adopted Sabbathkeeping through the influence of Joseph Bates in 1849. Together with H. S. Case, Bowles seems to have held a leadership position in the Jackson congregation as well as being a traveling preacher in Michigan and neighboring states up to the time of his death in 1853.

J. C. Bowles's acquaintance with the Whites dated back to their correspondence during the autumn of 1849. Bowles is mentioned in two of Ellen White's visions of 1852 and 1853. Although appreciating his good intentions in working with the Jackson members, she called him to account for his "oppressive exalted" leadership style.

See: 1850 U.S. Federal Census, "John C. Bowles," Michigan, Jackson County, Jackson, p. 336; J. Whitmore, "From Bro. Whitmore," *Review,* Oct. 4, 1853, p. 103; J. C. Bowles, "Letter From Br. Bowles," *Voice of Truth,* Sept. 24, 1845, p. 464; James White to "Beloved Brother Bowles," Nov. 8, 1849; J. C. Bowles, "Dear Brother White," *Present Truth,* September 1849, p. 32; search term "Bowles" in *Review and Herald* online collection, www.adventistarchives.org; Ellen G. White, Lt 2, 1852 (June 2); Ms 1, 1853 (June 2).

BOYER, Elijah (1821-1903) and **Mary** (1823-1898)

Church members from Erie County, New York. Mary Boyer became a Sabbathkeeper about 1851, followed within a year or two by Elijah. The Boyers were farmers and attended the church in Mill Grove/Alden, Erie County, for the remainder of their lives. There is no mention of the Boyers in Ellen White's writings outside of a letter to "Sister Below" on January 1, 1856, in which she sent her greetings to the Boyers and acknowledged a donation they had made.

See: Ellen G. White, Lt 9, 1856 (Jan. 1); M. Boyer, "From Sister Boyer," *Review*, Sept. 13, 1853, p. 79; obituary, "Elijah Boyer," *Review*, Jan. 14, 1904, p. 23; 1850 U.S. Federal Census, "Elijah Boyers" [*sic*], New York, Erie County, Alden, p. 161; H. Perry Smith, ed., *History of the City of Buffalo and Erie County With Illustrations and Biographical Sketches of Some of Its Prominent Men and Pioneers* (Syracuse, N.Y.: D. Mason & Co., 1884), vol. 1, p. 717; Louise G. Walker, *William Gallop, Revolutionary Soldier* (Chicago: n.p., 1973), p. 19.

BRACKETT, Ezra (1805-1889) and **Mary D.** (1807-1882)

When she was about 50 years of age, Mary Brackett (née Davison), daughter of an influential banker and industrialist, left the Baptist Church to become a Sabbatarian Adventist in 1857. She "stood alone for more than a year" as the sole Sabbathkeeper in Convis, Michigan, before others joined her. Her husband, Ezra Brackett, a pioneer settler in Convis, "was not connected with the S.D.A. church." According to his obituary, Ezra was nevertheless "a believer in the prominent doctrines of this people, and an observer of the Sabbath." Despite his ambivalent relation to the church, Brackett took an active part in the landmark conference on church organization held at Battle Creek in 1860. In 1869 he was a member of a committee set up to build a church in Convis. The Bracketts received incidental mention in Ellen White's 1859 diary in connection with a visit she made to Convis.

See: Obituary: "Ezra Brackett," *Review*, May 21, 1889, p. 335; obituary: "Mary D. Brackett," *Review*, Mar. 7, 1882, p. 158; Henry F. Thomas, *A Twentieth Century History of Allegan County, Michigan* (New York: Lewis Pub. Co., 1907), pp. 87, 88; Herbert I. Brackett, *Brackett Genealogy: Descendants of Anthony Brackett of Portsmouth and Captain Richard Brackett of Braintree. With Biographies of Immigrant Fathers, Their Sons, and Others of Their Posterity* (Washington, D.C.: [author], 1907), p. 566; "Business Proceedings of B.C. Conference," *Review*, Oct. 9, 1860, pp. 161-163; *ibid*., Oct. 23, 1860, p. 178; H. B. Peirce, *History of Calhoun County, Michigan: With Illustrations Descriptive of Its Scenery, Palatial Residences, Public Buildings, Fine Blocks, and Important Manufactories, From Original Sketches by Artists of the Highest Ability*, p. 154; Ellen G. White, Ms 6, 1859 (entries for Apr. 9, 10, 23).

BRACKETT, Louisa (née **FOSS**) (1824-1861) and **Benjamin** (1821-after 1880)

Louisa Brackett was a sister of Millerite visionary Hazen Little Foss. Louisa's brother Samuel Hoyt Foss was married to Ellen White's sister **Mary Plummer** (née **Harmon**) **Foss.** On several journeys in 1845 Louisa accompanied Ellen, who later recollected, "My constant and faithful companion at this time was Louisa Foss, a sister of Samuel Foss, the husband of my sister Mary." Louisa married Benjamin Brackett, a cooper from New Gloucester, Maine, in 1852. She died in 1861 shortly after the birth of her third child. No evidence has been found that Louisa Foss became a Sabbathkeeper. Neither she nor her husband is mentioned in the *Review*.

See: George Thomas Little, *The Descendants of George Little, who came to Newbury, Massachusetts, in 1640* (Auburn, Maine: the author, 1882), pp. 290, 291; Herbert I. Brackett, *Brackett Genealogy: Descendants of Anthony Brackett of Portsmouth and Captain Richard Brackett of Braintree. With Biographies of Immigrant Fathers, Their Sons, and Others of Their Posterity* (Washington, D.C.: [author], 1907), p. 207; Ellen G. White, *Life Sketches,* p. 77.

BRAZEE (BRISSEE), Cornelius (c. 1808-1890) and **Emily C.** (c. 1821-1889)

Church members and farmers from Fulton and Herkimer counties, New York. Emily Brazee's mother, Betsey Cady, and possibly Emily herself, had, while living in New Bedford, Massachusetts, first started to keep the Sabbath in the 1840s through their contacts with Joseph Bates.

In 1852 James and Ellen White visited Emily Brazee and her husband, Cornelius, then living in Stratford, New York. In a report published in the *Review* James White entertained the "hope that [Cornelius] . . . will soon join his companion in observing the fourth commandment." Ellen White's only mention of the Brazee family is found in a diary entry from 1859, where she expressed her pleasure at receiving a letter from "Emily Brissee." "I have long wanted to hear from Emily. She still holds on to the truth. Her husband is converted; keeps the Sabbath with her."

See: Obituary: "Betsey Cady," *Review,* Mar. 24, 1874, p. 119; "Our Tour West," *Review,* Feb. 17, 1852, p. 94; Ellen G. White, Ms 6, 1859 (Apr. 18 entry); 1850 U.S. Federal Census, "Emily Brisee," New York, Fulton County, Stratford, p. 244; Mary M. De Bolt, ed., *Lineage Book: National Society of the Daughters of the American Revolution* (Washington, D.C.: The Society, 1925), vol. 76, p. 33.

BRIGHAM, William Henry (c. 1819-1866) and **Polly A.** (c. 1831-after 1866)

W. H. Brigham, a carpenter from Lorraine, New York, is first mentioned in the *Review* in 1852. The Brighams are referred to only once in Ellen White's writings. In Lt 16, 1859, she called S. W. Rhodes, a well-known preacher of the early 1850s, to account for the poor counsel he had offered the Brighams, the counsel having exacerbated rather than helped solve their problems.

See: Obituary: "William H. Brigham," *Review,* July 10, 1866, p. 47; obituary: "Wm. Henry Brigham," *Review,* May 29, 1866, p. 207; "William H. Brigham," in *Vital Records of Jefferson County, 1847, 1848, and 1849: Town of Lorraine,* http://jefferson.nygenweb.net/vreclorr.htm (Jan. 8, 2010); 1850 U.S. Federal Census, "William H. Brigham," New York, Jefferson County, Lorraine, p. 367; Ellen G. White, Lt 16, 1859 (Oct. 28).

BUCK, Harry G. (1822-1902) and Jane Eliza (1823-1918)

Harry Buck, born in New York State, preached for the Wesleyan Methodists for several years before he and Jane became Sabbathkeepers about 1852. From 1854 to 1859 Buck preached widely, together with other evangelists, in New York, Vermont, and Canada East. Problems seem to have attended his work, however, for in 1861 Ellen White wrote him a very frank letter regarding his unwillingness "to learn or submit to your brethren" and his, at times, "harsh, hard spirit." The upshot of the letter was that "in your present condition . . . [God] will not accept your labors." Some months later Harry Buck confessed his faults publicly through a letter to the *Review* editor, but there is no evidence that he returned to itinerant ministry. He did, however, remain an active church member for the rest of his life, first in Buck's Bridge church, New York, where he was ordained as an elder in 1862, and, from about 1864, in the Monterey, Michigan, church.

See: Obituary: "Harry G. Buck," *Review,* May 6, 1902, p. 23; obituary: "Jane Eliza Buck," *Review,* Oct. 31, 1918, p. 15; obituary: "Harriet King Rumery" (Buck), *Review,* Mar. 6, 1913, p. 22; H. G. Buck, "From Bro. Buck," *Review,* July 16, 1861, p. 55; search term "H. G. Buck" in *Review and Herald* online collection, www.adventistarchives.org; Ellen G. White, Lt 18, 1861 (Jan. 19).

BUCKLAND, Curtis P. (1804-1891) and Eliza (1806-1889)

Church members and farmers from Orleans County, New York. According to his obituary, "about the year 1853 [C. P. Buckland] received the S. D. Adventist doctrines through reading." In the early years the Bucklands hosted monthly district meetings and tent meetings on their farm. "Many a time they entertained and provided for as many as fifty under his roof." Ellen White's only mention of the Bucklands was in connection with a tent meeting held by the Whites on the Bucklands' farm in 1859.

See: Obituary: "Curtis P. Buckland," *Review,* Feb. 3, 1891, p. 79; obituary: "Eliza Buckland," *Review,* Nov. 26, 1889, p. 750; Philip L. Cobb, *A History of the Cobb Family* (Cleveland: Cobb, 1907), p. 184; Ellen G. White, Ms 7, 1859 (entries for Aug. 18-22); J. W. [James White], "Eastern Tour," *Review,* Sept. 1, 1859, p. 116.

BURTON, Samuel G. (c. 1805-after 1880) and Lydia A. (c. 1818-after 1880)

Little is known of Samuel Burton's connection to the Sabbatarian Adventists. A farmer and blacksmith from Pittsfield, later Mayfield, Maine, Burton is mentioned in the *Review* only in 1855 and 1857. The *Review* did not carry his obituary. It is quite possible that he remained with the movement for only a few years. The Whites paid a brief visit to the Burton family in 1855. Ellen described Samuel Burton as a "poor brother with nine children," and the family as "real good people."

See: Search term "Burton" in *Words of the Pioneers;* 1840 U.S. Federal Census, "Samuel

G. Burton," Maine, Somerset County, Pittsfield, p. 210; 1850 U.S. Federal Census, "Samuel P. Burton" [*sic*], Maine, Somerset County, Pittsfield, p. 94; 1860 U.S. Federal Census, "Simon G. Burton" [*sic*], Maine, Somerset County, Mayfield, p. 20; 1880 U.S. Federal Census, "Samuel Burton," Maine, Somerset County, Mayfield, p. 4; Ellen G. White, Lt 2, 1855 (Aug.).

BURWELL, Anna Lucretia. See **KING, Anna Lucretia.**

BURWELL, Anthony Lee (c. 1806-1873) and **Achsah** (1810-1886)

Church members and farmers, originally from Panton, Vermont, later settling in Parma, Michigan. The Burwells took part in the Millerite movement and became Sabbathkeepers at some point between 1850 and 1852. During the 1850s their property doubled in value, perhaps as a result of new opportunities in connection with their move to Michigan in 1856. Ellen White wrote two letters to Anthony Burwell in 1857 cautioning him against becoming ensnared in materialism.

See: Obituary: "Anthony L. Burwell," *Review*, Jan. 28, 1873, p. 55; obituary: "Achsah Burwell," *Review*, June 8, 1886, p. 366; Herbert Cornelius Andrews, Sanford Charles Hinsdale, and Alfred L. Holman, *Hinsdale Genealogy: Descendants of Robert Hinsdale of Dedham, Medfield, Hadley, and Deerfield, With an Account of the French Family of De Hinnisdal* (Lombard, Ill.: A. H. Andrews, 1906), pp. 148, 384; 1850 U.S. Federal Census, "Anthony L. Burwell," Vermont, Addison County, Panton, p. 263; 1860 U.S. Federal Census, "Anthony Burwell," Michigan, Jackson County, Parma, p. 19; Ellen G. White, Lt 1, 1857 (Jan. 28); Lt 2, 1857 (Oct. 21).

BUTLER, Ezra Pitt (1796-1875) and **Sarah** (1799-1866)

Parents of **George Ide Butler**, who served as General Conference president 1871-1874 and 1880-1888. Ezra Pitt's father, who had the same name, was governor of Vermont (1826-1828). Ezra married Sarah Grow in 1819. According to his obituary, he was "a very zealous worker in the '44 movement." Sarah became a Sabbathkeeper in 1848, her husband following her two or three years later. E. P. Butler was ordained for ministry in 1853, although his subsequent participation in public ministry was quite limited.

Ellen White's major comment on Butler relates to his participation in several conferences in New Hampshire and Vermont in October and November 1851. Apparently Butler belonged to the small faction that, despite the warnings of the Whites, expected the Second Coming in October 1851 and doubted the visions of Ellen White. During the course of the conferences, however, Butler radically revised his position, declaring publicly, "I believe them [the visions] to be of God, am a full believer in the visions, so you may know where to find me."

Together with several other Sabbathkeeping Adventist families from New England, Butler with his family migrated westward in 1856 to Waukon, Iowa, and farmed there for most of the remainder of his life. Butler's move to Iowa seems to have coincided with a decline in his religious experience. In 1863 he wrote of "the stupidity and indifference that has rested upon me for six years." In 1868 J. N. Andrews despaired of Butler, that the Waukon church was suffering from some of his theological notions that he was pressing "to a ridiculous extent . . . and disfellowshipping all who did not make it a test of salvation." Nevertheless, by 1869 things had improved. "I think I can say something encouraging of Father," wrote his son, G. I. Butler, to James White. "He acts very different towards us all—attends meetings regularly, takes part, confesses he has been led by Satan in the course he has pursued." Butler's last years were spent with his daughter in Battle Creek, Michigan.

See: Obituary: Ezra P. Butler, *Review,* Dec. 9, 1875, p. 183; obituary: Sarah G. Butler, *Review,* Sept. 18, 1866, p. 127; George W. Davis, *John Grow of Ipswich: John Groo (Grow) of Oxford* (Washington, D.C. [?]: Davis, 1913), p. 76; Ellen G. White, Lt 8, 1851 (Nov. 12); E. P. Butler, "From Bro. Butler," *Review,* Apr. 7, 1863, p. 151; J. N. Andrews to "Brother and Sister White," July 3, 1868; G. I. Butler to James and Ellen White, Feb. 3, 1869. For a survey of E. P. Butler's family background, see Emmett K. Vande Vere, *Rugged Heart: The Story of George I. Butler,* pp. 9-13.

BUTLER, George Ide (1834-1918) and (first wife) **Lentha Ames** (1826-1901) and (second wife) **Elizabeth Jane** (1845-1927)

An administrator and evangelist, George I. Butler was born in Vermont. His grandfather, Ezra Pitt Butler, had been governor of Vermont, and his parents, **Ezra Pitt** and **Sarah G. Butler**, were pioneer Sabbatarian Adventists who had been active in William Miller's movement of the 1840s. George, on the other hand, had skeptical tendencies in his youth and was not converted until he was 22 years old. In 1859, while living in Iowa, he married Lentha Lockwood, who had taken part in the Millerite movement and had started to keep the Sabbath about 1846.

Described in an obituary as having "splendid executive ability," G. I. Butler was elected president of the Iowa Conference in 1865 before even being licensed as a minister. For the next 23 years, often concurrently, Butler served as president of various church entities: Iowa Conference (1865-1872, 1876-1877, 1879-1882, 1885-1886), Missouri Conference (1877-1882), General Conference (1871-1874, 1880-1888) and the Seventh-day Adventist Publishing Association (1881-1889).

The last two years of Butler's General Conference presidency, 1886-1888, were times of personal crisis as he faced emerging teachings championed by A. T. Jones and E. J. Waggoner. Butler (and many with him) insisted that their interpretation of the "law" in Galatians 3:24 and their focus on righteousness through Christ gave aid to critics of the Sabbath and undermined traditional Adventist respect for the ten-commandment law. Using the leverage of his presidential office, Butler sought to oppose the "new" teachings and to enlist Ellen White's support. When her backing did not materialize and she openly supported Jones and Waggoner at the 1888 Minneapolis General Conference session, Butler, broken in health, promptly resigned his office. He spent the next 13 years in retirement running a fruit farm in Bowling Green, Florida, and nursing Lentha, who had become partially paralyzed following a stroke about 1891. Following her death in 1901,

Butler was quickly coopted for the presidency of the Florida Conference (1901-1904) and the Southern Union Conference (1902-1907). His second marriage, in 1907, was to a widow, Elizabeth Jane Grainger (née Work), earlier a teacher at Healdsburg College and missionary to Japan, together with her husband, W. C. Grainger.

"I never had more unbounded faith in the Testimonies than now," Butler exclaimed in 1882. Earlier, in the mid-1870s, as president of the Iowa Conference, he had vigorously supported the visions against the attacks of the Marion Party. Even when Butler himself became the object of censure in a testimony, he was open to accept it. Thus, when in 1875 he received a testimony that he interpreted as a call for his resignation as General Conference president, Butler reacted with alacrity: "My mind was settled before the reading of the testimony was finished. I resigned at once." The testimonies he received during the theological crises of 1886-1888, however, were a much more severe test for Butler. For a time, in 1888, Ellen White even classed him with those "who appear to be defenders of the Testimonies, but are their real assailants." Finding himself unsupported and even opposed by Ellen White on the issues of the law in Galatians and the new focus on righteousness in Christ, Butler refused to budge. In response to an 1888 letter from Ellen White pointing out his part in the Galatians dispute, Butler retorted, "I have not, Sister White, been able to see the justice of your letter of April 5, 1887, and never expect to." Not until five years later did Butler begin to admit that he may have been on the wrong side on some of those issues. For Lentha, it was an even longer struggle. "My poor wife," Butler wrote in 1904, "never could get her feelings fully brought around until just a little while before her death." Looking back over his life experiences in 1906, Butler remarked to J. H. Kellogg, "I have had Testimonies, I tell you, that shaved [me] to the very quick . . . and it takes a lot of study before you can really come to the point of cheerfully accepting them." Unlike Kellogg, however, Butler retained his confidence in the testimonies of Ellen White, declaring in his old age, in 1907, "I do not suppose there is anyone who believes them any more strongly than I do."

See: Obituary: "George I. Butler," *Review,* Aug. 8, 1918, p. 2; "George Ide Butler," *Review,* Aug. 29, 1918, pp. 14-16; obituary: "Lentha Ames Butler," *Review,* Dec. 3, 1901, p. 990; obituary: "Elizabeth Jane Butler," *Review,* June 28, 1928, p. 22; G. I. Butler to Ellen G. White, June 28, 1882 and Oct. 1, 1888; G. I. Butler to James White, Mar. 29, 1875; G. I. Butler to "Uncle Stephen" [S. N. Haskell], Apr. 22, 1893; G. I. Butler to J. H. Kellogg, Mar. 7, 1906, as in Emmett K. Vande Vere, *Rugged Heart,* p. 126; G. I. Butler to F. E. Belden, June 20, 1907; Ellen G. White, Lt 18, 1888 (Dec. 11); E. G. White, *Testimony for the Church,* No. 25 (Battle Creek, Mich.: Steam Press of the Seventh-day Adventist Pub. Assn., 1875), p. 72 [special edition, original at Center for Adventist Research, Andrews University, Berrien Springs, Mich.] For a general account of G. I. Butler's life, see Emmett K. Vande Vere, *Rugged Heart: The Story of George I. Butler.*

BYINGTON, John (1798-1887) and (first wife) **Mary Priscilla** (c. 1803-1830) and (second wife) **Catherine** (1803-1885)

Self-supporting minister and first president of the General Conference of Seventh-day Adventists. John was born in Vermont and in the early 1830s moved to Buck's Bridge,

New York. An active lay member and licensed "exhorter" in the Methodist Episcopal Church, Byington was also an abolitionist and joined the breakaway Methodist Wesleyan Church when it seceded over the slavery issue in 1843. In 1852 Byington became a Sabbatarian Adventist, and in 1855 built one of the earliest Sabbatarian churches on his property.

Having already served as minister in the Methodist Wesleyan Church for a few years prior to becoming an Adventist, Byington conducted services in Buck's Bridge and, from about 1856, was called upon to preach farther afield, including a Michigan itinerary in 1857. In 1858, following a request from James White, Byington relocated to Michigan, buying a farm in Newton township, just a few miles south of Battle Creek. Until within a few months of his death in 1887, Byington traveled widely among the Michigan churches, supporting his ministry from the proceeds of his farm. His administrative talents were also recognized: he was often given committee responsibilities and served as the first president of the General Conference from 1863 to 1865.

The only two extant letters from Ellen White to John Byington both date from 1859 and deal with a major crisis in his life. Having heeded James White's call to move to Michigan in October 1858, Byington became despondent when the move entailed serious financial loss. He became particularly unhappy with James White when he heard that White had raised funds to buy a house for Joseph Bates. Byington felt he was being treated unfairly, descended into depression, and for about a year—judging from the absence of reports in the *Review*—appears to have stopped his ministerial travels. Ellen White's letters, written in the summer of 1859, were both stern and entreating, and within weeks Byington was back on his preaching itineraries.

See: Obituary: "John Byington," *Review,* Jan. 25, 1887, pp. 57, 58; obituary: "Catherine Byington," *Review,* Mar. 17, 1885, p. 175; Ellen G. White, Lt 2, 1859 (June 21); Lt 28, 1859 (June/July); Herbert Cornelius Andrews, Sanford Charles Hinsdale, and Alfred L. Holman, *Hinsdale Genealogy: Descendants of Robert Hinsdale of Dedham, Medfield, Hadley, and Deerfield, With an Account of the French Family of De Hinnisdal* (Lombard, Ill.: A. H. Andrews, 1906), pp. 150, 151; Grace Amadon, "The First President of the General Conference," *Review,* June 22, 1944, pp. 6, 7; John O. Waller, "John Byington of Bucks Bridge," *Adventist Heritage,* July 1974, pp. 5-13, 65-67.

BYINGTON, John Fletcher (1832-1872) and **Martha Louisa (née SMITH)** (1834-1920)

Printer, schoolteacher, dentist, physician, and son of **John Byington**, first president of the General Conference, John Fletcher Byington became a Sabbathkeeping Adventist in 1852. By 1853 he was working as an apprentice at the *Review and Herald* printing office in Rochester, New York. Ellen White wrote in August 1853, "Stephen Belden and Fletcher Byington do not return from the office until 10, 12, 2 or 3 o'clock. They have labored uncommonly hard of late."

Byington continued his work at the *Review* "for some years," but during the 1850s he also taught school intermittently. In 1855 he taught at the first school to be operated by Sabbatarian Adventists in Buck's Bridge, New York, and in 1858 at a similar school in Battle Creek, Michigan. The same year he married Martha Smith, daughter of **Cyrenius** and **Louisa Smith.** He graduated from the Homoeopathic Medical College of Cleveland,

Ohio, in 1863 and entered into private medical practice. For about one year he served at the Western Health Reform Institute in Battle Creek. An action taken by the directors on May 27, 1867, stated that "the wages of Dr. Byington be fixed at $15 per week." According to his obituary, he died in 1872 "of cerebro-spinal meningitis . . . in the 40th year of his age."

J. F. Byington boarded with the Whites while at Rochester. Years later Ellen White wrote appreciatively of "Brother Fletcher Byington, who was a member of my family for years. He seemed like a brother, and we were thoroughly united in the truth." The only negative comment by Ellen White concerned Byington's involvement around 1860 in the general resentment shown by *Review* workers against James White.

See: Obituary: "Dr. J. F. Byington," *Review,* June 25, 1872, p. 15; obituary: "Martha Louisa King," *Review,* Oct. 14, 1920, p. 31; Ellen G. White, Lt 7, 1853 (Aug. 24); Lt 28, 1859 (June/July); Lt 7, 1860 (June); Lt 174, 1906 (June 7); Grace Amadon, "The First President of the General Conference: John Byington, Farmer-Preacher," *Review,* June 22, 1944, p. 7; James White, "School at Battle Creek," *Review,* Jan. 14, 1858, p. 80; C. Smith, J. P. Kellogg, "A School in Battle Creek," *Review,* Oct. 14, 1858, p. 168; *Records of the Board of Directors of the Health Reform Institute at Battle Creek, Mich., April 25, 1867-Oct. 8, 1876* (Berrien Springs, Mich.: Center for Adventist Research, n.d.), p. 23; Herbert Cornelius Andrews, Sanford Charles Hinsdale, and Alfred L. Holman, *Hinsdale Genealogy: Descendants of Robert Hinsdale of Dedham, Medfield, Hadley, and Deerfield, With an Account of the French Family of De Hinnisdal* (Lombard, Ill.: A. H. Andrews, 1906), pp. 272, 273.

CARMAN, John Frost (1827-1923) and **Maria Louisa** (1829-1916)

A prosperous farmer and active layman from Benton Township, Eaton County, Michigan, John Carman became a Sabbathkeeping Adventist in 1855 through the preaching of J. B. Frisbie in nearby West Windsor. His wife, Maria Louisa (née Potter), came from one of the most influential families of Eaton County. John Carman took the initiative in building the first Seventh-day Adventist church in Potterville, dedicated in 1870. During the 1870s and 1880s he used his administrative skills in the service of the church, serving on numerous committees of the Michigan Conference.

The earliest record of Carman's contact with Ellen White is found in her 1859 diary, where she told of his request that the Whites come to his area to preach. Subsequently the Whites visited the Carmans on numerous occasions. According to John Carman's daughter, Cora Viola, their home became a retreat for the Whites from the pressures of Battle Creek, a special room being built for their use.

See: Obituary: "John Frost Carman," *Review,* May 10, 1923, p. 22; obituary: "Maria Louisa Potter Carman," *Review,* Nov. 16, 1916, p. 22; S. C. Courter, "Extracts of Letters," *Review,* July 10, 1855, p. 8; 1870 U.S. Federal Census, "John Carman," Michigan, Eaton County, Benton, p. 11; *The Past and Present of Eaton County, Michigan, Historically, Together With Biographical Sketches of Many of Its Leading and Prominent Citizens and Illustrious Dead* (Lansing, Mich.: Michigan Historical Publishing Association, 1880[?]), pp. 495, 496; James White, "Report From Bro. White," *Review,* May 14, 1867, p. 271; J. H. Waggoner, "Dedication at Potterville, Eaton Co.," *Review,* Jan. 18, 1870, p. 30; search term "Carman" in *Review and Herald* online collection, www.adventistarchives.org; Ellen G. White, Ms 5, 1859 (Feb. 5 entry); Arthur W. Spalding, *Footprints of the Pioneers* (Washington, D.C.: Review and Herald, 1947), pp. 205, 206.

CARPENTER, Caroline. See WEED, Caroline and Eber.

CASE, Hiram S. (1814-1882) and Rebecca Ann (1816-1887)

Hiram Case was one of the founders of the *Messenger* Party, an 1850s splinter movement from Sabbatarian Adventism. Born in New York State, Hiram and Rebecca Case moved in the 1830s to Michigan, where Hiram worked as a blacksmith and later engaged in farming.

Although he gives no exact details, Case preached either for the Millerites or one of the subsequent Adventist groups in the 1840s. Not satisfied, however, with the teachings of the major Adventist groups, he readily accepted Sabbatarian Adventism when a traveling preacher, Samuel Rhodes, presented it to him in 1850. Shortly after his conversion Case began a vigorous program of itinerant preaching in several states, during which he was the first to advocate Sabbatarian Adventism in Ohio and Wisconsin. Theologically Case was among the earliest (1850) to interpret the two horns of the lamblike beast of Revelation 13 in terms of Protestantism and republicanism.

Hiram Case's ministry lasted less than three years. According to Ellen White's analysis in several letters written in 1853, Case's mentor, Samuel Rhodes, had influenced him negatively, in particular by Rhodes' harshness toward persons both within and outside the church and by his financial extravagance. Matters came to a head in June 1853, when Ellen White publicly reproved Hiram Case and his supporter, Charles P. Russell, for their callous treatment of Abigail Palmer, a member of the Jackson, Michigan, group. At the same time she appealed to Case to "make thorough work. Dig deep and confess from the bottom . . . and you will not be so likely to go astray again."

For a while it looked as if Case might accept the admonition and alter course. In a letter to the *Review* some weeks later, in August 1853, he acknowledged his failings, asking "the forgiveness of all my brethren and sisters." The reconciliation was not to last long, however, and by early 1854 Case had lost both his ministerial office and his church membership. H. S. Case reacted by becoming a founding member of the break-off *Messenger* Party and joining the publishing committee of its paper, the *Messenger of Truth,* which focused on attacking the visions of Ellen White and the leadership of James White.

Little is known about Case's religious leanings after the *Messenger* Party collapsed about 1857. James White, writing in 1858, described him as "run out as a preacher, and fishing on the lakes." Any intimation in this description that Case was poverty-stricken, however, is not borne out by the census records of 1860, which show Hiram and Rebecca as farmers owning a substantial $4,000 in real estate. By 1862 they had also inherited further property after the death of Hiram's father.

See: Headstone for Hiram S. Case and Rebecca A. Case, Pioneer Cemetery, Hartford, Van Buren County, Michigan, www.usgwarchives.net/mi/vanburen/photos/tombstones/pioneer/case113002gph.jpg (Jan. 28, 2011); *The Northwestern Reporter, Vol. 44, Containing All the Decisions of the Supreme Courts of Minnesota, Wisconsin, Iowa, Michigan, Nebraska,*

North Dakota, South Dakota (St. Paul: West Pub. Co., 1890), pp. 578, 579; 1850 U.S. Federal Census, "Hiram Case," Michigan, Ionia County, Lyons, p. 157; 1860 U.S. Federal Census, "H. S. Case," Michigan, Clinton County, DeWitt, p. 191; H. S. Case, "Letter From Bro. Case," *Present Truth,* November 1850, p. 85; Ellen G. White, Lt 3, 1853 (June 29); Lt 6, 1853 (Aug. 3); Lt 9, 1853 (Dec. 5); Ms 1, 1853 (June 2); H. S. Case, "From Bro. Case," *Review,* Aug. 28, 1853, p. 64; J. W. [James White], "A Sketch of the Rise and Progress of the Present Truth," *Review,* Jan 14, 1858, p. 77. For an account of Case's separation from the Sabbatarian Adventists, seen from the eyes of the *Messenger* Party, see J. B. Bezzo, "H. S. Case," *Messenger of Truth,* Nov. 2, 1854, pp. [2-4].

CHAMBERLAIN, Mary Ann (née **BILL**) (1819-1900) and **Ezra L'Hommedieu** (1798-1855)

Mary Ann and Ezra Chamberlain were among the first Adventists in Connecticut to keep the Sabbath. After Ezra died in 1855, Mary, who was his second wife and more than 20 years his junior, studied medicine and homeopathy and received her M.D. from the University of Michigan. She subsequently served as doctor at the recently established Western Health Reform Institute in Battle Creek, Michigan, for several years up to 1875. While there Ellen White commended her for serving with "earnestness and energy for small pay." Later she worked at the Rural Health Retreat (which became St. Helena Sanitarium) in St. Helena, California, 1883-1884. During this period, however, Ellen White challenged Mary Chamberlain on her use of "little homeopathic doses for almost every ailment. . . . I was obliged to tell her that this practice of depending upon medicine, whether in large or small doses, was not in accordance with the principles of health reform."

Ellen and James White first met the Chamberlains in 1848 in response to Ezra's letter urging the Whites to attend a conference in Rocky Hill, Connecticut (later designated the first of the "Sabbath and Sanctuary Conferences"). During the next two or three years Ezra Chamberlain featured quite prominently in the Sabbatarian movement at conferences, as a traveling preacher, and as agent for the *Review* in Connecticut. Apparently, however, he was not very effective as a speaker. Ellen White received visions in 1849 and 1852 showing that "it was not his duty to travel" and that "he was not one of the messengers." Existing records indicate that during his few remaining years, till his death in 1855, Chamberlain's sphere of activity was mostly limited to the vicinity of his hometown.

See: Obituary: "Mary A. Chamberlain," *Review,* Apr. 17, 1900, p. 256; Lillian Hubbard Holch, ed., *Sizer Genealogy: A History of Antonio Dezocieur Who Changed His Name to Anthony Sizer,* pp. 205, 206, 208; obituary: "E.L.H. Chamberlain," *Review,* Jan. 24, 1856, p. 134; Health Reform Institute (Battle Creek, Mich.), "Minutes of the Health Reform Institute Board: Selections, 1867-1897" (Berrien Springs, Mich.: Center for Adventist Research, Andrews University, n.d.), minutes for Sept. 19, 1875; "St. Helena Sanitarium: Golden Jubilee 1878-1928," Ellen G. White Estate, DF 14, p. 13; Ellen G. White, Lt 10, 1850 (Mar. 18); Lt 4, 1852 (Oct. 25); Lt 26a, 1889 (Mar. 2); *The Health Reform and the Health Institute* (PH138), p. 32; *Spiritual Gifts [vol. 2],* pp. 91, 93; SDAE, s.v. "E.L.H. Chamberlain."

CHAPEL, Levi R. (1816-1901) and **Jane Eliza** (1818-1903)

Levi and Eliza Chapel took "an active part in the movement of 1843-44." According to one source, Levi Chapel also expected the Advent in 1845, and in a letter to his grandparents written July 15, 1845, "bids them goodbye forever, for he is lookin [*sic*] for the world to end." The Chapels became Sabbatarian Adventists before 1851, though the exact year is uncertain.

Levi Chapel, born in Massachusetts, migrated with his family to Oswego County, New York, in 1823. Listed variously as carpenter, grocer, and farmer in the censuses, he also served as postmaster for East Palermo, New York, for some time in the 1860s. He was an active layperson, being district leader for the Tract and Missionary Society in the 1880s, and on occasion serving on various committees of the New York Conference.

Ellen White mentioned the Chapels in connection with a crisis that their home church in Palermo underwent during the late 1850s. After the "Laodicean" call to the churches to "be zealous . . . and repent" (Rev. 3:19) had taken hold among Sabbatarian Adventists in 1856/1857, some members had interpreted this as a call to watch for faults among fellow members rather than to repent of their own shortcomings. This had led to internal dissension in the Palermo church. Levi and Eliza Chapel were admonished for the prominent part they had played in the troubles.

See: Mary Shaw Green, *The History of Levi Greene of Rhode Island, Massachusetts, New York, Michigan: And His Descendants* (Adrian, Mich.: Adrian College Press, 1944), pp. 10, 11, 27, 28; obituary: "L. R. Chapel," *Review*, Jan. 7, 1902, p. 14; obituary: "Eliza Chapel," *Review*, Mar. 17, 1903, p. 23; 1900 U.S. Federal Census, "Levi R. Chapel," New York, Oswego County, Palermo Town, p. 229B; search terms "L. R. Chapel" and "J. E. Chapel" in *Review and Herald* online collection, www.adventistarchives.org; Ellen G. White, Lt 8, 1857 (July 19); Lt 2, 1858 (c. 1858); Lt 17, 1859 (Oct. 28).

CHAPIN, Roderick R. (c. 1816-before 1880) and **Desdemona** (1812-after 1891)

Listed as a "pedlar" and "farmer" in the censuses of 1850 and 1860, R. R. Chapin was an active layman-preacher in the period 1850-1853, living in Rochester, New York, and vicinity. By 1854 notices appeared in the *Review* indicating that R. R. Chapin had joined the offshoot group of Hiram Case and C. P. Hall. The October and November 1854 issues of the *Messenger of Truth* (periodical of the *Messenger* Party) contained letters from Chapin rejecting Ellen White's visions and charging that Sabbatarian Adventists were making them a test of fellowship.

Ellen White's only mention of Chapin occurred in a vision account from 1850 (Ms 5, 1850 [July 29]). The vision indicated that already by 1850 Chapin had been "in darkness," from which God had rescued him "as a bird is rescued from the snare of the fowler." It is not known whether the "darkness" referred to in 1850 involved the same issues that three years later led to his break with the movement. Chapin's name is also connected with the publication of the purported "Camden vision" of Ellen White, which sought to show her close ties to an extreme shut-door position.

See: 1850 U.S. Federal Census, "Roderick Chapin," New York, Monroe County, Greece, p. 154; 1860 U.S. Federal Census, "R. R. Chapin," New York, Monroe County, Sweden, p. 2; search word "Chapin" in *Words of the Pioneers*; R. R. Chapin, "Who Are the Remnant?" *Messenger of Truth,* Oct. 19, 1854, p. [2]; R. R. Chapin, in *Messenger of Truth,* Oct. 19, 1854, p. [4]; R. R. Chapin, "To the Publishing Committee," *Messenger of Truth,* Nov. 30, 1854, p. [3]; Ellen G. White, Ms 5, 1850 (July 29); *The Rochester Directory for the Year Beginning July 1, 1891* (Rochester, N.Y.: Drew, Allis & Company, 1891). For further information on the *Messenger* Party and the "Camden vision," see SDAE, s.v. "*Messenger* Party"; EGWEnc, s.v. "*Messenger* Party" and "Camden Vision."

CHASE, Lewis (1814-1896) and **Almira** (1816-1881)

A Methodist farmer-minister from New York, Lewis Chase became a Sabbatarian Adventist about 1852. There is some evidence from the *Review* that he subsequently preached in his home area, around Sandy Creek and Boylston, New York. After 1863, however, there is no further mention of Lewis Chase or "L. Chase" in the *Review,* suggesting that he severed his contact with the Adventists. In her 1859 diary Ellen White wrote of a meeting in Mannsfield, New York, where "Brethren Chase and Bailey . . . opened their mouths and glorified God."

See: Phyllis Smith Oyer, *Oyer and Allied Families: Their History and Genealogy* (Rochester, Interlaken, N.Y.: Heart of the Lakes Publishing, 1988), p. 46; Glenn F. Thibault, "Thibault and Chase of New England and N.Y.," November 2004, RootsWeb, http://worldconnect.genealogy.rootsweb.com (Dec. 18, 2006); 1850 U.S. Federal Census, "Lewis Chase," New York, Oswego County, Boylston, p. 187; search term "Chase" in *Review and Herald* online collection, www.adventistarchives.org; C. B. Preston, "From Bro. Preston," *Review,* Nov. 11, 1858, p. 199; Ellen G. White, Ms 8, 1859 (Oct. 23 entry).

CHASE, Mary S. (née **WHITE**) (1810-1889) and **Daniel** (1798-after 1873)

A native of Palmyra, Maine, Mary S. White, an older sister of James White's, married Daniel Chase of Fairfield, Maine, in 1831. In the early 1840s Mary joined the Millerite movement together with her parents and some other family members. About 1866 (or 1869—her obituary is ambiguous on this point) she became a Sabbathkeeper. Whether for this or other reasons, her husband became "abusive." As a result Mary Chase left Daniel in the early 1870s and moved to Battle Creek, Michigan. It appears that for the remainder of her life Mary Chase lived either with James and Ellen White or in accommodation provided by them in Battle Creek. Several of Ellen White's letters after James's death in 1881 describe her efforts to arrange housing for Mary and to solicit financial help from Mary's brother, John W. White.

Ellen White was fond of Mary Chase. "Our hearts run together like two drops of water," she exclaimed in 1855. Later the bitter relations with her husband tended to create a general negativity in Mary. Surviving letters from Ellen White to Mary Chase from the 1870s focus on her need to break with dejection and embrace a positive faith in God.

See: Robert M. Sherman, Ruth W. Sherman, and Robert S. Wakefield, *Mayflower Families Through Five Generations: Descendants of the Pilgrims Who Landed at Plymouth, Mass., December 1620* (Plymouth, Mass.: General Society of Mayflower Descendants, 2005), vol. 20, part 2, p. 423; obituary: "Mary S. Chase," *Review,* Sept. 10, 1889, p. 575; Ellen G. White, Lt 2, 1870 (Mar. 2); Lt 6, 1873 (Feb. 6); Lt 30, 1884 (Nov. 21); Lt 61, 1884 (Nov. 27); Lt 19, 1889 (Jan. 8); Lt 2, 1855 (Aug.); Lt 28, 1877 (Oct. 26).

CLAFLIN, Nancy J. (née HILDRETH) (1814-1899) and (first husband) John Post (?-1841) and (second husband) Andrew Claflin (1814-1877)

Nancy Claflin, born in Vermont, lived for many years in Norfolk, New York; after Andrew's death, she lived in Bloomington, Illinois. Nancy Claflin became a Sabbatarian Adventist about 1852. The enthusiasm she had for her faith is shown in fervent letters to the *Review* and a long series of receipts for her subscriptions to the church paper. Her obituary in 1899 has the heading "Had Read Every Number of the *Review.*" Ellen White mentioned that Nancy Claflin attended some meetings held by the Whites in Buck's Bridge, New York, in 1859. Little is known about Andrew Claflin, who, Nancy reports, had joined her in keeping the Sabbath by 1853.

See: Obituary: "Nancy J. Claflin," *Review,* Dec. 26, 1899, p. 844; John Goodwin Locke, *Book of the Lockes: A Genealogical and Historical Record of the Descendants of William Locke, of Woburn, With an Appendix Containing a History of the Lockes in England, and Also of the Family of John Locke, of Hampton, N.H., and Kindred Families and Individuals* (Boston and Cambridge: James Munroe and Company, 1853), p. 154; Charles Henry Wight, *Genealogy of the Claflin Family, Being a Record of Robert Mackclothian, of Wenham, Mass., and of His Descendants 1661-1898* (New York: Press of William Green, [1903]), pp. 144; 1850 U.S. Federal Census, "Andrew Claflin," New York, St. Lawrence County, Norfolk, p. 154; 1870 U.S. Federal Census, "Andrew Claflin," New York, St. Lawrence County, Norfolk, p. 1; Nancy Claflin, "From Sister Claflin," *Review,* June 23, 1853, p. 24; Nancy Claflin, "From Sr. Claflin," *Review,* Jan. 1, 1857, p. 71; Ellen G. White, Ms 8, 1859 (Oct. 19 entry).

CLARKE, Joseph (c. 1818-after 1901) and Sarah (c. 1827-1898)

Active laypersons, administrators, and pioneer educators among freedmen of Texas. First mentioned in the *Review* in 1855, Joseph and Sarah Clarke were farmers in Portage, Ohio. There is some evidence that both of them also taught school in the vicinity. Joseph Clarke was perhaps best known for the scores of short, practical articles that he contributed to the *Review* and *Youth's Instructor* for more than 40 years. In Ellen White's only preserved letter to Joseph Clarke she affirmed him in his writing ministry: "Much of your time, I was shown, would be occupied in writing, and improving opportunities of doing good to others." He also served as secretary of the Ohio Conference in the 1860s and of the Missouri Conference in the 1880s.

Sarah Clarke served as secretary of the Missouri Tract Society in the early 1880s. In 1878, with the blessing of the General Conference, but self-financed, the Clarkes opened a small school for freedmen in Dallas County, Texas, one of the very earliest such ventures by Seventh-day Adventists. After leaving Texas the following year, they settled near Lowry City, Missouri. In 1885 the Clarkes headed up the city mission in St. Louis, Missouri, for some months.

See: Obituary, "Mrs. Joseph Clarke," *Review,* Mar. 1, 1898, p. 146; 1850 U.S. Federal Census, "Joseph Clark," Ohio, Wood County, Liberty, p. 129; 1880 U.S. Federal Census, "Joseph Clark," Missouri, St. Claire County, Butler, p. 19; search terms "Joseph Clarke" and "Sarah Clarke" in *Review and Herald* online collection, www.adventistarchives.org; Ellen G. White, Lt 9, 1868 (Mar. 22).

COLLINS, Deborah L. (1839-1852)

Deborah was the daughter of **Philip** and **Nancy Collins**, of Dartmouth, Massachusetts. A letter from Ellen White to Deborah in 1850, then age 9, and her brother **Gilbert,** 13, shows the personal interest Ellen White took in their spiritual welfare. Deborah Collins died at age 13 "of canker-rash, after an illness of two and a half days."

See: Obituary: "Deborah L. Collins," *Review,* Dec. 23, 1852, p. 128; Ellen G. White, Lt 7, 1849 (Sept.).

COLLINS, Gilbert N. (1836-1905) and **Arline F.** (1847-1927)

An elder of the New Bedford, Massachusetts, church for many years, Gilbert Collins also served on various New England Conference committees. At age 12, during the winter of 1848-1849, Gilbert become seriously ill with whooping cough and "wasted almost to a skeleton." At the request of his parents, **Philip** and **Nancy Collins**, Ellen and James White came to their home in Dartmouth, Massachusetts, and "earnestly besought the Lord to spare his life." After about eight days the Whites returned to Dartmouth to find Gilbert having "gained four pounds in flesh" and "the household rejoicing in God." Later in life Gilbert Collins became a successful manufacturer, and Ellen White encouraged him to give generously to various church projects, in particular to the New England Sanitarium in Melrose, Massachusetts. The details of Collins' responses to these appeals are not known, except that his last will included a bequest of $1,000 to the New England Sanitarium.

See: Obituary: "Gilbert N. Collins," *Review,* June 29, 1905, p. 23; "Arline F. Collins," 1900 U.S. Federal Census, Massachusetts, Bristol County, Dartmouth, p. 144B; *W. A. Greenough Co.'s 1927 New Bedford and Fairhaven Directory* (Boston: W. A. Greenough Co., 1927), p. 203; James White to Hastings, Feb. 25, 1849; Ellen G. White, *Spiritual Gifts [vol. 2],* pp. 108, 109; Lt 33, 1897 (June 9); Lt 6, 1902 (Jan. 3); Lt 305, 1904 (Aug.); Lt 341, 1904 (Dec. 22); Lt 29, 1905 (Jan. 1); Lt 23, 1905 (Jan. 17); A. E. Place, "Fund for the New England Sanitarium," *Atlantic Union Gleaner,* Aug. 9, 1905, p. 374.

COLLINS, Philip (c. 1809-1859) and **Nancy** (c. 1809-1882)

Among the earliest Sabbatarian Adventists in the country, Philip and Nancy Collins (née Biss), of Dartmouth, Massachusetts, were persuaded to keep the Sabbath by reading T. M. Preble's tract in early 1845. Their acquaintance with James White can be traced back to 1846. The dramatic healing of their son, **Gilbert N. Collins,** in 1849 after prayer and anointing by Ellen and James White deepened the ties between the two families. After the death of Philip Collins in 1859, Ellen White noted in her diary, "His loss is deeply felt, not only by his family, but by all the church."

See: Obituary: "Philip Collins," *Review,* June 23, 1859, p. 39; obituary: "Gilbert N. Collins," *Review,* June 29, 1905, p. 23; obituary: "Nancy Collins," *Review,* June 13, 1882, p. 382; obituary: "Rachel C. Ashley," *Atlantic Union Gleaner,* Feb. 18, 1903, p. 90; *Volume II—Marriages,* in *Vital Records of Dartmouth, Massachusetts, to the Year 1850* (Boston: New England Historic Genealogical Society, 1930), pp. 63, 121; T. M. Preble, *A Tract, Showing That the Seventh Day Should Be Observed as the Sabbath, Instead of the First Day "According to the Commandment"* (Nashua, N.H.: Murray and Kimball, 1845); James White to "Brother Collins," Aug. 26, 1846; Ellen G. White, *Spiritual Gifts [vol. 2],* pp. 108, 109; Ms 7, 1859 (Sept. 16 entry).

CORNELL, James (1832-1897) and **Roxanna** (1837-1895)

James Cornell was born in Ripley, New York, and moved with his family to Tyrone, Michigan, in 1834 or 1835. His better-known older brother, **Merritt E. Cornell**, a prominent evangelist, became a Sabbatarian Adventist in 1852, and it is possible that James also made that decision about the same time.

In 1857 James Cornell married Roxanna Bacheller. Roxanna, originally from Vermont, had worked at the Review and Herald press since 1852, first in Rochester, New York, and later in Battle Creek, Michigan, until her marriage. Roxanna was very well acquainted with Ellen and James White, having boarded in their home during the Rochester years, together with her brother **John Warren Bacheller** and mother, Cynthia Bacheller. James Cornell was a shoemaker and lived in several locations in Michigan. In 1876 the Cornells moved to Texas, but both their business and their health suffered; when Ellen and James White visited them in 1878, they found James earning "but little" and "suffering with rheumatism," while Roxanna had been "almost dead with asthma." "I gave each of the Cornell girls a dress," recounted Ellen White. "I cannot see want and misery and enjoy the comforts of life." Encouraged and led by James White, the Cornells, together with several other Adventist families, left Texas in April 1879, traveling by mule-drawn caravan through Indian Territory and Kansas, arriving in Boulder, Colorado, some six weeks later. The Cornells appear to have spent their remaining years in Boulder.

Ellen White wrote several serious letters of admonition to Roxanna and to James. In 1879 she compared James's life to "the barren fig tree, destitute of fruit" and made a strong call for a "most thorough reformation in the parents and children." That he heeded this call is suggested in James Cornell's obituary, which notes that "his religious experience during the last few years has been especially bright."

See: Obituary: "James Cornell," *Review,* Mar. 8, 1898, p. 162; obituary: "Roxanna Cornell," *Review,* Dec. 10, 1895, p. 799; obituary: "Cynthia Bacheller," *Review,* Jan. 15, 1884, p. 47; 1880 U.S. Federal Census, "James Cornell," Colorado, Boulder County, Boulder, p. 18; Frederick Clifton Pierce, *Batchelder, Batcheller Genealogy* (Chicago: W. B. Conkey, 1898), p. 577; Franklin Ellis, *History of Livingston Co., Michigan: With Illustrations and Biographical Sketches of its Prominent Men and Pioneers* (Philadelphia: Everts & Abbott, 1880), p. 396; Everett N. Dick, "For Health and Wealth: The Birth of Seventh-day Adventism in Colorado," *Adventist Heritage,* September-November 1982, pp. 18-27; Ellen G. White, Lt 8, 1856 (Jan. 21); Lt 63, 1878 (Dec. 26); Lts 37, 38, 39, 1879 (c. 1879, Jan. 16, c. 1879).

CORNELL, Merritt E. (1827-1893) and **Angeline M. A.** (1828-1901)

An ardent evangelist and debater, Merritt E. Cornell, originally from Chili, New York, preached widely in many states of the Union from 1852 to the 1870s. He married Angeline Lyon, daughter of **Henry** and **Deborah Lyon**, in 1849. After an earlier affiliation with an Adventist group headed by Joseph Marsh, the Cornells became Sabbatarians in 1852 following contacts with Joseph Bates. Cornell's evangelism in the 1850s was in the mid-West, expanding in the 1860s to include New England. In the early 1870s he preached for three years in California and, for a short time (1878-1879), in Colorado.

The work of the Cornells in the 1870s was overshadowed by two regrettable episodes, both made public in the columns of the *Review.* In 1871 Merritt Cornell revealed that Angeline had become "a confirmed spiritualist," and in 1876 a General Conference session ascertained that "Eld. M. E. Cornell has for several years past been guilty of immoral conduct." Most of Ellen White's letters to M. E. Cornell were written during this period and dealt with his grave moral problems, but also sought to set him on a path to restoration. Subsequently, for many years, Cornell did not serve in public ministry. In 1890 his ministerial credentials were restored, and he ministered in Michigan for the remaining three years of his life. Angeline had already publicly renounced her spiritualist beliefs in 1876.

See: Obituary: "Merritt E. Cornell," *Review,* Jan. 23, 1894, p. 63; obituary: "Angeline M. A. Cornell," *Review,* Jan. 7, 1902, p. 14; Michigan Pioneer and Historical Society, Historical Collections. *Collections and Researches Made by the Michigan Pioneer and Historical Society* (Lansing, Mich.: Robert Smith & Co., State Printers and Binders, 1896), vol. 26, pp. 53, 54; "To Whom It May Concern," *Review,* June 13, 1871, p. 208; "Fourteenth Annual Session of the General Conference of S. D. Adventists," *Review,* Oct. 5, 1876, p. 106; "Confession and Declaration of Faith," *Review,* Nov. 23, 1876, pp. 166, 167; Ellen G. White, Lt 23, 1871 (Dec. 27); Lt 29, 1872 (Oct. 1872); Lts 52, 53, 54, 55, 1876 (c. 1876).

CORNELL, Myron J. (1829-1920) and **Cornelia A.** (1836-1922)

An active layperson and the younger brother of prominent evangelist **Merritt E. Cornell,** Myron Cornell and his wife, Cornelia (née Lyon), moved to Battle Creek, Michigan, in 1856 and resided there for the rest of their lives. Myron Cornell engaged in various lines of business in Battle Creek before settling down on a nearby farm in his old age.

At some point after their move to Battle Creek, Myron became a Sabbatarian Adventist, possibly in 1859, when J. N. Loughborough notes in his diary that "Bro. White . . . baptized Myron and others." There are a number of mentions of Cornelia Lyon in the *Review* going back to 1853, so it is probable that she had become a Sabbathkeeper several years earlier than her husband. In 1861 Myron Cornell was chosen to be a deacon in the newly organized Battle Creek church, a position that he held till his death. The denomination drew extensively on his administrative talents. Among many other assignments, he served on the executive committee of the Michigan Conference, was a director of the Health Reform Institute, and sat on the board of Cedar Lake Industrial Academy.

Myron Cornell's solid reputation and administrative ability no doubt explain why in 1897 Ellen White gave Cornell the power of attorney to care for her business affairs in Michigan. Thus, in 1902, she wrote from St. Helena, California, asking him "to inquire if the outstanding debts for the rent of my house in Battle Creek have been collected." Earlier, in 1869, Ellen White had written several searching testimonies during a time of crisis when Cornelia Cornell, with others, had joined forces to level unfounded charges against the Whites.

See: Obituary: "Myron J. Cornell," *Review,* Feb. 17, 1921, p. 22; obituary: "Cornelia Cornell," *Review,* Aug. 10, 1922, p. 22; *Battle Creek and Marshall City Directories . . . for 1883* (Coldwater, Mich.: A. Nedham & Co., 1882), p. 41; 1870 U.S. Federal Census, "M. J. Cornell," Michigan, Calhoun County, Battle Creek, Ward 3, p. 15; J. N. Loughborough, 1859 Diary (Center for Adventist Research, Andrews University), entry for Jan. 1, 1859; search terms "Myron J. Cornell," "M. J. Cornell," and "Cornelia Lyon" in *Review and Herald* online collection, www.adventistarchives.org; Ellen G. White, Lt 155, 1897 (1897); Lt 165, 1902 (Oct. 23); Lts 9, 10, 13, 1869 (July 7, Aug. 15, Sept. 24).

COTTRELL, John Harvey (1817-1881) and **Maryette** (1816-1879)

John H. Cottrell was one of the founding members of the church in Mill Grove, New York, in 1851. He was listed as a farmer in available census records. According to J. N. Loughborough, the first evangelistic tent meetings in New York were held "on the farm of Bro. Harvey Cottrell" in Mill Grove in June 1855. He was the brother of well-known Seventh-day Adventist writer and preacher **Roswell Fenner Cottrell**.

Although Ellen White would have been personally acquainted with the Cottrells from her visits to Mill Grove in the early 1850s, there is no existing correspondence between them. However, in a letter to a friend in Mill Grove, Ellen White mentioned "Brother Harvey and family" as among those she missed and hoped to see again.

The most substantial mention of John Cottrell in Ellen White's writings is a paragraph in her "Testimony for the Mill Grove Church," in which she pointed out problems in his relation to the church in Mill Grove while at the same time recognizing that he and his wife "desire to press fully with the body and do the whole will of God."

See: Roy F. Cottrell, "A Brief Sketch of Cottrell Family History," unpublished manuscript (n.p., 1965), pp. 6, 13 (copy in DF 439 at Ellen G. White Estate, Silver Spring, Md.); obituary, "J. H. Cottrell," *Review*, July 19, 1881, p. 62; obituary, "Maryette Cottrell," *Re-*

view, Jan. 15, 1880, p. 46; 1850 U.S. Federal Census, "John H. Cottrell," New York, Erie County, Newstead, p. 212; 1860 U.S. Federal Census, "John H. Cottrell," New York, Erie County, Newstead, p. 41; J. N. Loughborough, "Recollections of the Past—No. 12," *Review*, Mar. 3, 1885, pp. 137, 138; Ellen White to Sister Below, Lt. 9, 1856 (Jan. 1); Ellen White, "Testimony for the Mill Grove Church," Ms 3, 1861 (c. 1861).

COTTRELL, Roswell Fenner (1814-1892) and **Catherine M.** (1818-1899)

A writer, poet, and minister, Roswell Cottrell was born into a Seventh Day Baptist home, his father being a Seventh Day Baptist preacher. At age 19 Roswell moved with his family to western New York, where he remained most of his life. About 1835 he married Catherine M. Harvey at Mill Grove, New York, and for 10 years taught in public schools in the area. Cottrell was rather ambivalent to the Second Advent preaching of the Millerites. Although personally sympathetic to much of their teaching, he could not join a movement that showed very little interest in even investigating the claims of Sabbatarians. Cottrell's dilemma was resolved when he subsequently came into contact with the Sabbatarian Adventist movement. "After some nine months [of] careful and cautious examination," he "arrived at the decision" and joined the new movement in 1851, together with his family.

Roswell Cottrell was ordained as a minister in 1854, preaching in western New York and in Pennsylvania, and pioneering in Canada West. He also served briefly as president of the New York Conference (1868-1869). But it was as a writer of articles and tracts that he made his mark. "As a speaker," notes his obituarist, "his ability was fair. As a writer, it was . . . superlative." According to one estimate, Cottrell contributed 1,692 items to the *Review*, ranging from theological analysis to exhortation to poetry. In 1864 the New York and northern Pennsylvania Conference voted, in view of "the labors of Bro. R. F. Cottrell in writing for the *Review*," to pay his salary "the same as though he were engaged in preaching." Of his theological contributions he is remembered most for his involvement in the debate over church organization in the early 1860s. However, the *Seventh-day Adventist Encyclopedia* cites Cottrell as an important contributor to Seventh-day Adventist theological development in a wide number of areas (see, e.g., articles entitled "Covenant," "Death," "Humanity, Doctrine of," "Probation," "Religious Liberty," "Sin"). Some of his poetry was set to music and has appeared in a range of Adventist hymnals up to the present.

Roswell and Catherine Cottrell were strong supporters of the visions of Ellen White. In 1855 their names headed a list of 13 Mill Grove members who maintained that "if the visions are not of God, they will surely come to nought. . . . But we have not been able to discover anything in them which conflicts with . . . the law and the testimony." In 1858 Roswell Cottrell wrote an introduction to volume 1 of Ellen White's *Spiritual Gifts*, which has remained a classic Seventh-day Adventist statement on the biblical bases for testing prophetic claims and on the continuation of the gift of prophecy beyond New Testament times.

See: Obituary: "R. F. Cottrell," *Review*, Apr. 19, 1892, p. 253; obituary: "Cathrane [*sic*] M. Cottrell," *Review*, Jan. 16, 1900, p. 46; West Ridgeway Cemetery, Town of Ridgeway, Orleans County, New York, www.rootsweb.ancestry.com/~nyorlean/wridgec2.htm (Aug. 21,

2009); Raymond F. Cottrell, "The Sabbath in the New World," in Kenneth A. Strand, ed., *The Sabbath in Scripture and History* (Washington, D.C.; Review and Herald, 1982), p. 255; James R. Nix, *Early Advent Singing*, pp. 75, 155, 157; Roy Franklin Cottrell, "The Cottrell Family Genealogy and Sketches" (Berrien Springs, Mich.: Center for Adventist Research, Andrews University), pp. 11, 12; Roswell F. Cottrell, "From Bro. Cottrell," *Review*, Nov. 25, 1851, p. 54; A. Lanphear, J. M. Aldrich, "Third Annual Report of the N.Y. and Northern Pa. Conference of the Seventh-day Adventists," *Review*, Oct. 25, 1864, p. 174; R. F. Cottrell, C. M. Cottrell, et al., "Letter From the Church at Mill Grove, N.Y., to Elder J. M. Stephenson," *Review*, Dec. 18, 1855, p. 93.

CRAIG, Stephen B. (1819-1904) and (first wife) **Miranda B.** (c. 1821-1863) and (second wife) **Marilla S.** (1833-1905)

Originally from New Hampshire, Stephen Craig came to Monroe County, New York, sometime before 1850 and farmed in the Hamlin/Parma area for more than 50 years. Of Millerite background, he was first mentioned in the *Review* in 1852 and was for many years an elder or deacon in the Parma Seventh-day Adventist Church. J. N. Andrews officiated at the funeral of Stephen Craig's first wife, Miranda, who died at 42 after having a leg amputated. Of Marilla, Craig's second wife, it is said that she was "actively engaged" in the Parma church. The Craigs received only incidental mention in Ellen White's writings. In 1859 she listed their names among others who attended a conference in nearby Carlton, New York.

See: Obituary: "Stephen B. Craig," *Review*, Apr. 7, 1904, p. 23; obituary: "Miranda B. Craig," *Review*, Feb. 24, 1863, p. 103; obituary: "Marilla S. Craig," *Review*, June 8, 1905, p. 31; 1850 U.S. Federal Census, "Stephen Craig," New York, Monroe County, Clarkson, p. 165; 1900 U.S. Federal Census, "Stephen B. Craig," New York, Monroe County, Parma, p. 14A; search term "S. B. Craig" in *Words of the Pioneers*; Ellen G. White, Lt 3, 1859 (Sept. 1).

CRAMER, Christopher G. (1809-1873) and (first wife) (unknown) and (second wife) **Mary** (?-died before 1850) and (third wife) **Jane Electa** (1828-1892)

Born in New York, Christopher Cramer moved to Michigan about 1844 and became a Sabbathkeeping Adventist about 1853 while living in Grand Rapids. A carpenter by trade, Cramer gave generously to various church causes. In her 1859 diary Ellen White mentioned the hospitality and help she received from Christopher Cramer and his son **James I. Cramer** while she was passing through Grand Rapids.

In his later years Ellen White warned Christopher Cramer that although he had "loved the truth," he had "not been sanctified by the truth." As a result of his "overbearing" manner, his wife, Jane, "who was a true Christian of fine sensibilities," had become dispirited. Ellen White appealed to him to "make haste to correct your errors." Christopher Cramer is buried in Wright, Michigan, where he spent his last years.

See: Obituary: "Christopher G. Cramer," *Review,* July 15, 1873, p. 39; obituary: "Jane Cramer," *Review,* May 3, 1892, p. 287; obituary: "James I. Cramer," *Review,* Sept. 3, 1914, p. 23; Thomas B. Wilson, *Ontario Marriage Notices* (Lambertville, N.J.: Clearfield, 1982; reprint, Baltimore: Genealogical Pub. Co., Inc., 1997), p. 52; search term "Cramer" in *Review and Herald* online collection, www.adventistarchives.org; 1850 U.S. Federal Census, "Christopher Cramer," Michigan, Kent County, Grand Rapids, p. 179; 1870 U.S. Federal Census, "Christopher Cramer," Ottawa County, Wright, p. 31; Ottawa County Cemetery Records, Vol. II, pp. 174-297, 1972, Advent Cemetery, Wright Township, Section 19, p. 275; Ellen G. White, Ms 5, 1859 (entries for Jan. 19, Jan. 24); Ms 8, 1859 (entry for Nov. 14); Ms 19, 1868 (c. 1868).

CRAMER, James I. (1832-1914) and **Sarah A.** (1833-1915)

James Cramer and Sarah Scott became Sabbatarian Adventists about 1853, shortly before their marriage. In her 1859 diary Ellen White reports that she stayed overnight at the Cramers' home in Grand Rapids, Michigan. By the following year, 1860, the Cramers had moved to nearby Wright, Michigan, and stayed there for the rest of their lives. In 1861 James was elected a deacon in the Wright church. In the census records he is listed as "carpenter" and "farmer." It is probable that the "Brother and Sister Cramer" to whom Ellen White wrote in 1873 concerning their spiritual struggles and dangers were in fact James and Sarah Cramer.

See: Ottawa County Cemetery Records, Vol. II, pp. 174-297, 1972, Advent Cemetery, Wright Township, Section 19, p. 275; obituary: "James I. Cramer," *Review,* Sept. 3, 1914, p. 23; obituary: "Sarrah [*sic*] Scott Cramer," *Review,* Nov. 4, 1915, p. 22; search term "Cramer" in *Review and Herald* online collection, www.adventistarchives.org; 1860 U.S. Federal Census, "James Cramer," Michigan, Ottawa County, Wright, p. 121; Ellen G. White, Ms 5, 1859 (Jan. 18 entry); Lt 16, 1873 (Nov. 25).

CRANSON, Samuel T. (1822-1855) and **Mary Jane** (c. 1825-1860); (daughter) **Lucretia** (1847-1879)

A former Methodist minister, Samuel T. Cranson, of Tompkins, Michigan, became a Sabbathkeeping Adventist in 1853 and began to preach for that movement within a few months. The *Review* carried notices of his preaching activities in Michigan for the next two years until his untimely death in 1855, aged 33.

Although correcting him on some points, Ellen White spoke highly of S. T. Cranson: "He was self-denying, self-sacrificing, beloved of God." After his death Mary Jane and her three children relocated in Battle Creek under difficult circumstances. In 1859 Ellen White wrote of Sister Cranson "that she has not received that heartfelt sympathy that her case required" from the church in Battle Creek. "I saw that widows should ever be cared for, especially those whose husbands . . . have fallen while engaged in His work." Later that same year Mary Jane died of "consumption" at age 35. The three orphaned children were cared for by the family of George W. Amadon, a worker at the Review and Herald press. Oldest of the children was Lucretia, age 12, who later married Dudley Marvin Canright, prominent Seventh-day

Adventist leader who, some years after Lucretia's death, left the church and became its severest critic.

See: S. T. Cranson, "From Bro. Cranson," *Review,* Apr. 14, 1853, pp. 190, 191; "Western Tour," *Review,* July 7, 1853, p. 29; obituary: "Samuel T. Cranson," *Review,* May 1, 1855, p. 222; obituary: "Mary Jane Cranson," *Review,* Sept. 18, 1860, p. 143; obituary: "The Death of Sister Canright," *Review,* Apr. 3, 1879, p. 108; Carrie Johnson, *I Was Canright's Secretary* (Washington, D.C.: Review and Herald, 1971), p. 18; Ellen G. White, Ms 4, 1859 (c. July 1859).

CRAWFORD, Marion Concordia (née **STOWELL**) (1829-1913) and (first husband) **Delos Lagrange Truesdail** (1829-1892) and (second husband) **Franklin A. Crawford** (1827-1902)

Marion Stowell and her brother **Lewis Oswald Stowell**, of Paris, Maine, were the first among future Seventh-day Adventists in Maine to keep the Sabbath, after reading a Sabbath tract by T. M. Preble in the spring of 1845. During the early 1850s Marion Stowell taught school at the home of Sabbatarian preacher George W. Holt in Oswego, New York, and subsequently was a district school teacher in Warren, Illinois. She married Delos Truesdale in 1860. The Truesdales brought up at least two orphans, one of whom, M. Bessie DeGraw Sutherland, later became a well-known Seventh-day Adventist educator. In 1894, after the death of her first husband, Marion married a childhood friend, Franklin Crawford, a prosperous Episcopalian businessman from Kankakee, Illinois.

An active layperson throughout her life, Marion Stowell Crawford had a wide network of persons to whom she sent Adventist literature. After the death of Franklin Crawford, Marion was left with substantial assets, which she liberally used to support a number of church projects, including schools, sanitariums, and work in the Southern states. She also lent money to Ellen White in order to help speed up the production of White's books.

Marion Stowell first met Ellen White (then Harmon) in the summer of 1845, when Ellen visited Paris, Maine. During the next few years Marion visited the Whites several times both in Maine and in New York, traveled with them on occasion, and saw Ellen White in vision "nearly a score of times." Marion had firsthand acquaintance with the outbreak of fanaticism in 1845 among some Adventists in Paris, and denied later claims that Ellen White was herself involved in the fanaticism. Some of Marion Stowell's testimony on this issue was published by John N. Loughborough and others, and can also be found in Ellen White's earliest autobiography.

See: Obituary: "Marion Stowell Crawford," *Review,* Dec. 18, 1913, p. 1230; W.H.H. Stowell, *The Stowell Genealogy: A Record of the Descendants of Samuel Stowell of Hingham, Mass.* (Rutland, Vt.: Tuttle Co., 1922), p. 366; Mrs. M. C. Stowell Crawford, "A Letter From a Veteran Worker," *Southern Watchman,* Apr. 25, 1905, p. 278; T. M. Preble, *A Tract, Showing That the Seventh Day Should Be Observed as the Sabbath, Instead of the First Day "According to the Commandment"* (Nashua, N.H.: Murray and Kimball, 1845); *Portrait and Biographical Record of Kankakee County, Illinois, Containing Biographical Sketches of Prominent and Representative Citizens, Together With Biographies of All the Governors of the State and of the Presidents of the United States* (Chicago: Lake City Pub. Co., 1893), pp. 311, 312; Episcopal

Church, *Journal of the Forty-Eighth Annual Convention of the Diocese of Chicago* (Chicago: Skeen and Stuart, 1885), p. 78; SDAE, s.v. "M. Bessie De Graw Sutherland"; J. N. Loughborough, *Rise and Progress of the Seventh-day Adventists,* p. 119; M. C. Stowell Crawford to Ellen G. White, Oct. 9, 1908; Ellen G. White, *Spiritual Gifts [vol. 2],* p. 301.

CURTIS, Robert G. (c. 1812-after 1880) and **Mercy A.** (1818-1907)

Robert G. Curtis, farmer/fisherman, and his wife, Mercy A. Curtis, received several mentions in published and unpublished sources in connection with Ellen White's visits to Topsham, Maine, in the 1840s. According to later accounts by Mrs. M. C. Truesdail and Mrs. Frances Lunt, it was during a vision in the "Curtiss" home in 1845 that Ellen Harmon held aloft their family Bible, weighing 18.5 pounds [8 kilos], "and texts of Scripture were pointed out by her as she turned from leaf to leaf, while her eyes were looking upward, and away from the book."

Ellen White recalled how, during a visit to Topsham in 1845, Mercy Curtis was present and participated in the faith healing of Frances Howland. In November 1846 Ellen White's well-known "astronomy vision," which convinced Joseph Bates of the genuineness of her visions, took place in "Bro. C's humble dwelling" in Topsham, which, according to J. N. Loughborough, was the "house of Mr. Curtiss." At a conference held in Topsham in September 1849 Ellen White addressed a short testimony to "Sister Curtis" while in vision. According to Mercy Curtis's obituary, both she and Robert "accepted the Adventist faith in 1843, . . . were among the first to embrace the Sabbath," and "were firm till the end of life."

See: Obituary: "Mercy A. Curtis," *Review,* Dec. 12, 1907, p. 31; 1840 U.S. Federal Census, "Robert G. Curtis," Maine, Lincoln County, Topsham, p. 13; 1860 U.S. Federal Census, "Robert G. Curtiss [*sic*]," Maine, Sagadahoc, Topsham, p. 9; 1880 U.S. Federal Census, "Robert G. Curtis," Maine, Sagadahoc County, Topsham, p. 18B; J. N. Loughborough, *The Great Second Advent Movement,* pp. 238, 257, 258; Ellen G. White, *Spiritual Gifts [vol. 2],* pp. 42, 83; Ms 5, 1849 (Sept. 23).

CUSHMAN, Horace (1796-1870) and **Mary** (c. 1797-1874)

Originally a farmer from Vermont, Horace Cushman was first mentioned in the *Review* in 1851, while he lived in Milton, New York. Several conferences and meetings were held in his house during the period 1851-1852, and Ellen White received a vision while staying in his home in 1851. Nothing further is heard of Horace Cushman after May 1853 for reasons unknown. It should be noticed that the grave moral failings attributed to "Horace Cushman" in Lts 17, 32, and 32a, 1861, clearly apply to Horace Cushman's son, Horace Cushman, Jr., and not to the father.

See: Henry Wyles Cushman, *A Historical and Biographical Genealogy of the Cushmans: The Descendants of Robert Cushman, the Puritan, From the Year 1617 to 1855* (Boston: Little, Brown, and Company, 1855), pp. 355, 567, 568; *Genealogical Death Indexing System,* Michigan Department of Community Health (see "Horace Cushman" and "Mary Cushman"), www.mdch.

state.mi.us/gendisx (Nov. 14, 2008); 1850 U.S. Federal Census, "Horrace [*sic*] Cushman," New York, Saratoga County, Milton, p. 449; search term "Cushman" in *Review and Herald* online collection, www.adventistarchives.org; Ellen G. White, Lt 4, 1851 (July 21), note 9; Lt 17, 1861 (Jan. 17).

CZECHOWSKI, Michael Belina (1818-1876) and (first wife) **Marie Virginie** (c. 1821-1870) and (second wife) **Wilhenmina (née SCHIRMER)** (?-?)

The first Seventh-day Adventist missionary to Europe, M. B. Czechowski was a former Franciscan monk, priest, and militant Polish nationalist. Disillusioned by laxity and corruption in the Catholic Church, Czechowski left the priesthood in 1850. In the same year he married Marie Virginie Delavouet and in 1851 emigrated to the United States, arriving in New York on September 3 aboard the *Yorktown*. Within a year Czechowski had come into contact with the Baptists in Canada East and subsequently became a Baptist preacher for about three years among French Canadians in northern New York.

Czechowski's first contact with Sabbatarian Adventism was in 1856 when he heard James White and others preach in Perry's Mills, New York. His baptism the following year and move to Battle Creek created quite a stir of anticipation among Adventist leaders. By the summer of 1858 he was appointed to preach among the French-speaking groups in northern New York that he had previously worked with as a Baptist preacher. James White appealed for donations from *Review* readers to help the poverty-stricken Czechowski family pay off a mortgage and get settled.

Together with several other preachers Czechowski did creditable work in the border areas of New York, Vermont, and Canada, but after less than two years, in 1860, he left his post and moved to New York City, without consulting Battle Creek leaders or local colleagues. Aiming to start a city mission in New York, Czechowski rented property, ran up high bills, and then appealed for donations through the *Review* to cover the costs. When in addition it became apparent after about a year that his city mission was yielding scant results, church leaders, while never doubting Czechowski's zeal and ardor, began to question his financial management capabilities and general trustworthiness. Thus when by the early 1860s he began seriously petitioning church leadership to sponsor him to start a mission in Europe, there were doubts on all sides. As J. N. Andrews explained some years later: "We thought him not at that time prepared for so responsible an undertaking. We therefore requested him to wait. . . . We did not think him a prudent manager." In a similar vein, Ellen White appealed to Czechowski in 1861: "Hold yourself ready to follow the opening providence of God, but you should not mark out a course for yourself."

As it turned out, Czechowski was not willing to wait or take counsel, and with his relations with Battle Creek strained he ultimately turned to non-Sabbatarian Adventists (in particular the Advent Christians) for financial aid to pursue his European plans. It was a dubious tactic, since Czechowski did not make it clear to the Advent Christians that he was still an earnest Seventh-day Adventist, whereas they assumed that his break with Battle Creek was also a doctrinal one. The tactic backfired within a few years of his arrival in Italy in 1864. By 1869 *The World's Crisis,* main organ of the Advent Christians, warned its readers that Czechowski "has been receiving our contributions to raise up a company of Jewish Sabbathkeepers." Donations soon dried up, and since no funds were forthcoming from Battle Creek either, Czechowski's mission experienced severe financial difficulties during its final years before his death in 1876 in Vienna. Nevertheless his years in Europe produced some very solid results on which J. N. Andrews was able to build when he arrived in Switzerland in 1874 as the first "official" Seventh-day Adventist missionary to Europe. Writing in 1870 with a tinge of regret, James White saw the hand of Providence in it all: "While we acknowledge the hand of God in this, we feel humbled . . . that in consequence of our fears to trust money with Bro. Czechowski, and our lack of care to patiently counsel him as to its proper use, God used our most decided opponents to carry forward the work."

Most of the information in the above sketch has been taken from the well-documented collection of essays *Michael Belina Czechowski 1818-1876,* edited by Rajmund Ladyslaw Dabrowski and B. B. Beach. See also *Passenger Lists of Vessels Arriving at New York, New York, 1820-1897* (National Archives Microfilm Publication M237, Microfilm Roll: M237_104), records of the U.S. Customs Service, Record Group 36; National Archives, Washington, D.C., as in Ancestry.com database online. For specific quotations above, see J. N. Andrews, "The Case of Eld. M. B. Czechowski," *Review,* July 8, 1873, p. 29; Ellen G. White, Lt 31, 1861 (c. 1861); L. T. Cunningham, *World's Crisis,* Dec. 22, 1869, p. 54; [James White], "Cause in Switzerland," *Review,* Jan. 11, 1870, pp. 21, 22.

DAVIS, Charles (1815-1884) and **Harriet** (1818-after 1884)

Church members and farmers from Woodstock, Maine, later Paris, Maine. Charles, probably with his wife, joined the Millerite movement in 1842 and by January 1846 had begun to keep the Sabbath. His name appeared on Maine Conference committees in the 1860s, and there is mention of meetings being held at his home. Ellen and James White visited the Davises' home in 1851 and found them "strong in all the present truth."

See: Obituary, "Charles Davis," *Review,* June 17, 1884, p. 399; William B. Lapham, *History of Woodstock, Me., With Family Sketches and an Appendix* (Portland: Stephen Berry, 1882), p. 242; search term "Davis" in *Review and Herald* online collection, www.adventistarchives.org; 1850 U.S. Federal Census, "Charles Davis," Maine, Oxford County, Woodstock, p. 204; 1880 U.S. Federal Census, "Charles Davis," Maine, Oxford County, Paris, p. 17; Ellen G. White, Lt 10, 1851 (May 18, 19).

DAY, John C. (c. 1811-after 1880) and **Phebe** (c. 1821-after 1880)

John C. Day, a carpenter from Massachusetts, participated in the Millerite movement and became a Sabbathkeeping Adventist in 1851. He wrote several theological articles for the *Review* in 1853-1854 and traveled, at least locally, as a preacher. His ambitions as a preacher collided with Ellen White's vision of September 1852, according to which Day "has been mistaken and thought that God had a greater work for him to do than He had ever laid upon him." John Day subsequently defected to the oppositional (though also Sabbatarian) *Messenger* Party in 1854 or 1855 and wrote against the Whites in the *Messenger of Truth.* By October 1856, however, Day reversed his position, writing a confessional letter to the *Review* asking for forgiveness "of the entire church."

Ellen White's vision two years later, in December 1858, in which J. C. Day and certain others were described as "changeable" and "wavering," met its fulfillment when, in the early 1860s, Day again left the Seventh-day Adventists and joined the early stages of the offshoot Marion Party, which became the Church of God (Seventh Day). In a letter to the *Hope of Israel,* in 1864 he vented his bitterness at being "cast off" because he and others "have dared to express their doubts as to the inspiration of E. G. White's visions."

See: 1880 U.S. Federal Census, "John C. Day," Massachusetts, Worcester County, Ashburnham, p. 24; Thomas W. Baldwin, *Vital Records of Cambridge, Massachusetts, to the Year 1850* (Boston: Wright & Potter Print Co., 1914), vol. 2, p. 112; John C. Day, "Letter From Bro. Day," *The Jubilee Standard,* July 10, 1845, p. 144; J. C. Day, *Hope of Israel,* Apr. 23, 1864, as in Richard C. Nickels, *A History of the Seventh Day Church of God* (Portland, Oreg.: the author, 1977), p. 44; John C. Day, "Letter From Bro. Day," *Review,* Oct. 9, 1856, p. 184; Ellen G. White, Lt 4, 1852 (Oct. 25); Ms 2, 1858 (Dec. 27).

DAY, John S. (1830-1894) and **Ruth D.** (1831-1892)

Originally from New York, John S. Day settled in Monterey, Michigan, in 1851 and became a Sabbatarian Adventist in 1856 together with his wife. Besides his work as a farmer, John Day served his township as justice of the peace and school inspector at various times, as well as being an active leader in his local church and beyond.

Ellen White regarded John Day highly, and there are several records of the Whites' visiting the Day family while in Monterey. "His interest is in the truth and he considers nothing too dear to sacrifice for the truth," she wrote in 1860. When Day hit a spiritual low in 1869, she entreated him to awaken to his precarious condition: "I wish to alarm you. I wish to arouse you to action. I wish to entreat of you to seek God while He invites you to come to Him that you may have life."

See: Obituary: "John S. Day," *Review,* Apr. 17, 1894, p. 255; obituary: "Ruth Day," *Review,* Nov. 8, 1892, p. 703; Anonymous, *History of Allegan and Barry Counties, Michigan: With Illustrations and Biographical Sketches of Their Prominent Men and Pioneers* (Philadelphia: D. W. Ensign & Co., 1880), p. 288; Ellen G. White, Ms 4, 1860 (Dec.); Ms 5, 1859 (various entries); Ms 6, 1859 (various entries); Ms 8, 1859 (various entries); Ms 9, 1862 (Nov.); *Testimony for the Churches at Allegan and Monterey* (Battle Creek, Mich.: Seventh-day Adventist Pub. Assn., 1869), pp. 10-15; 1860 U.S. Federal Census, "John S. Day," Michigan, Allegan County, Monterey, p. 141.

DICKINSON, Preston (1807-1868) and **Celesta B.** (1806-1869)

Born in Massachusetts and Connecticut respectively, Preston and Celesta Dickinson appear to have moved to Michigan in the 1830s. According to the 1850 census Preston was a mason by trade. Both Preston and Celesta were drawn to Millerite Adventism in the

1840s. They later became Sabbathkeepers after Joseph Bates visited Jackson, Michigan, in July 1849. On August 4 the Dickinsons, along with 15 others, became the first Adventists to celebrate the Sabbath in Michigan. The Dickinsons received only passing mention in the writings of Ellen White. The single substantial comment was the reproof found in Lt 6, 1856 (c. 1856), related to their dealings with future son-in-law **Smith Moses Kellogg** and his parents.

See: Obituary: "Preston Dickinson," *Review*, May 12, 1868, p. 350; obituary: "Celesta B. Dickinson," *Review*, July 20, 1869, p. 31; Timothy Hopkins, *The Kelloggs in the Old World and the New*, vol. 2, p. 1315; 1850 U.S. Federal Census, "Preston Dickinson," Michigan, Jackson County, Jackson, p. 328; G. W. Amadon, "Interesting Item of History: When and How the Sabbath Truth Was First Introduced Into the State of Michigan," *Review*, Nov. 11, 1890, p. 695.

DODGE, Abram A. (1817-1892) and **Caroline Elizabeth** (1830-1915)

The Dodges were active laypersons from Jackson, Michigan (early 1850s), later living in Battle Creek and Coopersville, in the same state. Although not a preacher, Abram Dodge was remembered by J. N. Loughborough for his "faithfulness . . . in carrying the workers from place to place in his carriage." Dodge was a businessman, a dealer in musical instruments, and a clock repairer. He also employed his financial and administrative talents for the church. When the Review and Herald press was moved from Rochester, New York, to Battle Creek, Michigan, in 1855, Dodge played a central role in organizing the move. He was also an agent for the Review and Herald during his years in Jackson.

Soon after their marriage in 1851, Abram and Caroline (daughter of well-known pioneer **Cyrenius Smith**) traveled to a conference in Camden, New York. There they met Ellen and James White for the first time and became firm friends with them. Some of their correspondence has been preserved. Years later, in 1872, Ellen White felt constrained to defend Caroline against unjust accusations: "If there was a precious, God-fearing woman in Battle Creek, it was Sister Dodge."

See: Obituary: "Abram A. Dodge," *Review*, May 31, 1892, p. 351; obituary: "Caroline Dodge," *Review*, Sept. 23, 1915, p. 21; Glenn and Jean Davis, compilers, "Records of Cyrenius Smith and R. M. Kilgore Families" (Berrien Springs, Mich.: Center for Adventist Research, 198?); 1860 U.S. Federal Census, "A. A. Dodge," Michigan, Calhoun County, Battle Creek, p. 24; 1880 U.S. Federal Census, "Abram A. Dodge," Michigan, Ottawa County, Coopersville, p. 22B; J. N. Loughborough, "Illinois," *Review*, Apr. 26, 1892, p. 268; *Calhoun County Business Directory for 1869-70* (Battle Creek, Mich.: E. G. Rust, 1869), pp. 267, 329; J. B. Frisbie and A. A. Dodge, "Meeting in Battle Creek," *Review*, Oct. 2, 1855, p. 56; [Notice re. A. A. Dodge and Wm. M. Smith], *Review*, Aug. 4, 1853, p. 48; James White's letters to Abram Dodge (mostly business) of July 26, 1853, July 31, 1853, Aug. 20, 1855; Ellen G. White, Lt 4, 1851 (July 21); Lt 9, 1851 (Dec. 21); Lt 5, 1853 (July 5); Lt 6, 1853 (Aug. 3); Lt 3, 1872 (Feb. 1).

DREW, Hiram (c. 1810-after 1880) and **Martha** (c. 1814-1880)

Born in Canada, Hiram Drew subsequently farmed in Jackson and Ottawa counties in Michigan. The date of Drew's joining the Sabbatarian Adventists is not known, but he was disfellowshipped during the winter of 1853-1854. By October 1854 he was listed as a member of the "publishing committee" of the *Messenger of Truth,* the journal of the breakaway *Messenger* Party.

Hiram Drew received brief mention by Ellen White in August 1853 in connection with his part in the growing rebellion among some members in Jackson and Sylvan, Michigan, against the leadership of the Whites—a rebellion that later led to the formation of the *Messenger* Party. Hiram Drew's supporters later claimed that "the hand of fellowship" had been wrongfully withdrawn "from Bro. Hiram Drew, after he had confessed all but the visions."

See: 1880 U.S. Federal Census, "Hiram Drew," Michigan, Ottawa County, Georgetown, p. 22; 1850 U.S. Federal Census, "Hiram Drew," Michigan, Jackson County, Henrietta, p. 382; J. B. Bezzo, "Test of Fellowship," *Messenger of Truth,* Oct. 19, 1854, p. [3]; Ellen G. White, Lt 6, 1853 (Aug. 3); Eli Bugbee et al., "Withdrawal of Fellowship," *Messenger of Truth,* Nov. 30, 1854, p. [4].

EDSON, Hiram (1806-1882) and (first wife) **Effa** (1810-1839) and (second wife) **Esther Marier** (1816-1893)

Hiram Edson is best known for his reminiscences of the occasion, soon after the Great Disappointment of October 22, 1844, when he "saw distinctly" that the "cleansing" of the sanctuary (Dan. 8:14) and the "coming" of the bridegroom (Matt. 25:6) did not indicate the Second Advent as the Millerites had proclaimed, but referred to pre-Advent events in the heavenly sanctuary. He further related how his insight provided the impetus for intensive study by O.R.L. Crosier, F. B. Hahn, and him, resulting in the seminal article by Crosier some months later in March 1845, "to all who are waiting for redemption . . . ," published in the *Day-Dawn.* Edson's account (the "Edson manuscript") is undated and probably dates to late in his life, but if reliable, it indicates that key elements of Seventh-day Adventist sanctuary theology owe Edson a large intellectual debt.

Hiram Edson became a Sabbathkeeper as a result of Joseph Bates's visit to western New York, probably in 1846. In 1848 the third in the series of "Sabbatarian Bible Conferences" took place at Edson's farm in Port Gibson, New York. He was a member of the publishing committee of the *Advent Review* in 1850, and throughout the 1850s preached widely in New York, Pennsylvania, and Canada. The Edsons generously supported the emerging Sabbatarian movement. In one instance, in 1852, they advanced $650 from the proceeds of the sale of their farm in Port Byron, New York, in order to facilitate the purchase of the young movement's first press. Hiram Edson was given ministerial credentials in 1870, but increasing ill-health prevented further itinerant preaching. His final years were marked by theological differences with church leaders, the details of which are uncertain, leading for a time to a break with the church. A reconciliation took place before his death in 1882.

Ellen White, who had known the Edsons since 1848, wrote with appreciation of their devotion. "I saw that God regarded the sacrifice made by him and Sister Edson. They had sacrificed for the good of the cause of God and had left their pleasant house and farm . . . to advance the cause of present truth." Some years after his death, Ellen White, while recognizing Hiram Edson's theological lapses in old age, nevertheless pronounced him "a good man, beloved of all who knew him."

See: James R. Nix, "The Life and Work of Hiram Edson" (term paper, Andrews University, 1971); Merlin D. Burt, "The Extended Atonement View in the *Day-Dawn* and the Emergence of Sabbatarian Adventism," *Andrews University Seminary Studies* 44, no. 2 (2006): 331-339; *idem*, "The *Day-Dawn* of Canandaigua, New York: Reprint of a Significant Millerite Adventist Journal," *Andrews University Seminary Studies* 44, no. 2 (2006): 317-330; Ellen G. White, Lt 16, 1861 (Aug. 8); Lt 49, 1894 (Aug. 3).

EVANS, D. T. (c. 1826-after 1910) and (first wife) **Lucinda** (c. 1823-1871) and (second wife) **Lucia** (c. 1826-1881) and (third wife) **Caroline** (c. 1835-after 1920)

D. T. Evans (his first name given in various sources as "Derrick" or "Dimick") was a minister from Vermont who became a Sabbatarian Adventist about 1851, his wife, Lucia (née Horr), following some years later. Evans started preaching in Vermont and Canada East about 1858. He was ordained to the ministry in 1860, the first Seventh-day Adventist minister to be ordained in Canada. Although recognizing his talents, Ellen White was shown in vision in 1859 that for a variety of reasons, Evans could best serve the church by preaching only on a part-time basis while continuing to work at his trade (shoemaker), thus supporting his family without depleting scarce church financial resources. It appears that Evans did not follow this counsel fully, since Ellen White pointed out the same problems five years later, in 1864. Subsequently the *Review* contains occasional reports of D. T. Evans' preaching activity up to 1879. He appears to have moved from Vermont in the late 1870s and spent the remainder of his life in Nebraska and Wisconsin.

See: Denis Fortin, *Adventism in Quebec,* pp. 75, 76 (see under "Daniel T. Evans"); *Walton's Vermont Register and Farmers' Almanac for 1871* ([Claremont, N.H.]: Claremont Manufacturing Co., 1871), p. 63; obituary: "Lucinda Evans," *Review,* July 4, 1871, p. 23; obituary: "Lucia Evans," *Review,* Feb. 7, 1882, p. 94; A. S. Hutchins, "Our Visit to Canada," *Review,* Nov. 13, 1860, p. 205; search term "D. T. Evans" in *Review and Herald* online collection, www.adventistarchives.org; Ellen G. White, Lt 21, 1859 (Sept.); *Testimonies for the Church,* vol. 1, pp. 448, 449 ("Brother C").

EVERTS, Elon (c. 1807-1858) and **Maria** (c. 1810-1856)

A traveling preacher from Vermont, Elon Everts is first mentioned in the *Review* in

1851. From 1852 to his death in 1858 Everts' preaching schedule and reports, as found in the *Review*, give evidence of a vigorous ministry centered in Vermont until 1855, and after that in Illinois. He was ordained to the ministry together with J. N. Andrews and others in 1853, at one of the earliest recorded ordination services among Sabbathkeeping Adventists. In the area of Adventist theology Everts is noted as the first writer to use the expression "investigative judgment."

A little more than two years before his death at age 51, Everts and his family moved west to Illinois, bought land, and increased in prosperity. Most of Ellen White's interaction with the family dates from this period. In an article about the Evertses (without actually using the name) written shortly after Elon's death, Ellen White revealed the dramatic struggle between materialistic pursuit and spirituality within the Everts family. Even after Elon became convicted through personal testimonies from Ellen White that he ought to resume wholehearted evangelism and donate part of his large lands to support the fledgling Sabbatarian movement, his wife and teenage daughter adamantly opposed such a plan, and Everts could not bring himself to cross their wishes.

When his wife, Maria, died in 1856, Everts still hesitated to oppose the entreaties of his daughter not to donate any property. Two years later, in 1858, Everts himself died. The net result, as Ellen White noted in an article poignantly entitled "A Warning," was that Everts "left his large property to his daughter. Nothing was bestowed upon the cause of God. . . . Satan had it just as he wanted it at his death."

See: Obituary: "My dear companion," *Review*, Nov. 6, 1856, p. 7; obituary: "Elon Everts," *Review*, Mar. 11, 1858, p. 135; 1850 U.S. Federal Census, "Maria Everts," Vermont, Addison County, New Haven, p. 187; Ellen G. White, "A Warning," *Review*, Apr. 15, 1858, p. 174; Lt 14, 1857 (July 12); Lt 5, 1857 (Nov. 22); search term "Everts" in *Words of the Pioneers*; Paul A. Gordon, *The Sanctuary, 1844, and the Pioneers*, p. 87.

FARNSWORTH, John P. (1834-1918) and (first wife) **Frances Jennette** (c. 1834-1868) and (second wife) **Laura L.** (c. 1846-1870) and (third wife) **Amelia M.** (1843-1930)

John Farnsworth was the eldest son of William Farnsworth, from Washington, New Hampshire, who was among the very first Adventists to keep the seventh-day Sabbath. In 1864 John married Frances Jennette Stevens, originally from Paris, Maine, a sister-in-law to prominent church leaders Uriah Smith and John Nevins Andrews.

John Farnsworth came to Iowa in the early 1860s, engaging in farming, and later owning grocery businesses in Waukon and Radcliff. By 1887 Farnsworth had moved to Kansas and in 1892 to Longmont, Colorado, where he spent his final years. He was an active church member, serving several times as a district leader for the Tract and Missionary Society in Iowa, Kansas, and Colorado.

Frances Stevens came to Waukon, Iowa, with her parents in 1856. The Stevens family, as well as some other Sabbatarian families that moved to Waukon about the same time, was skeptical of the visions of Ellen White and generally disapproving of the leadership of James White (see, for example, Lt 8, 1860 [June 11]). John Farnsworth, writing to Ellen White from Waukon in 1862, notes that "if you said VISION to some . . . you would feel and see a repulsation [*sic*] very soon." It is possible that Farnsworth had been influenced by the Waukon Adventists. He admits in the same letter to "the unbelief I had in the Testimony the Lord has given you" although heartily declaring his subsequent change of heart on the matter.

The only extant letter from Ellen White to J. P. Farnsworth was written 10 months after Frances' death at age 34. Regarding his plans for remarriage, Ellen White urged great caution because of his overbearing ways, through which the life of his first wife had been "sacrificed."

See: Obituary: "John P. Farnsworth," *Review,* Jan. 16, 1919, p. 31; obituary: "Frances Jennette Farnsworth," *Review,* Feb. 25, 1868, p. 174; obituary: "Laura L. Farnsworth," *Review,* Jan. 3, 1871, p. 23; obituary: "Amelia Farnsworth," *Review,* May 22, 1930, p. 28; J. P. Farnsworth to E. G. White, Jan. 9, 1862; *History of Washington, New Hampshire, From 1768 to 1886,* p. 398; 1880 U.S. Federal Census, "J. P. Farnsworth," Iowa, Allamakee County, Waukon, p. 8; search term "J. P. Farnsworth" in *Review and Herald* online collection, www.adventistarchives.org; Ellen G. White, Lt 21, 1868 (Oct. 7).

FERGUSON, Justus (c. 1831-1878) and **Lucretia** (c. 1833-after 1880)

The Fergusons were farmers living in Wright Township, Ottawa County, Michigan, having an association with the Seventh-day Adventist Church, but the exact relationship is uncertain.

While attending meetings in Wright in 1859, the Whites visited the home of Justus and Lucretia Ferguson. They lived close to the Sabbatarian Adventist meetinghouse, and the Whites "had a profitable season of conversation and prayer" with them. There is very little information on the Fergusons in available church sources. Ellen White refers to them as "Brother and Sister Ferguson" and Justus Ferguson's obituary appears in the *Review.* However, the same obituary pointedly refers to him as "Mr. Ferguson," with no mention of his association with the church. This strongly suggests that Justus Ferguson was not a church member in 1878, at the time of his death, even though he may have been one earlier. Nothing is known of Lucretia Ferguson's relation to the church after 1859.

See: Obituary: "Justus Ferguson," Feb. 7, 1878, p. 47; 1860 U.S. Federal Census, "Justen Furgeson [*sic*]," Michigan, Ottawa County, Wright, p. 122; 1880 U.S. Federal Census, "Lucretia Ferguson," Michigan, Ottawa County, Wright, p. 33; Ellen G. White, Ms 6, 1859 (May 1 entry); *Illustrated Historical Atlas of the Counties of Ottawa and Kent, Mich.* (Chicago: H. Belden & Co., 1876), p. xviii.

FINCH, Truman P. (1822-1890) and **Mary Sophrona** (1824-1913)

Church members from New York, later living in Michigan, Wisconsin, Minnesota, and Kansas. Mary Finch came from a Millerite background and had begun to keep the Sabbath as early as 1845, according to her obituary. Truman Finch, a carpenter, apparently became a Sabbatarian Adventist in the late 1840s, about the same time as his marriage to Mary. A number of enthusiastic letters and reports from the Finches to the *Review* witness to their active participation in church work in the various places they settled. There are also reports of Truman's involvement in the Kansas Tract Society and Mary's colporteur work in her late 70s and beyond. Ellen White's only mentions of Truman Finch are in reference to the internal conflict at the church in Roosevelt, New York, in the late 1850s. His name is mentioned, among several other members, as causing problems by his "faultfinding spirit."

See: Obituary: "Truman P. Finch," *Review,* Sept. 9, 1890, p. 559; obituary: "Mary Saphrona [*sic*] Wells," *Review,* Feb. 20, 1913, p. 189; search term "Truman" in *Review and Herald* online collection, www.adventistarchives.org; 1880 U.S. Federal Census, "Truman Finch," Minnesota, Mower County, Rose Creek, p. 29; Ellen G. White, Lt 8, 1857 (July 19); Lt 2, 1858 (c. 1858); Lt 17, 1859 (Oct. 28).

FISHER, John (c. 1789-after 1859)

A Baptist minister of Dutch background who briefly joined the Sabbatarian Adventist movement during 1858-1859. Though nearly 70 years old in 1858, Fisher, "with the ardor of youth," translated a Sabbath tract of 100 pages into Dutch and planned to work among his countrymen in western Michigan, in the area around Holland. Unfortunately, by 1859 Fisher was in deep conflict with the church in nearby Monterey. Ellen White was present at a church meeting in Monterey in January 1859 when "Father Fisher's case" was discussed. The conflict, at least in part, seems to have been over Ellen White's visions.

See: M. E. Cornell, "Meetings at Stony Creek, Mich.," *Review,* Apr. 8, 1858, p. 165; Joseph Bates, Uriah Smith, "The Conference," *Review,* May 27, 1858, pp. 12, 13; J. W. [James White] [Notice], *Review,* July 8, 1858, p. 64; John Fisher, "From Bro. Fisher," *Review,* Aug. 12, 1858, p. 102; Ellen G. White, Ms 5, 1859 (entries for Jan. 15, 17); James White, "The French Mission," *Review,* Feb. 17, 1859, p. 104.

FLANDERS, Samuel W. (c. 1822-1888) and **Elizabeth M.** (c. 1826-after 1888)

According to his obituary, Samuel W. Flanders, a farmer and brick mason from Canaan, Maine, became a Sabbathkeeper as early as 1845, while his wife "embraced the truth shortly after her husband did." Flanders appears to have played a leading role in the Canaan congregation, arranging conferences and acting as local agent for the *Review.*

Apart from writing of being invited to a meal at the Flanders home in 1855, Ellen White mentioned them only incidentally. The two families would, however, probably have met on a number of occasions, since the Flanderses lived only a few miles from James White's parental home in Palmyra, Maine.

See: Obituary: "Samuel W. Flanders," *Review,* Aug. 28, 1888, p. 559; 1880 U.S. Federal Census, "Samuel W. Flanders," Maine, Somerset County, Pittsfield, p. 26; Ellen G. White, Lt 2, 1855 (Aug.); search term "S. W. Flanders" in *Words of the Pioneers.*

FOLSOM, Paul (c. 1818-?) and **Margaret** (c. 1820-?)

A "confectioner" living in Somerville, just outside Boston, Massachusetts, Paul Folsom was first mentioned in the *Review* in 1851. For the next 13 years his home was an important center for Sabbatarian Adventists in the Boston area, both as a place for meetings and conferences and as a temporary home for visiting preachers, including James and Ellen White. Folsom himself served on planning committees and traveled as a delegate to conferences in Maine and Battle Creek, Michigan. There is some evidence that he did occasional lay preaching, or "exhorting."

Paul Folsom's involvement with the church came to a rather sudden halt in 1864. The precipitating factor, according to Ellen White, appears to have been a "testimony of reproof" she sent to Paul and Margaret Folsom, probably in the autumn of 1864. "I am sad that you have despised the testimony given you of Heaven," Ellen White wrote in October 1864. Although the testimony in its entirety has not been preserved, it is possible that an undated document, classified as "Lt 18, 1864," is a fragment of the original testimony. In November 1864 the Whites visited the Folsoms briefly, but there was no resolution, and by January 1865 J. N. Loughborough, also on a visit, reported "that Bro. Folsom had chosen to go with the world, and leave the obedience of God's commandments, which he still acknowledges to be truth."

See: 1850 U.S. Federal Census, "Paul Folsom," Massachusetts, Middlesex County, Medford, p. 448; 1860 U.S. Federal Census, "Paul Folsom," Massachusetts, Middlesex County, Somerville, p. 76; J. N. Loughborough, "Report From Bro. Loughborough," *Review,* Feb. 7, 1865, pp. 84, 85; search term "Folsom" in *Review and Herald* online collection, www.adventistarchives.org; Ellen G. White, Lt 7, 1864 (Oct. 14); Lt 18, 1864 (c. 1864); Elizabeth Knowles Folsom, *Genealogy of the Folsom Family* (Rutland, Vt.: Tuttle Pub. Co., Inc., 1938), vol. 1, p. 418.

FOSS, Louisa. See **BRACKETT, Louisa.**

FOSS, Mary Plummer (née **HARMON**) (1821-1912) and **Samuel Hoyt** (1817-1888)

The third-oldest sister of Ellen White, Mary married Samuel Foss, a farmer, in 1842. They settled in Poland, Maine, and later West Minot, Maine. Samuel's brother, Hazen Little Foss, on hearing Ellen relate her early visions in 1845, disclosed that he had received almost identical visions but had refused to relate them publicly, for which he felt condemned.

Soon after Ellen received her first vision in December 1844, Mary invited Ellen to visit her in Poland, Maine. While there, as Ellen recalled it in 1890, Mary "asked me to go" to a Millerite meeting at Macquires Hill. This suggests that Mary, like several others in the Harmon family, was a part of the Millerite Adventist movement in the mid-1840s. For many years Ellen sent her Seventh-day Adventist papers and books. On a visit to Maine in 1875 Ellen and James attended a camp meeting together with Mary and Samuel. "We hope the truth which they . . . heard preached," Ellen commented, "will result finally in their conversion to the truth." Although there is no evidence that Samuel ever became a Sabbathkeeper, in letters written after his death Mary speaks of observing the Sabbath. The correspondence between Ellen and Mary during the 1890s and beyond indicates that Mary, while often discouraged because of her isolation, continued a practicing Seventh-day Adventist until her death, although there is no evidence of her having been formally entered into church books.

See: George Thomas Little, *The Descendants of George Little, Who Came to Newbury, Massachusetts in 1640* (Auburn, Maine: the author, 1882), p. 290; James R. Nix, "Ellen G. White's Family" (Silver Spring, Md.: Ellen G. White Estate, 2005); Ellen G. White, Lt 82a, 1888 (Nov. 29); Lt 37, 1890 (Dec. 22); Lt 35, 1875 (Oct. 22); Lt 55, 1893 (Feb. 21); SDAE, s.v. "Hazen Foss"; search term "Foss" in *Review and Herald* online collection, www.adventistarchives.org; Mary Foss to Ellen White, Dec. 15, 1895; Sept. 15, 1891; June 19, 1892.

FOY, John Quincy (1843-1924) and **Mary** (1863-1949)

Born in Brunswick, Maine, John Foy was a gardener at Battle Creek Sanitarium and lay preacher. His parents, John Green and Dorcas Foy, were among the earliest Adventists in Maine to keep the Sabbath. At age 14 Foy traveled to Battle Creek, Michigan, to learn the printing trade at the Review and Herald Publishing Association. Because of illness he left the press in the 1860s and worked for some years on Ira Abbey's farm in New York before returning to Battle Creek in the 1880s to spend his remaining working life as gardener at the sanitarium. An active layperson, the *Review* records his engagement in tract and temperance societies and lay preaching. In 1884 Foy married Mary Staines, who worked for more than 50 years as nurse and nursing administrator at Battle Creek Sanitarium before retiring in 1933.

Ellen White makes only incidental mention of John Foy, but there is evidence that he stayed for some time with the Whites when he first came to Battle Creek as a teenager. The 1860 census lists "John Q. Foy" as a member of the White household, and some reminiscences by W. C. White suggest that Foy lived with them well before that.

See: Obituary: "John Quincy Foy," *Review*, Mar. 5, 1925, p. 23; 1850 U.S. Federal Census, "Dorcas Foy," Maine, Cumberland County, Brunswick, p. 232; obituary: "John G. Foy," *Review*, Feb. 26, 1861, p. 119; search term "Foy" in *Review and Herald* online collection, www.adventistarchives.org; 1870 U.S. Federal Census, "John Q Foy," New York, Madison County, Brookfield, p. 2; obituary: "Daniel Palmer," *Review*, Sept. 18, 1894, p. 607; obituary: "Mary Staines Foy," *Review*, June 30, 1949, p. 20; Michigan State Medical Society, *Medical History of Michigan. Compiled and Edited by a Committee, C. B. Burr, M.D., Chairman, and Published Under the Auspices of the Michigan State Medical Society* (Minneapolis and Saint Paul: Bruce Pub. Co., 1930), vol. 2, pp. 658, 659; 1860 U.S. Federal Census, "John Q Foy," Michigan, Calhoun County, Battle Creek, p. 6; W. C. White, "Sketches and Memories of James and Ellen G. White: XXVI. The Conference of 1856," *Review*, Jan. 9, 1936, p. 8.

FRASER, Jane ("Jenny"). See ROGERS, Jane and Sanford.

FRISBIE, Elihu (1785-1859) and Esther (c. 1784-1858)

Parents of pioneer Michigan preacher **Joseph B. Frisbie**, Elihu and Esther Frisbie moved from New York in 1837 or 1838 to the newly established township of Sylvan, in Washtenaw County, Michigan. Elihu, a merchant, opened the first store in Sylvan Center. At 72 years of age, in 1857, he became a Sabbathkeeping Adventist, following his son J. B. Frisbie, who had begun preaching for the young movement in 1853. Whether Esther Frisbie also joined the Sabbatarians is not known. Ellen White notes Elihu's accidental death in her 1859 diary.

See: Obituary: "E. Frisbie," *Review,* June 9, 1859, p. 23; 1850 U.S. Federal Census, "Elihu Frisbe [*sic*]," Michigan, Washtenaw County, Sylvan, p. 292; *History of Washtenaw County, Michigan,* pp. 754, 756, 778; E. Frisbie, "From Bro. Frisbie," *Review,* Aug. 27, 1857, p. 135; Ellen G. White, Ms 6, 1859 (May 18 entry).

FRISBIE, Joseph Birchard (1816-1882) and Delphia Jane (1830-1908)

J. B. Frisbie began preaching for the Protestant Methodist Church in 1843 and was ordained in 1846. In 1852, while engaged in a series of public debates with Joseph Bates on the Sabbath issue in Sylvan, Michigan, he conceded that Bates had the stronger position. Delphia Jane began to keep the Sabbath as a result of these meetings, but Joseph Frisbie hesitated some months before taking a firm stand in March 1853. Later the same year he began preaching for the Sabbatarian Adventists, and for the rest of the decade traveled widely in Michigan, enjoying considerable success in raising new groups of believers. The 1860s and 1870s were more problematic for Frisbie. Theological doubts removed him from ministry for extended periods, as did struggles with chronic ill-health.

The only existing letters from Ellen White to J. B. Frisbie date from the early 1860s. These war years were a time of crisis for Frisbie, according to his friend and obituary writer, John Byington. "Doubts came into his mind," and for a time he even "ceased the observance of the Sabbath." Ellen White counseled Frisbie in 1864 that "if you are not in a condition to bind up and strengthen the church, your place is at home or attending to your temporal matters." There was also a time Frisbie's "mind was thrown into a train of doubt" about the visions of Ellen White. Nevertheless, these doubts were surmounted, and Frisbie's son, W. E. Frisbie, recalls his father's strong affirmation in 1882, the year of his death, that "there was no doubt in his mind but that Mrs. White was an inspired prophet of God."

See: Obituary: "Joseph Birchard Frisbie," *Review,* Nov. 21, 1882, p. 735; obituary: "Delphia Jane Frisbie," *Review,* Feb. 6, 1908, p. 31; *History of Washtenaw County, Michigan,* p. 778; Leo Van Dolson, "Elder J. B. Frisbie: S.D.A. Pioneer in Michigan" (term paper,

Andrews University, 1965), p. 32; EGWEnc, s.v. "Joseph Birchard Frisbie"; Ellen G. White, Lt 10, 1864 (c. 1864); Lt 11, 1862 (Nov. 9).

GEROULD, Lyman (1819-1887) and **Sophia** (1826-1897)

Originally a Freewill Baptist, Lyman Gerould, together with Sophia, became a Sabbathkeeper in 1857 or 1858. Sometime in the 1840s he appears to have come to Kent County, Michigan, and was one of the earliest settlers in Caledonia Township. At various times in the 1850s Gerould held the offices of township supervisor and justice of the peace.

On at least two occasions Ellen White stayed with the Gerould family in Caledonia. "Brother and Sister Gerould seem to know how to make pilgrims at home," wrote James White on one of those occasions. Lyman Gerould was commended by Ellen White for his faithfulness in the Caledonia church but also corrected for his impatience with members who differed from him.

See: Obituary: "Lyman Gerould," *Review,* May 24, 1887, p. 334; obituary: "Sophia Gerould Devereaux," *Review,* Dec. 7, 1897, supp., p. 2; *History of Kent County, Michigan; Together With Sketches of Its Cities, Villages and Townships, Educational, Religious, Civil, Military, and Political History; Portraits of Prominent Persons, and Biographies of Representative Citizens* (Chicago: Chas. C. Chapman & Co., 1881), pp. 641, 642, 644, 645; Ellen G. White, Ms 5, 1859 (Jan. 26 entry); Ms 6, 1859 (Apr. 28 entry); Lt 12, 1861 (Dec.); Ms 3, 1863 (July 22); J. W. [James White], "Report From Bro. White," *Review,* May 12, 1859, p. 197.

GLOVER, Charles Smith (1814-1898) and (first wife) **Jane** (1815-1873) and (second wife) **Clarissa E.** (1826-1905)

According to J. N. Loughborough's account, Charles Glover returned from prospecting gold in California in the early 1850s to find that his wife, Jane, had converted to Sabbatarian Adventism during his absence. "On Friday she was preparing to keep the Sabbath. . . . As it neared sundown, she explained matters to him . . . and he said, 'I will keep the day with you!'"

The Glovers were enthusiastic laypersons. In 1853 their farm in Sylvan, Michigan, was the venue for meetings attracting several hundred persons, and in 1854 they spontaneously gave $35 toward the $200 needed to purchase the first tent for public evangelism. The same year Charles Glover was ordained as a deacon in the Sylvan church. His administrative talents were employed through the years as he served on a variety of committees of the Michigan and Kansas conferences.

Charles Glover professed in 1862 that even though "his name had been paraded in the public print, by our enemies, as a 'vision lover,'" yet he "was not ashamed of the visions, nor to own that he loved them." On a personal level the Glovers and the Whites seem to have got along well together. Thus, in 1860, while James White was away from home, Ellen and her children stayed a week with the Glovers, who had now moved to Newton, near Battle Creek, Michigan. "They took great pains to make us happy," Ellen observed. Later, in 1873, when the family had moved again to Kansas, Charles Glover happened to meet the Whites in Colorado while he was there on business and ended up spending several weeks with them at their borrowed mountain retreat. Testimonies from Ellen White to the Glovers in 1861 focused on fostering the spiritual development of their children.

See: Obituary: "Charles S. Glover," *Review,* May 24, 1898, p. 339; obituary: "Jane Glover," *Review,* July 1, 1873, p. 23; obituary: "Clarissa E. Glover," *Review,* Dec. 7, 1905, p. 23; F. C. Gilbert, "Israel's Jubilee and Its Present-Day Lessons," *Review,* July 24, 1924, p. 7; M. E. Cornell, "Report of Meetings," *Review,* Feb. 11, 1862, p. 85; search term "Glover" in *Review and Herald* online collection, www.adventistarchives.org; *Daughters of the American Revolution Lineage Book* (1930), vol. 113, p. 154. J. N. Loughborough, *Rise and Progress,* pp. 199, 200; Ellen G. White, Lt 14, 1860 (Nov. 19); Lt 1a, 1861 (Jan. 24); Lt 9, 1861 (Oct. 12); *History of Washtenaw County, Michigan,* p. 1396.

GODSMARK, Richard (1822-1905) and **Huldah Jane** (c. 1818-1899)

Richard Godsmark married widow Huldah J. Lane in 1852 and built up a flourishing farm about seven miles [11 kilometers] north of Battle Creek, in Bedford Township. After becoming Sabbathkeeping Adventists in 1853, the Godsmarks donated generously to a long succession of church projects through the years. According to Uriah Smith, the Godsmark home also became known for its hospitality, "a welcome place to which brethren and sisters, and employees of the Office, would often resort to spend an evening, or . . . a few hours' recreation." In Ellen White's diary there are several mentions of enjoyable short visits to the Godsmarks in Bedford. Both of Richard Godsmark's stepsons, Elbert B. Lane and Sands H. Lane, as well as his son, Otho C. Godsmark, became evangelists and church administrators.

See: Obituary: "Richard Godsmark," *Review,* Feb. 16, 1905, p. 23; U. S. [Uriah Smith], "Another Sad Reminder," *Review,* Mar. 28, 1899, p. 208; 1870 U.S. Federal Census, "Peter [*sic*] Godsmark," Michigan, Calhoun County, Bedford, p. 21; search term "Godsmark" in *Review and Herald* online collection, www.adventistarchives.org; Ellen G. White, Ms 5, 1859 (Mar. 23, 24 entries); Lt 6, 1866 (Dec. 8); Ms 16a, 1885 (July 23 entry); Ms 19, 1889 (Mar. 5 entry); Lt 65, 1889 (Mar. 28); Mark Bovee, "Richard Godsmark"; Arthur Whitefield Spalding, *Origin and History,* vol. 1, p. 277.

GORHAM, Elizabeth (c. 1813-after 1873) and **Henry M.** (?-after 1850)

In a number of letters written between 1849 and 1851 to friends in New Ipswich, New Hampshire, Ellen White included warm greetings and words of encouragement to "Sister Gorham." Most likely she was Elizabeth Gorham of Mason, New Hampshire, who lived about five miles [eight kilometers] east of New Ipswich. Little is known about her relation to the church except that "Elizabeth Gorham" and "E. Gorham" are listed in *Review* subscriber lists throughout the 1850s and as late as 1873. Census evidence suggests that she was divorced from her husband, Henry Gorham, a physician, sometime after 1850.

See: Ellen G. White, Lt 5, 1849 (Apr. 21), note 25; search word "Gorham" in *Words of the Pioneers*; 1850 U.S. Federal Census, "Henry M. Gorham," New Hampshire, Hillsborough County, Mason, p. 300; 1860 U.S. Federal Census, "Henry M. Gorham," New Hampshire, Strafford County, Somersworth, p. 122; 1860 U.S. Federal Census, "Elizabeth Gorham," New Hampshire, Hillsborough County, Mason, p. 11.

GORSLINE, Richard (c. 1806-1864)

A "carman" by trade and member of the Sabbathkeeping Adventist group in Oswego, New York. In 1850, while Ellen White also lived in Oswego, she was instructed in vision that Gorsline had "wounded and torn the hearts of God's people" and should be disfellowshipped "unless he changed his course entirely." Records suggest a positive outcome, with Gorsline becoming a faithful member, and leaving a legacy of $470.87 to the church.

See: 1850 U.S. Federal Census, "Richard Gorsline," New York, Oswego, Oswego City, 2nd Ward, p. 171; Elias Goodwin, "A Hard Case," *Review,* Jan. 24, 1854, p. 7; search term "Gorsline" in *Words of the Pioneers*; Ellen G. White, Ms 5, 1850 (July 29); James White, *An Appeal to the Working Men and Women,* p. 52.

GRAHAM, Andrew (c. 1836-after 1883) and (first wife) Abigail (c. 1840-1862) and (second wife) Sophronia (c. 1838-1871) and (third wife) Amelia A. (c. 1850-1883)

Born in Scotland, Andrew Graham became a Sabbatarian Adventist, together with his brothers **Bruce** and **William Henry**, while living in Berlin, Connecticut, in the early 1850s. Various censuses list him as "mechanic" and "farmer." In the 1860s he moved to Battle Creek, Michigan. In May 1867 the directors of the Western Health Reform Institute appointed Graham to be superintendent "for one year." He seems to have continued his employment at the Institute for several years after that, but probably not as superintendent.

In her 1859 diary Ellen White notes a visit to Andrew Graham and his family in Berlin, Connecticut. The Graham brothers seem to have been involved in fanaticism in their local meetings, for which Ellen White admonished them. In 1868 Ellen White assigned some of the responsibility for the major troubles at the Western Health Reform Institute to Andrew Graham's "want of proper oversight."

See: E.L.H. Chamberlain, "Receipts," *Review,* Aug. 11, 1853, p. 56; 1850 U.S. Federal Census, "Andrew Graham," Connecticut, Hartford County, Berlin, p. 53; 1870 U.S. Federal Census, "Andrew Graham," Michigan, Calhoun County, Battle Creek, p. 21; 1880 U.S. Federal Census, "Andrew Graham," Michigan, Saginaw County, Swan Creek, p. 3; obituary: "Abby Graham," *Review,* Apr. 29, 1862, p. 175; obituary: "Sophronia Graham," *Review,* July 18,

1871, p. 39; obituary: "Amelia A. Graham," *Review,* May 22, 1883, pp. 334, 335; Health Reform Institute (Battle Creek, Mich.): "Minutes of the Health Reform Institute Board: Selections, 1867-1897" (Berrien Springs, Mich.: Center for Adventist Research, Andrews University, n.d.), May 5, 1867, May 22, 1867; Ellen G. White, *Testimony for the Church at Battle Creek by Ellen G. White* (Battle Creek, Mich.: Steam Press of the Seventh-day Adventist Pub. Assn., 1868), pp. 45, 46; Ms 7, 1859 (Sept. 2 entry); Lt 7, 1859 (Sept. 24); Lt 19, 1859 (Oct. 4).

GRAHAM, **Bruce** (1833-1919) and (first wife) **Lavina** (c. 1835-1870) and (second wife) **Caroline V.** (1849-1928)

Originally from Scotland, Bruce Graham became a Sabbatarian Adventist, together with his brothers **Andrew** and **William Henry**, while living in Berlin, Connecticut, in the early 1850s. He later lived in Battle Creek, Michigan, before moving sometime during the 1870s to Franklin County, Massachusetts, where he farmed for most of the remainder of his life. An active layperson, he is described in his obituary as a "leader in different companies of believers with which he was connected." In 1858 he married Lavina Thayer, and in 1884 Caroline Prior.

In her 1859 diary Ellen White notes that she and James "took dinner with Brother Bruce Graham" while on a visit to Berlin, Connecticut. She also mentions the death of Graham's first wife, Lavina, in 1870. James White spoke at her funeral in Battle Creek. Ellen White admonished the Graham brothers for their apparent involvement in fanaticism in Berlin during the 1850s.

See: Obituary: "Bruce Graham," *Review,* Aug. 7, 1919, p. 29; obituary: "Lavina Graham," *Review,* Jan. 31, 1871, p. 55; obituary: "Caroline V. Graham," *Review,* Mar. 1, 1928, p. 22; Bruce Graham, "Communications," *Review,* May 29, 1856, p. 46; 1870 U.S. Federal Census, "Bruce Graham," Michigan, Calhoun County, Battle Creek, Ward 3, p. 32; 1880 U.S. Federal Census, "Bruce Graham," Massachusetts, Franklin County, Buckland, p. 2; Ellen G. White, Ms 7, 1859 (Sept. 2 entry); Lt 7, 1859 (Sept. 24); Lt 19, 1859 (Oct. 4); Lt 22, 1870 (Dec. 16).

GRAHAM, **William Henry** (1831-1925) and **Mary A.** (1834-1908)

Church members and farmers. Born in Scotland, William Graham became a Sabbatarian Adventist, together with his brothers **Andrew** and **Bruce**, while living in Berlin, Connecticut, in the early 1850s. For about 20 years he was a member of the Berlin church, also serving as deacon. After moving to Massachusetts in 1871, he left the church but remained supportive. William and Mary's daughter, Ella May, was in the first graduating class of South Lancaster Academy and later married F. C. Gilbert, pioneer Adventist evangelist to the Jews. William Graham rejoined the church through baptism in 1924, some months before his death. His wife, Mary, remained a member throughout her life.

In her 1859 diary Ellen White mentions a visit to William Graham and his wife in Berlin. She admonished the Graham brothers for their apparent involvement in fanaticism in their local meetings.

See: Obituary: "William Henry Graham," *Review,* July 2, 1925, p. 22; obituary: "Mary A. Graham, *Review,* July 30, 1908, p. 23; obituary: "Ella May Gilbert," *Review,* Feb. 17, 1944, p. 19; "Receipts," *Review,* Feb. 3, 1852, p. 88; 1870 U.S. Federal Census, "William Graham," Connecticut, Tolland County, Mansfield, p. 9; Ellen G. White, Ms 7, 1859 (Sept. 2 entry); Lt 7, 1859 (Sept. 24); Lt 19, 1859 (Oct. 4).

GRANT, Harrison (1821-1901) and **Chloe S.** (1821-1904)

Later to become president of the Minnesota Conference, Harrison Grant had converted to Millerite Adventism in his youth after hearing a series of lectures by William Miller in Vermont. In 1844 he married Chloe S. Pierson, and both became Sabbathkeepers about 1858. In 1861 or 1862 they moved from Vermont to Minnesota, where they spent the next 30 years. From 1863, when the Minnesota Conference was first organized, Grant served on the executive committee, and from 1870 to 1883 as conference president. Ellen White's only mention of Harrison Grant is in her account of a visit to Roxbury, Vermont, in 1859, when the Whites received hospitality at his home.

See: Obituary: "Harrison Grant," *Review,* Apr. 2, 1901, p. 219; obituary: "Chloe S. Grant," *Review,* May 19, 1904, p. 23; search terms "H. Grant" and "Harrison Grant" in *Review and Herald* online collection, www.adventistarchives.org; Ellen G. White, Lt 30, 1859 (Oct. 12); Ms 8, 1859 (Oct. 11 entry).

GRANT, Walter (1814-after 1880) and (first wife) **Nancy E.** (1821-1877) and (second wife) **Jane** (c. 1832-after 1880)

Walter ("farmer," "house painter") and Nancy Grant lived in Bedford, a few miles north of Battle Creek, Michigan, and later in Battle Creek. Their marriage appears to have broken up in the 1860s. The 1870 census does not list Nancy in the Walter Grant household.

An 1858 reference in the *Review* to "Walter Grant, Battle Creek" and a number of receipts published in the *Review* for "W. Grant" in the period 1853 to 1863 are the main published traces of Walter Grant's connection to Adventists. Because of the problems indicated below, it is almost certain that he separated from the church sometime in the 1860s, leaving the question open whether he rejoined later. Nancy Grant, according to her obituary, continued a "faithful and consistent member" of the Battle Creek church until her death in 1877. Ellen White's main mentions of Walter and Nancy Grant are found in a letter written about 1864 in which she speaks in plain language about Walter's extramarital relationship with a "Mrs. Munsel" and the devastating effect this had on Nancy.

See: Obituary: "Nancy E. Grant," *Review,* Feb. 15, 1877, p. 55; 1850 U.S. Federal Census, "Walter Grant," Michigan, Calhoun County, Bedford, p. 103; 1870 U.S. Federal Census, "Walter Grant," Michigan, Calhoun County, Battle Creek, Ward 1, p. 56; 1880 U. S. Federal Census, "Jane Grant," Michigan, Calhoun County, Battle Creek, Ward 1, p. 15; A. S. Hutchins, *Review,* Aug. 12, 1858, p. 104; search word "W. Grant" in *Words of the Pioneers*; Ellen G. White, Lt 12, 1864 (c. 1864).

GREGORY, John (c. 1826-?) and Esther C. (c. 1829-1862)

The Gregorys were farmers from Parma, Michigan, who became Sabbathkeeping Adventists in 1859, having been instructed by Joseph Bates. While on a short visit to nearby Jackson in April 1859 Ellen White met the Gregorys, noting in her diary that they had "recently commenced to keep the Sabbath. May the Lord enable them . . . to persevere." Before Esther Gregory's death three years later, at age 33, she requested that the Whites attend her funeral, but this, for some reason, did not happen. John Gregory's movements or connection with the Seventh-day Adventist Church after his wife's death are not known.

See: 1860 U.S. Federal Census, "Jno. Gregory," Michigan, Jackson County, Parma, p. 21; obituary: "Esther C. Gregory," *Review,* Apr. 29, 1862, p. 175; Ellen G. White, Ms 6, 1859 (Apr. 2 entry).

GURNEY, Heman Stetson (1818-1896) and Ann Eliza (1831-1921)

Heman Gurney, a blacksmith and lay preacher from Massachusetts, is most remembered for his enthusiastic participation in the closing stages of the Millerite movement and the early stages of Sabbatarian Adventism. In the spring of 1844 Gurney accompanied Joseph Bates, both of abolitionist convictions, on a risky evangelistic foray into slaveholding areas of Maryland. After Bates became a Sabbatarian Adventist in the spring of 1845, Gurney was one of his first converts and participated in several of the Sabbath and Sanctuary Conferences of 1848.

In 1853 Heman Gurney married Ann Eliza (Gifford) Randall, a widow, and daughter of William Gifford, friend of Joseph Bates and fellow Millerite and temperance advocate. They moved to Jackson, Michigan, in 1856 and to Memphis, Michigan, in 1865. In both places Gurney was elected church elder and was active in lay preaching. In 1869-1870 he served as president of the Michigan Conference. Through the years he contributed a large number of short, pithy articles and letters to the *Review,* which the editor, James White, appreciated: "We want more articles, short, and to the point, like Bro. Gurney's . . ."

In his article "Recollections of Early Advent Experience" Gurney gives some insights into his views on the visions of Ellen White. It appears that he first met 18-year-old Ellen Harmon (White) early in 1846 when she came to Advent Hall in New Bedford, Massachusetts, to relate her visions. Like his mentor, Joseph Bates, Gurney was cautious about accepting their authenticity. "I wished to prove all things," he relates, and subsequently traveled to the Harmon home in Portland, Maine, to make enquiries, visited "a number of weeks with the [Harmon] family and in their vicinity and became convinced that . . . God had called sister [*sic*] Harmon to an important work." Acting on his conviction before returning to Massachusetts, Gurney shared the cost with James White of republishing Ellen Harmon's earliest visions in April 1846 in the broadside *To the Little Remnant Scattered Abroad.* After this he continued, "I often met sister [*sic*] Harmon. . . . I have seen her in holy vision often. I have been encouraged by the visions, and sharply reproved by them [see Ms 11, 1850 (Dec. 25)]. . . . I never have doubted their inspiration."

See: Obituary: "Herman [*sic*] S. Gurney," *Review,* Sept. 8, 1896, pp. 577, 578; obituary: "Ann Eliza Gifford," *Review,* Mar. 3, 1921, p. 23; Benjamin Shurtleff, *Descendants of William Shurtleff of Plymouth and Marshfield, Massachusetts, vol. 1* (Revere, Mass.: no publisher, 1912), p. 360; [James White], "This Week's *Review,*" *Review,* May 3, 1864, p. 180; H. S. Gurney, "Recollections of Early Advent Experience," *Review,* Jan. 3, 1888, p. 2; search term "H. S. Gurney" in *Review and Herald* online collection, www.adventistarchives.org. For a survey of Heman Gurney's association with Joseph Bates, see George R. Knight, *Joseph Bates,* pp. 60-64, 80, 81, 121, 122.

HADDEN, Lewis (1819-1893) and **Mary E.** (c. 1824-after 1893)

Lewis and Mary E. Hadden are listed among the original members of the Otsego, Michigan, Seventh-day Adventist Church, organized by Joseph Bates in 1861. They had moved to Otsego from New York in the 1850s. There is reference to an "L. Hadden" in the *Review* as early as 1857.

Lewis Hadden is probably the "Brother Hatten" who, according to Ellen White's diary, was present at Sabbatarian meetings in Otsego on January 8 and 9, 1859, when there was a tense standoff with the followers of Gilbert Cranmer. Hadden remained a member of the Otsego church until his death in 1893.

See: Ellen G. White, Ms 5, 1859 (Jan. 9 entry); obituary, "Lewis Hadden," *Review,* Oct. 3, 1893, p. 627; 1870 U.S. Federal Census, "Mary Hadden," Michigan, Allegan County, Otsego, p. 12; *History of Allegan and Barry Counties, Michigan,* p. 305; search term "Hadden" in *Review and Herald* online collection, www.adventistarchives.org.

HARDY, William J. (1823-1888) and **Eliza** (1820-1890)

Thought to be the first African-American to be elected to public office in Michigan, William J. Hardy was a leading member of the Seventh-day Adventist Church in the Gaines-Caledonia area. He was born in New York, and his family moved to Michigan in 1827. According to some sources, Hardy, after his father's death, was, when only 6 or 7 years old, bound out as an indentured servant for some years. By 1846 he was able to purchase his own farm in Gaines, which by the time of the 1870 census was valued at a very respectable $7,500.

William Hardy, preceded by his wife, Eliza (née Watts), became a Sabbatarian Adventist in 1857 and remained a key member of his local church for the rest of his life. After the Michigan legislature in 1870 endorsed the Fifteenth Amendment, giving the vote to African-American men, William Hardy began to run for various public offices in Gaines Township. Although disadvantaged by his race, unpopular church affiliation, and by running on a Republican ticket in an area dominated by Democrats, Hardy was elected supervisor of Gaines Township in 1872.

Ellen White was impressed by the Hardy family when she paid a brief visit in 1859: "We were heartily welcomed by the family. A good dinner was soon in readiness for us. . . . This is a colored family. Although the house is poor and old, everything is arranged with neatness and exact order. The children are well behaved, intelligent, and interesting." Problems of disunity, however, at times beset the church in Gaines and

Caledonia in the 1860s, and several times during that decade Ellen White cautioned William and Eliza Hardy over their part in the troubles.

See: Obituary: "Wm. J. Hardy," *Review*, June 19, 1888, pp. 398, 399; 1870 U.S. Federal Census, "William Hardy," Michigan, Kent County, Gaines, p. 4; [Birth and death dates of Eliza Hardy] www.migenweb.net/kent/cemeteries/gaines/blain/1995go.html (Oct. 17, 2010); Franklin Everett, *Memorials of the Grand River Valley* (Chicago: Chicago Legal News Co., 1878), p. 29 ("Biographical Sketches" section); Randall Maurice Jelks, *African Americans in the Furniture City: The Struggle for Civil Rights in Grand Rapids* (Urbana and Chicago: University of Illinois Press, 2006), pp. 1-5, 15-20; Ellen G. White, Ms 5, 1859 (Jan. 25 entry); Lt 22, 1861 (Jan. 22); Ms 3, 1863 (July 22); Ms 10, 1868 (c. 1868); "Byington and Amadon Diaries, 1857-1912" (Berrien Springs, Mich.: Center for Adventist Research, Andrews University, n.d.), John Byington diary, Oct. 5, 1857, entry.

HARMON, John B. (1815-1883) and (first wife) **Dorcas N.** (?-c. 1842) and (second wife) **Abigail** (c. 1824-c. 1850) and (third wife) **Lucy J.** (1829-1911)

John B. Harmon was Ellen G. White's older brother. Born in Portland, Maine, he married Dorcas N. Gould in 1836 and soon left Maine. Their first son was born in Georgia in 1838. The following year the Harmons moved to the village of Portage, in St. Charles County, Missouri, on the banks of the Mississippi River, where John Harmon apparently worked as "boatman" during the 1840s. By 1850 the Harmons moved across the river to Jersey County, Illinois. John Harmon probably remained in that general area for the rest of his life, apart from some time spent in Iowa in the mid 1850s. According to the 1860 census he had turned to farming, and by 1870 he owned real estate valued at a comfortable $10,000. Dorcas died young, probably in her 20s, as did his second wife, Abigail Bagby, whom John Harmon married in 1843. Whether Lucy J. Bagby, his third wife, was a sister of Abigail is not known, but they both came from Virginia.

From available records it appears that Ellen White only met her brother John once after he left Maine in the 1830s. On July 22, 1859, while at home in Battle Creek, Michigan, she noted in her diary, "My brother that I have not seen for twenty years came from Illinois with his wife to visit us." By 1873 Ellen had lost contact with John, having written repeatedly but receiving no replies. In 1879 the Whites planned to visit John Harmon while en route from Texas to Michigan, but subsequent events defeated their plans. Finally, some time before 1883, there were plans afoot for John to come to California to visit Ellen. "I had so many fond hopes that he would come west," Ellen wrote to her sister. "He gave me this encouragement in his last letter." Unfortunately, John Harmon's death intervened. According to obituary information supplied by Mary Plummer Foss, John Harmon joined the Methodist Episcopal Church about 10 years before his death.

See: Artemas C. Harmon, ed., *The Harmon Genealogy*, p. 79; 1840 U.S. Federal Census,

"Jno. B. Harmon," Missouri, Saint Charles County, Portage, p. 11; 1850 U.S. Federal Census, "John B. Harman," Illinois, Jersey County, Township 8, Range 13, p. 92; 1870 U.S. Federal Census, "John B. Harmon," Illinois, Calhoun County, Hardin, p. 10; "Bagby, Abigail" in Jordan Dodd, *Missouri Marriages to 1850* (database online), (Provo, Utah: Ancestry.com Operations, Inc., 1997); *History of Greene and Jersey Counties, Illinois* (Springfield, Ill.: Continental Historical Co., 1885), p. 364; James White to "Edson and Emma," Mar. 8, 1879; James White to W. C. White, Feb. 20, 1879; Ellen G. White, Ms 7, 1859 (July 22 entry); Lt 2a, 1873 (Jan. 21); Lt 10, 1883 (Apr. 8); M. P. Foss to Ellen White, May 19, 1883.

HARMON, Robert (1786-1866) and **Eunice** (c. 1787-c. 1863)

Parents of Ellen G. White. Born in Maine, Robert Harmon and Eunice Gould were married in Portland, Maine (then part of Massachusetts) in 1810. They were members of the Methodist Episcopal Church, where "they held prominent connection," according to James White. Robert and Eunice, together with several of their children, accepted the Second Advent teaching of William Miller in the early 1840s, for which they were cut off from the Methodist Church in 1843. Although remaining Adventists, the Harmons rejected the extremism that broke out among some Adventists in Portland, Maine, in 1845 and for a time left their home in Portland in order to be free of such influence.

Ellen Harmon and James White stayed with the Harmons for a little more than a year after marrying in August 1846, and it was during this period that the Whites began to keep the Sabbath. By 1848 Robert and Eunice had also become Sabbathkeepers (see notes on Lt 3, 1847 [July 13]).

In their old age Robert and Eunice Harmon left Maine and spent their remaining years living with or near their daughters, Ellen White and **Sarah Belden,** and their son, **John B. Harmon**. From about 1855 to 1862 they stayed in Battle Creek, Michigan, where both Ellen and Sarah lived with their families. In the early 1860s the Harmons moved to Greene County, Illinois, probably to live with John Harmon. Here Eunice died, probably in December 1863, about the same time that Ellen and James's oldest son, Henry Nichols White, died (Dec. 8, 1863). After his wife's death, Robert Harmon spent the remaining three years of his life with Sarah and Stephen Belden, by then living in Connecticut. Ellen White visited her father shortly before his death. In her diaries and other writings she frequently expressed her devotion to her parents.

For a discussion of the dates of birth of Robert and Eunice Harmon as well as a study of the genealogy of Eunice, see Roger D. Joslyn, "Gould Ancestry of Ellen Gould (Harmon) White," prepared for the Ellen G. White Estate (Silver Spring, Md.: 2002-2003); see also obituary: "Eunice Harmon," *Review,* Jan. 26, 1864, p. 71; Ellen G. White, "They Sleep in Jesus," *Review,* Apr. 21, 1868, p. 297; Ellen G. White, Lt 3, 1847 (July 13); Lt 8, 1856 (Jan. 21); Lt 29, 1861 (Nov. 13); Artemas C. Harmon, ed., *The Harmon Genealogy,* p. 41; James White to "Dear Brother and Sister," Aug. 26, 1848; James White and Ellen G. White, *Life Sketches* (1880), p. 130; Ellen G. White, *Spiritual Gifts [vol. 2],* p. 50.

HARMON, Sarah B. See BELDEN, Stephen T. and Sarah B.

HARRIS, William (c. 1803-1873) and Lydia (c. 1808-after 1873)

A carpenter from the hamlet of Centreport, near Port Byron, New York, William Harris became a Millerite about 1842 and a Sabbathkeeper in 1847. There are indications that he did some lay preaching in the 1850s. The first recorded meeting of the Harris family with Ellen and James White was in August 1848. In response to prayer Lydia Harris was "greatly relieved" of her chronic catarrh and left off the use of snuff as treatment. Two years later, in 1850, the Whites lived at the Harris home during August and September while James published the first four issues of the *Advent Review* in nearby Auburn. Dramatic healings of 1-year-old Edson and of James took place in their home during this period.

See: Obituary: "William Harris," *Review*, Apr. 22, 1873, p. 151; 1850 U.S. Federal Census, "William Harris," New York, Cayuga County, Mentz, p. 97; Wm. Harris, "From Bro. Harris," *Review*, Feb. 5, 1857, p. 110; William Harris, "From Bro. Harris," *Review*, Sept. 10, 1857, p. 151; "Conferences," *Advent Review*, November 1850, p. 72; Ellen G. White, *Spiritual Gifts [vol. 2]*, pp. 99-100, 136-143; Ellen G. White, Lt 8, 1850 (Aug. 4).

HART, Josiah Rice (1817-1858) and Orvilla (1810-1861)

Josiah Hart of Northfield, Vermont, married Orvilla Webster in 1839. After becoming a Sabbatarian Adventist in 1850, he began to preach in his home state. Following his ordination in 1853, Hart became very active in tent evangelism throughout New England and New York. In 1856, together with fellow evangelist Elon Everts, he moved with his family westward to Round Grove, Illinois. For the next two years, until his death of typhoid fever at 41, Hart, often accompanied by Everts, traveled widely in Illinois, Wisconsin, and Iowa holding public meetings.

In his early days as a Sabbatarian Adventist, Hart strongly opposed the visions of Ellen White and supported the minority view that the Second Advent would take place in the autumn of 1851. Ellen White wrote in 1851 of Stephen Smith and Josiah Hart that they "had filled the minds of many with prejudice against us." The turning point came at the conferences held in Bethel and Waterbury, Vermont, in November 1851, where "hearty confessions were made by Brother Hart and others." In 1856 David Arnold described Hart as "a strong one on the visions," and that he had "labored hard and long" (and unsuccessfully) to convince James White "that they were a test" (i.e., a test of fellowship).

See: Obituary: "Josiah Hart," *Review*, Sept. 2, 1858, p. 127; obituary: "Orvilla Hart," *Review*, Mar. 19, 1861, p. 143; William Holcomb Webster and Melville Reuben Webster, *History and Genealogy of the Gov. John Webster Family of Connecticut With Numerous Portraits and Illustrations* (Rochester, N.Y.: E. R. Andrews Printing Co., 1915), vol. 2, p. 574; search term "Hart" in *Words of the Pioneers*; Ellen G. White, Lt 8, 1851 (Nov. 12); D. Arnold to M. Crawford, Feb. 3, 1856.

HASKELL, Lewis (1801-1882) and **Salina** (c. 1803-1891)

Originally from Vermont, Lewis and Salina Haskell settled in New York about 1841. They connected with William Miller's Second Advent movement in 1843 and became Sabbathkeepers about 1851. Their house in Norfolk, New York, became the meeting place for Seventh-day Adventists in that area for the next 40 years. The Haskells received incidental mention in Ellen White's 1859 diary.

See: Obituary: "Lewis Haskell," *Review,* Aug. 22, 1882, p. 542; obituary: "Salina Haskell," *Review,* Apr. 7, 1891, p. 222; 1860 U.S. Federal Census, "Lewis Haskell," New York, St. Lawrence County, Norfolk, p. 21; Ellen G. White, Ms 8, 1859 (Oct. 19 entry).

HASKELL, Stephen Nelson (1833-1922) and (first wife) **Mary E.** (1812-1894) and (second wife) **Hetty** (1857-1919)

Stephen and Mary Haskell, both from Massachusetts, converted to Sabbatarian Adventism in 1853. Ordained a minister in 1868, Stephen Haskell became president of the New England Conference in 1870. From that time till 1911 he served frequently as president of the California, Maine, and New England conferences and sat on the General Conference Committee. At various times during the 1880s and 1890s he undertook church assignments in Europe, southern Africa, and Australia.

Stephen Haskell's first wife, Mary How, was among the founders in 1869 of the Vigilant Missionary Society, which engaged in literature distribution and home visitation and was a forerunner of the extensive Tract and Missionary societies later organized by Stephen. His second wife, Hetty Hurd, whom he married while in Australia in 1897, had long experience as a teacher of Bible Instructors in America, England, and South Africa. For two years they served on the faculty of the newly formed Avondale College in Australia before returning to the United States in 1899, where they worked together on city evangelism and other projects.

During his early years of self-supporting ministry S. N. Haskell took a dim view of Ellen and James White. "My mind became very much prejudiced against them," Haskell recalled in 1870, attributing his bias to the fact that he had become "acquainted with those who were their enemies." His negativity during the late 1850s was confirmed in Ms 2, 1858, where Ellen White wrote of Stephen Haskell as having "scattered evil" and "been at work to destroy confidence in the visions and in those who have the charge of the work at Battle Creek." By 1862 he seemed to have undergone a change of mind, writing positively in the *Review,* for the first time, of the value of "the gift of prophecy, in correcting wrongs." In time Haskell became a staunch supporter and personal friend of Ellen White's, who, in turn, came to appreciate his talents as a preacher and administrator. "Brother Haskell is an excellent laborer," she reported after hearing him preach in 1874. Years later, in 1897, Ellen White expressed her high regard for Stephen and Hetty Haskell for their services at Avondale College. "He [Stephen Haskell] presents truth in a clear, simple, earnest manner. . . . As matron and teacher, Sister Haskell could not be excelled. She is firm as a rock to principle." It was fitting that Stephen Haskell was chosen to preach the sermon at Ellen White's funeral in 1915.

See: Obituary: "Stephen N. Haskell," *Review,* Dec. 14, 1922, p. 17; obituary: "Mary E. Haskell," *Review,* Feb. 20, 1894, p. 127; obituary: "Mrs. S. N. Haskell," *Review,* Nov. 20, 1919, pp. 24, 25; "From Bro. Haskell," *Review,* Aug. 19, 1862, p. 95; S. N. Haskell, "Responses to the Above," in John Nevins Andrews et al., *Defense of Elder James White and Wife,* p. 33; Ellen G. White, Ms 2, 1858 (Dec. 27); Lt 35, 1874 (June 22); Lt 99, 1897 (Aug. 19). For a major biography of S. N. Haskell, see Ella M. Robinson, *S. N. Haskell: Man of Action.*

HASTINGS, Emma A. (1841-1865)

Daughter of **Leonard** and **Elvira Hastings,** of New Ipswich, New Hampshire, close friends of Ellen and James White. She was probably baptized by James White in 1850. She wrote several short articles and letters for the *Youth's Instructor.* She died at age 23, of "erysipelas and typhoid fever."

See: Obituary: "Emma A. Hastings," *Review,* Mar. 21, 1865, p. 127; Ellen G. White, *Spiritual Gifts [vol. 2],* p. 112; Emma A. Hastings, "From Emma A. Hastings," *Youth's Instructor,* March 1854, p. 24; Emma A. Hastings, "We Are Going Home," *Youth's Instructor,* March 1859, p. 24; Emma A. Hastings, "Religion," *Youth's Instructor,* August 1859, p. 1; Emma A. Hastings, "Rest in Heaven," *Youth's Instructor,* May 1860, p. 37; Emma A. Hastings, "Let him That Thinketh He Standeth, Take Heed Lest He Fall," *Youth's Instructor,* May 1862, p. 39; Charles H. Chandler, *The History of New Ipswich, New Hampshire, 1735-1914,* p. 457.

HASTINGS, Harriet Arabella (c. 1834-1854)

Oldest daughter of **Leonard** and **Elvira Hastings**, who were close friends of Ellen and James White. She was baptized by James White in 1850. When her mother died in 1850, Harriet, about 16 years old, assumed major responsibilities for her younger siblings. She received several letters of encouragement from Ellen White. Harriet died at age 20 of tuberculosis.

See: Obituary: "Harriet A. Hastings," *Review,* Sept. 5, 1854, p. 31; Ellen G. White, *Spiritual Gifts [vol. 2],* p. 112; Lt 8, 1849 (May 29); Lt 8, 1850 (Aug. 4); Lt 7, 1851 (July 27); Lt 3, 1851 (Aug. 11).

HASTINGS, Leonard (1803-1883) and (first wife) **Elvira** (c. 1808-1850) and (second wife) **Martha** (c. 1819-1888)

Pioneer laypersons from New Ipswich, New Hampshire, and early friends of Ellen and James White. Elvira Hastings is said to have become "a full believer" in Ellen White's visions by 1847. Ellen White devoted several pages of her autobiographical account in *Spiritual Gifts* to a description of the dramatic events that attended her visit to the Hastings family in 1849.

Leonard Hastings, a New Ipswich farmer, not only pioneered the Seventh-day Adventist message in his own area but was later given a ministerial license by the New England Conference in 1875 and preached further afield. He also served as vice president of the New England Tract and Missionary Society for a period in the 1870s.

See: Obituary: "Leonard W. Hastings," *Review,* June 5, 1883, p. 367; W. [James White], "Our Tour East," *Advent Review,* August 1850 (No. 1), p. 14; obituary: "Martha C. Hastings," *Review,* July 3, 1888, p. 431; Charles H. Chandler, *The History of New Ipswich, New Hampshire, 1735-1914,* pp. 288, 457; James White to "Sister Hastings," Aug. 22, 1847; Ellen G. White, *Spiritual Gifts [vol. 2],* pp. 109-113; S. N. Haskell, "The New England Conference," *Review,* Sept. 16, 1875, p. 86; L. W. Hastings, "Report of the General Quarterly Meeting of the N. E. Tract and Missionary Society," *Review,* Apr. 1, 1875, p. 110.

HASTINGS, Sarah Amelia (c. 1839-before 1918)

Daughter of well-known Sabbatarian pioneer **Leonard W. Hastings**, Sarah Hastings was baptized by James White in 1850. During her teenage years she wrote a number of spiritual appeals in articles and letters published in the *Youth's Instructor* and *Review.* Ellen and James White were close friends of the Hastings family and appealed to the children to give their lives to God after the death of their mother in 1850. In her 1859 diary Ellen White mentions a brief meeting with "Amelia Hastings" in Somerville, Massachusetts. No sources have been found relating to Sarah Hastings after 1860, except for the information in her brother Frederick Hastings' obituary, that Sarah, together with four of her siblings, all died before 1918 and had all died Seventh-day Adventists.

See: 1850 U.S. Federal Census, "Sarah A. Hastings," New Hampshire, Hillsborough County, New Ipswich, p. 273; 1860 U.S. Federal Census, "Amelia Hastings," Massachusetts, Middlesex County, Somerville, p. 77; W. [James White], "Our Tour East," *Advent Review,* August 1850, pp. 14, 15; "Sr. Amelia Hastings Writes From New Ipswich . . . ," *Youth's Instructor,* May 1853, p. 62; Amelia S. Hastings, "From Amelia S. Hastings," *Youth's Instructor,* March 1854, pp. 23, 24; S. A. Hastings, "Experience," *Youth's Instructor,* October 1858, p. 78; S. A. Hastings, "Jesus Pities," *Youth's Instructor,* February 1859, pp. 10, 11; S. A. Hastings, "Chastening," *Youth's Instructor,* August 1859, p. 62; S. A. Hastings, "Lo, I Am With You Alway," *Youth's Instructor,* December 1859, p. 95; S. A. Hastings, "A Death Scene," *Youth's Instructor,* February 1860, p. 15; S. A. Hastings, "Extracts From Letters," *Review,* May 20, 1858, p. 7; James White to "My Dear Afflicted Brother," Mar. 18, 1850; Ellen G. White, Lt 10, 1850 (Mar. 18); Ms 7, 1859 (Sept. 14 entry); obituary: "Frederick Hastings," *Review,* June 6, 1918, p. 21.

HEWETT, Oren (c. 1805-1855)

From 1850 to his death in Rochester, New York, in 1855, the *Review* contains frequent receipts for Oren Hewett and includes two or three articles from his pen. One of the articles suggests that Hewett did some lay preaching.

Little is known for certain about Oren Hewett's background or full identity. One possibility is that he is the "Brother Hewit" from Dead River, Maine, who made a dramatic appearance in 1850 at a meeting in Paris, Maine, where Ellen White received a vision. However, there is currently insufficient evidence to make that connection decisively.

Oren Hewett's name can be tied with greater plausibility to two other events related to Ellen White. First is the letter she received in 1851 from "Bro. Hewett" asking whether she had "seen in vision it is wrong to use tobacco," Second is A. T. Jones's claim in 1893 that "Brother O. Hewitt" was present at Ellen White's vision in Ballston, New York, in 1852 and had "secured" a written copy of it.

See: Obituary: "Oren Hewett," *Review,* May 1, 1855, p. 222; search terms "Hewett" and "Hewitt" in *Words of the Pioneers*; Ellen G. White, Lt 28, 1850 (Nov. 27); Lt 5, 1851 (Dec. 14); Ms 2, 1852 (Mar. 14); A. T. Jones, "The Third Angel's Message—No. 24," *General Conference Daily Bulletin,* Mar. 26, 1893, p. 518.

HEWITT, David (1805-1878) and Olive (1809-1876)

Best known as the first converts to Sabbatarian Adventism in Battle Creek, David and Olive Hewitt had settled in Battle Creek, Michigan, in the 1830s. Variously listed as a "peddler" and grocer, David Hewitt, and most probably his wife, connected with the Millerite movement in the 1840s and began keeping the Sabbath in 1852 after being contacted by Joseph Bates.

Most earlier historical accounts, following suggestions by J. N. Loughborough, considered David Hewitt noteworthy because he was "one of the earliest non-Millerites to join the movement." However, a letter from David Hewitt published in the Adventist (Millerite) journal *Voice of Truth* in 1845 provides unmistakable evidence of his earlier Millerite background. An occasional lay preacher, Hewitt is also well known for being the first to move, during committee deliberations in 1860, that the name "Seventh-day Adventist" be given to the emerging movement.

Although little is said of David Hewitt in Ellen White's writings, his wife, Olive, received occasional mention. "Sister Hewitt was a good woman, beloved of God and faithful," she maintained in an 1872 letter, defending Olive Hewitt against those who had unjustly censured her in a church disciplinary hearing.

See: Virginia Hewitt Watterson, *Descendants of Captain Thomas Hewitt of Stonington, Connecticut, Compiled by Virginia Hewitt Watterson* (Carlsbad, Calif.: 1996), p. 96; "Death of David Hewitt," Battle Creek *Daily Journal,* Feb. 6, 1878, p. 4; obituary: "Sister Hewitt," *Review,* Nov. 30, 1876, p. 175; 1840 U.S. Federal Census, "David Hewitt," Michigan, Calhoun County, Battle Creek, p. 186; James M. Thomas, *Battle Creek City Directory, for 1871 and 1872, With a Historical Sketch of the City, Past and Present* (Battle Creek, Mich.: Review and Herald Steam Book and Job Printing House, 1871), p. 22; J. N. Loughborough, *The Great Second Advent Movement,* pp. 548, 549; SDAE, s.v. "David Hewitt"; Arthur Whitefield Spalding, *Origin and History of Seventh-day Adventists,* vol. 1, p. 255; David Hewitt to "Bro. Marsh," *Voice of Truth,* Sept. 3, 1845, p. 443; Ellen G. White, Lt 3, 1872 (Feb. 1). For an extensive collection of source documents on David Hewitt, see Glenn Davis and Jean Davis, "Notebook, Vol. 1," deposited at Historic Adventist Village, Battle Creek, Michigan.

HILLIARD, Aaron Henderson (c. 1820-1875) and **Lydia Ann** (c. 1819-1883)

Formerly a "class leader" in the Wesleyan Methodist Church, Aaron Hilliard and his wife, Lydia, became Sabbatarian Adventists about 1852 while living in Buck's Bridge, New York. Aaron's uncle **John Byington,** who was also living in Buck's Bridge at the time, later became the first General Conference president of the Seventh-day Adventist Church.

In 1853 the first Sabbatarian Adventist elementary school was opened in the Hilliard home, taught by John Byington's daughter Martha D. Byington. In 1859 the Hilliards moved to a farm near Otsego, Michigan, where they became charter members of the Otsego church when it was organized in 1861, and where Aaron served as church elder. The Hilliards' home in Otsego is best remembered by Seventh-day Adventist historians as the place where Ellen White received her comprehensive vision on health reform in 1863.

See: Obituary: "Aaron H. Hilliard," *Review,* Sept. 2, 1875, p. 71; obituary: "Lydia Ann Hilliard," *Review,* Sept. 25, 1883, p. 622; obituary: "Edward Hilliard," *Review,* Dec. 24, 1936, p. 21; *History of Allegan and Barry Counties, Michigan*, p. 305; "Extracts From Records of the Wesleyan Methodist Church, Morley, New York," Ellen G. White Estate, DF 1030-d; Ellen G. White, "Questions and Answers," *Review,* Oct. 8, 1867, p. 260; search term "Hilliard" in *Review and Herald* online collection, www.adventistarchives.org.

HILLIARD, Henry (1815-1892) and (first wife) **Pheba** (c. 1818-c. 1855) and (second wife) **Lucinda C.** (c. 1828-1887)

An active layperson, Henry Hilliard, originally from Vermont, spent most of his working life farming in the Buck's Bridge-Madrid area of northern New York. He was first mentioned in the *Review* in 1854 and was, until the 1870s, a leading member and lay preacher at the Buck's Bridge church. He also served on various committees of the New York Conference and was active in the Tract and Missionary societies in New York and Michigan.

Lucinda Hilliard is of particular historical interest in that she probably taught at the earliest Sabbatarian Adventist school before her marriage to Henry Hilliard. According to Grace Amadon, this pioneering home school in Buck's Bridge was first taught by her mother, **Martha D. Amadon**, in 1853, but in 1854 "Lucinda Paine" took over and taught the school "in Henry Hilliard's parlor." According to her mother's obituary, Lucinda Hilliard's maiden name was "Payne." Despite the difference in spelling, it is likely that "Lucinda Paine" and "Lucinda Payne" were the same person, especially since the school was conducted in 1854 in the home of Henry Hilliard, whom Lucinda subsequently married.

In several places Ellen White mentioned the hospitality she received at the home of Henry and Lucinda Hilliard. "We always find rest in that pilgrim's home" she wrote in 1863. In 1881 Ellen White told of Lucinda's spiritual depression and of speaking "words . . . that brought comfort to her mind."

See: Obituary: "Henry Hilliard," *Review,* Mar. 15, 1892, p. 175; obituary: "Lucinda Hilliard," *Review,* May 10, 1887, p. 303; 1850 U.S. Federal Census, "Pheba (?) Hulliard [*sic*]," New York, St. Lawrence County, Madrid, p. 285; 1860 U.S. Federal Census, "Lucinda Hilliard," New York, St. Lawrence County, Madrid, p. 34; *History of St. Lawrence Co., New York, With Illustrations and Biographical Sketches of Some of Its Prominent Men and Pioneers* (Philadelphia: L. H. Everts & Co., 1878), p. 257; Grace Amadon, "The First President of the General Conference: John Byington, Farmer-Preacher," *Review,* June 22, 1944, pp. 6, 7; obituary: "Anna Payne," *Review,* Dec. 15, 1868, p. 279; search term "Hilliard" in *Review and Herald* online collection, www.adventistarchives.org; Ellen G. White, Lt 7, 1863 (Nov. 5); Ms 8, 1859 (Oct. 18 entry); Ms 12, 1868 (Jan. 2 entry); Lt 1, 1881 (Apr. 22).

HOLLAND, Robert (c. 1834-1876) and **Elizabeth** (c. 1837-after 1880)

Originally from New York, Robert Holland was known mainly as an early teacher in the first church school in Battle Creek, Michigan. Receipts in the *Review* suggest that Robert Holland joined the Sabbathkeeping Adventists about 1854. In 1856 or 1857 (sources disagree on the date and on some other points), Holland taught at the small Adventist school in Battle Creek, which had been started in 1855. His tenure at the school was brief, because of, according to some accounts, parent dissatisfaction with his lax discipline. Subsequently Holland continued his teaching career in Caledonia, Michigan, but by 1870 the census listed him as a "pedlar" in Napoleon, Michigan. Ellen White's only mention of Robert Holland was a diary notation from 1859, written in Battle Creek: "Had a conversation with Robert Holland in the evening."

For a careful examination of the sometimes conflicting sources on Robert Holland's time as teacher in Battle Creek, see Wilbur Arthur Burton, "A History of the Mission of Seventh-day Adventist Education, 1844-1900" (Ph.D. diss., Kansas State University, 1987), pp. 41-43. See also 1860 U.S. Federal Census, "Robert Holland," Michigan, Kent County, Caledonia, p. 157; 1870 U.S. Federal Census, "Robert Holland," Michigan, Jackson County, Napoleon, p. 22; 1880 U.S. Federal Census, "Elizabeth How," Michigan, Jackson County, Napoleon, p. 14; search term "Holland" in *Review and Herald* online collection, www.adventistarchives.org; photo: Gravestone of Robert L. Holland, Oak Grove Cemetery, Napoleon, Jackson County, Michigan, www.findagrave.com (Dec. 3, 2008); Ellen G. White, Ms 5, 1859 (Feb. 7 entry).

HOLLIS, Nelson A. (1806-1885) and **Polly** (c. 1815-after 1885)

A Vermont farmer and clock repairer, Nelson Hollis preached for the Millerites in the mid-1840s. In 1849 he became a Sabbathkeeper, and for the next two or three years the *Review* carried reports of his preaching itineraries, mostly in Vermont. For reasons largely unknown, Hollis almost severed his connection with the movement in 1857. However, according to his obituary in 1885, "he still clung to the Sabbath" and "for the last few years he appeared to be gaining ground." In 1851 the perilous spiritual condition of Nelson Hollis was shown to Ellen White in vision. He had been involved in spreading a number of accusations that James White was misappropriating "church" funds for personal use.

See: 1860 U.S. Federal Census, "Nelson A. Hollis," Vermont, Caledonia County, Wheelock, p. 119; 1870 U.S. Federal Census, "Nelson A. Hollis," Vermont, Caledonia County, Wheelock, p. 1; Harvey Childs, "From Bro. Harvey Childs," *Present Truth,* December 1849, p. 39; W. [James White], "Our Tour East," *Advent Review,* August 1850 (No. 1), pp. 14, 15; G. W. Holt, "From Bro. Holt," *Review,* July 22, 1852, p. 46; S. Pierce, "Conference in Wolcott, Vt.," *Review,* Mar. 5, 1857, p. 144; obituary: "Nelson A. Hollis," *Review,* Apr. 14, 1885, p. 239; Theodore A. Bingham, *The Bingham Family in the United States, Especially of the State of Connecticut* (Easton, Pa.: Bingham Association, 1927), vol. 2, p. 289; Ellen G. White, *Spiritual Gifts [vol. 2],* pp. 145-147; Lt 6, 1851 (Apr. 1).

HOLT, George W. (1812-1877) and **Elizabeth** (c. 1815-after 1880)

Described by James White in 1849 as "a man who has stood like a pillar in all the truth since 1843, and a powerful preacher of the truth," George W. Holt was first mentioned as a Sabbathkeeper in 1848. During the 1850s and early 1860s Holt preached widely and effectively in New England and the Midwest.

George Holt was close to Ellen and James White during the early years, traveling and preaching with them on many occasions. Nevertheless, he seemed to have become increasingly estranged from the Whites. Ellen White wrote of several vision-based messages of reproof that she conveyed to Holt regarding his "ungovernable" family members who "were a source of trouble and vexation everywhere they lived" and who undercut Holt's influence as an evangelist. However, "instead of receiving" the vision "and acting on the light God had given him, his feelings rebelled against it . . . [and] he did not reform." A crisis came in 1858 when Holt began actively to "stir up wrong feelings" among the believers in Ohio, saying that "he believed the visions, but that . . . [Ellen White] was influenced by others in writing them." Although he wrote a confession, published in the *Review* in 1861, Holt did not engage in public ministry during the last 14 years of his life.

See: Obituary: "Geo. W. Holt," *Review,* Feb. 21, 1878, p. 63; James White to "Brother Bowles," Oct. 17, 1849; James White to "My Dear Brother," July 2, 1848; search term "Holt" in *Words of the Pioneers*; Arthur L. White, *Ellen G. White: The Early Years,* pp. 434-437; Ellen G. White, *Testimonies for the Church,* vol. 1, pp. 234-235; Ms 8, 1863 (May); G. W. Holt, "From Bro. Holt," *Review,* May 14, 1861, p. 207.

HOWARD, Daniel (1818-1898) and (first wife) Clarissa (1819-1865) and (second wife) Elvira (c. 1831-1896)

Daniel and Clarissa Howard were church members who farmed near Northfield, Vermont. In 1859, while passing through the area, the Whites stayed overnight with the Howards, who lived, Ellen White noted, in "a very pleasant place on the top of the mountain." In 1863 the family moved to Minnesota, where Clarissa died 18 months later "of consumption." Daniel Howard married Elvira Arnold in 1866.

See: Obituary: "Clarissa Howard," *Review,* Feb. 14, 1865, p. 95; Heman Howard, *The Howard Genealogy: Descendants of John Howard of Bridgewater, Massachusetts, From 1643 to 1903* (Brockton, Mass.: Standard Printing Co., 1903), p. 137; 1860 U.S. Federal Census, "Daniel Howard," Vermont, Washington County, Northfield, p. 220; 1880 U.S. Federal Census, "Daniel Howard," Minnesota, Dodge County, Wasioja, p. 33; Ellen G. White, Ms 8, 1859 (entries for Oct. 11, 12); Lt 30, 1859 (Oct. 12).

HOWELL, John (c. 1820-1861) and Lucinda S. (later BURDICK) (c. 1828-after 1908)

Although an Advent Christian minister in later years, in 1845 John Howell had identified closely with the minority "Bridegroom" shut door Adventists. He publicly renounced this position in early 1846 and returned to majority Adventist views. Amid the Adventist theological controversies of the late 1840s and the 1850s, Howell sided with the conditionalists and joined the Advent Christians.

In Ellen White's memoirs John Howell was remembered mostly for the active role he played in 1845 in attempting to discredit her visions. Howell's wife, Lucinda T. Howell (later Burdick), was also an active opponent of Ellen White. In the 1870s some of her charges were published in the Advent Christian press.

See: Obituary: "Bro. Howell Sleeps in Jesus," *The World's Crisis,* Jan. 8, 1862, p. 66; 1860 U.S. Federal Census, "John Howell," Vermont, Rutland County, Poultney, p. 243; David Tallmadge Arthur, "Come Out of Babylon," p. 334; Lucinda S. Burdick, "Statement of Mrs. Lucinda Burdick, Concerning the Shut Door [and the] Visions of Ellen G. Harmon, 1908," Ellen G. White Estate, DF 330; Miles Grant, *The True Sabbath: Which Day Shall We Keep? An Examination of Mrs. Ellen White's Visions* (Boston: Advent Christian Publication Society, 1874), p. 71; John Howell, "Letter From Bro. Howell," *Voice of Truth,* Jan. 21, 1846, pp. 30, 31; John Howell, "Notices," *The Bible Advocate,* Nov. 11, 1847, p. 112; Ellen G. White, *Spiritual Gifts [vol. 2],* pp. 49, 50.

HOWLAND, Stockbridge (1801-1883) and Louisa M. (1806-1897)

The Howlands were close friends of James and Ellen White, and were among the earliest Adventists in Maine to adopt Sabbathkeeping. According to their respective obituaries, Louisa (née Morse) and Stockbridge Howland began to keep the Sabbath in the spring of 1845, i.e., about the same time as Joseph Bates. Earlier they had been active supporters of the Millerite Adventist movement and had "generously imparted of their substance to forward the work" to the point that they were "in close circumstances," as Ellen White put it. Unsympathetic local authorities probably feared that the Howlands' zealous generosity would result in penury and that the family would become a public charge, so Stockbridge, like some other Millerites, was for a time placed under a guardian to handle his business affairs.

Records indicate that a number of meetings and conferences were held at the Howlands' home in Topsham, Maine, during the 1840s and 1850s. Stockbridge Howland, a millwright by trade, also served as local agent for Review and Herald publications and sat on the "tent committee" for Maine. In 1869 or 1870 the Howlands moved to Allegan, Michigan, and later to Battle Creek in the same state, where they stayed the remainder of their lives. During this period Stockbridge was frequently appointed as a delegate to General Conference sessions.

In the late 1840s and early 1850s especially, when Ellen and James White were struggling with poverty and exhausting responsibilities, the Howlands were remarkably supportive. Thus, after the birth of Henry White, the Howlands shared their house with the Whites for six months during the winter of 1847-1848 while James worked at manual jobs in the vicinity. Some months later, in November 1848, because of 1-year-old Henry's fragile health and the arduous travel schedules facing the Whites, the Howland family volunteered to look after Henry. It was an arrangement that was to last for five years. James and Ellen White were ever after grateful for their help. "We are not able to express the gratitude we owe that dear family" wrote James in 1853. Some of the many letters from James and Ellen to the Howlands during the five years they cared for Henry have been preserved and contain valuable biographical information.

See: Obituary: "Stockbridge Howland," *Review*, Apr. 17, 1883, p. 254; obituary: "Louisa M. Howland," *Review*, Mar. 9, 1897, p. 160; Abner Morse, *Memorial of the Morses; Containing the History of Seven Persons of the Name Who Settled in America in the Seventeenth Century With a Catalogue of Ten Thousand of Their Descendants* (Boston: William Veazie, 1850), p. 134; J. N. Loughborough, *The Great Second Advent Movement,* p. 170; Ellen G. White, *Spiritual Gifts [vol. 2],* pp. 87, 104-108; 1870 U.S. Federal Census, "Howland, Stockbridge," Michigan, Allegan County, Allegan, p. 31; James White, "Eastern Tour," *Review,* Nov. 1, 1853, p. 133; search term "Howland" in *Review and Herald* online collection, www.adventistarchives.org.

HOWLETT, John (1796-1892) and **Caroline** (c. 1811-1861)

John Howlett emigrated from England to Canada East in 1834. A former Methodist minister, Howlett, together with his wife, accepted William Milller's teachings in 1843, and in 1859 they became Sabbatarian Adventists. A few months later the Howletts met James and Ellen White at a conference in Berkshire, northern Vermont. Ellen White noted in her diary that "Brother Howlett, an old Methodist minister, spoke. He spoke with fervor and intelligence." Of his wife, Ellen White wrote, "Sister Howlett arose . . .

and gave a most stirring exhortation." Caroline Howlett died two years later, aged about 50, but John Howlett lived to 96. He died in Battle Creek, Michigan.

See: Obituary: "John Howlett," *Review,* Nov. 29, 1892, p. 751; obituary: "Sister Howlet," *Review,* June 18, 1861, p. 31; obituary: "Elizabeth Cross-Clark," *Review,* Sept. 10, 1925, p. 21; Denis Fortin, *Adventism in Quebec,* pp. 79, 80, 98; 1871 Canada Census, "John Howlet," Quebec, Sutton, p. 58; Sister C. Howlet, "Extracts From Letters," *Review,* Oct. 16, 1860, p. 175; Ellen G. White, Ms 8, 1859 (Oct. 15 entry); Ms 9, 1862 (Nov.).

HUNGERFORD, Sealey (Seley) P. (1811-1868) and (first wife) **Mary Ann** (1816-1857) and (second wife) **Cynthia** (1822-1875)

Church members from Bedford, later Ross, Michigan. Born in Massachusetts and New York, respectively, Sealey Hungerford and Mary Ann Gilbert married in 1832 and migrated to Michigan at some point before 1840 and engaged in farming. After Mary Ann's death in 1857, Sealey married her sister Cynthia.

Judging from receipts appearing in the *Review* and from Mary Ann's obituary, the Hungerfords became Sabbathkeepers by 1853 or early 1854 while living in Bedford. Some months later, in the summer of 1854, Ellen White gave serious counsel to Sealey Hungerford. His life "did not show the fruits of a Christian" and "brought a reproach upon the cause." Little is known about Sealey after this except that he continued his *Review* subscription to within a few years of his death in 1868.

See: Geoffrey Gilbert, *Gilberts of New England: Part I. Descendants of John Gilbert of Dorchester* (Victoria, British Columbia: 1959), pp. 202, 204; obituary: "Mary Hungerford," *Review,* Aug. 13, 1857, p. 119; 1850 U.S. Federal Census, "Seley [*sic*] P. Hungerford," Michigan, Calhoun County, Bedford, p. 99; 1860 U.S. Federal Census, "Seely [*sic*] Hungerford," Michigan, Kalamazoo County, Ross, p. 23; search term "Hungerford" in *Review and Herald* online collection, www.adventistarchives.org; Ellen G. White, Lt 8, 1854 (July).

HUTCHINS, Alfred S. (1823-1894) and (first wife) **Esther M.** (1834-1860) and (second wife) **Abigail ("Abbie") D.** (1836-1902)

A minister and administrator, Alfred Hutchins was honored by his obituarist as "almost . . . the father of the [Vermont] Conference" for his long and devoted service in that state dating back to 1852. Just prior to that time he had been a minister in the Freewill Baptist Church for five years. From 1852 to the early 1860s A. S. Hutchins preached widely in New England, New York, Michigan, Illinois, Pennsylvania, and Canada East. For the next 20 years his efforts were more focused on Vermont, where he also served as conference president from 1875 to 1885. Hutchins suffered from poor health during much of his working life and spent protracted periods receiving treatment at the sanitarium in Battle Creek, Michigan.

A. S. Hutchins married Esther M. Barrows, also of Vermont, probably in 1855 or

1856. Esther came from a family with Millerite background and had been baptized a Sabbatarian Adventist by Joseph Bates in 1849 or 1850. After her marriage she assisted Alfred in his evangelistic work and accompanied him on his travels, for which she was later commended by Ellen White. Esther died at age 26 in 1860. Alfred subsequently married Esther's sister, Abigail Barrows.

Hutchins was a firm supporter of the visions of Ellen White, even when he was the object of censure. His faith was especially tested in 1864 when he received a testimony of reproof for being too "exacting" and "fault-finding" in his pastoral work. Ellen White urged Hutchins "to comfort and entreat the church and lay aside the whip." Some months later in a short article to the *Review* he humbly craved "for wisdom to improve under the chastening rod," probably a reference to his own recent experience.

See: Obituary: "A. S. Hutchins," *Review,* July 17, 1894, p. 458; obituary: "Esther M. Hutchins," *Review,* June 5, 1860, p. 23; obituary: "A. D. Hutchins," *Review,* May 13, 1902, p. 31; Arthur H. Locke, *A History and Genealogy of Captain John Locke [1627-1696] of Portsmouth and Rye, N.H., and His Descendants Also of Nathaniel Locke of Portsmouth and a Short Account of the History of the Lockes in England* (Concord, N.H.: Rumford Press, 1916?), p. 115; Pekka Ilmari Tahti, "'The Father of the Vermont Conference,' The Study of Alfred S. Hutchins, One of the First Pioneers of the Seventh-day Adventist Church" (Berrien Springs, Mich.: Seventh-day Adventist Theological Seminary, Andrews University, 1975); Ellen G. White, Lt 10, 1863 (Nov. 28); Lt 5, 1864 (Feb. 22); A. S. Hutchins, "Guarding the Wrong Point," *Review,* June 14, 1864, p. 1; Denis Fortin, *Adventism in Quebec,* pp. 75-77, 82-84, 95, 96, 114, 116.

INMAN, Eldad (c. 1814-after 1880) and (first wife) **Catharine** (1813-1864) and (second wife) **Rebecca** (1819-after 1880)

Farmers from Cass County, Michigan, Eldad and Catharine Inman started keeping the Sabbath in 1858. Ellen White met Eldad Inman, apparently for the first time, in Monterey, Michigan, in January 1859. "It seems to me," she noted in her diary, that "he has too much of the minister about him, . . . prays lengthy, and exhorts lengthy." It is possible that Inman questioned the visions, because in the same diary entry Ellen White mentioned that "Father Fisher read to him [Inman] a long piece he had written against the visions." Little is known of Inman's subsequent course, but receipts and subscriptions to the *Review* in his name continued into the late 1870s, indicating his continuing relationship with the church.

See: 1860 U.S. Federal Census, "Eldad Inman," Michigan, Cass County, La Grange, p. 13; 1870 U.S. Federal Census, "Eldad Inman," Michigan, Berrien County, Benton, p. 43; 1880 U.S. Federal Census, "Eldad Innman [*sic*]," Michigan, Allegan County, Manlius, p. 20; obituary: "Catharine Inman," *Review,* Apr. 26, 1864, p. 175; E. Inman to "Bro. Smith," *Review,* July 15, 1858, p. 71; Ellen G. White, Ms 5, 1859 (Jan. 17 entry); search term "Inman" in *Review and Herald* online collection, www.adventistarchives.org.

IRVING, Agnes. See IRVING, William and Catherine.

IRVING, William (c. 1813-1859) and Catherine (c. 1818-?) and (daughter) Agnes (c. 1842-1891)

William Irving, a farmer from Ross, Michigan, became a Sabbathkeeper about 1857. In 1859 Ellen White described the family as "poor. . . . Their crops have failed. They have breadstuff to buy and nothing to buy with." William Irving died in 1859 at age 46 of tuberculosis, leaving Catherine and several children.

James and Ellen White helped the Irving family with gifts of clothing and money. They also employed Agnes (Agnes Nye), one of the Irving daughters, in their home for some months in 1859 and launched an appeal on behalf of the bereaved family through the newly founded paper, *The Good Samaritan,* in December 1859.

See: Obituary, "William Irving," *Review,* June 9, 1859, p. 23; 1860 U.S. Federal Census, "Catherine Irving," Michigan, Kalamazoo County, Ross, p. 25; Ellen G. White, Ms 5, 1859 (Jan. 6 entry); Ellen G. White, "From My Diary," *The Good Samaritan,* December 1859, pp. 5, 6; Harriet N. Smith et al., "Widow Cranson," *The Good Samaritan,* February 1860, p. 12; Washington Gardner, *History of Calhoun County, Michigan; a Narrative Account of Its Historical Progress, Its People, and Its Principal Interests* (New York: Lewis Pub. Co., 1913), vol. 2, p. 1151.

JONES, Charles (1822-1904) and (first wife) Sarah A. (c. 1824-1882) and (second wife) Jane Cordelia (1831-1910)

A Millerite in his youth and a carpenter by trade, Charles Jones moved to Monterey, Michigan, in 1853, with his wife, Sarah. In 1854 they became Sabbathkeeping Adventists under the preaching of M. E. Cornell. Jones subsequently served as elder of the Monterey church for 40 years. In 1862 the Monterey church "voted that Bro. Charles Jones take the oversight of the building of the new meeting house."

Among the Monterey members was the aged Joseph Bates, who spent his last 12 years in Monterey. Before Bates's death in 1872 Ellen White entrusted Charles Jones with ensuring that Bates did not overtax his strength by traveling and preaching. There is evidence that Jones held the visions of Ellen White in high regard. When, in 1860, her "Testimony for Monterey" included some straight counsel to the Jones family on the upbringing of their son, Charles's response, recorded in the Monterey church minutes, was that he "believed evry [*sic*] word of the testimony." Later, in the mid-1870s, when W. H. Littlejohn created serious division among the churches in Monterey and vicinity by accusations against Ellen White, Charles Jones was among her firm supporters.

See: 1860 U.S. Federal Census, "Charles Jones," Michigan, Allegan County, Monterey, p. 140; 1900 U.S. Federal Census, "Charles Jones," Michigan, Allegan County, Monterey,

p. 15A; obituary: "Charles Jones," *Review,* Mar. 24, 1904, p. 23; obituary: "Sarah A. Jones," *Review,* May 2, 1882, p. 286; obituary: "Jane Cordelia Jones," *Review,* Dec. 29, 1910, p. 23; "Records of the Seventh-day Adventist Church, Monterey, Michigan [1860-1880]," minutes for Jan. 6, 1861, and Jan. 5, 1862 (Berrien Springs, Mich.: Center for Adventist Research, Andrews University, n.d.), pp. 7, 26; Ellen G. White, Lt 2, 1872 (Feb. 12); Ms 4, 1860 (Dec.); Lt 16, 1875 (June 6).

JONES, Leander M. (1824-1902) and (first wife) **Harriet** (c. 1818-1869) and (second wife) **Caroline M.** (c. 1843-?)

Leander Jones, a carpenter from Monterey, Michigan, became a Sabbathkeeper in 1856, probably together with Harriet. Jones was an active and leading member of his local church. He and his family appear to have been close friends of the Whites. In her diaries Ellen White mentioned several occasions on which the Whites stayed at the Jones home while visiting Monterey. This probably explains James White's fond comment made in 1866: "We stopped at our old home, in the family of Bro. L. M. Jones, where, as usual, we received every possible act of kindness." Jones married Caroline in 1870 after the death of his first wife.

See: Obituary: "L. M. Jones," *Review,* Jan. 28, 1902, p. 62; obituary: "Harriet Jones," *Review,* June 22, 1869, p. 206; 1870 U.S. Federal Census, "Leander M. Jones," Michigan, Allegan County, Allegan, p. 31; Ellen G. White, Ms 5, 1859 (entries for Jan. 13-16); Ms 8, 1859 (Nov. 18 entry); Ms 16, 1868 (entries for May 2-9); James White, "Report From Bro. White," *Review,* June 19, 1866, p. 20; search term "L. M. Jones" in *Words of the Pioneers.*

JONES, Orrin B. (1825-1883) and **Elizabeth** (c. 1830-after 1883)

A carpenter and builder by trade, Orrin Jones and his brothers, **Leander M. Jones** and **Charles Jones**, also carpenters, settled in Monterey, Michigan, in the mid-1850s. Charles had a Millerite Adventist background, so it is possible that Orrin Jones shared the same experience. He became a Sabbatarian Adventist in 1857 and was chosen as deacon of the Monterey church in 1861, in which year he also supervised the construction of a two-story brick building to house the Review and Herald press in Battle Creek.

In the early 1870s Orrin Jones was again called upon to erect additional press buildings and the three-story Battle Creek College. James White was impressed with the quality of Jones's work and in 1875 called for him to come out to Oakland, California, to construct a building for the newly established press (later "Pacific Press"). In the face of complaints from local Adventist carpenters who could see no reason to import labor from the East, James White endorsed Jones for his "ability and faithfulness." As a result, Orrin and his brother, Charles, spent two years in the Oakland-San Francisco area engaged in several building projects for the church. On returning to Michigan, Orrin Jones supervised the construction in 1877-1878 of a four-story brick building later known as the Battle Creek Sanitarium.

There are no known letters from Ellen White to Orrin Jones. A few mentions are found, such as eating breakfast at Jones's house in 1859 and an account of a sailing excursion with the Jones brothers and others in San Francisco Bay in 1876. "The wind was blowing strong and I never enjoyed anything as much in my life," Ellen White reported.

See: Obituary: "Orrin B. Jones," *Review*, Aug. 28, 1883, p. 559; 1860 U.S. Federal Census, "Elizabeth Jones," Michigan, Allegan County, Monterey, p. 140; [news item] *Signs of the Times*, Mar. 25, 1875, p. 160; "Records of the Seventh-day Adventist Church, Monterey, Michigan [1860-1880]," minutes for Nov. 9, 1861 (Berrien Springs, Mich.: Center for Adventist Research, Andrews University, n.d.), p. 22; J. N. Loughborough, "Conference Address," *Review*, Oct. 19, 1876, p. 122; J. W. [James White], "How We Found Things," *Review*, Oct. 21, 1875, p. 124; search term "O. B. Jones" or "Orrin B. Jones" in *Review and Herald* online collection, www.adventistarchives.org; Ellen G. White, Ms 8, 1859 (Nov. 18 entry); Lt 5, 1876 (Apr. 11).

JONES, Victor ("Victory") V. (c. 1826-?) and (first wife) **Elizabeth L.** (1833-1908) and (second wife) **Emily** (fl. 1863)

Born in New York State, Victor Jones settled in Monterey, Michigan, in 1856 and soon joined the growing band of Sabbatarian Adventists in the village. Victor and Elizabeth Jones struggled with poverty, and in 1857 Ellen White upbraided wealthier church members in Monterey for not giving the Jones family more support and encouragement.

A crisis occurred in September 1860 when the Monterey church disfellowshipped Victor Jones, probably for his use of alcohol, to which he had a propensity. A few months later Ellen White sent him a stirring appeal. "You are a kind husband and father when your reason is not perverted by strong drink. . . . We feel deeply for you. We cannot leave you to perish." Shortly thereafter Jones was reinstated to church fellowship. Problems, however, reappeared, and by 1864 Elizabeth had divorced Victor and married a wealthy Adventist neighbor, **George T. Lay**. The dubious circumstances leading up to this marriage and the damage the whole affair had caused the church in Monterey were the subject of Ellen White's Ms 2, 1863 (June 6) and Lt 2, 1864 (c. 1864). Records indicate that Victor Jones married Emily Donalson in 1863, but no information on his life after that date has been found.

See: 1860 U.S. Federal Census, "Victor Jones," Michigan, Allegan County, Monterey, p. 142; *History of Allegan and Barry Counties*, pp. 289, 290; obituary: "Elizabeth L. Lay," *Review*, Sept. 10, 1908, p. 23; "Victor V. Jones" in Jack and Marianne Dibean, *Calhoun County, Michigan, Dibean Marriage Index* (2003-2008), http://files.usgwarchives.org/mi/calhoun/vitals/marriages/dbn-feb-2011-j.txt (Oct. 14, 2011); "Records of the Seventh-day Adventist Church, Monterey, Michigan [1860-1880]," minutes for Sept. 15, 1860, and Mar. 3, 1861 (Berrien Springs, Mich.: Center for Adventist Research, Andrews University, n.d.), pp. 4, 9; Ellen G. White, Lt 9, 1857 (Oct.); Lt 1, 1861 (Jan.).

KELLOGG, Albert (1836-1913) and **Lucina** (1840-1916)

Albert Kellogg was the third son of **John Preston Kellogg** and a half brother of John

Harvey Kellogg. Albert first joined Sabbathkeeping Adventists in Tyrone, Michigan, in 1853. In 1854, with the beginning of tent evangelism in Michigan, he apparently served as "tent master" for a time. His occupations included "grocer," "gardener," and "broom maker." Albert married Lucina Ashley in the early 1860s, but census records indicate that they were separated or divorced by 1900.

In letters written to the Kelloggs in the 1850s and 1860s Ellen White related visions given her regarding the family. In a letter from about 1861 she counseled Albert regarding his relationship with his father and on his lack of spiritual devotion. In a subsequent letter written a few years later she wrote that Albert had not heeded the earlier admonition, and she cautioned him on allowing his business pursuits to overshadow his spiritual life.

See: Obituary: "Albert Kellogg," *Review,* May 29, 1913, p. 527; obituary: "Lucina Ashley," *Review,* Apr. 20, 1916, p. 22; Timothy Hopkins, *The Kelloggs in the Old World and the New,* vol. 1, p. 636; 1870 U.S. Federal Census, "Albert Kellog [*sic*]," Michigan, Ottawa County, Wright, p. 8; 1880 U.S. Federal Census, "Albert Kellogg," Michigan, Kalamazoo County, Kalamazoo, p. 38; 1900 U.S. Federal Census, "Lusina Kellogg," Michigan, Calhoun County, Battle Creek, Ward 3, Precinct 2, p. 4A; 1910 U.S. Federal Census, "Albert Kellogg," Michigan, Gratiot County, Washington, p. 11A; Ellen G. White, Lt 6, 1856 (c. 1856); Lt 15, 1861 (c. 1861); Lt 17, 1864 (c. 1864).

KELLOGG, John Preston (1807-1881) and (first wife) **Mary Ann** (1811-1841) and (second wife) **Ann Janette** (1824-1893)

An active layperson and financial benefactor, J. P. Kellogg was the father of Dr. Merritt Gardner Kellogg, Dr. John Harvey Kellogg, Will Keith Kellogg of cereal fame, and 13 other children. J. P. Kellogg migrated from Massachusetts to Michigan in 1834, eventually settling in Battle Creek in 1856 for the remainder of his life. Together with his second wife, Ann, he became a Sabbathkeeper in 1852.

Successful in both farming and, later, broom manufacturing, Kellogg liberally supported the young Sabbatarian movement with donations and loans. J. N. Loughborough related how in the early 1850s Kellogg sold his farm "for the sole purpose of having means to use in advancing the work." He liberally supported the young movement with donations and investments in such major ventures as the establishment of the Review and Herald press in Battle Creek in 1855 and the support of the Health Reform Institute, which opened in 1866. Kellogg's financial and administrative talents were also tapped, as he served on the board of directors of the Health Reform Institute and on a number of committees, including the publishing committee of the Seventh-day Adventist Publishing Association.

Several testimonies from Ellen White to J. P. Kellogg survive from the 1850s and 1860s. One recurring theme was Kellogg's tendency to gloominess: "You forget the good and can only see the evil and the dark." She urged him to "turn from these things and believe in God." In another letter (c. 1864) she warned Kellogg that he had become "too much engrossed" in his business to the detriment of his spiritual health and to the neglect of his family. In her diaries and letters of 1859 and 1860 Ellen White mentioned several enjoyable visits with Kellogg's second wife, Ann. Elsewhere Ann was described as a "good . . . kind and tender mother" who looked after John Preston's children from his first marriage "as if they were flesh of her flesh."

See: Obituary: "J. P. Kellogg," *Review,* May 31, 1881, p. 350; SDAE, s.v. "John Preston Kellogg"; Richard W. Schwarz, *John Harvey Kellogg, M.D.,* pp. 13-17; J. N. Loughborough, *The Great Second Advent Movement,* pp. 287, 561; Timothy Hopkins, *The Kelloggs in the Old World and the New,* vol. 1, pp. 288, 636; Ellen G. White, Lt 18, 1860 (Nov. 2); Lt 15, 1861 (c. 1861); Lt 17, 1864 (c. 1864).

KELLOGG, Smith Moses (1834-1927) and **Maria Susan** (c. 1837-1911)

Born in Hadley, Massachusetts, Smith M. Kellogg was the son of **John Preston Kellogg** and half brother of John Harvey Kellogg. He attended Oberlin College for a time in his youth and in 1858 married Maria Dickinson, daughter of **Preston** and **Celesta Dickinson**, who were among the first group of Adventists to keep the Sabbath in Michigan. Smith Kellogg engaged in various types of business enterprise, including broom manufacture and patent medicines in Michigan, Wisconsin, and Illinois. The last 23 years of his life he was blind. Smith and Maria Kellogg remained church members throughout their lives. Smith is listed as a "licentiate" minister in the 1888 *Seventh-day Adventist Yearbook.*

Smith Kellogg is mentioned in three letters from Ellen White to his parents in the 1850s and 1860s. She acknowledged that Smith had caused his parents much grief by his course of action in his youth and in his marriage, but she counseled them in 1861 that "Smith has been trying to return to the Lord" and urged the parents to bring about a reconciliation. In the same letter she gave a positive assessment of Maria: "Maria loves God. She loves the truth and will be a help to Smith."

See: Obituary: "Smith M. Kellogg," *Review,* Feb. 9, 1928, p. 22; Timothy Hopkins, *The Kelloggs in the Old World and the New,* vol. 2, p. 1315; M. G. Kellogg, *Notes Concerning the Kellogg's* [*sic*] (Battle Creek, Mich.: n.p., 1927, reprint 1990), pp. [119, 120]; *Seventh-day Adventist Yearbook* (Battle Creek, Mich.: Review and Herald Publishing House, 1888), p. 3; 1870 U.S. Federal Census, "Smith M. Kellogg," Michigan, Branch County, Union, p. 24; Ellen G. White, Lt 6, 1856 (c. 1856); Lt 15, 1861 (c. 1861).

KELSEY, Eunice Rebecca (1820-1906) and **Asa Post H.** (1818-1857)

Asa and Eunice Kelsey settled in Leroy Township, near Battle Creek, Michigan, prior to 1840 and became Sabbathkeepers in 1852. According to Eunice Kelsey's obituary, "it was from Brother Kelsey's sawmill that lumber was secured for the erection of the first church building" in Battle Creek (1855). Eunice was left a widow in 1857 with four children, and Ellen White wrote caringly in her 1859 diary, "I feel the deepest sympathy for this devoted widow."

Eunice Kelsey's older daughter, Hannah Louise, married Edwin R. Jones, minister and church administrator in Michigan, Colorado, and the West Coast. Her younger daughter, Mary Ellen, married James and Ellen White's son **William Clarence White** in 1876. Ellen White developed a warm relationship with Eunice and often referred to her fondly as "Mother Kelsey" in her diaries and correspondence.

See: Obituary: "Eunice Rebecca Kelsey," *Review,* June 21, 1906, p. 23; obituary: "A.P.H. Kelsey," *Review,* Aug. 13, 1857, p. 119; Edward A. Claypool and Azalea Clizbee, *A Genealogy of the Descendants of William Kelsey Who Settled at Cambridge, Mass., in 1632; at Hartford, Conn., in 1636; and at Killingworth, Conn., in 1663* (Bridgeport, Conn.: Marsh Press, Inc., 1947), vol. 3, pp. 622, 623, 785, 786; Ellen G. White, Ms 5, 1859 (Mar. 2 entry); SDAE, s.v., "Mary (Kelsey) White."

KING, Anna Lucretia (née BURWELL) (1844-1931) and James Henry (1842-1922)

In letters to Anna's parents, **Anthony** and **Achsah Burwell**, Ellen White showed great concern and anxiety for the spiritual welfare of Anna during her teenage years. She subsequently became a lifelong Seventh-day Adventist.

See: Obituary: "James Henry King," *Review,* Dec. 7, 1922, p. 22; obituary: "Anna Lucretia King," *Review,* Mar. 5, 1931, p. 28; Herbert Cornelius Andrews et al., *Hinsdale Genealogy: Descendants of Robert Hinsdale of Dedham, Medfield, Hadley and Deerfield, With an Account of the French Family of De Hinnisdal* (Lombard, Ill.: A. H. Andrews, 1906), pp. 148, 384; Ellen G. White, Lt 1, 1857 (Jan. 28); Lt 2, 1857 (Oct. 21); search terms "Anna L. Burwell" and "A. L. Burwell" in *Review and Herald* online collection, www.adventistarchives.org.

LAMSON, David Henry (1835-1897) and Elizabeth Louise (1838-1926)

An ordained minister originally from New York, D. H. Lamson preached widely throughout the Michigan Conference for more than 20 years and in Nebraska and Indiana during the last four years of his life. After his ordination in 1871 he frequently served on conference and General Conference committees. Elizabeth (née Chappell) taught public school before her marriage to David Lamson in 1857. One of their daughters, Mary Elizabeth Lamson, later became preceptor at Emmanuel Missionary College, now Andrews University, where the present women's residence hall is named in her honor.

Of the two extant letters from Ellen White to D. H. Lamson, one is of special interest, having been written shortly after the 1888 General Conference session in Minneapolis, Minnesota. D. H. Lamson was among those leading ministers who opposed Ellen White, E. J. Waggoner, and A. T. Jones on the issue of righteousness by faith, which was the focus of the session. Among other concerns raised in the letter, Ellen White was clearly trying to bring about a change of mind and heart in Elder Lamson on this issue.

See: Obituary: "David Henry Lamson," *Review,* Oct. 26, 1897, p. 687; obituary:

"Elizabeth Louise Chappell," *Lake Union Herald*, June 23, 1926, p. 5; search term "D. H. Lamson" in *Review and Herald* online collection, www.adventistarchives.org; U. S. [Uriah Smith], "The Michigan Camp-Meeting," *Review*, Sept. 19, 1871, p. 108; SDAE, s.v. "Mary Elizabeth Lamson"; Bert Haloviak, "From Righteousness to Holy Flesh: Judgment at Minneapolis" (Takoma Park, Md.: 1987), chap. 6, p. 21 [www.adventistarchives.org/doc_info.asp?DocID=17757]; Ellen G. White, Lt 10, 1856 (Jan.); Lt 48, 1888 (Dec. 13).

LAMSON, Joseph Bradley (c. 1829-1870) and **Drusilla** (c. 1831-1919)

J. B. Lamson, farmer and active layman from the Rochester, New York, area, was elected treasurer of the New York Conference when it was first organized in 1862. Drusilla (née Orton) was widowed at 39 when her husband died in 1870 of "quick consumption and typhoid fever." Her father, **Jonathan T. Orton**, had been murdered just four years earlier, in 1866.

In the late 1870s Drusilla Lamson was employed at Battle Creek Sanitarium as matron. Ellen White's *Testimony for the Physicians and Helpers of the Sanitarium* pointed to several weaknesses in her work. In particular, she had failed to uphold "the distinct and separate character" of the sanitarium.

In 1893 Drusilla Lamson wrote to J. N. Loughborough, giving her eyewitness testimony confirming Ellen White's vision experiences. Nevertheless, Dudley M. Canright claimed that "Mrs. Lamson and Miss Fellows, both matrons of the sanitarium, lost faith in the doctrine." This may explain why Drusilla Lamson's obituary does not appear in the *Review* at her death in 1919.

See: Obituary, "J. B. Lamson," *Review*, Feb. 15, 1870, p. 71; SDAE, s.v. "New York Conference"; Ellen G. White, *Testimony for the Physicians and Helpers of the Sanitarium* (n.p., c. 1879), pp. 7, 8, 77, 78, 91; J. N. Loughborough, *The Great Second Advent Movement*, p. 208; D. M. Canright, *Seventh-Day Adventism Renounced*, p. 64.

LANDON, Warren E. (1824-1913) and (first wife) **Mary F.** (1824-1883) and (second wife) **Adeline E.** (1828-after 1900)

A blacksmith by trade, Warren Landon spent most of his life in Connecticut after moving from Vermont in his early years. Although initially "opposed bitterly" by his wife, he left the Baptist Church in 1853 and became a Sabbatarian Adventist, soon to be joined by Mary. Scattered notices in the *Review* indicate that Warren Landon was an active layperson, holding meetings in his house, paying for extra copies of the *Review* to share with friends and relatives, and occasionally serving on various New England Conference committees in the 1880s. The only extant letter from Ellen White relating to the Landons dates from 1859, in which she counseled them to exercise "decision and firmness in the government of their children."

See: Norton William Jipson, *A History & Genealogy of the Descendents* [*sic*] *of John Jepson, of England and Boston, Mass., Through His Son John's Two Sons William and Micah, 1610-1917* (Janesville, Wis.: The Gazette Press, 1917), p. 41; obituary: "Warren E. Landon," *Atlantic Union Gleaner,* Feb. 5, 1913, p. 6; obituary: "Mary F. Landon," *Review,* Feb. 5, 1884, p. 94; 1850 U.S. Federal Census, "Warren E. Landon," Connecticut, Hartford County, Farmington, p. 344; 1900 U.S. Federal Census, "Adeline E. Landon," Connecticut, Windham County, Ashford, p. 6B; search term "Landon" in *Review and Herald* online collection, www.adventistarchives.org; "Letter From W. E. Landon," *Review,* July 24, 1856, p. 95; Ellen G. White, Lt 7, 1859 (Sept. 24).

LANE, James (1807-1880) and **Sarah** (1810-1905)

Church members living in Convis Township, Michigan, employed as innkeepers and farmers. James and Sarah Lane, immigrants from England, were among the first four settlers in their area, arriving in 1835. Relations with local Indians were tenuous. At one point a band of Indians broke down the door of their tavern and made off with a keg of brandy while the Lane family cowered in the attic. James Lane became prominent in township affairs. The establishment of Convis Township in 1837 took place in the Lane house, and James frequently held civic office in the years that followed.

Sarah Lane became a Sabbathkeeping Adventist in 1857 and was among the charter members when the Convis Seventh-day Adventist Church was organized in 1861. James Lane did not become a member till later; the exact date is not known. He continued to operate a tavern until 1862. After James's death in 1880, Uriah Smith noted in the obituary that Lane had joined the Convis church "a few years ago." Sarah Lane received only incidental mention in the writings of Ellen White, who noted in her 1859 diary that "Sister Lane . . . came from Convis to the meeting at Battle Creek."

See: Obituary: "James Lane," *Review,* Aug. 26, 1880, p. 158; obituary: "Sarah Lane," *Review,* Apr. 6, 1905, p. 23; H. B. Peirce, *History of Calhoun County, Michigan,* pp. 153-155; Ellen G. White, Ms 6, 1859 (Apr. 23 entry).

LAY, George Talbot (1822-1901) and (first wife) **Mary Exene** (1825-1862) and (second wife) **Elizabeth L.** (1833-1908)

A wealthy landowner and business entrepreneur from Monterey and Allegan, Michigan, George Lay had a checkered relationship with the Seventh-day Adventist Church. Baptized together with Mary in 1856 by Joseph Bates, he was active in the Monterey church for a few years and was elected church deacon.

Troubles began when, after Mary's death, he married a recent divorcé, **Elizabeth L. Jones,** in 1864, under dubious circumstances. He did this despite the pleas of Ellen White in 1863 that the proposed marriage would damage not only his own reputation but also that of the local church. According to an investigating church committee, George Lay "recklessly burnt" his copy of this manuscript. For a few years he was separated from church fellowship, but Ellen White made strong efforts to reclaim him in 1868. "Rode over to Brother George Lay's," she wrote in a diary entry on May 9, 1868. "Had an interview with his family. Prayed with them and left them weeping, all broken down before the Lord."

Following Ellen White's intervention in 1868, George Lay returned to church fellowship for a few years. In 1872 he was elected vice president of the Missionary and Tract Society for the Michigan and Indiana Conference. However, by 1874 George Lay had again relapsed, and from available documentation he seems from then on to have remained outside the church until within a year or two of his death in 1901. Much of his disinterest, according to Ellen White, was because of his total absorption with his business and wealth. By 1880 George Lay was the largest landowner in Monterey, and in 1883 he helped to organize the Michigan Buggy Company in Kalamazoo, serving as its vice president until his death.

In 1885, when George Lay was in his early 60s, Ellen White reminded him that his "sun passed its meridian some time ago and is now rapidly declining," and she appealed to him "from this hour" "to be the Lord's." She also cautioned him not to "force from His reluctant hand destruction of your property or affliction of your person." The latter warning probably came to George Lay's mind when, in 1896, the Michigan Buggy factory burned down with a loss of $63,000. The factory was rebuilt and enlarged, but again it burned to the ground, with a loss of $249,000. Insurance covered only a fraction of the losses. The warnings and ensuing disasters may explain why George Lay subsequently returned to the church. On receiving this news, Ellen White wrote a warm letter to Lay in 1900. "I have heard that you have commenced once more to serve the Lord. I am more glad than I can tell you."

See: Obituary: "George T. Lay," *Review,* Apr. 16, 1901, p. 256; obituary: "Mary E. Lay," *Review,* Dec. 16, 1862, p. 23; obituary: "Elizabeth L. Lay," *Review,* Sept. 10, 1908, p. 23; J. N. Loughborough, George W. Amadon, "Decision of the Committee in the Case of George T. Lay, c. 1864," Ellen G. White Estate, DF 287; "75-50-25 years ago," *Review,* Feb. 27, 1947, p. 2; *History of Allegan and Barry Counties, Michigan,* pp. 285, 288-290; David Fisher and Frank Little, *Compendium of History and Biography of Kalamazoo County, Mich.* (Chicago: A. W. Bowen & Co., 1906), pp. 276, 277; Ellen G. White, Ms 2, 1863 (June 6); Ms 16, 1868 (May 9 entry); Lt 58, 1874 (Nov. 4); *Testimonies for the Church,* vol. 5, pp. 349-354; Lt 15, 1900 (Feb. 1).

LAY, Horatio S. (1828-1900) and **Julia M.** (1831-1893)

Horatio Lay served as medical director of the Western Health Reform Institute in Battle Creek, Michigan, from the time of its opening in 1866 to 1870. He also edited the first Seventh-day Adventist health journal, the *Health Reformer,* from 1866 to 1868. Lay was listed as a medical student in the *Catalogue of the Officers and Students in the Western Reserve College 1848-9.* From 1850 to 1864 he practiced medicine in Allegan, Michigan, and then spent two years on the staff of "Our Home Hygienic Institute" in Dansville, New York, which emphasized features of health reform such as vegetarianism and hydrotherapy.

Some of the reasons for Lay's dismissal from the health institute in 1870 are suggested in a February 13 letter from Ellen White to "Brother and Sister Lay." There is no mention of medical incompetence, but rather, among other things, of Horatio's domestic problems, which had diverted his time and attention from the work of the institute. Lay felt he had been unfairly treated, and several years of spiritual decline followed after he returned to his former practice in Allegan. "Brother Lay, you were shown me enshrouded in darkness," Ellen White wrote in 1872. "The love of the world has taken control of your entire being." Even more gloomy was her assessment in 1874: "In regard to Dr. Lay, the testimonies have spoken plainly in his case. He must answer to God for his course. . . . I do not think we can do him or George [his brother, **George T. Lay**] any good."

H. S. Lay gained a medical degree from Detroit Medical College in 1877, and in 1880 the Lays moved to the more salubrious climate of Petoskey in northern Michigan. Positive reports started to come to the *Review* of Dr. Lay's missionary work in that area. "He has felt much cast down in the past. The Lord has now revealed His Spirit to him, and he is greatly blessed," G. I. Butler testified in 1884. The following year Lay was given ministerial credentials, and for the next decade and more, until ill-health slowed him down, he was active in ministry and evangelism in northern Michigan. "Dr. Lay has made great improvements. He is a good man," Ellen White enthused during an extended summer visit to Petoskey in 1890.

See: Obituary: "Julia M. B. Lay," *Review,* Sept. 12, 1893, p. 591; obituary: "Horatio S. Lay," *Review,* Mar. 13, 1900, p. 176; *Catalogue of the Officers and Students in the Western Reserve College 1848-9* (Hudson, Ohio: Western Reserve College, 1848), p. 8; *History of Allegan and Barry Counties, Michigan,* pp. 158, 159; G. I. B. [George I. Butler], "Camp-Meeting Notes," *Review,* Sept. 9, 1884, p. 584; search term "H. S. Lay" in *Review and Herald* online collection, www.adventistarchives.org; Ellen G. White, Lt 30, 1870 (Feb. 13); Lt 1a, 1872 (Jan. 11); Lt 61, 1874 (Nov. 11); Lt 100, 1890 (Aug. 11).

LEIGHTON, George (1812-1902) and (first wife) **Rocksilda** (c. 1812-1867) and (second wife) **Emily** (1822-after 1900)

A farmer and stonemason from Otsego, Michigan, George Leighton became a Sabbatarian Adventist with his wife, Rocksilda, about 1856 or 1858 (sources disagree). They were charter members of the Otsego church, in which George served as elder until his death. George Leighton assisted in the construction of the Review and Herald, college, and sanitarium buildings in Battle Creek.

Ellen White makes only incidental mention of Leighton. In 1859 she stayed with the Leighton family in Otsego over a weekend, and in 1861 Leighton came to Battle Creek to get the Whites' "cellar fixed."

See: Obituary: "George Leighton," *Review,* Dec. 30, 1902, p. 23; obituary: "Rocksilda Leighton," *Review,* Sept. 24, 1867, p. 238; Henry F. Thomas, *A Twentieth Century History of Allegan County, Michigan* (New York: Lewis Pub. Co., 1907), p. 594; 1900 U.S. Federal Census, "George Leighton," Michigan, Allegan County, Otsego, p. 33; Ellen G. White, Ms 5, 1859 (entries for Jan. 7, 8); Lt 6, 1861 (June 17).

LILLIS, Henry (c. 1807-after 1860) and Eliza (c. 1811-after 1860)

A carpenter living in Oswego, New York, in the 1850s and 1860s, Henry Lillis is most likely the "Lillis" of Oswego mentioned in several Sabbatarian sources of the early 1850s. Ellen White held a meeting in his house in 1850. In 1851, during another meeting in his house, Lillis, apparently of a rash temperament, threatened O.R.L. Crozier that "if he did not go out of his house he would put him out." Crozier, who by this time opposed the Sabbatarian Adventists, complained bitterly of this mistreatment in the *Advent Harbinger.* Ellen White is reported to have reproved Lillis for his rashness.

Sometime between 1854 and 1855 Henry Lillis joined the breakaway *Messenger* Party. Loughborough recorded that he, Cottrell, and the Whites held a meeting in Oswego in 1855, which Lillis disturbed by distributing the dissident party's paper, the *Messenger of Truth.* The last mention of Lillis is in a report in 1858 by James White on the decline of the *Messenger* Party in which he notes that Lillis had become a Spiritualist.

See: 1850 U.S. Federal Census, "Henry Lillis," New York, Oswego County, Oswego, Ward 3, p. 190; 1860 U.S. Federal Census, "Henry Lillies [*sic*]," New York, Oswego County, Oswego, Ward 4, p. 45; Ellen G. White, Lt 8, 1850 (Aug. 4); "The Cause Wounded," *Review,* Aug. 19, 1851, p. 11; O.R.L. Crozier, "Brief Tour: Oswego-Auburn-Seneca Falls-Geneva," *Advent Harbinger and Bible Advocate,* Aug. 16, 1851, p. 70; J. N. Loughborough, *The Great Second Advent Movement,* p. 325; J. W. [James White], "A Sketch of the Rise and Progress of the Present Truth," *Review,* Jan. 14, 1858, p. 77; SDAE, s.v. "*Messenger* Party."

LINDSAY, John M. (c. 1807-1895) and Eliza A. (1816-1890)

Active laypersons from Newfane Township, near Olcott, in western New York. Arriving by ox team from the eastern part of the state in the early 1830s, the Lindsays belonged to the Methodist Episcopal Church and were successful farmers. In 1852 they became Sabbathkeepers and made generous financial contributions to the fledgling movement. At various times during the 1860s and early 1870s John M. Lindsay served on several New York Conference and New England Conference committees. One of the Lindsays' sons, Harmon Lindsay, later served as General Conference treasurer.

Ellen White wrote affectionately of John and Eliza as "faithful burden-bearers in the cause of God." She made particular mention of when, in 1865, the Lindsays came to Rochester, New York, to pray on a daily basis at the bedside of James White, who was seriously ill after his first stroke.

See: Obituary: "John M. Lindsay," *Review,* May 28, 1895, p. 351; obituary: "Eliza A. Lindsay," *Review,* May 13, 1890, p. 303; Edward T. Williams, *Niagara County New York: One Hundred of the Most Wonderful Regions in the World; a Concise Record of Her Progress and People, 1821-1921, Published During Its Centennial Year: Historical* (Chicago: J. H. Beers & Company, 1921), vol. 2, p. 651; *History of Niagara County, N.Y., with Illustrations Descriptive of Its Scenery, Private Residences, Public Buildings, Fine Blocks, and Important Manufactories, and Portraits of Old Pioneers and Prominent Residents* (New York: Sanford & Co., 1878), p. 281; search term "J. M. Lindsay" in *Review and Herald* online collection, www.adventistarchives.org; Ellen G. White, *Testimonies for the Church,* vol. 3, p. 57 ("Brother and Sister I"); *Life Sketches,* p. 171.

LOBDELL, Edward (1817-1883)

Originally a Methodist, Edward Lobdell, a brickmason from Portland, Maine, joined one of the Adventist bodies in 1854. He united with the Sabbatarian Adventists in 1858 after attending public meetings held by James White and J. N. Loughborough in Portland. James White openly praised Lobdell in the *Review* for his generous financial support of various church ventures. Three brief visits by the Whites to Edward Lobdell are recorded. He did not marry.

See: Obituary: "Edward Lobdell," *Review,* Apr. 24, 1883, p. 271; 1870 U.S. Federal Census, "Edward Lobdell," Maine, Cumberland County, Portland, Ward 7, p. 38; search term "Lobdell" in *Review and Herald* online collection, www.adventistarchives.org; J. W. [James White], "Good," *Review,* Jan. 22, 1861, p. 80; *idem,* "Pacific Publishing Association," *Review,* May 27, 1875, p. 176; Ellen G. White, Ms 7, 1859 (Sept. 19 entry); Lt 39a, 1880 (Aug. 26); Lt 42, 1880 (Sept. 22); J. N. Loughborough, "Sketches of the Past—No. 112," *Pacific Union Recorder,* Feb. 23, 1911, p. 1.

LOCKWOOD, Ransom G. (1824-1897) and (first wife) Mary (?-1851) and (second wife) Aurora (1827-1902)

The Lockwoods were close, trusted friends of Ellen and James White, who on various occasions looked after the Whites' children and property in their absence.

Ransom Lockwood, originally from Vermont, became a Sabbathkeeper about 1850. Little is known about his first wife, Mary Adams, who died in her youth, but his second wife, Aurora Butler, was the sister of **George I. Butler**, future General Conference president, and granddaughter of Ezra Butler, eleventh governor of Vermont. Aurora and her family had Millerite roots and began to keep the Sabbath about 1850. She married Ransom Lockwood, a "chair maker," in 1852. By 1859 they had relocated to Battle Creek, Michigan, where they remained for the most part until the 1880s, when they moved to California. For a number of years Aurora Lockwood supervised the "folding" department at the Review and Herald press.

On meeting Aurora Lockwood in 1859, Ellen White noted in her diary that "she is a choice sister, beloved of God and highly respected of all the church." Records indicate that during the summers of 1868 and 1869 the Lockwoods were entrusted to look after the White home and farm in Greenville, Michigan, while the Whites were absent on extended travels. From 1884 to 1888 the Lockwoods undertook similar responsibilities at Ellen White's houses in Healdsburg and St. Helena, California. In 1888 she fondly described "Brother and Sister Lockwood" as "ever kind, sympathetic and true." The bulk of the extant correspondence between the Lockwoods and Ellen White dates from this period and concerns mainly practical matters regarding the houses, orchards, etc. There is also discussion of spiritual matters, in particular, regarding their involvement in E. P. Daniels' controversial revival meetings.

See: Obituary: "Ransom G. Lockwood," *Review,* Sept. 21, 1897, p. 607; obituary: "Aurora Butler Lockwood," *Review,* Jan. 28, 1902, p. 63; *A Brief History and Genealogical Sketch of the First Daniel Griswold of Springfield, Vermont* (Springfield, Vt.: Stiles' Reporter Job Printing Rooms, 1880), p. 22; 1860 U.S. Federal Census, "Ransom G. Lockwood," Michigan, Calhoun County, Battle Creek, p. 23; Ellen G. White, Ms 5, 1859 (Mar. 1 entry); Lt 22, 1868 (Oct. 20); Lt 11, 1869 (Sept. 1); Lt 27, 1888 (May 29). On the Lockwoods' involvement with Daniels, see, for example, R. G. Lockwood to E. G. White, Sept. 22, 1885, Oct. 1, 1885; A. B. Lockwood to E. G. White, Oct. 21, 1885; Ellen White, Lt 10, 1885 (Nov. 4); Lt 36, 1886 (Mar. 16).

LOTHROP, Howard (c. 1805-after 1880) and **Olive** (c. 1807-after 1880)

Howard Lothrop, then living in Eaton, Canada East, was first mentioned in the *Review* in 1850. From 1851 to 1853 Lothrop was active as a Sabbatarian preacher in Canada East as well as undertaking an extensive preaching tour of Vermont, Massachusetts, and Rhode Island. Ellen White, however, was shown in vision in 1852 that Lothrop "had traveled too extensively" and that the effect of his preaching was not positive. On several occasions he was reproved by the Whites for "fanaticism," and he subsequently joined the breakaway *Messenger* Party. After the collapse of that movement, there was some speculation in the *Review* that Howard Lothrop had turned up in Minnesota claiming to be a bona fide Sabbatarian Adventist preacher. James White took the occasion, in 1861, to remind church members to demand identification papers of unknown visiting ministers in order to expose "impostors."

See: 1851 Canada East Census, "Howard Lathrop [*sic*]," Canada East (Quebec) Sherbrooke County, Eaton, p. 41; 1860 U.S. Federal Census, "Howard Lotrop [*sic*]," Minnesota, Goodhue County, Roscoe, p. 112; 1880 U.S. Federal Census, "Howard Lothrop," Minnesota, Goodhue County, Roscoe, p. 10; Ellen G. White, Lt 4, 1852 (Oct. 25); W. [James White], "Our Tour East," *Advent Review,* August 1850 (No. 1), p. 15; search term "Lothrop" in *Words of the Pioneers*; "Organization," *Review,* Aug. 27, 1861, p. 100; SDAE, s.v. "*Messenger* Party."

LOUGHBOROUGH, John Norton (1832-1924) and (first wife) **Mary J.** (1832-1867) and (second wife) **Maggie A.** (c. 1840-1875) and (third wife) **Anna Mariah** (1840-1907)

Pioneer evangelist, administrator, and author of the first history of the Seventh-day Adventist Church, John Loughborough was born in Victor, New York, and began lay preaching for non-Sabbatarian Adventists in 1848, just before his seventeenth birthday.

In 1852 he accepted the seventh-day Sabbath and immediately began to advocate the new teaching. Ordained in 1854, Loughborough preached widely in the Midwest, New York, and the Eastern states before D. T. Bourdeau and he pioneered the Adventist work in California in 1868. His subsequent service included the presidencies of the California Conference (1873-1878 and 1887-1890), Nevada Association (1878), Upper Columbia Conference (1884-1885), and Illinois Conference (1891-1895). Loughborough is also remembered as one of the earliest Adventist workers sent to England, from 1878 to 1883.

Ellen White's working association with Loughborough spanned some six decades. She valued him as a zealous worker "willing to . . . endure any and every privation," and, in the area of administration, as "a safe financier" and capable fund-raiser. In the years of crisis following 1888 she saw in Loughborough "a Caleb . . . bearing a decided testimony in the face of unbelief and doubts" and as a leader who "stood firmly for the testimonies."

Ellen White's letters to John Loughborough were a blend of obvious goodwill together with a completely frank disclosure of his weaknesses. On the question of administration, for example, there was frequent mention of Loughborough's unwillingness to delegate. "Be careful not to feel that you must have every part of [the work] under your immediate supervision and control," she urged. "Let others develop. Give them a chance to work. Censure them not."

John Loughborough's first wife, Mary J. Walker, was admonished in her younger years by Ellen White for her lack of consecration. Mary seems to have taken the admonition to heart. "I believe Mary is doing the best she can," Ellen affirmed in 1865. Mary died in childbirth two years later at age 35. John then married Maggie A. Newman in 1868 just before launching out on a pioneer mission to California, but she also died in her mid-30s, some six years later. John Loughborough also outlived his third wife, Anna Mariah Driscoll, an accountant. She served as auditor and treasurer in several institutions and conferences, as well as matron of the Rural Health Retreat in St. Helena, California (later St. Helena Hospital).

See: J. N. Loughborough, *Rise and Progress of the Seventh-day Adventists*; obituary: "Elder J. N. Loughborough," *Review,* June 19, 1924, p. 17; obituary: "Mary J. Loughborough," *Review,* July 2, 1867, p. 40; obituary: "Maggie A. Loughborough," *Review,* Apr. 29, 1875, p. 143; search term "A. M. Loughborough" in *Review and Herald* online collection, www.adventistarchives.org; Ellen G. White, Lt 30, 1880 (May 26); Lt 10, 1886 (Dec. 1); Lt 20, 1890 (Oct. 7); Lt 40, 1879 (c. 1879); Ms 3, 1858 (Mar.); Lt 11, 1865 (c. 1865). For a lengthy series of more than 140 largely autobiographical articles, see J. N. Loughborough, "Sketches of the Past," *Pacific Union Recorder,* starting Oct. 17, 1907, p. 1, and continuing intermittently until 1914.

LOVELAND, Reuben (1807-c. 1898) and **Belinda** (1812-1906)

The Lovelands were active laypersons from Johnson, Vermont, and friends of Ellen and James White. Belinda Loveland (née Boutwell), earlier a Methodist and Millerite, became a Sabbathkeeper about 1850. She wrote in 1857, "My companion and children embraced this truth with me." For years Sabbath meetings and conferences were held in the Loveland home. The Lovelands gave generously and frequently to various church causes. According to Belinda's obituary, "in the early days of the message they sacrificed their home farm for the advancement of the message, and moved onto a back lot." Reuben Loveland at times served on various committees of the Vermont State Conference. In 1884 Ellen White wrote of "our aged Bro. and Sr. Loveland" that they "have let their light shine day by day in steady beams."

See: J. B. Loveland and George Loveland, *Genealogy of the Loveland Family in the United States of America From 1635 to 1895 Containing the Descendants of Thomas Loveland of Wethersfield, Now Glastonbury, Connecticut* (Fremont, Ohio: I. M. Keeler & Son, 1895), vol. 3, p. 184; obituary: "Belinda Loveland," *Review,* Mar. 22, 1906, p. 23; Belinda Loveland, "From Sister Loveland," *Review,* June 11, 1857, p. 46; E. G. White, "Notes of Travel," *Review,* Nov. 11, 1884, p. 705. For receipts of donations and mentions of Reuben Loveland's committee appointments, see search term "Loveland" in *Review and Herald* online collection, www.adventistarchives.org.

LUNT, Noah Norton (1821-1902) and (first wife) **Rebecca E.** (c. 1828-1851) and (second wife) **Sarah H.** (1833-1868) and (third wife) **Frances** (1830-after 1910)

Noah Lunt, a carpenter from Maine, was an active layperson, first as a Millerite Adventist, later as a Seventh-day Adventist. According to J. N. Loughborough's obituary of Noah Lunt, he was "arrested and put in prison for preaching the [Millerite] message." Support for this claim is found in William Lapham's *History of Paris, Maine . . .*, published in 1884: "Noah Lunt was arrested and taken before Judge Cole, Apr. 2 [1845] charged with disturbing the peace by calling at persons' houses in the night time and preaching that 'the church and the world were rejected of God.'"

Loughborough also recorded that Noah Lunt was among a group of 60 persons in Portland, Maine, who in January 1845 heard Ellen White relate the vision she had received the month before, and that he began to keep the Sabbath in 1846. Until about 1865 he worshipped with Sabbathkeepers in Portland, then lived in Battle Creek, Michigan, for many years before finally settling in Oakland, California, in the early 1880s. In all three places he served as church elder. Ellen White appears to have appreciated his qualities as a preacher, for in 1890 she suggested to O. A. Olsen, then General Conference president, that Noah Lunt, together with J. N. Loughborough, "come to Michigan and work in this state," a suggestion that was never implemented.

Noah Lunt's first two wives, Rebecca and Sarah Chamberlain, were sisters, and both died young. His third wife, Frances Howland, was the daughter of **Stockbridge** and **Louisa Howland**. In her autobiographical writings Ellen White called Frances Howland "a very dear friend of mine" and recalled the occasion in 1845 when Frances was dramatically healed of rheumatic fever after prayer by Ellen and others. It was also Frances Howland who later had the main care of the Whites' infant son, Henry, during the five years that he spent with the Howland family.

See: Obituary: "Noah Norton Lunt," *Review,* Jan. 28, 1902, p. 63; obituary: "Sarah Lunt," *Review,* June 2, 1868, p. 382; Thomas S. Lunt, *Lunt. A History of the Lunt Family in America* (Salem, Mass.: Salem Press Co., 1914), p. 186; William Berry Lapham, *History of Paris, Maine,* p. 171; 1900 U.S. Federal Census, "Frances H. Lunt," California, Alameda County, Oakland City, p. 8A; James White, "Eastern Tour," *Review,* Nov. 1, 1853, p. 133; Ellen G. White, Lt 20, 1890 (Oct. 7); James White and Ellen G. White, *Life Sketches* (1880), p. 199.

LYON, Henry (1796-1872) and Deborah (1796-1874)

Born in New York State, Henry and Deborah Lyon moved to Michigan in the 1820s. When Plymouth Township in Wayne County was organized in 1827, Henry Lyon was elected tax assessor, a position he held on several occasions in the following years, also serving as township clerk for two years. The Lyons were apparently Adventists of the "age-to-come" persuasion, followers of Joseph Marsh prior to becoming Sabbathkeeping Adventists in 1852. The same year they sold their farm in Plymouth and moved to Battle Creek in 1853.

Henry Lyon is remembered in particular for his contributions to the reorganization of the Review and Herald publishing house and its relocation from Rochester, New York, to Battle Creek in 1855. Financing and promoting the *Review* single-handedly had taken a heavy toll on James White's health by 1855, and he was determined to bring about change. He suggested, among other things, that a finance committee be appointed to carry full financial responsibility for the publishing work, a committee on which Henry Lyon subsequently served. When the decision was made to relocate the press to Battle Creek, Lyon was one of four Michigan persons who invested $300 of personal money to raise the $1,200 needed to buy a plot of land and erect a building to house the press. Three years earlier the Lyons had sold their Plymouth farm for $4,000, which gave them the means to contribute generously to church projects.

Henry and Deborah Lyon receive only incidental mention in the writings of Ellen White. The one exception is a testimony, written some months after Henry's death in 1872, directed to their son-in-law, **Merritt E. Cornell,** and daughter, **Angeline Cornell,** containing reproof for neglecting to look after Henry and Deborah in their sickness and old age.

See: Obituary: "Henry Lyon," *Review,* May 28, 1872, p. 191; obituary: "Deborah Lyon," *Review,* Mar. 10, 1874, p. 103; Sidney Elizabeth Lyon, *Lyon Memorial: Families of Connecticut and New Jersey* (Detroit: Graham Print Co., 1907), p. 301; Silas Farmer, *History of Detroit and Wayne County and Early Michigan: A Chronological Cyclopedia of the Past and Present,* Township and Biographical Edition (Detroit: S. Farmer & Co., 1890), p. 1341; Henry Lyon, "From Bro. Lyon," *Review,* Sept. 16, 1852, pp. 79, 80; Uriah Smith, *Vindication of the Business Career of Elder James White* (Battle Creek, Mich.: Steam Press of the Seventh-day Adventist Pub. Assn., 1863), p. 21; Ellen G. White, Lt 29, 1872 (c. 1872). For a survey of events surrounding the move of the press from Rochester to Battle Creek, see Virgil Robinson, *James White,* pp. 111-115.

MARTIN, John (1820-1889) and Clara M. (c. 1829-1880)

A carpenter and farmer, born in either Vermont or New York (the sources are contradictory), John Martin and his wife, Clara, born in Canada East, appear to have spent most of their lives in northern Vermont, although during their final years they moved to Otsego, Michigan. John Martin had been an active layman in the Millerite movement of the 1840s and was first mentioned in the *Review* in 1851. According to his obituary, Martin was "among the first to embrace the light on the Sabbath question." Ellen White's only mention of the Martins was in connection with her journey in 1859, together with James, to Berkshire, in northern Vermont, where they stayed two nights in the Martin home.

See: Obituary: "John Martin," *Review,* Sept. 3, 1889, p. 559; obituary: "Clara M. Martin," *Review,* Feb. 26, 1880, p. 142; 1860 U.S. Federal Census, "John Martin," Vermont, Franklin County, Berkshire, p. 28; 1870 U.S. Federal Census, "John Martin," Vermont, Franklin County, Enosburgh, p. 24; 1880 U.S. Federal Census, "John Martin," Michigan, Allegan County, Otsego, p. 19; search terms "J. Martin" and "John Martin" in *Words of the Pioneers*; Ellen G. White, Ms 8, 1859 (entries for Oct. 14, 16).

MASTEN, Luman V. (c. 1829-1854)

Luman Masten was hired by James White in April 1852 to oversee printing operations at the newly acquired *Review* press in Rochester, New York. He lived with the Whites for most of his time in Rochester. Impressed with his hard work, Ellen White wrote that "he has overdone often." Of no particular church affiliation when hired, he was amazed by the faith of fellow employees and other believers in Rochester: "So different, were they, from any [other Christians] that I had ever before seen, that I was struck with astonishment." Some months later he was "brought almost to death" by cholera. Declaring that he would become a Sabbathkeeper if his life was spared, he made a startling recovery following the prayer of believers. Masten continued his work at the *Review* and wrote several stirring testimonies for the paper before he died of "consumption" 18 months later, on March 1, 1854, "aged about 25 years."

See: Obituary: "L. V. Masten," *Review,* Mar. 14, 1854, p. 63; L. V. Masten, "Communication From Bro. Masten," *Review,* Nov. 25, 1852, p. 108; 1850 U.S. Federal Census, "Luman Maston" [*sic*], New York, Saratoga County, Saratoga Springs, p. 200; J. N. Loughborough, *Rise and Progress,* p. 169; Ellen G. White, Lt 7, 1853 (Aug. 24).

MCCANN, Harriet (née **Harmon)** (1813-1876) and **Samuel** (c. 1812-c. 1874)

Sister of Ellen G. White. About 14 years older than Ellen, Harriet Harmon had left home and married while Ellen was still a young child and many years before the Harmon family became Millerite Adventists. According to Maine census records, Harriet and Samuel McCann lived in Poland (1840, 1850), Sanford (1860), and Saco, Maine (1870). The 1860 census lists Samuel as a "clergyman," and another account notes that a "Samuel McCann" served as minister of the Christian Church in Sanford and Lebanon in the early 1860s.

Harriet McCann experienced much personal tragedy. In 1874 Ellen White wrote of Harriet's "life of trial in watching over one child after another who has died with consumption—three in number—then the many years she watched over her husband until he died." Harriet herself succumbed to the disease in 1876. Ellen paid at least three visits to the McCann family during the early 1870s.

Harriet McCann never became a Seventh-day Adventist. A year or so before Harriet's death, Ellen White worried that there was no "religious influence in the [McCann] family. No family prayer, and no blessing asked at the table. A godless, prayerless house!" Nevertheless, during Ellen's last visit to her sister in September 1875, she wrote, "I felt such strong desire to gather my sister in my arms and shield her from the anguish of physical prostration she endures daily; but Jesus loves her better than I can. I leave her in His tender arms of love."

See: 1850 U.S. Federal Census, "Samuel McCann," Maine, Cumberland County, Poland, p. 34; 1860 U.S. Federal Census, "Samuel McCan [*sic*]," Maine, York County, Sanford, p. 19; 1870 U.S. Federal Census, "McCann, Samuel," Maine, York County, Saco, p. 114; Edwin Emery, *The History of Sanford, Maine, 1661-1900* (Fall River, Mass.: William Morrell Emery, 1901), p. 140; Artemas C. Harmon, ed., *The Harmon Genealogy*, p. 41; *City of Saco,* Maine., *Deaths, 1868-1891,* p. 14, www.sacomaine.org/dyer/deaths/DEATHS-18681891.pdf (Sept. 13, 2012). Ellen G. White, Lt 50, 1874 (Sept. 2); Lt 31, 1875 (Sept. 3).

MCPHERSON, Samuel A. (c. 1823-1898) and (first wife) **Polly M.** (c. 1824-1863) and (second wife) **Sarah** (c. 1842-after 1898)

Samuel and Polly McPherson, well-to-do farmers from Wright, Michigan, probably both became Sabbatarian Adventists in 1858. The McPhersons were generous donors to church projects, and for a time, in the early 1870s, Samuel McPherson was a director of the Western Health Reform Institute in Battle Creek, Michigan.

Samuel McPherson and a fellow church member, Brother Cramer, were somewhat of a rarity among fellow Adventists in that they held pro-slavery views, and moreover they defended them vigorously among church members, causing division. Ellen White upbraided both of them in an 1867 testimony. "Your political views are at fault. They are not in harmony with God's Word and are not in union with the body of Sabbathkeeping believers. . . . These brethren cannot receive the approval of heaven while they lack sympathy for the oppressed slave."

See: Obituary: "Samuel A. McPherson," *Review,* Feb. 28, 1899, p. 142; obituary: "P. M. McPherson," *Review,* Mar. 17, 1863, p. 127; 1860 U.S. Federal Census, "Polly McFerson," Michigan, Ottawa County, Wright, p. 121; 1870 U.S. Federal Census, "McPherson, Sarah," Michigan, Ottawa County, Polkton, p. 14; search term "McPherson" in *Review and Herald* online collection, www.adventistarchives.org; Ellen G. White, Ms 8, 1867 (c. 1867).

MEAD, Stephen Newell (1820-1888) and **Sarah Phelps** (1833-1920)

The Meads were among the earliest Adventists to become Sabbathkeepers in

Washington, New Hampshire. Newell Mead (who seems to have favored using his middle name) was a farmer and, according to James White, "a successful teacher of penmanship and music." In the early 1840s Newell joined the Millerite group in Washington. Over the next few years a number of these Adventists also began to keep the Sabbath. The exact year when Mead became a Sabbatarian Adventist is disputed. His obituary writer dated it to 1850, but others placed the event several years earlier, perhaps 1845 or even 1844. Sarah joined the Sabbathkeepers not long after her marriage to Newell in December 1849. The Meads remained lifelong members of the church in Washington.

Two incidents in particular are recorded of Ellen White's relationship with the Meads. In 1851 Sarah Mead, who was "afflicted with a slow fever," requested Ellen and James White, who were visiting Washington, to pray for her. Ellen White reports that she "anointed her with oil" and joined with four others in prayer, after which Sarah Mead "was healed every whit and fell prostrate by the power of God." In 1868 Ellen and James White organized an appeal on behalf of the Meads, who were unable to work because of the prolonged sickness of Sarah and a near-fatal fall from a barn roof that left Newell in feeble health and chronic depression.

See: Obituary: "S. Newell Mead," *Review,* Mar. 13, 1888, p. 175; obituary: "Sarah Phelps Mead," *Review,* Apr. 14, 1921, p. 22; James White, "Eastern Tour," *Review,* Jan. 28, 1868, p. 104; *History of Washington, New Hampshire, From 1768 to 1886,* p. 535; search term "Mead" in *Review and Herald* online collection, www.adventistarchives.org; Ellen G. White, Lt 8, 1851 (Nov. 12). For an evaluation of the question of when Newell Mead and other Adventists in Washington became Sabbatarians, see Arthur Whitefield Spalding, *Origin and History of Seventh-day Adventists,* vol. 1, pp. 397-400.

MEAD, Thomas B. (1827-1861) and **Mary Jane** (1834-1890)

According to James White, Thomas Mead, born in Washington, New Hampshire, "was among the first who embraced the third message in New Hampshire." It is possible that Mead became a Sabbathkeeper as early as 1844 or 1845 together with William Farnsworth, his brother-in-law, and other Adventists in Washington.

At some point before March 1857 Thomas Mead worked at the Review and Herald press, but he contracted tuberculosis and could not continue. Ellen White noted in her diary on March 4, 1859, that "we assembled at Brother T. Meade's [in Battle Creek] to pray for him . . . . He is fast going down, and unless God in mercy raises him, he will go down into the grave." James and Ellen White assisted the Mead family financially and helped raise funds for them through appeals in the *Review* and *The Good Samaritan*. The Meads moved to Waukon, Iowa in 1859 where Thomas died two years later, aged 33.

Before her marriage to Thomas Mead, Mary Jane (nee Patten) became a Sabbathkeeper (1851) and worked at the *Review* office in Rochester, New York during the winter of 1852-1853. After the death of Thomas Mead she married Robert Sawyer. At various time Mary served as matron of the Battle Creek sanitarium and matron of the Pacific Press boarding house in California.

See: History of Washington, New Hampshire, from 1768 to 1886: A Facsimile of the 1886 Edition with a New Foreword by Ronald Jager and Grace Jager, 1886 (Claremont, N.H.: Claremont Manufacturing Co., 1886; reprint, Washington, N.H.: Washington History Committee, 1976), 534, 535; Obituary: "Mary Jane Sawyer," *Review*, May 27, 1890, 335; Obituary: "Thomas B. Mead," *Review*, Aug. 27, 1861, 103; *SDAE,* s. v. "Farnsworth, William," "Washington, New Hampshire, Church"; John Nevins Andrews, *Defense of Elder James White and Wife* (Battle Creek, Mich.: Steam Press, 1870), 19; Ellen G. White, Ms 5, 1859 (Mar. 4 entry); search term "Mead" in *Words of the Pioneers*; J. W. [James White], "The Poor," *The Good Samaritan*, Dec. 1859, 7.

MILES, Alonzo (c. 1818-after 1870) and **Martha** (c. 1825-after 1870)

The earliest mention of Alonzo Miles in the *Review* dates to 1852, when James and Ellen White conducted meetings on his farm in Boylston, New York. He was an active layperson, raising small groups of believers both in the Boylston area and in Plainfield, Illinois, where he had moved by 1853. By 1854, however, Alonzo and Martha Miles became involved with the *Messenger* Party with its rejection of Ellen White's special role and criticism of James White's leadership. There is no further reference to Alonzo Miles until 1859, by which time the Mileses had returned to New York and had also changed their minds regarding Ellen White and the now-defunct *Messenger* Party. The Whites met Alonzo and Martha and ate supper with them in October 1859. Ellen White noted in her diary: "Brother and Sister Miles once joined the *Messenger* [Party], and turned from us and sought to injure us, but now they sob out their repentant prayers and beg God to forgive them." As available church sources make no mention of the Alonzo Miles family after 1860, it is likely that they did not remain with the church.

See: 1850 U.S. Federal Census, "Alonzo Miles," New York, Oswego County, Boylston, p. 188; 1860 U.S. Federal Census, "Alonzo Miles," New York, Jefferson County, Ellisburg, p. 46; 1870 U.S. Federal Census, "Alonzo Miles," Kansas, Shawnee County, Auburn, p. 1; James White, "Boylston Meeting," *Review*, Sept. 2, 1852, p. 72; Alonzo Miles, "Dear Bro. White," *Review*, May 26, 1853, p. 8; A. Miles, "Dear Brn. of the Publishing Committee," *Review*, Dec. 5, 1854, pp. 125, 126; Ellen G. White, Ms. 8, 1859 (Oct. 22 entry); SDAE, s.v. "*Messenger* Party."

NARAMORE, John (c. 1820-c. 1897) and **Eliza A. C.** (1830-1914)

John Naramore, a dentist from Rochester, New York, and his wife, Eliza, were reported in a February 1859 issue of the *Review* to have "lately embraced the truth." Ellen White corresponded with "Doctor Naramore" on several occasions and incorporated portions of one of her letters into a general article appearing in the *Review*. It would appear, however, that the Naramores' association with Sabbathkeeping Adventists was short-lived. There was a flurry of letters and donations from John Naramore in the *Review* during 1859, but silence after March 1860.

See: 1870 U.S. Federal Census, "Naramore, John," New York, Monroe County, Rochester, Ward 7, p. 61; *The Rochester Directory . . . for the Year Beginning July 1, 1897* (Rochester, N.Y.: Drew Allis Co., 1897), p. 519; 1900 U.S. Federal Census, "Naramore, Eliza,"

New York, Monroe County, Rochester, Ward 6, p. 11A; *Rochester Directory for the Year Beginning July 15, 1914* (Rochester, N.Y.: Drew Allis Co., 1914), p. 822; R. F. C. [R. F. Cottrell], "Report From Bro. Cottrell," *Review*, Feb. 3, 1859, p. 85; search term "Naramore" in *Words of the Pioneers*; Ellen G. White, Ms 5, 1859 (entries for Jan. 3, Feb. 21); Ms 6, 1859 (Apr. 15 entry); Lt 18, 1859 (Apr. 14); cf. "The Sinner's Trials," *Review*, Apr. 28, 1859, pp. 181, 182.

NICHOLS, Henry Otis (1828-1917) and (first wife) **Harriet** (1836-1880) and (second wife) **Harriet L.** (1853-1917)

A close acquaintance of Ellen White's in his youth, Henry Nichols was the son of **Otis** and **Mary Nichols.** During 1845-1846, while Henry was in his late teens and probably living at home, the Nicholses opened up their home in Dorchester, Massachusetts, for Ellen Harmon (White) for some eight months while she traveled in the vicinity relating her visions. In a poignant autobiographical account Ellen White recalls how in late 1846 or early 1847, after she had returned to Maine and fallen dangerously ill, the Nicholses sent Henry "bringing things for my comfort." During a prayer session for her recovery, "Bro. Henry commenced praying . . . and with the power of God resting upon him . . . laid his hands upon my head, saying, 'Sister Ellen, Jesus Christ maketh thee whole,' and fell back prostrated by the power of God. I believed that the work was of God, and the pain left me. My heart was filled with gratitude and peace."

No doubt as a token of their friendship with the Nichols family, James and Ellen White named their first son Henry Nichols White. According to the reminiscences of Charles F. Stevens, Henry Nichols assisted James White with the publishing of the *Review* during the winter of 1850-1851 in Paris, Maine. Several poems and letters to the editor from Henry Nichols were published in the *Review* during the early 1850s in addition to subscription receipts, etc. Little is heard, however, of Henry Nichols, after 1855. The reason, Ellen White explained in 1862, was that "doubts and difficulties [were] thrown into Henry Nichols' mind, which have destroyed his interest and faith in the visions and in us." Ironically, she maintained that it was J. N. Andrews, later a strong supporter of the visions, a General Conference president, and first official Seventh-day Adventist missionary to Europe, who instilled the doubts into Henry Nichols' mind "at the time of the removal of the Office," i.e., in 1855 when the *Review* office was moved from Rochester, New York, to Battle Creek, Michigan. (J. N. Andrews, under influence from his family, had doubts about the authenticity of the visions for a period of time during the 1850s.) Writing in 1903 to Henry Nichols, Ellen White made it fairly clear that Nichols subsequently abandoned Sabbathkeeping for many years, but began to keep it again in his old age, shortly before 1903. Whether he then continued to keep the Sabbath till his death in 1917 is not known.

See: In the Footsteps of the Pioneers (Silver Spring, Md.: Ellen G. White Estate, 1990), p. 51; J. G. Swift and Harrison Ellery, *The Memoirs of Gen. Joseph Gardner Swift . . . to Which is Added a Genealogy of the Family of Thomas Swift of Dorchester, Mass.* (Worcester, Mass.: Press of F. S. Blanchard & Co., 1890), p. 40 (of the genealogy section); C. F. Stevens, "From the Oldest Reader of the 'Review,'" *Review*, Aug. 21, 1919, p. 27; Ellen G. White, *Spiritual Gifts [vol. 2],* p. 84; Lt 11, 1862 (Nov. 9); "To Brother J. N. Andrews and Sister H. N. Smith" (PH016), p. 19; Lt 99, 1903 (May 24).

NICHOLS, Otis (1798-1876) and (first wife) **Sally Orne** (1803-1824) and (second wife) **Mary** (c. 1800-1868)

The Nicholses were early public supporters of the visions of Ellen Harmon (White). Of Millerite background, Otis and Mary Nichols were prosperous farmers from Dorchester, Massachusetts, who opened their home to provide a base for Ellen Harmon during her travels in Massachusetts to relate her visions during the autumn and winter of 1845-1846. "I made my home at the house of Bro. O. Nichols," Ellen wrote later. "They were attentive to my wants, and generously supplied me with means to travel." Otis Nichols personally drove Ellen Harmon and her companions to meet with various Adventist groups in the Boston and New Bedford areas, groups which were often hostile to the visions.

In April 1846 Otis Nichols wrote a letter to William Miller that included a lengthy section making his case for the genuineness of Ellen Harmon's visions. The continuing financial support of the Nicholses was of considerable importance to the impoverished James and Ellen White as they struggled to build up the emergent movement. Ellen White later recalled of Otis Nichols that "for several years nearly all the means necessary to bear our expenses came from his purse."

Although there is no record of Otis Nichols' being a preacher, he did author a number of theological articles, published in the *Review* during the 1850s and early 1860s. He is also remembered for publishing the first Sabbatarian Adventist prophetic chart in 1850. Some historians believe that Nichols was an engraver and lithographer by trade, but contemporary census and tax records available to this study list him solely as "farmer."

See: Sherman Leland, *The Leland Magazine, or a Genealogical Record of Henry Leland, and His Descendants* (Boston: Wier & White, 1850), p. 176; E. O. Jameson, *The Biographical Sketches of Prominent Persons and the Genealogical Records of Many Early and Other Families in Medway, Mass. 1713-1886* (Millis, Mass.: E. O. Jameson, 1886), p. 122; obituary: "Mary Nichols," *Review,* Feb. 11, 1868, p. 142; obituary: [notice re. death of O. Nichols], *Review,* July 27, 1876, p. 40; Ellen G. White, *Spiritual Gifts [vol. 2],* pp. 68, 69; "They Sleep in Jesus," *Review,* Apr. 21, 1868, p. 297. For general surveys of Otis Nichols' life, see Clifton L. Taylor, "The Robert Morris of the Advent Movement," *Review,* June 13, 1963, pp. 7, 8; SDAE, s.v. "Otis Nichols."

ORTON, Alva (1845-1917) and **Valerie E.** (1843-after 1900)

Ellen and James White were close acquaintances of Alva Orton's parents, **Jonathan** and **Caroline Orton,** at whose home in Rochester, New York, the Whites often received hospitality. Alva Orton is listed as a police officer living in Buffalo, New York, in the 1880 census and later as a merchant in Brooklyn, New York. His obituary is found in the *Review,* suggesting that he ended his days a church member.

After Jonathan Orton's murder in 1866, Ellen White appears to have had a special concern for Alva Orton and his wife. After meeting the Ortons at a wedding in 1868, she reflected, "God gave me a testimony for the two just united in marriage, but more especially were my remarks directed to Alva Orton and wife. I entreated them to live for self no longer, but consecrate themselves to God."

See: 1880 U.S. Federal Census, "Alva H. Orton," New York, Erie County, Buffalo, p. 10; 1900 U.S. Federal Census, "Albah H. Orton [*sic*]," New York, Kings County, Brooklyn, Ward 22, p. 1A; obituary: "Alva H. Orton," *Review,* Mar. 29, 1917, p. 21; Ellen G. White, Ms 12, 1868 (Jan. 9 entry).

ORTON, Jonathan T. (c. 1811-1866) and **Caroline** (c. 1813-1873)

Jonathan Orton was a prominent layperson from Rochester, New York, a hackman by trade. John N. Loughborough, an early friend, credited Orton with introducing him to public meetings held by Sabbathkeeping Adventists in Rochester in 1852.

James and Ellen White became well acquainted with the Ortons during the period 1852-1855 when the *Review* was published in Rochester. During this time the Ortons, together with some other families in the area, became disaffected with the leadership of James White and the testimonies of Ellen White. They "would not receive reproof and counsel . . . and they determined to separate themselves from us."

In 1856 the Ortons moved west to Waukon, Iowa, which for a few years became somewhat of a center of anti-White sentiment. Their attitude to the Whites, however, appears to have changed fairly soon after that, probably as a result of the important visit of the Whites to Waukon in December 1856. Within a year Jonathan and Caroline Orton had moved back to Rochester and seem to have been fully supportive of Ellen and James White in the years that followed. In December 1865, for example, the Ortons joined other Rochester members in several prayer sessions daily for three weeks for the recovery of James White from the major stroke he had suffered some months earlier.

In March 1866 Jonathan Orton was brutally murdered. The perpetrator was never found. In later memoirs J. N. Loughborough connected Orton's death with a vision shown Ellen White on December 25, 1865, in which Satan was "angry with this company who have continued for three weeks praying earnestly" for James White, and "is now determined to make a powerful attack upon them." It is likely that this is the same vision that Ellen White described and commented on in Manuscript 6, 1865. More recently, on the basis of newspaper and other sources, it has been proposed that Orton's murder was likely a revenge killing.

See: Obituary: "Bro. Orton," *Review,* Mar. 27, 1866, p. 135; obituary: "Caroline Orton," *Review,* May 13, 1873, p. 175; 1850 U.S. Federal Census, "Jonathan Orton," New York, Monroe County, Rochester, Ward 7, p. 317; J. T. Orton, "From Bro. Orton," *Review,* Feb. 12, 1857, p. 118; Ronald D. Graybill, "The Murder of Jonathan Orton," *Insight,* Dec. 5, 1978, pp. 8-12; William F. Peck, *History of the Police Department of Rochester, N.Y., From the Earliest Time to May 1, 1903* (Rochester, N.Y.: Rochester Police Benevolent Association, 1903), p. 116; J. N. Loughborough, *Rise and Progress,* pp. 270, 271; *idem,* "Recollections of the Past—No. 3," *Review,* Feb. 12, 1884, p. 107; search term "Orton" in *Review and Her-*

ald online collection, www.adventistarchives.org; Ellen G. White, *Testimony to the Church at Battle Creek* (PH123) (Battle Creek, Mich.: Steam Press, 1872), p. 75; *Spiritual Gifts [vol. 2]*, pp. 217-222; Ms 6, 1865 (Apr. 9).

PALMER, Dan R. (1817-1897) and **Abigail** (1823-1902)

Born in Sodus, New York, Dan Palmer moved to Jackson, Michigan, in 1838. Dan Palmer, and probably his wife, Abigail (née Wilmoth), came from a Millerite background and, together with other Adventists in Jackson, became Sabbatarians through their contact with Joseph Bates on his first visit to Jackson in 1849. Historical sources disagree on whether the Palmers were Bates's first converts, prior to the rest of the Jackson Adventists. Having arrived in Jackson "with only $30 in his pocket," Dan Palmer built up a flourishing blacksmithing business.

Dan and Abigail are remembered for giving generously to almost every church project for which appeal was made, including the purchase of the first evangelistic tent in 1854, the construction of a building to house the *Review* office in 1855, large donations for the Western Health Reform Institute, the mission to Europe, and the James White Memorial home in 1891. Dan's financial acumen was also put to use. He served on a financial committee of three who were charged with moving the *Review* office to Battle Creek, as well as on the Michigan tent committee, the board of directors of the Health Reform Institute, and several other assignments.

When visiting Jackson, James and Ellen White often stayed with the Palmers. Although they were firm supporters of Ellen White and her visions, an incident in 1853 involving Abigail Palmer's hasty temperament led to very serious consequences. Mrs. Palmer was accused by some fellow believers of insulting a neighbor by calling her a "bitch," and they demanded that church discipline be applied. Mrs. Palmer vigorously denied the charges, and the Jackson group became bitterly divided between her accusers and defenders. During this state of affairs Ellen White received a vision reproving Abigail Palmer's unchristian spirit but revealing that she had not, in fact, used the offensive term, and reprimanding those who had harshly condemned her. Rather than settling the matter, some of those reproved in Jackson, nearby Sylvan, and beyond now turned against the authority of the visions themselves, ultimately resulting in the first offshoot movement from the Sabbatarian Adventists, the *Messenger* Party.

See: Horace Wilbur Palmer, *Palmer Families in America: Lt. William Palmer of Yarmouth, Mass. and His Descendants of Greenwich, Conn.* (Neshanic, N.J.: Neshanic Printing Co., 1966), vol. 1, p. 816; obituary: "Dan R. Palmer," *Review*, Jan. 26, 1897, p. 64; obituary: "Mrs. D. R. Palmer," *Review*, Dec. 23, 1902, p. 23; *History of Jackson County, Michigan* (Chicago: Inter-State Pub. Co., 1881), p. 686; search term "D. R. Palmer" in *Review and Herald* online collection, www.adventistarchives.org; Arthur Whitefield Spalding, *Footprints of the Pioneers* (Washington, D.C.: Review and Herald, 1947), pp. 139-146; G. W. Amadon, "Interesting Item of History," *Review*, Nov. 11, 1890, p. 695; SDAE, s.v. "Michigan Conference."

PEABODY, William (1791-1866) and **Hannah** (1787-1876)

Born in Canada, William Peabody came to New York State as a child. He was a soldier in the War of 1812. In the early 1840s he became a Millerite Adventist and in 1853 started to keep the Sabbath. It appears that his wife remained a member of the Methodist Episcopal Church throughout her life.

William Peabody was a successful farmer, one of the wealthiest Sabbatarian Adventists of the 1850s, with real estate valued at $15,000 in the 1850 census. In 1859, when Peabody was 68, Ellen White reminded him that he "had but a short time to work and lay up your treasure in heaven." He gave generously to a multitude of church causes and at his death in 1866 left legacies to the publishing and health work totaling more than $2,000.

Just before her death in 1855, Annie R. Smith published a book of poems, including one "respectfully dedicated to Wm. Peabody," which contains the lines:

"Desires, above his needs, were all denied,
His will, subdued, to Heaven's decrees resigned."

See: Obituary: "William Peabody," *Review,* Jan. 22, 1867, p. 82; Selim Hobart Peabody, *Peabody (Paybody, Pabody, Pabodie) Genealogy* (Boston: Charles H. Pope, 1909), p. 117; Chapman Brothers, *Portrait and Biographical Album of Barry and Eaton Counties, Michigan* (Salem, Mass.: Higginson Book Co., 1891), pp. 792, 793; 1850 U.S. Federal Census, "Wm. Peabody," New York, Monroe County, Wheatland, p. 245; Annie Rebekah Smith, *Home Here and Home in Heaven: With Other Poems* (Rochester, N.Y.: Advent Review Office, 1855), pp. 89-91; search term "Peabody" in *Review and Herald* online collection, www.adventistarchives.org; Ellen G. White, Lt 4, 1859 (Sept. 2).

PEARSALL, Alfred B. (1823-1895) and **Adaline** (1823-1906)

The Pearsalls were church members from Michigan who emerged from the Millerite movement to become Sabbathkeepers about 1852. Until about 1858 the Pearsalls lived in Grand Rapids but then settled in Battle Creek for most of their remaining working lives. A. B. Pearsall owned a house-painting and sign-painting business and was active in the 1850s as a local church agent for the *Review.* Two letters from Ellen White to the Pearsalls are known, one in response to their queries regarding parenting and one in which Alfred was admonished for being "too familiar with the sisters," thus bringing "a reproach upon the cause."

See: Obituary: "A. B. Pearsall," *Review,* Mar. 19, 1895, p. 191; obituary: "Adalign [*sic*] Pearsall," *Review,* July 12, 1906, p. 23; Clarence E. Pearsall et al., *History and Genealogy of the Pearsall Family in England and America* (San Francisco: H. S. Crocker, 1928), vol. 3, p. 1282; search term "Pearsall" in *Words of the Pioneers*; *Calhoun County Business Directory for 1869-70* (Battle Creek, Mich.: E. G. Rust, 1869), p. 127; Ellen G. White, Lt 4, 1853 (June 30); Lt 3, 1854 (July 12).

PECKHAM, Job B. (1823-1859) and **Sophronia** (1825-1887)

In 1850 Ellen White saw in vision that Sophronia Peckham, from Volney, New York, must "break loose" from the secular influence of her husband, Job B. Peckham, which had "dragged her down." When Job Peckham died at age 35, Ellen White noted that according to Sophronia, her husband had "embraced the Sabbath before his sickness" and that "she has hopes in his death." Some years after Job's death, Sophronia married widower Samuel W. Rhodes, a well-known minister during the 1850s.

See: Ellen G. White, Ms 7a, 1850 (Aug. 24); Ms 6, 1859 (May 18 entry); "Job B. Peckham," *RootsWeb* (Mount Pleasant Western Cemetery, Volney, Osweo Co., N.Y., 2000), www.rootsweb.ancestry.com/~nyoswego/cemeteries/mtpleasantwestvol4.html (Oct. 20, 2011); obituary: "Sophronia L. Rhodes," *Review,* Jan. 17, 1888, p. 46.

PHILLIPS, Daniel C. (c. 1813-1882) and (first wife) **Amanda** (c. 1812-1859) and (second wife) **Mary** (c. 1843-1884)

A lay preacher from Vermont, Daniel Phillips participated in the Millerite movement in the 1840s, along with his first wife, Amanda. Daniel Phillips' decision to join the Sabbatarian Adventists, and probably that of his wife also, was made at meetings that James and Ellen White held in Bethel, Vermont, in 1851. Numerous reports in the *Review* during the 1850s chronicle Phillips' preaching engagements in Vermont and beyond.

Ellen White's testimonies to Daniel Phillips initially encouraged him to expand his evangelistic exploits. By the end of the 1850s, however, she was shown that his performance among the churches did not justify a full-time traveling ministry funded by church members, and he was counseled to continue as a self-supporting lay preacher. After the death of Amanda in 1859, Daniel Phillips appears to have gone through a period of spiritual crisis, as attested by Ellen White's letters of 1862-1864 concerning his sharp business dealings with church members and an unwise romantic entanglement. He spent his final years in Wellsville, New York. His second wife, Mary Oviatt, was an enthusiastic lay worker and for several years served as secretary-treasurer of the Pennsylvania Tract and Missionary Society. Her brother, D. B. Oviatt, later served as president of the Pennsylvania Conference.

See: Obituary: "D. C. Phillips," *Review,* July 11, 1882, p. 446; obituary: "Amanda Phillips," *Review,* Mar. 24, 1859, p. 143; obituary: "Mrs. D. C. Phillips," *Review,* Feb. 3, 1885, p. 78; "Death of Mrs. D. C. Phillips (Mary Oviatt Phillips)," Wellsville *Daily Reporter,* Jan. 2, 1885, www.alleganycountynylocalhistory.com/Obituaries/obitflders/Phillips-Mary Oviatt.htm (Oct. 20, 2011); search terms "D. C. Phillips" and "Mrs. D. C. Phillips" in *Review and Herald* online collection, www.adventistarchives.org; "Mrs. D. C. Phillips," *Seventh-day Adventist Year Book* (Battle Creek, Mich.: Seventh-day Adventist Pub. Assn., 1883), p. 15; SDAE, s.v. "D. B. Oviatt," "Pennsylvania Conference"; Ellen G. White, *Spiritual Gifts, [vol. 2],* p. 147; Lt 15, 1857 (c. 1857); Lt 2, 1862 (Jan. 20); Lt 4, 1864 (Jan. 12, 1864).

PIERCE, Henry Harlow (1833-1901) and **Esther Ann** (1837-1908)

A carpenter from Allegan County, Michigan, H. H. Pierce became a Sabbathkeeping Adventist in the mid-1850s and was elder of the Allegan church for some years. In 1859 he married Esther Morse, who had been a Sabbathkeeper since about 1849. He later helped in the construction of the Battle Creek ("Dime") Tabernacle. In 1879 the family moved to Boulder, Colorado, where meetings were held in the Pierce home until a church was built in 1881. In 1883 and 1884 Pierce served as treasurer of the newly formed Colorado Conference. He received only incidental mention in the writings of Ellen White.

See: Obituary: "Henry Harlow Pierce," *Review,* Nov. 12, 1901, p. 742; obituary: "Esther Ann Pierce," *Review,* Jan. 14, 1909, p. 23; 1860 U.S. Federal Census, "Henry H. Pierce," Michigan, Calhoun County, Battle Creek, p. 25; *History of Allegan and Barry Counties, Michigan,* p. 162; SDAE, s.v. "Colorado Conference"; *Seventh-day Adventist Yearbook* (Battle Creek, Mich.: Seventh-day Adventist Pub. Assn., 1884), p. 24; Ellen G. White, Ms 5, 1859 (Feb. 3, 12 entries); Ms 4, 1860 (Dec.).

PIERCE, Stephen (1804-1883) and **Almira** (1806-1875)

Minister, conference administrator, and writer, Stephen Pierce and his wife, Almira, were both born in Cavendish, Vermont. They held Millerite convictions in the 1840s but apparently never separated from the Baptist Church until they became Sabbathkeepers in 1852. These facts make it unlikely that Stephen Pierce participated in the formative theological discussions and Sabbath Conferences of the mid- and late 1840s, as some historians have concluded on the basis of Ellen White's recollections in 1903 (Ms 135, 1903 [Nov. 4]).

Pierce was a corresponding editor for the *Review* for several years in the 1850s. With the coming of conference organization in the early 1860s, he served as president of the Vermont Conference (1863-1865) and of the Minnesota Conference (1865-1870). About 1857 Ellen White wrote to Pierce that he had too little confidence in his own success, urging him to "arouse, arouse," because "your gift is needed." Pierce's subsequent notable service as minister and administrator suggests that he took this encouragement to heart.

In the area of theology the names Stephen Pierce and Ellen White are perhaps most commonly associated with the intense denominational discussions from 1886 to 1888 on whether the "schoolmaster" law of Galatians 3:24 referred to the moral law of the Ten Commandments or the ceremonial law. Uriah Smith and G. I. Butler argued for the traditional ceremonial law position, buttressing their view with the claim that this was the position Ellen White adopted as early as the mid-1850s when she, in turn, had become convinced by the arguments of Stephen Pierce. Whether Pierce held to an exclusive ceremonial law stance in the mid-1850s is, however, open to doubt. An article written by Pierce in 1856 appears to present a broader view, encompassing both the moral and ceremonial laws.

See: Obituary: "Stephen Pierce," *Review,* Oct. 9, 1883, p. 637; obituary: "Almira Pierce," *Review,* Jan. 13, 1876, p. 15; Ellen G. White, Lt 15, 1857 (c. 1857); Stephen Pierce, "From Bro. Pierce," *Review,* Jan. 20, 1853, p. 143. On the presumed relationship of the views of Stephen Pierce and Ellen White on the law in Galatians, see, for example, David P. McMahon, *Ellet Joseph Waggoner: The Myth and the Man* (Fallbrook, Calif.: Verdict Publications, 1979), pp. 51, 53, 86-89; Timothy E. Crosby, "Ellen G. White and the Law in Galatians: A Study in the Dynamics of Present Truth" (term paper, Andrews University, 1979); George R. Knight, *From 1888 to Apostasy: The Case of A. T. Jones* (Washington, D.C.: Review and Herald, 1987), pp. 23-27; S. P. [Stephen Pierce], "Answer to Bro. Merriam's Question Respecting the Law of Gal. iii . . . ," *Review,* Oct. 8, 1857, pp. 180, 181.

POOLE, Ezra A. (c. 1807-1894) and **Sally Marilla** (1819-after 1900)

Earlier a Congregationalist clergyman, Ezra Poole became a Millerite Adventist in the early 1840s. He joined the Sabbatarian Adventists in 1850 and soon after began to preach for them, mostly in Lincklaen, New York, and vicinity. Surprisingly, the *History of Chenango and Madison Counties* lists Ezra Poole as pastor of the Lincklaen Seventh Day Baptist Church from 1856 to 1859. A letter to the *Review* in 1858 explained that the Sabbatarian Adventists in Lincklaen "hold their meetings each Sabbath afternoon in the meeting house of the Seventh-day [*sic*] Baptists, where Bro. Poole preaches to the latter in the morning and then meets with the Advent brethren in the afternoon." Although his preaching seems to have been mostly local, his administrative talents had a wider impact. Among other responsibilities, he served on a committee set up in 1852 to raise funds for the first *Review* printing press and to oversee "the financial concerns of the paper." In 1860 Poole was active in the debate at a general conference in Battle Creek over the adoption of "Seventh-day Adventist" as the denominational name. It was his motion "that we *call ourselves* Seventh-day Adventists" that finally passed after withdrawal of David Hewitt's initial motion "that we *take the name* of Seventh-day Adventists" (italics supplied).

Ezra Poole and his wife are briefly mentioned by Ellen White in 1854 as having been deeply hurt by the severity and "overbearing spirit" of Samuel W. Rhodes, a traveling preacher of some prominence in the early 1850s. It is also likely that, despite the disparity in spelling, the "Brother Pool" referred to in Letter 11, 1862 (Nov. 9), is Ezra Poole. He is there counseled that he "has lost sense of the greatness" of the work and needs to "move with more energy and decision."

See: Obituary: "Elder Ezra A. Poole," *Review,* Apr. 3, 1894, p. 223; James H. Smith, *History of Chenango and Madison Counties, New York, With Illustrations and Biographical Sketches of Some of Its Prominent Men and Pioneers* (Syracuse, N.Y.: D. Mason & Co., 1880), p. 486; Benj. Hostler, "From Bro. Hostler," *Review,* Aug. 26, 1858, p. 118; search term "Poole" in *Words of the Pioneers*; "The Conference," *Review,* Mar. 23, 1852, p. 108; "Business Proceedings of B. C. Conference," *Review,* Oct. 16, 23, 1860, pp. 169, 170, 179; 1860 U.S. Federal Census, "Ezra A. Poole," New York, Chenango County, Lincklaen, p. 339; 1880 U.S. Federal Census, "Pool [*sic*], Ezra A.," New York, Chenango County, Lincklaen, p. 5; 1900 U.S. Federal Census, "Marilla Pool" [*sic*], New York, Chenango County, Lincklaen, p. 5b; Ellen G. White, Ms 6, 1854 (Feb. 19); Lt 11, 1862 (Nov. 9).

PRESTON, Almira (Elmira) (née **BARNES**) (1811-1888) and (second husband) **John S.** (c. 1804-1879)

A church member originally of Camden, New York, Almira M. Preston became a Sabbathkeeper against the strong opposition of her farmer-husband, John S. Preston, in the late 1840s or early in 1850.

The only recorded interaction between Ellen White and Almira Preston occurred in

June 1851 during the Whites' visit to Camden. The account in *Spiritual Gifts* tells of Mrs. Preston's dramatic escape from her husband to attend the meeting at which the Whites were present. For reasons not fully known, the Camden members had disfellowshipped Mrs. Preston. A vision given Ellen White while she was visiting there emphasized the unfairness and uncharitableness of their behavior. It was well received by the members. Almira Preston subsequently moved to Illinois but remained an enthusiastic church member until the time of her death, as evidenced by her frequent letters to the *Review* and an appreciative obituary. There is evidence that her husband, John S. Preston, overcame his antipathies and became a Seventh-day Adventist.

See: Obituary: "Almira Preston," *Review,* July 17, 1888, p. 463; obituary: "John S. Preston," *Review,* Oct. 30, 1879, p. 151; 1870 U.S. Federal Census, "John S. Preston," Illinois, Ogle County, Marion, p. 17; Ellen G. White, *Spiritual Gifts [vol. 2],* pp. 150, 151; Ms 2, 1851 (June 23); Ms 2a, 1851 (June 23); search term "Preston" in *Words of the Pioneers.* Part of the above account depends on the identity of Almira Preston with "E. P." in *Spiritual Gifts [vol. 2],* pp. 150, 151. See Ms 2, 1851 (June 23), note 1, for discussion.

PRESTON, Chandler Bristol (1806-1891) and **Eliza Ann** (1810-1883)

Church members and former Millerites from Camden, New York, later Palermo, New York. Eliza Preston and probably also her husband became Sabbathkeepers in 1848. Ellen and James White stayed with the Prestons while visiting Camden during the winter of 1848-1849 and likely also during their visit in June 1851. Ellen White gave a gripping account of the second visit, in which Chandler Preston's brother, **John S. Preston**, also living in Camden but at this time vehemently opposed to the Sabbatarian Adventists, tied up his wife to prevent her attending the meetings. Only one letter from Ellen White to the Prestons is known to have survived.

See: Goldie Satterlee Moffatt, *Satterlee-Ley-Ly & Allied Families Genealogy* (Middleboro, Mass.: Chedwato Service, 1971), p. 220; obituary: "Chandler B. Preston," *Review,* Nov. 17, 1891, p. 719; obituary: "Eliza A. Preston," *Review,* May 1, 1883, p. 286; obituary: "John S. Preston," *Review,* Oct. 30, 1879, p. 151; C. B. Preston, [Receipts], *Day-Star,* June 6, 1846, p. 4; Ellen G. White, *Spiritual Gifts [vol. 2],* pp. 124, 126, 150; Lt 1, 1851 (Oct. 19).

PRIOR, Edward (c. 1815-?) and **Georgianna** (c. 1820-1850s)

Originally from England, Edward and Georgianna Prior settled in Camden, New York, where Edward was listed as "laborer" in the 1850 census. In June 1851 Ellen White reprimanded the Sabbathkeepers in Camden for disfellowshipping the Priors. They "had erred greatly. . . . It was an awful thing to reject one of God's children." The Priors were apparently reinstated. Georgianna Prior died at some point before 1860. Ellen White attributed her death to certain Camden members who had influenced her "against . . . obtaining medical aid." Ellen White rebuked those members as "fanatical in the extreme."

See: 1850 U.S. Federal Census, "Edward Prior," New York, Oneida County, Camden, p. 244. Ellen G. White, *Spiritual Gifts [vol. 2],* pp. 134, 135; Ms 2a, 1851 (June 23); Lt 1, 1851 (Oct. 19).

RALPH, Richard (1812-1897) and (first wife) **Minerva** (c. 1815-1854) and (second wife) **Sarah F.** (1832-1920)

Active laypersons from Berlin, Connecticut. The mentions of Richard Ralph by James and Ellen White in the late 1840s and early 1850s suggest that he was a traveling preacher during that period. The U.S. censuses of the period 1850-1880 list his occupation as shoemaker, "roofing buildings," and farmer. His first wife, Minerva, died in 1854, leaving six children.

Ellen White recounted her interaction with Richard and Minerva Ralph on two or three occasions in 1849. Most notable was their involvement in the dramatic healing of "Sister Penfield" and Richard Ralph's speaking "in a new tongue," interpreted to mean that Ralph and Hiram Edson should seek to reclaim Samuel W. Rhodes for public ministry.

See: Obituary, "Richard Ralph," *Review,* Oct. 5, 1897, p. 639; obituary, "The Companion of Bro. R. Ralph," *Review,* Oct. 17, 1854, p. 79; obituary, "Sarah F. Ralph," *Review,* Dec. 30, 1920, p. 14; Sherman W. Adams, *The History of Ancient Wethersfield, Connecticut: Comprising the Present Towns of Wethersfield, Rocky Hill and Newington: and of Glastonbury Prior to Its Incorporation in 1693, From Date of Earliest Settlement Until the Present Time, With Extensive Genealogies and Genealogical Notes on Their Families* (New York: Grafton Press, 1904), vol. 2, p. 538; 1850 U.S. Federal Census, "Richard Ralph," Connecticut, Hartford County, Berlin, p. 256; 1860 U.S. Federal Census, "Richard Ralph," Connecticut, Hartford County, Berlin, p. 31; 1870 U.S. Federal Census, "Richard Ralph," Connecticut, Hartford County, Berlin, p. 31; "Receipts for *Review and Herald,*"*Review,* Jan. 10, 1878, p. 16 ; Ellen G. White, *Spiritual Gifts [vol. 2],* p. 116; "Beloved Brethren, Scattered Abroad," *Present Truth,* December 1849, p. 35; Lt 8, 1849 (May 29).

RATELLE, Marguerite (née **DION**) (1829-1923) and **Joseph** (1820-after 1900)

Marguerite Ratelle, at one time a neighbor of the Whites in Battle Creek, Michigan, is mentioned in Ellen White's 1859 diary. At the time, the young Ratelle family was poverty-stricken, two children had died, Mrs. Ratelle's health was "very poor," and she had begun to "spit blood." Ellen and other neighbors assisted with clothing for Mrs. Ratelle's baby. Ellen White also gave a Bible to Elmira, the oldest daughter, age 10. Although Marguerite Ratelle never became a Seventh-day Adventist, she recalled in her old age that her friendship with the Whites had been "a pleasant one despite their religious differences." Her daughter, Elmira, on the other hand, became a lifelong and active Adventist.

See: "In Battle Creek Over 63 Years: Mrs. Marguerite Ratelle, Who Is 90, Recalls Early Day Experiences," newspaper account, Oct. 2, 1919, in Ross Coller Collection, Willard Library, Battle Creek, Michigan; "Aged Resident Dies in Indiana: Mrs. Margarette Ratelle, 94, Receives Call," newspaper article, Jan. 24, 1923, in Ross Coller Collection, Willard Library, Battle Creek, Michigan; "Mrs. Chapman, B. C. Resident 82 years, Dies," newspaper article, Mar. 12, 1937, in Ross Coller Collection, Willard Library, Battle Creek, Michigan; 1910 U.S. Federal Census, "Marguerite Ratell [*sic*]," Michigan, Calhoun County, Battle Creek, Ward 3, p. 4B; obituary: "Mrs. Elmira Chapman," *Lake Union Herald*, Mar. 30, 1937, p. 10; Ellen G. White, Ms 5, 1859 (Feb. 28, Mar. 1 entries).

RHODES, Samuel W. (c. 1810-1883) and (first wife) **Betsey E.** (?-1867) and (second wife) **Sophronia L.** (1825-1887)

Samuel Rhodes was an effective Millerite lecturer in upstate New York in the early 1840s but retired in confusion and discouragement after the disappointment of 1844. Encouraged by a vision of Ellen White's in 1849, Hiram Edson and Richard Ralph, under dramatic circumstances, sought Rhodes out from his isolation. Rhodes accepted the Sabbatarian message and immediately began to travel and preach.

During his first year Rhodes traveled to Illinois and Wisconsin, becoming the first Sabbatarian Adventist to preach in those states, also speaking in Michigan, Indiana, Canada East, and New England. Throughout the early 1850s he kept up a punishing schedule of travel and preaching appointments, but from 1852 onward there were continuing reports in the *Review* that Rhodes's health was suffering. Complaints started surfacing in the mid-1850s of Rhodes's severity and harshness, a result, perhaps, of his deteriorating health. Ellen White sent him several letters of admonition and reproof, but the problems persisted, and in 1860 Rhodes resigned as minister. He continued, however, to be a supportive member of the church till the end of his life, as evidenced by the many subscriptions and donations recorded in the *Review*. Samuel Rhodes's second wife, Sophronia, was the widow of **Job B. Peckham**.

See: Arthur Whitefield Spalding, *Footprints of the Pioneers* (Washington, D.C.: Review and Herald, 1947), pp. 148-156; 1870 U.S. Federal Census, "Saml. W. Rhodes," Michigan, Allegan County, Allegan, p. 59; Samuel W. Rhodes, "A Cheering Revival," *The Midnight Cry*, Oct. 5, 1843, p. 51; search term "S. W. Rhodes" in *Review and Herald* online collection, www.adventistarchives.org; obituary: "Betsey E. Rhodes," *Review*, Nov. 19, 1867, p. 358; obituary: "Sophronia L. Rhodes," *Review*, Jan. 17, 1888, p. 46; Ellen G. White, Ms 1, 1853 (June 2); Ms 6, 1854 (Feb. 19); Lt 16, 1859 (Oct. 28); Lt 5a, 1861 (Apr. 5).

ROGERS, Jane (née **FRASER**) (1821-1896) and **Sanford** (1830-1917)

Born in Scotland, Jane Fraser emigrated to the United States about 1846. In 1852 she became a Sabbatarian Adventist and shortly thereafter was employed as a domestic helper by James and Ellen White, then based in Rochester, New York, until her marriage to Sanford Rogers in 1862. Sanford was a carpenter, born in New York, who had joined the Sabbathkeeping Adventists in 1856. In 1861 he expressed his desire to join in tent evangelism, and apparently he spent a number of years as a lay preacher while still practicing his trade. In 1881, while living in Indiana, Sanford was ordained as a minister. From 1881 to 1890 he ministered in California, probably most of the time in St. Helena, where he also served for a while as "treasurer" at the Rural Health Retreat (later St. Helena Sanitarium).

Ellen White clearly found Jane to be dependable and efficient during the years she worked in the White household, especially so in looking after the children during the Whites' frequent travels. "An excellent baby tender," Ellen asserted in a letter to James in 1860. When, some 20 years later, Ellen met Jane Rogers again in California, she evidently enjoyed Jane's company, at one point taking Jane on an escorted trip to local churches. At the same time several testimonies from Ellen White to Jane and Sanford Rogers pointed out their character weaknesses, particularly in letters written to Sanford in 1890 in connection with his resignation and return to Michigan. Notable also is Ellen's letter of sympathy to Sanford Rogers after Jane's death.

See: Obituary: "Janey [*sic*] Rogers," *Review,* June 30, 1896, p. 415; obituary: "Sanford Rogers," *Review,* June 21, 1917, p. 22; 1870 U.S. Federal Census, "Rogers, Sanford," Michigan, Calhoun County, Battle Creek, Ward 3, p. 31; James Sawyer, "Systematic Benevolence," *Review,* Feb. 12, 1861, p. 104; J. O. Corliss, "Indiana Camp-Meeting," *Review,* Oct. 11, 1881, p. 235; search terms "S. Rogers" and "Sanford Rogers" in *Review and Herald* online collection, www.adventistarchives.org; Ellen G. White, "Among the Churches—Healdsburg," *Signs of the Times,* Jan. 19, 1882, p. 32; "Among the Churches—St. Helena," *Signs of the Times,* Jan. 26, 1882, p. 44; Lt 12a, 1860 (Oct.); Lt 22a, 1890 (Feb. 9); Lt 58, 1890 (Mar. 1); Lt 1c, 1890 (May 28); Lt 101, 1897 (Nov. 8).

ROOT, Ephraim Henry (1828-1906) and **Hezzy** (1832-1913)

President of the Michigan Conference from 1872 to 1876, and holding a number of other church leadership positions, Ephraim Root, of Wright, Michigan, became a Sabbathkeeping Adventist in 1858. His wife, Hezzy, took the same stand within a year or two. Within months of E. H. Root's becoming a Sabbatarian in 1858, the first meetinghouse in Wright was built on his land. In 1868 the first officially designated Seventh-day Adventist "camp-meeting" was held on the Root farm.

In 1861 Ephraim Root was elected elder of Wright church, and in 1874 he was ordained to the ministry. Root's administrative skills led to his serving frequently on the Michigan Conference executive committee from 1869 till the end of the century and holding the conference presidency 1872-1876. During the 1870s and 1880s he was heavily engaged on both district and state levels in the leadership of the Michigan Tract and Missionary Society, and for some years in the 1870s he served on the board of the Western Health Reform Institute.

The Whites stayed with Ephraim and Hezzy Root on numerous occasions when visiting Wright. The best known of these visits was a six-week stay December 1867 to January 1868 while James White was recovering from his first major stroke. Ellen White wrote of the Roots, "We were kindly received by this dear family and as tenderly cared for as Christian parents can care for invalid children."

See: Obituary: "Ephraim Henry Root," *Review,* Jan. 17, 1907, p. 23; obituary: "Hezzy Streeter Root," Apr. 10, 1913, p. 358; SDAE, s.v. "Michigan Conference"; Arthur Whitefield Spalding, *Footprints of the Pioneers* (Washington, D.C.: Review and Herald, 1947), pp. 196, 197; search term "E. H. Root" in *Review and Herald* online collection, www.adventistarchives.org; Ellen G. White, *Testimonies for the Church,* vol. 1, p. 570.

ROSS, Alexander (1810-1888) and (first wife) Caroline (c. 1810-1866) and (second wife) Melissa S. (1832-1915)

A blacksmith and farmer, Alexander Ross settled in Oswego County, New York, about 1834. He shared in the Millerite disappointment of 1844 and subsequently became a Sabbathkeeper, although the exact date is unknown. It probably predated August 1848, when Ross, according to J. N. Loughborough's account, attended the Volney Conference.

Ross had leadership potential, and there are indications in the *Review* that he did some lay preaching and was influential in his local church at Roosevelt. However, Ellen White's testimonies to Alexander Ross indicate personal and spiritual difficulties, which thwarted his potential. Among the problems mentioned were his reliance on "dreams and impressions," indifference to health reform, and a prolonged feud with his brother, **Manley Ross**, which had been "a reproach to the cause of God." Ross had also publicly embarrassed the church by his open support for the pro-slavery South in the early stages of the Civil War. He later retracted his position and expressed regret, but the damage had already been done.

Caroline Ross died in 1866, having "made no outward profession of religion," according to her obituary, although during her last year she had "become more in favor with the cause of present truth." Melissa, Alexander's second wife, joined the Seventh-day Adventist Church in the early 1860s. There are reports in the *Review* that she was an able speaker, especially on prophetic topics. Nevertheless, Ellen White did not encourage either Melissa or Alexander Ross to go on speaking tours of Adventist churches, but if anything, to venture to reach the unchurched. Whether Melissa Ross took offense at the 1872 testimony is not known, but her obituary states that "for some years she was not in perfect harmony with the people of God on the question of the spirit of prophecy," although "before her death she expressed confidence in the Testimonies."

See: Obituary: "Alexander Ross," *Review,* June 12, 1888, p. 383; obituary: "[Wife of] A. Ross," *Review,* Oct. 30, 1866, p. 175; obituary: "Melissa S. Ross," *Review,* Dec. 2, 1915, p. 22; 1850 U.S. Federal Census, "Caroline Ross," New York, Oswego County, Schroeppel, p. 268; J. N. Loughborough, "Recollections of the Past—No. 12," *Review,* Mar. 3, 1885, p. 138; Alex. Ross, "From Bro. Ross," *Review,* Apr. 21, 1863, p. 167; search terms "A. Ross" and "Alexander Ross" in *Review and Herald* online collection, www.adventistarchives.org; R. O. Damon, "Adams Center, N.Y.," *Review,* Nov. 21, 1871, p. 182; Ellen G. White, Ms 2, 1856 (May 27); Lt 24, 1862 (c. 1862); *Testimony to the Church* (PH159) (1872), pp. 78, 79, 81-84, 87.

ROSS, Manley T. (1824-1911) and Susanna (1825-1906)

Manley Ross, a blacksmith from Schroeppel, New York, and his wife, Susanna, started to keep the Sabbath in 1848. Before a church was built in nearby Roosevelt, meetings were held in their home, and James and Ellen White are said to have stayed with them when visiting the area.

Of Manley Ross, Ellen White wrote that he "intended to be true and right" but had a "fretful, unhappy temperament" and was involved in some of the dissension among Roosevelt members. The conflict between Manley and his brother and fellow church member **Alexander Ross** was a "reproach to the cause of God."

See: Obituary: "Manley Ross," *Review,* Mar. 16, 1911, p. 23; obituary: "Susanna Moyer Ross," *Review,* Nov. 15, 1906, p. 23; 1850 U.S Federal Census, "Manly Ross," New York, Oswego County, Schroeppel, p. 268; 1900 U.S. Federal Census, "Many [*sic*] Ross," New York, Oswego County, Volney, p. 8; Ellen G. White, Lt 2, 1858 (c. Mar.); Lt 16, 1861 (Aug. 3); *Testimony to the Church* (PH159) (1870), p. 81.

RUMERY, Sylsbre R. (1820-1884) and (first wife) **Nancy M.** (?-before 1848) and (second wife) **Betsey Jane** (1826-1916)

Church members from Monterey, Michigan. The Rumerys, who were of Methodist Episcopalian background, became Sabbathkeepers in 1856 or 1857. Sylsbre Rumery remained a church member for a number of years, but appears to have severed his connection in the 1870s and "made no profession of religion at the time of his death," according to his obituary. The Rumerys were well-to-do farmers, and Sylsbre held various important civic positions in Monterey throughout the years. As early as 1857 Ellen White pointed out to Sylsbre that "for years you have loved money better . . . than God." She made strong appeals to Rumery in 1860 and 1868, and while he did make serious efforts at reform, in the long run there appears to have been little change to his materialistic bent. Betsey Rumery remained a church member throughout her life. Jeremiah L. Rumery, Sylsbre's son by his first wife, subsequently served as elder and also as a treasurer of the Monterey church.

See: Portrait and Biographical Record of Kalamazoo, Allegan, and Van Buren Counties, Michigan (Chicago: Chapman Bros., 1892), pp. 710, 711; obituary: "Sylsbre Rumery," *Review,* Dec. 2, 1884, p. 766; obituary: "Betsie Lay Rumery," *Review,* June 15, 1916, p. 22; 1870 U.S. Federal Census: "Sylsbre Rumery," Michigan, Allegan County, Monterey, p. 13; Jack and Marianne Dibean, *Calhoun County, Michigan, Dibean Marriage Index*, 2003-2011, http://files.usgwarchives.net/mi/calhoun/vitals/marriages/dbn/dbn-feb-2011-l.txt (Oct. 20, 2011); *History of Allegan and Barry Counties, Michigan,* p. 288; Ellen G. White, *Testimony for the Churches at Allegan and Monterey* (PH099) (1869), pp. 29-41; Lt 9, 1857 (Oct.); Ms 4, 1860 (Dec.); Ms 16, 1868 (entries for May 8, 9).

RUSSELL, Charles P. (c. 1810-1879) and **Eunice** (c. 1810-after 1880)

Charles P. Russell is best known as one of the founders of the *Messenger* Party, the first offshoot movement from the Sabbatarian Adventists in the mid-1850s. Charles and

Eunice Russell, originally from New York State, settled in Jackson County, Michigan, about 1835. After a stint as a hotelkeeper, Charles Russell became established for many years as a "glove maker" in Jackson.

In 1843 or 1844 the Russells joined the Millerite Adventists in Jackson, and they became Sabbathkeepers following Joseph Bates's first visit to Jackson in 1849. Although some later historians claim that Charles Russell was a preacher, J. N. Loughborough, who knew Russell personally, speaks of him only as a church "brother." Russell later claimed that his break with the church in 1853 was a result of what he called "those vain visions" of Ellen White. Other accounts hold that the breaking point was not so much the visions themselves but the fact that Russell and Hiram S. Case became incensed when they were rebuked by a vision in the summer of 1853 for their severity in a church discipline case involving Abigail Palmer. They reacted with an open and concerted campaign against the Whites and joined others in organizing the *Messenger* Party, which survived till about 1857.

Three extant issues of *The Messenger of Truth,* house organ of the *Messenger* Party, indicate that Charles Russell was a member of the publishing committee. Little is known of Russell's religious endeavors after the breakup of the *Messenger* Party. According to his obituary in the Jackson *Weekly Citizen,* Russell "remained firm" "in the advent faith" to the end of his life. J. N. Loughborough adds that he gave up keeping the Sabbath three years before his death.

See: 1860 U.S. Federal Census, "Charles P. Russell," Michigan, Jackson County, Jackson, Ward 1, p. 15; 1880 U.S. Federal Census, "Eunice Russell," Michigan, Jackson County, Jackson, p. 15; U.S. Census Mortality Schedules, Michigan, Jackson, 1850-1885, Record for Charles P. Russell, Persons Who Died During the Year Ending May 31, 1880; *Report of the Pioneer Society of the State of Michigan, Together With Reports of County, Town, and District Pioneer Societies,* Pioneer Collections (Lansing, Mich.: W. S. George & Co., Printers and Binders, 1883), vol. 4, p. 272; J. N. Loughborough, "Sketches of the Past—82," *Pacific Union Recorder,* Nov. 11, 1909, p. 2; C. P Russell, "A Confession," *Messenger of Truth,* Oct. 19, 1854, p. [2]; "Death of a Pioneer," Jackson *Weekly Citizen,* Dec. 5, 1879, p. 5.

RUSSELL, Lester (1814-1898) and (first wife) **Ordelia** (c. 1820-before 1860) and (second wife) **Paulina P.** (1819-1898)

It is not known what year Lester Russell, a farmer and carpenter from Otsego, Michigan, became a Sabbatarian Adventist, but he submitted an affirmative letter to the *Review* in 1856, and two references to an "L. Russell" appear dating back to 1853. Numerous receipts in the *Review* through the years attest to his generosity to various church causes.

In her diary Ellen White related a visit to Otsego in January 1859, when the Sabbatarians were locked out of the Baptist meetinghouse and their meetings were relocated to "Brother Russell's house." Russell's strong support of the visions is clear from Gilbert Cranmer's account of his confrontation with Russell in 1858 over the authority of the visions. Cranmer finally responded to Russell with the words "Perhaps Mrs. White's visions are proof to you, but they are not to me."

See: Obituary: "Lester Russell," *Review,* Jan. 24, 1899, p. 62; obituary: "P. P. Russell," *Review,* Aug. 16, 1898, p. 530; 1850 U.S. Federal Census, "Ordelia Russell," Michigan, Allegan County, Otsego, p. 47; 1860 U.S. Federal Census, "Lester Russell," Michigan, Allegan County, Otsego, p. 54; 1870 U.S. Federal Census, "Lester Russell," Michigan, Allegan County, Otsego, p. 4; Lester Russell, "From Bro. Russell," *Review,* Dec. 25, 1856, p. 62; search term "Russell" in *Words of the Pioneers*; Ellen G. White, Ms 5, 1859 (Jan. 9 entry); Richard C. Nickels, *A History of the Seventh Day Church of God,* vol. 1, p. 36.

SAXBY, William L. (1827-1876) and **Euphemia H.** (1826-1902)

William and Euphemia Saxby, from Vermont and New York, respectively, became Adventists in the late 1840s and accepted the seventh-day Sabbath through the preaching of Joseph Bates in 1852 while living in Springfield, Massachusetts. William Saxby, a tinsmith and farmer, was an active layman through whom his brother-in-law **Augustin C. Bourdeau** and Stephen N. Haskell, later church leaders, became Sabbatarians in the 1850s. Around 1859 the Saxbys moved to Vermont, and in 1862-1863 William fought with the 1st Vermont Cavalry in the Civil War. It is possible that his war engagement coincided with a decline of faith. His obituary speaks of "a marked change in his course, . . . a desire to draw near to God" as he neared his death. The Saxbys received incidental mention in Ellen White's 1859 diary. The Whites were entertained at their home in Salem, Massachusetts, while holding meetings there.

See: Obituary: "W. L. Saxby," *Review,* Apr. 6, 1876, p. 111; Willard H. Saxby, "Father's Experience," *Review,* Mar. 8, 1917, p. 17; obituary: "Euphemie [*sic*] H. Saxby," *Review,* Oct. 7, 1902, p. 23; 1860 U.S. Federal Census, "William L. Saxby," Vermont, Franklin County, Enosburgh, p. 43; Stephen N. Haskell, Mary E. Haskell, "From Bro. and Sr. Haskell," *Review,* Feb. 6, 1855, p. 175; S. B. Horton, "Another Pioneer Laid to Rest," *Review,* Aug. 17, 1916, p. 16; *Civil War Research Database.* 2006, www.ancestry.com/search/rectype/military/cwrd/main.aspx (Dec. 11, 2006); *Report of the Adjutant & Inspector General of the State of Vermont From October 1, 1863 to October 1, 1864* (Montpelier: Walton's Steam Press, 1864), p. 211.

SCOTT, Mary A. (1820-1904) and **David W.** (1818-after 1904)

Mary Scott came to the United States from England as a child, married in the mid-1840s, and settled in Convis, Michigan, during the 1850s. On the day of her baptism, April 23, 1859, Mary was invited to dinner at the home of James and Ellen White in Battle Creek, Michigan. In 1863 Ellen White described David Scott as a "kind husband" but "not one" with Mary "in faith," and indications are that he never joined the Seventh-day Adventist Church. In 1863, at a time when Mary Scott was deeply disturbed over an alleged theft by a fellow church member, Ellen White wrote to admonish her to submit such matters to the church board and not let it ruin her spiritual experience.

See: Obituary: "Mary A. Scott," *Review,* Jan. 19, 1905, p. 23; 1860 U.S. Federal Census, "Mary Scott," Michigan, Calhoun County, Convis, p. 180; 1900 U.S. Federal Census, "Mary

A. Scott," Michigan, Calhoun County, Marshall, Ward 2, p. 10B; Ellen G. White, Ms 6, 1859 (Apr. 23 entry); Lt 5, 1863 (July 6).

SEELEY (SEELY), David Ross (1811-1901) and (first wife) **Laura** (c. 1822-1860) and (second wife) **Ellen Amelia** (1830-1907)

Laura Seeley began to keep the Sabbath in 1851, the first Adventist in Rochester, New York, to do so. David, a blacksmith, followed his wife in 1852, but not without first opposing her almost to the point of divorce. "I made up my mind that we should have to part" he wrote in a gripping testimony to the *Review*. The Seeleys both came out of the Millerite movement and were active laypersons in Rochester after becoming Sabbatarians.

James and Ellen White knew the Seeley family well, having lived next door to them in Rochester for a time in the early 1850s. David Seeley witnessed Ellen White in vision in 1854, his testimony of this event appearing in J. N. Loughborough's book *The Great Second Advent Movement*. On a return visit to Rochester in 1859, Ellen White found Laura Seeley very ill. "Poor afflicted soul!" Ellen exclaimed in her diary. Laura died the following year of "paralysis," age 38. After Laura's death David moved to Illinois and then Iowa. His second marriage was to Ellen Amelia Bannister Childs.

See: Obituary: "David Ross Seeley," *Review,* Nov. 12, 1901, p. 742; obituary: "Laura Seely," *Review,* June 5, 1860, p. 23; obituary: "Ellen Amelia Seeley," *Review,* Feb. 28, 1907, p. 23; Adelaide Keith Merrill, *The Keith Book* (Minneapolis: Lynd Press, 1934), p. 176; Sister Seely, "Letters," *Review,* Nov. 25, 1851, p. 55; David Seely, "Communication From Bro. Seely," *Review,* Nov. 25, 1852, p. 109; search term "Seely" in *Words of the Pioneers*; Ellen G. White, Lt 7, 1854 (July); Ms 7, 1859 (Aug. 23 entry); J. N. Loughborough, *The Great Second Advent Movement,* pp. 208, 209; 1860 U.S. Federal Census, "David Seely," Illinois, Whiteside County, Mount Pleasant, p. 296; 1870 U.S. Federal Census, "David Seeley," Iowa, Fayette County, Westfield, p. 27; 1900 U.S. Federal Census, "David Seeley," Iowa, Fayette County, Fayette, p. 12A.

SHARP, William D. (1830-1910) and **Sarah F.** (c. 1831-1910)

While visiting Green Springs, Ohio, in 1858, James and Ellen White stayed at the home of William Sharp, a carpenter, and his wife, Sarah. "They have recently embraced the truth," Ellen wrote to a friend. "Seem to be first-rate people." Though this appears to be the only reference to William and Sarah Sharp in her writings, Ellen White, while in Australia during the 1890s, developed a friendship with their daughter, Ida Ellen, and her husband, Edward Harmon Gates. The Gateses, pioneer missionaries to the South Pacific, sailed on the first voyage of the *Pitcairn* in 1890 and became well acquainted with Ellen White during visits to Australia.

See: Obituary: "William D. Sharp," *Review,* Jan. 5, 1911, p. 23; 1870 U.S. Federal Census, "Wm. D. Sharp," Ohio, Sandusky County, Green Creek, p. 53; 1910 U.S. Federal Census, "William D. Sharpe," Michigan, Calhoun County, Battle Creek, Ward 3, p. 6A; SDAE, s.v. "Edward Harmon Gates"; Ellen G. White, Lt 1, 1858 (Mar. 3); Ms 29, 1892 (Feb. 15 entry); Lt 49, 1892 (Dec. 23).

SMITH, Cyrenius (1804-1874) and **Louisa** (1806-1881)

Cyrenius Smith was born in Windsor, Vermont, and Louisa, née Sawyer, came from Lynn, Massachusetts. Cyrenius' father, Asahel Smith, had fought in the Revolutionary War in the late 1770s. After some years spent in Niagara County, New York, the Smiths bought land near Jackson, Michigan, where they farmed from the mid-1830s to 1855. In the 1840s they connected with the Millerite Adventist movement, and in 1849, following a visit by Joseph Bates to Jackson, they were among the first Adventists in Michigan to adopt Sabbathkeeping.

Cyrenius Smith's enthusiasm for his new faith is unmistakable in his first letter to the *Review* in 1850: "All that the Lord has placed in my hands is on the altar. . . . I send you fifty dollars to use in the cause of the Lord." In 1852, according to J. N. Loughborough, the Smiths sold their farm in order to free up cash to use for church projects. In 1855, when funds were needed to erect a building to house the Review and Herald press in Battle Creek, Michigan, Smith joined with others to lend $300 toward the project. His administrative talents were put to good use in the years following 1855, when the Smith family moved to Battle Creek. For several years Cyrenius Smith served on the publishing committee of the *Review* as well as sitting on the Michigan Conference executive committee in the 1860s.

In 1859/1860 the Smiths' attitude toward the visions of Ellen White, and toward James White in particular, hit a temporary low point. Letter 32, 1859 (July 9), suggests that the Smiths would not accept a testimony of reproof that they had received from Ellen White, and in the summer of 1860 a full-scale crisis of relations erupted between several church leaders, including Cyrenius Smith and James White. A special council was called in Battle Creek in June 1860 to work out a solution. Smith apparently retreated from his position, as seen in the resulting report: "At this council very humble acknowledgments were made by . . . Uriah Smith, and also by Bro. Cyrenius Smith, who has occupied an extremely faithless position in regard to the visions." Relations improved, and in 1863 Smith testified to the detractors of James White that for the 11 or 12 years he had dealt with him, White's course had been "one of unexceptionable integrity and benevolence."

See: Obituary: "Cyrenius Smith," *Review,* June 30, 1874, p. 23; obituary: "Louisa Smith," *Review,* Jan. 10, 1882, p. 30; Glenn and Jean Davis, compilers, "Records of Cyrenius Smith and R. M. Kilgore Families" (Berrien Springs, Mich.: Center for Adventist Research, Andrews University, 198?); Henry E. Perkins, *A New Edition of the Record of the Family of Roswell Smith* (Rutland, Vt.: Tuttle Co., 1921), p. 37; "Bro. C. Smith of Jackson, Mich.," *Review,* December 1850, p. 16; J. N. Loughborough, "Uncle Elkins and His Nephews," *Review,* Jan. 12, 1897, p. 18; Ellen G. White, Lt 32, 1859 (July 9); S. T. Belden et al., *To Brother J. N. Andrews and Sister H. N. Smith* (PH016) (n.p., 1860); Uriah Smith, *Vindication of the Business Career of Elder James White* (Battle Creek, Mich.: Steam Press of the Seventh-day Adventist Pub. Assn., 1863), p. 26; search terms "C. Smith" and "Cyrenius Smith" in *Review and Herald* online collection, www.adventistarchives.org.

SMITH, Stephen (1806-1889) and Matilda (1809-1891)

Stephen and Matilda Smith, from New Hampshire, became Sabbathkeepers about 1850. Although he did some lay preaching in the 1850s, Stephen Smith had a troubled relationship with the church and subsequently allied himself to offshoot movements in opposition to Seventh-day Adventism and the visions of Ellen White. Some sources suggest that Matilda Smith, unlike her husband, remained a Seventh-day Adventist until her death.

About 1842 Stephen and Matilda Smith joined the Millerite Adventist movement. According to his obituary, Stephen Smith gave himself "to the work of publicly proclaiming the second coming of Christ." The Smiths subsequently became Sabbathkeepers and remained so the rest of their lives. However, there were other doctrinal issues on which Stephen Smith was at odds with the new movement. These included, at an earlier stage, his belief in some sort of "spiritual" rather than literal Second Coming, his later support for 1854 as the date for the Second Coming, and his rejection of the visions of Ellen White.

These consequent tensions with the Sabbatarian Adventist movement led to periodic crises. In 1851 Smith was excluded from fellowship but was readmitted in 1852 after having "fully confessed and renounced" his errors. In 1854 Smith left the movement again but sought readmission in 1857, when in midwinter he "waded twelve miles through the snow on foot to confess his past wrongs." However, by the following year he was out again "in his rebellion" and remained so until a few years before his death, when, in 1885, he returned to the church with the self-described words "another rebel has surrendered."

There is no record of Stephen Smith's acknowledging the authenticity of Ellen White's visions before 1885. As early as 1851 Ellen White noted at a meeting in Washington, New Hampshire, that "all acknowledged their faith in the visions except Brother Butler and S. Smith." In 1857 Smith confessed that he had "had particular hatred towards Bro. and Sr. White." During the mid-1850s Smith was sympathetic to the *Messenger* Party, and from the 1860s to the Marion Party (later Church of God [Seventh Day]), both of which, although Sabbatarian, were offshoot movements from Seventh-day Adventism and were strongly opposed to the visions. In a dramatic turnaround in 1885, Stephen Smith testified that he had come to the place "where I firmly believe they [the testimonies of Ellen White] are all of God," acknowledging the truthfulness of a personal testimony he had received 28 years earlier, but which he had chosen not to read until that time, having "locked it up in my trunk."

See: Obituary: "Stephen Smith," *Review,* Jan. 28, 1890, p. 63; obituary: "Matilda Smith," *Review,* June 2, 1891, p. 351; *History of Washington, New Hampshire,* pp. 611, 612; E. W. Farnsworth to Ellen G. White, July 15, 1885; "Returning to the Ranks," *Review,* Feb. 19, 1857, p. 126; A. S. Hutchings, "Communication From Bro. Hutchins," *Review,* Mar. 12, 1857, p. 152; "Bro. Stephen Smith," *Review,* Nov. 25, 1852, p. 112; letter from "Bro. J. Stowell," *Review,* Apr. 18, 1854, p. 102; 1850 U.S. Federal Census, "Stephen Smith," New Hampshire, Sullivan County, Lempster, p. 58; Ellen G. White, Lt 8, 1851 (Nov. 12); Ms 2, 1858 (Dec. 27).

SMITH, Uriah (1832-1903) and Harriet Newall (1831-1911)

Editor and author, Uriah Smith was born in New Hampshire. As a boy he participated in the closing stages of the Millerite movement and was baptized as a Sabbatarian Adventist in 1852. Because of his literary skill Smith was invited to join the Review and Herald office in 1853, rapidly rising to the position of editor by 1855. In 1857 Uriah married Harriet Stevens, a coworker, the daughter of **Cyprian** and **Almira Stevens**. Until his death in 1903 Smith served, with only brief interruptions, as either editor or associate editor of the *Review.*

Best known of the many books Smith authored were his expositions on the prophecies of Revelation (*Thoughts . . . on the Book of Revelation,* 1867) and Daniel (*Thoughts . . . on the Book of Daniel,* 1873). These two books were later combined into one volume, went through several editions, and are still in print. Uriah Smith also served in various administrative positions, most notably as executive secretary of the General Conference for a total of about 20 years, and taught Bible subjects at Battle Creek College.

Uriah Smith was connected with Ellen White as a friend and colleague for 50 years and was one of the staunchest defenders of her prophetic gift, as evidenced in many articles and books. His biographer, Eugene Durand, notes that despite his public defense, Smith sometimes found it difficult to accept testimonies of warning and reproof directed at himself. Durand gives examples of Smith initially rejecting or denying the accuracy of such personal testimonies but later confessing that they had been right on target. Uriah's wife, Harriet, the recipient of a number of strong reproofs from Ellen White in the 1850s and 1860s, remained a faithful member of the Battle Creek church to the time of her death.

See: Eugene F. Durand, *Yours in the Blessed Hope, Uriah Smith,* pp. 281-296; obituary: "In Memoriam," *Review,* Mar. 10, 1903, pp. 3-7; obituary: "Harriet N. Smith," *Review,* Mar. 30, 1911, p. 23.

SMITH, William (c. 1808-after 1872) and Laura (1810-1872)

The Smiths were farmers and church members from Convis, Michigan. Laura Smith became a Sabbathkeeper about 1857, but her husband, William, struggled for some time before taking that step. While on a visit to Convis in 1859, Ellen White noted in her diary that "Brother Smith is convinced that the seventh day is the Sabbath, but the cross stands in his way. He fears his children." Nevertheless, when the Convis Seventh-day Adventist church was organized in 1861, William Smith was listed among the charter members, and there are several notices in the *Review* of monthly district meetings held in his home during the 1860s. About 1865 Ellen White admonished Smith over his continued use of tobacco while also appealing to Convis church members to "exercise a kind forbearance to Brother Smith" in his struggle.

See: 1870 U.S. Federal Census, "William Smith," Michigan, Calhoun County, Convis, p. 8; James White, *An Appeal to the Working Men and Women in the Ranks of Seventh-day Adventists,* p. 36; obituary: "Laura Smith," *Review,* June 25, 1872, p. 15; Ellen G. White, Ms 6, 1859 (Apr. 10 entry); Ms 4, 1865 (c. 1865); H. B. Peirce, *History of Calhoun County, Michigan,* vol. 1, p. 154; J. N. Loughborough, "Appointments," *Review,* Nov. 20, 1866, p. 200; John Sisley, "Monthly Meeting in Convis, Mich.," *Review,* June 25, 1867, p. 28; J. H. Waggoner, "Monthly Meeting at Convis," *Review,* June 23, 1868, p. 13.

SPERRY, Charles W. (c. 1820-1861) and **Rachel Ann** (c. 1831-1863)

Pioneer preacher Charles W. Sperry and his wife, Rachel Ann, were both from Vermont, came from a Millerite background, and became Sabbathkeepers in 1851-1852. Soon after this, Charles, earlier a schoolteacher, began an intensive preaching ministry, mostly in Vermont and New York. In 1853 he was "ordained to the work of the gospel ministry" together with J. N. Andrews and A. S. Hutchins, in one of the earliest ordination services of the Sabbatarian movement. His ministry lasted only nine years until his untimely death in 1861, at age 41.

"I saw that Charles and Rachel Ann both were beloved of God. I saw that Charles was a precious, chosen vessel," Ellen White wrote in 1856. She later consoled Rachel at the loss of her husband with the words "He fell like a soldier; he died at his post." Nevertheless, Ellen White was impressed that Charles Sperry's death was a premature one, that "had he worked with reference to health he might have lived to have labored until the present time."

See: Obituary: "Charles W. Sperry," *Review,* Oct. 1, 1861, p. 143; obituary: "Rachel Ann Sperry," *Review,* Nov. 24, 1863, p. 207; H. B. Peirce, *History of Calhoun County, Michigan,* vol. 2, pp. 1167, 1168; search term "Sperry" in *Words of the Pioneers*; "Eastern Tour," *Review,* Nov. 15, 1853, p. 148; Ellen G. White, Lt 11, 1856 (Apr.); Lt 8, 1861 (Sept. 26); Ms 3, 1868 (June 12).

STEVENS, Angeline S. See **ANDREWS, John Nevins** and **Angeline.**

STEVENS, Cyprian (1795-1858) and **Almira T.** (c. 1803-1873)

Among the earliest Sabbatarian Adventists in the state of Maine, the Stevenses were the parents-in-law of **J. N. Andrews** and **Uriah Smith**. For more than 30 years Cyprian and Almira farmed in Paris, Maine, before moving west to Waukon, Iowa, in 1856, where Cyprian died two years later from a rattlesnake bite.

During the spring of 1845 several Adventist families in Paris, including Cyprian and Almira Stevens, became Sabbathkeepers after studying T. M. Preble's tract on the Sabbath, published in March 1845. Together with a certain segment of ex-Millerites in Maine after the disappointment of 1844, Cyprian Stevens descended for a time into rank fanaticism, including religious crawling. His son, Charles F. Stevens, later to become a Seventh-day Adventist minister and administrator, recalled that local authorities in Paris took his brothers and sisters from their parents for a time, "except myself who was the youngest," placing them with other families in the area "who were supposed to know how to train them up in the way they should go."

The Stevens family did not take kindly to testimonies of reproof received from Ellen

White, nor to James White's leadership during the Whites' stay in Paris in 1850-1851. Their opposition continued through the 1850s. "They have despised reproof, despised the visions," wrote Ellen White in 1860. She also noted that two of the Stevens daughters married eminent church leaders (Angeline married **J. N. Andrews** and Harriet married **Uriah Smith**), thus spreading their views of the visions and of James White to the very core of church leadership. By the early 1860s, however, various members of the Stevens family appear to have had a change of heart. "I no [*sic*] that I have not taken that stand on the visions for years past as I should," Almira acknowledged in a letter to Ellen White in 1862, and in a letter to the *Review* editor some months later she thanked the Lord "for the strait testimonies that He has sent us through Sister White."

See: Obituary: "Cyprian Stevens," *Review,* Oct. 28, 1858, p. 183; obituary: "Almira T. Stevens," *Review,* Mar. 3, 1874, p. 95; William Berry Lapham, *History of Paris, Maine,* p. 733; "General Conference Proceedings, Sixth Meeting . . . ," *General Conference Bulletin,* Apr. 8, 1901, p. 116; T. M. Preble, *A Tract, Showing That the Seventh Day Should Be Observed as the Sabbath, Instead of the First Day; "According to the Commandment"* (Nashua, N.H.: Murray and Kimball, 1845); M. S. Crawford, "Extracts From Letter of M. S. Crawford to W. C. W." dated "c. Oct. 9, 1908," Ellen G. White Estate, DF 439; Charles F. Stevens, [Recollections], Smith/Bovee Collection (Berrien Springs, Mich.: Center for Adventist Research, Andrews University), p. 5; Almira Stevens to Ellen White, Jan. 23, 1862; Almira T. Stevens, "From Sister Stevens," *Review,* July 29, 1862, p. 71; Ellen G. White, Lt 8, 1860 (June 11). For a survey of relations between the Stevens and Andrews families of Paris and James and Ellen White, see Ron Graybill, "The Family Man," in Harry Leonard, ed., *J. N. Andrews: The Man and the Mission,* pp. 16-19.

STEVENS, Harriet Newall. See **SMITH, Uriah** and **Harriet Newall.**

STONE, Albert (1803-c. 1893) and (first wife) **Lurena** (1803-1868) and (second wife) **Ayer** (c. 1805-after 1880)

A farmer-preacher from Vermont, Albert Stone began preaching in his early 20s, probably for the Baptists. About 1840 Lurena adopted the Second Advent teachings of William Miller, for which "the Baptists dropped her name from their records." Albert Stone took the same step and went on to preach for the Millerites and mainstream Adventists until about 1852. In 1853 the Stones became Sabbathkeepers. Albert continued preaching, mostly in northern Vermont, for the remainder of his long life. He was also active in the Vermont Conference, serving as its first "chairman" when the conference was organized in 1862. A son, Charles Wesley Stone, served as secretary of the General Conference, assistant editor of the *Review and Herald,* and teacher at Battle Creek College in the late 1870s and early 1880s. Albert Stone received only incidental mention in the writings of Ellen White.

See: 1850 U.S. Federal Census, "Albert Stone," Vermont, Franklin County, Berkshire,

p. 214; "Editorial Notes," *General Conference Bulletin,* Feb. 22, 1895, p. 308; obituary: "Lurena Stone," *Review,* May 5, 1868, p. 334; 1880 U.S. Federal Census, "Ayer Stone," Vermont, Lamoille County, Eden, p. 16; Lewis Cass Aldrich, ed., *History of Franklin and Grand Isle Counties, Vermont: With Illustrations and Biographical Sketches of Some of the Prominent Men and Pioneers* (Syracuse, N.Y.: D. Mason & Co., 1891), p. 457; Albert Stone, "Communications," *Review,* Aug. 4, 1853, p. 47; search term "Stone" in *Review and Herald* online collection, www.adventistarchives.org; SDAE, s.v. "Northern New England Conference," "Charles Wesley Stone."

STOWELL, Harriet Augusta. See **BARTON, Harriet Augusta.**

STOWELL, Lewis Barnard (1793-1886) and **Laura B.** (1805-1868)

Lewis and Laura Stowell were among the first Adventists in Maine to become Sabbathkeepers. Lewis Stowell had served as a corporal in the War of 1812 and later became a merchant in Paris, Maine. Laura, née Tuell, was a schoolteacher before her marriage and is said to have been "a public speaker of unusual ability." Her cousin, Sidney Perham, served as a member of the U.S. House of Representatives from 1863 to 1869 and was governor of Maine from 1871 to 1874. The Stowells left Maine in 1854 and settled in Illinois, later Wisconsin.

Lewis and Laura Stowell took part in the Millerite movement of the early 1840s. During the spring of 1845 their 15-year-old daughter, **Marian C. Stowell**, together with her brother, **Lewis Oswald Stowell,** studied a Sabbatarian tract by T. M. Preble, and became, perhaps not the first Adventists in Maine to keep the Sabbath, but the first of those Adventists who would later become Seventh-day Adventists. Their parents, as well as several other families in Paris, soon followed their lead.

In later reminiscences Marian Stowell strongly suggested that her parents, along with some other Paris Sabbatarians, were for a while caught up in some of the fanaticism and theological confusion that followed the disappointment of October 1844. She recalled that short-term visionaries such as Dorinda Baker and Mary Hamlin stayed in their house for two or three months, probably in 1845. By 1849 Lewis Stowell was again involved in theological entanglements. Ellen White was shown in vision that "Brother Stowell of Paris was wavering upon the shut door," causing her and James to visit Stowell and other Paris members for a week of meetings. As a result "Brother Stowell was established in the shut door and all the present truth he had doubted." It is the only major mention of Lewis Stowell in Ellen White's writings. Both Lewis and Laura Stowell went on to become lifelong members of the church.

See: Obituary: "Lewis B. Stowell," *Review,* Jan. 4, 1887, p. 14; obituary: "Laura Stowell," *Review,* May 12, 1868, p. 350; W.H.H. Stowell, *The Stowell Genealogy: A Record of the Descendants of Samuel Stowell of Hingham, Mass.* (Rutland, Vt.: Tuttle Co., 1922), pp. 365-367; Mrs. M. C. Stowell Crawford, "A Letter From a Veteran Worker," *Southern Watchman,* Apr. 25, 1905, p. 278; T. M. Preble, *A Tract, Showing That the Seventh Day Should Be Observed as the Sabbath, Instead of the First Day; "According to the Commandment"*

(Nashua, N.H.: Murray and Kimball, 1845); Marian Stowell Crawford to "Sister White," Oct. 9, 1908; Ellen G. White, Lt 5, 1849 (Apr. 21).

STOWELL, Lewis Oswald (1828-1918) and Mary Melissa (1839-1899)

Lewis Oswald Stowell and his sister **Marian C. (Stowell) Crawford** are best known for being the first of future Seventh-day Adventists in Maine to adopt Sabbathkeeping. It was in the spring of 1845 that these teenagers from Paris, Maine, began to keep the Sabbath after studying a tract by T. M. Preble. They were soon joined by their parents, **Lewis Barnard** and **Laura B. Stowell**, and several other families in the area.

Oswald Stowell (he was known by his middle name) joined the staff at the *Review* printing office in Rochester, New York, in 1852, operating the hand press and boarding with James and Ellen White. He apparently left *Review* employ in 1855 or earlier, since there is no record of Stowell's moving to Battle Creek when the press moved there in 1855. For the next 30 or so years he was a farmer in Illinois while remaining an active layperson and giving generously to church causes. Several poems by Mary Stowell were published in the *Review*. The 1910 census revealed that the widowed Oswald Stowell was living with his daughter, Cora Belle, and her husband, Albion Fox Ballenger, in Riverside, California. By this time A. F. Ballenger, previously a prominent Seventh-day Adventist minister, writer, and editor, had apostatized. Stowell, however, did not adopt Ballenger's variant doctrinal views, as his obituary writer pointed out: "Brother Stowell remained a firm believer in every principle of the message till the hour of his death."

Two striking incidents involving Ellen White and Oswald Stowell have been recorded. In the first, Oswald, age 21, was present at a conference in Topsham, Maine, in 1849 at which Ellen White received a vision. According to an observer, Ellen White, while in vision, "laying the Bible on Oswell Stowell," uttered an admonition including the words "let not its pages be closed, read it carefully." Three years later, in 1852, while living with the Whites in Rochester, Oswald was suffering "from a very severe attack of pleurisy, and had been given up by the physician to die," according to J. N. Loughborough's account. Following prayer by the Whites, Loughborough, and several others at Oswald's bedside, and after anointing with oil by James White, Oswald "was instantly healed."

See: Obituary: "Lewis Oswald Stowell," *Review*, Oct. 17, 1918, p. 12; obituary: "Mary Melissa Stowell," *Review*, Jan. 30, 1900, p. 78; W.H.H. Stowell, *The Stowell Genealogy: A Record of the Descendants of Samuel Stowell of Hingham, Mass.* (Rutland, Vt.: Tuttle Co., 1922), pp. 614, 615; Mrs. M. C. Stowell Crawford, "A Letter From a Veteran Worker," *Southern Watchman*, Apr. 25, 1905, p. 278; T. M. Preble, *A Tract, Showing That the Seventh Day Should Be Observed as the Sabbath, Instead of the First Day; "According to the Commandment"* (Nashua, N.H.: Murray and Kimball, 1845); "The Review and Herald," *Review*, Oct. 14, 1852, p. 96; search term "Stowell" in *Review and Herald* online collection, www.adventistarchives.org; 1910 U.S. Federal Census, "Stowell, Oswald," California, Riverside County, West Riverside Township, p. 4A; SDAE, s.v. "Albion Fox Ballenger"; J. N. Loughborough, *The Great Second Advent Movement*, p. 318; Ellen G. White, Ms 5, 1849 (Sept. 23).

STOWELL, Marion Concordia. See CRAWFORD, Marion Concordia (Stowell).

STREET, Sherman A. (c. 1827-1888) and Sarah Jane (1834-1915)

A farmer from Eaton County, Michigan, Sherman Street is first mentioned in Sabbatarian sources in 1856. He married Sarah Jane Love in 1855. In 1859 Sherman traveled to Battle Creek, Michigan, with J. F. Carman, to urge James and Ellen White to come and preach in their home area. Ellen White recorded their visit in her diary.

See: Obituary: "Sarah Jane Love Street," *Review,* Mar. 25, 1915, p. 22; Gilbert Warren Chapin, *The Chapin Book of Genealogical Data, With Brief Biographical Sketches, of the Descendants of Deacon Samuel Chapin* (Hartford, Conn.: Chapin Family Association, 1924), vol. 2, p. 1594; 1860 U.S. Federal Census, "Sherman A. Street," Michigan, Eaton County, Benton, p. 118; Ellen G. White, Ms 5, 1859 (Feb. 5 entry).

TAYLOR, Charles O. (1817-1905) and (first wife) Matilda W. (c. 1824-1880) and (second wife) Mary Jane (1838-1913)

C. O. Taylor, a minister from New York State, is most remembered for his pioneer evangelism in the southeastern United States. Both he and his brother, Daniel T. Taylor, participated in the Millerite movement and subsequently became clergymen in different branches of Adventism, with Daniel Taylor becoming an Advent Christian preacher and writer. Charles Taylor started to keep the Sabbath in 1852 and was ordained as a minister in 1857. After serving many years in New York, in 1876 Charles and Matilda Taylor embarked on several years of itinerant and pioneering evangelism in Georgia, the Carolinas, Alabama, and Mississippi. Records indicate that Charles Taylor addressed some Black audiences, although most of his meetings were with Southern Whites.

Ellen White appreciated Charles Taylor's good qualities ("Brother Taylor's spirit is precious in the sight of the Lord"), but she also conveyed messages of reproof on occasion. In 1868 she censured him for being "selfish in regard to means" to the point that he had exploited his domestic hired help. Perhaps most interesting is an 1872 testimony addressed to Taylor and several other ministers in New York in which they were upbraided for going "over and over the same ground among the churches" and were urged instead "to go out in new fields and labor to bring souls into the truth." There may be a connection between this testimony and the Taylors' bold venture four years later to leave their native New York and become the first denominational workers to enter Georgia, and be among the first to work in other states in the Southeast.

See: Obituary: "Chas. O. Taylor," *Review,* Sept. 7, 1905, pp. 19, 20; obituary: "M. W. Taylor," *Review,* Nov. 4, 1880, p. 302; obituary: "Mary Jane Haskell Taylor," *Re-*

view, Sept. 4, 1913, p. 862; SDAE, s.v. "South Atlantic Conference," "Charles O. Taylor," "Daniel T. Taylor"; search term "C. O. Taylor" in *Review and Herald* online collection, www.adventistarchives.org; Ellen G. White, Lt 31, 1861 (c. 1861); Lt 16, 1868 (June 20); *Testimony to the Church* (1872) (PH159), pp. 63, 64.

TEMPLE, Elizabeth (c. 1808-1884) and (first husband) **James L.** (c. 1814-before 1862) and (second husband) **Ransom HICKS** (1802-1872)

Elizabeth Temple was an active layperson in Boston and a physician. The earliest mention of Elizabeth Temple in church records dates from 1849, when she experienced a remarkable healing following prayer and anointing by a small group of believers, including Ellen and James White. Ellen White described Elizabeth Temple as "very poor," taking in "washing to earn means to sustain her family" and married to a "confirmed drunkard." Yet 20 years later, in a striking turnaround, Elizabeth Temple, of 41 Shawmut Ave., Boston, was registered in the 1869 *Boston Directory* as a "physician," and with a substantial $12,000 in real estate holdings, according to the 1870 census. That it was the same Elizabeth Temple as the one healed in 1849 is confirmed by the mention in the *Review* that Sabbath services were held in 1870 at "Sr. Temple's, 41 Shawmut Avenue, Boston."

After Elizabeth Temple became a woman of some means, Ellen White sent at least two testimonies reminding her that she had not "borne well the test of prosperity" and was "robbing God in tithes and offerings." To one of these letters Mrs. Temple responded publicly in the *Review,* acknowledging that the testimony was "true." On the positive side, Elizabeth showed her devotion to the church by opening up her home for church services for many years and for the frequent hospitality she showed to visiting preachers, including James and Ellen White when they were in Boston.

Given her positive contributions to the church, it is surprising that Elizabeth Temple's second marriage, in the late 1860s, was to Ransom Hicks. A fairly well-known oppositional figure, Ransom Hicks had joined the offshoot *Messenger* Party in the 1850s and continued to write against Seventh-day Adventists in the 1860s. There are hints, however, that Mrs. Temple may have become estranged from the church following misunderstandings over a large donation that she had made in 1864. Nevertheless, by the end of 1868 her problems with the church were cleared up, and Elizabeth decisively broke with Ransom by divorcing him.

See: Obituary: "Elizabeth Temple," *Review,* Feb. 24, 1885, p. 127; 1850 U.S. Federal Census, "James L. Temple," Massachusetts, Suffolk County, Boston, Ward 10, p. 343; Ellen G. White, *Spiritual Gifts [vol. 2],* pp. 109, 110; Lt 5, 1849 (Apr. 21); Lt 25, 1868 (Dec. 2); Lt 39, 1874 (July 6); Lt 34, 1897 (June 8); *The Boston Directory . . . 1869* (Boston: Sampson, Davenport, & Co.), p. 595; 1870 U.S. Federal Census, "Elizabeth Temple," Massachusetts, Suffolk County, Boston, Ward 10, p. 234; search term "E. Temple" and "Elizabeth Temple" in *Review and Herald* online collection, www.adventistarchives.org; "Sr. E. Temple . . . to Sr. White," *Review,* Mar. 2, 1869, p. 79; N. Orcutt, "Report of Labor," *Review,* Aug. 2, 1870, p. 51. On Ransom Hicks, see *First Record Book of the Society of Colonial Dames in the State of Rhode Island and Providence Plantation* (Providence, R.I.: Snow & Farnham, Printers, 1897), p. 126; "From Bro. Hicks," *Messenger of Truth,* Nov. 2, 1854, p. [4]; "A Correction," *Review,* May 14, 1867, p. 275; "Personal," *Review,* Oct. 4, 1864, p. 148; John Nevins Andrews et al., *Defense of Elder James White and Wife,* pp. 17, 18.

TENNEY, Elizabeth (née WHITE) (1818-1885) and Thomas Boynton (1800-1875)

Elizabeth Tenney was a sister of **James Springer White**'s. Born in Palmyra, Maine, she married Thomas Tenney, from nearby St. Albans, in 1851. Thomas, a farmer, served several times as a member of the Maine legislature. In 1852 James White refers to the Tenneys as "Bro. and Sr. Tenney," which suggests that they were associated with the Sabbatarian Adventists. If that was the case, it was not a lasting association, since death notices of both Thomas and Elizabeth appear in Congregationalist publications. Thomas Tenney is there commended as "a strict keeper of the Sabbath" (i.e., Sunday).

Whatever her relationship to the Adventist Church may have been, Elizabeth Tenney, or "Lizzie," as she was affectionately called, appears to have had a very good personal relationship with James and Ellen White. The two families made a special effort to meet when the Whites visited central Maine. At least six such occasions are on record. In 1871 Thomas came to hear Ellen White speak at a camp meeting in nearby Skowhegan. Probably the last meeting of Ellen with Elizabeth took place in 1876 after Elizabeth's husband had died and left her living in very meager circumstances with in-laws. "I felt not a little indignant," wrote Ellen White. "Lizzie sleeps in an unfinished open stairway. . . . I said when I saw it, my sister Lizzie shall never live in such a place like this." Exactly what action Ellen White subsequently took is not known, but it does illustrate Ellen's warm feelings for her sister-in-law.

See: M. J. Tenney, *The Tenney Family or the Descendants of Thomas Tenney of Rowley, Massachusetts, 1638-1904* (Concord, N.H.: Rumford Press, 1904), p. 167; *General Conference of the Congregational Churches in Maine—Forty-ninth Annual Meeting, Maine Missionary Society, Sixty-eighth Anniversary* (Bangor: Barr & Robinson, 1875), p. 95; *General Conference of the Congregational Churches in Maine, Sixtieth Anniversary, Maine Missionary Society, Seventy-ninth Anniversary* (Bangor: John H. Bacon, Printers, 1886), p. 97; "Eastern Tour," *Review,* Oct. 14, 1852, p. 96; 1860 U.S. Federal Census, "Thomas B. Tenney," Maine, Somerset, St. Albans, p. 42; 1870 U.S. Federal Census, "Thomas B. Tenney," Maine, Somerset, St. Albans, p. 14; search terms "Tenney" and "Tenny" in *Words of the Pioneers*; Ellen G. White, Lt 13, 1871 (Sept. 2); Lt 47, 1876 (July).

THOMPSON, Jesse (1795-1858) and Nabby Maria (1805-1866)

Born in Andover, New Hampshire, Jesse Thompson was ordained as an "evangelist" for the Christian Connection in 1821. He married Maria Gilbert in 1822. By the late 1820s they had settled in Ballston, New York, where they lived for the remainder of their lives. According to Ellen White, Jesse Thompson "preached twenty years" with the Christian Connection "before he embraced the second advent doctrine." In 1840 he was a delegate to the first Millerite General Conference and was listed among the "ministers" attending the 1841 General Conference. Through the preaching of George W. Holt in early 1851, Jesse and Maria connected with the Sabbatarian Adventists. Shortly thereafter, during the summer of 1851, they extended their hospitality to James and Ellen White, who stayed in their home for several weeks before moving to nearby Saratoga Springs. An important conference dealing with the future of the publishing work was held in the Thompson house in 1852. The last mention of Jesse Thompson in the *Review* was in 1854.

See: John R. Eastman, *History of the Town of Andover, New Hampshire, 1751-1906* (Concord, N.H.: Rumford Printing Co., 1910), p. 401; Francis Bacon Trowbridge, *The Champion Genealogy: A History of the Descendants of Henry Champion of Saybrook and Lyme, Connecticut, Together with Some Account of Other Families of the Name* (New Haven, Conn.: the author, 1891), p. 295; Dave Bixby, "Briggs Cemetery, Town of Ballston," n.d., http://saratogany genweb.com/brigscem.htm (Sept. 13, 2011); Geo. W. Holt, "Letter From Bro. Holt," *Review,* March 1851, p. 56; Gerald Wheeler, *James White,* p. 66; "The Conference," *Review,* Mar. 23, 1852, p. 108; Ellen G. White, Lt 7, 1851 (July 27); "Conference. Names of Members and Contributors," *Signs of the Times* (Himes), Nov. 1, 1840, p. 120; "General Conference," *Signs of the Times* (Himes), Dec. 1, 1841, p. 131; search term "Thompson" in *Review and Herald* online collection, www.adventistarchives.org.

TOWLE, John R. (1812-after 1885) and **Mary M.** (1818-after 1885)

A former minister, born in New Hampshire, John Towle became an Adventist around 1848 and a Sabbathkeeper probably in 1852. He married Mary M. Brooks in 1834. Despite his ministerial background, Towle was not highly regarded as a Sabbatarian preacher. At a conference in 1853 at New Haven, Vermont, "all were agreed in expressing their disapproval" of Ezra Eastman and J. R. Towle. "While they travel from place to place (doing no real good, but, rather, harm), apparently to get their living, they are unworthy the confidence of the people of God." A vision given Ellen White some weeks later confirmed this appraisal. Towle did not break his association with the Sabbatarian movement after this setback, however. For six years the *Review* carried a continuing record of his subscriptions, donations, and letters (including a letter of "confession" in 1856) until 1859, after which there is no further record of him. The 1880 census listed John Towle as a "minister" living in Walker, Iowa.

See: George Hiram Greely, *Genealogy of the Greely-Greeley Family* (Boston: Frank Wood, Printer, 1905), p. 398; William Allen Wallace, *The History of Canaan, New Hampshire* (Concord, N.H.: Rumford Press, 1910), p. 640; 1880 U.S. Federal Census, "John R. Towle," Iowa, Linn County, Walker, p. 20; 1885 Iowa State Census, "John R. Towle," Linn County, Walker, p. 35; [J. R. Towle], "Bro. J. R. Towle Writes From Woodbury, Vt.," *Review,* June 10, 1852, p. 24; J. R. Towle, "A Confession of Faults," *Review,* Dec. 11, 1856, p. 46; "Eastern Tour," *Review,* Nov. 15, 1853, pp. 148, 149; Ellen G. White, Lt 11, 1853 (Dec. 3); search term "Towle" in *Words of the Pioneers.*

TREADWELL, William (1831-1904) and **Lurana Lucretia** (1834-1917)

William Treadwell, a carpenter from Palermo, New York, was first mentioned in the *Review* in 1852, the same year that he married Lurana Blinn. Available sources indicate that he was an active layperson, involved in giving Bible studies, occasional lay preaching, leading out in Tract and Missionary Society work in his district, and serving on New York Conference committees.

"In the early days of the message," William Treadwell's obituary related, "Brother and Sister White, Brother Andrews, and others were made welcome at his home." The only extant mentions of William Treadwell in Ellen White's writings alluded to his part in the damaging "church trials" and internal conflicts in the Roosevelt church during the late 1850s.

See: Obituary: "William Treadwell," *Review,* Sept. 22, 1904, p. 23; obituary: "Lurana Lucretia Treadwell," *Review,* Sept. 6, 1917, p. 22; 1860 U.S. Federal Census, "William Treadwell," New York, Oswego County, Palermo, p. 39; search term "Treadwell" in *Review and Herald* online collection, www.adventistarchives.org; Ellen G. White, Lt 8, 1857 (July 19); Lt 2, 1858 (c. 1858).

TUBBS, Ira B. (1800-1882) and (first wife) **Hannah** (c. 1800-1872) and (second wife) **Amelia L.** (c. 1808-1892)

Church members and farmers in Wright Township, Michigan. Ira and Hannah Tubbs became Sabbathkeepers in 1857 under the preaching of J. B. Frisbie. Ellen White mentioned Ira Tubbs once in her 1859 diary in connection with a visit to Wright. "We called on Brother Tubbs. Spent a few hours in profitable conversation."

See: Obituary: "Ira Tubbs," *Review,* Oct. 17, 1882, p. 654; obituary: "Hannah Tubbs," *Review,* Oct. 15, 1872, p. 143; obituary: "Amelia Tubbs," *Review,* June 28, 1892, p. 415; 1850 U.S. Federal Census, "Ira Tubbs," Michigan, Ottawa County, Wright, p. 16; 1880 U.S. Federal Census, "Ira B. Tubbs," Michigan, Ottawa County, Wright, p. 14; Ellen G. White, Ms 6, 1859 (May 1 entry).

WAGGONER, Joseph Harvey (1820-1889) and **Maryetta** (1823-1908)

A prominent early Adventist editor, author, and evangelist, Joseph H. Waggoner was born in Pennsylvania and married Maryetta Hall in 1845. Among their 10 children was Ellet J. Waggoner, who, with A. T. Jones, was prominent in the 1888 righteousness by faith revival. At the time of their conversion to Sabbatarian Adventism in the winter of 1851-1852, Waggoner was editor of the newspaper *Sauk County Democrat* in Baraboo, Wisconsin. Within a few months he began to propagate his new faith. Too poor to afford transportation, Waggoner often undertook his early evangelistic journeys on foot. "Brn. Phelps and Waggoner," James White reported in 1854, "have traveled many hundred miles on foot to get the truth before the people." After 1855 his preaching itineraries took him to various Midwestern states, and later, in the mid-1870s, to California. Waggoner was also a lucid and prodigious writer, publishing several hundred articles and a number of theological books, including *The Nature and Tendency of Modern Spiritualism* (1857),

The Atonement (1884), and *From Eden to Eden* (1890). After James White's death he also composed the (anonymous) "Appendix" to *Life Sketches . . . of Elder James White, and His Wife, Mrs. Ellen G. White"* (1888).

Despite the domestic turmoil of his last decade, as outlined below, it was during these years that Joseph Waggoner made some of his most important contributions. From 1879 to 1886 he edited the West Coast paper *Signs of the Times,* first as "resident editor" and from 1881 as editor in chief. In 1885 his zeal for health reform resulted in the publication of the *Pacific Health Journal,* of which he was both founder and editor. During the same year Waggoner was largely instrumental in founding and editing the *American Sentinel,* devoted to issues of religious liberty. Then from 1887 to 1889 he closed his lifework in Switzerland as editor in chief of French and German denominational papers.

Ellen White thought highly of Joseph Waggoner's abilities. "You have a valuable gift in laboring in truth and doctrine," she told Waggoner in 1872, and in 1886 she described him as "a man blessed with superior light and knowledge, endowed with great capacity for good." Yet his potential for church service was undermined by his turbulent domestic life, and it was on this matter that the bulk of Ellen White's letters to Joseph Waggoner focus. Much of the responsibility for the discord, especially during the early years of their married life, Ellen White placed on Maryetta. Of Joseph she wrote in 1860, "You have tried every means in your power to remove every cause of fretfulness from your wife . . . but in vain. . . . The influence of her continual fretfulness and finding fault is ruinous to your children." Among other things Ellen counseled Joseph to "decidedly rule your own house." Although Maryetta publicly confessed her wrongs in the columns of the *Review* in 1861, she appears not to have changed her ways, and by the late 1860s was involved in an adulterous affair. Joseph subsequently took Maryetta back—an unwise move against which Ellen protested in 1872.

Matters took a decided turn for the worse in the early 1880s when Joseph Waggoner was working as editor at the Pacific Seventh-day Adventist Publishing Association in Oakland, California. Although later maintaining that adultery was never involved, Waggoner embarked on an affair with a local church member, Mrs. Mary Charlotte ("Lottie") Chittenden, that continued for several years. By 1882 Ellen White was aware of the situation, but rather than recommending Waggoner's termination, she sent him several warnings and appeals to break off the relationship. Unfortunately his promises to do so were not fulfilled, and by 1885 the situation had reached crisis proportions. Under pressure from both G. I. Butler, General Conference president, and Ellen White, Waggoner finally left Oakland and Mary Chittenden in mid-1886 and returned to his wife and home in Burlington, Michigan, where he stayed for almost a year in a limbo state, his future undecided. George Butler remained unconvinced of the sincerity of Joseph Waggoner's confessions and felt the church should "purge the camp" of Waggoner and others of his ilk. While she was also anxious about the depth of Waggoner's repentance, in April 1887 Ellen White urged that mercy be introduced into the equation. "If we err, let it be on the side of mercy rather than on the side of condemnation and harsh dealing." Butler yielded to Ellen White's position, and shortly thereafter Waggoner left for Europe to serve as editor for what was to be the final two years of his life.

See: Obituary: "Joseph Harvey Waggoner," *Review,* Sept. 3, 1889, pp. 558, 559; obituary: "Mariette Waggoner," *Review,* Mar. 5, 1908, p. 23; Harry Ellsworth Cole, *A Standard History of Sauk County, Wisconsin* (Chicago: Lewis Pub. Co., 1918), vol. 1, p. 443; [James White], "Western Tour," *Review,* July 4, 1854, p. 172; search term "J. H. Waggoner" in *Re-*

view and Herald online collection, www.adventistarchives.org.; Ellen G. White, Lt 3, 1872 (Feb. 1); Lt 51, 1886 (Sept. 6); Lt 4, 1860 (Apr. 19); Lt 16, 1887 (Apr. 21); J. H. Waggoner to Ellen White, June 28, 1882; J. H. Waggoner to "Mary Ette," in G. I. Butler to Ellen White, [1885]; G. I. Butler to Ellen White, Aug. 23, 1886; W. C. White to J. H. Waggoner, Dec. 29, 1886; J. H. Waggoner to W. C. White, Feb. 23, 1888; Woodrow Whidden, *E. J. Waggoner: From the Physician of Good News to the Agent of Division* (Hagerstown, Md.: Review and Herald, 2008), pp. 20-37, 51-53, 100, 319-321. On the identity of Mrs. Chittenden, see 1870 U.S. Federal Census, "Mary C. Chittenden," California, San Francisco, Ward 9, p. 182; obituary: "Lottie Chittenden," *Review*, Dec. 15, 1896, p. 803; obituary: "Charles Redfield Chittenden," *Pacific Union Recorder*, Nov. 28, 1934, p. 6.

WEED, Caroline (née **CARPENTER)** (1838-1909) and **Eber** (1841-1913)

Caroline Carpenter became a Sabbathkeeper in 1856 and was a close friend of Mary Loughborough's. She appeared to have worked for a time at the *Review* office in Battle Creek, Michigan, before her marriage to Eber Weed in 1865. He had recently been mustered out of the 13th Michigan Infantry, in which he fought during the closing months of the Civil War. Eber Weed subsequently became a lifelong church member and was ordained as an elder.

Ellen White made several mentions of "Carrie" Carpenter in her correspondence, most extensively in a letter to John and Mary Loughborough in 1860. This letter showed concern at the direction Carrie's life was taking and counseled Mary on her relationship with Carrie.

See: Obituary: "Carrie Carpenter Weed," *Review*, Sept. 9, 1909, p. 23; obituary: "Eber Weed," *Review*, June 19, 1913, p. 599; *Record of Service of Michigan Volunteers in the Civil War, 1861-1865* (Kalamazoo, Mich.: Ihling Bros. & Everard, 1903?), vol. 13, p. 152; search term "E Weed" in *Review and Herald* online collection, www.adventistarchives.org; Ellen G. White, Lt 6, 1860 (Apr. 15).

WHEELER, Frederick (1811-1910) and **Lydia** (1814-1886)

Although available sources are somewhat contradictory, according to several accounts Frederick Wheeler, a Millerite Adventist preacher from New Hampshire, began to keep the seventh-day Sabbath in the spring of 1844 through his contact with Rachel Oakes, a Seventh Day Baptist. If so, Wheeler was the first Millerite preacher to adopt the Sabbath, earlier than T. M. Preble, another Millerite minister who became a Sabbatarian some months later, in August 1844.

Frederick Wheeler was born in Acton, Massachusetts, and married Lydia Proctor in 1832. From about 1838 to 1857 they lived in Washington, New Hampshire, or nearby Hillsborough. About 1840 Frederick Wheeler was ordained as a minister in the Methodist Episcopal Church, and in 1842 he accepted the Second Advent teachings of William Miller. Whether or not he was excluded from the Methodist Church for his Millerite beliefs is not known, but by 1844 he was ministering to a group of Millerites in Washington when Rachel Oakes convinced him to become a Sabbatarian. His wife, Lydia, did not take that step until 1850.

From about 1851 Frederick Wheeler preached widely throughout the New England States. In 1857 the family moved to Brookfield, New York, and he continued itinerant preaching in New York State for the next three or four years. In 1861 the Wheelers left Brookfield, probably because of strained relationships with Ira Abbey (see below), and moved to a farm in West Monroe, New York. From then on Frederick Wheeler preached mostly locally in Oswego County.

In 1890, when Frederick Wheeler was approaching 80 years of age, Ellen White respectfully classed him among the "aged standard-bearers." The only known rough patch in the relationship between the Whites and Wheeler occurred during the early 1860s. In 1861 Wheeler refused for a while to support James White in his drive for church organization. Also in 1861 Frederick and Lydia Wheeler received a testimony of reproof from Ellen White, focusing on their hypercritical attitude toward fellow church member and neighbor Ira Abbey, while failing to notice more serious problems in their own family. For a year or so Frederick Wheeler refused to acknowledge the rebuke and began to spread his doubts about the visions to others. He subsequently changed his mind and published a "Confession" in the *Review,* in which he reaffirmed his belief that the visions "are from the Lord." Another letter from Wheeler to the *Review* published in 1867 suggests that problems had continued to fester for several years.

See: Obituary: "Frederick Wheeler," *Review,* Nov. 24, 1910, p. 15; obituary: "L. P. Wheeler," *Review,* Mar. 30, 1886, p. 206; William Lawrence Proctor and Dolly Pauline Howard Proctor, *A Genealogy of Descendants of Robert Proctor of Concord and Chelmsford, Mass.* (Ogdensburg, N.Y.: Republican & Journal Print, 1898), p. 69; Merlin Burt, ". . . Sabbatarian Adventism From 1844 to 1849," pp. 53, 54; search terms "Frederick Wheeler," "F. Wheeler," *Review and Herald* online collection, www.adventistarchives.org; "Organization," *Review,* Aug. 27, 1861, p. 100; F. Wheeler, "From Bro. Wheeler," *Review,* Aug. 27, 1861, p. 103; F. Wheeler, "Confession," *Review,* Dec. 3, 1861, p. 7; F. Wheeler, "Note from Bro. Wheeler," *Review,* Nov. 19, 1867, p. 360; Ellen G. White, Ms 33, 1890 (Oct. 11); Lt 20, 1861 (Aug.); Lt 13, 1862 (Jan. 13). For a discussion of sources dealing with the date when Frederick Wheeler and the Millerite group in Washington, New Hampshire, began Sabbathkeeping, see Arthur Whitefield Spalding, *Origin and History of Seventh-day Adventists,* vol. 1, pp. 399, 400.

WHIPPLE, John G. (1817-1902) and **Sarah B.** (1822-1905)

Sarah Butler, older sister of **George I. Butler**, twice General Conference president, married John G. Whipple in 1849. They were comfortably situated in Perry's Mills, Clinton County, New York, with a farm and other property worth $3,700 according to the 1860 census. In the 1860s they moved to Battle Creek, Michigan, where J. G. Whipple operated a grocery business for many years. Both Sarah and John Whipple came from Millerite backgrounds, began to observe the Sabbath about 1852, and were active lay members in their area. Tent meetings were held on their farm in 1855. In the 1860s and 1870s J. G. Whipple's name appears on various conference and publishing committees.

Both James and Ellen White commended the Whipples—by all indications quite well off—for their generosity toward the poverty-stricken preacher M. B. Czechowski in the period 1858-1861. However, some years later, in an 1868 testimony, Ellen White pointed out that "love of the world has . . . eaten out true godliness" and she appealed to the Whipples to "divest yourselves of selfishness and make thorough work for eternity."

See: Obituary: "John G. Whipple," *Review,* Sept. 30, 1902, p. 23; obituary: "Sarah B. Whipple," *Review,* June 22, 1905, p. 23; George W. Davis, *John Grow of Ipswich: John Groo (Grow) of Oxford* (Washington, D.C.: n.p., 1913), p. 76; 1860 U.S. Federal Census, "John G. Whipple," New York, Clinton County, Champlain, p. 59; 1870 U.S. Federal Census, "J. G. Whipple," Michigan, Calhoun County, Battle Creek, p. 14; 1880 U.S. Federal Census, "J. G. Whipple," Michigan, Calhoun County, Battle Creek, p. 61; C. W. Sperry, "From Bro. Sperry," *Review,* Mar. 19, 1857, p. 158; search term "Whipple" in *Words of the Pioneers*; James White, "Bro. M. B. Czechowski," *Review,* Dec. 30, 1858, p. 48; Ellen G. White, Lt 31, 1861 (c. 1861); Lt 16, 1868 (June 20).

WHITE, Anna (c. 1829-1854)

Editor, youngest sister of **James Springer White**. In 1852, while living in Rochester, New York, Ellen White was shown in vision "that we should open the way for my husband's brother Nathaniel and sister Anna to come and live with us." Neither were Sabbathkeepers, but both "came into the truth cautiously, yet understandingly" after settling in Rochester. Both were in poor health on arrival in November 1852, and Nathaniel died of tuberculosis within six months. Anna, however, rallied, and, showing considerable literary talent, became editor of the *Youth's Instructor* in January 1854. She also compiled *Hymns for Youth and Children,* which was published a few months later. Unfortunately, Anna White subsequently suffered a relapse and died of tuberculosis in November 1854, age 25.

See: Obituary: "Anna White," *Review,* Dec. 12, 1854, p. 135; 1850 U.S. Federal Census, "Anna White," Maine, Somerset County, Palmyra, p. 21; "To Our Young Readers," *Youth's Instructor,* Jan. 1854, p. 4; "Hymns for Youth and Children," *Review,* Apr. 25, 1854, p. 112; Ellen G. White, *Spiritual Gifts [vol. 2],* p. 173.

WHITE, Henry Nichols (1847-1863)

Eldest son of James and Ellen White, born in Gorham, Maine. Published sources focus on two crisis periods in Henry White's short life—his infancy and his last sickness. During his first 14 months Henry twice came close to death through serious illness. Each time he was dramatically healed after prayer. These crises brought into sharp relief the conflict between Henry's welfare and the constant travel and hardships of James and Ellen White during this early stage of the movement. After much heartache they made the decision to leave Henry with trusted friends, the family of Stockbridge Howland, in Topsham, Maine, where he lived from the age of 1 to 6.

When Henry caught pneumonia at age 16 and became convinced that he would not survive, he was distressed, not so much over his impending death as over the fact that he did not feel spiritually prepared to die. "Remember that the death-bed is a poor place to prepare for an inheritance in the second life," he implored his young friends in a dictated message from his bedside. In the few days that remained, Henry set about "pleading with God for pardon and acceptance," after which "he seemed to enjoy peace of mind and the blessing of God." A sketch of Henry White's life, together with a gripping account of his last sickness, was subsequently published. Advertised as being "of the deepest interest to every youth," it sold by the thousands.

See: Obituary: "Henry N. White," *Review,* Dec. 29, 1863, p. 39; *An Appeal to the Youth: Funeral Address of Henry N. White, at Battle Creek, Mich., Dec. 21, 1863* (Battle Creek, Mich.: Steam Press, 1864), pp. 26, 28; Ellen G. White, *Spiritual Gifts [vol. 2],* pp. 89, 90, 104-107; J. W. [James White], "Books! Books!!" *Review,* Jan. 28, 1868, p. 108; Arthur L. White, *Ellen G. White: The Progressive Years,* pp. 59-62, 70-72.

WHITE, James Edson (1849-1928) and (first wife) **Emma L.** (1848-1917) and (second wife) **Rebecca** (1884-1953)

Second son of James and Ellen White, James Edson White was best known for his pioneering mission work among African-Americans in the Southern states. He was also a successful author and educator. Born in Rocky Hill, Connecticut, he spent his early years in Battle Creek, Michigan. Eager for further education, Edson (he was known by his middle name) studied commercial subjects and took medical courses in New Jersey and at the University of Michigan, Ann Arbor, during his late teens and early 20s. At various times during this period he worked at the Review and Herald press in Battle Creek, learning the printing trade. In 1870 he married Emma McDearmon.

In 1874 Edson was invited to join the staff of the soon-to-be-launched Pacific Seventh-day Adventist Publishing Association in Oakland, California. Starting as a bookkeeper, he later became one of the directors. His five-year tenure at the press, however, was not a great success. His tendency toward unrealistic business expansion on borrowed money led to several financial crises for the press and to his termination in 1879 or early 1880. However, Edson White's years in California were not without their successes. His musical and printing talents combined in the compilation of two Adventist hymnals in 1878—*Hymns of Praise for Use at Lectures and Revival Meetings* and *Song Anchor: A Choice Collection of Favorites for Sabbath School and Praise Service.* Emma helped with some of the typesetting of the music. This beginning led to Edson's compiling of five further hymnals. While in California he also worked actively for the improvement and organization of Sabbath schools. In 1877 he was elected superintendent of the California State Sabbath School Society, the first such state society. Later, during the 1880s, he served several years on the executive committee of the General (International) Sabbath School Association in Battle Creek.

After leaving denominational employment at the Pacific SDA Publishing Association, Edson worked mainly as an independent book publisher from 1880 to 1893, although he experienced little financial success. Toward the end of this period he went through a spiritual decline, finally declaring himself "not at all religiously inclined" in a letter to his mother in the summer of 1893. Shortly thereafter, however, Edson experienced reconversion, sold his business, and from 1895 to 1899 led an innovative mission to Mississippi, focusing on the African-American population. He established literacy classes (some taught by Emma) and schools, creating the goodwill that opened the way for churches to be established. Much of the financing for the initial venture came from the sale of *The Gospel Primer,* a book of Bible stories Edson wrote in 1894 that doubled as a reading primer for the schools and literacy classes. It was the first of several similar children's books White wrote during the next decade or so in order to help fund the Southern work. Some titles, such as *Best Stories From the Best Book* and *The Gospel Primer,* sold by the hundreds of thousands. He also authored major books for adults, such as *The Coming King,* which had similar sales and were translated into other languages.

The scores of extant letters from Ellen White to her son Edson make for gripping reading. There can be little doubt that the letters of appeal and encouragement Edson received from his mother during his years of struggle in the 1880s and early 1890s were instrumental in his spiritual revival in 1893 and his return to church work. Ellen's letters to her son demonstrated "tough love," not hesitating to point out his weaknesses (such as lack of fiscal responsibility), but all the while assuring him of her constant love and concern.

Edson and Emma White had no children. In 1922, five years after Emma's death, Edson married Rebecca Landon Segerhorn (née Burrill), who had a son, Alfred B., from her previous marriage to a Mr. Segerhorn. In the early 1930s, after Edson's death, Rebecca married a Mr. Stephenson from Chico, California.

See: Obituary: "James Edson White," *Review,* July 5, 1928, p. 22; obituary: "Emma L. White," *Review,* Aug. 30, 1917, p. 21; J. E. White to W. C. White, Oct. 11, 1873; "California State Sabbath School Society," *Review,* Nov. 8, 1877, p. 151; Ellen G. White, Lt 123, 1893 (June 21). No full-length biography of Edson White has been published, but the following accounts provide useful information: Ronald D. Graybill, *Mission to Black America. The True Story of Edson White and the Riverboat* Morning Star (Mountain View, Calif.: Pacific Press, 1971); Alta Robinson, "James Edson White: Innovator," in George R. Knight, ed., *Early Adventist Educators* (Berrien Springs, Mich.: Andrews University Press, 1983), pp. 137-158. Regarding Rebecca's marriage to Marcus Landon, see "Items," *Canadian Union Messenger,* Jan. 26, 1905, p. 15; to Segerhorn, "Rebecca M. Segerhorn," 1920 U.S. Federal Census, California, Butte County, Chico, p. 3A; to Stephenson, "Rebecca Stephenson," [Rebecca Burrill], Ancestry.com. *California Death Index, 1940-1997* [database online], Provo, Utah, Ancestry.com Operations, Inc., 2000.

WHITE, James Springer (1821-1881) and **Ellen Gould** (1827-1915)

Cofounder of the Seventh-day Adventist Church, together with Ellen Gould White, his wife, and Joseph Bates. Bòrn in Palmyra, Maine, James White preached for the Millerite Adventists in the early 1840s. In 1846 he married Ellen Harmon, and soon thereafter the Whites became Sabbatarians. They had four sons, of whom **James Edson White** and **William Clarence White** survived into adulthood.

James White was recognized especially for his leadership qualities, pioneering publishing work, and business acumen. He established two publishing houses (Review and Herald, Pacific Press) and founded the major papers of the new movement, *Present Truth* (1849), *Second Advent Review and Sabbath Herald* (1850), *Youth's Instructor* (1852), and *Signs of the Times* (1874), being editor of all of them at various times. When subsequently the Seventh-day Adventist Publishing Association was organized in 1861, White served as its president until his death in 1881, except for a period of ill health (1865-1868). For a total of 10 years during the 1860s and 1870s, James White served as

General Conference president and was prominent in the establishment of Battle Creek College in 1874.

The Whites' marriage was an unusual one in that both filled major leadership roles in the emerging church. Modern scholarship has not supported the contention of D. M. Canright, early critic of Seventh-day Adventism, that James dominated the marriage. However, the last years of their marriage were complicated by the effects of several strokes that James suffered, beginning in 1865. Although he was repeatedly able to recover mentally from the strokes and continue to provide effective church leadership, on the emotional level James at times became depressed, irritable, and hypercritical, something that negatively impacted his relationship with coworkers as well as with Ellen. "I can but dread . . . James's changeable moods, his strong feelings, his censures," Ellen confided to her close friend Lucinda Hall in 1876.

Through the years Ellen made heroic efforts to help her husband regain his physical and emotional health, but during the last five or six years of James's life his moods became so difficult that at times this prompted her to respond in ways that led her later to apologize for anything she had said that caused him grief or distress. His negative moods also made it difficult for Ellen to write in peace or to meet speaking appointments, and at times she agonized over whether or not it was her duty to work apart from James for a period to carry out her felt duties to the church. Ellen's absences from James in 1874 (two months), 1876 (two months), 1878 (three to four months) and 1880 (five months) were at least in part because of such concerns. Throughout these difficult years, however, the underlying affection between Ellen and James is clearly evident from their correspondence.

See: Obituary: "Fallen at His Post," *Review,* Aug. 9, 1881, pp. 104, 105; obituary: "The Life and Labors of Mrs. Ellen G. White," *Review,* July 29, 1915, pp. 3-5; Dudley Marvin Canright, *Life of Mrs. E. G. White,* pp. 63-79; Ronald D. Graybill, "The Power of Prophecy," pp. 24, 10, 11, 25; Ellen G. White, Lt 64, 1876 (May 10). For general biographies of James White, see Virgil Robinson, *James White,* and Gerald Wheeler, *James White: Innovator and Overcomer.* Useful biographical information is also found in Andrew Gordon Mustard, *James White and SDA Organization,* and the first three volumes of Arthur L. White's biography of Ellen G. White: *Ellen G. White: The Early Years; Ellen G. White: The Progressive Years,* esp. pp. 424-445; and *Ellen G. White: The Lonely Years.*

WHITE, John (1785-1871) and **Betsey** (1788-1871)

Parents of **James Springer White**. John White settled in Palmyra, Maine, in 1806 and married Betsey Jewett about 1809. They had nine children, three of whom became clergymen: **John Whitney** (Methodist Episcopal), Samuel (Baptist), and James Springer (Seventh-day Adventist). After 51 years of farming in Palmyra, John and Betsey White moved west, probably in 1857, and stayed for a year and a half with their son John Whitney in Zanesville, Ohio. At the end of 1858 or early in 1859 they moved to Battle Creek, Michigan, where they stayed for the rest their lives. For some years they lived in a house just across the road from James and Ellen White. During their final months of frailty and illness John and Betsey moved in with James and Ellen to receive proper care.

John and Betsey White's transition toward Seventh-day Adventism was a protracted one, starting in the early 1840s when they were convicted by the Second Advent preaching of William Miller. During the 1850s they struggled over the issue of Sabbathkeeping. In 1855 Ellen White noted that her mother-in-law "longed to keep the Sabbath," whereas John was still undecided. By 1859, however, even John had made his decision, and Ellen happily reported that "Father and Mother White" "have embraced the Sabbath and are coming right along into all the present truth." Even after this date, however, John White retained his membership with the Christian Connection church, as he had for the previous 40 years or so.

It is possible that John had residual difficulties with Seventh-day Adventist teachings, as at least during the 1860s his son John Whitney White, Methodist clergyman in Ohio, made energetic efforts to turn his father against Seventh-day Adventism. Thus in an 1866 letter to his father, after an indirect critique of the visions of Ellen White, John Whitney concluded that "the whole thing [Seventh-day Adventist Church] will die out and be forgotten as sect or church in 15 years. . . . Most cincerly [*sic*] do I thank God that you and mother have kept clear of the whole business and I trust you will." For whatever reasons, in his will of 1864, as modified in 1867, John White declared his preference that his funeral be conducted by a Christian Connection clergyman. As it turned out, in 1871 both John and Betsey's funerals were conducted by Seventh-day Adventist ministers. Because of the scarcity of evidence, it is hard to determine whether this indicated further changes in their religious views during their final years.

The most detailed and best documented biography of John and Betsey White is James R. Nix, "John and Betsey (Jewett) White," in *Palmyra, Maine: 200th Anniversary, Bicentennial 1807-2007*, 2nd ed. (Palmyra [Rockland, Maine]: Penobscot Press, 2007), pp. 145-151. A useful collection of source documents, including the wills of John White, is found in Glenn Davis and Jean Davis, "Notebook, Vol. 1," deposited at Historic Adventist Village, Battle Creek, Michigan. See also: obituary: "Betsey White" ("My Mother"), *Review,* Jan. 24, 1871, pp. 45, 47; obituary: "John White" ("The Venerable Dead"), *Review,* July 18, 1871, p. 36; John Williams White to "Dear Grandfather and Mother," Aug. 20, 1866; Methodist Episcopal Church, *Minutes of the Annual Conferences of the Methodist Episcopal Church for the Year 1856* (New York: Carlton & Porter, 1856), p. 112; John Whitney White to "Dear Father," Nov. 7, 1866; Ellen G. White, Lt 2, 1855 (Aug.); Lt 31, 1859 (Feb. 21).

WHITE, John Whitney (1812-1886) and **Anna Catherine** (1818-after 1885)

John W. White was a Methodist Episcopal clergyman and the oldest brother of **James Springer White**. Of the five White brothers that survived to maturity, three became clergymen: John Whitney (Methodist Episcopal), Samuel Shepard (Baptist), and James Springer (Seventh-day Adventist). In 1833 John White settled in Ohio, and in the same year he joined the Methodist Episcopal Church. In 1834 he was licensed to preach, and he continued in active ministry in Ohio until his retirement in 1874. In 1840 he married Anna Catherine Williams. Their son, John Williams White, subsequently became a professor of Greek at Harvard University.

The surviving correspondence of John W. White reveals a somewhat ambivalent relationship with James and Ellen White. In letters to other family members John could be dismissive and derisive of James and his Adventist beliefs. On the other hand, it does not appear that John expressed such opinions to James or Ellen but sought friendly relations. He was especially grateful for the way James and Ellen had looked after his parents, John and Betsey White, during the last 10 or so years of their lives when they lived in Battle Creek, Michigan. "May God reward you a thousand fold," he wrote to James and Ellen after the death of Betsey White in 1871. There are signs that his critical views mellowed with time. "I rejoice to hear that poor sinners are coming to Christ in your midst," he let James know in 1872, and in 1880 he expressed his admiration for the "contributions of your people to Church, Educational, Missions and Sabbath School Enterprise" that he had read about in a General Conference report. After James's death in 1881 at age 60, John wrote, in a letter to Ellen, of James: "He was a man of wonderful energy, but not of philosophy enough to have grown aged and feeble. . . . There are some men that can't retire." John placed Ellen in the same category: "Look at yourself still working. . . . God bless you, Ellen."

See: Almira Larkin White, *Genealogy of the Descendants of John White of Wenham and Lancaster, Massachusetts, 1638-1900* (Haverhill, Mass.: Chase Brothers, Printers, 1900), vol. 2, pp. 503, 504; *History of Franklin and Pickaway Counties, Ohio, With Illustrations and Biographical Sketches* ([Cleveland]: Williams Bros., 1880), p. 432; Joshua Lawrence Chamberlain, ed., *Universities and Their Sons: History, Influence and Characteristics of American Universities, with Biographical Sketches* (Boston: R. Herndon Co., 1898), vol. 3, pp. 2, 3; J. W. White to "Sister Anna," June 1, 1846; J. W. White to "Dear Father," Mar. 28, 1866; J. W. White to "Dear Father," Nov. 7, 1866; J. W. White to "Dear Bro.," Jan. 9, 1871; J. W. White to "Dear Bro.," Jan. 22, 1872; J. W. White to "Dear Bro.," Jan. 16, 1880; J. W. White to "My Dr. Sister Ellen," May 13, 1882.

WHITE, Nathaniel (1831-1853)

A younger brother of **James Springer White**, Nathaniel White died at age 21 of tuberculosis. Most of what is known of Nathaniel's life is found in the tract *A Brief Account of the Last Sickness and Death of Nathaniel White,* published by James White. At age 10, during the Millerite awakening, Nathaniel was "soundly converted," as James White puts it, but after "the great declension, about 1844," he lost interest in religion. Instead he focused on becoming "a man in the world; to get an education and fill some high station."

In Nathaniel's late teens his health started to fail. According to his sister **Anna White**, he began to spit blood during the winter of 1851-1852. Refusing to be intimidated by his illness, Nathaniel left his parents' farm in Palmyra, Maine, in the summer of 1852 and set off for Boston, Massachusetts, where he got a job. He worked for months, even though he became increasingly weak to the point that he had to hang on to the staircase railings at his boardinghouse to avoid falling backward. He later admitted that he "murmured against God and thought it was cruel he could not have strength."

A turning point came in October 1852, when James White had an emotional meeting with Nathaniel in Boston, followed by an invitation for Nathaniel to join James and Ellen in Rochester, New York, with the hope that he might regain his health and possibly assist in the *Review* office. The next month Nathaniel arrived in Rochester, together with his sister, Anna, also afflicted by tuberculosis. Although Nathaniel's health continued to fail despite the prayers of the Rochester group, his Christian faith revived in the months before his death. On the day of his death, May 6, 1853, he confided to Ellen White, "I now feel reconciled to my sickness. I know that it is the only thing that will save me. I will praise the Lord, if he can save me through affliction."

See: Obituary: "Nathaniel White," *Review*, May 26, 1853, p. 8; J. White, *A Brief Account of the Last Sickness and Death of Nathaniel White, Who Died May 6th, 1853* (Rochester, N.Y.: *Advent Review* Office, 1853), esp. pp. 3, 11; Almira Larkin White, *Genealogy of the Descendants of John White of Wenham and Lancaster, Massachusetts, 1638-1900* (Haverhill, Mass., Chase Brothers, Printers, 1900), vol. 2, p. 502; Anna White to "Dear Brother and Sister Tenney," Mar. 6, 1853.

WHITE, William Clarence (1854-1937) and (first wife) **Mary** (née **KELSEY**) (1857-1890) and (second wife) **Ethel May** (née **LACEY**) (later **Currow**) (1873-1969)

Administrator, editorial and personal assistant to Ellen White, secretary of Ellen G. White Estate, and third son of James and Ellen White. Gifted in administration, by age 21 William White had already been elected president and business manager of the Pacific Seventh-day Adventist Publishing Association. For the next 20 years the focus of his contributions lay in the area of church and institutional administration in America, Europe, and Australia. His particular strength was in the planning and organization of new institutions and church structures. Modern scholarship credits much of White's administrative success to the mentorship of his mother. Besides taking counsel from his mother on a range of administrative issues, evidence indicates that even in White's major innovative contributions, notably the introduction of the "union" level of church administration in the 1890s, he was responding to the insights that his mother had received in vision.

In addition to his administrative responsibilities, after the death of James White in 1881 William became increasingly involved with assisting his mother in the work of editing and publishing her writings. Responding to Ellen White's encouragement, by the end of the 1890s White had divested himself of most of his administrative posts in order to devote himself more fully to supervising his mother's editorial staff, assisting with her voluminous correspondence, etc.

William's first wife, Mary, employed her editorial skills in the offices of the *Signs of the Times* and the *Youth's Instructor* and assisted Ellen White in preparing her book manuscripts for the press. After a three-year battle with tuberculosis, contracted during her mission service in Europe with William, she died in 1890, age 33, leaving him with the care of his two daughters, Ella (age 8), and Mabel (age 3). Five years later he married Ethel May Lacey, of Tasmania. Another daughter and four sons were born of this union.

White's close association with his mother led to allegations that he dominated the relationship and that on occasion he "manipulated" his mother's testimonies to further his personal agenda. Careful examination of the main allegations, including White's supposed influence over his mother on the issue of righteousness by faith at the 1888 General Conference session, indicates that the charges are not sustained.

See: Obituary: "William Clarence White," *Review*, Oct. 21, 1937, pp. 21, 22; obituary:

"Mary Kelsey White," *Review,* July 8, 1890, p. 430; obituary: "Ethel May Lacey White Currow," *Review,* Oct. 23, 1969, p. 6; Jerry Allen Moon, *W. C. White and Ellen G. White*; SDAE, s.v. "Mary (Kelsey) White," "May Lacey White Currow."

WILCOX, Henry H. (1819-1911) and (first wife) **Diadama** (c. 1825-1892) and (second wife) **Eliza Anna** (c. 1822-1896) and (third wife) **Mary A.** (1859-?)

Born in Oswego County, New York, Henry Wilcox was originally a member of the Methodist Episcopal Church and a shoemaker by trade. He first became acquainted with Sabbatarian Adventists about 1854 and in 1860 began "lecturing on the prophecies" in northern New York. Among his earlier contacts were two brothers, Francis McLellan Wilcox and Milton Charles Wilcox—not related to Henry—later editors of the *Review* and *Signs of the Times*, respectively. Henry was ordained to the ministry in 1881.

In 1890 Ellen White counted Wilcox among the "old standard-bearers" with whom "we have been acquainted . . . for the last forty years." Her earliest mention of him is in 1859, when she with her husband "ate our luncheon at Brother Wilcox's" while attending meetings in Mannsville, New York.

See: J. W. Lair, "Life Sketch of Elder H. H. Wilcox," *Review,* Oct. 12, 1911, p. 15; obituary: "Diadama Wilcox," *Review,* Sept. 6, 1892, p. 575; obituary: "Eliza Wilcox," *Review,* Apr. 21, 1896, p. 255; "Receipts," *Review,* Aug. 22, 1854, p. 16; obituary: "Milton Charles Wilcox," *Review,* Nov. 14, 1935, p. 21; F. M. Wilcox, "New York Conference," *Review,* Sept. 29, 1910, p. 17; Ellen G. White, Ms 41, 1890 (Oct. 11 entry); Ms 8, 1859 (Oct. 22 entry); SDAE, s.v. "Francis McLellan Wilcox," "Milton Charles Wilcox."

WILCOX, John Y. (1834-1910) and (first wife) **Mary S.** (c. 1823-1877) and (second wife) **Annie K.** (1845-after 1900)

John Wilcox, an engraver and farmer from Connecticut, became a Sabbathkeeper partly through the efforts of James and Ellen White during their visits to Rocky Hill, Connecticut, in 1848 and 1849. He was baptized by James White. During the late 1850s, for reasons not known, some church members in the Berlin, Connecticut, area took vehement exception to the marriage plans of John Wilcox and Mary North. Ellen White was shown, however, that John and Mary "were made to believe that they had greatly sinned where there was no sin. Their thinking of marriage might have been injudicious; further than this they were not guilty, and the treatment of Mary was cruel in the extreme." The marriage went ahead a year or two later, and both of their sons became lifelong church workers.

See: Obituary: "John Y. Wilcox," *Review,* May 12, 1910, p. 23; obituary: "Mary S. Wilcox," *Review,* July 5, 1877, p. 15; 1900 U.S. Federal Census, "Annie K. Wilcox," New Hampshire, Sullivan County, Washington, p. 2; 1860 U.S. Federal Census, "John Y. Wilcox," Connecticut, Middlesex County, Cromwell, p. 25; 1870 U.S. Federal Census, "John Wilcox," Connecticut, Hartford County, Berlin, p. 21; J. N. Loughborough, *The Great Second Advent Movement,* p. 224; J. Y. Wilcox, "Extracts From Letters," *Review,* June 12, 1860, p. 31; obituary: "Henry Clark Wilcox," *Review,* Mar. 31, 1949, p. 20; obituary: "Charles F. Wilcox," *Review,* Dec. 30, 1954, p. 23; Ellen G. White, Lt 19, 1859 (Oct. 4).

WILKINSON, Diantha (née **BENEDICT)** (1833-1907) and **James M.** (1837-1908)

Diantha Benedict, together with her parents, **Joseph** and **Millie Benedict**, joined the Sabbatarian Adventist movement about 1857 while living in Michigan. In 1859 and probably beyond, James and Ellen White occasionally employed Diantha in their home and at the *Review* office in Battle Creek, to help support the Benedict family. In 1861 Diantha married James M. Wilkinson. Ellen White cautioned Diantha and her mother for their tendency to take sides openly with erring church members who had received church discipline, thus undermining the church.

See: Obituary: "Diantha Benedict Wilkinson," *Review,* Feb. 6, 1908, p. 31; obituary: "James M. Wilkinson," *Review,* Mar. 26, 1908, p. 23; Henry Marvin Benedict, *The Genealogy of the Benedicts in America* (Albany: Joel Munsell, 1870), p. 155; D. Benedict, "From D. Benedict," *Youth's Instructor,* April 1858, p. 30; Ellen G. White, Ms 6, 1859 (June 12-17 diary entries); Ms 6, 1862 (c. 1862).

WOODRUFF, Azmon (1802-1889) and (first wife) **Elizabeth Norton Hart** (1796-1851) and (second wife) **Harriet Newell Cole** (1823-1870) and (third wife) **Elizabeth Barber Pierce** (later **DeGarmo)** (1801-1891)

A brother of Wilford Woodruff, fourth president of the Church of Jesus Christ of Latter-day Saints (LDS), Azmon Woodruff was a Seventh-day Adventist for almost 20 years before returning to the LDS Church.

In 1833 Azmon and his younger brother, Wilford, were baptized into the LDS church in Richland, Oswego, New York, and the following year Azmon was ordained as a local elder. Whereas Wilford stayed with the LDS movement, eventually reaching high office, Azmon left the church in 1834. Receipts and letters appearing in the *Review* indicate that Azmon Woodruff joined the Sabbatarian Adventist movement about 1851 and left about 1870, subsequently rejoining the LDS church in Utah. His brother, Wilford, noted with satisfaction in 1876 that he "had the privilege of going into a baptismal font with my eldest brother, Azmon Woodruff, and my children, to redeem our dead." Both Azmon's second and third wives were Sabbathkeepers for a number of years: in the case of Elizabeth B. (née Pierce), from 1851 until 1871, when she was disfellowshipped from the West Monroe, New York, Seventh-day Adventist Church "in consequence of departing from the doctrines of the Bible and embracing 'Mormon views' and being baptized into the same."

In 1858 Ellen White responded to a letter from Woodruff (not extant) in which he apparently expressed concern about "wrangling and strife" among members in Oswego County, New York.

See: 1850 U.S. Federal Census, "Elizabeth N. Woodruff," New York, Oswego County, Richland, p. 234; 1850 U.S. Federal Census, "Elizabeth Degarmo," New York, Oswego County, Parish, p. 5; 1870 U.S. Federal Census, "Harriet Woodruff," New York, Oswego County, West Monroe, p. 95; search terms "Azmon Woodruff," "Elizabeth Norton Woodruff," "Harriet Newell Woodruff," and "Elizabeth Barber Woodruff" in www.findagrave.com; Matthias Foss Cowley, *Wilford Woodruff, Fourth President of the Church of Jesus Christ of Latter-Day Saints, History of His Life and Labors* (Salt Lake City, Utah: The Deseret News, 1909), p. 4; Alfred Andrews, *Memorial, Genealogy, and Ecclesiastical History of First Church, New Britain, Conn.* (Chicago: A. H. Andrews, 1867), p. 283; Richard E. Bennett, "Line Upon Line, Precept Upon Precept: Reflections on the 1877 Commencement of the Performance of Endowments and Sealings for the Dead," *BYU Studies* 44, no. 3 (2005): 59; Lyman D. Platt, "Early Branches of the Church of Jesus Christ of Latter-day Saints 1830-1850," *Nauvoo Journal* 3 (1991): 38; "S.D.A. Church Book, West Monroe, N.Y." (undated), Ellen G. White Estate, DF 285c, entry for Dec. 11, 1871; Ellen G. White, Lt 2, 1858 (Mar.); search term "Woodruff" in *Review and Herald* online collection, www.adventistarchives.org.

APPENDIX A

UNAUTHENTICATED VISIONS ATTRIBUTED TO ELLEN G. WHITE

The Ellen G. White Estate has identified five documents of uncertain origin purporting to be accounts of visions Ellen White received between the dates of March 1850 and March 1852. The term apocryphal has sometimes been applied to these unauthenticated documents. Even in her own day, Ellen White met unfounded reports, garbled testimonies, and misstatements regarding what she had actually said or written, as evidenced by her comments published in *Testimonies for the Church* (vol. 5, pp. 692-696) and *Testimonies to Ministers* (p. 57).

In 1931 these and other unauthenticated documents were transferred to the Ellen G. White Estate Document File No. 103 to distinguish them from the regular manuscript file for one or more of the following reasons:

1. They were of uncertain origin, meaning that no Ellen White handwritten original was known to exist. The copies were derived from secondhand or thirdhand sources, and/or supportive records were lacking.
2. Their dating conflicted with known itineraries or was otherwise unverifiable.
3. They contained unusual or questionable content when compared with authenticated documents.

In 1956, when asked about the authenticity of one of these accounts, Arthur L. White, then secretary of the Ellen G. White Estate, replied, "We can neither attest to its accuracy nor can we say positively that certain elements were not based on something Ellen White wrote" (A. L. White to M. D. Lewis, Oct. 23, 1956). This more or less described the official status of these documents until 1987, when the White Estate staff restudied the collection, evaluated the evidence for and against each record, and compared the content and language of the disputed visions with a computer database of Ellen White's authentic writings.

The White Estate recognized that the mere absence of an Ellen White original does not necessarily discredit the authenticity of a vision. Yet it was decided that if there was reliable evidence to accept the essential content of any of these visions, a disclaimer relating to the accuracy of expression or wording should accompany the account, since only copies exist (and often with numerous variants).

The five remaining unauthenticated visions are listed below, with brief summaries of their content and current White Estate evaluations:

Ms 1, 1850—April 15, no year given, circa 1849-1851, Dartmouth, Massachusetts, at the home of Richard Ashley. A description of "the state of the churches" and a call to "come out of her, my people." Evaluation: No Ellen White original exists, and no supporting evidence has been found. The account remains unauthenticated.

Ms 8, 1850—August 24, 1850, no place given; concerns the need for rebaptism of believers since 1844. Evaluation: No Ellen White original exists, and 10 variants are known. All but half a sentence of the text is found in other authenticated Ellen White writings under dates of July 29 (Ms 5, 1850) and August 4 (or 24), 1850 (Ms 7 [7a], 1850, and *Early Writings,* pp. 59, 60; *Christian Experience and Views,* pp. 47, 48), to which the reader is referred.

Ms 9, 1850—October 23, 1850, Dorchester, Massachusetts; describes the "gathering time," the 1843 chart, and the future Sabbath conflict. Evaluation: No Ellen White original exists. Fifteen variants are known. Ellen White was in Dorchester on this date. Almost the entire first paragraph appears in *Present Truth,* November 1850, under the date of September 23, 1850, and all but three sentences are found in Ms 15, 1850, to which the reader is referred as a more reliable account of the vision.

Ms 3, 1851—April 27, 1851, Paris, Maine; a series of phrases apparently spoken in vision as reported by an unidentified observer. Evaluation: There is no supporting evidence for a vision on this date. It is probable, however, that the account represents notes taken by one who witnessed the vision. The account remains unauthenticated.

Ms 1a, 1851—June 29, 1851, Camden, New York; concerns the relationship between God's people and the ungodly. Evaluation: No Ellen White original exists. The vision has long been disputed because of its strong shut-door sentiments. (See entry "Camden Vision" in *The Ellen G. White Encyclopedia.*) Two variants are known. The date conflicts with Ellen White's itinerary, as records indicate that the Whites were in Camden only from June 18 to June 23 (see itinerary published in *Review and Herald,* June 9, 1851). The only source for the vision is a copy provided by R. R. Chapin, one of Ellen White's opposers. Uriah Smith responded to controversial phrases cited from the "Camden vision" in *The Visions: Objections Answered* (1868), suggesting that he might have accepted the authenticity of the vision, but that suggestion is tempered by his comment that he has referenced all shut-door expressions "that are *claimed* to have been given through any vision, either published or unpublished" (p. 28; italics supplied). Additionally, by this time (June 1851) Ellen White had abandoned the view that probation had closed for all non-Millerites—the shut door was understood to apply only to those who had willfully rejected the Second Advent message (see Lt 4, 1850 [Feb. 18]), and introductory article "The 'Shut Door' and Ellen White's Visions"). The White Estate views the evidence currently available as insufficient to establish that the report of the purported vision is genuine.

APPENDIX B

ELLEN G. WHITE AND RELIGIOUS ENTHUSIASM IN EARLY ADVENTIST EXPERIENCE[1]

Merlin D. Burt

1

During the years immediately preceding the 1844 disappointment, and to a lesser degree in the next few years, Ellen (Harmon) White[2] and other early Adventists were involved with intense charismatic-like experiences. These experiences included outbursts of spiritual rapture in the form of shouted exclamations of praise, prayer, and testimony; physical prostration under the influence of the Holy Spirit; and on at least one occasion, holy laughter. In Ellen White's experience, shouts of praise and physical prostration were often the precursors of visions or physical healing. Such physical manifestations were familiar occurrences up until about 1860. For Ellen White and many other Adventists, physical demonstration was a part of their spiritual heritage. Methodists, Christian Connectionists, Baptists, and many frontier groups frequently had dramatic physical and emotional activity as a part of their worship of God.

The American Religious Background That Influenced Adventists

Ellen White grew up in a devout Methodist family influenced by the environment of early-nineteenth-century New England revivalism. It is against this backdrop that one can better understand the style of expression that she and other early Adventists exhibited in their worship and social interactions.

The first decades of the nineteenth century saw the movement known as the Second Great Awakening. During this time revivals swept back and forth across America. It is estimated that participation in churches grew from approximately 40 percent to about 75 percent of the population between 1800

Merlin D. Burt, Ph.D., is Director of the Center for Adventist Research and the Ellen G. White Estate Branch Office at Andrews University.

[1] This article is based on a paper first presented at the Ellen G. White Estate Historical/Theological Consultation held June 17-19, 1998, at the Seventh-day Adventist General Conference office in Silver Spring, Maryland. The term *Adventist* in this article refers to the wider body of those who had been a part of the Millerite movement, in distinction from the later-emerging "Seventh-day Adventist" denomination.

[2] Ellen Harmon married James White on August 30, 1846. Her maiden name is sometimes used in this article when referring to her pre-1846 experiences.

to 1835.[3] In the aftermath of the American Revolution people asserted their freedom and independence in all areas of life. The more traditional American churches such as Congregationalists and Presbyterians had to confront a loss of ecclesiastical authority. This reaction against conventional lifeless religious practice, together with a disdain for the formal clergy, led many Americans to believe that "common people" were more sensitive to spiritual things than were the "elite." In the political realm, Federalism, with its rich and privileged class, was being challenged by radical Jeffersonian ideas of independence and self-determination. These and other factors led to rampant religious experimentation. Any approach that connected with the needs of common people became popular. The most popular and growing religious group in America during this time was the Methodists.

Methodism's Rise in America

In the wake of the American Revolution the Anglican Church, with the king of England as its head, was generally shunned. Methodism began as a "religious society" nominally connected to the Anglican Church, and many expected that the movement would collapse in America. John Wesley, founder of Methodism, was a vocal opponent of the Revolution. At the outbreak of hostilities he recalled all but one of the Methodist clergy. This left a vacuum that was soon filled with American lay preachers. This "native" leadership overcame the perception that Methodists were linked to Anglicans.

In 1784 John Wesley directed in the formation of the American Methodist Episcopal Church. Francis Asbury became the bishop and central figure in the American church. His goal was to restore the "apostolic order of sacrifice and itinerancy" among clergy. Thus he organized various lay ministers into "circuit riders," who traveled through an assigned territory preaching and establishing churches. Asbury insisted that a ministerial calling required the laying aside of worldly trappings of dress, deportment, and financial security. In fact, if a preacher chose to marry and/or settle down for any reason, he lost his membership in the Methodist Connection. Asbury said, "We must suffer *with* if we labor *for* the poor."[4] The circuit preacher's personal and popular spirituality, combined with true piety, inspired phenomenal church growth. By 1820 Methodists had surpassed Baptists as the largest denomination in America.

The rustic and untrained Methodist preachers had little concern for proper religious style or process. American church historian Winthrop S. Hudson has noted that Methodists were known as "shouting Methodists" because of their religious enthusiasm and demonstration.[5] The frequent exclamations of

---

[3] Winthrop S. Hudson and John Corrigan, *Religion in America,* p. 130.

[4] Francis Asbury, in the *Arminian Magazine* (London, 1784), p. 681, quoted in Nathan O. Hatch, *The Democratization of American Christianity,* p. 85.

[5] Winthrop S. Hudson, "Shouting Methodists," *Encounter,* Winter 1968, pp. 73-84.

"Glory, glory, glory," "Hallelujah," and "Amen" were integral to Methodist worship.

American revivalism received new energy around the turn of the nineteenth century with the emergence of the camp meeting movement. Beginning in Kentucky, the camp meeting phenomenon swept across America. Thousands gathered for spiritual renewal, and physical demonstrations of enthusiasm were a hallmark of the meetings. These demonstrations often included weeping, shouting, running, jumping, jerking, laughing, and even, in some cases, barking. The "excesses" of the camp meeting experience caused the more traditional churches to express stern disapproval.

Methodists, on the other hand, with their unrefined itinerates, found the camp meeting to be an ideal means of evangelism and renewal. Within a few years after the turn of the nineteenth century, camp meetings had become the special domain of Methodists. As time passed, they took on more and more of a Methodist style. By the 1830s some of the more dramatic "excesses" had been filtered out of Methodist camp meetings, but still camp meetings remained a place where participants could lose some of their inhibitions and devote a period of time to prayer and spiritual exercises. Camp meetings became an important fixture in the annual cycle of Methodist church life.

By the 1830s Charles Finney, the great revivalist of the Second Great Awakening, brought the camp meeting to town with his "protracted meetings." He instituted his "new measures," which included (1) praying for people in public by name, (2) allowing women to pray and testify in public to mixed audiences, (3) appointing a pew in the front of the church as the "anxious bench," and (4) establishing the inquiry room, where the minister could meet people and talk with them. Finney's innovations opened the door for greater religious expression in local congregations. His practices were widely accepted across America and directly impacted Methodist experience.

Another pivotal figure in mid-nineteenth-century Methodism was Phoebe Palmer. Palmer's father was a personal convert of John Wesley's. About 1835 Phoebe Palmer, at her home in New York City, instituted the Tuesday evening meetings for the "promotion of holiness." These meetings and others like them would have a profound effect on American religious experience in general and more particularly on Methodist experience.

Palmer taught that giving one's personal testimony in public was not only important but also vital for the development of Christian holiness. She believed that without personal testimony, religious life, irrespective of gender, would slide into apostasy.[6] Thus testimonies with the accompanying emotional content became for many a natural and necessary part of religious practice. Palmer was somewhat sympathetic to the Millerite movement, though she

---

[6] Melvin Easterday Dieter, *The Holiness Revival of the Nineteenth Century,* pp. 22-28.

rejected the setting of dates for the Second Coming.[7] She was a friend of Charles Fitch's and corresponded with William Miller. In 1844 she wrote the powerful Advent hymn "Watch, Ye Saints."

The "Christian Connection"

After Methodists, Baptists were the largest denomination in North America. The Baptists' more informal, spontaneous, and simple style of worship made them popular among working-class citizens. As the years passed, there was a "settling down" among many of the Baptist clergy. They endeavored to be more respectable in education, preaching style, dress, and civic involvement. This change offended many Baptists, among whom was a man named Elias Smith. A man of deep convictions, Smith rejected the growing respectability of Baptists and argued that denominational names and distinctions were the great evil that prevented Christians from coming together in apostolic unity. Smith said that "Christians" should restore the experience of the New Testament church in all its particulars. Consequently he forsook the Baptist Church and established, with the participation of a Freewill Baptist named Abner Jones, the New England branch of the "Christian Connection."

"Christians" had no creed but the Bible and were strictly congregational in style, with a free and dynamic form of worship. While Smith and Jones were the main leaders in New England, there were similar but separate "Christian" movements in other parts of the country. By the 1840s the New England "Christian" churches, in loose connection with Freewill Baptists, had become a significant religious group. While Ellen White came from a Methodist background, both of the other two principal founders of the Seventh-day Adventist Church, James White and Joseph Bates, were active ministers in the "Christian" Church.

James White and the Christian Connection

When the Advent movement arose in the 1830s, it found a ready acceptance among Methodists, "Christians," and Freewill Baptists. With their emphasis on obeying the Bible message, along with their free style and openness to the leading of the Spirit, they readily listened to the Advent message. Not surprisingly, Adventist worship tended to reflect the more dynamic style of these churches.

The account by James White of a Christian Connection conference in 1843 is a typical example. He recalled "a good Brother Clark," who "ever seemed to have resting upon him a solemn sense of the great day of God near at hand." As they were singing the chorus of the Advent hymn "You Will See Your Lord a-Coming," Brother Clark "would rise, strike

---

[7] Richard Wheatley, *The Life and Letters of Mrs. Phoebe Palmer,* pp. 511-515.

his hands together over his head, and shout 'Glory!' and immediately sit down." James White noted that "Brother Clark's solemn appearance and sweet shouts seemed electrifying. Many were in tears, while responses of 'Amen' and 'Praise the Lord' were heard from almost everyone who loved the Advent hope."[8] These types of demonstrations became the rule rather than the exception among Adventists, who were often from a "Christian," Methodist, or Baptist background.

Ellen White's Methodist Environment

Ellen White's father, Robert, was an active leader in the Methodist congregation in Portland, Maine. Methodists believed sanctification was an instantaneous work of grace that progressed through the rest of one's life. It was sometimes called the "second blessing," or the "second work of grace." Sanctification was not a state of sinless perfection but rather the presence of perfect love and right intentions, or an "entire conformity to the will of God." This "blessing" was something that the young Ellen earnestly coveted. She wrote: "The belief that Christ's coming was near stirred my soul to seek more earnestly for the sanctification of the Spirit of God."[9] At her uncle's home in Portland she found the freedom she sought: "As I prayed, the burden and agony of soul that I had so long endured left me, and the blessing of the Lord descended upon me like the gentle dew. I praised God from the depths of my heart. Everything seemed shut out from me but Jesus and His glory, and I lost consciousness of what was passing around me. The Spirit of God rested upon me with such power that I was unable to go home that night. When I awakened to realization, I found myself cared for in the house of my uncle."[10]

Ellen White recalled that when she was "first struck down, some of those present were greatly alarmed, and were about to run for a physician," but Ellen's mother, Eunice, who was familiar with the "wonderful power of God," told them not to be concerned.[11]

For six months following this blessing not a shadow clouded the teenager's mind, nor did she, to her knowledge, "neglect one known duty."[12] Those six months continued during 1843, as Adventists were expecting the return of Jesus at any time. Years later Ellen White described the testimony she gave at a Methodist class meeting shortly after the above-mentioned experience: "I told the story of my great suffering under the conviction of sin, how I had at length received the blessing so long sought, an entire conformity to the will of God."[13]

---

[8] James White, *Life Incidents,* p. 107.
[9] Ellen G. White, "Life Sketches" manuscript, p. 52.
[10] *Ibid.,* pp. 41, 42.
[11] *Ibid.,* p. 42.
[12] Ellen G. White, *Life Sketches,* p. 39.
[13] Ellen G. White, *Testimonies for the Church,* vol. 1, p. 35.

During the six-month period following her "blessing," Ellen gave her testimony whenever she could. The night after receiving her great blessing at her uncle's home, she bore public testimony in an Adventist meeting, probably held in Portland's Beethoven Hall: "The simple story of Jesus' love to me fell from my lips with perfect freedom, and my heart was so happy to be liberated from its bondage of dark despair that I lost sight of the people around me and seemed to be alone with God. I found no difficulty in expressing my peace and happiness, except for the tears of gratitude that choked my utterance as I told of the wondrous love that Jesus had shown me."[14]

Levi Stockman, a Methodist turned Millerite preacher, was so affected by Ellen's testimony that he "wept aloud," praising God for the blessing given to the girl so recently overcome with discouragement and fear.

On the occasions that Ellen shared her testimony, she was "greatly blessed." She wrote, "At times the Spirit of the Lord rested upon me with such power that my strength was taken from me. This was a trial to some. . . . Many could not believe that one could be so overpowered by the Spirit of God as to lose all strength."[15] They thought Ellen's demonstrations were from "over-wrought feelings" rather than the Holy Spirit.

Experiences With the Pearson Family

During the months preceding the 1844 disappointment evening prayer meetings were held in different localities of Portland to accommodate the many who wished to attend the Second Advent gatherings. A family named Pearson opposed Ellen's falling down in the Spirit. Soon, however, at one of the Adventist area meetings, one of the Pearson family members was "prostrated as one dead." The young man's relatives "stood weeping around him, rubbing his hands and applying restoratives. At length he gained sufficient strength to praise God, and quieted their fears by shouting with triumph."[16] The young man was unable to return home that night. The result was a new faith on the part of the Pearson family in the genuineness of Ellen's experience.

At another meeting Ellen White wrote of Pearson's apology: "The brother who had opposed me [H. Pearson] then rose, and with tears confessed that his feelings in regard to me had been all wrong. He humbly asked my forgiveness, and said, 'Sister Ellen, I will never again lay a straw in your way. God has shown me the coldness and stubbornness of my heart, which He has broken by the evidence of His power. I have been very wrong.' Then . . . he said, 'When Sister Ellen seemed so happy, I would think, Why don't I feel like that?' Why doesn't Brother Rich receive some such evidence? For I was convinced that he

---

[14] Ellen G. White, "Life Sketches" manuscript, p. 44.

[15] Ellen G. White, "Mrs. Ellen G. White: Her Life, Christian Experience, and Labors," *Signs of the Times,* Mar. 16, 1876, p. 116.

[16] *Ibid.*

was a devoted Christian, yet no such power had fallen upon him. I offered a silent prayer that, if this was the holy influence of God, Brother Rich might experience it this evening.'"[17]

Almost immediately after Pearson finished uttering this prayer, "Brother Rich" fell, prostrated by the power of God, crying, "Let the Lord work!" Rich then proceeded to make a confession of his doubt and unbelief.

Ellen White recalled that a few weeks after the above testimony, "the large family of Brother P[earson] were engaged in prayer at their own house" and "the Spirit of God swept through the room and prostrated the kneeling suppliants." Ellen's father "came in soon after and found them all, both parents and children, helpless under the power of the Lord."[18] Summarizing her experience, Ellen White wrote: "There had never been a question as to my perfect sincerity, but many had thought me young and [impressionable], and that it was my duty to restrain my feelings, which they regarded as the effect of excitement. But all [my] opposers were now brought to see their mistake and confess that the work was indeed of the Lord."[19]

The Experience of Samuel Brown and Other Millerite Adventists in Portland

Besides the Pearson family and Brother Rich, other Millerite Adventists in Portland experienced the same dramatic physical manifestations. On one occasion Levi Stockman was preaching in Beethoven Hall, where the Millerites often met. Elder Brown, a Christian minister in whose church Ellen had previously shared her testimony, was on the platform with Elder Stockman. Brown was deeply moved by the sermon. "Suddenly," Ellen White remembered, "his countenance grew pale as the dead, he reeled in his chair, and Elder Stockman caught him in his arms just as he was falling to the floor, and laid him on the sofa behind the desk, where he lay powerless until the discourse was finished. He then arose, his face still pale, but shining with light from the Son of righteousness, and gave a very impressive testimony."[20]

This man, usually slow of speech, had a solemn manner, and was generally free of any excitement. But on this occasion he had new power as he "warned sinners and his brother ministers to put away unbelief." An invitation to respond

---

[17] Ellen G. White, "Life Sketches" manuscript, p. 65. Possibly either George H. Rich or Gardner Rich. Both were members of the Portland Adventist Conference held in October 1841. See "Report of the Proceedings of the Third Session of the General Conference, Expecting the Advent of the Lord, Held in Portland, Maine, October 12-14, 1841," *Signs of the Times,* Nov. 1, 1841, p. 113.

[18] Ellen G. White, "Mrs. Ellen G. White: Her Life, Christian Experience, and Labors," *Signs of the Times,* Mar. 16, 1876, p. 116.

[19] *Ibid.*

[20] Ellen G. White, "Mrs. Ellen G. White: Her Life, Christian Experience, and Labors," *Signs of the Times,* Mar. 23, 1876, pp. 124, 125.

was made, and hundreds did. A sea captain jumped to his feet and, with tears running down his face, "involuntarily raised his hat, and swung it above his head with the free movement of an old sailor, and in the abandonment of his joy, shouted, 'Hurrah for God! I've enlisted in His crew, He is my Captain! Hurrah for Jesus Christ!'" He then sat down overpowered with emotion. Other testimonies were shared. As the meeting adjourned (at a late hour) and the people returned to their homes, voices could be heard from various quarters praising God. Ellen White recollected, "No one who attended these meetings can ever forget those scenes of deepest interest."[21]

While Methodist, "Christian," and Free-will Baptist meetings (whether Millerite or not) had demonstrations such as have been described, the focus of their religious meetings was not excitement but rather surrender of the life to God and a careful study of the Bible. Their worship was very message-centered. It focused on practical Christian living and holiness of life. There was nothing superficial about it. The physical demonstrations of weeping, shouting, and losing strength were to them a natural outgrowth of the moving of the Spirit of God. A deep solemnity pervaded all that happened. The salvation of sinners was the goal of all they did.

Religious Enthusiasm in Ellen G. White's Experience After Being Called to Prophetic Ministry

Ellen White received her first vision in December 1844. While we do not have an eyewitness account of her physical condition during her first vision, we do have many such accounts of later visions. M. G. Kellogg reported an 1853 vision thus: "As Sister White gave that triumphant shout of 'Glory! g-l-o-r-y! g-l-o-r-y!' which you have heard her give so often as she goes into vision, Brother White arose and informed the audience that his wife was in vision."[22] J. N. Loughborough, who saw Ellen White in vision scores of times, noted that "in passing into vision she gives three enrapturing shouts of 'Glory!' which echo and re-echo, the second, and especially the third, fainter." Continuing, Loughborough said that "for about four or five seconds she seems to drop down like a person in a swoon, or one having lost his strength; she then seems to be instantly filled with superhuman strength, sometimes rising at once to her feet and walking about the room."[23]

Those present during a vision were usually deeply affected. There was a strong sense of the presence of God. Often there was weeping and praising of God. Because Ellen White's open or public visions contained the elements of shouting and a loss of strength, it is not surprising that physical demonstrations were more common and accepted in early Adventist meetings.

---

[21] *Ibid.*
[22] Arthur L. White, *Ellen G. White: Messenger to the Remnant,* p. 22.
[23] *Ibid.*

In the years immediately following the 1844 disappointment Ellen White frequently mentioned cases of illness and prayers for divine healing. Often God responded by bringing either instantaneous healing or the beginning of recovery. Not surprising, such times of healing were also accompanied by dramatic manifestations of shouted praise and physical prostration.

Ellen White's public visions continued for some 40 years until 1884. She continued to have visions after this date but not in public settings. During the latter years of her life she more commonly received divine direction through dreams given during the night.[24]

Ellen White's Interaction With Fanatics During 1845 and 1846

Early in Ellen White's prophetic experience, she frequently encountered different types of fanaticism. Her understanding of its danger increased, particularly after a vision she received during her first trip to New Hampshire and Vermont,[25] sometime in the late winter or early spring of 1845.

Public sentiment increasingly turned against Adventists in Maine as many disposed of their possessions because of their fervent anticipation of Christ's return in the spring of 1845. Non-adventists in Bangor, Orrington, and other places in Maine had the Adventists' property placed under the control of local selectmen to prevent it from being sold and the owner being left without a home and thus becoming a burden to the community. Another public concern was the "no work" doctrine embraced by some former Millerites in the region. Because they felt that Christ would come in just weeks or months, some saw no need to work. In fact, they felt that to work would be a denial of faith. Town officials feared that the Adventist citizens would become public charges, since the state of Maine's settlement laws dictated that town officials and taxpayers were legally required to support their poor.[26]

Of particular interest is the report of the arrest and trial of local Adventist leader Israel Dammon, first printed in the *Piscataquis Farmer* and then the Portland, Maine, *Tri-Weekly Argus*.[27] These accounts were copied across New England and at least as far west as Ohio.[28] Ellen Harmon and James White were mentioned by several witnesses at the trial, which led to their being

---

[24] J. N. Loughborough, "Study of the Testimonies, No. 2," *Review and Herald Extra: Daily Bulletin of the General Conference,* Jan. 29, 30, 1893, p. 20; Herbert E. Douglass, *Messenger of the Lord,* pp. 135-137.

[25] Ellen G. White, Ms 10, 1859 (c. 1859).

[26] Jean F. Hankins, "'Every Town Shall Maintain Their Own Poor': New England's Settlement Laws," *Maine History,* Fall 2000, pp. 169-185.

[27] Trial of Elder I. Dammon: Reported for the Piscataquis Farmer," *Piscataquis Farmer,* Mar. 7, 1845, p. 1; "The Horrors of Millerism: Trial of Israel Dammon," *Tri-Weekly Argus,* Mar. 14, 1845, p. 1.

[28] "The Fruits of Millerism," New York *Observer,* Mar. 22, 1845, p. 47; "The Horrors of Millerism," *Ontario Repository,* Mar. 26, 1845, p. 2.

branded as fanatics. According to the report, on February 15, 1845, Dammon and another man from Exeter named "Elder Hall" led out in a meeting in the home of James Ayer in Atkinson, Maine.[29] About 25 people gathered, at least in part, to hear Ellen Harmon give an account of her visions. Also present was Dorinda Baker, a young single woman, age 23 or 24, who also professed to receive visions. Community sentiment was strong against Adventists, and when the news that people from out of town were present spread, the sheriff investigated and arrested Israel Dammon.

The trial occurred at the courthouse in Dover, Maine, on February 17, 1845. James White and Ellen Harmon were not present, nor were they charged in connection with the trial. The plaintiff, Hartford J. Rowe, was a farmer who charged that Dammon was an "idler" and a "vagabond" going from "place to place, begging." He further asserted that Dammon was a "common railer or brawler, neglecting his calling, or employment, misspending his earnings, and . . . [not providing] for the support of himself [and] family." Dammon pleaded not guilty to the charges.[30] The attorneys for the prosecution were C. P. Chandler and H.G.O. Morrison; the defense attorney was J. S. Holmes. Holmes, a Mason by profession, was certainly not a supporter of Adventists, though he did support the free practice of religion. In later years he remembered the case as "one of the grandest defenses of religious toleration and freedom" that he had ever seen.[31] Though Dammon was convicted and sentenced to 10 days in the House of Correction, Holmes appealed the ruling, and according to Dammon, "the warrant was quashed" and he was "acquitted without date."[32]

During February 1845 former Millerite Adventists were only beginning to differentiate themselves into opposing groups. Why Jesus had not come was the burning question on most Adventists' minds. Ellen Harmon and James White clearly embraced the "Bridegroom" concept[33] as an answer and were promoting the continued relevance of the October 1844 movement. They understandably associated with other Adventists who shared this view and influenced others to accept it. Their presence at the Atkinson meeting did not mean that they supported the fanatical elements that led to Dammon's arrest.[34]

Given Ellen White's later emphatic statements against fanaticism, it is

---

[29] Ellen G. White, *Spiritual Gifts [vol. 2]*, pp. 40, 41; "Trial of Elder I. Dammon: Reported for the Piscataquis Farmer," *Piscataquis Farmer*, Mar. 7, 1845, p. 1.

[30] *Ibid.*

[31] John F. Sprague, Esq., "James Stuart Holmes: The Pioneer Lawyer of Piscataquis County," *Bangor Historical Magazine* 4, July 1888-June 1889, p. 34, quoted in Bruce Weaver, "Incident in Atkinson: The Arrest and Trial of Israel Dammon," *Adventist Currents*, April 1988, p. 24; for the most detailed evaluation of the Dammon trial, see James R. Nix, "Another Look at Israel Damman."

[32] Israel Dammon to Samuel Snow, *Jubilee Standard*, June 5, 1845, p. 104.

[33] See introductory article "The 'Shut Door' and Ellen White's Visions." The "Bridegroom" view had been first published in the *Advent Mirror* only a few weeks before the Dammon event.

[34] See James R. Nix, "Another Look at Israel Damman."

surprising to think of her interacting with and supporting people who seemed to be imbalanced. However, in the context of the dynamic experiences of Adventists and other Christian groups at the time, it is more understandable. Also, the newspaper report was not a transcript of the trial but rather a reporter's observations and thus contained incomplete and perhaps biased information.

For James White and Ellen Harmon the fanatical excesses apparently seemed less important initially than a shared faith in the 1844 experience. Though they did interact with and support Dammon at the time of the meeting mentioned above, they came to oppose the spiritualizing views that he and others embraced.[35]

Spiritualizers

Another Millerite Adventist, Orlando Squires, began publication of the *Voice of the Shepherd* in Utica, New York, during March 1845. This paper spiritualized almost every tangible aspect of Christian belief. These included rejecting a literal heaven,[36] a literal destruction of the world by fire,[37] a literal resurrection,[38] a literal "body of Jesus in the universe of God," and a literal Second Coming.[39] The *Voice of the Shepherd* proposed that all of these were accomplished in a spiritual sense within the Christian's own experience. This spiritual "Second Coming" they understood to have occurred at the time of the disappointment in the fall of 1844.

Ellen White's third major vision, in which she was shown the new earth (spring 1845), directly countered the spiritualizing view. She was transported to the future and walked with Jesus and the saints in the earth made new. There were literal trees, grass, animals, and food. Jesus was a real person, as were the resurrected saints.[40] She and others who became Sabbatarian Adventists did all in their power to oppose the spiritualizers.

Extreme Literalization

A second type of fanaticism Ellen White was forced to confront was extreme literalization. This included such views as extreme voluntary humility. Some believed that to follow Jesus' command to become as little children, they should show their humility by creeping upon the ground. Some began to creep rather than walk when they went on errands into town. In South Paris, Maine, Cyprian Stevens got down in front of a stagecoach full of passengers.

---

[35] Ellen G. White, Lt 2, 1874 (Aug. 24).
[36] Orlando Squires, "Where is Heaven?" *Voice of the Shepherd,* March 1845, pp. 4, 5.
[37] C. H. Fenton, "The Harvest of the Earth," *Voice of the Shepherd,* March 1845, p. 1.
[38] S. Fenton, "The Resurrection," *Voice of the Shepherd,* March 1845, p. 8.
[39] Orlando Squires, "This Same Jesus," *Voice of the Shepherd,* March 1845, p. 5.
[40] White, *Spiritual Gifts [vol. 2],* pp. 52-55.

It frightened the horses and angered the driver, who plied the whip on Stevens so severely that he ended up bruised and bleeding.[41]

Extreme Sanctification

A third type of fanaticism confronted by Ellen White was extreme sanctification, sometimes called "holy flesh." This fanaticism came to the Millerite movement in 1842 through John Starkweather, who served briefly as associate pastor with Joshua V. Himes at the Chardon Street Chapel in Boston.[42] Starkweather held that when a person was converted and blessed with the "gift" of sanctification, one's inclinations, desires, and impressions became holy and pure. His view denied the continued presence of the sinful nature and led to many bizarre and shameful actions by its adherents.

During the first half of 1845 a similar form of fanaticism was active in Maine. William H. Hyde, the 17-year-old son of a Portland bookseller, is one example. Hyde became involved with Adventists who were advocating that they "show their love for one another" in a familiar way. They believed that men and women could remain pure and lie together innocently on the same bed.[43] At the time, Hyde was staying in Topsham, Maine, north of Portland. Probably during April 1845 he contracted a serious case of bloody dysentery. After two weeks of severe illness, the physicians concluded that Hyde's case was almost hopeless. He sent for James White, Ellen Harmon, and some others to come and pray for him. They appealed for him to renounce his fanaticism and let them take him away from those who were influencing him. Hyde agreed, was taken to a different home in Topsham, and humbly confessed. During earnest prayer the Holy Spirit "rested" on him and all present. Believing that he was healed, Hyde arose and sat down to a full "farmer's" meal. Ellen White recollected that "his recovery was perfect and lasting."[44]

Animal Magnetism

A fourth type of fanaticism met by Ellen White was "animal magnetism," or mesmerism. In the United States during the mid-nineteenth century animal magnetism was a popular philosophy of healing. Originated by Viennese physician Franz Anton Mesmer (1734-1815), it taught that an invisible magnetic fluid permeates the universe. Mesmer theorized that disease produced an imbalance of this fluid within the human body, which could be cured

---

[41] Marion C. Stowell Crawford to Ellen G. White, Oct. 9, 1908.

[42] Josiah Litch, "Protest," *The Midnight Cry,* Sept. 14, 1843, p. 29; Sylvester Bliss et al., *Defence of Elder Joshua V. Himes,* pp. 7, 8, 11, 12; see also George R. Knight, *Millennial Fever,* pp. 174-177.

[43] "Notes From a Talk With Mrs. E. G. White, Dec. 12, 1906," Ellen G. White Estate, DF 733-c.

[44] *Ibid.;* James and Ellen G. White, *Life Sketches* (1888), pp 200, 201.

through the use of magnets and electrical current. He eventually abandoned the use of magnets and proposed that the "healer's body," "permeated with animal magnetism, could redirect the patient's magnetic fluid without the use of magnets." The goal was to induce a "crisis" by altering the subject's mental state through fever, delirium, convulsions, uncontrolled weeping, and nervous twitches. Mesmer saw these manifestations as healthy symptoms of healing. Suggestibility and dominance were used to produce a trance and thus realign the body.[45] James Braid (1795-1860) later redefined the term *mesmerism* as hypnotism, and Mesmer became known as the father of modern hypnosis.[46]

During 1845 Joseph Turner, a leading Adventist minister and editor in Maine, adopted this theory and began to hypnotize people, particularly young girls and women. At a meeting in Poland, Maine, Turner tried to mesmerize, or hypnotize, Ellen White. She recalled: "He had his eyes looking right out of his fingers, and his eyes looked like snake's eyes, evil."[47] Her experiences in confronting this man, together with her visionary guidance, placed her in opposition to all hypnotic mind-controlling modalities that removed a person's God-given mental independence and freedom. In later life Ellen White wrote directly and specifically on this topic.: "It is not God's purpose that any human being should yield his mind and will to the control of another, becoming a passive instrument in his hands. . . . He is not to look to any human being as the source of healing. His dependence must be in God."[48]

In 1845 Ellen White was prompted through visions to confront Turner on repeated occasions. He in turn became her determined adversary, following her from place to place seeking to undermine her influence. Turner later denied being involved in this fanaticism, but in 1848 Joseph Bates confirmed it.[49]

Other Fanatical Views

Beyond these more clearly definable types of fanaticism, Ellen White confronted other erroneous ideas and demonstrations during 1845 and 1846. For instance, a few were teaching that people should cut off their hair, while others said it was wrong to eat anything grown that year. One man, named Hewitt, thought he was to eat nothing but sugar.[50]

While Ellen White was sympathetic to certain forms of religious

---

[45] Irving Kirsch et al., "Introduction to Clinical Hypnosis," in *Handbook of Clinical Hypnosis,* p. 5; John C. Burnham, "Franz Anton Mesmer," *International Encyclopedia of Psychiatry, Psychology, Psychoanalysis, and Neurology,* vol. 7, p. 213.

[46] Henry Alan Skinner, *The Origin of Medical Terms,* p. 186.

[47] Ellen G. White, Ms 131, 1906 (Aug. 13).

[48] Ellen G. White, *The Ministry of Healing,* p. 242.

[49] Joseph Bates, *A Vindication of the Seventh-day Sabbath,* pp. 15-17.

[50] Extracts from a letter of Marion C. Stowell Crawford to W. C. White, Oct. 14, 1908; Ellen G. White, Ms 131a, 1906 (c. 1906).

demonstration, she was consistently opposed to the mixed-gender aspect of foot washing and the salutation kiss.[51] Once a man came up to her in a meeting and said: "The Lord tells me, Sister White, that I must wash your feet."

"The Lord tells me," she responded, "that you have no business with my feet at all. When my feet are washed, it will be by a sister, not by any man." The man then began to "cry and cry and cry and cry." Ellen told him, "I wouldn't use up my strength in that way, because it doesn't make any more impression on me than the barking of a dog, not a bit."[52]

Fanaticism is an affliction of the sincere who become misguided and lose a biblical and reasoned basis for their faith and practice. Later in life Ellen White observed: "We have found in our experience that if Satan cannot keep souls bound in the ice of indifference, he will try to push them into the fire of fanaticism. When the Spirit of the Lord comes among His people, the enemy seizes his opportunity to work also upon different minds and lead them to mingle their own peculiar traits of character with the work of God. Thus there is always danger that they may allow their own spirit to mingle with the work and that unwise moves may be made."[53]

In the uncertainty and confusion of Millerite Adventism following the 1844 disappointment, Ellen White's prophetic gift helped to stabilize and preserve a core group of people who retained faith in the prophetic significance of 1844 and later adopted the teaching of the seventh-day Sabbath. Her visions consistently opposed the more radical or fanatical aspects of Adventism in the confusing months following the 1844 disappointment. This did not mean, however, that she was opposed to sometimes-exuberant religious expression.

Religious Enthusiasm Not Connected to Fanaticism

Nonfanatical religious enthusiasm was relatively common in the years following the Disappointment. Various examples of shouting and exclamations of praise and physical prostration are found in Ellen White's writings from this early era. In one instance Spirit-prompted laughter is mentioned, as a woman was "set entirely free" from her "sunken and discouraged" state.[54] Such enthusiastic expression should be viewed in the context of a struggling new movement. Early Adventists were willing to give up everything in light of their expectation of the soon coming of Jesus.

---

[51] Ellen G. White, "Early Experiences in Meeting Fanaticism," Ms. 10, 1859 (c. 1859); *idem, A Sketch of the Christian Experience and Views of Ellen G. White,* pp. 7, 8; *idem,* Lt 2, 1874 (Aug. 24); J. N. Andrews, "Testimonials," September 1874 (Silver Spring, Md.: Ellen G. White Estate); Marion C. S. Truesdail, L. O. Stowell, W. A. Barton, C. C. Chase, P. F. Chase, and L. B. Stowell, "Testimonial," Aug. 17, 1875, Ellen G. White Estate.

[52] Ellen G. White and Clarence C. Crisler, 1906 interview, Ellen G. White Estate, DF 733-c.

[53] Ellen G. White, Lt 34, 1889 (Jan. 4); see also *idem, Mind, Character, and Personality,* vol. 1, p. 38.

[54] Ellen G. White, Lt 12, 1850 (Aug. 15).

From her statements it is clear that Ellen White believed physical responses such as shouting, weeping, laughter, and prostration were valid when prompted by the Holy Spirit. While the experiences she described occurred most commonly during the early years following 1844, there are examples at least into the 1870s.[55] Beginning in the 1850s, however, cautioning statements appeared that became stronger and more numerous over the course of her ministry. For example:

1850: "I saw that we should strive at all times to be free from unhealthy and unnecessary excitement. I saw that there was great danger of leaving the Word of God and resting down and trusting in exercises. I saw that God had moved by His Spirit upon your company in some of their exercises and their promptings; but I saw danger ahead."[56]

1860: "Repeatedly have they been slain by the power of God, and while the impression remains, all is well; but when the impression wears away, the same wrong feelings return, self rises, because they did not make thorough work."[57]

c. 1861: "I saw that religion does not consist in making a noise. . . . To be a Christian is to be Christlike, and the habit Brother Hungerford has of shouting is no evidence that he is a Christian, for his shouting is regarded by God as no shouting. Half of the time he himself knows not what he is shouting at."[58]

1890: "The peace of Christ is not a boisterous, untamable element made manifest in loud voices and bodily exercises. The peace of Christ is an intelligent peace, and it does not make those who possess it bear the marks of fanaticism and extravagance. It is not a rambling impulse, but an emanation from God. When the Saviour imparts His peace to the soul, the heart will be in perfect harmony with the Word of God; for the Spirit and the Word agree."[59]

1896: "Persons may, under certain influences of the moment, be full of ecstasies; for chords are touched whose vibrations are pleasing to the natural taste. But these persons will have to learn that this is not the religion of Jesus Christ. When the circumstances change which so elated them, the depression and want of stimulus is felt, as the drunkard feels the want of the stimulus of the intoxicating cup."[60]

---

[55] See, for example, Ellen G. White, Lt 20, 1872 (Dec. 7), published in *idem, Manuscript Releases,* vol. 21, pp. 239, 240.

[56] Ellen G. White, "Vision at Paris, Maine," Ms 11, 1850 (Dec. 25).

[57] Ellen G. White to Brother John [Andrews], Lt 8, 1860 (June 11); see also "To Brother J. N. Andrews and Sister H. N. Smith" [PH016], p. 10.

[58] Ellen G. White to Brothers and Sisters at Bedford, Lt 14, 1861 (c. 1861), published in *idem, Manuscript Releases,* vol. 21, pp. 364-366.

[59] Ellen G. White, in *Signs of the Times,* May 19, 1890, p. 290.

[60] Ellen G. White, "Conformity to the World," *Review and Herald,* July 28, 1896, p. 465.

1908: "In this stage of our history we must be very careful to guard against everything that savors of fanaticism and disorder. We must guard against all peculiar exercises that would be likely to stir up the minds of unbelievers, and lead them to think that as a people we are led by impulse, and delight in noise and confusion accompanied by eccentricities of action. . . . Such experiences will come to us from time to time. Let us give no place to strange exercisings, which really take the mind away from the deep movings of the Holy Spirit. God's work is ever characterized by calmness and dignity."[61]

The Mackin Experiences[62]

The setting for Ellen White's 1908 statement above is her interaction with Ralph and Mary Mackin, Adventist church members from Ohio. The Mackins had requested an interview with Ellen White to describe their spiritual experiences, which included prophetic messages, speaking in tongues, "extemporaneous" singing, and casting out demons.

During the interview Ellen White listened cautiously, recounted incidences from her early experiences, and expressed openness to unexpected workings of the Holy Spirit. She told them, "In the future we shall have special tokens of the influence of the Spirit of God—especially at times when our enemies are the strongest against us. The time will come when we shall see some strange things; but just in what way—whether similar to some of the experiences of the disciples after they received the Holy Spirit following the ascension of Christ—I cannot say."[63]

But Ellen White repeatedly warned the Mackins about relying upon such experiences instead of the evidences of God's Word. She stated: "We must go to the people with the solid Word of God; and when they receive that Word, the Holy Spirit may come, but it always comes, as I have stated before, in a way that commends itself to the judgment of the people. In our speaking, our singing, and in all our spiritual exercises, we are to reveal that calmness and dignity and godly fear that actuates every true child of God. . . . It is through the *Word*—not feeling, not excitement—that we want to influence the people to obey the truth."[64]

Describing her interview in a letter to church leader S. N. Haskell, Ellen White elaborated on her concerns: "I said further that before the end we

---

[61] Ellen G. White to Elder S. N. Haskell, Lt 338, 1908 (Nov. 26), published in *idem, Selected Messages,* book 2, pp. 41, 42.

[62] While the focus of this article is religious enthusiasm in early Adventist history, Ellen White made frequent mention of her post-Millerite experiences in her interview with the Mackins. Her reflections and counsel are pertinent to understanding her more fully developed views toward charismatic experiences.

[63] Ellen G. White, "Report of Interview," Ms 115, 1908 (Nov. 12), published in *idem, Selected Messages,* book 3, pp. 363-375.

[64] *Ibid.*

would see strange manifestations by those who professed to be led by the Holy Spirit. There are those who will treat as something of great importance these peculiar manifestations, which are not of God, but which are calculated to divert the minds of many away from the teachings of the Word. . . . In the last days the enemy of present truth will bring in manifestations that are not in harmony with the workings of the Spirit, but are calculated to lead astray those who stand ready to take up with something new and strange."[65]

Not long after her interview Ellen White wrote to the Mackins about instruction she received in "visions of the night," making clear that their exhibitions were "not in accordance with the genuine work of the Holy Spirit."[66] And to those who had been influenced by their experience, she cautioned, "True religion does not demand great bodily demonstrations such as some of you have had the misfortune to witness here. These are no evidence of the presence of the Spirit of God."[67]

A summarizing statement by Ellen White on how to relate to religious enthusiasm was written several years earlier in 1901: "Careful management on all points is needed, so that we shall neither run into the fire of fanaticism nor drift into formalism, which will freeze our own souls and the souls of others. We need more of the good, old-fashioned religion which leads a man to walk humbly before God."[68]

Summary

In order for us to understand early Adventist religious enthusiasm it is necessary to understand the spirit and attitudes existing in North America during the first half of the nineteenth century. The American Revolution produced a tremendous optimism combined with a spirit of freedom and independence. As Americans pushed west, a frontier disposition became increasingly dominant. The aristocratic Federalist Party began to fall into disfavor, while the popular ideas of freedom and individuality promoted by Thomas Jefferson were embraced. At the same time the older authoritarian state-sponsored Congregational and Presbyterian churches were seen to be out of harmony with the new American freedom and the needs of the common people. The result was the rise of the Baptist Church, followed rapidly by the even more popular Methodist Episcopal Church.

About the same period the Christian Connection Church was growing

---

[65] Ellen G. White, Lt 338, 1908 (Nov. 26), published in *idem, Selected Messages,* book 2, pp. 41, 42.

[66] Ellen G. White, Lt 358a, 1908 (Dec. 11), published in *idem, Selected Messages,* book 2, pp. 44-46.

[67] Ellen G. White, Ms 97, 1909 (Oct. 16), published in *idem, Sermons and Talks,* vol. 1, pp. 397-405.

[68] Ellen G. White, "Labors in California," *Review and Herald,* Feb. 12, 1901, p. 97.

to be an important force in shaping popular religious thought. Contributing to the religious shift toward freedom and experimentation particularly within the Methodist Church were the camp meeting movement, the ideas of Phoebe Palmer, and the general mood of revival in America. The new "democratic" Christianity of Methodism, the Christian Connection Church, and others had a more demonstrative style of religious expression. Shouting, weeping, laughing, and losing strength—among other exercises—were usually seen as demonstrations of the moving of the Holy Spirit.

The Advent movement in America found its greatest attraction among the new and popular religious groups. Millerite Adventists brought with them from their previous churches their manner of worship expression, including sometimes physical exuberance. The message of Jesus' imminent return intensified all aspects of their spiritual experience. They studied their Bibles intensely, gave testimonies intensely, and prayed intensely, committing their lives and belongings entirely to God. Yet amid that intensity, a deep sense of seriousness pervaded. Levity was absent. There was no time for anything that did not speak to the spiritual needs of the human soul. Clear and solid preaching of the Bible message and its requirements was always emphasized.

Before the 1844 disappointment Ellen White's experience, like that of her fellow believers, frequently included expressions of religious enthusiasm. Most common were shouting and physical prostration under the Holy Spirit's power. Ellen White reported several examples of shouting and prostration among her fellow Adventists as the great prophetic date approached.

After the Disappointment many of the scattered former Millerites were comforted and instructed by the prophetic messages Ellen White received. Her public visions usually began with the shout of "Glory, glory, glory," followed by physical prostration. Up through the 1850s, James and Ellen White, with the rest of the coalescing movement, frequently expressed themselves with shouts of praise and a loss of physical strength. These exclamations were not in any way flippant or frivolous. Early Adventists battled daunting spiritual challenges and frequent physical illness. The physical demonstrations reported by Ellen White and others were clearly believed to be genuine workings of the Holy Spirit in response to God's physical and spiritual deliverance.

The confusion following the Millerite disappointment led to various forms of fanaticism. Ellen White consistently opposed this fanaticism and suffered significant opposition because of her interactions with fanatics. The key identifiable theological orientations of fanatics included spiritualizing, extreme literalizing, extreme sanctification, and mesmerism. She was opposed by the fanatics themselves as well as by the broader Adventist leaders for associating with those of a fanatical disposition. Her reason for interacting with fanatics was her concern to help those who were within her sphere of influence who still had confidence that something of prophetic significance had happened in October 1844. It was her prophetic guidance that helped protect the "little flock" of believers during the difficult first years following the 1844 disappointment.

Beginning in 1850 Ellen White wrote of the dangers of imbalance and an undue dependence upon physical manifestations of the Spirit's power. She urged a worship environment that would commend itself "to thoughtful, intelligent minds," rather than "create only disgust in the minds of unbelievers."[69] Adding to her concerns were revelations that *counterfeit* exercises would be introduced to lead believers away from God's Word as the only reliable criterion of genuine experience and truth. These warnings intensified over the course of her ministry, and suggest a leading away from reliance on forms of religious enthusiasm that were common to the spiritual heritages of early Adventists.

Ellen White's fully developed teachings on the subject of charismatic-like experiences instruct believers that while they should be open to the Holy Spirit working in surprising ways, they should not *seek* or *rely* upon physical and emotional exercises. She repeatedly pointed to the Word of God as the solid foundation of the Christian's experience, and to conformity to its teachings as the safest evidence of the Spirit's presence. "When the Spirit of God moves upon the heart," Ellen White wrote, "it causes the faithful, obedient child of God to act in a manner that will commend religion to the good judgment of sensible-minded men and women."[70]

---

[69] Ellen G. White, "Blessed Are the Pure in Heart," *General Conference Bulletin,* Apr. 23, 1901, p. 421, published in *idem, Selected Messages,* book 2, p. 35.

[70] Ellen G. White, "Who Are the Sanctified?" *Signs of the Times,* Feb. 28, 1895, p. 4.

BIBLIOGRAPHY OF WORKS CITED

Adams, Daniel. *Arithmetic*. New York: Collins and Brother, 1861.

Ahlstrom, Sydney E. *A Religious History of the American People*. New Haven, Conn.: Yale University Press, 1972.

Alger, Linda Andrews. "The Lane-Godsmark Family." Term paper, Center for Adventist Research, Andrews University, n.d.

"Allegan SDA Church: 1863-1976." Berrien Springs, Mich.: Center for Adventist Research, Andrews University, n.d.

Andrews, Angeline Stevens. "Diary." Loma Linda, Calif.: Archives and Special Collections, Loma Linda University,

Andrews, John Nevins, et al. *Defense of Elder James White and Wife: Vindication of Their Moral and Christian Character*. Battle Creek, Mich.: Steam Press, 1870.

Armstrong, David, and Elizabeth Metzger Armstrong. *The Great American Medicine Show*. New York: Prentice Hall, 1991.

Arthur, David Tallmadge. "'Come Out of Babylon': A Study of Millerite Separatism and Denominationalism, 1840-1865." Ph.D. diss., University of Rochester, 1970.

Bates, Joseph. *An Explanation of the Typical and Anti-Typical Sanctuary, by the Scriptures. With a Chart*. New Bedford. Mass.: Press of Benjamin Lindsey, 1850.

———. *The Opening Heavens*. New Bedford, Mass.: Benjamin Lindsey, 1846.

———. *A Seal of the Living God: A Hundred Forty-four Thousand, of the Servants of God Being Sealed, in 1849*. New Bedford, Mass.: Benjamin Lindsey, 1849.

———. *Second Advent Waymarks and High Heaps, or a Connected View, of the Fulfillment of Prophecy, by God's Peculiar People, From the Year 1840 to 1847*. New Bedford, Mass.: Benjamin Lindsey, 1847.

———. *The Seventh Day Sabbath: A Perpetual Sign, From the Beginning, to the Entering Into the Gates of the Holy City, According to the Commandment*. New Bedford, Mass.: Benjamin Lindsey, 1846.

———. *The Seventh Day Sabbath: A Perpetual Sign From the Beginning, to the Entering Into the Gates of the Holy City, According to the Commandment*, 2nd ed., rev. and enl. New Bedford, Mass: Benjamin Lindsey, 1847.

———. *A Vindication of the Seventh-day Sabbath, and the Commandments of God*. New Bedford, Mass.: Benjamin Lindsey, 1848.

Belden, S. T., et al. *To Brother J. N. Andrews and Sister H. N. Smith*. N.p., 1860.

Bettmann, Otto L. *The Good Old Days—They Were Terrible!* New York: Random House, 1974.

Bliss, Sylvester, et al. *Defence of Elder Joshua V. Himes*. Boston: Chardon Street Church, 1851.

"Book of Records of the Seventh-day Advent Church in Otsego, Allegan County, Michigan, Otsego, Michigan." Berrien Springs, Mich.: Center for Adventist Research, Andrews University, n.d.

Bovee, Mark. "Richard Godsmark: A Man of God Who Left His Mark in the Battle

Creek Area." Adapted from article appearing in the Battle Creek *Enquirer and News,* May 10, 1964. Berrien Springs, Mich.: Center for Adventist Research, Andrews University, n.d.

Bruinsma, Reinder. *Seventh-day Adventist Attitudes Toward Roman Catholicism 1844-1965.* Berrien Springs, Mich.: Andrews University Press, 1994.

Bunyan, John. *The Pilgrim's Progress.* Harmondsworth, England: Penguin, 1959.

Burt, Merlin, ed. *"Ellen White and Current Issues" Symposium.* Berrien Springs, Mich.: Center for Adventist Research, Andrews University, 2005.

———. "The Historical Background, Interconnected Development, and Integration of the Doctrines of the Sanctuary, the Sabbath, and Ellen G. White's Role in Sabbatarian Adventism From 1844 to 1849." Ph.D. diss., Andrews University, 2002.

Byington, Martha. 1857 diary. Berrien Springs, Mich.: Center for Adventist Research, Andrews University.

Cadwallader, E. M. *A History of Seventh-day Adventist Education.* 4th ed. Payson, Ariz.: Leaves-of-Autumn Books, 1958, 1975.

Canright, D. M. *Life of Mrs. E. G. White: Seventh-day Adventist Prophet, Her False Claims Refuted.* Cincinnati: Standard Pub. Co., 1919.

———. *Seventh-Day Adventism Renounced.* Chicago: Fleming H. Revell, 1889.

Carroll, Bret E. *Spiritualism in Antebellum America.* Bloomington, Ind.: Indiana University Press, 1997.

Caruso, John Anthony. *The Great Lakes Frontier: An Epic of the Old Northwest.* Indianapolis: Bobbs-Merrill, 1961.

Chandler, Charles H. *The History of New Ipswich, New Hampshire, 1735-1914: With Genealogical Records of the Principal Families.* Fitchburg, Mass.: Sentinel Print. Co., 1914.

Chilson, Adriel, ed. *Miracles in My Life: Autobiography of Adventist Pioneer J. N. Loughborough.* Angwin, Calif.: Heritage Publications, n.d.

Clayburn, Jon K., ed. *Rochester's Adventist Heritage.* New York: Adventist History Project, 2002.

Cole, Harry Ellsworth. *A Standard History of Sauk County, Wisconsin.* Chicago: Lewis Pub. Co., 1918. Vol. 1.

Comba, Emilio. *History of the Waldenses of Italy.* London: Truslove & Shirley, 1889.

Coon, Roger W. *The Great Visions of Ellen G. White.* Hagerstown, Md.: Review and Herald, 1992. Vol. 1.

Coulter, Robert. *Story of the Church of God (Seventh Day).* Denver: Bible Advocate Press, 1983.

Cutter, William Richard. *Genealogical and Family History of Southern New York and the Hudson River Valley.* New York: Lewis Historical Pub. Co., 1913. Vol. 3.

Dabrowski, Rajmund L., and B. B. Beach, eds. *Michael Belina Czechowski 1818-1876: Results of the Historical Symposium About His Life and Work Held in Warsaw, Poland, May 17-23, 1976, Commemorating the Hundredth Anniversary of His Death.* Warsaw: Znaki Czasu Pub. House, 1979.

Damsteegt, P. Gerard. *Foundations of the Seventh-day Adventist Message and Mission.* Grand Rapids: Eerdmans Pub. Co., 1977.

Dartmouth, Massachusetts, "Copy of Sheet From Dartmouth New Bedford Church Clerk's Record." Berrien Springs, Mich.: Center for Adventist Research, Andrews University, 1861[?].

Davis, Moshe. *America and the Holy Land.* Westport, Conn.: Praeger, 1995.

Dederen, Raoul, ed. *Handbook of Seventh-day Adventist Theology.* Hagerstown, Md.: Review and Herald, 2000.

Delafield, D. A. *Ellen G. White in Europe.* Washington, D.C.: Review and Herald, 1975.

Dickens, Charles. *Pictures From Italy. American Notes.* London: Chapman & Hall, 1880.

Dieter, Melvin Easterday. *The Holiness Revival of the Nineteenth Century.* 2nd ed. Lanham, Md.: Scarecrow Press, 1996.

Douglass, Herbert E. *Dramatic Prophecies of Ellen White.* Nampa, Idaho: Pacific Press, 2007.

———. *Messenger of the Lord: The Prophetic Ministry of Ellen G. White.* Nampa, Idaho: Pacific Press, 1998.

Dowell, Thomas. *Farewell to the Outward Bound. Addressed to Members of the Church of England by One of Her Ministers.* Second ed., enl. London: Longman, Brown, Green, and Longmans, 1850.

Dunbar, Will, and George S. May. *Michigan: A History of the Wolverine State.* Third ed. Grand Rapids: Eerdmans, 1995.

Durand, Eugene F. *Yours in the Blessed Hope, Uriah Smith.* Washington, D.C.: Review and Herald, 1980.

Edson, Hiram. *The Time of the End: Its Beginning, Progressive Events, and Final Termination.* Auburn, N.Y.: Henry Oliphant, 1849.

Ellen G. White Estate. *A Critique of the Book* Prophetess of Health. Washington, D.C.: Ellen G. White Estate, 1976.

———. "I'd Like to Ask Sister White . . ." Washington, D.C.: Review and Herald, 1965.

Engs, Ruth C. *Clean Living Movements: American Cycles of Health Reform.* Westport, Conn.: Praeger, 2000.

Ferris, Roger H. "The Ordinances of Foot Washing and the Lord's Supper in the Seventh-day Adventist Denomination." Term paper, Seventh-day Adventist Theological Seminary, 1957.

Fletcher, W. W. *The Reasons for My Faith.* Sydney: William Brooks & Co., Ltd., 1932.

Fortin, Denis. *Adventism in Quebec: The Dynamics of Rural Church Growth 1830-1910.* Berrien Springs, Mich.: Andrews University Press, 2004.

———, and Jerry Moon, eds. *Ellen G. White Encyclopedia.* Hagerstown, Md.: Review and Herald, 2013. (Abbreviated as EGWEnc.)

Froom, LeRoy Edwin. *The Conditionalist Faith of Our Fathers.* Washington, D.C.: Review and Herald, 1965-1966. 2 vols.

———. *The Prophetic Faith of Our Fathers.* Washington, D.C.: Review and Herald, 1950-1954. 4 vols.

Gaustad, Edwin S., ed. *The Rise of Adventism: Religion and Society in Mid-Nineteenth Century America.* New York: Harper & Row, 1974.

Gordon, Paul A. *The Sanctuary, 1844, and the Pioneers.* Hagerstown, Md.: Review and Herald, 1983.

Graybill, Ronald D. "The Power of Prophecy: Ellen G. White and the Women Religious Founders of the Nineteenth Century." Ph.D. diss., Johns Hopkins University, 1983.

Greenleaf, Floyd. *In Passion for the World; A History of Seventh-day Adventist Education.* Nampa, Idaho: Pacific Press, 2005.

Greenslade, S. L., ed., *The West From the Reformation to the Present Day. The Cambridge History of the Bible.* Cambridge: Cambridge University Press, 1963. Vol. 3.

Hale, A. *Herald of the Bridegroom! in Which the Plagues That Await the Enemies of the*

King Eternal Are Considered; and the Appearing of Our Lord to Gather His Saints Is Shown to Be the Next Event Before Us, by a Scriptural Exhibition of the Order of Events From the Fall of the Papacy Down to the Establishment of the Everlasting Kingdom. Boston: Joshua V. Himes, 1843.

Haller, John S. *Medical Protestants: The Eclectics in American Medicine, 1825-1939.* Carbondale, Ill.: Southern Illinois University Press, 1994.

Hardinge, Mervyn G. *A Physician Explains Ellen White's Counsel on Drugs, Herbs, and Natural Remedies.* Hagerstown, Md.: Review and Herald, 2001.

Harmon, Artemas C., ed. *The Harmon Genealogy Comprising All Branches in New England*. Washington, D.C.: Gibson Bros, 1920.

Haskell, Stephen N. *The Cross and Its Shadow.* South Lancaster, Mass.: Bible Training School, 1914.

Hastings, James, ed. *Encyclopaedia of Religion and Ethics.* Edinburgh: T. & T. Clark, 1908-1926.

Hatch, Nathan O. *The Democratization of American Christianity.* New Haven: Yale University Press, 1989.

Herzog, Johann Jakob, and Philip Schaff, eds. *The New Schaff-Herzog Encyclopedia of Religious Knowledge.* New York, London: Funk and Wagnalls, 1908-1914.

Himes, Joshua V., ed. *Views of the Prophecies and Prophetic Chronology, Selected From Manuscripts of William Miller, With a Memoir of His Life.* Boston: Joshua V. Himes, 1842.

History of Allegan and Barry Counties, Michigan: With Illustrations and Biographical Sketches of Their Prominent Men and Pioneers. Philadelphia: D. W. Ensign & Co., 1880.

History of Washington, New Hampshire, From 1768 to 1886: A Facsimile of the 1886 Edition With a New Foreword by Ronald Jager and Grace Jager. Claremont, N.H.: Claremont Manufacturing Co., 1886. (Reprint, Washington N.H.: Washington History Committee, 1976.)

History of Washtenaw County, Michigan; Together With Sketches of Its Cities, Villages and Townships, Educational, Religious, Civil, Military, and Political History; Portraits of Prominent Persons, and Biographies of Representative Citizens. Chicago: Chas. C. Chapman & Co., 1881.

Holbrook, Frank B., ed. *Symposium on Revelation: Introductory and Exegetical Studies. Book 1.* Silver Spring, Md.: Biblical Research Committee, General Conference of Seventh-day Adventists, 1992.

Holch, Lillian Hubbard, ed. *Sizer Genealogy: A History of Antonio Dezocieur Who Changed His Name to Anthony Sizer.* Brooklyn, N.Y.: Bowles-Printer, 1941.

Hopkins, Timothy. *The Kelloggs in the Old World and the New.* San Francisco: Sunset Press and Photo Engraving Co., 1903. Vol. 1.

Horn, Siegfried H. ed. *Seventh-day Adventist Bible Dictionary*, revised ed. Hagerstown, Md.: Review and Herald, 1979.

Hudson, Winthrop S., and John Corrigan. *Religion in America: An Historical Account of the Development of American Religious Life.* 5th ed. Upper Saddle River, N.J.: Prentice Hall, 1992.

The Jewett Family of America: Year Book of 1912-1913. Rowley, Mass.: The Jewett Family Association of America, 1913[?].

Julian, John, ed. *A Dictionary of Hymnology: Setting Forth the Origin and History of Christian Hymns of All Ages and Nations.* Rev. ed. New York: John Murray, 1907.

Kachuba, John B. *Ghosthunting Ohio*. Cincinnati: Emmis Books, 2004.

Kirsch, Irving, et al. *Handbook of Clinical Hypnosis*. Washington, D.C.: American Psychological Association, 1993.

Knight, George R. *Ellen White's World: A Fascinating Look at the Times in Which She Lived*. Hagerstown, Md.: Review and Herald, 1998.

———. *Joseph Bates: The Real Founder of Seventh-day Adventism*. Hagerstown, Md.: Review and Herald, 2004.

———. *Millennial Fever and the End of the World: A Study of Millerite Adventism*. Boise, Idaho: Pacific Press, 1993.

———. *Organizing to Beat the Devil: The Development of Adventist Church Structure*. Hagerstown, Md.: Review and Herald, 2001.

———. *Reading Ellen White: How to Understand and Apply Her Writings*. Hagerstown, Md.: Review and Herald, 1997.

———. *A Search for Identity*. Hagerstown, Md.: Review and Herald, 2000.

———. *Walking With Ellen White*. Hagerstown, Md.: Review and Herald, 1999.

Kovacs, Judith L., et al. *Revelation: The Apocalypse of Jesus Christ*. Malden, Mass.: Blackwell Pub., 2004.

Kreiger, Barbara, with Shalom Goldman. *Divine Expectations, an American Woman in 19th-Century Palestine*. Athens, Ohio: Ohio University Press, 1999.

Kurtz, Paul. *The Transcendental Temptation: A Critique of Religion and the Paranormal*. Buffalo: Prometheus, 1986.

Lake, Jud. *Ellen White Under Fire*. Nampa, Idaho: Pacific Press, 2010.

Land, Gary, ed. *The World of Ellen G. White*. Hagerstown, Md.: Review and Herald, 1987.

Lapham, William Berry. *History of Paris, Maine, From Its Settlement to 1880*. Paris, Maine: printed for the authors, 1884.

Lee, Jairyong. "Faith and Works in Ellen G. White's Doctrine of the Last Judgment." Ph.D. diss., Seventh-day Adventist Theological Seminary, Andrews University, 1985.

Leonard, Harry, ed. *J. N. Andrews: The Man and the Mission*. Berrien Springs, Mich.: Andrews University Press, 1985.

Lindén, Ingemar. *1844 and the Shut Door Problem*. Uppsala, Sweden: Almqvist & Wiksell, 1982.

Litch, Josiah. *Prophetic Expositions; or a Connected View of the Testimony of the Prophets Concerning the Kingdom of God and the Time of Its Establishment (Vol. 1)*. Boston: Joshua V. Himes, 1842.

Lorenz, Felix A. "A Study of Early Adventist Interpretations of the Laodicean Message With Emphasis on the Writings of Mrs. E. G. White." B.Div. thesis, Seventh-day Adventist Theological Seminary, 1951.

Loughborough, J. N. *The Church, Its Organization, Order, and Discipline*. Washington, D.C.: Review and Herald, 1907.

———. "Diary." Berrien Springs, Mich: Center for Adventist Research, Andrews University, 1859.

———. *The Great Second Advent Movement*. Washington D.C.: Review and Herald, 1905. Also: Adventist Pioneer Library reprint, 1992.

———. *Rise and Progress of the Seventh-day Adventists*. Battle Creek, Mich.: General Conference Association of the Seventh-day Adventists, 1892.

Margo, Robert A. *Wages and Labor Markets in the United States, 1820-1860*. Chicago:

University of Chicago Press, 2000.

The Mennonite Encyclopedia. Hillsboro, Kans.: Mennonite Brethren Pub. House, 1955-1990.

Miller, William. *Evidence From Scripture and History of the Second Coming of Christ About the Year 1843; Exhibited in a Course of Lectures.* Boston: J. V. Himes, 1842.

———. *A Trilogy, by William Miller.* Boston: Joshua V. Himes, 1842; reprint, Payson, Ariz: Leaves-of-Autumn Books, 1985.

The Millerites and Early Adventists. Ann Arbor, Mich.: University Microfilms International, 1978.

Moon, Jerry. *W. C. White and Ellen G. White: The Relationship Between the Prophet and Her Son*. Berrien Springs, Mich.: Andrews University Press, 1993.

Morgan, Douglas. *Adventism and the American Republic.* Knoxville: University of Tennessee Press, 2001.

Mustard, Andrew G. *James White and SDA Organization: Historical Development, 1844-1881.* Andrews University Seminary Doctoral Dissertation Series. Berrien Springs, Mich.: Andrews University Press, 1987. Vol. XII.

Neufeld, Don F., ed. *Seventh-day Adventist Encyclopedia*, rev. ed. Hagerstown, Md.: Review and Herald, 1996. 2 vols. (Abbreviated as SDAE.)

Neuffer, Julia. "The Gathering of Israel: A Historical Study of *Early Writings,* pp. 74-76." Washington, D.C.: Biblical Research Committee, General Conference of Seventh-day Adventists, n.d.

Newhall, Beaumont. *The Daguerreotype in America*. 3rd ed. New York: Dover Publications, 1976.

Nichol, Francis D. *Ellen G. White and Her Critics.* Washington, D.C.: Review and Herald, 1951.

———. *The Midnight Cry.* Washington, D.C.: Review and Herald, 1945.

———, ed. *The Seventh-day Adventist Bible Commentary.* Rev. ed. Washington, D.C.: Review and Herald, 1953-1957, 1976-1980.

Nickels, Richard C. *A History of the Seventh Day Church of God*. N.p., 1977.

———. *Six Papers on the History of the Church of God*. 2nd ed. Neck City, Mo.: Giving and Sharing, 1993.

Nix, James R. "Another Look at Israel Damman." Unpublished paper, Ellen G. White Estate, 2004. Also: www.whiteestate.org/issues/israel_damman.html.

———. *Early Adventist Singing.* Hagerstown, Md.: Review and Herald, 1994.

———. "From Vision to Printed Page." Ellen G. White Estate Document File 52. Unpublished paper, Ellen G. White Estate, 2001.

———. "John and Betsey (Jewett) White." Unpublished paper, Ellen G. White Estate, 2006.

———. "The Life and Work of Moses Hull." Term paper, Seventh-day Adventist Theological Seminary, Andrews University, 1971.

———. "Robert Harmon." Unpublished paper, Ellen G. White Estate, 1991.

Noorbergen, Rene. *Ellen G. White: Prophet of Destiny.* New Canaan, Conn.: Keats Pub. Inc., 1972.

Numbers, Ronald L. *Prophetess of Health: Ellen G. White and the Origins of Seventh-day Adventist Health Reform.* 3rd ed. Grand Rapids: Eerdmans Pub. Co., 2008.

Olson, Robert W. "The 'Shut Door' Documents." Silver Spring, Md.: Ellen G. White Estate, 1982.

Pedersen, Gunnar. "The Soteriology of Ellen G. White Compared With the Lutheran

Formula of Concord: A Study of the Adventist Doctrine of the Final Judgment of the Saints and Their Justification Before God." Ph.D. diss., Andrews University, 1995.

Pereyra, Elbio. "Marriage, Divorce, and Remarriage in the Writings of Ellen G. White." Unpublished manuscript, Ellen G. White Estate, 1987.

Peirce, H. B. *History of Calhoun County, Michigan: With Illustrations Descriptive of Its Scenery, Palatial Residences, Public Buildings, Fine Blocks, and Important Manufactories, From Original Sketches by Artists of the Highest Ability.* Philadelphia: L. H. Everts & Co., 1877. Reprint: Mount Vernon, Ind.: Windmill Pub., Inc., 1998.

Poehler, Rolf J. "'. . . and the Door Was Shut': Seventh-day Adventists and the Shut-Door Doctrine in the Decade After the Great Disappointment." Unpublished paper, Seventh-day Adventist Theological Seminary, 1978.

Poirier, Tim. "Exhibits Regarding the Work of Ellen White's Literary Assistants." Ellen G. White Estate Document File 1049-b. Unpublished paper, Ellen G. White Estate, 1990.

"Records of the Seventh-day Adventist Church, Monterey, Michigan [1860-1880]." Berrien Springs, Mich.: Center for Adventist Research, Andrews University, n.d.

Reiber, Donald D. "An Investigation Into the Development of Feet Washing Among Advent Believers From 1844 to 1860." Term paper, Andrews University, 1963.

Rice, George E. *Luke, a Plagiarist?* Mountain View, Calif.: Pacific Press, 1983.

Ripley, George, and Charles A. Dana, eds. *The New American Cyclopaedia: A Popular Dictionary of General Knowledge.* New York: D. Appleton and Co., 1862.

Robinson, Dores Eugene. *The Story of Our Health Message: The Origin, Character, and Development of Health Education in the Seventh-day Adventist Church.* Third ed. Nashville: Southern Pub. Assn., 1943, 1955, 1965.

Robinson, Ella M. *S. N. Haskell: Man of Action.* Washington, D.C.: Review and Herald, 1967.

Robinson, Virgil. *James White.* Washington, D.C.: Review and Herald, 1976.

Rosenberg, Charles E. *The Cholera Years: The United States in 1832, 1849, and 1866.* Chicago: University of Chicago Press, 1987.

Rosenberg, Chaim M. *The Great Workshop: Boston's Victorian Age.* Charleston, S.C.: Arcadia Pub., 2004.

Schaefer, Richard A. *Legacy: Daring to Care.* Centennial ed. Loma Linda, Calif.: Legacy, 2005.

Schwarz, Richard W. *John Harvey Kellogg, M.D.: Pioneering Health Reformer.* Hagerstown, Md.: Review and Herald, 2006.

———, and Floyd Greenleaf. *Light Bearers: A History of the Seventh-day Adventist Church.* Rev. ed. Nampa, Idaho: Pacific Press, 2000.

Seventh-day Adventists Answer Questions on Doctrine. Annotated ed. Berrien Springs, Mich.: Andrews University Press, 2003.

Shaw, Horace John. "A Rhetorical Analysis of the Speaking of Mrs. Ellen G. White, a Pioneer Leader and Spokeswoman of the Seventh-day Adventist Church." Ph.D. diss., Michigan State University, 1959.

Skinner, Henry Alan. *The Origin of Medical Terms.* Baltimore: Williams & Wilkins, 1949.

Sloane, Eric. *Our Vanishing Landscape.* New York: Funk and Wagnalls, 1955. Reprint: Mineole, N.Y.: Dover Publications, 2004.

Smith, Andrew F. *The Tomato in America: Early History, Culture, and Cookery.* Columbia,

S.C.: University of South Carolina Press, 1994.

Smith, Timothy L. *Revivalism & Social Reform: American Protestantism on the Eve of the Civil War.* Baltimore:Johns Hopkins University Press, 1980.

Smith, Uriah. *In Memoriam. A Sketch of the Last Sickness and Death of Elder James White, Who Died at Battle Creek, Michigan, August 6, 1881, Together With the Discourse Preached at His Funeral.* Battle Creek, Mich.: 1881.

———. *The Visions of Mrs. E. G. White, a Manifestation of Spiritual Gifts According to the Scriptures.* Battle Creek, Mich.: Steam Press of the Seventh-day Adventist Pub. Assn., 1868.

Spalding, Arthur Whitefield. *Origin and History of Seventh-day Adventists.* Washington, D.C.: Review and Herald, 1961-1962. 4 vols.

Steadman, Philip, and Gerrylynn K. Roberts. *American Cities and Technology: Wilderness to Wired City.* New York: Routledge, 1999.

Strayer, Brian E. "Early Advent Waymarks in Jackson, Michigan: Parts I & II." Unpublished manuscript, Adventist Heritage Center, Andrews University, 1985.

Syme, Eric Douglas. *A History of SDA Church-State Relations in the United States.* Mountain View, Calif.: Pacific Press, 1973.

Taves, Ann. *Fits, Trances, & Visions: Experiencing Religion and Explaining Experience From Wesley to James.* Princeton, N.J.: Princeton University Press, 1999.

Thompson, Alden. *Escape From the Flames: How Ellen White Grew from Fear to Joy—and Helped Me Do It Too.* Nampa, Idaho: Pacific Press, 2005.

Timm, Alberto R. *The Sanctuary and the Three Angels' Messages: Integrating Factors in the Development of Seventh-day Adventist Doctrines.* Berrien Springs, Mich.: Adventist Theological Society Publications, 1995.

———. "The 1,290 and 1,335 Days of Daniel 12." Biblical Research Institute, General Conference of Seventh-day Adventists, 2002.

Turner, R. Edward. *Proclaiming the Word: The Concept of Preaching in the Thought of Ellen G. White.* Berrien Springs, Mich.: Andrews University Press, 1980.

Vande Vere, Emmett K. *Rugged Heart: The Story of George I. Butler.* Nashville: Southern Pub. Assn., 1979.

———. *The Wisdom Seekers.* Nashville: Southern Pub. Assn., 1972.

Vyhmeister, Nancy, ed. *Women in Ministry: Biblical and Historical Perspectives.* Berrien Springs, Mich.: Andrews University Press, 1998.

Wellcome, Isaac C. *History of the Second Advent Message and Mission, Doctrine and People.* Yarmouth, Maine: the author, 1874.

Wheatley, Richard. *The Life and Letters of Mrs. Phoebe Palmer.* New York: W. C. Palmer, 1881.

Wheeler, Gerald. *James White: Innovator and Overcomer.* Hagerstown, Md.: Review and Herald, 2003.

Whidden II, Woodrow W. *Ellen White on Salvation.* Hagerstown, Md.: Review and Herald, 1995.

———. "The Soteriology of Ellen G. White. The Persistent Path to Perfection, 1836-1902." Ph.D. diss., Drew University, 1989.

White, Arthur L. "Ellen G. White and the Shut Door Question." Silver Spring, Md.: Ellen G. White Estate, 1982.

———. *Ellen G. White: The Australian Years, 1891-1900.* Washington, D.C.: Review and Herald, 1983.

———. *Ellen G. White: The Early Elmshaven Years, 1900-1905.* Washington, D.C.:

Review and Herald, 1981.
———. *Ellen G. White: The Early Years, 1827-1862.* Washington, D.C.: Review and Herald, 1985.
———. *Ellen G. White: The Later Elmshaven Years, 1905-1915.* Washington, D.C.: Review and Herald, 1982.
———. *Ellen G. White: The Lonely Years, 1876-1891.* Washington, D.C.: Review and Herald, 1984.
———. *Ellen G. White: Messenger to the Remnant.* Washington, D.C.: Review and Herald, 1954.
———. *Ellen G. White: The Progressive Years, 1862-1876.* Washington, D.C.: Review and Herald, 1986.
———. *Ellen White, Woman of Vision.* Hagerstown, Md.: Review and Herald, 2000.
———. *The Ellen G. White Writings.* Washington, D.C.: Review and Herald, 1973.
White, Ellen G., *The Adventist Home.* Nashville: Southern Pub. Assn., 1952.
———. *An Appeal to the Youth: Funeral Address of Henry N. White at Battle Creek, Mich. Dec. 21, 1863: Brief Narrative of His Life, Experience, and Last Sickness: His Mother's Letters, Etc.* Battle Creek, Mich.: Steam Press of the Seventh-day Adventist Pub. Assn., 1864.
———. *Child Guidance.* Hagerstown, Md.: Review and Herald, 1954, 1982.
———. *Counsels on Health and Instruction to Medical Missionary Workers.* Mountain View, Calif.: Pacific Press, 1923.
———. *Counsels on Speech and Song.* Nampa, Idaho: Pacific Press, 1988.
———. *The Desire of Ages.* Oakland: Pacific Press, 1898.
———. *Early Writings of Ellen G. White.* Hagerstown, Md.: Review and Herald, 1945.
———. *Education.* Mountain View, Calif.: Pacific Press, 1903.
———. *Evangelism as Set Forth in the Writings of Ellen G. White.* Washington, D.C.: Review and Herald, 1946.
———. *The Great Controversy Between Christ and Satan.* Mountain View, Calif.: Pacific Press, 1911.
———. *In Heavenly Places.* Washington, D.C.: Review and Herald, 1967.
———. *Last Day Events: Facing Earth's Final Crisis.* Nampa, Idaho: Pacific Press, 1992.
———. "Life Sketches: The Christian Experience, Views, and Labors of Ellen G. White in Connection With the Rise and Progress of the Third Angel's Message." Silver Spring, Md.: Ellen G. White Estate, Inc., n.d. Cited as "Life Sketches" manuscript.
———. *Life Sketches of Ellen G. White: Being a Narrative of Her Experience to 1881 as Written by Herself; With a Sketch of Her Subsequent Labors and of Her Last Sickness Compiled from Original Sources.* Mountain View, Calif.: Pacific Press, 1915.
———. *Manuscript Releases From the Files of the Letters and Manuscripts Written by Ellen G. White.* Silver Spring, Md.: Ellen G. White Estate, 1981-1993. 21 vols.
———. *Medical Ministry: A Treatise on Medical Missionary Work in the Gospel.* Mountain View, Calif.: Pacific Press, 1932.
———. *Mind, Character, and Personality: Guidelines to Mental and Spiritual Health.* Nashville: Southern Pub. Assn., 1977. 2 vols.
———. *The Ministry of Healing.* Nampa, Idaho: Pacific Press, 1905.
———. *Our High Calling.* Washington, D.C.: Review and Herald, 1961.
———. *Prayer.* Nampa, Idaho: Pacific Press, 2002.
———. *Reflecting Christ.* Hagerstown, Md.: Review and Herald, 1985.
———. *Selected Messages From the Writings of Ellen G. White.* Washington, D.C.: Review

and Herald, 1958, 1980. Books 1-3.
———. *Sermons and Talks.* Silver Spring, Md.: Ellen G. White Estate, 1990, 1994. 2 vols.
———. *A Sketch of the Christian Experience and Views of Ellen G. White.* Saratoga Springs, N.Y.: James White, 1851.
———. *Spalding and Magan's Unpublished Manuscript Testimonies of Ellen G. White.* Payson, Ariz: Leaves-of-Autumn Books, 1985.
———. *The Spirit of Prophecy,* vol. 1: *The Great Controversy Between Christ and His Angels and Satan and His Angels.* Battle Creek, Mich.: Steam Press of the Seventh-day Adventist Pub. Assn., 1870.
———. *Spiritual Gifts [vol. 1]. The Great Controversy Between Christ and His Angels, and Satan and His Angels.* Battle Creek, Mich.: James White, 1858.
———. *Spiritual Gifts [vol. 2]. My Christian Experience, Views and Labors in Connection With the Rise and Progress of the Third Angel's Message.* Battle Creek, Mich.: James White, 1860.
———. *Supplement to the Christian Experience and Views of Ellen G. White.* Rochester, N.Y.: James White, 1854.
———. *Testimonies for the Church.* Mountain View, Calif.: Pacific Press, 1948. 9 vols.
———. *Testimonies on Sexual Behavior, Adultery, and Divorce.* Silver Spring, Md.: Ellen G. White Estate, 1989.
———. *Testimonies to Ministers and Gospel Workers.* Mountain View, Calif.: Pacific Press, 1923.
———. *Testimony for the Church,* No. 4. Battle Creek, Mich.: Steam Press of the Review and Herald Office, 1857.
———. *This Day With God.* Washington, D.C.: Review and Herald, 1979.
———. *The Truth About Angels.* Boise, Idaho: Pacific Press, 1996.
———. *Welfare Ministry: Instruction in Christian Neighborhood Service.* Washington, D.C.: Review and Herald, 1952.
White, James. *An Appeal to the Working Men and Women in the Ranks of Seventh-day Adventists.* Battle Creek, Mich.: Steam Press of the Seventh-day Adventist Pub. Assn., 1872.
———. *A Brief Account of the Last Sickness and Death of Nathaniel White, Who Died May 6th, 1853.* Rochester, N.Y.: *Advent Review* Office, 1853.
———, ed. *Brother Miller's Dream.* Oswego, N.Y.: n.p., 1850.
———, ed. *Health: Or How to Live.* Battle Creek, Mich.: Steam Press of the Seventh-day Adventist Pub. Assn., 1865.
———, comp. *Hymns, for God's Peculiar People, That Keep the Commandments of God, and the Faith of Jesus.* Oswego, N.Y.: Richard Oliphant, 1849.
———. *Life Incidents, in Connection With the Great Advent Movement, as Illustrated by the Three Angels of Revelation XIV.* Battle Creek, Mich.: Seventh-day Adventist Pub. Assn., 1868.
———, ed. *A Word to the "Little Flock."* Brunswick, Maine: [James White], 1847. Facsimile reproduction: Washington, D.C.: Review and Herald, 1944.
———, and Ellen G. White. *Life Sketches. Ancestry, Early Life, Christian Experience, and Extensive Labors, of Elder James White, and His Wife, Mrs. Ellen G. White.* Battle Creek, Mich.: Steam Press of the Seventh-day Adventist Pub. Assn., 1880, 1888.
White, W. C. "Memories and Records." Ellen G. White Estate Document File 256. Silver Spring, Md.: Ellen G. White Estate, n.d.
Wilson, James Michael. "Enthusiasm and Charismatic Manifestations in Sabbatarian

Adventism With Applications for the Seventh-day Adventist Church of the Late Twentieth Century." D.Min. diss., Andrews University, 1995.

Wolman, Benjamin B., ed. *International Encyclopedia of Psychiatry, Psychology, Psychoanalysis, and Neurology.* New York: Aesculapius Pub., 1977.

Wood, George B. *A Treatise on the Practice of Medicine.* 5th ed. Philadelphia: J. B. Lippincott and Co., 1858. Vol. 1.

Words of the Pioneers: A Collection of Early Seventh-day Adventist Writings. Loma Linda, Calif: Adventist Pioneer Library, 1995. CD Version 2.0.

Wright, Robert E. *Hamilton Unbound: Finance and the Creation of the American Republic.* Westport, Conn.: Praeger, 2002.

Zackrison, Edwin Harry. "Seventh-day Adventists and Original Sin: A Study of the Early Development of the Seventh-day Adventist Understanding of the Effect of Adam's Sin on His Posterity." Ph.D. diss., Seventh-day Adventist Theological Seminary, Andrews University, 1984.

Unless otherwise indicated, all correspondence cited is from the Ellen G. White Estate archives.

LIST OF CORRESPONDENTS

GENERAL INDEX

Note: The letters and manuscripts of Ellen White, together with the annotations, have been indexed, but not the introductory articles or appendixes. Names of persons, places, and selected topics are combined in this one index. A separate list of correspondents is found on page 947. The list of visions and places Ellen White traveled is not complete, but includes only those mentioned in the letters, manuscripts, and notes.

Abbreviations and Type

- EGW = Ellen G. White
- n, nn = footnote, footnotes
- Personal names printed in bold type indicate that the name is included in the biographical sketches

A

B

D

M

S

U

V

W

Y

Wisconsin
Waukon
Volney
Madison
Dubuque
Iowa
Chicago
Round Grove
Illinois
N
nw
ne
W
E
sw
se
S